THE *unofficial* GUIDE®
^{TO} Walt Disney World®

2022

BOB SEHLINGER *and* LEN TESTA

(Walt Disney World® is officially known as Walt Disney World® Resort.)

Please note that prices fluctuate in the course of time and that travel information changes under the impact of many factors that influence the travel industry. We therefore suggest that you write or call ahead for confirmation when making your travel plans. Every effort has been made to ensure the accuracy of information throughout this book, and the contents of this publication are believed to be correct at the time of printing. Nevertheless, the publishers cannot accept responsibility for errors or omissions, for changes in details given in this guide, or for the consequences of any reliance on the information provided by the same. Assessments of attractions and so forth are based upon the authors' own experiences; therefore, descriptions given in this guide necessarily contain an element of subjective opinion, which may not reflect the publisher's opinion or dictate a reader's own experience on another occasion. Readers are invited to write the publisher with ideas, comments, and suggestions for future editions. There is a risk of contracting COVID-19 in any public space. The Unofficial Guides are not liable for any illness or injury. Consult a physician regarding your risk factors before booking travel.

The Unofficial Guides
An imprint of AdventureKEEN
2204 First Ave. S., Ste. 102
Birmingham, AL 35233

Cover design by Scott McGrew

Text design by Vertigo Design and Annie Long

To contact us from within the United States, please call 888-604-4537 or fax 205-326-1012. You may also email us at info@theunofficialguides.com; on social media, you may contact us at TheUnofficialGuides on Facebook; @TheUGSeries on Twitter, Instagram, and Pinterest; and TheUnofficialGuideSeries on YouTube.

AdventureKEEN also publishes its books in a variety of electronic formats. Some content that appears in print may not be available in electronic formats.

ISBN: 978-1-62809-123-6; eISBN: 978-1-62809-124-3

Distributed by Publishers Group West

Manufactured in the United States of America

5 4 3 2 1

CONTENTS

INTRODUCTION

▌ FOR *the* LOVE *of* DISNEY

DEAR READER, we've been writing *The Unofficial Guide to Walt Disney World* for 36 years. You've really got to love a place to cover it for that long—and we do. Millions of you do too. Comments like these arrive at our office every day:

> *"Disney World was definitely the most magical and the best family vacation we ever had."*

> *"Holiday of a lifetime. Meticulous planning required, but amazing."*

> *"We've already booked another trip."*

Disney's theme parks are among the world's greatest man-made vacation destinations. At their best, they combine unparalleled imagination and storytelling with new technologies, all presented with optimism and an unwavering faith in humanity. Walt Disney World in particular is essentially a purpose-built city: a place designed to entertain, amaze, and inspire.

▌ WHY DISNEY WORLD NEEDS *a* 750-PAGE GUIDEBOOK

WE KNOW WHAT YOU'RE THINKING. The child-rearing classic *What to Expect When You're Expecting* clocks in at 656 pages, and a typical version of the King James Bible is around 1,200. Does the advice needed for Walt Disney World really fall somewhere between childbirth and God's manual for living?

If it's your first time, yes.

The thing that surprises most new visitors to Walt Disney World is that a Disney vacation requires much more planning and effort than most other vacations they've had.

Why? The main reason is capacity. Around 60,000 people visited Disney World's Magic Kingdom theme park in a normal, pre-pandemic day. Most of them would eat at its most popular restaurant—Be Our

Guest—if they could get in. But the restaurant can serve only a tiny fraction of those who want to dine there. Visitors who can't get into Be Our Guest often end up at restaurants with worse food, higher prices, or both.

Capacity also affects Disney World's popular rides: For some rides, there are far more people who want to ride than the ride can handle. As a result, some visitors will wait just 10 minutes to experience a ride, and others will wait 80 minutes or more for the same attraction on the same day.

Don't panic. If you love theme parks, Disney World is as good as it gets—the best in the small-*w* world. If you arrive without knowing a thing about the place and make every possible mistake, chances are about 90% that you'll have a wonderful vacation anyway.

The job of a guidebook is to give you a heads-up regarding opportunities and potential problems. We're certain we can help you turn a great vacation into an absolutely fabulous one.

A mom from Streator, Illinois, who was amazed at the size of the *Unofficial Guide,* came back saying this:

> It had been 10 years since we'd been to WDW, and I was shocked by how much your book grew. After going, I'm surprised that it's so small.

WHAT MAKES THIS BOOK DIFFERENT?

THE ADVICE IN THIS BOOK is different from what you'll find on the internet or in other books, in three important ways.

First, the team that produces this book is totally independent of the Walt Disney Company, Walt Disney World, and all other members of the Disney corporate family. We don't accept free trips, gifts, special favors, or other compensation from Disney in exchange for our coverage; we pay for everything we review. Disney doesn't request, influence, edit, or approve anything you'll read here.

In this guide, we represent and serve you, the reader. If a restaurant serves bad food, a gift item is overpriced, or a ride isn't worth the wait, we say so. In the process, we hope to make your visit more fun and rewarding.

Second, we use data, science, and technology to help solve problems that you'll encounter in Walt Disney World. In many ways, the Disney theme parks are the quintessential system: the ultimate in mass-produced entertainment, the most planned and programmed environment anywhere. Lines for rides and restaurants form in predictable ways at predictable times, for example. That makes it possible for us to study them.

You may be surprised that Disney-related questions like "How can I wait less in line?" or "What rides should my kids try?" are active areas of research in schools around the world; similar problems pop up in businesses every day. The authors and researchers who write this book have years—some have decades—of academic and professional experience in these areas and use them to benefit you.

The third way this book is different is the amount of time and money that goes into making it. Disney research is the full-time job of most of our core team. Over the years, we've spent millions of dollars reviewing and analyzing Disney World's hotels, rides, lines, and restaurants.

No other book or website commits the people, skills, or budget to do anything like the research you'll find in these pages. The only other organization that does comparable analysis of Disney World is Disney itself. And we will tell you what it won't.

HOW *to* USE THIS BOOK

THE BEST WAY TO USE THIS BOOK is to read in order the first few pages of each chapter, to get a feel for the kinds of questions the chapter answers. Then read in depth the chapters most important to you.

We've organized the chapters so that they appear in the same sequence and timeline that you'll use to plan and take your trip. For example, Part Two contains advice on what you need to know to start planning your trip. The next few chapters guide you through choosing a hotel, finding good places to eat, and picking the best rides and entertainment in the parks.

Each chapter starts with **Key Questions,** a list of the most common and important queries that visitors have about Walt Disney World (and Universal Orlando). For each question, we've listed where in the chapter to find the answers. Here's an example:

KEY QUESTIONS ANSWERED IN THIS CHAPTER

- Where can I find a planning checklist and timeline? *(pages 26–31)*
- What are the six most important tips for avoiding lines at Disney World? *(page 49)*
- What is the Genie+ ride-reservation system, and how do I use it? *(page 59)*

If you don't recognize a term such as *Genie+,* you should read that section of the chapter—it's probably important.

Of course, each chapter answers many more questions than the ones shown on the first page. We suggest skimming each chapter's boldfaced section headings to see if a particular topic is relevant to your family.

Some subjects, such as how Disney accommodates guests in wheelchairs, are relevant across multiple parts of your vacation. These subjects are usually covered in depth in one chapter (in this case, Part Eight, "Special Tips for Special People"), with cross-references in other chapters when they're needed.

Many topics are discussed in depth. For example, Disney World has hundreds of attractions, from simple spinning things you find at your local town carnival to massive super-headliners, the likes of which you've never seen. Understanding the scale of these rides, and how they're run, will help you decide what's worth your time. And if you visit another theme park later, you'll know what to look for when planning that trip too.

If you use the guide like an encyclopedia or dictionary—say, you look something up in one of the indexes then go to the cited page—you may overlook information presented in previous sections that is vital to understanding the subject. Likewise, if you skip or skim over explanatory material in the introductory chapters, that might lead to a misunderstanding later on.

YOUR UNOFFICIAL WALT DISNEY WORLD TOOLBOX

WHEN IT COMES TO WALT DISNEY WORLD, a couple with two toddlers in diapers needs different advice than a party of seniors going to the EPCOT International Flower & Garden Festival. Likewise, adults touring without children, families with kids of varying ages, and honeymooners all require their own special guidance.

To meet the needs of our diverse readers, we've created the comprehensive guide before you. We call *The Unofficial Guide to Walt Disney World,* at 744 pages, the "Big Book." It provides the detailed information that anyone traveling to Walt Disney World needs in order to have a super vacation. It's our cornerstone.

As thorough as we try to make the main guide, though, there just isn't sufficient space for all the tips and resources that may be useful to certain readers. Therefore, we've developed three additional guides that provide information tailored to specific visitors.

Here's what's in the toolbox:

The Unofficial Guide to Disney Cruise Line, by Erin Foster with Len Testa and Ritchey Halphen, presents advice for first-time cruisers; money-saving tips for booking your cruise; and detailed profiles for restaurants, shows, and nightclubs, along with deck plans and thorough coverage of the ports visited by Disney Cruise Line.

The Unofficial Guide to Walt Disney World with Kids, by Bob Sehlinger and Liliane J. Opsomer with Len Testa, presents detailed planning and touring tips for a family vacation, along with more than 20 family touring plans not included in the Big Book.

The Unofficial Guide to Universal Orlando, by Seth Kubersky, is the most comprehensive guide to Universal Orlando Resort in print. At more than 400 pages, it's the perfect tool for understanding and enjoying Universal's ever-expanding complex consisting of theme parks, a water park, resort hotels, nightclubs, and restaurants. The guide includes field-tested touring plans that will save you hours of standing in line.

CORRECTIONS, UPDATES, AND BREAKING NEWS

LOOK FOR THESE at **TouringPlans.com;** see page 23 for a complete description of the site.

LETTERS AND COMMENTS FROM READERS

MANY OF YOU WHO USE *The Unofficial Guide to Walt Disney World* write us to comment or share your own strategies for visiting Disney World. Your feedback is frequently incorporated into future editions of the *Unofficial Guide* and has contributed immeasurably to its ongoing improvement. If you write us or complete our reader survey, rest assured that we won't release your name or address to any mailing-list companies, direct-marketing advertisers, or other third parties.

unofficial **TIP**
If you're up for having your comments quoted in the *Guide,* be sure to tell us where you're from.

Speaking of comments, from the thousands of letters, emails, and surveys we receive, only about 1 in 8 contains comments. Of these, only a small percentage are substantive and well stated. In other words, quotable comments are like gold to us. If a comment on a particular subject hits the nail on the head, it's unlikely (though it happens) that we'll receive a more well-written and more incisive one. If a better comment isn't forthcoming, the older one remains in the next edition because it best serves our readers.

Online Reader Survey

Our website hosts a questionnaire you can use to express opinions about your Walt Disney World visit. Access it here: touringplans.com /walt-disney-world/survey. This questionnaire lets every member of your party, regardless of age, tell us what they think about attractions, hotels, restaurants, and more.

You can also print out the reader survey and mail it to us at the following address:

Reader Survey
The Unofficial Guide to Walt Disney World
2204 First Ave. S., Ste. 102
Birmingham, AL 35233

Finally, if you'd like to review this book on Amazon, go to tinyurl .com/wdw2022reviews.

How to Contact the Authors

Bob Sehlinger and Len Testa
The Unofficial Guide to Walt Disney World
2204 First Ave. S., Ste. 102
Birmingham, AL 35233
info@theunofficialguides.com
Facebook: TheUnofficialGuides | Twitter: @TheUGSeries

When you write, please put your mailing address on both your letter and your envelope—the two sometimes get separated. It's also a good idea to include your phone number. If you email us, please tell us where you're from.

THE *UNOFFICIAL GUIDE* TEAM

ALLOW US TO INTRODUCE THE PEOPLE who work on this book, except for our dining critic, who shall remain anonymous:

- **BOB SEHLINGER** Author and publisher • **LEN TESTA** Coauthor
- **FRED HAZELTON** Statistician • **DAVID DAVIES TouringPlans.com** webmaster
- **JIM HILL** Disney Dish contributor • **TRAVIS BRYANT TheUnofficialGuides.com** webmaster
- **KAREN TURNBOW, PhD** Child psychologist

DATA COLLECTORS	Sue Pisaturo	**EDITORIAL, ART, AND PRODUCTION**
Chantale Brazeau	Laurel Stewart	
Shane Grizzard	Darcie Vance	• **KATE JOHNSON, HOLLY CROSS**
Cliff Myers	Mary Waring	Managing editors
Ivonne Ramos	Deb Wills	• **ANNIE LONG** Text design
Darcie Vance		• **SCOTT McGREW** Cover design
Rich Vosburgh	**HOTEL INSPECTORS**	• **STEVE JONES, CASSANDRA POERTNER** Cartography
Kelly Whitman	Seth Kubersky	
CONTRIBUTING WRITERS	Ritchey Halphen	• **TAMI KNIGHT, CHRIS ELIOPOULOS** Cartoonists
Rich Bernato	Kristen Helmstetter	
Christina Harrison	Lillian Macko	• **POTOMAC INDEXING** Indexers
Brian McNichols	Richard Macko	(**Joanne Sprott**, team leader)
Liliane J. Opsomer	Darcie Vance	

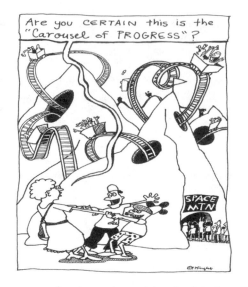

Are you CERTAIN this is the "Carousel of PROGRESS"?

Steve Bloom is the voice of reason in the wilderness that is statistical analysis. Gerelyn Reaves answers email better than we could and generally keeps everyone in line. Seth Kubersky is our Universal Orlando guru, assisted by food consigliere Derek Burgan. Brad Huber developed the latest version of our Lines app, and Julia Mascardo keeps the TouringPlans blog running. Tom Bricker does fabulous theme park photography for the TouringPlans blog. Todd Perlmutter, Bryan Klinck, and EJJ skillfully debugged our touring plan software. Lines's chat is moderated by the fabulous Weasus, Heather, and Camsdad, missoverexcited, and PrincipalTinker.

We'd like to say thanks to these folks for their assistance with fact-checking and research: Ashley Arthur, Robert Bloom, Shannon Bohn, Dani Dennison, Anne Densk, Alyssa Drake, Erin Foster, Becky Gandillon, Scott Gustin, Erin Jenkins, Richard and Lillian Macko, Lauren Macvane, David McDonough, Sarah McWhorter, Susan Roberts McWilliams, Lauren Musni, and Carlye Wisel. Thanks also to Jamie Holding and his GitHub repository (github.com/cubehouse/themeparks). Thanks to John Tierney, who, as far as we know, did not acquire his "data collection" skills during stints in Eastern Europe working for three-letter US government agencies.

Finally, to everyone at Walt Disney Parks and Resorts who follows our research from a distance in this special, weird relationship, even if they can't say it: We love you too.

THE IMPORTANCE OF BEING SERIOUS

SOME ARE ASTONISHED that seemingly intelligent adults would spend so much time on critical analyses of theme park rides. If you've ever heard "You're going to Disney *again?*" from a relative, try explaining to complete strangers your theory that Mrs. Potts is an unreliable narrator. But most of us wouldn't think twice about reading *Consumer Reports* before buying a car or a major appliance. And Disney World costs more than a dishwasher.

Beyond that, the Disney corporation is immensely powerful—it has enough money, talent, and time to do almost anything its executives desire. When Disney's marketing says its theme parks and restaurants are "world-class" and its artists are "legends," it's important to hold it accountable for those words, if they are to mean anything at all.

The best way to do that is to point out whether the things Disney wants to sell you meet the standards it has set for itself. When we say that Rise of the Resistance at Disney's Hollywood Studios is the best theme park ride Disney has made in at least 30 years, it's because we believe it meets the highest of Disney's ideals dating back to Walt himself. Likewise, if you read us kvetching about a cartoon-based roller coaster in EPCOT, or that the adjective *regal* means "fit for a king" and absolutely shouldn't be used in the name of a post-Colonial American restaurant next to an attraction literally dedicated to the republic, it's because those things don't make sense in the stories that Disney has already established. And as Disney says, it all begins with a story.

THE IMPORTANCE OF BEING GOOFY

AT THE SPECIAL EVENTS MEETING, Bert Standup announced excitedly, "We're having a company hoops contest."

"Is that like a cast member basketball tournament?" asked Joe Potash, security chief for special events.

"No," Bert responded, "it's a contest open to all cast members to suggest ways we can make guests jump through more hoops. We already have some good entries. They're judged on guest inconvenience, generating revenue, and how hard they are to comprehend."

"Like what?" Joe wanted to know.

"Well, we have one suggestion that does away with all point-to-point transportation. For example, if you were at Port Orleans and wanted to go to the Magic Kingdom, you'd have to transfer at the Animal Kingdom Lodge."

"Won't that make guests late for dining reservations?" the food and beverage exec (Food Dude) wanted to know.

"That's the beauty part," said Bert. "We'll have point-to-point van transportation for $10 a head."

He continued, "We can extend this concept to attractions where you'd have to transfer to a different boat in the middle of The Jungle Cruise. Also, at theme park parking lots, we can arrange three tram transfers en route to the park entrance."

"If we do it, we should put a concession stand at the transfer points. Make a note," the Food Dude said.

"Here's a good one," Bert commented. "Program all the parks' drinking fountains so guests have to sign in with a Disney app and answer three trivia questions to get a drink."

"I like that," the marketing director chimed in. "Should we also require drinking fountain reservations made 60 days before the guest's visit?"

"No," Bert replied, "but we could take the drinking fountains offline periodically to goose sales for bottled water."

Bert pulled another entry. "Some suggestions are silly, like converting the Dumbo flying elephants from automatic transmission to stick shift. And you know those little sealed packages of ketchup and mustard like they give out at Casey's Corner hotdog eatery in the Magic Kingdom? Well, one entry suggests that we make them twice as hard to open."

"They're already about impossible to open. I always have to use my teeth," offered Doris, the caterer. "If we make them twice as *easy* to open, guests will squirt mustard all over themselves. That would be hilarious."

"Any way to further complicate getting a boarding group for Rise of the Resistance?" an attractions supervisor wanted to know.

Bert furled his brow. "The operations folks who dreamed all that up are gone. Three have been institutionalized, and one is missing in the Amazon rainforest. No one is left who understands it, much less knows how it works. If you can figure it out, let me know."

And so it goes…

What makes writing about Walt Disney World so much fun is that the Disney people take everything so seriously. Day to day, they debate momentous decisions with far-ranging consequences: Will Pluto look silly in a silver cape? Have we gone too far with The Little Mermaid's cleavage? With the nation's drug problem a constant concern, should we have a dwarf named Dopey?

Unofficially, we think having a sense of humor is important. This guidebook has a one, and you'll need one too—not to use the book but to have the most fun possible at Walt Disney World. Think of the *Unofficial Guide* as a private trainer to help get your sense of humor in shape. It will help you understand the importance of being goofy.

UNOFFICIAL GUIDE UPDATES

We expect this 2022 edition to be available through fall 2022. The first set of updates was done in the summer of 2021 and incorporates Disney's current operating procedures at press time, including what we know about new programs like Genie+ ride-reservation system, for those of you planning trips in the next few months. An up-to-date summary of book changes is available at tinyurl.com/wdwupdates.

DISNEY WORLD *in the* POST-COVID VACCINE ERA

WALT DISNEY WORLD CLOSED on March 15, 2020, for 118 days as the novel coronavirus swept through the country. When it reopened on July 11, 2020, its theme parks and resorts implemented a series of new safety procedures designed to keep employees and guests as safe as possible. Some of these procedures, such as temperature screenings before entering the parks and requiring masks to be worn outdoors, have been discontinued now that a significant share of the US population has been vaccinated. For the foreseeable future, Disney requires all guests to wear masks indoors, regardless of vaccination status.

Other changes have been retained, and Disney is using the pandemic as an opportunity to modify others. Among the changes that appear to be more or less permanent are:

- Requiring guests to make an advance reservation to enter a park on a specific date (see page 28)
- Requiring guests to use their mobile phones when ordering from counter-service restaurants (see page 279)
- Limiting the ability to "hop" between parks (see page 71)

unofficial **TIP** We'll reiterate key COVID-related information throughout the following chapters and highlight it with our own masked Wuffo character (at left), but we've tried to centralize the essentials here to avoid overloading the remainder of the book with COVID callouts.

Disney has also used the pandemic as an excuse to end outright certain popular pre-COVID programs or to change them in a way that costs more money. Among these are:

- Extra Magic Hours for resort guests (replaced by Early Theme Park Entry and Extended Evening Theme Park hours; see page 38)
- The FastPass+ ride-reservation system (replaced by Lightning Lane, Genie+, and Individual Attraction Selections; see page 59)
- The Magical Express bus service (see page 420)
- Complimentary Magic Bands for resort guests (see page 78)
- The Disney Dining Plan (see page 206)

Finally, Disney has greatly simplified and made common many of its restaurant menus. That saves Disney money on food costs and labor, but it results in limited dining options for guests.

Other changes will be phased out as travel returns to normal levels and Disney replaces the employees they laid off during the pandemic. Nightly fireworks have already returned to the Magic Kingdom and EPCOT, and Disney has indicated that park capacity limits should be lifted by fall 2021, and all of Disney's hotels will be open by mid-December of 2021.

All up-close character greetings and many stage shows with live performers remain closed. We expect stage shows to return once Disney and the performers union figure out appropriate safety measures for offstage areas. Up-close character greetings should return as well—they're too integral a part of the Disney theme park experience not to—but the health risks may be prohibitive until children under age 12 are vaccinated. We think some live shows that were closed during the pandemic, such as Voyage of the Little Mermaid, may never reopen.

WHAT'S OPEN *at* WALT DISNEY WORLD

THEME PARKS All four of the theme parks are open daily, opening and closing at staggered times to reduce demand on Disney's bus service, which is short on drivers. Operating hours have been reduced from pre-pandemic levels: Expect the parks to be open around 10–14 hours daily during summer and holidays, and 9–12 hours at other times.

Almost all theme park attractions are open. Up-close character greetings and large parades have been suspended. Except for private VIP tours, Disney's guided tours, such as Keys to the Kingdom, are also suspended.

A few counter-service and sit-down restaurants remain closed. See Part Six, "Dining," for more details.

HOTELS AND RESORTS All the Disney hotels will be open by mid-December 2021 and are accepting reservations. Some resort activities and recreation are limited or suspended. See Part Five, "Accommodations," for more details.

TRANSPORTATION Disney's buses, monorails, boats, and Skyliner are running between the theme parks, resorts, and Disney Springs. A few monorail, bus, and boat routes remain closed or altered. See Part Nine, "Arriving and Getting Around," for more details.

WATER PARKS Blizzard Beach is open daily, 11 a.m.–6 p.m. Typhoon Lagoon didn't have an opening date at press time. We expect it to be open by summer 2022.

DINING, SHOPPING, AND NIGHTLIFE All of Disney Springs' restaurants and stores are open, and most are operating at or near 100% of pre-pandemic capacity. Dining reservations are still recommended. Restaurants will encourage you to read menus using your smartphone. Contactless payments (that is, not cash) are encouraged throughout Walt Disney World. See Part Six, "Dining In and Around Disney World," and Part Seventeen, "Disney Springs, Shopping, and Nightlife," for more details.

RECREATION, SPAS, AND BEHIND-THE-SCENES TOURS Disney's golf courses are open. Other recreational activities, spas, and behind-the-scenes tours remain closed. We think it's unlikely that hands-on experiences, such as spa treatments, or large-group park tours will return to the parks as they were. Thus, we've decided not to cover these topics in this edition.

PART ONE

WALT DISNEY WORLD: *An* OVERVIEW

KEY QUESTIONS ANSWERED IN THIS CHAPTER

- What is Walt Disney World? *(see below)*
- How big is Walt Disney World? *(see below and next page)*
- What's the difference between the Magic Kingdom and EPCOT? *(pages 12-13)*
- Are Universal and Disney the same? Where are the Harry Potter rides? *(page 21)*
- What do these new words and acronyms mean? *(page 22)*

▌ WHAT IS DISNEY WORLD?

WE MAY BE BIASED, but we think Walt Disney World (WDW), in Orlando, Florida, is the best collection of theme parks on Earth. Its combined size, quality, and ambition go far beyond that of any other amusement park or theme park you may have seen.

If this is your first visit, you're probably familiar with Disney World through Disney's theme park advertising. It's great at showing families enjoying exciting rides and meeting its famous characters. But 30-second ads don't convey where to find those rides and characters.

Walt Disney World has four theme parks. If you're familiar with any of them, it's probably the **Magic Kingdom**—the first one built and the one most people think of when they hear the words *Disney World*. The other three theme parks are **EPCOT, Disney's Hollywood Studios,** and **Disney's Animal Kingdom.**

Walt Disney World also contains two water parks, **Blizzard Beach** and **Typhoon Lagoon.** But there's more: over three dozen hotels and a campground; more than 100 restaurants; a massive year-round sports center; an outdoor mall/entertainment/hotel complex called **Disney Springs;** six convention centers; four golf courses; and an array of spas, recreation options, and other activities.

HOW BIG IS WALT DISNEY WORLD?

WALT DISNEY WORLD IS HUGE—around 43 square miles, about double the size of Manhattan and slightly smaller than Miami.

For easy reference, we (and Disney) use the theme parks as rough guides to locations within Walt Disney World. The **Magic Kingdom Resort Area,** for example, is about 7 square miles and contains the Magic Kingdom theme park and nearby hotels, restaurants, golf courses, and entertainment. The **EPCOT Resort Area** is roughly 1.5 square miles and contains the EPCOT theme park, nearby hotels and restaurants, and so on. Most of these areas are separated by miles of barely developed Central Florida swampland.

The areas are so far apart that it's not possible to walk between them. Instead, you'll usually get around via the Walt Disney World transportation system's fleet of buses, boats, cars, monorail trains (monorails), and aerial trams. In fact, Disney World's bus system is the third largest in Florida, behind Jacksonville's and Miami's. The Disney transportation system is so large that Part Nine of this book is dedicated to it.

Because of Walt Disney World's size, it would probably take around two weeks to explore most of it. Most families don't have two weeks to spare, so we'll tell you the best things to see in the time you have.

THE MAJOR THEME PARKS

The Magic Kingdom

When most people think of Walt Disney World, they think of the Magic Kingdom, opened in 1971. It consists of **Cinderella Castle** and adventures, rides, and shows featuring the Disney cartoon characters. It's only one element of Disney World, but it remains the heart.

The Magic Kingdom is divided into six "lands" arranged around a central hub. First you come to **Main Street, U.S.A.,** which connects the Magic Kingdom entrance with the hub. Arranged clockwise around the hub are **Adventureland, Frontierland, Liberty Square, Fantasyland,** and **Tomorrowland.** The Magic Kingdom has more rides, shows, and entertainment than any other WDW theme park. A comprehensive tour takes two days; a tour of the highlights can be done in one full day.

Five hotels—**Bay Lake Tower,** the **Contemporary** and **Grand Floridian Resorts, Polynesian Village,** and **The Villas at the Grand Floridian**—are connected to the Magic Kingdom by monorail and boat. Three other hotels—**Shades of Green** (for the US military and their families), **Wilderness Lodge** (incorporating the **Boulder Ridge Villas** and **Copper Creek** time-share units), and **Fort Wilderness Resort & Campground**—are located nearby but are served by boat and bus instead of monorail.

EPCOT

Opened in October 1982, EPCOT is twice as big as the Magic Kingdom and comparable in scope. It has two major areas: **Future World** consists of pavilions concerning human creativity, technological advancement, and—increasingly—cartoon characters; **World Showcase,** arranged around a 40-acre lagoon, presents the architectural, social, and cultural heritages of almost a dozen nations, each country represented by replicas of famous landmarks and settings familiar to world travelers.

The EPCOT resorts—the **BoardWalk Inn & Villas, Dolphin, Swan, Swan Reserve, Yacht & Beach Club Resorts,** and **Beach Club Villas**—are within a 5- to 15-minute walk of the International Gateway, the World Showcase entrance to the theme park. The hotels are also linked to EPCOT and Disney's Hollywood Studios by boat and walkway. EPCOT is connected to the Magic Kingdom and its hotels by monorail. An elevated ski lift–like gondola system called the **Skyliner** links EPCOT and Disney's Hollywood Studios to Disney's Pop Century, Art of Animation, Caribbean Beach, and Riviera Resorts.

Disney's Hollywood Studios

Opened in 1989 in an area a little larger than the Magic Kingdom, Disney's Hollywood Studios (DHS) has two main sections. One area, occupying about 50% of the Studios, is a theme park focused on the motion picture, music, and television industries. Park highlights include a re-creation of Hollywood and Sunset Boulevards from Hollywood's Golden Age, several rides and musical shows, and a movie stunt show.

The other half of DHS is two immersive lands based on popular Disney film franchises: **Toy Story Land** opened in 2018 with two highly themed but relatively simple rides for children. **Star Wars: Galaxy's Edge**, which opened in August 2019, has two state-of-the-art, large rides for older children, teens, and adults.

DHS is connected to other Walt Disney World areas by highway, boat, and Skyliner but not by monorail. Guests can park in DHS's pay parking lot or commute by bus; guests at EPCOT resort hotels can reach DHS by boat, on foot, or by Skyliner.

Disney's Animal Kingdom

About five times the size of the Magic Kingdom, Disney's Animal Kingdom combines zoological exhibits with rides, shows, and live entertainment. The park is arranged in a hub-and-spoke configuration somewhat like the Magic Kingdom. A lush tropical rainforest serves as Main Street, funneling visitors to **Discovery Island,** the park's hub. Dominated by the park's central icon, the 14-story-tall, hand-carved **Tree of Life,** Discovery Island offers services, shopping, and dining. From there, guests can access the themed areas: **Africa, Asia,** and **DinoLand U.S.A.** Discovery Island, Africa, and DinoLand U.S.A. opened in 1998, followed by Asia in 1999. Africa, the largest themed area at 100 acres, is home to free-roaming herds in a re-creation of the Serengeti Plain.

Pandora—The World of Avatar, based on James Cameron's 2009 film *Avatar,* is the most significant recent expansion. Its biggest draws may be the animals and scenery—including "floating mountains" and glow-in-the-dark plants—which Disney has replicated from the movie. See Part Thirteen for full details.

Disney's Animal Kingdom has its own parking lot and is connected to other Walt Disney World destinations by the Disney bus system. Although no hotels lie within Animal Kingdom proper, the **All-Star Resorts, Animal Kingdom Lodge & Villas,** and **Coronado Springs Resort** are all nearby.

THE WATER PARKS

DISNEY WORLD HAS TWO MAJOR WATER PARKS: **Typhoon Lagoon** and **Blizzard Beach.** Opened in

COVID *tip*
The Blizzard Beach water park was open at press time, while no opening date was available for Typhoon Lagoon.

continued on page 18

South Orlando

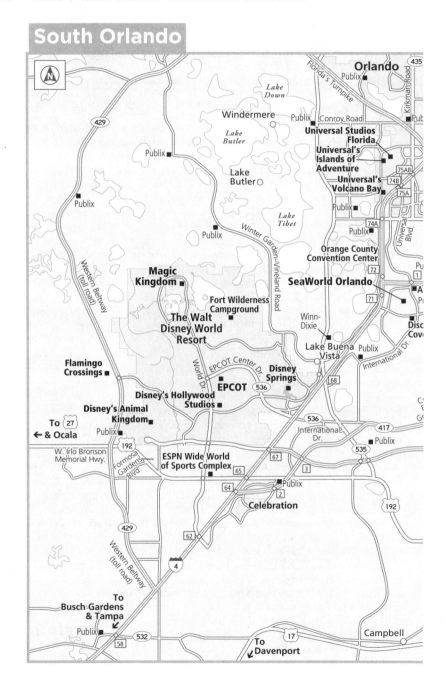

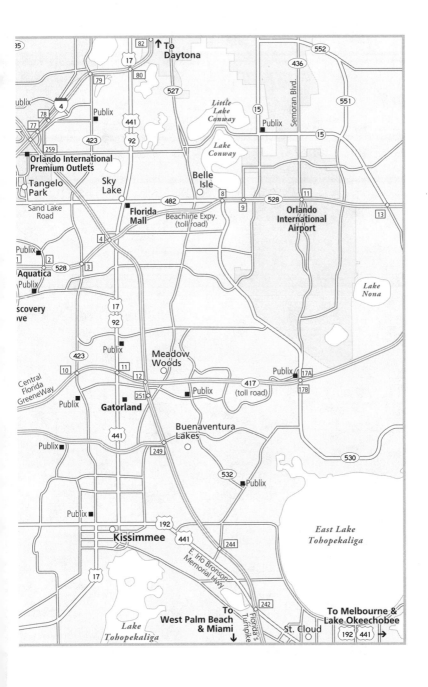

Walt Disney World

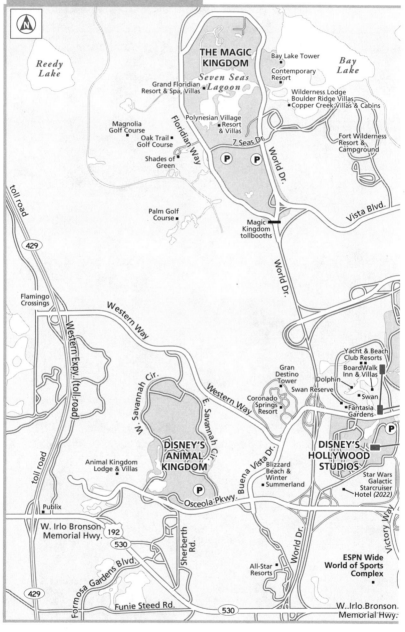

Reedy Lake

THE MAGIC KINGDOM

Seven Seas Lagoon

Bay Lake Tower
Contemporary Resort

Bay Lake

Grand Floridian Resort & Spa, Villas

Wilderness Lodge
Boulder Ridge Villas
Copper Creek Villas & Cabins

Magnolia Golf Course

Polynesian Village Resort & Villas

Oak Trail Golf Course

7 Seas Dr.

Fort Wilderness Resort & Campground

Shades of Green

Floridian Way

toll road

429

Palm Golf Course

Magic Kingdom tollbooths

World Dr.

Vista Blvd.

World Dr.

Flamingo Crossings

Western Way

Yacht & Beach Club Resorts

BoardWalk Inn & Villas

Gran Destino Tower

Dolphin

Swan Reserve

Swan

Coronado Springs Resort

Fantasia Gardens

W. Savannah Cir.

E. Savannah Cir.

Western Way

DISNEY'S ANIMAL KINGDOM

DISNEY'S HOLLYWOOD STUDIOS

Animal Kingdom Lodge & Villas

Buena Vista Dr.

Blizzard Beach & Winter Summerland

Star Wars Galactic Starcruiser Hotel (2022)

toll road

Publix

W. Irlo Bronson Memorial Hwy. 192

530

Osceola Pkwy.

Sherberth Rd.

World Dr.

Victory Way

All-Star Resorts

ESPN Wide World of Sports Complex

429

Formosa Gardens Blvd.

Funie Steed Rd.

530

W. Irlo Bronson Memorial Hwy.

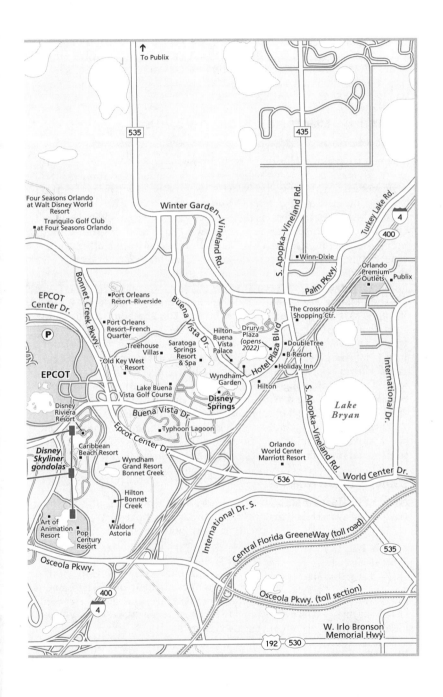

To Publix

535

435

Four Seasons Orlando
at Walt Disney World
Resort

Tranquilo Golf Club
at Four Seasons Orlando

Winter Garden–Vineland Rd.

S. Apopka–Vineland Rd.

Turkey Lake Rd.

4

400

Palm Pkwy.

Winn-Dixie

Orlando
Premium
Outlets

Publix

EPCOT
Center Dr.

Bonnet Creek Pkwy.

Port Orleans
Resort–Riverside

Port Orleans
Resort–French
Quarter

Buena Vista Dr.

The Crossroads
Shopping Ctr.

Hilton
Buena
Vista
Palace

Drury
Plaza
(opens
2022)

Hotel Plaza Blvd.

DoubleTree

B Resort

Holiday Inn

Treehouse
Villas

Saratoga
Springs
Resort
& Spa

P

Old Key West
Resort

EPCOT

Wyndham
Garden

Hilton

Lake Buena
Vista Golf Course

Disney
Springs

Disney
Riviera
Resort

Buena Vista Dr.

International Dr.

Lake
Bryan

Typhoon Lagoon

**Disney
Skyliner
gondolas**

Caribbean
Beach Resort

Wyndham
Grand Resort
Bonnet Creek

Epcot Center Dr.

Orlando
World Center
Marriott Resort

S. Apopka–Vineland Rd.

World Center Dr.

536

Hilton
Bonnet
Creek

International Dr. S.

Art of
Animation
Resort

Pop
Century
Resort

Waldorf
Astoria

Central Florida GreeneWay (toll road)

535

Osceola Pkwy.

Osceola Pkwy. (toll section)

400

4

W. Irlo Bronson
Memorial Hwy.

192   530

continued from page 13

1989, Typhoon Lagoon is distinguished by a wave pool capable of making 6-foot waves. Blizzard Beach opened in 1995 and features more slides. Both parks pay great attention to atmosphere and aesthetics. Typhoon Lagoon and Blizzard Beach have their own parking lots and can be reached by Disney bus.

OTHER WALT DISNEY WORLD VENUES

Disney Springs

Themed to evoke a Florida waterfront town, Disney Springs encompasses four areas, each with shopping, dining, and entertainment: the **Marketplace,** on the east; the **West Side,** on (surprise!) the west; **The Landing,** on the waterfront; and **Town Center.**

The Marketplace contains the country's largest store selling Disney-character merchandise; upscale resort-wear and specialty shops; and numerous restaurants. The West Side is a diverse mix of nightlife, shopping, dining, and notable entertainment. That entertainment includes a dedicated **Cirque du Soleil** show found only at Disney World, although an opening date has not been announced.

The Landing offers additional shopping and arguably the best dining options in Disney Springs. These include **The Boathouse,** an upscale waterfront seafood eatery with better steaks than anything nearby; **Morimoto Asia,** a high-quality, midpriced table-service restaurant from Iron Chef Masaharu Morimoto; **Chef Art Smith's Homecomin',** a restaurant from celebrity chef and Florida native Art Smith that features local farm-to-table ingredients, traditional Southern cooking, and excellent cocktails; and **Wine Bar George,** serving tasty Mediterranean small plates and a well-curated list of affordable wines.

Disney Springs includes three multistory parking garages, with short walks to the middle of the action. It is also accessible via Disney transportation from Disney resort hotels and theme parks.

Disney's BoardWalk

Near EPCOT, the BoardWalk is an idealized replication of a 1930s East Coast waterfront resort. Open all day, the BoardWalk features upscale restaurants, shops and galleries, a brewpub, and an ESPN sports bar. In the evening, a nightclub with dueling pianos and a DJ dance club join the lineup. Both are for guests age 21 and up only. There's no

COVID *tip*
The dance club was closed at press time

admission fee for the BoardWalk, but the piano bar levies a cover charge at night. This area is anchored by the **BoardWalk Inn & Villas,** along with its adjacent convention center.

The BoardWalk is within walking distance of the EPCOT resorts, EPCOT's International Gateway, and Disney's Hollywood Studios. Boat transportation is available to and from EPCOT and Disney's Hollywood Studios, the Skyliner connects the BoardWalk to the Studios and the hotels on its route, and buses serve other Walt Disney World locations.

Disney Cruise Line: The Mouse at Sea

Disney launched (literally) its own cruise line in 1998 with the 2,400-passenger *Disney Magic.* Three more ships were added, and three more will join the soon-to-be seven-ship fleet starting in 2022. Most cruises depart from Port Canaveral, Florida (about a 90-minute drive from Walt Disney World), or from Miami on three-, four-, and seven-night itineraries. Bahamian and Caribbean cruises include a day at **Castaway Cay,** Disney's 1,000-acre private island. Cruises can be packaged with a stay at Disney World. Disney offers a free online video at disneyplanning.com to help familiarize you with Disney Cruise Line cruises.

To get the most out of your cruise, check out *The Unofficial Guide to Disney Cruise Line,* by Erin Foster with Len Testa and Ritchey Halphen.

WHAT'S NEW AT WALT DISNEY WORLD

Disneyland is something that will never be finished. It's something that I can keep developing. It will be a live, breathing thing that will need change.

—Walt Disney

WHAT WALT SAID OF DISNEYLAND is also true of Disney World. The table on pages 21–22 shows all the major construction projects that have been completed at Walt Disney World in the last 2, 5, and 10 years.

THE PEOPLE OF WALT DISNEY WORLD

DISNEY'S EMPLOYEES are called **cast members.** How you're treated by the ones you encounter can make or break a vacation. Fortunately, Disney staff often go the extra mile to make your visit special, as the following three readers report.

First, from a family from Pawnee, Illinois, who was assisted in a health emergency:

On our first day at the resort, our 6-year-old grandson woke up with a deep cough, fever, and kind of wheezing. Our daughter-in-law contacted the desk and found that WDW provided a shuttle to a local prompt-care facility. As it turned out, the shuttle wasn't available, so they called a cab instead and covered the cost! Our grandson was able to be seen by a physician and received medication that allowed him to get better and salvage the trip. We can't say enough about what the staff and WDW did for us that day! They were terrific!

A family from St. Joseph, Michigan, had this to relate:

We had a very unexpected and wonderful surprise waiting in our stroller after the Country Bear Jamboree. *Out of nearly 30 strollers, ours had been visited by Santa Mickey while we were in the show. We came out to a stroller decorated with silly bands, Christmas ornaments, and a snowman Mickey plush toy. Our 5-year-old son, not to mention the rest of our party, were delighted. Just another way that WDW goes one more step to make a magical experience.*

Finally, from a suburban Philadelphia family:

At Expedition Everest, I witnessed expert handling of a group of teenage line-jumpers by Disney staff. Once they reached the loading

continued on page 21

WHAT'S NEW AT WALT DISNEY WORLD SINCE YOUR LAST VISIT

LAST 2 YEARS

- Disney ended its free Magical Express bus service between Orlando International Airport and the Walt Disney World Resort.

- Disney's free FastPass+ ride reservation system was replaced by a paid system called Genie+ and Lightning Lane

- Disney ended its Extra Magic Hours program for resort guests. Extra Magic Hour Mornings were cut to 30 minutes, but expanded to all four theme parks in a program called Early Theme Park Entry. Extra Magic Hour Evenings were replaced by Extended Evening Theme Park Hours, but only for guests at Deluxe and DVC resorts.

- Disney ended its complimentary Magic Band program for Disney World resort guests.

- **EPCOT** opened a new nighttime show called **_Harmonious_** in October 2021, along with **Remy's Ratatouille Adventure,** a sit-down ride based on the Pixar film _Ratatouille_. A roller coaster based on Marvel's _Guardians of the Galaxy_ might open in 2022.

- The **Magic Kingdom** debuted a new nighttime show, **_Disney Enchantment,_** featuring fireworks and digital projection technology that extends special effects from Cinderella Castle to Main Street, U.S.A. A new ride based on the _Tron_ films is also in the works for Tomorrowland, possibly opening in 2022.

- Hollywood Studios opened **Mickey and Minnie's Runaway Railway,** an immersive 3D ride through the new Mickey Mouse cartoon universe.

- A _Star Wars_–themed hotel, **Star Wars: Galactic Starcruiser,** opens in 2022 with two-day role-playing adventures that start at $4,800 per couple.

LAST 5 YEARS

- The land **Star Wars: Galaxy's Edge** opened at **Disney's Hollywood Studios (DHS),** with two new state-of-the-art rides, and _Star Wars_–themed dining options.

- **Disney's Riviera Resort,** a Disney Vacation Club property, opened in 2019 adjacent to the Caribbean Beach Resort. Connecting the Riviera to EPCOT and DHS is the new **Disney Skyliner** elevated gondola system, which also links Disney's Pop Century, Art of Animation, and Caribbean Beach Resorts with each other and those theme parks.

- **Disney's Coronado Springs Resort** opened the 15-story **Gran Destino Tower** in 2019, with more-upscale guest rooms and dining options.

- **Hollywood Studios** opened **Toy Story Land,** with two new rides: **Alien Swirling Saucers** is a variation on an amusement park spinning ride, while **Slinky Dog Dash** is a mild roller coaster that's more fun than it might seem at first glance.

- The remodeling of **Disney's Animal Kingdom** is complete with **Pandora—The World of Avatar,** with two new attractions and glowing "bioluminescent" plants. The adventurous restaurant **Tiffins** opened with the accompanying **Nomad Lounge.** The nighttime spectacular **Rivers of Light** debuted but has since been discontinued. Other nighttime activities like the **evening Kilimanjaro Safaris** (temporarily suspended) and multiple entertainment acts, also debuted.

- At the **Magic Kingdom,** the longtime fireworks spectacular _Wishes_ was replaced by the fantastic **_Happily Ever After_** (which was replaced by **_Disney Enchantment_** in 2021).

- **EPCOT** unveiled the **Festival of the Arts,** which runs from mid-January to February.

- **Hollywood Studios** began the road toward **Star Wars: Galaxy's Edge** with **Star Wars Launch Bay** and **_Star Wars: A Galactic Spectacular,_** a themed fireworks show.

- **Copper Creek Villas & Cabins** at **Disney's Wilderness Lodge Resort** opened, adding refurbished Disney Vacation Club rooms and two-bedroom cabins along Bay Lake, as well as the new **Geyser Point Bar & Grill.**

LAST 10 YEARS

- **New Fantasyland** opened in the **Magic Kingdom,** comprising **Seven Dwarfs Mine Train; Under the Sea: Journey of the Little Mermaid; Enchanted Tales with Belle;** and **Be Our Guest Restaurant.** Also at the Magic Kingdom, **Jungle Navigation Co. Skipper Canteen** offers table-service dining in Adventureland with all the whimsy of the Jungle Cruise, and **Festival of Fantasy** became the new daytime parade.

WHAT'S NEW AT WALT DISNEY WORLD SINCE YOUR LAST VISIT *(continued)*

LAST 10 YEARS *(continued)*

- The **FastPass+** ride-reservation system, with online and mobile apps, replaced the paper-based Fastpass system in use since 1998.

- **MagicBands,** flexible, RFID-enabled bracelets, were introduced as a form of admission and a way to use FastPass+ reservations, pay for food and merchandise, and more.

- **EPCOT** saw the opening of **Frozen Ever After,** a ride themed on the popular film *Frozen.*

- *For the First Time in Forever: A Frozen Sing-Along Celebration* opened at **DHS.**

- **Disney's Polynesian Villas & Bungalows** opened, adding studios, suites, and over-the-water two-bedroom bungalows on Seven Seas Lagoon. The nearby **Villas at Disney's Grand Floridian Resort & Spa** also opened with studios and one-, two-, and three-bedroom suites.

- **Disney's Art of Animation,** a Value resort, opened with many one-bedroom suites.

continued from page 19

> *area, cast members ushered them aside in a very calm and friendly fashion, causing no apparent disruption. I didn't see where they were ushered or what happened next, but I did not see them board the ride. It was as if they were never there.*

▌▌ UNIVERSAL ORLANDO

LIKE WALT DISNEY WORLD, the Universal Orlando Resort consists of two theme parks, a water park, several hotels, dozens of restaurants, and other entertainment venues. It sits about 14 miles east of Walt Disney World, just off I-4.

Both resorts are owned by media companies: Comcast owns Universal, and the Walt Disney Company owns Walt Disney World. Thus, admission tickets bought for Disney World can't be used at Universal, and vice versa.

Because they're owned by different companies, Disney and Universal are generally viewed as direct competitors—the time and money you spend in one place are time and money not spent in the other. In reality, we think the Disney and Universal parks complement each other; if you're in Orlando for themed entertainment, it's worth visiting both.

Universal's big claims to fame are its spectacular lands themed to the *Harry Potter* film franchise: **Harry Potter and the Forbidden Journey** at **Universal's Islands of Adventure (IOA)** and **Harry Potter and the Escape from Gringotts** at **Universal Studios Florida (USF)**. Both are highly detailed areas with amazing technology and beloved characters. (Len has never seen the films or read the books yet happily spent 6 hours exploring just Diagon Alley.) And Universal continues to expand, adding more hotels and rides to its almost 1,000 acres of land. Its new high-speed coaster, **VelociCoaster,** is the best of its kind in Orlando.

Universal is a high-quality alternative to Walt Disney World, so we cover its basics in this guide. For an in-depth guide to everything Universal has to offer, try *The Unofficial Guide to Universal Orlando,* by Seth Kubersky.

POCKET TRANSLATOR FOR COMMON DISNEY AND UNIVERSAL ABBREVIATIONS

IT MAY COME AS A SURPRISE to many, but Walt Disney World has its own somewhat peculiar language. Below are some abbreviations and slang you're likely to bump into, both in this guide and in the larger Disney (and Universal) community.

COMMON ABBREVIATIONS AND WHAT THEY STAND FOR	
ADR Advance Dining Reservation	**I-DRIVE** International Drive (a major Orlando thoroughfare)
BG Boarding group (for RoTR)	**IOA** Universal's Islands of Adventure theme park
CM Cast member	**MDE** My Disney Experience mobile app
DCL Disney Cruise Line	**RoTR** Star Wars: Rise of the Resistance ride
DDV Disney Deluxe Villas	**TTC** Ticket and Transportation Center
DHS Disney's Hollywood Studios	**USF** Universal Studios Florida theme park
DSRA Disney Springs Resort Area	**WDI** Walt Disney Imagineering
DTS Disney Transportation System	**WDTC** Walt Disney Travel Company
DVC Disney Vacation Club	**WDW** Walt Disney World
ETPE Early Theme Park Entry (formerly Extra Magic Hours, or EMH)	

THE DISNEY LEXICON IN A NUTSHELL
ADVENTURE Ride	**ATTRACTION** Ride or theater show
ATTRACTION HOST Ride operator	**AUDIENCE** Crowd
BACKSTAGE Behind the scenes, out of view of customers
CAST MEMBER Employee
CHARACTER Disney character impersonated by an employee
COSTUME Work attire or uniform	**DARK RIDE** Indoor ride
DAY GUEST Any customer not staying at a Disney resort
DRC Disney Reservation Center
FACE CHARACTER A character who doesn't wear a head-covering costume (Snow White, Cinderella, Jasmine, and the like)
GENERAL PUBLIC Same as day guest
GREETER Employee positioned at an attraction entrance	**GUEST** Customer
HIDDEN MICKEYS Frontal silhouette of Mickey's head worked subtly into the design of buildings, railings, golf greens, attractions, and just about anything else
OFF-SITE HOTEL A hotel located outside of Walt Disney World's boundaries
ON-SITE HOTEL A hotel located inside Walt Disney World's boundaries and served by Disney's transportation network
ONSTAGE In full view of customers
PRESHOW Entertainment at an attraction before the feature presentation
RESORT GUEST A customer staying at a Disney resort
ROLE A cast member's job
SOFT OPENING The opening of a park or attraction before its stated opening date
TRANSITIONAL EXPERIENCE An element of the queuing area and/or preshow that provides information essential to understanding the attraction

PLANNING *before* YOU LEAVE HOME

Visiting Walt Disney World is a bit like childbirth—you never really believe what people tell you, but once you have been through it yourself, you know exactly what they were saying!

—Hilary Wolfe, a mother and
Unofficial Guide reader from Swansea, Wales

GATHERING INFORMATION

IN ADDITION TO USING THIS GUIDE, we recommend that you visit our sister website, **TouringPlans.com.** The companion blog posts breaking news for Walt Disney World, Universal Orlando, Disney Cruise Line, and Disneyland.

TouringPlans.com complements and augments the information in our books, and it provides real-time personal services that are impossible to build into a book. The book is your comprehensive reference source; TouringPlans.com is your personal concierge. Sign up for free here: touringplans.com/walt-disney-world/join/basic.

With that free access, you'll be able to create custom touring plans, follow them in the parks, and get updates to them if conditions change while you're there. You'll also find up-to-the-minute information on attractions, shows, restaurants, crowds, park hours, and more.

A few parts of the site require a small subscription fee to access, such as a detailed, day-by-day crowd calendar or a service that sends your hotel room request directly to Disney. That fee covers the costs of the extra people, technology, and external services that it takes to provide them, beyond what's needed for the books.

Below is a brief rundown of some things you'll find on the site. If this looks like a long advertisement, it's because we still receive many requests each year asking us for tools and information—such as where to find ticket discounts—that are already available on the site for free.

TICKET DISCOUNTS A free customizable search helps you find the cheapest tickets for your specific needs. A typical family of four saves around $130 on average by purchasing admission from one of our recommended ticket wholesalers.

CUSTOM TOURING PLANS The best and most efficient touring plans are found in these guidebooks. They've been used by hundreds of thousands of families over the years, usually with excellent results. They depend, however, on your arriving at the park before opening. For some families with children, and for those who bristle at rising early while on vacation, being on hand for park opening is a nonstarter. In those cases, and for others with unique circumstances, we provide custom touring plans online.

If getting up early isn't an issue, you can customize the plans in this book by simply skipping any attractions that don't interest you.

A DETAILED 365-DAY CROWD CALENDAR FOR EACH THEME PARK Subscribers can see which parks will be the least crowded every day of their trip, using a 1–10 scale. You can also view historical crowd data and check the accuracy of our predictions.

HOTEL-ROOM VIEWS AND ONLINE EMAIL SERVICE We have photos of the views from every hotel room in Walt Disney World—more than 35,000 images in all—and we'll give you the exact wording to use for requesting a specific room. For subscribers, we'll even automatically email your request to Disney before you arrive. A mother who used the service writes:

> *The send-ahead feature was wonderful! We got a room with a GORGEOUS river view! My husband's jaw dropped when he saw what our view was like! He immediately gave me a big high-five. Thanks!*

Disney tries to accommodate your request, but its ability to do that depends on variables we can't control. Most of the requests we send on behalf of readers are honored in full or partially, but sometimes Disney just can't make it work. Feel fortunate if you get what you asked for.

GENIE+/LIGHTNING LANE INFORMATION When it's offered, the site shows every Lightning Lane and Individual Attraction reservation available.

ANSWERS TO YOUR TRIP-PLANNING QUESTIONS Our online community includes tens of thousands of Disney experts and fans willing to help with your vacation plans. Ask questions and offer your own helpful tips.

LINES APP Our in-park app, Lines, is available on the Apple App Store and the Google Play Store. For years, Lines has been the highest-rated Disney World app for Apple and Android devices—higher than even

Disney's own apps. Designed to accompany you in the park, Lines has lots of interesting, free features and provides ride and park information that Disney doesn't, including:

- **Posted and actual wait times at attractions.** Lines is the only Disney-parks app that displays both posted wait times and the actual times you'll wait in line. The wait time you see posted outside of a ride is sometimes much longer than the real wait time, often because Disney's trying to do crowd control. With Lines, you can make better decisions about what to see.

- **"Ride now or wait" recommendations.** Lines shows you whether ride wait times are likely to get longer or shorter. If you find a long line at a particular attraction, Lines tells you the best time to come back.

- **Real-time touring plan updates while you're in a park.** Lines automatically updates your custom touring plan to reflect actual crowd conditions at a given moment. You can also restart your plan and add or change attractions, breaks, meals, and more.

The *Unofficial Guide* and TouringPlans.com, along with the Lines app, are designed to work together as a comprehensive planning and touring resource.

This mom from St. Louis used all of the tools in our toolbox:

The Unofficial Guide *was the perfect place to start planning our vacation (actually our honeymoon). After reading the book, I had a good idea of what hotels I was interested in, and I had must-do and must-eat places somewhat picked out. I then took the knowledge from the book and switched to the website to personalize our touring plans and use as a reference when needed. The book and the website together made our trip INCREDIBLE.*

A mother from Lexington, South Carolina, echoes the sentiments of the mom above:

The Lines app and the personalized touring plans were unbeatable! If we missed a step or took extra time on something, it was so easy to catch right back up. The book allowed me to preplan our entire trip, from what to pack to what to see and eat. It was priceless. We traveled during Thanksgiving week, so the parks were at very high crowd levels. The planning allowed us to maximize the use of our time and quietly rejoice that we weren't the ones standing in line for hours.

Our other website, **TheUnofficialGuides.com,** is dedicated to news about our guidebooks and features a blog with posts from *Unofficial Guide* authors. You can also sign up for the **"Unofficial Guides Newsletter,"** which contains even more travel tips and special offers. Next, we recommend that you obtain the following:

1. **WALT DISNEY WORLD RESORT VACATION-PLANNING VIDEOS** Disney has online videos advertising Walt Disney World's offerings at disneyplanning.com. You can access videos about Disney Cruise Line and other Disney destinations from the same website.

2. **GUIDE FOR GUESTS WITH DISABILITIES** An overview of services and options for guests with disabilities is available at disneyworld.disney .go.com/guest-services/guests-with-disabilities; at Guest Relations when entering the parks; at resort front desks; and at wheelchair-rental areas (locations are listed in each theme park chapter).

3. **VISIT ORLANDO DEALS** If you're considering lodging outside Disney World or think you might patronize out-of-the-World attractions and restaurants, obtain a Free Vacation Planning Kit and the *Orlando Official*

Visitors Guide (both free) from the **Visit Orlando Official Visitors Center.** The discounts cover hotels, restaurants, ground transportation, shopping malls, dinner theaters, and Disney and non-Disney theme parks and attractions. For more information, view the deals at visitorlando .com and click on "Offers." Or call ☎ 407-363-5872 from 8 a.m. to 8 p.m. Eastern time year-round. You can also download the Visit Orlando app and sign up for emails on the website.

YOUR DISNEY TRIP-PLANNING TIMELINE, AKA THE QUICK-START GUIDE TO USING THE *GUIDE*

AS YOU GO THROUGH THIS BOOK, you'll see many references to date-specific planning milestones for your trip: As we went to press, you could make Disney park reservations for dates through January 2023 and dining reservations 60 days before your arrival. And you might be wondering about other milestone dates that are important to know for your Disney trip.

Starting on the next page is a comprehensive timeline that represents the major research, decisions, and tasks that come into play when preparing for a typical Walt Disney World vacation. Next to each milestone, we've put a reference to the section in this book that has the information you need for that milestone, and/or links to our website and blog for additional material like photos or videos.

Most Disney trips involve about a dozen important dates to remember. If you've started planning more than 11 months before your trip, you'll have plenty of time to do research ahead of those dates. If you've decided to visit Disney World within the next couple of months, you'll want to move a bit quicker.

Do you really need to do this? Absolutely—the demand for park reservations and restaurants can easily outstrip their capacity, and you may not get to experience them without planning and reservations. Consider that in July 2021 Disney's Hollywood Studios and Magic Kingdom showed no available park reservations for several days around Thanksgiving, Christmas and New Year's Eve—four to five months in advance. And a hot restaurant such as Be Our Guest, running at full speed, can serve lunch to a tiny percentage of people who want to eat there.

Making park and dining reservations as soon as possible is vital if you want to eat at nice restaurants and avoid hours-long waits at popular rides. Other reservations, such as those for spas or recreational activities, aren't currently offered. When they are, they can frequently be made when you arrive in Orlando, especially if you're visiting during a slower time of year or if you're flexible with the date or time of your appointment. But your best bet is to research early and make reservations as soon as Disney allows.

How to Plan in a Hurry

We get variations on this email a lot:

> *OMG! Our first Disney trip is in three weeks, and I just found out about the* Unofficial Guide. *I had no idea about all the preparation I should have done! What do I do?*

Three weeks is plenty of time. You'll still want to go through the timeline below, because those steps are important, if not mandatory— you'll just have a more compressed schedule.

If your preferred places to eat are already booked, check out our guide on page 276 that shows highly rated alternatives to hard-to-get restaurants. Also check **TouringPlans.com** for advice.

You'll also want to follow the touring plans in the back of this book—they're your insurance against long waits in line. The plans suggest which ride reservations to get and when. If our recommendations aren't available, our free touring plan software can make alternative suggestions and work with whatever Lightning Lane reservations you can get.

12–9 Months Before Your Trip

You may already have a general idea of when you want to visit Disney World. What the trip will cost you, however, can be a surprise. Take a couple of evenings to plan a budget and an approximate time of year to travel, and to narrow down your hotel choices.

- **Establish a budget.** See pages 66–68 in Part Four for an idea of how much Disney vacation you can get for $2,000–$4,000, for various family sizes. More information is available at tinyurl.com/2000-disney-vacation.

- **Check health department advice from your home state,** plus that of Florida and any other state where you'll spend more than 24 hours, at tiny url.com/ushealthdepts. While no quarantines or vaccine mandates were in effect as we went to press, things may change, and this gives you an idea of whether you'll need to add days to self-quarantine on either side of your trip.

- **Figure out when to go and where to stay.** Begin researching resorts (see Part Five) and the best times of year to visit to avoid crowds (see page 34). Our own Erin Foster has devised an excellent method for finding the best vacation dates for your family. See her planning blog at tinyurl.com /planningwdw.

- **Brush up on discounts.** Disney releases certain discounts around the same time every year. Check mousesavers.com for a list of these regular discounts, when they're usually announced, and the travel dates they cover at tinyurl.com/wdw-historic-discounts. Also see our section on hotel discounts beginning on page 91 in Part Five.

- **Create an account at My Disney Experience** (see page 33). You'll need it to make park, hotel, dining, and ride reservations later.

- **Make a preliminary hotel reservation.** This typically requires a deposit equal to one night's cost and guarantees you a room. (It also opens up a separate pool of park reservations to you.) You can change or cancel without penalty for several months while you continue your research.

- **Disney Vacation Club** (DVC) members can make reservations at their home resorts starting 11 months before their trip. See page 94 for information on how to rent points from a DVC member.

- **Investigate whether trip insurance makes sense for your situation.** If you'll be traveling to Disney World during peak hurricane season (August and September), it might be worthwhile. Third-party policies, such as those from insuremytrip.com, are usually cheaper than Disney's trip insurance and are often more comprehensive.

- **If you're not a US citizen, make sure your family's passports and visas are in order.** Passports typically need to be valid for six months beyond your travel dates. An electronic US visa is typically good for two years from the date of issue, if you need one. See esta.cbp.dhs.gov/esta for details. As of 2020, you must apply for a visa at least 72 hours prior to arrival.

9–7 Months Before Your Trip

Now is the time to start thinking about where you'll be eating and what you want to do in the theme parks.

- **Purchase your park admission** at least this far in advance (see pages 70–74 for ticket details and add-ons). Our Least Expensive Ticket Calculator will find you the best discounts on Disney tickets: touringplans.com /walt-disney-world/ticket-calculator.
- **Link your tickets to your My Disney Experience account,** so you can make park reservations now (see next item) and dining reservations at the 60-day mark.
- **Make park reservations.** Disney World requires you to make a theme park reservation in addition to purchasing valid admission to that park. At press time, reservations were available through at least January 2023. Visit disneyworld.disney.go.com/park-reservations to get started.
- **Disney Vacation Club** members can make resort reservations outside their home resorts starting seven months before their trip.
- **Check the best days to visit each park.** Use our Disney World Crowd Calendar to select the parks you'll visit on each day of your trip: touring plans.com/walt-disney-world/crowd-calendar.

6–4 Months Before Your Trip

Familiarize yourself with Disney's rides, shows, and attractions, and start planning what you'll see each day. This will help you identify potential bottlenecks, which you can address using our touring plans and Disney's Lightning Lane/Genie/Genie+/Individual Attraction Selections programs.

- **Review the attractions and shows** at the Magic Kingdom (page 459), EPCOT (page 507), Disney's Animal Kingdom (page 542), and Disney's Hollywood Studios (page 571).
- **Make a list of must-see attractions in each park.** If you're unsure whether your child should experience a particular attraction, see our Small-Child Fright Potential Table on pages 390–392. Every attraction is listed. A table on page 394 lists height requirements for the attractions. Finally, you can preview attractions on YouTube at tinyurl.com/wdw-ride-videos.
- **Review our touring plans** (see page 710) and use them to begin putting together a touring strategy for each park. You can also use our touring plan software: See touringplans.com/walt-disney-world/touring-plans. By starting now, you'll be able to see what attractions would benefit from Lightning Lane ride reservations (if available). You'll also see whether you'll need the Park Hopper option on your theme park tickets, which you'll purchase later.

180 Days Before Your Trip

Now you can start making tour, spa, and other reservations. These timelines may change (perhaps to 60 days in advance) once these activities return.

- **Make reservations for the following** (all temporarily suspended):
    Theme park tours: ☎ 407-WDW-TOUR (939-8687)
    Recreational activities such as boating: ☎ 407-WDW-PLAY (939-7529)
    Spa treatments: ☎ 407-WDW-SPAS (939-7727)
    Bibbidi Bobbidi Boutique (page 664): ☎ 407-WDW-STYL (939-7895)
- **Get familiar with Disney World restaurants** (see Part Six). When Disney's dining reservation system opens at your 60-day mark, you can make

reservations. See touringplans.com/walt-disney-world/dining for current menus and prices at every Disney restaurant, all searchable.

- **Also get familiar with the Disney Dining Plan** (temporarily suspended, but Disney says it will return; see Part Five, page 206). If you're planning to stay at a Disney hotel, you'll need to figure out if the plan will save you money on the restaurants you've identified.

120 Days Before Your Trip

As your vacation approaches, it's time to make concrete arrangements for your days in the theme parks.

- **Save money on stroller rentals in the parks** (if needed) by renting from a third-party company; see page 384 for our recommendations. You can also **save on wheelchair and ECV rentals** this way; see page 406 for details and recommendations.
- **Recheck the health department advice for your home state,** plus those of Florida and any other state in which you'll spend more than 24 hours, at tinyurl.com/ushealthdepts.
- As we went to press, Disney had not implemented any specific policies around vaccination status for its guests, such as requiring vaccinations for indoor dining. But **make copies of your COVID vaccination cards,** including on your phone, in case things change.

60 Days Before Your Trip

- **Make reservations for sit-down dining** beginning at 5:45 a.m. Eastern time online at disneyworld.disney.go.com/dining, or at 6:45 a.m. by phone (see page 271 for tips): ☎ 407-WDW-DINE (939-3463). If you're staying at a Walt Disney World resort, you can make reservations for up to 10 days of your trip today. You have a better chance of getting what you want if you use the website instead of calling.
- **Revisit the economics of the Disney Dining Plan** (temporarily suspended, but it will return) after you've made dining reservations, to verify it's still worth the money. If not, call Disney to drop it from your reservation.
- **Start a walking regimen** to prepare for the 7–10 miles per day you may be walking in the parks. See page 374 for more on that.
- **Try a ride-hailing service** like Lyft or Uber. These services are often the fastest way to get between your hotel and the airport or theme parks, and they're cheaper than taxis. Download one of these apps to your smartphone, create an account, and take a short trip in your hometown to become familiar with how they work.
- **If you decide not to go to Disney World,** you typically have 30 days to cancel most Disney vacation packages without a penalty; room-only reservations can be canceled without a penalty until six days before your trip. See page 89 for a review of Disney's cancellation policies, as they may be more flexible during the pandemic. Otherwise, you can start your online check-in at Disney resorts 60 days before you arrive.

45 Days Before Your Trip

- **Final payment for room-only reservations** is due if you book online within 45 days of arrival (payment of room-only reservations booked farther out isn't due until check-in).
- **Order your MagicBands** (page 78) if desired.
- **If you're flying,** make arrangements for your transfer between the airport and your hotel (see page 420).
- **If you want to switch resorts** or make additional dining reservations, now is a good time to check, owing to cancellations at the 45-day mark.

- **Recheck the quarantine policies for your home state,** plus those of Florida and any other state in which you'll spend more than 24 hours, at tinyurl.com/ushealthdepts.
- **Travelers age 2 and up** entering the United States from another country (including returning US citizens), make an appointment to get a coronavirus test no more than three days prior to entering the United States.

30 Days Out

- **Send your room request to Disney.** We can do this for you automatically. See tinyurl.com/wdw-hotel-fax for details.
- **Final payment is due for Disney vacation packages.**
- **Sign up for Disney's Disability Access Service** (DAS; see page 405) between 30 and 2 days before your trip. You'll be able to make two ride reservations in advance. See tinyurl.com/DAS-at-WDW for more details.
- **Confirm park hours** and finish preliminary touring plans.
- **Download our Lines app** so you can follow your touring plan and get updates in the parks: touringplans.com/disney-world-app.
- **Arrange to stop delivery of mail and newspapers.**
- **Arrange for pet or house sitters.**

2 Weeks Out

- **Arrange grocery delivery to your resort** (see Part Ten, page 458).
- **If you're flying to the US from another country,** complete the **Advance Passenger Information and Secure Flight** (**APIS**) process at least 72 hours before your flight. You should be able to do this through your airline's website; otherwise, make sure your travel agent has your information. You'll need to provide the address where you'll be staying in the United States, so have that information handy when you complete this form.
- **Check that you have enough prescription medication.**
- **Triple-check the health department advice for your home state,** plus those of Florida and any other state in which you'll spend more than 24 hours, at tinyurl.com/ushealthdepts.

6 Days Out

- This is typically your last chance to **cancel Disney room-only reservations booked *online*** without a penalty. Call ☎ W-DISNEY (407-934-7639).
- **Check the weather forecast** for Orlando: tinyurl.com/wdw-weather.
- **Start packing.** See touringplans.com/blog/tag/packing-tips for our tips.

5 Days Out

- This is typically your last chance to **cancel Disney room-only reservations booked *by phone or travel agent*** without a penalty. Call ☎ 407-W-DISNEY.

4 Days Out

- **Purchase Disney's Memory Maker photo package** (see page 455) at least three days in advance to ensure that all photos are linked as soon as you arrive. You'll also get a discount if you buy your package in advance.

3 Days Out

- **Travelers age 2 and up** entering the United States from another country (including returning US citizens) must obtain negative coronavirus test results no more than three days prior to entering the United States.

The Day Before

- **Check in to your airline online.**

- **Finish Disney resort online check-in,** if you haven't already done so: disneyworld.disney.go.com/trip/online-resort-check-in.
- **Cancel any unneeded dining or baby- or pet-sitting reservations.**
- **Do one last check of park hours and weather.**

DISNEY ONLINE: OFFICIAL AND OTHERWISE

A SET OF HIGH-TECH ENHANCEMENTS to Disney's theme parks and hotels, officially known as **MyMagic+,** includes optional rubber wristbands (**MagicBands**) with embedded computer chips that function as admission tickets and hotel keys; MyMagic+ also encompasses Disney's dining reservation system and Genie+ ride-reservation system.

MyMagic+ requires you to make detailed decisions about every day of your trip, sometimes months in advance, if you want to visit popular parks and avoid long waits in line (see the previous section for a complete trip-planning timeline). Disney's requirement that you make park reservations means you must decide in advance which theme park you want to visit on each day of your trip, and restaurant reservations require you to know the exact time you want to eat, and where, two months before you arrive.

The Walt Disney World website (disneyworld.com) and mobile app are the glue that binds all of this together. Because you must plan so much before you leave home, we cover the basics of both the website and the app in the next section. While we may provide navigational instructions here, note that Disney's web designers move things around all the time, so you may have to hunt around to find some features. More information about theme park reservations is on page 74; MagicBands starts on page 82; details on how Genie, Genie+, Lightning Lane, Individual Attraction Selections, and Virtual Queues work start on page 63.

My Disney Experience at DisneyWorld.com

In this area of the Disney website (disneyworld.disney.go.com/plan), you can make park, hotel, dining, ride, and some recreation reservations; buy admission; and get park hours, attraction information, and much more.

TECHNICAL PROBLEMS A Google search for "My Disney Experience issues" returns around *86 million* results (not kidding). Disney's app and website frequently don't work as intended and often require human intervention to fix, so if you find yourself in a digital pickle, call ☎ 407-939-4357 in the US or ☎ 0800 16 90 749 in the UK for help.

BEFORE YOU BEGIN Set aside at least 30–40 minutes to complete this process. Make sure you have the following items on hand:

- A valid admission ticket or confirmation number for everyone in your group
- Your hotel-reservation number, if you're staying on-site
- A computer, smartphone, or tablet connected to the Internet
- An email account that you can access easily while traveling
- A schedule of the parks you'll be visiting each day, including arrival and departure times and the times of any midday breaks
- The dates, times, and confirmation numbers of any dining or recreation reservations you've made

If you're coordinating travel plans with friends or family who live elsewhere, you'll also need the following information:

- The names and (optional) email addresses of the people you're traveling with
- A schedule of the parks they are visiting on each day of their trip, including their arrival, departure, and break times
- The dates and times of any dining or recreation reservations they have made

GETTING STARTED Go to disneyworld.disney.go.com/plan and click "Create Account." You'll be asked for your email address, along with your name, billing address, and birth date. (Disney uses your billing address to send your hotel-reservation information, if applicable, and to charge your credit card for anything you purchase.)

Once you've created an account, the website will display a page with links to other steps in the planning process. These steps are described next. It's worth noting that the steps below apply only to the first time you sign into Disney's website—for some reason, the website shows you different screens and options when you sign in after that. In those cases, click the "My Disney Experience" icon in the upper-right corner of the page, and look for wording like that below.

DISNEY HOTEL INFORMATION If you're staying at a Disney hotel, select "Resort Hotel" and then "Link Reservation." Enter your reservation number. This associates your My Disney Experience (MDE) account with your hotel stay in Disney's computer systems. If you've booked a travel package that includes theme park admission, Disney computers will automatically link the admission to your MDE account, allowing you to skip the "Linking Tickets" step below. If you've booked a Disney hotel through a third-party site like Expedia, that site should send you a Disney reservation number to use here. Note that it can take up to a week for third-party sites to send Disney your booking information, so plan ahead accordingly.

REGISTER FRIENDS AND FAMILY Click the "Family & Friends" icon; then enter the names and ages of everyone traveling with you. You can do this later, too, but you'll need this information when you make your park and dining reservations.

LINKING TICKETS You will need to have purchased theme park tickets for each member of your group and linked them to each member's MDE profile before making some reservations.

If you haven't purchased your tickets, do so now. Disney's website doesn't have the cheapest prices for theme park tickets of three or more days. See pages 75–77 for where to find better deals. Once purchased, you can add these tickets to MDE just like tickets bought directly from Disney.

If you've already purchased tickets but have not linked them, click the "Park Tickets" widget, then click on "Link Tickets," and follow the instructions.

MAKING DINING RESERVATIONS Click the "Dining" icon then the "Make a Reservation" link to get started. (You may have to reenter your travel dates.) A list of every Walt Disney World eatery will be displayed. Use the filtering criteria at the top of the page to narrow the list.

Once you've settled on a restaurant, click the restaurant's name to check availability for your preferred dining time and the number of people in your party. If space is available and you want to make a reservation, you'll need to indicate which members of your party will be joining you. You'll also need to enter a credit card number to hold your reservation. If you want to make other dining reservations, you'll need to repeat this process for every reservation.

My Disney Experience Mobile App

In addition to its website, Disney offers a companion app on the Apple App Store and Google Play Store called My Disney Experience. It includes park hours, attraction operating hours and descriptions, wait times for buses, restaurant hours with descriptions and menus, the ability to make dining and Lightning Lane reservations online, GPS-based directions, counter-service meal ordering, the locations of park photographers, and more.

unofficial **TIP**
My Disney Experience is optimized for the latest phones and tablets, so some features, including mobile ordering, may not be available on all devices.

Our Recommended Websites

Searching online for Disney information is like navigating an immense maze for a tiny piece of cheese: You may find a lot of dead ends before you get what you want. Our picks follow.

BEST Q&A SITE Walt Disney World's **Mom's Panel** consists of mothers chosen from among 10,000-plus applicants. The panelists have a website, **DisneyWorldMoms.com,** where they offer tips and discuss how to plan a Disney World vacation. Several moms have specialized experience in areas such as Disney Cruise Line, runDisney, and traveling with sports groups; some speak Spanish, French, and Portuguese too.

BEST MONEY-SAVING SITE MouseSavers (mousesavers.com) keeps an updated list of discounts for use at Disney World resorts. These discounts are separated into categories such as "For the general public" and "For residents of certain states." Anyone who calls or books online can use a current discount. The savings can be considerable—as much as 40% in some cases. MouseSavers also offers deals on rental cars and non-Disney hotels in the area, along with a calendar showing when Disney sales typically launch.

BEST SITE FOR CAR-RENTAL DEALS AutoSlash (autoslash.com) will use every available discount code for every car company in Orlando to find you the best car-rental deal. See page 423 for more on car rentals.

BEST GENERAL UNOFFICIAL WALT DISNEY WORLD WEBSITE Besides TouringPlans.com, **AllEars.net** is the first website we recommend to friends who want to make a trip to Disney World. Updated several times a week, the site includes breaking news, tons of photos, Disney restaurant menus, resort and ticket information, tips for guests with special needs, and more. We also check **wdwmagic.com** for news and happenings around Walt Disney World.

SOCIAL MEDIA YouTube is an excellent place to find videos of Disney and other Central Florida attractions. **Facebook, Twitter,** and **Instagram** are popular places for Disneyphiles to gather online and share tips and

photos. Walt Disney World's official social-media outlets are facebook
.com/waltdisneyworld, twitter.com/waltdisneyworld, and instagram.com
/waltdisneyworld.

BEST DISNEY DISCUSSION BOARDS There are tons of these; among the
most active boards are **disboards.com; forums.wdwmagic.com;** our own
forum.touringplans.com; and, for Brits, **thedibb.co.uk** (DIBB stands for
"Disney Information Bulletin Board").

WHEN *to* GO *to* WALT DISNEY WORLD

SELECTING THE TIME OF YEAR FOR YOUR VISIT

IN BOTH PRE- AND POST-PANDEMIC TIMES, Walt Disney World
is busiest from the weekend before Christmas Day until the first weekend in January. Next busiest are spring break (early March–early April,
plus the week before Easter when Easter is later); Thanksgiving week;
and February during Presidents' Day and Mardi
Gras. You'll also see shorter bursts of crowds on
three-day weekends, such as Columbus Day.

*un*official **TIP**
See tinyurl.com
/planningwdw for a
handy worksheet to
help with this step.

The least busy time *historically* is Labor Day
through the beginning of October (but see our
caveats following). The last two weeks of October and the first week of November are usually
less crowded than average, as are the weeks after Thanksgiving and
before Christmas. The weeks between late April and Memorial Day
have lower crowds than the weeks on either side. Aside from being
asphalt-melting hot, July normally brings throngs of tourists from
South America who are on their winter holiday; summer crowds were
highest in 2019 between mid-July and mid-August.

Late February, early April, and early June are dicey. Crowds ebb
and flow according to school vacation schedules and the timing of
Mardi Gras and Presidents' Day weekend.

The rule of thumb is that Walt Disney World is less crowded (and
less expensive) when kids are in school. That said, Disney has become
adept at loading off-peak periods with special events, conventions,
food festivals, and the like; discounts on rooms and dining during
slower periods also figure in, as does the number of employees Disney
decides to use in the parks.

New rides and Disney's new park-reservation system also affect
crowds. In the weeks immediately after Disney opens a new ride,
expect it to be more difficult than normal to get reservations for that
park, and for the park to hit its capacity limit.

In short: The World can be packed at any time, and you'll need to
look beyond the time of year to pinpoint the least crowded dates. For
a calendar of scheduled Disney events, see tinyurl.com/wdwevents.

Off-Season Touring

We strongly recommend going to Disney World in the fall, winter, or
spring because of the milder weather, generally smaller crowds, and
deeper discounts. However, these benefits come with some trade-offs.

The parks often close early during the off-season because of lower crowds. This drastically reduces touring hours. Even when crowds are small, it's difficult to see big parks such as the Magic Kingdom between 9 a.m. and 7 p.m. Early closing may mean no evening entertainment. And because these are slow times, some rides and attractions may be closed. Finally, Central Florida temperatures fluctuate wildly during late fall, winter, and early spring; daytime highs in the 40s and 50s aren't uncommon. Still, it's so much easier to see the parks during the off-season that we'd advise taking children out of school for a Disney World visit. See page 372 for the pros and cons of this approach.

If this isn't possible, we want to make clear that you can have a wonderful experience regardless of when you go. Our advice, irrespective of season, is to arrive early at the parks and avoid the crowds by using one of our touring plans. If lines are low, kick back and forget the plans.

DON'T FORGET AUGUST Kids go back to school pretty early in Florida (and in a lot of other places too). This makes mid- to late August a good time for families who can't vacation during the off-season.

A New Jersey mother of two school-age children spells it out:

The end of August is the PERFECT time to go (just watch out for hurricanes; it's the season). There were virtually no wait times, 20 minutes at the most.

A family from Roxbury, New Jersey, agrees:

I recommend the last two weeks of August for anyone traveling there during the summer. We have visited twice during this time of year and have had great success touring the parks.

PLANNING FOR FLORIDA WEATHER

Why is the world's best theme park in the world's worst climate?

—A reader from Clackamas, Oregon

LONG BEFORE WALT DISNEY WORLD, tourists visited Florida year-round to enjoy the temperate tropical and subtropical climates. The best weather months generally are October, November, March, and April (see the table on page 37). Fall is usually dry, whereas spring and summer are wet. Rain is possible anytime, usually in the form of scattered thunderstorms. An entire day of rain is unusual.

Y'all need to give statistical weight to rides with outdoor waits in the heat (we went in August). For instance, just because the Guide *says to get in line for Runaway Railway at 1 p.m., I'm not going to do that because it's too hot at that time of day.*

—A reader from Sugar Land, Texas

SUMMER TEMPERATURES CAN FEEL LIKE 120°F Did you know that air temperature is measured in the shade? So if your phone's weather app says it's 95°F in Orlando, it's warmer if you're standing in the sun, and hotter still if you're wearing dark-colored clothing.

Florida's humidity makes the heat feel worse because it prevents your perspiration from evaporating to cool you off. Meteorologists use something called the Heat Index to express the combined effect of heat and humidity as a temperature reading we can understand. During summer in the Magic Kingdom, you'll commonly feel Heat Index temperatures above 110°F, and we've measured highs of up to 122°F. How hot is that? A steak cooked rare is considered done at 130°F.

CROWD CALENDAR

DISNEY WORLD'S ATTENDANCE was almost 59 million in 2019—that's an average of around 161,000 guests per day. Tips for avoiding crowds is the most frequent request we get. Besides which month or week to visit, readers want to know the best park to visit on each day of their stay.

Expect Disney to regularly adjust things like resort discounts, park capacity, and park hours. Because of that, it's not possible to include an accurate calendar in this book. To make things easier for you (and us), we provide at TouringPlans.com a calendar covering the next year (click "Crowd Calendar" on the home page). For each date, we offer a crowd-level index based on a 1–10 scale, with 1 being least crowded and 10 being most crowded. Our calendar is based on how long you'll wait in line and takes into account all holidays, special events, and more, as described in the next section.

Keeping the online Crowd Calendar updated requires year-round work. Thus, we have to charge a modest subscription fee. Much of the rest of the website is free, and owners of the current edition of this guide are eligible for a substantial discount on the subscription. See pages 23–25 for more information about our website.

Even on a "slow" day, you may see waits of 60 minutes or more for popular rides such as Seven Dwarfs Mine Train at the Magic Kingdom, Flight of Passage at the Animal Kingdom, Test Track at EPCOT, and Mickey and Minnie's Runaway Railway at Disney's Hollywood Studios.

A Braintree, Massachusetts, woman cautions:

> It should be emphasized that parks can still feel really crowded on a low-crowd day, especially the Magic Kingdom. But you will notice the difference when you see the wait times for the rides. Anyone expecting to have room to roam freely in certain parts of the Magic Kingdom on a low-attendance day will be disappointed. The same is true for Animal Kingdom: We went there on a "low" attendance day in the afternoon, and it was extremely congested and difficult to walk through some areas of the park.

HOW WE DETERMINE CROWD LEVELS AND BEST DAYS A number of factors contribute to the models we use to predict both crowd levels and the best days to visit each theme park.

Data we use to predict crowd levels:

- Historical wait times from the same time period in past years
- Historical theme park hours from the same time period in past years
- Future hotel-room bookings in the Orlando area
- Disney's special-events calendar (for example, the Magic Kingdom's Halloween and Christmas parties)

WALT DISNEY WORLD CLIMATE

	JAN	FEB	MAR	APR	MAY	JUN	JUL	AUG	SEP	OCT	NOV	DEC
AVERAGE DAILY HIGH												
	70°F	73°F	77°F	82°F	86°F	91°F	92°F	89°F	86°F	82°F	76°F	72°F
AVERAGE DAILY HEAT INDEX (COMBINED EFFECT OF HEAT AND HUMIDITY)												
	68°F	73°F	77°F	87°F	96°F	108°F	113°F	115°F	106°F	90°F	77°F	73°F
AVERAGE DAILY TEMPERATURE												
	60°F	63°F	67°F	72°F	77°F	80°F	81°F	81°F	79°F	74°F	67°F	63°F
AVERAGE DAILY HUMIDITY												
	71%	68%	65%	64%	65%	75%	79%	80%	80%	73%	71%	73%
AVERAGE RAINFALL PER MONTH												
	2.3"	2.0"	2.5"	2.2"	2.8"	6.8"	6.2"	6.7"	5.6"	2.7"	1.4"	2.0"
NUMBER OF DAYS OF RAIN PER MONTH												
	5	5	5	5	7	14	16	17	14	8	4	4

Source: climate-data.org

- Legal holidays in the United States
- Public-school schedules, weighted by distance from Florida and tourism rates

We also collect thousands of wait times from every ride in every Disney park every day, including posted and actual times. *Popular Science* did a nice article on the data science behind our predictions; read it at popsci.com/touring-plan-app-disney-lines.

SUMMER AND HOLIDAY CROWDS

MANY FOLKS HAVE NO CHOICE concerning the time of year they visit Disney World. Much of this book, in fact, is dedicated to making sure those readers who visit during busier times enjoy their experience. Armed with knowledge and some strategy, you can have a great time whenever you visit.

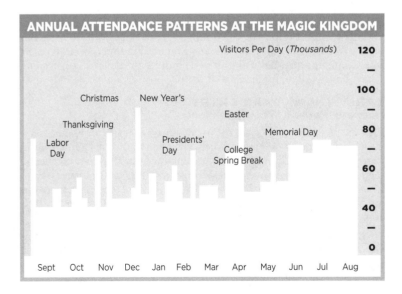

To put things in perspective, early summer (up to about June 8) and late summer (after August 15) are not as crowded as midsummer. Disney World experiences its highest demand during holiday periods. If you visit during spring break or a major holiday, the first thing you need to know is that the theme parks' guest capacity is not infinite. Disney allocates park capacity so that guests staying at its hotels and those who have bought date-specific tickets in advance have priority for park reservations. If you're not staying in the World, you may find yourself on the outside looking in, as did this Dahlonega, Georgia, family:

> Because we planned our July visit late, there were no park reservations available for the Magic Kingdom or Hollywood Studios on any of the 5 days of our trip. We couldn't get a Rise of the Resistance reservation because of that. We didn't have park-hopping tickets, so we ended up at EPCOT and Animal Kingdom every. single. day.

The reader might have done well by purchasing the park-hop option and by checking each morning whether day-of park reservations were available for the Magic Kingdom and Studios. The point is that you should commit to obtaining park reservations well in advance of your trip.

Christmas and New Year's at the Theme Parks

Don't expect to see all the attractions in a single day of touring at any park. That said, Disney's Animal Kingdom is usually the least crowded park during the winter holidays, especially on New Year's Eve. EPCOT is a good choice too, because it has about twice the land and typically lower crowds than the Magic Kingdom. (It also has fewer attractions, but many of them are high-capacity shows and rides.)

New Year's Eve is the busiest day of the year at The Magic Kingdom. The park stages New Year's Eve fireworks on both December 30 and December 31 for those who either wish to see fireworks in multiple parks or don't wish to be caught in the crowds. If you stay until midnight, expect it to take 1–3 hours to get back to your hotel by bus or car. We suggest getting a room at a Magic Kingdom monorail resort (the Contemporary, Bay Lake Tower, Grand Floridian, or Polynesian), which have walking paths as well.

EARLY THEME PARK ENTRY
(formerly Morning Extra Magic Hours)

EARLY THEME PARK ENTRY (Early Entry) is a perk for families staying at Walt Disney World resort hotels, including the Swan, Dolphin, Swan Reserve, Shades of Green, the Four Seasons, the Disney Springs hotels, and the Hilton hotels in Bonnet Creek. Those resort guests can enter any of Disney's four theme parks 30 minutes earlier than the official park-operating hours on any day of the week. This perk began on October 1, 2021, and replaces the Extra Magic Hours program that ran until early 2020.

WHAT'S REQUIRED? A valid ticket or MagicBand, along with a reservation for that theme park on that day, are required to enter the park. If you haven't yet checked into your Disney hotel, make sure you have your reservation linked to your My Disney Experience account.

WHEN IS EARLY ENTRY OFFERED? Early Entry is offered every day at all four Disney theme parks.

HOW DOES EARLY ENTRY WORK? Eligible resort guests (see above) are invited to enter any theme park 30 minutes before the general public. During this time, guests should be able to enjoy select attractions. In the Magic Kingdom, for example, you should find attractions open in Fantasyland and Tomorrowland at least.

In practice, we think Disney might let guests into the parks more than 30 minutes ahead of official park opening, especially on days with high attendance. For that reason, we think on-site guests who want to experience Early Entry should arrive at their park's entrance an hour before official opening: You'll be at the front of the line inside the park, ready to go.

During holidays and other busy times, the Magic Kingdom opens to regular guests at 8 a.m. and Early Entry begins at 7:30 a.m., so you'll need to be at the Magic Kingdom entrance no later than 7 a.m. You won't be alone, but because relatively few people are willing to get up that early for a theme park, your first few hours in the parks will be (pardon us) magical.

How Early Entry Affects Attendance at the Theme Parks

Early Entry should affect theme park attendance much less than the previous Extra Magic Hours program because Extra Magic Hours was offered only at one or two parks per day. When Animal Kingdom offered morning Extra Magic Hours sessions on Monday, for example, rides at that park had longer waits throughout the day because of the additional guests who arrived early to take advantage of their perk and stayed all day.

That incentive to visit a specific park on a specific day is removed with Early Entry because it's offered at every park every day. That should spread out Disney resort guests more evenly among the parks, while still providing an on-site benefit for Disney to dangle in front of potential hotel customers.

If you're staying at a Disney resort, remember these three things about Early Entry:

1. The Magic Kingdom has more attractions open for Early Entry than any other park. We think the Magic Kingdom's Early Entry, coupled with a good touring plan, is the most worthwhile of any park.

2. Early Entry will be useful at EPCOT for the new attractions Remy's Ratatouille Adventure and Guardians of the Galaxy: Cosmic Rewind.

3. Should Disney's Hollywood Studios' Star Wars: Rise of the Resistance ever get a standby line, it would be almost mandatory to use Early Entry at DHS to avoid long waits.

WHAT'S THE CATCH? The primary disadvantage of Early Entry for on-site guests is that they must now get up an extra half-hour early to beat the crowds. And that's mitigated somewhat (for now) by the staggered park opening times.

Off-site guests are considerably disadvantaged by the new Early Entry program. With the old EMH schedule, off-site guests could level the playing field by simply avoiding the park that offered morning

EMH. If that park was EPCOT, then it was still possible to stay at an inexpensive hotel, get up early, and be at the front of the pack when the Magic Kingdom's rides opened.

With Early Entry, off-site guests are guaranteed to have thousands of on-site guests already in front of them at any theme park they visit on any day. When EPCOT opens a new ride like Guardians of the Galaxy, it's a safe bet that its line will be hours long well before the first off-site guest even sets foot inside the park.

To mitigate the effect of Early Entry on off-site guests, we've added off-site versions of our touring plans to this book. Be aware, however, that even with an optimal touring plan, off-site guests may wait for up to an extra hour or more in line per day than on-site guests, due to the head start that on-site guests have.

EXTENDED EVENING THEME PARK HOURS
(formerly Evening Extra Magic Hours)

EXTENDED EVENING THEME PARK HOURS is the limited revival of the former Evening Extra Magic Hours program, which was discontinued in 2020. Typically held on one night per week for each park, Extended Evening Theme Park Hours allows guests staying at Disney's Deluxe and DVC resorts—and only those guests—2 extra hours in that park after official closing. Thus, if the Magic Kingdom closes at 9 p.m. to regular guests, the park will operate Extended Hours from 9 to 11 p.m. for guests at a Disney Deluxe or DVC resort only.

As we went to press, Extended Hours was set to begin the first week of October 2021. The Magic Kingdom was scheduled to have Extended Hours on Wednesdays, and EPCOT on Mondays; no other park had days scheduled.

Disney will likely set up checkpoints throughout the park, such as the entrance to each land, to verify that guests entering the area are eligible for the program. Disney will likely scan your MagicBand or plastic ticket to verify your resort.

Most theme park attractions should be open during Extended Hours, although we'd be surprised if the Studios' Rise of the Resistance ride participated.

The downside to Extended Hours versus Early Theme Park Entry is that the attractions' lines may be full of regular guests for a substantial part of the Extended Hours. For example, if EPCOT closes to regular guests at 9 p.m. and the line for Remy's Ratatouille Adventure is 60 minutes at 9 p.m., then the first half of Extended Hours will be used to process guests who got in line before the park closed. That materially diminishes the benefit of Extended Hours. Of course, you could get in line for Remy at 10:59 p.m. and still ride, but you'd end up staying extra late to do so.

THE WALT DISNEY WORLD CALENDAR

DISNEY CELEBRATES SPECIAL EVENTS throughout the year. Some events commemorate major holidays, while others have been designed specifically by Disney to boost attendance during otherwise-slow times of year.

JANUARY Usually held the second weekend after New Year's (it's January 5–9 in 2022), the **Walt Disney World Marathon** pulls in more runners and their families every year. Information on all Disney running events can be found at rundisney.com.

Another winter event is the **EPCOT International Festival of the Arts.** Running from the first full week of January until the third full week of February, the festival, which is included as part of your park admission, features art (some of it Disney-themed), food, entertainment, and workshops to further your creative skills. See page 674 for more information.

FEBRUARY Black History Month is celebrated throughout Walt Disney World with displays, artisans, storytellers, and entertainers.

In 2022, **Presidents' Day** is Monday, February 21, and **Mardi Gras** is Tuesday, March 1. These holidays increase attendance starting the weekend before.

MARCH At the **EPCOT International Flower & Garden Festival,** which runs March–July, expert horticulturists showcase exotic floral displays and share gardening tips. The 30 million blooms from some 1,200 species will make your eyes pop. The festival features food and beverage kiosks, making it more like fall's International Food & Wine Festival (see below), only with flowers. See page 288 for more information on both festivals.

APRIL Easter is April 17, 2022. Because Easter is late in 2022, expect late March to be peak spring break season. The weeks on either side of Easter will also draw crowds.

Disney usually announces a **"free" Disney Dining Plan** promotion in mid- to late April for travel dates usually starting in August. See page 206 for more details.

JUNE Gay Days, an unofficial gathering of lesbian, gay, bisexual, transgender, and queer (LGBTQ) people from around the world, has been happening annually at Walt Disney World since 1991. Organizers say previous Gay Days have attracted close to 200,000 visitors and their friends and families. For additional information, visit gaydays.com.

AUGUST "Fall" begins in mid-August as far as Walt Disney World is concerned. **Disney's After Hours Boo Bash,** at the Magic Kingdom, is typically held on 30+ select nights between mid-August and November 1, from 9 p.m. to midnight (guests with tickets can get into the park starting at 7 p.m.). The festivities include trick-or-treating in costume, parades, live music, storytelling, and a fireworks show. See page 80 for more information.

Those who say Christmas is the most wonderful time of year have never been to the **EPCOT International Food & Wine Festival.** Usually held in the World Showcase from mid-July to late November, the celebration represents 25 nations and cuisines. Before 2020, the event included demonstrations, wine seminars, tastings, and opportunities to see some of the world's top chefs; many activities are included in EPCOT admission, though some workshops and tastings are by reservation only and cost more than $100. There's no word yet on whether

continued on page 43

WALT DISNEY WORLD PHONE NUMBERS

General Information ☎ 407-824-4321 or 407-824-2222

General Information for the Hearing-Impaired (TTY) ☎ 407-827-5141

Accommodations/Reservations ☎ 407-934-7639

Advent Health Centra Care (urgent-care clinic) Kissimmee ☎ 407-390-1888
Lake Buena Vista ☎ 407-934-2273   Universal–Dr. Phillips ☎ 407-291-8975

All-Star Movies Resort ☎ 407-939-7000

All-Star Music Resort ☎ 407-939-6000

All-Star Sports Resort ☎ 407-939-5000

AMC Movies at Disney Springs ☎ 407-827-1308

Animal Kingdom Lodge & Villas Jambo House ☎ 407-938-3000
Kidani Village ☎ 407-938-7400

Art of Animation Resort ☎ 407-938-7000

Beach Club Resort ☎ 407-934-8000

Beach Club Villas ☎ 407-934-8000

Blizzard Beach Information ☎ 407-560-3400

BoardWalk Inn & Villas ☎ 407-939-6200

Caribbean Beach Resort ☎ 407-934-3400

Car Rentals ☎ 407-824-3470, ext. 1

Contemporary Resort & Bay Lake Tower ☎ 407-824-1000

Convention Information ☎ 321-939-7129

Coronado Springs Resort ☎ 407-939-1000

Dining Advance Reservations ☎ 407-939-3463

Disabled Guests Special Requests ☎ 407-939-7807

Disney Institute ☎ 407-824-7997 or 321-939-4600

Disney Springs Information ☎ 407-939-6244

ESPN Wide World of Sports Complex ☎ 407-939-1500

Fantasia Gardens Miniature Golf ☎ 407-560-4870

Fort Wilderness Resort & Campground ☎ 407-824-2900

Golf Reservations and Information ☎ 407-939-4653

Grand Floridian Resort & Spa/Grand Floridian Villas ☎ 407-824-3000

Group Camping ☎ 407-939-7807

Guided-Tour Information ☎ 407-939-8687

Guided VIP Solo Tours ☎ 407-560-4033

House of Blues Tickets & Information ☎ 407-934-2583

Lost and Found *(for articles lost yesterday or before; for same day, go to Guest Relations, front desk, or disneyworld.com/lostandfound)* ☎ 407-824-4245

Merchandise Guest Services ☎ 877-560-6477

Old Key West Resort ☎ 407-827-7700

WALT DISNEY WORLD PHONE NUMBERS *(continued)*

Outdoor Recreation Reservations & Information ☎ 407-939-7529

Polynesian Village Resort ☎ 407-824-2000

Polynesian Village Villas ☎ 407-824-3500

Pop Century Resort ☎ 407-938-4000

Port Orleans Resort–French Quarter ☎ 407-934-5000

Port Orleans Resort–Riverside ☎ 407-934-6000

Riviera Resort ☎ 407-828-7030

Resort Dining ☎ 407-939-3463

Saratoga Springs Resort & Spa, Treehouse Villas ☎ 407-827-1100

Security Routine ☎ 407-560-7959; urgent ☎ 407-560-1990

Shades of Green Resort ☎ 407-824-3400 or 407-824-3600

Telecommunication for the Deaf Reservations (TTY) ☎ 407-827-5141

Walt Disney Travel Company ☎ 407-939-6244

Walt Disney World Dolphin ☎ 407-934-4000

Walt Disney World Swan ☎ 407-934-3000

Walt Disney World Swan Reserve ☎ 407-934-3000

Walt Disney World Ticket Inquiries ☎ 407-939-7679

Weather Information ☎ 407-827-4545

Wilderness Lodge/Boulder Ridge & Copper Creek Villas ☎ 407-824-3200

Winter Summerland Miniature Golf ☎ 407-560-3000

Wrecker Service (7 a.m.–11 p.m.; if closed, call Security) ☎ 407-824-0976

Yacht Club Resort ☎ 407-934-7000

continued from page 41

these will be back for 2022. See page 288 for more information about the festival.

NOVEMBER The **Wine and Dine Half-Marathon** early in this month revolves around a 13.1-mile race that ends with a nighttime party amid the EPCOT International Food & Wine Festival. The 2021 event was on November 5.

DECEMBER The annual **Disney Parks Christmas Day Parade,** televised on December 25, is usually taped at the Magic Kingdom in November or the first week of December. The parade ties up pedestrian traffic on Main Street, U.S.A., all day.

EPCOT's holiday celebration, called the **EPCOT International Festival of the Holidays,** typically runs late November–late December. The festival includes food booths similar to those present in World Showcase during the Food & Wine and Flower & Garden Festivals.

DISNEY'S VERY MERRIEST AFTER HOURS CHRISTMAS PARTY This event takes place from 9 p.m. to midnight (after regular hours; guests can get into the park starting at 7 p.m.) on 20+ evenings in November and December. The event includes attractions, holiday-themed stage shows featuring Disney characters, cookies and hot chocolate, performances of a special holiday-themed fireworks show, carolers, "a magical snowfall on Main Street," white lights on Cinderella Castle, and holiday-themed live entertainment. See page 81 for more details.

IMPORTANT WALT DISNEY WORLD ADDRESSES

GENERAL INFORMATION
WDW Guest Communications, PO Box 10040, Lake Buena Vista, FL 32830-0040
☎ 407-560-2544
wdw.guest.communications@disneyworld.com or guest.services@disneyworld.com
General online help: disneyworld.disney.go.com/help/email

CONVENTION AND BANQUET INFORMATION
Walt Disney World Resort South
PO Box 10000, Lake Buena Vista, FL 32830-1000
☎ 321-939-7129
disneymeetings.com

MERCHANDISE MAIL ORDER (Guest Service Mail Order)
PO Box 10070
Lake Buena Vista, FL 32830-0070
☎ 877-560-6477
merchandise.guest.services@disneyparks.com

WALT DISNEY WORLD CENTRAL RESERVATIONS
☎ 407-W-DISNEY (934-7639)

WALT DISNEY WORLD YOUTH PROGRAMS
☎ 877-WD-YOUTH (939-6884)
disneyyouth.com

WALT DISNEY WORLD TICKET MAIL ORDER
☎ 407-566-4985
ticket.inquiries@disneyworld.com

MAKING *the* MOST *of* YOUR TIME

◼ ALLOCATING TIME

THE VACATION THAT FIGHTS BACK

A WHIRLWIND TOUR of Disney's four theme parks and two water parks takes at least **six full days** and a level of stamina more often associated with running a marathon. A British gentleman, thinking we exaggerated, measured how far he walked and found this:

> Our visits to the theme parks were spread over five days, during which my wife and I (ages 51 and 55) walked a total of 68 miles for an average of 13 miles per day!

At Walt Disney World, less is more. Take the World in small doses, with plenty of swimming, napping, reading, and relaxing in between. If you don't see everything, you can always come back.

An articulate Anchorage, Alaska, teen and her family found out the hard way the importance of building in time to decompress:

> We crammed our schedule a little too full, with seven parks—Disney, Universal, and SeaWorld—in eight full days. My older sisters would speed-walk from attraction to attraction while my parents straggled behind trying to keep up, while I was caught in the middle, both wanting to get to the next ride as fast as I could and wanting just to spend some quality time with my parents. No family should spend more than two consecutive days at the parks without a low-key day in the middle. I wish I'd known this going in.

It's exhausting to rise at dawn and run around a theme park for 8–10 hours day after day. Sooner or later (usually sooner), you hit the wall. To avoid that, use these two tips alone or in combination:

1. Take at least a morning off (preferably the entire day) after two consecutive days in the parks.

2. Return to your hotel for a 3- to 5-hour break each day you're in the theme parks.

The keys to those sleep-in days are to set up a touring plan (see page 52) and visit over multiple days. To get you started, we've created **late-start touring plans** for Animal Kingdom. Check them out at tinyurl.com/sleepin-animalkingdom.

This Arlington, Virginia, family recommends taking it slow and easy:

We spent eight days in Disney, and it was totally worth it. A longer trip, believe it or not, eliminates the happy death march—we cut our stress by 90%. Each day, we took some sort of break: a morning swim, an afternoon nap, a sit-down snack in a restaurant. The end result was that the kids got to see/ride everything they wanted without exhausting themselves (or us)—or spending most of their days in line. And we had almost zero tantrums (really!).

The rest of this section will help you decide which park to start at, when to arrive, how to build breaks and naps into your schedule, and what to do on the first and last days of your trip.

WHICH PARK TO SEE FIRST?

THIS QUESTION IS LESS OBVIOUS than it appears, especially if your party includes children or teenagers. If kids see the Magic Kingdom first, they expect the same experience at the other parks. At EPCOT, they're often disappointed (as are many adults) by the educational orientation of the older Future World attractions. And children may not find Animal Kingdom as exciting as the Magic Kingdom or Hollywood Studios—real animals, after all, can't be programmed to entertain on cue.

First-time visitors should see Animal Kingdom first; it's educational, but its live animals provide a change of pace.

See EPCOT second, if you're visiting for at least four days. Like Animal Kingdom, most of EPCOT's experiences are not based on Disney's film and TV characters, so you'll be able to enjoy it without having been preconditioned to think of Disney entertainment as solely fantasy or adventure.

Next, see Disney's Hollywood Studios (DHS), which helps you transition from the educational EPCOT and Animal Kingdom to the fanciful Magic Kingdom.

We recommend saving the Magic Kingdom for last, although we recognize that for many readers the Magic Kingdom is synonymous with Walt Disney World.

OPERATING HOURS

AS OF PRESS TIME, the Disney World website publishes preliminary park hours around 75–90 days in advance, but schedule adjustments can happen at any time, including the day of your visit. Check disneyworld .com or call ☎ 407-939-5277 for the exact hours before you arrive. Off-season, parks may be open as few as 11 hours (8 a.m.–7 p.m.). At busy times (particularly holidays), they may operate for more than 12 hours. Disney staggers each park's opening and closing times to limit the demand on its transportation systems. Animal Kingdom usually opens first, typically at 8 a.m., followed by the Magic Kingdom (9 a.m.), Hollywood Studios (9 or 10 a.m.), and EPCOT (10 or 11 a.m.).

Closing Time

Rides and attractions shut down at approximately the official closing time. Some shopping venues, such as Main Street, U.S.A., in the Magic Kingdom, remain open 30 minutes to an hour after the rest of the park has closed.

Official Opening Versus Real Opening

When you check the website or call, you're given "official hours." On many days, the parks open to day guests a bit earlier. If the official hours are 8 a.m.–7 p.m., for instance, Animal Kingdom may start admitting day guests into the park and onto rides at 7:30 a.m., possibly earlier during busier times.

THE PRACTICALITY OF RETURNING TO YOUR HOTEL FOR REST

MANY READERS WRITE ABOUT the practicality of departing the theme park for a nap and swim at the hotel.

A dad from Sequim, Washington, made the following request:

I would like to see nearness to the parks emphasized in your accommodation guide. We tried going back to the hotel for midday breaks, but it was too time-consuming. By the time you got to the car, negotiated traffic, rested, and reversed the process to get back to the park, it took 2–3 hours for a short rest and was not worth it!

In Part Five, "Accommodations," we publish a chart (pages 252–263) that provides the commuting times to each of the Disney theme parks from many popular hotels within 20 miles of Walt Disney World. Before the pandemic, our advice to the reader above would have been to allocate 4–5 hours for a break to remain rested and relaxed. But it's difficult to recommend a 4- or 5-hour break these days, as the parks may be open only 11 or 12 hours. A better option is to cut your day short: sleep late and arrive later, or arrive earlier and leave earlier for a nap. In fact, Disney's staggered park openings are excellent guidelines: arrive early at Animal Kingdom and Magic Kingdom, then leave for naps when you're tired. Sleep in on the mornings you want to visit Disney's Hollywood Studios and EPCOT.

How long will it take you to get from a theme park to your hotel by car? At Animal Kingdom, Hollywood Studios, and EPCOT, you can get to your car in the parking lot in about 15–20 minutes. From the Magic Kingdom, it will take you 30–35 minutes. Obviously, if you're at the farthest point from the park entrance when you decide to return to the hotel, it will take longer. But from most places in the parks, the times above are correct. Once in your car, you'll be able to commute to most US 192 hotels, all Disney World hotels, all Lake Buena Vista hotels, and most hotels along the I-4 corridor and south International Drive (I-Drive) in 20 minutes or less. It will take about the same time to reach hotels on I-Drive north of Sand Lake Road and in the Universal Orlando area. So, for most people, the one-way commute will average 35–40 minutes.

ARRIVAL AND DEPARTURE DAYS: WHAT TO DO WHEN YOU HAVE ONLY HALF A DAY

ON ARRIVAL AND DEPARTURE DAYS, you will probably have only part of a day for touring or other recreational pursuits. It's a common problem: You roll into the World about 1 p.m., excited and ready to go—but where?

The first question: Do you feel comfortable using a full day's admission to the parks when you have less than a full day to tour? The incremental cost to add another day of admission is under $20 if you're visiting for four or more days but $90 and up if you're there for only one to three days. The availability of park reservations, your arrival time, and the parks' closing times are also considerations. If you even think you might want to visit a park on your first or last day, make a park reservation just in case. There's no charge to do so, and you can cancel at any time.

Opting for a Partial Day at the Theme Parks

If you decide to use one day's admission on a half day or less, refer to our **Lines** app for the least crowded park to visit and to see which parks have reservations available.

One option—if you can reach the park before 1 p.m. and stay until closing (usually 7 p.m.)—is Disney's Animal Kingdom, which requires the least amount of time to tour. You'll find short lines for Avatar Flight of Passage, Kilimanjaro Safaris, and Expedition Everest on all but the busiest days of the year.

Another option is to experience Disney's Hollywood Studios' secondary attractions, such as Star Tours—The Adventures Continue, any live shows and entertainment, and shopping on your partial day, leaving your full day for the park's rides.

Whenever you arrive at a theme park after noon, you should go to higher-capacity attractions where waiting time is relatively brief, even during the most crowded part of the day. Our clip-out Touring Plan Companions in the back of the book list attractions in each of the Disney parks that require the least waiting during the most crowded part of the day. Although the lines for these attractions may seem humongous, they move quickly.

Alternatives to the Theme Parks on Arrival Day

Before you head out for fun on arrival day, you must check in, unpack, and buy admissions, and you will probably detour to the grocery or convenience store to buy snacks, drinks, and breakfast food. At all Disney resorts and many non-Disney hotels, you can't occupy your room until after 3 p.m. (4 p.m. for DVC resorts); however, many properties will check you in, sell you tickets, and store your luggage before that hour.

The least expensive way to spend your arrival day is to check in, unpack, do your chores, and relax at your hotel swimming pool.

Another daytime option is a trip to a **water park** (see Part Sixteen, "The Water Parks," for details). Any one that stays open past 5 p.m.

is worth a look because the crowds at all parks clear out substantially after 4 p.m. If the park is open late and you get hungry, you'll find ample fast food.

If none of the above options sound appealing, consider minigolf (expensive in Walt Disney World, more reasonable outside it) or the entertainment lineup at Disney Springs (see Part Seventeen, page 660).

In the Evening

Dinner provides a great opportunity to plan the next day's activities. If you're hungry for entertainment too, consider **Disney Springs**. It includes **Cirque du Soleil** (page 664) and **Raglan Road** (page 343), an Irish pub with live music and good food, both best appreciated by adults.

Departure Days

Departure days don't seem to cause as much consternation as arrival days. If you want to visit a theme park on your departure day, Animal Kingdom is usually the first to open, and it's easier to get into and out of than Magic Kingdom. Get up early and be at the park when it opens. If you have plenty of time, check out and store your luggage with the bell desk or in your car. Or, if you can arrange a late checkout, you might want to return to your hotel for a shower and change of clothes before departing.

HOW *to* AVOID LONG WAITS *in* LINE

LONG LINES ARE USUALLY THE TOP COMPLAINT among theme park guests—not the quality of the rides, the cost to get in, or the food. It's fair to say that the *Unofficial Guide* was written to save you time in line. It's the thing the book is most famous for, and the thing most of our day-to-day work revolves around.

There are six keys to avoiding long lines at Disney World:

1. Decide in advance what you really want to see.
2. Arrive early.
3. Know what to expect when you arrive.
4. Use a touring plan.
5. Understand how standby queues, boarding groups/Virtual Queues, Individual Attraction purchases, Disney's Genie and Genie+, and Disney's Lightning Lane work to supplement the touring plan.
6. Use the single-rider line if one is available.

We elaborate on each these in the remainder of this chapter.

1. DECIDE IN ADVANCE WHAT YOU REALLY WANT TO SEE

DISNEY'S ATTRACTIONS RANGE from midway-type rides that you can get at your local carnival to high-tech extravaganzas found nowhere else on earth. To help you decide which to see, we describe the theme parks and their attractions in detail. In each description, we include our evaluation of the attraction, and the opinions of Disney

World guests are expressed as star ratings, with five stars being the highest rating. Our evaluation also uses the following hierarchy of categories to compare the size and scope of the different attractions:

SUPER-HEADLINERS The best attractions the theme park has to offer. Mind-boggling in size, scope, and imagination, they represent the cutting edge of attraction technology and design. When you get back from Walt Disney World and people ask, "Did you go on so-and-so?" this is what they'll be talking about.

HEADLINERS Multimillion-dollar, full-scale, themed adventures and theater presentations that are modern in technology and design and employ a full range of special effects.

MAJOR ATTRACTIONS More modestly themed adventures, but ones that incorporate state-of-the-art technologies. Or larger-scale attractions of older design.

MINOR ATTRACTIONS Midway-type rides, small "dark" rides (cars on a track, zigzagging through the dark), small theater presentations, transportation rides, and elaborate walk-through attractions.

DIVERSIONS Exhibits, both passive and interactive, including playgrounds, video arcades, and street theater.

Not every attraction fits neatly into these descriptions, but it's a handy way to compare any two. Remember that bigger and more elaborate doesn't always mean better. Peter Pan's Flight, a minor attraction in the Magic Kingdom, continues to be one of the park's most beloved rides. Likewise, for many young children, no attraction, regardless of size, surpasses Dumbo.

A Word About Disney Thrill Rides

Readers of all ages should try to be open-minded about Disney "thrill rides." Compared to those at other theme parks, the Disney attractions are quite tame, with more emphasis on sights, atmosphere, and special effects than on the motion, speed, or feel of the ride. While we suggest you take Disney's pre-ride warnings seriously, we can tell you that guests of all ages report enjoying rides such as Soarin' Around the World, Tower of Terror, Big Thunder Mountain, and Splash Mountain.

Rock 'n' Roller Coaster and Expedition Everest, however, are a different story. Both are serious coasters that are faster and more intense than Space Mountain or Big Thunder Mountain.

Mission: Space, a high-tech simulation ride at EPCOT, is a toss-up (pun intended)—it absolutely has the potential to make you sick. After many guest incidents, Disney made half of the ride a tamer, no-spin experience, one that's less likely to launch your lunch.

2. ARRIVE EARLY! ARRIVE EARLY! ARRIVE EARLY!

THIS IS THE MOST IMPORTANT KEY to efficient touring and avoiding long lines. First thing in the morning, there are no lines and fewer people. The same four rides you experience in 1 hour in the early morning at the Magic Kingdom can take as long as 3 hours after 10:30 a.m.

Eat breakfast before you arrive; don't waste prime touring time sitting in a restaurant.

You gain a big advantage if you're already past the turnstiles when the park opens. While everyone else is stuck in line waiting for the people ahead to find their admission media and figure out how the turnstiles work, the lucky few (hundreds) already in the park will be in line for their first attraction. You'll probably be done and on your way to your second before many of them are even in the park, and the time savings accrue throughout the rest of the day.

The earlier a park opens, the greater your advantage. This is because most vacationers won't make the effort to rise early and get to a park before it opens. Fewer people are willing to make an 8 a.m. opening than a 9 a.m. opening. If you visit during midsummer and are staying at a Disney resort, arrive at the turnstiles 60 minutes before official opening (to take advantage of the Early Theme Park Entry for Disney hotel guests), or 30 minutes if you're not staying at a Disney resort (to get into the park at official opening time).

During holiday periods, Disney resort guests should arrive 60–70 minutes early, and off-site guests, 40–50 minutes early. By arriving, we mean be at the turnstiles at the recommended time. Consider that you'll have to clear security before advancing to the turnstiles.

Many readers share their experiences about getting to the parks before opening. From a Pennsylvania mom of two:

> Be there at rope drop. *I went during one of the slowest times of the year, and the morning I didn't wake up for rope drop I was able to experience less than half of what I did the other days.*

A reader from Kingsley, Pennsylvania, notes that the secret of rope-dropping was becoming more widely known before the shutdown:

> *Rope-dropping is not the advantage that it used to be as crowds have increased. As recently as five years ago, you could be at rope drop for Splash Mountain, Big Thunder Mountain, Pirates of the Caribbean, and The Haunted Mansion, and they would all be close to walk-ons. That's not the case anymore. On an average day, if you rope-drop Splash Mountain, you'll wait 20 minutes unless you're right up front, and Big Thunder Mountain will have a 35-minute wait when you get off Splash Mountain. The Haunted Mansion will have a 30-minute wait by 10 a.m. Even Pirates will have a 20-minute wait within the first hour.*

Even with more people rope-dropping, it's still the best free strategy for seeing the most popular attractions with minimal waits.

If getting the kids up earlier than usual makes for rough sailing, don't despair. You'll have a great time no matter when you get to the park. Many families with young children have found that it's better to accept the relative inefficiencies of arriving at the park a bit late than to jar the children out of their routine. In our guide especially for families, *The Unofficial Guide to Walt Disney World with Kids,* we provide a number of special touring plans (including touring plans for sleepyheads) that we don't have room for in this guide.

3. KNOW WHAT TO EXPECT WHEN YOU ARRIVE

BECAUSE MOST OF THE TOURING PLANS are based on being present when the theme park opens, you need to know about opening procedures. Disney transportation to the parks begins 1–1½ hours before official opening. The parking lots open about an hour before the park does. Each park has an entrance plaza outside the turnstiles, where you'll remain until the parks open.

Disney typically allows guests into the parks roughly 30–60 minutes before official opening time. This prevents dense crowds from forming around the admission turnstiles. Once inside the park, guests are typically held at various points in the park until the official opening, a process called rope drop for historical reasons. Once the park is open, you can walk immediately to your first attraction.

4. USE A TOURING PLAN

SINCE THE FIRST EDITION of the *Unofficial Guide,* minimizing our readers' waits in line has been a top priority. We know from research that theme park patrons base their overall satisfaction on the number of attractions they're able to experience. Thus, we developed field-tested touring plans: step-by-step itineraries that allow readers to experience as many attractions as possible with the least amount of waiting.

unofficial **TIP**
The facts and figures in our books come from years of data collection and analysis by expert statisticians, programmers, field researchers, and lifelong Disney enthusiasts.

We're confident that the touring plans in this book can save you up to 4 hours or more of standing in line, and they allow you to see more attractions. How do they do this? The answer is *science.*

You may be surprised to learn that avoiding lines in theme parks is like everyday situations faced by companies around the world. For example, it's almost the exact problem FedEx and UPS have when trying to deliver packages efficiently (you're the driver; the rides you want to ride are the customers that need to be visited; and the time you spend walking and waiting in line is the travel time to the next customer.)

Because this kind of problem is common, it gets studied widely in schools and corporations, mainly in the fields of mathematics, operations research, and computer science. Bob used his experience teaching college operations research to come up with the first Disney touring plans in this book. Years later, Bob helped Len while Len was writing his master's thesis on efficient computer techniques for this kind of problem. It was their chocolate-and-peanut-butter moment.

In the years since, we've assembled a full-time team of data scientists, programmers, and researchers, and spent millions of dollars, to figure out how to avoid lines at Disney World.

This research has been recognized by both the travel industry and academe, having been cited by such diverse sources as *Popular Science, The Atlanta Journal-Constitution, The Dallas Morning News,* the Mathematical Association of America, *Money, The New York Times,* Operations Research Forum, *Travel Weekly, USA Today,* and *Wired,* along with the BBC, CBS News, Fox News, and the Travel Channel. The methodology behind our touring plans was also used as a case study in the 2010 book *Numbers Rule Your World,* by Kaiser Fung, professor of statistics at New York University.

So that's a touring plan: a step-by-step guide to avoiding lines, just for you, that is supported by a team of well-funded, obsessive, Disney science–y types with lots and lots of computers.

We get a ton of reader mail—98% of it positive—commenting on our touring plans. First, from a mother who planned a last-minute trip:

> We rode all of the main attractions in EPCOT, Magic Kingdom, and Hollywood Studios over a three-day period, and we didn't wait more than 10 minutes for any ride—and this was during spring break!

An Ohio family felt the wind in their sails:

> The whole time we were in the Magic Kingdom, following the touring plan, it seemed that we were traveling in front of a hurricane— we'd wait 10 minutes or so for an attraction (or less—sometimes we just walked right on), but when we got out and started moving on to the next one, we could see the line building for what we just did.

From a Noblesville, Indiana, couple:

> LOVE the touring plans. They work. I was skeptical.

A family of four from Louisville, Kentucky, had this to say:

> If there is one cult in this world I could join, it would be the staff of the Unofficial Guide. I tell everyone going to Disney to use this book and the awesome app. Years ago, we tried to convince friends to use the book, but they were scared off by the highly structured nature of the touring plans. We happened to see them at Disney during a late summer afternoon. Our family had enjoyed a full day with lots of rides and no more than a 20-minute wait. They had been on two total rides, standing in line over 1½ hours each time. They were miserable, and already considering escaping back to the hotel.

A mom from Warren, Arkansas, gave the touring plans a shot:

> This is our fifth family trip to WDW, and this was my first time to use a touring plan. I have read the books and been a member of Lines for years. However, I never bought into the demands of the touring plan. After this last trip, I am officially a fan! I cannot express to you how much better our trip was since we followed a plan. We accomplished more in the first hour of Magic Kingdom than we used to accomplish in 3 hours. My family will use touring plans from now on.

From a Monroe, Michigan, family of 10:

> I have always read the Unofficial Guide but never paid much mind to the touring plan section. This trip there were 10 of us in total going to the parks! We decided to give the plans a try so that we weren't standing around saying, "What do you want to do next?" Oh, my goodness! How have we survived without the plans? We got to do every attraction that everyone in the group wanted, with minimal crying from the 2- and 4-year-old nieces.

A woman from Westminster, Colorado, chimed in with this:

> I love the Unofficial Guides. I love the humor, and I feel like I get a real idea of what to expect. When I first told my family I wanted to use the touring plans to maximize our theme park experience, they thought I

was crazy. I secretly cut the plans out of the book and stowed them in my day pack, then urged us in the direction of the plans. After the first day they were shocked at how much we got done and how few huge lines we had to wait in. When I told them that we had actually followed your touring plans, they happily followed them the rest of the trip. It made a huge difference with the crowds and heat of summer!

A 30-something mom of two from Oconomowoc, Wisconsin, found that the touring plans fanned the flames of *amour*:

My husband was a bit doubtful about using a touring plan, but on our first day at Magic Kingdom, after we'd done all the Fantasyland attractions and ridden Splash Mountain twice before lunch, he looked at me with amazement and said, "I've never been so attracted to you."

A woman from Smithville, Tennessee, used the touring plans as a litmus test for her fiancé:

Your book has helped me plan two amazing trips to Disney World. My first trip there, I went in blind. My second trip, I discovered your book and used your touring plans. My third trip, I used the app you created and had the best trip of my life! My fiancé just informed me that we can't go "every year." I think I'm going to have to break it off with him.

Finally, from an Edmonds, Washington, family who used the touring plans for Universal's Islands of Adventure:

This trip was the first time we were actually going to leave the property (gasp!) and go to Universal, and I was very happy that you included a touring plan for Islands of Adventure. It worked like a charm! I've always wondered how it feels to follow your plans not ever having seen the park before, and now I know—it was easy!

Variables That Affect the Success of the Touring Plans

The plans' success will be affected by how early you arrive at the parks; how quickly you move from ride to ride; when and how many breaks you take; when, where, and how you eat; and whether you have young children in your tour group, among other factors. **Rider Switch** (page 395), also known as "baby swap," among other things, inhibits families with little ones from moving expeditiously among attractions. Plus, some folks simply cannot conform to the plans' "early to rise" conditions, as this reader from Cleveland Heights, Ohio, recounts:

Our touring plans were thrown totally off by one member who could not be on time for opening. Even in October, this made a huge difference in our ability to see attractions without waiting.

UNEXPECTED RIDE CLOSURES Some things are beyond your control. Tops among these are rides that don't open on time or stop running suddenly during the day. For example, Test Track, an automobile-based thrill ride at EPCOT, can run about 30 cars at a time. But it's a decades-old, outdoor ride with fragile technology that doesn't seem to handle Florida's humid mornings very well.

About twice a week, Test Track will unexpectedly open late or stop running while the staff work to get it going again. They might begin

ATTRACTIONS THAT FREQUENTLY EXPERIENCE OUTAGES			
NAME OF ATTRACTION AND THEME PARK	Likelihood ride is **down** at some point in first hour park is open	Likelihood ride is **down** at some point **during the day**	Median outage duration in minutes
SPLASH MOUNTAIN (Magic Kingdom)	48%	72%	49 min.
STAR WARS: RISE OF THE RESISTANCE (Hollywood Studios)	29%	76%	53 min.
TEST TRACK (EPCOT)	25%	75%	25 min.
PIRATES OF THE CARIBBEAN (Magic Kingdom)	19%	41%	42 min.
MICKEY AND MINNIE'S RUNAWAY RAILWAY (Hollywood Studios)	19%	61%	40 min.
THE MANY ADVENTURES OF WINNIE THE POOH (Magic Kingdom)	19%	62%	35 min.
EXPEDITION EVEREST (Animal Kingdom)	17%	44%	46 min.
THE HAUNTED MANSION (Magic Kingdom)	17%	47%	19 min.

the ride with 10 or 20 cars before going to full capacity; on these days, you'll have a long wait even if you're among the first in line.

Most Disney attractions run reliably for days on end. A few experience chronic outages. When a major ride breaks down during the middle of the day, the thousands of guests who would have been on that ride head for the others that are still running.

Our touring plans consider ride reliability when choosing which attraction to visit first each morning. The EPCOT plans usually visit Soarin' first, for example, because there's a decent chance that walking to Test Track or Frozen Ever After would be a waste of time and effort, and Remy requires a Virtual Queue reservation.

If you're following a touring plan on our Lines app, you can tap the "Optimize" button to have the plan adjusted automatically to avoid the problem areas.

If you're following a printed touring plan, it's safe to assume that a ride outage will affect your plan at some point during the day. Our advice is to check the My Disney Experience app or the Lines app for current wait times throughout the rest of the park and then adjust your plan accordingly.

WEATHER AND STAFFING Two things we can't predict are the weather and how Disney will staff its rides. When lightning or heavy rains are close, Disney will close many (if not all) outdoor rides for safety. The effect on ride wait times when this happens is similar to a set of unexpected ride breakdowns, as described above.

Also, Disney will occasionally cut a ride's staffing or hourly capacity, typically to save money. We're pretty sure—because we've counted how many people exited the attractions per hour—that this has happened many times over the past few years; it's likely to keep happening too, but it's unpredictable.

THEATER SHOWS Another variable is your arrival time for a theater show: You'll wait from the time you arrive until the end of the presentation in progress. The sooner you arrive after the show in progress has started, the longer you'll wait; conversely, the later you arrive, the shorter your wait will be.

Customize Your Touring Plans

The attractions included in our touring plans are the most popular, as determined by more than 1 million reader surveys. If you've never been to Walt Disney World, we suggest using the plans in this book. Not only are they the best our program can produce, but they've also been field-tested by hundreds of thousands of families. They'll ensure that you see the best Disney attractions with as little waiting in line as possible.

If you are a return visitor, your favorite attractions may be different. One way to customize the plans is to go to **TouringPlans.com** to create personalized versions. Tell the software the date, time, and park you've chosen to visit, along with the attractions you want to see. Your custom plan will tell you, for your specific travel date and time, the exact order in which to visit attractions to minimize your waits in line. Our touring plans also support Rider Switch on thrill rides (see page 395). Besides attractions, you can schedule meals, breaks, character greetings, and more. You can even tell your plans how fast you plan to walk, and they'll make the necessary adjustments.

Our custom touring plans get rave reviews from readers and website subscribers. From an Edmonton, Alberta, reader:

> We love the ability to personalize the touring plans! Because we rarely arrive at park opening, we can't use the ones printed in the book. The personalized plans let us reduce wait times and eliminate arguing about what we are going to do next. Everyone can see their "big" attraction coming up on the plan, and we know we'll get to them all.

From a mother of two from Halifax, Nova Scotia:

> I was hesitant to pay additional money to get the TouringPlans.com membership, but boy, am I glad I did! My husband was hesitant about needing to have a plan for the park, but when we got there and he saw how we beat all the lines by following it and using the [suggested ride reservations] in the book, he was happy we had the plan. We also used the Lines app in the park to see the waiting times for rides, which were much more accurate than the Disney posted times. Next time we go to Disney World, the very first thing we will do is get a website membership!

(As a reminder, you can create touring plans for free on the website. See page 24 for details.)

From an Alexandria, Virginia, mom:

> The touring plans helped make our vacation perfect! We visited WDW over spring break, the week before Easter. It was CROWDED. We saw signs for 90- to 120-minute waits on some of the rides. Using our touring plans, we only waited for 30 minutes once. Other than that, our longest wait was 20 minutes, and most of our other waits were 0–10 minutes. We would have had a completely different vacation without the touring plans. They were lifesavers!

From a couple across the pond in London:

The personalized touring plans and the Lines app worked really well. In our five days at the parks, we managed to ride everything we wanted to multiple times. Even though there were posted waits of up to and over 120 minutes for some rides at peak times, we very rarely waited more than 15 minutes, and most times we just walked straight up to the rides.

Finally, from a Chelsea, Alabama, reader:

The book and the personal touring plans are like a one–two punch. Between them we were completely covered.

Alternatively, some changes are simple enough to make on your own. If a plan calls for an attraction you're not interested in, simply skip it and move on to the next one. You can also substitute similar attractions in the same area of the park. If a plan calls for, say, riding Dumbo and you'd rather not, but you would enjoy the Mad Tea Party (which is not on the plan), then go ahead and substitute that for Dumbo. As long as the substitution is a similar attraction (substituting a show for a ride won't work) and is pretty close to the attraction called for in the touring plan, you won't compromise the overall effectiveness of the plan.

A family of four from South Slocan, British Columbia, found they could easily tailor the touring plans to meet their needs:

We amended your touring plans by taking out the attractions we didn't want to do and just doing the remainder in order. It worked great, and by arriving before the parks opened, we got to see everything we wanted, with virtually no waits!

As did a Jacksonville, Florida, family:

We used a combination of the Two-Day Touring Plan for Parents with Small Children and the Two-Day Touring Plan for Adults. We were able to get on almost everything with a 10-minute wait or less.

What to Do If You Lose the Thread

If unforeseen events interrupt a plan:

1. If you're following a touring plan in our Lines app (touringplans.com/lines), just press "Optimize" when you're ready to start touring again. The app will figure out the best possible plan for the remainder of your day.

2. If you're following a printed touring plan, skip a step on the plan for every 20 minutes' delay. For example, if you lose your phone and spend an hour hunting for it, skip three steps and pick up from there.

3. Forget the plan and organize the remainder of your day using the standby wait times listed in Lines or the Clip-Out Touring Plan Companions in the back of this book.

"Bouncing Around"

Disney generally tries to place its popular rides on opposite sides of the park. In the Magic Kingdom, for example, the most popular attractions are positioned as far apart as possible—in the north, east, and west corners of the park—so that guests are more evenly distributed throughout the day.

It's often possible to save a lot of time in line by walking across the park to catch one of these rides when crowds are low. Some readers object to this crisscrossing. A woman from Decatur, Georgia, told us she "got dizzy from all the bouncing around." Believe us, we empathize.

In general, our touring plans recommend crossing the park only if you'll save more than 1 minute in line for every 1 minute of extra walking. (If you prefer some other trade-off, our touring plan software can help.)

We sometimes recommend crossing the park to see a newly opened ride; in these cases, a special trip to visit the attraction early avoids much longer waits later. Also, live shows, especially at the Studios, sometimes have performance schedules so at odds with each other (and the rest of the park's schedule) that orderly touring is impossible.

If you want to experience headliner attractions in one day without long waits, you can see those first (requires crisscrossing the park) or hope to squeeze in visits during the last 2 hours the park is open (may not work).

If you have two days to visit the Magic Kingdom, use its Two-Day Touring Plan (see page 721–722). It spreads the popular attractions over two mornings and works great even when the parks close early.

Touring Plan Rejection

We suggest sticking to the plans religiously, especially in the mornings, if you're visiting during busy times. The consequence of touring spontaneity in peak season is hours of standing in line. However, some folks don't respond well to the regimentation of a touring plan. If you encounter this problem with someone in your party, roll with the punches, as this Maryland couple did:

> The rest of the group was not receptive to the use of the touring plans. I think they all thought I was being a little too regimented about planning this vacation. Rather than argue, I left the touring plans behind as we ventured off for the theme parks. You can guess the outcome.

A reader from Royal Oak, Michigan, ran into trouble by not getting her family on board ahead of time:

> The one thing I will suggest is if one member of the family is doing most of the research and planning (like I did), that they communicate what the book/touring plans suggest. I failed to do this and it led to some, shall we say, tense moments between my husband and me on our first day. However, once he realized how much time we were saving, he understood why I was so bent on following the touring plans.

That said, if you're a type-A planner, relax and be prepared for surprises and setbacks. It's easy to get overwhelmed with all of this, as this woman from Trappe, Pennsylvania, reflected:

> I had been planning for this trip for two years and researching it using guidebooks, websites, videos, and information from WDW. On night three of our trip, I ended up taking an unscheduled trip to the ER. When the doctor asked what seemed to be the problem, I responded, "I don't know—but I can't stop shaking and I can't stay

here very long, because I have to get up in a couple hours to go to Disney's Hollywood Studios." Diagnosis: an anxiety attack caused by my excessive itinerary.

One of our all-time favorite letters came from an Omaha, Nebraska couple. One of them was a planner, and one clearly wasn't. They were both experienced negotiators, as their letter shows:

We created our own 4.25 x 5.5 guidebook for our trip that included a number of pages from the TouringPlans.com website. This was the first page:

THE TYPE-A SPOUSE'S BILL OF RIGHTS
1. We will not see everything in one vacation, and any attempt to do so may be met with blunt trauma.
2. Len Testa will not be vacationing with us. His plans don't schedule time for benches. Ours may.
3. We may deviate from the touring plans at some point. Really.
4. Even if it isn't on the Disney Dining Plan, a funnel cake or other snack may be purchased without a grouchy face from the nonpurchasing spouse.
5. Sometimes, sitting by the pool may sound more fun than going to a park, show, or other scheduled event. On this vacation, that will be fine.
6. "But I thought we were going to . . . " is a phrase that must be stricken from the discussion of any plans that had not been previously discussed as a couple.
7. Other items may be added as circumstances dictate at the parks.

It was a much happier vacation with these generally understood principles in writing.

Early Theme Park Entry, Extended Hours, Special Events, and the Touring Plans

Disney announced a new program called Early Theme Park Entry (aka Early Entry; see page 38) to replace the Extra Magic Hours program that ran until 2020. With Early Entry, Disney resort guests are admitted to all four Disney theme parks 30 minutes before official park opening. Off-site resort guests who enter the parks will find thousands of on-site guests already ahead of them in lines.

To mitigate the effect of Early Entry on off-site guests, we've added off-site versions of our touring plans to this book. And our free touring plan software (see touringplans.com/walt-disney-world/touring-plans) will optimize touring plans that begin up to an hour before official park opening.

As of mid-2021, Disney ran special, holiday-themed events in the Magic Kingdom from August through December. These events typically run from 9 p.m. to midnight. All require the purchase of separate tickets to attend.

5. UNDERSTAND STANDBY QUEUES, BOARDING GROUPS/VIRTUAL QUEUES, GENIE+, LIGHTNING LANE, AND INDIVIDUAL ATTRACTION ACCESS

PRIOR TO 2021, Disney ran a *free* ride-reservation system called FastPass+ which allowed you to reserve a spot on an attraction at a theme park for a specific day and time. You could book a reservation up to two months in advance. When your reservation arrived, you went to the attraction, got in a line separate from the regular ("standby") line, and were given priority access to get on the ride. In practice, the wait to use a FastPass+ was often around 20% of the wait in the standby line.

The original goal of FastPass+ was to increase guest satisfaction—Disney knew that guests who used it were more satisfied than guests who did not. That increase in guest satisfaction was apparently so important that Disney reportedly spent over $1 billion on the implementation of FastPass+ and related technology. The problem, from Disney management's perspective, was that it was hard to translate an increase in guest satisfaction—through shorter waits in line—into more money for shareholders.

Disney's current management decided to make this trade-off much clearer, by charging money to wait less. The result is an unprecedented, complex system for navigating Disney's theme parks. There are now at least six different Disney processes for waiting in line at rides. Each method has its own set of rules, and often those rules are put in place for Disney's benefit, not yours. We think that this complexity is intentional—some guests will simply give up trying to figure out how it all works and throw money at Disney to make it simpler. (If you're familiar with the term *dark pattern* in user interface design, this is a theme park example.)

Here are the ways you can wait in line at Walt Disney World:

STANDBY QUEUES This is what most people are familiar with: You get in a line, such as for Magic Carpets of Aladdin, and you wait some number of minutes until you ride. It doesn't cost anything, and the wait-time sign in front of the attraction gives you some idea of how long you're going to wait.

As we went to press, only two rides in Walt Disney World might not operate a daily standby queue: Rise of the Resistance at Disney's Hollywood Studios and Remy's Ratatouille Adventure in EPCOT. Those attractions may use boarding groups (see below) on some days.

COST: Standby queues are free with park admission.

BOARDING GROUPS/VIRTUAL QUEUES A boarding group, also known as a Virtual Queue, is a virtual line without a specific return time. Boarding groups may be used at Rise of the Resistance at Disney's Hollywood Studios and Remy's Ratatouille Adventure in EPCOT. Here's how it works: You first make a park reservation for whatever park holds the ride you want to ride. At exactly 7 a.m. on the day of your visit, you'll use My Disney Experience (MDE) to request a boarding group for that ride. If you're successful, you'll get a boarding group number (e.g., 57) and a rough estimate of how long you must wait until your boarding group is called (e.g., 250 minutes).

You need to be fast and lucky: Boarding groups for Rise of the Resistance are typically allocated for the entire day within 10 seconds of 7 a.m. So many people are trying to get a boarding group that it's essentially a lottery as to who gets in. And if anything goes wrong, your chances are almost certainly gone. A second group of reservations is available at 1 p.m., using the same process. These afternoon reservations are less likely to be called to ride, however.

If the ride is running smoothly, boarding groups typically start getting called within 30 minutes of park opening, beginning with boarding group 1. The MDE app will display the current range of boarding groups that are able to ride now. When your group is called, the app will alert you so you can return.

Boarding groups are used at rides that Disney thinks are likely to break down often. Because new rides may not have worked out all their bugs, Disney isn't confident that it can give guests a specific time to return and ride. For example, suppose Disney gave you a specific time of 1–2 p.m. to ride Rise of the Resistance. If Rise of the Resistance breaks down and is unavailable between 1 and 2 p.m., then at 2 p.m., the ride must accommodate everyone who didn't get to ride between 1 and 2, plus everyone who was scheduled to ride between 2 and 3 p.m. There's not enough ride capacity to do that (and Disney doesn't want to run the ride at half capacity in anticipation of it either). Boarding groups solve this problem by not attaching a specific return time to your virtual wait.

An issue with boarding groups (when used) is that you won't be able to ride Rise or Remy unless your first park of the day is the Studios or EPCOT (i.e., if you plan to park-hop to EPCOT or the Studios, you'll have almost no chance of riding those parks' headliner rides for free).

COST: Boarding groups are free with park admission and reservations.

GENIE+ AND LIGHTNING LANE *(aka paid FastPass+)* Genie+ is a paid version of Disney's recent FastPass+ system. Built as a feature in the My Disney Experience app, using Genie+ costs $15 per person, per day. You can purchase the Genie+ option before your trip or on specific days of your visit. If purchased in advance, the $15 fee is charged for every person who'll use Genie+, for every day of your trip. Thus, if you have a family of four and are visiting the Disney parks for five days, the advance cost of Genie+ is $15 × 4 × 5 = $300. If purchased on specific days, you can choose the days and members of your family that will use Genie+.

Paying for Genie+ allows you to make reservations that work similar to the old FastPass+ system: At participating rides, Genie+ will show you the next available return time at each attraction, such as 1–2 p.m., 1:15–2:15 p.m., and so on You'll pick the attraction whose return time works best for your day. (At press time, Disney had not indicated that you'll have the ability to select a specific return time; you'll get only what's "next" at each attraction.) When you return to ride, you'll use the Lightning Lane—a separate line that's shorter than the standby line. As with FastPass+, guests in the Lightning Lane are given priority to board. Almost all the attractions that offered FastPass+ now offer Lightning Lane. It's possible that shows that offered Fast Pass+ before will not participate in Genie+.

The number of Lightning Lane reservations available is limited, so Lightning Lane doesn't eliminate the need to arrive early. With Fast Pass+, Disney would normally allocate 75%–80% of a ride's hourly capacity to FastPass+ riders. In practice, that meant Disney put three or four people from the FastPass+ line on the ride for every one person it took from the standby line. But even with a separate line for Fast Pass+ riders, people often waited 30 minutes or more in the FastPass+ line once they returned to ride.

Disney hasn't said how much of each ride's capacity is now for sale. But because Genie+ costs real money, we believe Disney will want to set a limit on how long people will wait in the Lightning Lane—something like 25%–35% of the posted wait for the standby line.

Lightning Lane passes are offered only on the day of your visit. That differs from FastPass+, where you could make a ride reservation up to 60 days before your visit. Thus, it's possible for a ride to run out of Lightning Lane passes or desirable return times before you arrive at the park.

Guests staying at Disney's resorts can make reservations starting at 7 a.m., while off-site guests can make reservations when the park they're visiting opens officially. As we went to press, 7 a.m. was also the time at which you needed to make boarding group reservations for Rise of the Resistance and Remy's Ratatouille Adventure. We're not sure why Disney has scheduled two critical, mutually exclusive tasks for the exact same time of day, but we expect one of those times to change.

Speaking of boarding groups, Lighting Lane isn't available on rides that may use boarding groups, so you won't be able to pay to get a return window for Rise of the Resistance or Remy's Ratatouille Adventure. For those, you'll need Individual Attraction Access.

Lightning Lane Guidelines

- Park tickets must be activated at the park turnstiles before being used to obtain Lightning Lane return times, so you can't send one family member into the park while the others snooze.

- Don't use Lightning Lane unless it can save you 30 minutes or more at an attraction or if the ride is distributing immediate return times.

- If you arrive after a park opens, obtain a return time for your preferred Lightning Lane attraction first thing.

- Always check the Lightning Lane return period before obtaining your reservation. Keep an eye out for attractions whose Lightning Lane return time is immediate, or at least sooner than the standby wait.

- Don't depend on Lightning Lane or Individual Attraction Access being available for popular attractions (especially Rise of the Resistance and Remy's Ratatouille Adventure, plus Tron and Guardians of the Galaxy when they open) after noon during busier times of the year.

- Make sure everyone in your party has their own Lightning Lane return time. Reservations are tied to each individual admission pass and may not be transferred.

- You can obtain a second Lightning Lane return time as soon as you redeem your first at the attraction's entrance.

- Maximize efficiency by always obtaining a new Lightning Lane return time for the next attraction while waiting to board the previous one.

- Be mindful of your Lightning Lane return time, and plan intervening activities accordingly. You may use your Lightning Lane entry 5 minutes before its start time and up to 15 minutes after it expires. This unadvertised grace period is typically the only exception allowed to your return window.

- Attractions may not dispense Lightning Lane reservations while they are closed for technical difficulties or special events.

- If an attraction is unavailable due to technical difficulties during your return window, your Lightning Lane automatically converts to a Replacement Lightning Lane pass. Replacement passes remain valid for use until closing time at that attraction (if it reopens) or at selected other Lightning Lane attractions in the same park. If the original return window was near closing time, the Replacement pass may be valid the next day.

- You may hold only one Genie+ Lightning Lane reservation at a time, and/ or up to two reservations for individual Lightning Lane attractions. The only exception to this rule is a Replacement Lightning Lane reservation; there is no limit to the number of those you can simultaneously hold.

- You may want to pick one member of your party to handle everyone's tickets and Lightning Lane reservations on their phone. This gives your group the option of splitting up but still retaining access to each other's plans; however, each person must still use their own ticket to enter the park or redeem Lightning Lane reservations.

COST: $15 per person per day.

INDIVIDUAL ATTRACTION ACCESS   The idea here is that you'll pay even more to get on a new or very popular ride. If you didn't get a boarding group for Rise of the Resistance and you still want to ride or if you want to avoid a 2-hour wait at Slinky Dog Dash, Disney will offer you a chance to ride at a price, using Individual Attraction Access.

Purchasing an Individual Attraction Access pass should be as simple as pressing a button in the MDE app. Passes are sold on a per-person basis, and guests are limited to two purchases per day. When it's your time to ride, you'll be directed to the Lightning Lane to board.

Individual Attraction Access is a separate program from Genie and Genie+. You don't need to purchase Genie+ to purchase Individual Attraction Access. Likewise, purchasing Individual Attraction Selections does not get you access to the other attractions in the Genie+ portfolio.

At press time, Disney hadn't said which attractions will participate in Individual Attraction Access. We think this is a reasonable guess for late 2021 and into early 2022:

- **Magic Kingdom** Seven Dwarfs Mine Train, Space Mountain. Tron may replace Space Mountain when it opens.
- **EPCOT** Remy's Ratatouille Adventure, Test Track. Guardians of the Galaxy may replace Test Track when it opens
- **Hollywood Studios** Rise of the Resistance, Slinky Dog Dash
- **Animal Kingdom** Avatar Flight of Passage, Kilimanjaro Safaris

COST: Disney hadn't released prices at press time. Based on the cost of similar passes at Disneyland Paris, we expect an Individual Attraction Access pass to cost anywhere from $4 to $50 per person per ride. Prices may vary by attraction, day of year, and time of day.

DISNEY GENIE Disney announced the Genie itinerary-planning feature of the My Disney Experience app in 2019 and said little more about it for the next two years. Originally, Genie sounded a lot like our computer-optimized touring plans: You tell Genie what rides you want to ride, and Genie told you the order in which you should ride those rides to minimize your wait in line.

COST: We think the basic version of Genie will be free.

6. USE THE SINGLE-RIDER LINE *(if available)*

THIS TIME-SAVER, a line for individuals riding alone, is available at Test Track at EPCOT; Expedition Everest at Animal Kingdom; and Rock 'n' Roller Coaster and *Millennium Falcon:* Smugglers Run at the Studios. The objective is to fill odd spaces left by groups that don't quite fill the ride vehicle. Because there aren't many singles and most groups are unwilling to split up, single-rider lines are usually shorter.

PART FOUR

MAKING *the* MOST *of* YOUR MONEY

KEY QUESTIONS ANSWERED IN THIS CHAPTER

- What kind(s) of tickets do I need for Disney World? *(page 70)*
- Where can I find ticket discounts? *(page 75)*
- What are MagicBands, and how do they work? *(page 78)*
- Which special events are worth the extra cost? *(page 80)*

There is more to Orlando than Disney World. And that's a good thing, because increasingly, the only people who get to rub elbows with Mickey Mouse are rich ones.

—Sandra Tan, staff writer, *Buffalo News*

ALLOCATING MONEY

HOW MUCH DOES A DISNEY VACATION COST?

EVERY YEAR, WE HEAR FROM tens of thousands of families who are either planning or just back from a Disney vacation, and we talk with travel agents who hear from thousands more. The thing that surprises these families the most is how expensive their trip turned out to be.

So that you know what you're dealing with up front, we've created the table on pages 66–68. It shows how much Disney vacation you get for $1,500, $2,000, $3,000, and $4,000, for families of various sizes. Most cells in the table contain a list of options, such as the type of hotel at which you stay or the restaurants at which you dine. These options illustrate the trade-offs you should consider when planning your trip—and there *will* be trade-offs. Here's an example for a family of two adults and one child with a $2,000 budget, excluding transportation:

OPTION A Two full days at a Disney's theme park, two counter-service meals and one sit-down meal each day, and one night at a Disney Deluxe resort

OPTION B Three days at Disney's theme parks, three counter-service meals each day, and three nights at a budget off-site motel

In this case (and in general), your choice is between (1) a nicer hotel or (2) a longer trip, including more time in the parks, plus more nights in a cheaper hotel. You may also get better meals every day.

If you'd like to plug in your own numbers, you can download our spreadsheet at tinyurl.com/wdwyouget2022. Ticket prices are based on Disney's August 2021 costs and include tax. All hotel prices are quoted for summer nights in 2022 and include tax. These prices are likely 15%–20% higher than what you'll pay—at press time, Disney had not released discounts for summer 2022.

Here are the assumptions we made to go along with actual prices from Disney's website:

- Children are ages 3–9; adults are ages 10 and up.
- The cost of Base Tickets comes from Disney's website, reflects the average of the minimum and maximum price, and includes tax.
- One night at a non-Disney budget hotel—the GreenPoint Hotel Kissimmee—booked through the hotel, costs $86.58.
- One night at Disney's Pop Century Resort (the cheapest Disney Value resort at the time) costs $194.96 on the WDW website.
- One night at Disney's Coronado Springs Resort (the cheapest Disney Moderate resort at the time) costs $290.26 using Disney's website.
- One night at Disney's Animal Kingdom Lodge (the cheapest Disney Deluxe/Disney Vacation Club resort at the time) costs $518.07 using Disney's website.
- A day's worth of counter-service meals, plus one snack, costs $53.66 for adults and $39.12 for kids.
- A counter-service breakfast and lunch, a snack, and a table-service meal costs $86.45 per adult and $54.14 per child.

In most places in the table, theme park admission ranges from 35% to 60% of the cost of a trip, regardless of family size. If you're not staying at a Deluxe resort, it's safe to assume that ticket costs will take half of your budget (again, excluding transportation).

It's a different story for off-site hotels, which lack services like free shuttles and extra time in the theme parks. Excellent third-party resorts, such as the **Sheraton Vistana** and the **Marriott Harbour Lake,** offer *two-bedroom* rates up to 65% less than those of Disney's cheapest one-bedroom Deluxe hotels. It helps considerably if you have a car, even if you factor in the cost of gas.

How to Save $600 on Your Trip

This guide describes many techniques for saving money on a Walt Disney World vacation, including finding an inexpensive hotel, discounts on third-party admission tickets, and budget-friendly restaurants. Sometimes, however, you can do all of that and *still* need to cut your budget.

TouringPlans.com blogger **Kristi Fredericks** has you covered with six simple ways to save almost $600 on your Disney vacation.

For each of these tips, assume a family of four traveling to Walt Disney World for a one-week (six-day, seven-night) vacation. Our sample family includes two adults and two children ages 3 and 9.

continued on page 69

WHAT YOU PAY AND WHAT YOU GET AT WDW

• 2 ADULTS/$4,000

BUDGET OPTION ($4,052)
• 10 days theme park admission, parking
• 10 sit-down dinners
• 10 nights at a budget off-site motel

VALUE OPTION ($3,810)
• 8 days theme park admission
• 8 counter-service meals
• 9 nights at a Disney Value resort

MODERATE OPTION ($3,937)
• 7 days theme park admission
• 7 counter-service meals
• 7 nights at a Disney Moderate resort

DELUXE OPTION ($3,900)
• 5 days theme park admission
• 2 counter-service meals, 3 sit-down dinners
• 4 nights at a Disney Deluxe resort

• 2 ADULTS, 2 KIDS/$4,000

BUDGET OPTION ($4,150)
• 6 days theme park admission, parking
• 4 counter-service meals, 2 sit-down dinners
• 6 nights at a budget off-site motel

VALUE OPTION ($4,051)
• 5 days theme park admission
• 5 sit-down meals
• 5 nights at a Disney Value resort

MODERATE OPTION ($3,929)
• 4 days theme park admission
• 4 counter-service meals
• 4 nights at a Disney Moderate resort

DELUXE OPTION ($3,896)
• 3 days theme park admission
• 1 counter-service meal, 2 sit-down dinners
• 3 nights at a Disney Deluxe resort

• 2 ADULTS, 1 KID/$4,000

BUDGET OPTION ($4,096)
• 9 days theme park admission, parking
• 9 counter-service meals
• 9 nights at a budget off-site motel

VALUE OPTION ($3,908)
• 6 days theme park admission
• 6 counter-service meals
• 7 nights at a Disney Value resort

MODERATE OPTION ($3,995)
• 6 days theme park admission
• 6 counter-service meals
• 5 nights at a Disney Moderate resort

DELUXE OPTION ($4,187)
• 4 days theme park admission
• 4 sit-down dinners
• 4 nights at a Disney Deluxe resort

• 3 ADULTS/$4,000

BUDGET OPTION ($3,936)
• 8 days theme park admission, parking
• 8 counter-service meals
• 8 nights at a budget off-site motel

VALUE OPTION ($4,051)
• 5 days theme park admission
• 5 counter-service meals
• 5 nights at a Disney Value resort

MODERATE OPTION ($3,929)
• 4 days theme park admission
• 4 counter-service meals
• 4 nights at a Disney Moderate resort

DELUXE OPTION ($3,896)
• 3 days theme park admission
• 1 counter-service meal, 2 sit-down dinners
• 3 nights at a Disney Deluxe resort

• 3 ADULTS, 1 KID/$4,000

BUDGET OPTION ($4,067)
• 6 days theme park admission, parking
• 6 counter-service meals
• 6 nights at a budget off-site motel

VALUE OPTION ($3,965)
• 4 days theme park admission
• 1 counter-service meal, 3 sit-down dinners
• 4 nights at a Disney Value resort

MODERATE OPTION ($4,006)
• 4 days theme park admission
• 4 counter-service meals
• 4 nights at a Disney Moderate resort

DELUXE OPTION ($3,990)
• 3 days theme park admission
• 1 counter-service meal, 2 sit-down dinners
• 3 nights at a Disney Deluxe resort

• 2 ADULTS/$3,000

BUDGET OPTION ($3,066)
• 9 days theme park admission, parking
• 9 counter-service meals
• 8 nights at a budget off-site motel

VALUE OPTION ($2,937)
• 6 days theme park admission
• 6 counter-service meals
• 6 nights at a Disney Value resort

MODERATE OPTION ($3,082)
• 5 days theme park admission
• 5 counter-service meals
• 5 nights at a Disney Moderate resort

DELUXE OPTION ($3,015)
• 4 days theme park admission
• 4 counter-service meals
• 3 nights at a Disney Deluxe resort

• 2 ADULTS, 1 KID/$3,000

BUDGET OPTION ($3,096)
• 6 days theme park admission, parking
• 6 counter-service meals
• 5 nights at a budget off-site motel

VALUE OPTION ($2,894)
• 4 days theme park admission
• 4 sit-down dinners
• 4 nights at a Disney Value resort

MODERATE OPTION ($2,985)
• 4 days theme park admission
• 4 counter-service meals
• 3 nights at a Disney Moderate resort

DELUXE OPTION ($2,920)
• 3 days theme park admission
• 3 sit-down dinners
• 2 nights at a Disney Deluxe resort

WHAT YOU PAY AND WHAT YOU GET AT WDW *(continued)*

• 2 ADULTS, 2 KIDS/$3,000

BUDGET OPTION ($3,108)
- 4 days theme park admission, parking
- 4 counter-service meals
- 3 nights at a budget off-site motel

VALUE OPTION ($3,022)
- 3 days theme park admission
- 3 sit-down dinners
- 3 nights at a Disney Value resort

MODERATE OPTION ($3,117)
- 3 days theme park admission
- 2 counter-service meals, 1 sit-down dinner
- 3 nights at a Disney Moderate resort

DELUXE OPTION ($3,017)
- 2 days theme park admission
- 2 sit-down dinners
- 3 nights at a Disney Deluxe resort

• 3 ADULTS/$3,000

BUDGET OPTION ($2,979)
- 5 days theme park admission, parking
- 5 counter-service meals, 1 sit-down dinner
- 5 nights at a budget off-site motel

VALUE OPTION ($2,971)
- 4 days theme park admission
- 4 counter-service meals
- 4 nights at a Disney Value resort

MODERATE OPTION ($3,062)
- 4 days theme park admission
- 4 counter-service meals
- 3 nights at a Disney Moderate resort

DELUXE OPTION ($2,737)
- 3 days theme park admission
- 3 counter-service meals
- 2 nights at a Disney Deluxe resort

• 3 ADULTS, 1 KID/$3,000

BUDGET OPTION ($2,615)
- 5 days theme park admission, parking
- 5 sit-down dinners
- 5 nights at a budget off-site motel

VALUE OPTION ($3,134)
- 3 days theme park admission
- 3 sit-down dinners
- 3 nights at a Disney Value resort

MODERATE OPTION ($3,080)
- 3 days theme park admission
- 3 counter-service meals
- 3 nights at a Disney Moderate resort

DELUXE OPTION ($3,056)
- 2 days theme park admission
- 2 counter-service meals
- 3 nights at a Disney Deluxe resort

• 3 ADULTS, 1 KID/$2,000

BUDGET OPTION ($2,028)
- 2 days theme park admission, parking
- 2 sit-down dinners
- 3 nights at a budget off-site motel

VALUE OPTION ($2,005)
- 2 days theme park admission
- 1 counter-service meal, 1 sit-down dinner
- 2 nights at a Disney Value resort

MODERATE OPTION ($2,082)
- 2 days theme park admission
- 2 counter-service meals
- 2 nights at a Disney Moderate resort

DELUXE OPTION ($2,020)
- 2 days theme park admission
- 2 counter-service meals
- 1 night at a Disney Deluxe resort

• 2 ADULTS, 2 KIDS/$2,000

BUDGET OPTION ($1,868)
- 2 days theme park admission, parking
- 2 sit-down dinners
- 2 nights at a budget off-site motel

VALUE OPTION ($2,047)
- 2 days theme park admission
- 2 counter-service meals
- 3 nights at a Disney Value resort

MODERATE OPTION ($2,043)
- 2 days theme park admission
- 2 counter-service meals
- 2 nights at a Disney Moderate resort

DELUXE OPTION ($1,980)
- 2 days theme park admission
- 2 counter-service meals
- 1 night at a Disney Deluxe resort

• 3 ADULTS/$2,000

BUDGET OPTION ($2,021)
- 3 days theme park admission, parking
- 3 counter-service meals
- 3 nights at a budget off-site motel

VALUE OPTION ($2,091)
- 2 days theme park admission
- 2 counter-service meals
- 3 nights at a Disney Value resort

MODERATE OPTION ($2,043)
- 2 days theme park admission
- 2 counter-service meals
- 2 nights at a Disney Moderate resort

DELUXE OPTION ($1,871)
- 2 days theme park admission
- 2 sit-down dinners
- 1 night at a Disney Deluxe resort

continued on next page

continued from previous page

WHAT YOU PAY AND WHAT YOU GET AT WDW *(continued)*

• 2 ADULTS/$2,000

BUDGET OPTION ($2,077)
- 5 days theme park admission, parking
- 5 counter-service meals
- 4 nights at a budget off-site motel

VALUE OPTION ($1,914)
- 3 days theme park admission
- 3 counter-service meals
- 4 nights at a Disney Value resort

MODERATE OPTION ($2,005)
- 3 days theme park admission
- 3 counter-service meals
- 3 nights at a Disney Moderate resort

DELUXE OPTION ($1,938)
- 2 days theme park admission
- 2 sit-down meals
- 2 nights at a Disney Deluxe resort

• 2 ADULTS, 1 KID/$2,000

BUDGET OPTION ($1,962)
- 3 days theme park admission, parking
- 3 counter-service meals
- 3 nights at a budget off-site motel

VALUE OPTION ($1,863)
- 2 days theme park admission
- 2 sit-down dinners
- 3 nights at a Disney Value resort

MODERATE OPTION ($1,987)
- 2 days theme park admission
- 2 counter-service meals
- 2 nights at a Disney Moderate resort

DELUXE OPTION ($1,796)
- 2 days theme park admission
- 2 sit-down dinners
- 1 night at a Disney Deluxe resort

• 2 ADULTS/$1,500

BUDGET OPTION ($1,540)
- 3 days theme park admission, parking
- 3 counter-service meals
- 4 nights at a budget off-site motel

VALUE OPTION ($1,524)
- 3 days theme park admission
- 3 counter-service meals
- 2 nights at a Disney Value resort

MODERATE OPTION ($1,482)
- 2 days theme park admission
- 2 sit-down dinners
- 2 nights at a Disney Moderate resort

DELUXE OPTION ($1,420)
- 2 days theme park admission
- 2 sit-down dinners
- 1 night at a Disney Deluxe resort

• 2 ADULTS, 1 KID/$1,500

BUDGET OPTION ($1,497)
- 2 days theme park admission, parking
- 1 counter-service meal, 1 sit-down dinner
- 3 nights at a budget off-site motel

VALUE OPTION ($1,506)
- 2 days theme park admission
- 2 counter-service meals
- 2 nights at a Disney Value resort

MODERATE OPTION ($1,487)
- 2 days theme park admission
- 1 counter-service meal, 1 sit-down dinner
- 1 night at a Disney Moderate resort

DELUXE OPTION ($1,087)
- 1 day theme park admission
- 1 sit-down dinner
- 1 night at a Disney Deluxe resort

• 2 ADULTS, 2 KIDS/$1,500

BUDGET OPTION ($948)
- 1 day theme park admission, parking
- 1 sit-down dinner
- 1 night at a budget off-site motel

VALUE OPTION ($1,036)
- 1 day theme park admission
- 1 sit-down dinner
- 1 night at a Disney Value resort

MODERATE OPTION ($1,512)
- 1 day theme park admission
- 2 counter-service meals
- 2 nights at a Disney Moderate resort

DELUXE OPTION ($1,264)
- 1 day theme park admission
- 1 counter-service meal
- 1 night at a Disney Deluxe resort

• 3 ADULTS/$1,500

BUDGET OPTION ($1,456)
- 2 days theme park admission, parking
- 1 counter-service meal
- 2 nights at a budget off-site motel

VALUE OPTION ($1,449)
- 2 days theme park admission
- 1 counter-service meal, 1 sit-down dinner
- 1 night at a Disney Value resort

MODERATE OPTION ($1,446)
- 2 days theme park admission
- 2 counter-service meals
- 1 night at a Disney Moderate resort

DELUXE OPTION ($1,107)
- 1 day theme park admission
- 1 counter-service meal
- 1 night at a Disney Deluxe resort

• 3 ADULTS, 1 KID/$1,500

BUDGET OPTION ($1,072)
- 1 day theme park admission, parking
- 1 sit-down dinner
- 2 nights at a budget off-site motel

VALUE OPTION ($1,469)
- 1 day theme park admission
- 1 counter-service meal, 1 sit-down dinner
- 2 nights at a Disney Value resort

MODERATE OPTION ($1,460)
- 1 day theme park admission
- 1 sit-down dinner
- 2 nights at a Disney Moderate resort

DELUXE OPTION ($1,284)
- 1 day theme park admission
- 1 counter-service meal
- 1 night at a Disney Deluxe resort

continued from page 65

TIP #1: BRING YOUR OWN RAINGEAR

Disney World can be a rainy place no matter what time of year you visit. Bring your own rain ponchos instead of buying at the parks to save some dough.

DON'T Buy 2 adult ponchos x $10 and 2 kids' ponchos x $9 = **$38**
DO Buy 4 ponchos at local dollar store = **$4**
SAVINGS $38 – $4 = **$34**

TIP #2: BUY TICKETS IN ADVANCE

Disney adds a $21.30 surcharge to every ticket of three days or longer that is bought at its theme parks. Why? Because it can; it knows that you're not likely to turn the kids around and leave once you're that close.

DON'T Wait until you get to the parks to buy tickets.
DO Buy tickets in advance either from Disney or from one of our recommended ticket wholesalers (see page 76).
SAVINGS $21.30 x 4 tickets = **$85.20**

TIP #3: BRING YOUR OWN STROLLER

Our sample family will need a stroller for their 3-year-old in the parks, and it's handy to have a stroller for the airport and resort areas as well. Remember that most airlines will gate-check your stroller for free.

DON'T Rent a stroller for $15 per day (length-of-stay rate) x 6 days = **$90**
DO Buy 1 umbrella stroller on Amazon = **$28**
SAVINGS $90 – $28 = **$62**

TIP #4: DRINK FREE WATER

All Disney restaurants will give you a free cup of ice water. Instead of wasting money and calories on sugary drinks, this is an easy way to save some cash. For our sample family, let's assume that everyone wants to drink something other than water at breakfast and that the kids' meals will include a drink at lunch and dinner. Only the adults will drink free water, and only at lunch and dinner.

DON'T Buy 1 beverage at $3.99 each x 2 adults x 2 meals x 6 days = **$96**
DO Drink free water = **$0**
SAVINGS $96 – $0 = **$96**

TIP #5: BRING YOUR OWN SNACKS

It's amazing how much you can save by bringing your own nonperishable snacks into the park. A zip-top plastic bag filled with cereal bars, granola, raisins, and crackers goes a long way toward staving off hunger.

DON'T Buy 1 snack at $4 each x 4 people x 2 times x 6 days = **$192**
DO Bring your own snacks = **$35**
SAVINGS $192 – $35 = **$157**

TIP #6: EAT BREAKFAST IN YOUR ROOM

This saves you time and a small fortune. Let's assume our family will grab two coffees and two milks from their hotel's food court each morning, so we won't include beverages in either cost.

DON'T Buy one $12 breakfast platter + one $6 yogurt parfait + two $7 kids' Mickey waffle meals x 6 days = **$192**
DO Bring your own breakfast, including paper bowls, napkins, plastic spoons, cereal, breakfast pastries, mini-doughnuts, and cereal bars = **$40**
SAVINGS $192 – $40 = **$152**

TOTAL SAVINGS **$586.20** *(about $98 per day)*

FOUR MORE TIPS FROM BOB

1. Buy your admission online from one of the sellers on page 74. Get tickets only for the number of days you plan to visit, skipping any add-ons.

2. Book a hotel outside of Walt Disney World. Hotels on US 192 (Irlo Bronson Memorial Highway) are usually the least expensive. Or consider renting a vacation home (see discussion starting on page 222) if you have four or more people in your group.

3. Avoid parking fees by using your hotel's shuttle service or by taking a Disney bus from the water parks (where—for the moment—parking is free) to a Disney hotel, then to a theme park. This suggestion takes a lot of time, so do it only if you're budgeting to the penny.

4. Buy discounted Disney-brand apparel and souvenirs from one of Orlando's two **Disney Character Warehouse** outlets (tinyurl.com/disneyoutlets).

WALT DISNEY WORLD ADMISSION TICKETS

DISNEY OFFERS MORE THAN 7,000 theme park ticket options, ranging from the humble **1-Day Base Ticket,** which is good for a single day's entry into one Disney theme park, to the blinged-out **Incredi-Pass,** good for 365 days of admission into every Disney theme park and more attractions. See the table on pages 72–73 for a summary of the most common admission types.

A theme park reservation is required for each day you plan to use your theme park tickets. Make reservations as far in advance as possible. Capacity is limited, and buying park tickets, even directly from Disney and for specific dates, doesn't guarantee that you'll get a park reservation. Thus, there's a risk that you could purchase tickets that cannot be used, especially during busier times of the year.

If you purchased tickets and were planning to use them between March 12 and July 11, 2020, Disney automatically extended those tickets to be used on any date through September 26, 2021. If you didn't plan visit before September 26, 2021, you can apply the value of the unused portion of your tickets to new tickets bought after that date. If those options don't work for you, then you can ask Disney for a refund by calling ☎ 407-939-1289.

DATE-BASED PRICING AND OTHER SURCHARGES

DISNEY INTRODUCED DATE-BASED PRICING for multiday theme park tickets in late 2018, following its switch to date-based pricing of single-day tickets in 2016. Now they're more like hotel-room or airline-ticket pricing, where the price of the ticket changes based on the days of the year you're traveling.

Tickets are now generally most expensive when children are out of school: Christmas and other holidays, spring break, and summer vacation. Less-expensive tickets are generally available during non-holiday periods when children are in school and during months subject to inclement weather: January and February, for example, and peak hurricane season in September.

You must tell Disney the first date you plan to visit a theme park or water park. Your ticket price will be based on that starting date, the number of days you plan to visit theme parks or water parks, and whether you plan to visit more than one theme park per day.

If you need to move your vacation dates from more-expensive to less-expensive days, Disney will not refund the difference in ticket prices—but they will charge you the incremental cost if you need to move from less-expensive to more-expensive days.

TICKET ADD-ONS

THREE TICKET ADD-ON OPTIONS are available with your park admission, each at an additional cost:

PARK HOPPER Lets you visit more than one theme park per day. The cost is about $69–$91 (including tax) on top of the ticket price. The longer your stay, the more affordable it is: As an add-on to a 7-Day Base Ticket, for example, the flat fee works out to $13 a day for park-hopping privileges; as an add-on to a 2-Day Base Ticket, the fee works out to $40 a day. If you want to visit the Magic Kingdom in the morning and eat at EPCOT in the evening, this is the feature to request. At press time, guests must make a reservation for the first park they wish to visit, and they must enter that park first. Guests will not be allowed to hop to the second park until 2 p.m., though that is subject to change.

WATER PARK AND SPORTS This $75 (including tax) option provides daily entry to Disney's two water parks (Blizzard Beach and Typhoon Lagoon), the Oak Trail Golf Course, Fantasia Gardens and Winter Summerland minigolf, and the ESPN Wide World of Sports Complex.

PARK HOPPER PLUS The Park Hopper Plus option combines the Park Hopper and Water Park and Sports add-ons. This option costs $91–$112 more than a Base Ticket, including tax, which is cheaper than the combined cost of the two options purchased separately.

You can't change how many Park Hopper/Water Park/PHP admissions you can buy with either option; the number is fixed, and unused days aren't refundable. You can, however, skip Park Hopper/Water Park/PHP entirely and buy an individual admission to any of the venues above—that's frequently the best deal if you're not park-hopping and want to visit just Typhoon Lagoon and/or Blizzard Beach once.

If you buy a ticket but then decide later that you want to add the Park Hopper/PHP option, you can do so. Disney doesn't prorate the cost: If you add Park Hopper/PHP on the last day of your trip, you'll pay the same price as if you'd bought it before you left home.

WHEN TICKETS EXPIRE
(for tickets dated August 13, 2021, and later)

ALONG WITH IMPLEMENTING date-based pricing, Disney has shortened the amount of time you have to use your tickets. Whereas previously all tickets expired 14 days from the date of first use, ticket expiration is now based on how many days you're visiting the theme parks and water parks, as shown in the table on page 74.

WDW THEME PARK TICKET OPTIONS

	1-DAY	2-DAY	3-DAY	4-DAY	5-DAY	
USE WITHIN: 1 DAY	4 DAYS	5 DAYS	7 DAYS	8 DAYS	
BASE TICKET AGES 3-9						
ALL PARKS: $111-$164	$216-$319	$321-$461	$419-$578	$446-$611	
—	($108-$160/day)	($107-$154/day)	($105-$144/day)	($89-$122/day)	
BASE TICKET AGE 10+						
ALL PARKS: $116-$169	$226-$330	$336-$476	$437-$597	$466-$631	
—	($113-$165/day)	($112-$159/day)	($109-$149/day)	($93-$126/day)	

Base Ticket admits guest to one theme park each day of use. Tickets must be used within the number of days shown in the "Use Within" row above.

FLEXIBLE DATES *(add-on)*					
AGES 3-9: $0-$53 AGE 10+: $0-$53	$5-$109 $6-$109	$4-$144 $5-$145	$4-$163 $6-$165	$5-$170 $6-$171	

Flexible Dates allows you to start using your ticket on any day of the year, through December 31, 2021. In addition, tickets expire 14 days after first use.

PARK HOPPER					
AGES 3-9: $180-$233 AGE 10+: $185-$239	$296-$399 $306-$410	$401-$541 $416-$556	$509-$669 $528-$687	$536-$701 $557-$721	

Park Hopper option entitles guest to visit more than one theme park on each day of use. See page 75 for details.

WATER PARK AND SPORTS					
AGES 3-9: $185-$224 AGE 10+: $191-$244	$296-$368 $306-$378	$406-$505 $421-$520	$492-$625 $511-$644	$520-$671 $540-$691	

Water Park and Sports entitles you to a specified number of visits (between 1 and 10) to a choice of entertainment and recreation venues. It's a flat $75 fee to add to any ticket for any age and any ticket length.

PARK HOPPER PLUS					
AGES 3-9: $201-$255 AGE 10+: $207-$260	$335-$421 $345-$431	$443-$562 $458-$577	$535-$685 $554-$704	$562-$722 $582-$742	
1 visit	2 visits	3 visits	4 visits	5 visits	

Park Hopper Plus option entitles guest to a specified number of visits (1-10) to a choice of entertainment and recreation venues, plus the Park Hopper option above. PHP tickets expire 1 day later than the "Use Within" days above.

Example: If you purchase a basic 4-Day Base Ticket and specify that you'll start using it on June 1, 2021, you must complete your four theme park visits by midnight June 7, 2021. *Once you start using your ticket, any unused admissions expire even if you don't use them.*

If you purchase a ticket and don't use any of it before it expires, you can apply the amount paid for that ticket toward the purchase of a new ticket at current prices, providing the new ticket's price is the same cost (or more) of the expired ticket.

ANNUAL PASSES

ANNUAL PASSES PROVIDE UNLIMITED USE of the major theme parks for one year. Passholders can add on a year of water park access for an additional $105 on top of the prices shown. Four versions are available (prices are for age 3 and up and include tax):

NOTE: ALL TICKET AND ADD-ON PRICES INCLUDE 6.5% SALES TAX.				
6-DAY	**7-DAY**	**8-DAY**	**9-DAY**	**10-DAY**
9 DAYS	10 DAYS	12 DAYS	13 DAYS	14 DAYS
BASE TICKET AGES 3–9				
$459–$625	$473–$640	$496–$656	$513–$669	$530–$680
($77–$104/day)	($68–$91/day)	($62–$82/day)	($57–$74/day)	($53–$68/day)
BASE TICKET AGE 10+				
$480–$646	$494–$662	$518–$679	$536–$692	$554–$704
($80–$108/day)	($71–$95/day)	($65–$85/day)	($60–$77/day)	($55–$70/day)
Park choices are Magic Kingdom, EPCOT, Disney's Hollywood Studios, or Disney's Animal Kingdom.				
FLEXIBLE DATES (add-on)				
$5–$171 $6–$172	$7–$174 $6–$174	$8–$169 $7–$168	$11–$165 $9–$163	$12–$162 $10–$160
In essence, the Flexible Dates option prices your ticket as the most expensive possible under Disney's pricing scheme, plus a small surcharge.				
PARK HOPPER				
$550–$716 $571–$736	$563–$730 $585–$752	$586–$747 $609–$769	$603–$759 $627–$782	$620–$770 $644–$794
Park choices are any combination of Magic Kingdom, EPCOT, Disney's Hollywood Studios, or Disney's Animal Kingdom on each day of use.				
WATER PARK AND SPORTS				
$575–$740 $596–$761	$593–$756 $615–$778	$624–$777 $647–$799	$635–$788 $658–$811	$644–$798 $668–$822
Choices are Disney's Blizzard Beach water park, Disney's Typhoon Lagoon water park, Oak Trail Golf Course, ESPN Wide World of Sports Complex (if open), and Fantasia or Winter Summerland minigolf.				
PARK HOPPER PLUS				
$575–$740 $596–$761	$593–$756 $647–$799	$624–$777 $630–$791	$635–$788 $658–$811	$644–$798 $668–$822
6 visits	7 visits	8 visits	9 visits	10 visits
Choices are Disney's Blizzard Beach water park, Disney's Typhoon Lagoon water park, Oak Trail Golf Course, ESPN Wide World of Sports Complex (if open), or Fantasia Gardens or Winter Summerland minigolf.				

- The **Pixie Dust Pass** ($425; Florida residents only) allows for holding up to three simultaneous park reservations. The Pixie Dust Pass has the most blockout dates—dates when the pass cannot be used: almost all weekends are off-limits, plus a week or two around every major holiday, and chunks of time around minor holidays.

- The **Pirate Pass** ($744; Florida residents only) includes four simultaneous park reservations. Has fewer blockout dates on weekends than the Pixie Dust Pass. Retains the blockout dates for every major and minor holidays.

- The **Sorcerer Pass** ($957; Florida residents and Disney Vacation Club members only) includes five simultaneous park reservations. The only blockout dates are the Wednesday to Sunday around Thanksgiving, and December 18–31 in 2021.

- The **Incredi-Pass** ($1,383; available to everyone) includes five simultaneous park reservations and has no blockout dates.

WHEN TICKETS EXPIRE

Number of Days on Base Ticket	How Many Days Till Ticket Expires From First Use (without Park Hopper Plus option)	How Many Days Till Ticket Expires From First Use (with Park Hopper Plus option)
1	Expires after first use	Expires 1 day after first use
2	4 days	5 days
3	5 days	6 days
4	7 days	8 days
5	8 days	9 days
6	9 days	10 days
7	10 days	11 days
8	12 days	13 days
9	13 days	14 days
10	14 days	15 days

Holders of all Annual Passes also get perks, including free parking; hotel, dining, and merchandise discounts; and seasonal offers such as a dedicated entrance line at the parks. The passes are not valid for special events. As we went to press, stand-alone water park Annual Passes were not offered. See disneyworld.com/passes for more information about all Annual Pass options.

Note: Due to COVID-19, a theme park reservation is required for each day you plan to use your theme park tickets. Purchasing an Annual Pass doesn't guarantee you a theme park reservation.

WHERE TO PURCHASE DISNEY WORLD TICKETS

unofficial **TIP**
If you order physical tickets in advance, allow enough time for them to be mailed to your home.

PASSES ARE AVAILABLE at Disney resorts and theme parks and at Disney Stores and disney world.com for the prices shown above. (If you purchase on arrival, you will incur a $21.30-per-ticket surcharge for tickets of three days or longer.)

If you're trying to keep your vacation costs to an absolute minimum, consider using an online ticket wholesaler such as **Tripster** (☎ 888-590-5910; tripster.com) or **Boardwalk Ticketing** (boardwalkticketing.com), especially for trips of three or more days in the parks. All tickets are brand new, and the savings can easily exceed $200 for a family of four. Vendors will provide you with electronic tickets just like Disney does, so you'll be able to make park reservations immediately through the My Disney Experience website.

You might be wondering why Disney gives third-party wholesalers such large discounts on tickets. The answer is volume. Disney knows most visitors will pay full price for tickets, so there's no incentive to offer them a discount. However, Disney also knows that there are lots of shoppers who will visit only if they can get a deal. Disney uses third-party wholesalers to offer discounted tickets to those shoppers, so it doesn't have to offer discounts to the general public. It's a win-win-win: The discount shoppers get their deal, Disney maximizes its revenue, and third-party companies earn a little bit too.

Tripster offers discount tickets for almost all Central Florida attractions, including Disney, Universal, and SeaWorld. Boardwalk Ticketing offers them only for Disney. Discounts for the major theme parks range from about 6% to 12%; tickets for other attractions are more deeply discounted.

Finally, tickets are available at some non-Disney hotels and shopping centers and through independent ticket brokers. Because Disney admissions are only marginally discounted in the Walt Disney World–Orlando area, the chief reason for you to buy from an independent broker is convenience. Offers of free or heavily discounted tickets abound, but the catch is that they generally require you to attend a time-share sales presentation.

Where *Not* to Buy Tickets and Passes

In addition to the many authorized resellers of Disney admissions, a number of unauthorized ones exist. They buy unused days on legitimately purchased park passes and resell them as if they were brand new.

unofficial **TIP**
Also steer clear of passes offered on eBay and Craigslist.

These resellers insist that you specify the exact days you plan to use the ticket. They already know, of course, how many days are left on the pass and when it expires. If you tell them that you plan to use it tomorrow and the next two days, then they'll sell you a ticket that has three days left on it and expires in three days. Naturally, because they don't tell you this, you assume that the usual five-day expiration period applies from the date of first use. In the case of your tickets, however, the original purchaser triggered the five-day expiration period. Skip a day instead of using the pass on the next three consecutive days, and you'll discover to your chagrin that it has expired.

HOW TO SAVE MONEY ON DISNEY WORLD TICKETS

DISNEY'S DATE-BASED PRICING SCHEME is the most complicated system it has ever used for ticket purchases—so complicated, in fact, that we wrote a computer program to analyze all the options and to look for loopholes in the new pricing rules. Visit **TouringPlans.com** and try our **Ticket Price Comparison Tool** (tinyurl.com/ug-ticketcalculator). It aggregates ticket prices from Disney and a number of online ticket vendors. Answer a few questions relating to the size of your party and the parks you intend to visit, and the calculator will identify your four cheapest ticket options. It will also show you how much you'll save versus buying at the gate.

The program will also make recommendations for considerations other than price. For example, annual passes might cost more, but Disney often offers substantial resort discounts and other deals to annual pass holders. These resort discounts, especially during the off-season, can more than offset the price of the pass.

Our Ticket Calculator will automatically use all of the tips below, and more. If you'd rather do the heavy lifting yourself (please don't), here's what you'll need to consider:

1. BUY PARK TICKETS BEFORE YOU GET TO THE PARKS. As mentioned previously, if you buy at the theme parks, Disney adds a surcharge of $21.30 to park tickets with three or more days of admission.

2. BUY FROM A THIRD-PARTY WHOLESALER. As we've noted, Disney contracts with third-party ticket vendors to offer discounts to price-sensitive consumers who'll visit only if they are able to get a "deal." By using other companies, Disney doesn't have to offer those discounts directly to people who'd visit anyway. These vendors sign contracts with Disney and provide exactly the same tickets you'd purchase at Walt Disney World. See "Where to Purchase Disney World Tickets," page 74, for vendors we recommend.

3. MEMBERS OF THE US MILITARY AND FLORIDA RESIDENTS GET SPECIAL DISCOUNTS. Disney's recent deal for US military personnel included a 4-Day Park Hopper for $315, substantially less than the $687 regular price. Florida resident discounts aren't as steep, but they're better than anything the general public gets.

4. SET YOUR TICKET'S START DATE EARLIER THAN YOUR ARRIVAL DATE. Suppose you're visiting for a long weekend (Thursday–Sunday) and you're buying four-day tickets. You'd naturally pick Thursday as your ticket's start date. But remember that four-day park tickets are valid for seven days. If you're visiting at the start of a busy (i.e., expensive) season, setting your ticket start date to Monday or Tuesday can save around $8 per ticket.

5. BUY A SEPARATE WATER PARK TICKET INSTEAD OF THE WATER PARK AND SPORTS ADD-ON IF YOU'RE VISITING ONLY ONE WATER PARK. The break-even point on the Water Park and Sports option is two water-park visits.

6. VISIT A WATER PARK ON YOUR FIRST OR LAST DAY. Let's say your Disney World trip starts at the end of a busy period and you're already planning one water park visit. Visiting the water park on your first day allows you to set your theme park start date one day later, saving around $3 per ticket. The same advice works in reverse: If your trip ends at the beginning of a busy season, go to the water park on the last day of your trip.

Ticket Deals for Canada Residents

Disney often discounts theme park admission for Canada residents by setting the Canadian dollar at par with the United States dollar. The exchange rate as of this writing is $1 CAD equals $0.80 USD, so this deal effectively boosts the value of the Loonie by around 25%. Visit disneyworld.disney.go.com/en_CA/special-offers to see the latest offers.

Ticket Deals for United Kingdom Residents

In the UK, Disney offers advance-purchase tickets that aren't available in the United States. As we went to press, you can get 14-Day **Ultimate Tickets** for £439 for adults and £419 for kids—the same price as a 7-Day Ultimate Ticket. Ultimate Tickets provide unlimited admission to major and minor parks along with park-hopping privileges to the major parks. Ultimate Tickets expire 14 days after first use. To find out more, call ☎ 0800-169-0730 UK or 407-566-4985 US (Monday–Friday, 9 a.m.–8 p.m.; Saturday, 9 a.m.–7 p.m.; and Sunday, 10 a.m.–4 p.m.), or see disneyholidays.co.uk/walt-disney-world or the **Disney Information Bulletin Board** at thedibb.co.uk.

Discounts Available to Certain Groups and Individuals

DISNEY VACATION CLUB Members get a discount on annual passes.

CONVENTION-GOERS Disney World, Universal Orlando, SeaWorld, and other Orlando-area parks sometimes set up a web link cited in convention materials allowing you to purchase discounted afternoon and evening admissions.

DISNEY CORPORATE SPONSORS If you work for one of these, you may be eligible for discounted admissions or perks at the parks. Check with your workplace's employee-benefits office.

FLORIDA RESIDENTS get substantial savings on virtually all tickets. You'll need to prove Florida residency with a valid driver's license or state identification card.

MILITARY, DEPARTMENT OF DEFENSE, CIVIL SERVICE Active-duty and retired military, Department of Defense (DOD) civilian employees, some civil-service employees, and dependents of these groups can buy Disney multiday admissions at a 9%–10% discount. Military personnel can buy discounted admission for nonmilitary guests if the military member accompanies the nonmilitary guest. If a group seeks the discount, at least half of the members of the group must be eligible for the military discount.

DISNEY YOUTH EDUCATION SERIES Disney runs daily educational programs for K–12 students; these programs also offer substantial ticket discounts (but with substantial restrictions). See disneyyouth.com.

Special Passes

Go to **MouseSavers.com** for information on passes that are not known to the general public and are not sold at any Walt Disney World ticket booth. For details, see tinyurl.com/wdwdiscounttix.

DISNEY TICKET PRICE INCREASES

DISNEY USUALLY RAISES TICKET PRICES once or twice a year. Hikes were announced in February 2020, March 2019, February and September 2018, February 2014–2017, June 2011–2013, and August 2006–2010. We expect a price increase in late 2021 or early 2022.

unofficial **TIP**
Save money on tickets by planning ahead—buy them before the next price increase.

Prices on all tickets went up an average of almost 6% in 2020, 4% in 2019, 9% in 2018, and 7% in 2017. Year-over-year hikes averaged around 5% earlier in this decade. If you're putting together a budget, assume an increase of around 8% per year to be safe.

FOR ADDITIONAL INFORMATION ON TICKETS

IF YOU HAVE A QUESTION OR CONCERN regarding admissions that can be addressed only with a person-to-person conversation, call **Disney Ticket Inquiries** at ☎ 407-566-4985 or email ticket.inquiries@ disneyworld.com. If you call, be aware that you may spend considerable time on hold; if you email, know that it can take up to three days to get a response. In contrast, the ticket section of the Walt Disney World website, disneyworld.disney.go.com/tickets, is refreshingly straightforward in showing how ticket prices break down.

TICKETS AND MAGICBANDS

WE'VE USED THE WORD *TICKET* to describe that thing you carry around as proof of your admission to the park. In fact, Disney admission media come in three forms—none of which is a ticket.

One admission medium is a rubber wristband about the size and shape of a small wristwatch. Called a **MagicBand,** it contains a tiny radio frequency identification (RFID) chip, on which is stored a link to the record of your admission purchase in Disney's computers. Your MagicBand also functions as your Disney hotel-room key, and it can (optionally) work as a credit card for most food and merchandise purchases. MagicBands are available for purchase for about $13 each if you're staying off-site, or about $5 if you're staying on-site.

Each member of your family gets his or her own MagicBand, each with a unique serial number. The wristbands are removable, resizable, and waterproof, and they have ventilation holes for cooling. Eleven colors are available: black, blue, green, mint green, orange, pink, purple, red, yellow, dark gray, and gray (the default). You can choose your colors and personalize your bands when you order them at the Disney World website. More customized bands are available throughout the parks.

Some guests, particularly those with hand- or wrist-mobility issues, find using the MagicBand physically challenging. To help with this, the center portion of the band (essentially a puck the size of a quarter) is removable. The puck can then be placed on a lanyard or clipped on a bag, making it easier to maneuver.

Along with the wristband, each family member will be asked to select a four-digit personal-identification number (PIN) for purchases. See below for details.

If you don't want a MagicBand, you're staying off-property, or you bought your admission from a third-party vendor, your second "ticket" option is a **Key to the World (KTTW) Card,** which is a flexible, credit card–size piece of plastic with an embedded RFID chip.

Your third option is to use the **My Disney Experience** (MDE) app on your Bluetooth-enabled smartphone. This option allows you to "tap" your smartphone for admission at park entrances, in the same way you tap your phone for payments at stores and restaurants.

Of these three options, we think the MagicBands and KTTW Cards are the fastest and easiest to use. The main problem with using the MDE app is that it's far slower to take out your phone, open the app, and find the right screen to do what you want. And that's assuming you don't have to connect to Wi-Fi, log into the app, or remember the password you used.

RFID for Payment, Genie+, Hotel-Room Access, and Photos

Disney's hotel-room doors have RFID readers, allowing you to enter your room simply by tapping your wristband or KTTW Card against the reader, or by telling the MDE app to open the door. RFID readers are also installed at virtually every Disney cash register on-property, allowing you to pay for food, drinks, and souvenirs by tapping your MagicBand/KTTW Card against the reader. We expect Disney to allow the MDE app to handle ride reservations and payments by 2022. To complete a purchase, you'll be asked to verify your identity by entering your PIN on a small keypad.

COVID *tip*
Disney strongly encourages guests to use contactless methods of payment throughout the World. These include MagicBands, ApplePay, Google Pay, credit cards, and debit cards.

We think the MDE app will require that you enable Bluetooth transmitting and receiving for tickets, photos, ride reservations, and payments. Doing so will allow your location to be tracked while you're using the app.

If you're using Disney's **Memory Maker** service (see page 455), your MagicBand/KTTW Card serves as the link between your photos and your family. Each photographer carries a small RFID reader, against which you tap your MagicBand, KTTW Card, or (eventually) your phone after having your photo taken. The computers that run the Memory Maker system will link your photos to you, and you'll be able to view them on the Disney World website.

Disney's onboard ride-photo computers incorporate RFID technology too. As you begin down the big drop near the finale of Splash Mountain, for example, sensors read the serial number on your MagicBand (or detect the Bluetooth signal sent from the MDE app on your phone) and pass it to Splash Mountain's cameras. When those cameras snap your family plunging into the briar patch, they attach your MagicBands' serial number to the photo, allowing you to see your ride photos together after you've returned home. Because ride sensors may not pick up the signal from an RFID card or a phone sitting in a wallet or purse, we think onboard ride photos require MagicBands.

PRIVACY CONCERNS Many people are understandably wary of multinational corporations tracking their movements. As noted earlier, guests who prefer not to wear MagicBands or not to download the MDE app can instead obtain KTTW Cards, which are somewhat harder to track (RFID-blocking wallets are available online). Disney says guests who opt out of MagicBands and the MDE app don't get the full range of ride experiences, though, so there's a trade-off.

OPTIONAL EXPENSES

WHICH SPECIAL EVENTS ARE WORTH THE MONEY?

AS A WAY TO "SELL" THE SAME THEME PARK RIDES multiple times per day, Disney constantly experiments with offers of extra time in the parks that require buying separate admission. For example, the Magic Kingdom has hosted (before the pandemic) a pre-opening event, regular park hours, and then another event after the park closed to regular guests, all on the same day.

The scope of the events varies: Morning events usually include access to all the rides in just one land, plus breakfast. Evening events typically include most of a park's attractions. Holiday-themed events are held in the evening and include special entertainment, parades, fireworks, and decorations in addition to access to almost all the park's rides; complimentary snacks are also offered. (Guests with tickets to evening events are usually admitted to the parks starting around 4 p.m., allowing them to catch a few extra hours in the parks too.)

Disney restricts the number of tickets sold for these events, from a few hundred at the morning events to less than 30,000 (we've heard) for the Halloween and Christmas events (those estimates are pre-pandemic and probably lower as of 2021). As a result, wait times for rides at most of these are usually 15 minutes or less. Hyperpopular rides, such as Avatar Flight of Passage or Mickey and Minnie's Runaway Railway, will undoubtedly have longer waits, but nothing like those during the day. The trade-off for the money, therefore, is shorter lines (and often unique entertainment). We think all the events have some value to guests with limited time. To help you decide whether they are worth the cost, we've summarized each below, in the (rough) order we think they're worth. In addition, each theme park chapter includes a table showing which attractions are best experienced during these events.

Finally, as we discuss in Part Seven, children rate character greetings and these events' parades and fireworks higher than almost every ride in these parks. If you're looking for good entertainment with short lines for your children, start here.

1. MICKEY'S AFTER HOURS BOO BASH HALLOWEEN PARTY (Magic Kingdom; 9 p.m.–midnight; select days mid-August–November 1; 2021 ticket prices were $137–$212 per person). With holiday-themed characters and performers, the Magic Kingdom's Halloween parade is the best in Walt Disney World. The event also includes decorations throughout the park; special (often rare) character sightings; fireworks; and occasional, light retheming of a few attractions, plus a boatload of candy if you're interested.

2. MAGIC KINGDOM AFTER HOURS (not offered at press time; Magic Kingdom; 3 hours after regular park closing; select Mondays and Thursdays; $137 per person). Yes, it's $137 for 3 hours in the park, but the high cost keeps crowds low. Most rides will have wait times of 5 minutes or less, meaning that the number of rides you can visit depends largely on how fast you can walk between them and how long the rides last.

3. DISNEY'S VERY MERRIEST AFTER HOURS (Magic Kingdom; 7 p.m.–midnight; select days early November–late December; $180–$265 per person—those aren't typos). Like the Halloween party, the Christmas party offers holiday decorations and a special parade and fireworks, plus unique shows and live performances by the Disney characters. We like the Halloween parade and character greetings better.

4. ANIMAL KINGDOM AFTER HOURS (not offered at press time; Animal Kingdom; 3 hours after regular park closing; days of week vary; $137 per person). If you can't get up early for Avatar Flight of Passage and you're visiting during a busy time of year, this is the most direct way to experience the ride (multiple times!) with short waits. Plus, nighttime rides on Kilimanjaro Safaris (if offered) and Expedition Everest are vastly different than during the day.

ACCOMMODATIONS

The BASIC CONSIDERATIONS

LOCATING A SUITABLE HOTEL OR CONDO is critical to planning any Walt Disney World vacation. The basic question: whether
to stay at a hotel located inside Disney World
("on-site") or not ("off-site").

> *unofficial* **TIP**
> We recommend that most
> readers' first choice for
> lodging be an on-site hotel
> at Walt Disney World (or
> Universal Orlando). The
> incremental extra cost is
> generally more than offset
> by the room quality, ameni-
> ties, transportation, and
> theme park benefits.

Around 86% of *Unofficial Guide* readers
stay on-site during their trips. Beyond the convenience and the amenities, readers say they
enjoy "being in the Disney bubble"—that is,
the special magic and peace of mind associated with staying inside Walt Disney World.
"I feel more a part of everything and less like
a visitor," one guest writes. We agree.

The primary reasons to stay off-site are cost
and space. Walt Disney World room rates vary
from about $118 on a slow weeknight at what Disney calls its Value
resorts to almost $2,200 per night during the holidays at its Deluxe
properties. Outside the World, clean, bare-bones motel rooms can be
had for as little as $80 a night. Lodging prices can change, but it's pos-
sible to get a hotel room comparable to one at a midtier Disney resort

for half the cost during holidays, or a room twice the size for the same money, all within a 15-minute drive of the parks.

There are advantages to staying outside Disney World and driving or taking a hotel shuttle to the theme parks. Meals can be less expensive, and rooming outside the World makes you more receptive to other Orlando-area attractions and eating spots. **Universal Studios** and **Universal's Islands of Adventure, Kennedy Space Center Visitor Complex, SeaWorld,** and **Gatorland** are well worth your attention.

Because Walt Disney World is so large, some off-property hotels are actually closer in both time and distance to many of the theme parks than are some Disney resorts. Check our Hotel Information Chart on pages 252–263, which lists commuting times from both Disney and non-Disney hotels.

If you have young children, read Part Seven, "Walt Disney World with Kids," before choosing lodging. Seniors, couples on a honeymoon or romantic holiday, and disabled guests should read the applicable sections of Part Eight, "Special Tips for Special People," before booking.

Finally, if you're looking for the cheapest room possible on the premise that "it's just a place to sleep," please read our discussion on page 104 first. Our research indicates that most people are happier *not* booking the cheapest room, even when they take the extra cost into account.

THE LATEST IN LODGING

AS WE WERE GOING TO PRESS, Disney was offering limited hotel discounts in the second half of 2021, we assume in an attempt to balance hotel capacity with demand, in order to maximize revenue. But there are still opportunities to stretch your lodging budget.

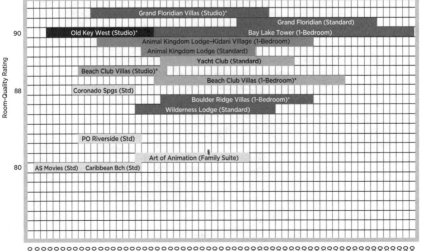

WDW Accommodations by Room Quality and Price Point

Room-Quality Rating

Price per Night (Low–High)   *Disney Vacation Club properties*

If you're planning to stay at a Disney Moderate or Deluxe hotel, it's possible to get an equivalent or superior room by renting DVC points instead of paying cash for the room. In the chart on the previous page, for example, note that it's often less expensive to rent a one-bedroom villa at Animal Kingdom Lodge than it is to pay cash for a standard room. Likewise, a one-bedroom villa at Bay Lake Tower is often less expensive than a standard room at one of the Grand Floridian's outer buildings. See page 94 for an explanation of how to rent DVC points.

Over the past two years, we've spent considerable time researching the one area in which Disney is not yet price-competitive: **family suites** and **villas.** We've tried a dozen new, non-Disney contenders, and the very best have been added to this chapter. Almost all of them offer a whole lot more space than Disney does, and for a whole lot less money. All come highly rated by *Unofficial Guide* readers, and most are within a 15-minute drive of the parks. See "The Best Hotels for Families Outside Walt Disney World," page 228, to find out more.

Before the pandemic hit, a major hotel-refurbishment project was underway ahead of Walt Disney World's 50th anniversary in 2021. Some properties, such as **Pop Century Resort** and **All-Star Movies,** have already dramatically improved their rooms; others, such as **Wilderness Lodge,** have expanded their restaurants and amenities. COVID led Disney to pause most of its scheduled refurbishments; likewise, **Universal Orlando**'s building spree was slowed. We expect these projects to resume in late 2021 or early 2022.

THE BENEFITS OF STAYING IN THE WORLD

GUESTS WHO STAY on Disney property enjoy privileges and amenities unavailable to those staying off-site. Though some of these perks are advertising gimmicks, others are real and potentially valuable.

Here are the benefits and what they mean:

unofficial **TIP**
If you're flying to Orlando and staying on-property, Disney's free transportation network—coupled with ride-hailing services like Lyft and Uber—means you won't need to rent a car.

1. CONVENIENCE Commuting to the theme parks using the Disney transportation system is easy, especially if you stay in a hotel connected by monorail, boat, or Skyliner.

2. EARLY ACCESS TO ATTRACTION AND RESTAURANT RESERVATIONS Guests at Disney resorts can make **Genie+** reservations (see page 61) starting at 7 a.m.; off-site guests must wait until the park opens. Guests staying on-property can also make dining reservations 60 days before they arrive and then an additional 10 days into their trip.

3. EARLY THEME PARK ENTRY Disney resort guests—along with guests of the **Swan, Dolphin, Swan Reserve, Shades of Green, Signia by Hilton Orlando Bonnet Creek, Waldorf Astoria Orlando, Four Seasons,** and **Disney Springs Resort Area** hotels—enjoy extra time in the theme parks not available to the general public. In many cases, this means shorter waits in line for Disney's most popular rides. See page 38 for details.

4. EXTENDED EVENING HOURS Guests staying at Disney Deluxe resorts and Disney Vacation Club (DVC) properties, plus the Dolphin, Swan, Swan Reserve, and Shades of Green, get 2 extra hours in the theme parks after they close to regular guests. At the time of this writing,

WDW RESORT PRIVILEGES AT A GLANCE

HOTEL	GENIE+ RESERVATIONS	RESTAURANT RESERVATIONS	EARLY THEME PARK ENTRY	EXTENDED P.M. HOURS
Disney resort hotels and Disney Vacation Club (DVC) properties	Starting at 7 a.m.	Up to 70 days out	Yes	Deluxe, DVC only
Disney Springs Resort Area hotels*	Park opening	60 days out	Yes	No
Four Seasons Orlando	Park opening	60 days out	Yes	No
Shades of Green	Park opening	60 days out	Yes	Yes
Signia Bonnet Creek	Park opening	60 days out	Yes	No
Swan, Dolphin, and Swan Reserve	Park opening	60 days out	Yes	Yes
Waldorf Astoria Orlando	Park opening	60 days out	Yes	No
Non-WDW hotels	Park opening	60 days out	No	No

Disney Springs Resort Area (DSRA) hotels are B Resort & Spa, DoubleTree Suites by Hilton, Hilton Orlando Buena Vista Palace, Hilton Orlando Lake Buena Vista, Holiday Inn Orlando–Disney Springs, and Wyndham Garden Lake Buena Vista.

Dining note: All table-service restaurants at Disney Springs and the Swan and Dolphin are independently owned and run, as are a handful of other restaurants scattered around the parks (such as Patina Restaurant Group's Tutto Italia and Via Napoli at EPCOT). These non-Disney-owned restaurants take Advance Reservations (see page 271), but many also accept reservations directly or through OpenTable.com, meaning (1) they may have tables available even when Disney says they don't and (2) depending on the restaurant, you may not have to prebook with a credit card or pay a no-show fee when you make reservations outside of the Disney system.

Extended Evening Hours were offered one day per week at the Magic Kingdom and EPCOT only. See page 40 for details.

5. SEPARATE POOL OF PARK RESERVATIONS The **Disney Park Pass** reservation system holds a certain number of reservation slots to be used only by Disney resort guests. Thus, even if no park reservations remain for (off-site) Annual Pass holders or (off-site) guests with dated tickets, Disney resort guests might still be able to get reservations. This is a big advantage, especially if you're trying to get into Disney's Hollywood Studios during busier times of the year.

6. FREE PARKING AT THE THEME PARKS Disney resort guests with cars pay nothing to park in theme park lots—this saves you $25 per day. Be aware, though, that Disney charges for overnight parking at its hotels (see page 117 for details and exceptions).

7. GOLFING PRIVILEGES Disney guests get priority tee times at the on-property golf courses.

8. NO RESORT FEES Unlike most hotels outside of Walt Disney World, the on-site hotels don't charge a nebulous nightly resort fee (versus a parking fee) on top of their advertised rates.

THE PROS AND CONS OF STAYING ON-SITE

1. COST Realistically, you should expect to pay **$100–$175 per night** (including taxes and fees), depending on the time of year, for a clean, safe, everything-in-working-order hotel room near Walt Disney World.

Disney's cheapest hotel rooms compare favorably with non-Disney rooms within this price range. Rooms at the **Pop Century Resort,** for example, cost $162–$361 (before discounts) throughout the year, *plus* they have convenient transportation and perks such as separate park reservations. In addition, Pop Century has completed a major stylish refurbishment. For an incremental cost of around $66–$129 per night (again, before discounts), we think Pop Century is the best Value choice for most readers.

Off-site hotels and homes are often better deals for families looking for more space, or high-end lodging and service, for the same money. For instance, Disney's cheapest family suite, at the **Art of Animation Resort,** sleeps six and costs $428–$764 per night. A comparable room at the **Sonesta ES Suites Lake Buena Vista** costs around $170–$305 per night, depending on the time of year. Renting a three-bedroom condo in Kissimmee is even cheaper: around $150–$250 per night. You can afford a longer trip with those savings—a fact that more than offsets the advantage of park reservations.

Similarly, the cheapest room at Disney's flagship **Grand Floridian Resort & Spa** costs between about $737 and $1,080, depending on the date of stay. The cheapest room at the **Four Seasons Resort Orlando** (adjacent to Walt Disney World) is at the upper end of that range. But the Four Seasons room is larger and better in every way, with restaurants generally as good as or better than the Grand Flo's, along with superior customer service.

Our ratings of hotel quality, cost, and commuting times to the theme parks include hotels both in and out of the World (see How the Hotels Compare, pages 248–251, and the Hotel Information Chart, pages 252–263).

2. EASE OF ACCESS Even if you do stay in Walt Disney World, you're dependent on some mode of transportation. It may be less stressful to use the Disney transportation system, but with the single exception of commuting to the Magic Kingdom, the fastest, most efficient, and most flexible way to get around is usually a car. If you're at EPCOT, for example, and you want to take your cranky kids back to Disney's Contemporary Resort for a nap, forget the monorail. You'll get back much faster by car.

A Raynham, Massachusetts, reader who stayed at Caribbean Beach Resort writes:

> *Even though the resort is on the Disney bus line, I recommend renting a car if it fits your budget. The buses don't go directly to many destinations, and often you have to switch buses. Getting a bus back to the hotel after a hard day can mean a long wait in line.*

Readers complain about problems with the Disney transportation system more than most topics. The following comments from a from Columbus, Ohio, reader are typical:

> *Sometimes it felt like we were visiting Mass Transit World instead of Walt Disney World. More and more of our energy was devoted to planning for getting from point A to point B than there had been in the past. I've never rented a car on-property, but after this trip I might have to consider it.*

Although it exists exclusively for the use and benefit of Walt Disney World guests, the Disney transportation system is nonetheless public, and users must expect inconveniences: conveyances that arrive and depart on their schedule, not yours; the occasional need to transfer; multiple stops; time lost loading and unloading passengers; and, generally, the challenges of using and managing a large, complex transportation network.

If you plan to have a car, consider this: Walt Disney World is so large that some destinations within the World can be reached more quickly from off-property hotels than from Disney hotels. For example, lodgings on US 192 (near the so-called Walt Disney World Maingate) are closer to Disney's Hollywood Studios, Animal Kingdom, and Blizzard Beach water park than many hotels inside Disney World.

Traffic on I-4 is the largest potential problem with staying at an off-site hotel, especially if you're coming or going during rush hours. Thus, the closer your off-site hotel is to Disney property, the less risk there is in being stuck in I-4 traffic. Secondary roads, such as Turkey Lake Road, Palm Parkway, International Drive, and Universal Boulevard, can help get you around that traffic; look for shortcuts in Part Nine, "Arriving and Getting Around."

A Kentucky dad overruled his family about staying at a Disney resort and is glad he did:

> My wife read in another guidebook that it can take 2 hours to commute to the parks if you stay outside Walt Disney World. I guess it could take 2 hours if you stayed in Tampa, but from our hotel on US 192, we could commute to any of the parks except the Magic Kingdom and have at least one ride under our belt in about an hour.

For commuting times from specific non-WDW hotels, see our Hotel Information Chart on pages 252–263.

3. FOOD COSTS Many off-site hotels' prices include some sort of free (often prepackaged) breakfast, ranging from fruit and pastries to pancakes, microwavable waffles, bacon, and eggs. The Disney hotels don't. Depending on how hungry your family is in the morning, eating breakfast at your off-site hotel can save you a minimum of $5–$15 per person per day versus breakfast in the parks.

Beyond breakfast, if you have a large family that chows down like cattle on a finishing lot, you may likewise do better staying outside the World, where food is a lot less expensive.

4. YOUNG CHILDREN Although the hassle of commuting to most non-World hotels is only slightly (if at all) greater than that of commuting to Disney hotels, a definite peace of mind results from staying in the World. Regardless of where you stay, make sure you get your young children back to the hotel for a nap each day.

5. SPLITTING UP If you're in a party that will probably split up to tour (as frequently happens in families with teens or children of widely varying ages), staying in the World offers more transportation options and, thus, more independence. Mom and Dad can take the car and return to the hotel for a relaxed dinner and early bedtime while the teens remain in the park for extra rides.

6. VISITING OTHER ORLANDO-AREA ATTRACTIONS If you also plan to visit Universal Orlando, SeaWorld, Kennedy Space Center, or other area attractions, it may be more convenient to stay outside of Walt Disney World.

The DISNEY RESORTS

DISNEY RESORTS 101

BEFORE YOU MAKE ANY DECISIONS, understand these basics regarding Disney resorts.

Disney groups its resorts into four main categories: **Value, Moderate, Deluxe,** and **Deluxe Villa.** It's a handy system that we'll use in discussing both Disney and off-site hotels. A fifth category, **Campground,** is exclusive to **Fort Wilderness Resort**'s campsites. (**Star Wars: Galactic Starcruiser** isn't yet classified as a hotel; Disney calls it an "experience.")

unofficial **TIP**
Understand that Disney Reservation Center and Walt Disney Travel Company representatives don't have detailed personal knowledge of the resorts.

Value resorts have the lowest rates of any Disney-owned hotels, along with the smallest rooms and most limited amenities.

Moderate resorts are a step up from the Values in guest-room quality, amenities, and cost. Disney also classifies **The Cabins at Fort Wilderness Resort** as a Moderate resort.

Deluxe resorts are Disney's top-of-the-line hotels, boasting extensive theming, luxurious rooms, and superior on-site dining, recreation, and services.

Disney Deluxe Villa (DDV) resorts, also known as **Disney Vacation Club (DVC) resorts,** offer suites, some with full kitchens. DDV/DVC resorts, several of which are attached to Deluxe resorts, equal or surpass Deluxe resorts in quality. They can also be a better value.

2. MAKING RESERVATIONS Whether you book your hotel room through Disney, a travel agent, the internet, a tour operator, or an organization like AAA, you can frequently save by reserving the room exclusive of any vacation package. This is known as a **room-only reservation.** Though later on in this chapter we'll scrutinize the advantages and disadvantages of buying a package (see page 202), we'll go ahead and tell you now that Disney World packages at list price rarely save you any money (although they can certainly be convenient).

unofficial **TIP**
If you must book by phone, call before 11 a.m. or after 3 p.m. Eastern.

We recommend that you book your trip at the Walt Disney World website (disneyworld.com) instead of calling the Disney Reservation Center (DRC) at ☎ 407-W-DISNEY (934-7639). Not only is booking online much faster than booking by phone, but DRC reservationists are also focused on selling you a Walt Disney Travel Company package. Even if you insist that all you want is the room, they'll try to persuade you to bundle it with some small extra, like a minigolf pass, so that your purchase can be counted as a package—this lets Disney apply various restrictions and cancellation policies that you wouldn't be saddled with if you bought just the room by itself.

CANCELLATION POLICIES Regarding cancellation, know that there are some trade-offs. If you book a package and then cancel 2–29 days before arrival, you lose your $200 deposit. If you cancel a day or less before arrival, you lose the entire package cost, including your airfare and insurance. If you reserve only a room and cancel fewer than five days before arrival (six days if you booked through Disney's website), you lose your deposit of one night's room charge, which can easily be more than $200 if you booked at a Moderate, Deluxe, or DDV resort. Further, Disney imposes a $50 fee, plus a $15 processing fee, for changing your package's details, including adjusting travel dates, moving to a cheaper resort, or adding a discount code, 30 days or fewer before your trip.

If you have to book by phone rather than online, tell the agent up front what you want in terms of lodging, and make sure to get a *room-only rate quote*. Then tell the agent what you're looking for in terms of park admissions. When you've pinned down your room selection and lodging costs, ask the agent if he or she can offer you any deals that beat the à la carte prices. But don't be swayed by little sweeteners included in a package unless they have real value for you. If the first agent you speak to isn't accommodating, hang up and call back—DRC has hundreds of agents, some more helpful than others.

When dealing with Disney reservations, a careful shopper from West Lafayette, Indiana, advises both wariness and toughness:

> *Making reservations through* ☎ *407-W-DISNEY is like buying a car: You need to know the sales tricks, have a firm idea of what you want, and be prepared to walk away if you don't get it at a price you're willing to pay.*

If you need specific information, call the resort directly, ask for the front desk, and pose your question before phoning the DRC (the person who answers your call almost certainly won't be at the hotel's front desk, but they'll know who to ask). If your desired dates aren't available, keep calling back or checking online. Something might open up.

3. YOUR HOTEL-ROOM VIEW Rates at Disney hotels vary from season to season (see page 93) and from room to room according to view. Furthermore, each Disney resort has its own seasonal calendar that varies depending on the resort instead of that tired old 12-months-of-the-year thing that the rest of us use. But as confusing as Disney seasons can be, they're logic personified compared with the panoply of guest-room views that the resorts offer. Depending on the resort, you can choose standard views, courtyard views, water views, pool views, lagoon views, nature views, garden views, theme park views, or savanna views, among others.

Standard view, the most ambiguous category, crops up at about three-fourths of Disney resorts. It's usually interpreted as a view of infrastructure or unremarkable scenery. At Animal Kingdom Lodge, for example, you have savanna views, pool views, and standard views. Savanna views overlook the replicated African veldt, pool views overlook the swimming pool, and value and standard views offer stunning vistas of . . . rooftops and parking lots.

With a standard view, however, you can at least pinpoint what you *won't* be seeing. Every resort defines views of water differently. At the Grand Floridian Resort & Spa, for example, rooms with views of Seven Seas Lagoon are sensibly called lagoon-view rooms, while those with views of the marina or pools are known as garden-view rooms.

Zip over to the Yacht Club Resort, another Deluxe property. Like the Grand Floridian, the Yacht Club is on a lake and has a pool and a marina. Views of all three are lumped into one big "water" category—anything wet counts! But wait, what's the view of the lake, pool, or waterfall called at the Wilderness Lodge? You guessed it: "courtyard."

Our favorite water views are at the Contemporary Resort's South Garden Wing, which extends toward Bay Lake to the east of the giant A-frame. Rooms in this three-story structure, such as room 6109, afford some of the best lake vistas in Disney World (see tinyurl.com /contemporary6109 for a view from one of these rooms). Many rooms are so near the water, in fact, that you could spit a prune pit into the lake from your window. And their category? Garden views.

For many readers, a good view is essential to enjoying their hotel room. Getting the view you want, however, doesn't necessarily mean that you'll have the *experience* you want, as a Rochester, New York, couple points out:

> We stayed in the Conch Key building at the Grand Floridian. The view was lovely, but we could hear the boat's horn blasting every 20 minutes, 7 a.m.–midnight. It was obnoxious and kept us up.

It's worth noting that scoring a Grand Floridian room with a view of the Magic Kingdom can require excruciatingly specific verbiage, as a mom from Pontefract, England, attests:

> We stayed at the Grand Floridian and paid extra for a Magic Kingdom view. I was soooo disappointed when all I could see from the balcony was Space Mountain. I was so looking forward to sitting on the balcony with a glass of wine and watching the fireworks. Next time I'll ask for a view of Cinderella Castle—not just a Magic Kingdom view.

We could go on and on, but pinning Disney down on precisely what will be outside your window is the point. In our discussion of individual resorts later in this chapter, we'll tell you which rooms have the best views.

Our website's **Hotel Room Views** project uses more than 35,000 photos to show the view you get from every hotel room in Walt Disney World, plus instructions on how to request each specific room. It uses interactive maps for every building in every resort, so you can search for rooms by cost, view, walking distance, noise, handicap accessibility, and more. As you read this chapter, visit touringplans.com/walt-disney-world/hotels to see photos of the rooms we recommend.

unofficial **TIP**
Disney will guarantee connecting rooms if your party includes more kids than adults. (In Disney terms, *adjoining rooms* are next to each other, and *connecting rooms* have a door between them.)

4. HOW TO GET THE ROOM YOU WANT Disney won't guarantee a specific room when you book but will post your request on your reservation record. The easiest way to make a request is to use our Hotel Room Views tool, described above. Select the room you want, and we'll automatically email your request to Disney 30 days before you arrive.

Our experience indicates that making a request with just a single room number confuses Disney's reservationists; as a result, they're unsure where to place you if the room you've asked for is unavailable. To increase your odds of getting the room you want, tell the reservationist (or your travel agent) *to the letter* what characteristics and amenities you desire.

Be politely assertive when speaking to the Disney agent. At Port Orleans Riverside, for example, rooms with king beds have options for standard-, garden-, pool-, preferred-, and river-view rooms. If you want to overlook the river, say so; likewise, if you want a pool view, speak up. Similarly, state clearly such preferences as a particular floor, a room near restaurants, or a room away from elevators and ice machines. If you have a long list of preferences, type it in order of importance and email, fax, or snail-mail it to the hotel. Include your contact information and your reservation-confirmation number. Be brief, though: We're told that Disney's reservation system has a limited amount of space to store what you write.

It will be someone from Disney's Centralized Inventory Management team, or the resort itself, who actually assigns your room. Call back in a few days to make sure your preferences were posted to your record.

> *un**official* **TIP**
> A week or two before you arrive, call your resort's front desk. Call late in the evening when they're not so busy, and reconfirm the requests that by now should be appearing in their computers.

We'll provide the information needed for each resort to frame your requests, including a resort map and our recommendations for specific rooms or buildings. A dash (–) indicates a range of rooms.

Readers say our hotel-request service works about two out of three times. Disney's room assigners tell us that the most common reasons for not getting the exact room requested are as follows:

- **Someone is already in the requested room.** This is common during holidays and other busy times. It helps to list several alternatives.

- **Asking to get into your room early (before 3 or 4 p.m.).** Unless you say otherwise, the front desk will assume that any room currently available overrides your earlier requests.

- **Listing only rooms that are more expensive than the one you paid for.** It doesn't hurt to ask for an upgrade, but make sure you've given the room assigners a fallback option based on what you've bought.

- **Unclear requests.** We've read multipage requests with sentences about room preferences embedded in paragraphs relating the life stories of everyone in the group, and requests with enough picky stuff to rule out every room in the hotel. Make sure that your requests are *succinct* and *realistic*.

HOW TO GET DISCOUNTS ON LODGING

THERE ARE SO MANY GUEST ROOMS in and around Disney World that competition is brisk, and everyone, including Disney, wheels and deals to fill them. Disney, however, has its own atypical way of managing its room inventory. To uphold the brand integrity of its hotels, Disney prefers to use inducements rather than discounts per se. For example, Disney has included Free Dining (see page 205) if you reserve a certain number of nights at rack rate, or offered special deals only by email to returning guests. Consequently, many of the strategies for obtaining discounted rates in most cities and destinations don't work well for Disney hotels. We'll explore these strategies in-depth when we discuss booking

WHAT IT COSTS TO STAY IN THE DISNEY SPRINGS RESORT AREA	
B Resort & Spa $111–$243	DoubleTree Suites by Hilton Orlando $123–$333
Hilton Orlando Buena Vista Palace $153–$338	Hilton Orlando Lake Buena Vista $133–$365
Holiday Inn Orlando–Disney Springs Area $89–$275	Wyndham Garden Lake Buena Vista $89–$309

COSTS PER NIGHT OF DISNEY HOTEL ROOMS, 2021 *(rack rate)*	
Rates are for standard rooms except as noted.	
ALL-STAR RESORTS	$112–$285
ALL-STAR MUSIC RESORT FAMILY SUITES	$300–$581
ANIMAL KINGDOM LODGE	$434–$759
ANIMAL KINGDOM VILLAS *(studio, Jambo House/Kidani Village)*	$416–$759
ART OF ANIMATION FAMILY SUITES	$428–$764
ART OF ANIMATION RESORT	$188–$353
BAY LAKE TOWER AT CONTEMPORARY RESORT *(studio)*	$608–$1,011
BEACH CLUB RESORT	$504–$883
BEACH CLUB VILLAS *(studio)*	$504–$883
BOARDWALK INN	$555–$943
BOARDWALK VILLAS *(studio)*	$555–$943
BOULDER RIDGE VILLAS *(studio)*	$424–$826
CARIBBEAN BEACH RESORT	$240–$432
CONTEMPORARY RESORT *(Garden Wing)*	$518–$882
COPPER CREEK VILLAS & CASCADE CABINS *(studio)*	$524–$826
CORONADO SPRINGS RESORT	$232–$400
DOLPHIN *(Sheraton)*	$559–$1,371
FORT WILDERNESS RESORT & CAMPGROUND *(cabins)*	$414–$789
GRAN DESTINO TOWER	$280–$532
GRAND FLORIDIAN RESORT & SPA	$737–$1,214
GRAND FLORIDIAN VILLAS *(studio)*	$737–$1,115
OLD KEY WEST RESORT *(studio)*	$429–$705
POLYNESIAN VILLAGE RESORT	$618–$1,053
POLYNESIAN VILLAS & BUNGALOWS *(studio)*	$618–$1,053
POP CENTURY RESORT	$162–$330
PORT ORLEANS RESORT *(French Quarter & Riverside)*	$256–$418
RIVIERA RESORT *(studio)*	$429–$738
SARATOGA SPRINGS RESORT & SPA *(studio)*	$430–$701
STAR WARS: GALACTIC STARCRUISER *(opens spring 2022)*	$4,800+
SWAN *(Westin)*	$531–$1,029
SWAN RESERVE *(Autograph Collection)*	$451–$811
TREEHOUSE VILLAS	$1,007–$1,825
WILDERNESS LODGE	$430–$831
YACHT CLUB RESORT	$504–$883

non-Disney hotels near Walt Disney World; for the moment, though, here are some tips for getting price breaks at Disney properties.

One of our major research projects for this edition was to identify sellers with the steepest discounts on Disney hotel rooms. Those best discounts are almost certainly found through sites that offer last-minute, one- to four-night DVC deals—where *last-minute* typically means within 90 days. If you're willing to stay at any Disney hotel as long as it's a great deal, see "Rent Disney Vacation Club Points" on page 94 for the details.

Note: Discounts may be limited to a certain number of rooms and/ or for certain dates. Rooms at deep discounts tend to get snatched up quickly, so don't take too long to decide what you want to do.

1. LOOK FOR SEASONAL SAVINGS Save 15%–35% per night or more on a Disney hotel room by visiting during the slower times of year. However, Disney has so many seasons in its calendar that it's hard to keep up; plus, the dates for each "season" vary among resorts. Disney also changes the price of its hotel rooms with the day of the week, charging more for the same room on Friday and Saturday nights. The rate hikes can range from $36 to more than $100 or more per room, per night.

2. ASK ABOUT SPECIALS If you're booking online, Disney's website will display discounts available to the general public for your dates. Look for the words *special offer* near the top of the page, in the section that asks whether you're booking a room-only or package deal. You must click on the particular special to get the discount; otherwise, you may be charged the full rack rate.

If you're booking by phone, ask the reservationist what special deals or discounts are available at Disney hotels during the time of your visit. Being specific and assertive paid off for a Warren Township, New Jersey, dad:

> *Your tip on asking Disney employees about discounts was invaluable. They will not volunteer this information, but by asking, we saved almost $500 on our hotel room.*

A family from West Springfield, Massachusetts, discovered that if you keep on shopping even after you've booked, your efforts can really pay off:

> *I booked our trip online with Disney using a special-offer discount we had received in the mail. Two months before our trip, and after I had already paid in full, Disney ran a special that was even better than the one I had booked. I gave them a call, and they politely, quickly, and efficiently credited the difference.*

Be aware that specials can include discounts on vacation packages in addition to discounts on rooms. Discounts on park admission or dining packages (see "Keep an Eye Out for Free Dining" in "Disney Lodging for Less," page 205) can be substantial, depending on the number of people in your traveling party or where you're staying. Finally, see our coverage of **Magical Vacations Travel** discounts, starting on page 98.

3. CHECK MOUSESAVERS This awesome Disney-travel website (mousesavers.com) maintains an updated list of discounts and reservation codes for Disney resorts. The codes are separated into categories such as "for anyone," "for residents of certain states," and "for Annual Pass holders." Anyone calling ☎ 407-W-DISNEY (934-7639) can use a current code and get the discounted rate. Discounts for the general public also appear on Disney's website (see "Ask About Specials," previous page), but Mouse Savers shows you targeted discounts that Disney's website may not.

MouseSavers also maintains an informative historical list of when past discounts were released and what they encompassed; see mouse savers.com/historicalwdwdiscounts.html. You can also sign up for the MouseSavers newsletter, with discount announcements, Disney news, and exclusive offers not available to the general public.

4. INVESTIGATE INTERNET SELLERS The online travel sellers **Expedia** (expedia.com), **Hotwire** (hotwire.com), **Priceline** (priceline.com), and **Travelocity** (travelocity.com) offer discounted rooms at Disney hotels, but usually at a price approximating the going rate obtainable from the Walt Disney Travel Company or Walt Disney World Central Reservations. Most breaks are in the 7%–25% range.

In late summer 2021, Hotwire was offering Pop Century rooms at $94 per night with tax versus $186 on Disney's website, and Coronado Springs rooms at $122 per night versus $280 directly through Disney. Another good website to check is Priceline's Express Deals. *Always check these websites' prices against Disney's.* See tinyurl.com/ugprice linetips for the latest on these deals.

5. RENT DISNEY VACATION CLUB POINTS The **Disney Vacation Club** (**DVC**) is Disney's time-share program. DVC members buy a number of "points" annually that they use to pay for their Disney accommodations. Sometimes members elect to "rent" (sell) their points instead of using them in a given year. Though Disney is not involved in the transaction, it allows DVC members to make these points available to the general public.

The going rental rate for points is $13–$18 per point, depending on the resort and time of year, when you deal with members directly; third-party brokers charge $18–$20 per point for hosting the buying-and-selling market, and offering credit card payments.

Renting a studio for six nights during summer season 2022 at Animal Kingdom Lodge & Villas currently costs $3,105 with tax if you're paying with cash. The same room costs a DVC member 20 points. If you rented those points at $20 per point, that studio would cost you $1,200—a savings of more than $1,900.

We think renting a one-bedroom villa is a good alternative for families looking for extra space, at not much more cost than a regular hotel room. For example, a 344-square-foot standard room at Animal Kingdom Lodge cost around $3,105 for six nights during summer 2021. It consists of one main room for everyone and a bathroom.

A one-bedroom villa at Animal Kingdom Lodge, however, is around 629 square feet, with a full kitchen and separate bedroom, living room, and bath. It rents for 132 points, or $2,640 at $20 per point. That's a savings of $465 with 80% more space, a private bedroom, two bathrooms, and a full kitchen.

Likewise, if you're a family of six people or more, a two-bedroom villa at Animal Kingdom Lodge sleeps eight. While it costs around

$615 per night (at $20 per point), a family suite at Art of Animation costs $581 (without discounts). For $34 more per night, you get more than double the space—1,170 square feet of space at Animal Kingdom versus 565 at Art of Animation—and better amenities.

As mentioned previously, you have two options when renting points: Go through a third-party broker or deal directly with a DVC member. For a fixed rate of around $20 per point, **David's Vacation Club Rentals** (dvcrequest.com) will match your request for a specific resort and dates to its available supply. David's per-point rate is higher than if you did the legwork yourself, but they take requests months in advance, and they notify you as soon as something becomes available; plus, they takes credit cards. We've used David's for huge New Year's Eve events and last-minute trips, and it's tops.

In addition to David's, some readers, like this one from St. Louis, have had good results with **The DVC Rental Store** (dvcrentalstore.com):

> *We rented DVC points for this trip through the DVC Rental Store, and we had a wonderful experience. Unlike David's, they don't make you pay the entire cost upon booking. For our stay at Boulder Ridge Villas, we paid just over half what we were planning to pay for the Wilderness Lodge.*

LAST-MINUTE DVC DEALS The website **DVCReservations.com** emails a newsletter roughly every week with steeply discounted DVC rooms available within the next 90 days. These discounts are, by a wide margin, the best generally available deals you can find on Disney hotel rooms: typically 35%–60% off Disney's rates. For example, we've seen $251 per night for a 465-square-foot studio villa at Polynesian Village Resort, while Disney's website quoted $711. For reference, that $251 per night was just $50 more than Disney was charging for a 260-square-foot room at its Pop Century Value resort the same nights.

The best last-minute discounts are on one- and two-bedroom villas at **Old Key West** and **Saratoga Springs Resorts:** as low as $310 per night for a 714-square-foot one-bedroom and $520 per night for 1,075-square-foot two-bedrooms. Those are better rates than Disney was offering for a standard room at its Moderate and Deluxe resorts, which have less than half the space of the DVC units.

You're most likely to find these last-minute rentals for stays of one to four nights. If you're willing to switch resorts every couple of nights, though, you can easily make a week of it.

When you deal directly with the selling DVC member, you pay him or her directly, such as by certified check (few members take credit cards). The DVC member makes a reservation in your name and pays Disney the requisite number of points. Arrangements vary, but again, the going rate is around $13–$18 per point. Trust is required from both parties. Usually your reservation is documented by a confirmation sent from Disney to the owner and then passed along to you. Though the deal you cut is strictly up to you and the owner, you should always insist on receiving the aforementioned confirmation before making more than a one-night deposit.

We suggest checking online at one of the various Disney discussion boards (such as MouseOwners.com or Disboards.com) if you're not picky about where you stay and when you go and you're willing to put in the effort to ask around. If you're trying to book a particular resort, especially during a busy time of year, there's something to be said for the low-hassle approach of a points broker.

When you're looking at these sites, keep in mind that Disney World has 12 DVC resorts, also known as Disney Deluxe Villas (DDV): **Animal Kingdom Villas, Bay Lake Tower at the Contemporary Resort, Beach Club Villas, BoardWalk Villas, Boulder Ridge Villas, Copper Creek Villas & Cascade Cabins, Grand Floridian Villas, Old Key West Resort, Polynesian Villas & Bungalows, Riviera Resort, Saratoga Springs Resort & Spa,** and **Treehouse Villas at Saratoga Springs.** Construction on a 13th, **Reflections—A Disney Lakeside Lodge,** started before it was suspended during the pandemic.

6. CRACK THE (PIN) CODE Disney maintains a list of recent Walt Disney World visitors as well as those who have inquired about a Disney World vacation. During slow times of the year, Disney will send these folks direct mail and emails with personalized discounts. Each offer is uniquely identified by a long string of letters and numbers called a PIN code. This code is required to get the discount—thus, it can't be shared—and Disney will verify that the street or email address that the code was sent to is yours.

> *un*official **TIP**
> To enhance your chances of receiving a PIN-code offer, you need to get your name and street or email address into the Disney system.

To get your name into the Disney system for a PIN code, call ☎ 407-W-DISNEY (934-7639) and request written info. If you've been to Disney World before, your name and address will, of course, already be on record, but you won't be as likely to receive a PIN-code offer as you would by calling and requesting that information be mailed to you.

Or go to disneyworld.com and sign up to automatically be sent offers and news at your email address. You might also consider getting a **Disney Rewards Visa Card,** which entitles you to around two days' advance notice when a discount is released (visit disney.go.com/visa for details).

7. DISNEY-SPECIALIST TRAVEL AGENTS Disney vacations are so popular that entire travel agencies specialize in just Disney theme park trips and cruises. Even large, general-travel agencies such as AAA often have dedicated agents with specialized, up-to-date knowledge of what's going on at the parks.

Three obvious situations where it makes sense to engage a travel agent are as follows:

1. This is one of your first trips to Walt Disney World and you'd like to talk to someone objective in person.

2. You're looking to save time in evaluating several different what-if scenarios, such as which of two discounts saves the most money.

3. You want someone else to keep checking if a better deal than what you already have comes along.

We can't emphasize enough how much time (and money) a travel agent will save you in those last two scenarios. If you're trying to compare, say, the cost difference between a Value and a Moderate resort with a particular discount that may not be available at all resorts on all dates, you could easily spend an hour working through different combinations to find the best deal. We think most people give up far before finishing, potentially wasting a lot of money. Good travel agents will do this for you at no charge (because they'll earn a commission from Disney when you book through them).

Travel agents save so much time in these scenarios that we use them ourselves. Even if the agent can't beat a deal we've found on our own, we let him or her book it anyway if it's commissionable, to nurture the relationship.

So which are the best Disney-specialist travel agents? Each year we ask our readers to rate the travel agents who helped them plan their Disney vacations. Our survey asks two questions:

1. Is this agent an expert on Walt Disney World?
2. Would you use this agent again?

For this edition, we received surveys about more than 1,750 agents. The top 11 agents for 2022 are as follows:

- **SUE PISATURO** of **Small World Vacations** (sue@smallworldvacations.com) is our Empress of Travel and a longtime friend of and contributor to this guide.
- **Darren Wittko** (darren@magicalvacationstravel.com) made our readers' list for the eighth year in a row.
- **Mike Rahlmann** (mike.rahlmann@themagicforless.com) appears on the list for the sixth straight time.
- Being recognized for the fourth consecutive year are **Wendy Ott** (wendy@smallworld vacations.com) and **Darcy Phelps** (darcy@magicalvacationstravel.com).
- **Holly Biss** (holly@magicalvacationstravel.com) makes her third appearance on our list.
- **Alissa Almeida-Yngve** (alissa@smallworldvacations.com), **Dawn Speno** (dawn@small worldvacations.com), and **Sharon Iocono** (sharon@magicalvacationstravel.com) all made the list for the second time.
- **Gina Akin** (gina@touringplans.com) and **Michelle McKnight** (michelle@touringplans .com) made the list for the first time.

Our reader-survey results indicate that for Walt Disney World, you'll be much more satisfied using a travel agent who specializes in Disney and much more likely to recommend those agents to a friend. While the agents listed above are among the ones most consistently recommended in our surveys, you'll find good Disney specialists throughout the country if you prefer to work with someone close to home. We suggest asking your travel agency if they have agents who specialize in Disney vacations.

8. ORGANIZATIONS AND AUTO CLUBS Disney has developed time-limited programs with some auto clubs and organizations. AAA, for example, can often offer discounts on hotels and packages comparable to those that Disney offers its Annual Pass holders. Such deals come and go, but the market suggests there will be more. If you're a member of AARP, AAA, or any travel or auto club, ask whether the group has a program before shopping elsewhere.

9. ROOM UPGRADES Sometimes a room upgrade is as good as a discount. If you're visiting Disney World during a slower time, book the least-expensive room your discounts will allow. Checking in, ask very politely about being upgraded to a water-view or pool-view room. A fair percentage of the time, you'll get one at no additional charge or at a deep discount. Understand, however, that a room upgrade should be considered a favor. Hotels are under no obligation to upgrade you, so if your request is not met, accept the decision graciously. Also, note that suites at Deluxe resorts are exempt from discount offers.

10. MILITARY DISCOUNTS Shades of Green Armed Forces Recreation Center, near the Grand Floridian Resort & Spa, offers luxury accommodations at rates based on a service member's rank, as well as attraction tickets to the theme parks (see our profile on page 141). For rates and other information, call ☎ 888-593-2242 or see shadesofgreen.org.

11. YEAR-ROUND DISCOUNTS AT THE SWAN AND DOLPHIN RESORTS Government workers, teachers, nurses, military, and AAA and *Entertainment Coupon Book* members can save on rooms at the Dolphin or Swan (when space is available, of course). Call ☎ 888-828-8850 or visit swandolphin.com and click on "Special Offers."

Our Favorite Money-Saving Find: Magical Vacations Travel

Magical Vacations Travel (**MVT**) is a travel agency with a unique approach. It commits to Disney to sell a certain number of rooms (for example, 10 rooms at three nights each) during a certain time period, and it can't return any unsold rooms. In return, Disney sells MVT those hotel rooms at rates below what's offered to the general public.

MVT also lets clients cancel, with refunds, using Disney's standard cancellation policy—that is, up to 5 or 6 days in advance rather than the 30-day policy it's held to in its contract. That's part of the risk that MVT accepts in return for being able to offer less-expensive rooms. If you can work with the available dates, the savings can be amazing.

At the time of this writing, MVT's rates seem to be at least 10% lower than the cheapest discounted rate Disney is offering to the general public. As we were going to press, for instance, MVT had theme park–view rooms at Disney's Contemporary Resort for $595 per night for fall 2021, around 43% lower than the rate Disney was quoting on its website ($1,043) for the same room on the same date.

A disclaimer: We have no relationship of any kind with MVT. Rather, we just think they have an interesting, innovative business model. If you try MVT, let us know how they worked for you.

CHOOSING A WALT DISNEY WORLD HOTEL

IF YOU WANT TO STAY IN THE WORLD but you don't know which hotel to choose, the most important factors to consider are as follows:

1. Room quality (below)	**5.** Location/distance from parks (page 105)
2. Transportation (page 101)	**6.** Theme (page 106)
3. Cost (page 102)	**7.** Dining options (page 108)
4. Pools and amenities (page 104)	**8.** The size of your room vs. the size of your group (page 109)

1. ROOM QUALITY Many Disney hotel rooms are among the best designed and appointed anywhere. Plus, they're maintained much better than the average hotel room in Orlando. All rooms, for instance, have free Wi-Fi and in-room mini refrigerators, along with coffee makers in the DVC units.

HOTEL	ROOM-QUALITY RATING	
RIVIERA RESORT	**95**	DOLPHIN	**87**
GRAND FLORIDIAN VILLAS	**93**	POLYNESIAN VILLAGE RESORT	**87**
GRAND FLORIDIAN RESORT & SPA	**92**	PORT ORLEANS RESORT-FRENCH QUARTER	**87**
BAY LAKE TOWER	**91**	ANIMAL KINGDOM LODGE	**86**
BOARDWALK INN	**91**	ANIMAL KINGDOM LODGE-JAMBO HOUSE (*studio*)	**86**
CONTEMPORARY RESORT	**91**	
GRAN DESTINO TOWER	**91**	BEACH CLUB VILLAS (*studio*)	**86**
OLD KEY WEST RESORT	**91**	WILDERNESS LODGE	**86**
SHADES OF GREEN	**91**	BOULDER RIDGE VILLAS (*studio*)	**84**
YACHT CLUB RESORT	**91**	
ANIMAL KINGDOM LODGE-KIDANI VILLAGE (*studios*)	**90**	SARATOGA SPRINGS RESORT & SPA (*studio*)	**84**
COPPER CREEK VILLAS & CASCADE CABINS	**90**	PORT ORLEANS RESORT-RIVERSIDE	**83**
FORT WILDERNESS CABINS	**90**	ALL-STAR MOVIES RESORT	**80**
TREEHOUSE VILLAS	**90**	ART OF ANIMATION RESORT (*standard room*)	**80**
BEACH CLUB RESORT	**89**	
BOARDWALK VILLAS (*studio*)	**89**	CARIBBEAN BEACH RESORT	**80**
SWAN	**89**	POP CENTURY RESORT	**80**
CORONADO SPRINGS RESORT	**88**	ALL-STAR MUSIC AND ALL-STAR SPORTS RESORTS	**73**
POLYNESIAN VILLAS & BUNGALOWS (*studio*)	**88**	

Note: Swan Reserve and Star Wars: Galactic Starcruiser weren't open at press time.

As Disney refurbishes its hotel rooms, it also reexamines how modern families use these spaces. As a simple example, new rooms have between 5 and 10 built-in USB charging ports to accommodate everyone's cell phones and tablets. Other changes are much more substantial.

Not surprisingly, many readers rate Disney's Deluxe and DVC rooms highest for quality, but some Value and Moderate rooms rate even higher than some Deluxe and DVC rooms. The text that follows provides context for these room-quality ratings.

In addition, the chart above shows how current Walt Disney World hotels stack up for quality. Note that many hotels were undergoing refurbishment in late 2019 and that all of Walt Disney World was closed for several months in 2020, so our survey results may reflect ratings for the old and the new rooms combined.

VALUE RESORTS Room quality is highest at **Pop Century** and **All-Star Movies,** where the entire room configuration has changed recently. Carpet has been replaced with vinyl "hardwood" flooring. Queen beds are now standard, and king beds are still available. More interesting is that in rooms with two queen beds, one bed folds into the wall during the day, exposing a desk. That frees up around 36 square feet of space in these 260-square-foot rooms—around 14% in all. In addition, bathrooms at Pop and Movies are brighter and more open, and more storage is available in the living areas.

Art of Animation's room quality is in the middle of the pack for the Disney Value resorts. Rooms are clean and functional, but because the resort opened in 2012, they're not yet old enough to need the updates that Pop and Music have gotten.

All-Star Music and **All-Star Sports** have the oldest room designs in the Value category. These rooms are also the cheapest, but that's not necessarily a bad thing: We think the mattresses, pillows, and bathrooms here are of much better quality than the average Orlando budget hotel's—just not as good as the ones at Movies or Pop.

MODERATE RESORTS Readers rate the rooms at **The Cabins at Fort Wilderness Resort** the highest of any Moderate resort. They're more like small mobile homes, with a separate living room, kitchen, and bedroom.

Readers rate rooms at **Coronado Springs** and **Port Orleans French Quarter** next highest in this category. Rooms at Coronado have been modernized with vinyl "hardwood" floors, plenty of desk space, excellent lighting, and doors separating the bathroom area from the main living space. Rooms at French Quarter have similar flooring but don't have the newest storage or bathroom makeovers. We think French Quarter's rooms are rated highly because this resort is the smallest and most intimate of the Moderates, and that atmosphere carries over into the room ratings.

Port Orleans Riverside and **Caribbean Beach** have the lowest-rated Moderate rooms. All rooms in Riverside have vinyl flooring. One section, Alligator Bayou, has an updated bathroom design and a new drop-down twin bed that fits a fifth child. However, the furniture design in these rooms is rustic (to fit the theming) and lacks the modern conveniences found in the updated Value resorts. The same can be said for Caribbean Beach's rooms—while some have undergone updates (vinyl floors, new furniture), the bathroom layout and storage options feel dated.

Disney's most recent addition to the Moderate category is **Gran Destino Tower** at Coronado Springs, which offers some of the best-designed bathrooms in this category. Even better, Gran Destino's Club Level rooms—with access to the fabulous private **Chronos Club** lounge—are the cheapest Club Level rooms on-property. If you're looking to try one of these rooms, Gran Destino is a great place to start.

DELUXE RESORTS Rooms at the **Grand Floridian Resort & Spa** are rated the highest in this category. These are among the largest and well appointed anywhere on Disney property. Rooms include textured carpeting along with plenty of storage, desk, and bathroom space.

Other above-average Deluxe rooms are found at the **Contemporary** and **Yacht Club Resorts** and **Disney's BoardWalk Inn.** Those at the **Beach Club Resort** and the **Swan** are rated average. Below-average rooms are found at the **Polynesian Village Resort** and the **Dolphin.** The lowest-rated Deluxe rooms are found at **Animal Kingdom Lodge–Jambo House** and **Wilderness Lodge.** These rooms are the smallest in the Deluxe category, and we think that's the most significant factor here. (Rooms at the Polynesian Village and Contemporary Resorts were updated in summer 2021 and are too new to have reader ratings.)

Animal Kingdom Lodge & Villas, BoardWalk Inn, and **Wilderness Lodge,** along with the **Contemporary, Grand Floridian, Polynesian Village,** and **Yacht & Beach Club Resorts** and **Gran Destino Tower** at Coronado Springs, boast **Club Level** (concierge) floors. Benefits include personalized trip planning and a lounge stocked with small bites to graze on. This Basking Ridge, New Jersey, reader, however, found the snacks on the skimpy side:

> We found the Club Level food offerings limited and carefully metered out. Tiny plates were replenished slowly. Given that Club Level is a significant extra expense, we didn't appreciate being told how much we could eat and when.

DVC RESORTS Disney's highest-rated rooms are found at its time-share resorts. At the top of this list are the rooms at **Riviera Resort** and **The Villas at Disney's Grand Floridian Resort & Spa.** Setting aside the Victorian decor, these are the most luxurious rooms in any Disney-owned hotel on-site. Ranked just below the Grand Flo Villas is **Old Key West Resort.** Its rooms are large, very functional, and quiet, plus they've been updated recently.

Almost all other DVC resorts have rooms rated above average: **Bay Lake Tower, Animal Kingdom Lodge–Kidani Village, Copper Creek Villas & Cascade Cabins at Wilderness Lodge, Treehouse Villas at Saratoga Springs,** and **BoardWalk Villas.**

Readers rated the rooms at **Saratoga Springs Resort & Spa** and **Boulder Ridge Villas at Wilderness Lodge** as below average. We agree that they're not as good as rooms at other DVC resorts—in particular, the room layout, decor, and furnishings at Boulder Ridge suffer compared with the other DVC complexes at Wilderness Lodge, the **Copper Creek Villas** and **Cascade Cabins.** Saratoga Springs' rooms are being refurbished in 2021, but even pre-refurb these were nice rooms relative to what you'll find in the Orlando area in general.

Disney's newest DVC resort, the **Riviera,** opened in late 2019. With large stylish rooms, above-average on-site dining, and Skyliner access to EPCOT and Hollywood Studios, the Riviera is a positive (if pricey) addition to Disney's resort lineup.

2. TRANSPORTATION If you're going to be driving, your Disney hotel's transportation isn't especially important unless you plan to spend most of your time at the Magic Kingdom. (Disney transportation is usually more efficient than your car in this case because it bypasses the Transportation and Ticket Center, the Magic Kingdom's transportation hub, and deposits you at the theme park entrance.) If you haven't decided whether you want a car for your Disney vacation, see "How to Travel Around the World" (page 430).

The hotels that our readers rate highest for Disney transportation are **Polynesian Village, Grand Floridian, Contemporary, Wilderness Lodge, Port Orleans French Quarter, Riviera, Art of Animation,** and **Pop Century.** The Polynesian and Grand Floridian connect to the Magic Kingdom and EPCOT by monorail; the Contemporary is a short walk from the Magic Kingdom too. These resorts use buses to get to other destinations on-property.

Art of Animation (AOA) and Pop Century's transportation is primarily bus service to most

unofficial **TIP**
If you plan to use Disney transportation to visit all four major parks and one or both of the water parks, book a centrally located resort that has good transportation connections. The EPCOT resorts and the **Polynesian Village, Caribbean Beach, Art of Animation, Pop Century,** and **Port Orleans Resorts** fill the bill.

destinations on-property. The Skyliner connects AOA and Pop with the Caribbean Beach and Riviera Resorts, Disney's Hollywood Studios, and EPCOT.

Readers rated the following resorts as below average for transportation: The **Swan, Dolphin, Coronado Springs, Old Key West, Port Orleans Riverside, Saratoga Springs/Treehouse Villas, Animal Kingdom Lodge,** and **Caribbean Beach.** The bus service at Coronado, Port Orleans, and Saratoga Springs makes multiple internal stops at these resorts, which increases the time it takes to get where you're going. The Swan and Dolphin's separate bus service runs slightly less often than Disney's own buses. Animal Kingdom Lodge, meanwhile, is among the most remote resorts in Walt Disney World.

3. COST Hotel rooms start as low as $118 a night at the All-Stars and top out above $2,100 at the Grand Floridian. The table on page 92 shows the cost per night for various Disney hotel rooms.

Disney's **Value resorts** are the least-expensive on-site hotels. Because they're popular, they have four separate, unofficial price categories:

- The **All-Star Movies, Music,** and **Sports Resorts** are Disney's oldest and least-expensive Value resorts. Non-discounted rates for standard rooms here are $118–$254 per night.

- **Pop Century Resort** sits in the middle of the Value price range—about $45 per night more than the All-Stars. Pop Century is the most popular Disney World resort among *Unofficial Guide* readers.

- **Art of Animation Resort** has the largest rooms, best food court, and best pools in this category. Standard rooms here cost about $70–$90 per night more than those at the All-Stars.

- Two-room **Family Suites** are available at the All-Star Music and Art of Animation Resorts, from around $300 to $764 per night with tax.

While All-Star Movies and Pop Century are older and less expensive than Art of Animation, they've had extensive room renovations that make them among the most attractive and functional on-property. In terms of room quality, they're better and cheaper than Art of Animation's standard rooms.

The next most expensive tier includes Disney's **Moderate resorts.** Like the Values, these have different price points:

- **Caribbean Beach Resort** was the first Moderate resort when it opened in 1988. Prices here range from $240 to $432 per night. **Coronado Springs Resort** is priced about $10 less per night.

- **Port Orleans Riverside** and **Port Orleans French Quarter Resorts** are the most popular in this category. Standard rooms cost $256–$418 per night.

- **Gran Destino Tower** is the newest entry in the Moderates category. Located on the grounds of Coronado Springs Resort, this 15-story tower has standard rooms starting at $280–$532 per night.

- **The Cabins at Fort Wilderness Resort** are unique in the Moderate category. These small, mobile home–like accommodations sleep up to six people and include a small kitchen. Rates range from $414 to $789 per night.

Rates at Disney's **Deluxe resorts** vary depending on room size and the hotel's location relative to the theme parks:

- The **Walt Disney World Swan** (Westin), **Walt Disney World Dolphin** (Sheraton), and **Swan Reserve** (Autograph Collection) are usually the least-expensive Deluxe hotel rooms on-property. They're not owned by Disney, and they cater to convention traffic as much as families, giving them a different feel from the other hotels. These hotels are within walking distance of EPCOT and Disney's Hollywood Studios.

- The smallest and least-expensive Disney-owned Deluxe hotel rooms are found at **Wilderness Lodge** and **Animal Kingdom Lodge.** Both hotels have excellent theming; Animal Kingdom Lodge has excellent dining as well.

- The next tier of Deluxe prices applies to the EPCOT resorts: the **Yacht Club, Beach Club,** and **BoardWalk Inn**. These are arranged around Crescent Lake, with a short walk to EPCOT and a slightly longer walk to Disney's Hollywood Studios.

- Slightly more expensive are the **Polynesian Village** and **Contemporary Resorts.** Both opened in 1971 and are a short walk or monorail ride from the Magic Kingdom and EPCOT. The Polynesian Village has excellent theming. Along with its easy access to two theme parks, its location makes it easy to visit any hotel restaurant along the Magic Kingdom monorail loop.

- Finally, Disney's most expensive standard hotel rooms are found at the **Grand Floridian Resort & Spa,** Disney World's flagship hotel.

IS IT MORE THAN A PLACE TO SLEEP? Many families headed to Walt Disney World opt for the Value resorts, not so much because of the lower cost but because, in their words, "it's just a place to sleep." But do those families feel the same way at the end of their trip? We put together an experiment to find out.

Since 2019, we've surveyed more than 16,000 families about the brand of hotel they typically stay at when *not* vacationing at Walt Disney World. We categorized those hotels as follows:

- **Budget:** Days Inn, Motel 6, Super 8, etc.
- **Moderate:** Best Western, Hampton Inn, Holiday Inn Express, etc.
- **Upscale:** Crowne Plaza, Radisson, SpringHill Suites, Wyndham, etc.
- **Luxury:** Four Seasons, Ritz-Carlton, Waldorf Astoria, etc.

We grouped Disney's hotels into Disney's own Value, Moderate, Deluxe, and DVC categories. Then we asked the families three questions, each on a five-point scale:

- How satisfied were you with your Disney hotel?
- Would you recommend this hotel to a friend?
- Would you stay at this hotel again?

Here's how the results shook out among those families who were "very satisfied" with their Disney hotel, would recommend it to a friend, and would stay at that hotel again:

TYPE OF HOTEL TYPICALLY CHOSEN	DISNEY VALUE (% Positive Responses)	DISNEY MODERATE (% Positive Responses)	DISNEY DELUXE (% Positive Responses)	DVC/DDV (% Positive Responses)
Budget	75%	69%	78%	77%
Moderate	72%	67%	77%	79%
Upscale	71%	67%	79%	78%
Luxury	70%	71%	79%	77%

The takeaway? No matter what kind of hotel you stay at outside of Walt Disney World, **you'll probably be most satisfied at a Disney Deluxe or DVC resort.** So even if you stay at a low-cost Microtel Inn on other trips, you'll still be happier if you stay at Animal Kingdom Lodge instead of Port Orleans.

After doing these surveys for 30 years, we're convinced that most people add the words "for the money I paid" to the end of every question we ask. So when you read the survey results on pages 118–119, it's safe to assume that they take into account the higher cost of the hotel rooms. If you have the budget, we think you'll have a better trip by booking a Deluxe hotel or DVC.

4. POOLS AND AMENITIES Disney's **Yacht & Beach Club Resorts** share the highest-rated pool in Walt Disney World. Called **Stormalong Bay,** it includes a lazy river with sand bottom and an elaborate waterslide that begins from a pirate ship beached on Crescent Lake. Stormalong Bay is so popular that guests must show proof they're staying at the resort before being admitted to the pool area.

The **Polynesian Village**'s volcano-themed pool also gets top marks from readers. It's large and attractive, with convenient food and bar options. At night, you can lounge in the pool with a tropical drink and watch the Magic Kingdom fireworks too.

The pools at **Art of Animation** are also rated above average. Like the Poly's, Animation's pools are well themed and have convenient bar and food options.

DISNEY RESORT POOL RATINGS

1. YACHT & BEACH CLUB RESORTS & BEACH CLUB VILLAS (*shared complex*) ★★★★★
2. GRAND FLORIDIAN RESORT & SPA, VILLAS ★★★★½
3. ANIMAL KINGDOM VILLAS (*Kidani Village*) ★★★★½
4. SARATOGA SPRINGS RESORT & SPA/TREEHOUSE VILLAS ★★★★½
5. WILDERNESS LODGE & BOULDER RIDGE/COPPER CREEK VILLAS ★★★★½
6. ANIMAL KINGDOM LODGE & VILLAS (*Jambo House*) ★★★★
7. PORT ORLEANS RESORT ★★★★
8. CORONADO SPRINGS RESORT/GRAN DESTINO TOWER ★★★★
9. DOLPHIN ★★★★
10. SWAN ★★★★
11. POLYNESIAN VILLAGE, VILLAS, & BUNGALOWS ★★★★
12. BAY LAKE TOWER ★★★★
13. CARIBBEAN BEACH RESORT ★★★★
14. RIVIERA RESORT ★★★★
15. BOARDWALK INN & VILLAS ★★★½
16. CONTEMPORARY RESORT ★★★½
17. ALL-STAR RESORTS ★★★
18. ART OF ANIMATION RESORT ★★★
19. OLD KEY WEST RESORT ★★★
20. FORT WILDERNESS RESORT & CAMPGROUND ★★★
21. POP CENTURY RESORT ★★★
22. SHADES OF GREEN ★★★

Note: The Swan Reserve was not open at press time; the *Star Wars* resort will not have a pool.

DISNEY RESORT AMENITIES					
RESORT	SUITES	CONCIERGE FLOOR	NUMBER OF ROOMS	ROOM SERVICE (full)	FITNESS CENTER
ALL-STAR RESORTS	•	—	5,406	—	—
ANIMAL KINGDOM LODGE	•	•	972	•	•
ANIMAL KINGDOM VILLAS	•	•*	458	•	•
ART OF ANIMATION RESORT	•	—	1,984	—	—
BAY LAKE TOWER	•	—	295	•	•
BEACH CLUB VILLAS	•	—	282	•	•
BOARDWALK INN	•	•	378	•	•
BOARDWALK VILLAS	•	—	532	•	•
CARIBBEAN BEACH RESORT	—	—	1,536	—	—
CONTEMPORARY RESORT	•	•	655	•	•
CORONADO SPRINGS RESORT	•	•	1,839	•	•
DOLPHIN	•	—	1,509	•	•
FORT WILDERNESS CABINS	—	—	409	—	—
GRAN DESTINO TOWER	•	•	545	•	•
GRAND FLORIDIAN RESORT & SPA, VILLAS	•	•	1,016	•	•
OLD KEY WEST RESORT	•	—	761	—	•
POLYNESIAN VILLAGE, VILLAS, & BUNGALOWS	•	•	866	•	—
POP CENTURY RESORT	—	—	2,880	—	—
PORT ORLEANS RESORTS	—	—	3,056	—	—
RIVIERA RESORT	—	—	300	•	•
SARATOGA SPRINGS RESORT & SPA	•	—	1,260	—	•
SHADES OF GREEN	•	—	586	•	•
STAR WARS: GALACTIC STARCRUISER (opens in 2022)	•	—	100	•	—
SWAN	•	—	758	•	•
SWAN RESERVE	•	—	349	•	•
TREEHOUSE VILLAS	•	—	60	•	•
WILDERNESS LODGE & BOULDER RIDGE/COPPER CREEK VILLAS	•	•	889	•	•
YACHT & BEACH CLUB RESORTS	•	•	1,211	•	•

*Jambo House only

Readers rate the pools as below average at these resorts: **BoardWalk, Contemporary, All-Star Music, All-Star Sports,** and the **Swan.** Of these, our opinion is that all but the BoardWalk have relatively generic pool offerings, and are often crowded.

See the tables opposite and above for specific resort pool ratings and a summary of the amenities offered by each resort.

5. LOCATION AND DISTANCE FROM THE THEME PARKS Once you've determined your budget, think about what you want to do at Walt Disney World. Will you go to all four theme parks or concentrate on one or two?

The resorts closest to the Magic Kingdom include the **Grand Floridian** and its **Villas;** the **Contemporary** and **Bay Lake Tower;** and the **Polynesian Village, Villas, & Bungalows.** All are served by the monorail and walking paths, so staying at one of these resorts also gets you access to more dining options, many of which are among Disney World's best.

Next closest to the Magic Kingdom, **Wilderness Lodge & Boulder Ridge/Copper Creek Villas,** along with **Fort Wilderness Resort & Campground,** are linked to the Magic Kingdom by boat and to everywhere else in the World by rather convoluted bus service.

The most centrally located hotels in Walt Disney World are the EPCOT resorts—the **BoardWalk Inn, BoardWalk Villas, Yacht & Beach Club Resorts, Beach Club Villas, Swan, Dolphin,** and **Swan Reserve**—and **Coronado Springs/Gran Destino Tower,** near Disney's Animal Kingdom. The EPCOT resorts are within easy walking distance of Disney's Hollywood Studios and EPCOT's International Gateway. Besides giving you easy theme park access, staying at one of these hotels gets you access to a wide variety of restaurants. EPCOT hotels are best for guests planning to spend most of their time at EPCOT or DHS. Coronado Springs is convenient for driving to EPCOT, Hollywood Studios, Animal Kingdom, or Blizzard Beach water park.

Caribbean Beach, Riviera, Pop Century, and **Art of Animation Resorts** are just south and east of EPCOT and DHS. All are connected to EPCOT and DHS by the Skyliner and to everything else by bus.

The Disney resorts along Bonnet Creek, which offer quick access to Disney Springs and its top restaurants, include **Old Key West Resort, Saratoga Springs Resort & Spa** and its **Treehouse Villas,** and the two **Port Orleans Resorts.** On an adjacent 70-acre parcel of non-Disney land called **Bonnet Creek Resort** are the **Waldorf Astoria Orlando;** the **Signia by Hilton Orlando Bonnet Creek;** and two **Wyndham** properties, **Club Wyndham Bonnet Creek** and its more luxurious sibling, the **Wyndham Grand Orlando Resort Bonnet Creek.**

The Bonnet Creek Resort occupies a sort of gray area between on- and off-property: The hotels are as close to the theme parks as Disney's own, offer transportation to the parks and Disney Springs, and are every bit as good as Disney's best—and often at around half the price. Further muddying the waters, guests of the Signia and Waldorf get Early Theme Park Entry privileges (as do guests of the **Four Seasons Resort Orlando,** adjacent to Fort Wilderness Resort). We profile two of the four Bonnet Creek Resort properties in "Hotels Outside Walt Disney World" (pages 238 and 239).

6. THEME With a few exceptions, each Disney hotel is designed to make you feel that you're in a special place or period of history. Some resorts carry off their theming better than others, and some themes are more exciting. See the table on the opposite page for a summary of each resort's theme.

Readers rate the resorts in the next four paragraphs tops for theming:

Animal Kingdom Lodge & Villas replicates grand safari lodges of Kenya and Tanzania and overlooks its own African-style game preserve. By far the most exotic Disney resort, it's made to order for couples on romantic getaways and for families with children.

Wilderness Lodge & Boulder Ridge/Copper Creek Villas is visually extraordinary, reminiscent of a grand early-20th-century national park lodge. The lobby opens eight stories to a timbered ceiling supported by giant columns of bundled logs. One look eases you into the woodsy wilderness theme. Wilderness Lodge is a great choice for couples and seniors and is heaven for children.

DISNEY HOTELS BY THEME
ALL-STAR RESORTS Movies, music, and sports
ANIMAL KINGDOM LODGE & VILLAS African game preserve
ART OF ANIMATION RESORT Disney's animated films
BAY LAKE TOWER Upscale, ultramodern urban hotel
BEACH CLUB RESORT & VILLAS New England beach club of the 1870s
BOARDWALK INN East Coast boardwalk hotel of the early 1900s
BOARDWALK VILLAS East Coast beach cottage of the early 1900s
CARIBBEAN BEACH RESORT Caribbean islands
CONTEMPORARY RESORT The future as perceived by past and present generations
CORONADO SPRINGS RESORT Northern Mexico and the American Southwest
DOLPHIN "Modern" (read: early-1990s-vintage) Florida resort
GRAN DESTINO TOWER Spanish/Moorish influences
GRAND FLORIDIAN RESORT & SPA, VILLAS Turn-of-the-20th-century luxury hotel
OLD KEY WEST RESORT Relaxed Florida Keys vibe
POLYNESIAN VILLAGE RESORT, VILLAS, & BUNGALOWS Hawaii–South Seas
POP CENTURY RESORT Popular-culture icons from various decades of the 20th century
PORT ORLEANS RESORT–FRENCH QUARTER Turn-of-the-19th-century New Orleans
PORT ORLEANS RESORT–RIVERSIDE Old Louisiana bayou-side retreat
RIVIERA RESORT Mediterranean beach resort in the South of France
SARATOGA SPRINGS RESORT & SPA 1880s Victorian lake
STAR WARS: GALACTIC STARCRUISER *Star Wars*-themed adventure (*opens 2022*)
SWAN What modern looked like 30 years ago
SWAN RESERVE Brand-new resort with a true 21st-century design aesthetic
TREEHOUSE VILLAS Disney-rustic vacation homes with modern amenities
WILDERNESS LODGE & BOULDER RIDGE/COPPER CREEK VILLAS Grand national park lodge of the early 1900s
YACHT CLUB RESORT New England seashore hotel of the 1880s

Likewise dramatic, the **Polynesian Village, Villas & Bungalows** conveys the feeling of the Pacific Islands. It's great for romantics and families. Many waterfront rooms on upper floors offer a perfect view of Cinderella Castle and the Magic Kingdom fireworks across Seven Seas Lagoon.

Port Orleans Resort–French Quarter does a good (albeit sanitized) job of capturing the architectural essence of its New Orleans inspiration. **Port Orleans Resort–Riverside** likewise succeeds with its early-19th-century Louisiana bayou setting.

Unofficial Guide readers rate the following resorts as below average for theming: the **All-Star Resorts, Pop Century, Saratoga Springs** and **Treehouse Villas,** the **Contemporary Resort** (before its 2021 renovation) and **Bay Lake Tower,** and the **Swan** and **Dolphin.**

The **All-Star Resorts** have 15 themed areas: 5 celebrate sports (surfing, basketball, tennis, football, and baseball), 5 recall Hollywood films, and 5 have musical motifs. The resort's design, with entrances shaped like giant Dalmatians, Coke cups, footballs, and the like, is pretty adolescent, sacrificing grace and beauty for energy and novelty. Guestroom decor is reminiscent of a teenage boy's bedroom.

Pop Century Resort is pretty much a clone of the All-Star Resorts, only here the giant icons symbolize decades of the 20th century (Big Wheels, 45-rpm records, silhouettes of people doing period dances, and such), and period memorabilia decorates the rooms.

Saratoga Springs Resort & Spa, supposedly representative of an upstate New York country retreat, looks like what you'd get if you crossed the Beach Club with the Wilderness Lodge. When it comes to the resorts inspired by Northeastern hotels (including the **Yacht and Beach Clubs**), thematic distinctions are subtle and thus lost on many guests.

The **Contemporary, Bay Lake Tower, Swan, Swan Reserve,** and **Dolphin** are essentially themeless though architecturally interesting. The original Contemporary Resort is a 15-story A-frame building with monorails running through the middle. An update in 2021 adds characters from Pixar's *The Incredibles*. The Swan and Dolphin are massive yet whimsical; designed by Michael Graves, they're excellent examples of early-1990s "entertainment architecture," but they lack any references to Disney theme parks, films, or characters.

7. DINING OPTIONS The best resorts for dining quality are **Animal Kingdom Lodge & Villas** and the **Grand Floridian Resort & Villas.** Three of Walt Disney World's top 10 sit-down restaurants are found at Animal Kingdom Lodge: **Jiko—The Cooking Place, Sanaa,** and **Boma—Flavors of Africa.** The Grand Floridian holds Walt Disney World's very best restaurant, **Victoria & Albert's,** and five of its other restaurants all place within the top 25 of our reader surveys. (At press time, however, Jiko and Victoria & Albert's remained closed.) The Grand Floridian is also a short monorail ride from the **California Grill** at the Contemporary Resort, another top venue. If high-quality dining is a top priority for your Walt Disney World trip and these two resorts fit in your budget, we think they're excellent choices.

unofficial **TIP**
The best resort lounges are the DVC-only **Top of the World** at Bay Lake Tower (make friends with an owner for access), **Victoria Falls** at Animal Kingdom Lodge, and **Trader Sam's** at the Polynesian. Honorable mention goes to the **Territory Lounge** at Wilderness Lodge and **Crew's Cup** at the Yacht Club.

The best resorts for dining quality *and* selection are the EPCOT resorts: the **Beach Club Villas, BoardWalk Inn & Villas, Dolphin, Swan,** and **Yacht and Beach Club Resorts.** (We expect the **Swan Reserve** to follow suit.) Each has good sit-down restaurants, and each is within easy walking distance of the others as well as the dining options available in EPCOT's World Showcase section. However, on-site quick-service options are limited for all but the BoardWalk & Villas, and readers rate these hotels below average for quick-service options. If quick, simple breakfasts and lunches are what you're after, stay elsewhere.

unofficial **TIP**
If you stay at an EPCOT resort, you have more than 30 restaurants within a 5- to 12-minute walk.

The only other hotels in Disney World with similar access to a concentrated area of good restaurants comprise the **Disney Springs Resort Area.** In addition to restaurants in the hotels themselves, **B Resort & Spa, DoubleTree Suites, Hilton Orlando Buena Vista Palace, Hilton Orlando Lake Buena Vista, Holiday Inn Orlando, Saratoga Springs Resort & Spa,** and **Wyndham Garden Lake Buena Vista** are all within walking distance of restaurants in Disney Springs. As with the EPCOT resorts, though, many readers complain about the difficulty in finding quick, tasty breakfast and lunch options at these hotels.

Hotels rated as below average for dining include **Fort Wilderness Resort & Campground** and **Caribbean Beach Resort.** Because Fort Wilderness caters primarily to guests who are cooking for themselves, on-site dining options are limited, and not just in terms of the menu selections: The restaurants' remote location, near the shore of Bay Lake, makes them a hassle to get to from most parts of the resort—so unless you've brought a car or you're renting a bike or golf cart, count on a *long* walk or bus ride to get something to eat. And despite extensive efforts to upgrade its dining offerings, Caribbean Beach remains one of Walt Disney World's lowest-rated resorts overall.

8. ROOM SIZE How much space you get inside a Disney hotel room almost always depends on how much you pay. The size of a standard (or studio) room at Disney's resorts varies from 260 square feet at the Value resorts to 440 square feet at the Deluxe **Grand Floridian Resort** to 460 square feet for a studio at the **Polynesian Villas** DVC resort. The diagrams on pages 110–114 show the size and layout of typical rooms at each Disney property.

It's no surprise that readers rate larger rooms better than smaller ones. At the top of this list are rooms at **Old Key West,** Disney's first DVC resort, which are larger than most. Also scoring well are the rooms at the **Grand Floridian Villas**—we're not kidding when we say that the showers here are large enough that you can hear an echo. And although they don't score well in most other categories, the rooms at the **Fort Wilderness Cabins** and Saratoga Springs' **Treehouse Villas** are popular with readers in terms of sheer space.

There are two exceptions to the "More Money, More Space" mantra: Standard rooms in the main buildings of **Animal Kingdom Lodge** and **Wilderness Lodge** are 344 square feet—the smallest of any Deluxe resort, and closer in size to the rooms at many Moderate resorts than Deluxes. Readers rate these among the lowest for space. The other rooms rated lowest for space are at Disney's Value resorts.

Standard rooms at the **Riviera** include a two-person, 225-square-foot option that's small enough to necessitate a fold-down bed. They're almost certainly the worst rooms on Disney property, and we recommend skipping them.

STANDARD ROOMS THAT SLEEP FIVE (plus one child under age 3 in a crib) are found at the following resorts:

- **DELUXE** Beach Club, BoardWalk Inn, Contemporary, Grand Floridian, Polynesian, Yacht Club
- **MODERATE** Caribbean Beach, Port Orleans Riverside (Alligator Bayou only)

FAMILY SUITES sleep six people and are found exclusively at **All-Star Music** and **Art of Animation Resorts.** The All-Star versions are basically two Value rooms stuck together; those at Art of Animation, however, were designed from the ground up and are slightly larger (and nicer). Family Suites at both resorts have two bathrooms.

continued on page 114

DISNEY DELUXE RESORTS

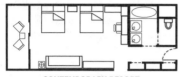

CONTEMPORARY RESORT
Typical room, 394 square feet;
accommodates 5 guests
plus 1 child under age 3 in a crib

POLYNESIAN VILLAGE RESORT
Typical room, 415 square feet;
accommodates 5 guests
plus 1 child under age 3 in a crib

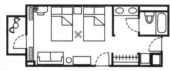

BOARDWALK INN
Typical room, 371 square feet;
accommodates 5 guests
plus 1 child under age 3 in a crib

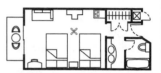

GRAND FLORIDIAN RESORT & SPA
Typical room, 440 square feet;
accommodates 5 guests
plus 1 child under age 3 in a crib

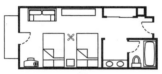

BEACH CLUB RESORT
Typical room, 381 square feet;
accommodates 5 guests
plus 1 child under age 3 in a crib

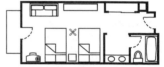

YACHT CLUB RESORT
Typical room, 381 square feet;
accommodates 5 guests
plus 1 child under age 3 in a crib

WILDERNESS LODGE
Typical room, 344 square feet;
accommodates 4 guests
plus 1 child under age 3 in a crib

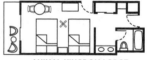

ANIMAL KINGDOM LODGE
Typical room, 344 square feet;
accommodates 4 guests
plus 1 child under age 3 in a crib

COPPER CREEK VILLAS & CASCADE CABINS

Studio (sleeps 4): 345 sf (*gray area*)
1-bedroom (sleeps 4): 761 sf
2-bedroom (sleeps 8): 1,105 sf
Cabin (2 bedrooms; sleeps 8): 1,737 sf
Grand Villa (3 bedrooms; sleeps 12): 3,204 sf

DISNEY DELUXE VILLA RESORTS

**BAY LAKE TOWER
AT CONTEMPORARY RESORT**
Studio: 339 square feet (*gray area*);
1-bedroom: 803 sf; **2-bedroom:** 1,152 sf
Grand Villa: 2,044 square feet

**OLD KEY WEST
RESORT**
Studio: 376 square feet (*gray area*);
1-bedroom: 942 square feet; **2-bedroom:** 1,333
square feet; **Grand Villa:** 2,202 square feet

**TREEHOUSE VILLAS
AT SARATOGA SPRINGS
RESORT & SPA**
3-bedroom:
1,074 square feet

BOARDWALK VILLAS
Studio: 412 square feet (*gray area*);
1-bedroom: 814 square feet; **2-bedroom:** 1,236
square feet; **Grand Villa:** 2,491 square feet

**THE VILLAS AT
GRAND FLORIDIAN RESORT & SPA**
Studio: 374 square feet (*gray area*)
1-bedroom: 844 square feet
2-bedroom lock-off: 1,232 square feet

DDV GUEST-OCCUPANCY LIMITS

Studios: 4 at all but Boulder Ridge Villas (5),
Grand Floridian (5), Polynesian (5),
and Riviera (2 for Tower Studios,
5 for Deluxe Studios)

- **1-bedroom villas:** 4 at Beach Club,
Saratoga Springs, and Boulder Ridge;
4 or 5 at Animal Kingdom Lodge
(Jambo House); 5 everywhere else

- **2-bedroom villas and bungalows:**
8 or 9 at Animal Kingdom Lodge
(Jambo House); 9 at Animal Kingdom
Lodge (Kidani Village), Bay Lake Tower,
BoardWalk, Old Key West, and Riviera; 9 or
10 at Grand Floridian; 8 everywhere else

- **3-bedroom and Grand Villas:**
9 at Treehouse Villas; 12 everywhere else

Note: To all these limits you may add
1 child under age 3 in a crib.

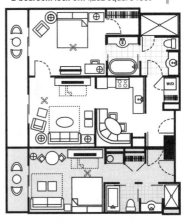

DISNEY DELUXE VILLA RESORTS
(continued)

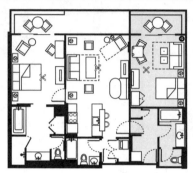

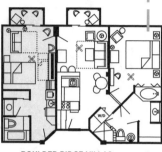

BOULDER RIDGE VILLAS
Studio: 356 square feet *(gray area)*
1-bedroom: 727 square feet
2-bedroom: 1,080 square feet

ANIMAL KINGDOM VILLAS–JAMBO HOUSE
Studio: 316–365 square feet *(gray area)*
1-bedroom: 629–710 sf; **2-bedroom:** 945–1,075 sf
Grand Villa: 2,349 square feet

ANIMAL KINGDOM VILLAS–KIDANI VILLAGE
Studio: 366 square feet *(gray area)*
1-bedroom: 807 square feet
2-bedroom: 1,173 square feet
Grand Villa: 2,201 square feet

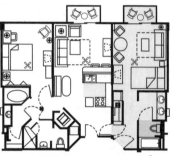

BEACH CLUB VILLAS
Studio: 356 square feet *(gray area)*
1-bedroom: 726 square feet
2-bedroom: 1,083 square feet

SARATOGA SPRINGS RESORT & SPA
Studio: 355 square feet *(gray area)*
1-bedroom: 714 square feet
2-bedroom: 1,075 square feet
Grand Villa: 2,113 square feet

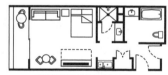

POLYNESIAN VILLAGE VILLAS
Studio: 460 square feet

POLYNESIAN VILLAGE BUNGALOWS
1,650 square feet

DISNEY DELUXE VILLA RESORTS
(continued)

DISNEY'S RIVIERA RESORT
Deluxe Studio:
423 square feet (*gray area*)
1-bedroom: 813 square feet
2-bedroom lock-off:
1,246 square feet
3-bedroom: 2,530 square feet

DISNEY'S RIVIERA RESORT,
TOWER STUDIO
225 square feet,
accommodates 2 guests
plus 1 child under age 3 in a crib

DISNEY MODERATE RESORTS

CORONADO SPRINGS RESORT
Typical room, 314 square feet;
accommodates 4 guests
plus 1 child under age 3 in a crib

CARIBBEAN BEACH RESORT
Typical room, 314 square feet;
accommodates 5 guests
plus 1 child under age 3 in a crib

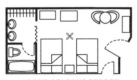

PORT ORLEANS RESORT–
FRENCH QUARTER
Typical room, 314 square feet;
accommodates 4 guests
plus 1 child under age 3 in a crib

PORT ORLEANS RESORT–RIVERSIDE
Typical room, 314 square feet;
accommodates 5 guests
plus 1 child under age 3 in a crib.
Alligator Bayou has trundle bed for
child (54" long) at no extra charge.

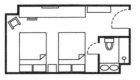

CORONADO SPRINGS RESORT,
GRAN DESTINO TOWER

Typical room, 375 square feet;
accommodates 4 guests plus
1 child under age 3 in a crib

DISNEY VALUE RESORTS

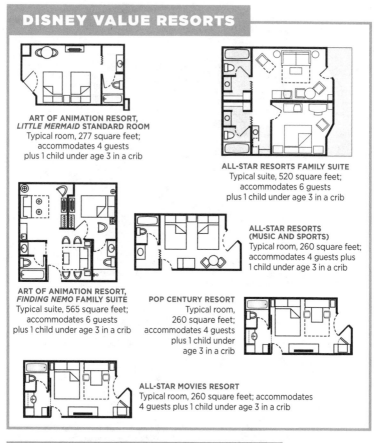

ART OF ANIMATION RESORT,
***LITTLE MERMAID* STANDARD ROOM**
Typical room, 277 square feet;
accommodates 4 guests
plus 1 child under age 3 in a crib

ALL-STAR RESORTS FAMILY SUITE
Typical suite, 520 square feet;
accommodates 6 guests
plus 1 child under age 3 in a crib

**ALL-STAR RESORTS
(MUSIC AND SPORTS)**
Typical room, 260 square feet;
accommodates 4 guests plus
1 child under age 3 in a crib

ART OF ANIMATION RESORT,
***FINDING NEMO* FAMILY SUITE**
Typical suite, 565 square feet;
accommodates 6 guests
plus 1 child under age 3 in a crib

POP CENTURY RESORT
Typical room,
260 square feet;
accommodates 4 guests
plus 1 child under
age 3 in a crib

ALL-STAR MOVIES RESORT
Typical room, 260 square feet; accommodates
4 guests plus 1 child under age 3 in a crib

FORT WILDERNESS RESORT

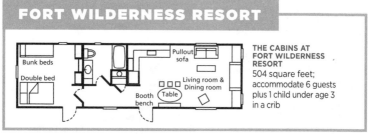

Bunk beds

Double bed

Pullout sofa

Living room &
Dining room

Booth bench

Table

**THE CABINS AT
FORT WILDERNESS
RESORT**
504 square feet;
accommodate 6 guests
plus 1 child under age 3
in a crib

continued from page 109

The **Fort Wilderness Cabins** also sleep six, but they have just one bathroom each.

HOW WE INSPECT HOTELS

WE EVALUATE SEVERAL HUNDRED hotels in the Walt Disney World area to compile the *Unofficial Guide*'s list of lodging choices. If a hotel has been renovated or has refurbished its guest rooms, we reinspect it, along with any new hotels, for the next edition of the *Guide*.

THE QUIETEST ROOMS AT WALT DISNEY WORLD

All-Star Music Buildings 5 and 6, rooms facing west

All-Star Sports Building 3, rooms facing west; building 2, rooms facing north

Bay Lake Tower Any room is good here—rooms are the quietest in WDW

Beach Club Easternmost hallways, rooms facing east

Beach Club Villas Rooms facing southeast

BoardWalk Inn All rooms facing courtyard, just east of main lobby

Caribbean Beach Trinidad South, buildings 35 and 38, rooms facing lake

Port Orleans Riverside Alligator Bayou, buildings 26 and 28, rooms facing east; Acadian House, north wings, rooms facing west

Port Orleans French Quarter Building 1, rooms facing water; building 7, north wing, rooms facing water; building 6, north wing, rooms facing water

Treehouse Villas Any room is good

Wilderness Lodge/Copper Creek Villas Middle of northernmost wing, rooms facing northwest (woods)

Boulder Ridge Villas Southernmost part of the building, water-view rooms facing east

Hotels reporting no improvements are rechecked every two years. We inspect most Disney-owned hotels every 6–12 months, and no less than once every couple of years.

Pipe Down Out There!

The most common complaint that Walt Disney World–area hotel guests make regarding their rooms is excessive noise. A well-designed room blocks noise coming from both your neighbor's television and the pool across the resort.

The hotels with the best exterior soundproofing are **Saratoga Springs,** the **Riviera, Contemporary, Grand Floridian, Gran Destino Tower,** and the **Yacht Club.**

Hotels with the least exterior soundproofing are **Caribbean Beach, All-Star Movies,** both **Port Orleans Resorts, Art of Animation'**s *Little Mermaid* rooms, and the **Polynesian Village** (but not the Villas).

The **Riviera** and **Gran Destino Tower** are newer resorts, and it looks like Disney specifically addressed soundproofing when installing those exterior doors. At the other end of the list, the **Polynesian Village** and **Port Orleans Resorts** have performed consistently poorly in our tests over the years. Your best bet here might be to ask for a remote, corner room without a connecting interior door.

Room soundproofing, however, is only half of the story; the other half, as any good real estate agent knows, is location, particularly as it relates to guest traffic. A pool-view room at any resort, for instance, is likely to pick up a lot more noise than an upper-floor corner room.

With all of these factors in mind, we set out to determine the amount of external noise affecting every single room at Walt Disney World. We took into account factors including the floor level, pedestrian traffic, proximity to public spaces, and number of nearby rooms.

Illustration: Chris Eliopoulos

Take the northwest-facing rooms in buildings 4 and 5 of Disney's **All-Star Music Resort:** They overlook the extreme end of a parking lot, well away from most public spaces. There's little pedestrian traffic here, and the rooms themselves are well soundproofed—a recipe for quiet, or so we thought. But as it turns out, the remoteness of this location isn't lost on Disney: It's where (before the pandemic) the diesel buses are warmed up in the morning before servicing the three All-Stars.

Our research indicates that quiet rooms can be found in almost any resort, regardless of price point. For readers who put peace and quiet at the top of their lists, we've listed the 12 quietest spots among all WDW resorts in the table on the previous page.

Let There Be Light!

In addition to sound, we measure the amount of light available in three key areas of each hotel room: at the bathroom vanity or sink, at the desk or work area, and in bed. (If you have dark hair and tried to brush it in a dimly lit bathroom, especially one with dark walls, you'd understand why this is important.) The good news is that Disney has been steadily improving the lighting throughout most of its resorts. The **Contemporary Resort** sets the standard: Light at the desk measures well above the recommended level for office or school work. Light at the bathroom vanity is brighter than normal daylight. Other resorts with good lighting include the **Riviera, Wilderness Lodge,** and **All-Star Movies.** Resorts that didn't do well in our lighting test include **BoardWalk Villas** and **Port Orleans Riverside.** If you think you'll need to get work done while at Walt Disney World, consider staying at a hotel with good lighting.

unofficial **TIP**
Check the My Disney Experience app before you get in a long check-in line— sometimes the app will be updated with your room number even if you didn't get a text or email alert.

Check-in and Checkout

Up to 60 days before you arrive, you can log on to mydisneyexperience.com to complete the check-in process, make room requests and dining reservations, and note events such as birthdays and anniversaries that you're celebrating during your trip. Depending on how much information you provide to the site before your trip, your resort check-in can be eliminated or streamlined considerably in a variety of ways.

DIRECT-TO-ROOM CHECK-IN If you provide the website with a credit card number, a PIN for purchases, and your arrival and departure times, Disney will send you an email or text confirmation that your check-in is complete. Next, Disney will email or text you with your room number a few hours before you arrive at your resort, allowing you to go straight to your room without stopping at the front desk.

ONLINE CHECK-IN If you've checked in online but you haven't added a credit card or PIN to your account, you'll still be able to bypass the regular check-in desk and head for the Online Check-In Desk to finish the check-in process. *Note:* Online check-in should be completed at least 24 hours before you arrive.

AT THE FRONT DESK At the Value resorts, such as All-Star Sports, which get lots of tour and sports-team traffic, Disney has separate check-in areas for those groups, leaving the huge main check-in desk free for regular travelers. A cast member also roams the lobby and can issue an "all hands on deck" alert when lines develop.

The arrival of a busload of guests can sometimes overwhelm the front desk of Deluxe resorts, which have smaller front desks and fewer agents, but this is the exception rather than the rule.

If your room is unavailable when you arrive, Disney will either give you a phone number to call to check on the room or will offer to call or send a text message to your cell phone when it's ready.

At some resorts, checkout is a snap: Your bill will be prepared and emailed, affixed to your doorknob, or slipped under your door the night before you leave. If everything is in order, you have only to pack up and depart.

A Kutztown, Pennsylvania, reader jumped through the hoops, but to no avail:

> Did online check-in, but when we got to the resort, there was no sep-
> arate line for this—we had to stand in line with people doing regu-
> lar check-in.

EARLY CHECK-IN Official check-in time is 3 p.m. at Disney hotels and 4 p.m. for DVC time-shares. Note that if you check in early and you ask for a room that's ready, that request will cancel out any previous one you've made.

HOUSEKEEPING SERVICE As of summer 2021, Disney's housekeeping service visits rooms every other day.

OVERNIGHT PARKING FEES Disney charges resort guests a fee to park overnight. Each resort category has a different pricing structure:

- **Value:** $15 per night
- **Moderate:** $20 per night
- **Deluxe and DVC (for non-DVC members):** $25 per night

Guests staying at the campground section of **Disney's Fort Wilderness Resort** still get free standard parking, with each campsite providing a parking space for one vehicle.

Disney Vacation Club members aren't charged for overnight parking if they're staying at a DVC property. Members also get to park free when they use vacation points to stay at a non-DVC Disney resort hotel.

Day guests who visit the Disney resorts to eat, shop, use recreational facilities, and the like can still park free (again, valet parking costs extra). Day parking in the theme parks also remains free for guests staying on-property.

Complimentary overnight self-parking is available for

- Guests with disabilities
- Cast members staying as guests
- Guests traveling as part of some groups or conventions

READERS' RESORT REPORT CARD

EACH YEAR, SEVERAL THOUSAND READERS send in responses to our surveys. The Resort Report Card on the next page documents

READERS' 2021 DISNEY RESORT REPORT CARD

RESORT	OVERALL
ALL-STAR MOVIES RESORT	B-
ALL-STAR MUSIC RESORT	B-
ALL-STAR SPORTS RESORT	C
ANIMAL KINGDOM LODGE (JAMBO HOUSE)	B
ANIMAL KINGDOM VILLAS (JAMBO HOUSE)	B
ANIMAL KINGDOM VILLAS (KIDANI VILLAGE)	B
ART OF ANIMATION RESORT	B
BAY LAKE TOWER (CONTEMPORARY RESORT)	B
BEACH CLUB RESORT	B
BEACH CLUB VILLAS	B
BOARDWALK INN	B
BOARDWALK VILLAS	B
BOULDER RIDGE VILLAS (WILDERNESS LODGE)	B
CARIBBEAN BEACH RESORT	B
CONTEMPORARY RESORT	B
COPPER CREEK VILLAS & CABINS (WILDERNESS LODGE)	B
CORONADO SPRINGS RESORT	B
DOLPHIN	C+
FORT WILDERNESS RESORT (CABINS)	B
FORT WILDERNESS RESORT (CAMPSITES)	B-
GRAND FLORIDIAN RESORT & SPA	B
OLD KEY WEST RESORT	B
POLYNESIAN VILLAGE RESORT	B
POLYNESIAN VILLAS & BUNGALOWS	B
POP CENTURY RESORT	B-
PORT ORLEANS RESORT-FRENCH QUARTER	B
PORT ORLEANS RESORT–RIVERSIDE	B
RIVIERA RESORT	B
SARATOGA SPRINGS RESORT & SPA	B
SHADES OF GREEN	B
SWAN	C+
TREEHOUSE VILLAS (SARATOGA SPRINGS)	B-
THE VILLAS AT GRAND FLORIDIAN RESORT & SPA	B+
WILDERNESS LODGE	B
YACHT CLUB RESORT	B
Average for Disney Hotels	**B**
Average for Off-Site Hotels	**C**

Note: The Swan Reserve and Star Wars: Galactic Starcruiser weren't open at press time.

their opinions of the Walt Disney World resorts as well as the Swan, the Dolphin, and Shades of Green. Room Quality reflects readers' satisfaction with their rooms, while Check-In Efficiency rates the speed and ease of check-in. Quietness of Room measures how well, in the guests' perception, their rooms are insulated from external noise. Shuttle Service rates Disney bus, boat, and/or monorail service to and from the hotels. Pool reflects readers' satisfaction with the resorts' swimming

ROOM QUALITY	CHECK-IN EFFICIENCY	QUIETNESS OF ROOM	SHUTTLE SERVICE	POOL	STAFF	FOOD COURT
B	B+	B	C+	B	B+	C-
B-	B	B	C	B	A-	C
C	A-	B	C	B	B	D+
A-	B	B	C	B	A	B-
B+	A	B-	C	A-	A	F
A-	B+	A	C	B	A	D
B	B+	C+	B	B	A-	C
A-	A-	A-	C	B	A-	C
B+	B	B-	C	A-	A-	D
B	B+	B	C+	A-	B	D
A	A-	B	C	B	A	D
B+	A	B	B-	B	A-	D
B	A	B+	B	A-	A-	C
B	A-	B	C	B	A-	C-
A-	A-	B	B-	B	A-	C
A-	A-	B	B-	B	A	C
A-	B	B	C	B	B	D+
B	B	B-	C	B	B-	C
B+	B	A	C	C+	B	C
B+	A	C	B	C	C	F
A	B+	B	B	B	A	C+
A	A-	B	C	B	A	D
B	B	B	B	B+	A-	C
B	A-	B	B	A-	A	C
B	B	C	B	B-	B+	D+
B	B+	B	C+	B	A-	C
B	B	B	C	B	B	C
A-	A	A	B	B	A	C
B	A-	A-	C	B	A-	C
A	A-	B	C	B+	A	C
B	B	C+	C-	B	B	C-
B+	B	A	C-	B-	A	B-
A	A-	A	B	B	B+	B
B	A-	B	C	B	A	C
A-	B+	C	C	A-	B	D
B	**B+**	**B**	**C**	**B**	**A-**	**C-**
B	**B-**	**C**	**F**	**D**	**B-**	**F**

pools. Staff measures the friendliness and helpfulness of the resort's employees, and Dining rates the overall food quality and value.

Readers have ranked Disney resorts about the same over the past seven years, with most properties receiving an overall B rating. Also for a seventh consecutive year, bus transportation and dining options are the areas where Disney scores lowest. Check-in processing is an area where they do better than most.

UNOFFICIAL PICKS FOR DISNEY ON-SITE RESORTS

● **ADULTS**

VALUE: Pop Century For the nostalgic decor and new room designs

MODERATE: Port Orleans French Quarter For its theming and small, intimate size

DELUXE: Grand Floridian For excellent service and access to good sit-down restaurants

● **GROUPS OF FIVE OR MORE**

VALUE: Art of Animation Newest suites with two baths

MODERATE: Port Orleans Riverside One or two connecting rooms in Alligator Bayou

DELUXE: Old Key West Two-bedroom villa (booked with DVC rental points)

● **FAMILIES WITH YOUNG KIDS**

VALUE: Art of Animation Kids will delight in the architecture and themed pools.

MODERATE: Port Orleans French Quarter Kid-friendly, smaller-scale resort

DELUXE: Animal Kingdom Lodge Fantastic scenery and chances to see animals

● **FAMILIES WITH OLDER KIDS**

VALUE: Pop Century A lively pool scene means meeting new friends. Very teen-friendly food court, with Art of Animation's within walking distance.

MODERATE: Fort Wilderness There's plenty of opportunity to independently explore this massive resort, plus having a kitchen means you won't have to take out a second mortgage to feed the bottomless pits that are teen stomachs.

DELUXE: Yacht & Beach Clubs For Stormalong Bay and easy access to EPCOT and Disney's Hollywood Studios

---

Off-site hotels are, on average, rated slightly lower than Disney hotels, with problems noted in food courts and transportation. As noted earlier in this chapter, we think these ratings justify the premium that Disney charges at many of its hotels.

Putting It All Together: Reader Picks for Best and Worst Resorts

For the seventh year in a row, **The Villas at Disney's Grand Floridian Resort & Spa** took the top spot in our reader survey, getting top marks for room quality and quietness. In second place is **Disney's Riviera Resort,** loved by readers for its staff, room quality, and check-in process. The **Boulder Ridge** DVC units place third, and regular (cash) rooms at **Grand Floridian Resort & Spa** come in fourth. We think readers got this absolutely correct.

The rankings for **Animal Kingdom Lodge–Jambo House** were almost certainly colored by the resort's restaurant closures during the pandemic. While the DVC part of Jambo House was open, the Lodge's main restaurants, Boma and Jiko, were closed, with shortened hours for the resort's one grab-and-go location. (*Note:* Jiko remains closed at press time.) During one of our stays, the only food available was at the pool bar, and even then, you had to know to ask for it: Resort signage suggested taking the bus to Kidani Village to eat. That lack of dining options dragged Jambo House down to the middle of the pack for this year's surveys. We expect Animal Kingdom to rate higher in next year's surveys.

The highest-rated Disney Moderate resorts are **Port Orleans–French Quarter** and the **Fort Wilderness Cabins.** Both properties have unique aspects: French Quarter is Disney's smallest Moderate resort, and the relatively small crowds at the pool and food court probably add to its appeal. The Fort Wilderness Cabins are likely Disney's most unusual accommodations. The remote setting is definitely part of Fort Wilderness's charm. The highest-rated Disney Value resort is **Art of Animation.**

The lowest-rated Disney resorts are the three **All-Star Resorts,** plus the **Swan** and **Dolphin.** The All-Stars are Disney's least-expensive properties, and the unrefurbished rooms at Music and Sports have the lowest room-quality ratings of any on-site hotel. The Swan and Dolphin are rated low for transportation to the parks and for dining options. We think readers are spot-on with those assessments.

READER RATINGS EXCLUDING AIRPORT-SHUTTLE SCORES In our latest survey, we asked readers about Disney's Magical Express shuttle service between Orlando International Airport and the Disney hotels. Because Magical Express ends service on December 31, 2021, it's worth wondering how much the reader rankings will change when it's gone. Not

WOULD YOU STAY AT THIS HOTEL AGAIN?	WOULD YOU RECOMMEND THIS HOTEL TO A FRIEND?
RESORT % would definitely stay again	**RESORT** % would definitely recommend
Shades of Green **99%**	The Villas at Grand Floridian Resort **98%**
Animal Kingdom Villas–Jambo House **98%**	Polynesian Villas & Bungalows **94%**
The Villas at Grand Floridian Resort **98%**	Animal Kingdom Villas–Jambo House **93%**
BoardWalk Villas **97%**	Polynesian Village Resort **92%**
Copper Creek Villas (Wilderness Lodge) **97%**	Wilderness Lodge **92%**
Port Orleans French Quarter **96%**	Bay Lake Tower (Contemporary Resort) **91%**
Bay Lake Tower (Contemporary Resort) **95%**	BoardWalk Inn **91%**
Beach Club Villas **95%**	Fort Wilderness Resort (Cabins) **91%**
Polynesian Villas & Bungalows **94%**	Port Orleans French Quarter **91%**
Wilderness Lodge **94%**	Yacht Club Resort **91%**
Beach Club Resort **93%**	Beach Club Resort **90%**
BoardWalk Inn **93%**	Boulder Ridge Villas (Wilderness Lodge) **90%**
Yacht Club Resort **93%**	Copper Creek Villas (Wilderness Lodge) **90%**
Old Key West Resort **92%**	Riviera Resort **90%**
Pop Century Resort **92%**	Animal Kingdom Lodge–Jambo House **89%**
Riviera Resort **92%**	Animal Kingdom Villas–Kidani Village **89%**
Swan **92%**	Beach Club Villas **89%**
Dolphin **91%**	Old Key West Resort **89%**
Polynesian Village Resort **91%**	Pop Century Resort **89%**
Saratoga Springs Resort & Spa **91%**	BoardWalk Villas **88%**
Art of Animation Resort **90%**	Grand Floridian Resort & Spa **88%**
Fort Wilderness Resort (Campsites) **90%**	Shades of Green **88%**
Grand Floridian Resort & Spa **90%**	Fort Wilderness Resort (Campsites) **87%**
Animal Kingdom Lodge–Jambo House **89%**	Art of Animation Resort **86%**
Boulder Ridge Villas (Wilderness Lodge) **89%**	Contemporary Resort **86%**
Fort Wilderness Resort (Cabins) **89%**	Saratoga Springs Resort & Spa **85%**
Animal Kingdom Villas–Kidani Village **88%**	Swan **85%**
Coronado Springs Resort **88%**	Coronado Springs Resort **84%**
Caribbean Beach Resort **87%**	Port Orleans Riverside **84%**
All-Star Movies Resort **86%**	Caribbean Beach Resort **83%**
All-Star Music Resort **86%**	Dolphin **82%**
Contemporary Resort **86%**	Treehouse Villas (Saratoga Springs) **82%**
Port Orleans Riverside **85%**	All-Star Movies Resort **79%**
All-Star Sports Resort **77%**	All-Star Music Resort **75%**
Treehouse Villas (Saratoga Springs) **60%**	All-Star Sports Resort **66%**
Average for WDW hotels 90%	**Average for WDW hotels** 87%
Average for off-site hotels 84%	**Average for off-site hotels** 74%

Note: The Swan Reserve was not open at press time.

much, as it turns out: The **Grand Floridian Villas** and **Riviera** still end up on top, and the **All-Stars, Swan,** and **Dolphin** still end up at the bottom. Some resorts in the middle of the pack switch places, but there's no statistical significance to the differences.

In addition to the Reader Report Card, we list in the table on the previous page the percentage of readers responding "Definitely" to the questions **"Would you stay at this hotel again?"** and **"Would you recommend this hotel to a friend?"** Percentages of 97 or above in response to the first question and 94 or above in response to the second are considered Above Average; percentages of 82 or below in response to the first question and 79 or below in response to the second are considered Below Average.

For each hotel profiled in the following pages, we include these two percentages, plus the overall reader ratings, expressed as letter grades, from the 2021 Disney Resort Reader Report Card (pages 118–119).

WALT DISNEY WORLD HOTEL PROFILES

FOR MORE INFORMATION on the Disney resorts, including photos and videos, check out our website, **TouringPlans.com.**

As we were going to press, Disney World's bus transportation network was suffering from a lack of drivers. This shortage has substantially increased the transportation time between some resorts and theme parks, to the point where Disney resorts are reminding their guests that they can drive their own cars and park free at the theme parks. That's not a sign of confidence in your transportation system's capacity.

The simplest way to reduce your transportation wait is to walk—for example, from the Polynesian, Grand Floridian, or Contemporary to the Magic Kingdom, or from any EPCOT resort to EPCOT or Disney's Hollywood Studios. The next best alternative is to get a taxi or ride-hailing service to drop you off at the closest resort to the park you're visiting and walk over. Driving your own car or taking a Disney bus is the next best option. Boats and the Skyliner may take the longest to get you to park opening.

THE MAGIC KINGDOM RESORTS

Disney's Grand Floridian Resort & Spa

(See **tinyurl.com/ug-grandfloridian** *for extended coverage.)*

Unofficial Guide Reader-Survey Results

Percentage of readers who'd stay here again	90% (*Average*)
Percentage of readers who'd recommend this resort to a friend	88% (*Average*)
Overall reader rating	B

QUICK TAKE: *The Grand Floridian Resort, its Villas in particular, is one of the highest-rated resorts in Walt Disney World. It also has many sit-down restaurants that are rated in the top 20 of our reader surveys. If the Villas are within your budget, your only big decision is whether to stay there or at Animal Kingdom Lodge & Villas (see page 174).*

Grand Floridian Resort & Spa and Grand Floridian Villas

WALT DISNEY WORLD'S FLAGSHIP HOTEL was inspired by grand Victorian resorts such as the Hotel del Coronado in San Diego and Mount Washington Resort in New Hampshire. A complex of four- and five-story white-frame buildings, the Grand Floridian integrates verandas, intricate latticework, dormers, and turrets beneath a red-shingle roof to capture the most distinctive elements of 19th-century ocean-resort architecture. Covering 40 acres along Seven Seas Lagoon, the Grand Floridian offers lovely pools, white-sand beaches, and a marina.

The 867 guest rooms, with wood trim and soft goods (curtains, linens, towels, and the like) in tones of deep red, gold, and tan, are luxurious, though we think the mocha-colored walls are a little dreary at night. The woodwork, marble-topped sinks, and ceiling fans amplify the Victorian theme. Large by any standard, the typical room is 440 square feet (dormer rooms are smaller) and furnished with two queen beds, a daybed, and a small desk with chair. Many rooms have a balcony. All rooms have a Keurig coffee maker, a large dresser with mini-fridge, and a wall-mounted TV.

GRAND FLORIDIAN RESORT & SPA

STRENGTHS	WEAKNESSES
• High staff-to-guest ratio	• Most expensive WDW resort
• Excellent dining options for adults	• Self-parking is $25/night *and* across the street
• Large rooms with daybeds	
• Very good on-site spa	• Public areas often blocked by wedding parties
• Fantastic kids' *Alice in Wonderland*–themed splash area	• Noise from Magic Kingdom, boat horns, and whistles
• Boat and monorail transportation to the Magic Kingdom, plus a pedestrian walkway	• Bus transportation to DHS, Animal Kingdom, water parks, and Disney Springs is shared by the other monorail resorts
• Diverse recreational options	
• Close to Palm, Magnolia, and Oak Trail Golf Courses	

Bathrooms are large, with plenty of counter space and fluffy towels. Two shelves under the sink provide a small amount of storage. A 1,500-watt, wall-mounted hair dryer is provided, but it's not very powerful, so bring your own if you have lots of hair. Water pressure in the shower is probably less than what you get at home but still enough to rinse out shampoo suds. A separate dressing area next to the bathroom includes two sinks and enough counter space to fit most of your toiletries. Combined with the bathroom, this allows three people to get dressed at the same time.

With a high ratio of staff to guests, service is outstanding. The hotel is connected directly to the Magic Kingdom by monorail, boat, and a pedestrian walkway, and to other Disney World destinations by bus. Walking time to the monorail-, boat-, and bus-loading areas from the most remote guest rooms is about 7–10 minutes. It takes about 15–20 minutes on the pedestrian walkway to get to the Magic Kingdom turnstiles from the farthest points of the Grand Floridian.

The resort has several full-service restaurants, though the fine-dining **Victoria & Albert's** wasn't open at press time. Others are a short monorail ride or walk away.

The Grand Floridian's **Senses Spa,** modeled after the spas on the Disney Cruise Line ships, is one of the best in the Orlando area, but it was still closed as we went to press. In addition, the resort's pools are among the nicest on Disney property. The **Courtyard Pool,** large enough that local waterfowl mistake it for a lake, has a zero-entry ramp for small children to splash in. Cabanas are available to rent here too. An *Alice in Wonderland*–themed splash area sits between the main building and the Villas. If your kids like water, this is the place to be.

*un*official **TIP**
In 2022 the Grand Floridian will convert all 200 guest rooms in its Big Pine Key building to DVC studios. This will reduce the number of rooms available for cash-paying guests.

The rest of the Grand Floridian's grounds are maintained to an extremely high standard. It's a lovely place to walk around during the evening, with romantic light levels and charming background music. A stroll from the marina, past the resort's main buildings, and over to the Polynesian Village for a nightcap is a nice way to end the evening.

Most reader comments concerning the Grand Floridian are positive. First, from a Durham, North Carolina, mother of two preschoolers:

The Grand Floridian pool with the waterslide was a big hit with our kids. They also loved taking the boat across the lagoon to return from the Magic Kingdom.

Speaking of pools, a father of two from Minneapolis had this specific concern:

The concrete surrounding the Grand Floridian's beach pool gets very hot. Walking from pool chair to pool was a very painful experience and one that could have been avoided with proper materials [for example, heat-reducing concrete].

GOOD (AND NOT-SO-GOOD) ROOMS AT THE GRAND FLORIDIAN *(See* tinyurl.com/gfroomviews *for photos.)* The resort is spread over a peninsula that juts into Seven Seas Lagoon. In addition to the main building, there are five dispersed rectangular buildings. Most of the rooms have a balcony, and most balconies are enclosed by a rail that affords good visibility. Dormer rooms, just beneath the roof in each building, have smaller enclosed balconies that limit visibility when you're seated. Most dormer rooms, however, have vaulted ceilings and a coziness that compensates for the less-desirable balconies.

The main building used to be a hub of activity well into the night, hosting everything from jazz bands to life-size gingerbread houses at Christmas. All of those activities have been suspended during the pandemic, which makes the main building much quieter.

If you want to be near the bus and monorail, most of the restaurants, and shopping, ask for a room in the main building (all Club Level rooms). The best rooms are **4322–4329** and **4422–4429,** which have full balconies and overlook the lagoon in the direction of the beach and the Polynesian Village. Other excellent main-building rooms are **4401–4409,** with full balconies overlooking the marina and an unobstructed view of Cinderella Castle across the lagoon.

Before the pandemic, nightly entertainment that took place in the lobby could be heard from some rooms—possibly to the detriment of your sleep:

The Grand Floridian has a six-person band that plays every night until almost 10 p.m. Our room faced the lobby, and the music kept us up when we tried to go to bed.

Of the four lodges, two—**Boca Chica** and **Conch Key**—have one long side facing the lagoon and the other facing inner courtyards and swimming pools. At Conch Key, full-balcony rooms **7229–7231, 7328, 7329, 7331, 7425–7429,** and **7431** offer vistas across the lagoon to the Magic Kingdom and castle. Room **7427** is just about perfect. Less-expensive rooms in the same building that offer good marina views are **7212, 7312, 7412–7415, 7417, 7419, 7421, 7513–7515,** and **7517.** (Grand Floridian room numbers are coded. Take room 7213: 7 is the building number, 2 is the floor, and 13 is the room number.) In Boca Chica, ask for a lagoon-view room on the first, second, or third floor. A few garden-view rooms in Boca Chica have views obstructed by a poolside building. These are the worst views from any Grand Floridian room.

The two remaining buildings, **Sugar Loaf Key** (Club Level) and **Sago Key,** face each other across the marina. The opposite side of Sugar Loaf Key faces a courtyard, while the other side of Sago Key faces a finger of the lagoon and a forested area. These views are pleasant but not in the same league as those from the rooms listed previously. Exceptions are end rooms in Sago Key that have a view of the lagoon and Cinderella Castle (rooms **5139, 5144, 5145, 5242–5245,** and **5342–5345**).

THE VILLAS AT DISNEY'S GRAND FLORIDIAN RESORT & SPA

(See **tinyurl.com/ug-gfvillas** *for extended coverage.)*

Unofficial Guide Reader-Survey Results

Percentage of readers who'd stay here again	98% (*Average*)
Percentage of readers who'd recommend this resort to a friend	98% (*Average*)
Overall reader rating	B+

THIS DISNEY DELUXE VILLA PROPERTY opened in the fall of 2013. Readers have rated it the best Disney World resort for seven years in a row. If the Average designation for the Villas' "would stay again" and "would recommend to a friend" survey results seems to contradict the high percentages, that's because we receive relatively few surveys about this resort compared with others. Thus, the margin of error for the Villas' survey results is slightly higher than for other properties. Put another way: We're pretty sure that readers think the Villas are fantastic—we just don't have enough surveys to prove it with math.

Decorated in neutral tones, with mostly green and red accent colors, the rooms are the nicest at any DDV property. Most have vaulted living-room ceilings and faux-wood balconies or porches. Those balconies stretch the entire length of the room, giving everyone enough space for a good view.

Studios have a kitchenette with minifridge, sink, and drip coffee maker, while the larger rooms have full kitchens. Those feature a stainless-steel oven range, with the dishwasher and refrigerator tucked behind white wood panels that match the glass-door cabinets. Other amenities in the full kitchens include a full-size drip coffee maker, a toaster, frying pans, and the usual set of plates, glasses, cups, and cutlery. Also in the kitchen are a banquette seat and a table with room for six.

The living room has a sofa that seats three comfortably; an upholstered chair and ottoman; a coffee table; and a large, flat-panel TV. The sofa converts into a bed that sleeps two; a cabinet below the TV hides a small pull-down bed. We'd use these beds for kids, not adults.

Studio rooms have a queen bed in addition to the folding options listed above. One-bedroom villas have a king bed along with the folding options; two-bedroom villas have a king bed in one room and two queen beds in the other, plus the folding options; the Grand Villa's third bedroom has an additional two queen beds.

The one- and two-bedroom units and the Grand Villa bedrooms are outfitted with a large writing desk, a flat-panel TV with DVD player, two nightstands with convenient electric plugs, and a side chair. They also have large walk-in closets.

Bathrooms are large, with marble tile and flat-panel TVs built into the mirrors. Studio bathrooms have a separate toilet and shower area; in the one-bedroom configuration, a tub and dressing area sit adjacent to the bedroom. The bathroom and shower are connected by a pocket door, allowing two groups of people to get dressed at the same time. The tiled shower looks as if it could comfortably hold eight people should the need arise. It also has a rain showerhead mounted in the ceiling in addition to a wall-mounted faucet.

The villas have their own parking lot next to the building but no on-site dining. Within walking distance, however, are the restaurants of both the main Grand Floridian and the Polynesian Village, giving you a bit more variety than at other Magic Kingdom resorts. Room service is available from the Grand Floridian's in-room dining menu. Rates are high, as you might expect, but renting DVC points helps in that regard.

GOOD (AND NOT-SO-GOOD) ROOMS AT THE GRAND FLORIDIAN VILLAS *(See* tinyurl.com/gfvillaviews *for photos.)* Rooms **1X14**, **1X16**, and **1X18** face the Magic Kingdom and have views of Space Mountain and the castle; **1X14** has probably the best views of any room in all of the Villas. (*X* indicates a floor number.)

Even-numbered rooms **1X02–1X12** face west, toward the Polynesian Village and Seven Seas Lagoon, and afford a good view of the nightly water pageant as it floats by.

Rooms **1X15, 1X17, 1X19–1X22, 1X24, 1X26,** and **1X28** face Disney's Wedding Pavilion, the parking lot, the monorail, and landscaping. Odd-numbered rooms **1X03–1X13** and **1X25, 1X27,** and **1X29** look out onto pool facilities and landscaping.

South-facing rooms in Big Pine Key look out over the Seven Seas Lagoon, although mature trees and landscaping partially block those views from many upper-floor rooms. Rooms **9X41–9X47** may have views of the Magic Kingdom fireworks.

Disney's Polynesian Village Resort, Villas & Bungalows

(See map on page 128; see tinyurl.com/ug-poly *for extended coverage.)*

STRENGTHS	
• Walking distance to EPCOT monorail	• Close to Palm, Magnolia, and Oak Trail Golf Courses
• Most family-friendly dining on the monorail loop	**WEAKNESSES**
• Fun South Seas theme	• No spa or exercise facilities (guests must use those at the Grand Floridian)
• Boat and monorail transportation to the Magic Kingdom	• Noise from boat horns and whistles
• Among the best Club Levels of the Deluxe resorts	• $25/night self-parking (except DVC areas)
	• Bus transportation to DHS, Animal Kingdom, water parks, and Disney Springs

Unofficial Guide **Reader-Survey Results**

Percentage of readers who'd stay here again	91% *(Average)*
Percentage of readers who'd recommend this resort to a friend	92% *(Average)*
Overall reader rating	B

SOUTH PACIFIC TROPICS ARE RE-CREATED at this Deluxe resort, which consists of two- and three-story Hawaiian longhouses situated around

Polynesian Village Resort, Villas & Bungalows

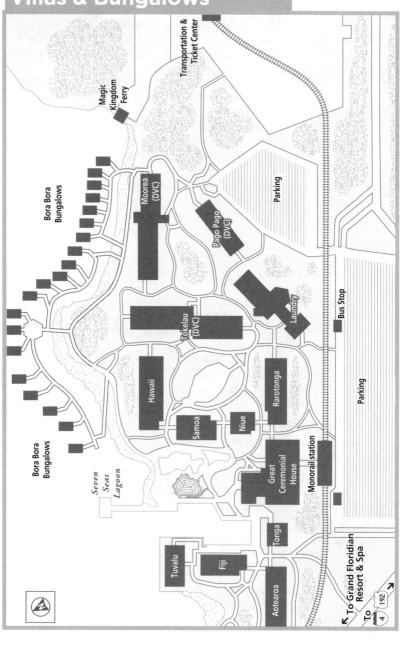

the four-story **Great Ceremonial House,** which contains restaurants, shops, and an atrium lobby with slate floors and many species of tropical plants. Buildings feature wood tones, including exposed roof beams and tribal-inspired geometric inlays in the cornices.

Spread across 39 acres along Seven Seas Lagoon, the resort, which has fewer than 500 standard hotel rooms, has three white-sand beaches, some with volleyball courts. Its pool complex likewise captures the South Pacific theme. There is no dedicated fitness center, but guests are welcome to use the Grand Floridian's facilities, just a quarter-mile walk or 2-minute monorail ride away. Landscaping is superb—garden-view rooms are generally superior to equivalent rooms at other resorts.

The Polynesian Village's **Moorea, Pago Pago,** and **Tokelau** buildings are part of Disney's time-share program (described in the next section).

Except for the three aforementioned buildings, the resort opened with the Magic Kingdom in 1971. The most recent room refurbishments were completed in summer 2021, adding bright, island-themed murals and subtle references to characters from Disney's *Moana*.

We're always suspicious when Disney adds characters to anything, as it's often an attempt to distract from something else. But this is one of Disney's better room-renovation projects in recent memory, and the *Moana* additions work well with the resort's theme. As before, most rooms have two queen beds, a sofa, a reading chair, a large dresser with plenty of shelf space, and a wall-mounted TV. A minifridge and coffee maker sit between two large closets near the doorway and opposite the bathroom area. The closets are spacious and light. Lighting throughout the room, including that for the desk and beds, has improved.

The Poly's bathrooms have also been redone. Two large sinks offer plenty of counter space. A spacious, glass-enclosed shower provides good-to-excellent water pressure. (*Note:* We're pretty sure that most bathrooms have only showers, not bathtubs, so if a tub is important to you, ask your travel agent or Disney about it when booking.) The new bathroom layout includes a door between the toilet and sink area, plus another separating the entire bathroom from the rest of the room. This allows three people to get dressed at once—an improvement over the old bathroom design.

The Polynesian Village has an on-site monorail station, and all rooms are within easy walking distance of the monorail station at the Transportation and Ticket Center. Easily accessible by monorail are full-service restaurants at the Grand Floridian and Contemporary Resorts, as well as restaurants in the Magic Kingdom. Bus service is available to other Disney destinations, and boat service takes you to the Magic Kingdom. Walking time to the bus and on-site monorail stations from the most remote rooms is 8–11 minutes. The pedestrian walkway between the Poly and Grand Floridian continues to the Magic Kingdom—it's about 1.5 miles from the farthest point at the Poly to the Magic Kingdom turnstiles.

The Poly's transportation options are a major draw for some readers:

We stay at the Polynesian Village because it offers the best transportation. You can walk to a direct monorail to both the Magic Kingdom and EPCOT, the water taxi can be a fast option, and the bus service to other parks is fairly direct.

A Maryland family found the room soundproofing lacking, confirming our own research:

We took towels from the pool and stuffed them under the door to deaden the noise coming from the connecting room.

Unofficial Guide correspondents Dawn and Taylor gave us this scoop about self-parking:

The parking situation here was INSANE! People were circling like vultures—like what you'd see at the mall on Black Friday.

The Polynesian Village has two lounges, with **Trader Sam's Grog Grotto** being the more themed. Modeled after the famed bar of the same name at the Disneyland Hotel, Trader Sam's serves whimsical (and potent) cocktails and tasty appetizers, along with interactive art and "artifacts" stuffed into every available inch of space. We love it ourselves, although in this Hartford, Wisconsin, reader's eyes, it's not special enough to warrant a stay at the resort:

> *unofficial* **TIP**
> During busier times of the year, it can take several hours to get a table at Trader Sam's.

After I stayed at Animal Kingdom Lodge in a savanna-view room, the Polynesian Village was a letdown. The proximity to the Magic Kingdom is nice, and Trader Sam's was awesome, but otherwise it was nothing extraordinary. They need to step it up for what they charge.

GOOD (AND NOT-SO-GOOD) ROOMS AT POLYNESIAN VILLAGE RESORT *(See* tinyurl.com/polyroomviews *for photos.)* The Polynesian Village's 11 guest-room buildings, or longhouses, are spread over a long strip of land bordered by the monorail on one side and Seven Seas Lagoon on the other. All buildings have first-floor patios and third-floor balconies. The older buildings, which comprise more than half of the resort's rooms, have faux balconies on their second floors. (The newer buildings offer full balconies on both the second and third floors, and patios on the first.) A small number of patios in the first-floor rooms have views blocked by mature vegetation, but these patios provide more room than do the balconies on the third floor. If views are important and you're staying in one of the eight older longhouses, ask for a third-floor room.

The Great Ceremonial House contains most of the restaurants and shops, as well as the resort lobby, guest services, and bus and monorail stations. The longhouses most convenient to the Great Ceremonial House—**Fiji,** the **Tonga suites, Rarotonga, Niue,** and **Samoa**—offer views of the swimming complex, a small marina, or inner gardens (possibly with the monorail). There are no lagoon views except for oblique views from the upper floors of Fiji, Samoa, and Tuvalu; Aotearoa; and a tunnel view from Tonga. Samoa, however, by virtue of its proximity to the main swimming complex, is a good choice for families who plan to spend time at the pool. If your children are under age 8, request a first-floor room on the volcano-pool side of Samoa.

You can specifically request a lagoon- or Magic Kingdom–view room at the Polynesian Village, provided you're willing to pay extra. The best of these rooms are on the third floor in **Tuvalu** and, if you're staying in a Club Level (concierge) room, the third floor in **Hawaii.**

In addition to second-floor rooms in the older buildings (the ones with fake balconies), we also advise against booking the monorail-side (south-facing) rooms in **Rarotonga** and **Aotearoa**. Garden-view rooms here are especially nice, but the monorail, though quiet, runs within spitting distance.

Many first-floor rooms in **Hawaii (1501–1518)** are garden- or lagoon-view rooms; their scenery is blocked by the over-the-water bungalows. These rooms still offer a chance to see the evening fireworks, however, and are a little less expensive than similar rooms on higher floors.

Tuvalu, Fiji, and **Aotearoa** are the most distant accommodations from the bus stop. For large strollers or wheelchair access, take the ferry to the Magic Kingdom.

POLYNESIAN VILLAS & BUNGALOWS

Unofficial Guide Reader-Survey Results

Percentage of readers who'd stay here again	94% (*Average*)
Percentage of readers who'd recommend this resort to a friend	94% (*Average*)
Overall reader rating	B

THE TOKELAU, MOOREA, AND PAGO PAGO longhouses hold DVC studio rooms that sleep five and are the largest studios in Walt Disney World's DVC inventory. They also have two bathrooms: The smaller bath has a small sink and step-in shower; the larger has a toilet, sink, and bath–shower combination. This allows three people to get ready simultaneously. The studios also include kitchenettes.

While these studios are functionally similar to the Poly's standard rooms, they have enough small touches to make them different, including recessed ceilings, more stone and tile work in the baths, and a slightly darker color scheme.

The Polynesian's 20 over-the-water **Bora Bora Bungalows** sit in front of Hawaii, Tokelau, and Moorea. Connected to land by a wood walkway, these two-bedroom bungalows offer stunning views of the Magic Kingdom fireworks and of Seven Seas Lagoon and its nightly Electrical Water Pageant. Not surprisingly, those stunning views come with stunning prices—up to $5,528 per night.

Let's start with the positives: The bungalows are well built, with topnotch design elements from top to bottom. The bedrooms are spacious, the beds are the best on Disney property, the bathrooms are gorgeous, and the showers will make you feel as happy as anything nonsentient is capable of. The open kitchen design works wonderfully, and you could easily host a good-size party inside. The floors are spotlessly clean, with interesting slate and rug textures, so you'll want to run around barefoot. Hell, the doorbell plays a different chime every time you ring it. And yeah, the views are spectacular.

The bungalows' two fatal flaws: price and location. First of all, 160 DVC points for a one-night stay is equivalent to about $3,000 in cash at the time of this writing. Check-in is at 4 p.m. and checkout at 11 a.m., so a 19-hour stay costs about $158 an hour.

Problem was, we couldn't check in at 4—we never got our room assignment by text, email, or phone. It wasn't until we walked back to the front desk at 5 p.m. that we finally got our bungalow. The 75 minutes we couldn't use it amounted to about $200 in lost time—almost enough to pay for an entire night at Saratoga Springs. And nobody said a word about it.

The first "Are you out of the room yet?" knock on our door came before 9 a.m. We're not kidding.

Then there's the ferry horn. We were in 7019, the second-closest bungalow to the Transportation and Ticket Center (TTC) ferry dock. A ferry leaves here about every 12 minutes, from about 30–45 minutes before the park opens until an hour after closing. Every time a ferry departs, it has to sound a warning horn so that nearby craft know it's coming.

The sound of the horn is akin to an air-raid siren: loud enough to stop indoor conversation in its tracks. Reading, watching TV, getting a baby to nap? Forget it. You simply can't hear or think above the noise.

If the bungalows were on the other side of the Poly's marina, we could *almost* justify selling a gently used organ to stay here again, but between the stratospheric prices and that hellish horn, we just can't. If you're determined to stay here anyway, shoot for one of **bungalows 7001–7005,** which are farthest from the TTC.

The Polynesian Villas have a separate parking lot close to their longhouses. Dining and transportation are shared with the main resort.

GOOD (AND NOT-SO-GOOD) ROOMS AT THE POLYNESIAN VILLAS
Because there are a few quirks in the way Disney categorizes room views here, it's possible to snag a Magic Kingdom view from a garden-view room. The second- and third-floor rooms in **Tokelau (2901–2928, 2939–2948, 3901–3928,** and **3939–3948)** offer the best shot at getting side views of Cinderella Castle and the fireworks, although readers report that palm trees may block some second-floor views. First-floor rooms (**1901–1913** and **1939–1948**) may also have landscaping blocking some views; on the upside, the patios provide room to move to find a better spot.

The second and third floors in **Moorea** have rooms with lagoon and Magic Kingdom views; those that face north see the Magic Kingdom. Avoid **Pago Pago**'s southeast-facing rooms (**1X01–1X12**)—these look onto the parking lot and monorail.

If you plan to spend a lot of time at EPCOT, **Moorea** and **Pago Pago** are good choices because they're within easy walking distance of the TTC and the EPCOT monorail. Even if you're going to the Magic Kingdom, it's a shorter walk from Moorea and Pago Pago to the TTC and Magic Kingdom monorail than to the monorail station at the Great Ceremonial House.

Disney's Wilderness Lodge, Boulder Ridge Villas, and Copper Creek Villas & Cascade Cabins

(See **tinyurl.com/ug-wlodge** *for extended coverage.)*

Unofficial Guide **Reader-Survey Results**

Percentage of readers who'd stay here again	94% (*Average*)
Percentage of readers who'd recommend this resort to a friend	92% (*Average*)
Overall reader rating	B

QUICK TAKE: *Hotel rooms at the lodge, DVC rooms at Boulder Ridge Villas, and (if it's in your budget) the Cascade Cabins are our picks.*

Wilderness Lodge & Boulder Ridge/Copper Creek Villas

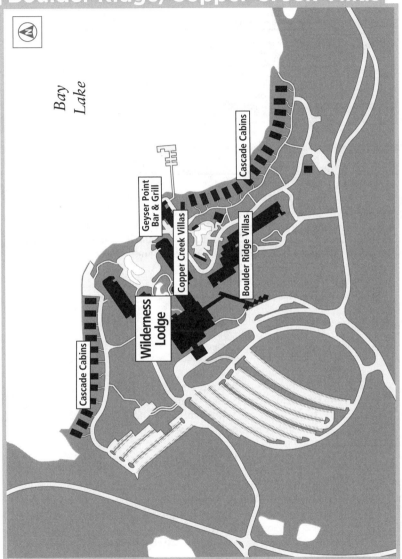

THIS DELUXE RESORT is inspired by grand, rustic Arts and Crafts lodges of the early 20th century—think The Ahwahnee in Yosemite National Park and the Grove Park Inn in Asheville, North Carolina. Situated on the shore of Bay Lake, the lodge consists of an eight-story central building augmented by two seven-story guest wings, a wing of studio and one- and two-bedroom condominiums, and 26 lakeside cabins. The hotel features exposed timber columns, log cabin–style

WILDERNESS LODGE & BOULDER RIDGE/COPPER CREEK VILLAS

STRENGTHS	WEAKNESSES
• National park lodge theme is a favorite of kids and adults alike	• Transportation to Magic Kingdom is by bus or boat only
• Along with Animal Kingdom Lodge, it's the least-expensive Disney Deluxe resort	• $25/night self-parking (except DVC areas)
• Excellent lounge for adults	• Noise from main building's lobby can be heard inside nearby rooms
• Close to recreational options at Fort Wilderness	• Bus transportation to Magic Kingdom sometimes shared with Fort Wilderness
• Great views from guest rooms	• Smallest rooms and baths of Disney's Deluxe resorts
• Rooms with bunk beds available	
• Exceptionally peaceful location and public areas (Villas)	

facades, and dormer windows, along with an 82-foot-tall stone fireplace in the lobby. Outside, there's a beach and a delightful pool modeled on a mountain stream.

We use the admittedly clunky "Wilderness Lodge & Boulder Ridge/ Copper Creek Villas" to refer to the entire complex, including its timeshare units, which are available to the general public when not being used by DVC members. (In reality, the full name would be something like "Disney's Wilderness Lodge, Boulder Ridge Villas, and Copper Creek Villas & Cascade Cabins"—but that's what happens when you pay a marketing team by the pound.) Here's what the various names mean:

- **Disney's Wilderness Lodge** refers to the hotel (that is, the non-time-share) component of the main building (the lodge), which opened in 1994.

- **Boulder Ridge Villas** (Boulder Ridge for short) refers to time-share rooms in an adjacent building that opened in 2000.

- **Copper Creek Villas & Cascade Cabins** (Copper Creek for short) refers to DVC time-share rooms in the main building (Copper Creek Villas) and the lakeside Cascade Cabins, both opened in 2017.

The lodge's guest rooms were last refurbished in 2012. Darkly stained Mission-style furniture is complemented by soft goods in burnt umber and blue, accented with American Indian–inspired patterns. Carved-wood headboards, rough-hewn armoires, and rustic light fixtures create a log cabin atmosphere.

Typical rooms have two queen-size beds; some rooms have one queen plus bunk beds or two queens plus a queen sleeper sofa. Rooms with a single king-size bed are also available. All rooms have a table and chairs, a dresser, a TV, a two-sink vanity just outside the bathroom, a minifridge, and a coffee maker. Rooms on the ground floor have patios; rooms above have balconies.

The pool area features a children's water-play area and a pool bar.

Dining choices encompass two full-service restaurants plus the outdoor **Geyser Point** bar and restaurant. More dining options are available via a short boat ride to the Contemporary or Fort Wilderness.

The resort is connected to the Magic Kingdom by boat and to other parks by bus. Your best bet for catching the first boat is to send someone out to the boat dock about 90 minutes before the Magic Kingdom's official opening time. If a line has started to form but has fewer than 30 people, get in line. If the line is longer than that, consider taking a bus or ride-hailing service to the park. Boat service may be suspended during storms, so if it's raining or rain looks likely, Disney will provide buses. Walking time to buses and boats from the remotest rooms is 5–8 minutes.

A Boone County, Indiana, reader thinks transportation is a weak spot:

To paraphrase Mark Twain, rumors that Wilderness Lodge's trans-portation problems have been resolved are greatly exaggerated—it's an easy boat ride to the Magic Kingdom, but bus trips to the Studios and Animal Kingdom take nearly an hour, which is just inexcusable.

A mom from Oklahoma City concurs:

During our most recent stay, transportation from Wilderness Lodge to the parks was the worst we have ever experienced in all our trips to WDW. We waited more than an hour for a boat to the Magic Kingdom; then, after it finally showed up and loaded, we made an unexplained trip to Fort Wilderness and loaded 26 more people. It took 90 minutes to get to the Magic Kingdom! The bus system wasn't much better—it's nearly impossible to get to the parks before opening.

GOOD (AND NOT-SO-GOOD) ROOMS AT WILDERNESS LODGE *(See* tinyurl.com/wlroomviews *for photos.)* The lodge is shaped like a very blocky letter V. The main entrance and lobby are at the closed end of the V. Next are middle wings that connect the lobby to the parallel end sections, which extend to the open part of the V. The V's open end flanks pools and gardens and overlooks Bay Lake directly or obliquely. Avoid rooms on the fourth, fifth, and sixth floors numbered 67–99; these overlook the main lobby and pick up every whoop, holler, and shout from the boisterous Whispering Canyon Cafe downstairs. The noise makes it difficult to get to sleep before Whispering Canyon closes, usually at 10 p.m.

The better rooms are on floors four, five, and six, toward the V's open end. On the very end of the northernmost V, rooms **4000–4003, 5000–5003,** and **6000–6003** offer a direct frontal view of Bay Lake through some tall trees. Toward the end of the V on the parallel wings but facing inward, odd-numbered rooms **4005–4023, 5005–5023,** and **6005–6023** face the courtyard but have excellent oblique lake views. Even-numbered rooms **5004–5034** and **6004–6034** face the Cascade Cabins, woodlands northwest of the lodge, and, beyond the woodlands, the Magic Kingdom.

Odd-numbered rooms **5035–5041** and **6035–6041,** on the lake end of the parallel middle wings, offer a direct but distant view of the lake, with pools and gardens in the foreground.

Standard-view rooms **X042–X066** are some of the cheapest in the main building, with views of parking lots, service areas, and such, and the Cascade Cabins in the foreground. Avoid these on the fourth floor. On the fifth and sixth floors, however, these rooms afford views of the Magic Kingdom fireworks and are more expensive. (Seventh-floor rooms are Club Level—that is, expensive.)

The rooms listed previously afford the most desirable views, but if you can't score one, you're pretty much assured of a woodland view or a room fronting the faux rocks and creek in the V's inner court-yard. Club Level rooms on the seventh floor aren't recommended: Only those facing the Magic Kingdom have nice views, and even those have a service area in the foreground. Almost all rooms at Wilderness Lodge have balconies.

COPPER CREEK VILLAS & CASCADE CABINS

Unofficial Guide Reader-Survey Results

Percentage of readers who'd stay here again	97% *(Average)*
Percentage of readers who'd recommend this resort to a friend	90% *(Average)*
Overall reader rating	B

SOME ROOMS IN THE LODGE'S MAIN BUILDING are DVC units—Disney calls these Copper Creek Villas. Options include studios and one-, two-, and three-bedroom villas. The studios have kitchenettes, while most one- and two-bedroom villas have full kitchens (the one-bedroom we stayed in had a galley kitchen). All rooms have vinyl "hardwood" floors, modern furniture including a table and chairs, a coffee maker, and a microwave. Bathrooms are spacious, although sink space is limited; storage is plentiful otherwise.

Copper Creek rooms have less theming than those in the rest of the lodge—with another color of paint and different knickknacks, they could be rooms at Saratoga Springs or Animal Kingdom Lodge. Nonetheless, readers give these rooms an A for quality. In fact, they're so well appointed and comfortable that they highlight the need for refurbishments at the older Boulder Ridge Villas.

We've also stayed at the lakeside Cascade Cabins. Their floor plan (see page 110) is similar to that of the Bora Bora Bungalows at Polynesian Village. Room quality and views are excellent—and they'd better be at these prices: more than $4,400 per night in peak season.

We prefer the cabins over the bungalows, as does this Iowa City, Iowa, reader:

> *Loved the cabin at Copper Creek—better value than the Polynesian bungalows. Quiet and well arranged, but close to everything.*

GOOD (AND NOT-SO-GOOD) ROOMS AT COPPER CREEK VILLAS These rooms are in the main building's southeast wing. Avoid rooms **X100–X106,** which overlook the lobby. Odd-numbered rooms **X107–X133** face the interior courtyard and pool. Studios **X119** have a nice view of the lake in the distance. Even-numbered rooms **X108–X134** face the Boulder Ridge Villas, a garden area, and woods. Rooms on the sixth floor are high enough for you to see the lake past Boulder Ridge and the Cascade Cabins in the foreground.

GOOD (AND NOT-SO-GOOD) ROOMS AT CASCADE CABINS Guests in cabins **8001–8006** get to watch boats glide to the Magic Kingdom, while cabins **8023–8026** offer excellent fireworks views.

BOULDER RIDGE VILLAS

Unofficial Guide Reader-Survey Results

Percentage of readers who'd stay here again	89% *(Average)*
Percentage of readers who'd recommend this resort to a friend	90% *(Average)*
Overall reader rating	B

ALSO PART OF THE DVC TIME-SHARE PROGRAM, the 136 Boulder Ridge Villas are studio and one- and two-bedroom units in a freestanding building to the right of the lodge. Studios have kitchenettes; one- and two-bedroom villas have full kitchens. The rustic decor features pine furniture, textured rugs, curtains, and woodland creatures from Disney's *Bambi* decorating the pillows and bedding. Boulder Ridge has its own pool but shares restaurants and other amenities with the main lodge.

The villas' studios have fold-down sleeper sofas. All villas have armoires and flat-panel TVs, and one- and two-bedroom units have stainless-steel kitchen appliances.

We think more updates are needed. This reader from Buffalo, New York, agrees:

> *Absolutely hated the room at Boulder Ridge—any Hampton Inn I've ever stayed at for half the price had better rooms. The furniture was mismatched and outdated, the rugs were worn, and the pullout sofa bed was worse than the one we owned in the 1970s! Most upsetting, there were no grab bars in the showers, which are a hotel-industry safety standard. Perhaps because the bathroom was so small, Disney figured we could just hold on to the walls?*

A Plymouth, Massachusetts, family found a way to make the room more comfortable:

> *The sofa bed was improved greatly after we requested an additional mattress for it. We couldn't use the sofa, but the extra mattress made for a much better night's sleep.*

GOOD (AND NOT-SO-GOOD) ROOMS AT BOULDER RIDGE VILLAS Except for a few rooms overlooking the pool, these rooms offer woodland views. The best are odd-numbered rooms **X531–X563** on floors three through five, which open to the lake (northeast) side of the resort (you usually can't see the lake, though). Rooms on the opposite side of the same wing offer similar views, but with some roads and parking lots visible, and with traffic noise.

Disney's Contemporary Resort & Bay Lake Tower

(See map on page 138; see **tinyurl.com/ug-contemporary** for extended coverage.)

STRENGTHS	WEAKNESSES
• Iconic architecture; the only hotel that the monorail goes *through*	• Overpriced, especially so-called Magic Kingdom–view rooms that mostly look out onto parking lots
• Large rooms with views of Bay Lake	
• Bay Lake Tower rooms are the quietest in all of Walt Disney World	• Refurbished rooms are a downgrade, with decor that's lazy and uninspired
• Easy walk to the Magic Kingdom	• $25/night self-parking (except DVC areas)
• Excellent staff/service	• Very small studios in Bay Lake Tower sleep no more than 2 people comfortably
• Convenient parking	
• Best lounge at Walt Disney World (Top of the World, Bay Lake Tower)	• Hallway decor at Bay Lake Tower can feel institutional
• Recreation options on Bay Lake	• Bus transportation to Hollywood Studios, Animal Kingdom, the water parks, and Disney Springs is shared with the other monorail resorts
• Boat service to Fort Wilderness Resort & Campground	

Unofficial Guide **Reader-Survey Results** *(continued on next page)*

Percentage of readers who'd stay here again	86% *(Average)*

Contemporary Resort & Bay Lake Tower

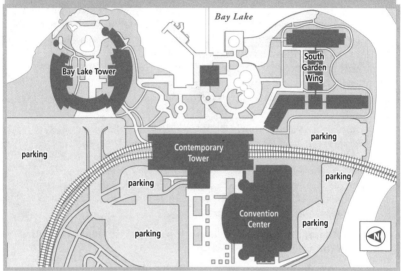

Bay Lake

South Garden Wing

Bay Lake Tower

parking

Contemporary Tower

parking

parking

parking

parking

Convention Center

parking

parking

Unofficial Guide **Reader-Survey Results** *(continued from previous page)*

Percentage of readers who'd recommend this resort to a friend	86% (*Average*)
Overall reader rating	B

NOTE: *This year's Contemporary reader ratings were based on stays before the summer 2021 refurbishment.*

THIS 655-ROOM DELUXE RESORT ON BAY LAKE is unique in that its A-frame design permits the Magic Kingdom monorail to pass through the structure's cavernous atrium. A 90-foot mosaic depicts American Indian children and nature. The off-white central tower is augmented by a three-story Garden Wing fronting Bay Lake to the south and by Bay Lake Tower, a 295-room, 15-story Disney Deluxe Villa development, to the north.

Standard rooms in the A-frame afford fantastic views of Bay Lake or the Magic Kingdom, and all have balconies. At 394 square feet each, they're only slightly smaller than equivalent rooms at the Grand Floridian Resort.

Rooms in the Contemporary's main building were refurbished in the summer of 2021, adding characters from Pixar's *The Incredibles* films. Off-white walls, bedspreads, and flooring are joined by carpets and couches in bold reds and other accent colors. Bathrooms have been remodeled as well, with a continuous countertop featuring two sinks and plenty of storage. The shower–tub combination remains standard, and it's all enclosed by glass sliders. References to *The Incredibles* are found on soft goods and posters and in hidden spots around the room.

Our main criticism of the Contemporary's refurbishment is that it's devoid of style, taste, and imagination. It's no secret that Disney tries to shoehorn characters into every available space around the World, whether they're needed or not. It's also not a secret that Disney cuts corners by standardizing everything, from the same white bedspreads in every room in every resort to common bathroom designs. In some cases, like the new rooms at Disney's Polynesian Village Resort, those two forces can still produce interesting rooms whose design melds with the resort's overall look and feel.

In the case of the Contemporary, Disney had a chance to make this into one of America's great midcentury-themed hotels, and they didn't—even though there are plenty of places they could have drawn inspiration from. Take the TWA Hotel at New York City's JFK International Airport, for instance: Its rooms are miniature masterpieces of midcentury modern design in small spaces. And a 2-hour drive from Disney's headquarters in Burbank puts you in Palm Springs, the spiritual home of the midcentury modern aesthetic, where you can't walk a block without running into fabulous retro architecture and furniture.

What Disney has "designed" for the Contemporary is just lazy— it's the same generic ideas they've been putting into every recent hotel. Compare the look of the Contemporary's restyled rooms with those of the TWA Hotel (twahotel.com) or even the Motel 6 Anaheim Maingate, near Disneyland (tinyurl.com/anaheimmotel6), and ask yourself if the Contemporary is $400–$600 better per night. If you ask us, it's not. What Disney's *really* selling these days at the Contemporary is just walking-distance access to the Magic Kingdom.

Dining options abound at the Contemporary. On the first floor is **Steakhouse 71**, a new restaurant specializing in grilled meats. **Contempo Cafe,** a counter-service restaurant on the fourth floor's Grand Canyon Concourse, serves upscale sandwiches, salads, and flatbread pizzas. **Chef Mickey's,** also on the fourth floor, hosts a popular character buffet at breakfast. On the 15th floor, the award-winning **California Grill** serves contemporary American cuisine.

The pool has slides for kids and cabanas for rent. The resort also has a few shops. The Contemporary is within easy walking distance of the Magic Kingdom; monorail transportation is available to both the Magic Kingdom and EPCOT. Other destinations can be accessed by bus or boat. Walking time to transportation loading areas from the most remote rooms is 6–9 minutes.

GOOD (AND NOT-SO-GOOD) ROOMS AT THE CONTEMPORARY RESORT (*See* tinyurl.com/crroomviews *for photos.*) The Contemporary has two hotel buildings: the A-frame tower and the **Garden Wing**. Rooms in the A-frame overlook either Bay Lake and the marina and swimming complex on one side or the parking lot, with Seven Seas Lagoon and the Magic Kingdom in the background on the other. Except for most second- and third-floor rooms in the Garden Wing, each room has a balcony with two chairs and a table. If you stay on the Magic Kingdom side of the A-frame, ask for a room on the ninth floor or higher. The parking lot and connecting roads are less distracting there (see tinyurl.com/cr-room4848 as an example). On the Bay Lake side, the view is fine from all floors, though higher floors are preferable.

In the Garden Wing, all ground-floor rooms have patios. Only end rooms on the second and third floors facing Bay Lake have full balconies; all other rooms have balconies only a foot deep. Also, keep in mind that the Garden Wing is a fair walk from the restaurants, shops, front desk, guest services, and monorail station in the A-frame.

There's a lot of boat traffic in the lake and canal alongside the Garden Wing. Nearest the lake, and quietest, are rooms **6116–6123, 6216–6223,** and **6316–6323.** At the water's edge, but noisier, are rooms **6107–6115, 6207–6215,** and **6307–6315.** Flanking the canal connecting Bay Lake and Seven Seas Lagoon are rooms **5128–5151, 5228–5251,** and **5328–5351.** All of these have nice canal and lake views, which subject them to some daytime noise from passing watercraft, but the whole area is exceptionally quiet at night.

The Garden Wing also has rooms facing the marina, pool, and playground; these work well for families with kids. The views don't compare with views from the rooms previously listed, but ground-floor rooms **5105–5127** and **6124–6130** provide easy access to the pool.

In addition to offering some of the most scenic and tranquil guest rooms in Disney World, the Garden Wing likewise contains some of the most undesirable ones. Avoid rooms ending with numbers **52–70**— almost all of these look directly onto a parking lot.

BAY LAKE TOWER AT DISNEY'S CONTEMPORARY RESORT
(See **tinyurl.com/ug-blt** *for extended coverage.*)

Unofficial Guide Reader-Survey Results

Percentage of readers who'd stay here again	95% *(Average)*
Percentage of readers who'd recommend this resort to a friend	91% *(Average)*
Overall reader rating	B

OPENED IN 2009, this 15-story, 295-unit DDV resort consists of studios and one- and two-bedroom villas as well as two-story, three-bedroom Grand Villas with views of Bay Lake and the Magic Kingdom. Laid out in a semicircle, Bay Lake Tower is connected to the Contemporary by an elevated, covered outdoor walkway and shares the main resort's monorail service.

Rooms are well appointed, with flat-panel TVs, DVD players, mini-fridges, microwaves, and coffee makers. Brightly colored accessories, paintings, and accent walls complement an otherwise-neutral color scheme. Wood tables and granite countertops add a natural touch. Each room has a private balcony or patio. The rooms we've stayed in tested as the quietest on Disney property.

Studios sleep up to four people and include one queen-size bed and one double sleeper sofa. The part of the studio with the bed, sofa, and TV measures about 170 square feet and feels small with just two people; four would be an adventure.

One-bedroom villas sleep five people (the living room's chair and sofa fold out to sleep three) and provide a formal kitchen, a second bathroom, and a living room in addition to the studio bedroom.

The two-bedroom villas—our pick for the best of the standard rooms—sleep nine and include all of the kitchen amenities found in a one-bedroom, plus an extra bathroom. One of the baths is attached to a second bedroom with two queen beds or a queen plus a sleeper-size sofa. As with the one-bedrooms, a sofa bed and sleeper chair in the living room provide extra places to snooze, though they're best suited for small children. Bathrooms in the two-bedroom villas are a bit more spacious than those in the one-bedrooms. One odd feature in the baths (also found at other DVC resorts) is a folding door separating the tub from the master bedroom.

The two-story Grand Villas sleep 12 and include four bathrooms, the same master-bedroom layout, and two bedrooms with two queen beds apiece. An upstairs seating area overlooking the main floor provides a sleeper sofa and chair. Two-story windows offer unparalleled views of Bay Lake or the Magic Kingdom—with unparalleled prices to match.

Bay Lake Tower has its own check-in desk as well as its own private pool and pool bar, plus a small fire pit on the beach. Its **Top of the World Lounge** (currently closed) is the best bar on Disney property, but, alas, it admits only DVC owners and their guests. If need be, offer to buy an owner a round of drinks in exchange for an invite.

A 1-mile jogging path loops around Bay Lake Tower and the Contemporary's Garden Wing. Dining, transportation, and other recreational activities are shared with the Contemporary Resort.

Besides room quietness, readers give Bay Lake an A rating for room quality and staff service. This Minnesota family of four loved it:

> *We had a studio with a Magic Kingdom view. The balcony was a private oasis where my husband and I would relax and watch the fireworks together after the kids were asleep. On our second night he looked at me and said, "We're always going to stay here."*

GOOD (AND NOT-SO-GOOD) ROOMS AT BAY LAKE TOWER *(See* **tinyurl .com/blt-roomviews** *for photos.)* If you're paying for a Magic Kingdom view, request a room on an upper level—above the seventh floor, at least—if you don't want to look out on the parking lot. Even-numbered rooms **XX06–XX16** have the best viewing angle of the park. Rooms **XX24–XX30** may technically be described as having Magic Kingdom views, but they're oriented toward the Contemporary, and you have to turn the other way to see the park.

Shades of Green

(See map on page 142; see **tinyurl.com/ug-shades** *for extended coverage.)*

STRENGTHS	WEAKNESSES
• Large guest rooms	• No theming to speak of
• Discount tickets for military personnel with ID	• Room decor is nondescript
• Quiet setting	• Limited on-site dining
• Views of golf course from guest rooms	• Limited bus service
• Convenient self-parking	• Daily parking fee ($24)
• Swimming complex, fitness center	• No free parking at theme parks
• On-site car rental (Alamo; currently unavailable)	

Unofficial Guide **Reader-Survey Results**

Percentage of readers who'd stay here again	99%	*(Above Average)*
Percentage of readers who'd recommend this resort to a friend	92%	*(Average)*
Overall reader rating	B	

ORIGINALLY OWNED BY DISNEY, Shades of Green was called The Golf Resort when it opened in 1973 and renamed The Disney Inn in 1986. In 1994 Disney reached an agreement with the U.S. Army Family and

Shades of Green

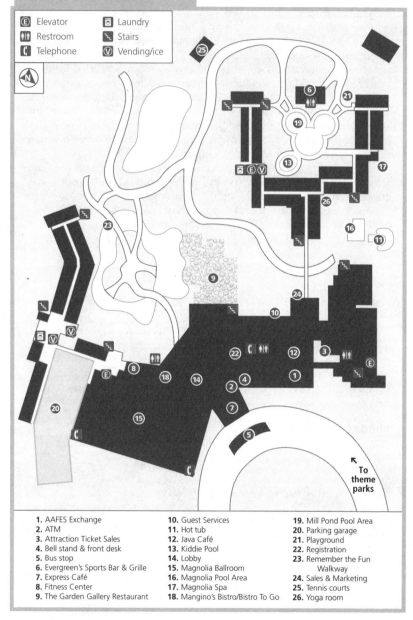

Ⓔ Elevator	ⒶLaundry	
🚻 Restroom	⬆ Stairs	
📞 Telephone	Ⓥ Vending/ice	

1. AAFES Exchange
2. ATM
3. Attraction Ticket Sales
4. Bell stand & front desk
5. Bus stop
6. Evergreen's Sports Bar & Grille
7. Express Café
8. Fitness Center
9. The Garden Gallery Restaurant
10. Guest Services
11. Hot tub
12. Java Café
13. Kiddie Pool
14. Lobby
15. Magnolia Ballroom
16. Magnolia Pool Area
17. Magnolia Spa
18. Mangino's Bistro/Bistro To Go
19. Mill Pond Pool Area
20. Parking garage
21. Playground
22. Registration
23. Remember the Fun Walkway
24. Sales & Marketing
25. Tennis courts
26. Yoga room

Morale, Welfare, and Recreation Command (Army MWR) to lease the property as an official Armed Forces Recreation Center. In 1996 the Army MWR purchased the property outright; Disney, however, still owns the land on which the resort is located.

Shades of Green is open to active and retired US servicemembers (including reservists) and their families, among other qualifying groups. Civilians may accompany eligible military personnel as their guests. (For details, see shadesofgreen.org/about-shades-green/eligibility.) If you're planning a holiday visit or a long weekend here, we recommend booking as early as possible—up to seven months in advance. Guests at Shades of Green are eligible for Disney's Early Theme Park Entry and Extended Evening Hours.

COVID *tip*

At the time of this writing, Shades of Green guests must wear masks in indoor public spaces and on the resort's shuttle buses.

Shades of Green consists of one three-story and one five-story building nestled among three golf courses that are open to Disney guests. At 455 square feet each, the 586 guest rooms at Shades of Green are larger than those at the Grand Floridian.

On its Frequently Asked Questions page, the website states that "Shades of Green would be comparable to the Disney Deluxe Resorts." While the rooms are certainly large, nicely appointed, and immaculately maintained, not to mention a great value for those who qualify to stay here, they're indistinguishable from the rooms at any number of decent midpriced hotels. There's no discernible theming or "wow" factor. The dining options are fine but not amazing. Service, on the other hand, is superb—definitely up to the Deluxe standard.

Standard rooms have two queen-size beds, a single sleeper sofa, a minifridge, a table and two chairs, and a TV. Junior suites sleep six with three queen beds, one in the living area. Family suites sleep eight with three queen sleeper sofas and a king bed; these suites also have two bathrooms. All rooms have a patio or balcony.

A military mom from Loganville, Georgia, wishes we loved Shades of Green as much as she does:

> We loved our stay at Shades of Green. I know it's only for military personnel, but I feel like you could say a little more about it. The rooms are huge. The pools are fantastic. Kids 4 and younger eat for less than $4, and the buffet is better than a typical chain—when I can feed my family of five for about $60, that's pretty awesome. They have fun themed nights all week and occasional kids' activities too.

Another mom, this one from Plainfield, Indiana, makes the case for exploring all of your lodging options:

> While it's true that SOG is often a good deal, military families should still do some comparison shopping. Room rates are tiered based on rank—the higher your rank, the higher the rate. Definitely check into military rates at Disney properties, and also check out the **Armed Forces Vacation Club** for condos near WDW [see afvclub.com for participating Orlando-area properties]. We rented a two-bedroom, two-bath condo with a full kitchen and pool for seven nights, and it cost us less than two nights at a Disney hotel.

Shades of Green has two pools. The **Mill Pond Pool** features a tiered waterslide, while the **Magnolia Pool** has a zero-entry feature as well as a splash-and-play area and hot tubs.

Restaurants include **Mangino's,** an Italian eatery; the **Garden Gallery** buffet (closed at press time); three quick-service options (**Bistro to Go,**

Express Café, and **Java Café**); and **Evergreen's,** a sports bar and grill. The **Army & Air Force Exchange Service,** comparable to a convenience store or hotel gift shop, sells Disney merchandise in addition to snacks, soft drinks, alcohol, tobacco, and over-the-counter medicines.

Transportation to all theme parks is by bus; a transfer is required to almost all destinations. Walking time to the bus-loading area from the most remote rooms is about 5 minutes. Readers including this Lancaster, Ohio, woman report that bus service is a sore spot:

> Please, please, please stress to your readers how awful the transportation system is—there is no direct access to the Magic Kingdom or EPCOT, and the buses that go directly to the other parks run only once an hour. If you want to go back to your room midday, plan for an hour to an hour and a half of travel time there and then back to the park.

A Bloomington, Indiana, family advises that it's faster to just use Disney transportation:

> You can walk to the Polynesian Village to ride the monorail, bypassing the TTC to get to the Magic Kingdom.

(During our summer 2021 visit, we saw signs at Shades of Green that guided guests to the Magic Kingdom walkways via the Polynesian Village and Grand Floridian.)

You don't have to worry much about bad room views or locations at Shades of Green: Except for a small percentage that overlook the entrance road and parking lot, most offer views of the golf courses that surround the hotel or views of the swimming area. Note, however, that a few rooms are located a good ways from the elevators. When you reserve, make your preference known.

THE EPCOT RESORTS

THE EPCOT RESORTS ARE POSITIONED around Crescent Lake between EPCOT and Disney's Hollywood Studios (but closer to EPCOT). Both theme parks are accessible by boat and on foot. No EPCOT resort offers transportation to EPCOT's main entrance, and it's between 0.7 and 1.1 miles to walk, depending on the hotel and route. As a Greenville, South Carolina, mom reports, this can be a problem:

> The only transportation to EPCOT is by boat or foot. There's no bus to take you to the front gates. We had to walk through the International Gateway and all the way to the front of EPCOT to ride Future World attractions. And if we finished EPCOT at the end of the day near the front entrance, the only way back home was a long hike through Future World and the International Gateway.

A reader from Emporia, Kansas, overcame this obstacle:

> We had no transportation to the front gate of EPCOT for arrival before opening. So we decided to do early entry at Magic Kingdom (7 a.m.), take in one popular attraction, and then catch the monorail [temporarily suspended] to EPCOT. Worked like a charm. We were at EPCOT by 8:20 a.m.

The **Skyliner** (see page 438) connects EPCOT's International Gateway with Disney's Hollywood Studios. If you're staying at the Beach Club, taking the Skyliner may be faster than walking.

Disney's Yacht & Beach Club Resorts and Beach Club Villas

(See map on page 146; see tinyurl.com/ug-yacht *and* tinyurl.com/ug-beach *for extended coverage.)*

STRENGTHS	WEAKNESSES
• Best pool complex of any WDW resort	• $25/night self-parking (except DVC areas)
• Excellent staff/service	• Views and balcony size are hit-or-miss
• Walking distance to EPCOT's International Gateway	• Bus service to Magic Kingdom, Animal Kingdom, water parks, and Disney Springs is shared with other EPCOT resorts
• Close to many BoardWalk and EPCOT dining options	• No three-bedroom Grand Villas at the Beach Club Villas
• Well-themed public spaces	• Beach Club Villas have fewer baths per bedroom than newer DVC/ DDV properties
• Bright and attractive guest rooms	
• Boat and Skyliner transportation to DHS	

Unofficial Guide **Reader-Survey Results**

Percentage of readers who'd stay here again YC: 93%; BC: 93% (*both Average*)
Percentage of readers who'd recommend this resort to a friend YC: 91%; BC: 90% (*both Average*)
Overall reader rating YC: B; BC: B

THESE ADJOINING DELUXE RESORTS are similarly themed. Both have clapboard facades with whitewashed-wood trim. The Yacht Club is painted a subdued gray, the Beach Club a brighter blue. The Yacht Club has a nautical theme with model ships and antique navigational instruments in public areas. The Beach Club is embellished with beach scenes in foam-green and white. Both have themed lobbies, with a giant globe in the Yacht Club's and sea horse fixtures in the Beach Club's. The resorts face the 25-acre Crescent Lake and share an elaborate swimming complex.

There are 635 rooms and 21 suites at the Yacht Club and 576 rooms at the Beach Club, plus 282 studio and one- and two-bedroom DVC units at the Beach Club Villas. Most rooms are 381 square feet and have two queen-size beds, a sofa, a desk and chair, a dresser, a wall-mounted TV, a minifridge, and a coffee maker (Yacht Club's is Keurig). The Yacht Club's rooms are decorated in white with blue and brass accents, while the Beach Club's are decked out in summery tans and blues. The most recent Yacht Club refurbishment also replaced carpeting with vinyl "hardwood" floors, freshening the rooms' look; Beach Club's redo kept the carpeted floors. Some rooms have full balconies; many rooms have mini balconies.

The Beach Club Villas evoke seaside Victorian cottages. Studio accommodations have kitchenettes; one- and two-bedroom villas have full kitchens. Like the Yacht Club (but unlike the Beach Club), the Villas got faux-hardwood laminate flooring in its most recent redo, as well as updated bathrooms. Other decor is like the Beach Club's.

As is the case with all DVC/DDV properties, the villas are available to the general public depending on availability. They share restaurants, pools, and other amenities with the main Yacht & Beach Club.

A Portsmouth, Rhode Island, reader with a big family likes the Villas' refresh:

> *The Beach Club Villas update was well done. Very nice-looking rooms, stylish baths, and plenty of accessible outlets, including 16 USB ports in a two-bedroom villa.*

Yacht & Beach Club Resorts and Beach Club Villas

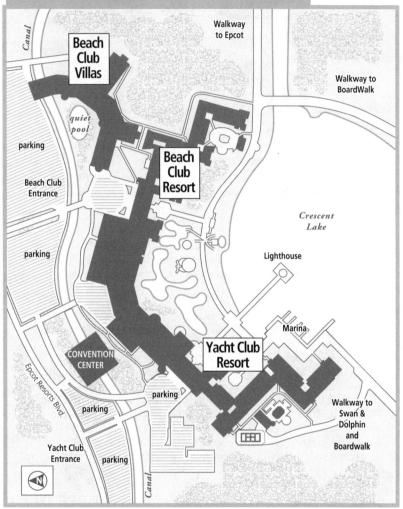

A reader from Altadena, California, likewise appreciates the Yacht Club's upgrades:

> *The refurbished rooms at Yacht Club are lovely. The laminate floors are not noisy at all—if we had neighbors above us, we never heard them. Soundproofing on the balcony is good.*

As Disney Deluxe resorts, both the Yacht Club and the Beach Club provide excellent service. Nine restaurants and lounges are within walking distance of EPCOT and the BoardWalk. Our previous complaint about a lack of good quick-service dining at Beach Club was partially addressed by expanding the existing grab-and-go area that was carved out of a retail space.

Transportation from these resorts to other destinations is by bus, boat, or Skyliner. Walking time to the transportation loading areas from the most remote rooms is 7 minutes.

Although the Yacht & Beach Club Resorts are situated along Crescent Lake, opposite Disney's BoardWalk, only a relatively small percentage of rooms actually overlook the lake dead-on—many additional rooms have lake views from the side but actually face a courtyard or garden. To complicate matters, the resorts don't differentiate between a room with a lake view and one overlooking a swimming pool, pond, or canal. There's only one category for anything wet: lagoon or pool view. To see specific views from these rooms for yourself, go to tinyurl .com/yacht-roomviews or tinyurl.com/beach-roomviews.

The Beach Club consists of a long main building with several wings protruding toward Crescent Lake; viewed from the lake, the Beach Club adjoins the Yacht Club on the left and spreads toward EPCOT on the right. The main building and the various wings range from three to five stories. Most rooms have full or mini balconies or, on the ground floor, patios. Full balconies are big enough for a couple of chairs, while mini balconies are about 6 inches deep (stand at the rail or sit in a chair inside the room). Top-floor rooms often have enclosed balconies set into the roof. Unless you're standing, visibility is somewhat limited from these dormer balconies. Our **Hotel Room Views** describe each room's balcony type.

We receive a lot of mail about the Yacht & Beach Club. First, from a Wayland, Massachusetts, mom of two:

This was the first time we stayed at the Beach Club, and for us the amazing pool complex was worth the extra money. Several nights we climbed to the top of the waterslide as the sun was setting, and it was an incredible sight—truly a memorable experience!

This family (no hometown given) got a chilly reception, however:

Families with kids should not stay at the Beach Club during the winter. Based on an experience at the Polynesian Village in December, we anticipated that Stormalong Bay would be warm enough to swim in—it was not. This was a terrible disappointment to our kids. The resort's location is divine (I loved walking to France for breakfast), but the pool situation made me bitter about the cost of this place.

A reader from Danbury, Connecticut, advises that "standard" rooms at the Beach Club are anything but:

The term standard rooms *at Beach Club means many things. Some standard rooms have one queen bed and one daybed, or two queen beds and a writing desk, two queen beds and a daybed, and so on. There are also variations in the sizes of the balconies: Some rooms have a full balcony with two chairs; others have a reduced-size balcony with two chairs squeezed in or a tiny, one-person balcony with just enough room to step outside.*

GOOD (AND NOT-SO-GOOD) ROOMS AT THE BEACH CLUB RESORT *(See* tinyurl.com/beach-roomviews *for photos.)* The Beach Club's better views are from rooms that have full balconies, and from those that overlook the lake. Other good rooms include those facing woods, with

EPCOT in the background. The woods-facing rooms are the resort's most peaceful accommodations, both in terms of lack of noise and attractive scenery. These rooms are also the nearest to EPCOT's International Gateway entrance if you're walking, but the farthest from the resort's main pool area, lobby, and restaurants.

Of the remaining rooms, most face courtyards, with some of these providing oblique views of the lake and others overlooking parking lots and the resort's front entrance.

The following are our recommendations for good rooms at the Beach Club Resort. All room numbers are four digits, with the first digit specifying the floor and the remaining three digits specifying the room number.

Heads-up: The Beach Club will charge you for a water view if there's so much as a birdbath in sight. If you're going to spend the money, get a *real* water view.

WATER-VIEW ROOMS WITH FULL BALCONIES FACING THE LAKE   Odd-numbered rooms **2641–2645**; suite **2647**; **3501–3507**; **3699–3725**; **4607–4623**; or Club Level rooms **5699–5725**

STANDARD-VIEW ROOMS WITH FULL BALCONIES FACING THE WOODS AND EPCOT   Even-numbered rooms **2512–2530, 2578–2596, 3512–3530,** or **4532–4596**

GOOD (AND NOT-SO-GOOD) ROOMS AT THE YACHT CLUB RESORT *(See* tinyurl.com/yacht-roomviews *for photos.)* When you look at the Yacht Club from Crescent Lake, the resort is connected to the Beach Club on the right and angles toward the Dolphin hotel on the left. All Yacht Club rooms offer full balconies or, on the ground floor, patios. Rooms with the best views are as follows (the higher the last three digits in the room number, the closer to lobby, main pool area, and restaurants):

ROOMS WITH FULL BALCONIES FACING THE LAKE, WITH THE BOARDWALK INN IN THE BACKGROUND   Odd-numbered rooms **2001–2009, 2043–2065, 2123–2137, 2157–2163; 3001–3009, 3043–3065, 3123–3137, 3157–3163; 4057–4065, 4123–4137, 4157–4163;** or Club Level rooms **5161, 5163,** or **5241**

FIFTH-FLOOR ROOMS DIRECTLY FACING EPCOT   Rooms **5195–5199** or **5153**

STANDARD-VIEW FOURTH-FLOOR ROOMS FACING EPCOT   Rooms **4195–4199** or **4153**

Some other rooms face the BoardWalk or EPCOT across Crescent Lake, but they're inferior to the rooms just listed.

Avoid standard-view rooms at either resort *except* for rooms **3512–3536** and **4578–4598** at the Beach Club; these overlook a dense pine thicket. In addition to offering a nice vista for a standard-view rate, these are the closest rooms to EPCOT available at any resort on Crescent Lake.

Finally, Yacht Club room **1102** is unusual in that it has a wet bar in the main living area, along with the other recent room refurbishments. Its bathroom is slightly smaller than the typical Yacht Club room's, but the main living area is also furnished with a sofa bed, so perhaps that's where the space went. This may be a test remodel or DVC room—in any case, if you stay here, let us know how you like it.

BEACH CLUB VILLAS

Unofficial Guide **Reader-Survey Results** *(continued on next page)*

Percentage of readers who'd stay here again	95% *(Average)*

Percentage of readers who'd recommend this resort to a friend	89% (*Average*)
Overall reader rating	B

THIS DISNEY DELUXE VILLA PROPERTY is purportedly inspired by grand Atlantic seaside homes of the early 20th century. In point of fact, there's little to differentiate the Beach Club Villas from the Yacht & Beach Club Resorts, or from the parts of the BoardWalk Inn & Villas that don't front the BoardWalk.

Configured roughly in the shape of a fat Y or slingshot, the Beach Club Villas are set back away from the lake adjoining the front of the Beach Club Resort. Arrayed in connected four- and five-story taffy-blue sections topped with cupolas, the villas are festooned with white woodwork and slat-railed balconies. The effect is clean, breezy, and evocative . . . though of what exactly we're not sure.

Accommodations include studios, which have a kitchenette, a queen bed, a single pull-down bed, and a sleeper sofa, and one- and two-bedroom villas with full kitchens. The rooms are a bit small but attractively decorated in neutral shades accented by seashore-themed art.

A Springfield, Illinois, reader found her studio villa somewhat lacking in terms of space and amenities:

(1) There's very little space to unpack and store clothes. Drawer space is minimal, which left me living out of my suitcase. (2) No full-length mirror, which is inconvenient not to have when you have one at home. (3) The pullout vanity mirror is not height-adjustable.

Regarding her last point, we've also seen the vanity mirrors mounted at different heights in different bathrooms.

We don't like the Beach Club Villas as much as the Copper Creek Villas, which are newer and better appointed, or the villas of Old Key West Resort, which are roomier, more luxurious, and more private. The Beach Club Villas have their own modest swimming pool but otherwise share the restaurants, facilities, and transportation options of the adjoining Yacht & Beach Club Resorts. The villas' strengths and weaknesses include all of those listed for the Yacht & Beach Club Resorts. Additional strengths include laundry and kitchen facilities in the one- and two-bedroom units, and self-parking directly adjacent to the building. The villas' one additional weakness is that they offer no lake views.

GOOD (AND NOT-SO-GOOD) ROOMS AT THE BEACH CLUB VILLAS *(See* tinyurl.com/bcv-roomviews *for photos.)* Although the studios and villas are attractive and livable, the location of the Beach Club Villas— between parking lots, roads, and canals—leaves much to be desired. Rooms facing the pool offer a limited view of a small canal but are subject to traffic noise. Ditto for the rooms on the northeast side, but they don't face the pool. Only southeast-facing rooms provide both a scenic landscape (woods) and relative relief from traffic noise. The nearby road is two lanes only, and traffic noise probably won't bother you if you're indoors with the balcony door closed, but for the bucks you shell out to stay at the villas, you can easily find nicer, quieter accommodations elsewhere on Disney property. If you elect to stay at the Beach Club Villas, go for odd-numbered rooms **225–251, 325–351, 425–451,** and **525–551.**

Disney's BoardWalk Inn & Villas

(See **tinyurl.com/ug-bwinn** *for extended coverage.)*

STRENGTHS	
• Walking distance to EPCOT's International Gateway and Disney's Hollywood Studios	• $25/night self-parking (except DVC areas)
• Excellent staff/service	• Limited quick-service dining options suitable for kids
• Unique garden suites	• Not as many rooms overlook the BoardWalk as you might think
• Vast selection of dining options for adults	
• Fitness center is larger than Yacht & Beach Club's	• Bus service to Magic Kingdom, Animal Kingdom, water parks, and Disney Springs is shared with other EPCOT resorts
• Carnival pool is whimsical	
WEAKNESSES	• BoardWalk Villas have fewer baths per bedroom than newer DVC/DDV properties
• Long, confusing hallways	
• Some may find room theming overly fussy	

***Unofficial Guide* Reader-Survey Results**

Percentage of readers who'd stay here again	93% *(Average)*
Percentage of readers who'd recommend this resort to a friend	91% *(Average)*
Overall reader rating	B

ON CRESCENT LAKE across from the Yacht & Beach Club, the Board-Walk Inn is another of Disney's Deluxe resorts. The complex is a detailed replica of an early-20th-century East Coast beach boardwalk. Facades of hotels, diners, and shops create an inviting and exciting waterfront skyline. Think HBO's *Boardwalk Empire* minus the icky criminal element.

In reality, the BoardWalk Inn & Villas comprise a single integrated structure behind the facades. Restaurants and shops occupy the boardwalk level, while accommodations rise to six stories above. The inn and villas share a pool featuring an old-fashioned amusement park theme; there are also two quiet pools for adults.

The BoardWalk Inn's 378 Deluxe rooms measure 371 square feet each. Most contain two queen-size beds with hardwood headboards, an upholstered daybed, a cherry desk and chair, a minifridge, a coffee maker, and ceiling fan. Decor includes yellow-and-white-striped wallpaper, green carpet, and blue-and-gray curtains. Closet space exceeds that of rooms in other Deluxe resorts. Most rooms have balconies.

Readers give the inn high marks for room quality and check-in efficiency. Service is excellent. The complex is within walking distance of EPCOT and is connected to other destinations by bus and boat. Walking time to transportation loading areas from the most remote rooms is 5–6 minutes. It's about a 5-minute walk to the Skyliner's International Gateway station at EPCOT, if you'd rather use that to get to the Studios.

This Iowa City, Iowa, family stayed at the BoardWalk:

> We were surprised that so relatively few rooms at the BoardWalk Inn have interesting views. The one couple in our group who actually had a view of the boardwalk said it was noisy.

As is the case with several other Disney resorts, readers report that the BoardWalk's bus service is inefficient. This comment is typical:

> The bus to Animal Kingdom and Magic Kingdom was the worst. We almost missed a dinner reservation for which we'd left 1½ hours early.

BoardWalk Inn & Villas

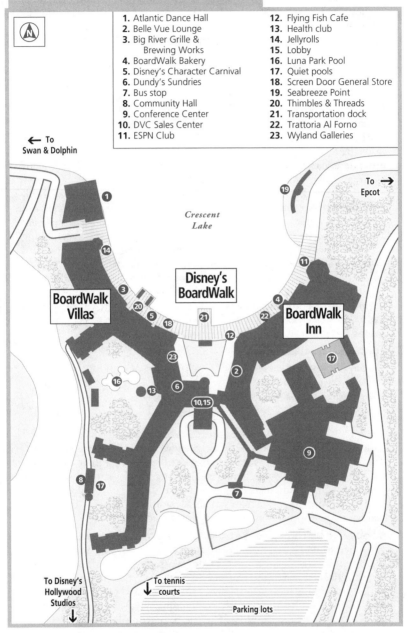

1. Atlantic Dance Hall
2. Belle Vue Lounge
3. Big River Grille & Brewing Works
4. BoardWalk Bakery
5. Disney's Character Carnival
6. Dundy's Sundries
7. Bus stop
8. Community Hall
9. Conference Center
10. DVC Sales Center
11. ESPN Club
12. Flying Fish Cafe
13. Health club
14. Jellyrolls
15. Lobby
16. Luna Park Pool
17. Quiet pools
18. Screen Door General Store
19. Seabreeze Point
20. Thimbles & Threads
21. Transportation dock
22. Trattoria Al Forno
23. Wyland Galleries

← To Swan & Dolphin

To → Epcot

Crescent Lake

Disney's BoardWalk

BoardWalk Villas

BoardWalk Inn

To Disney's Hollywood Studios ↓

↓ To tennis courts

Parking lots

GOOD (AND NOT-SO-GOOD) ROOMS AT THE BOARDWALK INN *(See* tinyurl.com/bwi-roomviews *for photos.)* The complex consists of several wings that radiate from the lobby complex, in a rough H shape. Crescent Lake and the pedestrian BoardWalk itself are to the north, the entrance is to the south, and the canal that runs to Disney's Hollywood Studios is to the west. If you book a BoardWalk room through Disney's agents or website, *water view* means Crescent Lake and the BoardWalk area only; views of the canal or pool are considered standard view. But if you book a villa through a DVC member or the DVC website, the same canal and pool are called garden or pool view, and the view of the BoardWalk is cleverly called a BoardWalk view.

Most rooms have a balcony or patio, although balconies on the standard upper-floor rooms alternate between large and medium. The BoardWalk Inn & Villas each share about half the frontage on the promenade, which overlooks Crescent Lake. The promenade's clubs, stores, and attractions are spread about equally between the two sections, leading to similar levels of noise and commotion. However, the inn side is closer to EPCOT and the nearby access road; this means easier access to that theme park, but also more road noise.

Otherwise, the inn is actually less noisy than the more expensive villas; there's one tranquil, enclosed courtyard, and another half-enclosed area with a quiet pool (where BoardWalk's Garden Suites are). There are many rooms to avoid at the inn, starting with rooms overlooking access roads and parking lots, and rooms looking down on the roof of the adjacent conference center. And although the aforementioned quiet rooms face courtyards, the views are pretty ho-hum. When you get right down to it, the only rooms with decent views are those fronting the promenade and lake, specifically odd-numbered rooms **3213–3259** and **4213–4259.** We're told by Disney insiders that most of these rooms are reserved more than 10 months ahead.

BOARDWALK VILLAS

Unofficial Guide Reader-Survey Results

Percentage of readers who'd stay here again	97% (*Average*)
Percentage of readers who'd recommend this resort to a friend	88% (*Average*)
Overall reader rating	B

THE 532 BOARDWALK VILLAS are decorated in pastels—lots of green and pink, with neutral carpets—and bright tiles in the kitchens and baths. Villas measure 412–2,491 square feet (studio through three-bedroom) and sleep 4–12. Many villas have full kitchens, laundry rooms, and whirlpool tubs; most rooms have balconies. The studio and two-bedroom units tend to be more expensive than similar accommodations at Old Key West and Saratoga Springs—you're paying for the address.

GOOD (AND NOT-SO-GOOD) ROOMS AT THE BOARDWALK VILLAS Most villas overlook a canal to the west, with the Swan resort and its access road and parking lots on the far side. Worse are the rooms that front BoardWalk's entrance and car lots. As at the inn, the villas offer only a handful of rooms with good views. Odd-numbered rooms **3001–3047, 4001–4047,** and **5001–5047** afford dynamic views of the promenade and Crescent Lake, with EPCOT in the background. Rooms **X05, X07, X13, X15, X29,** and **X31** are studios. They're a little noisy if you open your balcony door but otherwise offer a glimpse of one of Walt Disney World's more happening places.

Promenade-facing villa rooms have noise issues identical to those of their inn counterparts. The midsection of the canal-facing villas looks out onto the **Luna Park Pool,** which gets extremely noisy during the day. Some quieter villas located away from the promenade have views of the canal and a partially enclosed quiet pool. Rooms on the opposite side of this wing are almost as quiet; their downside is that they face the BoardWalk's parking lot.

The Walt Disney World Swan, Swan Reserve & Dolphin

(See map on page 154; see **tinyurl.com/ug-swan** *and* **tinyurl.com/ug-dolphin** *for extended coverage.)*

STRENGTHS	WEAKNESSES
• Best-priced location on Crescent Lake	• Conventioneers may be off-putting to vacationing families
• The hotels participate in the Marriott Loyalty program	• Daily resort ($35/night, plus tax) and parking fees ($35/night)
• Good on-site and nearby dining	• No Disney Dining Plan
• Only hotels within walking distance to minigolf (Fantasia Gardens)	• Non-Disney bus service runs less often than that of other resorts
• Large variety of upscale restaurants	• Architecture that was on the cutting edge decades ago now looks dated and cheesy (Swan, Dolphin)
• On-site car rental (Alamo, National)	
• Very nice pool complex	• Self-parking is quite distant from the hotels' entrances
• Impressive public spaces	• Tiny bathrooms (Swan)
• Walking distance to both EPCOT International Gateway and DHS	• Spotty front-desk service and housekeeping (Swan)

Unofficial Guide Reader-Survey Results

Percentage of readers who'd stay here again Swan: 92% (*Above Average*); Dolphin: 91% (*Average*)
Percentage of readers who'd recommend this resort to a friend Swan: 85% (*Average*); Dolphin: 82% (*Average*)
Overall reader rating C+ (*Swan and Dolphin*)

QUICK TAKE: *A respectable percentage of readers said they would stay at the Dolphin again; all things considered, however, it rates below average among Disney resorts (see pages 248–251). If you're spending your own money versus using Marriott points, we recommend almost any other Deluxe, Moderate, or DVC resort over the Dolphin. The Swan Reserve, across the street from the Swan, should open in fall 2021.*

OPENED IN 1990, THE SWAN AND DOLPHIN face each other on either side of an inlet of Crescent Lake. The Swan Reserve is located across the street from the Swan and Dolphin. Although they're inside Walt Disney World and Disney handles their reservations, they're managed by Sheraton (Dolphin) and Westin (Swan), and the Swan Reserve is part of the Autograph Collection. As such, they can be booked directly through Marriott as well as through Disney.

All three resorts are served by Disney transportation to the theme parks and participate in Early Theme Park Entry and Extended Evening Hours, but they don't participate in the Disney Dining Plan.

The Dolphin's main building is a 27-story turquoise triangle. This central A-frame, with large wings extending from both sides and four smaller arms from its rear, is attached to a large conference center. Perched on the roof, at the edge of each main wing, are two 56-foot-tall dolphins balanced vertically, with their tails in the air.

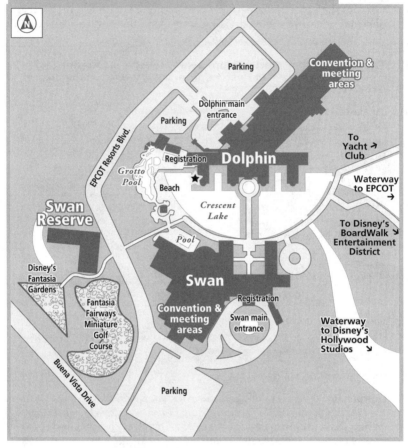

Swan, Swan Reserve & Dolphin

Parking

Convention & meeting areas

Dolphin main entrance

Parking

Registration

Dolphin

Grotto Pool

Beach

Crescent Lake

To Yacht Club

Waterway to EPCOT

To Disney's BoardWalk Entertainment District

Swan Reserve

Pool

Disney's Fantasia Gardens

Fantasia Fairways Miniature Golf Course

Swan

Convention & meeting areas

Registration

Swan main entrance

Waterway to Disney's Hollywood Studios

Buena Vista Drive

EPCOT Resorts Blvd.

Parking

Whereas the Dolphin is pointy, the Swan is rounded: Its gently arching main building rises 12 stories and is flanked by two 7-story towers, with two 47-foot-tall swans adorning its roof.

The last renovation of the hotels' guest rooms and lobby areas was completed in 2018. Key upgrades included new bedding and carpets, more electrical outlets, new AC units, and new TVs. In addition to updated decor, the Dolphin lobby has a larger bar area, **Phins,** and a grab-and-go restaurant, **Fuel.**

The Dolphin's rooms incorporate light wood, gray carpeting, and taupe draperies. Oversize upholstered headboards buttress Westin's plush Heavenly Beds, and minimal art adorns the walls. A dresser and desk with desk chair round out the furnishings. All rooms have coffee makers, and some have balconies. The baths in most rooms have step-in showers.

The Swan's standard rooms are similar to but are, in our opinion, more attractive than the Dolphin's. Heavenly Beds make for ultracomfy sleeping. The reading light is great in or out of bed. A flat-panel TV sits on the dresser. The bathrooms, small for Disney, have step-in showers and limited counter space.

Because these hotels aren't run by Disney, service is less relentlessly cheerful than elsewhere on-property. Readers rate the Dolphin's check-in service as below average.

Be warned: Both resorts will nickel-and-dime you to death. Each tacks on a $35-per-day resort fee (plus tax) and another $35 per day for self-parking. Whatever rate you're quoted at either resort, count on another $75 per day in miscellaneous costs.

The two hotels collectively house more than a dozen restaurants and lounges and are within easy walking distance of EPCOT and the BoardWalk. They're also connected to other destinations by bus and boat. Walking time from the most remote rooms to the transportation loading areas is 7–9 minutes. These readers from Houston say the Swan is the slightly easier of the two to navigate:

> While the Dolphin is closer to EPCOT, we prefer the Swan because it's easier and more straightforward to walk from the hotel to the park and vice versa. The Dolphin has a very narrow, winding sidewalk that doesn't look like it gets much traffic.

This Nashua, New Hampshire, couple gives the shared pool complex high marks:

> Neither the Disney nor the Swan and Dolphin website depicts how great the pool complex is. Not only are there multiple pools, a waterslide, and maybe the best poolside bar in all of Disney World, there's also a wonderfully green, restful grotto-in-tropical-forest theme.

SWAN RESERVE This 14-story hotel, scheduled to open in early fall 2021, is adjacent to Disney's Fantasia Gardens minigolf course. The resort will have 349 guest rooms and suites, some with views of either EPCOT or Hollywood Studios. Standard rooms sleep four and are around 330 square feet, 16 square feet larger than a Disney Moderate.

As a smaller resort, the Swan Reserve will have one full-service restaurant (featuring Mediterranean cuisine), a pool, and a fitness center. Bus service is provided to Disney's theme parks, water parks, and Disney Springs, and the Swan and Dolphin are a short walk across the street.

GOOD (AND NOT-SO-GOOD) ROOMS AT THE SWAN AND DOLPHIN *Note:* The Swan and Dolphin are configured very differently, and because of their irregular shapes, it's easier to discuss groups of rooms in relation to exterior landmarks and compass directions rather than by room numbers. When speaking with a Disney (or Sheraton/Westin) reservationist, use the following tips and descriptions.

THE SWAN East-facing rooms offer prime views, particularly in the upper half of the seven-story wing above Il Mulino New York restaurant. From this vantage point, you overlook a canal and Disney's Board-Walk, with EPCOT in the distance. Balcony rooms on floors five, six, and seven cost an additional $50 and up per night, versus the least-expensive rooms.

On the downside, rooms in the wing nearest the main section have the southern portion of their views obscured by the building's easternmost portion, which juts east beyond the seven-story wing.

There are some east-facing rooms on that portion of the main section, sans balconies. Lofty palm trees obscure the views from east-facing rooms below the fourth floor. The best rooms with views of EPCOT are **626** and **726**.

North-facing rooms afford views of the Dolphin and (generally) of the courtyard, except for north-facing rooms on the easternmost portion of the main section, which look across Crescent Terrace to the BoardWalk; these afford angled views of EPCOT and are buffered by palms on the lowest three floors.

The few north-facing rooms at the end of the Swan's two eight-story wings directly overlook Crescent Lake, with the bulk of north-facing rooms situated in the main section and overlooking the courtyard, which has greenery, fountains, and an indoor café in its center. Courtyard-facing rooms are subject to noise from below, though never much.

Above the eighth floor, north-facing rooms in the main section overlook roofs of the shorter wings. In these rooms, height enhances the vista from your window, but only near the center of the hotel is the view not seriously marred by rooftops below.

North-facing main-section rooms have more-direct views of the Dolphin across the lake than courtyard-facing rooms in either eight-story wing. Guests in most wing rooms, however, can see the lake at an angle.

Most courtyard-facing rooms have balconies; 224 rooms are so equipped, and these balconies offer panoramic 180-degree views. Of course, from most rooms at the Swan, part of any 180-degree view will include another section of the hotel.

The Swan's worst views are from the **west-facing rooms** above the fourth floor, which overlook the unsightly roof of the hotel's western wing. The northernmost rooms in the wing directly above Kimonos restaurant are an exception—their balconies overlook the pool and the beach on Crescent Lake's western shore. Rooms **680–691** offer nice pool views.

Above the Swan's main entrance, **south-facing rooms** overlook the parking lot, with forest and the Hollywood Studios in the distance. However, the canal is also visible to the east. These rooms lack balconies.

THE DOLPHIN If you want a room with easy access to shopping, dining, and transportation to and from the parks, almost any Dolphin room will do. The shuttle (outside the main entrance) and the boat dock are equidistant from the main front and rear exits. Restaurants and shopping are primarily on the first and third floors.

If, however, you also want a view of something besides parking-lot asphalt, your choices narrow considerably. Rooms in the Dolphin with pleasant views are in **the four arms on the rear of the building.** Rooms on all arms sport balconies from the first through fourth floors, then offer alternating balconies or windows on floors five through nine.

One of the Dolphin's best views overlooks the **Grotto Pool,** on the far west side of the building. An artificial beach with a small waterfall is visible from rooms at the very end of the large west wing. None of these rooms has a balcony. A better bet would be to ask for a room on the far west side of the first rear arm. These outer rooms have balconies and are more removed from the pool. Rooms on the inner, west part of that arm overlook a bladderwort-encrusted reflecting pool.

Between the second and third arms looms the monstrous **Dolphin fountain;** the better room choices here are located on the top two floors. Here, from arm two, you can see the BoardWalk (including nighttime fireworks at EPCOT), and from arm three you can see the Grotto Pool. Otherwise, you may "enjoy" a view of massive green-concrete fish scales.

Arms three and four are situated around a **reflecting pool.** A concern for rooms in this area is that the ferry toots its horn every time it approaches and departs the dock. Its path runs right by these rooms, and the horn blows just as it passes.

The **Crescent Lake** side of arm four, and the small jut of the large Dolphin wing perpendicular to it, offer arguably the best views. You have an unobstructed view of the lake and EPCOT fireworks; a fine BoardWalk view for people-watching; and, from higher floors, a view of the beach at Beach Club. There's ferry noise, but these rooms still have the most going for them. The best of the best in this arm are rooms **8015, 7015, 5015, 4015,** and **3015.**

Disney's Caribbean Beach Resort

(See map on page 158; see **tinyurl.com/ug-caribbean** *for extended coverage.)*

STRENGTHS	WEAKNESSES
• Colorful Caribbean theme	• Check-in is far from rest of resort
• Rooms with *Pirates of the Caribbean* and *Finding Nemo* themes	• $20/night self-parking (except DVC areas)
	• Dining gets low marks from readers
• Lakefront setting	• Multiple bus stops make it slow to go anywhere
• Large food court	
• Child-size Murphy beds in select rooms increase capacity to 5 people	• Some "villages" are a good distance from restaurants and shops
	• No elevators

Unofficial Guide Reader-Survey Results

Percentage of readers who'd stay here again	87% *(Below Average)*
Percentage of readers who'd recommend this resort to a friend	83% *(Below Average)*
Overall reader rating	B

CARIBBEAN BEACH WAS DISNEY'S first Moderate resort when it opened in 1998. It consists of two dozen colorful, two-story motel-style buildings, separated into five areas named for Caribbean islands: **Aruba, Barbados, Jamaica, Martinique,** and **Trinidad.**

Most of the 1,536 guest rooms measure 314 square feet and are outfitted with two queen beds; a fold-down Murphy bed is also available in select rooms. Except as noted below, decor is distinguished by neutral beach tones, bright tropical accent colors, and furnishings of dark wood and rattan. Sliding doors separate the grooming area from the main room. Together with the bathroom, this allows three people to get ready at once. All rooms have a dresser, small table with chairs, minifridge, coffee maker, TV, and plenty of storage. Rooms don't have balconies, but the access passageways are external and have railings.

Rooms in Trinidad have a *Pirates of the Caribbean* theme and cost about $70–$100+ more than comparable ones elsewhere in the resort. Soft goods and headboards in some non-*Pirates*-themed rooms have a subtle *Finding Nemo* theme.

Caribbean Beach Resort & Riviera Resort

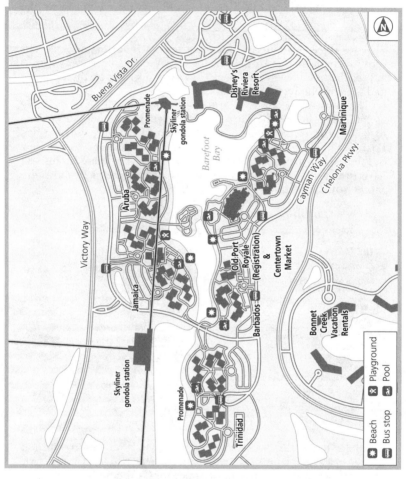

The refurbished **Old Port Royale** building houses the check-in desk, restaurants, and shops. A food court has counter-service and grab-and-go options; **Sebastian's Bistro** is a sit-down restaurant with waterfront tables.

Caribbean Beach's on-site dining remains a weakness with readers. This Bismarck, North Dakota, reader, for example, thinks the counter-service dining logistics need work:

> Not a fan of the queue area in the food court—who thought that was a good idea? Two checkout lanes for a resort that big? The grab-and-go area is way too small.

South and east of EPCOT and Hollywood Studios, Caribbean Beach offers transportation to all Disney World destinations by bus and to EPCOT and the Studios by **Skyliner**. Caribbean Beach has access to two Skyliner stations: one south of Jamaica and one north of Aruba at the Riviera Resort; bus service runs between the Skyliner stations and the resort villages.

Walking time to the transportation-loading area from Caribbean Beach's most remote rooms is 7–9 minutes, and readers rate Disney bus service here as below average. Seriously consider bringing a car—this 20-something couple from Kansas City, Missouri, wished they had:

> Caribbean Beach's bus service is horrendous. It often felt like there was only one bus running at a time, and we experienced several 30-plus-minute waits. The bus circled the entire resort—which is huge—before it headed out, so if you were unlucky enough to be at one of the last stops during a rush to the parks, the bus would pass right by if it was full. On multiple occasions, we arrived at the bus stop an hour or more before our dining reservations, but we still found ourselves running past the park gates to make it to the restaurant on time!

A mom from Fenton, Michigan, likewise found bus service lacking:

> We recommend renting a car and/or paying for a preferred room location, especially during the hotter months. The buses just take way too long with all the stops, and it was a long hike to the food court and pools in the heat.

GOOD (AND NOT-SO-GOOD) ROOMS AT CARIBBEAN BEACH RESORT *(See* tinyurl.com/cbrroomviews *for photos.)* The five "islands," or groups of buildings clustered around Barefoot Bay, are identical. The two-story motel-style structures comprising each island are arranged in various ways to face courtyards, pools, the bay, and so forth. Except for the theme, the setup is very similar to the one at Coronado Springs Resort (page 178). The verdant landscaping features lots of ferns and palm trees, especially in the courtyards.

In general, corner rooms are preferable because they have more windows. Standard-view rooms face either parking lots or courtyards, and the usual broad interpretation of water views is in play here. Beyond that, your main choices will revolve around your preference for proximity to (or distance from) Old Port Royale's check-in desk and restaurants, pools, parking lots, pirates, or beaches on Barefoot Bay. Each island has direct access to at least one beach, playground, bus stop, and parking lot.

Martinique, next to the main pool and playground at Old Port Royale, is also closest to the Riviera, whose dining options are vastly superior to those at Caribbean Beach.

Aruba and **Jamaica** are similar to Martinique, but guests must cross a footbridge from here to Old Port Royale. Aruba buildings 54, 55, and 56, along with Jamaica building 41, are closest to the two Skyliner stations.

With just three buildings, **Barbados** gets noise from surrounding roads and from rambunctious kids at Old Port Royale next door.

The quietest island, and the farthest from resort facilities, is **Trinidad.** It has its own playground, and its beach looks across Barefoot Bay onto wild, undeveloped Florida forest—a rarity on Disney property.

When it comes to the view from your room, avoid standard views: All look onto a parking lot, road, or tiny garden. Water views overlook swimming pools or Barefoot Bay; pool views are less than enchanting, not to mention the pools are noisy.

What you want are **bay views.** Rooms that fill the bill in Martinique, Barbados, and Trinidad catch the afternoon sun; bay-view rooms in Aruba and Jamaica catch the morning sun. Because we like the sun at our back in the evening, we always go for rooms **4246–4252** in **Jamaica** or **5256–5260** and **5541–5548** (but not 5542 or 5545) in **Aruba.** If you don't mind the sun in your eyes during cocktail time, rooms **2254–2256, 2413–2416,** and **2445–2448** in Martinique are good bets, as are lake-facing rooms **3533–3534, 3853–3858,** and **3949** in Trinidad. We're not crazy about any room in **Barbados.**

Disney's Riviera Resort

See map on page 158; see **tinyurl.com/ug-drr** *for extended coverage.)*

STRENGTHS	
• Stylish, well-appointed rooms	• Easy walk to Caribbean Beach and its pretty views
• Skyliner to EPCOT and Hollywood Studios	**WEAKNESSES**
• On-site dining and bar	• Expensive
• Child play area near main pool	• Tower studios are small and dark

Unofficial Guide **Reader-Survey Results**

Percentage of readers who'd stay here again	92% *(Average)*
Percentage of readers who'd recommend this resort to a friend	90% *(Average)*
Overall reader rating	B+

THE RIVIERA IS THE NEWEST DVC resort at Walt Disney World. Themed to evoke glamorous beach resorts in the South of France, it has 300 guest rooms, including studios and one-, two-, and three-bedroom villas, spread over nine floors. Though it's on land that used to belong to Caribbean Beach, a Moderate resort, Disney has positioned the Riviera to be as upscale as the Grand Floridian—with service, amenities, and prices to match.

Rooms at the Riviera are some of our favorite at Disney World, with white walls and off-white accents, beige carpets, and furniture in neutral tones. Faux-wood vinyl laminate covers the floors, except in the bedrooms, which have carpet. As with other DVC resorts, deluxe studio accommodations have kitchenettes, while the one-, two-, and three-bedroom villas have full kitchens. We like the villas quite a bit—they're bright, comfortable, and modern, even if the theme is understated.

The Riviera has a unique room type among DVC resorts that we like considerably less: the **tower studio,** which accommodates two guests. These rooms measure about 225 square feet—the smallest on Disney property, and small enough that they require the room's single bed to fold into the wall when not in use. Disney may have found a lower limit on how small it can make hotel rooms, and these are *too* small. In fact, when Len visited two friends staying in one of these rooms, one of them stood in the bathroom to maintain what felt like normal social distance—there's just not a lot of space here.

Beyond the size, the tower studio rooms are dim during the day and dismal at night. The most cheerful space in the studio is the bathroom because of the better lighting. There's little doubt that these are the worst rooms for the money in Walt Disney World.

In addition to otherwise-posh rooms and amenities and high-end restaurants, the Riviera boasts easy access to EPCOT and Disney's Hollywood Studios. The resort sits about 1,500 feet from World Showcase, affording park-facing rooms on high floors excellent views of both EPCOT's and the Studios' evening entertainment. The Riviera's restaurants have similar views.

Of course, Disney charges a premium for these views: Rack rates run $429–$738 per night for tower studios; $642–$1,025 for deluxe studios, depending on the date and the view; $911–$1,415 for one-bedroom villas; $1,443–$2,541 for two-bedroom units; and $2,892–$4,677 for three-bedroom villas.

The Riviera's restaurants include **Primo Piatto,** an excellent counter-service eatery with grab-and-go options; **Le Petit Café,** a morning-coffee-and-pastry bar that serves wine in the evening; and **Bar Riva,** a pool bar. **Topolino's Terrace,** the sit-down restaurant, is a Disney Signature venue that serves fixed-price character breakfasts for kids and upscale dinners for grown-ups.

Other amenities include two pools and a fitness center. The main **Riviera Pool** offers play areas for children, while the **Beau Soleil Pool** is the quiet pool. The Riviera Resort is connected to EPCOT and Disney's Hollywood Studios by **Skyliner** and to the rest of Walt Disney World by bus.

THE BONNET CREEK RESORTS

Not to be confused with the Disney resorts that follow, the **Bonnet Creek Resort** *is a 70-acre hotel, golf, and convention complex located along Bonnet Creek. Although it's adjacent to and accessible from Walt Disney World, the resort is not owned by Disney. Two of its four hotels are reviewed in "Hotels Outside Walt Disney World" (pages 238 and 239).*

Disney's Saratoga Springs Resort & Spa
Treehouse Villas at Disney's Saratoga Springs Resort & Spa

(See maps on pages 162 and 165; see tinyurl.com/ug-ssr *for extended coverage.)*

SARATOGA SPRINGS RESORT & SPA

STRENGTHS	WEAKNESSES
• Often available at discounted rates or as a DVC/DDV rental	• On-site dining is limited for a resort of this size
• Attractive main pool; multiple well-themed quiet pools with snack bars	• Theme is dull compared with those of other Disney resorts
• Closest resort to Disney Springs	• Fewer baths per bedroom than newer DVC/DDV properties
• Convenient parking	
• Only WDW-owned resort with dedicated golf (Lake Buena Vista Golf Course)	• Bus service can take some time to get out of the (huge) resort
• Grocery options in gift shop	
• Very nice spa and fitness center	

Unofficial Guide **Reader-Survey Results** *(continued on next page)*

Percentage of readers who who'd stay here again	92% *(Average)*

Saratoga Springs Resort & Spa

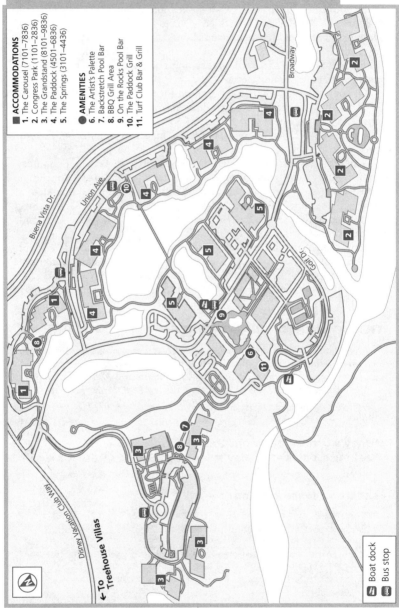

ACCOMMODATIONS
1. The Carousel (7101–7836)
2. Congress Park (1101–2836)
3. The Grandstand (8101–9836)
4. The Paddock (4501–6836)
5. The Springs (3101–4436)

AMENITIES
6. The Artist's Palette
7. Backstretch Pool Bar
8. BBQ Grill Area
9. On the Rocks Pool Bar
10. The Paddock Grill
11. Turf Club Bar & Grill

Boat dock
Bus stop

Unofficial Guide **Reader-Survey Results** *(continued from previous page)*

Percentage of readers who'd recommend this resort to a friend	84% *(Below Average)*
Overall reader rating	B

QUICK TAKE: *In 2021 Saratoga Springs completed a massive two-year renovation project, which likely boosted its reader-survey results this* *year. Treehouse Villas, meanwhile, is the lowest-rated Disney Deluxe Villa resort, both in terms of readers who would stay here again or recommend it to a friend. The key issue seems to be bus transportation, which is extremely inconvenient to use due to the resort's remoteness.*

SARATOGA SPRINGS HAS A THEME described by Disney as recalling a Victorian-era retreat in upstate New York. A DDV resort, its 1,260 studio and one-, two-, and three-bedroom villas are located across the lake from Disney Springs. Most buildings were constructed around 2004, while the fitness center and check-in building are older. An adjacent 60-unit DDV complex, **Treehouse Villas at Disney's Saratoga Springs Resort & Spa,** opened in 2009.

The color scheme of the villas' newly renovated rooms tends toward neutral earth tones, with faux-teak vinyl floors in the living rooms and dark-brown patterned carpets in the bedrooms. Kitchen cabinets are white, while appliances are stainless steel. New furnishings and soft goods are more refined than the last iteration. Chairs, sofas, and tables are likewise more modern and less bulky, though you'd be hard-pressed to identify even the slightest bit of theming; this decor could be at any one of a dozen Disney hotels. A fold-down child's bed sits beneath the wall-mounted TV in the living room. Bathrooms, with color accent walls, are spacious in all but the studios, where they compare with those in any other hotel room.

Saratoga Springs guests can use Disney transportation, their cars, or an on-property walking path to get to Disney Springs.

Readers tend to be more critical of Saratoga Springs than other Disney resorts. The positive comments frequently mention the quiet rooms, proximity to Disney Springs, and quality of the spa and fitness center. Those were enough for this reader:

> *We loved Saratoga Springs! It was comfortable, beautiful, and quiet, with a quick walk to the dock for the boat to Disney Springs.*

This reader from Mount Holly, New Jersey, agrees:

> *We were absolutely floored at how much we loved our stay at Saratoga Springs. Our first couple of days were in Congress Park, which was perfectly lovely. Then we moved (because we had two reservations) to a Paddock building immediately next to the pool, the bus stop, and the walkway to the main building. We truly enjoyed the time we spent there.*

The fitness center is by far the best at Walt Disney World. **Senses Spa** (currently closed), like its counterpart at the Grand Floridian, echoes the spas of the same name on Disney Cruise Line's ships. Service is very good, plus this Senses location is easier to get to than the one at the Grand Floridian if you're staying east of the World.

Surrounded on three sides by a golf course, Saratoga Springs is the only Disney-owned resort that affords direct access to the links (the military-only **Shades of Green** also provides golf on-property).

The top reader complaints about Saratoga Springs have to do with transportation. These comments from an Arlington Heights, Illinois, family are typical:

> *Buses started running just 45 minutes before park opening. We had to make multiple stops inside the resort, and because of Saratoga's*

size and distance to the parks, we arrived at the park only about 15 minutes before opening. We faced instant 60-plus-minute waits for the top attractions despite our best efforts.

A couple from Peru, Indiana, had a variety of complaints:

Saratoga Springs is our least favorite resort. We didn't enjoy the theming, and unless you have a car, getting around by bus is a real hassle. The food court is very small and the food expensive. Also, checkout was very slow, and our room seemed smaller than comparable rooms at BoardWalk Villas and Old Key West.

GOOD (AND NOT-SO-GOOD) ROOMS AT SARATOGA SPRINGS RESORT & SPA *(See* tinyurl.com/ug-saratogasprings *for photos.)* This resort's sprawling size puts some of its best rooms very far away from the main lobby, restaurants, and shops. If you don't have a car, the best rooms are those in **The Springs,** numbered **3101–3436** and **3501–3836.** Ask for a room toward the northeast side of these buildings (away from the lobby), as the southwest rooms border a well-traveled road. Avoid rooms **4101–4436**—a pedestrian walkway running behind the patios gets a lot of use in the early morning from guests who are heading to breakfast.

If you have a car or don't mind a longer walk to the lobby, rooms **1101–1436** and **2501–2836** in **Congress Park** offer quietness, a view of Disney Springs, and a relatively short walk to the bus stop. Also good are rooms **4501–4826, 6101–6436,** and **6501–6836** in **The Paddock.** Also in The Paddock, avoid rooms on the northeast side of its **5101–5435** building, as well those as the northwest side of its **5501–5836** building—these border a swimming pool and bus stop.

In addition to being quiet, rooms **1101–1436** of **Congress Park** and rooms **6101–6436** and **6501–6836** of **The Paddock** afford the closest walks to Disney Springs.

TREEHOUSE VILLAS

STRENGTHS	WEAKNESSES
• Spacious stand-alone three-bedroom villas	• Long distance from Saratoga Springs services such as check-in and dining
• Quiet location	
• Historical connection to the Treehouses from the 1970s	• Kids may find all that quiet boring
	• Lackluster pool
• Innovative round design feels more spacious than other villas with the same square footage	• Limited number of units makes the Treehouses among the most difficult accommodations to book at WDW
	• Only two baths per villa
	• Bus travelers connect through Saratoga Springs

Unofficial Guide **Reader-Survey Results**

Percentage of readers who who'd stay here again	60% *(Below Average)*
Percentage of readers who'd recommend this resort to a friend	82% *(Below Average)*
Overall reader rating	B–

THIS COMPLEX OF 60 three-bedroom villas lies between Old Key West Resort and the Grandstand section of Saratoga Springs proper, with a separate entrance off Disney Vacation Club Way. The treehouses are bordered by Lake Buena Vista Golf Course to the northeast and a waterway to the southwest that feeds into Village Lake.

Treehouse Villas at Saratoga Springs Resort & Spa

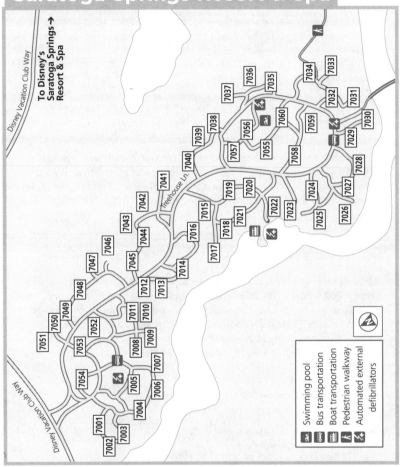

Disney Vacation Club Way

To Disney's
Saratoga Springs
Resort & Spa →

Treehouse Ln.

Disney Vacation Club Way

Swimming pool
Bus transportation
Boat transportation
Pedestrian walkway
Automated external
defibrillators

   The villas stand on stilts 10 feet off the ground, with ramps providing wheelchair access. Surrounded by a densely wooded landscape, each villa is an eight-sided structure with three bedrooms and two full bathrooms covering about 1,074 square feet.

   Villas hold nine people, about the same number as comparably sized rooms at other DDV resorts. The master and second bedrooms have queen beds; the third bedroom has bunks; and the living room has a sofa bed and sleeper chair, both more appropriate for kids than adults.

   The interior of each villa is decorated with natural materials: stone floors in the kitchen, granite countertops, and stained-wood furniture. End tables, picture frames, and bunk beds are made from rustic logs. Bathrooms, outfitted in modern tile, have showers and tubs, along with a decent amount of counter space. Showers can be cramped, as noted on the following page.

The three-bedroom Treehouses usually cost about $50–$300 more per night than a comparable two-bedroom villa and $700–$800 *less* than a standard three-bedroom villa elsewhere at Saratoga Springs. The trade-off for that third Treehouse bedroom is giving up some space elsewhere. In particular, beware the master-bath shower, next to the tub in an enclosed glass wall: Tilt down to shave your legs or grab a bottle of shampoo, and you could bang your head on the side of the tub.

A Columbus, New Jersey, family thinks a stay at Treehouse Villas is money well spent:

We give Treehouse Villas five stars for value. With nine people in our party, our villa saved us about $700–$1,000 per night. The three bedrooms and pullout couch comfortably slept our group, plus having a great eat-in kitchen helped us save money on breakfast.

A walking path connects the complex to the rest of Saratoga Springs; Treehouse guests can use all of the main resort's facilities. Two dedicated bus stops serve the Treehouses, but transportation is nevertheless a weakness. This West Warwick, Rhode Island, reader felt stranded:

Transportation is abhorrent—and I actually had some idea what to expect (i.e., taking one bus at the villas to another bus at the main resort). The Treehouses are nice in and of themselves, but I would suggest not staying here if going to the parks is your main objective.

GOOD (AND NOT-SO-GOOD) ROOMS AT TREEHOUSE VILLAS Treehouses **7024–7034** and **7058–7060** are closest to one of the villas' two dedicated bus stops and the walkway to Saratoga Springs; **7026–7033** also have water views. Treehouses **7001–7011** and **7045–7054** are closest to the other bus stop; **7020–7023** are closest to the boat docks. Finally, Treehouses **7035–7037, 7055, 7056,** and **7060** surround the pool.

Disney's Old Key West Resort

*(See **tinyurl.com/ug-okwest** for extended coverage.)*

STRENGTHS	
• Largest villas of the DVC/DDV resorts	• Gift shop with grocery selection
• Often available at discounted rates or as a DVC rental	• Convenient parking
• Mature landscaping	**WEAKNESSES**
• Homey, well-themed lounge (The Gurgling Suitcase)	• Multiple bus stops
	• No elevators in many buildings
• Close to Lake Buena Vista Golf Course	• Highway noise
• Boat service to Disney Springs	• Fewer baths per bedroom than newer DVC/DDV properties
	• Mediocre on-site dining

Unofficial Guide **Reader-Survey Results**

Percentage of readers who'd stay here again	92% (*Average*)
Percentage of readers who'd recommend this resort to a friend	90% (*Average*)
Overall reader rating	B

OLD KEY WEST WAS THE FIRST Disney Vacation Club property. It's a favorite among readers and *Unofficial Guide* staff for its room quality and quiet surroundings. An Erie, Pennsylvania, reader thinks it's Walt Disney World's best-kept secret:

Old Key West Resort

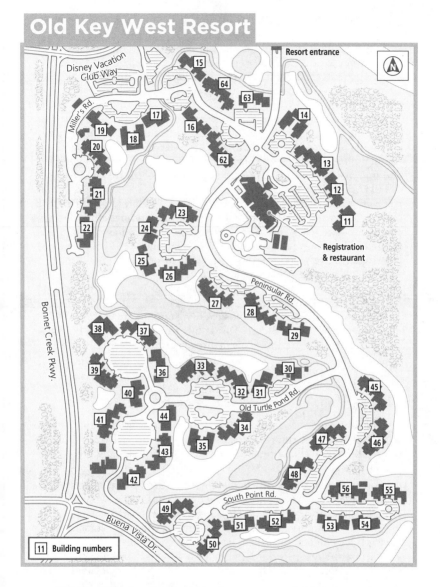

Old Key West has the most spacious rooms and the easiest access to your car—right outside your door! There are a number of small, almost private pools, so you don't have to go to the main pool to swim.

The resort is a large aggregation of two- to three-story buildings modeled after Caribbean-style residences and guesthouses of the Florida Keys. Set subdivision-style around a golf course and along Bonnet Creek, the buildings are arranged in small, neighborhood-like clusters. They feature pastel facades, white trim, and shuttered windows. **Conch Flats Community Hall** houses the check-in area along with a full-service restaurant, fitness center, marina, and sundries shop. Each cluster of accommodations has a quiet pool; Conch Flats is home to the main pool, featuring a waterslide in the shape of a giant sandcastle.

Old Key West boasts some of the roomiest accommodations at Walt Disney World, with all rooms having been refurbished in 2018. Studios are 376 square feet; one-bedroom villas, 942; and two-bedroom villas, 1,333. Studios contain two queen-size beds, a table and two chairs, and an extra vanity outside the bathroom. One-bedroom villas have a king-size bed in the master bedroom, a queen-size sleeper sofa in the living room, a laundry room, and a full kitchen with coffee maker. Two-bedroom villas feature a king-size bed in the master bedroom, a queen-size sleeper sofa and fold-out chair in the living room, and two queen beds in the second bedroom. Closets are large enough to hold your entire wardrobe.

Studios and villas are tastefully decorated. The latest refurbishment toned down the Key West beach theme while adding subtle Disney characters—we like it. Kitchen cabinets and TVs, along with the living room and bedroom furniture, were also upgraded. One-bedroom and larger villas have wood flooring instead of carpet.

Each villa has a private balcony that opens to views of the golf course, the landscape, or a waterway. The waterway views are among the best in Walt Disney World.

Transportation and lack of on-site dining options are Old Key West's main weaknesses with readers. This family from Basingstoke, England, also found that the groundskeepers often get started early in summer:

We enjoyed our stay at Old Key West, but we would not return as we found it a bit noisy. Crews were leaf-blowing at 6:40 one morning, and the rooms are not soundproofed well at all. We also found the quick-service breakfast offerings very limited.

Old Key West is connected by boat to Disney Springs (and by bus when the boat isn't running). Transportation to other Disney destinations is by bus. Walking time to the transportation loading areas from the most remote rooms is about 6 minutes.

GOOD (AND NOT-SO-GOOD) ROOMS AT OLD KEY WEST RESORT *(See* tinyurl.com/oldkeywest-roomviews *for photos.)* Old Key West is huge, with 49 three-story villa buildings spread over about 100 acres. Views are nice from almost all villas; all multiroom villas and some studios have a large balcony furnished with a table and chairs.

Because the resort is bordered by busy Bonnet Creek Parkway and even busier Buena Vista Drive, the best villas are those located as far from the road noise as possible. For quiet isolation and a lovely river view, ask for **building 46** or **45,** in that order. For nice lake and golf-course views away from roads and close to restaurants, recreation, the marina, the main swimming complex, and shopping, ask for **building 13.** Nearby, **buildings 12** and **11** are likewise quiet and convenient; they offer primarily golf-course views. The next-best choices are **buildings 32** and **34;** the former looks onto a lake, with the golf course in the background, while the latter faces the golf course, with tennis courts to the left and a lake to the right. Avoid **buildings 19–22, 38, 39, 41, 42,** and **49–54,** which border Bonnet Creek Parkway and Buena Vista Drive and get their attendant noise.

Finally, if you want to use your balcony without the sun in your face, use the map on page 167 to check out the position of your building relative to sunrise and sunset. If you want to use your balcony in the afternoon, ask for an east-facing building. Conversely, request a west-facing building if you primarily want to use your balcony in the morning. We like to enjoy a drink on the balcony in the afternoon or evening, so we ensure shade by asking for an east-facing villa.

Disney's Port Orleans Resort: French Quarter and Riverside

(See maps on pages 170 and 172; See **tinyurl.com/ug-por** *and* **tinyurl.com/ug-pofq** *for extended coverage.)*

A MODERATE RESORT, Port Orleans is divided into two sections. The smaller, southern part is called the **French Quarter;** the larger section is labeled **Riverside.** French Quarter is this year's top Moderate, both overall and in terms of readers who said they'd stay there again, and it tied with another Moderate, the Fort Wilderness Cabins, regarding whether readers would recommend it to a friend.

PORT ORLEANS RESORT–FRENCH QUARTER

STRENGTHS	
• Excellent staff/service	• Short walk to Port Orleans Riverside's restaurants and bars
• Most compact of the WDW Moderate resorts	• Good place to walk or run for fitness
• One bus stop	**WEAKNESSES**
• Live entertainment in Scat Cat's Club	• Ho-hum pool
• Beignets in food court!	• Shares bus service with Port Orleans Riverside during slower times of year
• Attractively themed lobby	• No full-service dining

Unofficial Guide **Reader-Survey Results**

Percentage of readers who'd stay here again	96% *(Average)*
Percentage of readers who'd recommend this resort to a friend	91% *(Average)*
Overall reader rating B *(Highest-rated Disney Moderate resort)*	

CONSISTING OF SEVEN THREE-STORY guest-room buildings next to the Sassagoula River, the 1,008-room French Quarter section is a sanitized Disney version of New Orleans's Vieux Carré. The prim pink-and-blue guest buildings are festooned with wrought iron filigree, shuttered windows, and old-fashioned iron lampposts.

The centrally located **Mint** contains the registration area and food court. The registration desk features a vibrant Mardi Gras mural and old-fashioned bank-teller windows. **Doubloon Lagoon** surrounds a colorful fiberglass creation depicting Neptune riding a sea serpent.

Rooms at Port Orleans French Quarter measure 314 square feet. Most are outfitted with two queen beds, a table and two chairs, a dresser–credenza, a minifridge, a coffee maker, and a vanity outside the bathroom. With their hardwood floors, cherry headboards, purple accent fabrics, and cherrywood credenzas, the rooms are themed but tasteful. A privacy curtain separates the dressing area from the rest of the room, allowing three people to get ready at once. No rooms have balconies, but iron-railed accessways on each floor provide a good (though less private) substitute.

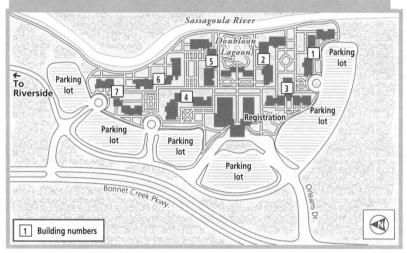

Port Orleans Resort–French Quarter

Sassagoula River

Doubloon Lagoon

Parking lot

To Riverside

Parking lot

Parking lot

Parking lot

Parking lot

Parking lot

Registration

Bonnet Creek Pkwy.

Orleans Dr.

1 | Building numbers

Most readers really like Port Orleans French Quarter. Some, such as this Raleigh, North Carolina, family, rate it even higher than many Deluxe resorts:

We stayed at the Polynesian Village in 2017, but we loved French Quarter! The updated rooms were great and the resort was so easy to navigate.

Note that there's no full-service restaurant—just a food court that can get overwhelmed, as this Waxahachie, Texas, reader discovered:

The French Quarter food court was a disaster on the night we checked in. We waited 18 minutes for our order.

The closest full-service eatery is in the adjacent Riverside section, a 15-plus-minute walk away. The commute to restaurants in other hotels may be 40–60 minutes each way.

Disney buses link the French Quarter to all Disney World destinations. Walking time to bus-loading areas from the most remote French Quarter rooms is 5 minutes or less.

GOOD (AND NOT-SO-GOOD) ROOMS AT PORT ORLEANS RESORT– FRENCH QUARTER *(See* tinyurl.com/pofq-roomviews *for photos.)* Seven guest-room buildings flank the pool, Guest Relations building, and bus stop. The best views are from rooms facing the river and pine forest on the opposite bank. Wings of **buildings 1, 2, 5, 6,** and **7** flank the river and provide the best river views in all of Port Orleans. River-view rooms in **buildings 1, 6,** and **7** are a long walk from French Quarter public facilities, but they're the most tranquil. Families with children should request river-view rooms in **buildings 2** and **5,** nearest the swimming complex. Make sure the reservationist understands that you're requesting a room with a river view, not just a water view. All river-view rooms are also water-view rooms but not vice versa. Note that standard-view rooms look onto a courtyard or a parking lot.

The following are the best river-view rooms in each building:

BUILDING 1 Rooms **1127-1132, 1227-1232** (a tree blocks some of the view in **1229** and **1230**), or **1327-1332**

BUILDING 2 Rooms **2227-2232** (landscaping blocks some of the view in **2129** and **2130**), or **2327-2332**

BUILDING 5 Rooms **5118-5123, 5218-5225,** or **5318-5325**

BUILDING 6 Rooms **6123-6129, 6138-6139, 6145-6148, 6223-6226, 6233-6240, 6245-6248, 6323-6329, 6335-6340,** or **6345-6348**

BUILDING 7 Rooms **7142-7147, 7242-7247,** or **7342-7347**

Note that room **6X23** in building 6 is a corner room with two windows, one of which faces the river. But Disney puts it in the less expensive garden-view category.

PORT ORLEANS RESORT–RIVERSIDE

STRENGTHS	
• Interesting narrative to theming	• Close driving distance to the Magic Kingdom
• Disney princess–themed rooms in Magnolia Bend	• Good place to walk or run for fitness
• Live entertainment in River Roost Lounge	• Recreation options (bikes, boats)
• A Moderate resort that can sleep five, the fifth in a Murphy bed, at Alligator Bayou	**WEAKNESSES**
• Very nice feature pool	• Multiple bus stops; may share service with Port Orleans French Quarter during slower times of year

Unofficial Guide **Reader-Survey Results**

Percentage of readers who'd stay here again	85% (*Average*)
Percentage of readers who'd recommend this resort to a friend	84% (*Average*)
Overall reader rating B (*Lowest-rated Disney Moderate resort*)	

THIS RESORT DRAWS ON THE LIFESTYLE and architecture of Mississippi River communities in early-19th-century Louisiana. Spread along the Sassagoula River, which encircles **Ol' Man Island** (the section's main swimming area), Riverside is subdivided into two more themed areas: **Magnolia Bend,** which features plantation-style architecture, and **Alligator Bayou,** featuring tin-roofed rustic (imitation) wooden buildings. "Mansions" in Magnolia Bend are three stories tall, while guesthouses in Alligator Bayou are a story shorter. Riverside's food court houses a working cotton press powered by a 32-foot waterwheel.

Each of Riverside's 2,048 rooms is 314 square feet. Most provide one king or two queen beds, a table and two chairs, a minifridge and coffee maker, and two pedestal sinks outside the bathroom.

Disney refurbished rooms in Alligator Bayou in 2019. These rooms, along with those at Caribbean Beach, are unique among Disney Moderates in that they sleep five people; the fifth bed is a Murphy-style fold-down, more suitable for kids than adults. Rooms feature hickory-branch tables, and all have vinyl "hardwood" floors. Bathrooms have increased shelf space and a curtain separator that allows three people to get ready at once.

Rooms in Magnolia Bend are more conventional, with light-green walls, chestnut-colored wood furnishings, and olive carpets. Bathroom lighting seems to have been improved, and a small shelf above the dual-sink countertop provides additional storage space.

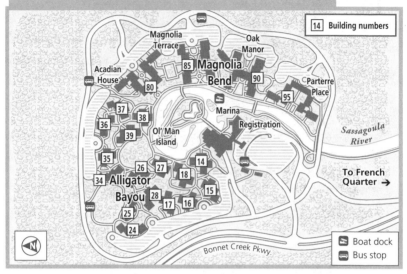

Port Orleans Resort–Riverside

Oak Manor and **Parterre Place** in Magnolia Bend contain exclusively Disney princess–themed rooms, similar in concept to the Disney-themed rooms at Caribbean Beach Resort. Port Orleans Riverside's rooms are themed to *The Princess and the Frog,* with appearances by Tiana's other princess friends. These rooms cost around $50 more per night than standard rooms.

Disney buses link Riverside to all Disney World destinations. Walking time to bus-loading areas from the most remote rooms is 5 minutes or less. Unfortunately, bus service is one of readers' biggest gripes about Riverside. First from a Scottsdale, Arizona, reader:

> *The buses were very crowded, hot, and sweaty. It was a fight just to get on in the morning, and we often had to wait for a second bus.*

Next, from a Delmar, Delaware, mom:

> *Port Orleans Riverside has some of the worst bus service on-property. One day a bus to a park takes 20 minutes; two days later, going to the exact same park, you will experience a long, leisurely drive around the loop, then make a stopover at French Quarter, followed by finally getting to the park about 45 minutes later or more. Utter madness!*

A big fan of Port Orleans Riverside says she won't be going back:

> *I absolutely love Port Orleans Riverside and have stayed here four times. But as lovely as it is, I'm always very disappointed with the bus service to and from the Magic Kingdom. You have people trying to leave early enough to make it to their dining reservations, but whoever schedules the buses doesn't seem to care. And the service coming back from the park is nothing short of abominable: Every single night, I waited more than 35 minutes in a large crowd only to have to stand on the bus. It is for this reason that I will not go back to this beautiful resort.*

Don't throw Port Orleans Riverside under the bus (pun intended). Simply rent a car or use a ride-hailing service, and get off the bus, Gus.

Finally, the resort's size can be overwhelming to some guests, as this reader from Pensacola, Florida, writes:

> *It was our first extended stay at Port Orleans Riverside, and we found the resort to be too big and the pathways too confusing. We were situated 0.5 mile from the lobby/food court, which made taking advantage of our refillable mugs a somewhat-arduous task.*

GOOD (AND NOT-SO-GOOD) ROOMS AT PORT ORLEANS RIVERSIDE RESORT *(See* tinyurl.com/por-roomviews *for photos.)* Riverside is so large that we use bicycles whenever we visit there. All told, there are 20 guest-room buildings (not counting flanking wings on two buildings). Divided into two sections, **Alligator Bayou** and **Magnolia Bend,** the resort is arranged around two pine groves and a man-made watercourse that Disney calls the Sassagoula River.

Magnolia Bend consists of four three-story, grand plantation–style complexes named **Acadian House, Magnolia Terrace, Oak Manor,** and **Parterre Place.** Though Magnolia Bend is on the river, only about 15% of the guest rooms have an unobstructed view of the water. Most rooms overlook a courtyard or parking lot. Trees and other vegetation block the view of many rooms actually facing the river. The best views in Magnolia Bend are from the third-floor river side of Acadian House (building 80), which overlooks the river and Ol' Man Island: rooms **8414–8419.**

To the south are Magnolia Terrace (building 85) and Oak Manor (building 90), each in an H shape. They're nearer the front desk, restaurant, lounge, and shopping complex than Acadian House. Continuing south, Parterre Place (building 95) has a number of rooms facing the river, but most views are blocked by trees or extend to the parking lot on the opposite shore. Try **9537–9540, 9573–9576, 9737–9739,** and **9773–9776.** In general, with the few previous exceptions, if you want a nice river view, opt for Port Orleans French Quarter.

Alligator Bayou, the other part of Port Orleans Riverside, forms an arch around the resort's northern half. Sixteen smaller, two-story guest-room buildings, set among pine groves and abundant gardens, offer a cozy alternative to the more-imposing structures of the Magnolia Bend section of Riverside and of Port Orleans French Quarter. If you want a river view, ask for a second-story water-view room in **building 27** or **38. Building 14** also offers some river-view rooms and is convenient to shops, the front desk, and the restaurant, but it's in a noisy, high-traffic area. A good compromise for families is **building 18.** It's insulated from traffic and noise by landscaping, but it's also next to a satellite swimming pool and within an easy walk of the lobby and restaurant.

Disney's official Riverside map shows two green areas north of the river bend in Alligator Bayou—these are dried-up lakes that are now richly forested with pine. Though out of sight of water, these offer the most peaceful and serene accommodations in the entire Port Orleans Resort. In this area, we recommend **buildings 26, 25,** and **39,** in that order. Note that these buildings are somewhat distant from the resort's central facilities, and there's no adjacent parking. In Alligator Bayou, avoid **buildings 15, 16, 17,** and **24,** all of which are subject to traffic noise from nearby Bonnet Creek Parkway.

THE ANIMAL KINGDOM RESORTS
Disney's Animal Kingdom Lodge & Villas:
Jambo House and Kidani Village
(See tinyurl.com/ug-aklodge *for extended coverage.)*

ANIMAL KINGDOM LODGE & VILLAS–JAMBO HOUSE

STRENGTHS	WEAKNESSES
• Magnificent lobby	• Few counter-service dining options
• Excellent on-site sit-down dining options	• Jambo House villas are smaller than those at Kidani Village
• Large, beautiful feature pool	• Rooms are among the smallest of the Deluxe resorts
• On-site cultural and nature programs	• Erratic bus service
• Best theming of any Disney hotel	• No direct non-bus transportation to any theme park

Unofficial Guide **Reader-Survey Results**

Percentage of readers who'd stay here again	89% *(Average)*
Percentage of readers who'd recommend this resort to a friend	89% *(Average)*
Overall reader rating	B

QUICK TAKE: *Rooms here are rated among the highest in any Disney hotel. The resort also has three of the five highest-rated sit-down restaurants in our reader surveys. If it fits in your budget, Animal Kingdom Lodge & Villas is the first on-property resort you should consider.*

IN THE SOUTHWESTERNMOST CORNER OF THE WORLD, adjacent to Disney's Animal Kingdom theme park, Animal Kingdom Lodge opened in 2001. The resort is divided into **Jambo House,** which comprises both regular hotel rooms and DVC/DDV units, and the all-DVC **Kidani Village.** The section below describes Jambo House; Kidani Village coverage follows.

Designed by Peter Dominick of Wilderness Lodge fame, the resort fuses African tribal architecture with the rugged style of grand East African national park lodges. Five-story thatched-roof guest-room wings fan out from a vast central rotunda housing the lobby. Public areas and about half of the rooms offer panoramic views of a private 21-acre wildlife preserve, punctuated with streams and elevated *kopje* (rock outcrops) and populated with some 200 free-roaming hoofed animals and 130 birds.

Most of the lodge's 972 guest rooms measure 344 square feet and boast hand-carved furnishings and richly colored soft goods. Standard amenities include a flat-panel TV, table with two chairs, ceiling fan, minifridge, and coffee maker. Behind each headboard sits faux mosquito netting. The bathrooms have animal-themed wallpaper, two sinks, and a large mirror. Almost all rooms have full balconies.

Jambo House also has DDV studios and one-, two-, and three-bedroom villas. Most are slightly smaller than at neighboring Kidani Village—anywhere from 50 square feet for a studio to more than 200 square feet smaller for a two-bedroom unit. The three-bedroom Grand Villas at Jambo House are an exception, larger than those in Kidani at 148 square feet. Jambo's lowest-priced one-bedroom rooms sleep four; standard, savanna, and Club Level rooms sleep five.

Animal Kingdom Lodge & Villas

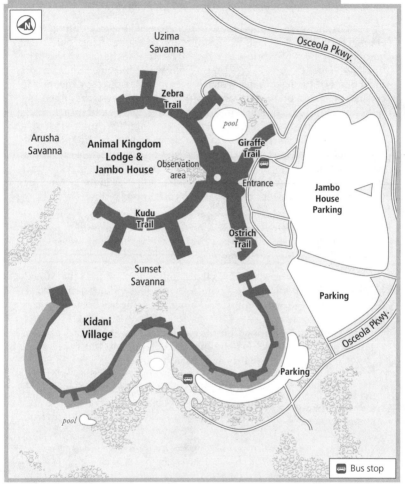

Uzima
Savanna

Osceola Pkwy.

Zebra
Trail

pool

Arusha
Savanna

Animal Kingdom
Lodge &
Jambo House

Observation
area

Giraffe
Trail

Entrance

Jambo
House
Parking

Kudu
Trail

Ostrich
Trail

Sunset
Savanna

Parking

Kidani
Village

Osceola Pkwy.

Parking

pool

🚌 Bus stop

A Murfreesboro, Tennessee, mom loved everything but the room size:

*We wanted to love staying at Animal Kingdom Lodge. We found the
setting unique, the staff exceptional, and the common areas breath-
takingly gorgeous. Loved all three table-service restaurants. Location
wasn't an issue since we had a car, and the pool was fabulous. However, the rooms are really small for the price. We were especially dis-
mayed at the commode/shower area—we had to sit on the commode
in order to have room to shut the door. Unfortunately, the room size
and bathrooms dropped us from "love" to "like."*

From a New Jersey mom:

*Animal Kingdom Lodge was wonderful, but the rooms were some-
what disappointing. While we loved the theme, ambience, staff, and
amazing savanna view, the room was small and had terrible storage.*

There were only two dresser drawers for four people—the room could have used another dresser and under-sink storage. Even a few strategically placed shelves would have been helpful.

Besides theming, Jambo House's strength is its upscale dining: readers place all 3 of the sit-down restaurants at Animal Kingdom Lodge among Walt Disney World's top 10. At the top of the list is **Jiko—The Cooking Place** (closed at press time). Twin wood-burning ovens are the focal point of the restaurant, which serves meals inspired by the myriad cuisines of Africa. **Boma—Flavors of Africa,** the family restaurant, serves a buffet breakfast and dinner with food prepared in an exhibition kitchen featuring a wood-burning grill and rotisserie. Tables are under thatched roofs. (**Sanaa,** the third restaurant, is a short walk away at Kidani Village.) **Victoria Falls,** a delightful mezzanine lounge overlooking Boma, rounds out the hotel's sit-down service. **The Mara,** the lone quick-service place, can get crowded, even with extended hours. A family from New Canaan, Connecticut, found the resort's restaurants a draw:

The restaurants at Animal Kingdom Lodge are great. We had lunch at Sanaa, which featured fantastic food and awesome views of the animals on the savanna. The Mara's counter-service options were way better than anything we found in the Magic Kingdom.

Uzima Springs serves drinks, salads, and snacks next to the resort's huge, elaborate pool. Other amenities include a village marketplace, outdoor movies shown nightly, and a nightly campfire hosted by African cast members.

The **Starlight Safari** wildlife tour is for guests age 8 and up. The 1-hour tour costs $74.17 including tax per person and takes place nightly at 8:30 and 10 p.m.

COVID *tip*

At press time, the Starlight Safari tour was temporarily suspended.

Jambo House is connected to the rest of Walt Disney World by bus, but because of the resort's remote location, you should seriously consider having a car if you stay there. This family from Downers Grove, Illinois, concurs:

We stayed at Animal Kingdom Lodge knowing we were going to have minimal park time. The distance from the parks was noticeable— the buses were packed, with standing passengers the norm, and the posted wait times for the next bus were only a guide. We wouldn't recommend staying here if you were planning to go to the parks on a daily basis.

This Baltimore mom found transportation the resort's weakest aspect:

Animal Kingdom Lodge was a calm oasis with peaceful hotel rooms, but it's too hard to access the Magic Kingdom from there, either by car or by bus.

GOOD (AND NOT-SO-GOOD) ROOMS AT AKL–JAMBO HOUSE *(See* tinyurl.com/akl-roomviews *for photos.)* A glance at the resort map tells you where the best rooms and villas are. **Kudu Trail** and **Zebra Trail,** two wings branching from the rear of Jambo House, form a semicircle around the central wildlife savanna. Along each wing are seven five-story buildings, with accommodations on floors two through five. Five buildings on each wing form the semicircle, while the remaining two buildings jut away from the center. The best rooms—on floors three and four, facing into the circle—are high enough to survey the entire savanna yet low enough to let you appreciate the ground-level detail of this amazing wildlife exhibit; plus, these rooms offer the easiest access to the lobby and restaurants. Second-floor rooms really can't take in the panorama, and fifth-floor rooms are a little too high for intimate views of the animals. Most of the fourth-floor rooms in Jambo House are reserved for Club Level guests, and the fifth and sixth floors house the DDV units.

Most rooms in the outward-jutting buildings, as well as rooms facing away from the interior, also survey a savanna, but one not as compelling as that of the inner circle. On the Zebra Trail, the first two buildings plus the first jutting building provide savanna views on one side and look onto the swimming complex on the other.

Less attractive still are two smaller wings, **Ostrich Trail** and **Giraffe Trail,** branching from either side of the lodge near the main entrance. Some rooms on the left side of Ostrich Trail (see map on page 175) overlook a small savanna. Rooms on the opposite side of the same buildings overlook the front entrance. Least desirable is Giraffe Trail, extending from the right side of the lobby: Its rooms overlook either the pool (water view) or the resort entrance (standard view). A Portage, Indiana, family begs to differ with our assessment, however:

> We stayed in a pool-view room in Giraffe Trail and loved it. The view was beautiful, even without animals (which you can see elsewhere). The proximity to the pool, lobby, and restaurants was great, and we saved about $500 over what we would've spent on a savanna view.

ANIMAL KINGDOM VILLAS–KIDANI VILLAGE

STRENGTHS	
• Nice pool with excellent splash area	• Close to Jambo House amenities and restaurants
• Underground parking close to elevators	• Great fitness room
• Beautiful, understated lobby	**WEAKNESSES**
• Sanaa restaurant is an *Unofficial Guide* favorite	• Savanna views can be hit-or-miss
	• Erratic bus service
• Beautiful Grand Villas sleep 12	• No quick-service dining options other than pool bar

Unofficial Guide **Reader-Survey Results**

Percentage of readers who'd stay here again	88% (*Average*)
Percentage of readers who'd recommend this resort to a friend	89% (*Average*)
Overall reader rating	B

CONSISTING OF A SEPARATE BUILDING shaped like a backward 3, Kidani Village has 324 DDV units, a dedicated savanna, a well-themed pool and splash zone, and **Sanaa,** a top-rated sit-down restaurant combining Indian and African cuisines. Other amenities include a fitness center; an arcade; a gift shop; and tennis, shuffleboard, and basketball courts. Kidani Village is connected to Jambo House by a half-mile walking trail; DDV guests at either resort can use the facilities at both.

As noted previously, Kidani Village has studios and one-, two-, and three-bedroom villas. Except for the three-bedroom units, most rooms are larger than their counterparts at Jambo House by anywhere from 50 square feet (for a studio) to more than 200 square feet (for a two-bedroom unit). Kidani's villas also have one more bathroom for the one-, two-, and three-bedroom units. Because of the difference in area, one-bedroom units in Kidani Village can accommodate up to five people, and two-bedroom units can hold up to nine with a sleeper chair in the living room.

Having stayed at Kidani Village more than a dozen times, we think it's quiet and relaxed. The lobby and rooms have a smaller, more personal feel than Jambo House's. The exterior isn't anything special: It's basically a set of green rectangles with oversize African-themed decorations attached. Kidani's distance from Jambo House makes it feel especially remote. The bus stops are a fair distance from the main building, too, and it's easy to head in the wrong direction when you're coming back from the parks at night.

GOOD (AND NOT-SO-GOOD) ROOMS AT AKL-KIDANI VILLAGE *(See* **tinyurl.com/kidani-roomviews** *for photos.)* The best views in Kidani Village are from the north-facing rooms near the bottom and middle of the backward 3. Try rooms **7X38–7X44, 7X46–7X52, 7X06–7X11, 7X68–7X82,** and **7X61–7X67** (*X* indicates numbers 0–9). These overlook the savanna next to Jambo House's Kudu Trail rooms and beyond into undeveloped woods. West- and south-facing rooms in the bottom half of Kidani Village overlook the parking lot; west-facing rooms in the top half have either pool or savanna views.

Disney's Coronado Springs Resort

(See **tinyurl.com/ug-coronado** *for extended coverage.)*

STRENGTHS	WEAKNESSES
• Most sophisticated room decor of the Moderate resorts	• Conventioneers may be off-putting to vacationing families
• Setting is beautiful at night	• Some rooms are a long distance from check-in, lobby, and restaurants
• Themed swimming area with waterslides	
• Large feature pool	• Multiple bus stops
• On-site business center	
• Best public Wi-Fi at any Disney resort	

Unofficial Guide **Reader-Survey Results**

Percentage of readers who'd stay here again	88% (*Average*)
Percentage of readers who'd recommend this resort to a friend	84% (*Average*)
Overall reader rating	B

NEAR ANIMAL KINGDOM, Coronado Springs Resort is Disney's only midpriced convention property. Inspired by northern Mexico and the American Southwest, the resort is divided into four separately themed areas. The two- and three-story **Ranchos** call to mind Southwestern cattle ranches, while the two-story **Cabanas** are modeled after Mexican beach resorts. The multistoried **Casitas** embody elements of Spanish architecture found in Mexico's great cities.

The **Gran Destino Tower** serves as the lobby for all of Coronado Springs, and the rooms in this 15-floor building are nicer than those in the rest of the resort. (The idea, we hear, is to appeal to companies reluctant to put their executives in Moderate hotel rooms.)

Coronado Springs Resort

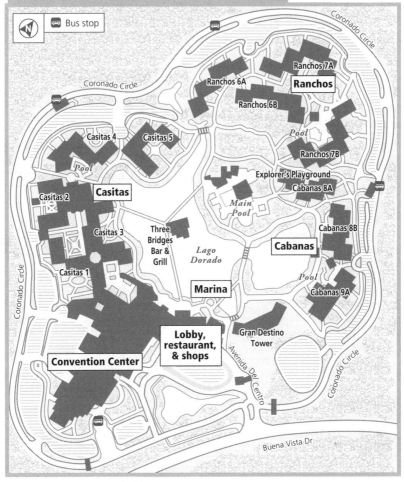

This vast resort, surrounding a 22-acre lake, has three small pools and one large swimming complex. The main pool features a reproduction of a Mayan step pyramid with a waterfall cascading down its side.

Most of the 1,839 rooms in the Ranchos, Cabanas, and Casitas measure 314 square feet and contain two queen beds, a desk with an excellent working area, a chair, a minifridge, a coffee maker, and a vanity outside the bathroom. Sliding doors divide the main living area from the sinks, allowing three people to get ready at the same time. Bathrooms have plenty of storage. Rooms are decorated with a subtle Southwestern theme, in a desert-landscape palette. No rooms have balconies.

The 545 rooms in Gran Destino Tower range from standard issue to deluxe, one-bedroom, and presidential suites. The public areas showcase a vibrant mix of Spanish and Moorish design, with bold colors and large, open spaces.

Gran Destino's standard rooms are almost 20% larger than those in the rest of the resort. They have vinyl "hardwood" floors, large windows, good lighting, and lots of desk and storage space; rooms are also equipped with a minifridge and a Keurig coffee maker. Bathrooms have plentiful lighting and shelf space, two sinks, a huge shower, and separate areas for grooming and the toilet, allowing three people to get ready at the same time. Our one criticism is that there's little theming: The rooms barely differ from those at other Disney resorts.

Our favorite thing about Gran Destino is the relatively low cost of Club Level rooms, which get you access to the **Chronos Club** lounge. Standard rates for these rooms run $200–$300 per night less than the next-cheapest Club Level room on-property, and limited-time discounts made the price even better. The Chronos Club has fantastic views, good food throughout the day, and a friendly staff. If you're looking for a little pampering on vacation, Gran Destino's Club Level rooms are probably the best value in Walt Disney World.

Perhaps because Coronado Springs is geared to conventions, getting actual work done here is easier than at any other Disney Moderate resort. Lighting above the desk provides excellent illumination of the work area. Wi-Fi is available throughout the resort.

Coronado Springs has four full-service restaurants and a food court, plus two bars. One of those full-service restaurants, **Toledo—Tapas, Steak & Seafood,** is in Gran Destino Tower. An over-water bar called **Three Bridges Bar & Grill** sits in the middle of Coronado Springs' 22-acre lake, connected to the resort by—drum roll—three bridges. Even with these additions, though, dining capacity and choices may be just adequate for a resort this big. We suggest having a car to expand your options.

The resort is connected to other Disney destinations by bus only. Walking time from the most remote rooms to the bus stop is 8–10 minutes. Bus service is the other of Coronado Springs' weaknesses. This Oklahoma City family's comments are representative:

> The buses took at least 30–45 minutes to arrive at the parks and/or resort. The queues for the bus would be filled with guests, and they still wouldn't send another.

Beyond transportation, reader opinions of Coronado Springs are split. A family from Cumming, Georgia, was disappointed:

> The convention center really interferes with a family vacation— everyone we met there was working and wanted to talk about work while we were trying to get away from work!

A Chester, Virginia, mother had a very different experience:

> Coronado Springs was absolutely fabulous. The staff was friendly, the kids loved the pool, and we all loved the market. It was nice and quiet at night. There were many convention guests, but they didn't interfere with our trip.

Coronado Springs was the Disney Moderate resort of choice for this Kansas City, Kansas, family:

> On our previous three trips, we stayed at Pop Century, and I was curious if a Moderate resort was worth the extra money. At first the

size of Coronado Springs was daunting, but we quickly settled into a routine and figured out the bus routes (bus service was really the only major drawback). The room was spacious, and the door separating the living area from the bath vanity was very useful because I was able to get ready in the morning without waking the kids. The kids really enjoyed the pool area, and I thought it was better themed than Pop Century. Overall, I thought the resort was worth the price difference.

A family from Indianapolis liked the swimming pools:

The pool at Coronado Springs was excellent—the kids loved the slide! We also utilized the smaller pool close to our room—it was good for the kids to relax before bedtime.

GOOD (AND NOT-SO-GOOD) ROOMS AT CORONADO SPRINGS RESORT *(See* tinyurl.com/csr-roomviews *for photos.)* As convention hotels go, Coronado Springs is kind of an odd duck. Whereas at comparable hotels everything is centrally located and the guest rooms are in close proximity to each other, the rooms here are spread around a huge lake called **Lago Dorado.** If you're assigned a room on the opposite side of the lake from the meeting area and restaurants, plan on an 11- to 15-minute hike every time you leave your room.

Coronado Springs' main lobby is inside **Gran Destino Tower.** To its west is **El Centro**, which contains shops, restaurants, and a conference center. There are three accommodation "communities."

If you think of Coronado Springs as a clock face, El Centro is at the 6 o'clock position. Moving clockwise around the lake beyond El Centro, the **Casitas** are located near the lobby, restaurants, shops, and convention center, in the 7 through 9 o'clock positions. Standard-view rooms face parking lots or a courtyard. Water-view rooms cover pools, the lake, and so on. For a good view of Lago Dorado, book one of these rooms:

3220-3223, 3241-3259, 3267-3273, or 3281-3287

3320-3383 *(except* 3324, 3330-3335, 3360-3365, 3374-3380, and 3384-3387)

3420-3423, 3425-3429, 3436-3459, 3466-3473, 3480-3482, or 3487

4461-4464

5202-5212

5303-5304 or 5311-5312

5400-5402, 5405-5410, 5413, or 5423-5463 *(except* 5450)

Next come the **Ranchos,** which are set back from the lake at the 11, 12, and 1 o'clock positions. The desert theme translates to lots of cactus and gravel, not much water or shade, and almost no good views. The Ranchos are a hike from everything but the main swimming area. Rooms **6X00-6X04** afford the best views.

The **Cabanas** are at 2, 3, and 4 o'clock. Lake-view rooms we recommend here include the following: **8129-8131** and **8142-8147; 8500-8510, 8550-8553,** and **8573** *(except* 8505, 8507, and 8509).

Finally, **Gran Destino Tower** is at 5 o'clock, close to El Centro. Even-numbered rooms face EPCOT and Hollywood Studios, and guests on upper floors can see those parks' fireworks shows. Odd-numbered rooms at Gran Destino have a view of the resort's lake.

Disney's All-Star Resorts: Movies, Music, and Sports

(See **tinyurl.com/ug-allstars** *for extended coverage.)*

STRENGTHS	WEAKNESSES
• Least expensive of the Disney resorts	• Most likely Disney resorts to host large school groups
• Family suites at All-Star Music are less expensive than those at Art of Animation	• Sports and Music are Disney's lowest-rated resorts
• Convenient parking	
• Lots of pools	• Older rooms (Sports and Music) feel small and dated
• Lovely landscaping, if you know where to look (Music)	• No full-service dining; food courts often overwhelmed at mealtimes
• In-room pizza delivery (currently unavailable)	• All three resorts share buses during slower times of year; bus stops often crowded
	• $15/night parking fee

Unofficial Guide **Reader-Survey Results**

Percentage of readers who'd stay here again Movies: 86% (*Average*); Music: 86% (*Below Average*); Sports: 77% (*Below Average*)
Percentage of readers who'd recommend this resort to a friend Movies: 79% (*Below Average*); Music: 77% (*Below Average*); Sports: 66% (*Below Average*)
Overall reader rating Movies: B; Music: B; Sports: C+

QUICK TAKE: *The All-Stars came in dead last in this year's reader survey, with All-Star Sports earning the lowest percentages of readers who'd stay at a particular Value resort again or recommend it to a friend. That said, a turnaround is already underway. Disney refurbished All-Star Movies' rooms in 2019, and the results are fantastic. Disney hasn't said how long it will take to complete the renovations at the other resorts—we don't expect anything to get started before mid-2022 at the earliest.*

DISNEY'S ORIGINAL VERSION of a budget resort features three distinct themes executed in the same hyperbolic style. Spread over a vast expanse, the resorts comprise 30 three-story motel-style guest-room buildings. Although the three resorts are neighbors, each has its own lobby, food court, and registration area.

All-Star Sports features huge sports equipment: bright football helmets, tennis rackets, and baseball bats—all taller than the buildings they adorn. Similarly, **All-Star Music** features 40-foot guitars, maracas, and saxophones, while **All-Star Movies** showcases giant popcorn boxes and icons from Disney films.

The food courts function well for their size and purpose. Lobbies are loud (in both decibels and brightness) and cartoonish, with checkerboard walls; photographs of famous athletes, musicians, or film stars; and a dedicated area for kids to watch Disney shows and movies while parents are checking in.

Each resort has two main pools; Music's are shaped like musical instruments (the **Piano Pool** and the guitar-shaped **Calypso Pool**), and one of Movies' is star-shaped. All six pools feature plastic replicas of Disney characters, some shooting water pistols.

At 260 square feet, standard rooms at the All-Star Resorts are very small—the same size as the ones at Pop Century Resort and slightly smaller than Art of Animation's standard rooms. All-Star rooms are so

All-Star Resorts

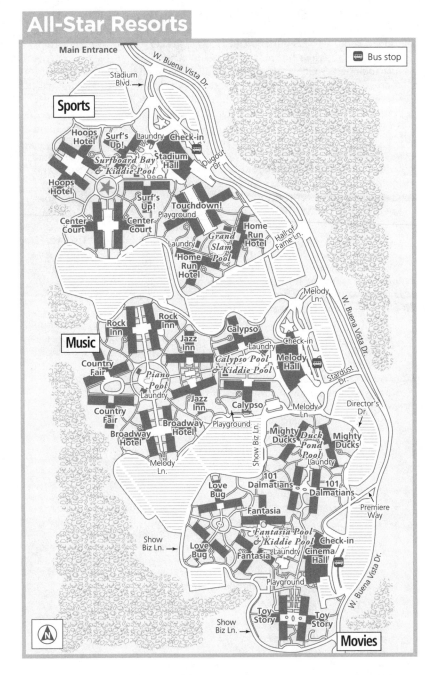

small, in fact, that a family of four attempting to stay in one room might redefine *family values* by week's end. (*And just remember they give you 60 square feet per person in prison. —Len*)

All of the All-Star Movies buildings have been refurbished. These rooms include vinyl "hardwood" floors, sleek modern storage units, queen beds, 10 USB outlets, and a coffee maker. One of the beds folds into the wall when not being used, converting into a table; two chairs are included. Space has been freed under the fixed bed for storage. The bathroom remodel swaps out plastic shower curtains for sliding glass doors, new showerheads, and tile walls. The grooming area is vastly improved, with modular shelving, improved lighting, and increased counter space. Another sliding door separates the bath from the main living space, allowing three people to get ready at the same time.

Older rooms are found throughout All-Star Sports and All-Star Music. These include two double beds or one king bed, a minifridge (no coffee maker), a separate vanity area, and a table and chairs. Bathrooms have curved shower rods. Except for artwork and bathroom wallpaper, all older rooms in these two resorts are furnished identically. No rooms have balconies, either in the older or refreshed rooms.

Due to the low staff-to-guest ratio, service is mediocre. Also, there are no full-service restaurants, and the bus ride from the remote All-Stars to a sit-down restaurant at another resort is about 45 minutes one-way (there is, however, a McDonald's about 0.25 mile away). Bus service to the theme and water parks is pretty efficient. Walking time to the bus stop from the most remote guest rooms is about 8 minutes.

If space is an important consideration for your Disney vacation, you may want to budget enough for a bigger room at another resort— Art of Animation's standard rooms, at least. Also, All-Star Sports and Music are the noisiest Disney resorts: Though rooms are well sound-proofed, we still use a white-noise app when we stay here. Be aware, however, that while the All-Stars suffer compared with other Disney properties, you're better off here than at most hotels you'll find in Kissimmee or Lake Buena Vista for $130 per night or less.

We receive a lot of letters commenting on the All-Star Resorts. This family from Poplar Grove, Illinois, loved the new Movies rooms:

> We stayed in a newly refurbished room at Pop Century; then we moved to All-Star Movies for two nights. Both were wonderful—we loved the new layouts, and there was plenty of space, even with all of our gear—but All-Star Movies felt a bit more upscale.

A Baltimore family had a similarly positive experience:

> We were pleasantly surprised by All-Star Movies. Yes, the rooms are small, but the overall magic there is amazing. The lobby played Disney movies, which is perfect if you get up early and the buses aren't running yet. Customer service was impeccable.

A Canadian family had a not-so-positive experience:

> The Guide didn't prepare us for the large groups of students who take over the resorts. They're very noisy and pushy when it comes to getting on buses. Our scariest experience was when we tried getting on a bus and got mobbed by about 100 students.

ALL-STAR MUSIC FAMILY SUITES In the Jazz and Calypso Buildings, the 192 suites measure roughly 520 square feet, slightly larger than the Fort Wilderness Cabins but slightly smaller than Art of Animation's

Family Suites. Each suite, formed from the combination of two formerly separate rooms, includes a kitchenette with minifridge, microwave, and coffee maker. Sleeping accommodations include a queen bed in the bedroom, plus a pullout sleeper sofa, a chair bed, and an ottoman bed. We're not sure we'd let adult friends (ones we want to keep, anyway) use the sofa bed or the chair or ottoman beds, but they're fine for kids. A hefty door separates the two rooms.

The All-Star Music Family Suites have flat-panel TVs as well as two baths—one more than the Fort Wilderness Cabins. The suites cost up to 25% less than the cabins and about 20% less than Art of Animation's Family Suites, but they don't have the kitchen space or appliances to prepare anything more than rudimentary meals. If you're trying to save money by eating in your room, the cabins are your best bet. If you just want a little extra space and somewhere to nuke your Pop-Tarts in the morning, the All-Star suites are just fine.

Reader comments about the Family Suites are generally positive, albeit measured. First, from a North Carolina family of five:

> It was so nice to have a place to unwind without the kids at night, along with two bathrooms and extra kitchen space. My only issue was that we weren't comfortable leaving the kids on the foldouts because they're right next to the front door; plus, my husband and I didn't want to be confined to the bedroom from the time we put the kids to bed, so we slept on a foldout. The first night was hell, but the second night we took the mattresses off the pullout chair and ottoman and put them on top of the mattress on the couch— MUCH better!

From a Skokie, Illinois, family of five:

> We found the All-Star Music Family Suite to be very roomy. Our teenagers and preteen were quite comfortable on the pullout sofa, chair, and ottoman. Having the two bathrooms was a must, and the kitchen area had lots of shelf space for the food we had delivered from Garden Grocer [see page 458]. Our only complaint is that from 7:30 a.m. until midnight there's music playing. The rooms are soundproofed but not enough; we had to use earplugs.

GOOD (AND NOT-SO-GOOD) ROOMS AT THE ALL-STAR RESORTS
(See tinyurl.com/asmo-roomviews, tinyurl.com/asmu-roomviews, *and* tinyurl .com/assp-roomviews *for photos.*) Although the layouts of the All-Star Resorts' Movies, Music, and Sports sections are different, the three buildings are identical T-shaped, three-story, three-winged structures. The buildings are further grouped into pairs, generally facing each other and sharing a common subtheme (for example, there's a *Toy Story* pair in the Movies section). In addition to being named by theme, such as *Fantasia,* the buildings are numbered 1–10 in each section. Rooms are accessed via a motel-style outdoor walkway, but each building has an elevator.

unofficial **TIP**
Music 5654 may be the best room at the All-Star Resorts. This third-floor corner room overlooks a small pond in a wooded area behind the resort. See tinyurl.com/music5654 for a photo of the view.

Parking is plentiful, all of it in sprawling lots buffering the three sections. A room near a parking lot means easier loading and unloading but also unsightly views of the lot. The resort offers a luggage service, but it often takes up to an hour for your bags to arrive.

To avoid a parking-lot vista, request a room facing a courtyard or pool. The trade-off is noise. The sound of cars starting in the parking lot is no match for shrieking children or hooting teenagers in the pool. And don't count on a good view of the pool, even if your room faces it. The buildings' themed facade decorations are placed on their widest face—the top of the T—which is also the side facing the pool or courtyard. In some cases, as with the surfboards in the Sports section, these significantly obstruct the view. Floodlights are also trained on these facades, so if you step out of your room at night to view the action below, looking down may result in temporary blindness.

The sort of traveler you are should dictate the room you request. If you choose an All-Star Resort because you'd rather spend time and money at the parks, book a room near the bus stop, your link to the rest of the World. Note that buses leave from the central public buildings of each section, which are near the larger, noisier pools. If you're planning to return to your room for an afternoon nap, request a room farther from the pools. Also consider an upper-story room to minimize foot traffic past your door.

On the other hand, if you choose All-Star for its kid-friendly aspects, consider roosting near the action. A bottom-floor room provides easy pool access, and a room looking out on a courtyard or pool allows you to keep an eye on children playing outside.

For travelers without young children (infants excluded), the best bets for privacy and quiet are rooms in buildings that overlook the forest behind the resort: **buildings 2** and **3** in **All-Star Sports** and **buildings 5** and **6** in **All-Star Music.** Interior-facing rooms in these buildings (and their partners) also fill the bill because they overlook courtyards farthest from the large pools. The courtyards vary with theme but are generally only mildly amusing.

If you're traveling with kids, opt for a section and building with a theme that appeals to them. Often, that will be a film, but it might be a sport. If you're staying in Home Run Hotel, for instance, don't forget the ball and gloves to maximize the experience (just keep games of catch away from the pool). Older elementary- and middle-school children will probably want to spend hotel time in or near the bigger pools. Periodically, however, cadres of teenagers—too cool for their younger siblings—effectively commandeer the smaller secondary pools.

Playgrounds are tucked behind Cinema Hall, next to building 9, in **All-Star Movies;** between the backs of buildings 9 and 10 in **All-Star Music;** and between buildings 6 and 7 in **All-Star Sports.** Rooms facing these are ideal for families with children too young or timid for the often-chaotic larger pools. In All-Star Movies, the playground is nearer to the food court than to any rooms.

The following tip from a former All-Star Resorts cast member from Fayetteville, Georgia, illustrates just how big these resorts are:

Rooms at the far end of the Mighty Ducks building of All-Star Movies are closer to the All-Star Music food court, pool, and buses than to All-Star Movies' own facilities. Follow the walkway from the Ducks building north to All-Star Music's Melody Hall.

Disney's Pop Century Resort
(See **tinyurl.com/ug-popcentury** *for extended coverage.)*

POP CENTURY RESORT

STRENGTHS	WEAKNESSES
• Theming is fun for anyone over 35	• Theming may be lost on kids and teens
• Our favorite pool bar of the Value resorts	• Small rooms that are the same size as All-Stars' but slightly more expensive
• One bus stop	
• Skyliner connection to DHS and EPCOT	• Bus stops at theme parks are a long distance from park entrances
• Queen beds; stylish, modern room design	
• Convenient parking	• $15/night parking fee

Unofficial Guide **Reader-Survey Results**

Percentage of readers who'd stay here again	92% *(Average)*
Percentage of readers who'd recommend this resort to a friend	89% *(Average)*
Overall reader rating	B–

ON CENTURY DRIVE, near the ESPN Wide World of Sports, is Pop Century Resort. A near-clone of the All-Star Resorts, it consists of four-story motel-style buildings arrayed around a central pool, food court, and registration area. Decorative touches make the difference: Where the All-Stars display larger-than-life icons from movies, music, and sports, and Art of Animation is inspired by Disney cartoons, Pop Century draws its icons from decades of the 20th century and their attendant fads and

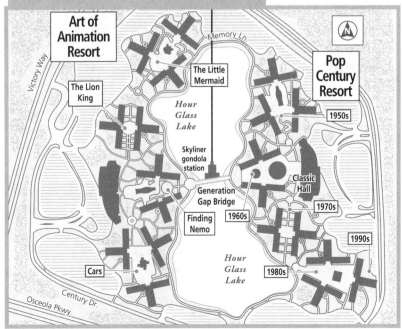

Pop Century Resort & Art of Animation Resort

fancies: building-size Big Wheels, Hula-Hoops, and the like, punctuated by silhouettes of folks doing the jitterbug and the twist.

Running $162–$361 per night, guest rooms at Pop Century are small, at 260 square feet. On the upside, a major refurbishment has given Pop Century the best rooms of any Disney Value resort. For the second straight year, Pop is the No. 1 Value property among readers who say they would stay at a particular Disney resort again.

The refurbishment replaced carpet with a modern hardwood-floor look. IKEA-style storage nooks and space-saving touches are everywhere. A particular feature we love is that the second bed in the room is a fold-down option, as at Art of Animation. When the bed isn't in use, it disappears into the wall, freeing floor space (and turning into a desk). The bulky armoire–TV stand has been replaced by built-in shelving and a wall-mounted monitor. The bathroom overhaul provides lots more shelf space, plenty of storage, and a modern shower.

The public areas at Pop Century feature 20th-century period furniture and decor, rolled up in a saccharine "those were the days" theme. A food court, bar, playground, pools, and so on emulate the All-Star versions in size and location. A lake separating Pop Century from the Art of Animation Resort offers water views not available at the All-Stars.

Another Pop Century difference from the All-Stars has merchandise retailers located with fast-food concessions in a combination dining–shopping area. As at the All-Stars and Art of Animation, there's a bar but no full-service restaurant. Art of Animation's food court is a short walk over a bridge from many Pop rooms; at press time, however, both locations had the same menu. Because of the limited dining options, we recommend having a car—which will cost you $15 per night to park.

The resort is connected to Walt Disney World by bus and the **Skyliner.** Readers rate Pop's bus service relatively low. Pop Century shares a Skyliner station with the Art of Animation (AOA) Resort. The Skyliner connects Pop and AOA with the Caribbean Beach and Riviera Resorts, and it's the main Disney transportation to Hollywood Studios and EPCOT. (Disney adds bus service to EPCOT and DHS during busy times.) On average, the Skyliner is more efficient than the bus system for getting between these resorts and theme parks. However, lines can form at Pop's Skyliner station anywhere from 90 minutes to 2 hours before opening at Hollywood Studios. We think it's far less hassle to drive, take a ride-hailing service, or call a taxi.

Besides transportation, we receive many complaints from readers about poor soundproofing between Pop Century's rooms—something that the refurbishment didn't address. As with most hotel rooms, we recommend having a white-noise machine or app available.

A reader from Dublin, Georgia, likes Pop for several reasons:

(1) There's a lake and a view of fireworks. (2) The courtyards have Twister and neat pools for little children. (3) Pop's dinner entrées are among the best bargains and the best food anywhere. (4) The layout is convenient to the food court. (5) Bus transportation is better than anywhere else, including Grand Floridian! (6) Where else do the cast members do the shag to oldies?

From a Jackson, Mississippi, family:

We loved the newly remodeled rooms at Pop Century—they are very modern-looking and have loads of storage space. But while there was no noise from rooms next to or above us, the noise directly outside was disturbing.

A Beaver Dam, Wisconsin, family had the same "good room, bad soundproofing" experience:

The remodeled room was very nice. We liked the Murphy bed and extra bathroom counter space. The only downside was when we left the parks in the afternoon to take a nap—the loudspeaker in the pool area made it hard to rest in our room nearby.

A Springfield, Illinois, dad also gives Pop Century a mixed review:

We wanted something different from All-Star Movies, so we gave Pop Century a shot. Believe the noise complaints—it's like the walls were made of papier-mâché. Although the bus service was great and the pool was nice, we'll be back at All-Star Movies the next time around.

A hungry Schnecksville, Pennsylvania, reader thought the best thing about Pop Century was the Art of Animation Resort next door (that is, when the food court menus are different):

We stayed at Pop but found our access to AOA to be invaluable. The AOA food court was by far superior to Pop's—it had separate lines at individual stations for things like burgers or pasta bowls. At Pop, there were no separate lines like this, and the station with burgers, strips, and fries was always busy.

An Austin, Texas, couple had this comment:

The Pop Century food court at late-dinner time (9 p.m. and beyond) continues to be a hellscape and will drain any remaining life force in your body faster than you could ever imagine.

unofficial **TIP**
We don't recommend Pop Century's so-called preferred rooms, which are closer to the main pool and lobby and cost about $12–$22 more than standard. They probably save only 5 minutes of walking per day and subject you to more noise from guests walking past your room.

GOOD (AND NOT-SO-GOOD) ROOMS AT POP CENTURY RESORT *(See* tinyurl.com/pop-roomviews *for photos.)* The best rooms for both view and convenience are the lake-view rooms in **buildings 4** and **5** in the **1960s** area. Another option, though with a less compelling view, would be rooms in the same building facing east, toward the registration and food-court building. Next-best choices would be the east-facing rooms of **building 3** in the **1950s**, and of **building 6** in the **1970s**. Avoid south-facing rooms in **1980s building 7** and **1990s building 8**; Both are echo chambers for noise from nearby Osceola Parkway.

Disney's Art of Animation Resort
(See map on page 187; see **tinyurl.com/ug-artofanimation** *for extended coverage.)*

OPENED IN MAY 2012, Disney's Art of Animation is a Value resort across Hour Glass Lake from Pop Century. It was originally designed to be part of Pop Century and represent the years 1900–1949, but recessions and a then-glut of hotel rooms prevented Disney from ever completing construction. When the time came for a new Value resort,

ART OF ANIMATION RESORT

STRENGTHS	WEAKNESSES
• Exceptional theming, particularly *Cars* and *Lion King* areas	• Most expensive Value resort
• Best pool of the Value resorts	• Terrible in-room mobile reception
• Family Suites are innovatively designed and themed	• The number of made-to-order meals available at the food court can mean long waits in line
• Interior hallways in some buildings	• The resort's standard rooms are rarely discounted
• Skyliner connection to DHS and EPCOT	
• Walking trail around Hour Glass Lake and connecting bridge to Pop Century	• Poor soundproofing
• Just one bus stop	• $15/night parking fee

Unofficial Guide **Reader-Survey Results**

Percentage of readers who'd stay here again	90% (*Average*)
Percentage of readers who'd recommend this resort to a friend	86% (*Average*)
Overall reader rating	B-

Disney switched the theme to its animated movies, which still fit in well with the pop-culture motif across the lake.

As at Pop Century, Art of Animation's standard rooms are housed in four-story buildings and exterior-facing walkups, with themed swimming pools and a food court. Most of the resort's accommodations, however, are suites similar to those at Disney's All-Star Music Resort: 1,120 suites versus 864 standard rooms. The suite buildings have interior hallways to the rooms instead of the exterior walkways found at Disney's other Value resorts.

Art of Animation's suites are around 565 square feet, about what you'd get by combining two standard rooms into one suite. Each suite has a master bedroom, a living room, two full bathrooms, and a kitchenette with minifridge, microwave, and coffee maker. Sleeping accommodations include a queen bed in the bedroom, a sleeper sofa, and a living room table that converts into a full-size bed. The bedroom and living room have flat-panel TVs.

This family from McKinney, Texas, found that the suites' second bathroom sped things up in the morning:

> With two teenagers, the extra space and second bathroom were absolutely worth the additional cost. Imagine being able to get ready for a park day twice as fast!

Slightly larger than comparable rooms at other Value resorts, standard rooms are 277 square feet and include one king bed or two doubles, a flat-panel TV, a minifridge, and a table and chairs.

The theming incorporates characters from four Disney animated films: **Cars, Finding Nemo, The Lion King,** and **The Little Mermaid.** All but the *Little Mermaid*–themed rooms are suites. As at Pop Century, large, colorful icons stand in the middle of each group of buildings; here, though, they represent film characters rather than pop culture touchstones. Giant murals stretch the length of each exterior structure— the *Cars* buildings, for example, each display a four-story panoramic vista of the American desert, with the movie's iconic characters in the middle, while the *Lion King* buildings capture a single verdant jungle scene.

Readers complain, however, about the long walk from the *Little Mermaid*–themed buildings to the food court and front desk. A pooped reader from Illinois offered this:

> Only two reasons to stay in a Little Mermaid *room at Art of Animation: (1) There is a die-hard* Little Mermaid *fan in your party who will make your trip miserable if you don't get this room. (2) You don't feel you will walk enough in the parks and you want to add an extralong trek to/from the bus, main pool, restaurant, gift shop, and front desk.*

Three of the four sets of themed buildings have pools. Like the other Value resorts, Art of Animation has a central building—here called **Animation Hall**—for check-in and bus transportation; it also houses the resort's food court, **Landscape of Flavors;** a gift shop; and a video-game arcade.

Most of the comments concerning Art of Animation are positive. A Collingswood, New Jersey, reader says:

> I was skeptical about Art of Animation. From pics it looked like it was going to be a child's dream but not necessarily an adult's. I was wrong—it's incredible! For a Value resort, it feels more like a Deluxe. The room was awesome—great layout, and having two bathrooms was so nice. The Big Blue Pool and the Cozy Cone Pool are great. Landscape of Flavors impressed me too—so many options for fresh, delicious comfort food as well as exotic fare.

As is the case with many Disney resorts, readers give low marks to Art of Animation's bus transportation. This comment from an Ambler, Pennsylvania, family sums it up:

> Art of Animation was incredibly practical for a family of five. Only issues are with transportation, which was AWFUL! We were there during a busy week, but even on slower days, buses were impossible. We ended up driving almost everywhere.

As at Pop Century, the **Skyliner** is the main Disney transportation option from AOA to EPCOT and Disney's Hollywood Studios, and in the morning lines form to get to Hollywood Studios starting around 90 minutes to 2 hours before park opening. (Disney adds bus service to EPCOT and DHS during busy times.) Your best bet is to drive or take a ride-hailing service or taxi to the Studios. Access to the rest of Walt Disney World is on buses.

Noise and soundproofing are likewise issues. A Guyton, Georgia, mom comments:

> The room was very poorly soundproofed. I heard snoring and bathroom noises from other rooms that I should not have been able to hear. One afternoon my toddler and I returned to the room for a nap—I suppose housekeeping was cleaning the room above ours, but it sounded like someone was bowling up there.

GOOD (AND NOT-SO-GOOD) ROOMS AT ART OF ANIMATION *(See* tinyurl .com/animation-roomviews *for photos.)* The quietest suites are south- and east-facing rooms in **buildings 3** (*Cars*), **4** (*Finding Nemo*), and **6** (*The Lion King*). The quietest standard rooms are east-facing rooms in

building 8 and south-facing rooms in **building 7** (both *The Little Mermaid*). Avoid northwest-facing rooms in **building 1** and southwest-facing rooms in **building 10,** which face the Disney bus route and Art of Animation's bus stops.

Star Wars: Galactic Starcruiser *(opens 2022)*

THE GALACTIC STARCRUISER is a live-action role-playing experience that happens to come with a hotel room. In this case, the experience includes two nights in a *Star Wars*–themed hotel, where you interact with characters from that movie series' universe, learn how to wield a lightsaber, and aid the Resistance in their battle against evil.

The best way to think about the Galactic Starcruiser is as a cruise ship that doesn't float. As on cruise ships, everyone checks in to and out of the Starcruiser on the same day, for the same two-day itinerary. Likewise, a daily schedule shows what you'll be doing at any given time, including assigned seating times for meals. One half of one day is spent in Galaxy's Edge, to ride Rise of the Resistance and *Millennium Falcon:* Smugglers Run.

The Galactic Starcruiser will have 100 rooms: 94 standard cabins and 6 suites. Stays will include meals and nonalcoholic beverages, with plenty of upsell options. Rates will start at $4,800 per couple and nearly $6,000 for a family of four.

INDEPENDENT HOTELS OF THE DISNEY SPRINGS RESORT AREA

THE SIX HOTELS of the Disney Springs Resort Area (DSRA) were created back when Disney had far fewer of its own. These hotels—the **B Resort & Spa, DoubleTree Suites by Hilton Orlando–Disney Springs Area,** the **Hilton Orlando Buena Vista Palace,** the **Hilton Orlando Lake Buena Vista,** the **Holiday Inn Orlando–Disney Springs Area,** and the **Wyndham Garden Lake Buena Vista**—are chain affairs with minimal or nonexistent theming, though the Buena Vista Palace is fairly upscale. Several properties have shifted their focus to convention and business travelers. A new **Drury Inn** remains under construction at Disney Springs, with work seeming to be slowed or delayed.

AMENITIES AT THE DSRA RESORTS					
HOTEL	**CHILDREN'S PROGRAMS**	**DINING**	**KID-FRIENDLY**	**POOL(S)**	**RECREATION**
B Resort & Spa	None	★★★½	★★½	★★½	★★★
DoubleTree Suites	None	★★	★★★	★★½	★★½
Hilton Orlando BV Palace	★★★★	★★	★★★½	★★★½	★★★★
Hilton Orlando LBV	None	★★½	★★½	★★★	★★½
Holiday Inn Orlando	★★★	★★	★★	★★★	★★
Wyndham Garden LBV	★★½	★★½	★★★	★★★	★★★

The main advantages to staying in the DSRA are as follows:

- The ability to pay for your stay with hotel rewards points instead of money
- The same Early Theme Park Entry benefits extended to Disney resort guests
- Being within walking distance of Disney Springs

The Wyndham Garden, Buena Vista Palace, and Holiday Inn are an easy 5- to 15-minute walk from the Marketplace, on the east side of

Disney Springs. Guests at B Resort & Spa and DoubleTree Suites are about 10 minutes farther.

Disney transportation can be accessed at Disney Springs, though the bus service is notoriously slow due to the number of stops throughout the resort complex. Although all of the DSRA hotels offer shuttles to the theme parks, the service is provided by private contractors and is somewhat inferior to Disney transportation in frequency of service, number of buses, and hours of operation. A Denver family of five, for example, found that the Hilton Orlando Lake Buena Vista's shuttle service fell short:

> The transportation, provided by Mears, was unreliable. It did a better job of getting guests back to the hotel from the park than getting them to the park from the hotel. Shuttles from the hotel were randomly timed and went repeatedly to the same parks—skipping others and leaving guests to wait for up to an hour.

All of these hotels are easily accessible by car and are only marginally farther from the Disney parks than several of the Disney resorts.

DSRA hotels, even the ones focused on business and convention travelers, try to appeal to families. Some have pool complexes rivaling the ones at the Disney resorts, while others offer a food court or all-suite rooms. A few sponsor character meals and organized kids' activities; all have counters for buying Disney tickets, and most have Disney gift shops. On the downside, the rooms in many hotels are outdated.

unofficial **TIP**
DSRA hotels do *not* have access to Extended Evening Hours, Disney bus transportation, or the Disney Dining Plan.

The Value Proposition

As noted previously, Disney extends some of the same benefits to the DSRA hotels as it does to its own hotels. Those benefits—such as Early Theme Park Entry—add to the DSRA value proposition.

To explore the question of value further, we looked at the cost of rooms at each DSRA hotel, plus Disney's Pop Century and Caribbean Beach Resorts, for weeklong stays June 11–15 and August 13–17, 2022, for a family of two adults and two children. We used every publicly available discount as long as it didn't affect our ability to cancel a reservation. Here's what we found:

Our benchmarks were (1) rates for a standard, 260-square-foot room at **Pop Century:** $938 and $912 for those dates in June and August 2022; and (2) rates for a standard, 314-square-foot room at **Caribbean Beach** for the same dates: $1,358 and $1,373. Prices include all fees and taxes.

At the time of this writing, rates for the 250-square-foot rooms at **B Resort** are $1,085 for stays in both June and August—about $35–$43 per night more expensive than at Pop Century. Along with higher cost, that assumes you're going to take B's free resort shuttle to the parks, and that shuttle service gets very low ratings from readers. If you're going to drive yourself to the parks, add another $25 to park your car at the B and $25 to park at Disney's theme parks per day. Do that and it costs $85–$93 more per night to stay at the B, plus Pop Century is a better resort. What's more, the B Resort doesn't seem to have a widely used rewards program, so most people aren't using points for a stay.

Rates at the **Hilton Orlando Buena Vista Palace** are currently $1,450 ($363 per night) for a 400-square-foot room. That's as big as a Disney Deluxe resort at Moderate prices—but the Buena Vista Palace isn't as nice as a Disney resort. *A Disney Value or Moderate resort is the better choice here.* Similarly, the **Hilton Orlando**'s rates are $1,212 for both sample dates we checked, about $75 per night more expensive than Pop Century. We think Pop is a better choice, even if the Hilton's rooms are slightly larger.

The other three resorts' rooms are larger than Pop Century's, too, ranging from the **Wyndham Garden**'s 312 square feet to 360 square feet at the **Holiday Inn.** At press time, all three resorts' prices were between $610 and $845 for those stays, or up to 35% less than Pop Century's rooms, and about half the cost of a room at Caribbean Beach. As we explained with the B Resort on the previous page, that cost savings between the cheaper DSRA hotels and Pop Century assumes you're going to use the DSRA shuttle service, which is inferior to Disney's bus service, and assumes that you don't have a car. Once you factor in the cost of having a car or the hassle of using DSRA transportation, Pop Century is a better choice than paying cash for almost any DSRA hotel.

All of this said, if you're using a hotel's rewards-program points to pay for your stay, then the resorts with loyalty programs are a good value—you can save anywhere from $610 to $938 versus staying at Pop. That's a lot of money. Also, **DoubleTree**'s 540-square-foot suites' rates cost considerably less than comparably sized Disney suites. If you can pay with points, the DoubleTree is a no-brainer.

Finally, when you're looking at room rates on the DSRA website, note that they don't include nightly self-parking, resort fees, or taxes. These can add $48–$64 per night to the cost of your room, as shown in the following table.

ADDITIONAL FEES AT THE DSRA RESORTS (INCLUDES TAX)				
HOTEL	**SELF-PARKING**	**RESORT FEE**	**INTERNET**	**TOTAL PER DAY**
B Resort & Spa	$23	$32	Free	$55
DoubleTree Suites	$23	$23	Free*	$45
Hilton Orlando BV Palace	$22	$35	Free	$57
Hilton Orlando LBV	$22	$35	Free	$57
Holiday Inn Orlando	$20	$33	Free	$53
Wyndham Garden LBV	$20	$24	Free	$44

*After joining free Hilton Honors program

B Resort & Spa ★★★½

1905 Hotel Plaza Blvd.
☎ 407-828-2828 or
866-759-6832
bhotelsandresorts.com
/b-resort-and-spa

LOCATED WITHIN WALKING DISTANCE of shops and restaurants and situated 5 miles or less from the Disney parks, the 394-room B Resort & Spa targets couples, families, groups, and business travelers.

Decorated in cool blues, whites, and grays, guest rooms and suites afford views of downtown Orlando, area lakes, and theme parks. Along with B Resorts–exclusive Blissful Beds, each room is outfitted with sleek modern furnishings and a large interactive flat-panel TV. Additional touches include a minifridge and gaming consoles (available on request). Some rooms are also equipped with bunk beds, kitchenettes, or wet bars.

We enjoyed our most recent stay at B Resort quite a bit. Our standard room was spotlessly clean, and the room decor is fun without being faddish. The bathroom is spacious, with plenty of storage. The glass shower is well designed and has good water pressure. There's absolutely nothing wrong with this hotel at this price point, except for the terrible traffic you have to endure every night because of Disney Springs. And that's a shame because it's not the hotel's doing. If the B were on the other side of Disney Springs, we'd gladly stay here again.

A mom from Tennessee also likes the B Resort, especially when the rooms are on sale:

The vibe of B Resort was great—like a knockoff of the W, very bright and modern. The restaurant was great, and the zero-entry pool was good. The resort has a more adult feel, but I never felt out of place with my son. I found a deal on Orbitz for around $310 for three nights, with taxes and fees. If choosing between the B and Pop Century for a short stay, I'd take B Resort hands-down.

Amenities include free Wi-Fi, a spa, a beauty salon, and a fitness center. The main restaurant, **American Kitchen,** serves a modern-upscale take on classic comfort food. Guests can also choose from a poolside bar and grill; **The PickUp,** a grab-and-go shop off the lobby that serves breakfasts, snacks, picnic lunches, and ice cream; and in-room dining 6–11 a.m. and 5 p.m.–midnight. (*Note:* Spa and salon services, the poolside bar and grill, and in-room dining are all temporarily unavailable.)

Other perks: a zero-entry pool with interactive water features; a kids' area; loaner iPads for business guests; **Monscierge,** a touchscreen concierge and destination guide in the lobby; and more than 25,000 square feet of meeting and multiuse space. Though it's not served by Disney transportation, B Resort provides bus service to the parks and other Disney venues. A resort fee of $32 per day applies.

DoubleTree Suites by Hilton Orlando–Disney Springs Area ★★★½

THIS GIANT WHITE BUNKER of a hotel is the only all-suite establishment on Disney property. What it lacks in atmosphere and creative attributes, it makes up for in convenience and comfort. Within walking distance of Disney Springs, the 229 suites are spacious for a family, although the decor is startling, with no apparent theme.

2305 Hotel Plaza Blvd.
☎ 407-934-1000
doubletreeguestsuites.com

Amenities include a safe, hair dryer, minifridge, microwave, coffeepot, foldout sofa bed, and two TVs (bedroom and living room).

Children will enjoy a free chocolate-chip cookie and a small playground. The heated pool, children's pool, and whirlpool spa are moderate in size; a minus is that traffic noise from I-4 can be heard faintly from the pool deck. The tiny fitness center, game room, four tennis courts, and outdoor bar are adjacent to the pool. High-speed internet and a business center in the lobby are convenient for those on working holidays. The EverGreen Cafe serves breakfast, lunch, and dinner.

The DoubleTree is the farthest DSRA hotel from Disney Springs—a little over 0.5 mile to the closest entrance and a mile to its center, so figure on a 15- to 20-minute walk each way. If you're headed to the Magic Kingdom, the DoubleTree's bus service may drop you off at the Transportation and Ticket Center instead of the Magic Kingdom bus stop, adding another 10 minutes or so each way to your commute. We recommend budgeting $15 each way for a Lyft or Uber to the Contemporary or Grand Floridian instead.

Hilton Orlando Buena Vista Palace ★★★

1900 E. Buena Vista Dr.
Lake Buena Vista
☎ 407-827-2727
buenavistapalace.com

HILTON BOUGHT THIS PROPERTY in 2016 and has invested substantially in renovating it. That said, you should stay somewhere else. Rates approach $275 per night thanks to a resort fee of $35 and $22 self-parking—that's about the same as a Disney Moderate resort, only this Hilton isn't nearly as nice.

An inspection in mid-2018 had us in a room whose smell can be most charitably described as musty. And while some room features had been upgraded—an all-glass shower with decent water pressure, for example—the hotel's public-facing spaces show signs of wear and neglect (such as room numbers missing from exterior doors).

The resort's key strength is its outdoor recreation: a float lagoon and two heated pools, as well as private cabanas. Two restaurants and a minimarket are on-site.

Hilton Orlando Lake Buena Vista ★★★★

1751 Hotel Plaza Blvd.
☎ 407-827-4000
hilton-wdwv.com

ALTHOUGH THE HILTON'S resort fees are outrageous and the decor is dated, the rooms are clean, comfortable, and nicer overall than those at some other DSRA hotels. On-site dining includes **Benihana,** part of the Japanese steakhouse-sushi chain, as well as a grab-and-go market and a poolside café. The Disney-character breakfast held here on Sundays pre-COVID remains temporarily suspended. The two heated pools are matched with a kids' spray pool. A fitness center and game room are on-site, as is a 24-hour market. There are no organized kids' programs.

Starting rates at the Hilton can exceed $380 per night—within a few dollars of the top rate at a Disney Moderate. If you're paying cash,,we think the Moderates are a better option.

Holiday Inn Orlando–Disney Springs Resort Area ★★★½

1805 Hotel Plaza Blvd.
☎ 407-828-8888 or
888-465-4329
hiorlando.com

LAST RENOVATED IN 2018, the Holiday Inn's rooms are clean and comfortable. The rest of the hotel looks like any midpriced hotel anywhere in the country, with tower rooms grouped around an atrium and wing rooms overlooking the pool. Disney Springs is a short walk away.

The totally upgraded 360-square-foot rooms feature pillow-top beds with triple sheeting and firm or soft pillows. Each room has a 49- or 55-inch flat-panel HDTV and free high-speed internet. The bathrooms are clean and well designed, the nicest in any DSRA resort; amenities include granite countertops and showerheads with a choice of comfort sprays.

Palm Breezes Restaurant serves breakfast and dinner at reasonable prices; the restaurant service remains temporarily suspended, so the lounge currently offers an à la carte breakfast. The grab-and-go in the lobby sells quick snacks and sandwiches. Other amenities include a large and well-kept zero-entry pool, along with a whirlpool spa in the pool area. A separate entrance brings you into the convention center, ballroom, and meeting room areas, with a business center nearby.

If Disney's Value hotels are sold out, the Holiday Inn is worth considering.

Wyndham Garden Lake Buena Vista ★★★½

1850-B Hotel Plaza Blvd.
☎ 407-842-6644
wyndhamlakebuena
vista.com

THE MAIN REASON TO STAY at the Wyndham Garden is the short walk to Disney Springs. The lobby is bright and airy, and check-in service is friendly. Rooms are larger than most and have in-room refrigerators. Pool-facing rooms in the hotel's wings have exterior hallways that overlook the pool and center courtyard; these hallways can be noisy during summer. Elevators are unusually slow—it's probably faster to walk to the second and third floors, assuming you're up for the exercise.

The Wyndham Garden's pool and room soundproofing have gotten good marks in our reader surveys over the last three years, but only 71% of readers say they'd stay at this Wyndham again, and just 67% would recommend it to a friend. That's worse than all Disney resorts except Caribbean Beach. As with most off-site resorts, transportation and quick-service dining options score low. Also, readers rate staff service at the Wyndham Garden lower than that at any resort, Disney-owned or not, in Walt Disney World.

CAMPING AT WALT DISNEY WORLD

DISNEY'S FORT WILDERNESS RESORT & CAMPGROUND is a spacious area for tent and RV camping. Fully equipped, air-conditioned prefabricated log cabins are also available for rent.

Tent/Pop-Up campsites provide water, electricity, and cable TV and run $89–$179 a night depending on season. **Full Hook-Up** campsites have all of the amenities above, accommodate large RVs, and run $118–$219 per night. **Preferred Hook-Up** campsites for tents and RVs add sewer connections and run $126–$242 per night. **Premium** campsites add an extra-large concrete parking pad and run $137–$250 a night. Disney says all campsites accommodate up to 10 people. Free parking for one vehicle is included in the nightly rate.

Sites are level and provide picnic tables, waste containers, grills, and free Wi-Fi. Fires are prohibited except in grills. Pets are permitted in some loops for a $5 fee per night but aren't allowed in tents or pop-up trailers.

Campsites are arranged on loops accessible from one of three main roads. There are 28 loops, with loops **100–2100** for tent and RV campers and loops **2200–2800** offering cabins at $414–$789 per night. The RV sites are roomy by eastern-US standards, with the Premium and Full Hook-Up campsites able to accommodate RVs more than 45 feet long, but tent campers will probably feel a bit cramped. (Note that tent stakes cannot be put into the concrete at the Premium sites.) On any given day, 90% or more of campers are RVers.

Fort Wilderness offers arguably the widest variety of recreational facilities and activities of any Disney resort. Among them are two video arcades; nightly campfire programs; Disney movies; a dinner theater (temporarily closed); two swimming pools; a beach; walking paths; bike, boat, canoe, golf-cart, and kayak rentals; horseback riding; wagon rides; and tennis, basketball, and volleyball courts. There are multiple dining options, including a full-service restaurant, a food truck, and a tavern. Comfort stations with toilets, showers, pay phones, ice machine, and laundry facilities are within walking distance of all campsites.

If you're in the mood to walk, a path near **Pioneer Hall** leads to the Wilderness Lodge area. This flat, paved walkway is about 0.75 mile long and is a great place to see deer and other woodland creatures. It also provides easy access to the restaurants at Wilderness Lodge.

Access to the Magic Kingdom is by boat from Fort Wilderness Landing and to EPCOT by bus, with a transfer at the Transportation and

Ticket Center (TTC) to the EPCOT monorail. Boat service may be suspended during thunderstorms, in which case Disney will provide buses. An alternative route to the Magic Kingdom is by internal bus to the TTC, then by monorail or ferry to the park. Transportation to all other Disney destinations is by bus. Motor traffic within the campground is permitted only when entering or exiting. Get around within the campground by bus, golf cart, or bike, the latter two available for rent.

For tent and RV campers, there's a fairly stark trade-off between sites convenient to pools, restaurants, trading posts, and other amenities and those that are scenic, shady, and quiet. RVers who prefer to be near guest services, the marina, the beach, and the restaurant and tavern should go for loops **100, 200, 700,** and **400** (in that order); note, however, that loops 100 and 400 are nearest ongoing hotel construction (see below). Loops near the campground's secondary facility area with pool, trading post, bike and golf-cart rentals, and campfire program are **1400, 1300, 600, 1000,** and **1500,** in order of preference.

If you're looking for a tranquil, scenic setting among mature trees, we recommend loops **1800, 1900, 1700,** and **1600,** in that order, and the west-side sites on the **700** loop. The best loop of all—and the only one to offer both a lovely setting and proximity to key amenities—is **300.** The best loops for tents and pop-up campers are **1500** and **2000,** with 1500 being nearest a swimming pool, a convenience store, and the campfire program.

With the exception of loops **1800** and **1900,** avoid sites within 40 yards of the loop entrance—these are almost always flanked by one of the main traffic arteries within Fort Wilderness. Further, sites on the outside of the loop are almost always preferable to those in the center. RVers should note that all sites are back-ins and that the loop access roads are pretty tight and narrow.

Before the pandemic, Disney had started building a 900-room hotel called **Reflections—A Disney Lakeside Lodge** in the northwest section of Fort Wilderness, just west of Tri-Circle-D Ranch on the site of the old River Country water park. Construction appears to be paused, but it could restart at any time. That construction may affect access to the exercise trail, and daytime construction activity may be heard in loops 100, 400, 700, and 800.

Fort Wilderness Cabins

RENTAL CABINS OFFER a queen bed and bunk bed in the only bedroom, augmented by a pullout sofa bed in the living room. There's one small bathroom with shower and tub.

These prefab log cabins (classified as Disney Moderate resorts) are warm and homey, but the stem-to-stern interior wood paneling and smallish windows make for rather dark accommodations at night. If construction is happening in the northwest part of Fort Wilderness, the noise shouldn't reach the cabin loops.

All cabins have air-conditioning, TVs, fully equipped kitchens, and dining tables. Housekeeping is provided every other day.

Most readers are crazy about the cabins, giving them A ratings for room quality, check-in efficiency, quietness, and staff. The cabins tied for the No. 1 spot among Disney Moderate resorts for positive

FORT WILDERNESS RESORT & CAMPGROUND

STRENGTHS	WEAKNESSES
• Informality	• Isolated location
• Children's play areas	• Complicated bus service
• Best recreational options at WDW	• Confusing campground layout
• Special day and evening programs	• Lack of privacy
• Campsite amenities	• Very limited on-site dining options
• Shower and toilet facilities	• Crowding at beaches and pools
• *Hoop-Dee-Doo Musical Revue* show (temporarily suspended)	• Small baths in cabins
• Convenient self-parking	• Extreme distance to store and restaurant facilities from many cabins and campsites
• Off-site dining via boat at the Magic Kingdom	

Unofficial Guide Reader-Survey Results (Cabins/Campsites)

Percentage of readers who'd stay here again 89%/90% (*Average*)	
Percentage of readers who'd recommend this resort to a friend 91%/87% (*Average*)	
Overall reader rating B/B–	

responses to the survey question "Would you recommend this resort to a friend?" (Port Orleans–French Quarter was the other.)

A Wappingers Falls, New York, family writes:

We stayed at Fort Wilderness in a cabin because (1) we wanted a separate bedroom area; (2) we wanted a kitchen; (3) our kids are very lively, and the cabins were apart from each other so we wouldn't disturb other guests; and (4) we thought the kids might meet other children to play with. The cabins worked out just right for us. The kids had a ball chasing the little lizards and frogs, kicking around pinecones, sitting on the deck to eat ice pops, and sleeping in bunk beds.

A mother of two from Albuquerque, New Mexico, offers this:

We stayed in a cabin and liked having all the space and the full kitchen. However, the pool nearest our cabin (a quarter mile away!) never even had a lifeguard. I had hoped to be able to send the kids to swim when we needed some time to ourselves, but with the distance and lack of lifeguards, there was no way to do that.

A mother of two from Mechanicsville, Virginia, puts Fort Wilderness on a pedestal:

This is the only resort where you're encouraged to go outside and play! You can bike, swim, hike the nature trail, ride a horse, rent a boat, play volleyball, go to the beach, attend a character sing-along and marshmallow roast followed by a classic Disney movie, enjoy multiple playgrounds, play tennis, take a romantic carriage ride, take your first pony ride, and see a wild turkey. Don't forget the view of the fireworks from the beach or the up-close water light parade. With all of this stuff, much of it free or very affordable, who needs the parks?

Bus service at Fort Wilderness leaves a lot to be desired—so much so, in fact, that we wouldn't stay there unless we had our own car. To go anywhere, you first have to catch an internal bus that makes many, many stops. If your destination is outside Fort Wilderness, you then must transfer to a second bus. To complicate things, buses serving

Fort Wilderness Resort & Campground

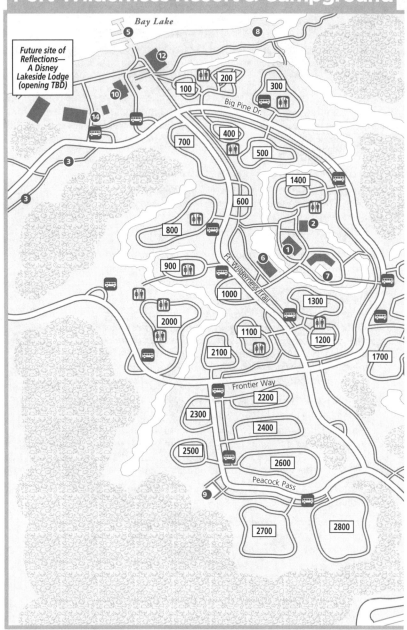

destinations outside the campground depart from two locations, the **Reception Outpost** and **Pioneer Hall.** This means you must keep track of which destinations each transfer center serves.

A Washington, D.C., family of five writes:

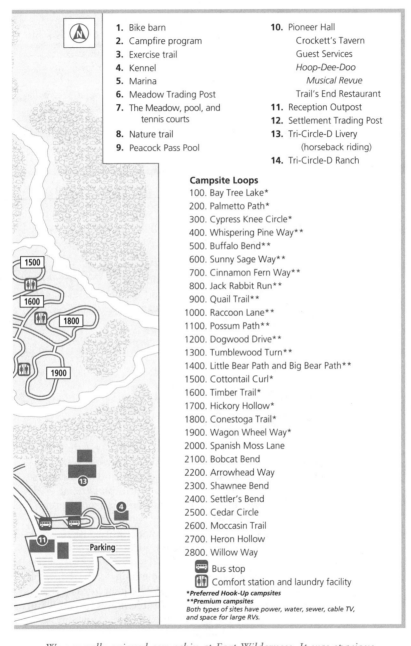

1. Bike barn
2. Campfire program
3. Exercise trail
4. Kennel
5. Marina
6. Meadow Trading Post
7. The Meadow, pool, and tennis courts
8. Nature trail
9. Peacock Pass Pool
10. Pioneer Hall
    Crockett's Tavern
    Guest Services
    Hoop-Dee-Doo
    Musical Revue
    Trail's End Restaurant
11. Reception Outpost
12. Settlement Trading Post
13. Tri-Circle-D Livery (horseback riding)
14. Tri-Circle-D Ranch

Campsite Loops
100. Bay Tree Lake*
200. Palmetto Path*
300. Cypress Knee Circle*
400. Whispering Pine Way**
500. Buffalo Bend**
600. Sunny Sage Way**
700. Cinnamon Fern Way**
800. Jack Rabbit Run**
900. Quail Trail**
1000. Raccoon Lane**
1100. Possum Path**
1200. Dogwood Drive**
1300. Tumblewood Turn**
1400. Little Bear Path and Big Bear Path**
1500. Cottontail Curl*
1600. Timber Trail*
1700. Hickory Hollow*
1800. Conestoga Trail*
1900. Wagon Wheel Way*
2000. Spanish Moss Lane
2100. Bobcat Bend
2200. Arrowhead Way
2300. Shawnee Bend
2400. Settler's Bend
2500. Cedar Circle
2600. Moccasin Trail
2700. Heron Hollow
2800. Willow Way

Bus stop
Comfort station and laundry facility

Preferred Hook-Up campsites
Premium campsites
Both types of sites have power, water, sewer, cable TV, and space for large RVs.

We generally enjoyed our cabin at Fort Wilderness. It was spacious, with bunk beds for the kids, a separate room for the parents to sleep, and a kitchen. We were very surprised and disappointed, though, when we figured out that we couldn't get anywhere in the resort in a timely fashion without either bikes or a golf cart—otherwise, you spend your day waiting for buses. A quick trip to the pool or the counter-service diner was impossible.

A reader from Minneapolis found that feeding her crew was a bit of a challenge:

The cabins are beautiful and quiet, but you really need to bring your own food. To get to the restaurants, it was over a mile on the bus, not to mention the choices were limited: The buffet looked pretty good but cost $32 per person, while the takeout place had just a few unhealthy options and nowhere to sit except outside. We were hoping the store would have something, but that was very limited as well— honestly, you'd have better luck at a gas station.

An Augusta, Georgia, family has this transportation tip:

Regular boat service to the Magic Kingdom from Fort Wilderness doesn't start until 30 minutes before park opening. We chose to ride a boat to the Contemporary and walk to the Magic Kingdom so we could get there earlier. (A boat captain did tell us that they send one boat at 7 a.m. to get people to the MK for early dining reservations.)

If you rent a cabin or camp in a tent or RV, particularly in fall or spring, keep abreast of local weather conditions.

A number of independent campgrounds and RV parks are convenient to Walt Disney World. See **Camp Florida** (campflorida.com/regions /central-florida) for listings.

HOW *to* EVALUATE *a* WALT DISNEY WORLD TRAVEL PACKAGE

HUNDREDS OF WALT DISNEY WORLD package vacations are offered each year. Some are created by the Walt Disney Travel Company, others by airlines, independent travel agents, and wholesalers. Almost all include lodging at or near Disney World plus theme park admissions. Packages offered by airlines include air transportation.

Prices vary seasonally; mid-March–Easter, summer, and holiday periods are the most expensive. Off-season, you can negotiate great discounts, especially at non-Disney properties. Airfares and car rentals are cheaper off-peak too.

Almost all package ads are headlined something to the effect of "5 Days at Walt Disney World from $645." The key word is *from:* The rock-bottom price includes the least desirable hotels; if you want better or more-convenient digs, you'll pay more—often much more.

Packages offer a wide selection of hotels. Some, like the Disney resorts, are very dependable. Others run the gamut of quality. Checking two or three independent sources is best. Also, before you book, ask how old the hotel is and when the guest rooms were last refurbished. Locate the hotel on a map to verify its proximity to Disney

World. If you won't be driving a car, make sure the hotel has adequate shuttle service.

Packages with non-Disney lodging are much less expensive. But guests at Disney-owned properties (and several third-party hotels that operate inside Disney World's boundaries) get free parking and extra time at the parks and access to Disney transportation. See page 85 for a list of which benefits Disney extends to third-party hotels.

Packages should be a win–win proposition for both the buyer and the seller. The buyer makes just one phone call and deals with one sales-person to set up the whole vacation. The seller, likewise, deals with the buyer only once.

Because selling packages is efficient and the packager often can buy package components in bulk at discount, the seller's savings in operating expenses are sometimes passed on to the buyer. In practice, however, the seller may not pass on those savings: Packages are sometimes loaded with extras that cost the packager almost nothing but run the package's price sky-high.

Choose a package that includes features you're sure to use—you'll pay for all of them whether you use them or not. If price is more important than convenience, call around to see what the package would cost if you booked its components on your own. If the package price is less than the à la carte cost, the package is a good deal. If costs are about equal, the package probably is worth it for the convenience. Much of the time, however, you'll find you save significantly by buying the components individually.

CUT TO THE CHASE

IT'S MUCH FASTER TO BOOK A DISNEY RESORT ROOM online than it is to call Disney reservations (☎ 407-W-DISNEY [934-7639]). If you call, you'll be subjected to a minute or so of recordings covering recent park announcements—press 0 to skip this. Next you'll go through about 5–10 minutes of answering more than a dozen recorded questions, asking you everything from your name and home address to the salutation you prefer. Slog on through, though, if you actually want to make a reservation. (When the question "How many times have you been to Walt Disney World?" pops up, answering "zero" may route you to an additional survey for "first-timers.") Unfortunately, there doesn't seem to be a way to bypass these questions by pressing 0.

WALT DISNEY TRAVEL COMPANY PACKAGES

DISNEY'S TRAVEL-PACKAGE PROGRAM mirrors the admission-ticket program. Here's how it works: You begin with a base package room and tickets. Tickets can be customized to match the number of days you intend to tour the theme parks and range in length from 2 to 10 days. (*Note:* the 1-Day Base Ticket isn't eligible for packages.) As with theme park admissions, the package program offers strong financial incentives to book a longer stay. "The longer you play, the less you pay per day," is the way Disney puts it, borrowing a page from Sam Walton's concept of the universe. An adult 1-Day Base Ticket (including tax) costs $116–$169,

continued on page 206

DISNEY LODGING FOR LESS

Sarah Stone, *webmaster for* **MouseSavers** *(mousesavers.com; see pages 33 and 93), might know more about Disney hotel packages than anyone on the planet. Here are her money-saving suggestions.*

- **BOOK ROOM-ONLY.** It's frequently a better deal to book a room-only reservation instead of buying a vacation package. Disney likes to sell vacation packages because they're easy and profitable. When you buy a package, you're typically paying a premium for the convenience, but you can often save money by putting together your own package. It's not hard—just book room-only at a resort and buy your passes, meals, and extras separately.

  Disney doesn't break down the individual prices of the components of its packages, but direct comparison shows that Disney prices these components the same as if you'd purchased them separately at full price, plus a small extra "package fee." What Disney doesn't tell you, though, is that these components can often be purchased separately at a discount—and those discounts aren't always reflected in the prices of Disney's package. (Sometimes Disney does offer package-only discounts, but those are relatively rare, with the exception of Free Dining—see the next page.)

  Disney's packages often include coupons and sometimes small bits of merchandise like luggage tags, but the cash value of those extras is minimal. Also, packages require a $200 deposit and full payment 30 days in advance, and they have stringent change and cancellation policies. In contrast, booking room-only requires a deposit of one night's room rate with the remainder due at check-in. Your reservation can be changed or canceled for any reason until six days before check-in.

- **USE DISNEY'S DISCOUNTS TO REDUCE YOUR ROOM-ONLY OR PACKAGE RATE.** Disney uses discount programs to push unsold rooms at certain times of year and occasionally offers packages that include resort discounts or value-added features. Check a website like MouseSavers to learn about discounts that may be available for your vacation dates. Some discounts are available to anyone, while others are just for Florida residents, Annual Pass holders, and so on.

  Discounts aren't always available from Disney for every hotel or every date, and they typically don't appear until two to six months in advance. The good news is that you can usually apply a discount to an existing reservation. Just call the Disney Reservation Center at ☎ 407-W-DISNEY (934-7639) or contact a Disney-savvy travel agent, and ask whether any rooms are available at your preferred hotel for your preferred dates using the discount.

  In addition, other travel sellers sometimes tack on an additional discount on top of Disney's or offer a small discount on rooms that Disney doesn't typically discount. These discounts vary constantly, but you can check Mouse Savers for the latest ways to score additional stackable discounts.

- **BE FLEXIBLE.** Finding a discount on a room or package is a little like shopping for clothes at a discount store: If you wear a size extra-small or extra-large, or you like green when everyone else is wearing pink, you're a lot more likely to score a bargain. Likewise, resort discounts are available only when Disney has excess rooms to fill. You're more likely to get a discount during less popular times (such as value season) and at larger or less popular resorts—Animal Kingdom Lodge and Old Key West Resort, for instance, seem to have discounted rooms available more often than the other Disney resorts do. On the other hand, really popular resorts and room types, like the *Little Mermaid* rooms at Art of Animation and the Royal Rooms at Port Orleans Riverside, are often excluded from discounts because Disney can fill them at full price.

- **BE PERSISTENT.** This is the most important tip. Disney allots a certain number of rooms to each discount. Once the discounted rooms are gone, you won't get that rate unless someone cancels. Fortunately, people change and cancel reservations all the time. If you can't get your preferred dates or hotel with one discount, try another one (if available) or keep checking back first thing in the morning to check for cancellations—the system resets overnight, and any reservations with unpaid deposits are automatically released for resale.

- **KEEP AN EYE OUT FOR FREE DINING.** One of Disney's most popular package bargains, the Free Dining promotion has been offered since 2005 during less-busy times of year. When you purchase a full-price room and full-price tickets for each person in the room, you get a Disney Dining Plan for your entire stay. The trick is choosing one of Disney's cheapest rooms and enjoying all that free food.

  If you choose a Value resort, you get the Quick Service Dining Plan; if you choose a Deluxe resort, you get the standard plan. The plan included with a Moderate resort varies from year to year depending on how many rooms Disney has to fill. You can always pay the difference to upgrade, say, from Quick Service to a standard plan or from standard to Deluxe, but you don't get a discount on the upgrade charge.

  Free Dining is usually offered September–November (a slow time due to heat, humidity, hurricane season, and kids going back to school), with blackouts for holidays; sometimes it's also offered in late August, early December, or other times during the year.

  Some years Disney has offered a similar discount, usually called **Stay, Play & Dine,** which requires buying a full package with a dining plan. As with other package discounts, Disney doesn't tell you which components it's discounting, but our analysis shows that Stay, Play & Dine is primarily a discount on the dining plan (usually 40%–60% off) combined with an otherwise-full-price hotel room and tickets. Sometimes there is also a very small discount on the hotel rate for some room types. This discount has typically been offered in February–May, with blackouts for holidays and spring-break season.

  Of course, Free Dining isn't really free—you still have to pay full price for your tickets and your room(s), and you could possibly get a better deal by taking advantage of other discounts. For example, where a family of three or four staying in a Value resort will usually find Free Dining to be the best deal available, a couple staying in a Deluxe resort will often do better with a hotel discount instead. *Bottom line:* Check out a variety of discount options to make sure you're getting the best deal.

  Finally, if you're not a fan of the regimented nature of Disney's dining plans, Free Dining may not hold much appeal, so consider how much it's worth to have the freedom to eat the way you want.

NOTE: *At the time of this writing, dining plans are still suspended at Walt Disney World, and obviously Free Dining and other packages with dining discounts aren't going to be offered until the plans return. We feel confident that dining plans will, in fact, return; they're far too popular for Disney to eliminate. And the Free Dining discount is similarly exceptionally popular— the lure of "free" food is strong. Disney has offered it so far every year except 2020 and 2021 (when dining plans weren't being offered).*

continued from page 203

depending on the day of your visit, whereas if you buy a 7-Day Base Ticket, the average cost per day drops to $70–$95 depending on the days you visit. You can purchase options to add on to your Base Tickets, such as hopping between theme parks or visiting the water parks or ESPN Wide World of Sports. (See page 70 for more details on ticket pricing.)

With Disney travel packages, you can avoid paying for features that you don't intend to use—you need not purchase a package with theme park tickets for the entire length of your stay. Rather, you can choose to purchase as many days of admission as you intend to use. On a one-week vacation, for example, you might want to spend only five days in the Disney parks, saving one day each for Universal Orlando and SeaWorld. (That is, even if your Disney hotel stay is seven days, you can buy admission tickets lasting anywhere from 2 to 10 days; the ticket length doesn't need to match your hotel stay length.) Likewise, if you don't normally park-hop, you can purchase multiday admissions that don't include the Park Hopper feature. Best of all, you can buy the various add-ons at any time during your vacation.

Before we inundate you with a boxcar of options and add-ons, let's begin by defining the basic components of a Disney travel package:

- One or more nights of accommodations at your choice of any Disney resort. Rates vary with lodging choice: The Grand Floridian is usually the most expensive, and the All-Star, Pop Century, and Art of Animation Resorts are the least expensive.
- Base Ticket for the number of days you tour the theme parks (must be at least 2-Day Base Tickets for travel packages)
- Unlimited use of the Disney transportation system
- Free day parking at the theme parks
- Official Walt Disney Travel Company luggage tag (one per person)

Disney Dining Plans

Note: *Dining plans were unavailable at press time, but Disney has said they'll return, probably in 2022. Prices and other information in the following section are from 2020, the last time the plans were offered. In the meantime, Disney has offered the UK market a set of dining credits worth $36–$68 per person, per day, for select dates in 2022. That might be a model for the US as well, because it provides more flexibility when choosing dining venues.*

Disney offers dining plans to accompany its ticket and travel-package programs. They're available to all Disney resort guests *except* those staying at the Swan, the Dolphin, the Swan Reserve, the hotels of the Disney Springs Resort Area, and Shades of Green. Guests must also purchase a travel package from Disney or an authorized Disney travel agent (not through an online reseller), have Annual Passes, or be members of the Disney Vacation Club (DVC) to participate in the plan. Except for DVC members, a three-night minimum stay is typically also required. Overall cost is determined by the number of nights you stay at a Disney resort.

You must purchase a Disney package vacation to be eligible for a dining plan, as a family of five from Waldron, Michigan, found out the hard way:

> We read through the Unofficial Guide *and saw that it said not to book a package during slow season. We were overwhelmed with the*

decisions that we had to make, so we booked the resort first and then the tickets. Then we wanted the dining plan, but they wouldn't add it because we had already booked everything separately.

DISNEY DINING PLAN Disney offers three dining plans. We'll cover the standard Disney Dining Plan first, and then explain the two variations.

The standard plan provides, for each member of your group (age 3 and up), for each night of your stay, one counter-service meal, one full-service meal, and two snacks at participating Disney dining locations and restaurants, including room service at some Disney resorts (type "Disney Dining Plan Locations" into your favorite search engine to find sites with the entire list).

The plan also includes one refillable drink mug per person, per package, but it can be filled only at Disney-resort counter-service restaurants. For guests age 10 and up, the price for 2020 was $78, tax included; for guests ages 3–9, the price was $30.50 per night, tax included. Children younger than age 3 eat free from an adult's plate.

For instance, if you're staying for three nights, you'll be credited with three counter-service meals, three full-service meals, and six snacks for each member of your party. All of these meals are placed in a group account. The meals in your account can be used by anyone in your group, on any combination of days, so you're not required to eat every meal every day. This means that, for example, that you can skip a full-service meal one day and have two on another day.

The counter-service meal includes

- An entrée (a sandwich, dinner salad, pizza, or the like) or a complete combo meal (such as a burger and fries) plus drink; breakfast is typically a combo platter with eggs, bacon or sausage, potatoes, a biscuit, and a drink

The full-service sit-down meals include

- An entrée or a complete combo meal, plus drink
- A dessert (except breakfast)

If you're dining at a buffet, the full-service meal includes the food and beverages. Tax is included in the dining plan, but tips are not. Beverage choices include soda, coffee, or tea; one milkshake, smoothie, or specialty hot chocolate; or, for guests age 21 and older, one beer, glass of wine, or cocktail from a predetermined list.

A snack can be any of several single-serving items such as a pretzel or bottle of water. They are often specifically marked as Dining Plan snacks on menus and may include the following:

- A frozen ice-cream novelty, ice pop, or fruit bar
- A scoop of popcorn
- A 12-ounce coffee, hot chocolate, or hot tea
- A prepackaged container of milk or juice
- A piece of whole fruit
- A bag of snacks
- A 20-ounce bottle of Coca-Cola, Sprite, or Dasani water
- A 20-ounce fountain soft drink

Disney's top-of-the-line restaurants (aka **Disney Signature Restaurants**), along with **Cinderella's Royal Table,** the **dinner shows,** regular **room service,** and **in-room pizza delivery,** count as two full-service meals on the standard dining plan.

In addition to the preceding, the following rules apply:

- Everyone staying in the same resort room must participate in the Disney Dining Plan.
- Children ages 3–9 must order from the kids' menu, if available. This rule is occasionally relaxed at Disney's counter-service restaurants, enabling older kids to order from the adult (age 10+) menu.
- Alcoholic and specialty beverages are included in the plan.
- A full-service meal can be breakfast, lunch, or dinner. The greatest savings occur when you use your full-service-meal credits for dinner.
- The dining plan expires at midnight **on the day you check out** of your Disney resort. **Unused meals are nonrefundable.**
- Neither the Disney Dining Plan nor Disney's Free Dining promotion (see page 205) can be added to a discounted room-only reservation.

QUICK-SERVICE DINING PLAN This plan includes meals, snacks, and drinks at most counter-service eateries and outdoor carts in Walt Disney World. The cost (including tax) is $55.01 per day for guests age 10 and up, $26 per day for kids ages 3–9. The plan includes two counter-service meals and two snacks per day, in addition to one refillable drink mug per person, per package (eligible for refills only at counter-service locations in your Disney resort).

DISNEY DINING PLAN PLUS This plan offers a choice of two full- or counter-service meals per day at any participating restaurant. It also includes two snacks per day and a refillable drink mug. The Plus Plan costs $94.60 for adults and children age 10 and up and $35 for children ages 3–9 for each night of your stay (prices include tax).

DISNEY DELUXE DINING PLAN This plan offers a choice of full- or counter-service meals for three meals a day at any participating restaurant. In addition to the three meals a day, the plan also includes two snacks per day and a refillable drink mug. The Deluxe Plan costs $119 for adults and children age 10 and up and $47.50 for children ages 3–9 for each night of your stay (prices include tax).

Not only does the Deluxe Dining Plan cost a lot of money, it costs a lot of time, as a dad from Hudson Falls, New York, explains:

> The Deluxe Dining Plan gave us a chance to try new restaurants, but it felt like most of our trip revolved around food: get to the restaurant, wait to be seated, order drinks, wait, get drinks, wait, order meals, wait, get meals, wait, order dessert, wait, get dessert, wait, get the check, wait, give the waitstaff your room card, wait, figure out the tip, and wait. We lost 4½–6 hours a day just on eating, plus the travel time.

In addition to dining plans, the vacation packages include sweeteners, such as a free round of miniature golf and discounts on spa treatments, salon services, and recreational activities like water sports.

Disney ceaselessly tinkers with the dining plans' rules, meal definitions, and participating restaurants. Here are some recent examples:

- You can exchange a sit-down meal credit for a counter-service meal, though doing this even once can negate any savings you get from using a plan in the first place.
- At sit-down restaurants, you can substitute dessert for a side salad, cup of soup, or fruit plate.
- You may exchange one sit-down or counter-service meal credit for three snacks at a counter-service location, as long as you do so within the same transaction. Exchanging a sit-down credit for three snacks is not a good deal.

- Some counter-service restaurants don't differentiate between adult and child meal credits. If you have two adult credits and two child credits on your account, you may purchase four adult counter-service meals with the credits.

Finally, you can usually use your credits to pay for the meals of people who aren't on *any* dining plan. We've heard of sporadic instances of Disney not allowing this, but we think they're instances of confusion about what the dining-plan rules actually say: The rules say that meals can't be transferred, but they say nothing about meals being *shared*— as if that could even be enforced.

To ensure that everybody knows the rules, it might help to carry a printout of them with you—see disneyworld.disney.go.com/guest -services/disney-dining-plan. As long as someone enrolled in the dining plan tells the server in advance that he or she plans to redeem the appropriate number of credits and then orders the meals for the diners who aren't enrolled, everything should be on the up and up. Should a server or manager tell you that the rules prohibit meal sharing, just point out that your copy of the rules doesn't say that.

THINGS TO CONSIDER WHEN EVALUATING THE DISNEY DINING PLAN
About 9 out of 10 readers who've used the Disney Dining Plan would do so again, according to our reader surveys. The plan has been one of the most requested of Disney's package add-ons since its introduction; families report that their favorite aspect is the peace of mind that comes from knowing their meals are paid for ahead of time, rather than having to keep track of a budget while they're in the parks. Families also enjoy the communal aspect of sitting down together for a full meal, without having to worry about who's picking up the food or doing the dishes.

Costwise, however, it's difficult for many families to justify using the plan. If you prefer to always eat at counter-service restaurants, you'll be better off with the Quick Service Plan. You should also avoid the Disney Dining Plan if you have finicky eaters, you're visiting during holidays or summer, or you can't get reservations at your first- or second-choice sit-down restaurants. In addition, if you have children age 10 and up, be sure they can eat an adult-size dinner at a sit-down restaurant every night; if not, you'd probably come out ahead just paying for everyone's meals without the plan.

If you opt for the plan, skipping one full-service meal during a visit of five or fewer days can mean the difference between saving and losing money. In our experience, having a scheduled sit-down meal for every day of a weeklong vacation can be mentally exhausting, especially for kids. One option might be to schedule a meal at a Disney Signature Restaurant, which requires two full-service credits, and have no scheduled sit-down meal on another night in the middle of your trip, allowing everyone to decide on the spot if they're up for something formal.

As already noted, many of the most popular restaurants are fully booked as soon as their reservation windows open. If you're still interested in the Disney Dining Plan, book your restaurants as soon as possible, typically 60 days before you visit. Then decide whether the plan makes economic sense. For more on Advance Reservations, see Part Six.

If you're making reservations to eat at Disney hotels other than your own, having a car allows you to easily access all the participating restaurants. When you use the Disney transportation system, dining at the various resorts can be a logistical nightmare. Those without a car may want to weigh the immediate services of a taxi or ride-hailing service—typically $16–$33 each way across Disney property, versus a 50- to 75-minute trip on Disney transportation each way.

When Disney offers **Free Dining** discounts, typically in September but earlier in 2019, it generally charges rack rate for the hotel. (*Note:* Free Dining was unavailable in 2021; see page 205.) Room-only discounts are often available at these times, too, meaning you should work out the math to see which discount works best for you. For an example of how to do this, see tinyurl.com/ug-freedining.

In most cases we examined, Free Dining was a better deal for families of two adults and up to two kids under age 10 staying at a Value or Moderate resort. The break-even point at a Deluxe resort depended on whether the kids ate like adults. An option instead of doing this math yourself is to have a travel agent do it for you.

Readers who have tried the Disney Dining Plan had varying experiences, but frustration seems to be a common refrain. A New Hampshire family comments:

> *Dining plans are NOT for us. Keeping track of the meals, figuring out what you can and can't buy, and rushing around on the last day trying to use up what's left is just too stressful. We'd rather just buy what we want, when and where we want it.*

A reader from The Woodlands, Texas, laments that the plan has altered the focus of her vacation:

> *I want to have fun. I don't want to be locked into a tight schedule, always worrying about where we need to be when it's time to eat. And I don't want to eat when I'm not hungry just because I have a reservation somewhere.*

On the upside, here's what a Tennessee mother of a 3-year-old has to say:

> *We LOVED the dining plan. It was wonderful to not have to stress every day about trying to keep up with a budget for food. The plan turned out to be a fantastic deal for us, especially because we did four character meals that would have cost at least $400 otherwise.*

A dad from Belmont, Massachusetts, is a fan of the Quick Service Dining Plan:

> *If you'll be eating Disney food, the counter-service plan is a good option. You get two counter-service meals and two snacks per person, per day, and even though kids' meals are cheaper, there's no distinction when you order—kids can order [more-expensive] adult meals.*

But a mom from Orland Park, Illinois, comments on the difficulty of getting Advance Reservations:

> *It's next to impossible to get table reservations anywhere good. I don't enjoy planning my day exclusively around eating at a certain restaurant at a certain time—but that is what you must do months in advance if you want to eat at a good sit-down restaurant in Disney.*

Echoing the mom above is a reader from San José, California, who *wasn't* on the dining plan:

I was told that most of the sit-down restaurants don't even take walk-ins anymore. Sure enough, even though my vacation was still a ways away, a lot of my restaurant choices were unavailable. I had to rearrange my entire schedule to fit the open slots at the restaurants I didn't want to miss.

To the two readers above we say, "Where there's a will—and internet access—there's a way!" For more information, see pages 275–276 in Part Six.

Many readers report that Disney cast members are more knowledgeable about the dining plan than they used to be, but a mom from Texarkana, Arkansas, begs to differ:

We had a 2-year-old, who was supposed to be able to eat free, plus a 5-year-old and four adults. Some restaurants would let me order my 2-year-old a free kids' meal, but others would not. Either the staff is completely confused about the dining plan or the inconsistencies are on purpose. Either way, it made the dining part of our trip very frustrating!

The addition of alcohol to the Dining Plan has precipitated some (*hic*) confusion, as a Carp, Ontario, family relates:

At some places, we were entitled to an alcoholic beverage AND a dessert, and at some places it was either/or. At still other places, we were entitled to neither an alcoholic beverage NOR a dessert because they didn't start serving alcohol till later in the day. Even the servers didn't seem to know what was included. Our hostess at 'Ohana told me I couldn't have a cocktail with dinner, but our server said I could.

A Land O' Lakes, Florida, dad bumped into this problem:

We had some trouble with our Deluxe Dining Plan being invalidated after checkout, though it was supposed to be valid until midnight of our checkout date. That was annoying, because calls to the resort were needed to verify the meals left on our passes for The Crystal Palace and for some snacks later.

Another reader encountered the problem in reverse:

While your park tickets are activated on the day of your arrival, it turns out that your dining plan isn't activated until someone at the hotel checks you in. Nothing in Disney's emails or literature lets you know this. We were unable to use our dining plan for breakfast or snacks until Wilderness Lodge decided it was time to check us in. Fortunately, we had a credit card we could use for breakfast and snacks. Then we had to spend an hour dealing with the front desk to reverse the credit card charges and deduct our meal credits.

Reader Tips for Getting the Most Out of the Plan

A mom from Radford, Virginia, shares the following tip:

Warn people to eat lunch early if they have dinner reservations before 7 p.m. Disney doesn't skimp on food—if you eat a late lunch (where, by the way, they feed you the same ungodly amount of food), you WILL NOT be hungry for dinner.

And a Lawrence, Kansas, mom offers another:

The quick-service meals aren't really designated for kids or adults when they ring you up and subtract the food from your plan. I wish I'd have known early on that if they couldn't see I had a child under age 9, I could have ordered a regular meal and gotten more food. We figured that out toward the end and started ordering bigger meals for our 7-year-old (we saved the leftovers to share later).

A mom from Brick Township, New Jersey, found that the dining plan streamlined her touring:

We truly enjoyed our Disney trip, and this time we purchased the dining plan. This was great for the kids because we did a character-dining experience every day. This helped us in the parks because we didn't have to wait in line to see characters—instead, we got all of our autographs during our meals.

A Saskatoon, Saskatchewan, dad of three says to watch snack vendors like a hawk:

We had a problem with a vendor who charged us meal service for each of the ice cream bars we purchased. This became evident at our final sit-down meal, when we didn't have any meal vouchers left. Check the receipts after every purchase!

DOING THE MATH

COMPARING A DISNEY TRAVEL PACKAGE with purchasing the package components separately is a breeze.

1. Pick a Disney resort and decide how many nights you want to stay.
2. Next, work out a rough plan of what you want to do and see so you can determine the admission passes you'll require.
3. When you're ready, call the Disney Reservation Center (DRC) at ☎ 407-W-DISNEY (934-7639) and price a package with tax for your selected resort and dates. The package will include both admissions and lodging. It's also a good idea to get a quote from a Disney-savvy travel agent (see page 96).
4. Now, to calculate the costs of buying your accommodations and admission passes separately, call the DRC a second time. This time, price a room-only rate for the same resort and dates. Be sure to ask about the availability of any special deals. While you're still on the line, obtain the prices, with tax, for the admissions you require. If you're not sure which of the various admission options will best serve you, consult our free Ticket Calculator at **TouringPlans.com.**
5. Add the room-only rates and the admission prices. Compare this sum to the DRC quote for the package.
6. Check for deals and discounts on packages and admission.

Regarding the economics of the dining plan, it's illustrative to know how the cost of one day on the plan is spent on each component. We'll spare you the math, but an approximate value for each item across every 2020 Disney Dining Plan is as follows:

- Each counter-service meal is worth **$18.**
- Each table-service meal is worth **$41.**
- Every snack is worth around **$3–$4.**
- The refillable mug is worth **$2–$3,** depending on trip length.
- A specialty drink is worth around **$6.**

THROW ME A LINE!

IF YOU BUY A PACKAGE FROM DISNEY, don't expect the reservationists to help you sort out your options. Generally, they respond only to your specific questions, ducking queries that require an opinion. A reader from North Riverside, Illinois, complains:

> My wife made two phone calls, and the representatives from WDW were very courteous, but they answered only the questions posed and were not eager to give advice on what might be most cost-effective. I feel a person could spend 8 hours on the phone with WDW reps and not have any more input than you get from reading the literature.

If you can't get the information you need from Disney, get in touch with a good travel agent (see page 96). Chances are that the agent can help you weigh your options.

Purchasing Room-Only Plus Passes Versus a Package

Sue Pisaturo of **Small World Vacations** (smallworldvacations.com), a travel agency that specializes in Walt Disney World, also thinks there's more involved in a package-purchase decision than money.

> Should you purchase a Walt Disney World package or buy all the components of the package separately? There's no single answer to this confusing question.
> A Walt Disney World package is like a store-bought prepackaged kids' meal, the kind with the little compartments filled with meat, cheese, crackers, drink, and dessert: You just grab the package and go. It's easy, and if it's on sale, why bother doing it yourself? If it's not on sale, it still may be worth the extra money for convenience.
> Purchasing the components of your vacation separately is like buying each of the meal's ingredients, cutting them up into neat piles, and packaging the lunch yourself. Is it worth the extra time and effort to do it this way? Will you save money if you do it this way?
> You have two budgets to balance when you plan your Disney World vacation: time and money. Satisfying both is your ultimate goal. Research and planning are paramount to realizing your Disney vacation dreams. Create your touring plans before making a final decision with regard to the number of days and options on your theme park passes. Create your dining itinerary (along with Advance Reservations, if possible) to determine if the Disney Dining Plan can save you some money.

HOTELS *outside* WALT DISNEY WORLD

SELECTING AND BOOKING A HOTEL OUTSIDE WALT DISNEY WORLD

LODGING COSTS OUTSIDE Disney World vary greatly. If you shop around, you can find a clean motel with a pool within 5–20 minutes of the World for as low as $50 a night with tax (but see our caveat on page 247). Discounts abound, particularly for AAA and AARP members.

There are four primary out-of-the-World areas to consider:

1. INTERNATIONAL DRIVE AREA This area, about 15–25 minutes northeast of the World, parallels I-4 on its eastern side and offers a wide selection of hotels and restaurants. Prices range $46–$439 per night. The chief drawbacks are terribly congested roads, countless traffic signals, and inadequate access to westbound I-4. While I-Drive's biggest bottleneck is its intersection with Sand Lake Road, the mile between Kirkman and Sand Lake Roads is almost always gridlocked, which increases the odds that you'll hit traffic going to a theme park in the morning, returning in the evening, or both.

Regarding traffic on International Drive (known locally as I-Drive), a conventioneer from Islip, New York, weighed in with this:

> When I visited Disney World last summer, we wasted huge chunks of time in traffic on I-Drive. Our hotel was in the section between the big McDonald's at Sand Lake Road and Volcano Bay at Universal Boulevard. There are practically no left-turn lanes in this section, so anyone turning left can hold up traffic for a long time.

Traffic aside, a man from Ottawa, Ontario, sings the praises of his I-Drive experience:

> International Drive is the place to stay when going to Disney. There are plenty of discount stores, boutiques, restaurants, mini putts, and other entertainment facilities, all within walking distance of remarkably inexpensive accommodations and a short drive away from Walt Disney World.

I-Drive hotels are listed on the **Visit Orlando** website: visitorlando.com/places-to-stay (click "International Drive Area").

2. LAKE BUENA VISTA AND THE I-4 CORRIDOR A number of hotels are along FL 535 and west of I-4 between Disney World and I-4's intersection with Florida's Turnpike. They're easily reached from the interstate and are near many restaurants, including those on International Drive. The **Visit Orlando** website (see above and page 25) lists most of them. For some traffic-avoidance tips, see our discussion on I-4 in Part Nine, page 426. This area includes Disney's value-priced **Flamingo Crossings** resort complex (see page 242).

3. US 192 (IRLO BRONSON MEMORIAL HIGHWAY) This is the highway to Kissimmee, to the southeast of Walt Disney World. In addition to large full-service hotels, some small, privately owned motels often offer a good value. Several dozen properties on US 192 are nearer Disney parks than are more expensive hotels inside the World. The number and variety of restaurants on US 192 is remarkable, compensating for the area's primary shortcoming: the lack of truly high-end resorts.

Locally, US 192 is called **Irlo Bronson Memorial Highway;** the section to the east and west of I-4 and the Disney Maingate is designated as Irlo Bronson Memorial Highway West. The highway has numbered mile markers that simplify navigation if you know which marker is closest to your destination.

Though traffic is heavy on Irlo Bronson west of the Maingate, it doesn't compare with the congestion found east of the Maingate and I-4 between mile markers 8 and 13. This section can—and should—be avoided by using **Osceola Parkway,** a partial toll road that parallels Irlo Bronson to the north and terminates in Disney World at the entrance to Animal Kingdom. No tolls are required to use Osceola Parkway on Disney property.

Hotels on US 192 and in Kissimmee are listed at the **Experience Kissimmee** website (experiencekissimmee.com); you can also order a copy of its newsletter by calling ☎ 407-569-4800.

4. UNIVERSAL ORLANDO AREA In the triangular area bordered by I-4 on the southeast, Vineland Road on the north, and Turkey Lake Road on the west are Universal Orlando and the hotels most convenient to it. Running north–south through the middle of the triangle is **Kirkman Road,** which connects to I-4. On the east side of Kirkman are several independent hotels and restaurants. Universal hotels, theme parks, and CityWalk are west of Kirkman. Traffic in this area is not nearly as congested as on nearby International Drive, and there are good interstate connections in both directions.

DRIVING TIME TO THE PARKS FOR VISITORS LODGING OUTSIDE WALT DISNEY WORLD

OUR HOTEL INFORMATION CHART on pages 252–263 shows the commuting time to the Disney theme parks from each hotel listed. Those commuting times represent an average of several test runs. Your actual time may be shorter or longer depending on traffic, road construction (if any), and delays at traffic signals.

The commuting times in our Hotel Information Chart show conclusively that distance from the theme parks is not necessarily the dominant factor in determining commuting times. Among those we list, the hotels on Major Boulevard opposite the Kirkman Road entrance to Universal Orlando, for example, are the most distant (in miles) from the Disney parks. But because they're only one traffic signal from easy access to I-4, commuting time to the parks is significantly less than for many closer hotels.

Note that times in the chart differ from those in the Door-to-Door Commuting Times chart in Part Nine. The latter compares using the Disney transportation system with driving your own car *inside* Walt Disney World. These times include actual transportation time plus tram, monorail, or other connections required to get from the parking lots to the entrance turnstiles. The hotel chart's commuting times, in contrast, represent only the driving time to and from the entrance of the respective parking lot of each park, with no consideration for getting to and from the parking lot to the turnstiles.

Add to the commuting times in the Hotel Information Chart a few minutes for paying your parking fee and parking. Once you park at the Transportation and Ticket Center (Magic Kingdom parking lot), it takes 20–30 minutes more to reach the Magic Kingdom via monorail or ferry, including security and health checks. To reach EPCOT from its parking lot, add 7–10 minutes. At Disney's Hollywood Studios and Animal Kingdom, the lot-to-gate transit is 5–15 minutes. If you

Hotel Concentrations Around Walt Disney World

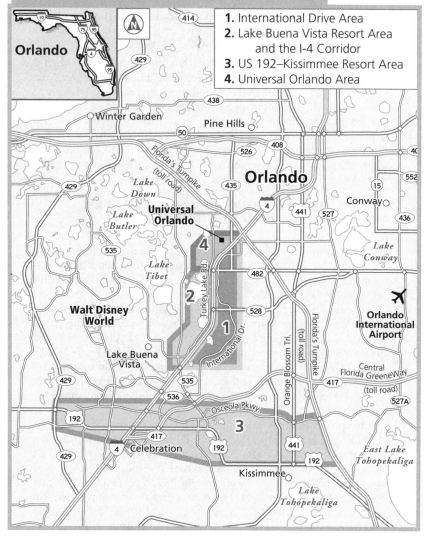

Orlando

1. International Drive Area
2. Lake Buena Vista Resort Area and the I-4 Corridor
3. US 192–Kissimmee Resort Area
4. Universal Orlando Area

haven't purchased your theme park admission in advance, tack on another 10–20 minutes.

If you're headed to the Magic Kingdom from off-site, you could put the park's standard $25 parking fee toward a Lyft or Uber that drops you off at **Disney's Contemporary Resort,** which is a 5-minute walk to the park. Doing that will save you 20–70 minutes of parking, trams, security checks, and monorails or ferries. It will save you almost as much time when leaving too.

International Drive & Universal Areas

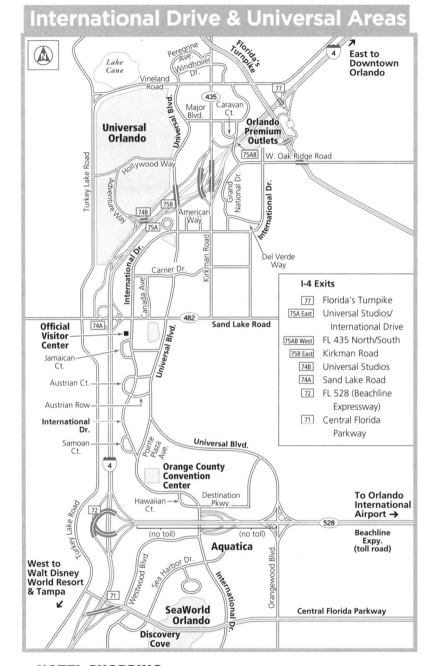

HOTEL SHOPPING

OTAs Online travel agencies (**OTAs**) sell travel products from a wide assortment of suppliers, often at deep discounts. These sites include

continued on page 220

Lake Buena Vista Resort Area & the I-4 Corridor

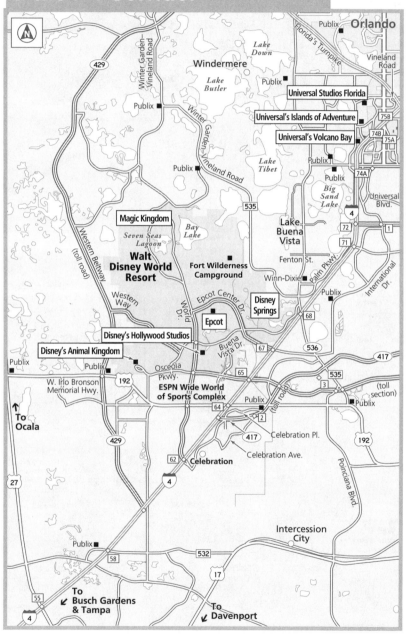

US 192–Kissimmee Resort Area

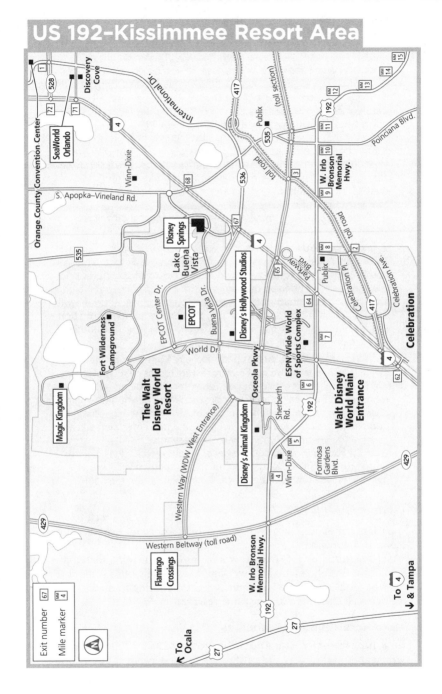

SIX QUICK TIPS FOR BOOKING THE HOTEL YOU WANT

1. START WITH GOOGLE MAPS Search for hotels close to your destination—for example, "hotels within 3 miles of Walt Disney World." (Google thinks the center of Walt Disney World is a patch of land to the right of World Drive as you pass EPCOT Center Drive. Most Disney resorts are within a 3-mile radius of that point.)

You can also search by walking distance, as in "hotels within a 10-minute walk of Disney Springs." A map will show nearby hotels, although it will also show a wider geographic area, so you'll have to zoom in, sometimes several times, using the plus sign (+) to adequately differentiate the hotels and see where they are in relation to Disney Springs.

Once Google Maps knows you're looking for hotels, it will prompt you to enter your check-in and checkout dates.

2. IDENTIFY YOUR OPTIONS The hotels displayed on the map will show a blue block containing an advertised rate—look for the closest hotel with the best rate. Placing your cursor over the block (but not clicking on it) will bring up the name and star rating of the hotel, along with some other information. If you click on the block, a column will appear on the left side of the page with more-in-depth information, including rate quotes from various OTAs and other sites. Included will be the names of similar hotels nearby.

3. OPTIONAL: GET IN THE BLOCK If you're attending a meeting or event that has large numbers of reserved rooms managed by the event's or meeting's sponsor, we recommend booking within that room block if you can afford it. Room blocks represent high-volume business for hotels, and sponsors can often leverage this volume for goodies such as catered events, hospitality suites, entertainment, and other extras that make your stay more enjoyable.

If the rooms in the block are beyond your means, don't be afraid to book outside the block if you must; the sponsor will have anticipated at least a few such bookings in contracting with the hotel.

continued from page 217

such familiar names as **Travelocity, Orbitz, Priceline, Expedia, Hotels .com,** and **Hotwire.**

The better-known OTAs draw a lot more web traffic than a given hotel's (or even hotel chain's) website. Most hotels offer some sort of "lowest-price guarantee" on their websites, offering to match or beat a price seen elsewhere for the same reservation.

More Hotel-Hunting Resources

NEW, INDEPENDENT, AND BOUTIQUE-HOTEL DEALS While chain hotels worry about sales costs and profit margins, independent and boutique hotels are concerned about making themselves known to the traveling public. The market is huge, and it's increasingly hard for such hotels to get noticed, especially when they're competing with major chains.

Independent and boutique hotels work on the premise that if they can get you through the front door, you'll become a loyal customer;

4. CHECK BOOKING.COM Once you've found one or more hotels that satisfy your location and rate criteria, check it/them out on booking.com to see which seller(s) is offering the best rates for your dates. Though you can spend days rooting around the web looking at different sellers, it's largely a waste of time—one check on booking.com is all you need. If the rates you find here seem higher than those you've seen elsewhere, it's because booking.com includes taxes in its quotes up-front. Also, note that rates quoted are for the entire length of your stay.

5. SEE IF THE HOTEL CAN BEAT ONLINE DEALS Every time a room is booked through a third party, whether that's an OTA or a content site like TripAdvisor, the hotel makes less money. Therefore, before you book a room, take the best deals you've found online and call the hotel directly (don't call the national reservations number).

Ask for a rate quote for your travel days—if it's higher than what you've found online, tell the hotel representative so without quoting your best online rate: "I've found lots of better rates online, and I know that your hotel will make a lot more on the reservation if I book directly with you. Can you offer me a better rate than what I've found?" If the representative comes back in the affirmative, pin her down regarding exactly what kind of room that rate gets you. Also get the rep's name and note the time of the call.

6. CHECK THE HOTEL'S WEBSITE Go to the website and investigate what kind of room you'll get at the quoted rate. If you're fine with what you see, call the hotel back and book. If you have any special room preferences, make sure they get noted on your reservation. We also usually ask about the age of the hotel, construction or renovations at the hotel or nearby, road noise, and Wi-Fi availability.

In addition, this is a good opportunity to ask about potential hidden charges such as taxes, resort fees, and fees for parking and internet. Hotels are notorious for tacking these on without disclosing them in their advertised rates.

thus, deeply discounted rates are part of their marketing plan to build a client base. Because such hotels get lost on the big OTA sites and on search engines like Kayak and Google, they've jumped on the flash-sale bandwagon. Offering almost-irresistible rates on daily-coupon sites like **Groupon,** the independents can get their product in front of thousands of potential guests.

These offers are very generous but also time-limited; if you're in the market, though, you'll be hard-pressed to find better deals. Groupon subscribers, for example, can bid on or secure coupons for rooms that are often as much as 50% cheaper than the hotel's standard rate—and the discounts frequently include perks such as meals, free parking, waived resort fees, shopping vouchers, spa services, and entertainment. On Groupon's homepage (groupon.com), click "Getaways" under the "Hotels and Travel" category, or just wait for Getaway coupons by email as part of your free subscription.

AIRBNB This service (airbnb.com) connects travelers with owner-hosted alternative lodging all over the world, from spare bedrooms in people's homes to private apartments, vacation homes, and even live-in boats.

We find Airbnb less useful in Orlando for a couple of reasons. First, Orlando has an enormous supply of vacation-home rentals and hotel rooms, which keeps prices down for lodging around Walt Disney World. Second, Disney's incentives for staying on-property—including free airport transportation—are hard to beat. That said, Kissimmee appears to be a rapidly growing market for Airbnb. If you find a good property this way, let us know.

Be Careful Out There: Hotel Scams

In a very persuasive scam that's been metastasizing to hotels all over the country, a guest receives a phone call, purportedly from the front desk, explaining that a computer glitch has occurred and that the hotel needs the guest's credit card information again to expedite checkout.

Here's what you need to know: (1) A legit hotel won't ask you to provide sensitive information over the phone, and (2) a legit hotel *especially* won't call you in the middle of the night to get it out of you. If this happens to you, hang up and contact hotel security.

Another scam involves websites that look very polished and official and may even include the logos of well-known hotel brands. The scammers will happily sell you a room, paid for in advance with your credit card, and then email you credible-looking confirmation documents. Problem is, they never contacted the hotel to make the booking, *or* they made the booking but failed to pay the hotel.

unofficial **TIP**
Never click a pop-up that routes you to a third-party hotel site, regardless of how good the deal sounds or how slick the website looks.

CONDOMINIUMS AND VACATION HOMES

BECAUSE CONDOS TEND TO BE part of large developments (frequently time-shares), amenities such as swimming pools, playgrounds, game arcades, and fitness centers often rival those found in the best hotels. Generally speaking, condo developments don't have restaurants, lounges, or spas. In a condo, if something goes wrong, someone will be on hand to fix the problem. Vacation homes rented from a property-management company likewise will have someone to come to the rescue, although responsiveness tends to vary vastly from company to company. If you rent directly from an owner, correcting problems is often more difficult, particularly when the owner doesn't live in the same area as the rental home.

In a vacation home, all the amenities are self-contained (in planned developments, there may be community amenities available as well). Depending on the specific home, you might find a small swimming pool, hot tub, two-car garage, family room, game room, and even a home theater. Features found in both condos and vacation homes include full kitchens, laundry rooms, TVs, and DVD players. Interestingly, though almost all freestanding vacation homes have private pools, very few have backyards. This means that, except for swimming, the kids are pretty much relegated to playing in the house.

Time-share condos are clones when it comes to furniture and decor, but single-owner condos and vacation homes are furnished and decorated in a style that reflects the owner's taste. Vacation homes, usually one- to two-story houses in a subdivision, very rarely afford interesting views (though some overlook lakes or natural areas), while condos, especially the high-rise variety, sometimes offer exceptional ones.

How the Vacation-Home Market Works

In the Orlando–Walt Disney World area, just prior to the pandemic, there were more than 26,000 rental homes, including stand-alone homes, single-owner condos—that is, not time-shares—and townhomes. The same area had about 128,000 hotel rooms. Almost all the rental homes are occupied by their owners for at least a week or two each year; the rest of the year, owners make the homes available for rent. Some owners deal directly with renters, while others enlist the assistance of a property-management company.

Incredibly, about 700 property-management companies operate in the Orlando–Kissimmee–Walt Disney World market. Most are mom-and-pop outfits that manage an inventory of 10 homes or fewer (probably fewer than 70 companies oversee more than 100 rental homes).

Some homes are made available to wholesalers, vacation packagers, and travel agents in deals negotiated either directly by the owners or by property-management companies on the owners' behalf. A wholesaler or vacation packager will occasionally drop its rates to sell slow-moving inventory, but more commonly the cost to renters is higher than when dealing directly with owners or management companies: Because most wholesalers and packagers sell their inventory through travel agents, both the wholesaler/packager's markup and the travel agent's commission are passed along to the renter. These costs are in addition to the owner's cut and/or the fee for the property manager.

Along similar lines, logic may suggest that the lowest rate of all can be obtained by dealing directly with owners, thus eliminating an intermediary. Although this is sometimes true, it's more often the case that property-management companies offer the best rates. With their marketing expertise and larger customer base, these companies can produce a higher occupancy rate than can the owners themselves. What's more, management companies, or at least the larger ones, can achieve economies of scale unavailable to owners when it comes to maintenance, cleaning, linens, and even acquiring furniture and appliances (if a house is not already furnished). The combination of higher occupancy rates and economies of scale adds up to a win–win situation for owners, management companies, and renters alike.

Location, Location, Location

The best vacation home is one that's within easy commuting distance of the theme parks (see the map on the following pages). If you plan to spend some time at Universal, SeaWorld, and the like, you'll want something just to the northeast of Walt Disney World (between the World and Orlando). If you plan to spend most of your time in the World, the best selection of vacation homes is along US 192 to the south of the park.

Rental-Home Developments Near WDW

Abbey/West Haven 7	Crystal Cove 5	Highland Park 10	Millbrook Manor 9	Rolling Hills 10
Acadia Estates 10	Cumbrian Lakes 5	Highlands Reserve 9	Mission Park 9	Royal Oaks 5
Ashley Manor 7	Cypress Lakes 3	Hillcrest Estates 9	Montego Bay 5	Royal Palm Bay 5
Aviana 7	Cypress Pointe Forest 7	Indian Creek 10	Oak Island Cove 10	Royal Palms 8
Aylesbury 8	Davenport Lakes 9	Indian Point 5	Oak Island Harbor 10	Runaway Beach Club 5
Bahama Bay 9	Doral Woods 6	Indian Ridge 10	Oakpoint 7	Sanctuary at
Bass Lake Estates 5	Eagle Pointe 5	Indian Ridge Oaks 10	Orange Lake 10	West Haven 7
Bass Lake US 27 9	Emerald Island 10	Indian Wells 1	Orange Tree 9	Sandy Ridge 10
Bella Piazza 9	Encantada 9	Island Club West 9	The Palms 9	Santa Cruz 7
Bella Trae 7, 8	Esprit/Fairways 9	Laguna Bay 5	Paradise Woods 7	Seasons 5
BellaVida 5	Fiesta Key 5	Lake Berkley 5	Pines West 8	Shire at West Haven 7
Bentley Oaks 7	Flamingo Lakes 3	Lake Davenport 9	Pinewood 7	Silver Creek 9
Blue Heron Beach 1	Florida Pines 9	Lake Wilson	Providence 4	Solana 9
Briargrove 7	Floridays 2	Preserve 7	Regal Palms 9	Southern Dunes 8
Bridgewater	Formosa Gardens 10	Lakeside 4	Remington Golf Club 4	St. James Park 6
Crossing 7	Four Corners 9	Legacy Dunes 9	Retreat at West Haven 7	
Bridgewater Town Ctr. 7	Glenbrook 9	Legacy Park 9	Reunion 7	
Buenaventura Lakes 4	Golden Oaks 1	Liberty Village 5	Remington Point 4	
Calabay Parc 9	Grand Palms 9	Lighthouse Key Resort 9	Ridgewood Lakes 8	
Calabay Tower Lake 8	Grand Reserve 7	Lindfields 9	Robbins Rest 7	
Calabria 9	Greater Groves 9	Loma Linda 7		
Cane Island 5	Hamilton Reserve 5	Loma Vista 4		
ChampionsGate 7, 8	Hamlet at West Haven 7	Lucaya Village Resort 5		
Chatham Park 5	Hampton Lakes 9	Magic Landings 4		
Clear Creek 9	Happy Trails 9	Manors at Westridge 9		
Club Cortile 5	Highgate Park 9	Marbella 8		
Country Creek 5	High Grove 9	Meadow Woods 4		
Countryside Manor 6				
Creekside 5				
Crescent Lakes 6				

Practically all of the vacation rentals in Orange County are in the **Floridays** and **Vista Cay** developments. By our reckoning, about half the rental homes in Osceola County and all the rental homes in Polk County are too far away for commuting to be practical. You might be

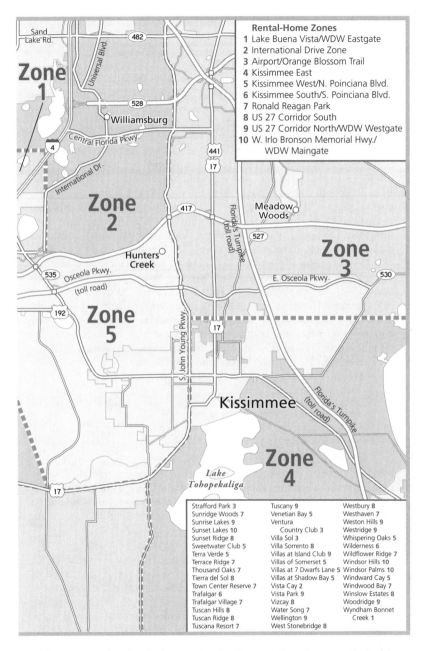

Rental-Home Zones

1 Lake Buena Vista/WDW Eastgate
2 International Drive Zone
3 Airport/Orange Blossom Trail
4 Kissimmee East
5 Kissimmee West/N. Poinciana Blvd.
6 Kissimmee South/S. Poinciana Blvd.
7 Ronald Reagan Park
8 US 27 Corridor South
9 US 27 Corridor North/WDW Westgate
10 W. Irlo Bronson Memorial Hwy./
   WDW Maingate

Strafford Park 3	Tuscany 9	Westbury 8
Sunridge Woods 7	Venetian Bay 5	Westhaven 7
Sunrise Lakes 9	Ventura	Weston Hills 9
Sunset Lakes 10	Country Club 3	Westridge 9
Sunset Ridge 8	Villa Sol 3	Whispering Oaks 5
Sweetwater Club 5	Villa Sorrento 8	Wilderness 6
Terra Verde 5	Villas at Island Club 9	Wildflower Ridge 7
Terrace Ridge 7	Villas of Somerset 5	Windsor Hills 10
Thousand Oaks 7	Villas at 7 Dwarfs Lane 5	Windsor Palms 10
Tierra del Sol 8	Villas at Shadow Bay 5	Windward Cay 5
Town Center Reserve 7	Vista Cay 2	Windwood Bay 7
Trafalgar 6	Vista Park 9	Winslow Estates 8
Trafalgar Village 7	Vizcay 8	Woodridge 9
Tuscan Hills 8	Water Song 7	Wyndham Bonnet
Tuscan Ridge 8	Wellington 9	Creek 1
Tuscana Resort 7	West Stonebridge 8	

able to save a few bucks by staying farther out, but the most desirable homes to be found are in **Vista Cay** and in developments no more than 10 miles south of Universal's main entrance, from west of John Young Parkway to east of the FL 429 Western Beltway.

To get the most from a vacation home, you need to be close enough to commute in 20 minutes or less to your Orlando destination. This will allow for naps, quiet time, swimming, and dollar-saving meals you prepare yourself.

Shopping for a Vacation Home

There are three main types of websites in the home-rental game: those for property-management companies, which showcase a given company's homes and are set up for direct bookings; individual owner sites; and third-party listing sites, which advertise properties available through different owners and sometimes management companies as well. Sites in the last category will usually refer prospective renters to an owner's or management company's site for reservations.

We've found that most property-management sites are poorly designed and will test your patience to the max. You can practically click yourself into old age trying to see all the homes available or figure out where on earth they are. Nearly all of them claim to be "just minutes from Disney." (By that reasoning, we should list our own homes: They're also just minutes from Disney—570 minutes, to be exact!)

Many websites list homes according to towns (such as Clermont, Lake Buena Vista, Windermere, and Winter Garden) or real estate developments (including Eagle Pointe, Floridays, Golden Oak, and Vista Cay) in the general Universal area, none of which you're likely to be familiar with. The information that counts is the distance of a vacation home or condo from Universal; for that, you often must look for something like "4 miles from Universal" embedded in the home's description.

The best websites provide the following:

- Numerous photos and in-depth descriptions of individual homes
- Detailed reviews of the homes, along with the dates of stay
- Overview maps or text descriptions that reflect how far specific homes or developments are from Walt Disney World
- The ability to book the rental home of your choice on the site
- An easy-to-find phone number for bookings and questions

The best sites are also easy to navigate, let you see what you're interested in without your having to log in or divulge any personal information, and list memberships in such organizations as the Better Business Bureau and the **Florida Vacation Rental Management Association** (VRMA; visit fvrma.org for the association's code of ethics).

Recommended Websites

After checking out dozens upon dozens of sites, here are the ones we recommend. All of them meet the criteria listed above. (For the record, we elected not to list some sites that met our criteria but whose homes are too far away from Walt Disney World.)

Florida Dream Homes (floridadreamhomes.com) has a good reputation for customer service and has photos of and information about the homes in its online inventory.

Vacation Rentals by Owner (vrbo.com) is a nationwide vacation-homes listing service that puts prospective renters in direct contact with owners. The site is straightforward and always lists a large number of rental properties in Celebration, Disney's planned community situated about 8–10 minutes from the theme parks. Two similar listing services with good websites are **Vacation Rentals 411** (vacationrentals411.com) and **Last Minute Villas** (lastminutevillas.net).

Visit Orlando (visitorlando.com) is the website to check if you're interested in renting a condominium at one of the many time-share developments (click on "Places to Stay" at the site's home page). You can call the developments directly, but going through this site allows you to bypass sales departments and escape their high-pressure invitations to sit through sales presentations. The site also lists hotels, vacation homes, and campgrounds.

Making Contact

Once you've found a vacation home you like, check the website for a Frequently Asked Questions page. If there's not one, here are some of the things you'll want to ask the owner or rental company.

1. How close is the property to Walt Disney World?
2. Is the home or condominium that I see on the internet the one I'll get?
3. Is the property part of a time-share development?
4. Are there any specials or discounts available?
5. Is everything included in the rental price, or are there additional charges? What about taxes?
6. How old is the property I'm interested in? Has it been refurbished recently?
7. What is the view from the property?
8. Is the property near any noisy roads?
9. What is your smoking policy?
10. What is your pet policy?
11. Is the pool heated? If yes, is there an extra charge for the heating?
12. Is there a fenced backyard where children can play?
13. How many people can be seated at the main dining table?
14. Is there a dedicated land phone line at the property to ensure a reliable connection to 911 and other emergency services?
15. Is high-speed internet available?
16. Are linens and towels provided?
17. How far are the nearest supermarket and drugstore?
18. Is childcare available?
19. Are there restaurants nearby?
20. Is transportation to the parks provided?
21. Will we need a car?
22. What is required to make a reservation?
23. What is your change/cancellation policy?
24. When is checkout time?
25. What will we be responsible for when we check out?
26. How will we receive our confirmation and arrival instructions?
27. What are your office hours?
28. What are the directions to your office?
29. What if we arrive after your office has closed?
30. Whom do we contact if something goes wrong during our stay?
31. How long have you been in business?
32. Are you licensed by the state of Florida?
33. Do you belong to the Better Business Bureau and/or the Florida VRMA?

We frequently receive letters from readers extolling the virtues of renting a condo or vacation home. This endorsement by a New Jersey family of five is typical:

> *I cannot stress enough how important it is if you have a large family (more than two kids) to rent a house for your stay! We stayed at Windsor Hills Resort, 1.5 miles from the Disney Maingate. It took us about 10 minutes to drive there in the a.m., and we had no traffic issues at all.*

THE BEST HOTELS FOR FAMILIES OUTSIDE WALT DISNEY WORLD

WHAT MAKES A SUPER FAMILY HOTEL? Spacious rooms, an in-room fridge, a great pool, free breakfast, and kids' activities, for starters.

Narrowed from hundreds of properties, the hotels profiled in the next section, listed by zone and alphabetically, are the best we've found in each area of Orlando. Some of our picks are expensive, others are more reasonable, and some are a bargain. All understand a family's needs.

The best square feet for your lodging dollar are often found in an off-site suite. Suites have the advantage of separate bedrooms, allowing tired family members to rest while others can stay up if they like.

Unofficial Guide readers give low ratings to most off-site hotels' park-transportation options. Though all hotels profiled offer some type of shuttle to the theme parks, some offer very limited service, so call the hotel before you book and ask what the shuttle schedule will be when you visit. Likewise, most off-site hotels' restaurants won't meet the needs of a family staying for a week, so plan to go elsewhere for variety.

unofficial **TIP**
Check the resort's room photos to make sure you're booking an actual suite with multiple rooms. Some hotels with *suites* in their name or *all-suite* in their description are little more than slightly larger, single-space-for-everyone rooms with a microwave.

Ten Bangs for Your Hotel Buck

For this edition, we stayed at 10 villa-style resorts outside of Walt Disney World; some are profiled in the following section. Our goal was to assess the value for money paid, with a focus on space, amenities, and transportation to the parks. All 10 properties provided clean, comfortable rooms at reasonable prices for their size (bit see our caveat below). We recommend the following six, with **Margaritaville Resort Orlando** being the one we'd suggest first:

- Club Wyndham Cypress Palms
- Homewood Suites by Hilton (Flamingo Crossings)
- JW Marriott Orlando Bonnet Creek Resort & Spa
- Margaritaville Resort Orlando
- Marriott's Cypress Harbour
- Marriott's Imperial Palm Villas

Homewood Suites is profiled on page 242 and Margaritaville on page 240. **Marriott's Cypress Harbour, Marriott's Imperial Palms,** and **Club Wyndham Cypress Palms** are similar to **Marriott's Harbour Lake,** profiled on page 237.

The next four, while acceptable, are either more expensive than or not as nice as comparable off-site hotels, or they have marketing departments that hounded us repeatedly after our stay:

- Aloft Orlando Lake Buena Vista
- Grand Beach (Diamond Resorts)
- Caribe Royale Orlando
- Home2Suites by Hilton (Flamingo Crossings)

INTERNATIONAL DRIVE & UNIVERSAL AREAS

Hard Rock Hotel Orlando   ★★★★½

Rate per night $362–$603. **Pool** ★★★★. **Fridge in room** Yes. **Shuttle to parks** Yes (Universal, SeaWorld, Discovery Cove, Aquatica, Volcano Bay). **Maximum number of occupants per room** 3 (king)/ 5 (double queen). **Comments** Pets welcome ($100/night flat fee, 2 max). Parking $28/day. **Survey results** 95% of *Unofficial Guide* readers would stay here again; 91% would recommend this resort to a friend.

5800 Universal Blvd.
☎ 407-503-2000 or
888-464-3617
hardrockhotels.com
/orlando

FOR YOUNGER ADULTS and families with older kids, the Hard Rock Hotel is the hippest place to lay your head. It's also the closest Universal Orlando resort to the theme parks. The exterior has a California Mission theme, with white stucco walls, arched entryways, and rust-colored roof tiles. Inside, the lobby's walls are decorated with enough concert posters, costumes, and musical instruments to start an outpost of the Rock and Roll Hall of Fame (ask the front desk about a self-guided memorabilia tour). The eight floors hold 650 rooms and 29 suites, with the rooms classified as Standard, Deluxe, and Club Level.

Standard rooms are 375 square feet, slightly larger than rooms at Disney's Moderate resorts and a bit smaller than most Disney Deluxe rooms. Decor is distinguished by light-gray walls and linens, pastel furniture, and colorful retro-inspired accents. Furnishings include two queen beds along with a flat-panel TV, a refrigerator, a coffee maker, and an alarm clock with an iPhone docking port. A six-drawer dresser and separate closet with sliding doors ensure plenty of storage space. In addition, most rooms have a reading chair and a small desk with two chairs. An optional rollaway bed, available at an extra charge, allows standard rooms to sleep up to five people.

Each room's dressing area features a sink and hair dryer. The bathroom is probably large enough for most adults to get ready in the morning while another person gets ready in the dressing area.

Deluxe rooms with king beds are around 400 square feet and can accommodate up to three people with an optional rollaway bed rental. These rooms feature a U-shaped sitting area in place of the second bed, and the rest of the amenities are the same as in standard rooms. Deluxe queen rooms are 500 square feet and can hold up to five people using a pullout sofa.

Situated in the middle of the resort's C-shaped main building, the 12,000-square-foot pool includes a 250-foot waterslide, a sand beach, and underwater speakers so you can hear the music while you swim. Adjacent to the pool are a fountain play area for small children, a sand-volleyball court, hot tubs, and a poolside bar. On-site dining includes **The Kitchen,** a casual full-service restaurant open for breakfast, lunch, and dinner, featuring American food such as burgers, steaks, and salads. **The Palm Restaurant** is an upscale steakhouse that's open for dinner only, while the lobby's **Velvet Lounge** hosts intimate concerts. And, of course, the world's largest **Hard Rock Cafe** is just a short distance away at Universal CityWalk.

While it's not exactly cheap—self-parking alone is $28 per night—the Hard Rock is a good value compared with, say, Disney's Yacht & Beach Clubs. What you're paying for here is a short walk to the theme parks and Universal Express Unlimited first, and the room second.

Hilton Grand Vacations at SeaWorld ★★★★

6924 Grand Vacations Way
☎ 407-239-0100
tinyurl.com/seaworldhgv

Rate per night $170–$492. **Pool** ★★★★. **Fridge in room** Yes. **Shuttle to parks** Yes (Universal, SeaWorld). **Maximum number of occupants per room** 2 (studio)/8 (3-bedroom suite). **Comments** Guests get front-of-line access to some SeaWorld rides. **Survey results** 88% of *Unofficial Guide* readers would stay here again; 80% would recommend this resort to a friend.

ACROSS THE STREET FROM SEAWORLD, Hilton Grand Vacations is within a 15-minute drive of both Walt Disney World and Universal Orlando. While that means spending more time in a car, you get a lot more room for your money: one-bedroom suites are 878 square feet, compared with around 520 for Disney's Value Family Suites and Fort Wilderness Cabins. Grand Vacations' one-bedroom averages $280 per night in the summer—about $40–$100 per night less than Disney's cheapest family suite, at All-Star Music. In fact, Grand Vacations' 1,225-square-foot, two-bedroom suite is often less than Disney's cheapest suite. Plus, Grand Vacations has free parking.

Unofficial Guide readers give this Hilton an A for room quality and a solid B for room quietness. Studios have kitchenettes. Suites come equipped with a washer and dryer; kitchen with utensils, dishwasher, oven/range, microwave, and coffee maker; plus flat-panel TVs. One-bedroom suites have a sofa bed and one bathroom, two-bedroom suites have two baths, and three-bedroom suites have three. The decor isn't the most modern, but it is bright, clean, functional, and comfortable.

Amenities include three pools with cabanas, a fitness center, a kids' playground, basketball and tennis courts, and a business center. One sit-down and one counter-service/grab-and-go restaurant serve guests 6:30 a.m.–11 p.m.

Loews Portofino Bay Hotel ★★★★½

5601 Universal Blvd.
☎ 407-503-1000 or
888-464-3617
loewshotels.com
/portofino-bay-hotel

Rate per night $389–$618. **Pools** ★★★★. **Fridge in room** Yes. **Shuttle to parks** Yes (Universal, SeaWorld, Discovery Cove, Aquatica, Volcano Bay). **Maximum number of occupants per room** 3 (king)/ 5 (double queen). **Comments** Pets welcome ($100 flat fee, 2 max). Parking $28/day. **Survey results** 80% of *Unofficial Guide* readers would stay here again; 83% would recommend this resort to a friend.

UNIVERSAL'S TOP-OF-THE-LINE HOTEL evokes the Italian seaside city of Portofino, complete with a man-made Portofino Bay past the lobby. To Universal's credit, the layout, color, and theming of the guest-room buildings are a good approximation of the architecture around the harbor in the real Portofino (Universal's version has fewer yachts, however).

Inside, the lobby is decorated with pink-marble floors, white wood columns, and arches. The space is airy and comfortable, with side rooms featuring seats and couches done in bold reds and deep blues.

Most guest rooms are 450 square feet, larger than most at Disney's Deluxe resorts, and have either one king bed or two queens. King rooms sleep up to three people with an optional rollaway bed; the same option allows queen rooms to sleep up to five. Two room-view options are available: Garden rooms look out over the landscaping and trees (many of these are the east-facing rooms in the resort's east wing; others face one of the three pools); bay-view rooms face either west or south and overlook Portofino Bay.

Rooms come furnished with a flat-panel LCD TV, a minifridge, an alarm clock with USB charging ports, and a coffee maker. Other amenities include a small desk with two chairs, a comfortable reading chair with lamp, a chest of drawers, and a standing closet. As at all Universal on-site hotels, Wi-Fi is free in guest rooms and the lobby, though you can pay $15 per day for higher speeds. Beds are large, plush, and comfortable.

The guest bathrooms are the best on Universal property. The shower has enough water pressure to strip the paint from old furniture, not to mention an adjustable spray nozzle that varies the water pulses to simulate everything from monsoon season in the tropics to the rhythmic thumps of wildebeest hooves during migrating season.

Portofino Bay has three pools, the largest of which, the **Beach Pool,** is on the west side of the resort. Two smaller quiet pools sit at the far end of the east wing and to the west of the main lobby. The Beach Pool has a zero-entry design and a waterslide themed after a Roman aqueduct, plus a children's play area, hot tubs, and a poolside bar and grill. The **Villa Pool** has private cabanas for that Italian Riviera feeling. Rounding out the luxuries are the **Mandara Spa,** a complete fitness center, a business center, and a video arcade.

On-site dining includes three sit-down restaurants serving Italian cuisine, including **BiCE,** a sit-down, upscale dinner place; a deli that serves pizza; and a coffee/gelato bar. While we like BiCE quite a bit, some of the food prices at the other venues go well beyond what we'd consider reasonable, even for a theme park hotel.

Portofino Bay has some of Universal's best rooms, but the prices at the upper end put it on par with the Ritz-Carlton—something its good points can't quite justify. On the other hand, Portofino Bay is significantly cheaper than the resorts along Disney's monorail—and the Ritz isn't a short walk from The Wizarding World.

Loews Royal Pacific Resort ★★★★½

Rate per night $327–$545. **Pools** ★★★★. **Fridge in room** Yes. **Shuttle to parks** Yes (Universal, SeaWorld, Discovery Cove, Aquatica, Volcano Bay). **Maximum number of occupants per room** 3 (king)/5 (double queen). **Comments** Microwaves available for $15/day. Character breakfast on Saturday (by reservation; temporarily suspended at press time). Pets welcome ($100 flat fee, 2 max). Parking $28/day.
Survey results 93% of *Unofficial Guide* readers would stay here again; 91% would recommend this resort to a friend.

6300 Hollywood Way
☎ 407-503-3000 or
888-464-3617
loewshotels.com
/royal-pacific-resort

YOU MAY BE TEMPTED, as we were initially, to write off the Royal Pacific as a knockoff of Disney's Polynesian Village Resort. There are similarities, but the Royal Pacific is attractive enough, and has enough strengths of its own, for us to recommend that you try it for yourself.

Guests enter the lobby from a walkway two stories above an artificial stream that surrounds the resort. Once you're inside, dark teakwood accents contrast nicely with the enormous amount of light coming in from the windows and three-story A-frame roof. Palms line the walkway through the lobby, and through these you see that the whole lobby surrounds an enormous outdoor fountain.

The 1,000 rooms are spread among three Y-shaped wings attached to the main building. Standard rooms are 335 square feet—about the size of a room at Disney's Moderate resorts—and have one king or two queen beds. King rooms sleep up to three people with an optional rollaway bed; queen rooms sleep five with that rollaway bed. The beds, fitted with 300-thread-count sheets, are very comfortable.

Rooms have modern monochrome wall treatments and carpets, accented with boldly colored floral graphics, and include a flat-panel TV, a minifridge, a coffee maker, an alarm clock, and several USB-equipped power outlets. Other amenities include a small desk with two chairs, a comfortable reading chair, a chest of drawers, and a large closet. A dressing area with sink is separated from the rest of the room by a wall. Next to the dressing area is the bathroom, with a tub, shower, and toilet. While they're acceptable, the bathroom and dressing areas at the Royal Pacific are our least favorite in the upscale Universal resorts.

As at the Hard Rock, the Royal Pacific's zero-entry pool includes a sand beach, a volleyball court, a play area for kids, a hot tub, and cabanas for rent, plus a poolside bar and grill.

Amenities include a 5,000-square-foot fitness facility, a business center, a video arcade, a full-service restaurant, a sushi bar, two bars, and a weekly luau (temporarily suspended at press time). **Islands Dining Room,** serving Pacific Rim and traditional fare, is open for breakfast and dinner and has a play area for kids. **Jake's American Bar** is open for lunch, dinner, and late-night eats, while the poolside **Bula Bar & Grille** offers wraps, sandwiches, burgers, salads, and fruity drinks.

Loews Sapphire Falls Resort ★★★★

6601 Adventure Way
☎ 407-503-5000 or
888-464-3617
loewshotels.com
/sapphire-falls-resort

Rate per night $226–$350. **Pools** ★★★★. **Fridge in room** Yes. **Shuttle to parks** Yes (Universal, SeaWorld, Discovery Cove, Aquatica, Volcano Bay). **Maximum number of occupants per room** 3 (king)/ 5 (double queen). **Comments** Microwaves available for $15/day. Pets welcome ($100 flat fee, 2 max). Parking $26/day. **Survey results** 92% of *Unofficial Guide* readers would stay here again, and 92% would recommend this resort to a friend.

UNIVERSAL'S FIFTH ON-SITE LOEWS HOTEL brought a sunny Caribbean vibe to the moderately priced market when its 1,000 rooms opened in the summer of 2016. Sandwiched between Royal Pacific and Cabana Bay—both physically and pricewise—Sapphire Falls sports all the amenities of Universal's three deluxe hotels, including water-taxi transportation to the parks, with the crucial exception of complimentary Universal Express privileges.

Water figures heavily here: The namesake falls form the scenic centerpiece of the resort. The 16,000-square-foot, zero-entry main pool features a white-sand beach, a waterslide, children's play areas, a fire pit, and cabanas for rent. A fitness room holds a sauna and hot tub.

For dinner, **Amatista Cookhouse** offers table-service Caribbean dining, with an open kitchen and waterfront views. **Dhrum Club Kantine** serves tapas-style small plates near the pool bar's fire pit. **New Dutch Trading Co.** is an island-inspired grab-and-go marketplace. **Strong Water Tavern** in the lobby specializes in rum and deserves its own paragraph in this review. Strong Water serves tasty, island-inspired tapas from a menu longer than you'd expect. It's one of our favorite on-site restaurants and a great way to end your night. Try the ceviche.

Sapphire Falls also has 131,000 square feet of meeting space and a business center. Walkways connect to a parking structure that in turn connects to the meeting facilities at Royal Pacific, making these sister properties ideal for conventions. And that leads us to our main critique of the resort: Aside from the lobby and pool, the public areas feel like those of a standard convention hotel.

The rooms range from 364 square feet in a standard queen or king room to 529 square feet in the 36 Kids' Suites to up to 1,358 square feet in the 15 Hospitality Suites. All rooms have HDTVs, minifridges, and coffee makers. We like these a bit better than those at Aventura, but they're more expensive too.

Sheraton Vistana Villages Resort Villas ★★★★

12401 International Dr.
☎ 407-238-5000
tinyurl.com/vistana
villagesresort

Rate per night $179–$359. **Pool** ★★★★. **Fridge in room** Yes. **Shuttle to parks** No. **Maximum number of occupants per room** 6

(2-bedroom suite). **Survey results** 96% of *Unofficial Guide* readers would stay here again; 87% would recommend this resort to a friend.

THIS IS ONE OF TWO SHERATON VISTANA properties in Orlando that are favorites of *Unofficial Guide* readers (the other is the **Sheraton Vistana Resort Villas** in Lake Buena Vista, profiled on page 237). The 1,100-square-foot, two-bedroom villas are the rooms to get. While that's double the size of a Disney one-bedroom Family Suite, rack rates are much less than Disney's, ranging from $265 per night during summer to $299 per night at Christmas.

Suites have fully equipped kitchens and a washer and dryer. All rooms have a private balcony or patio. The resort has two pools, including one zero-entry for kids; a fitness center; and a business center.

This family from Bedford, Texas, really enjoyed their stay:

> I highly recommend Vistana Villages—it's the best value for the money. Plenty of space for everyone to spread out, great pools, and fantastic location—it was 10 minutes to EPCOT and Hollywood Studios and 5 minutes to Disney Springs, and lots of restaurants were nearby.

The Vistana Villages are about a 15-minute drive from Walt Disney World (and you don't have to take I-4!) and 20 minutes to Universal Orlando.

Universal's Aventura Hotel ★★★½

Rate per night Standard rooms, $164–$278; Kids' Suites, $289–$503. **Pools** ★★★½. **Fridge in room** Yes. **Shuttle to parks** Yes (Universal, SeaWorld, Discovery Cove, Aquatica, Volcano Bay). **Maximum number of occupants per room** 4 (double queen or king with pullout)/6 (Kids' Suites). **Comments** Parking $18/day. **Survey results** 86% of *Unofficial Guide* readers would stay here again; 80% would recommend this resort to a friend.

6725 Adventure Way
☎ 407-503-6000 or
888-464-3617
loewshotels.com/universals
-aventura-hotel

OPENED IN SUMMER 2018, the Aventura Hotel is Universal Orlando's sixth resort and second so-called Prime Value–priced option. The curvilinear glass-and-steel tower evokes beachfront hotels of the 1950s. The 600 rooms range from 238 square feet for standard king rooms that sleep four to 575 square feet for Kids' Suites that sleep five. Decor is streamlined and minimalist, in keeping with the midcentury-modern architectural cues.

Aventura's standard rooms, about 22 square feet smaller than those at Disney's Value resorts, have vinyl "hardwood" floors. Beds are comfortable and all of the electronics work, but our shower curtain didn't extend far enough down, resulting in a wet floor every time someone showered.

Kids' Suites are distinguished by sleeping areas rather than special theming: Mom and Dad get a bedroom with a king bed, while kids get a separate room with two twin beds. Plus, the living room couch converts to a deluxe bed with memory-foam mattress. All rooms have a coffee maker, iron and ironing board, flat-panel TV, and minifridge.

Reader ratings for Aventura are lower than those for almost all Disney and Universal resorts. In particular, Aventura lags behind in room quietness and food-court quality. We understand the rating for the food court—it feels small and disjointed, with lots of small stations. We think Cabana Bay (see next profile) is a better value-priced option overall.

Food-and-drink options include **Bar 17 Bistro,** an expansive rooftop restaurant and lounge with fantastic views (great in the cooler months); the food court; lobby and pool bars; and a **Starbucks.** Rounding out the amenities are a pool with a separate kids' splash area, a fitness center, a virtual reality game room, a gift shop with Universal-themed swag, and supervised children's activities. Aventura guests enjoy early admission to The Wizarding World of Harry

Potter at both theme parks as well as Volcano Bay (but not free Universal Express privileges).

Universal's Cabana Bay Beach Resort ★★★★

6550 Adventure Way
☎ 407-503-4000 or
888-464-3617
loewshotels.com
/cabana-bay-hotel

Rate per night Standard rooms, $164–$278; suites, $214–$358. **Pools** ★★★★. **Fridge in room** Yes. **Shuttle to parks** Yes (Universal, Sea-World, Discovery Cove, Aquatica, Volcano Bay). **Maximum number of occupants per room** 4 (standard)/6 (suite). **Comments** Parking $18/day. **Survey results** 82% of *Unofficial Guide* readers would stay here again; 80% would recommend this resort to a friend.

OPENED IN SPRING 2014, Cabana Bay was Universal's first on-site hotel aimed at the value and midpriced markets. But whereas Disney's Value resorts use kid-friendly oversize characters and bright colors, Cabana Bay went with a sleek midcentury-modern theme. It was an immediate hit, running at high occupancy levels from the day it opened. Disney's current redesign of its Value rooms is a direct result of Cabana Bay's success. The resort has proved so popular, in fact, that Universal has added two towers with 400 rooms that afford views of Universal's Volcano Bay water park.

Befitting a classy Rat Pack retreat in Palm Springs or Las Vegas, Cabana Bay's retro-hip 1950s style includes lots of windows, bright colors, and period-appropriate lighting and furniture. Kids will love the two large, well-themed pools (one with a lazy river), the video arcade, and the vintage cars parked outside the lobby. Adults will appreciate the sophisticated kitsch of the decor, the multiple lounges, and the on-site **Starbucks.** We think Cabana Bay is an excellent choice for price- and/or space-conscious families.

The hotel's closest competitor in the Orlando area is Disney's Art of Animation Resort, and the two share many similarities. Both have standard rooms and family suites. At 430 square feet per suite, Cabana Bay suites are about 135 square feet smaller than comparable suites at AOA and have just one bathroom. We found them well appointed for two to four people per room (though not for the six Loews claims as its capacity). Rack rates for the suites run about $130–$200 per night less than Art of Animation's.

Each family suite has a small bedroom with two queen beds, divided from the living area and kitchenette by a sliding screen; a foldout sofa in the living area provides additional sleeping space. (Standard rooms also have two queen beds.) The bath is divided into three sections: toilet, sink area, and shower room with additional sink. The kitchenette has a microwave, coffee maker, and minifridge. A bar area provides extra seating for quick meals, and a large closet has enough space to store everyone's luggage. Built-in USB charging outlets for your devices are a thoughtful touch.

Recreational options include the 10-lane **Galaxy Bowl** ($12.99 per person with shoe rental; registered hotel guests only, same-day in-person reservations required), poolside table tennis and billiards, and a **Jack LaLanne Fitness Center.** (Fitness centers aren't found at any Disney Value or Moderate resort except Coronado Springs.) Outdoor movies are shown nightly near the pool.

In addition to the Starbucks, a food court with seating shows 1950s TV clips. **Swizzle Lounge** in the lobby, two pool bars, in-room pizza delivery, and Galaxy Bowl round out the on-site dining options. The **Universal Studios Store** is the largest hotel store in the resort and stocks candy and clothes exclusive to Cabana Bay.

Unlike the pricier Universal resorts, Cabana Bay offers no watercraft service to the parks—it's either take the bus or walk. A pedestrian bridge connects Cabana Bay to CityWalk and the rest of Universal Orlando, but we recommend the bus for most visitors. Cabana Bay guests are eligible for Early Park Entry at Universal but not free Universal Express privileges.

The biggest complaints we hear about Cabana Bay are that wait times to check in during midafternoon are often excessive (try to arrive early or late) and that housekeeping services can sometimes be inconsistent.

Universal's Endless Summer Resort   ★★★½

Rate per night Standard rooms, $113–$223; suites, $168–$278. **Pool** ★★★. **Fridge in room** Yes. **Shuttle to parks** Yes (Universal, SeaWorld, Discovery Cove, Aquatica, Volcano Bay). **Maximum number of occupants per room** 4 (standard)/6 (suite). **Comments** Parking $15/day. **Survey results** Endless Summer is the highest-rated value-priced resort at both Universal Orlando and Walt Disney World; 92% of *Unofficial Guide* readers would stay here again; 94% would recommend this resort to a friend.

Dockside Inn and Suites:
7125 Universal Blvd.
☎ 407-503-8000
loewshotels.com
/dockside-inn-and-suites
Surfside Inn and Suites:
7000 Universal Blvd.
☎ 407-503-7000
loewshotels.com
/surfside-inn-and-suites

UNIVERSAL'S LATEST HOTEL COMPLEX consists of two value-priced resorts: **Surfside Inn and Suites,** which opened in June 2019, and **Dockside Inn and Suites,** which opened in late 2020.

Surfside Inn has 360 standard rooms and 390 two-bedroom suites, while Dockside Inn has 577 standard rooms and 723 two-bedroom suites. With both hotels open, Universal has almost doubled the number of its on-site value rooms. Both resorts' color schemes include pale blues and greens, with lots of white. Bright ocean- and surf-themed art hangs on the walls. Room sound-proofing is excellent, which is a surprise at this price, and there are plenty of under-shelf hooks on which to hang things, though only a handful of drawers for stowing your clothes. Our biggest nitpick is the poor quality of the soft goods—foam pillows and polyester-blend bath towels should be illegal.

Standard rooms are around 313 square feet and have vinyl "hardwood" floors, two queen beds, a chair, minifridge, coffee maker, iron, and ironing board. They're about the size of a Disney Moderate room at Disney Value prices: about $100–$145 per night cheaper than a Moderate. That's quite a savings.

Two-bedroom suites are 440 square feet and include a kitchenette with picnic-style table and microwave, plus one bathroom. *Two-bedroom* is a misnomer, though: The suite comprises one main room with two beds and a separate room with another bed. That's about 65–80 square feet smaller—and one less bathroom than—Disney's Family Suites. Universal's suites, however, are roughly $150–$240 cheaper per night, which pays for a *lot* of park admission.

The pools are unusually shallow (maximum depth 4 feet) and lack waterslides. Unfortunately, Endless Summer guests are forbidden to crash the pools at the non-Value resorts. Each hotel includes a well-stocked free fitness room, plus a **Universal Studios Store** and a video arcade. Full-service dining isn't offered, but cafeteria-style food courts, lobby and pool bars, **Starbucks** cafés, and pizza delivery are all available. Between the two hotels, we think Surfside has a slight edge owing to its smaller, more manageable size, but Dockside has a few improved amenities and food options.

Because Endless Summer is on the opposite side of International Drive and I-4 from the rest of Universal Orlando, walking to the parks from the resort isn't practical, so a fleet of free buses is provided, servicing both the parking hub (from which you walk to CityWalk and the theme parks) and direct to Volcano Bay. The ride from here is actually slightly shorter than the one from Cabana Bay; travel time is barely 5 minutes each way, and the entire trip (including walking and waiting to depart) takes about 15 minutes.

As at Cabana Bay, guests at Endless Summer get free early admission to Universal's theme parks but not free Universal Express.

LAKE BUENA VISTA & I-4 CORRIDOR

10100 Dream Tree Blvd.
☎ 407-313-7777 or
800-267-3046
fourseasons.com/orlando

Four Seasons Resort Orlando at Walt Disney World Resort ★★★★★

Rate per night $613–$1,355. **Pools ★★★★★. Fridge in room** Yes. **Shuttle to parks** Yes (Disney). **Maximum number of occupants per room** 4 (3 adults or 2 adults + 2 children). **Comments** The best deluxe hotel rooms, staff service, and pool complex in Walt Disney World, if not Orlando. Character breakfast on Saturday (by reservation). **Survey results** Not enough to rate.

WITH 444 GUEST ROOMS, THE FOUR SEASONS is simultaneously the largest hotel in the Four Seasons chain and the smallest on Disney property. It's also the best deluxe resort in the area, offering comfort, amenities, and personal service that far surpass anything that the Disney-branded Deluxe resorts offer.

Standard rooms average around 500 square feet and have either one king bed with a sleeper sofa or two double beds (a crib is available in double rooms). Amenities include two flat-panel TVs (one is in the mirror above the bathroom sink!), a coffee maker, a minifridge, a work desk with two chairs, and Bluetooth speakers. In keeping with the room's gadget-friendly spirit, each nightstand has four electrical outlets and two USB ports. Bathrooms have glass-walled showers, a separate tub, marble vanities with two sinks, mosaic-tile floors, hair dryers, and lighted mirrors.

Most rooms have an 80-square-foot balcony with table and chairs—perfect for your morning coffee or an evening nightcap. Standard-view rooms look out onto the resort's lawns, gardens, and nearby homes in Golden Oak. Lake-view rooms—which overlook the lake, the Tom Fazio–designed Tranquilo Golf Club, or the pool—cost about $250 more per night than standard-view rooms. Park-view rooms, on floors 6–16, cost up to $700 *more* per night than standard-view rooms and offer views of the Magic Kingdom's nightly fireworks; EPCOT-view suites are available as well.

The 5-acre pool area is the best—and least crowded—on Disney property, with an adult pool, a family pool, an 11,000-square-foot lazy river, and a splash zone with two 242-foot waterslides. To put this in perspective, the Four Seasons' pool area is about twice as large as Stormalong Bay at the Yacht & Beach Club Resorts, but with only a third as many guests. Private cabanas rent for around $150–$300 per day.

Capa, a Spanish-themed rooftop restaurant, serves seafood and steaks (open 6–10 p.m.; dress is resort casual, and reservations are recommended). **Ravello,** on the first floor, serves American breakfasts (6:30–11 a.m.) and Italian dinners (5:30–10 p.m.; reservations are recommended, and dress is smart casual); it also offers a character breakfast on Saturdays. **PB&G (Pool Bar and Grill)** serves barbecued meats and salads by the main pool (11 a.m.–6 p.m.).

At the hotel's Disney Planning Center, Four Seasons staff can help guests with reservations or any other Disney needs. Disney will also deliver your in-park purchases to the Four Seasons, and staying here qualifies you for Early Theme Park Entry.

The hotel has a full-service spa and fitness center, as well as a beautiful late-checkout lounge that allows use of the showers and bathrooms in the spa.

Marriott's Harbour Lake ★★★★

Rate per night 1-bedroom suites, $229–$469; 2-bedroom suites, $259–$499. **Pool** ★★★★. **Fridge in room** Yes. **Shuttle to parks** No. **Maximum number of occupants per room** 4 (1-bedroom)/ 8 (2-bedroom). **Comments** Significantly higher rated than other suite hotels in Lake Buena Vista. **Survey results** 98% of *Unofficial Guide* readers would stay here again; 92% would recommend this resort to a friend.

7102 Grand Horizons Blvd.
☎ 407-465-6100
tinyurl.com/harbourlake

HARBOUR LAKE IS A FAVORITE of *Unofficial Guide* readers, with good deals on one- and two-bedroom villas within a 15-minute drive of both Disney World and Universal. The resort's theme seems to be a cross between Key West and Nantucket, with architectural elements and color palettes from both.

Room categories include studios and one- and two-bedroom villas, the latter being the ones to request. These include bedrooms separated from the living areas, a fully equipped kitchen, a sofa, a reading chair, a dining table and chairs, and a washer and dryer. The master bedroom has a king bed, while the two-bedroom villa's second bedroom has two queens. The earth-tone decor isn't memorable, but it is modern and comfortable. Counter space around the bathroom sinks is a bit sparse, but there's plenty of storage elsewhere. Water pressure is acceptable. Most rooms have a balcony or patio.

Rates for the 1,082-square-foot two-bedroom villas are $259–$469 per night, including taxes and fees—that's up to $200 per night cheaper than Disney's Art of Animation Family Suites during the off-season, with more than double the space. Rates for the 800-square-foot one-bedroom villas are even cheaper, at $229–$469 per night.

The pools are top-notch, with a pirate ship, waterslides, and excellent play areas for smaller children. The resort also has an on-site fitness center and 18-hole minigolf course. On-site dining is limited to a bar and grill and a grab-and-go outpost, so be prepared to do some grocery shopping or eating out.

Sheraton Vistana Resort Villas ★★★★

Rate per night 1-bedroom villas, $147–$327; 2-bedroom villas, $200–$360. **Pools** ★★★½. **Fridge in room** Yes. **Shuttle to parks** Yes (Disney). **Maximum number of occupants per room** 4 (1-bedroom)/8 (2-bedroom). **Comments** Though they're time-shares, the villas are rented nightly as well. **Survey results** 99% of *Unofficial Guide* readers would stay here again; 93% would recommend this resort to a friend.

8800 Vistana Centre Dr.
☎ 407-239-3100 or
866-208-0003
tinyurl.com/sheratonresortlbv

THE SHERATON VISTANA is deceptively large, stretching across both sides of Vistana Centre Drive. Because Sheraton's emphasis is on selling the time-shares, the rental angle is little known. But families should consider it; it's one of Orlando's best off–Disney World properties.

The spacious villas offer 850-square-foot one-bedroom and 1,025-square-foot two-bedroom models. Decorated in beachy pastels offset by dark wood finishes, each villa has a full kitchen (including fridge, microwave, oven/range, dishwasher, toaster, and coffee maker, with an option to prestock with groceries and laundry products), a washer and dryer, TVs in the living room and each bedroom (one with DVD player), a stereo with CD player in some villas, a separate dining area, and a private patio or balcony in most villas.

The grounds feature seven swimming pools (three with bars); four playgrounds; two restaurants; game rooms; fitness centers; a minigolf course; sports-equipment rentals (including bikes); and courts for basketball, volleyball, tennis, and shuffleboard. A mind-boggling array of activities for kids (and adults) ranges from crafts to games and sports tournaments.

Of special note: Vistana is highly secure, with locked gates bordering all guest areas, so children can have the run of the place without parents worrying about them wandering off. The one downside: noise, both above (from the flight path of a helicopter-tour company) and below (from International Drive). Bring a white-noise machine or app for better sleep.

Signia by Hilton Orlando Bonnet Creek ★★★★

14100 Bonnet Creek Resort Ln.
☎ 407-597-3600
hiltonbonnetcreek.com

Rate per night $250–$385. **Pool** ★★★★½. **Fridge in room** Yes. **Shuttle to parks** Yes (Disney). **Maximum number of occupants per room** 4. **Comments** $45/night resort fee. Parking $30/day. Guests are eligible for Early Theme Park Entry benefits. **Survey results** Not enough survey results to rate.

THE SIGNIA IS ONE of our favorite non-Disney hotels in Lake Buena Vista, and the value for the money beats anything in Disney's Deluxe category. Behind Caribbean Beach and Pop Century Resorts, this Hilton property is much nicer than the two in the Disney Springs Resort Area.

Standard rooms measure around 414 square feet—comparable to Disney Deluxes—and have either one king bed or two queen beds. Mattresses and linens are very comfortable. Other features include a 37-inch flat-panel TV, spacious work desk, small reading chair with floor lamp, nightstand, and digital clock. A coffee maker, a minifridge, and an ironing board and iron are all standard, along with free Wi-Fi.

Bathrooms have tile floors, and some have glassed-in showers. Unfortunately, the layout isn't as up-to-date as other hotels'—where many upscale hotel bathrooms have two sinks, the Signia's have just one. And where modern bathroom configurations often include a dressing area separate from the bath and a separate water closet for the commode, everything is in the bathroom here.

Public areas are stylish and spacious. Families will enjoy the huge zero-entry pool, complete with waterslide, as well as the 3-acre lazy river. Even better, the staff runs arts-and-crafts activities poolside during the day, allowing parents to grab a quick swim and a cocktail. Pool-facing cabanas are also available for rent at around $300–$400 per day. A nice fitness center sits on the ground floor.

The Signia participates in the neighboring Waldorf Astoria's **WA Kids Club** (temporarily closed) for children ages 5–12. A daytime program is available 10:30 a.m.–2:30 p.m., and an evening program is available 6–10 p.m. on Friday and Saturday. Price is $75 for the first child, $25 for each additional child.

The Signia and the Waldorf boast more than a dozen restaurants and lounges between them, with options including an upscale steakhouse, Italian, sushi, tapas, a coffee bar, an American bistro, and breakfast buffets. Hours are usually 7–11:30 a.m. for breakfast, 11:30 a.m.–5 p.m. for lunch, and 5–10 p.m. for dinner. Reservations are recommended for the fancy places.

Sonesta ES Suites Lake Buena Vista ★★★★½

8751 Suiteside Dr.
☎ 407-238-0777
tinyurl.com
/sonestalbv

Rate per night 1-bedroom suites, $169–$259; 2-bedroom suites, $174–$299. **Pool** ★★★. **Fridge in room** Yes. **Shuttle to parks** Yes (Disney, Universal). **Maximum number of occupants per room** 4 (1-bedroom suites)/8 (2-bedroom suites). **Comments** Free grab-and-go breakfast. **Survey results** 95% of *Unofficial Guide* readers would stay here again; 87% would recommend this resort to a friend.

WE FOUND THIS GEM through our reader surveys, which named this the best off-site hotel near Walt Disney World in 2016. Having stayed there, we agree. It's so inexpensive that we'd recommend the two-bedroom suites for families as small as two or three people.

The best values are the 750-square-foot, two-bedroom suites, at rates less than you'd pay for a Disney Moderate resort. For that we got two separate bedrooms on opposite ends of the suite. One bedroom has a king bed, the other two doubles. A sleeper sofa is standard in both the one-and two-bedroom layouts. The one-bedroom suites measure around 550 square feet.

Each bedroom has its own full bathroom. Between the bedrooms are a living room, dining area, and full kitchen with dishwasher, range, microwave, and fridge as well as plates, cups, glasses, cutlery, and basic pots and pans. There's a big-screen TV in the living room and smaller ones in each bedroom.

Other amenities include free Wi-Fi and a free grab-and-go breakfast. Service was excellent. Be aware that the Sonesta is so popular that it's unlikely your room will be ready much before the 4 p.m. check-in time.

Located about 0.5 mile from the Disney Springs Resort Area, just around the corner on South Apopka–Vineland Road, the Sonesta ES is about a 10-minute drive to the Disney Springs parking garages and about 19 minutes to the Magic Kingdom parking lot. Two nearby shopping centers are easily walkable from your room.

Waldorf Astoria Orlando ★★★★½

Rate per night $353–$735. **Pool** ★★★★. **Fridge in room** Yes. **Shuttle to parks** Yes (Disney). **Maximum number of occupants per room** 4 plus child in crib. **Comments** Good alternative to the Disney Deluxe resorts; $45/night resort fee. **Survey results** Not enough to rate.

14200 Bonnet Creek Resort Ln.
☎ 407-597-5500 or
800-925-3673
waldorfastoriaorlando.com

THE WALDORF ASTORIA is between I-4 and Pop Century Resort, near the Signia by Hilton at the back of the Bonnet Creek Resort property. Getting here requires a GPS or good directions, so be prepared with those before you travel. Once you arrive, however, you'll know the trip was worth it. Beautifully decorated and appointed, the Waldorf is more elegant than any Disney resort. Service is excellent, and the staff-to-guest ratio is far higher than at Disney properties.

At just under 450 square feet, standard rooms feature either two queen beds or one king. A full-size desk allows you to get work done if it's absolutely necessary, and rooms also have flat-panel TVs, high-speed internet, and Wi-Fi (included with the resort fee). The bathrooms are spacious and gorgeous, with cool marble floors, glass-walled showers, separate tubs, and enough counter space for a Broadway makeup artist.

Amenities include a fitness center, a spa, a golf course, six restaurants, and two pools (including a zero-entry pool for kids). Shuttles service the Disney parks about every half hour (see www.bonnetshuttle.com for schedule). Runners will like the relative solitude—it's about a 1-mile round-trip to the nearest busy road.

US 192 AREA

Gaylord Palms Resort & Convention Center
★★★★½

Rate per night $352–$409. **Pool** ★★★★. **Fridge in room** Yes. **Shuttle to parks** Yes (Disney, free; other parks, $21/person round-trip). **Maximum number of occupants per room** 4. **Comments** Along with a handful of other hotels, the Gaylord Palms is probably the closest you'll get to Disney-level extravagance out of the World. $30/night resort fee. Parking $28/day. **Survey results** Not enough to rate.

6000 W. Osceola Pkwy.
☎ 407-586-0000
gaylordpalms.com

THIS UPSCALE RESORT, with its colossal convention facility, caters to business clientele, but it's still a nice (if pricey) family resort. Hotel wings are defined by the three themed glass-ceilinged atria they overlook. **Key West**'s design is reminiscent of island life in the Florida Keys; **Everglades** is an overgrown spectacle of shabby swamp chic; and the immense central **St. Augustine** recalls Spanish Colonial Florida. Lagoons, streams, and waterfalls connect all three, and walkways and bridges abound. A fourth wing, **Emerald Bay Tower,** overlooks the Emerald Plaza shopping and dining area of the St. Augustine atrium. These rooms are the nicest and most expensive; they're mostly used by convention-goers. Though rooms have fridges, alarm clocks, and other perks such as high-speed internet, they work better as retreats for adults than for kids. However, children will enjoy the themed areas and the family pool (with water-squirting octopus). In-room childcare is available.

Holiday Inn Club Vacations at Orange Lake Resort ★★★★½

8505 W. Irlo Bronson Memorial Hwy.
☎ 407-477-7025 or 888-465-4329
tinyurl.com/holidayinnorangelake

Rate per night $132–$175. **Pools** ★★★★. **Fridge in room** Yes. **Shuttle to parks** Yes, for a fee (varies based on your destination). **Maximum number of occupants per room** Varies. **Comments** This is a time-share property, but if you rent directly through the resort instead of the sales office, you won't have to listen to any sales pitches. $15/night resort fee. **Survey results** 93% of *Unofficial Guide* readers would stay here again; 80% would recommend this resort to a friend.

YOU COULD SPEND YOUR ENTIRE VACATION never leaving this property about 6–10 minutes from the Disney theme parks. From its seven pools and mini water park to its golfing opportunities (36 holes of championship greens plus two 9-hole executive courses), Orange Lake offers an extensive menu of amenities and recreational opportunities. If you tire of lazing by the pool, try waterskiing, wakeboarding, tubing, fishing, or other activities on the 80-acre lake. There are also exercise programs, organized competitive sports and games, arts-and-crafts sessions, and miniature golf. Karaoke, live music, a Hawaiian luau, and movies at the resort cinema are some of the evening options.

The 2,412 units are tastefully decorated and comfortably furnished, ranging from suites and studios to three-bedroom villas, all with fully equipped kitchens. These rooms are massive and cheap: The 1,700-square-foot, three-bedroom villa sleeps 11 people and goes for as little as $255 a night. That's about the same as five—*five!*—Disney Moderate rooms, for less money.

If you'd rather not cook on vacation, try one of the seven restaurants scattered across the resort: two cafés, three grills, one pizzeria, and a fast-food place.

We reevaluated the resort after a reader noticed several negative reviews of the property on TripAdvisor, most mentioning room cleanliness. Our test room—a one-bedroom villa with washer and dryer and full kitchen for $136 per night with tax—was spotless, as were the rooms we got to peek into around the resort. As far as suites go, we like the **Sonesta ES Suites Lake Buena Vista** (see page 238) a bit better, but we'd stay at Orange Lake again.

Margaritaville Resort Orlando ★★★★

8000 Fins Up Circle
☎ 407-479-0950 or
855-995-9099
tinyurl.com
/margaritaville-fl

Rate per night Hotel rooms, $230–$440; cottages (1–8 bedrooms), $229–$2,120. **Pool** ★★★★. **Fridge in room** Yes (full kitchen). **Shuttle to parks** No. **Maximum number of occupants per room** 2 (standard room)/18 (8-bedroom cottage). **Survey results** Not enough to rate.

BEYOND OUR ABSOLUTE CERTAINTY that Margaritaville's restaurant would serve a Cheeseburger in Paradise, Jimmy Buffett's lyrics reveal few thoughts about hotel management. We were skeptical that this was going to be anything other than a standard hotel with some tropical prints and parrots. But Margaritaville is a well-designed, reasonably priced resort that's worth considering for large families and groups, especially those who aren't going to Walt Disney World every day.

Sitting on an impressive 300 acres of land, Margaritaville has two kinds of accommodations: The main building holds 186 standard rooms and suites, and another 187 one- to eight-bedroom vacation cottages sit around a central lake. (Construction of additional accommodations is scheduled in the future.)

An island/beach theme is consistent across the resort. Standard hotel rooms are 470 square feet, larger than any standard Disney Deluxe room. Amenities include vinyl floors, a microwave and coffee maker, and good lighting. Bathrooms are well lit and spacious, with walk-in glass showers and good water pressure.

Vacation cottages are freestanding homes, ranging from one-story, one-bedroom bungalows to three-story, eight-bedroom buildings that sleep up to 18 guests. The most notable thing about these cottages is that nothing feels cheap or underbuilt. The kitchen layout makes it easy to cook for large groups. The couches, chairs, and beds are comfortable. Bathrooms have good water pressure. The A/C blows cold. The lights and appliances work the way they're supposed to. And the homes we've stayed in have been spotlessly clean.

A 5-minute walk from the hotel lobby puts you in the middle of **Sunset Walk,** Margaritaville's dining and entertainment district, comprising 15 restaurants and bars with cuisines ranging from sushi to British pub to Memphis barbecue. We think it's worth visiting. There's also an on-site water park—**Island H2O Live!**—but we consider Universal's Volcano Bay a better value. A Publix supermarket is half a mile away. A free internal shuttle service links the hotel, cottages, and Sunset Walk.

If you're headed to Disney property from Margaritaville, you can avoid almost all of the US 192 traffic by taking Inspiration Drive to Black Lake Road to Osceola Parkway. That half-mile, traffic-free stretch of road puts you smack-dab between Animal Kingdom and Animal Kingdom Lodge, with clear, easy access to the rest of Walt Disney World.

Polynesian Isles Resort (Diamond Resorts) ★★★½

Rate per night 1-bedroom villas, $112–$298; 2-bedroom villas, $170–$355. **Pool** ★★★½. **Fridge in room** Yes (full kitchen). **Shuttle to parks** No. **Maximum number of occupants per room** 4 (1-bedroom)/6 (2-bedroom), plus child in crib. **Survey results** Not enough to rate.

3045 Polynesian Isles Blvd.
☎ 407-396-1622 or
800-925-3673
polynesianisle.com

LET'S START BY SAYING that the Polynesian Isles' rooms aren't the most modern and could use a good interior decorator. And the location, a few miles east of I-4 in Kissimmee, isn't the most upscale. But there are few other places in Orlando where you can get 1,500–1,600 square feet of space for less than $200 a night with tax. (Quantity, as they say, has a quality all its own.)

One-bedroom villas are 1,500 square feet and have one king bed and one sofa bed; two-bedroom villas are 1,600 square feet and have king, queen, and sofa beds. Both villa types are outfitted with a full kitchen, a dining room table with seating for six, upholstered chairs, and a TV. Bathrooms are large and clean, with decent water pressure and so-so lighting.

The resort's Polynesian theme is pulled off pretty well for something not in a theme park. Other amenities include tennis courts, a small basketball half-court, a very small fitness room, a playground, and a pool.

FLAMINGO CROSSINGS

Home2Suites by Hilton ★★★½

341 Flagler Ave.
☎ 407-993-3999
tinyurl.com/fc
-home2suites

Rate per night $140–$250. **Pool** ★★★★. **Fridge in room** Yes. **Shuttle to parks** Yes (Magic Kingdom only, $5). **Maximum number of occupants per room** 6, plus child in crib. **Survey results** Unavailable for this edition.

Homewood Suites by Hilton ★★★★

411 Flagler Ave.
☎ 407-993-3011
tinyurl.com/fc
-homewoodsuites

Rate per night $150–$250. **Pool** ★★★★. **Fridge in room** Yes. **Shuttle to parks** Yes (Magic Kingdom only, $5). **Maximum number of occupants per room** 4 (1-bedroom suite with king and pullout beds)/ 5 (1-bedroom suite with 2 queen and pullout beds), plus child in crib. **Survey results** Unavailable for this edition.

Residence Inn *(opens October 2021)*

Will consist of 1- and 2-bedroom suites.

2111 Flagler Ave.
☎ 407-993-3233
tinyurl.com/fc-residenceinn

SpringHill Suites ★★★★

13279 Hartzog Rd.
☎ 407-507-1200
tinyurl.com/fc-springhill

Rate per night $149–$199. **Pool** ★★★★. **Fridge in room** Yes. **Shuttle to parks** Yes (Magic Kingdom only, $5). **Maximum number of occupants per room** 6, plus child in crib. **Survey results** Not enough to rate.

TownePlace Suites ★★★★

13295 Hartzog Rd.
☎ 407-507-1300
tinyurl.com/fc-towneplace

Rate per night $146–$199. **Pool** ★★★★. **Fridge in room** Yes. **Shuttle to parks** Yes (Magic Kingdom only, $5). **Maximum number of occupants per room** 3 (1-bedroom suite)/5 (2-bedroom suite with 2 queen and pullout beds), plus child in crib. **Survey results** Not enough to rate.

FLAMINGO CROSSINGS IS LOCATED at the intersection of US 429 and Western Way—we're not exaggerating when we say it's less than 60 seconds from Disney property by car. Follow Western Way for a bit, and you'll end up at Coronado Springs Resort.

Five hotels are located here. Three are Marriott brands: **TownePlace Suites,** an extended-stay hotel; **Residence Inn** (opens fall 2021); and **SpringHill Suites.** Two are Hilton properties: **Home2 Suites** and **Homewood Suites.** All have 220–300 rooms. In terms of value, we'd rate them in this order (keeping in mind that the Residence Inn wasn't open at press time):

1. SpringHill Suites 2. Homewood Suites 3. TownePlace Suites 4. Home2Suites

The related hotels are adjacent and share parking, a huge pool complex, and gyms. Other amenities include practice fields and facilities—a nod to the sports groups that participate in events at the ESPN Wide World of Sports Complex. The lobbies are constantly abuzz with color-coordinated teens either preparing for or unwinding from some event.

Despite the potential for noise, our rooms were very quiet. They were also spotless. Our two-bedroom suite had a small, full kitchen, while our studio had a microwave and coffee maker. Both had only one bathroom, and we think the two-bedroom units could have used a second. Water pressure was better at the Marriott properties than the Hiltons.

In addition to being close to Disney property, the Flamingo Crossings hotels are about a 10-minute drive to a wide variety of suburban retailers on US 192, including a Publix, a Super Target, and tons of restaurants. That said, if you have a car or you aren't participating in anything at the Wide World of Sports Complex, we think any of the other resorts in the preceding section offer better value for the money.

HOTELS *and* MOTELS:
Rated and Ranked

IN THIS SECTION, WE COMPARE HOTELS in four main areas outside Walt Disney World (see page 214) with those inside the World.

In addition to Disney properties, we rate hotels in the four lodging areas defined earlier in this chapter. Additional hotels can be found at the intersection of US 27 and I-4, on US 441 (Orange Blossom Trail), and in downtown Orlando. Most of these require more than 30 minutes of commuting to Disney World and thus are not rated. We also haven't rated lodging east of Siesta Lago Drive on US 192. As mentioned earlier, if a hotel isn't listed in this section, the most likely reason is that the ones listed are better choices in terms of quality and price.

WHAT'S IN A ROOM?

EXCEPT FOR CLEANLINESS, state of repair, and decor, travelers pay little attention to hotel rooms. There is, of course, a clear standard of quality that differentiates Motel 6 from Holiday Inn, Holiday Inn from Marriott, and so on. Many guests, however, fail to appreciate that some rooms are better engineered than others. Making the room usable to its occupants is an art that combines both form and function.

Beyond decor, how livable is the room? In Orlando, for example, we've seen some beautifully appointed rooms that aren't well designed for human habitation. Even more than decor, your room's details and layout will make you feel comfortable and at home.

ROOM RATINGS

TO EVALUATE PROPERTIES FOR THEIR QUALITY, tastefulness, state of repair, cleanliness, and size of their standard rooms, we have grouped the hotels and motels into classifications denoted by stars—the overall star rating. Star ratings in this guide apply only to Orlando-area properties and don't necessarily correspond to ratings awarded by *Frommer's*, TripAdvisor, AAA, or other travel critics. Because stars have little relevance when awarded in the absence of recognized standards of comparison, we have tied our ratings to expected levels of quality established by specific American hotel corporations.

Overall star ratings apply only to room quality and describe the property's standard accommodations. For most hotels, a standard accommodation is a room with one king bed or two queen beds. In an all-suite property, the standard accommodation is either a studio or a one-bedroom suite. Ratings are assigned without regard to amenities such as restaurant(s), recreational facilities, and entertainment.

In addition to stars (which delineate broad categories), we use a numerical rating system—the room-quality rating. Our scale is 0–100, with 100 being the best possible rating and zero (0) the worst. Numerical ratings show the difference we perceive between one property and another. For instance, rooms at both **Clarion Suites Maingate** and **B Resort** are rated three and a half stars (★★★½). In the supplemental numerical ratings, the former is a 75 and the latter an 82. This means that within the ★★★½ category, B Resort has slightly nicer rooms than the Clarion Suites.

The location column identifies the area around Walt Disney World where you'll find a particular property. **WDW** means the hotel is inside Walt Disney World. A **1** means it's on or near International Drive. Properties on or near US 192 (aka Irlo Bronson Memorial Highway, Vine Street, and Space Coast Parkway) are indicated by a **3,** and those in the vicinity of Universal Orlando as **4.** All others are marked with **2** and for the most part are along FL 535 and the I-4 corridor, though some are in nearby locations that don't meet any other criteria.

The names of properties along US 192 also designate location (for example, the Holiday Inn Maingate West). The consensus in Orlando seems to be that the main entrance to Walt Disney World is the broad interstate-type road that runs off US 192. This is called the **Maingate.** Properties along US 192 call themselves Maingate East or West to differentiate their positions along the highway. So, driving southeast from Clermont or Florida's Turnpike, the properties before you reach the Maingate turnoff are called Maingate West, while the properties after you pass the Maingate turnoff are called Maingate East.

LODGING AREAS *(see maps on pages 216–219)*	
WDW Walt Disney World	
1 International Drive	**3** US 192 (Irlo Bronson Memorial Highway)
2 Lake Buena Vista and the I-4 Corridor	**4** Universal Orlando Area

Cost estimates are based on the hotel's published rack rates for standard rooms. Each **$** represents $50. Thus a cost symbol of **$$$** means that a room (or suite) at that hotel will be about $150 a night; amounts over $200 are indicated by **$ x 5** and so on.

We've focused on room quality and excluded location, services, recreation, or amenities. In some instances, a one- or two-room suite is available for around the same price as a single standard room.

OVERALL STAR RATINGS		
★★★★★	Superior rooms	Tasteful and luxurious by any standard
★★★★	Extremely nice rooms	What you'd expect at a Hyatt Regency or Marriott
★★★	Nice rooms	Holiday Inn or comparable quality
★★	Adequate rooms	Clean, comfortable, and functional without frills—like a Motel 6
★	Super-budget	These exist but are not included in our coverage

We add new properties and change ratings and rankings annually, some because of room renovations or improved maintenance or housekeeping. Conversely, lax housekeeping or poor maintenance can bring down ratings.

Before you shop for a hotel, consider this letter from a man in Hot Springs, Arkansas:

> *We canceled our room reservations to follow the advice in your book and reserved a hotel highly ranked by the* Unofficial Guide. *We wanted inexpensive, but clean and cheerful. We got inexpensive, but also dirty, grim, and depressing. The room spoiled the holiday for me aside from our touring.*

This letter was as unsettling to us as the bad room was to the reader—our integrity as travel journalists is based on the quality of the information we provide. When rechecking the hotel, we found our rating was representative, but the reader had been assigned one of a small number of threadbare rooms scheduled for renovation.

Be aware that some hotel chains use the same guest-room photo in promotional literature for all their hotels and that, consequently, the rooms at a specific property may bear no resemblance to the photo in question. When you or your travel agent calls, ask how old the property is and when the guest room you're being assigned was last renovated. If you're assigned a room that is inferior to your expectations, demand to be moved.

A WORD ABOUT TOLL-FREE TELEPHONE NUMBERS

AS WE'VE REPEATED SEVERAL TIMES in this chapter, it's essential to communicate with the hotel directly when shopping for deals and stating your room preferences. Most toll-free numbers are routed directly to a hotel chain's central reservations office, and the customer-service agents there typically have little or no knowledge of the individual hotels in the chain or of any specials those hotels may be offering. In our Hotel Information Chart (pages 252–263), therefore, we provide the hotels' local phone numbers rather than the toll-free numbers. We also provide local numbers for the Disney resorts in both the Hotel Information Chart and the Walt Disney World Phone Numbers table on pages 42–43, but note that Disney hotels must be booked through the Disney Reservation Center (☎ 407-W-DISNEY or 934-7639). After you've reserved your room, you can check online to make sure the reservation is in order.

THE 30 BEST HOTEL VALUES

IN THE CHART ON THE NEXT PAGE, we look at the best combinations of quality and value in a room. Rankings are calculated without consideration for location or the availability of restaurant(s), recreational facilities, entertainment, and/or amenities.

A reader wrote to complain that he had booked one of our top-ranked rooms in terms of value and had been very disappointed in the room. We noticed that the room the reader occupied had a quality rating of ★★½. Remember that the list of top deals is intended to give you some sense of value received for dollars spent. A ★★½ room at $60 may have the same *value* as a ★★★★ room at $120, but that doesn't mean the rooms will be of comparable *quality*. Regardless of whether it's a good deal, a ★★½ room is still a ★★½ room.

THE TOP 30 BEST DEALS

	HOTEL	LODGING AREA	OVERALL QUALITY	ROOM QUALITY	COST ($ = $50)
1	Star Island Resort & Club	3	★★★★	84	$$-
2	Hawthorn Suites by Wyndham Lake Buena Vista	2	★★★★	85	$$-
3	Shades of Green	WDW	★★★★½	91	$$+
4	Rodeway Inn Maingate	3	★★★½	65	$+
5	Quality Suites Turkey Lake South/ Lake Buena Vista	2	★★★½	77	$$-
6	Holiday Inn Orlando SW– Celebration Area	3	★★★★	83	$$
7	Mystic Dunes Resort & Golf Club (Diamond Resorts)	3	★★★★½	90	$$$-
8	Clarion Suites Maingate	3	★★★½	75	$$-
9	Vacation Village at Parkway	3	★★★★½	93	$$$-
10	Drury Inn & Suites Orlando	1	★★★★	85	$$+
11	Extended Stay America Convention Center/Westwood	1	★★★★½	84	$$+
12	Westgate Vacation Villas Resort	3	★★★★½	90	$$$
13	Rosen Inn at Pointe Orlando	1	★★★★	84	$$$-
14	DoubleTree by Hilton at the Entrance to Universal Orlando	4	★★★★	89	$$$-
15	Fairfield Inn & Suites Orlando Kissimmee/Celebration	3	★★★½	78	$$
16	Holiday Inn Club Vacations at Orange Lake Resort	3	★★★★½	94	$$$+
17	Courtyard Orlando Lake Buena Vista at Vista Centre	2	★★★★	89	$$$-
18	Holiday Inn Express & Suites Orlando at SeaWorld	1	★★★½	82	$$+
19	Rosen Plaza Hotel	1	★★★★½	91	$$$+
20	Marriott's Grande Vista	1	★★★★½	93	$$$+
21	SpringHill Suites Orlando at Flamingo Crossings	2	★★★★	85	$$$-
22	Parc Corniche Resort	1	★★★★½	90	$$$+
23	Holiday Inn Resort Orlando–Lake Buena Vista	2	★★★½	82	$$+
24	Rosen Centre Hotel	1	★★★★½	95	$$$$-
25	Sheraton Vistana Resort Villas, Lake Buena Vista	2	★★★★½	89	$$$
26	TownePlace Suites Orlando at Flamingo Crossings	2	★★★★	84	$$$-
27	Sheraton Vistana Villages Resort Villas, I-Drive	1	★★★★	87	$$$
28	Westgate Lakes Resort & Spa	2	★★★★½	92	$$$$-
29	Holiday Inn & Suites Across from Universal Orlando	4	★★★½	75	$$+
30	Staybridge Suites Orlando at SeaWorld	1	★★★★½	90	$$$-

$80 IS THE NEW $50 One of our major research projects over the past few years has been to find hotels with clean, safe, functional rooms that we could recommend to you for around $50 per night with tax.

Gentle reader, we found exactly one for this edition (see the table opposite). And we learned something along the way.

At the $50 price point, we frequently had to make compromises in either safety or functionality, or both. At one motel on International Drive, we were greeted with a sign advising that copies of our driver's licenses would be shared with local police (!). At another motel, our door lock was made of plastic and didn't include a dead bolt—we had to pack our belongings into the car every time we left the room. At a third, our game of "spot the meth lab" became "spot the one that's *not* a meth lab." We were too scared to stay the night. Most of the rooms we checked at this price point also had some sort of mechanical problem, from balky toilets to water shooting out of the faucet whenever you turned it on. On the upside, the staff we met were uniformly helpful, and most were downright cheerful.

Ultimately, we decided that **$80 per night** (with tax) is the bare minimum you should expect to pay for a clean, safe, not-sketchy hotel room near Disney property—the $50 rooms that made it into the book are rare exceptions to the rule and aren't really representative when it comes to quality.

Not convinced? Here's the experience of a Rockton, Illinois, reader who booked a $75-per-night hotel for a solo trip, based on the hotel's internet photos—after he'd emailed us personally and we quoted the section above:

> *The TV remote looked so dirty that every time I used it, I grabbed my hand sanitizer. The dead bugs on the walls contributed to the "this place is definitely a dump" feeling. My biggest issue was with the front door—even with the dead bolt locked, the gaps between the door and the jamb meant that if someone had really wanted to kick the door in, they'd have had no problem. Every time I left the room, I locked my stuff in the car trunk. There's no way in hell my wife would stay here. I'd happily pay $100 a night for a better option.*

If you find something cheaper than $80 per night that meets our criteria and isn't already listed here, please let us know.

HOW THE HOTELS COMPARE

HOTEL	LODGING AREA	OVERALL QUALITY	ROOM QUALITY	COST ($ = $50)
Four Seasons Resort Orlando at Walt Disney World Resort	WDW	★★★★★	98	$+ x 22
Disney's Riviera Resort	WDW	★★★★½	95	$- x 12
Rosen Centre Hotel	1	★★★★½	95	$$$$-
Gaylord Palms Resort & Convention Center	3	★★★★½	94	$ x 7
Holiday Inn Club Vacations at Orange Lake Resort	3	★★★★½	94	$$$+
Omni Orlando Resort at ChampionsGate	2	★★★★½	94	$$$$+
The Ritz-Carlton Orlando, Grande Lakes	1	★★★★½	94	$- x 14
Hard Rock Hotel Orlando	4	★★★★½	93	$ x 10
Marriott's Grande Vista	1	★★★★½	93	$$$+
Vacation Village at Parkway	3	★★★★½	93	$$$-
The Villas at Disney's Grand Floridian Resort & Spa	WDW	★★★★½	93	$ x 19
Waldorf Astoria Orlando	WDW	★★★★½	93	$+ x 10
Disney's Grand Floridian Resort & Spa	WDW	★★★★½	92	$ x 19
Hyatt Regency Grand Cypress	2	★★★★½	92	$$$$
JW Marriott Orlando Bonnet Creek Resort & Spa	WDW	★★★★	92	$- x 8
Loews Portofino Bay Hotel at Universal Orlando	4	★★★★½	92	$+ x 10
Westgate Lakes Resort & Spa	2	★★★★½	92	$$$$-
Bay Lake Tower at Disney's Contemporary Resort (*studios*)	WDW	★★★★½	91	$- x 17
Disney's Contemporary Resort	WDW	★★★★½	91	$ x 14
Disney's Old Key West Resort	WDW	★★★★½	91	$+ x 11
Disney's Yacht Club Resort	WDW	★★★★½	91	$ x 14
Rosen Plaza Hotel	1	★★★★½	91	$$$+
Shades of Green	WDW	★★★★½	91	$$+
The Cabins at Disney's Fort Wilderness Resort	WDW	★★★★½	90	$- x 12
Club Wyndham Bonnet Creek	WDW	★★★★½	90	$$$$$+
Copper Creek Villas & Cabins at Disney's Wilderness Lodge (*studios*)	WDW	★★★★½	90	$+ x 12
Cypress Pointe Resort	2	★★★★½	90	$$$$+
Disney's Animal Kingdom Villas (*Kidani Village, studios*)	WDW	★★★★½	90	$+ x 11
Loews Royal Pacific Resort at Universal Orlando	4	★★★★½	90	$+ x 9
Mystic Dunes Resort & Golf Club (Diamond Resorts)	3	★★★★½	90	$$$-
Orlando World Center Marriott	2	★★★★½	90	$$$$+
Parc Corniche Resort	1	★★★★½	90	$$$+
Sonesta ES Suites Lake Buena Vista	2	★★★★½	90	$$$$
Staybridge Suites Orlando at SeaWorld	1	★★★★½	90	$$$$-
Treehouse Villas at Disney's Saratoga Springs Resort & Spa	WDW	★★★★½	90	$+ x 10
Westgate Vacation Villas Resort	3	★★★★½	90	$$$
Club Wyndham Cypress Palms	3	★★★★	89	$$$$-

HOW THE HOTELS COMPARE *(continued)*

HOTEL	LODGING AREA	OVERALL QUALITY	ROOM QUALITY	COST ($ = $50)
Courtyard Orlando Lake Buena Vista at Vista Centre	2	★★★★	89	$$$−
Disney's Beach Club Resort	WDW	★★★★	89	$ x 14
Disney's BoardWalk Inn	WDW	★★★★	89	$ x 14
Disney's BoardWalk Villas	WDW	★★★★	89	$− x 15
DoubleTree by Hilton at the Entrance to Universal Orlando	4	★★★★	89	$$$−
Sheraton Vistana Resort Villas, Lake Buena Vista	2	★★★★	89	$$$
Walt Disney World Swan	WDW	★★★★	89	$$$$$
Disney's Coronado Springs Resort	WDW	★★★★	88	$− x 8
Disney's Polynesian Villas & Bungalows *(studios)*	WDW	★★★★	88	$− x 17
Hilton Grand Vacations at SeaWorld	1	★★★★	88	$$$+
Hilton Grand Vacations at Tuscany Village	1	★★★★	88	$$$+
Signia by Hilton Orlando Bonnet Creek	WDW	★★★★	88	$$$$$+
Marriott's Harbour Lake	2	★★★★	88	$$$$−
Rosen Shingle Creek	1	★★★★	88	$$$$$−
The Berkley Orlando	3	★★★★	87	$$$$
Disney's Polynesian Village Resort	WDW	★★★★	87	$− x 17
Disney's Port Orleans Resort–French Quarter	WDW	★★★★	87	$+ x 7
Hilton Orlando Lake Buena Vista	WDW	★★★★	87	$$$$+
Sheraton Vistana Villages Resort Villas, I-Drive	1	★★★★	87	$$$
Walt Disney World Dolphin	WDW	★★★★	87	$$$$$
Caribe Royale Orlando	2	★★★★	86	$$$$−
Disney's Animal Kingdom Lodge	WDW	★★★★	86	$+ x 11
Disney's Animal Kingdom Villas *(Jambo House, studios)*	WDW	★★★★	86	$ x 12
Disney's Beach Club Villas *(studios)*	WDW	★★★★	86	$ x 14
Disney's Wilderness Lodge	WDW	★★★★	86	$+ x 12
Grand Beach (Diamond Resorts)	2	★★★	86	$$$+
Liki Tiki Village	3	★★★★	86	$$$$−
Marriott's Imperial Palms Villas	2	★★★★	86	$$$$$$+
Walt Disney World Swan Reserve *(opens 2021)*	WDW	★★★★	86	$ x 16
Drury Inn & Suites Orlando	1	★★★★	85	$$+
Hawthorn Suites by Wyndham Lake Buena Vista	2	★★★★	85	$$−
Homewood Suites by Hilton Lake Buena Vista-Orlando	2	★★★★	85	$$$+
Homewood Suites by Hilton Orlando Theme Parks	1	★★★★	85	$$$+
Marriott's Cypress Harbour Villas	2	★★★★	85	$$$$$+
SpringHill Suites Orlando at Flamingo Crossings	2	★★★★	85	$$$−
Wyndham Grand Orlando Resort Bonnet Creek	WDW	★★★★	85	$$$$$+
Boulder Ridge Villas at Disney's Wilderness Lodge *(studios)*	WDW	★★★★	84	$− x 12
Disney's Saratoga Springs Resort & Spa	WDW	★★★★	84	$+ x 11

HOW THE HOTELS COMPARE *(continued)*

HOTEL	LODGING AREA	OVERALL QUALITY	ROOM QUALITY	COST ($ = $50)
Embassy Suites by Hilton Orlando Lake Buena Vista Resort	2	★★★★	84	$$$$-
Extended Stay America Convention Center/ Westwood	1	★★★★	84	$$+
Loews Sapphire Falls Resort at Universal Orlando	4	★★★★	84	$$$$$+
Margaritaville Resort Orlando	3	★★★★	84	$$$$-
Rosen Inn at Pointe Orlando	1	★★★★	84	$$$-
SpringHill Suites Orlando Lake Buena Vista South	3	★★★★	84	$$$
Star Island Resort & Club	3	★★★★	84	$$-
TownePlace Suites Orlando at Flamingo Crossings	2	★★★★	84	$$$-
Disney's Port Orleans Resort-Riverside	WDW	★★★★	83	$+ x 7
Holiday Inn Orlando SW-Celebration Area	3	★★★★	83	$$
Universal's Cabana Bay Beach Resort	4	★★★★	83	$$$$
B Resort & Spa	WDW	★★★½	82	$$$+
Clarion Inn & Suites Across from Universal	4	★★★½	82	$$$$$+
Hilton Orlando	1	★★★½	82	$$$$-
Holiday Inn Express & Suites Orlando at SeaWorld	1	★★★½	82	$$+
Holiday Inn Resort Orlando-Lake Buena Vista	2	★★★½	82	$$+
Homewood Suites by Hilton Orlando at Flamingo Crossings Town Center	2	★★★★	82	$$$+
Homewood Suites by Hilton Orlando- Nearest to Universal Studios	1	★★★½	82	$$$
Hyatt Place Orlando/Lake Buena Vista	2	★★★½	82	$$$-
Parkway International Resort	3	★★★½	82	$$$+
Universal's Aventura Hotel	4	★★★½	82	$$$$
Home2Suites by Hilton	2	★★★½	81	$$$
Homewood Suites by Hilton Orlando- International Drive/Convention Center	1	★★★½	81	$$$+
Universal's Endless Summer Resort: Dockside Inn & Suites	4	★★★½	81	$$$-
Universal's Endless Summer Resort: Surfside Inn & Suites	4	★★★½	81	$$$-
Delta Hotels by Marriott Lake Buena Vista	2	★★★½	80	$$$-
Disney's All-Star Movies Resort	WDW	★★★½	80	$$$$
Disney's Art of Animation Resort	WDW	★★★½	80	$$$$$$-
Disney's Caribbean Beach Resort	WDW	★★★½	80	$ x 7
Disney's Pop Century Resort	WDW	★★★½	80	$$$$$$-
Fairfield Inn & Suites Orlando Near SeaWorld	1	★★★½	80	$$$-
Fairfield Inn & Suites Orlando Near Universal	4	★★★½	80	$$$-
Polynesian Isles Resort (Diamond Resorts)	3	★★★½	80	$$$
Wingate by Wyndham Universal Studios & Convention Center	4	★★★½	80	$$$
WorldMark Orlando-Kingstown Reef	1	★★★½	80	$$+

HOW THE HOTELS COMPARE (continued)

HOTEL	LODGING AREA	OVERALL QUALITY	ROOM QUALITY	COST ($ = $50)
Holiday Inn Orlando–Disney Springs Resort Area	WDW	★★★½	79	$$$
Aloft Orlando Lake Buena Vista	2	★★★	78	$$$+
Fairfield Inn & Suites Orlando Kissimmee/Celebration	3	★★★½	78	$$
Meliá Orlando Suite Hotel at Celebration	3	★★★½	78	$$$$-
Residence Inn Near Universal Orlando	1	★★★½	78	$$$+
Holiday Inn Express & Suites/South Lake Buena Vista	2	★★★½	77	$$$-
Quality Suites Turkey Lake South/Lake Buena Vista	2	★★★½	77	$$-
Galleria Palms Kissimmee Hotel	3	★★★½	76	$$$-
Hampton Inn Orlando/Lake Buena Vista	2	★★★½	76	$$$
Staybridge Suites Royale Parc	3	★★★½	76	$$$-
Best Western Plus Universal Inn	4	★★★½	75	$ x 11
Clarion Suites Maingate	3	★★★½	75	$$-
Comfort Suites Maingate East	3	★★★½	75	$$+
DoubleTree Suites Orlando–Disney Springs Area	WDW	★★★½	75	$$$$-
Holiday Inn & Suites Across from Universal Orlando	4	★★★½	75	$$+
Silver Lake Resort	3	★★★½	75	$$$$-
Wyndham Garden Lake Buena Vista	WDW	★★★½	75	$$$
High Point World Resort	3	★★★	74	$$$
Hilton Orlando Buena Vista Palace	WDW	★★★	74	$$$$$-
Disney's All-Star Music Resort	WDW	★★★	73	$$$$+
Disney's All-Star Sports Resort	WDW	★★★	73	$$$$+
La Quinta Inn & Suites by Wyndham Orlando Universal Area	4	★★★	72	$$+
Comfort Suites Near Universal Orlando Resort	4	★★★	70	$$$-
Hampton Inn Universal	4	★★★	67	$$
Rodeway Inn Maingate	3	★★★	65	$+
Ramada by Wyndham Kissimmee Gateway	3	★★½	62	$$-

HOTEL INFORMATION CHART

Aloft Orlando Lake Buena Vista
★★★
7950 Palm Pkwy.
Orlando, FL 32836
☎ 407-778-7600
tinyurl.com/aloftorlandofl

LOCATION	2
ROOM RATING	78
COST ($ = $50)	$$$+
DAILY RESORT FEE	None

COMMUTING TIMES TO PARKS
(in minutes):

MAGIC KINGDOM	15:00
EPCOT	14:00
ANIMAL KINGDOM	19:00
DHS	12:00

B Resort & Spa ★★★½
1905 Hotel Plaza Blvd.
Lake Buena Vista, FL 32830
☎ 407-828-2828
bhotelsandresorts.com
/b-resort-and-spa

LOCATION	WDW
ROOM RATING	82
COST ($ = $50)	$$$+
DAILY RESORT FEE	$30.00

COMMUTING TIMES TO PARKS
(in minutes):

MAGIC KINGDOM	15:45
EPCOT	11:00
ANIMAL KINGDOM	15:00
DHS	12:45

Bay Lake Tower at Disney's Contemporary Resort *(studios)*
★★★★½
4600 N. World Dr.
Lake Buena Vista, FL 32830
☎ 407-824-1000
tinyurl.com/baylaketower

LOCATION	WDW
ROOM RATING	91
COST ($ = $50)	$- x 17
DAILY RESORT FEE	None

COMMUTING TIMES TO PARKS
(in minutes):

MAGIC KINGDOM	on monorail
EPCOT	11:00
ANIMAL KINGDOM	17:15
DHS	14:15

The Cabins at Disney's Fort Wilderness Resort ★★★★½
4510 N. Fort Wilderness Trl.
Lake Buena Vista, FL 32830
☎ 407-824-2900
tinyurl.com/ftwilderness

LOCATION	WDW
ROOM RATING	90
COST ($ = $50)	$- x 12
DAILY RESORT FEE	None

COMMUTING TIMES TO PARKS
(in minutes):

MAGIC KINGDOM	13:15
EPCOT	8:30
ANIMAL KINGDOM	20:00
DHS	14:00

Caribe Royale Orlando ★★★★
8101 World Center Dr.
Orlando, FL 32821
☎ 407-238-8000
cariberoyale.com

LOCATION	2
ROOM RATING	86
COST ($ = $50)	$$$$-
DAILY RESORT FEE	$25.00

COMMUTING TIMES TO PARKS
(in minutes):

MAGIC KINGDOM	11:00
EPCOT	10:00
ANIMAL KINGDOM	17:00
DHS	9:00

Clarion Inn & Suites Across from Universal ★★★½
5829 Grand National Dr.
Orlando, FL 32819
☎ 407-351-3800
tinyurl.com/clarionuniversal

LOCATION	4
ROOM RATING	82
COST ($ = $50)	$$$$$+
DAILY RESORT FEE	None

COMMUTING TIMES TO PARKS
(in minutes):

MAGIC KINGDOM	20:00
EPCOT	15:00
ANIMAL KINGDOM	18:00
DHS	17:00

Comfort Suites Maingate East
★★★½
2775 Florida Plaza Blvd.
Kissimmee, FL 34746
☎ 407-397-7848
comfortsuitesfl.com

LOCATION	3
ROOM RATING	75
COST ($ = $50)	$$+
DAILY RESORT FEE	None

COMMUTING TIMES TO PARKS
(in minutes):

MAGIC KINGDOM	17:00
EPCOT	16:00
ANIMAL KINGDOM	17:00
DHS	13:00

Comfort Suites Near Universal Orlando Resort ★★★
5617 Major Blvd.
Orlando, FL 32819
☎ 407-363-1967
tinyurl.com/csuniversal

LOCATION	4
ROOM RATING	70
COST ($ = $50)	$$$-
DAILY RESORT FEE	None

COMMUTING TIMES TO PARKS
(in minutes):

MAGIC KINGDOM	17:45
EPCOT	13:15
ANIMAL KINGDOM	16:15
DHS	15:15

Copper Creek Villas & Cabins at Disney's Wilderness Lodge *(studios)*
★★★★½
901 Timberline Dr.
Lake Buena Vista, FL 32830
☎ 407-824-3200
tinyurl.com/wdwcoppercreek

LOCATION	WDW
ROOM RATING	90
COST ($ = $50)	$+ x 12
DAILY RESORT FEE	None

COMMUTING TIMES TO PARKS
(in minutes):

MAGIC KINGDOM	by ferry
EPCOT	10:00
ANIMAL KINGDOM	15:15
DHS	13:30

Disney's All-Star Movies Resort
★★★½
1901 W. Buena Vista Dr.
Lake Buena Vista, FL 32830
☎ 407-939-7000
tinyurl.com/allstarmovies

LOCATION	WDW
ROOM RATING	80
COST ($ = $50)	$$$$
DAILY RESORT FEE	None

COMMUTING TIMES TO PARKS
(in minutes):

MAGIC KINGDOM	6:15
EPCOT	5:45
ANIMAL KINGDOM	4:15
DHS	5:15

Disney's All-Star Music Resort
★★★
1801 W. Buena Vista Dr.
Lake Buena Vista, FL 32830
☎ 407-939-6000
tinyurl.com/allstarmusicresort

LOCATION	WDW
ROOM RATING	73
COST ($ = $50)	$$$$+
DAILY RESORT FEE	None

COMMUTING TIMES TO PARKS
(in minutes):

MAGIC KINGDOM	6:15
EPCOT	5:45
ANIMAL KINGDOM	4:15
DHS	5:15

Disney's All-Star Sports Resort
★★★
1701 W. Buena Vista Dr.
Lake Buena Vista, FL 32830
☎ 407-939-5000
tinyurl.com/allstarsports

LOCATION	WDW
ROOM RATING	73
COST ($ = $50)	$$$$+
DAILY RESORT FEE	None

COMMUTING TIMES TO PARKS
(in minutes):

MAGIC KINGDOM	6:15
EPCOT	5:45
ANIMAL KINGDOM	4:15
DHS	5:15

*Irlo Bronson Memorial Highway

The Berkley Orlando ★★★★
8545 W. US 192*
Kissimmee, FL 34747
☎ 321-329-7000 or
877-686-5259
theberkleyorlando.com

LOCATION	3
ROOM RATING	87
COST ($ = $50)	$$$$
DAILY RESORT FEE	None
COMMUTING TIMES TO PARKS (in minutes):	
MAGIC KINGDOM	20:00
EPCOT	21:00
ANIMAL KINGDOM	16:00
DHS	16:00

Best Western Plus Universal Inn
★★★½
5618 Vineland Rd.
Orlando, FL 32819
☎ 407-226-9119
tinyurl.com/bwuniversal

LOCATION	4
ROOM RATING	75
COST ($ = $50)	$ x 11
DAILY RESORT FEE	None
COMMUTING TIMES TO PARKS (in minutes):	
MAGIC KINGDOM	17:30
EPCOT	13:00
ANIMAL KINGDOM	16:00
DHS	15:30

Boulder Ridge Villas at Disney's Wilderness Lodge (studios)
★★★★
901 Timberline Dr.
Lake Buena Vista, FL 32830
☎ 407-824-3200
tinyurl.com/wlvillas

LOCATION	WDW
ROOM RATING	84
COST ($ = $50)	$- x 12
DAILY RESORT FEE	None
COMMUTING TIMES TO PARKS (in minutes):	
MAGIC KINGDOM	by ferry
EPCOT	10:00
ANIMAL KINGDOM	15:15
DHS	13:30

Clarion Suites Maingate ★★★½
7888 W. US 192*
Kissimmee, FL 34747
☎ 407-390-9888
clarionsuiteskissimmee.com

LOCATION	3
ROOM RATING	75
COST ($ = $50)	$$-
DAILY RESORT FEE	$12.00
COMMUTING TIMES TO PARKS (in minutes):	
MAGIC KINGDOM	10:00
EPCOT	9:15
ANIMAL KINGDOM	7:00
DHS	9:00

Club Wyndham Bonnet Creek
★★★★½
9560 Via Encinas
Orlando, FL 32830
☎ 407-238-3500
wyndhambonnetcreek.com

LOCATION	WDW
ROOM RATING	90
COST ($ = $50)	$$$$$+
DAILY RESORT FEE	$28.00
COMMUTING TIMES TO PARKS (in minutes):	
MAGIC KINGDOM	8:00
EPCOT	6:00
ANIMAL KINGDOM	7:15
DHS	4:15

Club Wyndham Cypress Palms
★★★★
5324 Fairfield Lake Dr.
Kissimmee, FL 34746
☎ 407-397-1600
cypresspalms.com

LOCATION	3
ROOM RATING	89
COST ($ = $50)	$$$$-
DAILY RESORT FEE	None
COMMUTING TIMES TO PARKS (in minutes):	
MAGIC KINGDOM	15:15
EPCOT	15:00
ANIMAL KINGDOM	14:45
DHS	14:45

Courtyard Orlando Lake Buena Vista at Vista Centre ★★★★
8501 Palm Pkwy.
Orlando, FL 32836
☎ 407-239-6900
tinyurl.com/courtyardlbv

LOCATION	2
ROOM RATING	89
COST ($ = $50)	$$$-
DAILY RESORT FEE	$11.25
COMMUTING TIMES TO PARKS (in minutes):	
MAGIC KINGDOM	13:15
EPCOT	8:30
ANIMAL KINGDOM	11:30
DHS	11:00

Cypress Pointe Resort ★★★★½
8651 Treasure Cay Ln.
Orlando, FL 32836
☎ 407-597-2700
cypresspointe.net

LOCATION	2
ROOM RATING	90
COST ($ = $50)	$$$$+
DAILY RESORT FEE	$16.95
COMMUTING TIMES TO PARKS (in minutes):	
MAGIC KINGDOM	12:00
EPCOT	14:00
ANIMAL KINGDOM	13:00
DHS	12:00

Delta Hotels by Marriott Lake Buena Vista ★★★½
12490 S. Apopka–Vineland Rd.
Orlando, FL 32836
☎ 407-387-9999
tinyurl.com/deltaorlando

LOCATION	2
ROOM RATING	80
COST ($ = $50)	$$$-
DAILY RESORT FEE	None
COMMUTING TIMES TO PARKS (in minutes):	
MAGIC KINGDOM	19:00
EPCOT	4:00
ANIMAL KINGDOM	10:00
DHS	9:00

Disney's Animal Kingdom Lodge
★★★★
2901 W. Osceola Pkwy.
Lake Buena Vista, FL 32830
☎ 407-938-3000
tinyurl.com/aklodge

LOCATION	WDW
ROOM RATING	86
COST ($ = $50)	$+ x 11
DAILY RESORT FEE	None
COMMUTING TIMES TO PARKS (in minutes):	
MAGIC KINGDOM	8:15
EPCOT	6:15
ANIMAL KINGDOM	2:15
DHS	6:00

Disney's Animal Kingdom Villas
(Jambo House, studios) ★★★★
2901 W. Osceola Pkwy.
Lake Buena Vista, FL 32830
☎ 407-938-3000
tinyurl.com/akjambo

LOCATION	WDW
ROOM RATING	86
COST ($ = $50)	$ x 12
DAILY RESORT FEE	None
COMMUTING TIMES TO PARKS (in minutes):	
MAGIC KINGDOM	8:15
EPCOT	6:15
ANIMAL KINGDOM	2:15
DHS	6:00

Disney's Animal Kingdom Villas
(Kidani Village, studios) ★★★★½
3701 W. Osceola Pkwy.
Lake Buena Vista, FL 32830
☎ 407-938-7400
tinyurl.com/akkidani

LOCATION	WDW
ROOM RATING	90
COST ($ = $50)	$+ x 11
DAILY RESORT FEE	None
COMMUTING TIMES TO PARKS (in minutes):	
MAGIC KINGDOM	8:15
EPCOT	6:15
ANIMAL KINGDOM	2:15
DHS	6:00

HOTEL INFORMATION CHART (continued)

Disney's Art of Animation Resort
★★★½
1850 Animation Way
Lake Buena Vista, FL 32830
☎ 407-938-7000
tinyurl.com/artofanimationresort

LOCATION	WDW
ROOM RATING	80
COST ($ = $50)	$$$$$$-
DAILY RESORT FEE	None

COMMUTING TIMES TO PARKS
(in minutes):

MAGIC KINGDOM	12:00
EPCOT	10:00
ANIMAL KINGDOM	12:00
DHS	3:00

Disney's Beach Club Resort
★★★★
1800 EPCOT Resorts Blvd.
Lake Buena Vista, FL 32830
☎ 407-934-8000
tinyurl.com/disneybeachclub

LOCATION	WDW
ROOM RATING	89
COST ($ = $50)	$ x 14
DAILY RESORT FEE	None

COMMUTING TIMES TO PARKS
(in minutes):

MAGIC KINGDOM	7:15
EPCOT	5:15
ANIMAL KINGDOM	6:45
DHS	4:00

Disney's Beach Club Villas (studios)
★★★★
1800 EPCOT Resorts Blvd.
Lake Buena Vista, FL 32830
☎ 407-934-8000
tinyurl.com/beachclubvillas

LOCATION	WDW
ROOM RATING	86
COST ($ = $50)	$ x 14
DAILY RESORT FEE	None

COMMUTING TIMES TO PARKS
(in minutes):

MAGIC KINGDOM	7:15
EPCOT	5:15
ANIMAL KINGDOM	6:45
DHS	4:00

Disney's Contemporary Resort
★★★★½
4600 N. World Dr.
Lake Buena Vista, FL 32830
☎ 407-824-1000
tinyurl.com/contemporarywdw

LOCATION	WDW
ROOM RATING	91
COST ($ = $50)	$ x 14
DAILY RESORT FEE	None

COMMUTING TIMES TO PARKS
(in minutes):

MAGIC KINGDOM	on monorail
EPCOT	11:00
ANIMAL KINGDOM	17:15
DHS	14:15

Disney's Coronado Springs Resort
★★★★
1000 W. Buena Vista Dr.
Lake Buena Vista, FL 32830
☎ 407-939-1000
tinyurl.com/coronadosprings

LOCATION	WDW
ROOM RATING	88
COST ($ = $50)	$- x 8
DAILY RESORT FEE	None

COMMUTING TIMES TO PARKS
(in minutes):

MAGIC KINGDOM	5:30
EPCOT	4:00
ANIMAL KINGDOM	4:45
DHS	4:45

Disney's Grand Floridian Resort & Spa ★★★★½
4401 Floridian Way
Lake Buena Vista, FL 32830
☎ 407-824-3000
tinyurl.com/grandflresort

LOCATION	WDW
ROOM RATING	92
COST ($ = $50)	$ x 19
DAILY RESORT FEE	None

COMMUTING TIMES TO PARKS
(in minutes):

MAGIC KINGDOM	on monorail
EPCOT	4:45
ANIMAL KINGDOM	11:45
DHS	6:45

Disney's Pop Century Resort
★★★½
1050 Century Dr.
Lake Buena Vista, FL 32830
☎ 407-938-4000
tinyurl.com/popcenturywdw

LOCATION	WDW
ROOM RATING	80
COST ($ = $50)	$$$$$$-
DAILY RESORT FEE	None

COMMUTING TIMES TO PARKS
(in minutes):

MAGIC KINGDOM	8:30
EPCOT	6:30
ANIMAL KINGDOM	6:15
DHS	5:00

Disney's Port Orleans Resort–French Quarter ★★★★
2201 Orleans Dr.
Lake Buena Vista, FL 32830
☎ 407-934-5000
tinyurl.com/portorleansfq

LOCATION	WDW
ROOM RATING	87
COST ($ = $50)	$+ x 7
DAILY RESORT FEE	None

COMMUTING TIMES TO PARKS
(in minutes):

MAGIC KINGDOM	12:00
EPCOT	8:00
ANIMAL KINGDOM	16:15
DHS	12:30

Disney's Port Orleans Resort–Riverside ★★★★
1251 Riverside Dr.
Lake Buena Vista, FL 32830
☎ 407-934-6000
tinyurl.com/portorleansriverside

LOCATION	WDW
ROOM RATING	83
COST ($ = $50)	$+ x 7
DAILY RESORT FEE	None

COMMUTING TIMES TO PARKS
(in minutes):

MAGIC KINGDOM	12:00
EPCOT	8:00
ANIMAL KINGDOM	16:15
DHS	12:30

Disney's Yacht Club Resort
★★★★½
1700 EPCOT Resorts Blvd.
Lake Buena Vista, FL 32830
☎ 407-934-7000
tinyurl.com/yachtclubwdw

LOCATION	WDW
ROOM RATING	91
COST ($ = $50)	$ x 14
DAILY RESORT FEE	None

COMMUTING TIMES TO PARKS
(in minutes):

MAGIC KINGDOM	7:15
EPCOT	5:15
ANIMAL KINGDOM	6:45
DHS	4:00

DoubleTree by Hilton at the Entrance to Universal Orlando
★★★★
5780 Major Blvd.
Orlando, FL 32830
☎ 407-351-1000
doubletreeorlando.com

LOCATION	4
ROOM RATING	89
COST ($ = $50)	$$$-
DAILY RESORT FEE	None

COMMUTING TIMES TO PARKS
(in minutes):

MAGIC KINGDOM	19:00
EPCOT	14:15
ANIMAL KINGDOM	17:15
DHS	16:45

DoubleTree Suites by Hilton Orlando–Disney Springs Area
★★★½
2305 Hotel Plaza Blvd.
Lake Buena Vista, FL 32819
☎ 407-934-1000
doubletreeguestsuites.com

LOCATION	WDW
ROOM RATING	75
COST ($ = $50)	$$$$-
DAILY RESORT FEE	$23.00

COMMUTING TIMES TO PARKS
(in minutes):

MAGIC KINGDOM	13:00
EPCOT	8:30
ANIMAL KINGDOM	12:30
DHS	10:00

*Irlo Bronson Memorial Highway

Disney's BoardWalk Inn ★★★★
2101 N. EPCOT Resorts Blvd.
Lake Buena Vista, FL 32830
☎ 407-939-6200
tinyurl.com/boardwalkinn

LOCATION	WDW
ROOM RATING	89
COST ($ = $50)	$ x 14
DAILY RESORT FEE	None
COMMUTING TIMES TO PARKS (in minutes):	
MAGIC KINGDOM	7:15
EPCOT	5:30
ANIMAL KINGDOM	7:00
DHS	3:00

Disney's BoardWalk Villas ★★★★
2101 N. EPCOT Resorts Blvd.
Lake Buena Vista, FL 32830
☎ 407-939-6200
tinyurl.com/boardwalkvillas

LOCATION	WDW
ROOM RATING	89
COST ($ = $50)	$- x 15
DAILY RESORT FEE	None
COMMUTING TIMES TO PARKS (in minutes):	
MAGIC KINGDOM	7:15
EPCOT	5:30
ANIMAL KINGDOM	7:00
DHS	3:00

Disney's Caribbean Beach Resort ★★★½
1114 Cayman Way
Lake Buena Vista, FL 32830
☎ 407-934-3400
tinyurl.com/caribbeanbeachresort

LOCATION	WDW
ROOM RATING	80
COST ($ = $50)	$ x 7
DAILY RESORT FEE	None
COMMUTING TIMES TO PARKS (in minutes):	
MAGIC KINGDOM	8:00
EPCOT	6:00
ANIMAL KINGDOM	7:15
DHS	4:15

Disney's Old Key West Resort ★★★★½
1510 North Cove Rd.
Lake Buena Vista, FL 32830
☎ 407-827-7700
tinyurl.com/oldkeywest

LOCATION	WDW
ROOM RATING	91
COST ($ = $50)	$+ x 11
DAILY RESORT FEE	None
COMMUTING TIMES TO PARKS (in minutes):	
MAGIC KINGDOM	10:45
EPCOT	6:00
ANIMAL KINGDOM	14:30
DHS	10:30

Disney's Polynesian Village Resort ★★★★
1600 Seven Seas Dr.
Lake Buena Vista, FL 32830
☎ 407-824-2000
tinyurl.com/wdwpolyvillage

LOCATION	WDW
ROOM RATING	87
COST ($ = $50)	$- x 17
DAILY RESORT FEE	None
COMMUTING TIMES TO PARKS (in minutes):	
MAGIC KINGDOM	on monorail
EPCOT	8:00
ANIMAL KINGDOM	16:15
DHS	12:30

Disney's Polynesian Villas & Bungalows (studios) ★★★★
1600 Seven Seas Dr.
Lake Buena Vista, FL 32830
☎ 407-824-2000
tinyurl.com/wdwpolyvillage

LOCATION	WDW
ROOM RATING	88
COST ($ = $50)	$- x 17
DAILY RESORT FEE	None
COMMUTING TIMES TO PARKS (in minutes):	
MAGIC KINGDOM	on monorail
EPCOT	8:00
ANIMAL KINGDOM	16:15
DHS	12:30

Disney's Riviera Resort ★★★★½
1080 Esplanade Ave.
Lake Buena Vista, FL 32830
☎ 407-828-7030
tinyurl.com/disneyriviera

LOCATION	WDW
ROOM RATING	95
COST ($ = $50)	$- x 12
DAILY RESORT FEE	None
COMMUTING TIMES TO PARKS (in minutes):	
MAGIC KINGDOM	8:00
EPCOT	6:00
ANIMAL KINGDOM	7:15
DHS	4:15

Disney's Saratoga Springs Resort & Spa ★★★★
1960 Broadway
Lake Buena Vista, FL 32830
☎ 407-827-1100
tinyurl.com/saratogawdw

LOCATION	WDW
ROOM RATING	84
COST ($ = $50)	$+ x 11
DAILY RESORT FEE	None
COMMUTING TIMES TO PARKS (in minutes):	
MAGIC KINGDOM	14:45
EPCOT	8:45
ANIMAL KINGDOM	18:15
DHS	14:30

Disney's Wilderness Lodge ★★★★
901 Timberline Dr.
Lake Buena Vista, FL 32830
☎ 407-824-3200
tinyurl.com/wildernesslodge

LOCATION	WDW
ROOM RATING	86
COST ($ = $50)	$+ x 12
DAILY RESORT FEE	None
COMMUTING TIMES TO PARKS (in minutes):	
MAGIC KINGDOM	by ferry
EPCOT	10:00
ANIMAL KINGDOM	15:15
DHS	13:30

Drury Inn & Suites Orlando ★★★★
7301 W. Sand Lake Rd.
Orlando, FL 32819
☎ 407-354-1101
tinyurl.com/druryinnorlando

LOCATION	1
ROOM RATING	85
COST ($ = $50)	$$+
DAILY RESORT FEE	None
COMMUTING TIMES TO PARKS (in minutes):	
MAGIC KINGDOM	18:30
EPCOT	15:30
ANIMAL KINGDOM	20:15
DHS	18:00

Embassy Suites by Hilton Orlando Lake Buena Vista Resort ★★★★
8100 Lake St.
Orlando, FL 32836
☎ 407-239-1144
tinyurl.com/embassylbv

LOCATION	2
ROOM RATING	84
COST ($ = $50)	$$$$-
DAILY RESORT FEE	$24.95
COMMUTING TIMES TO PARKS (in minutes):	
MAGIC KINGDOM	12:45
EPCOT	8:00
ANIMAL KINGDOM	11:00
DHS	10:30

Extended Stay America Convention Center/Westwood ★★★★
6443 Westwood Blvd.
Orlando, FL 32821
☎ 407-351-1982
tinyurl.com/extendedstay
westwood

LOCATION	1
ROOM RATING	84
COST ($ = $50)	$$+
DAILY RESORT FEE	None
COMMUTING TIMES TO PARKS (in minutes):	
MAGIC KINGDOM	17:30
EPCOT	12:45
ANIMAL KINGDOM	15:45
DHS	15:30

HOTEL INFORMATION CHART (continued)

Fairfield Inn & Suites Orlando Kissimmee/Celebration ★★★½
6073 US 192*
Kissimmee, FL 34747
☎ 407-390-1532
tinyurl.com/fairfieldinnkissimmee

LOCATION	3
ROOM RATING	78
COST ($ = $50)	$$
DAILY RESORT FEE	None
COMMUTING TIMES TO PARKS *(in minutes)*:	
MAGIC KINGDOM	18:00
EPCOT	11:00
ANIMAL KINGDOM	14:00
DHS	6:00

Fairfield Inn & Suites Orlando Near SeaWorld ★★★½
10815 International Dr.
Orlando, FL 32821
☎ 407-354-1139
tinyurl.com/fairfieldsw

LOCATION	1
ROOM RATING	80
COST ($ = $50)	$$$-
DAILY RESORT FEE	None
COMMUTING TIMES TO PARKS *(in minutes)*:	
MAGIC KINGDOM	18:00
EPCOT	15:00
ANIMAL KINGDOM	17:00
DHS	15:00

Fairfield Inn & Suites Orlando Near Universal ★★★½
5614 Vineland Rd.
Orlando, FL 32819
☎ 407-581-5600
tinyurl.com/fairfielduniversal

LOCATION	4
ROOM RATING	80
COST ($ = $50)	$$$-
DAILY RESORT FEE	None
COMMUTING TIMES TO PARKS *(in minutes)*:	
MAGIC KINGDOM	17:30
EPCOT	12:45
ANIMAL KINGDOM	15:45
DHS	15:15

Grand Beach (Diamond Resorts) ★★★
8317 Lake Bryan Beach Blvd.
Orlando, FL 32821
☎ 407-238-2500
tinyurl.com/diamondgrandbeach

LOCATION	2
ROOM RATING	86
COST ($ = $50)	$$$+
DAILY RESORT FEE	$16.95
COMMUTING TIMES TO PARKS *(in minutes)*:	
MAGIC KINGDOM	15:00
EPCOT	11:00
ANIMAL KINGDOM	19:00
DHS	12:00

Hampton Inn Orlando/Lake Buena Vista ★★★½
8150 Palm Pkwy.
Orlando, FL 32836
☎ 407-465-8150
tinyurl.com/hamptoninnlbv

LOCATION	2
ROOM RATING	76
COST ($ = $50)	$$$
DAILY RESORT FEE	None
COMMUTING TIMES TO PARKS *(in minutes)*:	
MAGIC KINGDOM	12:45
EPCOT	8:00
ANIMAL KINGDOM	11:00
DHS	10:30

Hampton Inn Universal ★★★
5621 Windhover Dr.
Orlando, FL 32819
☎ 407-351-6716
tinyurl.com/hamptonuniversal

LOCATION	4
ROOM RATING	67
COST ($ = $50)	$$
DAILY RESORT FEE	None
COMMUTING TIMES TO PARKS *(in minutes)*:	
MAGIC KINGDOM	19:00
EPCOT	14:15
ANIMAL KINGDOM	17:15
DHS	16:45

Hilton Grand Vacations at SeaWorld ★★★★
6924 Grand Vacations Way
Orlando, FL 32821
☎ 407-239-0100
tinyurl.com/seaworldhgv

LOCATION	1
ROOM RATING	88
COST ($ = $50)	$$$+
DAILY RESORT FEE	$28.13
COMMUTING TIMES TO PARKS *(in minutes)*:	
MAGIC KINGDOM	17:00
EPCOT	12:30
ANIMAL KINGDOM	16:30
DHS	15:30

Hilton Grand Vacations at Tuscany Village ★★★★
8122 Arrezzo Way
Orlando, FL 32821
☎ 407-465-2600
tinyurl.com/hgvtuscany

LOCATION	1
ROOM RATING	88
COST ($ = $50)	$$$+
DAILY RESORT FEE	$25.00
COMMUTING TIMES TO PARKS *(in minutes)*:	
MAGIC KINGDOM	16:15
EPCOT	14:00
ANIMAL KINGDOM	17:00
DHS	16:30

Hilton Orlando ★★★½
6001 Destination Pkwy.
Orlando, FL 32819
☎ 407-313-4300
thehiltonorlando.com

LOCATION	1
ROOM RATING	82
COST ($ = $50)	$$$$-
DAILY RESORT FEE	$35.00
COMMUTING TIMES TO PARKS *(in minutes)*:	
MAGIC KINGDOM	24:00:00
EPCOT	17:00
ANIMAL KINGDOM	16:00
DHS	14:00

Holiday Inn Club Vacations at Orange Lake Resort ★★★★½
8505 W. US 192*
Orlando, FL 34747
☎ 407-477-7025
tinyurl.com/holidayinnorangelake

LOCATION	3
ROOM RATING	94
COST ($ = $50)	$$$+
DAILY RESORT FEE	$7.95
COMMUTING TIMES TO PARKS *(in minutes)*:	
MAGIC KINGDOM	8:45
EPCOT	8:30
ANIMAL KINGDOM	5:30
DHS	8:00

Holiday Inn Express & Suites Orlando at SeaWorld ★★★½
10771 International Dr.
Orlando, FL 32821
☎ 407-996-4100
tinyurl.com/holidaysw

LOCATION	1
ROOM RATING	82
COST ($ = $50)	$$+
DAILY RESORT FEE	None
COMMUTING TIMES TO PARKS *(in minutes)*:	
MAGIC KINGDOM	18:00
EPCOT	15:00
ANIMAL KINGDOM	17:00
DHS	15:00

Holiday Inn Express & Suites/South Lake Buena Vista ★★★½
5001 Calypso Cay Way
Kissimmee, FL 34746
☎ 407-997-1400
hieorlando.com

LOCATION	2
ROOM RATING	77
COST ($ = $50)	$$$-
DAILY RESORT FEE	$18.00
COMMUTING TIMES TO PARKS *(in minutes)*:	
MAGIC KINGDOM	22:00
EPCOT	15:00
ANIMAL KINGDOM	16:00
DHS	10:00

*Irlo Bronson Memorial Highway

Four Seasons Resort Orlando at Walt Disney World Resort
★★★★★
10100 Dream Tree Blvd.
Lake Buena Vista, FL 32836
☎ 407-313-7777
fourseasons.com/orlando

LOCATION	WDW
ROOM RATING	98
COST ($ = $50)	$+ x 22
DAILY RESORT FEE	None

COMMUTING TIMES TO PARKS
(in minutes):

MAGIC KINGDOM	9:00
EPCOT	8:00
ANIMAL KINGDOM	15:00
DHS	8:00

Galleria Palms Kissimmee Hotel
★★★½
3000 Maingate Ln.
Kissimmee, FL 34747
☎ 407-396-6300
gphkissimmee.com

LOCATION	3
ROOM RATING	76
COST ($ = $50)	$$$-
DAILY RESORT FEE	$9.99

COMMUTING TIMES TO PARKS
(in minutes):

MAGIC KINGDOM	8:15
EPCOT	7:30
ANIMAL KINGDOM	5:15
DHS	7:15

Gaylord Palms Resort & Convention Center ★★★★½
6000 W. Osceola Pkwy.
Kissimmee, FL 34746
☎ 407-586-0000
gaylordpalms.com

LOCATION	3
ROOM RATING	94
COST ($ = $50)	$ x 7
DAILY RESORT FEE	$34.95

COMMUTING TIMES TO PARKS
(in minutes):

MAGIC KINGDOM	9:00
EPCOT	8:45
ANIMAL KINGDOM	7:00
DHS	8:15

Hard Rock Hotel Orlando
★★★★½
5800 Universal Blvd.
Orlando, FL 32819
☎ 407-503-2000
hardrockhotels.com/orlando

LOCATION	4
ROOM RATING	93
COST ($ = $50)	$ x 10
DAILY RESORT FEE	None

COMMUTING TIMES TO PARKS
(in minutes):

MAGIC KINGDOM	21:45
EPCOT	17:00
ANIMAL KINGDOM	20:00
DHS	19:30

Hawthorn Suites by Wyndham Lake Buena Vista ★★★★
8303 Palm Pkwy.
Orlando, FL 32836
☎ 407-597-5000
hawthornlakebuenavista.com

LOCATION	2
ROOM RATING	85
COST ($ = $50)	$$-
DAILY RESORT FEE	None

COMMUTING TIMES TO PARKS
(in minutes):

MAGIC KINGDOM	20:15
EPCOT	15:30
ANIMAL KINGDOM	18:30
DHS	18:00

High Point World Resort ★★★
2951 High Point Blvd.
Orlando, FL 34747
☎ 407-396-9600
highpointresortorlando.com

LOCATION	3
ROOM RATING	74
COST ($ = $50)	$$$
DAILY RESORT FEE	None

COMMUTING TIMES TO PARKS
(in minutes):

MAGIC KINGDOM	21:00
EPCOT	11:00
ANIMAL KINGDOM	8:00
DHS	9:00

Hilton Orlando Buena Vista Palace
★★★
1900 E. Buena Vista Dr.
Lake Buena Vista, FL 32830
☎ 407-827-2727
buenavistapalace.com

LOCATION	WDW
ROOM RATING	74
COST ($ = $50)	$$$$$-
DAILY RESORT FEE	$35.00

COMMUTING TIMES TO PARKS
(in minutes):

MAGIC KINGDOM	16:00
EPCOT	11:15
ANIMAL KINGDOM	15:15
DHS	13:00

Hilton Orlando Lake Buena Vista
★★★★
1751 Hotel Plaza Blvd.
Lake Buena Vista, FL 32830
☎ 407-827-4000
hilton-wdwv.com

LOCATION	WDW
ROOM RATING	87
COST ($ = $50)	$$$$$+
DAILY RESORT FEE	$35.00

COMMUTING TIMES TO PARKS
(in minutes):

MAGIC KINGDOM	15:15
EPCOT	10:30
ANIMAL KINGDOM	14:30
DHS	12:15

Holiday Inn & Suites Across from Universal Orlando ★★★½
5916 Caravan Ct.
Orlando, FL 32819
☎ 407-351-3333
hiuniversal.com

LOCATION	4
ROOM RATING	75
COST ($ = $50)	$$+
DAILY RESORT FEE	None

COMMUTING TIMES TO PARKS
(in minutes):

MAGIC KINGDOM	19:00
EPCOT	14:15
ANIMAL KINGDOM	17:15
DHS	16:45

Holiday Inn Orlando SW– Celebration Area ★★★★
5711 W. US 192*
Kissimmee, FL 32830
☎ 407-396-4222
hicelebration.com

LOCATION	3
ROOM RATING	83
COST ($ = $50)	$$
DAILY RESORT FEE	$12.00

COMMUTING TIMES TO PARKS
(in minutes):

MAGIC KINGDOM	12:15
EPCOT	12:00
ANIMAL KINGDOM	10:15
DHS	11:30

Holiday Inn Orlando–Disney Springs Resort Area ★★★½
1805 Hotel Plaza Blvd.
Lake Buena Vista, FL 34746
☎ 407-828-8888
hiorlando.com

LOCATION	WDW
ROOM RATING	79
COST ($ = $50)	$$$
DAILY RESORT FEE	$22.00

COMMUTING TIMES TO PARKS
(in minutes):

MAGIC KINGDOM	15:30
EPCOT	10:45
ANIMAL KINGDOM	12:30
DHS	14:45

Holiday Inn Resort Orlando– Lake Buena Vista ★★★½
13351 FL 535
Orlando, FL 32821
☎ 407-239-4500
hiresortlbv.com

LOCATION	2
ROOM RATING	82
COST ($ = $50)	$$+
DAILY RESORT FEE	$24.95

COMMUTING TIMES TO PARKS
(in minutes):

MAGIC KINGDOM	10:45
EPCOT	6:00
ANIMAL KINGDOM	9:00
DHS	8:30

HOTEL INFORMATION CHART *(continued)*

Home2Suites by Hilton ★★★½
341 Flagler Ave.
Winter Garden, FL 32819
☎ 407-993-3999
tinyurl.com/fc-home2suites

LOCATION	2
ROOM RATING	81
COST ($ = $50)	$$$
DAILY RESORT FEE	None
COMMUTING TIMES TO PARKS *(in minutes)*:	
MAGIC KINGDOM	18:00
EPCOT	16:00
ANIMAL KINGDOM	10:00
DHS	15:00

**Homewood Suites by Hilton
Lake Buena Vista–Orlando** ★★★★
11428 Marbella Palm Ct.
Orlando, FL 32836
☎ 407-239-4540
tinyurl.com/homewoodsuiteslbv

LOCATION	2
ROOM RATING	85
COST ($ = $50)	$$$+
DAILY RESORT FEE	None
COMMUTING TIMES TO PARKS *(in minutes)*:	
MAGIC KINGDOM	18:00
EPCOT	12:00
ANIMAL KINGDOM	18:00
DHS	14:00

**Homewood Suites by Hilton
Orlando at Flamingo Crossings
Town Center** ★★★★
411 Flagler Ave.
Winter Garden, FL 34787
☎ 407-993-3011
tinyurl.com/fc-homewoodsuites

LOCATION	2
ROOM RATING	82
COST ($ = $50)	$$$+
DAILY RESORT FEE	None
COMMUTING TIMES TO PARKS *(in minutes)*:	
MAGIC KINGDOM	18:00
EPCOT	16:00
ANIMAL KINGDOM	10:00
DHS	15:00

**Hyatt Place Orlando/
Lake Buena Vista** ★★★½
8688 Palm Pkwy.
Orlando, FL 32836
☎ 407-778-5500
orlandolakebuenavista
.place.hyatt.com

LOCATION	2
ROOM RATING	82
COST ($ = $50)	$$$-
DAILY RESORT FEE	None
COMMUTING TIMES TO PARKS *(in minutes)*:	
MAGIC KINGDOM	18:00
EPCOT	13:00
ANIMAL KINGDOM	12:00
DHS	14:00

Hyatt Regency Grand Cypress
★★★★½
1 Grand Cypress Blvd.
Orlando, FL 32821
☎ 407-239-1234
grandcypress.hyatt.com

LOCATION	2
ROOM RATING	92
COST ($ = $50)	$$$$
DAILY RESORT FEE	$42.75
COMMUTING TIMES TO PARKS *(in minutes)*:	
MAGIC KINGDOM	13:30
EPCOT	8:45
ANIMAL KINGDOM	11:45
DHS	11:15

**JW Marriott Orlando Bonnet Creek
Resort & Spa** ★★★★
14900 Chelonia Pkwy.
Orlando, FL 32819
☎ 407-919-6300
tinyurl.com/jwmarriottorlandobc

LOCATION	WDW
ROOM RATING	92
COST ($ = $50)	$- x 8
DAILY RESORT FEE	$35.00
COMMUTING TIMES TO PARKS *(in minutes)*:	
MAGIC KINGDOM	15:00
EPCOT	12:00
ANIMAL KINGDOM	18:00
DHS	11:00

**Loews Royal Pacific Resort at
Universal Orlando** ★★★★½
6300 Hollywood Way
Orlando, FL 32819
☎ 407-503-3000
loewshotels.com/royal
-pacific-resort

LOCATION	4
ROOM RATING	90
COST ($ = $50)	$+ x 9
DAILY RESORT FEE	None
COMMUTING TIMES TO PARKS *(in minutes)*:	
MAGIC KINGDOM	20:00
EPCOT	15:15
ANIMAL KINGDOM	18:15
DHS	17:45

**Loews Sapphire Falls Resort at
Universal Orlando** ★★★★
6601 Adventure Way
Orlando, FL 34747
☎ 407-503-5000
loewshotels.com/sapphire
-falls-resort

LOCATION	4
ROOM RATING	84
COST ($ = $50)	$$$$$+
DAILY RESORT FEE	None
COMMUTING TIMES TO PARKS *(in minutes)*:	
MAGIC KINGDOM	20:00
EPCOT	15:00
ANIMAL KINGDOM	17:00
DHS	14:00

Margaritaville Resort Orlando
★★★★
8000 Fins Up Circle
Kissimmee, FL 32821
☎ 407-479-0950
tinyurl.com/margaritaville-fl

LOCATION	3
ROOM RATING	84
COST ($ = $50)	$$$$-
DAILY RESORT FEE	$25.00–$42.50
COMMUTING TIMES TO PARKS *(in minutes)*:	
MAGIC KINGDOM	15:00
EPCOT	14:00
ANIMAL KINGDOM	16:00
DHS	14:00

Marriott's Harbour Lake ★★★★
7102 Grand Horizons Blvd.
Orlando, FL 34747
☎ 407-465-6100
tinyurl.com/harbourlake

LOCATION	2
ROOM RATING	88
COST ($ = $50)	$$$$-
DAILY RESORT FEE	None
COMMUTING TIMES TO PARKS *(in minutes)*:	
MAGIC KINGDOM	18:00
EPCOT	13:30
ANIMAL KINGDOM	18:00
DHS	16:30

**Meliá Orlando Suite Hotel at
Celebration** ★★★½
225 Celebration Pl
Celebration, FL 34747
☎ 407-964-7000
tinyurl.com/meliacelebration

LOCATION	3
ROOM RATING	78
COST ($ = $50)	$$$$-
DAILY RESORT FEE	$27.24
COMMUTING TIMES TO PARKS *(in minutes)*:	
MAGIC KINGDOM	14:45
EPCOT	10:00
ANIMAL KINGDOM	13:00
DHS	12:30

**Mystic Dunes Resort & Golf Club
(Diamond Resorts)** ★★★★½
7600 Mystic Dunes Ln.
Celebration, FL 33896
☎ 407-396-1311
mystic-dunes-resort.com

LOCATION	3
ROOM RATING	90
COST ($ = $50)	$$$-
DAILY RESORT FEE	$24.95
COMMUTING TIMES TO PARKS *(in minutes)*:	
MAGIC KINGDOM	10:45
EPCOT	10:30
ANIMAL KINGDOM	7:45
DHS	10:00

*Irlo Bronson Memorial Highway

Homewood Suites by Hilton Orlando Theme Parks ★★★★
6940 Westwood Blvd.
Orlando, FL 32819
☎ 407-778-5888
tinyurl.com/homewoodorl

LOCATION	1
ROOM RATING	85
COST ($ = $50)	$$$+
DAILY RESORT FEE	None

COMMUTING TIMES TO PARKS (*in minutes*):

MAGIC KINGDOM	17:00
EPCOT	14:00
ANIMAL KINGDOM	13:00
DHS	14:00

Homewood Suites by Hilton Orlando–International Drive/ Convention Center ★★★½
8745 International Dr.
Orlando, FL 32821
☎ 407-248-2232
tinyurl.com/homewoodidrive

LOCATION	1
ROOM RATING	81
COST ($ = $50)	$$$+
DAILY RESORT FEE	None

COMMUTING TIMES TO PARKS (*in minutes*):

MAGIC KINGDOM	21:45
EPCOT	17:00
ANIMAL KINGDOM	20:00
DHS	19:30

Homewood Suites by Hilton Orlando–Nearest to Universal Studios ★★★½
5893 American Way
Orlando, FL 32836
☎ 407-226-0669
tinyurl.com/homewoodnearuni

LOCATION	1
ROOM RATING	82
COST ($ = $50)	$$$
DAILY RESORT FEE	None

COMMUTING TIMES TO PARKS (*in minutes*):

MAGIC KINGDOM	18:00
EPCOT	14:00
ANIMAL KINGDOM	20:00
DHS	20:00

La Quinta Inn & Suites by Wyndham Orlando Universal Area ★★★
5621 Major Blvd.
Orlando, FL 34787
☎ 407-313-3100
laquintaorlandomajorblvd.com

LOCATION	4
ROOM RATING	72
COST ($ = $50)	$$+
DAILY RESORT FEE	None

COMMUTING TIMES TO PARKS (*in minutes*):

MAGIC KINGDOM	18:00
EPCOT	13:15
ANIMAL KINGDOM	16:15
DHS	16:00

Liki Tiki Village ★★★★
17777 Bali Blvd.
Winter Garden, FL 32819
☎ 407-239-5000
likitiki.com

LOCATION	3
ROOM RATING	86
COST ($ = $50)	$$$$-
DAILY RESORT FEE	$19.95

COMMUTING TIMES TO PARKS (*in minutes*):

MAGIC KINGDOM	9:00
EPCOT	8:45
ANIMAL KINGDOM	5:15
DHS	8:15

Loews Portofino Bay Hotel at Universal Orlando ★★★★½
5601 Universal Blvd.
Orlando, FL 32819
☎ 407-503-1000
loewshotels.com/portofino -bay-hotel

LOCATION	4
ROOM RATING	92
COST ($ = $50)	$+ x 10
DAILY RESORT FEE	None

COMMUTING TIMES TO PARKS (*in minutes*):

MAGIC KINGDOM	21:45
EPCOT	17:15
ANIMAL KINGDOM	20:15
DHS	19:45

Marriott's Cypress Harbour Villas ★★★★
11251 Harbour Villa Rd.
Orlando, FL 32821
☎ 407-238-1300
tinyurl.com/marriottchv

LOCATION	2
ROOM RATING	85
COST ($ = $50)	$$$$$+
DAILY RESORT FEE	None

COMMUTING TIMES TO PARKS (*in minutes*):

MAGIC KINGDOM	15:00
EPCOT	13:00
ANIMAL KINGDOM	19:00
DHS	13:00

Marriott's Imperial Palms Villas ★★★★
8404 Vacation Way
Orlando, FL 32821
☎ 407-238-6200
tinyurl.com/marriottipv

LOCATION	2
ROOM RATING	86
COST ($ = $50)	$$$$$$+
DAILY RESORT FEE	None

COMMUTING TIMES TO PARKS (*in minutes*):

MAGIC KINGDOM	6:00
EPCOT	4:00
ANIMAL KINGDOM	6:00
DHS	4:00

Marriott's Grande Vista ★★★★½
5925 Avenida Vista
Orlando, FL 32821
☎ 407-238-7676
tinyurl.com/marriottsgrandevista

LOCATION	1
ROOM RATING	93
COST ($ = $50)	$$$+
DAILY RESORT FEE	None

COMMUTING TIMES TO PARKS (*in minutes*):

MAGIC KINGDOM	15:00
EPCOT	12:45
ANIMAL KINGDOM	15:45
DHS	15:15

Omni Orlando Resort at ChampionsGate ★★★★½
1500 Masters Blvd.
ChampionsGate, FL 32821
☎ 407-390-6664
tinyurl.com/omnichampionsgate

LOCATION	2
ROOM RATING	94
COST ($ = $50)	$$$$+
DAILY RESORT FEE	$35.00

COMMUTING TIMES TO PARKS (*in minutes*):

MAGIC KINGDOM	15:30
EPCOT	15:00
ANIMAL KINGDOM	15:00
DHS	14:30

Orlando World Center Marriott ★★★★½
8701 World Center Dr.
Orlando, FL 32821
☎ 407-239-4200
marriottworldcenter.com

LOCATION	2
ROOM RATING	90
COST ($ = $50)	$$$$+
DAILY RESORT FEE	$35.00

COMMUTING TIMES TO PARKS (*in minutes*):

MAGIC KINGDOM	9:45
EPCOT	5:00
ANIMAL KINGDOM	8:00
DHS	7:30

Parc Corniche Resort ★★★★½
6300 Parc Corniche Dr.
Orlando, FL 34747
☎ 407-239-7100
parccorniche.com

LOCATION	1
ROOM RATING	90
COST ($ = $50)	$$$+
DAILY RESORT FEE	$8.95

COMMUTING TIMES TO PARKS (*in minutes*):

MAGIC KINGDOM	21:00
EPCOT	18:00
ANIMAL KINGDOM	20:00
DHS	18:00

HOTEL INFORMATION CHART *(continued)*

Parkway International Resort
★★★½
6200 Safari Trl.
Kissimmee, FL 34746
☎ 407-396-6600
parkwayresort.com

LOCATION	3
ROOM RATING	82
COST ($ = $50)	$$$+
DAILY RESORT FEE	$13.95

COMMUTING TIMES TO PARKS
(in minutes):

MAGIC KINGDOM	8:30
EPCOT	8:15
ANIMAL KINGDOM	6:15
DHS	7:45

**Polynesian Isles Resort
(Diamond Resorts)** ★★★½
3045 Polynesian Isles Blvd.
Kissimmee, FL 32819
☎ 407-396-1622
polynesianisle.com

LOCATION	3
ROOM RATING	80
COST ($ = $50)	$$$
DAILY RESORT FEE	$14.95

COMMUTING TIMES TO PARKS
(in minutes):

MAGIC KINGDOM	14:30
EPCOT	14:15
ANIMAL KINGDOM	12:30
DHS	14:00

**Quality Suites Turkey Lake South/
Lake Buena Vista** ★★★½
9350 Turkey Lake Rd.
Orlando, FL 34747
☎ 407-351-5050
qualitysuitesorlandofl.com

LOCATION	2
ROOM RATING	77
COST ($ = $50)	$$-
DAILY RESORT FEE	$6.95

COMMUTING TIMES TO PARKS
(in minutes):

MAGIC KINGDOM	26:00:00
EPCOT	11:00
ANIMAL KINGDOM	17:00
DHS	16:00

Rodeway Inn Maingate ★★★
5995 W. US 192*
Kissimmee, FL 32819
☎ 407-396-4300
rodewayinnmaingate.com

LOCATION	3
ROOM RATING	65
COST ($ = $50)	$+
DAILY RESORT FEE	None

COMMUTING TIMES TO PARKS
(in minutes):

MAGIC KINGDOM	11:15
EPCOT	11:00
ANIMAL KINGDOM	9:15
DHS	10:30

Rosen Centre Hotel ★★★★½
9840 International Dr.
Orlando, FL 32819
☎ 407-996-9840
rosencentre.com

LOCATION	1
ROOM RATING	95
COST ($ = $50)	$$$$-
DAILY RESORT FEE	None

COMMUTING TIMES TO PARKS
(in minutes):

MAGIC KINGDOM	19:45
EPCOT	15:15
ANIMAL KINGDOM	18:15
DHS	17:45

Rosen Inn at Pointe Orlando
★★★★
9000 International Dr.
Orlando, FL 32819
☎ 407-996-8585
roseninn9000.com

LOCATION	1
ROOM RATING	84
COST ($ = $50)	$$$-
DAILY RESORT FEE	None

COMMUTING TIMES TO PARKS
(in minutes):

MAGIC KINGDOM	22:15
EPCOT	17:30
ANIMAL KINGDOM	20:30
DHS	20:00

**Sheraton Vistana Resort Villas,
Lake Buena Vista** ★★★★
8800 Vistana Centre Dr.
Orlando, FL 32821
☎ 407-239-3100
tinyurl.com/sheratonresortlbv

LOCATION	2
ROOM RATING	89
COST ($ = $50)	$$$
DAILY RESORT FEE	None

COMMUTING TIMES TO PARKS
(in minutes):

MAGIC KINGDOM	11:15
EPCOT	6:30
ANIMAL KINGDOM	9:30
DHS	9:00

**Sheraton Vistana Villages
Resort Villas, I-Drive** ★★★★
12401 International Dr.
Orlando, FL 34747
☎ 407-238-5000
tinyurl.com/vistanavillagesresort

LOCATION	1
ROOM RATING	87
COST ($ = $50)	$$$
DAILY RESORT FEE	None

COMMUTING TIMES TO PARKS
(in minutes):

MAGIC KINGDOM	11:15
EPCOT	6:30
ANIMAL KINGDOM	9:30
DHS	9:00

**Signia by Hilton Orlando
Bonnet Creek** ★★★★
14100 Bonnet Creek Resort Ln.
Orlando, FL 32821
☎ 407-597-3600
hiltonbonnetcreek.com

LOCATION	WDW
ROOM RATING	88
COST ($ = $50)	$$$$$+
DAILY RESORT FEE	$45.00

COMMUTING TIMES TO PARKS
(in minutes):

MAGIC KINGDOM	8:00
EPCOT	6:00
ANIMAL KINGDOM	7:15
DHS	4:15

**SpringHill Suites Orlando
Lake Buena Vista South** ★★★★
4991 Calypso Cay Way
Kissimmee, FL 34746
☎ 407-997-1300
tinyurl.com/springhillkiss

LOCATION	3
ROOM RATING	84
COST ($ = $50)	$$$
DAILY RESORT FEE	None

COMMUTING TIMES TO PARKS
(in minutes):

MAGIC KINGDOM	22:00
EPCOT	9:00
ANIMAL KINGDOM	11:00
DHS	10:00

Star Island Resort & Club ★★★★
5000 Avenue of the Stars
Kissimmee, FL 32821
☎ 407-997-8000
star-island.com

LOCATION	3
ROOM RATING	84
COST ($ = $50)	$$-
DAILY RESORT FEE	$14.19

COMMUTING TIMES TO PARKS
(in minutes):

MAGIC KINGDOM	15:45
EPCOT	15:15
ANIMAL KINGDOM	14:15
DHS	13:30

**Staybridge Suites Orlando at
SeaWorld** ★★★★½
6985 Sea Harbor Dr.
Orlando, FL 34746
☎ 407-917-9200
tinyurl.com/staybridgeseaworld

LOCATION	1
ROOM RATING	90
COST ($ = $50)	$$$$-
DAILY RESORT FEE	None

COMMUTING TIMES TO PARKS
(in minutes):

MAGIC KINGDOM	15:00
EPCOT	12:00
ANIMAL KINGDOM	14:00
DHS	12:00

*Irlo Bronson Memorial Highway

Ramada by Wyndham Kissimmee Gateway ★★½
7470 W. US 192*
Kissimmee, FL 32819
☎ 407-396-4400
ramadagateway.com

LOCATION	3
ROOM RATING	62
COST ($ = $50)	$$-
DAILY RESORT FEE	$4.00
COMMUTING TIMES TO PARKS *(in minutes):*	
MAGIC KINGDOM	5:00
EPCOT	9:00
ANIMAL KINGDOM	9:00
DHS	7:00

Residence Inn Near Universal Orlando ★★★½
5614 Major Blvd.
Orlando, FL 32837
☎ 407-313-1234
tinyurl.com/residenceinn
universalorlando

LOCATION	1
ROOM RATING	78
COST ($ = $50)	$$$+
DAILY RESORT FEE	None
COMMUTING TIMES TO PARKS *(in minutes):*	
MAGIC KINGDOM	18:00
EPCOT	14:15
ANIMAL KINGDOM	18:00
DHS	16:00

The Ritz-Carlton Orlando, Grande Lakes ★★★★½
4040 Central Florida Pkwy.
Orlando, FL 34747
☎ 407-206-2400
ritzcarlton.com/en/hotels/florida
/orlando

LOCATION	1
ROOM RATING	94
COST ($ = $50)	$- x 14
DAILY RESORT FEE	$40.00
COMMUTING TIMES TO PARKS *(in minutes):*	
MAGIC KINGDOM	23:00
EPCOT	18:15
ANIMAL KINGDOM	21:30
DHS	20:45

Rosen Plaza Hotel ★★★★½
9700 International Dr.
Orlando, FL 32819
☎ 407-996-9700
rosenplaza.com

LOCATION	1
ROOM RATING	91
COST ($ = $50)	$$$+
DAILY RESORT FEE	None
COMMUTING TIMES TO PARKS *(in minutes):*	
MAGIC KINGDOM	20:45
EPCOT	16:15
ANIMAL KINGDOM	19:15
DHS	18:45

Rosen Shingle Creek ★★★★
9939 Universal Blvd.
Orlando, FL 32830
☎ 407-996-9939
rosenshinglecreek.com

LOCATION	1
ROOM RATING	88
COST ($ = $50)	$$$$$-
DAILY RESORT FEE	None
COMMUTING TIMES TO PARKS *(in minutes):*	
MAGIC KINGDOM	24:00:00
EPCOT	17:00
ANIMAL KINGDOM	16:00
DHS	14:00

Shades of Green ★★★★½
1950 W. Magnolia Palm Dr.
Lake Buena Vista, FL 32821
☎ 407-824-3400
shadesofgreen.org

LOCATION	WDW
ROOM RATING	91
COST ($ = $50)	$$+
DAILY RESORT FEE	None
COMMUTING TIMES TO PARKS *(in minutes):*	
MAGIC KINGDOM	3:30
EPCOT	4:45
ANIMAL KINGDOM	9:30
DHS	6:15

Silver Lake Resort ★★★½
7751 Black Lake Rd.
Kissimmee, FL 32836
☎ 407-397-2828
silverlakeresort.com

LOCATION	3
ROOM RATING	75
COST ($ = $50)	$$$$-
DAILY RESORT FEE	None
COMMUTING TIMES TO PARKS *(in minutes):*	
MAGIC KINGDOM	8:15
EPCOT	8:00
ANIMAL KINGDOM	4:30
DHS	7:30

Sonesta ES Suites Lake Buena Vista ★★★★½
8751 Suiteside Dr.
Orlando, FL 34787
☎ 407-238-0777
tinyurl.com/sonestalbv

LOCATION	2
ROOM RATING	90
COST ($ = $50)	$$$$˜
DAILY RESORT FEE	$15.00
COMMUTING TIMES TO PARKS *(in minutes):*	
MAGIC KINGDOM	14:15
EPCOT	9:30
ANIMAL KINGDOM	12:30
DHS	12:00

SpringHill Suites Orlando at Flamingo Crossings ★★★★
13279 Hartzog Rd.
Winter Garden, FL 34746
☎ 407-507-1200
tinyurl.com/fc-springhill

LOCATION	2
ROOM RATING	85
COST ($ = $50)	$$$-
DAILY RESORT FEE	None
COMMUTING TIMES TO PARKS *(in minutes):*	
MAGIC KINGDOM	18:00
EPCOT	16:00
ANIMAL KINGDOM	10:00
DHS	15:00

Staybridge Suites Royale Parc ★★★½
5876 W. US 192*
Kissimmee, FL 34787
☎ 407-396-8040
tinyurl.com/staybridgeroyaleparc

LOCATION	3
ROOM RATING	76
COST ($ = $50)	$$$-
DAILY RESORT FEE	$13.00
COMMUTING TIMES TO PARKS *(in minutes):*	
MAGIC KINGDOM	11:15
EPCOT	11:00
ANIMAL KINGDOM	9:15
DHS	10:30

TownePlace Suites Orlando at Flamingo Crossings ★★★★
13295 Hartzog Rd.
Winter Garden, FL 32830
☎ 407-507-1300
tinyurl.com/fc-towneplace

LOCATION	2
ROOM RATING	84
COST ($ = $50)	$$$-
DAILY RESORT FEE	None
COMMUTING TIMES TO PARKS *(in minutes):*	
MAGIC KINGDOM	18:00
EPCOT	16:00
ANIMAL KINGDOM	10:00
DHS	16:00

Treehouse Villas at Disney's Saratoga Springs Resort & Spa ★★★★½
1960 Broadway
Lake Buena Vista, FL 32819
☎ 407-827-1100
tinyurl.com/saratogawdw

LOCATION	WDW
ROOM RATING	90
COST ($ = $50)	$+ x 10
DAILY RESORT FEE	None
COMMUTING TIMES TO PARKS *(in minutes):*	
MAGIC KINGDOM	12:45
EPCOT	7:15
ANIMAL KINGDOM	16:45
DHS	12:30

HOTEL INFORMATION CHART *(continued)*

Universal's Aventura Hotel ★★★½
6725 Adventure Way
Orlando, FL 32819
☎ 407-503-6000
loewshotels.com/universals
-aventura-hotel

LOCATION	4
ROOM RATING	82
COST ($ = $50)	$$$$
DAILY RESORT FEE	None

COMMUTING TIMES TO PARKS
(in minutes):

MAGIC KINGDOM	20:00
EPCOT	15:00
ANIMAL KINGDOM	17:00
DHS	14:00

Universal's Cabana Bay Beach Resort ★★★★
6550 Adventure Way
Orlando, FL 34747
☎ 407-503-4000
loewshotels.com/cabana-bay-hotel

LOCATION	4
ROOM RATING	83
COST ($ = $50)	$$$$
DAILY RESORT FEE	None

COMMUTING TIMES TO PARKS
(in minutes):

MAGIC KINGDOM	20:00
EPCOT	15:00
ANIMAL KINGDOM	17:00
DHS	14:00

Universal's Endless Summer Resort: Dockside Inn & Suites ★★★½
7125 Universal Blvd.
Orlando, FL 32819
☎ 407-503-8000
loewshotels.com/dockside-inn
-and-suites

LOCATION	4
ROOM RATING	81
COST ($ = $50)	$$$-
DAILY RESORT FEE	None

COMMUTING TIMES TO PARKS
(in minutes):

MAGIC KINGDOM	19:00
EPCOT	17:00
ANIMAL KINGDOM	22:00
DHS	16:00

Waldorf Astoria Orlando ★★★★½
14200 Bonnet Creek Resort Ln.
Orlando, FL 32830
☎ 407-597-5500
waldorfastoriaorlando.com

LOCATION	WDW
ROOM RATING	93
COST ($ = $50)	$+ x 10
DAILY RESORT FEE	$45.00

COMMUTING TIMES TO PARKS
(in minutes):

MAGIC KINGDOM	8:00
EPCOT	6:00
ANIMAL KINGDOM	7:15
DHS	4:15

Walt Disney World Dolphin ★★★★
1500 EPCOT Resorts Blvd.
Lake Buena Vista, FL 32830
☎ 407-934-4000
swandolphin.com

LOCATION	WDW
ROOM RATING	87
COST ($ = $50)	$$$$$
DAILY RESORT FEE	$35.00

COMMUTING TIMES TO PARKS
(in minutes):

MAGIC KINGDOM	6:45
EPCOT	5:00
ANIMAL KINGDOM	6:15
DHS	4:00

Walt Disney World Swan ★★★★
1200 EPCOT Resorts Blvd.
Lake Buena Vista, FL 32830
☎ 407-934-3000
swandolphin.com

LOCATION	WDW
ROOM RATING	89
COST ($ = $50)	$$$$$
DAILY RESORT FEE	$35.00

COMMUTING TIMES TO PARKS
(in minutes):

MAGIC KINGDOM	6:30
EPCOT	4:45
ANIMAL KINGDOM	6:15
DHS	4:00

Wingate by Wyndham Universal Studios & Convention Center ★★★½
5661 Windhover Dr.
Orlando, FL 38321
☎ 407-226-0900
wingateorlando.com

LOCATION	4
ROOM RATING	80
COST ($ = $50)	$$$
DAILY RESORT FEE	None

COMMUTING TIMES TO PARKS
(in minutes):

MAGIC KINGDOM	21:00
EPCOT	16:00
ANIMAL KINGDOM	19:00
DHS	18:00

WorldMark Orlando–Kingstown Reef ★★★½
12000 International Dr.
Orlando, FL 32830
☎ 407-597-2550
tinyurl.com/wmokingstownreef

LOCATION	1
ROOM RATING	80
COST ($ = $50)	$$+
DAILY RESORT FEE	None

COMMUTING TIMES TO PARKS
(in minutes):

MAGIC KINGDOM	18:00
EPCOT	15:00
ANIMAL KINGDOM	21:00
DHS	15:00

Wyndham Garden Lake Buena Vista ★★★½
1850-B Hotel Plaza Blvd.
Lake Buena Vista, FL 32821
☎ 407-842-6644
wyndhamlakebuenavista.com

LOCATION	WDW
ROOM RATING	75
COST ($ = $50)	$$$
DAILY RESORT FEE	$24.00

COMMUTING TIMES TO PARKS
(in minutes):

MAGIC KINGDOM	15:15
EPCOT	10:45
ANIMAL KINGDOM	14:45
DHS	12:15

*Irlo Bronson Memorial Highway

Universal's Endless Summer Resort: Surfside Inn & Suites ★★★½
7000 Universal Blvd.
Orlando, FL 32819
☎ 407-503-7000
loewshotels.com/surfside-inn-and-suites

LOCATION	4
ROOM RATING	81
COST ($ = $50)	$$$-
DAILY RESORT FEE	None

COMMUTING TIMES TO PARKS (in minutes):

MAGIC KINGDOM	19:00
EPCOT	17:00
ANIMAL KINGDOM	22:00
DHS	16:00

Vacation Village at Parkway ★★★★½
2975 Arabian Nights Blvd.
Kissimmee, FL 32830
☎ 407-396-9086
tinyurl.com/vacation-village-pkwy

LOCATION	3
ROOM RATING	93
COST ($ = $50)	$$$-
DAILY RESORT FEE	$30 (one-time)

COMMUTING TIMES TO PARKS (in minutes):

MAGIC KINGDOM	8:30
EPCOT	8:15
ANIMAL KINGDOM	6:45
DHS	7:45

The Villas at Disney's Grand Floridian Resort & Spa ★★★★½
4401 Floridian Way
Lake Buena Vista, FL 32821
☎ 407-824-3000
tinyurl.com/grandfloridianvillas

LOCATION	WDW
ROOM RATING	93
COST ($ = $50)	$ x 19
DAILY RESORT FEE	None

COMMUTING TIMES TO PARKS (in minutes):

MAGIC KINGDOM	on monorail
EPCOT	4:45
ANIMAL KINGDOM	11:45
DHS	6:45

Walt Disney World Swan Reserve
(opens 2021) ★★★★
1500 EPCOT Resorts Blvd.
Lake Buena Vista, FL 32819
☎ 407-934-3000
swandolphin.com

LOCATION	WDW
ROOM RATING	86
COST ($ = $50)	$ x 16
DAILY RESORT FEE	$35.00

COMMUTING TIMES TO PARKS (in minutes):

MAGIC KINGDOM	6:30
EPCOT	4:45
ANIMAL KINGDOM	6:15
DHS	4:00

Westgate Lakes Resort & Spa ★★★★½
9500 Turkey Lake Rd.
Orlando, FL 34747
☎ 407-345-0000
westgateresorts.com/lakes

LOCATION	2
ROOM RATING	92
COST ($ = $50)	$$$$-
DAILY RESORT FEE	$13.00

COMMUTING TIMES TO PARKS (in minutes):

MAGIC KINGDOM	17:30
EPCOT	14:30
ANIMAL KINGDOM	19:15
DHS	18:00

Westgate Vacation Villas Resort ★★★★½
7700 Westgate Blvd.
Kissimmee, FL 32819
☎ 407-239-0510
westgateresorts.com/vacation-villas

LOCATION	3
ROOM RATING	90
COST ($ = $50)	$$$
DAILY RESORT FEE	$13.00

COMMUTING TIMES TO PARKS (in minutes):

MAGIC KINGDOM	8:45
EPCOT	8:30
ANIMAL KINGDOM	5:45
DHS	8:00

Wyndham Grand Orlando Resort Bonnet Creek ★★★★
14651 Chelonia Pkwy.
Orlando, FL 32819
☎ 407-390-2300
tinyurl.com/wyndhamgrandbonnetcreek

LOCATION	WDW
ROOM RATING	85
COST ($ = $50)	$$$$$+
DAILY RESORT FEE	$28.00

COMMUTING TIMES TO PARKS (in minutes):

MAGIC KINGDOM	18:00
EPCOT	8:00
ANIMAL KINGDOM	15:00
DHS	10:00

DINING *in* AND *around* WALT DISNEY WORLD

KEY QUESTIONS ANSWERED IN THIS CHAPTER

READER SURVEYS *plus* EXPERT OPINIONS: *Our Approach to Dining*

WE'VE RECEIVED MORE THAN 76,000 SURVEYS about Walt Disney World restaurants in the past year, and almost 650,000 since 2018. We think that's more surveys than Yelp and TripAdvisor have gotten for the World over their entire lifetimes. *Combined.*

What makes the *Unofficial Guide* different from Yelp and others is that we display those surveys alongside objective reviews written by culinary experts. With these critical analyses, you get a consistent evaluation of the entire range of Disney dining options from people who've tried every restaurant, kiosk, and food stand in the World. We (Bob and Len) weigh in occasionally too. Here's how to use the reader surveys and critical reviews together.

> • *If a restaurant has earned 90% or better in our reader surveys and at least four stars (sit-down) or a B or better (counter-service) from our critics, make plans to visit.* Chances are good that you'll enjoy your meal. In EPCOT, for example, France's counter-service **Les Halles**

Boulangerie-Pâtisserie and Italy's **Via Napoli Ristorante e Pizzeria** sit-down restaurant both fit this profile.

• *Avoid restaurants that have earned 80% or less in our reader surveys and either three stars or less (sit-down) or a C or lower (counter-service) from our critics.* They're probably not worth your time or money. **Hollywood & Vine** and **PizzeRizzo** at Disney's Hollywood Studios are examples.

• *For restaurants where our reader surveys disagree with our critical analysis, read the review for an explanation.* An example is **The Edison** at Disney Springs. This upscale restaurant and nightclub has good food and friendly service, earning three stars from our critics. However, upon opening it was billed as an East Coast version of the swanky Los Angeles original, but it is decidedly not—instead, it was Disneyfied for mass appeal, dropping the L.A. location's sexy burlesque show and diluting its strict "dress to impress" requirements for guests. What's left isn't fancy enough for an adults' special evening out, yet it's too unusual for tourists just looking for a meal.

SURVEY RESULTS DEMYSTIFIED

FOR BOTH COUNTER-SERVICE and full-service restaurants, along with the restaurants mentioned in "Dining at Universal CityWalk" (see page 362), we list reader-survey results for each restaurant profiled, expressed as a percentage of positive responses.

The average positive (+) rating for all Disney counter-service restaurants is **88.5%** at a 95% confidence interval (CI). If that sounds overly technical, know this: In a nutshell it means that these ratings are derived from highly accurate data—thus, you can trust them in deciding whether a particular restaurant is worth a try or deserves a swipe-left.

We use the following categories to provide context for the percentages:

CATEGORY	IN LEN-SPEAK	IN ENGLISH
EXCEPTIONAL	+ rating is in top 10% of all restaurants in this category	Don't miss it
MUCH ABOVE AVERAGE	+ rating is in top 25% of all restaurants in this category	Really, really good
ABOVE AVERAGE	+ rating is in top 40% of all restaurants in this category	Worth a try
BELOW AVERAGE	+ rating is in bottom 40% of all restaurants in this category	Not the best, not the worst; if you just need a bite to eat, it's fine
MUCH BELOW AVERAGE	+ rating is in bottom 25% of all restaurants in this category	Skip it if you have other options
DO NOT VISIT	+ rating is in bottom 10% of all restaurants in this category	If you have functioning taste buds, it's a hard no

DINING *in* WALT DISNEY WORLD

THIS SECTION AIMS TO HELP YOU find good food without going broke or tripping over a culinary land mine. More than 200 restaurants—including around 90 full-service establishments, around 30 of which are inside the theme parks—operate within the World. These restaurants offer exceptional variety, serving everything from Moroccan lamb to Texas barbecue. Most restaurants are expensive, and many serve food that doesn't live up to the prices, but there are good choices to be found in every area of Walt Disney World.

PANDEMIC DINING OPTIONS AND EXPERIENCES

RESTAURANT OPERATIONS have changed during the pandemic:

- Many restaurant menus have been scaled back to a handful of selections, usually offered for the same price at both lunch and dinner.
- Most meals with Disney characters are either temporarily suspended or have eliminated direct character interactions.
- Disney's popular dining plans were not being offered as we went to press.
- The number of days in advance you can make dining reservations has shortened from 180 to 60.
- Disney recommends that you order counter-service restaurant meals in advance using the My Disney Experience app.
- Some buffets have been replaced with all-you-care-to-eat selections brought to your table, or with prix fixe menu options.

The lack of characters and buffets, and the simplified menus, has dramatically lowered the reader ratings of some Disney-owned restaurants. Restaurants operated by third parties, such as those at Disney Springs, seem to be operating with a similar number of menu options as they were before the pandemic. Quality at these restaurants is in line with pre-pandemic levels as well.

The rest of this chapter offers detailed advice on how to find the best Disney dining experiences. Here are a couple of quick tips to keep in mind, regardless of where you decide to eat:

- Place your counter-service restaurant order 30–45 minutes before you want to eat; that will allow the restaurant enough time to prepare your food before you arrive, and it will reduce your wait.
- Consider eating before noon or after 1 p.m. because it will be easier to find open tables at counter-service restaurants then.

GETTING IT RIGHT

ALTHOUGH WE WORK HARD to be fair, objective, and accurate, many readers, like this Charleston, West Virginia, woman, think we're overly critical of Disney dining:

> Get a life! It's crazy and unrealistic to be so snobbish about restaurants at a theme park. Considering the number of people Disney feeds each day, I think they do a darn good job. Also, you act so surprised that the food is expensive. Have you ever eaten at an airport? HELLO IN THERE? . . . Surprise, you're a captive! It's a theme park!

And a mom from Erie, Pennsylvania, strikes a practical note:

> Most of the food at Walt Disney World is OK. You pay more than you should, but it's more convenient to eat in Disney World than to try to find cheaper restaurants somewhere else.

As you may infer from these comments, researching and reviewing restaurants is no straightforward endeavor—to the contrary, it's fraught with peril and intrigue.

It's a Shill World: Disney and the Blogosphere

We could be wrong, but when it comes to dining reviews, we suspect that Disney plays favorites with blogs and websites they know are likely to provide positive coverage. Most of these sites rely on ad views to make money, so drawing in readers with exclusive content is a quid pro quo. Thus, the sites' primary goals are (1) not to offend Disney and (2) to show lots of ads to lots of people. (Keep in mind the lesson learned from Facebook: If you're not paying for something online, you're probably the product being sold to advertisers.)

Be especially skeptical of online opening-night "reviews" of new Disney restaurants. Representatives from social-media–driven sites show up to cover these events in droves; Disney, knowing this, stage-manages them with a gravitas worthy of a royal wedding, bringing in executive chefs to ensure perfection in everything from preparation to presentation.

This is unsustainable, of course. As soon as the blog posts go up, the chefs go back to their regular jobs, the accountants change the menu to ensure profits, and the regular kitchen staff is left to figure out things on their own. It's highly unlikely that the lavish dishes showcased on the blogs will actually make it to the restaurant's diners each night.

The *Unofficial* Difference

How, then, do we go about presenting the best possible dining coverage? At the *Unofficial Guide,* we begin with highly qualified culinary experts and then balance their opinions with those of our readers—which, by the way, don't always coincide. (Likewise, the coauthors' assessments don't always agree with those of our dining experts.)

> *unofficial* **TIP**
> Our research team has eaten at every restaurant, kiosk, bar, cart, and food stand in Walt Disney World many times.

In the spirit of democracy, we encourage you to fill out our online reader survey at touring plans.com/walt-disney-world/survey. If you'd like to share your dining experience in greater depth, we also invite you to write to us at the address on page 5 or shoot us an email at info@ theunofficialguides.com.

WHERE TO FIND GOOD MEALS

THE BEST CONCENTRATIONS OF SIT-DOWN RESTAURANTS in Walt Disney World are found at **Disney's Animal Kingdom Lodge; Disney's Grand Floridian Resort & Spa;** and the **Disney Springs** dining, shopping, and entertainment complex.

Animal Kingdom Lodge boasts 3 of the top 10 sit-down restaurants in Walt Disney World: **Boma—Flavors of Africa** (No. 3 overall out of more than 110 sit-down restaurants) is a beloved buffet favorite; **Jiko— The Cooking Place** (No. 6 overall out of 112; closed at press time) puts a lot of thought into its menu and has a good wine list; and **Sanaa** (No. 10; open) serves delicious African–Indian fusion dishes.

The Grand Floridian houses the best restaurant in Walt Disney World: **Victoria & Albert's** (closed at press time), which won its 20th consecutive AAA Five Diamond Award in early 2020. The food is extraordinary, of course, as is the service. Beyond V&A's, you'll find the **Grand Floridian Cafe** (No. 22; open) and the **1900 Park Fare** character buffet (No. 23; closed at press time). Within walking distance of the Grand Flo is the **Polynesian Village Resort**'s **Kona Cafe** (No. 31), with excellent breakfast options, and 'Ohana (No. 44; open), with family-style dining at breakfast and dinner; the Contemporary Resort's California Grill (No. 17; open) is a short monorail ride away too. If dining is an important part of your Disney World vacation and these resorts are within your budget (and the restaurants have reopened), we suggest staying at one of them.

The next best concentration of open restaurants is at the Contemporary Resort. Along with the California Grill (No. 17 overall), the Contemporary has a new sit-down restaurant called Steakhouse 71 (not yet open at press time), and the counter-service Contempo Cafe (88%; Average) is convenient for simple meals. If the Contemporary isn't an option, consider dining at Disney Springs.

Highlights at Disney Springs include Chef Art Smith's Homecomin' (No. 8), with excellent fried chicken, tasty cocktails, and luscious desserts. For seafood and steaks, try The Boathouse (No. 9). Disney Springs also has some of the World's top counter service, including The Polite Pig barbecue joint (No. 3 in this category), Earl of Sandwich (No. 13), and Blaze Fast-Fire'd Pizza (No. 14).

Disney Springs is also home to two of our favorite tapas restaurants. Wine Bar George (No. 2 overall) is run by a master sommelier who partnered with a chef to create a menu that pairs food and wine. It's the perfect choice for a glass or two and some small bites. Our other tapas favorite is Jaleo (No. 7), from celebrity chef José Andrés. Jaleo's menu of modern Spanish dishes is extensive and affordable. We wouldn't be surprised if fights broke out over the last bite of patatas bravas. The jamón ibérico is the stuff of dreams.

If the dining at Disney Springs sounds good to you, consider a stay at Disney's Saratoga Springs Resort & Spa. Many of the buildings are a short walk to Disney Springs.

Finally, in the theme parks, food at Disney's Animal Kingdom and EPCOT gets the highest marks.

▌▌ DISNEY DINING 101

WALT DISNEY WORLD RESTAURANT CATEGORIES

IN GENERAL, food and beverage offerings at Walt Disney World are defined by service, price, and convenience:

FULL-SERVICE RESTAURANTS Full-service restaurants are in all Disney resorts (except the Value resorts and Port Orleans French Quarter), all major theme parks, and Disney Springs. Disney operates most of the restaurants in the theme parks and its hotels, while contractors or franchisees operate the rest. Advance Reservations (see page 271) are recommended for most full-service restaurants.

CHARACTER MEALS As we went to press, five Walt Disney World restaurants have Disney characters in attendance during meals. Most of these meals were buffets before the pandemic; now you order from a fixed-price menu, some of which are all-you-care-to-eat. And most restaurants have a separate kids' menu featuring dishes such as hot dogs, burgers, chicken nuggets, pizza, and macaroni and cheese.

BUFFETS AND FAMILY-STYLE RESTAURANTS Most Walt Disney World buffets have been suspended during the pandemic, replaced with all-you-care-to-eat offerings from a daily fixed menu, brought to your private table by a server. For example, at Animal Kingdom's Tusker House, your party will be provided with several platters stacked high with meats, vegetables, pastas, and salads. You can ask for more (or less) of any item. We've tried several family-style restaurants since WDW reopened, and we've been pleasantly surprised at the food quality and quantity provided at most of them.

Advance Reservations are highly recommended for character meals and recommended for all other restaurants. Most credit cards are accepted. An automatic 18% gratuity is added to the bill for parties of six or more, but when the tipping is at *your* discretion, a North Carolina reader urges generosity with waitstaff:

> *I've seen diners leave a dollar or two per person. I've also heard of people protesting Disney's prices by leaving a small tip or none at all. This is unacceptable—these servers keep your drinks full, keep your plates clean, and check on you constantly. They deserve at least 15%–18%. If you can't afford to tip, you shouldn't eat there.*

FOOD COURTS Featuring a number of counter-service eateries under one roof, food courts can be found at Disney's Moderate and Value resorts. If you're staying at one of these resorts, chances are you'll eat once or twice a day at your hotel's food court. As we went to press, Disney had simplified and made common its food court menus across all of its resorts. Reader satisfaction ratings dropped considerably as a result—every food court except one has dropped to "Do Not Visit" status in those surveys.

DISNEY RESORT FOOD COURTS: Reader-Survey Ratings		
RESORT	FOOD COURT	POSITIVE RATING
All-Star Movies	World Premier Food Court	74% *(Do Not Visit)*
All-Star Music	Intermission Food Court*	83% *(Average)*
All-Star Sports	End Zone Food Court*	80% *(Below Average)*
Art of Animation	Landscape of Flavors	76% *(Do Not Visit)*
Caribbean Beach	Centertown Market	78% *(Do Not Visit)*
Coronado Springs	El Mercado de Coronado Food Court	61% *(Do Not Visit)*
Fort Wilderness	P & J's Southern Takeout	84% *(Much Below Average)*
Pop Century	Everything POP	78% *(Do Not Visit)*
Port Orleans French Quarter	Sassagoula Floatworks & Food Factory*	90% *(Much Above Average)*
Port Orleans Riverside	Riverside Mill Food Court*	82% *(Below Average)*

Closed at press time; survey results from 2019-2020

The closest thing to a food court at the theme parks is **Sunshine Seasons** at EPCOT; see "Fast Casual" on the next page and the full profile on page 301. Advance Reservations are neither required nor available at these restaurants.

COUNTER SERVICE Counter-service fast food is plentiful in all the theme parks and at the BoardWalk and Disney Springs. You'll find hot dogs, burgers, chicken sandwiches, salads, and pizza almost everywhere. They're augmented by special items that relate to the park's theme or the part of the park you're touring. In EPCOT's Germany, for example, counter-service bratwurst and beer are sold; in Frontierland in the Magic Kingdom, vendors sell smoked turkey legs.

Ordering meals ahead of time through the My Disney Experience app is preferred at all counter-service restaurants.

Most counter-service restaurants serve combo meals, but you can order any meal without the side to save some money. Counter-service prices are fairly consistent from park to park. You can expect to pay the same for your coffee or hot dog at Disney's Animal Kingdom as you would at Disney's Hollywood Studios.

FAST CASUAL Somewhere between burgers and formal dining are the establishments in Disney's fast casual category, including two in the theme parks: **Satu'li Canteen** in the Animal Kingdom and **Sunshine Seasons** in EPCOT.

VENDOR FOOD Vendors abound at the theme parks, Disney Springs, and the BoardWalk. Offerings include popcorn, ice-cream bars, churros, soft drinks, bottled water, and (in the theme parks) fresh fruit. Prices include tax; many vendors are set up to accept credit cards, charges to your room at a Disney resort, and the Disney Dining Plan (when it's offered). Others take cash only (look for a sign near the cash register).

DISNEY DINING PLANS

IF YOU WANT TO SIGN UP FOR one of Disney's prepaid dining plans, you must do so when you book your Disney resort room or package vacation; for this reason, we explore the topic in depth in Part Five, "Accommodations," starting

unofficial **TIP**
Disney dining plans remain temporarily suspended at press time, but Disney says they're coming back.

on page 82. These plans were not available as we went to press. They may not be widely available until restaurant capacity returns to pre-pandemic levels.

ADVANCE RESERVATIONS

GET PARK RESERVATIONS before you make dining reservations. Having a dining reservation inside a theme park doesn't provide access to that theme park—you still need a theme park reservation to get in. See page 74–75 for details on how to make a theme park reservation.

You can make reservations for Disney's sit-down restaurants, including those in the theme parks, as you can at most sit-down restaurants in your hometown. See the table on the next page for specifics.

The main difference between most hometown restaurants and Disney's, however, is that hundreds of people are trying to get reservations at Disney's popular restaurants at the instant they become available.

In fact, Disney's most popular restaurants can run out of reservations months in advance. Also, most Disney restaurants hold no tables at all—none—for walk-in guests. That means it's important to book your dining reservations as soon as you're able (typically 60 days before your visit). This section explains how it all works, and why.

ADVANCE RESERVATIONS: *The Official Line*

YOU CAN RESERVE THE FOLLOWING up to 60 days in advance:

AFTERNOON TEA AND CHILDREN'S PROGRAMS* at the Grand Floridian Resort & Spa

ALL DISNEY TABLE-SERVICE RESTAURANTS and character-dining venues

FANTASMIC! **DINING PACKAGE*** at Disney's Hollywood Studios

HOOP-DEE-DOO MUSICAL REVUE* at Fort Wilderness Resort & Campground

OGA'S CANTINA at Star Wars: Galaxy's Edge, Disney's Hollywood Studios

SPIRIT OF ALOHA DINNER SHOW** at the Polynesian Village Resort

Guests staying at Disney-owned resorts may make dining reservations for the entire length of their stay—up to 10 days—in a single booking up to 60 days in advance.

*Closed at press time

**Closed at press time; may be closed permanently

Behind the Scenes at Advance Reservations

Although they're called reservations, most dining reservations at Walt Disney World don't actually guarantee you a table at a specific time as they would at your typical hometown restaurant. Instead, Disney restaurants operate on what's known as a template system: Instead of scheduling Advance Reservations for actual tables, reservations fill time slots. The number of slots available is based on the average length of time that guests occupy a table at a particular restaurant, adjusted for seasonality.

unofficial **TIP**
Disney charges a $10- to $25-per-person penalty for missing an Advance Reservation or if you cancel on the day of the meal.

Here's a rough example of how it works: Let's say that Coral Reef Restaurant at EPCOT has 40 tables for four and 8 tables for six, and that the average length of time for a family to be seated, order, eat, pay, and depart is 40 minutes. Add 5 minutes to bus the table and set it up for the next guests, and the table is turning every 45 minutes. The restaurant then provides Disney's central dining-reservations system (**CDRS**) with a computer template of its capacity, along with the average amount of time that the table is occupied. Disney uses CDRS to process reservations both online and by phone.

Thus, when you use the website to make Advance Reservations for four people at 6:15 p.m., CDRS removes one table for four from its overall capacity for 45 minutes. The system template indicates that the table will be unavailable for reassignment until 7 p.m. (45 minutes later). And so it goes for all tables in the restaurant, each being subtracted from overall capacity for 45 minutes, then listed as available again, then assigned to other guests and subtracted again, and so on throughout the meal period.

CDRS tries to fill every time slot for every seat in the restaurant or come as close to filling every slot as possible; again, no seats are reserved for walk-ins. Templates are filled differently depending on the season and restaurant.

When you arrive at a restaurant having made Advance Reservations, your wait to be seated will usually be less than 20 minutes during peak hours and often less than 10 minutes. If you just show up unencumbered by a reservation, especially during busier seasons, expect to either wait 40–75 minutes or—more likely—be told that there are no tables available.

NO-SHOW PENALTIES Disney restaurants charge a no-show fee of $10–$25 per person; this has reduced the no-show rate to virtually zero, and these restaurants are booked every day according to their actual capacity. Note, however, the following:

- Only one person needs to dine at the restaurant for Disney to consider your reservation fulfilled, even if you have a reservation for more people.
- Some restaurants booked through **OpenTable.com** (see page 277) do not have no-show penalties.
- While Disney says it requires 24 hours' notice, you can cancel up until midnight of the day before your meal in many instances.

The upside to the no-show fee is that it generally makes booking easier closer to the date of your visit, as the fee discourages tentative plans.

GETTING ADVANCE RESERVATIONS AT POPULAR RESTAURANTS

TWO OF THE HARDEST RESERVATIONS TO GET in Walt Disney World these days are the lunch spots at Hollywood Studios' **Sci-Fi Dine-In Theater** and **Hollywood & Vine**. Why? The park is very popular because of the Star Wars and Toy Story attractions, and it doesn't have many good dining options. You'll have to put in some effort to secure Advance Reservation at these places, especially during busier times of year.

The easiest and fastest way to get a reservation is to go to disneyworld.disney.go.com/dining starting at 5:45 a.m. Eastern time, a full hour before phone reservations open. To familiarize yourself with how the site works, try it out a couple of days before you actually make reservations. You'll also save time by setting up a **My Disney Experience** account online (see page 33) before your 60-day booking window, making sure to enter any credit card information needed to guarantee your reservations.

If you live in California and you have to get up at 2:45 a.m. Pacific time to make a reservation, Disney couldn't care less: There's no limit to the number of hoops they can make you jump through if demand exceeds supply.

Disney's website is usually within a few seconds of the official time as determined by the federal government, accessible online at time.gov. Using this site, synchronize your computer *to the second* the night before your 60-day window opens, if your computer hasn't synchronized automatically already.

Early on the morning on which you want to make reservations, take a few moments to type the date of your visit into a word processor in MM/DD/YYYY format—for example, 11/16/2021 for November 16, 2021. Select the date, then copy it to your computer's clipboard. This will save you from having to retype the date when the site comes online.

Next, start trying the Disney website about 3 minutes before 5:45 a.m. You'll see a text box where you can specify the date of your visit: Click in the text box, select it (**Ctrl-A** on Windows or **Cmd-A** on Mac), and then paste in the date you copied earlier (**Ctrl-V** on Windows or **Cmd-V** on Mac; don't right-click to paste—every millisecond counts!); then press the tab key on your keyboard. You'll also see a place to specify the location (such as Magic Kingdom), the time of your meal, and your party size; you can fill in this information in ahead of time too. Then click "search times."

If your date isn't yet available, a message will appear saying, "There is a problem searching for reservations at this time" or something similar. If this happens, refresh the browser page and start over. If you don't see an error message, however, the results returned will tell you whether your restaurant has a table available.

Note that while you're typing, other guests are trying to make Advance Reservations too, so you want the transaction to go down as quickly as possible. Flexibility on your part counts—it's much harder to get seating for a large group, so give some thought to breaking your group into numbers that can be accommodated at tables for four. Also make sure you have your credit card out where you can read it.

Advance Reservations for **Cinderella's Royal Table,** character meals, and—when they're offered—the *Fantasmic!* **Dining Package** and the *Hoop-Dee-Doo Musical Revue* are actual reservations—that is, they require complete prepayment with a credit card at the time of the booking. The name on the booking can't be changed after the reservation is made. Reservations may be canceled, with the deposit refunded in full, by calling ☎ 407-WDW-DINE at least 48 hours before seating for these shows (versus 24 hours ahead for regular Advance Reservations). Disney will work with you in the event of an emergency.

If you don't have access to a computer at 5:45 a.m. on the morning you need to make reservations, be ready to call ☎ 407-WDW-DINE at 6:45 a.m. Eastern time and follow the prompts to speak to a live person. You may still get placed on hold if call volume is higher than usual, and you'll be an hour behind the early birds with computers. Still, you'll be well ahead of those who couldn't make it up before sunrise.

Note that if the Disney Dining Plan returns and you want to book a *Harmonious* or *Fantasmic!* package, Cinderella's Royal Table, or one of the dinner shows, you may be better off reserving by phone anyway. The online system may not recognize your table-service credits, but you can book and pay with a credit card, then call ☎ 407-WDW-DINE after 6:45 a.m. and have them credit the charge for the meal back to your card; be aware that this can be a potential hassle if you get an uncooperative cast member. When you get to Walt Disney World, you'll use credits from your dining plan to "pay" for the meal. (Sometimes the online system has glitches and shows no availability; in this case, call after 6:45 a.m. to confirm if the online system is correct.)

NEVER, NEVER, NEVER, NEVER GIVE UP Not getting what you want the first time you try doesn't mean the end of the story. A mom from Cincinnati advises persistence in securing Advance Reservations:

> I was crushed when I called and tried to reserve Chef Mickey's and couldn't. I decided not to give up and would go online once or twice a day to check reservations for Chef Mickey's and the other restaurants I wanted. It took me about a week, but sooner or later I ended up booking every single reservation I wanted except one.

A woman from Franklin, Tennessee, agrees:

> I started trying to get a reservation at Be Our Guest Restaurant about a month out from our vacation. By checking the website whenever I

THE REALITY OF GETTING LAST-MINUTE DINING RESERVATIONS

IF YOUR VACATION is more than 60 days out and you want to dine at a popular venue such as Be Our Guest Restaurant, following our advice below will get you the table you want more than 80% of the time.

The longer you wait, the more effort you'll have to put in to find a reservation. For example, if you're trying for an early breakfast at Be Our Guest within the next seven days, your chance of finding any table the first time you check is less than 3%, based on our tests. But if you have the time and patience to visit Disney's website around 30 times over the next week—nope, not a typo—you have a 50–50 shot at snapping up a last-minute cancellation.

Besides Sci-Fi Dine-In and Be Our Guest, the list below shows the restaurants where capacity and demand make finding a last-minute reservation more difficult. If you're planning a trip within the next 30 days, see page 276 for our recommended alternatives.

- **CHEF ART SMITH'S HOMECOMIN'** *(Disney Springs)* Exceptional fried chicken, desserts you'd slap your siblings to get more of, *and* the best cocktails in Disney Springs. Dinner reservations are hardest to get.
- **CHEF MICKEY'S** *(Contemporary Resort)* The food isn't anything special; neither is the venue. The draws are the Disney characters and the service, both of which are great.
- **GARDEN GRILL** *(The Land/EPCOT)* The only character meal in the park right now. Serves lunch and dinner.
- **HOLLYWOOD & VINE** *(Disney's Hollywood Studios)* One of the few character meals available in Walt Disney World, lunch here helps pass the time if you're waiting for your Rise of the Resistance boarding group to be called.
- **THE PLAZA RESTAURANT** *(Magic Kingdom)* The Plaza serves decent sandwiches in blessed air-conditioned comfort, but its small size makes it a difficult reservation to snag.
- **RAGLAN ROAD** *(Disney Springs)* Long regarded as one of Disney Springs' best restaurants, Raglan Road is tough to book for dinner.
- **T-REX** *(Disney Springs)* The theming and dinosaurs are the draw here, and it's aimed at children. Food quality isn't high, but portions are huge.

thought of it—morning, noon, and night—I ended up getting not only a lunch reservation but a dinner reservation!

LAST-MINUTE ADVANCE RESERVATIONS Because Advance Reservations require a credit card, and because a fee is charged for failing to cancel in time, you can often score a last-minute reservation. This is attributable to reservation holders who are tired or have last-minute conflicts calling in at the last moment to avoid paying the $10-per-head penalty. As long as the reservation holder calls to cancel before midnight the day before, he or she won't be charged. So your best shot at picking up a canceled reservation is to repeatedly call or visit disneyworld.disney.go.com /dining as often as possible between 10 and 11 p.m.

***STILL* CAN'T GET AN ADVANCE RESERVATION?** Go to the restaurant on the day you wish to dine, and try for a table as a walk-in. Yes, we've already told you this is a long shot—that said, you *may* be able to swing it between 2:30 and 4:30 p.m., the hours when most full-service restaurants are most likely to take walk-ins, if they do at all. Your chances of success increase during less-busy times of year or on cold or rainy days during busier seasons. If you don't mind eating late, see if you can get a table during the restaurant's last hour of serving.

Disney full-service restaurants in the theme parks can be very hard-nosed about walk-ins: Even if you walk up and see that the

GOOD RESTAURANTS WITH LAST-MINUTE AVAILABILITY

IF YOU CAN'T GET A RESERVATION FOR	TRY ONE OF THESE RESTAURANTS INSTEAD
CINDERELLA'S ROYAL TABLE (Magic Kingdom) CHEF MICKEY'S (Contemporary) BE OUR GUEST (Magic Kingdom)	**Liberty Tree Tavern** (Magic Kingdom; no characters) serves comfort-food classics in an interesting early-American setting. If you suddenly have a hankering for turkey and stuffing in the middle of summer, this is the place to get it. **Grand Floridian Café** (Grand Floridian Resort; no characters) serves a limited menu of mostly comfort food. Its post-reopening take on fried chicken is outstanding.
VICTORIA & ALBERT'S (Grand Floridian)	Our first choice for an adults' night out would be **Jiko—The Cooking Place** (Animal Kingdom Lodge), which has excellent food and an extensive wine list. If Jiko isn't available, the Contemporary Resort's **California Grill** is highly rated but very loud at dinner.
VIA NAPOLI RISTORANTE E PIZZERIA (Italy/EPCOT)	In EPCOT, try **Teppan Edo** (Japan) or the **Rose & Crown Dining Room** (United Kingdom). Outside of EPCOT, try **Trattoria al Forno** (BoardWalk).
RAGLAN ROAD or CHEF ART SMITH'S HOMECOMIN' (both Disney Springs)	In Disney Springs, adults should try **Wine Bar George**. The family-friendly **Boathouse** (Disney Springs) has a relatively large capacity, plus good steaks and seafood.

restaurant isn't busy, you may still need to use Disney's app or visit Guest Services to make a reservation, as was this Fayetteville, Georgia, reader's experience:

> We went to the Hollywood & Vine check-in podium at DHS to try for walk-in seating because it was an off time—3:30 p.m.—and we could see that the restaurant was virtually empty. But we were turned away for lack of availability. So we walked to Guest Services, obtained a reservation there, walked back to the podium, and were immediately checked in.

Landing an Advance Reservation for Cinderella's Royal Table at dinner is somewhat easier than at lunch (or at breakfast, when offered), but the price is $62 for adults and $37 for children ages 3–9 during peak times of year (prices vary seasonally by as much as $15–$20). Throw in tax and gratuity, and you're looking at around $260 for one meal for a family of four. But if you're unable to lock up a table for breakfast or lunch, a dinner reservation will at least get your kids inside the castle.

ALSO TRY OPENTABLE Several Disney World restaurants take reservations through the popular online-booking service **OpenTable** (open table.com; mobile app available for iOS and Android). The participating restaurants (subject to change) are listed in the table on the next page. If you're having trouble getting a dining reservation through the usual Disney channels, this option may be worth checking out. *A big bonus:* If you book through OpenTable, some restaurants won't subject you to the same no-show fee you'd have to pay through Disney if you missed your reservation without canceling. We should add, however, that OpenTable monitors no-shows and will chastise you by email if you fail to appear. Your account will be suspended if you no-show for four reservations within a year. Besides being the polite thing to do, it's a snap to cancel or change reservations on the website or app.

WDW RESTAURANTS BOOKABLE AT opentable.com *(subject to change)*

BONNET CREEK

Bull & Bear Steakhouse Waldorf Astoria Orlando

DISNEY SPRINGS

- **The Boathouse** The Landing • **City Works** West Side • **The Edison** Town Center
- **Enzo's Hideaway, Maria & Enzo's Ristorante** The Landing
- **Frontera Cocina** Town Center • **House of Blues** West Side • **Jaleo** West Side
- **Morimoto Asia** The Landing • **Paddlefish** The Landing • **Paradiso 37** The Landing
- **Planet Hollywood** Town Center
- **Raglan Road Irish Pub & Restaurant** The Landing • **Splitsville Restaurant** West Side
- **STK Steakhouse** The Landing • **Terralina Crafted Italian** The Landing
- **Wine Bar George** The Landing • **Wolfgang Puck Bar & Grill** Town Center

DISNEY HOTELS

- **Flying Fish** BoardWalk • **Maya Grill** and **Toledo—Tapas, Steak & Seafood** Coronado Springs • **Jiko—The Cooking Place** Animal Kingdom Lodge-Jambo House

SWAN AND DOLPHIN

- **Big River Grille & Brewing Works** BoardWalk • **Garden Grove** Swan
- **Il Mulino New York** Swan • **Shula's Steak House** Dolphin
- **Todd English's bluezoo** Dolphin

FOUR SEASONS RESORT ORLANDO

Capa, Plancha, and Ravello

THEME PARK RESTAURANTS AND ADMISSION

MANY FIRST-TIME VISITORS to Walt Disney World are surprised when making their Advance Reservations to learn that admission to a theme park, as well as theme park reservations, are required to eat at restaurants inside of it. The lone exception is **Rainforest Cafe** at Animal Kingdom, which can be entered from the parking lot just outside of the theme park; you must have admission and a park reservation, however, if you want to enter Animal Kingdom after you eat.

If you're booking a meal for a day when you weren't expecting to visit the parks, you'll need to check the restaurant's location to make sure it isn't in a theme park. Also, if you've visited a theme park earlier in the day that's different from the one in which your restaurant is located, you'll need to have purchased the **Park Hopper** option (page 71) in order to dine inside the second theme park.

DRESS

DRESS IS INFORMAL at most theme park restaurants, but Disney has a business casual dress code for some of its resort restaurants: khakis, slacks, or dress shorts with a collared shirt for men, and capris, skirts, dresses, and dress shorts for women; jeans may be worn by men and women if in good condition. Restaurants with this dress code are **Jiko—The Cooking Place** at Animal Kingdom Lodge, **Flying Fish** (closed at press time) at the BoardWalk, **California Grill** at the Contemporary Resort, **Monsieur Paul** (closed at press time) at EPCOT's France Pavilion, **Takumi-Tei** (closed at press time) at EPCOT's Japan Pavilion, **Cítricos** and **Narcoossee's** at the Grand Floridian, **Yachtsman Steakhouse** at the Yacht Club Resort, **Todd English's bluezoo** and **Shula's Steak House** at the Dolphin Hotel, **Il Mulino** at the Swan Hotel, and **Topolino's Terrace** at the Riviera Resort. **Victoria & Albert's** (closed at press time) at the

Grand Floridian is the only Disney restaurant that requires men to wear a jacket to dinner (they'll provide one if needed).

FOOD ALLERGIES AND DIETARY NEEDS

unofficial **TIP**
Be aware that there is a charge for canceling a meal with kosher or other special requests, to cover the extra cost of ordering the individual meal components.

IF YOU HAVE SPECIAL DIETARY NEEDS, make them known when you make your Advance Reservations. For more information, see Part Eight, "Special Tips for Special People." A Phillipsburg, New Jersey, mom reports her family's experience:

My 6-year-old has many food allergies. When making my Advance Reservations, I indicated these to the clerk. When we arrived at the restaurants, the staff was already aware of my child's allergies and assigned our table a chef who double-checked the list of allergies with us. The chefs were very nice and made my son feel very special.

A Milford, Pennsylvania, family advises patience:

Disney is great with allergies, but expect LOTS of waiting for someone to call a chef, wait for a chef, and wait for your food. Sit-down restaurants were actually faster than quick-service, which is ridiculous as there was always a line of allergy diners. There should be a separate kiosk or at least a call button so diners can call a chef themselves.

unofficial **TIP**
Many sit-down restaurants inside the theme parks have switched to using the same menus and prices for both lunch and dinner, so check before you go.

Healthful Food at Walt Disney World

Health-conscious choices such as fresh fruit are available at most fast-food counters and from vendors. Vegetarians, people who have diabetes, those requiring kosher meals, and anyone trying to eat healthfully should have no trouble finding something that meets their needs.

SIT-DOWN-RESTAURANT TIPS AND TRICKS

BEFORE YOU BEGIN EATING your way through the World, you need to know a few things:

1. Theme park restaurants rush their customers to make room for the next group of diners. Dining at high speed may appeal to a family with young, restless children, but for people wanting to relax, it's more like eating in a pressure chamber than fine dining.

2. Disney restaurants have comparatively few tables for parties of two, and servers are generally disinclined to seat two guests at larger tables. If you're a duo, you might have to wait longer—sometimes much longer—to be seated.

3. At full-service Disney restaurants, an automatic gratuity of 18% is added to your tab for parties of six or more—even at buffets where you serve yourself.

SPEAKING OF RESTAURANT PRICES While the inflation-adjusted cost of a one-day theme park ticket has increased about 73% since 2010, the average lunch entrée price at Le Cellier has gone from around $22 to around $50—an increase of 124%. For reference, the average meal cost in a US restaurant went up 33% during the same time, according to the Federal Reserve.

This comment from a New Orleans mom spells it out:

Disney keeps pushing prices up and up. For us, the sky is NOT the limit. We won't be back.

Fortunately, you're not limited to dining in the World. See "Dining Outside Walt Disney World," page 361.

MOBILE ORDERING

DISNEY STRONGLY RECOMMENDS mobile ordering at almost all of its in-park counter-service restaurants. Using the My Disney Experience (MDE) app, you place an order, pay for your meal online, choose a time to pick up your food, and notify the restaurant when you've arrived for that pickup. The app will tell you when your food is ready. Show that notification to a cast member, and you'll be directed to a specific window or line to collect your food, so you're an appropriate distance away from other guests doing the same thing. Be sure to keep your app updated to see the latest participating restaurants.

It can take restaurants 30 minutes or more to prepare your order once it's placed, and it may take another 5–10 minutes to pick it up. Plan to place your food order 30–40 minutes before you want to eat.

If you're unable to access the MDE app or use mobile ordering, speak with a cast member outside the restaurant. They'll usually provide a paper menu and individual access to a cashier for payment.

A Portsmouth, Rhode Island, family found that the mobile app flaked on them:

We used mobile ordering once for Pinocchio Village Haus. [The app] said we would be notified when our order was ready, but we never got notice, and after waiting for 10–15 minutes we went in and found our food had been ready the entire time and was now cold.

Lesson learned: If your order seems to be running behind and you haven't received an alert, check with a cast member.

TIPS FOR SAVING TIME AND MONEY

Even if you confine your meals to counter-service fare, you lose a lot of time getting food in the parks—not to mention the costs can add up fast (see the table on page 296). Here are some ways to minimize the time you spend hunting and gathering:

1. Eat breakfast before you arrive, either at a restaurant outside the World or from a stocked fridge or cooler in your room. This will save you a ton of time.

2. After a good breakfast, buy vendor snacks in the parks, or bring your own.

3. All theme park restaurants are busiest between 11:30 a.m. and 2:15 p.m. for lunch and between 6 and 9 p.m. for dinner. Avoid trying to eat during these hours, especially 12:30–1:30 p.m.

4. Many counter-service restaurants sell cold sandwiches. Buy a cold lunch minus drinks before 11:30 a.m., and carry it in small plastic bags until you're ready to eat (within an hour or so of purchase). Ditto for dinner. Buy drinks at the appropriate time from any convenient vendor.

5. If you're short on time and the park is closing early, just stay until closing and eat dinner outside the World before returning to your hotel. If the park stays open late, eat dinner about 4 or 4:30 p.m. at the restaurant of your choice. You should sneak in just ahead of the dinner crowd.

This Missouri mom shares her variations on our tips:

*We arrived at WDW with our steel cooler well stocked with milk and sandwich fixings. I froze a block of ice in a milk bottle, and we replenished it daily with ice from the resort ice machine. [**Note:** Loose ice and dry ice are prohibited in coolers inside the theme parks and water parks.] We ate cereal, milk, and fruit each morning, with boxed juices.*

Each child had a belt bag of his own, which he filled from a special box of goodies each day with things like packages of crackers and cheese and packets of peanuts and raisins. Each child also had a small, rectangular plastic water bottle that could hang on the belt. We filled these at water fountains before getting into lines.

We left the park before noon; ate sandwiches, chips, and soda in the room; and napped. We purchased our evening meal in the park at a counter-service eatery. We budgeted for both morning and evening snacks from a vendor but often didn't need them.

A Whiteland, Indiana, mom adds a tip of her own:

If you're traveling with younger kids, take a supply of small paper or plastic cups to split drinks, which are both huge and expensive.

CHARACTER DINING

CHARACTER DINING IS LIMITED throughout Walt Disney World during the pandemic. At press time, 5 restaurants, down from around 15 before, offer a chance to see Disney characters while you eat, and seating capacity at those restaurants has been cut. Those remaining restaurants have changed their menus and prices, too, and there are no up-close character photos, hugs, or interactions. But there's still enough demand for these character experiences that reservations for popular dining times can be hard to come by if you wait until a couple of weeks before your vacation to book.

What's more, if you want to book a character meal, you must provide Disney with a credit card number. Your card will be charged $10 per person if you don't show or cancel your reservation less than 24 hours in advance; you may, however, reschedule with no penalty. See "Getting Advance Reservations at Popular Restaurants" (page 271) for the full story.

At very popular character meals, like breakfast or dinner at **Chef Mickey's,** you're required to make a for-real reservation and guarantee it with a for-real deposit.

WHAT TO EXPECT

CHARACTER MEALS ARE BUSTLING AFFAIRS held in the largest full-service restaurants at the theme parks and on-property resorts, along with the Swan at Walt Disney World, select hotels in the Disney Springs Resort Area and Bonnet Creek Resort, and the Four Seasons.

Character breakfasts typically offer a fixed menu served family-style (in large skillets or platters at your table) or à la carte. The typical breakfast includes scrambled eggs; bacon and sausage; potato casserole; waffles, pancakes, or French toast; biscuits, rolls, or pastries; and fruit.

Character dinners range from a set menu to dishes ordered off the menu. Dinners, such as those at 1900 Park Fare at the Grand Floridian (closed at press time) and Chef Mickey's at the Contemporary Resort, separate the kids' fare from the grown-ups', though everyone is free to eat from both menus. Typically, the kids' menu includes burgers, hot dogs, pizza, fish sticks, chicken nuggets, macaroni and cheese, and peanut-butter-and-jelly sandwiches. Selections from the adult menu usually include prime rib or another carved meat, baked or broiled seafood, pasta, chicken, an ethnic dish or two, vegetables, potatoes, and salad.

At all meals, characters circulate around the room at a safe distance (sometimes behind a barrier) while you eat. During your meal, each of the three to five characters present will pause, wave, and pose for socially distant selfies with your family. Characters move slowly, and it's unlikely that you'll miss the characters when they swing by.

WHEN TO GO

AT PRESS TIME, only one in-park restaurant (Tusker House at the Animal Kingdom) and two at Disney resorts (Chef Mickey's at the Contemporary and Topolino's at the Riviera) offered character breakfasts.

Attending a resort's character breakfast usually prevents you from arriving at the theme parks in time for opening. Because early morning is best for touring and you don't want to burn daylight lingering over breakfast, we suggest the following strategies:

1. Go to a character dinner or lunch instead of breakfast. It will be a nice break.

2. Schedule the first seating for lunch, typically 11:30 a.m. Have a light snack such as cereal or bagels before you head to the parks for opening, hit the most popular attractions until 11:15 or so, and then head for brunch. That should keep you fueled until dinnertime, especially if you eat another light snack in the afternoon.

3. Go on arrival or departure day. The day you arrive and check in is good for a character dinner—not only is it a good way to ease into your trip, it can also help your children get acquainted with how they'll encounter characters at a distance in the parks. Similarly, scheduling a character breakfast on checkout day, before you head for the airport or begin your drive home, is a nice way to cap off the trip.

4. Go on a rest day. If you plan to stay five or more days, you'll probably take a day or half-day off from touring to rest or do something else. These are perfect days for a character meal.

If you book an in-park character breakfast, schedule yours for the first seating if the park opens at 9 a.m. or later. You'll be admitted to the park before other guests (admission and park reservations are still required) through a special line at the turnstiles. Arrive early to be among the first parties seated.

HOW TO CHOOSE A CHARACTER MEAL

MANY READERS ASK FOR ADVICE about character meals. This question from a Waterloo, Iowa, mom is typical:

Are all character meals pretty much the same or are some better than others? How should I go about choosing one?

CHARACTER-MEAL HIT PARADE

1. CHEF MICKEY'S   CONTEMPORARY
- MEALS SERVED Breakfast, dinner • SETTING ★★★
- CHARACTERS Mickey, Minnie, Donald, Goofy, Pluto
- TYPE OF SERVICE Family-style • FOOD VARIETY & QUALITY ★★★½
- NOISE LEVEL Very loud • CHARACTER-GUEST RATIO 1:56

2. GARDEN GRILL RESTAURANT   EPCOT
- MEAL SERVED Lunch, dinner • SETTING ★★★★
- CHARACTERS Mickey, Pluto, Chip 'n' Dale • TYPE OF SERVICE Family-style
- FOOD VARIETY & QUALITY ★★★½ • NOISE LEVEL Very quiet
- CHARACTER-GUEST RATIO 1:46

3. HOLLYWOOD & VINE   DISNEY'S HOLLYWOOD STUDIOS
- MEALS SERVED Breakfast (seasonal lunch and dinner) • SETTING ★★½
- CHARACTERS *Breakfast:* Disney Junior characters
  Seasonal lunch and dinner: Minnie, Mickey, Goofy, Pluto, Donald (and sometimes Daisy)
- TYPE OF SERVICE Family-style • FOOD VARIETY & QUALITY ★★★
- NOISE LEVEL Moderate • CHARACTER-GUEST RATIO 1:71

4. TOPOLINO'S TERRACE   RIVIERA RESORT
- MEALS SERVED Breakfast • SETTING ★★★★
- CHARACTERS Mickey, Minnie, Donald, Daisy
- TYPE OF SERVICE Fixed menu • FOOD VARIETY & QUALITY ★★★★
- NOISE LEVEL Moderate • CHARACTER-GUEST RATIO 1:45

5. CINDERELLA'S ROYAL TABLE**   MAGIC KINGDOM
- MEALS SERVED Lunch, dinner • SETTING ★★★★
- CHARACTERS Cinderella, Ariel, Aurora, Belle, Jasmine, Snow White, Fairy Godmother
- TYPE OF SERVICE Fixed menu • FOOD VARIETY & QUALITY ★★★
- NOISE LEVEL Quiet • CHARACTER-GUEST RATIO 1:26

6. THE CRYSTAL PALACE**   MAGIC KINGDOM
- MEALS SERVED Lunch, dinner • SETTING ★★★
- CHARACTERS Pooh, Eeyore, Piglet, Tigger • TYPE OF SERVICE Buffet
- FOOD VARIETY & QUALITY Breakfast ★★½ Lunch and dinner ★★★
- NOISE LEVEL Very loud
- CHARACTER-GUEST RATIO Breakfast, 1:67; lunch and dinner, 1:89

7. AKERSHUS ROYAL BANQUET HALL*   EPCOT
- MEALS SERVED Breakfast, lunch, dinner • SETTING ★★★★
- CHARACTERS 4–6 Disney princesses chosen from among Ariel, Belle, Jasmine, Snow White, Aurora, Mulan, and Cinderella
- TYPE OF SERVICE Family-style and menu (all you care to eat)
- FOOD VARIETY & QUALITY ★★★½ • NOISE LEVEL Loud
- CHARACTER-GUEST RATIO 1:54

Characters are subject to change, so check before you go.

In fact, some *are* better, sometimes much better. When we evaluate character meals, we look for the following:

1. THE CHARACTERS The meals feature a diverse assortment of characters. See our Character-Meal Hit Parade table above to find out

CHARACTER-MEAL HIT PARADE (continued)

8. 1900 PARK FARE* GRAND FLORIDIAN

- **MEALS SERVED** Breakfast, dinner • **SETTING** ★★★
- **CHARACTERS** *Breakfast:* Mary Poppins, Alice, Mad Hatter, Pooh, Tigger *Dinner:* Cinderella, Prince Charming, Lady Tremaine, the two stepsisters
- **TYPE OF SERVICE** Buffet
- **FOOD VARIETY & QUALITY** Breakfast ★★★ Dinner ★★★½
- **NOISE LEVEL** Moderate • **CHARACTER–GUEST RATIO** Breakfast, 1:54; dinner, 1:44

9. TUSKER HOUSE RESTAURANT DISNEY'S ANIMAL KINGDOM

- **MEALS SERVED** Breakfast, lunch, dinner • **SETTING** ★★★
- **CHARACTERS** Donald, Daisy, Mickey, Goofy, Pluto • **TYPE OF SERVICE** Fixed menu
- **FOOD VARIETY & QUALITY** ★★★ • **NOISE LEVEL** Very loud
- **CHARACTER–GUEST RATIO** 1:112

10. CAPE MAY CAFE** DISNEY'S BEACH CLUB

- **MEAL SERVED** Breakfast **SETTING** ★★★ • **CHARACTERS** Goofy, Donald, Minnie, Daisy
- **TYPE OF SERVICE** Buffet • **FOOD VARIETY & QUALITY** ★★½
- **NOISE LEVEL** Moderate • **CHARACTER–GUEST RATIO** 1:67

11. 'OHANA** POLYNESIAN VILLAGE

- **MEAL SERVED** Breakfast **SETTING** ★★
- **CHARACTERS** Lilo and Stitch, Mickey, Pluto • **TYPE OF SERVICE** Family-style
- **FOOD VARIETY & QUALITY** ★★½ • **NOISE LEVEL** Loud
- **CHARACTER–GUEST RATIO** 1:57

12. ARTIST POINT* WILDERNESS LODGE

- **MEAL SERVED** Dinner • **SETTING** ★★★½
- **CHARACTERS** Snow White, Dopey, Grumpy, the Evil Queen
- **TYPE OF SERVICE** Fixed menu with several choices
- **FOOD VARIETY & QUALITY** ★★★★
- **NOISE LEVEL** Quiet • **CHARACTER–GUEST RATIO** 1:35

13. TRATTORIA AL FORNO** DISNEY'S BOARDWALK

- **MEAL SERVED** Breakfast • **SETTING** ★★★½
- **CHARACTERS** Rapunzel, Flynn Ryder, Ariel, Prince Eric
- **TYPE OF SERVICE** Fixed menu with several choices
- **FOOD VARIETY & QUALITY** ★★★½
- **NOISE LEVEL** Quiet • **CHARACTER–GUEST RATIO** 1:50

14. GARDEN GROVE** SWAN

- **MEALS SERVED** Breakfast (Sat. and Sun.) • **SETTING** ★★½
- **CHARACTERS** Chip 'n' Dale, Goofy, Pluto • **TYPE OF SERVICE** Buffet
- **FOOD VARIETY & QUALITY** ★★½ • **NOISE LEVEL** Moderate
- **CHARACTER–GUEST RATIO** 1:198, but frequently much better

* Closed at press time

** Open, but no characters at press time

which characters are assigned to each meal. Most restaurants stick with the same characters; even so, check the lineup when you call to make your Advance Reservations.

2. ATTENTION FROM THE CHARACTERS At all character meals, Disney characters circulate at a safe distance from diners. How much time a character spends in camera range of you and your children depends primarily on the ratio of characters to guests. The more characters and fewer guests, the better. Because many character-meal venues never fill to capacity, the character-to-guest ratios in our Character-Meal Hit Parade table have been adjusted to reflect an average attendance. Even so, there's quite a range. The best ratio of currently open restaurants is at Garden Grill and Topolino's Terrace, where there's about one character to every 46 guests.

The worst ratio is theoretically at the Swan resort's **Garden Grove,** where there could be as few as 1 character for every 198 guests. We say *theoretically,* however, because in practice there are far fewer guests at Garden Grove than at character meals in Disney-owned resorts, and often more characters. (During one meal, some friends of ours were literally the only guests in the restaurant for breakfast and had to ask the characters to leave them alone so they could eat.)

A Jerseyville, Illinois, mom gives the characters high marks:

Our 7-year-old daughter wanted to have dinner with Sleeping Beauty, so we scheduled a princess dinner in the Norway Pavilion [before the pandemic]. The princesses were so accessible and took their time with our child, answering questions and smiling for pictures. In fact, our daughter told us she had the best day of her life.

An Indiana mother of two relates the importance of keeping tabs on the characters:

For character meals, take note of which characters are there when you arrive, and mentally check them off as they visit your table. If the last one or two seem slow to arrive, seek out the "character manager" and let him or her know ASAP.

3. THE SETTING Some character meals have exotic settings; for others, moving the event to an elementary-school cafeteria would be an improvement. Our table rates each meal's setting with the familiar scale of zero (worst) to five (best) stars. The **Garden Grill Restaurant** in The Land at EPCOT deserves special mention. Garden Grill is a revolving restaurant overlooking several scenes from the Living with the Land boat ride. Also at EPCOT, the popular Princess Storybook Dining (closed at press time) is held in the castlelike **Akershus Royal Banquet Hall.** Though **Chef Mickey's** at the Contemporary Resort is rather sterile in appearance, it affords a great view of the monorail running through the hotel. Themes and settings of the remaining character-meal venues, while apparent to adults, will be lost on most children.

4. THE FOOD Although some food served at character meals is quite good, most is just average. In variety, consistency, and quality, restaurants generally do a better job with breakfast than with lunch or dinner. To help you sort everything out, we rate the food at each character meal in our table using a five-star scale.

Most restaurants currently offer family-style service, in which all hot items are served from the same pot or skillet. A Texas mom notes:

The family-style meals are much better for character dining—at a buffet, you're scared to leave your table in case you miss a character or other action.

5. NOISE If you want to eat in peace, character meals are a bad choice. That said, some are much noisier than others. Our table gives you an idea of what to expect.

6. WHICH MEAL? Although breakfasts seem to be most popular, character lunches and dinners are usually more practical because they don't interfere with early-morning touring. During hot weather, a character lunch can be heavenly.

7. COST Dinners and lunches cost more than breakfasts. Meal prices vary considerably from the least expensive to the most expensive restaurant; they can also vary by as much as $15–$20 depending on the season. Breakfasts run about $28–$48 for adults and $17–$28 for kids ages 3–9. For character lunches and dinners, expect to pay around $55 for adults and $36 for kids. Little ones age 2 years and younger eat free.

8. ADVANCE RESERVATIONS (See "Advance Reservations: The Official Line," page 271, for details.) Though Advance Reservations are generally tough to get for in-demand restaurants, reservations for most character meals are easy to obtain even if you call only a couple of weeks before your trip, as long as you're not particular about the time you eat. **Garden Grill** and **Topolini's Terrace** are another story—for these, you'll need our strategy (see page 273). If you don't get what you want at first, keep trying, advises a London mother of two:

> When a booking window opens, many people overbook and then either get buyer's remorse or find alternative bookings and cancel. When my booking window first opened, I was able to book barely 20% of what I wanted, but within two to three weeks I had 100%.

9. CHECKING IT TWICE Disney occasionally shuffles the characters and theme of a character meal. If your little one's heart is set on Pooh and Piglet, getting Hook and Mr. Smee instead will just brand you forever as lame. Reconfirm all character-meal Advance Reservations three weeks or so before you leave home by calling ☎ 407-WDW-DINE (939-3463).

10. "FRIENDS" Some character meals advertise a main character and a varying cast of "friends"—for example, "Pooh and friends," meaning Eeyore, Piglet, and Tigger, or some combination thereof, or "Mickey and friends" with some assortment chosen from among Minnie, Goofy, Pluto, Donald, Daisy, Chip, and Dale.

11. THE BUM'S RUSH Most character meals are leisurely affairs, and you can usually stay as long as you want. An exception is Cinderella's Royal Table at the Magic Kingdom, when it has characters. Because Cindy's is in such high demand, the restaurant does everything short of pre-chewing your food to move you through, as this European mother of a 5-year-old can attest:

> We dined a lot, did three character meals and a few Signature restaurants, and every meal was awesome except for lunch with Cinderella. It was a rushed affair. We had barely sat down when the appetizers were thrown on our table, the princesses each spent just a few seconds with our daughter—almost no interaction—and the side dishes were cold. We were out of there within 40 minutes and felt very stressed. Considering the price, I cannot recommend it.

DISNEY DINING SUGGESTIONS

FOLLOWING ARE OUR SUGGESTIONS for dining at each of the major theme parks. If you want to try a full-service restaurant at one of the parks, be aware that the restaurants continue to serve after the park's official closing time.

unofficial **TIP**
All Magic Kingdom sit-down restaurants serve beer and wine with dinner.

THE MAGIC KINGDOM

OF THE PARK'S OPEN full-time full-service restaurants, the best are **Liberty Tree Tavern** in Liberty Square and the **Jungle Navigation Co. Ltd. Skipper Canteen** in Adventureland. Liberty Tree Tavern serves standard American family-style meals for lunch and dinner, while Skipper Canteen serves heartier food in a Jungle Cruise–themed environment. Both are rated as above average by readers.

The big draw at the pricey **Cinderella's Royal Table** is the setting—the food is average. **The Plaza Restaurant** on Main Street serves passable meals at more moderate prices than the other sit-down restaurants. Cinderella's is rated as average by readers, while The Plaza is below average.

The most popular restaurant in all of Walt Disney World is **Be Our Guest,** in Fantasyland; unfortunately, the food quality has taken a big dip in recent years, even as the prices have increased. The service seems to have slipped as well—this woman from Hartland, Wisconsin, recalls that she was served attitude instead of food:

> *I was unable to get a reservation for Be Our Guest. When I mentioned this to the cast member out front, she offered no suggestions, told me I couldn't go in just to look around, and said the fact that I couldn't get a reservation is "what makes it so special." In that moment, I just wanted to slap her.*

Readers rate Be Our Guest as much below average, and we agree it's an especially poor value for the money. Likewise, quality at the Crystal Palace has dropped since reopening—readers rate it as below average. Avoid **Tony's Town Square** on Main Street and (if it's open) **The Diamond Horseshoe**—these are among the worst restaurants in Walt Disney World.

AUTHORS' FAVORITE COUNTER-SERVICE RESTAURANT

- **Columbia Harbour House** Liberty Square
- **Pecos Bill Tall Tale Inn and Cafe** Frontierland

Columbia Harbour House is the best counter-service restaurant in the Magic Kingdom. Its menu focuses on seafood, with a tasty lobster roll, grilled salmon, and grilled shrimp all worth ordering, plus solid options for kids, vegans, and vegetarians. **Pecos Bill's** offers fajitas, nachos, burgers, rice bowls, and salads, including vegetarian options. The kids' menu includes a cheeseburger, rice bowls with pork or chicken, and mac and cheese.

If these two places don't do it for you, be prepared to make some compromises at the Magic Kingdom's other counter-service restaurants, all of which struggle to achieve average levels of quality. Be Our Guest's lunch offerings are now the same as at dinner—heavy and expensive—and it's hard to get reservations. Avoid **Pinocchio Village Haus,** where the food is bad enough that you'll question whether it was worth anything dying—plant or animal—to make it.

EPCOT

SINCE THE BEGINNING, dining has been an integral component of EPCOT's entertainment product. World Showcase has many more restaurants than attractions, and EPCOT has added bars, tapas-style eateries, and full-service restaurants faster than any park in memory.

EPCOT runs food festival booths almost every day of the year. Its annual Food & Wine Festival runs mid-July through late November; EPCOT's International Festival of the Holidays begins a few days later. Festival of the Arts follows that and lasts through late February, and then it's time for Flower & Garden from March through July.

unofficial **TIP**
EPCOT has 21 full-service restaurants: 3 in Future World and 18 in World Showcase. With a couple of exceptions, these are among the best restaurants at Walt Disney World, in or out of the theme parks.

While it's not the same as sitting inside a well-themed World Showcase pavilion, food booths have their pluses: There's a lot of variety from which to choose, the food quality can be quite good, and it's generally faster than a full sit-down meal.

As we were going to press, two new restaurants were scheduled to open in EPCOT: a space-themed restaurant named **Space 220** in Future World, and **La Crêperie de Paris** in the France Pavilion of World Showcase, which will offer both table and quick service.

FULL-SERVICE RESTAURANTS IN EPCOT	
FUTURE WORLD	
Coral Reef Restaurant The Seas	Garden Grill Restaurant The Land
WORLD SHOWCASE	
Akershus Royal Banquet Hall* Norway	San Angel Inn Restaurante Mexico
Biergarten Restaurant Germany	Spice Road Table Morocco
Chefs de France France	Takumi-Tei* Japan
La Hacienda de San Angel Mexico	Teppan Edo Japan
Le Cellier Steakhouse Canada	Tokyo Dining* Japan
Monsieur Paul* France	Tutto Gusto Wine Cellar Italy
Nine Dragons Restaurant China	Tutto Italia Ristorante Italy
Restaurant Marrakesh* Morocco	Via Napoli Ristorante e Pizzeria Italy
Rose & Crown Dining Room United Kingdom	
Coming soon: **Space 220 in Future World** and **La Crêperie de Paris** in the France Pavilion	

* Closed at press time

For the most part, EPCOT's restaurants serve decent food, though the World Showcase restaurants tend toward the timid when it comes to delivering authentic representations of their host nations' cuisine. While it's true that the less adventuresome diner can find steak and potatoes on virtually every menu, the same kitchens will happily serve up the real thing for anyone willing to ask.

An afternoon without dinner at World Showcase is like not having a date on the day of the prom. Each pavilion except the United States has a beautifully seductive ethnic restaurant. To tour these exotic settings and not partake is almost beyond the limits of willpower. Still, some restaurants are better than others.

EPCOT restaurants that combine attractive ambience and well-prepared food with good value are **Teppan Edo** (Japan)—the highest-rated restaurant in Walt Disney World over the past year—**Via Napoli Ristorante e Pizzeria** (Italy), **Rose & Crown Dining Room** (United Kingdom), **Spice Road Table** (Morocco), and **Garden Grill Restaurant** (The Land). Those that *don't* provide good value for the money include **Akershus Royal Banquet Hall** (Norway; closed at press time), **Coral Reef Restaurant** (The Seas), **Nine Dragons Restaurant** (China), **San Angel Inn Restaurante** (Mexico), and **Monsieur Paul** (France; closed at press time). Of course, some readers take issue with our assessments, as is the case with this Wilmington, North Carolina, couple:

> *We disagree that Monsieur Paul is overpriced. A similar meal would fetch a similar price in any foodie town, such as New York or Miami; therefore, we'd call it "foodie priced." If you want overpriced food at Disney World, pay $12.50 for a turkey leg.*

A Germantown, Tennessee, woman who ate at Via Napoli found the leisurely service uncharacteristic—and not in a good way:

> *We waited 40 minutes for dessert, which we wouldn't have bothered to order had it not been included in our Candlelight Processional dining package. On one hand, this more closely resembled what we experienced on a trip to the actual country of Italy versus the typical in-and-out experience of WDW restaurants. On the other hand, I don't believe Via Napoli was particularly striving for authenticity—it was just bad service.*

AUTHORS' FAVORITE COUNTER-SERVICE RESTAURANTS

• **Les Halles Boulangerie-Pâtisserie** *France* • **Kringla Bakeri og Kafe** *Norway*
• **Tangierine Café** *Morocco*

Les Halles Boulangerie-Pâtisserie in France is one of the highest-rated counter-service restaurants in Walt Disney World. It sells pastries, sandwiches, and quiches. The bread and pastries are made on-site, and the sandwiches are as close to actual French street food—in taste, portion size, *and* price—as you'll get anywhere in EPCOT. Another favorite is the chicken or lamb shawarma platter at Morocco's **Tangierine Café.** Besides juicy lamb, it comes with some of the best tabbouleh we've tasted in Florida.

In addition to these, we recommend the United Kingdom's **Rose & Crown Pub** for Guinness, Harp, and Bass beers, and the **Yorkshire County Fish Shop** for fresh fish-and-chips.

EPCOT FOOD FESTIVALS EPCOT hosts four major festivals per year. No matter what season or theme the festival has, food and drinks are the main draw.

For each festival, EPCOT runs small semipermanent, themed booths around World Showcase and Future World. The booths serve appetizer-size portions that fit the stand's theme and almost always serve beer and wine to go with the theme too. For example, **The Citrus Blossom** food booth at the 2021 Food & Wine Festival served Meyer lemon–poached lobster and a crispy citrus pork belly with kumquats and carrots.

These festivals give EPCOT's chefs a chance to experiment with new ingredients and flavor combinations. The food quality is generally very good, and sometimes amazing: Chefs from the Canada Pavilion have produced an outstanding honey-mascarpone cheesecake made with local wildflower honey—one of the best desserts we've had anywhere in Walt Disney World. It was perfect, and small enough to eat on the way to our next pavilion.

Besides our high opinion, readers rate the food quality of the booths at the Flower & Garden and Food & Wine festivals as above average.

Drinking Around the World (Showcase)

A popular adult pastime at EPCOT is to make a complete circuit of World Showcase, sampling the alcoholic drinks native to each nation. Here's a list of the don't-miss places.

LA CAVA DEL TEQUILA, MEXICO (93%/Above Average) The best bar in Walt Disney World and one of the best tequila bars in the United States is La Cava del Tequila, inside the pyramid of the Mexico Pavilion in the World Showcase. Its ever-changing menu has more than 200 kinds of tequila and mezcal, several margaritas, and various light appetizers. On weekends and during special events such as the Food &Wine Festival, Cinco de Mayo, and National Tequila Day (July 24), expect a wait to get a drink.

Most days La Cava has a tequila expert on hand to explain the different types and provide tasting notes. (Ask for Hilda or Humberto, both from Tequila in Jalisco, Mexico—tell them Len sent you.) If you happen to be at EPCOT during the fall Food & Wine Festival, sign up for a tequila tasting if they're offered. Done in small groups with flights of tequila, it will teach you how to appreciate this magical amber liquid that Len likens to "a hug, but from the inside." He regrets that many of his favorite La Cava stories are unsuitable for print.

CHOZA DE MARGARITA, MEXICO (92%/Above Average) The menu is limited—just five on-the-rocks and four frozen options, three beers, two nonalcoholic options, and small plates for snacking—but each item is intensely flavorful and delicious, making this a great spot to visit when La Cava del Tequila is full. The rocks margaritas are what we gravitate toward.

SAKE BARS, JAPAN (92%/Above Average) There are two sake bars in Japan—one is an outdoor kiosk on the walking path toward the back of the pavilion. The other is a small counter tucked into the back of the first floor of the Mitsukoshi department store. Both have decent, affordable selections of sakes. The ones in the department store can be purchased from a shelf right next to the bar table. We're still amazed these haven't turned into a waterside bar.

WEINKELLER, GERMANY (88%/Average) Decorated with stone, dark woods, and heavy chandeliers, Weinkeller serves wines by the glass (around $7). If you love sweet white wines, this is the place to be. Selections usually include a couple of Rieslings, a liebfraumilch, dessert wines, and ice wines. The bar has no seating and wasn't serving food at press time, but the wine pours are generous.

LES VINS DES CHEFS DE FRANCE, FRANCE (93%/Above Average) Les Vins is a small retail space that offers a variety of French wines, including Chardonnay and Merlot, plus cocktails with Grey Goose vodka.

ROSE & CROWN PUB, UNITED KINGDOM (96%/Much Above Average) It's a little brighter than many British pubs we've seen, but Rose & Crown serves a wide variety of ales, lagers, stouts, and ciders alongside traditional English pub fare such as fish-and-chips and sausage rolls. If you're wanting something stronger, the pub has Scotch whiskies and not-quite-in-the-UK Irish whiskeys. Service is cheerful and fast.

DISNEY'S ANIMAL KINGDOM

ALONG WITH EPCOT, Disney's Animal Kingdom has the best dining options of any Disney theme park. The food isn't particularly exotic, and a lot of it is counter-service, but the quality is superior to that found in the Magic Kingdom and Disney's Hollywood Studios.

The park's *Avatar*-themed **Satu'li Canteen** (97%/Exceptional) is Disney's answer to Chipotle's rice bowls—you pick a base of starch, grain, or lettuce and then add a protein and garnishes. The nearby **Pongu Pongu Lounge** (95%/Exceptional) serves drinks inspired by the film. If you need a drink and a place to gather yourself before venturing into Flight of Passage's multihour wait in line, stop at the **Nomad Lounge** (97%/Exceptional), which is on the way to Pandora from Discovery Island. The drinks here are well balanced and full of flavor, and the lounge's decor is pretty.

A Lodi, California, dad praises Satu'li Canteen:

> *Our favorite place to eat was, by far, Satu'li Canteen. I would honestly make a special trip just to eat there. First, the food was crazy good. Yes, they basically make a bowl of food and that's all they serve, but everything was so delicious I could mix and match my ingredients to create something new every time. Second, they make everything from scratch there on-site. I don't think I can stress enough how important this was to us, especially considering that our son has special dietary needs.*

Our choices for sit-down restaurants in the park include **Yak & Yeti Restaurant** (95%/Much Above Average) in Asia, serving familiar Asian and Indian dishes, and **Tusker House Restaurant** (90%/Above Average) in Africa, whose choices are much more interesting than most others at Disney. **Tiffins** (89%/Average) has declined in value over the past couple of years and is too expensive to recommend. Also stay away from the **Rainforest Cafe** (74%/Do Not Visit), which is among the lowest-rated restaurants in Walt Disney World.

Besides Satu'li Canteen, our two other favorite counter-service dining options in the park are **Flame Tree Barbecue** (95%/Much Above Average), serving house-made 'cue at waterfront dining pavilions, and **Harambe Market** (95%/Much Above Average) in Africa, serving rice bowls with chicken or ribs, plant-based "sausages," and salads.

AUTHORS' FAVORITE COUNTER-SERVICE RESTAURANTS

• **Flame Tree Barbecue** Discovery Island • **Satu'li Canteen** Pandora

DISNEY'S HOLLYWOOD STUDIOS

THE STUDIOS HAS THE LOWEST-RATED restaurants of any Walt Disney World theme park. There are only four dining options rated above average in the Studios. Two of those are **Starbucks** and **BaseLine Tap House** (95%/Much Above Average), a brewpub with a very limited food selection. The *Star Wars*–themed **Docking Bay 7 Food and Cargo** (93%/ Above Average) is a counter-service place with tasty chicken and a vegetarian option, while the upscale **Hollywood Brown Derby** serves steaks, chicken, and fish. Beyond that, readers rate the experience of ingesting packaged foods, popcorn, and booze higher than anything found in an actual restaurant.

What we think our reader surveys are saying here is that there are few restaurants in the Studios that combine good food, good service, an entertaining atmosphere, *and* reasonable prices—almost every place has at least one major flaw. **50s Prime Time Café** (87%/Average) is a sit-down restaurant where you sit in Mom's time-warp kitchen and scarf down meat loaf while watching clips of classic sitcoms. Recent menus have improved the food quality at the **Sci-Fi Dine-In Theatre** (87%/ Average), where you eat in fun little cars at a simulated movie. You won't find a more entertaining restaurant in Walt Disney World. **Hollywood & Vine** (76%/Much Below Average) features singing and dancing characters such as Minnie Mouse and friends at lunch and dinner. For simple Italian food, including flatbread pizzas, **Mama Melrose's Ristorante Italiano** (88%/Average) is fine; just don't expect anything fancy.

AUTHORS' FAVORITE COUNTER-SERVICE RESTAURANT

• **Docking Bay 7** *Galaxy's Edge*

The **Star Wars: Galaxy's Edge** land has two counter-service restaurants and one bar, plus a popcorn stand and a milk stand, both unique. **Docking Bay 7** (93%/Above Average) is the larger of the two counter-service restaurants and has indoor seating. It's also the best dining option in the park. Docking Bay 7 serves "intergalactic" chicken and ribs, plus a vegetarian kefta that's virtually identical to its meat-based counterpart. The other counter-service restaurant is **Ronto Roasters** (96%/Above Average), whose menu includes roasted meat wraps, lovingly prepared for breakfast, lunch, and dinner over an open fire by a droid.

Oga's Cantina (88%/Average), reminiscent of the bar from *A New Hope,* serves exotic alcoholic and nonalcoholic cocktails. Oga's is the only Galaxy's Edge restaurant that offers reservations, but they're difficult to get. If you can't get a reservation, try walking up in the last hour the park is open.

The land's two outdoor stands are **Kat Saka's Kettle** (59%/Do Not Visit), which offers tasty multiflavored popcorn, and **Milk Stand** (84%/ Below Average), which serves the films' famous blue and green milk. Both "milks" are actually vegan, made from coconut and rice.

Our general advice when it comes to the Studios is to eat a good breakfast before you get to the park. For lunch and dinner, go with the cheapest acceptable snacks or counter-service options to avoid wasting your money. If you have time, consider a 20-minute walk to one of the EPCOT resort restaurants for a sit-down meal.

FULL-SERVICE DINING FOR
FAMILIES WITH YOUNG CHILDREN

DISNEY RESTAURANTS OFFER AN EXCELLENT (though expensive) opportunity to introduce young children to the variety and excitement of ethnic food. No matter how formal a restaurant appears, rest assured that the staff is accustomed to fidgety, impatient, and often boisterous children. **Chefs de France** at EPCOT may be the only French restaurant in the US where most patrons wear shorts and T-shirts and at least two dozen young diners are attired in basic black . . . mouse ears.

unofficial **TIP**
Look for the **Mickey Check** icon on healthy menu items such as fresh fruit and low-fat milk.

Almost all Disney restaurants offer kids' menus, and all have booster seats and high chairs. Servers understand how tough it is for children to sit still for an extended period, and they'll supply little ones with crackers and rolls and serve your dinner much faster than in comparable restaurants elsewhere. Reader letters suggest that being served too quickly is more common than waiting too long.

A Saratoga Springs, New York, dad says timing is key when dining with younger kids:

> As a family with three girls all under the age of 10, we quickly discovered that no restaurant is worth dragging the family to after 8 p.m. The Disney Dining Plan forced us to bring three overtired children to a sit-down restaurant after 8 p.m. We ended up with at least two children sleeping on the chairs after ordering chicken nuggets for the second time that day. I would rather eat at a quick-service restaurant if it gets my family in bed by 9 p.m.

Good Walt Disney World Theme Park
Restaurants for Children

In **EPCOT,** preschoolers most enjoy **Biergarten Restaurant** in Germany, **San Angel Inn** in Mexico, and **Coral Reef Restaurant** at The Seas with Nemo & Friends Pavilion in Future World.

Biergarten combines a rollicking and noisy atmosphere with tasty, mostly familiar foods, including rotisserie chicken. A German oompah band entertains crowds at both lunch and dinner.

San Angel Inn is in the Mexico village marketplace. From the table, children can watch boats on the Gran Fiesta Tour drift beneath a smoking volcano. With a choice of quesadillas, tacos, and other familiar items, picky kids usually have no difficulty finding something to eat. (Be aware, though, that the service here is sometimes glacially slow.)

Coral Reef, with tables beside windows looking into The Seas' aquarium, offers a satisfying mealtime diversion for all ages. For those who don't eat fish, it also serves beef, chicken, and vegetarian options.

Biergarten offers reasonable value, plus good food. San Angel Inn is overpriced, though the food is pretty good. Coral Reef is overpriced and serves unmemorable food.

Be Our Guest and **Cinderella's Royal Table,** both in Fantasyland, are hot tickets in the **Magic Kingdom,** and reservations at both restaurants are often unobtainable. (At present, the only character at Be

Our Guest is the Beast.) Be Our Guest's quality has suffered lately, however, and it's no longer a good value. We think the best kids' fare is served at the **Liberty Tree Tavern** in Liberty Square.

At **Disney's Hollywood Studios,** all ages enjoy the atmosphere and entertainment at **Hollywood & Vine, Sci-Fi Dine-In Theater Restaurant,** and **50's Prime Time Cafe.**

The best full-service restaurant for kids at **Disney's Animal Kingdom** is **Yak & Yeti Restaurant.**

NOISE AT RESTAURANTS

RESTAURANTS ARE NOISY in and out of the World. A Palmyra, Pennsylvania, reader using the Disney Dining Plan shared this:

> We ate four times at Signature restaurants. The food was always good, and the check, with wine and tip, was always at least $150. However, the noise, especially at Le Cellier and Il Mulino, was overwhelming. WDW seems to have really skimped on the acoustics, even at Cítricos and the California Grill.

QUIET, ROMANTIC PLACES TO EAT

RESTAURANTS WITH GOOD FOOD and a couple-friendly ambience are rare in the theme parks. Only a handful of dining locales satisfy both requirements: an alfresco table at **Tutto Italia Ristorante,** the terraces at **Rose & Crown Dining Room** and **Teppan Edo,** and **Tokyo Dining,** all at EPCOT, and **The Hollywood Brown Derby** at Disney's Hollywood Studios. Waterfront dining is available at **Narcoossee's** at the Grand Floridian.

> *unofficial* **TIP**
> The **California Grill** at the Contemporary Resort and **Topolino's Terrace** at the Riviera have the best views at Walt Disney World.

Victoria & Albert's (closed at press time) at the Grand Floridian is the World's showcase gourmet restaurant; expect to pay big bucks. Other good choices for couples include **Jiko—The Cooking Place** and **Sanaa** at Animal Kingdom Lodge, and **Cítricos** at the Grand Floridian.

Eating later in the evening and choosing a restaurant we've mentioned will improve your chances for intimate dining; nevertheless, children—well behaved or otherwise—are everywhere at Walt Disney World, and there's no way to escape them. These honeymooners from Slidell, Louisiana, write:

> We made dinner reservations at some of the nicer Disney restaurants. We made sure to reserve past dinner hours, and we tried to stress that we were on our honeymoon. But in every restaurant we went to, we were seated next to large families. It's very difficult to enjoy a romantic dinner when there are small children crawling around under your table. Our suggestion: Seat couples without children together and families with kids elsewhere.

Meanwhile, a Canadian mom acknowledges that the upscale California Grill may not have been the best place to bring her little ones:

> We ate dinner on our last night at the California Grill. It was wonderful, but it's not a great place to take your kids. We were there from 7 to 10 p.m., and it was just too much for them.

WALT DISNEY WORLD DINNER THEATERS

WALT DISNEY WORLD RAN TWO dinner-theater shows before the pandemic: the Western-themed *Hoop-Dee-Doo Musical Revue* and the Hawaiian-themed *Spirit of Aloha Dinner Show.* Both have been suspended indefinitely, and the entertainers were laid off. *Hoop-Dee-Doo* was popular, and we expect it to return eventually.

MORE READER COMMENTS ABOUT WALT DISNEY WORLD DINING

EATING IS A POPULAR TOPIC among *Unofficial Guide* readers. In addition to participating in our annual restaurant survey, many readers share their thoughts. The following comments are representative.

Here's a 13-year-old girl from Omaha, Nebraska, who doesn't get bent out of shape over one bad meal:

> *Honestly, when was the last time you came home from Disney World and said, "Gosh, my vacation really sucked because I ate at a bad restaurant?"*

From a reader in the United Kingdom:

> *We had the most fantastic meal at California Grill. Being central London–living foodie-types, we're very hard to please, but the meal there really was second to none.*

Sanaa, in the Kidani Village section of Animal Kingdom Lodge, really impressed an Ellicott City, Maryland, family:

> *Sanaa is a beautiful restaurant with delicious and inexpensive (for Disney) food that you can't find anywhere else in Walt Disney World. We had a fabulous adults-only evening here, but I would bring children too, for an early dinner overlooking the savanna.*

Speaking of expensive food, this Superior, Wisconsin, reader noticed a pricing trend:

> *All the food is similarly priced. For example, all the main dishes in the nicer restaurants are between $35 and $55 for the most part. There are some outliers, but I was trying to find a nice, reasonably priced restaurant, and I couldn't. This is also true for the counter-service places: The prices are all similar, so finding a good deal is difficult. I get that they have you stuck there and can force you to buy the food—but still.*

A Columbus, Ohio, mom loved the character meal at Chef Mickey's:

> *Our favorite character dinner was Chef Mickey's. The kids were comfortable there, and the characters really spent time with our family getting pictures, being silly, and having fun. It was a great experience for the whole family. Was the food above and beyond? Nah. But the look on my 4-year-old's face when she saw Mickey was amazing.*

The following reader tried several character meals:

> **The Crystal Palace (no characters at press time; Magic Kingdom)** *A HUGE hit with my kids! We met Eeyore, Pooh, Tigger, and Piglet. The food was great too—lots of choices, and all done very well.*

Chef Mickey's (Contemporary Resort) *By far the best dining experience we had. And with it being Chef Mickey's, we of course got to meet Mickey, Minnie, Pluto, Goofy, and Donald. A must-do!*

Hollywood & Vine (Hollywood Studios) *We didn't care for this one at all—if it hadn't been for meeting the* Disney Junior *characters, we probably wouldn't have picked it. The food was subpar, but the worst was the seating and organization of the characters: Most of the tables were booths, which made it very hard for children to get in and out. There was no rhyme or reason to which way the characters were going, and the handlers were nowhere to be found.*

One mom in Columbia, South Carolina, was unimpressed with the character dinners:

Walt Disney World is becoming grossly overpriced. Major piece of advice: Unless your kids love character dining, skip ALL the sit-down restaurants.

And finally, Raglan Road at Disney Springs was a big hit with another mom of two, this one from Los Angeles:

Cannot say enough about this amazing Irish pub. The ambience, the food, and the entertainment were all absolutely top-notch.

COUNTER-SERVICE
Mini-Profiles

TO HELP YOU FIND TASTY FAST FOOD, we provide thumbnail profiles of the theme park counter-service restaurants, listed alphabetically by park. They're rated for quality, portion size, and value. All restaurants participate in the Disney Dining Plan (temporarily suspended) except where noted.

Mobile ordering (see page 279) through the My Disney Experience app is strongly recommended at all Disney counter-service restaurants.

Value ratings range from A to F, as follows:

A	Exceptional value; a real bargain
B	Good value
C	Fair value; you get exactly what you pay for
D	Somewhat overpriced
F	Extremely overpriced

See page 266 for a rundown of how the reader-survey percentages break down.

THE MAGIC KINGDOM

Aloha Isle

QUALITY Excellent **VALUE** B+ **PORTION** Medium **LOCATION** Adventureland
READER-SURVEY RESPONSES ➕ 98% (Exceptional)

Selections Soft-serve, ice-cream floats, pineapple juice.
Comments Located next to *Walt Disney's Enchanted Tiki Room.* The pineapple Dole Whip soft-serve is a world-famous Disney theme park treat.

THE COST OF COUNTER-SERVICE FOOD

BAGEL OR MUFFIN	$2.25–$2.95
BROWNIE	$4.30–$9
BURRITO BOWL	$11.75
CAKE OR PIE	$4.80–$6
CEREAL WITH MILK	$5
CHEESEBURGER WITH FRIES	$12–$17
CHICKEN BREAST SANDWICH	$12.50–$16
CHICKEN NUGGETS WITH FRIES	$10–$11
CHILDREN'S MEAL (various)	$6.20–$7.20
CHIPS	$3–$3.50
COOKIE	$2.30–$8
FRIED-FISH BASKET WITH FRIES	$11.50–$12.95
FRIES	$4.50–$6.50
FRUIT (whole)	$2.30–$4.20
FRUIT CUP/FRUIT SALAD	$4–$5.70
HOT DOG	$9–$13.50
ICE CREAM/FROZEN NOVELTIES	$5–$12.95
NACHOS WITH CHEESE	$5–$11.50
PB&J SANDWICH	$6.50 (kids' meal)–$10.50
PIZZA (personal)	$10.50–$12
POPCORN	$3–$7
PRETZEL	$5.80–$6.80
SALAD (entrée)	$10–$12
SALAD (side)	$3–$10
SMOKED TURKEY LEG	$12.50–$14.50
SOUP/CHILI	$4–$4.20
SUB/DELI SANDWICH	$7–$12.50
TACO SALAD	$10–$11
VEGGIE BURGER	$11.50–$13.50

THE COST OF COUNTER-SERVICE DRINKS

DRINK	SMALL	LARGE
BEER	$6.75	$13
BOTTLED WATER	$3.50	$5.50
COFFEE	$2.45	$5.75
LATTE	$4.25	$5.75
FLOAT, MILKSHAKE, OR SUNDAE	$4.50	$5.50
FRUIT JUICE	$4	$5
HOT TEA AND COCOA	$3.30	$5.25
MILK	$2	$3.60
SOFT DRINKS, ICED TEA, AND LEMONADE	$4	$5

Each person on a Disney Dining Plan gets a free mug, refillable at any Disney resort. If you're not on a dining plan, a refillable souvenir mug costs $20 including tax (free refills) at Disney resorts and around $12 at the water parks.

Be Our Guest Restaurant *(breakfast not currently available; Advance Reservations recommended when it is)*

QUALITY Excellent   **VALUE** C   **PORTION** Medium   **LOCATION** Fantasyland
READER-SURVEY RESPONSES ● 81% (Do Not Visit)

Selections *Breakfast:* Open-faced bacon-and-poached-egg sandwich with Brie, steel-cut oatmeal, cured meats and cheeses, scrambled egg whites with roasted tomatoes, signature croissant doughnuts.

Comments Declining food quality, high prices, and difficult-to-get reservations have taken their toll on Be Our Guest, whose reader ratings have dropped steeply in the past three years.

    Note: Though breakfast (8–10:30 a.m.) is technically counter-service (and not offered at press time), Be Our Guest is so popular that it's the only Disney restaurant that offers Advance Reservations for quick-service meals. If you have reservations, you can also preorder what you want to eat up to 30 days ahead. (See page 315 for our full-service profile.)

Casey's Corner

QUALITY Good   **VALUE** C   **PORTION** Medium   **LOCATION** Main Street, U.S.A.
READER-SURVEY RESPONSES ● 88% (Average)

Selections Hot dogs, corn dog nuggets, plant-based hot dogs, fries, brownies.

Comments Casey's corn dog nuggets are addictive, but Liberty Square Market (see the next page) has better hot dogs (when available).

Columbia Harbour House

QUALITY Good   **VALUE** B+   **PORTION** Medium   **LOCATION** Liberty Square
READER-SURVEY RESPONSES ● 92% (Much Above Average)

Selections Eat light with the grilled salmon with rice, indulge with fried shrimp and battered fish, or split the difference with the lobster roll. Other choices: fried chicken, grilled shrimp, New England clam chowder, salads, hush puppies, and seasonal cobbler or strawberry yogurt for dessert. For kids: shrimp skewer or grilled salmon.

Comments Columbia Harbour House is the highest-rated counter-service restaurant in the Magic Kingdom. The upstairs seating is far quieter than the seating downstairs.

Cosmic Ray's Starlight Cafe

QUALITY Fair-poor   **VALUE** C-   **PORTION** Large   **LOCATION** Tomorrowland
READER-SURVEY RESPONSES ● 82% (Much Below Average)

Selections Burgers, hot dogs, Greek salad, chicken sandwich, chicken strips, chili-cheese dog, Angus bacon cheeseburger, plant-based burger, chocolate Bundt cake for dessert. Kosher choices available on request.

Comments The same menu items appear at all three ordering stations. Cosmic Ray's is a crowded, high-volume restaurant where food quality and ambience are sacrificed in the name of just getting something to eat. The burgers' secret ingredient is indifference.

The Diamond Horseshoe *(seasonal)*

QUALITY Fair-poor   **VALUE** D   **PORTION** Medium–Large   **LOCATION** Frontierland
READER-SURVEY RESPONSES ● 56% (Do Not Visit)

Selections Sandwiches (pulled pork, brisket, grilled chicken); Cowboy Mac (mac and cheese with beef brisket and jalapeño-cheddar cornbread); Chuck Wagon Platters and family-style Saloon Feasts with pulled pork, brisket, or grilled chicken; apple cake, banana pudding, and cherry cheesecake for dessert; wine and beer.

Comments The Diamond Horseshoe is technically a table-service restaurant. We've stuck it here because it's open only sporadically, the hours are odd (1–7 p.m. the last time it was open), and, well, it's not very good. You'll be happier almost anywhere else that serves food.

The Friar's Nook

QUALITY Good	VALUE B	PORTION Medium–Large	LOCATION Fantasyland
READER-SURVEY RESPONSES ◔ 87% (Average)			

Selections Hot dogs; bacon-mac-and-cheese, sausage-and-gravy, or Buffalo chicken tots; creamy bacon mac and cheese.
Comments A good place for a snack.

Gaston's Tavern

QUALITY Good	VALUE C	PORTION Medium	LOCATION Fantasyland
READER-SURVEY RESPONSES ◔ 92% (Above Average)		NOT ON DISNEY DINING PLAN	

Selections Cinnamon rolls, cupcakes, LeFou's Brew (frozen apple juice with toasted-marshmallow flavoring).
Comments Very popular throughout the day. The cinnamon rolls are roughly the size of a barge. Ask for extra icing with yours.

Golden Oak Outpost
(seasonal)

QUALITY Good	VALUE B+	PORTION Medium	LOCATION Frontierland
READER-SURVEY RESPONSES ◔ 91% (Above Average)			

Selections Chicken strips, chili-cheese fries, chocolate chip cookies, bottled water and soft drinks.
Comments Bare-bones basic eats. The lemon-and-sweet-tea slushie will bring a smile to any Southerner's face.

Liberty Square Market

QUALITY Good	VALUE C	PORTION Medium	LOCATION Liberty Square
READER-SURVEY RESPONSES ◔ 91% (Above Average)		NOT ON DISNEY DINING PLAN	

Selections Mostly fresh fruit and packaged drinks and snacks. The pre-pandemic menu included fresh grilled hot dogs, which we hope come back soon.
Comments The setup looks like a couple of interns went to The Home Depot and lugged back the biggest barbecue grills they could find, but when the hot dogs are offered, these are the best in Walt Disney World. There's seating nearby, but none of it is covered.

The Lunching Pad

QUALITY Fair	VALUE C	PORTION Medium	LOCATION Tomorrowland
READER-SURVEY RESPONSES ◔ 83% (Below Average)			

Selections Bacon, egg, and cheese sandwich for breakfast; cheese-stuffed pretzel, frozen sodas, all-beef hot dogs, barbecue pork sandwich.
Comments The breakfast sandwiches are tasty, while the frozen carbonated drinks—cola or blue raspberry—are a treat in summer's heat.

Main Street Bakery
(Starbucks)

QUALITY Good	VALUE B	PORTION Medium	LOCATION Main Street, U.S.A.
READER-SURVEY RESPONSES ◔ 92% (Above Average)			

Selections Coffees, pastries, breakfast sandwiches.
Comments Extremely popular throughout the day, but the lines move fast.

Pecos Bill Tall Tale Inn and Cafe

QUALITY Good	VALUE C	PORTION Medium–Large	LOCATION Frontierland
READER-SURVEY RESPONSES ✪ 86% (Average)			

Selections Pork carnitas and chicken fajita platter with rice and beans; beef nachos; rice bowl with veggies; salad with or without chicken; churros, powdered cinnamon-sugar doughnut holes, and yogurt for dessert.

Comments Pecos Bill has taken a page from the menu at Chipotle. The Mexican fare is an improvement over the old burgers, but it's more expensive than and not quite as good as Chipotle's. The menu gets mixed reactions, like this one from a Mount Holly, New Jersey, reader:

We were less than impressed with the menu, though it was fine for staving off a "hanger" tantrum.

Perhaps in response, a basic cheeseburger was put back on the menu. If you're ordering the tacos or fajitas, ask for extra toppings.

Pinocchio Village Haus

QUALITY Fair-poor	VALUE D	PORTION Medium	LOCATION Fantasyland
READER-SURVEY RESPONSES ✪ 76% (Do Not Visit)			

Selections Flatbread pizzas; chicken strips; fries; Caesar salad; kids' meal of pizza, chicken strips, or PB&J.

Comments Your only reason to eat here instead of at Pecos Bill (see above) or Cosmic Ray's (page 297) would be if you had an inexplicable hankering for a bland flatbread pizza.

Tomorrowland Terrace Restaurant

(seasonal)

QUALITY Fair	VALUE C-	PORTION Medium–Large	LOCATION Tomorrowland
READER-SURVEY RESPONSES ✪ 87% (Average)			

Selections Varies.

Comments Ratings have improved over the past year, probably because the Terrace was serving the menu from Columbia Harbour House.

Tortuga Tavern

(seasonal)

QUALITY Fair	VALUE B	PORTION Medium–Large	LOCATION Adventureland
READER-SURVEY RESPONSES ✪ 68% (Do Not Visit)			

Selections Turkey legs, hot dogs, brisket sandwiches; rum cake for dessert.

Comments The eating area is large and shaded. Disney changes up the menu here from time to time. It's been Mexican and barbecue before.

EPCOT

L'Artisan des Glaces

QUALITY Excellent	VALUE C	PORTION Large	LOCATION France
READER-SURVEY RESPONSES ✪ 96% (Exceptional)	NOT ON DISNEY DINING PLAN		

Selections Ice-cream flavors change but can include vanilla, chocolate, coffee, coconut–white chocolate, mint chocolate, candied peanut with chocolate-peanut butter fudge, and cinnamon with caramelized pecans or apples. The dairy-free sorbet flavors may include mango, strawberry, and piña colada. Over-21s can enjoy two scoops in a martini glass, topped with Grand Marnier, rum, or whipped cream–flavored vodka.

Comments L'Artisan des Glaces serves the best ice cream at Disney World. The coconut in our coconut–white chocolate was freshly shaved. The macaron ice-cream sandwich is a gift from heaven.

La Cantina de San Angel

QUALITY Good **VALUE** B **PORTION** Medium–Large **LOCATION** Mexico
READER-SURVEY RESPONSES ✪ 88% (Average)

Selections Tacos with seasoned beef, chicken, or fried fish; fried cheese empanada; grilled chicken with Mexican rice, corn, cascabel sauce, and pickled onions; guacamole and chips; churros; margaritas. For kids, chicken tacos, empanadas, chicken tenders, or mac and cheese.

Comments A popular spot for a quick meal, with 150 covered outdoor seats. When it's extra busy, the back of La Hacienda de San Angel's dining room is opened for air-conditioned seating.

Fife & Drum Tavern

QUALITY Fair **VALUE** C **PORTION** Large **LOCATION** United States
READER-SURVEY RESPONSES ✪ 84% (Below Average)

Selections Turkey legs, hot dogs, popcorn, soft-serve ice cream, slushies, beer, alcoholic lemonade and root beer floats.

Comments Seating is available in and around the Regal Eagle Smokehouse, behind the Fife & Drum.

Les Halles Boulangerie–Pâtisserie

QUALITY Good **VALUE** A **PORTION** Small–Medium **LOCATION** France
READER-SURVEY RESPONSES ✪ 97% (Exceptional)

Selections The beautiful deli–bakery case is stocked with goodies such as sandwiches (ham and cheese; Brie, cranberry, and apple), imported-cheese plates, quiches, soups, and delicate pastries.

Comments Les Halles is the highest-rated counter-service restaurant in EPCOT and one of the best in the World. Breads and pastries are made on-site. For an authentic Parisian experience, grab a half-baguette (ask for extra butter) and eat it while you walk around France. Usually crowded all day.

Katsura Grill

QUALITY Good **VALUE** B **PORTION** Small–Medium **LOCATION** Japan
READER-SURVEY RESPONSES ✪ 83% (Average)

Selections Basic sushi; udon noodle bowls (vegetarian or shrimp tempura); pork ramen; chicken, beef, or shrimp teriyaki; chicken curry; edamame; miso soup; green tea cheesecake; teriyaki kids' plate; Kirin beer, sake, and plum wine.

Comments Possibly the loveliest spot to escape the EPCOT crowd and eat a quick meal outside.

Kringla Bakeri og Kafe

QUALITY Good–Excellent **VALUE** B **PORTION** Small–Medium **LOCATION** Norway
READER-SURVEY RESPONSES ✪ 93% (Above Average)

Selections Norwegian pastries and desserts, iced coffee, and imported beers and wines.

Comments Limited menu and hours. The School Bread (a sweet roll filled with custard and dipped in coconut) is popular. Shaded outdoor seating.

Lotus Blossom Café

QUALITY Fair **VALUE** C **PORTION** Medium **LOCATION** China
READER-SURVEY RESPONSES ✪ 76% (Do Not Visit)

Selections Pork and vegetable egg rolls, pot stickers, orange chicken, chicken fried rice, Mongolian beef with rice, caramel-ginger or lychee ice cream, plum wine, Tsingtao beer.

Comments The menu rarely changes, and the food remains a snooze.

Refreshment Outpost

QUALITY Good	VALUE B–	PORTION Small	LOCATION Between Germany and China
READER-SURVEY RESPONSES ✪ 87% (Average)			

Selections All-beef hot dogs, slushies, sodas, draft Safari Amber and other beers.

Comments The hot dogs here aren't bad at all, but there are plenty of better dining options within a few minutes' walk.

Refreshment Port

QUALITY Good	VALUE B–	PORTION Medium	LOCATION Near Canada
READER-SURVEY RESPONSES ✪ 92% (Average)			

Selections Poutine, chicken nuggets, unusual alcoholic drinks and beer.

Comments From croissant doughnuts to pork-belly Bloody Marys, you never know what you'll find here—but chances are that it will be good.

Regal Eagle Smokehouse: Craft Drafts & Barbecue

QUALITY Good	VALUE B	PORTION Large	LOCATION United States
READER-SURVEY RESPONSES ✪ 91% (Above Average)			

Selections Regional barbecue meat specialties, including Memphis smoked ribs, Kansas City chicken, North Carolina chopped pork, and Texas brisket, plus burgers, salads, and vegetarian options. Usually serves at least four different beers from around the country, plus hard ciders, wines, and specialty cocktails.

Comments A huge improvement over what was here before, Regal Eagle serves passable barbecue in hearty portions, with the Texas brisket (on garlic toast) being our favorite. If you're craving more, The Polite Pig at Disney Springs sets the standard in Walt Disney World.

Rose & Crown Pub

QUALITY Good	VALUE C+	PORTION Medium	LOCATION United Kingdom
READER-SURVEY RESPONSES ✪ 96% (Much Above Average)		NOT ON DISNEY DINING PLAN	

Selections Fish-and-chips; sausage roll and chips; Guinness, Harp, and Bass beers, as well as other spirits.

Comments Authentic British pub with ales, lagers, and stouts.

Sommerfest

QUALITY Fair	VALUE C	PORTION Medium	LOCATION Germany
READER-SURVEY RESPONSES ✪ 86% (Average)			

Selections Bratwurst, jumbo pretzel, cold beer.

Comments Tables are set up in the courtyard. Much of the food looks better than it tastes.

Sunshine Seasons

QUALITY Excellent	VALUE A	PORTION Medium	LOCATION The Land
READER-SURVEY RESPONSES ✪ 85% (Average)			

Selections Sunshine Seasons, a food court–like counter-service venue, consists of the following three areas: (1) wood-fired grills and rotisseries, with rotisserie chicken and wood-grilled fish with seasonal vegetables; (2) sandwiches, such as an amazing pulled pork and Cheddar on Texas toast, and a cheese flatbread option; and (3) the soup-and-salad shop, with soups made daily and unusual creations such as the Power Salad (quinoa, almonds, and chicken).

Comments The best spot in Future World for a quick meal, with enough variety for everyone in the family. Currently open for lunch and dinner.

Tangierine Café

QUALITY Good   **VALUE** B   **PORTION** Medium   **LOCATION** Morocco
READER-SURVEY RESPONSES ⊕ 88% (Average)

Selections Chicken and lamb shawarma; hummus; tabbouleh; lentil salad; couscous salad; vegetarian platter with hummus, tabbouleh, lentils, falafel, marinated olives, and pita bread; child's burger or chicken tenders; Moroccan wine and beer.

Comments Tangierine Café reopened just as we were going to press, and it's under new (Disney) management. This was one of the best quick-service places to eat in Walt Disney World before the pandemic and before the management change.

Traveler's Café *(Starbucks)*

QUALITY Good   **VALUE** B   **PORTION** Small   **LOCATION** West side of the border of World Showcase and Future World   **READER-SURVEY RESPONSES** ⊕ 85% (Average)

Selections Coffee drinks and teas; breakfast sandwiches and pastries.
Comments Relocated from Future World. The service is fast and efficient.

Yorkshire County Fish Shop

QUALITY Good   **VALUE** B+   **PORTION** Medium   **LOCATION** United Kingdom
READER-SURVEY RESPONSES ⊕ 97% (Exceptional)

Selections Fish-and-chips, Bass Pale Ale draft, and Harp Lager.
Comments There's usually a line for the crisp, hot fish-and-chips at this convenient fast-food window attached to the Rose & Crown Dining Room (see full-service profile on page 301). A tasty chicken-and-mushroom pie might be served during cooler months. Outdoor seating overlooks the lagoon.

DISNEY'S ANIMAL KINGDOM

Creature Comforts

(Starbucks)

QUALITY Good   **VALUE** C   **PORTION** Small   **LOCATION** Discovery Island near Africa
READER-SURVEY RESPONSES ⊕ 96% (Exceptional)

Selections Coffee drinks and teas; sandwiches and pastries.
Comments The fare is largely the same as you'd find at any other Starbucks, plus the occasional Animal Kingdom–themed treat.

Flame Tree Barbecue

QUALITY Excellent   **VALUE** B–   **PORTION** Large   **LOCATION** Discovery Island
READER-SURVEY RESPONSES ⊕ 95% (Exceptional)

Selections St. Louis–style ribs; smoked half-chicken; ribs and chicken sampler; pulled-pork sandwich; smokehouse chicken salad; mac and cheese with smoked pulled pork; plant-based sausage sandwich; child's plate of baked chicken drumstick, hot dog, or PB&J sandwich; fries and onion rings; Safari Amber beer, Bud Light, Mandarin orange vodka lemonade, and wine.

Comments Expanded outdoor seating provides more shaded space overlooking the water. One of our favorites for lunch.

Harambe Market

QUALITY Good   **VALUE** B   **PORTION** Large   **LOCATION** Africa
READER-SURVEY RESPONSES ⊕ 95% (Much Above Average)

Selections Grilled chicken or ribs served over rice and salad greens, salads, plant-based "sausage." Kids' selections include PB&J, chicken nuggets, and chicken and rice bowl.

Comments Plenty of shaded seating. Disney Imagineers modeled Harambe's marketplace setting after a typical real-life market in an African nation during the 1960s colonial era. We like the ribs and rice.

Kusafiri Coffee Shop and Bakery *(closed at press time)*

QUALITY Good	VALUE B	PORTION Medium	LOCATION Africa
READER-SURVEY RESPONSES ⊕ 94% (Much Above Average) NOT ON DISNEY DINING PLAN			

Selections Elephant ear pastries, giant cinnamon rolls, Danish, muffins, croissants, cookies, fruit cups, yogurt, coffee, cocoa, and juice. Sausage, egg, and cheese biscuit and spinach-feta quiche served until 10:30 a.m.

Comments The cinnamon roll is a favorite. Kosher items are available.

Pizzafari

QUALITY Fair	VALUE C	PORTION Medium	LOCATION Discovery Island
READER-SURVEY RESPONSES ⊕ 61% (Do Not Visit)			

Selections Shrimp flatbread; cheese, pepperoni, or sausage personal pizza; Caesar salad. For kids, mac and cheese, pasta with turkey marinara, cheese pizza, or PB&J. Cannoli cake for dessert.

Comments The pizza is profoundly unimpressive. One of the worst dining options in the park.

Restaurantosaurus

QUALITY Fair	VALUE C	PORTION Medium–Large	LOCATION DinoLand U.S.A.
READER-SURVEY RESPONSES ⊕ 88% (Average)			

Selections Angus bacon cheeseburger; chili-cheese hot dog; chicken nuggets; Cobb salad; breaded shrimp; plant-based spicy Southwestern burger; kids' chicken nuggets, cheeseburger, or PB&J.

Comments A wide variety of selections boosts these reader ratings. There's plenty of seating, but it's divided into rooms, so make sure to agree on where everyone's going to sit. A hard-to-find lounge next door serves adult beverages.

Royal Anandapur Tea Company *(closed at press time)*

QUALITY Good	VALUE B	PORTION Medium	LOCATION Asia
READER-SURVEY RESPONSES ⊕ 91% (Average) NOT ON DISNEY DINING PLAN			

Selections Wide variety of hot and iced teas, hot chocolate, and coffees (fantastic frozen chai); lattes and espresso; pastries.

Comments Halfway between Expedition Everest and Kali River Rapids, this is the kind of small, eclectic, Animal Kingdom–specific food stand that you wish other parks had. Around 10 loose teas from Asia and Africa can be ordered hot or iced.

Satu'li Canteen

QUALITY Good	VALUE A	PORTION Medium	LOCATION Pandora
READER-SURVEY RESPONSES ⊕ 97% (Exceptional)			

Selections The signature item is the customizable bowl. Start with a base of salad, red and sweet potato hash, rice and beans, or whole grains and rice. Add wood-grilled chicken, slow-roasted beef, chili-garlic shrimp, or chili-spiced fried tofu, and finish with a choice of sauces. The menu also offers steamed "pods": bao buns with a cheeseburger filling, served with root-vegetable chips and crunchy vegetable slaw. The children's menu choices are similar to the adults' menu.

Comments Breakfast served seasonally here, but if its not available, get the sausage, egg, and cheese biscuit next door at Pongu Pongu.

Yak & Yeti Local Food Cafes

QUALITY Fair	VALUE C	PORTION Large	LOCATION Asia

READER-SURVEY RESPONSES ➊ 92% (Above Average)

Selections Honey chicken with steamed rice, cheeseburger, teriyaki chicken salad, veggie tikka masala, Korean fried chicken sandwich, sweet-and-sour tempura shrimp, egg rolls, and fried rice. Kids' menu: chicken tenders, PB&J, or cheeseburger with carrot sticks and fresh fruit. Breakfast is American-style fare such as breakfast bowls and sausage-and-egg English muffins.

Comments For filling up when you're in a hurry. Expanded seating area behind the pickup windows.

DISNEY'S HOLLYWOOD STUDIOS

ABC Commissary

QUALITY Fair	VALUE D	PORTION Medium–Large	LOCATION Commissary Lane

READER-SURVEY RESPONSES ➊ 90% (Average)

Selections Pork carnitas or shrimp tacos, Buffalo chicken grilled cheese, Mediterranean salad with or without chicken, chicken club sandwich, shrimp or tofu curry rice bowl, plant-based burger, wine and beer. Some kosher.

Comments One of the few places to make substantial improvements in food quality during the pandemic. The Buffalo chicken grilled cheese and the shrimp tacos are the standout menu items.

Backlot Express

QUALITY Fair	VALUE C	PORTION Medium–Large	LOCATION Echo Lake

READER-SURVEY RESPONSES ➊ 90% (Average)

Selections One-third-pound Angus bacon cheeseburger, chicken strips, Cuban sandwich, Southwest salad, red pepper hummus with pita bread.

Comments Fun props, some used in movies, decorate this spacious eatery.

Catalina Eddie's

QUALITY Fair	VALUE C	PORTION Medium–Large	LOCATION Sunset Boulevard

READER-SURVEY RESPONSES ➊ 57% (Do Not Visit)

Selections Cheese and pepperoni pizzas, Caesar salad with or without chicken, strawberry shortcake verrine. Kids' menu includes cheese pizza and PB&J.

Comments Almost anything in the park—even a lemon-and-water cleanse, for that matter—is a better option.

Docking Bay 7 Food and Cargo

QUALITY Excellent	VALUE A	PORTION Medium	LOCATION Galaxy's Edge

READER-SURVEY RESPONSES ➊ 93% (Above Average)

Selections Smoked Kaadu Ribs, named after the creature Jar Jar Binks rode in *Episode I* but actually pork, are cut vertically to give them an alien appearance, then glazed with a sticky-sweet sauce and served with down-home blueberry corn muffins. Endorian Tip Yip (chicken) is roasted on a salad or compressed into cubes, deep-fried, and served with mac and cheese and roasted vegetables.

Vegans will rejoice at meatless menu items featuring Impossible Foods, while pescatarians can try the chilled Peka Tuna Poke.

Comments This is our choi for the best restaurant in Hollywood Studios. Most items here are above-average quality. The Tip Yip chicken is moist and flavorful, as are the vegetable kefta in the Felucian Garden Spread; the ribs, however, are difficult to eat. Also, if you have picky eaters in your crew, note that the kids' menu isn't particularly kid-friendly: In keeping with the idea that you're on an alien planet, many of the foods come in unfamiliar shapes and colors.

Dockside Diner

QUALITY Fair   **VALUE C**   **PORTION** Small–Medium   **LOCATION** Echo Lake
READER-SURVEY RESPONSES ✪ 83% (Below Average)

Selections Hot dogs with various topping options. Sides include Parmesan chips or pickled vegetables.

Comments Just reopened with a new menu at press time; we don't think this menu is going to last. Limited seating at nearby picnic tables.

Fairfax Fare

QUALITY Fair   **VALUE B**   **PORTION** Medium–Large   **LOCATION** Sunset Boulevard
READER-SURVEY RESPONSES ✪ 87% (Average)

Selections Assorted hot dogs and a Chicago-style hot dog salad.

Comments This is the best dining option in the area of Sunset Boulevard near Tower of Terror and Rock 'n' Roller Coaster.

Milk Stand

QUALITY Fair   **VALUE D**   **PORTION** Small   **LOCATION** Galaxy's Edge
READER-SURVEY RESPONSES ✪ 84% (Average)

Selections Frozen nondairy drinks, with or without alcohol.

Comments These plant-based beverages have the consistency of a smoothie. Green milk, as seen in *The Last Jedi,* has floral flavors; the blue drink from *A New Hope* tastes of melon and pineapple. These "milks" are expensive, so if you just *have* to try one, split it with a friend. The optional splash of booze—rum for blue milk, tequila for green—doesn't add anything but cost.

Oga's Cantina

QUALITY Fair   **VALUE D**   **PORTION** Medium   **LOCATION** Galaxy's Edge
READER-SURVEY RESPONSES ✪ 88% (Average)

Selections Alcoholic and nonalcoholic cocktails; wine and beer; Batuu Bits snack and a sampler platter with cured and roasted meats, cheese, and pork cracklings.

Comments This cantina, overseen by alien proprietor Oga Garra, will instantly remind fans of the Mos Eisley watering hole from *A New Hope.* A droid DJ—actually a recycled Captain Rex from the original Star Tours—spins an original 1980s-style synth-pop soundtrack. Nine signature alcoholic cocktails are on the menu. Draft craft beers and private-label wines are also served, as are nonalcoholic drinks (try the frozen cookie-crowned Blue Bantha).

Oga's has stayed packed from the moment it opened. Disney makes online reservations available up to 60 days in advance (see page 271), so be ready at your 60-day mark to grab one. If you can't get in, try showing up in the last hour the park is open for a possible walk-up spot. The later the park is open, the better your chances of getting in.

PizzeRizzo

QUALITY Poor   **VALUE D**   **PORTION** Large   **LOCATION** Grand Avenue
READER-SURVEY RESPONSES ✪ 84% (Below Average)

Selections Personal pizzas, meatball subs, and salads—none of them good. The too-doughy pizza's one accomplishment is that it manages to be both burned on top and underdone below.

Comments Rizzo's Deluxe Supreme Banquet Hall features an ongoing wedding reception, with a disco-heavy soundtrack. The upstairs decor might be the best part of the restaurant.

Ronto Roasters

QUALITY Good	VALUE B	PORTION Medium	LOCATION Galaxy's Edge
READER-SURVEY RESPONSES ✪ 96% (Exceptional)			

Selections Ronto Wrap (pita bread filled with roasted pork, grilled pork sausage, and slaw); pork rinds; nonalcoholic fruit punch. Breakfast wraps available too.

Comments A disgruntled smelting droid named 8D-J8 does the cooking, turning mysterious alien meats on a rotating spit as they roast beneath a recycled podracing engine. The sandwiches are delicious and filling.

Rosie's All-American Cafe

QUALITY Fair	VALUE C	PORTION Medium	LOCATION Sunset Boulevard
READER-SURVEY RESPONSES ✪ 82% (Below Average)			

Selections Cheeseburgers, chicken nuggets, fries, plant-based "lobster" roll; child's turkey sandwich or chicken nuggets with a yogurt smoothie and fruit; strawberry shortcake verrine or snacking sandwich cookie.

Comments A quick stop on the way to Tower of Terror or Rock 'n' Roller Coaster and close enough to eat with accompanying screams.

The Trolley Car Cafe *(Starbucks)*

QUALITY Good	VALUE B	PORTION Small	LOCATION Hollywood Boulevard
READER-SURVEY RESPONSES ✪ 93% (Above Average)			

Selections Coffee drinks and teas; breakfast sandwiches and pastries.

Comments Disney-themed Starbucks. The building is the real attraction: The pink-stucco Spanish Colonial exterior calls to mind old Hollywood; the industrial-style interior evokes a trolley-car switching station.

Woody's Lunch Box

QUALITY Excellent	VALUE A-	PORTION Medium-Large	LOCATION Toy Story Land
READER-SURVEY RESPONSES ✪ 91% (Average)			

Selections *Breakfast:* Lunch Box Tarts (think gourmet toaster pastries), breakfast bowl with scrambled eggs, potato barrels, and country gravy. *Lunch and dinner:* Sandwiches (barbecue brisket, smoked turkey, grilled three-cheese); tomato-basil soup; "totchos" (potato barrels smothered with chili, queso, and corn chips).

Comments Very limited seating and shade. Seasonal tarts are great.

DISNEY SPRINGS

Amorette's Patisserie

QUALITY Excellent	VALUE B	PORTION Small-Medium	LOCATION Town Center
READER-SURVEY RESPONSES ✪ 94% (Much Above Average)		NOT ON DISNEY DINING PLAN	

Selections Specialty cakes and pastries made by talented Disney chefs; Disney-themed 11-layer dome cake; sandwiches; Champagne.

Comments Don't miss Amorette's Petit Cake, a smaller portion of its signature cake with 11 layers of red velvet and chocolate cakes, cherry and chocolate mousses, raspberry jelly, and Italian butter cream.

Blaze Fast-Fire'd Pizza

QUALITY Excellent	VALUE A	PORTION Large	LOCATION Town Center
READER-SURVEY RESPONSES ✪ 94% (Above Average)			

Selections Specialty and build-your-own 11-inch pizzas with a selection of 40-plus fresh toppings and sauces; salads.

Comments Each fast-fired pizza is prepared in around 3 minutes after you select your toppings, Chipotle-style. Ignore the long line outside—it moves very quickly. Go light on the toppings for best results.

Chicken Guy!

QUALITY Fair	VALUE C	PORTION Large	LOCATION Town Center
READER-SURVEY RESPONSES ⊕ 89% (Average)			

Selections Fried chicken tenders, fries, mac and cheese.

Comments Chicken tenders and fries are the name of the game at Chicken Guy! (*Guy* refers to the restaurant's creator, celebrity chef Guy Fieri.) If you want to get adventurous, do it with the sauces, of which there are dozens to choose from. We think the food here is better than the rating—it's the lack of indoor seating that could be improved.

Cookes of Dublin

QUALITY Fair–Good	VALUE C-	PORTION Medium–Large	LOCATION The Landing
READER-SURVEY RESPONSES ⊕ 90% (Average)			

Selections Fried chicken tenders, burgers, fish-and-chips, and a specialty dip.

Comments Wait times can be on the high side, but even the pickiest eaters will like the excellent onion rings and chicken fingers.

D-Luxe Burger

QUALITY Good	VALUE C	PORTION Medium–Large	LOCATION Town Center
READER-SURVEY RESPONSES ⊕ 89% (Average)			

Selections Specialty burgers (The Southern, topped with a fried green tomato; veggie with mango salsa); hand-cut fries with a variety of dipping sauces (curry ketchup and garlic ranch are zesty and unique); gelato shakes (spiked and nonalcoholic).

Comments Burgers and fries take a little time, but the specialty options are worth the wait. Mobile ordering available.

Earl of Sandwich

QUALITY Good	VALUE B-	PORTION Small–Medium	LOCATION Marketplace
READER-SURVEY RESPONSES ⊕ 94% (Much Above Average)			

Selections Sandwiches, salads, wraps, soups; brownies and cookies.

Comments There's always a long line here, but it tends to move quickly. The sandwiches, while tasty, aren't anything you can't find at your local deli. It's been very highly rated by readers for many years.

Pepe by José Andrés *(closed at press time)*

QUALITY Good	VALUE B	PORTION Small	LOCATION West Side
READER SURVEY RESPONSES NA	NOT ON DISNEY DINING PLAN		

Selections Spanish sandwiches like bikinis, as well as gazpacho.

Comments Pepe is the first permanent location of José Andrés's popular food truck in Disney Springs.

Pizza Ponte

QUALITY Good	VALUE C	PORTION Medium	LOCATION The Landing
READER-SURVEY RESPONSES ⊕ 79% (Average)			

Selections Sandwiches, pizza by the slice, and Italian desserts such as cannoli and tiramisu.

Comments The platonic ideal of square pizza costs around $5 per slice and is found at Mama's Too at 105th and Broadway in Manhattan. Pizza Ponte isnt close to Mama's Too, but it's still above average even for New York. The prices (around $7–$8 per slice) might seem high, but the slices are large. If you want to build your own pizza, head over to Blaze Fast-Fire'd Pizza (see 306), where for about the same price, you can get a small pie that generally serves two.

The Polite Pig

QUALITY Good–Excellent **VALUE** A **PORTION** Medium **LOCATION** Town Center
READER-SURVEY RESPONSES ✪ 96% (Exceptional)

Selections Southern barbecue staples (pulled pork, ribs, smoked chicken); specialty veggie sides (barbecue cauliflower, grilled corn, whiskey-caramel Brussels sprouts); bourbon bar; cocktails and local beers on tap; homemade cakes and pies for dessert.

Comments A hybrid fast-casual/table-service restaurant, The Polite Pig offers a bit more than your standard quick-service spot. Barbecue smoked on-site is the name of the game, but the side dishes are not to be missed. Skip the sandwiches and split a few entrées (the pulled pork and ribs are our favorites) with sides; it's the best bang for your buck and offers a chance to try more of the outstanding appetizers (house-made giant pretzels, smoked wings) and delicious desserts.

Starbucks

QUALITY Good **VALUE** C **PORTION** Small **LOCATION** Marketplace
READER-SURVEY RESPONSES ✪ 94% (Above Average)

Selections Coffee drinks and teas; breakfast sandwiches and pastries.
Comments The fare is largely the same as you'd find at any other Starbucks.

FULL-SERVICE RESTAURANTS
In Depth

THE PROFILES IN THIS SECTION allow you to quickly check the cuisine, location, star rating, cost range, quality rating, and value rating of every full-service restaurant at WDW. Reservations for full-service restaurants are strongly recommended. See page 267 for information about dining during the pandemic.

The following profiles, including the reader ratings, reflect the menus and prices in use as we went to press. Although Disney isn't yet offering its popular dining plans, the profiles also include that information for when they return.

OVERALL RATING Ranging from one to five stars, this rating encompasses the entire dining experience: style, service, ambience, and food quality. Five stars is the highest rating attainable. Our star ratings don't correspond to those awarded by AAA, Mobil, Zagat, or other restaurant reviewers.

COST RANGE This tells you approximately how much you can expect to spend on a full-service entrée (appetizers, side dishes, soups and salads, desserts, drinks, and tips aren't included). Cost ranges are categorized as **inexpensive** (less than $13), **moderate** ($13–$23), or **expensive** ($24 and up).

QUALITY RATING Food quality is rated from one to five stars, five being the highest possible rating. The criteria are taste, freshness of ingredients, preparation, presentation, and the creativity of the food served. Price is no consideration.

VALUE RATING If, on the other hand, you're looking for both quality *and* value, then you should check this rating, which is also expressed as stars.

PAYMENT All Walt Disney World restaurants take the following credit cards: American Express, Diners Club, Discover, Japan Credit Bureau, MasterCard, and Visa. And unless otherwise noted, all accept the Disney Dining Plan.

RESTAURANTS OPENING IN 2021

La Crêperie de Paris
France, World Showcase, EPCOT; ☎ 407-939-3463

SUMMARY AND COMMENTS Generously sized savory and sweet crepes. Try the chèvre, spinach, and walnut savory crêpe for dinner, with the banana-filled crêpe for dessert.

Space 220
Future World East, EPCOT; ☎ 407-939-3463

SUMMARY AND COMMENTS This space-themed restaurant is being built between Mission: Space and Test Track. The idea is that you're dining on an international space station. Instead of traditional windows, huge digital displays will provide simulated views of Earth and stars.

Steakhouse 71
Contemporary Resort; ☎ 407-939-3463

SUMMARY AND COMMENTS On the ground floor of the Contemporary Resort, Steakhouse 71 seems like it'll be the lowest-common-denominator dining destination for the Magic Kingdom monorail resorts.

FULL-SERVICE RESTAURANT PROFILES

Akershus Royal Banquet Hall *(closed at press time)* ★★

NORWEGIAN/BUFFET	EXPENSIVE	QUALITY ★★	VALUE ★★★★
READER-SURVEY RESPONSES ⊕ 86% (Average)			

Norway, World Showcase, EPCOT; ☎ 407-939-3463

Reservations Required for breakfast and highly recommended for lunch and dinner. A credit card is required to reserve. **Dining Plan credits** 1 per person, per meal. **When to go** Anytime. **Cost range** Breakfast $53 (child $34), lunch and dinner $63 (child $41). Prices vary seasonally; check before you go. **Service** ★★★★. **Friendliness** ★★★★. **Parking** EPCOT lot. **Bar** Full service. **Wine selection** Good. **Dress** Casual. **Disabled access** Yes. **Customers** Theme park guests. **Character breakfast** Daily, 8–11:10 a.m. **Character lunch** Daily, 11:55 a.m.–3:30 p.m. **Character dinner** Daily, 4:55–8:35 p.m.

SETTING AND ATMOSPHERE The inside of Akershus looks like every child's vision of a fairy-tale castle: high ceilings, stone archways, sumptuous purple carpets, regal banners flying. What's mildly surprising, given the attention to authenticity elsewhere in EPCOT, is that it doesn't look more like the real Akershus Castle in Oslo, which has plain wooden floors; flat, simple

continued on page 314

WALT DISNEY WORLD RESTAURANTS BY CUISINE

CUISINE	LOCATION	OVERALL RATING	COST	QUALITY RATING	VALUE RATING
AFRICAN					
BOMA—FLAVORS OF AFRICA	Animal Kingdom Lodge–Jambo House	★★★★½	Exp	★★★★	★★★★
JIKO—THE COOKING PLACE	Animal Kingdom Lodge–Jambo House	★★★★½	Exp	★★★★	★★★
SANAA	Animal Kingdom Villas–Kidani Village	★★★★	Exp	★★★★	★★★★
JUNGLE NAVIGATION CO. LTD. SKIPPER CANTEEN	Magic Kingdom	★★★½	Inexp	★★★	★★★
TUSKER HOUSE RESTAURANT	Animal Kingdom	★★★	Mod	★★★	★★★
AMERICAN					
CALIFORNIA GRILL	Contemporary	★★★★★	Exp	★★★★★	★★★
CHEF ART SMITH'S HOMECOMIN'	Disney Springs	★★★★	Mod	★★★★	★★★½
THE HOLLYWOOD BROWN DERBY	DHS	★★★★	Exp	★★★★	★★★
TIFFINS	Animal Kingdom	★★★★	Exp	★★★★	★★★
STORY BOOK DINING WITH SNOW WHITE AT ARTIST POINT*	Wilderness Lodge	★★★½	Exp	★★★★	★★★½
WOLFGANG PUCK BAR & GRILL	Disney Springs	★★★½	Exp	★★★★	★★★½
CAPE MAY CAFÉ	Beach Club	★★★½	Exp	★★★½	★★★★
CITY WORKS EATERY AND POUR HOUSE	Disney Springs	★★★½	Mod	★★★	★★★
LIBERTY TREE TAVERN	Magic Kingdom	★★★½	Exp	★★★	★★★
BE OUR GUEST RESTAURANT	Magic Kingdom	★★★	Exp	★★★★	★★
WHISPERING CANYON CAFE	Wilderness Lodge	★★★	Exp	★★★½	★★★★
THE EDISON	Disney Springs	★★★	Exp	★★★½	★★★
GEYSER POINT BAR & GRILL	Wilderness Lodge	★★★	Mod	★★★½	★★★
HOUSE OF BLUES	Disney Springs	★★★	Mod	★★★½	★★★
ALE & COMPASS	Yacht Club	★★★	Mod	★★★	★★★
50'S PRIME TIME CAFE	DHS	★★★	Mod	★★★	★★★
GARDEN GRILL RESTAURANT	EPCOT	★★★	Exp	★★★	★★★
TUSKER HOUSE RESTAURANT	Animal Kingdom	★★★	Exp	★★★	★★★
THREE BRIDGES BAR & GRILL	Coronado Springs	★★★	Mod	★★★	★★½
BOATWRIGHT'S DINING HALL*	Port Orleans Riverside	★★★	Exp	★★★	★★
CINDERELLA'S ROYAL TABLE	Magic Kingdom	★★★	Exp	★★★	★★
OLIVIA'S CAFE	Old Key West	★★★	Exp	★★★	★★

*Closed at press time

WDW RESTAURANTS BY CUISINE (continued)

CUISINE	LOCATION	OVERALL RATING	COST	QUALITY RATING	VALUE RATING
T-REX	Disney Springs	★★★	Mod	★★	★★
THE CRYSTAL PALACE	Magic Kingdom	★★½	Exp	★★★½	★★★
PADDLEFISH	Disney Springs	★★½	Exp	★★★½	★★½
CHEF MICKEY'S	Contemporary	★★½	Exp	★★★	★★★
ESPN CLUB*	BoardWalk	★★½	Mod	★★★	★★★
HOLLYWOOD & VINE	DHS	★★½	Exp	★★★	★★★
1900 PARK FARE*	Grand Floridian	★★½	Exp	★★★	★★★
GRAND FLORIDIAN CAFE	Grand Floridian	★★½	Mod	★★★	★★
BEACHES & CREAM SODA SHOP	Beach Club	★★½	Mod	★★½	★★
FRESH MEDITERRANEAN MARKET	Dolphin	★★½	Mod	★★½	★★
SPLITSVILLE	Disney Springs	★★½	Mod	★★½	★★
RAINFOREST CAFE	Animal Kingdom and Disney Springs	★★½	Mod	★★	★★
GARDEN GROVE	Swan	★★	Exp	★★★	★★
TURF CLUB BAR & GRILL*	Saratoga Springs	★★	Exp	★★★	★★
SCI-FI DINE-IN THEATER RESTAURANT	DHS	★★	Mod	★★½	★★
BIG RIVER GRILLE & BREWING WORKS	BoardWalk	★★	Mod	★★	★★
THE FOUNTAIN	Dolphin	★★	Mod	★★	★★
THE PLAZA RESTAURANT	Magic Kingdom	★★	Mod	★★	★★
SPACE 220 (not open at press time)	EPCOT				
TRAIL'S END RESTAURANT*	Fort Wilderness Resort	★★	Exp	★★	★★
PLANET HOLLYWOOD	Disney Springs	★½	Mod	★★	★★
MAYA GRILL	Coronado Springs	★	Exp	★	★
BRITISH					
ROSE & CROWN DINING ROOM	EPCOT	★★★	Mod	★★★½	★★
BUFFET					
BIERGARTEN	EPCOT	★★	Exp	★★	★★★★
BOMA—FLAVORS OF AFRICA	Animal Kingdom Lodge-Jambo House	★★★★½	Exp	★★★★	★★★★
THE CRYSTAL PALACE	Magic Kingdom	★★½	Exp	★★★½	★★★
CAJUN					
BOATWRIGHT'S DINING HALL*	Port Orleans Riverside	★★★	Exp	★★★	★★
CHINESE					
NINE DRAGONS RESTAURANT	EPCOT	★★	Mod	★★	★★

WDW RESTAURANTS BY CUISINE (continued)

CUISINE	LOCATION	OVERALL RATING	COST	QUALITY RATING	VALUE RATING
COCKTAILS AND BAR BITES					
JOCK LINDSEY'S HANGAR BAR	Disney Springs	★★	Inexp	★★	★★
FRENCH					
LA CRÊPERIE DE PARIS (not open at press time)	EPCOT				
MONSIEUR PAUL*	EPCOT	★★★★	Exp	★★★★½	★★★
TOPOLINO'S TERRACE	Riviera	★★★★	Exp	★★★★	★★
BE OUR GUEST RESTAURANT	Magic Kingdom	★★★	Exp	★★★★	★★
CHEFS DE FRANCE	EPCOT	★★★	Exp	★★★	★★★
GERMAN					
BIERGARTEN	EPCOT	★★	Exp	★★	★★★★
GLOBAL					
PARADISO 37	Disney Springs	★★½	Exp	★★★	★★★
GOURMET					
VICTORIA & ALBERT'S*	Grand Floridian	★★★★★	Exp	★★★★★	★★★★
INDIAN/AFRICAN					
SANAA	Animal Kingdom Villas–Kidani Village	★★★★	Exp	★★★★	★★★★
IRISH					
RAGLAN ROAD	Disney Springs	★★★★	Mod	★★★½	★★★
ITALIAN					
TOPOLINO'S TERRACE	Riviera	★★★★	Exp	★★★★	★★
TUTTO ITALIA	EPCOT	★★★	Exp	★★★★	★★
VIA NAPOLI	EPCOT	★★★★	Exp	★★★½	★★★
TUTTO GUSTO WINE CELLAR	EPCOT	★★★½	Mod	★★★★	★★★
MARIA & ENZO'S RISTORANTE	Disney Springs	★★½	Exp	★★★½	★★★
TERRALINA CRAFTED ITALIAN	Disney Springs	★★★½	Mod	★★★	★★★
TRATTORIA AL FORNO	BoardWalk	★★★	Mod	★★★½	★★
IL MULINO NEW YORK	Swan	★★★	Exp	★★★	★★
MAMA MELROSE'S	DHS	★★½	Mod	★★★	★★
TONY'S TOWN SQUARE RESTAURANT	Magic Kingdom	★★½	Exp	★★★	★★
JAPANESE/SUSHI					
TAKUMI-TEI*	EPCOT	★★★★½	Exp	★★★★★	★★★½
KIMONOS	Swan	★★★★	Mod	★★★★	★★★
TEPPAN EDO	EPCOT	★★★½	Exp	★★★★	★★★
MORIMOTO ASIA	Disney Springs	★★★½	Exp	★★★½	★★★★
TOKYO DINING*	EPCOT	★★★	Mod	★★★★	★★★
MEDITERRANEAN					
CÍTRICOS	Grand Floridian	★★★½	Exp	★★★★½	★★★
FRESH MEDITERRANEAN MARKET	Dolphin	★★½	Mod	★★½	★★

*Closed at press time

WDW RESTAURANTS BY CUISINE *(continued)*

MEXICAN

CUISINE	LOCATION	OVERALL RATING	COST	QUALITY RATING	VALUE RATING
FRONTERA COCINA	Disney Springs	★★★½	Mod	★★★½	★★★
LA HACIENDA DE SAN ANGEL	EPCOT	★★★	Exp	★★★½	★★½
SAN ANGEL INN RESTAURANTE	EPCOT	★★★	Exp	★★★	★★
MAYA GRILL	Coronado Springs	★	Exp	★	★

MOROCCAN

CUISINE	LOCATION	OVERALL RATING	COST	QUALITY RATING	VALUE RATING
SPICE ROAD TABLE	EPCOT	★★★★	Exp	★★★★	★★★
RESTAURANT MARRAKESH*	EPCOT	★★★	Exp	★★½	★★

NORWEGIAN

CUISINE	LOCATION	OVERALL RATING	COST	QUALITY RATING	VALUE RATING
AKERSHUS ROYAL BANQUET HALL*	EPCOT	★★	Exp	★★	★★★★

PAN-ASIAN/POLYNESIAN

CUISINE	LOCATION	OVERALL RATING	COST	QUALITY RATING	VALUE RATING
TIFFINS	Animal Kingdom	★★★★	Exp	★★★★	★★★
MORIMOTO ASIA	Disney Springs	★★★½	Exp	★★★½	★★★★
'OHANA	Polynesian Village	★★★	Exp	★★★½	★★★
KONA CAFE	Polynesian Village	★★★	Mod	★★★	★★★★
TRADER SAM'S GROG GROTTO	Polynesian Village	★★★	Mod	★★★	★★★
YAK & YETI RESTAURANT	Animal Kingdom	★★★	Mod/Exp	★★½	★★

SEAFOOD

CUISINE	LOCATION	OVERALL RATING	COST	QUALITY RATING	VALUE RATING
NARCOOSSEE'S	Grand Floridian	★★★★½	Exp	★★★½	★★
FLYING FISH*	BoardWalk	★★★★	Exp	★★★★	★★★
THE BOATHOUSE	Disney Springs	★★★½	Exp	★★★	★★
TODD ENGLISH'S BLUEZOO	Dolphin	★★★	Exp	★★★★	★★
PADDLEFISH	Disney Springs	★★½	Exp	★★★½	★★½
CORAL REEF	EPCOT	★★½	Exp	★★	★★
SEBASTIAN'S BISTRO*	Caribbean Beach	★★	Exp	★★	★★★

SPANISH/TAPAS

CUISINE	LOCATION	OVERALL RATING	COST	QUALITY RATING	VALUE RATING
JALEO	Disney Springs	★★★★	Mod	★★★★	★★★★
TOLEDO	Coronado Springs	★★★½	Exp	★★★	★★½
THREE BRIDGES BAR & GRILL	Coronado Springs	★★★	Mod	★★★	★★½

STEAK

CUISINE	LOCATION	OVERALL RATING	COST	QUALITY RATING	VALUE RATING
SHULA'S STEAK HOUSE	Dolphin	★★★★	Exp	★★★★	★★
STK ORLANDO	Disney Springs	★★★½	Exp	★★★★	★★½
LE CELLIER STEAKHOUSE	EPCOT	★★★½	Exp	★★★½	★★★
STEAKHOUSE 71 (not open at press time)	Contemporary Resort				
YACHTSMAN STEAKHOUSE*	Yacht Club	★★½	Exp	★★★½	★★

WINE/SMALL PLATES

CUISINE	LOCATION	OVERALL RATING	COST	QUALITY RATING	VALUE RATING
WINE BAR GEORGE	Disney Springs	★★★★	Mod	★★★★	★★★★½

continued from page 309

ceilings; and painted brick arches. Disney's version is almost as ungodly expensive as the real thing, though, and you're apt to hear *norsk* spoken by your servers. Close enough for us. The saving grace is that most visitors don't realize that it is in fact a restaurant and walk right by.

HOUSE SPECIALTIES *Breakfast:* Smorgasbord of dilled salmon, mackerel, and goat cheese. *Lunch and dinner:* Taste of Norway (smorgasbord of meats, cheeses, seafood, and salads), herb-roasted chicken with potatoes, grilled salmon, cheese-and-spinach-stuffed pasta, and kjottkake (beef-and-pork meatballs served with mashed potatoes, vegetables, and lingonberry sauce). *For kids:* macaroni and cheese, grilled chicken, cheese pizza, salmon, and meatballs.

OTHER RECOMMENDATIONS Beer on tap, wine, aquavit cocktails.

SUMMARY AND COMMENTS Akershus has never been on our "you've just gotta try this" list, but if you have kids who love the Disney princesses, they won't be disappointed. There was a time when the Scandinavian-style buffet was noteworthy, but these days all of the attention in the kitchen goes to feeding families fast. As for the prices? You're paying for that princess face time.

Ale & Compass ★★★

AMERICAN	MODERATE	QUALITY ★★★	VALUE ★★★
READER-SURVEY RESPONSES ● 90% (Average)			

Yacht Club Resort; ☎ 407-939-3463

Reservations Recommended. **Dining Plan credits** 1 per person, per meal. **When to go** Anytime. **Cost range** Breakfast $13–$20 (child $7–$10), dinner $17–$34 (child $9–$13). **Service** ★★★½. **Friendliness** ★★★½. **Parking** Resort lot. **Bar** Full service. **Wine selection** Good. **Dress** Casual. **Disabled access** Yes. **Customers** EPCOT and hotel guests. **Breakfast** Daily, 7 a.m.–1:30 p.m. **Dinner** Daily, 5–9 p.m.

SETTING AND ATMOSPHERE This venue serves "Eastern seaboard eats." The large dining room is polished and pretty in a generic way, but there's no theme to speak of.

HOUSE SPECIALTIES For dinner, start with the cabernet-braised short ribs with roasted vegetables and end with the 12-layer chocolate cake.

OTHER RECOMMENDATIONS Breakfast selections include salted caramel–apple French toast, plus the usual combinations of eggs, bacon, pancakes, and waffles. Dinner features pastas, chicken, steaks, a good bacon–Vermont Cheddar burger, and a seafood pot pie with shrimp, scallops, crab, and sustainable fish. On the upside, vegetarians have two full-fledged meal options: the Protein Bowl (with quinoa, vegan Italian sausage, sweet potato, and Broccolini) and a pasta with mushrooms and other veggies.

SUMMARY AND COMMENTS The cuisine is advertised as "New England comfort food." Reader ratings have improved substantially in the past year, without compromising the diversity of the menu.

Beaches & Cream Soda Shop ★★½

AMERICAN	MODERATE	QUALITY ★★½	VALUE ★★
READER-SURVEY RESPONSES ● 92% (Much Above Average)			

Beach Club Resort; ☎ 407-939-3463

Reservations Highly recommended. **Dining Plan credits** 1 per person, per meal. **When to go** Lunch or dinner. **Cost range** $13–$17. **Service** ★★★. **Friendliness** ★★★★. **Parking** Hotel lot. **Bar** Beer, wine, hard floats. **Wine selection** Minimal. **Dress** Casual. **Disabled access** Yes. **Customers** Resort guests. **Hours** Daily, 11 a.m.–11 p.m.

SETTING AND ATMOSPHERE Casual eats and retro soda-fountain decor. Guests in bathing suits and flip-flops queue up for the burgers, sandwiches (Reuben, French dip, chicken), and piles of hot fries.

HOUSE SPECIALTIES Burgers and fries; chili and soup; hand-scooped ice cream, including the gargantuan $35 Kitchen Sink dessert, with five flavors of ice cream slathered with toppings.

OTHER RECOMMENDATIONS Root beer float.

SUMMARY AND COMMENTS Beaches & Cream exists mainly to give guests an excuse to eat all the things they're not supposed to. But hey, it's vacation—indulge! Seating is scarce during peak hours.

Be Our Guest Restaurant ★★½

FRENCH/AMERICAN   EXPENSIVE   QUALITY ★★★★   VALUE ★★
READER-SURVEY RESPONSES ✪ 81% (Much Below Average)

Fantasyland, Magic Kingdom; ☎ 407-939-3463

Reservations Highly recommended. **Dining Plan credits** 1 quick-service credit per person, per meal for breakfast (not currently offered); 2 table-service credits per person, per meal for lunch and dinner. **When to go** Lunch or dinner. **Cost range** Prix fixe lunch and dinner $62 (child $37). **Service** ★★★★. **Friendliness** ★★★★. **Parking** Magic Kingdom lot. **Bar** Wine and beer only. **Wine selection** Solid wine list with some French to match the restaurant's theme—from sparkling starters to a private-label wine sampler. A handful of popular California vintages are on the list as well. **Dress** Casual. **Disabled access** Yes. **Customers** Magic Kingdom guests. **Lunch** Daily, 11 a.m.–2:55 p.m. **Dinner** Daily, 3–9 p.m.

SETTING AND ATMOSPHERE Be Our Guest re-creates Beast's Castle from *Beauty and the Beast* with three themed rooms: the Grand Ballroom, the mysterious West Wing, and the pretty Castle Gallery. The rooms fill up fast, with a noise level to match the hordes (space for up to 550 seats). The lights are dimmed at lunch and dinner, which offers table service and a tad more serenity than breakfast. (See page 297 for counter-service profile.)

HOUSE SPECIALTIES French onion soup or charcuterie plate appetizers, roasted pork tenderloin with seasonal vegetables as an entrée.

OTHER RECOMMENDATIONS Filet mignon with Robuchon potatoes; pan-seared scallops with risotto.

SUMMARY AND COMMENTS Be Our Guest has been the most popular restaurant in Walt Disney World since it opened in 2012. Disney has tried to meet that demand in several ways, most notably adding breakfast in 2015 and switching to a common fixed-price menu for both lunch and dinner. These changes, especially the fixed-price menu, have led Be Our Guest to receive its worst survey ratings in six years—at the time of this writing, it's Below Average according to our criteria. The menu is heavy and expensive, it lacks enough choices to justify the cost, and service can be slow.

We've received quite a few reader comments about Be Our Guest with a common refrain of "just OK." First up, from Fletcher, North Carolina:

I got up early to snag this dinner reservation. The atmosphere was fun and unique, but the food really wasn't that special. I had the layered ratatouille, which was too salty. My son had experienced lamb for the first time at Boma the night before, so he ordered the roasted lamb. He was extremely disappointed by the portion size, which was really just a few bites. The Beast made several appearances during our meal, which was nice, but I felt the food should have been better.

A reader from Lincoln, Rhode Island, chimes in:

I was able to get reservations for Be Our Guest for breakfast and dinner. Unless you have to meet the Beast, skip dinner. While the food was good, the price for kids is ridiculous. And I don't know any kids who eat cheese in block form.

On a more positive note, this Lakeland, Florida, reader recommends Be Our Guest for breakfast if you're on the Disney Dining Plan:

Be Our Guest's breakfast is a great value because it counts as a quick-service meal. Besides good-size portions, you get a refillable basket of pastries, muffins, and croissants. They'll even pack up the goodies to go. [Note: Be Our Guest wasn't serving breakfast as we went to press, but there were strong rumors it was headed back.]

If you're looking for good food at comparable prices, **Liberty Tree Tavern** (page 336) is a better choice for lunch and dinner. For cheaper dining, **Main Street Bakery** (page 298) is a better choice for a fast breakfast. **Columbia Harbour House** (page 297), the highest-rated restaurant in the Magic Kingdom, makes a great stop for a quick lunch, or try **Pecos Bill** (page 299).

Biergarten Restaurant ★★

GERMAN/BUFFET	EXPENSIVE	QUALITY ★★	VALUE ★★★★
READER-SURVEY RESPONSES ◐ 85% (Average)			

Germany, World Showcase, EPCOT; ☎ 407-939-3463

Reservations Recommended. **Dining Plan credits** 1 per person, per meal. **When to go** Lunch or dinner. **Cost range** $46 (child $25). **Service** ★★★★. **Friendliness** ★★★★. **Parking** EPCOT lot. **Bar** Full service. **Wine selection** German. **Dress** Casual. **Disabled access** Yes. **Customers** Theme park guests. **Lunch** Daily, noon–3:55 p.m. **Dinner** Daily, 4–8 p.m.

SETTING AND ATMOSPHERE Biergarten is a hefty German restaurant set inside a nighttime Teutonic town square. You're seated at long tables lined up in rows emanating like the moon's rays from a central dance floor and stage. A lederhosen-clad oompah band plays and encourages diners to sing along. Tables are not shared between families, and there's plenty of space between occupied tables.

HOUSE SPECIALTIES Potato salad, traditional German sausages, and homemade spaetzle.

OTHER RECOMMENDATIONS Rotisserie chicken, braised red cabbage, and German beer.

ENTERTAINMENT AND AMENITIES Oompah band and German dancers perform throughout the day.

SUMMARY AND COMMENTS The buffet has returned, stacked with an astonishing amount of food of good quality. There are plenty of places in Walt Disney World where you could pay more for less. If you leave here hungry, ask your doctor about tapeworms. The lively 25-minute show (one every hour) and noisy dining room are part of the fun, especially for families. And kids seem to love the place.

Big River Grille & Brewing Works ★★

AMERICAN	MODERATE	QUALITY ★★	VALUE ★★
READER-SURVEY RESPONSES 76% ◐ (Much Below Average)			

BoardWalk; ☎ 407-751-1544

Reservations Recommended. **Dining Plan credits** 1 per person, per meal. **When to go** Lunch or dinner. **Cost range** $13–$28. **Service** ★★★. **Friendliness** ★★★★. **Parking** BoardWalk lot. **Bar** Full service. **Wine selection** Good. **Dress** Casual. **Disabled access** Yes. **Customers** Tourists. **Hours** Daily, 11 a.m.–11 p.m.

SETTING AND ATMOSPHERE Situated for prime people-watching on Disney's BoardWalk, the outdoor tables fill up fast on a pretty day. A minimalist interior focuses on the craft beer that is made on the premises, with glass walls allowing you to see the process as ales and lagers are microbrewed. The place is small—it seems like the huge copper brewing tanks take up more room than that allotted to the diners.

HOUSE SPECIALTIES Beer-cheese soup, baby back ribs with honey-chipotle barbecue sauce.

SUMMARY AND COMMENTS The food is just OK, but the popularity of craft beer makes Big River Grille a hot spot on the BoardWalk. House brews include a light lager, a robust ale, and seasonal choices. A good late-night-dining choice.

The Boathouse ★★★½

SEAFOOD   EXPENSIVE   QUALITY ★★★   VALUE ★★
READER-SURVEY RESPONSES ➊ 94% (Above Average; No. 9–rated restaurant in Walt Disney World)

The Landing, Disney Springs; ☎ 407-939-BOAT (2628)

Reservations Strongly recommended. **Dining Plan credits** 2 per person, per meal. **When to go** Lunch or dinner. **Cost range** $14–$55 (child $10). **Service** ★★★. **Friendliness** ★★★★. **Parking** Disney Springs Orange garage. **Bar** Full service. **Wine selection** Good. **Dress** Casual. **Disabled access** Yes. **Customers** Locals and Disney guests. **Hours** Daily, 11 a.m.–10 p.m.

SETTING AND ATMOSPHERE The first things you notice about The Boathouse, on the waterfront at Disney Springs, are the vintage American Amphicars (amphibious autos produced in the 1960s) and the Italian water taxis floating next to the front door—a multimillion-dollar fleet of 19 rare boats from private collectors, museums, and boat shows around the world. The airy restaurant seats up to 600 in nautically themed dining rooms (two private), as well as outdoors. The three bars include one built over the water and attached to more than 300 feet of boardwalk and docks.

HOUSE SPECIALTIES The menu changes daily, but there's seafood of every sort: a raw bar with fresh oysters, tuna, and wild-caught shrimp; lobster; fish and shellfish, including Florida seasonal varieties; and jumbo lump crab cake. There's also filet mignon, as well as ice-cream pie for dessert.

SUMMARY AND COMMENTS If you're not sure where to eat in Disney Springs, go to The Boathouse. Consistently good quality, especially with fresh seafood, made this restaurant the No. 2 highest-grossing independent restaurant in the United States in 2019 (Carmine's in Times Square was No. 1). The restaurant does enough volume that it has proprietary lines of oysters and rib eyes. While seafood is the star, the steaks are top-notch as well. Hop a ride in an Amphicar ($125 per car). Along with Chef Art Smith's Homecomin', it has the best service in Disney Springs.

A North Carolina family advises readers to save room—lots of room—for dessert:

By far the best meal was at The Boathouse in Disney Springs. Everyone's meal was superb—we all ordered seafood entrées. We had a mile-high ice-cream dessert designed to serve two. It was delicious and easily served all four of us.

Boatwright's Dining Hall *(closed at press time)* ★★★

AMERICAN/CAJUN   MODERATE/EXPENSIVE   QUALITY ★★★   VALUE ★★
READER-SURVEY RESPONSES ➊ 78% (Much Below Average)

Port Orleans Resort–Riverside; ☎ 407-939-3463

Reservations Highly recommended. **Dining Plan credits** 1 per person, per meal. **When to go** Early evening. **Cost range** $19–$36 (child $9–$12). **Service** ★★★★½. **Friendliness** ★★★★★. **Parking** Hotel lot. **Bar** Full service. **Wine selection** None. **Dress** Casual. **Disabled access** Yes. **Customers** Hotel guests. **Hours** Daily, 5–9 p.m.

SETTING AND ATMOSPHERE Situated between River Roost Lounge and Riverside Mill Food Court, just off of Port Orleans Riverside's lobby, Boatwright's features a simply appointed open dining room bathed in golden wood finishes, with diners feasting on New Orleans–inspired classics underneath a large boat skeleton. Always busy and a tad noisy, the restaurant serves dinner daily.

HOUSE SPECIALTIES The Mardi Gras pimento cheese fritters and the fried green tomatoes are the best appetizers. The best entrées are the shrimp and grits and the Nashville hot chicken (which isn't that hot).

OTHER RECOMMENDATIONS General Fulton's Prime Rib, slow-roasted in a chicory-coffee seasoning and served with mashed potatoes and horseradish cream.

SUMMARY AND COMMENTS The kitchen struggles with consistency when the restaurant is full. Stick to the basics.

Boma—Flavors of Africa ★★★★½

AFRICAN/BUFFET	EXPENSIVE	QUALITY ★★★★	VALUE ★★★★
READER-SURVEY RESPONSES ✪ 95% (Exceptional)			

Animal Kingdom Lodge & Villas–Jambo House; ☎ 407-939-3463

Reservations Highly recommended. **Dining Plan credits** 1 per person, per meal. **When to go** Breakfast or dinner. **Cost range** Breakfast $29 (child $16), dinner $49 (child $27). **Service** ★★★★½. **Friendliness** ★★★★. **Parking** Valet ($33) or hotel lot. **Bar** Full service. **Wine selection** All South African. **Dress** Casual. **Disabled access** Yes. **Customers** Hotel guests. **Breakfast** Daily, 7:30–11 a.m. **Dinner** Daily, 5–9:30 p.m.

SETTING AND ATMOSPHERE On the first floor of Animal Kingdom Lodge, Boma's huge dining room evokes an African marketplace, complete with thatched-roof ceilings. With so many tables and buffet dining stations, plus the massive open kitchen where guests can observe all the goings-on, the dining room can be loud during peak mealtimes. Still, large and small families alike find it welcoming.

HOUSE SPECIALTIES Boma's buffet takes guests to a culinary frontier full of rich flavors. Dishes represent regional cuisines from across Africa. Daily rotating entrées include carved African spice–crusted beef sirloin and whole-roasted salmon, plus a new recipe for slow-roasted ribs. Side dishes include spiced sweet potatoes, couscous, peanut rice, and Zulu cabbage. Cold prepared salads are ripe with fresh produce, ranging in flavor from sweet and sour (watermelon rind) to savory (lentils and hearts of palm). Boma's signature dessert, the Zebra Dome—a thin layer of white cake supporting an orb of Amarula cream-liqueur mousse, smothered with white chocolate ganache and drizzled with dark chocolate—has a cult following.

OTHER RECOMMENDATIONS A rotating selection of specialty soups—the carrot-ginger soup and Cape Malay lamb stew in particular are must-tries. Specialty dips and condiments such as Kalamata olive hummus, tamarind barbecue sauce, coriander chutney, and Masai Mara sauce (think a Kenyan pesto) will tickle taste buds as complements to any dish or bread. For breakfast, French toast bread pudding shines; made-to-order omelets and carved meats satisfy those in search of more American options.

SUMMARY AND COMMENTS Boma is consistently rated as one of the best restaurants in Walt Disney World—it's as much an attraction at the Animal Kingdom Lodge as, well, the animals. Boma's buffet includes fresh, seasonal, well-prepared offerings at each meal station. (Serving utensils are replaced very often these days.) And the value, at both breakfast and dinner, is almost impossible to beat. Advance Reservations are a must—walk-up tables here are few and far between.

California Grill ★★★★★

AMERICAN	EXPENSIVE	QUALITY ★★★★★	VALUE ★★★
READER-SURVEY RESPONSES ❂ 94% (Exceptional)			

Contemporary Resort; ☎ 407-939-3463

Reservations Highly recommended. **Dining Plan credits** 2 per person, per meal. **When to go** During evening fireworks. **Cost range** Dinner $32–$64 (child $11–$17). **Service** ★★★★★. **Friendliness** ★★★★★. **Parking** Hotel lot. **Bar** Full service. **Wine selection** Fantastic. **Dress** Dressy casual. **Disabled access** Yes. **Customers** Hotel guests and locals. **Dinner** Daily, 5–10 p.m.

SETTING AND ATMOSPHERE The beautiful California Grill remains one of the top choices for Disney dining, both for its remarkable view from the 15th floor of the Contemporary Resort and for its bustling open kitchen, which turns out spectacular fare. It can be crowded and noisy, filled with families who want a view of the Magic Kingdom fireworks, so book a table early or late for a somewhat quieter experience. A showstopping wine display comprises 1,600 bottles in a climate-controlled case just off the elevator. If you don't have a reservation, ask for a seat at the sushi bar, where you can order appetizers but not entrées, or the lounge, which serves the same menu as the restaurant.

HOUSE SPECIALTIES Try the braised beef short rib wonton if it's available. The plant-based Forbidden Roll might be the best sushi on the menu. Also try the pork tenderloin or oak-fired filet of beef. Outstanding wine list and craft cocktails.

ENTERTAINMENT AND AMENITIES Magic Kingdom fireworks are the star of the show and can be observed from the terrace—but only guests with dining reservations may watch from the Contemporary Resort's 15th floor.

SUMMARY AND COMMENTS In spite of the noise, California Grill is one of Walt Disney World's top dining experiences. The restaurant will debut a new dining concept in late 2021. Disney has't said what it'll entail. It's our guess that given the high ratings and high prices, Disney may not change much here.

Cape May Café ★★★

AMERICAN	EXPENSIVE	QUALITY ★★★	VALUE ★★★
READER-SURVEY RESPONSES ❂ 76% (Below Average)			

Beach Club Resort; ☎ 407-934-3358

Reservations Highly recommended. **Dining Plan credits** 1 per person, per meal. **When to go** Breakfast or dinner. **Cost range** Breakfast $25 (child $14), dinner $42 (child $25). Prices vary seasonally; check before you go. **Service** ★★★★★. **Friendliness** ★★★★★. **Parking** Hotel lot. **Bar** Full service. **Wine selection** Limited. **Dress** Casual. **Disabled access** Yes. **Customers** EPCOT and hotel guests. **Breakfast** Daily, 7:30–11:30 a.m. **Dinner** Daily, 5–9 p.m.

SETTING AND ATMOSPHERE Just off the lobby at the Beach Club, Cape May Cafe features nautical New England decor in two dining rooms and lots of comfortable seating.

HOUSE SPECIALTIES We couldn't identify anything special on our last visit.

SUMMARY AND COMMENTS Cape May Café is one of the Disney restaurants whose quality and ratings have suffered most during the pandemic. Switching to family-style dining from a buffet was always going to be a challenge, and the kitchen may not be configured properly for this kind of dining. Entrées include a seafood boil with shrimp, clams, and mahi mahi, and there's a "turf platter" with steak and chicken, but none of it is memorable. Better dining options include **Ale & Compass** (page 314) at Yacht Club and **Trattoria al Forno** (page 355) at BoardWalk Inn.

Le Cellier Steakhouse ★★★½

STEAK	EXPENSIVE	QUALITY ★★★½	VALUE ★★★
READER-SURVEY RESPONSES ➊ 90% (Average)			

Canada, World Showcase, EPCOT; ☎ 407-939-3463

Reservations Required. **Dining Plan credits** 2 per person, per meal. **When to go** Before 6 p.m. **Cost range** $34–$59 (child $11–$18). **Service** ★★★★. **Friendliness** ★★★★★. **Parking** EPCOT lot. **Bar** Full bar. **Wine selection** Canadian wines featured. **Dress** Casual. **Disabled access** Yes. **Customers** Theme park guests. **Lunch** Daily, noon–3:55 p.m. **Dinner** Daily, 4–9:30 p.m.

SETTING AND ATMOSPHERE Walk past the Canada Pavilion's pretty gardens into this small, darkened dining room, intended to evoke the look and feel of a wine cellar. Given the escalated prices, it doesn't feel upscale, with heavy wooden tables and no linens, but the crowd doesn't seem to mind—the steaks make up for the ambience. Service is "cheerful Canadian," meaning servers apologize to *you* if you spill something on *them*.

HOUSE SPECIALTIES Appetizer charcuterie plate that comes with an edible beef-fat candle—the idea is that you use the melted fat as a spread; AAA-Canadian filet mignon; Canadian Cheddar soup.

OTHER RECOMMENDATIONS For sides, share the five-cheese mac-and-cheese, the loaded mashed potatoes, or the poutine. For dessert, the warm pecan-brown butter tart. Excellent wine selection.

SUMMARY AND COMMENTS Le Cellier is another restaurant that has improved during the pandemic. It's still expensive, but the steaks are perfectly seasoned and cooked, with a beautiful char. Service is unrushed—it's possible for a full dinner to take 2 hours, so plan accordingly. The menu is the same at lunch and dinner.

Chef Art Smith's Homecomin' ★★★★

AMERICAN	MODERATE	QUALITY ★★★★	VALUE ★★★½
READER-SURVEY RESPONSES ➊ 95% (Exceptional; No. 8–rated restaurant in Walt Disney World)			

The Landing, Disney Springs; ☎ 407-560-0100

Reservations Highly recommended. **Dining Plan credits** 1 per person, per meal. **When to go** Lunch or dinner. **Cost range** $18–$32 (child $10). **Service** ★★★★. **Friendliness** ★★★★. **Parking** Disney Springs Orange garage. **Bar** Full service. **Wine selection** Modest. **Dress** Casual. **Disabled access** Yes. **Customers** Disney guests and locals. **Lunch and dinner** Daily, 11 a.m.–10 p.m. **Brunch** Saturday–Sunday, 9 a.m.–12:55 p.m.

SETTING AND ATMOSPHERE Florida farm-style decor with a reclaimed-wood-and-mason-jar vibe. Dining room chairs are covered in faux-burlap sacks. Florida born and raised, Art Smith is Oprah Winfrey's former private chef and is well known for his appearances on *Top Chef Masters* and *Iron Chef America.*

HOUSE SPECIALTIES The kitchen's specialty is fried chicken, optionally served with house-made sugar doughnuts. The Thigh High Chicken Biscuits appetizer very well may be one of the best food items on Disney property; be sure to check it out. The cocktails and desserts are fabulous.

OTHER RECOMMENDATIONS Beyond the fried chicken, the Art Burger is good; ask for the house-made pimento cheese instead of the menu's suggested slice of American. If you're from the South and live within driving distance of a barbecue restaurant, Homecomin's pork barbecue probably won't meet your standards (ours is Stamey's in Greensboro, North Carolina). Stick to the fried chicken and burgers and you'll be fine.

SUMMARY AND COMMENTS One of the best restaurants in Walt Disney World. If you can't get a table, try the bar.

Chef Mickey's ★★½

AMERICAN	EXPENSIVE	QUALITY ★★★	VALUE ★★★
READER-SURVEY RESPONSES ➕ 87% (Average)			

Contemporary Resort; ☎ 407-939-3463

Reservations Required. **Dining Plan credits** 1 per person, per meal. **When to go** Breakfast. **Cost range** Breakfast $42 (child $27), dinner $55 (child $36). Prices vary seasonally; check before you go. **Service** ★★★★. **Friendliness** ★★★★★. **Parking** Hotel lot. **Bar** Full service. **Wine selection** Fair. **Dress** Casual. **Disabled access** Yes. **Customers** Theme park guests. **Character breakfast** Daily, 7:30 a.m.–12:30 p.m. **Dinner** Daily, 5–10 p.m.

SETTING AND ATMOSPHERE Can you say *madhouse*? This big, open dining room with the monorail whizzing by overhead (inside the hotel) is a cacophony of children's and parents' voices. The food is secondary—everyone's here to see Mickey and his pals.

HOUSE SPECIALTIES Banana bread French toast, potato-cheese casserole with bacon and chives. At dinner, the gratin potato and farro wheat fried rice are better than average.

OTHER RECOMMENDATIONS All-you-care-to-eat family-style standard breakfast options, such as eggs, Mickey waffles, and bacon.

ENTERTAINMENT AND AMENITIES Character sightings.

SUMMARY AND COMMENTS As we went to press, meals were served family-style rather than as a buffet (the pre-pandemic version of the restaurant). Nothing on the dinner menu is as good as at EPCOT's Garden Grill or the Magic Kingdom's Liberty Tree Tavern, but you won't leave hungry, and the kids' choices will satisfy picky eaters. Best of all, nobody cares if the kids are loud.

Chefs de France ★★★

FRENCH	EXPENSIVE	QUALITY ★★★	VALUE ★★★
READER-SURVEY RESPONSES ➕ 88% (Average)			

France, World Showcase, EPCOT; ☎ 407-827-8709

Reservations Highly recommended. **Dining Plan credits** 1 per person, per meal. **When to go** Lunch or dinner. **Cost range** $25–$40 (child $9–$11.50); prix-fixe meal, $57. **Service** ★★★★★. **Friendliness** ★★★★★. **Parking** EPCOT lot. **Bar** Beer and cocktails. **Wine selection** Very good. **Dress** Casual. **Disabled access** Yes. **Customers** Theme park guests. **Lunch** Daily, 12:30–3 p.m. **Dinner** Daily, 4–8:55 p.m.

SETTING AND ATMOSPHERE It's like stepping into a busy bistro. The smells are delicious, with baguettes from the on-site bakery on every table. White cloth napkins and padded banquettes accentuate the classic bistro decor of the main dining room, where window tables make for fun people-watching on the World Showcase Promenade.

HOUSE SPECIALTIES Dishes inspired by the three French chefs for whom the restaurant is named: Paul Bocuse, Gaston Lenôtre, and Roger Vergé.

For the classic French experience, try the prix fixe menu with French onion soup topped with Gruyère for your appetizer and the Boeuf Bourguignon for your entrée.

OTHER RECOMMENDATIONS Ask your server for the vegetarian options.

SUMMARY AND COMMENTS The kitchen has struggled with the basics of food temperature and seasoning during our last couple of visits. The charcuterie plate isn't as good as the ones at Via Napoli or Le Cellier. Stick to the French onion soup and Boeuf Bourguignon.

Cinderella's Royal Table ★★★

AMERICAN	EXPENSIVE	QUALITY ★★★	VALUE ★★
READER-SURVEY RESPONSES ✪ 86% (Average)			

Cinderella Castle, Fantasyland, Magic Kingdom; ☎ 407-939-3463

Reservations Required; must prepay in full. **Dining Plan credits** 2 per person, per meal. **When to go** Early. **Cost range** $62 (child $37). Prices may vary seasonally; check before you go. **Service** ★★★★. **Friendliness** ★★★★. **Parking** Magic Kingdom lot. **Bar** Limited selection of sparkling wine by the glass and bottle. **Dress** Casual. **Disabled access** Limited. **Customers** Theme park guests. **Character lunch** Daily, 11 a.m.–2:55 p.m. **Character dinner** Daily, 3–9 p.m.

SETTING AND ATMOSPHERE A spiffy medieval banquet hall in the middle of Fantasyland. While the food is tasty, it's more about experiencing a meal in Cinderella Castle. Since reopening during the pandemic, only Cinderella makes an appearance. During our meal, that was three 3-minute circles along the outside walls of the dining area. Don't expect anything in the way of photos or interactions.

HOUSE SPECIALTIES Lunch and dinner have the same entrée selections: beef tenderloin, chicken breast, duck two ways, pan-seared scallops, or chickpea "fingers." For starters, try the charcuterie plate or the salad; for mains, the beef tenderloin comes with a Bordelaise sauce that should be sold by the bottle. Ask your server if you can sample each of the three desserts.

SUMMARY AND COMMENTS Food quality is better than average, it's less expensive than it was before (but still pricey), and service is good. For more on reserving a spot at the Royal Table, see page 273.

Cítricos ★★★½

MEDITERRANEAN	EXPENSIVE	QUALITY ★★★★½	VALUE ★★★
READER-SURVEY RESPONSES ✪ 81% (Average)			

Grand Floridian Resort & Spa; ☎ 407-939-3463

Reservations Required. **Dining Plan credits** 2 per person, per meal. **When to go** Dinner. **Cost range** $33–$53 (child $9–$16). **Service** ★★★★★. **Friendliness** ★★★★★. **Parking** Valet ($33); self-parking is deceptively far away. **Bar** Full service. **Wine selection** Very good. **Dress** Dressy casual. **Disabled access** Yes. **Customers** Hotel guests and locals. **Dinner** Daily, 5–9:30 p.m.

SETTING AND ATMOSPHERE Cítricos got a slight *Mary Poppins*–themed makeover before it reopened in 2021. The changes are subtle, though, and the restaurant feels upscale without being stuffy. The full-view show kitchen is still on display.

HOUSE SPECIALTIES The roulade of chicken belongs with rainbows and puppy dogs in the pantheon of things everyone should love. Sweet corn bisque; tilefish with chorizo "risotto"; house-made pasta.

OTHER RECOMMENDATIONS For starters, try the pork belly with plaintain croquette and salsa verde, or the smoked duck. The best dessert might be the orange blossom flan, a nice nod to the restaurant's name.

SUMMARY AND COMMENTS Cítricos is one of the few restaurants where our rating differs significantly from readers. Our rating is much higher, and the difference might be whether the reopened kitchen is able to deliver consistent quality night after night. Expect the menu to change often, and ask your server for their recommendations. If you can't get a reservation at Victoria & Albert's next door (see page 358; closed at press time), this is the next best thing we've eaten.

City Works Eatery and Pour House ★★★½

AMERICAN	MODERATE	QUALITY ★★★	VALUE ★★★
READER-SURVEY RESPONSES ⊕ 85% (Average)			

West Side, Disney Springs; ☎ 407-801-3730

Reservations Accepted. **Dining Plan credits** Not accepted. **When to go** Brunch, lunch, or dinner. **Cost range** $16–$38 (child $10–$11). **Service** ★★★★. **Friendliness** ★★★★. **Parking** Disney Springs Orange garage. **Bar** Full service. **Wine selection** Good. **Dress** Casual. **Disabled access** Yes. **Customers** Tourists. **Hours** Monday–Friday, 11 a.m.–10 p.m.; Saturday–Sunday, 10 a.m.–11 p.m.

SETTING AND ATMOSPHERE Indoor seating may be available; 17 outdoor seats can be very warm in the Florida sun.

HOUSE SPECIALTIES "A solid beer selection for brew nerds," says one of our resident beer experts. The fish tacos are a favorite.

SUMMARY AND COMMENTS City Works is a small chain of sports bars with an extensive list of beer taps. Its location near Cirque du Soleil means crowds before and after shows, once they resume. Food is standard for sports bars, with burgers and ribs.

Coral Reef Restaurant ★★½

SEAFOOD	EXPENSIVE	QUALITY ★★	VALUE ★★
READER-SURVEY RESPONSES ⊕ 84% (Below Average)			

The Seas with Nemo & Friends, Future World, EPCOT; ☎ 407-939-3463

Reservations Required. **Dining Plan credits** 1 per person, per meal. **When to go** Lunch. **Cost range** $24–$34 (child $11–$13). **Service** ★★★★. **Friendliness** ★★★★. **Parking** EPCOT lot. **Bar** Full service. **Wine selection** Good. **Dress** Casual. **Disabled access** Yes. **Customers** Theme park guests. **Lunch** Daily, 11:30 a.m.–3:30 p.m. **Dinner** Daily, 3:45–8 p.m.

SETTING AND ATMOSPHERE Though the decor could use a face-lift, you can't beat the view in this darkened dining room, which faces one of the world's largest saltwater aquariums; tiered seating gives everyone a pretty good view of the multitude of fishes (and sometimes Mickey in a scuba suit). The ethereal entryway gives the impression that you're going under the sea; special light fixtures throw ripple patterns on the ceiling.

HOUSE SPECIALTIES Lobster bisque, grilled rib eye, Chocolate Wave dessert. For kids, grilled fish, steak, chicken, or shrimp.

SUMMARY AND COMMENTS Not the best restaurant in EPCOT by a long shot, but Coral Reef is a great escape from the Florida sun. Grab a souvenir fish guide and check out the more than 2,000 sea creatures that call this place home—but that are probably not on the menu.

The Crystal Palace ★★½

AMERICAN	EXPENSIVE	QUALITY ★★★½	VALUE ★★★
READER-SURVEY RESPONSES ⊕ 78% (Much Below Average)			

Main Street, U.S.A., Magic Kingdom; ☎ 407-939-3463

Reservations Required. **Dining Plan credits** 1 per person, per meal. **When to go** Anytime. **Cost range** $39 (child $23). Prices vary seasonally; check before you go. **Service** ★★★. **Friendliness** ★★★★. **Parking** Magic Kingdom lot. **Bar** Wine and beer only. **Dress** Casual. **Disabled access** Yes. **Customers** Park guests. **Lunch** Daily, 11:30 a.m.–2:55 p.m. **Dinner** Daily, 3–9 p.m.

SETTING AND ATMOSPHERE A lunch visit to The Crystal Palace surrounds you with cool sunlight and decorative plants. The restaurant's white steel supports, arched ceilings, and glass roof (especially the atrium) are tributes to its namesake, built to house London's 1851 Great Exhibition—the first world's fair—and among the first structures to use plate glass in large quantities. Because of all the windows, the setting is less distinctive for dinner after dark.

HOUSE SPECIALTIES For appetizers, the seasonal salads are the best thing on the menu.

SUMMARY AND COMMENTS The Crystal Palace made a number of significant changes to reopen. Its buffet was replaced with a family-style menu, breakfast is no longer served, and characters no longer appear at meals.

The restaurant continues to have trouble maintaining its food quality. The crispy fried chicken is greasy, and the prime rib is tough and overcooked. The best of the bunch might be the plant-based Southern Fried Cauliflower, but nobody should have to pay $39 for albino broccoli. Likewise, the dessert portions are unusually small: one cupcake per table, which you're supposed to split among your group. *Really?*

Reader ratings for The Crystal Palace have dropped significantly with these changes. For the price of $39 per adult and $23 per child, we recommend **Liberty Tree Tavern** (see page 336) at the Magic Kingdom or **Garden Grill** (see page 327) at EPCOT instead.

The Edison ★★★

AMERICAN	EXPENSIVE	QUALITY ★★★½	VALUE ★★★
READER-SURVEY RESPONSES ◑ 79% (Below Average)			

The Landing, Disney Springs; ☎ 407-560-WATT (9288)

Reservations Recommended. **Dining Plan credits** 1 per person, per meal. **When to go** Dinner. **Cost range** $22–$42 (child $15). **Service** ★★★½. **Friendliness** ★★★★. **Parking** Disney Springs Orange garage. **Bar** Full service. **Wine selection** Good. **Dress** Casual. **Disabled access** Yes. **Customers** Tourists and locals on date night. **Dinner** Daily, 5–10 p.m.

SETTING AND ATMOSPHERE The concept: a 1920s electric company with high ceilings and themed rooms. Clips of black-and-white movies are projected onto some of the walls. With its steampunk aesthetic and abundance of gear imagery, the place has a distinct "Charlie Chaplin in *Modern Times*" vibe.

HOUSE SPECIALTIES The DB Clothesline Candied Bacon is the signature appetizer: four pieces of heavily smoked candied bacon and a few sprigs of rosemary clipped to a suspended string with clothespins. It's eminently Instagrammable—and that may be the entire point, because we don't know what the concept is supposed to be. The entrées are American comfort food: prime rib and burgers. The food is decent but pricey for what you get.

OTHER RECOMMENDATIONS Drinks are where The Edison shines. In addition to signature cocktails such as the Time Turner, made with Cruzan white rum, Campari, lime, pineapple, and orgeat (almond-flavored flower-water syrup), there are about 10 draft beers, along with bottled and canned beers and ciders; substantial wine offerings by the bottle and glass; a dozen vodkas; and almost as many varieties of gin, tequila, whiskey, and rum.

SUMMARY AND COMMENTS Beyond the bacon appetizer, we haven't identified a signature dish at The Edison, and it's not in the first or second tier of restaurants we'd recommend at Disney Springs. It's not a bad place for an after-dinner drink, but our experience in doing this is that service is terse.

ESPN Club *(closed at press time)* ★★½

AMERICAN/SANDWICHES	MODERATE	QUALITY ★★★	VALUE ★★★
READER-SURVEY RESPONSES ⊕ 82% (Below Average)			

BoardWalk; ☎ 407-939-1177

Reservations Accepted daily except for certain dates; see tinyurl.com/wdwespnclub for details. **Dining Plan credits** 1 per person, per meal. **When to go** Lunch or dinner. **Cost range** $15–$28 (child $9–$12). **Service** ★★★. **Friendliness** ★★★★. **Parking** BoardWalk lot. **Bar** Full service. **Wine selection** Minimal. **Dress** Casual. **Disabled access** Yes. **Customers** Tourists. **Hours** Monday–Friday, noon–11 p.m.; Saturday–Sunday, 11 a.m.–11 p.m. *Note:* There is a cover charge during big games.

SETTING AND ATMOSPHERE This is a sports bar to the nth degree, with basketball-court flooring, sports memorabilia, and more TV monitors than a network affiliate. The bar area features satellite sports-trivia video games. A large octagonal space with a wall of TVs serves as the main dining room.

HOUSE SPECIALTIES Burgers and chicken sandwiches, fish-and-chips, nachos with chicken or shrimp.

SUMMARY AND COMMENTS If you plan to watch a big sports event, go early—or run away—as the line often spills out the door and onto the sidewalks. It's incredibly noisy and fun, with large portions and decent quality. And don't worry about missing a play—there are even TVs in the restrooms.

50's Prime Time Cafe ★★★

AMERICAN	MODERATE	QUALITY ★★★	VALUE ★★★
READER-SURVEY RESPONSES ⊕ 87% (Average)			

Echo Lake, Disney's Hollywood Studios; ☎ 407-939-3463

Reservations Highly recommended. **Dining Plan credits** 1 per person, per meal. **When to go** Lunch or dinner. **Cost range** $17–$26 (child $10–$13). **Service** ★★★★★. **Friendliness** ★★★★★. **Parking** DHS lot. **Bar** Full service. **Wine selection** Good. **Dress** Casual. **Disabled access** Yes. **Customers** Theme park guests. **Lunch** Daily, 11 a.m.–3:55 p.m. **Dinner** Daily, 4–7 p.m.

SETTING AND ATMOSPHERE Dine in a 1950s kitchen stocked with antique fridges, laminate tabletops, sunburst clocks, and decoupage art made from preserved fruit. Black-and-white TVs play vintage sitcom clips while you wait for your entrées.

HOUSE SPECIALTIES Pot roast, fried chicken, meat loaf, plus a sampler platter with some of each; PB&J milkshake and other retro fare. Desserts are a strong point, with warm apple crisp and a chocolate–peanut butter layer cake being the highlights.

SUMMARY AND COMMENTS Though the restaurant is usually packed and noisy, the waitstaff makes it worthwhile, admonishing you just like Mom did to "Take your elbows off the table!" and "Green beans are nature's French fries."

Flying Fish *(closed at press time)* ★★★★

SEAFOOD	EXPENSIVE	QUALITY ★★★★	VALUE ★★★
READER-SURVEY RESPONSES ⊕ 89% (Average)			

BoardWalk; ☎ 407-939-3463

Reservations Highly recommended. **Dining Plan credits** 2 per person, per meal. **When to go** Dinner. **Cost range** $33–$59 (child $13–$23). **Service** ★★★★★. **Friendliness** ★★★★★. **Parking** Valet ($33) or Boardwalk hotel lot. **Bar** Full service. **Wine selection** Extensive. **Dress** Dressy casual. **Disabled access** Yes. **Customers** Hotel guests; locals. **Dinner** Daily, 5–9:30 p.m.

SETTING AND ATMOSPHERE Situated at the heart of the BoardWalk, Flying Fish takes diners under the sea for an upscale modern seafood dinner enveloped by classy deep blue– and silver-rich restaurant decor. The open kitchen and showcase bar entertain guests seated near the front of the bustling restaurant, with diners enjoying a more muted experience in the rear of the main dining room.

HOUSE SPECIALTIES Hokkaido scallops with antebellum grits shines on the seafood-dominant menu, though landlubbers will be perfectly content with the Angus filet mignon. Soup and salad, rotating frequently throughout every season, are solid ways to start any meal here, with both highlighting the freshest produce Florida has to offer. The oak-grilled salmon will hit all the high notes. Adroit bartenders craft specialty cocktails that pair with most meals, while a strong wine program complements every dish from start to finish. Complete your meal at Flying Fish with the visually striking and delicious Florida Sunset dessert or the always-competent chef's selection of artisanal cheeses.

OTHER RECOMMENDATIONS House fish specials are different every day and are accompanied by the freshest seasonal vegetables you can find at Walt Disney World.

SUMMARY AND COMMENTS A mainstay of Disney World's fine-dining roster, Flying Fish impresses with its upscale food and attentive service. The kitchen can sometimes force a slower-paced meal here, but the food is always worth the wait. Enjoy a fancy night out on the BoardWalk with an aperitif at neighboring **AbracadaBar** before settling into the Flying Fish dining experience.

The Fountain ★★

AMERICAN	MODERATE	QUALITY ★★	VALUE ★★
READER-SURVEY RESPONSES ✪ 67% (Much Below Average)			

Dolphin Hotel; ☎ 407-934-1609

Reservations Not accepted. **Dining Plan credits** Not accepted. **When to go** Lunch or dinner. **Cost range** $12–$18 (child $9–$11). **Service** ★★★★. **Friendliness** ★★★★. **Bar** Beer and wine only. **Wine selection** Limited. **Parking** Valet ($39) or hotel lot ($29), both free with validation. **Dress** Casual. **Disabled access** Yes. **Customers** Hotel guests. **Lunch and dinner** Thursday–Friday, 4–11 p.m.; Saturday–Sunday, noon–11 p.m.

SETTING AND ATMOSPHERE Informal soda-shop ambience.

HOUSE SPECIALTIES Hot dogs and burgers (including veggie and turkey burgers), milkshakes (we love the PB&J), and ice cream.

OTHER RECOMMENDATIONS Big salads, including seared salmon and chicken Caesar.

SUMMARY AND COMMENTS The Fountain probably isn't the best choice for calorie counters.

Fresh Mediterranean Market ★★½

MEDITERRANEAN/AMERICAN	MODERATE	QUALITY ★★½	VALUE ★★
READER-SURVEY RESPONSES ✪ 90% (Above Average)			

Dolphin Hotel; ☎ 407-934-1609

Reservations Recommended. **Dining Plan credits** Not accepted. **When to go** Breakfast or lunch. **Cost range** Breakfast $10–$29 (child $11–$18), lunch $14–$15. **Service** ★★★★. **Friendliness** ★★★★. **Parking** Valet ($39) or hotel lot ($29), both free with validation. **Bar** Beer, wine, and limited cocktails. **Wine selection** Limited. **Dress** Casual. **Disabled access** Yes. **Customers** Hotel guests. **Breakfast and lunch** Saturday-Wednesday, 7–11:30 a.m. Days of operation may vary according to hotel occupancy.

SETTING AND ATMOSPHERE A pleasant-enough room with floor-level windows. Ask for a veranda table if you want to have a quiet conversation away from the action in the open kitchen.

HOUSE SPECIALTIES *Breakfast:* Fresh pressed juices, made-to-order omelets, oatmeal, grits, sliced avocado, pastries, and mimosas. *Lunch:* Wraps, salads, smoothies, and wines by the glass.

OTHER RECOMMENDATIONS Crafted House Bloody Mary.

SUMMARY AND COMMENTS The menu is as spartan as the setting, but if you're looking for healthful and organic choices, this is the spot.

Frontera Cocina ★★★½

MEXICAN	EXPENSIVE	QUALITY ★★★½	VALUE ★★★
READER-SURVEY RESPONSES ✪ 77% (Below Average)			

Town Center, Disney Springs; ☎ 407-939-3463

Reservations Highly recommended. **Dining Plan credits** 1 per person, per meal. **When to go** Dinner. **Cost range** $19–$42.50 (children $9.50). **Service** ★★★★. **Friendliness** ★★★★. **Parking** Disney Springs Lime garage. **Bar** Full service. **Wine selection** Modest. **Dress** Casual. **Disabled access** Yes. **Customers** Disney guests and locals. **Lunch and dinner** Daily, 11 a.m.–11 p.m.

SETTING AND ATMOSPHERE Though the exterior presents with muted beige walls and white accents meant to evoke classic Florida waterfront architecture, bright pops of color from the centerpiece chandelier and bar accents highlight the sleek modern eatery's interior, made casual by exposed ductwork and cozy dark-wood furnishings. The open show kitchen and Wall of Fame shelves, packed with specialty liquors and wines, are bathed in natural sunlight from the large windows on nearly every wall, showcasing the springs and the patio from the back dining room.

HOUSE SPECIALTIES Tacos with carne asada or chipotle chicken, chicken enchiladas in red sauce, plantains, margaritas and specialty tequila flights.

OTHER RECOMMENDATIONS Guacamole, coconut-lime cuatro leches cake. The dessert menu is small; kids may be happier with a cupcake from nearby Sprinkles.

SUMMARY AND COMMENTS The menu often spotlights the flavors and ingredients of a particular region of Mexico. Frontera Cocina To Go, a walk-up window, serves two kinds of tacos, soft drinks, beer, and margaritas.

Garden Grill Restaurant ★★★

AMERICAN	EXPENSIVE	QUALITY ★★★	VALUE ★★★
READER-SURVEY RESPONSES ✪ 92% (Above Average)			

The Land, Future World, EPCOT; ☎ 407-939-3463

Reservations Required. **Dining Plan credits** 1 per person, per meal. **When to go** Anytime. **Cost range** $55 (child $36). Prices vary seasonally; check before you go. **Service** ★★★★. **Friendliness** ★★★★★. **Parking** EPCOT lot. **Bar** Wine, beer, and mixed drinks. **Wine selection** Fair. **Dress** Casual. **Disabled access** Yes. **Customers** Theme park guests. **Character lunch** 11:30 a.m.–3:30 p.m. **Character dinner** 3:45–8:30 p.m.

SETTING AND ATMOSPHERE With the popular Soarin' Around the World attraction nearby, the all-you-can-eat Garden Grill stays busy, even though the concept and the dining room have grown rather dated. Even so, it's a classic: The floor revolves slowly as you peer down into the unseen side of scenes from Living with the Land, the Land Pavilion's ride-through attraction (see page 523). At about the time you finish a meal, you've revolved once, past scenes of a desert, a rainforest, and a farm—an otherwise hidden view of inside the farmhouse. The constant crowing of a "rooster" and dog barks are questionable highlights.

Much more exciting for kids are the Disney characters—Mickey, Chip 'n' Dale, Pluto, and others make stops along the inner wall of the circular restaurant, far enough away to be safe but close enough for good photos.

HOUSE SPECIALTIES Grilled beef, chimichurri, turkey breast with stuffing and gravy, BBQ ribs, mashed potatoes, veggies, and salads made with ingredients from The Land's greenhouses. Dessert is a berry shortcake with whipped cream. Plant-based options available on request.

ENTERTAINMENT AND AMENITIES The view. Character dining at both meals. Free nonalcoholic beverages included with meals.

SUMMARY AND COMMENTS The food quality is, in our estimation, just OK. Nevertheless, readers really seem to like Garden Grill; we think the retro-Disney setting and the characters are at least as much of a draw as the food. If you can't get an Advance Reservation for one of the other character meals, this place is worth checking out.

Garden Grove ★★

AMERICAN	MODERATE	QUALITY ★★★	VALUE ★★
READER-SURVEY RESPONSES Not enough surveys to rate			

Swan Hotel; ☎ 407-934-1609

Reservations Recommended. **Dining Plan credits** Not accepted. **When to go** Breakfast or brunch. **Cost range** $14–$27 (child $7–$8). **Service** ★★★. **Friendliness** ★★★. **Parking** Valet ($39) or hotel lot ($29), both free with validation. **Bar** Full service. **Wine selection** Good. **Dress** Casual. **Disabled access** Yes. **Customers** Hotel guests, some locals, tourists. **Breakfast** Daily, 7 a.m.–2 p.m.

SETTING AND ATMOSPHERE A spacious dining room features a 25-foot faux oak tree in the center. When it's open at night, the lights are dimmed and the oak tree is illuminated with lanterns and twinkling lights.

HOUSE SPECIALTIES Familiar breakfast combinations, including waffles, French toast, and eggs.

SUMMARY AND COMMENTS Garden Grove isn't worth a special trip if you aren't staying at the Swan. But the room is pretty, and the food is plentiful.

Geyser Point Bar & Grill ★★★

AMERICAN	MODERATE	QUALITY ★★★½	VALUE ★★★
READER-SURVEY RESPONSES ◐ 96% (Above Average)			

Wilderness Lodge & Boulder Ridge/Copper Creek Villas; ☎ 407-939-3463

Reservations Not accepted. **Dining Plan credits** 1 per person, per meal. **When to go** Lunch or dinner. **Cost range** $10–$17 (child $7). **Service** ★★★½. **Friendliness** ★★★★. **Parking** Valet ($44) or hotel lot. **Bar** Full service. **Customers** Hotel guests. **Wine selection** Fair. **Lunch/dinner** 11 a.m.–11 p.m.

SETTING AND ATMOSPHERE Picturesque views of the resort's geyser and pool area along with Bay Lake. Geyser Point is a hybrid quick-service restaurant and table-service lounge, with both sharing the same lovely seating area. The main food offerings are counter service, but a substantial bar menu features imaginative drinks and hearty snacks.

HOUSE SPECIALTIES A step up from most standard quick-service fare, lighter lunch and dinner options include a turkey sandwich with cranberry mayo and an upgraded bison cheeseburger with Tillamook Cheddar and marionberry sauce that impresses without being stuffy or overpriced.

OTHER RECOMMENDATIONS The veggie-packed portobello salad can be ordered with salmon, chicken, or steak.

SUMMARY AND COMMENTS The quality of the food and the view of the resort area from any given table combine to create an upscale quick-service dining experience. Best of all, guests don't have to fuss with paper plates and trays of food in the busy dining area; ordered food is delivered to guests at their chosen tables on real dishes with nonplastic silverware (or neatly packaged in to-go containers, if so desired).

This family from London thinks Geyser Point is worth a quick boat or bus ride from the Magic Kingdom:

We found Geyser Point to be a brilliant place for lunch after a morning in the Magic Kingdom. Although not air-conditioned, it was still cool, very relaxing with nice views and comfortable chairs. Plus it's quick-service, but you get waited on.

Grand Floridian Cafe ★★½

AMERICAN	MODERATE	QUALITY ★★★	VALUE ★★
READER-SURVEY RESPONSES ⊕ 91% (Above Average)			

Grand Floridian Resort & Spa; ☎ 407-939-3463

Reservations Recommended. **Dining Plan credits** 1 per person, per meal. **When to go** Anytime. **Cost range** Breakfast and lunch $16–$27 (child $9–$12), dinner $16–$34 (child $10–$15). **Service** ★★★. **Friendliness** ★★★★. **Parking** Valet ($33); self-parking is far away. **Bar** Full service. **Wine selection** Good. **Dress** Casual. **Disabled access** Yes. **Customers** Hotel guests. **Breakfast** Daily, 7:30–11 a.m. **Lunch** Daily, 11:05 a.m.–2 p.m. **Dinner** Daily, 5–9 p.m.

SETTING AND ATMOSPHERE Light and airy decor with lots of sunlight, servers dressed in Victorian costumes, and pretty views of the pool and courtyard. Open three meals a day for casual dining.

HOUSE SPECIALTIES The extensive breakfast and lunch menu includes breakfast items—eggs Benedict, buttermilk pancakes, tomato-and-Feta quiche, and miso-glazed salmon—and lunch choices, such as the Lobster "Thermidor" Burger (a beef patty with lobster-Parmesan sauce). For dinner, the buttermilk-fried chicken remains outstanding. Other dinner options include miso-glazed salmon, the lobster burger, and New York strip.

OTHER RECOMMENDATIONS Any dessert the kitchen recommends.

SUMMARY AND COMMENTS A quick place to grab a tasty bite in a pleasantly themed room.

La Hacienda de San Angel ★★★

MEXICAN	EXPENSIVE	QUALITY ★★★½	VALUE ★★½
READER-SURVEY RESPONSES ⊕ 87% (Average)			

Mexico, World Showcase, EPCOT; ☎ 407-939-3463

Reservations Required. **Dining Plan credits** 1 per person, per meal. **When to go** Dinner. **Cost range** $22–$48 (child $10–$10.50). **Service** ★★★★. **Friendliness** ★★★★★. **Parking** EPCOT lot. **Bar** Full service. **Wine selection** Good. **Dress** Casual. **Disabled access** Yes. **Customers** Theme park guests. **Hours** Daily, 4 p.m.–park closing.

SETTING AND ATMOSPHERE Right along the waterfront in Mexico, La Hacienda is a primo spot for watching fireworks through the tall windows. The interior has authentic touches of Mexico in its lighting and decor.

HOUSE SPECIALTIES Excellent guacamole; queso fundido; carne asada–style New York strip; flank steak fajitas with bacon, poblano and bell peppers, cheese, and salsa; and fried-shrimp tacos with chipotle-lime aioli.

OTHER RECOMMENDATIONS For starters, try the flautas—fried tortillas with potato, chipotle chicken, cheese, and ranchero sauce. The margaritas are the real deal—or just go for a flight of fine tequila.

SUMMARY AND COMMENTS The menu is simple, but the quality is first rate. Also, one word: tequila.

Hollywood & Vine ★★½

AMERICAN	EXPENSIVE	QUALITY ★★★	VALUE ★★★
READER-SURVEY RESPONSES ✪ 76% (Much Below Average)			

Echo Lake, Disney's Hollywood Studios; ☎ 407-939-3463

Reservations Highly recommended. **Dining Plan credits** 1 per person, per meal. **When to go** Breakfast, lunch, or dinner. **Cost range** Breakfast $42 (child $27), lunch and dinner $55 (child $36). Prices may vary seasonally; check before you go. **Service** ★★★★. **Friendliness** ★★★★★. **Parking** DHS lot. **Bar** Full service. **Wine selection** Limited. **Dress** Casual. **Disabled access** Yes. **Customers** DHS guests. **Character breakfast** Daily, 8:30–10:30 a.m. **Lunch** Daily, 11:30 a.m.–3:55 p.m. **Dinner** Daily, 4–8 p.m.

SETTING AND ATMOSPHERE Just off Hollywood Boulevard, this 1940s-era diner has a sleek Art Deco design (think chrome and tile) that gets lost amid all the Disney-character frenzy. Breakfast includes characters from Disney Junior, such as Doc McStuffins and Fancy Nancy, while seasonal lunches and dinners feature Minnie, Mickey, Goofy, Pluto, and Donald (and sometimes Daisy), usually in holiday- or Hollywood-themed outfits, staying a safe distance from guests.

HOUSE SPECIALTIES At breakfast, the caramel monkey bread is essentially French toast raised to a higher dimension. At dinner, try the beef tenderloin, roasted turkey, mac and cheese with shrimp, or roasted pork. There's also a plant-based option, most recently an asparagus-and-truffle risotto.

SUMMARY AND COMMENTS The only value to be found here is at breakfast, especially if you have children who are fans of Disney Junior shows.

The Hollywood Brown Derby ★★★★

AMERICAN	EXPENSIVE	QUALITY ★★★★	VALUE ★★★
READER-SURVEY RESPONSES ✪ 93% (Above Average)			

Hollywood Boulevard, Disney's Hollywood Studios; ☎ 407-939-3463

Reservations Highly recommended. **Dining Plan credits** 2 per person, per meal. **When to go** Early evening. **Cost range** $20–$49 (child $8–$16). **Service** ★★★★★. **Friendliness** ★★★★★. **Parking** DHS lot. **Bar** Full service. **Wine selection** Very good. **Dress** Casual. **Disabled access** Yes. **Customers** Theme park guests. **Lunch** Daily, 11 a.m.–3:55 p.m. **Dinner** Daily, 4–7 p.m.

SETTING AND ATMOSPHERE An oasis of civility in the middle of a theme park, this is a replica of the original Brown Derby on Vine Street in Hollywood (the Wilshire Boulevard Brown Derby was the one shaped like a hat). The sunken dining room has a certain elegance, with tuxedoed waiters, curved booths, and white linen. Tall palm trees in huge pots stand in the center of the room and reach for the high ceiling. Ask for a seat on the second-level gallery; it's much quieter and affords good people-watching in the hectic main space.

HOUSE SPECIALTIES Cobb salad (named for Bob Cobb, owner of the original restaurant); the famous grapefruit cake made from the original Brown Derby recipe. Kids' menu includes beef filet, a fish special, and grilled chicken breast.

OTHER RECOMMENDATIONS The restaurant's signature burger might be the best in any Disney theme park, with pastrami, Gruyère cheese, heirloom tomato, fried egg, and cognac-based mustard. Order it medium-rare. Or try the Bell and Evans chicken breast with red pepper–and–Toma cheese polenta cakes and an amazing Madeira jus.

SUMMARY AND COMMENTS The Brown Derby is one of the top theme park restaurants at Disney World, and it has thrived during the pandemic. It's expensive, yes, but also a wonderful way to relax and regenerate. This reader from Montgomery, Alabama, recommends staying away from the entrées to save money:

I love The Hollywood Brown Derby. It's so nice to escape the parks, heat, and people in the refined, cool, quiet, and it doesn't have to cost much more than many other meals. I get the Cobb Salad, the lovely margarita flight, and the dessert trio.

If you don't have reservations, the patio lounge opens at 11 a.m. and is first come, first served, with a menu of small plates and cocktails, and it's a good place to have a drink and wait until your table is ready.

This reader from Hudson, New York, found the patio lounge a good venue for watching the Studios' live entertainment:

Our two favorite spots were the Nomad Lounge [see page 352] and the Brown Derby patio lounge! We sat just outside the door to the regular Brown Derby restaurant, so the air-conditioning from inside kept us cool midday in July. We also had a great view of the Star Wars *show from our spot!*

Drink choices are far more extensive than Disney's online menu might indicate and include various flights—martinis, margaritas, Champagnes, white and red wines, Scotches, and Grand Marnier vintages—along with wines by the bottle and by the glass, beer, and classic cocktails.

House of Blues Restaurant & Bar ★★★

REGIONAL AMERICAN   MODERATE   QUALITY ★★★½   VALUE ★★★
READER-SURVEY RESPONSES ✪ 90% (Average)

West Side, Disney Springs; ☎ 407-934-2583

Reservations Recommended. **Dining Plan credits** 1 per person, per meal. **When to go** Lunch or early dinner; weekend brunch. **Cost range** Brunch $13–$26, lunch and dinner $17–$32 (child $10). **Service** ★★★★. **Friendliness** ★★★. **Parking** Disney Springs Orange garage. **Bar** Full service. **Wine selection** Modest. **Dress** Casual. **Disabled access** Yes. **Customers** Blues lovers. **Brunch** Saturday–Sunday: 10 a.m.–2 p.m. **Lunch** Daily, 11:30 a.m.–3:55 p.m. **Dinner** Daily, 4–11 p.m.

SETTING AND ATMOSPHERE Adjacent to the Cirque du Soleil theater, House of Blues has a ramshackle look that's almost out of place in Disney Springs, but it's a solid stop for lunch or dinner before or after a show. And with its own separate concert hall, great live music, including the lively Sunday gospel brunch, should return once the pandemic is under control. A quick-service window (the Smokehouse), along with the outdoor bar and seating, draws passersby. But if you have time for a sit-down meal, the fabulous folk art in the restaurant is worth a look.

HOUSE SPECIALTIES Barbecue sandwiches (pulled pork and brisket), ribs, steaks, burgers, and shrimp and grits.

OTHER RECOMMENDATIONS Jambalaya and jalapeño cornbread.

SUMMARY AND COMMENTS Meat-centric menu on Disney Springs' West Side in a fun and casual setting.

Il Mulino New York ★★★

ITALIAN	EXPENSIVE	QUALITY ★★★	VALUE ★★
READER-SURVEY RESPONSES ⊕ 80% (Below Average)			

Swan Hotel; ☎ 407-939-3463

Reservations Recommended. **Dining Plan credits** Not accepted. **When to go** Dinner. **Cost range** $22–$48 (child $12–$16). **Service** ★★. **Friendliness** ★★. **Parking** Valet ($39) or hotel lot ($29), both free with validation. **Bar** Full service. **Wine selection** Good. **Dress** Dressy casual. **Disabled access** Yes. **Customers** Mostly hotel guests and conventioneers. **Hours** Daily, 5–11 p.m.

SETTING AND ATMOSPHERE A spin-off of the acclaimed Manhattan restaurant, Il Mulino takes an upscale-casual, downtown New York approach to Italian cuisine, with family-style platters for sharing. Tables are dark wood, and an open kitchen creates a bustle. You can request private dining in one of the smaller rooms.

HOUSE SPECIALTIES The cuisine focuses on Italy's Abruzzo region, with hearty pastas and big cuts of meat. Try the spaghetti carbonara or the veal saltimbocca. Risottos are well made; spaghetti with baby shrimp, scallops, clams, mussels, and calamari is well made but overpriced.

OTHER RECOMMENDATIONS Charcuterie, mussels in white wine, pizzas, sautéed jumbo shrimp, rib eye with sautéed spinach.

SUMMARY AND COMMENTS A predictable menu with a little bit of everything you would expect in a bustling Italian restaurant: pizza, pasta, meat, seafood. Il Mulino New York was perfect for conventioneers—but there aren't many left—so adventurous eaters may want to go elsewhere.

Jaleo by José Andrés ★★★★

SPANISH/TAPAS	MODERATE	QUALITY ★★★★	VALUE ★★★★
READER-SURVEY RESPONSES ⊕ 95% (Much Above Average; No. 7-rated restaurant in Walt Disney World)			

West Side, Disney Springs; ☎ 407-939-3463

Reservations Highly recommended. **Dining Plan credits** 2 per person, per meal. **When to go** Dinner. **Cost range** Tapas $12–$20 (child $10–$14). **Service** ★★★★. **Friendliness** ★★★★. **Parking** Disney Springs Orange garage. **Bar** Full bar with emphasis on Spanish drinks and wines. **Dress** Casual. **Disabled access** Yes. **Customers** Locals and Disney resort guests. **Hours** Monday–Wednesday, 4–9 p.m.; Thursday–Saturday, 4–10 p.m.

SETTING AND ATMOSPHERE Jaleo's entrance is an expansive, open space with tile mosaics and large-scale photo murals of iconic Spanish scenes on the walls. Warm colors from lighting in the kitchen and dining areas bathe the restaurant, reflecting off metal accents. The highlight is the paella pit and accompanying view into the kitchen—every time one of the massive paella dishes has finished cooking, the chefs ring a bell and the entire restaurant joins in the celebration.

HOUSE SPECIALTIES The restaurant serves Spain's famed aged ibérico ham. A selection of Spanish cheeses and, of course, traditional pan de cristal con tomate are both good first courses. Garlic shrimp and grilled chicken with garlic sauce burst with flavor, highlighting incredibly fresh produce and tons of herbs (with rosemary and cilantro at the fore). Our table nearly came to blows fighting over the last morsels of patatas bravas—fried potatoes topped with spicy tomato sauce and aioli. As for the paella, it's decent. The kitchen seems reluctant to serve the socarrat—the intensely flavorful crispy rice at the bottom of the paella pan—to Americans. To us that's like serving Thanksgiving turkey without the skin. Ask the waitstaff, though, and they'll bring you some.

OTHER RECOMMENDATIONS Drinks are on par with other Disney Springs restaurants in terms of pricing and quality: $12–$16 will get you a cocktail off Jaleo's varied drink menu, with beers in the $8–$9 range and a high-quality selection of vermouth. The wine menu is extensive, featuring a pretty nifty table at the front describing standard wine qualities and color-coding them on the subsequent menu.

SUMMARY AND COMMENTS This restaurant from celebrity chef José Andrés brings classic Spanish cuisine to Disney Springs' West Side neighborhood. We think Jaleo is one of the best restaurants in Disney Springs.

Jiko—The Cooking Place ★★★★½

AFRICAN/FUSION   EXPENSIVE   QUALITY ★★★★   VALUE ★★★
READER-SURVEY RESPONSES ✪ 96% (Exceptional)

Animal Kingdom Lodge & Villas–Jambo House; ☎ 407-939-3463

Reservations Required. **Dining Plan credits** 2 per person, per meal. **When to go** Dinner. **Cost range** $30–$57 (child $9–$17). **Service ★★★★★. Friendliness ★★★★★.** **Parking** Valet ($33) or hotel lot. **Bar** Full bar. **Wine selection** All South African. **Dress** Dressy casual. **Disabled access** Yes. **Customers** Hotel guests and locals. **Hours** Daily, 5:30–10 p.m.

SETTING AND ATMOSPHERE Bathed in a perpetual sunset, with metal birds soaring around, the main dining room is warm and inviting, accented by the central *jiko* ("cooking place" in Swahili), where chefs prepare many of the appetizers featured on the restaurant's seasonally rotating menu in view of a few lucky diners. As you enter, stop to gaze at the wine room. The bottles on display represent just a sample of the massive wine selection—the largest collection of South African wines available in any North American restaurant.

HOUSE SPECIALTIES Guests flock to Jiko for several dishes, among them the grilled wild-boar tenderloin appetizer, African spice–infused flatbreads, sustainable Vulcan-spiced fish, and oak-grilled filet mignon with South African red wine sauce and bobotie mac and cheese. The seasonally updated malva (mallow) pudding dessert highlights traditional African flavors on the sweet spectrum.

OTHER RECOMMENDATIONS Botswanan-style beef short ribs and Moroccan lamb tagine bring on the spices, while luscious seasonal soups like the curried cauliflower bisque start any meal off on the right foot. For those in search of vegan and vegetarian options, Jiko stands out as one of the few Disney Signature restaurants to offer dedicated options that are both satisfying and flavorful. A large selection of specialty teas and Kenyan press-pot coffee complement the excellent dessert selections.

SUMMARY AND COMMENTS Tucked away in a quiet corner of Animal Kingdom Lodge, Jiko is one of the true hidden gems of fine dining in Walt Disney World. Superb service in a nonfussy atmosphere can be tough to pull off, but Jiko does that and more, welcoming guests into the cooking place for a meal packed with truly unique flavors. Families will enjoy the dining room's perpetual sunset, while solo diners or small parties may want to take advantage of the cooking place's seating for both dinner and a show.

Jiko has remained good for a long time, even through the pandemic and chef and staff changes. The experience of this reader from Columbia, Missouri, is typical:

Jiko was fabulous! My husband and I went on a date and ended up sitting next to a nice family who had two younger kids with them. They were a bit loud, but we didn't mind. Near the end of our meal, the server brought us two complimentary martinis at the manager's request because of the "noisy" table nearby. That was good service even though we weren't inconvenienced. In fact, we shared our martinis with them and had a great conversation!

Jock Lindsey's Hangar Bar ★★

COCKTAILS AND BAR BITES	INEXPENSIVE	QUALITY ★★	VALUE ★★
READER-SURVEY RESPONSES ● 93% (Above Average)			

The Landing, Disney Springs; ☎ 407-939-3463

Reservations Not accepted. **Dining Plan credits** Not accepted. **When to go** Anytime. **Cost range** Appetizers $10.50–$22, alcoholic drinks $11.75–$16. **Service** ★★★★. **Friendliness** ★★★★. **Parking** Disney Springs Lime garage. **Bar** Full service. **Wine selection** OK; beer selection is better. **Dress** Casual. **Disabled access** Yes. **Customers** Theme park guests. **Hours** Daily, noon–10 p.m.

SETTING AND ATMOSPHERE The backstory: A 1940s-era airplane hangar belonging to Indiana Jones's indefatigable pilot has been converted to a bar. Naturally, references to Indy Jones and aviation suffuse the decor (a mammoth propeller dangling from the rafters, for example). Booth, bar, and table seating are available, all of it kid-friendly, as is covered outdoor seating.

HOUSE SPECIALTIES The wings, tacos, and flatbreads, while fancifully named, are standard-issue bar grub: Air Pirate's Pretzels are, well, pretzels, and Snakebite Sliders are miniburgers that you could get at virtually any chain "neighborhood grill."

OTHER RECOMMENDATIONS Creative cocktails such as the Hovito Mojito, made with Barsol Quebranta Pisco (a Peruvian brandy), fresh lime, mint, simple syrup, and club soda, and the Bedtime Story, made with Absolut Mandarin vodka, Domaine de Canton ginger liqueur, hibiscus syrup, fresh lemon juice, and iced tea.

SUMMARY AND COMMENTS With such touches as a sign that advises ARTIFACTS NO LONGER TAKEN AS PAYMENT, Jock Lindsey's is long on gimmicks—not a bad thing if you're a movie buff, but the food and drinks take a back seat to the gimmickry.

Jungle Navigation Co. Ltd. Skipper Canteen ★★★½

ASIAN/AFRICAN/LATIN	EXPENSIVE	QUALITY ★★★	VALUE ★★★
READER-SURVEY RESPONSES ● 93% (Much Above Average)			

Adventureland, Magic Kingdom; ☎ 407-939-3463

Reservations Highly recommended. **Dining Plan credits** 1 per person, per meal. **When to go** Lunch or dinner. **Cost range** $19–$34 (child $10–$13). **Service** ★★★★. **Friendliness** ★★★★. **Parking** Magic Kingdom lot. **Bar** Limited selection of beer and wine. **Dress** Casual. **Disabled access** Yes. **Customers** Magic Kingdom guests. **Lunch** Daily, 11:30 a.m.–2:55 p.m. **Dinner** Daily, 3–9 p.m.

SETTING AND ATMOSPHERE Posited as the home of off-duty Jungle Cruise skippers, Skipper Canteen offers guests an oasis from the theme park with three distinct dining rooms (and a boatload of corny jokes). The crew's mess hall features high ceilings, dark wooden fixtures, and souvenirs collected from skippers' travels bathed in stained glass window-tinted natural light. Behind a hidden bookcase (with highly amusing book titles), guests can visit the secret meeting room of the Society of Explorers and Adventurers, filled with posh fixtures, maps, and a beautiful collection of butterflies. The Jungle Room completes the dining set, with intimate seating near intricately carved wood bookshelves and colorful stained glass lamps.

HOUSE SPECIALTIES The menu features flavors from several world cuisines, with Asian influences in the char siu pork (a house favorite) and Korean barbecue–inspired crispy fried chicken. Latin flavors make their way into the grilled steak with adobo, as well as the house-made corn pancakes topped with pork and avocado cream. The Kungaloosh! chocolate cake with caramelized bananas will close out any meal with a smile.

OTHER RECOMMENDATIONS The pao de queijo cheese bread with dipping sauces. Plant-based dining is well represented here, with an emphasis on vegetables instead of "fake meat." Even the kids' menu satisfies across the board. The one dessert worth ordering is the Kungaloosh!

SUMMARY AND COMMENTS Skipper Canteen has fresh flavors and fine service. The menu decidedly doesn't cater to simpler tastes and aims higher than it can sometimes achieve, but any in-park restaurant that identifies its fish option as "not piranha" is OK in our book.

Kimonos ★★★★

JAPANESE	MODERATE	QUALITY ★★★★	VALUE ★★★
READER-SURVEY RESPONSES ✪ 94% (Much Above Average)			

Swan Hotel; ☎ 407-934-1792

Reservations Not accepted. **Dining Plan credits** Not accepted. **When to go** Dinner. **Cost range** Sushi rolls and appetizers à la carte $5.50–$20. **Service** ★★★★★. **Friendliness** ★★★★★. **Parking** Valet or hotel lot; validated for guests. **Bar** Full service. **Wine selection** Very good. **Dress** Casual. **Disabled access** Yes. **Customers** Hotel guests and locals. **Hours** Daily, 6–11 p.m.

SETTING AND ATMOSPHERE Sushi and nightly karaoke—what a combo! Go early if you want a zen experience with sushi and sake in the serene setting: dark teak tabletops and counters, tall pillars rising to bamboo rafters with rice-paper lanterns, and elegant kimonos that hang outstretched on the walls and between the dining sections. The chefs will greet you with a friendly welcome, and you'll be offered a hot towel to clean your hands.

HOUSE SPECIALTIES Both cooked and raw sushi and hot dishes. Classic rolls include California, tuna, and soft-shell crab; the Kimonos Roll features tuna, salmon, yellowtail, and wasabi mayo. Small plates include beef satay and chicken katsu.

SUMMARY AND COMMENTS The skill of the sushi artists is as much a joy to watch as is eating the wonderfully fresh creations. Excellent sake choices. Karaoke starts at 8:30 p.m.

Kona Cafe ★★★

POLYNESIAN/PAN-ASIAN	MODERATE	QUALITY ★★★	VALUE ★★★★
READER-SURVEY RESPONSES ✪ 90% (Above Average)			

Polynesian Village Resort; ☎ 407-939-3463

Reservations Highly recommended. **Dining Plan credits** 1 per person, per meal. **When to go** Anytime. **Cost range** Breakfast $12–$16 (child $6–$8), lunch $16–$32 (child $9–$11), dinner $16–$36 (child $9–$11). **Service** ★★★★. **Friendliness** ★★★★★. **Parking** Valet ($33) or hotel lot. **Bar** Full service. **Wine selection** OK. **Dress** Casual. **Disabled access** Yes. **Customers** Mostly hotel guests; some locals. **Breakfast** Daily, 7:30–11 a.m. **Lunch** Daily, 11:30–2 p.m. **Dinner** Daily, 5–10 p.m.

SETTING AND ATMOSPHERE Kona Cafe is the Polynesian Village's coffee shop, open three meals a day. Right next to the monorail station, the casual, open dining room is an easy ride from the Magic Kingdom by boat (or monorail to the Transportation and Ticket Center and walk) should you want to escape the park for lunch or dinner.

HOUSE SPECIALTIES *Breakfast:* Tonga Toast (French toast with bananas) is the most requested dish. *Lunch:* turkey banh mi, chicken stir-fry, noodle bowls with pork belly or vegetables, duck fried rice, and sushi rolls. *Dinner:* Sushi, tuna poke, Kona coffee–braised short rib.

OTHER RECOMMENDATIONS The kids' sushi makes for a great adult snack. Pot stickers. Desserts, served in small glasses, include Key lime, s'mores, tiramisu, banana, and coconut tapioca; Kona coffee served in a press pot.

SUMMARY AND COMMENTS The menu is themed to the island decor, and though the dining room isn't fancy by any stretch, the food is on a higher plane than your average java joint's.

Liberty Tree Tavern ★★★½

AMERICAN	EXPENSIVE	QUALITY ★★★	VALUE ★★★
READER-SURVEY RESPONSES ⊕ 91% (Above Average)			

Liberty Square, Magic Kingdom; ☎ 407-939-3463

Reservations Highly recommended. **Dining Plan credits** 1 per person, per meal. **When to go** Lunch or dinner. **Cost range** $39 (child $21). **Service** ★★★★. **Friendliness** ★★★★. **Parking** Magic Kingdom lot. **Bar** Limited selection of beer, wine, and hard cider. **Dress** Casual. **Disabled access** Yes. **Customers** Theme park guests. **Lunch** Daily, 11 a.m.–2:55 p.m. **Dinner** Daily, 3–9 p.m.

SETTING AND ATMOSPHERE With six individual rooms themed to key figures in the early history of the United States—Betsy Ross, Benjamin Franklin, Thomas Jefferson, John Paul Jones, Paul Revere, and George and Martha Washington—the Liberty Tree Tavern feels like a quaint and cozy Colonial home plunked down in a sprawling theme park. Appropriately creaky wooden staircases flank the central lobby, which can be quite busy during popular mealtimes.

HOUSE SPECIALTIES Most guests come (and return) to Liberty Tree for the All-You-Care-to-Enjoy Patriot's Platter, consisting of roasted turkey, carved pork roast, mashed potatoes, stuffing, seasonal vegetables, and house-made mac and cheese. Save room for the Ooey Gooey Toffee Cake.

OTHER RECOMMENDATIONS The Impossible Meat loaf, a plant-based dish served with mashed potatoes, seasonal vegetables, and mushroom gravy, is a tasty vegan option.

SUMMARY AND COMMENTS Always a solid standby for families in search of classic American fare, the tavern serves up high-quality food with good service at a quick pace—a luxury in the Magic Kingdom. It's very popular for both lunch and dinner, so reservations are sometimes hard to come by but are worth the effort to score: Liberty Tree Tavern still ranks as one of the top meals you can enjoy inside this park.

Mama Melrose's Ristorante Italiano ★★½

ITALIAN	MODERATE	QUALITY ★★★	VALUE ★★
READER-SURVEY RESPONSES ⊕ 87% (Below Average)			

Grand Avenue, Disney's Hollywood Studios; ☎ 407-939-3463

Reservations Highly recommended. **Dining Plan credits** 1 per person, per meal. **When to go** Lunch or dinner. **Cost range** $19–$33 (child $10–$11). **Service** ★★★. **Friendliness** ★★★★★. **Parking** DHS lot. **Bar** Full service. **Wine selection** Good. **Dress** Casual. **Disabled access** Yes. **Customers** Theme park guests. **Lunch** Daily, 11 a.m.–3:55 p.m. **Dinner** Daily, 4–7 p.m.

SETTING AND ATMOSPHERE Tucked at the back of Disney's Hollywood Studios, Mama Melrose's is easy to miss. This casual restaurant is inspired by red-sauce Italian joints as much as New York and L.A. movie scenes:

twinkling lights, red vinyl booths, and grapevines hanging from the rafters. Ambience is generally quiet unless it's peak season.

HOUSE SPECIALTIES Fresh mozzarella, campanelle with shrimp, flatbread "pizzas," seasonal pastas.

OTHER RECOMMENDATIONS Charred strip steak; tiramisu, Ghirardelli chocolate and cherry torte, and cannoli for dessert.

SUMMARY AND COMMENTS The food won't win any awards—the red sauce is a little heavy, for instance—but for family-style Italian, it's fine.

Maria & Enzo's Ristorante ★★★½

ITALIAN	EXPENSIVE	QUALITY ★★★½	VALUE ★★★
READER-SURVEY RESPONSES ⊕ 65% (Do Not Visit)			

The Landing, Disney Springs; ☎ 407-939-3463

Reservations Recommended. **Dining Plan credits** 1 per person, per meal. **When to go** Dinner. **Cost range** $28–$50 (child $14). **Service** ★★★½. Friendliness ★★★★. **Parking** Disney Springs Orange garage. **Bar** Full service. **Wine selection** Extensive. **Dress** Casual. **Disabled access** Yes. **Customers** Theme park guests. **Dinner** Daily, 5–10 p.m.

SETTING AND ATMOSPHERE This Italian trattoria is housed in an elegant Art Deco replica of a 1930s airline terminal. The airline motif is expertly rendered throughout, starting with a Passenger Check-In where you meet your wait-staff, clad in spiffy period flight-attendant uniforms. A smaller seating area called the First Class Lounge offers dining in a quieter setting.

HOUSE SPECIALTIES The extensive bar menu features aperitivi (including a Negroni), prosecco cocktails, and a variety of seasonal specialty drinks. The dishes consist primarily of Italian classics: appetizers such as polpet-tine (braised meatballs), fried calamari, and antipasti; pasta, steaks, and fish for the bulk of the entrées; and dessert mainstays, including cannoli, tarts, and gelato.

SUMMARY AND COMMENTS Excellent setting, mediocre food, high prices.

Maya Grill ★

MEXICAN/AMERICAN	EXPENSIVE	QUALITY ★	VALUE ★
READER-SURVEY RESPONSES Not enough surveys to rate			

Coronado Springs Resort; ☎ 407-939-3463

Reservations Highly recommended. **Dining Plan credits** 1 per person, per meal. **When to go** Dinner. **Cost range** $19–$27 (child $11). **Service** ★★★. **Friendliness** ★★★. **Parking** Hotel lot (free). **Bar** Full service. **Wine selection** Fair. **Dress** Casual. **Disabled access** Yes. **Customers** Hotel guests. **Hours** Thursday–Saturday, 5–10 p.m.

SETTING AND ATMOSPHERE The dining room, long in need of a redo, is intended to evoke the ancient world of the Maya, achieving "a harmony of fire, sun, and water." But the idea falls short. The kitchen is open to view—but so is the barren and starkly lit walkway outside.

HOUSE SPECIALTIES Tex-Mex and Nuevo Latino dinner fare, including a fajita skillet and slow-cooked pork with corn tortillas.

SUMMARY AND COMMENTS Maya Grill at the relatively overlooked Coronado Springs is owned by the same folks who run the restaurants at the Mexico Pavilion in EPCOT, but execution falls short here. Menu prices have come down somewhat, but $25 for fish tacos is still expensive.

Monsieur Paul (closed at press time) ★★★★

FRENCH	EXPENSIVE	QUALITY ★★★★½	VALUE ★★★
READER-SURVEY RESPONSES ⊕ 82% (Below Average)			

France, World Showcase, EPCOT; ☎ 407-939-3463

Reservations Required. **Dining Plan credits** 2 per person, per meal. **When to go** Late dinner. **Cost range** $39–$119 (child $13–$19). **Service** ★★★★. **Friendliness** ★★★★★. **Parking** EPCOT or BoardWalk lot; enter through the International Gateway. **Bar** Full service. **Wine selection** Good but pricey. **Dress** Dressy casual. **Disabled access** Elevator to second level. **Customers** Theme park guests. **Hours** Daily, 5:30–8:35 p.m.

SETTING AND ATMOSPHERE Light and modern, Monsieur Paul is tucked away at the France Pavilion. Access lies up a stairway lined with photos of legendary chef Paul Bocuse, whose son, Jérôme, owns and runs the restaurant, along with Chefs de France. Despite the relaxed ambience, the cuisine is upscale, with sublime sauces and classic preparations. Request a table at the windows to watch the world go by on World Showcase Lagoon. Seats just 120.

HOUSE SPECIALTIES Chef Bocuse's black-truffle soup, black sea bass in potato "scales," and roasted duck.

SUMMARY AND COMMENTS Monsieur Paul may be a bit formal and high-priced for many park guests, but if you can get past the sticker shock, this is *the* spot for a quiet dinner and conversation. Chef Nicolas Lemoyne, who worked at l'Auberge du Pont de Collonges in Lyon, France, wows diners with classic French tastes, including warm chocolate-almond cake with raspberry coulis. There's also a three-course fixed-price menu ($89 per person), along with a solid wine list. A rather grown-up kids' menu includes roasted salmon and grilled beef tenderloin.

Morimoto Asia ★★★½

JAPANESE/PAN-ASIAN **EXPENSIVE** **QUALITY** ★★★½ **VALUE** ★★★★
READER-SURVEY RESPONSES ➊ 88% (Average)

The Landing, Disney Springs; ☎ 407-939-6686

Reservations Recommended. **Dining Plan credits** 2 per person, per meal. **When to go** Dinner. **Cost range** $16–$66 (child $16). **Service** ★★★★. **Friendliness** ★★★★. **Parking** Disney Springs Lime garage. **Bar** Wine, beer, sake, cocktails. **Wine selection** Wide range by the glass or bottle. **Dress** Casual. **Disabled access** Yes. **Customers** Theme park guests and locals. **Lunch** Saturday and Sunday, noon–3 p.m. **Dinner** Sunday–Thursday, 4:30–9 p.m.; Friday and Saturday, 4:30–10 p.m.

SETTING AND ATMOSPHERE Orlando's version of a big-city club, with Japanese wood-tone highlights. Morimoto Asia expands beyond sushi and into a pan-Asian expedition, and in most cases he hits the mark. Quirky takes on Chinese, Japanese, and Korean dishes join a substantial sushi menu from the kitchen and upstairs sushi bar, where the chef makes frequent appearances. Fishing baskets and steel beads form the chandeliers, and a continuous white engineered-stone ribbon runs from the "secret" entrance to the Forbidden Lounge upstairs, creating the handrail, bar, and seating areas throughout the building and framing the glass-bottle lighting upstairs (a nod to the building's fictional beginnings as a bottling company). There are anime cartoons and graphic photographs throughout, framing the open kitchen.

HOUSE SPECIALTIES Pork dim sum; 24-hour-marinated, house-carved Peking duck; orange chicken; Morimoto spare ribs; Korean buri bop; lo mein and ramen noodles; sushi rolls and sashimi.

SUMMARY AND COMMENTS Iron Chef Masaharu Morimoto is famously hands-on with this restaurant, and it's not uncommon to see him in the kitchen or behind the sushi counter. We think this is one of the top restaurants in Disney Springs. The food is higher quality and more expensive than most hometown Chinese restaurants. We think this isn't what some guests expect, which may negatively affect the restaurant's ratings. If you're order-ing the Peking duck for yourself and the waitstaff says it serves two, the proper response is "Challenge accepted."

The outdoor terrace upstairs has what might be the best view of Dis-ney Springs lagoon, rising above the sometimes noisy crowd below. If you're in a hurry, the walk-up window outside and to the left of the entrance serves noodle bowls and other snacks. Prices range from $6 to $14, and outdoor seating is available.

Narcoossee's ★★★★½

SEAFOOD	EXPENSIVE	QUALITY ★★★½	VALUE ★★
READER-SURVEY RESPONSES ○ 90% (Average)			

Grand Floridian Resort & Spa; ☎ 407-939-3463

Reservations Required. **Dining Plan credits** 2 per person, per meal. **When to go** Early evening. **Cost range** $29–$54 (child $12–$18). **Service** ★★★★★. **Friendliness** ★★★★★. **Parking** Valet ($33); self-parking is deceptively far away. **Bar** Full service. **Wine selection** Good. **Dress** Dressy casual. **Disabled access** Yes. **Customers** Hotel guests and locals. **Dinner** Daily, 5–10 p.m.

SETTING AND ATMOSPHERE Situated on the waterfront of Seven Seas Lagoon at the far end of the Grand Floridian Resort, Narcoossee's may not amaze with its simple wood finishes and plain-bordering-on-sparse interi-ors, but the lagoon, Magic Kingdom views, and wraparound porch certainly bring a bit of ambience. Though the restaurant is slightly cramped and occasionally loud, the dim lighting and finely appointed tableware make for a romantic date night.

HOUSE SPECIALTIES It's hard to go wrong with any of the fresh seafood selections, and the butter-packed lobster is a particular favorite. Local shrimp shines in seasonal pasta dishes and appetizer shrimp and grits. Pan-seared Georges Bank day-boat scallops may also strike your fancy. For those sticking to land animals, the filet mignon is excellent, but sea-food really dominates the favorites here. For dessert, go for the banana cream tart.

OTHER RECOMMENDATIONS Maine lobster bisque and shrimp and crab cakes start any meal off well. Don't miss the loaded mashed potatoes—they're worth the splurge.

SUMMARY AND COMMENTS Narcoossee's, an oft-forgotten Signature res-taurant, outpaces its upscale competitors around Walt Disney World in delivering both impeccable service and outstanding food. You'll certainly pay a hefty price for a meal here, but the fresh ingredients shine every time.

Nine Dragons Restaurant ★★

CHINESE	MODERATE	QUALITY ★★	VALUE ★★
READER-SURVEY RESPONSES Not enough surveys to rate			

China, World Showcase, EPCOT; ☎ 407-939-3463

Reservations Not accepted. **Dining Plan credits** 1 per person, per meal. **When to go** Dinner. **Cost range** $18–$30 (child $9–$12). **Service** ★★★. **Friendliness** ★★★★. **Parking** EPCOT lot. **Bar** Full service. **Wine selection** Minimal. **Dress** Casual. **Disabled access** Yes. **Customers** Theme park guests. **Dinner** Tuesday–Saturday, 4:30–8:45 p.m.

SETTING AND ATMOSPHERE Nine Dragons' attractive interior—subdued wood tones, colorful lanterns, beautiful backlit glass sculptures from China—and efficient service create a respite from the bustle of World Showcase. Ask for a window seat for a view of passersby on the promenade.

HOUSE SPECIALTIES Crispy duck bao buns, honey-sesame chicken, salt-and-pepper shrimp.

OTHER RECOMMENDATIONS Stick to the appetizers and put the chili oil on everything. It's made in-house and should be sold as a souvenir.

SUMMARY AND COMMENTS You can usually get a table without a wait in the spacious dining room, and while Nine Dragons gets a bad rep for being pricey, we think the food and service are above average.

1900 Park Fare *(closed at press time)* ★★½

AMERICAN/BUFFET	EXPENSIVE	QUALITY ★★★	VALUE ★★★
READER-SURVEY RESPONSES ☉ 91% (Much Above Average)			

Grand Floridian Resort & Spa; ☎ 407-939-3463

Reservations Highly recommended. **Dining Plan credits** 1 per person, per meal. **When to go** Breakfast or dinner. **Cost range** Breakfast $45 (child $29), dinner $60 (child $39). **Service** ★★★★. **Friendliness** ★★★★. **Parking** Valet ($33); self-parking is deceptively far away. **Bar** Full service. **Wine selection** Limited. **Dress** Casual. **Disabled access** Yes. **Customers** Hotel and resort guests. **Character breakfast** Daily, 8–11:40 a.m. **Character dinner** Daily, 4–9 p.m.

SETTING AND ATMOSPHERE Everyone is here to see the Disney characters—the food and decor are afterthoughts, though the tables are set with linen and service is first-rate in the bright, cavernous, high-ceilinged room. An antique band organ, Big Bertha, periodically pumps out music to dine by.

HOUSE SPECIALTIES The buffet usually includes herb-crusted prime rib and Florida strawberry soup.

OTHER RECOMMENDATIONS A separate buffet for kids includes mac and cheese, pizza, chicken nuggets, and pasta.

ENTERTAINMENT AND AMENITIES Character dining with Mary Poppins, Pooh, Tigger, and Alice at breakfast, and Cinderella, Prince Charming, and others at dinner.

SUMMARY AND COMMENTS A good, relatively inexpensive choice for character dining, but too bright and loud for adults without children.

'Ohana ★★★

POLYNESIAN	EXPENSIVE	QUALITY ★★★½	VALUE ★★★
READER-SURVEY RESPONSES ☉ 81% (Below Average)			

Polynesian Village Resort; ☎ 407-939-3463

Reservations Highly recommended. **Dining Plan credits** 1 per person, per meal. **When to go** Breakfast or dinner. **Cost range** Breakfast $25 (child $14), dinner $55 (child $33). Prices vary seasonally; check before you go. **Service** ★★★★. **Friendliness** ★★★★★. **Parking** Hotel lot (free). **Bar** Full service. **Wine selection** Limited. **Dress** Casual. **Disabled access** Yes. **Customers** Resort guests. **Breakfast** Daily, 7:30 a.m.–noon. **Dinner** Daily, 3:30–10 p.m.

SETTING AND ATMOSPHERE Columns of carved tiki gods support the raised thatched roof in the center of 'Ohana's main dining room, while the dining tables, arranged in rows, resemble long, segmented surfboards.

HOUSE SPECIALTIES There's no menu to choose from—your only option is to ask for vegan or vegetarian options. With that decided, the food starts arriving and doesn't stop until you've had enough. Breakfast starts with seasonal fruit and pineapple-coconut "breakfast bread" (it's a Danish, really). Standard breakfast skillets include scrambled eggs, sausage, ham, potatoes, Mickey waffles, and biscuits; plant-based options are available too. At dinner, starters include honey-glazed chicken wings, fried pork dumplings, mixed green salads, and coconut-papaya scones and cheddar-bacon biscuits. The main course features teriyaki beef, peel-and-eat shrimp, roasted eight-way chicken, kielbasa sausage, noodles, and Broccolini, all placed on a lazy Susan in the center of the table.

SUMMARY AND COMMENTS Readers adore 'Ohana, which means "family." It's also an astounding amount of food that just keeps coming. Request a seat in the main dining room, where the fire pit is. Here's something to consider, though: 'Ohana tends to bring out your food at warp speed. This reader from Rochester, Minnesota, noticed it first:

Our dinner felt very rushed. The food quality was as expected—it just seemed like we were being timed.

The reader has a point—your server will bring food out as fast as you can eat it.

If you're dining with little ones, 'Ohana is *fabulous*—when our kids were very young, we would've donated a kidney to any server who brought our food to the table that fast. If, however, you're a group of grown-ups looking for a relaxed meal, 'Ohana will probably feel more akin to competitive eating than dinner, unless you ask your server to space out your courses a bit.

Olivia's Cafe ★★★

AMERICAN	EXPENSIVE	QUALITY ★★★	VALUE ★★
READER-SURVEY RESPONSES ◯ 93% (Above Average)			

Old Key West Resort; ☎ 407-939-3463

Reservations Recommended. **Dining Plan credits** 1 per person, per meal. **When to go** Lunch. **Cost range** Breakfast $14–$16 (child $6–$9), lunch $15–$34 (child $10), dinner $16–$37 (child $10). **Service** ★★★★. **Friendliness** ★★★★. **Parking** Hotel lot (free). **Bar** Full service. **Wine selection** Limited. **Dress** Casual. **Disabled access** Yes. **Customers** Resort guests. **Breakfast** Monday–Friday, 7:30–10:30 a.m. **Brunch** Saturday–Sunday, 7:30 a.m.–2 p.m. **Lunch** Monday–Friday, 11:30 a.m.–2 p.m. **Dinner** Daily, 5–9 p.m.

SETTING AND ATMOSPHERE Old Key West was the first Disney Vacation Club (DVC). Many DVC members consider Olivia's their home kitchen, and their photos decorate the walls. The decor is Disneyfied Key West, with pastels, mosaic-tile floors, potted palms, and tropical trees in the center of the room. Some outside seating looks out over the waterway. Tile, wood siding, and no tablecloths add up to one noisy dining room.

HOUSE SPECIALTIES *Breakfast:* Banana-bread French toast, omelets, waffles, pancakes. *Lunch:* Conch fritters and crab cakes, bacon cheeseburger and veggie burger, buttermilk chicken. *Dinner:* Slow-cooked prime rib, shrimp and pasta.

OTHER RECOMMENDATIONS Catch of the day, tofu and coconut curry, banana-bread pudding sundae, Key lime tart.

SUMMARY AND COMMENTS Brunch might be worth a special trip here. Unless you're staying at Old Key West, you might not know Olivia's exists—all the more reason to visit. Service is superfriendly, and the kitchen turns out tasty casual fare.

Paddlefish ★★½

AMERICAN/SEAFOOD	EXPENSIVE	QUALITY ★★★½	VALUE ★★½
READER-SURVEY RESPONSES ◯ 82% (Below Average)			

The Landing, Disney Springs; ☎ 407-934-2628

Reservations Recommended. **Dining Plan credits** 2 per person, per meal. **When to go** Lunch or dinner. **Cost range** $12–$48 (child $9–$15). **Service** ★★★★½. **Friendliness**

★★★★★. **Parking** Disney Springs Lime garage. **Bar** Full service. **Wine selection** Good. **Dress** Casual. **Disabled access** Yes. **Customers** Park guests, locals, fans of seafood. **Lunch** Daily, noon-3:55 p.m. **Dinner** Monday-Thursday, 4-9:30 p.m.; Friday-Saturday, 4-11 p.m.; Sunday, 4-10 p.m.

SETTING AND ATMOSPHERE Paddlefish has a modern aesthetic, making the stationary "steamship" seem more like a classy yacht than a classic paddleboat. Sleek design and muted colors inside don't distract from the views offered from the large picture windows at the sides and rear of the ship, overlooking her iconic paddlewheel. Outdoor seating on the first and third decks offers prime views of the area, but the true star of the restaurant is the rooftop bar, where you can enjoy an iconic Florida sunset with your cocktail.

HOUSE SPECIALTIES Crab guacamole. The crab fries (hand-cut and perfectly fried) are a solid choice for an appetizer if you're in search of fresh seafood. Ahi poke and ceviche will cool you down and tickle your palate on hot summer days.

OTHER RECOMMENDATIONS You can't go wrong with the lobster roll or the crab cakes, but the house burger might be the best thing on the menu.

SUMMARY AND COMMENTS **The Boathouse** (page 317), around the corner, has better food and better service. Readers apparently don't think it's worth it, and we agree.

Paradiso 37 ★★½

GLOBAL	EXPENSIVE	QUALITY ★★★	VALUE ★★★
READER-SURVEY RESPONSES ⊕ 67% (Do Not Visit)			

The Landing, Disney Springs; ☎ 407-934-3700

Reservations Recommended. **Dining Plan credits** 1 per person, per meal. **When to go** Lunch or dinner. **Cost range** $18-$38 (child $12). **Service** ★★★. **Friendliness** ★★★★. **Parking** Disney Springs Lime garage. **Bar** Full service. **Wine selection** Limited. **Dress** Casual. **Disabled access** Yes. **Customers** Theme park guests, locals. **Lunch** Daily, noon-3:55 p.m. **Dinner** Sunday-Thursday, 4-10 p.m.; Friday-Saturday, 4-11 p.m.

SETTING AND ATMOSPHERE Paradiso's outdoor seating is just as large as the inside's, with elevated terrace dining and a stage along the waterfront for live music performances. Those performances can get loud, so seating farther away is better. Ambience is festive and casual, with an open kitchen. The menu features dishes from North, Central, and South America. (The 37 in the name refers to the number of countries represented on the menu.)

HOUSE SPECIALTIES Argentinean skirt steak, Patagonian seared salmon, burgers, and the P37 Swirl, a margarita-sangria combo.

OTHER RECOMMENDATIONS Baja fish tacos.

SUMMARY AND COMMENTS Readers rate this as one of the worst restaurants in Walt Disney World. It must do an amazing bar business to stay in Disney Springs.

Planet Hollywood ★½

AMERICAN	MODERATE	QUALITY ★★	VALUE ★★
READER-SURVEY RESPONSES ⊕ 72% (Do Not Visit)			

Town Center, Disney Springs; ☎ 407-827-7827

Reservations Recommended. **Dining Plan credits** 1 per person, per meal. **When to go** Lunch or dinner. **Cost range** $16-$30 (child $10). **Service** ★★★. **Friendliness** ★★★. **Parking** Disney Springs Orange garage. **Bar** Full service. **Wine selection** Limited. **Dress** Casual. **Disabled access** Yes. **Customers** Tour groups, theme park guests. **Lunch** Daily, 11:30 a.m.-3:55 p.m. **Dinner** Sunday-Thursday, 4-11 p.m.; Friday-Saturday, 4-11:30 p.m.

SETTING AND ATMOSPHERE Wall projections and a house DJ take center stage in the typically loud and busy main dining room, but an outdoor patio offers seating with a view of Disney Springs in a much quieter atmosphere. Stargazers Lounge, outside on the ground-floor rear of the restaurant, features live music on select nights alongside a colorful constellation of alcoholic concoctions.

HOUSE SPECIALTIES Thanks to celebrity chef Guy Fieri, over-the-top burgers, including a burger topped with bacon mac and cheese, reign supreme. The signature Chicken Crunch remains a solid option. L.A. Lasagna (fried pasta tubes stuffed with ricotta and Bolognese and topped with roasted garlic cream and tomato-basil sauces), St. Louis–style barbecue ribs served on a mini picnic table, and the High Roller appetizer sampler served on a (nonfunctioning) Ferris wheel round out the highlights of the all-day menu.

OTHER RECOMMENDATIONS Salads, nachos, pasta, and steak, much like what you'd find at your neighborhood chain restaurant, make up much of the menu. Highly decorated milkshakes and individual desserts in jars occupy the dessert menu.

SUMMARY AND COMMENTS With high-quality food just a few steps away at Chef Art Smith's Homecomin', Blaze Fast-Fire'd Pizza, and D-Luxe Burger, we just don't think Planet Hollywood is worth your time or money.

The Plaza Restaurant   ★★

AMERICAN	MODERATE	QUALITY ★★	VALUE ★★
READER-SURVEY RESPONSES ⊕ 80% (Much Below Average)			

Main Street, U.S.A., Magic Kingdom; ☎ 407-939-3463

Reservations Recommended. **Dining Plan credits** 1 per person, per meal. **When to go** Lunch or dinner. **Cost range** $17–$23 (child $9–$11). **Service** ★★★★. **Friendliness** ★★★★. **Parking** Magic Kingdom lot. **Bar** Wine and beer only. **Dress** Casual. **Disabled access** Yes. **Customers** Theme park guests. **Lunch** Daily, 11 a.m.–2:55 p.m. **Dinner** Daily, 3–9 p.m.

SETTING AND ATMOSPHERE The Plaza, a quaint and cozy spot tucked away on a side street at the end of Main Street as you head to Tomorrowland, adds Art Nouveau touches to Main Street's Victorian theme. Decor aside, it's air-conditioned heaven on a sweltering Florida day.

HOUSE SPECIALTIES Roast beef sandwich, fried chicken sandwich with pickled onion, the Plaza Restaurant Sundae.

OTHER RECOMMENDATIONS Plaza turkey club sandwich. For kids, turkey sandwich, grilled chicken strips, cheeseburger, PB&J.

SUMMARY AND COMMENTS The Plaza isn't fine dining, but it was one of the first restaurants at the Magic Kingdom when the park opened in 1971. So go and enjoy an old-fashioned indulgence like a hot-fudge sundae. Because it's a small space, reservations are strongly suggested.

Raglan Road Irish Pub & Restaurant   ★★★★

IRISH	MODERATE	QUALITY ★★★½	VALUE ★★★
READER-SURVEY RESPONSES ⊕ 93% (Much Above Average)			

The Landing, Disney Springs; ☎ 407-938-0300

Reservations Recommended. **Dining Plan credits** 1 per person, per meal. **When to go** Monday–Saturday after 7 p.m. **Cost range** Brunch $14–$26 (child $8–$12), lunch and dinner $19–$29 (child $9–$12). **Service** ★★★½. **Friendliness** ★★★★★. **Parking** Disney Springs Lime garage. **Bar** Irish whiskeys and beers. **Wine selection** Better than a pub's but not extensive. **Dress** Casual. **Disabled access** Yes. **Customers** Tourists and locals. **Brunch** Saturday–Sunday, 10 a.m.–3 p.m. **Lunch** Monday–Friday, 11 a.m.–3 p.m. **Dinner** Sunday–Thursday, 3:05–10 p.m.; Friday–Saturday, 3:05–11 p.m.

SETTING AND ATMOSPHERE Many elements of this pub, including the bars (there are four), were handcrafted from hardwoods in Ireland and sent to the United States for reassembly ("lock, stock, and beer barrel," as the website advises). The venue is huge by Irish-pub standards, but the dark polished-wood paneling, as well as the snugs (small, private cubbyholes), preserves the feel of the traditional pub. The pentagonal main room sits beneath an impressive but very unpublike dome. In the middle of the room is a tall, tablelike platform accessible to Celtic dancers via a permanently attached short staircase. A modest bandstand is situated along the wall in front of a large pseudo-hearth. Branching from the cavernous domed center room are cozy dining areas and snugs.

HOUSE SPECIALTIES While you could order a burger, we recommend branching out and trying something different—say, Worth the Wait beef sandwich (12-hour braised beef with mushrooms, onions, and cheese). And of course, beer-battered fish-and-chips.

Brunch includes such whimsically named choices as Pork Hash Tagged (braised pork belly, scallions, and potato hash, with two fried eggs on top), the Hipsters Lament (smashed avocado, Irish bacon, and poached eggs on sourdough with chive butter), Irish breakfast (with pork, bacon, black and white pudding, roasted tomato, fried eggs, and potatoes), along with the requisite mimosas.

ENTERTAINMENT AND AMENITIES Though you could consider a great selection of Irish lagers and stouts an amenity, the real draw here is the Celtic music. A talented band plays daily. Starting in the early evening with a couple of superb acoustic sets, the band sets up as the diners filter out and the pub crawlers settle in. Celtic dancers fill the stage and dance on the aforementioned table to some of the numbers.

SUMMARY AND COMMENTS A night in a good Irish pub, Raglan Road included, is a joyous and uplifting experience. As the Irish say, it'll set you right up. A quick fish-and-chips can be had around the corner at **Cookes of Dublin** (page 307) if you're in a hurry.

Rainforest Cafe ★★½

AMERICAN	MODERATE	QUALITY ★★	VALUE ★★
READER-SURVEY RESPONSES ⊕ 75.5% (Do Not Visit; average of both locations)			

Animal Kingdom; ☎ 407-938-9100
Marketplace, Disney Springs; ☎ 407-827-8500

Reservations Recommended. **Dining Plan credits** 1 per person, per meal. **When to go** After the lunch crunch, in late afternoon, and before dinner hour. **Cost range** $16–$38 (child $11). **Service ★★★. Friendliness ★★★★. Parking** Animal Kingdom lot or Disney Springs Marketplace lot. **Bar** Full bar. **Wine selection** Limited. **Dress** Casual. **Disabled access** Yes. **Customers** Theme park guests, tourists, locals. **Hours** *Disney's Animal Kingdom: Lunch:* Daily, 10:30 a.m.–5 p.m.; *Dinner:* Daily, 5:05–7 p.m. *Disney Springs Marketplace:* Sunday, 11 a.m.–8 p.m.; Monday–Thursday, noon–8 p.m.; Friday–Saturday, 11 a.m.–9 p.m.

SETTING AND ATMOSPHERE It's always packed and there's usually a wait, but families flock to this now-familiar restaurant for big plates of food in a noisy dining room with lots to keep the kids entertained. Look for the giant volcano that can be seen, and heard, erupting all over the Marketplace; the smoke coming from the volcano is nonpolluting, in accordance with the restaurant's conservation theme. The dining room looks like a jungle (imagine all the silk plants in the world tacked to the ceiling), complete with animatronic elephants, bats, and monkeys (not the most realistic we've seen). There's occasional thunder and even some rainfall.

HOUSE SPECIALTIES House-made crab dip, Caribbean coconut shrimp, burgers, ribs, brownie cake with ice cream.

ENTERTAINMENT AND AMENITIES If you're willing to pay to avoid the long wait, stop by the day before and buy a Landry's Select Club membership for $25 (you get a $25 Welcome Reward back for joining). Present your card on the day you want to dine, and you'll be seated much faster (and earn points and sometimes discounts).

SUMMARY AND COMMENTS We've never been impressed by the Rainforest Cafes. The shopping and the kid appeal must be the attractions because it certainly isn't the food (or service). But the semisecret entrance into Animal Kingdom, hidden past the Rainforest gift shop, might be the best reason for its existence.

Restaurant Marrakesh *(closed at press time)* ★★★

MOROCCAN	EXPENSIVE	QUALITY ★★½	VALUE ★★
READER-SURVEY RESPONSES ✪ 88% (Average)			

Morocco, World Showcase, EPCOT; ☎ 407-939-3463

Reservations Highly recommended. **Dining Plan credits** 1 per person, per meal. **When to go** Lunch or dinner. **Cost range** Lunch $22–$36 (child $9–$12), dinner $22–$55 (child $9–$12). **Service** ★★★★½. **Friendliness** ★★★★★. **Parking** EPCOT lot. **Bar** Full service. **Wine selection** Limited. **Dress** Casual. **Disabled access** Yes. **Customers** Theme park guests. **Lunch** Daily, 11:30 a.m.–3:15 p.m. **Dinner** Daily, 3:30–9 p.m.

SETTING AND ATMOSPHERE Nestled in the far back corner of the Morocco Pavilion, Restaurant Marrakesh is pretty easy to miss from the outside but definitely wows once you step inside. A continuation of the ornate decorations of the Fez House courtyard near the front of the pavilion, Marrakesh's interior is palatial, complete with stucco carving, intricate wood inlays, and colorful tile mosaics. Plush carpet and dim lighting date the decor a bit, but guests may be too busy enjoying the hourly belly-dancing and traditional-music shows to notice.

HOUSE SPECIALTIES Entrées, such as the Mogador fish tagine and lemon chicken, truly shine above the muted flavors of the chicken and beef kebabs.

OTHER RECOMMENDATIONS The goat cheese and olive spread with tabbouleh and red pepper sauce is a hidden gem to share before an entrée or as a midafternoon snack. For lunch, try the beef brewat roll (akin to an egg roll, with ground beef and hints of cinnamon). Dessert isn't Marrakesh's strong suit, so stick to the baklava, or skip it in favor of alternate options at the nearby **Spice Road Table** (see page 348).

SUMMARY AND COMMENTS Restaurant Marrakesh rarely sees crowds outside of festival seasons with dining packages, so it's a good option if you're on the prowl for a prime walk-up or last-minute booking opportunity. Service is attentive but can border on formal, which may be off-putting for those wanting a more casual meal. The menu, while generally satisfying, rarely changes and features only faint efforts at spice-packed authentic cuisine nowadays. You may be better off with the more diverse flavors offered at Spice Road Table.

Rose & Crown Dining Room ★★★

BRITISH	MODERATE	QUALITY ★★★½	VALUE ★★
READER-SURVEY RESPONSES ✪ 90% (Above Average)			

United Kingdom, World Showcase, EPCOT; ☎ 407-939-3463

Reservations Highly recommended. **Dining Plan credits** 1 per person, per meal. **When to go** Lunch or dinner. **Cost range** $21–$27 (child $9–$12). **Service** ★★★★★.

Friendliness ★★★★★. **Parking** EPCOT lot. **Bar** Full bar with Bass, Guinness, and Harp beers on tap. **Wine selection** Limited. **Dress** Casual. **Disabled access** Yes. **Customers** EPCOT guests. **Lunch** Daily, 11:30 a.m.–3:30 p.m. **Dinner** Daily, 3:45–9 p.m.

SETTING AND ATMOSPHERE Pub in the front, dining room in the back. The pub hops with activity from open to close and has the look and feel of a traditional English watering hole: a large, cozy bar with rich wood appointments, beamed ceilings, and a hardwood floor. The adjoining dining room is rustic and simple.

HOUSE SPECIALTIES Fish-and-chips, bangers and mash (sausage and mashed potatoes), and shepherd's pie (the vegetarian version is delicious too), washed down with Bass ale.

OTHER RECOMMENDATIONS Trio of UK cheeses, Scotch egg (a hard-boiled egg with a deep-fried sausage coating), the Welsh Pub Burger with beer cheese sauce and beer-battered leeks, and the English trifle for dessert.

SUMMARY AND COMMENTS At dinnertime, the Rose & Crown is packed with folks appropriating tables for the EPCOT fireworks. The food is good, so branch out and try something new—you can always get fish-and-chips at the adjacent walk-up window, **Yorkshire County Fish Shop** (see page 302).

Sanaa ★★★★

INDIAN/AFRICAN	EXPENSIVE	QUALITY ★★★★	VALUE ★★★★
READER-SURVEY RESPONSES ⊕ 94% (Much Above Average)			

Animal Kingdom Lodge & Villas–Kidani Village; ☎ 407-939-3463

Reservations Highly recommended. **Dining Plan credits** 1 per person, per meal. **When to go** Lunch or dinner. **Cost range** Breakfast $10–$13 (child $5–$6), lunch $14–$28 (child $11–$13), dinner $19–$34 (child $11–$13). **Service** ★★★★. **Friendliness** ★★★★. **Parking** Valet ($33) or hotel garage. **Bar** Full service. **Wine selection** Good. **Dress** Casual. **Disabled access** Yes. **Customers** Theme park guests, locals, Disney Vacation Club guests. **Breakfast** Daily, 7–10 a.m. **Lunch** Daily, 11:30 a.m.–3 p.m. **Dinner** Daily, 5–10 p.m.

SETTING AND ATMOSPHERE A floor down from the Kidani Village lobby, Sanaa's casual dining room is inspired by African outdoor markets, with baskets, beads, and art on the walls. It's a cozy space, with 9-foot-tall windows that look out on the resort's savanna—giraffes, zebras, and other animals wander within yards of you as you dine.

HOUSE SPECIALTIES Starters include vegetable samosas and Indian-style breads (naan, onion kulcha, and paneer paratha) served with red-chile sambal, spicy jalapeño-lime pickle, coriander chutney, and cucumber raita. Entrées feature tandoori chicken, and plant-based options.

OTHER RECOMMENDATIONS African triple chocolate mousse.

SUMMARY AND COMMENTS Sanaa (sah-NAH) is a favorite of Disney cast members and locals—the flavors are addicting. It's not as upscale as **Jiko— The Cooking Place,** the resort's fine-dining restaurant (page 333), offering instead a casual take on African–Indian fusion cuisine. Sanaa serves a quick-service version of breakfast in the morning. Selections include hot foods such as eggs, waffles, and bacon, as well as a limited array of grab-and-go cold foods.

San Angel Inn Restaurante ★★★

MEXICAN	EXPENSIVE	QUALITY ★★★	VALUE ★★
READER-SURVEY RESPONSES ⊕ 87% (Average)			

Mexico, World Showcase, EPCOT; ☎ 407-939-3463

Reservations Highly recommended. **Dining Plan credits** 1 per person, per meal. **When to go** Lunch or dinner. **Cost range** $18–$36 (child $10). **Service** ★★★. **Friendliness** ★★★. **Parking** EPCOT lot. **Bar** Full service. **Wine selection** Limited. **Dress** Casual. **Disabled access** Yes. **Customers** Theme park guests. **Lunch** Daily, noon–3:55 p.m. **Dinner** Daily, 4–10 p.m.

SETTING AND ATMOSPHERE Step inside the Aztec pyramid in Mexico, navigate the busy marketplace, and end up at San Angel Inn, which overlooks a starry sky and the Gran Fiesta Tour boat ride. Its decor is inspired by the original San Angel Inn in Mexico City and is incredibly atmospheric—it really does feel like you're dining in an outdoor Mexican square.

HOUSE SPECIALTIES For appetizers try the tlayuda—a Oaxacan tostada with beans, chipotle chicken, avocado, and cheese—or the queso fundido (melted cheese with flour tortillas).

OTHER RECOMMENDATIONS Ribeye tacos should please almost anyone, but vegetarians might have the best dish on the menu in the vegetarian tqavos, with eggplant puree, oyster mushrooms, and a touch of truffle oil. Try the sweet corn ice cream for dessert.

SUMMARY AND COMMENTS The prices may be steep, but the menu goes beyond the typical tacos and such, offering regional dishes that are difficult to find in the States. Request a waterside table overlooking the boat ride for more room and a slightly quieter evening. The dining room is a cool, quiet respite from the theme park—but you might need a flashlight to read the menu.

Sci-Fi Dine-In Theater Restaurant ★★

AMERICAN	MODERATE	QUALITY ★★½	VALUE ★★
READER-SURVEY RESPONSES ✪ 87% (Average)			

Commissary Lane, Disney's Hollywood Studios; ☎ 407-939-3463

Reservations Highly recommended. **Dining Plan credits** 1 per person, per meal. **When to go** Lunch or dinner. **Cost range** $17–$25 (child $10–$12). **Service** ★★★★★. **Friendliness** ★★★★★. **Parking** DHS lot. **Bar** Full service. **Wine selection** Limited. **Dress** Casual. **Disabled access** Yes. **Customers** Theme park guests. **Lunch** Daily, 11 a.m.–3:55 p.m. **Dinner** Daily, 4–7 p.m.

SETTING AND ATMOSPHERE Walk through the doors and into the back of a simulated soundstage; then round the corner into a stage set that re-creates a drive-in from the 1950s, with faux classic cars instead of tables. Hop in, order, and watch campy black-and-white clips. It's a hoot.

HOUSE SPECIALTIES Same menu at lunch and dinner, with sandwiches, burgers, and pasta.

OTHER RECOMMENDATIONS The milkshakes are expensive but worth it. Burgers are also expensive; the Feature Film Burger, with cheddar, pork belly, and house-made mustard BBQ sauce on a brioche bun, is the best.

ENTERTAINMENT AND AMENITIES Clips of cartoons and vintage horror and sci-fi movies, such as *Attack of the 50 Foot Woman, Robot Monster,* and *The Blob.*

SUMMARY AND COMMENTS The kitsch is fun, but stick with simple fare like one of the burgers. Or just fill up on an appetizer and dessert.

Sebastian's Bistro ★★

LATIN/SEAFOOD	EXPENSIVE	QUALITY ★★	VALUE ★★★
READER-SURVEY RESPONSES ✪ 85% (Average)			

Caribbean Beach Resort; ☎ 407-939-3463

Reservations Recommended. **Dining Plan credits** 1 per person, per meal. **When to go** Dinner. **Cost range** $29 (child $17). **Service** ★★★. **Friendliness** ★★★★. **Parking** Hotel lot. **Bar**

Full service. **Wine selection** Limited. **Dress** Casual. **Disabled access** Yes. **Customers** Hotel guests. **Dinner** Sunday, Monday, and Thursday–Saturday, 5–9:30 p.m.

SETTING AND ATMOSPHERE Part of the remodeled Caribbean Beach dining area and named after the crab in *The Little Mermaid,* Sebastian's is remarkably understated for a Disney restaurant. White walls and tables are offset by blue-and-white chairs in two rooms with vaulted ceilings and plenty of windows to let in the sun.

HOUSE SPECIALTIES This family-style menu includes Caribbean Pull-Apart Rolls (warm bread with guava butter and caramelized onion jam), oven-roasted citrus chicken, slow-cooked mojo pork, grilled flank steak, cilantro rice and beans, vegetable curry, Broccolini, and coconut-pineapple bread pudding with caramel sauce and vanilla ice cream. There's also a plant-based menu option.

SUMMARY AND COMMENTS Unless you have no other options, walk over to the Riviera for better restaurants.

Shula's Steak House ★★★★

STEAK	EXPENSIVE	QUALITY ★★★★	VALUE ★★
READER-SURVEY RESPONSES ✪ 92% (Average)			

Dolphin Hotel; ☎ 407-934-1362

Reservations Highly recommended. **Dining Plan credits** Not accepted. **When to go** Dinner. **Cost range** $34–$69 (child $9–$14). *Note:* Everything is à la carte (that is, side dishes cost extra). **Service** ★★★★. **Friendliness** ★★★★. **Parking** Valet ($39) or hotel lot ($35), both free with validation. **Bar** Full service. **Wine selection** Good; expensive. **Dress** Dressy. **Disabled access** Yes. **Customers** Hotel guests and locals. **Dinner** Daily, 5–11 p.m.

SETTING AND ATMOSPHERE Shula's feels more like a men's club than a resort restaurant: dark woods, even darker lighting, framed black-and-white photos of football players, and high prices that get passed on to expense accounts.

HOUSE SPECIALTIES In a word, meat—really expensive but very high-quality meat. Only certified Angus beef is served: filet mignon, New York strip, cowboy rib eye, and porterhouse (including a 24-ounce cut).

OTHER RECOMMENDATIONS New Orleans–style shrimp, catch of the day.

SUMMARY AND COMMENTS Another restaurant that managed to regain its footing during the pandemic, Shula's is the place to go for steaks if you're staying in the EPCOT resort area.

Spice Road Table ★★★★

MOROCCAN	INEXPENSIVE	QUALITY ★★★★	VALUE ★★★
READER-SURVEY RESPONSES ✪ 90% (Above Average)			

Morocco, World Showcase, EPCOT; ☎ 407-939-3463

Reservations Not accepted. **Dining Plan credits** 1 per person, per meal. **When to go** Anytime; great spot for nightly fireworks when offered. **Cost range** Small plates $9–$15. **Service** ★★★★★. **Friendliness** ★★★★★. **Parking** EPCOT lot. **Bar** Full service. **Wine selection** Good. **Dress** Casual. **Disabled access** Yes. **Customers** EPCOT guests. **Hours** Daily, noon–10 p.m.

SETTING AND ATMOSPHERE A prime location for daytime people-watching and nighttime fireworks, Spice Road Table is situated directly along World Showcase Lagoon at the front of the Morocco Pavilion. The outdoor covered patio features excellent dining in plein air when Florida weather cooperates, and indoor seating provides colorful pops of modern Moroccan decor.

HOUSE SPECIALTIES Perfectly fried calamari and hummus fries stand out as favorites on the small-plates side of the menu.

OTHER RECOMMENDATIONS Lamb kefta with tzatziki offers a bit of punch and spice. Spiced shrimp and chicken may sound simple, but the accompanying sauces and sides elevate the otherwise pedestrian dish to the next level.

SUMMARY AND COMMENTS Food quality and service are good here. Appetizers and desserts pair excellently with the restaurant's extensive wine and cocktail lists. Service is attentive, and the casual atmosphere seems appropriate to the outdoor seating area and modern EPCOT.

Splitsville ★★½

AMERICAN	MODERATE	QUALITY ★★½	VALUE ★★
READER-SURVEY RESPONSES ⊕ 93% (Above Average)			

West Side, Disney Springs; ☎ 407-938-7467

Reservations Recommended. **Dining Plan credits** 1 per person, per meal. **When to Go** Lunch or dinner. **Cost range** $12–$26 (child $8). **Service** ★★½. **Friendliness** ★★★. **Parking** Disney Springs Orange garage. **Bar** Full service. **Wine selection** Don't expect Lafite Rothschild. **Dress** Casual. **Disabled access** Yes. **Customers** Tourists. **Lunch and dinner** Sunday–Thursday, 11 a.m.–10 p.m.; Friday–Saturday, 11 a.m.–11 p.m

SETTING AND ATMOSPHERE As part of a chain of combination restaurants and bowling alleys, Splitsville is loud, as you might expect, but there's plenty to see and room for rambunctious kids to roam while you wait for your food. Decor is vaguely midcentury modern, with Sputnik lamps and other space-age touches.

HOUSE SPECIALTIES The sushi—salmon, shrimp, tuna, crab, and various combinations thereof—is the best thing on the menu.

SUMMARY AND COMMENTS The menu is more spread-out than a 7/10 split: Burgers, pizza, seafood, Asian, and Mexican, along with assorted bar food, are represented. The only thing we'd order again is the sushi.

STK Orlando ★★★½

STEAK	EXPENSIVE	QUALITY ★★★★	VALUE ★★½
READER-SURVEY RESPONSES ⊕ 78% (Much Below Average)			

The Landing, Disney Springs; ☎ 407-917-7440

Reservations Highly recommended. **Dining Plan credits** 2 per person, per meal. **When to go** Weekend brunch and dinner. **Cost range** Brunch $21–$44, lunch $15–$45 (child $10–$17), dinner $40–$110 (child $10–$17). **Service** ★★★★. **Friendliness** ★★★★. **Parking** Disney Springs Orange garage. **Bar** Full service. **Wine selection** Not bad but not encyclopedic either. **Dress** Casual. **Disabled access** Yes. **Customers** Theme park guests. **Brunch** Saturday–Sunday, 11 a.m.–3 p.m. **Lunch** Monday–Friday, 11 a.m.–3 p.m. **Dinner** Sunday–Thursday, 4–10 p.m.; Friday–Saturday, 3–11 p.m.

SETTING AND ATMOSPHERE The turreted brick exterior, intended to evoke a turn-of-the-20th-century train station, couldn't be more different from the inside. A lower level houses a bar and seating area with a Las Vegas–ultralounge feel, complete with DJ and *lots* of noise. The quieter, less-glitzy upstairs has both indoor and outdoor seating.

HOUSE SPECIALTIES Duh—steaks, ranging from a $49 filet mignon to a $152, 34-ounce tomahawk. Sides include an indulgent macaroni and cheese, sweet corn pudding, and Parmesan-truffle fries.

SUMMARY AND COMMENTS STK is consistently rated as one of the worst dining experiences in Disney World: The steaks are good but overpriced, and they're inexplicably accompanied by a club DJ playing loud music. In Disney Springs, we recommend The Boathouse, Chef Art Smith's Home-comin', Jaleo, Wine Bar George, or Morimoto Asia instead.

Story Book Dining with Snow White at Artist Point
(closed at press time) ★★★½

AMERICAN	EXPENSIVE	QUALITY ★★★★	VALUE ★★★½
READER SURVEY RESPONSES ➕ 86% (Average)			

Wilderness Lodge & Villas; ☎ 407-939-3463

Reservations Recommended. **Dining Plan credits** 1 per person, per meal. **When to go** Dinner. **Cost range** $60 (child $39). **Service** ★★★★★. **Friendliness** ★★★★★. **Parking** Hotel lot. **Bar** Full service. **Wine selection** Decent array of reds and whites from the Pacific Northwest. **Dress** Dressy casual. **Disabled access** Yes. **Customers** Hotel guests. **Hours** Daily from 4 p.m., last seating 9 p.m.

SETTING AND ATMOSPHERE Understated Arts and Crafts decor takes inspiration from the Old Faithful Inn at Yellowstone National Park: massive landscape paintings, heavy wooden tables, cast-iron chandeliers.

HOUSE SPECIALTIES Appetizers include shrimp cocktail and mushroom bisque. Main courses include prime rib, pork shank, roast chicken, a fish dish, and a vegetarian option. For kids, there's pasta with red or cheese sauce, veggie steamed bun, prime rib, or grilled chicken.

SUMMARY AND COMMENTS Characters include Snow White, Dopey, Grumpy, and the Evil Queen—odd choices for a restaurant, as Snow White falls into a coma immediately after eating doctored food. (Apparently Disney's in on the joke, though, because there's a "Poison" Apple dessert.)

Takumi-Tei *(closed at press time)* ★★★★½

JAPANESE	EXPENSIVE	QUALITY ★★★★★	VALUE ★★★½
READER-SURVEY RESPONSES Not enough surveys to rate			

Japan, World Showcase, EPCOT; ☎ 407-939-3463

Reservations Highly recommended. **Dining Plan credits** 1 per person, per meal. **When to go** Dinner. **Cost range** $42–$120 (child $18–$29). **Service** ★★★★★. **Friendliness** ★★★★★. **Parking** EPCOT lot. **Bar** Full service. **Wine selection** Minimal. **Dress** Casual. **Disabled access** Yes. **Customers** EPCOT guests. **Dinner** Daily, 4–10 p.m.

SETTING AND ATMOSPHERE Takumi-Tei's decor celebrates five natural elements revered by Japanese craftsmen: water, wood, earth, stone, and *washi* (paper). The private dining room, home to traditional kaiseki dining, features a custom waterfall on its feature wall that is designed to look like it's flowing straight into the dining table.

HOUSE SPECIALTIES The menu rotates seasonally to reflect the freshest and most seasonal produce at the chef's disposal. The Hama no Kani ("Crab on the Beach") appetizer playfully combines two different crab preparations with frisée, heirloom tomato, and pickled watermelon. A-5 Wagyu beef—the most prized in the world—anchors the main-course menu, and while it's a significant spend, it makes for a meal unlike any other.

OTHER RECOMMENDATIONS Sashimi and nigiri with the freshest fish you'll ever taste; specialty desserts tailor-made for Instagramming, including the clear, perplexingly delicious Japanese water cake.

SUMMARY AND COMMENTS Filtering classical Japanese cookery through an upscale modern lens, Takumi-Tei treats diners to an indulgent retreat from the hustle and bustle of the theme park.

Teppan Edo ★★★½

JAPANESE	EXPENSIVE	QUALITY ★★★★	VALUE ★★★
READER-SURVEY RESPONSES ➕ 97% (Exceptional)			

Japan, World Showcase, EPCOT; ☎ 407-939-3463

Reservations Highly recommended. **Dining Plan credits** 1 per person, per meal. **When to go** Lunch or dinner. **Cost range** $26–$45 (child $16–$18). **Service** ★★★★★. **Friendliness** ★★★★★. **Parking** EPCOT lot. **Bar** Full service. **Wine selection** Limited. **Dress** Casual. **Disabled access** Via elevator. **Customers** EPCOT guests. **Lunch** Daily, noon–3:55 p.m. **Dinner** Daily, 4–9 p.m.

SETTING AND ATMOSPHERE Six Japanese dining rooms with grills on tables and entertaining chefs chopping, slicing, and dicing.

HOUSE SPECIALTIES Chicken, shrimp, beef, scallops, and Asian vegetables stir-fried on a teppanyaki grill by a knife-juggling chef.

ENTERTAINMENT AND AMENITIES Watching the teppanyaki chefs.

SUMMARY AND COMMENTS A popular dining option for families, Teppan Edo was the highest-rated restaurant in Walt Disney World over the past year. The food quality is comparable to what you'd get in a hometown teppan place. You'll get plenty to eat, and the starters include sushi, ribs, edamame, and miso soup. What's not to like?

Terralina Crafted Italian ★★★½

ITALIAN	MODERATE	QUALITY ★★★	VALUE ★★★
READER-SURVEY RESPONSES ✪ 78% (Below Average)			

The Landing, Disney Springs; ☎ 407-934-8888

Reservations Recommended. **Dining Plan credits** 1 per person, per meal. **When to go** Lunch or dinner. **Cost range** $15–$44 (child $7–$12). **Service** ★★★★. **Friendliness** ★★★★½. **Parking** Disney Springs Lime garage. **Bar** Full service. **Wine selection** Mostly Italian. **Dress** Casual. **Disabled access** Yes. **Customers** Disney Springs guests. **Lunch** Daily, noon–3:55 p.m. **Dinner** Sunday, 4–10 p.m.; Monday–Thursday, 4–9:30 p.m.; Friday–Saturday, 4–11 p.m.

SETTING AND ATMOSPHERE "Italian Lake District" is the restaurant's inviting theme, with stonework, hefty exposed wood beams, and warm colors. The waiting area has a beautiful fireplace and comfy leather chairs; an even better place to wait is the open-air bar.

HOUSE SPECIALTIES For appetizers, try the mozzarella-stuffed rice balls. For mains, try the gnocchi with pork ragù and shaved Parmesan or the eggplant Parmesan. For dessert, try the lemon panna cotta or the tiramisu.

SUMMARY AND COMMENTS If you're in the mood for Italian, Terralina, despite the lowest rating, is the best option in Disney Springs.

Three Bridges Bar & Grill at Villa del Lago ★★★

AMERICAN/SPANISH	EXPENSIVE	QUALITY ★★★	VALUE ★★½
READER-SURVEY RESPONSES ✪ 89% (Average)			

Coronado Springs Resort; ☎ 407-939-3463

Reservations You can join their wait list from the app, but they do not accept reservations. **Dining Plan credits** 1 per person, per meal. **When to go** Dinner. **Cost range** $15–$25 (child $10–$11). **Service** ★★★½. **Friendliness** ★★★★. **Parking** Coronado Springs lot. **Bar** Full service. **Wine selection** Mostly Spanish. **Dress** Casual. **Disabled access** Yes. **Customers** Hotel guests. **Dinner** Daily, 4:30 p.m.–midnight.

SETTING AND ATMOSPHERE At the crux of Coronado Springs Resort's three commuter bridges, this bar and grill floats in the middle of picturesque Lago Dorado, reflecting sunsets nightly and offering grand views of the complex's Gran Destino Tower. Lounge-style seating occupies half of the dining area, with a central bar and standard tables adjacent. Three Bridges is a happening spot even in the late afternoon.

HOUSE SPECIALTIES Stick to the basics: Szechuan peppercorn wings, Oaxacan cheese dip with chorizo, a fantastic house burger, ridiculously fresh tacos (with made-from-scratch tortillas). Portions aren't hefty, but they are enough to satisfy anyone looking to split a few snacks or grab a light meal. Specialty cocktails complement a hearty wine-and-beer selection.

OTHER RECOMMENDATIONS Hearty salads and harissa lamb chops are good main-dish choices.

SUMMARY AND COMMENTS Taking waterside dining to the next level, Three Bridges unites traditional bar fare with Spanish flair. Dishes are nicely executed and drinks are delightful at this beautiful island retreat.

Tiffins ★★★★

PAN-ASIAN/AMERICAN	EXPENSIVE	QUALITY ★★★★	VALUE ★★★
READER-SURVEY RESPONSES ⊕ 89% (Average)			

Discovery Island, Animal Kingdom; ☎ 407-939-3463

Reservations Highly recommended. **Dining Plan credits** 2 per person, per meal. **When to go** Lunch or dinner. **Cost range** $30–$65 (child $10–$15). **Service ★★★★**. **Friendliness ★★★★★**. **Parking** Animal Kingdom lot. **Bar** Full bar. **Wine selection** Excellent. **Dress** Casual. **Disabled access** Yes. **Customers** Theme park guests. **Lunch** Daily, noon–3:55 p.m. **Dinner** Daily, 4–7 p.m.

SETTING AND ATMOSPHERE Tiffins is tucked behind the Pizzafari counter-service restaurant on a walking path to the land of Pandora. Inside are three relatively small, quiet dining rooms, plus the **Nomad Lounge.** A wrap-around porch behind the dining rooms offers outdoor seating.

The decor is said to be inspired by the travel adventures of the Imagineers who built Animal Kingdom. You'll see artifacts from Asia and Africa lining the walls of one room, and giant butterflies in another. The main dining room's centerpiece is carved-wood sculptures.

HOUSE SPECIALTIES Appetizers include charred octopus and sweet corn soup. For entrées, try the whole fried sustainable fish or butter chicken. For dessert, the passion fruit tapioca is tasty.

OTHER RECOMMENDATIONS Skip the bread service.

SUMMARY AND COMMENTS We loved Tiffins when it first opened. But what was one of the best menus in any Disney theme park has been subjected to cost cutting, resulting in high prices that aren't justified by the food quality. That said, the Nomad Lounge next door is still an excellent place to relax with a drink and some light bites.

Todd English's bluezoo ★★★

SEAFOOD	EXPENSIVE	QUALITY ★★★★	VALUE ★★
READER-SURVEY RESPONSES ⊕ 86% (Average)			

Dolphin Hotel; ☎ 407-934-1609

Reservations Recommended. **Dining Plan credits** Not accepted. **When to go** Dinner. **Cost range** $18–$38 (child $10–$12). **Service ★★★★**. **Friendliness ★★★**. **Parking** Valet ($35) or hotel lot ($25), both free with validation. **Bar** Full service. **Wine selection** Excellent. **Dress** Dressy casual. **Disabled access** Yes. **Customers** Hotel guests, locals. **Hours** Daily, 5–11 p.m.

SETTING AND ATMOSPHERE A lovely yet slightly cold dining room swathed in blues with iridescent bubbles suspended from the lights. The name is courtesy of celebrity chef Todd English's son, who as a young boy saw an under-the-sea movie and said it looked like a "blue zoo." Open kitchen and a unique circular rotisserie that makes the fish being grilled on it seem to dance on the coals.

HOUSE SPECIALTIES Nightly fish selection (from the rotisserie), angus filet.

OTHER RECOMMENDATIONS New England–style clam chowder with salt-cured bacon, teppan-seared jumbo sea scallops.

SUMMARY AND COMMENTS The appetizers and desserts are above average, and you could fashion a good meal from just those. In fact, bluezoo's pastry chef, Laurent Branlard, is a two-time winner at the World Pastry Team Championships. It would be a disservice to the culinary arts not to order one of his desserts.

Tokyo Dining ★★★

JAPANESE	MODERATE	QUALITY ★★★★	VALUE ★★★
READER-SURVEY RESPONSES ⊕ 91% (Average)			

Japan, World Showcase, EPCOT; ☎ 407-939-3463

Reservations Highly recommended. Dining Plan credits 1 per person, per meal. When to go Lunch. Cost range $12–$24. Service ★★★★. Friendliness ★★★. Parking EPCOT lot. Bar Full service. Wine selection Limited. Dress Casual. Disabled access Yes. Customers Theme park guests. Lunch Daily, noon–3:45 p.m. Dinner Daily, 4–9 p.m.

SETTING AND ATMOSPHERE Gracious service and modern Asian decor distinguish this restaurant. There are no seats at the beautifully lit sushi bar, but the chefs are great entertainment for the entire dining room. Tables near the windows have a wonderful second-floor view of World Showcase.

HOUSE SPECIALTIES Sushi and sashimi.

SUMMARY AND COMMENTS The dining room is sleek; the sushi is super-fresh; and the overall experience is relaxing, congenial, and quintessentially Japanese.

Toledo—Tapas, Steak & Seafood ★★★½

SPANISH	EXPENSIVE	QUALITY ★★★	VALUE ★★½
READER-SURVEY RESPONSES Too new to rate			

Gran Destino Tower, Coronado Springs Resort; ☎ 407-939-3463

Reservations Recommended. Dining Plan credits 1 per person, per meal. When to go Dinner. Cost range $28–$89 (child $10–$14). Service ★★★★. Friendliness ★★★★. Parking Hotel lot. Bar Full service. Wine selection Mostly Spanish. Dress Casual. Disabled access Yes. Customers Hotel guests. Dinner Daily, 5–10 p.m.

SETTING AND ATMOSPHERE High atop Gran Destino Tower, Toledo envelops diners in a Cubist cloud heaven, complete with color-changing ceiling and trees reaching to the sky right beside several tables. A showcase bar anchors one side of the restaurant, while an open tapas kitchen greets guests at the far end of the dining room. The real attraction, though, is the massive wall of windows, offering views of some of Walt Disney World's most popular attractions and nighttime spectaculars.

HOUSE SPECIALTIES The highlight of our most recent visit was a grouper poached with what had to be a pound of butter, served with cauliflower, Cipollini onions, and braised Valencia oranges. The citrus helped cut through the richness of the grouper, and the sear on the fish was outstanding. Also try the Rioja-braised chicken—a deep wine reduction sauce elevates the entire dish.

OTHER RECOMMENDATIONS Like **Jaleo** (see page 332), Toledo has a robust tapas menu. Try the Rioja-braised chorizo sausage with wild onions. Avoid the pan tomate here, as it's better at Jaleo. For sides, the blistered shishito peppers are more than enough to share.

SUMMARY AND COMMENTS Toledo caters to park guests and convention-eers alike.

Tony's Town Square Restaurant ★★½

ITALIAN	EXPENSIVE	QUALITY ★★★	VALUE ★★
READER-SURVEY RESPONSES ✪ 80% (Much Below Average)			

Main Street, U.S.A., Magic Kingdom; ☎ 407-939-3463

Reservations Highly recommended. **Dining Plan credits** 1 per person, per meal. **When to go** Late lunch or early dinner. **Cost range** $21–$34 (child $10–$11). **Service** ★★★★. **Friendliness** ★★★★★. **Parking** Magic Kingdom lot. **Bar** Limited selection of beer and wine. **Dress** Casual. **Disabled access** Yes. **Customers** Theme park guests. **Hours** Daily, 11:30 a.m.–9 p.m.

SETTING AND ATMOSPHERE Just inside the Magic Kingdom on Main Street, with a glass-windowed porch that's wonderful for watching the action out-side, Tony's Town Square doesn't have good food, but it's a rite of passage for Disney fans—one *must* have a plate of spaghetti in the restaurant that commemorates *Lady and the Tramp*.

HOUSE SPECIALTIES Pizza, spaghetti with meatballs, shrimp fettuccine Alfredo, chicken parmigiana, Roman-style steak.

SUMMARY AND COMMENTS Tony's does a decent job with simple pasta (multigrain and gluten-free options available).

Topolino's Terrace—Flavors of the Riviera ★★★★

FRENCH/ITALIAN	EXPENSIVE	QUALITY ★★★★	VALUE ★★
READER-SURVEY RESPONSES ✪ 97% (Exceptional)			

Riviera Resort; ☎ 407-939-3463

Reservations Highly recommended. **Dining Plan credits** 2 per person, per meal. **When to go** Breakfast or dinner. **Cost range** Breakfast $42 (child $27); dinner $34–$54 (child $10–$17). **Service** ★★★★½. **Friendliness** ★★★★★. **Parking** Hotel lot. **Bar** Full service. **Dress** Dressy casual. **Disabled access** Yes. **Customers** Hotel and other Disney guests. **Breakfast** Daily, 7:30 a.m.–12:15 p.m. **Dinner** Daily, 5–9:30 p.m.

SETTING AND ATMOSPHERE The big feature of this rooftop restaurant is the fantastic view of EPCOT and Disney's Hollywood Studios, especially at night when those parks run their fireworks spectaculars. Beyond the windows, you'll find burgundy-and-cream carpets and dark wood tables and accents. In keeping with Disney's recent decorative trends, there's absolutely nothing here that's overtly tied to the Riviera.

HOUSE SPECIALTIES *Breakfast:* Sour cream waffle with roasted apples and orange-maple syrup; smoked salmon bagel. *Dinner:* Tomahawk veal chop with potato-onion gratin; bean cassoulet with mushrooms, vegetables, and plant-based "sausage."

OTHER RECOMMENDATIONS Lobster fettuccine, rigatoni pasta with chicken, Broccolini, and wild mushrooms.

SUMMARY AND COMMENTS There are seemingly no bad choices on this menu, and the service team is excellent. Breakfast features a socially distant parade of Disney characters including Mickey, Minnie, Donald, and Daisy.

Trader Sam's Grog Grotto ★★★

PAN-ASIAN	INEXPENSIVE	QUALITY ★★★	VALUE ★★★
READER-SURVEY RESPONSES ✪ 96% (Much Above Average)			

Polynesian Village Resort; ☎407-939-3463

Reservations Not accepted. **Dining Plan credits** Not accepted. **When to go** Dinner. **Cost range** $9.50–$15 (small plates only). **Service** ★★★. **Friendliness** ★★★★.

Parking Valet ($33) or hotel lot. **Bar** Full service. **Wine selection** Good. **Dress** Casual. **Disabled access** Yes. **Customers** Locals and Disney guests. **Hours** Daily, 3 p.m.–midnight (after 8 p.m., only guests age 21 and up are admitted).

SETTING AND ATMOSPHERE Off the Polynesian Village's main lobby and featuring views of the marina and Seven Seas Lagoon, this highly themed tiki bar has its own lore built in: It was started by Trader Sam, Adventureland's famous "head" salesman, who welcomes you to his enchanted South Seas hideaway to explore a menu of "magical tropical drinks and food."

HOUSE SPECIALTIES Cocktails are the stars, with names like Tahitian Torch and the over-the-top Uh-Oa!—Plantation Original Dark and Bacardi rums mixed with various fruit juices and served in a communal tiki bowl.

OTHER RECOMMENDATIONS Small plates include Hawaiian poke with Sriracha aioli, kalua pork tacos with shredded cabbage and pickled vegetables, roasted chicken and pork pâté banh mi sliders with pickled vegetables, Thai chicken flatbread, and the Headhunter Sushi Roll.

SUMMARY AND COMMENTS Trader Sam's is a hit with Disneyphiles, so get there early—there are just 50 seats inside and 80 on the patio.

Trail's End Restaurant *(closed at press time)* ★★

AMERICAN	EXPENSIVE	QUALITY ★★	VALUE ★★
READER-SURVEY RESPONSES ✪ 91% (Much Above Average)			

The Campsites at Fort Wilderness Resort; ☎ 407-939-3463

Reservations Highly recommended. **Dining Plan credits** 1 per person, per meal. **When to go** Breakfast or dinner. **Cost range** Breakfast $20 (child $12), dinner $30 (child $18). **Service** ★★★. **Friendliness** ★★★. **Parking** Resort lot. **Bar** Full-service bar next door. **Wine selection** Limited. **Dress** Casual. **Disabled access** Yes. **Customers** Fort Wilderness campers, theme park guests. **Breakfast** Sunday, Monday, and Thursday–Saturday, 7:30–noon. **Dinner** Sunday, Monday, and Thursday–Saturday, 4:30–9:30 p.m.

SETTING AND ATMOSPHERE Trail's End is what a restaurant would have looked like had America's settlers built one out of a log cabin. The interior features exposed log beams, oak tabletops, and walls hung with enough old-timey kitchen equipment to start a flea market.

HOUSE SPECIALTIES Breakfast features eggs, sausage, bacon, waffles, and pastries. Dinner includes salad, pecan-smoked brisket, rotisserie chicken andouille, fingerling potatoes, green beans, and corn on the cob.

SUMMARY AND COMMENTS With its "everything but the kitchen sink" philosophy, Trail's End offers something for everyone.

Trattoria al Forno ★★★

ITALIAN	MODERATE	QUALITY ★★★½	VALUE ★★
READER-SURVEY RESPONSES ✪ 90% (Much Above Average)			

BoardWalk; ☎ 407-939-3463

Reservations Highly recommended. **Dining Plan credits** 1 per person, per meal. **When to go** Breakfast or dinner. **Cost range** Breakfast $12–$21 (child $7–$9), dinner $19–$39 (child $12–$15). **Service** ★★★. **Friendliness** ★★★★. **Parking** BoardWalk lot. **Bar** Full service. **Wine selection** Good; all Italian. **Dress** Casual. **Disabled access** Yes. **Customers** Locals, Disney guests. **Breakfast** Daily, 7:30–11:30 a.m. **Dinner** Daily, 5–9 p.m.

SETTING AND ATMOSPHERE The space comprises three different dining areas, a private room in the back, and an open kitchen for watching the action. Our favorite spots are the formal dining room, right in front of the kitchen, or one of the booths at the back.

HOUSE SPECIALTIES *Breakfast:* Poached egg over polenta with fennel sausage; pancakes; steak and eggs; breakfast pizza (scrambled eggs, bacon, ham, sausage, bell peppers, and cheese). *Dinner:* Rigatoni Bolognese, chicken parmigiana, tiramisu.

SUMMARY AND COMMENTS The kitchen makes mozzarella cheese and rolls out fresh pasta daily. The wines represent Italy's major regions, with more than 30 available by the glass or quartino. Breakfast is one of the best on Disney property, even as the Disney characters are temporarily unavailable.

T-REX ★★★

AMERICAN	EXPENSIVE	QUALITY ★★	VALUE ★★
READER-SURVEY RESPONSES ○ 79% (Much Below Average)			

Marketplace, Disney Springs; ☎ 407-828-8739

Reservations Highly recommended. **Dining Plan credits** 1 per person, per meal. **When to go** Lunch or dinner. **Cost range** $19–$31 (child $11). **Service ★★★. Friendliness ★★★. Parking** Disney Springs Orange garage. **Bar** Full service. **Wine selection** Minimal. **Dress** Casual. **Disabled access** Yes. **Customers** Families. **Hours** Daily, 11 a.m.–9 p.m.

SETTING AND ATMOSPHERE Sensory overload in a cavernous dining room with life-size robotic dinosaurs, giant fish tanks, bubbling geysers, waterfalls, fossils in the bathrooms, and crystals in the walls. Volume: loud and louder.

HOUSE SPECIALTIES Megasaurus Burger.

SUMMARY AND COMMENTS Expect a wait unless there's an empty seat at the bar. But nobody's here just for the ordinary, overpriced food—it's non-stop "eatertainment," with kid-friendly food served in huge portions.

Turf Club Bar & Grill *(closed at press time)* ★★

AMERICAN	EXPENSIVE	QUALITY ★★★	VALUE ★★
READER-SURVEY RESPONSES ○ 86% (Average)			

Saratoga Springs Resort & Spa; ☎ 407-939-3463

Reservations Accepted. **Dining Plan credits** 1 per person, per meal. **When to go** Dinner. **Cost range** $20–$36 (child $9–$12). **Service ★★★. Friendliness ★★★★. Parking** Hotel lot. **Bar** Full service. **Wine selection** Good. **Dress** Casual. **Disabled access** Good. **Customers** Hotel guests. **Hours** Daily, 5–9:30 p.m.

SETTING AND ATMOSPHERE If you're looking for a quiet, out-of-the-way spot with decent food, Turf Club is a good bet. When the weather is nice, ask for an outdoor table; you can spot golfers on the adjacent Lake Buena Vista Golf Course and look across the way to Disney Springs. Just off the lobby of Saratoga Springs Resort, the dining room is equestrian-themed.

HOUSE SPECIALTIES Signature grilled romaine salad, prime rib.

OTHER RECOMMENDATIONS Sustainable fish.

SUMMARY AND COMMENTS Rarely crowded. The grilled romaine salad with Caesar dressing, balsamic reduction, and roasted tomatoes is one of Disney's best.

Tusker House Restaurant ★★★

AMERICAN/AFRICAN	EXPENSIVE	QUALITY ★★★	VALUE ★★★
READER-SURVEY RESPONSES ○ 90% (Above Average)			

Africa, Animal Kingdom; ☎ 407-939-3463

Reservations Required. **Dining Plan credits** 1 per person, per meal. **When to go** Anytime. **Cost range** Breakfast $42 (child $27), lunch and dinner $55 (child $36). Prices may vary seasonally; check before you go. **Service ★★★. Friendliness ★★★. Parking** Animal Kingdom lot. **Bar** Full-service bar next door. **Dress** Casual. **Disabled access** Yes. **Customers** Theme park guests. **Character breakfast** Daily, 8–10:30 a.m. **Character lunch** Daily, 11 a.m.–3:30 p.m. **Character dinner** Daily, 3:35–7 p.m.

SETTING AND ATMOSPHERE Tusker House's character meals feature socially distant Mickey, Donald, Daisy, and Goofy. The setting—inside the Harambe Village square—is plainer than promotional photos indicate, especially after dark. The food is surprisingly good, with spices and taste combinations you won't find at other character-dining spots.

HOUSE SPECIALTIES Roast pork, beef, and chicken.

SUMMARY AND COMMENTS Tusker House appeals not just to kids but also to grown-ups who appreciate more interesting dishes. This mom from Campobello, South Carolina, is a fan:

We had a supergood meal at Tusker House, probably the best of the entire trip.

Tutto Gusto Wine Cellar ★★★½

ITALIAN	EXPENSIVE	QUALITY ★★★★	VALUE ★★★
READER-SURVEY RESPONSES ✪ 88% (Average)			

Italy, World Showcase, EPCOT; ☎ 407-560-8040

Reservations Not accepted. **Dining Plan credits** Not accepted. **When to go** Dinner. **Cost range** $28–$39 (child $11). **Service** ★★★★. **Friendliness** ★★★½. **Parking** EPCOT lot. **Bar** Full service. **Wine selection** Large and diverse. **Dress** Casual. **Disabled access** Yes. **Customers** Theme park guests. **Hours** Daily, 1–7 p.m.

SETTING AND ATMOSPHERE Tutto Gusto is an intimate space with cozy fireplace-adjacent seating and unique wine-bottle chandeliers. Dark and cool as befits any wine cellar, it can be packed during the day with guests looking to cool off with a glass of one of 200-plus wines.

HOUSE SPECIALTIES Wine flights with three pours, plus quartinos and full bottles available for those wanting to settle in awhile. Shareable plates feature cheeses, charcuterie, marinated vegetables, and desserts.

SUMMARY AND COMMENTS Tutto Gusto serves light fare and high-quality wines in a beautifully quaint space. The standing bar area typically has a shorter wait than for tables at peak times.

Tutto Italia Ristorante ★★★

ITALIAN	EXPENSIVE	QUALITY ★★★★	VALUE ★★
READER-SURVEY RESPONSES ✪ 83% (Average)			

Italy, World Showcase, EPCOT; ☎ 407-939-3463

Reservations Highly recommended. **Dining Plan credits** 1 per person, per meal. **When to go** Midafternoon. **Cost range** $24–$39 (child $11). **Service** ★★★★. **Friendliness** ★★★★. **Parking** EPCOT lot. **Bar** Beer and wine only. **Wine selection** All Italian. **Dress** Casual. **Disabled access** Yes. **Customers** Theme park guests. **Hours** Daily, 1–7 p.m.

SETTING AND ATMOSPHERE Tutto Italia feels like a big restaurant in Rome or Milan, with murals of a piazza along the wall behind upholstered banquettes. It can get noisy—if the weather is nice, request an outside table.

HOUSE SPECIALTIES It's hard to identify anything as being done particularly well.

OTHER RECOMMENDATIONS Stick to the least-expensive menu items.

SUMMARY AND COMMENTS This should be one of the best Italian restaurants in Orlando, but it's not. Everything that happens inside Tutto Italia—from the cooking to the service—feels like it's done on autopilot. The food quality can't support the prices, even taking the Disney "bubble" cost premium into account: $34 for chicken parm is double what you'd pay in many neighborhood Italian joints and 30% more expensive than in Manhattan. Everything here needs to be done better.

Via Napoli Ristorante e Pizzeria ★★★★

ITALIAN   EXPENSIVE   QUALITY ★★★½   VALUE ★★★
READER-SURVEY RESPONSES ✪ 92% (Much Above Average)

Italy, World Showcase, EPCOT; ☎ 407-939-3463

Reservations Highly recommended. **Dining Plan credits** 1 per person, per meal. **When to go** Lunch or dinner. **Cost range** Entrées $28-$40, individual pizzas $21-$26, pizzas (serves 2-5) $38-$55. **Service ★★★★. Friendliness ★★★★. Parking** EPCOT lot. **Bar** Beer and wine only. **Dress** Casual. **Disabled access** Yes. **Customers** Theme park guests. **Hours** Daily, 11:30 a.m.-7 p.m.

SETTING AND ATMOSPHERE Three big pizza ovens, named after the three active Italian volcanoes—Etna, Vesuvio, and Stromboli—are the stars of the show in this loud, cavernous dining room.

HOUSE SPECIALTIES The best pizza in Walt Disney World.

SUMMARY AND COMMENTS The Carciofi (artichokes, fontina, and truffle oil) and four-cheese pies are our favorites.

Victoria & Albert's *(closed at press time)* ★★★★★

GOURMET   EXPENSIVE   QUALITY ★★★★★   VALUE ★★★★
READER-SURVEY RESPONSES ✪ 96% (Exceptional)

Grand Floridian Resort & Spa; ☎ 407-939-3463

Reservations Required; call at least 60 days in advance to reserve; must confirm special dietary needs by noon the day of your seating. **Dining Plan credits** Not accepted. **When to go** Dinner. **Cost range** Fixed price (not including tax or gratuity): main dining room and Queen Victoria's Room $235 (pairing $385), Chef's Table $250 (pairing $400). **Service ★★★★★. Friendliness ★★★★. Parking** Valet (free); self-parking is deceptively far away. **Wine selection** 700 on the menu, 4,200 more in the cellar. **Dress** Jacket required for men, evening wear for women. **Disabled access** Yes. **Customers** Hotel guests, locals. **Hours** Variable seating for main dining room 5:30-7:30 p.m., Queen Victoria's Room 5:30-7 p.m.; 1 seating at 5:30 p.m. for the Chef's Table. *Note:* No children under age 10 admitted except at Chef's Table.

SETTING AND ATMOSPHERE With just 14 tables in the main dining room, Queen Victoria's Room with seating for up to 8, and the 8-seat Chef's Table, this is the top dining experience at Walt Disney World. A consecutive winner of AAA's Five Diamond Award since 2000—the only restaurant in Central Florida so honored—Victoria & Albert's is lavish, and expensive, with Frette linens, Riedel crystal, and Christofle silver.

HOUSE SPECIALTIES The menu changes daily, but you might find Minnesota elk tenderloin, Alaskan salmon, local free-range chicken, Florida sturgeon caviar, and Australian Kobe-style beef on chef Scott Hunnel's menu. Pastry chef Kristine Farmer's desserts are divine.

SUMMARY AND COMMENTS Hunnel (a James Beard Award nominee) and his team prepare modern American cuisine with the best of the best from around the world. The main dining room and Queen Victoria's Room are whisper-quiet, but the Chef's Table is convivial and relaxed.

Whispering Canyon Cafe ★★★

AMERICAN   EXPENSIVE   QUALITY ★★★½   VALUE ★★★★
READER-SURVEY RESPONSES ✪ 86% (Average)

Wilderness Lodge & Boulder Ridge/Copper Creek Villas; ☎ 407-939-3463

Reservations Highly recommended. **Dining Plan credits** 1 per person, per meal. **When to go** Anytime. **Cost range** Breakfast $11-$22 (child $6-$13), lunch $14-$24 (child $16), dinner $19-$34 (child $9-$10). **Service ★★★★. Friendliness ★★★★. Parking** Hotel lot. **Bar** Full service. **Wine selection** Limited. **Dress** Casual. **Disabled access** Yes. **Customers** Hotel guests. **Breakfast** Daily, 7:30–11 a.m. **Lunch** Daily, 11:30 a.m.–2 p.m. **Dinner** Daily, 5–10 p.m.

SETTING AND ATMOSPHERE A big, open dining room just off the lobby, with whimsical Wild West decor.

HOUSE SPECIALTIES For breakfast, the all-you-can-eat skillet offers bacon, sausage, scrambled eggs, waffles, and buttermilk biscuits and gravy. For lunch and dinner, a big skillet loaded with barbecue pulled pork or ribs, roasted chicken, mashed potatoes, green beans, and corn is a crowd-pleaser. Three other skillet options are also available at dinner.

SUMMARY AND COMMENTS The all-you-can-eat skillets give hungry folks their money's worth.

Wine Bar George ★★★★

WINE/SMALL PLATES   MODERATE/EXPENSIVE   QUALITY ★★★★   VALUE ★★★★
READER-SURVEY RESPONSES ✪ 97% (Much Above Average; No. 2-rated restaurant in Walt Disney World)

The Landing, Disney Springs; ☎ 407-490-1800

Reservations Accepted. **Dining Plan credits** 1 per person, per meal. **When to go** Anytime. **Cost range** Brunch $16–$25, lunch $12–$19, dinner $28–$39, family-style entrées (serve 2 or more), $72–$75 (child $10). The midrange for wines is around $40 per bottle, and many wines by the glass run $8–$17. **Service** ★★★★. **Friendliness** ★★★★. **Parking** Disney Springs Lime garage. **Bar** Full service. **Wine selection** Wide-ranging—more than 140 wines in all—with a focus on affordability. **Dress** Casual. **Disabled access** Yes. **Customers** Disney Springs guests. **Brunch** Saturday–Sunday, 10:30 a.m.–2 p.m. **Lunch** Monday–Friday, noon–3 p.m. **Dinner** Monday–Wednesday, 3:05–9 p.m.; Sunday and Thursday, 3:05–9:30 p.m.; Friday–Saturday, 3:05–10 p.m.

SETTING AND ATMOSPHERE Decor is spare and industrial: exposed air vents, concrete floors, brick walls, and lots of windows. The focus of the ground floor is the central bar, with an elevated wine rack and seating for around 18 people; a dozen 6-person high-tops and four 4-person tables are also available. It's noisy here even before you add alcohol, but the second floor is much quieter, and it has outdoor as well as indoor seating.

HOUSE SPECIALTIES Tapas-style small bites made for sharing—we like the saganaki (cheese set on fire!). Entrées are limited, but a few are made for two or more—try the family-style skirt steak with roasted potatoes and seasonal vegetables.

OTHER RECOMMENDATIONS Many of the wines are available by the ounce, the glass, and the bottle, letting you create your own inexpensive wine-flight theme.

SUMMARY AND COMMENTS Owner-namesake George Miliotes is one of just 269 Master Sommeliers in the world. Miliotes is also committed to making great wines affordable: The wines we price-checked are offered at the industry-standard markup of two to three times the retail price, compared with several times that at other Disney restaurants.

The Basket, a counter-service window beneath the second-story terrace, serves European-style sandwiches, cheese, olives, hummus, charcuterie, cookies, and wines on tap—served to-go by the glass or carafe.

Wolfgang Puck Bar & Grill ★★★½

AMERICAN   EXPENSIVE   QUALITY ★★★★   VALUE ★★★½
READER-SURVEY RESPONSES ✪ 70% (Much Below Average)

Town Center, Disney Springs; ☎ 407-939-3463

Reservations Highly recommended. **Dining Plan credits** 1 per person, per meal. **When to go** Brunch, lunch, or dinner. **Cost range** Brunch $17–$31, lunch and dinner $16–$49. **Service** ★★★★. **Friendliness** ★★★★. **Parking** Disney Springs Orange garage. **Bar** Full service. **Dress** Casual. **Disabled access** Yes. **Customers** Locals and Disney resort guests. **Brunch** Saturday–Sunday, noon–3 p.m. **Lunch** Friday, noon–3 p.m. **Dinner** Sunday, 3:05–10 p.m.; Monday–Thursday, 4:30–10 p.m.; Friday–Saturday, 3:05–11 p.m.

SETTING AND ATMOSPHERE The decor—farmhouse chic meets brutalist modern architecture—melds the sleek style of the surrounding garage and over-the-top retail locations with the Florida-waterfront look of the rest of Town Center. An open kitchen draws the eye from the restaurant's front door, while exposed wood beams and a copper-accented pizza oven bring warmth to the restaurant's 250-seat interior, with an indoor bar offset from the main dining room. A slight outdoor seating area abuts one side of the restaurant's exterior, with the other side dedicated to a grab-and-go dessert and gelato window.

HOUSE SPECIALTIES The best appetizer is the calamari. For dinner, the chicken Wiener schnitzel and roasted half chicken are both good.

OTHER RECOMMENDATIONS Nothing here is bad, but the meats are better than the pastas, both of which are better than the pizzas.

SUMMARY AND COMMENTS Not the flashiest restaurant, but it has good food at decent (for Disney) prices. Also often easier to get into than other places in Disney Springs.

Yachtsman Steakhouse ★★½

STEAK	EXPENSIVE	QUALITY ★★★½	VALUE ★★
READER-SURVEY RESPONSES Not enough surveys to rate			

Yacht Club Resort; ☎ 407-939-3463

Reservations Highly recommended. **Dining Plan credits** 2 per person, per meal. **When to go** Dinner. **Cost range** $36–$59 (child $10–$17). *Note:* Everything is à la carte (that is, side dishes cost extra). **Service** ★★★★. **Friendliness** ★★★★. **Parking** Hotel lot. **Bar** Full service. **Wine selection** Very good. **Dress** Dressy casual. **Disabled access** Yes. **Customers** Hotel guests, locals. **Hours** Daily, 5–9:30 p.m.

SETTING AND ATMOSPHERE Wooden beams, white linens, and a view of the Yacht Club's sandy lagoon make Yachtsman feel light and airy rather than dark and masculine like the typical steakhouse. Beef is the star, of course, but there are other options on the menu.

HOUSE SPECIALTIES Bread service with roasted, sweet garlic.

SUMMARY AND COMMENTS We visited twice after Yachtsman reopened in early August 2021. Neither visit went well. The kitchen struggled with the basics of flavor and temperature. The prices are simply too high to accept for the quality of the food that's being produced here. Try Shula's over at the Dolphin instead.

Yak & Yeti Restaurant ★★★

PAN-ASIAN	EXPENSIVE	QUALITY ★★½	VALUE ★★
READER-SURVEY RESPONSES ✪ 95% (Much Above Average)			

Asia, Animal Kingdom; ☎ 407-939-3463

Reservations Highly recommended. **Dining Plan credits** 1 per person, per meal. **When to go** Dinner. **Cost range** $18–$33 (child $11). **Service** ★★★★. **Friendliness** ★★★★. **Parking** Animal Kingdom lot. **Bar** Full service. **Wine selection** Limited. **Dress** Casual. **Disabled access** Yes. **Customers** Theme park guests. **Hours** Daily, 10:30 a.m.–6:35 p.m.

SETTING AND ATMOSPHERE A rustic two-story Nepalese inn—with seating for hundreds. Windows on the second floor overlook the Asia section of the theme park.

HOUSE SPECIALTIES Lo mein noodle bowls, coconut shrimp, chicken tikka masala.

OTHER RECOMMENDATIONS Try the Korean fried chicken tenders or firecracker shrimp.

SUMMARY AND COMMENTS The fourth-highest-rated sit-down restaurant in Walt Disney World. Sitting at the bar with a Pink Himalayan cocktail and a basket of egg rolls is the perfect escape from Animal Kingdom madness.

DINING *Outside*
WALT DISNEY WORLD

UNOFFICIAL GUIDE RESEARCHERS LOVE good food and invest a fair amount of time scouting new places to eat. And because food at Walt Disney World is so expensive, we (like you) have an economic incentive for finding palatable meals outside the World. Alas, the surrounding area isn't exactly a culinary mecca. If you thrive on fast food and the fare at chain restaurants (Denny's, TGI Friday's, Olive Garden, and the like), you'll be as happy as an alligator at a chicken farm. But if you're in the market for a superlative dining experience, you'll find the pickings outside the World of about the same quality as those inside, only less expensive. Plus, some ethnic cuisines aren't represented in WDW restaurants.

IN OR OUT OF THE WORLD FOR THESE CUISINES?
AMERICAN Good selections both in and out of the World.
BARBECUE Better out of the World.
BUFFETS A toss-up—Disney buffets are expensive but offer excellent quality and variety. Out-of-World buffets aren't as upscale but are inexpensive.
CHINESE Better out of the World.
FRENCH Toss-up; good but expensive both in and out of the World.
GERMAN Passable but not great, in or out of the World.
ITALIAN Tie on quality; better value out of the World.
JAPANESE/SUSHI **Teppan Edo** in the Japan Pavilion at EPCOT is tops for teppanyaki (table grilling). For sushi and sashimi, try **Tokyo Dining** *(closed at press time)*, also in Japan, or visit **Morimoto Asia** at Disney Springs.
MEXICAN **La Hacienda de San Angel** at EPCOT is good but expensive, with more-affordable food right next door at the quick-service **La Cantina de San Angel.** For decent Tex-Mex, try **El Patron** outside the World.
MIDDLE EASTERN More choices and better value out of the World.
SEAFOOD Toss-up.
STEAK/PRIME RIB Try **The Boathouse** at Disney Springs or **The Capital Grille** on International Drive out of the World. For more-affordable but nevertheless-delicious wads o' meat, try one of the **Black Angus** steakhouses on FL 535 in Lake Buena Vista, on International Drive, or on West Irlo Bronson Memorial Highway in Kissimmee.

Among specialty restaurants both in and out of the World, Location and price will determine your choice. Our recommendations for specialty and ethnic fare served outside of the World are summarized in the table that starts on page 364.

Better restaurants outside the World cater primarily to adults. That's a plus, however, if you're looking to escape children or you want to eat in peace and quiet.

DINING IN UNIVERSAL CITYWALK

DINING AND SHOPPING are the focus at CityWalk, whose restaurants tend to cater more to adult tastes than the theme park restaurants do. Probably the best of the bunch is **The Cowfish**, but each restaurant has a couple of decent options if you know what to look for. One thing all of them have in common is noise: Your fussy toddler will have to fight to be heard in some of these places. Most restaurants at CityWalk and inside the parks use **Zomato** via universalorlando.com for online reservations, and you can make reservations for the other venues with **OpenTable** (see page 276).

ANTOJITOS (90%/Average) ☎ 407-224-2690; tinyurl.com/antojitos universal. The name means "little cravings," the Mexican equivalent of Spain's tapas, so it's only natural that the best dishes are the appetizers. Try the esquites, roasted corn on the cob with Cotija cheese and jalapeño mayo. Antojitos carries more than 200 tequila brands and makes a tasty margarita too.

BIGFIRE (93%/Above Average) ☎ 407-224-2074; tinyurl.com/bigfire citywalk. Bigfire replaced Emeril's in the summer of 2019. The decor features blazing hearths and open fire pits—both odd choices given Orlando's infamous humidity. The "elevated American fare" focuses on steaks and freshwater fish wood-grilled over open flames.

BOB MARLEY—A TRIBUTE TO FREEDOM (79%/Much Below Average) ☎ 407-224-3663; tinyurl.com/bobmarleyuniversal. Set in a replica of the singer's Jamaica home, the building is filled with memorabilia and photos showcasing his career and life. The Caribbean-inspired dishes—beef patties, yucca fries, oxtail stew, and such—aren't particularly memorable, but the laid-back atmosphere makes it worth a visit.

BUBBA GUMP SHRIMP CO. (82%/Average) ☎ 407-903-0044; bubba gump.com. A seafood-and-cocktails eatery, part of an international chain inspired by *Forrest Gump*. Shrimp and/or crab is in almost everything, with particular highlights of Mama Blue's shrimp gumbo and journey-worthy seafood hush pups.

THE COWFISH (93%/Above Average) ☎ 407-224-3663; tinyurl.com /thecowfishuniversal. Our readers say this is the best restaurant at CityWalk. An unusual combination of burger joint and sushi bar, Cowfish is a small chain out of North Carolina. It offers tasty food at reasonable prices. We like the burgers a bit more than the sushi. Try the crab Rangoon dip appetizer and the bacon coleslaw as a side. The servers are friendly, but food delivery is painfully slow at peak times because the kitchen is undersized for the multistory dining rooms.

HARD ROCK CAFE (79%/Much Below Average) ☎ 407-351-7625; hard rock.com. The best meals we've had here have consisted of drinks and appetizers or desserts. The entrées—burgers, sandwiches, steaks, and such—aren't especially memorable. More remarkable is the collection of music memorabilia, including a 1959 pink Cadillac revolving over the bar. It's the biggest such collection on display anywhere in the Hard Rock chain.

HOT DOG HALL OF FAME (91%/Average) ☎ 407-224-3663; tinyurl .com/hotdoguniv. The menu is inspired by the food from baseball stadiums around the US—Kayem dogs from Boston, Sabretts from New York—served on bleacher seating with broadcasts of live and classic baseball games.

JIMMY BUFFETT'S MARGARITAVILLE (81%/Below Average) ☎ 407-224-2155; margaritavilleorlando.com. A boisterous tribute to the head Parrothead. The focal point is a volcano that spews margarita mix instead of lava. The food is Floridian–Caribbean, so expect lots of seafood, jerk seasoning, and Key lime pie. If you're not a Buffett fan, it isn't worth a special trip.

NBC SPORTS GRILL & BREW (83%/Average) ☎ 407-224-3663; tinyurl .com/nbcsportsgrilluniversal. With nearly 100 HD screens, this is the go-to place at Universal to catch the latest game. The menu is surprisingly deep, with a large selection of burgers and beers (more than 100 of the latter, including one brewed exclusively for the restaurant).

PAT O'BRIEN'S (94%/Much Above Average) ☎ 407-224-2102; patobriens .com/orlando. Dueling pianos in the lounge, a full menu in the Courtyard Restaurant, those rum-filled Hurricanes throughout. Behind a facade that replicates the St. Peter Street original, Pat's offers NOLA classics (try the jambalaya) and massive sandwiches. The brick courtyard is a slice of the Big Easy, but noise levels are high during outdoor concerts nearby.

RED OVEN PIZZA BAKERY (86%/Average) ☎ 407-224-3663; tinyurl .com/redovenpizzabakery. Artisan pizza baked in a 900°F oven. Choose from white and red Neapolitan-style pies, made with San Marzano tomatoes, organic extra-virgin olive oil, buffalo mozzarella, fine-ground "00" flour, and filtered water. Pizzas run $13–$16 and serve two people.

TOOTHSOME CHOCOLATE EMPORIUM (87%/Average) ☎ 407-224-3663; tinyurl.com/toothsomekitchen. Candies, cakes, and ice-cream concoctions, along with steaks, salads, and sandwiches, served inside a whimsical Wonka-esque steampunk confectionery factory. Very highly rated by *Unofficial Guide* readers, though perhaps more for the theme than the food.

VIVO ITALIAN KITCHEN (89%/Average) ☎ 407-224-2318; tinyurl.com /vivoorl. CityWalk's third-highest-rated restaurant in our latest reader survey. Surprisingly good house-made pasta (Squid Ink Seafood is outstanding), interesting cocktails, and a 2-pound cannoli for dessert. Sit by the open kitchen and watch the show.

A food court located on CityWalk's upper level offers serviceable quick bites: **Bread Box Handcrafted Sandwiches, BK Whopper Bar, Fusion Bistro Sushi and Sake Bar, Menchie's Frozen Yogurt, Moe's Southwest Grill,** and **Panda Express.**

continued on page 366

Where to Eat Outside Walt Disney World

AMERICAN

- **THE RAVENOUS PIG** 565 W. Fairbanks Ave., Winter Park; ☎ 407-628-2333; theravenouspig.com; moderate–expensive. Closed Mondays. New American cuisine; an award-winning menu changes seasonally. Online ordering and curbside pickup.

- **SEASONS 52** 7700 W. Sand Lake Rd., Orlando; ☎ 407-354-5212; seasons52.com; moderate–expensive. Delicious, creative New American food that's low in fat and calories. Extensive wine list. Online ordering and curbside pickup.

- **SLATE** 8323 W. Sand Lake Rd., Orlando; ☎ 407-500-7528; slateorlando.com; moderate–expensive. Combines intimacy and casual dining with greater success than many Restaurant Row establishments. Grab a quick bite from the extensive menu or try heartier fare from the copper-clad wood oven. Delivery via Grubhub.

BARBECUE

- **BUBBALOU'S BODACIOUS BAR-B-QUE** 5818 Conroy Rd., Orlando (near Universal Orlando); ☎ 407-295-1212; bubbalous.com; inexpensive. Tender, smoky barbecue; tomato-based Killer Sauce. Online ordering. Delivery via DoorDash, Grubhub, and Uber Eats.

- **4 RIVERS SMOKEHOUSE** 874 W. Osceola Pkwy., Kissimmee, and six area locations; ☎ 844-474-8377; 4rsmokehouse.com; inexpensive. Closed Sundays. Award-winning brisket, plus fried okra, cheese grits, and collards. Outdoor seating available. Online ordering, curbside pickup, and drive-thru.

CARIBBEAN

- **BAHAMA BREEZE** 8849 International Dr., Orlando; ☎ 407-248-2499; 8735 Vineland Ave.; ☎ 407-938-9010; bahamabreeze.com; moderate. A creative and tasty take on Caribbean cuisine from the owners of Olive Garden and LongHorn Steakhouse. Patio seating available. Use call-ahead seating to check wait time. Online ordering.

CUBAN/SPANISH

- **COLUMBIA** 649 Front St., Celebration; ☎ 407-566-1505; columbiarestaurant.com; moderate/expensive. Authentic Cuban and Spanish creations, including paella and the famous 1905 Salad. One of our favorite places in Celebration. Outdoor seating available.

- **CUBA LIBRE** 9101 International Dr. at Pointe Orlando; ☎ 407-226-1600, cubalibre restaurant.com; moderate. Upscale, like Columbia above, it specializes in ceviches, tapas, and classic Cuban main courses ranging from $20 to $32. Salsa dancing until 2 a.m. on Fridays and 2:30 a.m. on Saturdays.

- **HAVANA'S CAFÉ** 8544 Palm Pkwy., Orlando; ☎ 407-238-5333, havanascubancuisine .com; moderate. Authentic homemade Cuban cuisine and Bob and Len's personal favorite. Reservations recommended. Outdoor seating available. Takeout available. Delivery via Uber Eats and Grubhub.

ETHIOPIAN

- **NILE ETHIOPIAN RESTAURANT** 7048 International Dr., Orlando; ☎ 407-354-0026; nileorlando.com; inexpensive–moderate. Authentic stews and delicious vegetarian dishes. Bob's favorite Orlando/WDW-area restaurant. Curbside pickup available. Delivery via Grubhub.

- **SELAM ETHIOPIAN & ERITREAN CUISINE** 5494 Central Florida Pkwy., Orlando; ☎ 407-778-3119; ethiopianrestaurantorlando.com; inexpensive–moderate. Closed on Tuesdays. The dishes here are a little spicier than the ones at Nile (see above). Specialties from Eritrea (Ethiopia's neighbor to the north) provide some nice variety. Outdoor seating available. Delivery via Grubhub, Uber Eats, and DoorDash.

GREEK

- **TAVERNA OPA ORLANDO** 9101 International Dr., Orlando; ☎ 407-351-8660; opaorlando.com; moderate. Try traditional Greek standouts like pastitsio, boureki, and moussaka, along with kebobs and seafood specialties cooked on a wood fire. Live entertainment many nights. Reservations available online or via OpenTable. Delivery via DoorDash and Uber Eats.

Where to Eat Outside Walt Disney World *(continued)*

INDIAN

• TABLA CUISINE 5847 Grand National Dr., Orlando; ☎ 407-248-9400; tablacuisine
.com; moderate. Within the Clarion Inn on I-Drive, but don't let that keep you away from
one of the better Indian restaurants in the area. The menu also includes Chinese and
Thai dishes. Online ordering, curbside pickup, and delivery available.

ITALIAN

• ANTHONY'S COAL FIRED PIZZA AND WINGS 8031 Turkey Lake Rd., Orlando;
☎ 407-363-9466; acfp.com; inexpensive. Pizzas, eggplant, wings, sandwiches, beer,
and wine. Online wait list and ordering. Delivery via Uber Eats.

• BICE RISTORANTE ORLANDO Loews Portofino Bay Hotel, Universal Orlando
Resort, 5601 Universal Blvd., Orlando; ☎ 407-503-1415; bice-orlando.com; expensive.
Authentic Italian and great wines. Reservations required. Outdoor seating available.

• PEPERONCINO CUCINA 7988 Via Dellagio Way, Orlando; ☎ 407-440-2856;
facebook.com/peperoncinoorlando; moderate. Calabrian chef Barbara Alfano runs a
tight and authentic kitchen, creating pastas and wood-fired pizza worthy of the name.
Reservations available. Outdoor seating available. Delivery via Uber Eats.

JAPANESE/SUSHI

• AKASAKA 7786 W. Sand Lake Rd., Orlando; ☎ 407-370-0007; akasaka-sushi.com;
moderate. A favorite sushi bar for locals. The tempura is popular too. Takeout available.
Delivery via DoorDash and Uber Eats.

• HANAMIZUKI 8255 International Dr., Suite 136, Orlando; ☎ 407-363-7200;
hanamizuki.us; moderate–expensive. Pricey but authentic. Takeout available. Delivery
via DoorDash, Grubhub, and Uber Eats.

• NAGOYA SUSHI 7600 Dr. Phillips Blvd., Ste. 66, in the very rear of The Marketplace
at Dr. Phillips; ☎ 407-248-8558; nagoyasushi.com; moderate. Closed Mondays; open
for lunch Tuesday–Sunday, noon–3 p.m.; for dinner Sunday and Tuesday–Thursday,
4:30–9:30 p.m. and Friday–Saturday, 4:30–10 p.m. Small, intimate restaurant with great
sushi and an extensive menu. Reservations available by phone or online. Takeout
available. Delivery via DoorDash and Uber Eats.

LATIN

• SOFRITO LATIN CAFE 8607 Palm Pkwy., Orlando; ☎ 407-778-4205; sofritocafe
.com; inexpensive. Located near the corner of FL 535 and Palm Parkway, Sofrito
specializes in comfort foods from Cuba, Colombia, Argentina, Chile, Puerto Rico, Peru,
Dominican Republic, Brazil, and Venezuela. The restaurant is modern but sterile. The best
play is to order takeout for pickup. Outdoor seating available. Delivery via DoorDash.

MEXICAN

• EL PATRON 12167 S. Apopka–Vineland Rd., Orlando; ☎ 407-238-5300; elpatron
orlando.com; moderate. Family-owned restaurant serving freshly prepared Mexican
dishes. Full bar. Weekend brunch buffet and weekday lunch buffet, with the buffet
now served by staff. Outdoor seating available. Online reservations, takeout, and
delivery available.

• EL TENAMPA MEXICAN RESTAURANT 4565 W. Irlo Bronson Memorial Hwy.,
Kissimmee; ☎ 407-397-1981; inexpensive. Family-owned, with an extensive menu of
authentic Mexican regional fare in a small, colorful room. Try their steak dish called
Arrachera el Tenampa. Outdoor seating available. Takeout and delivery available. Delivery also via DoorDash and Grubhub.

MOROCCAN

• MERGUEZ 11951 International Dr., Orlando; ☎ 407-778-4343; merguez.restaurant;
inexpensive. Bright, informal setting with adjacent alfresco option. Excellent and representative Moroccan specialties. Awesome bastillas and tagines. Couscous, following
the Moroccan custom, is served on Friday only. No alcohol sold. Outdoor seating
available. Takeout available. Delivery via Uber Eats.

NEW WORLD

• KNIFE AND SPOON 4012 Central Florida Pkwy., in the Ritz-Carlton Orlando; ☎ 407-
393-4333; grandelakes.com/dining/knife-and-spoon; expensive. Open Wednesday–
Saturday, 5:30–10 p.m. Led by award-winning chef John Tesar, the restaurant serves
seafood, in-house dry-aged steaks, and pastas. Reservations online or via OpenTable.

Where to Eat Outside Walt Disney World *(continued)*

PERUVIAN

• EL INKA GRILL 7600 Dr. Phillips Blvd., Orlando; ☎ 407-930-2810; elinkagrill.com; moderate. El Inka Grill features numerous ceviche and tiradito (thin raw fish marinated in citrus juice) preparations, including three ceviches that are grilled. Traditional Peruvian beef, fish, and chicken entrées run $17–$24 and most come with several sides. Portions are generous. Outdoor seating available. Takeout available. Delivery via DoorDash.

SEAFOOD

• CELEBRATION TOWN TAVERN 721 Front St., Celebration; ☎ 407-566-2526; thecelebrationtowntavern.com; moderate. Popular hangout for locals, featuring New England–style seafood. Clam chowder and lobster rolls are big hits. Outdoor seating available. Takeout available.

• OCEAN PRIME 7339 W. Sand Lake Rd., Orlando; ☎ 407-781-4880; ocean-prime .com; expensive. Elegant supper-club ambience; classic fare focusing on fresh seafood and perfectly cooked meats. Outdoor dining and piano bar. Dinner only. Reservations recommended. Takeout available. Delivery via DoorDash.

STEAK

• BULL & BEAR Waldorf Astoria Orlando, 14200 Bonnet Creek Resort Ln.; ☎ 407-597-5413; bullandbearorlando.com; expensive. Closed Mondays; open Tuesday–Sunday, 6–10 p.m. Classic steakhouse with a clubby ambience. The fried chicken is life-affirming. Reservations via phone, website, or OpenTable.

• THE CAPITAL GRILLE Pointe Orlando, 9101 International Dr., Orlando; ☎ 407-370-4392; thecapitalgrille.com; expensive. Dinner only. Dry-aged steaks, good wine list, and classic decor. Curbside pickup 5–9 p.m.

• TEXAS DE BRAZIL 5259 International Dr., Orlando; ☎ 407-355-0355; texasdebrazil .com; expensive. All you can eat in a Brazilian-style *churrascaria*. Filet mignon, sausage, pork, chicken, lamb, and more. Age 2 and under are free, ages 3–5 are $5, and ages 6–12 are half-price. Salad bar with 40-plus options temporarily unavailable, but salads are available to order. Takeout and delivery via website.

• VITO'S CHOP HOUSE (*closed at press time*) 8633 International Dr., Orlando; ☎ 407-354-2467; vitoschophouse.com; moderate. Upscale meatery with a taste of Tuscany. Specialty martini list, 850 wine selections, and a variety of cigars.

THAI

• THAI SILK 5532 International Dr., Orlando; ☎ 407-226-8997; thaisilkorlando.com; moderate. Acclaimed by Orlando dining critics for its authentic Thai dishes. Delicious vegetarian options; impressive wine list. Takeout available. Delivery via DoorDash, Grubhub, Postmates, or Uber Eats.

• THAI THANI 11025 International Dr., Orlando; ☎ 407-239-9733; thaithani.net; moderate. Specializes in Thai duck dishes.

TURKISH

• TURQUAZ TURKISH CUISINE AND HOOKAH BAR 5648 International Dr., Orlando; ☎ 407-309-5942; orlandoturkishcuisine.com; moderate. Closed Mondays; open Tuesday–Friday, 4 p.m.–midnight; Saturday–Sunday, 11 a.m.–midnight. Reflects Turkey's Mediterranean side. Outdoor seating available. Reservations by phone. Delivery via DoorDash.

continued from page 363

STRONG WATER TAVERN (95%/Exceptional) ☎ 888-503-5000; loews hotels.com/sapphire-falls-resort. Strong Water is at Universal's Sapphire Falls Resort, not CityWalk, but if you're a fan of rum and tasty tapas, it might be worth a trip. The menu features dozens of rums, mostly from the Caribbean, in individual glasses or regional flights. The Caribbean-influenced small-plates menu leans toward seafood but also includes chicken and beef at a quality better than you'd expect at a midpriced hotel. We're told all dishes are prepared on request from fresh ingredients.

BUFFETS AND MEAL DEALS OUTSIDE WALT DISNEY WORLD

BUFFETS, RESTAURANT SPECIALS, and discount dining abound in the area surrounding Walt Disney World, especially on US 192 (aka Irlo Bronson Memorial Highway) and along International Drive. Local visitor magazines, distributed free at non-Disney hotels and other places, are packed with advertisements and coupons for seafood feasts, Chinese buffets, Indian buffets, breakfast buffets, and a host of other specials. For a family trying to economize, some of the come-ons are mighty sweet. But are the places good? Is the food fresh, tasty, and appealing? Are the restaurants clean and inviting? Armed with little more than a roll of Tums, the *Unofficial* research team tried all the eateries that advertise heavily in the tourist magazines. Here's what we discovered. *Note:* To the best of our knowledge, the buffets in this section are still self-service unless stated otherwise.

CHINESE SUPER BUFFETS If you've ever tried preparing Chinese food, especially a stir-fry, you know that split-second timing is required to avoid overcooking. It's no surprise, then, that Chinese dishes languishing on a buffet lose their freshness, texture, and flavor in a hurry.

Ichiban Buffet (5269 W. Irlo Bronson Memorial Highway; ☎ 407-396-6668; 5529 International Dr.; ☎ 407-930-8889; ichibanbuffet .com) and **Hokkaido Chinese and Japanese Buffet** (12173 S. Apopka–Vineland Road; ☎ 407-778-5188; 5737 W. Irlo Bronson Memorial Highway; ☎ 407-396-0669; hokkaidobuffetorlando.co) are the best choices in their genre. Hokkaido buffets are comparable, so select whichever buffet is most convenient to you. And remember our intro: Selections dry out on buffets, so seek out a popular buffet, where dishes are replenished frequently.

INDIAN BUFFETS Indian food works better on a buffet than Chinese food; in fact, it actually improves as the flavors marry. In the Disney World area, most Indian restaurants offer a buffet at lunch only—not too convenient if you're spending your day at the theme parks. If you're out shopping or taking a day off, these Indian buffets are worth trying: **Aashirwad Indian Cuisine** (7000 S. Kirkman Road, at the corner of International Drive; ☎ 407-370-9830; aashirwadrestaurant.com); **Ahmed Indian Restaurant** (11301 S. Orange Blossom Trail; ☎ 407-856-5970; ahmedrestaurant.com); and **Woodlands Pure Vegetarian Indian Cuisine** (6040 S. Orange Blossom Trail; ☎ 407-854-3330; woodlandsusa.com), which isn't a buffet and has a very large menu.

CHURRASCARIAS A number of these South American–style meat emporiums have sprung up along International Drive. Our picks are **Café Mineiro** (6432 International Dr.; ☎ 407-248-2932; cafemineiro steakhouse.com), a Brazilian steakhouse north of Sand Lake Road, and **BoiBrazil Steakhouse** (5668 International Dr.; ☎ 407-354-0260; boibrazil.com). Both offer good food and good value. More expensive are the Argentinian churrasco specialties at **The Knife** (12501 FL 535; ☎ 321-395-4892; thekniferestaurant.com); be sure to try the sweetbreads, an Argentinean specialty rarely found in the United States. If you prefer chains, the pricey **Texas de Brazil** and **Fogo de Chão** also have locations in Orlando.

ITALIAN BUFFETS A relatively new buffet, **Oreganatta Italian Buffet** (6320 International Dr., Orlando; ☎ 407-985-4312) is advertising everywhere. It's a concept with a lot of potential, but our experience was disappointing. The average Cicis Pizza would do as well or better—and there are about half a dozen Cicis in the I-Drive, Kissimmee, and Lake Buena Vista areas. As we went to press, staff serve guests at Cicis buffets.

SEAFOOD AND LOBSTER BUFFETS These affairs don't exactly fall under the category of inexpensive dining. The main draw (no pun intended) is all the lobster you can eat. The problem is that, after a few minutes on the buffet line, lobsters make better tennis balls than dinner, so try to grab your lobster immediately after a fresh batch has been brought out.

Two lobster buffets are on I-Drive, and another two are on US 192. All four of them do a reasonable job, but we prefer **Boston Lobster Feast** (7702 W. Irlo Bronson Memorial Hwy.; ☎ 407-768-1166; 6071 W. Irlo Bronson Memorial Hwy.; ☎ 407-396-2606; 8731 International Dr., five blocks north of the Convention Center; ☎ 407-248-8606; bostonlobsterfeast.com). The International Drive Location is cavernous and noisy, which is why we prefer the Irlo Bronson location, where you can actually have a conversation over dinner. The I-Drive Location has ample parking, while the Irlo Bronson restaurant does not. Dining is expensive at both locations.

BREAKFAST AND ENTRÉE BUFFETS Most chain steakhouses in the area, including **Ponderosa** and **Golden Corral,** offer entrée buffets. All serve breakfast, lunch, and dinner. At lunch and dinner, you get the buffet when you buy an entrée, usually a steak; breakfast is a straightforward buffet (that is, you don't have to buy an entrée). As for the food, it's chain-restaurant quality but pretty good all the same. The prices are a bargain, and you can get in and out at lightning speed—important at breakfast when you're trying to get to the parks early. Some locations offer lunch and dinner buffets at a set price without your having to buy an entrée.

unofficial **TIP**
Most chain-restaurant breakfast buffets have a number of locations in the Disney World area, but their operating hours aren't always the same, so check online or call before you go.

In addition to the steakhouses, the WDW-area **Shoney's** also offers breakfast, lunch, and dinner buffets.

Local freebie visitor magazines are full of discount coupons for all of the previous restaurants.

A New Hampshire reader notes:

> You mention quite a few buffets for off-site dining, but it would have been nice to know their normal morning business hours. Some buffets (like Ponderosa) didn't open until 8 a.m. for breakfast. This is way too late if you're trying to get to the park [for a 9 a.m.] opening time.

DISNEY BUFFETS VS. OFF-SITE BUFFETS Most off-site buffets are long on selection but don't compare favorably with Disney buffets (when they're offered) in terms of quality; likewise, the setting and ambience of Disney buffets is generally superior. If you're trying to save money, however, non-Disney buffets offer excellent value. Though some dishes may be below par, you should find enough that's palatable to put together a more-than-acceptable meal. Just start with small samples to sort out the winners and losers; then go back for larger portions of your favorites.

One outstanding exception to the above is the **Café Osceola** buffet at Rosen Shingle Creek Resort (9939 Universal Blvd., Orlando; ☎ 407-996-9939; rosenshinglecreek.com/dining). Café Osceola specializes in carved meats.

MEAL DEALS Discount coupons are available for a wide range of restaurants. **Sonny's Real Pit Bar-B-Q** is a meat eater's delight. Among its offerings, the Family Feast, $57 per family of four, includes pulled pork, plus chicken, ribs, barbecue beans, slaw, fries, corn bread, and tea. The closest Sonny's Location to Walt Disney World and Universal is at 7423 S. Orange Blossom Trail in Orlando (☎ 407-859-7197; sonnysbbq.com). No coupons are available (or needed) for Sonny's, but they're available for other "meateries."

COUPONS Find discounts and two-for-one coupons for many of the restaurants mentioned in freebie visitor guides available at most hotels outside Walt Disney World. **Visit Orlando** (☎ 407-363-5800; visit orlando.com) offers discounts and information on its website and via phone. In Kissimmee, visit the **Osceola County Welcome Center and History Museum** (4155 W. Vine St.; ☎ 407-396-8644; osceolahistory .org; open Wednesday–Sunday, 10 a.m.–4 p.m.).

The Great Orlando Pizza Scam

Plenty of reputable local pizza joints deliver to hotels in and around the theme parks; many Disney and Universal resorts offer pizza delivery as well. But for a few years now, con artists have been distributing flyers advertising pizza delivery to hotel guests—they ask for your credit card number over the phone, but the pizza never arrives. Disregard any such flyers you find.

WALT DISNEY WORLD *with* KIDS

The **ECSTASY** *and the* **AGONY**

TRUE STORY: Bob was inspired to write the original *Unofficial Guide to Walt Disney World* after screwing up his family's first Disney trip. Len's didn't go any better.

It's safe to say that most of the *Guide,* and especially this chapter, is based on real-world experience: stuff we and our readers have learned by making every possible mistake in Walt Disney World. If you prepare the best you can and don't beat yourself up when something goes wrong, there will be moments of pure magic.

When it comes to Walt Disney World, parents and kids alike are likely to get revved up about a visit to this special place—all you have to do is watch a WDW commercial to see what we mean. But the reality of doing so, particularly during the summer, can be closer to agony than to ecstasy.

An Ohio mother who took her 5-year-old one summer recalls:

I felt so happy and excited before we went, but when I look back I think I should have had my head examined. The first day we went to the Magic Kingdom, it was packed. By 11 in the morning, we had walked so far and stood in so many lines that we were all exhausted. Kristy cried about going on anything that looked or even sounded scary and was frightened by all of the Disney characters (they're so big!) except Minnie and Snow White.

We got hungry about the same time as everyone else, but the lines for food were too long and my husband said we'd have to wait. By 1 in the afternoon, we were just plugging along, not seeing anything we were really interested in, but picking rides because the lines were short or because it was air-conditioned. At around 2:30, we finally got something to eat, but by then we were so hot and tired that it felt like we had worked in the yard all day. At the end, we were so P.O.'d and uncomfortable that we weren't having any fun.

Before you stiffen in denial, let us assure you that this family's experience is not unusual. Most young children are as picky about rides as they are about what they eat, and many preschoolers are intimidated by the Disney characters. Few humans (of any age) are mentally or physically equipped to march all day in a throng of 30,000-plus people in the Florida heat and humidity. And would it surprise you to learn that almost 60% of preschoolers said the thing they liked best about their Disney trip was the hotel swimming pool?

unofficial **TIP**
When considering a trip to Walt Disney World, think about whether your kids are old enough to enjoy what can be a very fun but taxing trip.

With good planning and a sense of humor, you'll be emailing us messages like this one from a Harrisburg, Pennsylvania, mom:

I knew it would be fun for my daughter, but what I didn't expect was just how much fun it would be for me.

REALITY TESTING: WHOSE DREAM IS IT?

REMEMBER WHEN YOU WERE A KID and you got that nifty remote-control car or collector Barbie for Christmas—the one you weren't allowed to play with? Did you wonder who the gift was really for? Ask yourself a similar question about your vacation to Walt Disney World. Whose dream are you trying to make come true: yours or your child's?

Young children are experts at reading their parents' emotions. When you ask, "Honey, how would you like to go to Disney World?" your child will respond more to your smile and enthusiasm than to any notion of what Disney World is all about. The younger the child, the more this holds true. From many preschoolers, you could elicit the same excitement by asking, "Sweetie, how would you like to go to Cambodia on a dogsled?"

So is your happy fantasy of introducing your child to Disney magic a pipe dream? Well, not necessarily—but you have to be open to reality testing. For example, would you increase the probability of a successful visit by waiting a year or two? Will your child have sufficient endurance and patience to cope with long lines and large crowds?

RECOMMENDATIONS FOR MAKING THE DREAM COME TRUE

WHEN YOU'RE PLANNING a Walt Disney World vacation with young children, consider the following:

AGE Although Disney World's color and festivity excite all children, and specific attractions delight toddlers and preschoolers, its entertainments are generally oriented to older kids and adults. Children should be a fairly mature 7 years old to *appreciate* the Magic Kingdom and Animal Kingdom, and a year or two older to get much out of EPCOT or Hollywood Studios.

Readers continually debate how old a child should be or the ideal age to go to Disney World. A Rockaway, New Jersey, mom writes:

> *Our hotel pool was the one and only thing our kids enjoyed. I had planned and saved for this trip for over a year, and I cried all week at the realization that our kids just wanted to swim.*

A Lawrenceville, Georgia, mother of two toddlers emphasizes the importance of maintaining your kids' regular schedule:

> *The first day, we tried your suggestion about an early start, so we woke the kids (ages 4 and 2) and hurried them to get going. BAD IDEA. This put them off-schedule for naps and meals the rest of the day.*

A Pennsylvania mom with two young kids recounts her experience:

> *Eighteen months is the absolute worst age to bring a child to Disney. They have no concept of waiting in lines, can't stand the heat, will not sit in a stroller, only want to be carried, and only want to go up and down the stairs outside of the attraction you want to ride. Expect lots of meltdowns, and good luck with the baby swap when they have to go to someone else. (Mom didn't get to do much.)*

WHEN TO VISIT Avoid the hot, crowded summer months, especially if you have preschoolers. Go in October, November (except Thanksgiving), early December, January, February, or May. If your children can't afford to miss school, try late August, before school starts; crowds and hotel rates should be lower. We should warn you, however, that staff shortages (which reduce the number of guests an attraction can handle in a day), special festivals and events, and attraction breakdowns can combine to make the parks seem crowded irrespective of the time of year. Concerning ride breakdowns, a mom from Springville, Alabama, says:

> *We had a lot of rides with tech problems: Pirates of the Caribbean, Winnie the Pooh, Avatar Flight of Passage, Peter Pan's Flight, and Spaceship Earth. VERY frustrating. We spent over 3 hours in line just for Flight of Passage. It made other rides less fun when a ride would just stop in the middle and lose the magic.*

If you have children of varying ages and they're good students, take the older ones out of school and visit during the cooler, less congested off-season. Most readers who have tried this at various times agree. A New Hampshire parent writes:

> *I took my grade-school children out of school for a few days to go during a slow time and highly recommend it. We communicated with the teachers about a month before traveling to seek their preference for whether classwork and homework should be completed before, during, or after our trip. It's so much more enjoyable to be at Disney when your children can experience rides and attractions and all that is Disney rather than standing in line.*

There's another side to this story, and we've received some well-considered letters from parents and teachers who don't think taking kids out of school is such a hot idea. From a father in Fairfax, Virginia:

My wife and I are disappointed that you seem to be encouraging families to take their children out of school to go to WDW. My wife is an eighth-grade teacher of chemistry and physics. She has parents pull their children, some honor-roll students, out of school for vacations, only to discover when they return that the students are unable to comprehend the material.

A Martinez, California, teacher offers a compelling analogy:

There are a precious 180 days for us as teachers to instruct our students, and there are 185 days during the year for Disney World. I've seen countless students during my 14 years of teaching struggle to catch up the rest of the year due to a week of vacation. The analogy I use with my students' parents is that it's like walking out of a movie after watching the first 5 minutes, then returning for the last 5 minutes and trying to figure out what happened.

But a teacher from Penn Yan, New York, sees things differently:

As a teacher and a parent, I disagree that it's horrible for a parent to take a child out for a vacation. If a parent takes the time to let us know that a child is going to be out, we help them get ready for upcoming homework the best we can. If the child is a good student, why shouldn't they go have a wonderful experience with their family?

If possible, ask your child's teacher for a list of topics they'll be covering while you're away. Have your child study these on the plane or in the car, during midday breaks, and at night before bed. Alternatively, if your school is using remote learning, do that in your hotel before heading to the parks.

BUILD NAPS AND REST INTO YOUR ITINERARY By a wide margin, the thing most parents say they learned during their first Disney visit was the importance of daily breaks and naps.

unofficial **TIP**
If you must rent a car to make returning to your hotel practicable, do it.

Why? The parks and crowds can be huge, and inevitably someone is going to run out of steam. And when that someone isn't happy, nobody's happy. Pushing the tired or discontented beyond their capacity will spoil the day for them *and* you. Go back to your hotel midday to rest and relax, then return to the park (or hop to another) in the late afternoon or early evening.

A family from Texas underlines the importance of naps and rest:

Probably the most important tip your guide gave us was going to the hotel to swim and regroup during the day. The parks became unbearable by noon—and so did my husband and boys. The hotel was an oasis that calmed our nerves! After about 3 hours of playtime, we headed out to a different park for dinner and a cool evening of fun.

Regarding naps, this mom doesn't mince words:

Take the book's advice, get out of the park, and take the nap, take the nap, TAKE THE NAP!

A mom from Chicago offers a suggestion:

With small children, two days on, one day off is helpful. We did three park days in a row, with travel days on either end, and our third day was a waste for the 5-year-old—she was tired and sick of walking, and she and I ended up only doing a few rides while everyone else went off and had fun. If I'd thought through that, we would have made one of the travel days a park day and had a pool day in the middle.

Be prepared for someone to get tired and irritable. Call time-out when it happens, and trust your instincts: What would feel best—another ride, an ice-cream break, or going back to the room for a nap?

WHERE TO STAY If you're going to take midday breaks, you'll be making two trips per day to the parks. The time and hassle involved in commuting to and from the parks will be less if your hotel is close by. This doesn't necessarily mean you have to lodge inside Disney World. Because the World is so geographically dispersed, many off-property hotels are closer to the parks than some Disney resorts (see our Hotel Information Chart, pages 252–263, showing commuting times from Disney and non-Disney hotels).

If you have young children, book a hotel that's within a 20-minute drive from the theme parks. If you want to stay in Walt Disney World, we recommend the **Polynesian Village & Villas, Grand Floridian & Villas,** or **Wilderness Lodge & Boulder Ridge/Copper Creek Villas** (in that order), if they fit your budget. The **Contemporary Resort, Bay Lake Tower, Polynesian Village & Villas,** and **Grand Floridian & Villas** are within walking distance of the Magic Kingdom; the downside is that they're expensive and the theming of some hotels may not appeal to kids.

For less expensive rooms, try **Port Orleans French Quarter.** The least expensive on-site rooms are the ones at the **All-Star Resorts. All-Star Music** and **Art of Animation** also have two-room Family Suites that can sleep as many as six and provide kitchenettes. Log cabins at **Fort Wilderness Resort & Campground,** along with the DVC resorts, are another option for families who need a little more space. Outside the World, check out our top hotels for families (see page 288), but know that many more good options exist.

BUILDING ENDURANCE Though most kids are active, their normal play usually doesn't condition them for the exertion required to tour a Disney park. Start family walks four to six weeks before your trip to get in shape. A mother from Wescosville, Pennsylvania, reports:

We had our 6-year-old begin walking with us a bit every day one month before leaving—when we arrived at Disney World, her little legs could carry her, and she had a lot of stamina.

From a Middletown, Delaware, mom:

You recommended walking for six weeks prior to the trip, but we began months in advance, just because. My husband lost 10 pounds, my daughter never once complained, and we met a lot of neighbors!

At the very least, run a little test, say a 6-mile walk or hike, to establish your family's baseline level of fitness. Be safe. Many find out the hard way that they're not as fit as they think. As a postscript, 6 miles is less ground than most cover in a Disney park.

SETTING LIMITS AND MAKING PLANS To avoid arguments and disappointments, establish guidelines for each day and get everybody committed. Include the following:

1. Wake-up time and breakfast plans
2. When to depart for the park
3. What to take with you
4. A policy for splitting the group or for staying together, and what to do if the group gets separated or someone is lost
5. What you want to see, including plans in the event that an attraction is closed or too crowded
6. A policy on what you can afford for snacks
7. How long you plan to tour in the morning and what time you'll return to your hotel to rest
8. When you'll return to the park and how late you'll stay
9. Dinner plans
10. A policy for buying souvenirs, including who pays (kids or parents)
11. Bedtimes

BE FLEXIBLE Any day at Disney World includes surprises; be prepared to adjust your plan. Listen to your intuition.

MAINTAINING SOME SEMBLANCE OF ORDER AND DISCIPLINE

DISCIPLINE AND ORDER are more difficult to maintain when traveling than at home because everyone is, as a Boston mom puts it, "in and out"—in strange surroundings and out of the normal routine. For kids, it's hard to contain the excitement and anticipation that pop to the surface in the form of fidgety hyperactivity, nervous energy, and (sometimes) acting out. Confinement in a car, plane, or hotel room only exacerbates things.

Once you're in the theme parks, it doesn't get much better. There's more elbow room, but there are also crowds, overstimulation, heat, and miles of walking. All this, coupled with marginal or inadequate rest, can lead to meltdowns in the most harmonious of families.

Sound parenting and standards of discipline practiced at home, applied consistently, will suffice to handle most situations on vacation. Still, you need to study the hand you're dealt when traveling. For starters, aside from being jazzed and ablaze with adrenaline, your kids may believe that rules followed at home can be suspended when away from it. Parents may reinforce this misguided intuition by being overly lenient in the name of keeping the peace.

While select house rules—cleaning your plate, going to bed at a set time—can safely be relaxed on vacation, tossing your normal approach to discipline out the window can precipitate major misunderstanding and possibly disaster.

Kids, being kids, are likely to believe that a vacation to Walt Disney World is intended just for them—and that can dramatically increase their sense of shock and hurt when you have to correct them or tell them no. An incident that would hardly elicit a pouty lip at home could well escalate to tears or defiance when traveling. It's important before you depart on your trip, therefore, to discuss the ground rules with your children, and to explore their wants and expectations as well.

According to *Unofficial Guide* child psychologist Karen Turnbow, PhD, addressing behavioral problems on the road begins with a clear-cut disciplinary policy at home, based on the following key concepts:

1. LET EXPECTATIONS BE KNOWN Discuss what you expect from your children as far as complying with parental directives, treatment of siblings, resolution of disputes, schedules (including waking up and bedtime), manners, staying together, and who pays for what.

2. EXPLAIN THE CONSEQUENCES OF NONCOMPLIANCE Be clear and firm: "If you do X (or don't do X), this is what will happen."

3. GIVE THEM A WARNING You're dealing with excited, expectant children, not machines, so it's important to issue a warning before meting out discipline. And by *warning,* we mean just one—multiple warnings without consequences not only undermine your credibility, but they also effectively put your child in control of things.

4. FOLLOW-THROUGH A corollary to the above: If you say you're going to do something, *do it.* Children must understand that you mean what you say.

5. CONSISTENCY Random discipline encourages random behavior, which in turn translates to a near total loss of parental control. Long-term, both at home and on the road, your response to a given situation or transgression must be both predictable and reliable.

Active Listening and a Feeling Vocabulary

Whining, tantrums, defiance, and holding up the group aren't just things your kids do to drive you nuts; they're also methods your kids use to communicate with you. Taken at face value, a fit may *seem* to be about the ice cream you refused to buy little Beulah, but there's almost always something deeper bubbling just beneath the surface. And as often as not, the root cause is a need for attention. This need is so powerful in some kids that they willingly subject themselves to punishment to get that attention—even if it's negative.

Getting at the root causes of unwanted behaviors involves two important concepts. **Active listening** involves not only being alert to what a child says but also tuning in to the context in which it's said, to the words used and possible subtext, to the child's emotional state and body language, and even to what's *not* said. Similarly, helping children develop a **feeling vocabulary** involves teaching them to express their emotions in words, not tantrums. If you've ever heard a parent encourage a child to "use your words," that's what we mean.

unofficial **TIP**
Teaching your kids to tell you clearly what they want or need will help make the trip more enjoyable for everyone.

Kids are almost never too young to start developing a feeling vocabulary. And helping your child to get in touch with—and to communicate—his or her emotions will stimulate you to focus on *your* feelings and mood states in a similar way. With persistence and effort, the whole family can achieve a vastly improved ability to communicate.

A Shelby, North Carolina, reader touts a resource for parents:

> *I use a therapy technique at work called the **Alert Program** that helps kids develop self-regulation skills, including a feeling vocabulary. The website (alertprogram.com) provides an explanation and additional resources [some for free, most for sale]. You can use many analogies to make it work, but an especially fun one is to use Disney characters: A child might feel like Winnie the Pooh if he's "just right," Tigger if he's hyper or needs a movement break, or Eeyore if he's feeling tired or sad.*

Dealing with Negative Behaviors

Until you and your child get the hang of active listening and a feeling vocabulary, you need to be careful not to become part of the problem—yelling, nagging, guilt-tripping, and getting physical only make things worse. Responding appropriately in a disciplinary situation requires thought and preparation, so keep the following in mind when your world blows up as you wait in line for Dumbo.

1. BE THE ADULT Most kids are practiced masters when it comes to pushing their parents' buttons. If you take the bait and respond with a tantrum of your own, you're no longer the adult in the room; worse, you suggest by your example that ranting and raving is acceptable behavior. No matter what happens, remind yourself, "I'm the adult here."

2. FREEZE THE ACTION Instead of responding to your kids' provocations in kind, and at a comparable maturity level, what you need to do is (to borrow a sports term) freeze the action. This usually means initiating a time-out (see "Frequent Acting Out," below). Find a place, preferably one that's private, to sit your child down, and refrain from talking until you've both cooled off.

3. ISOLATE THE CHILD Let the rest of the family go eat or explore without you, and arrange to meet up later. In addition to letting the others get on with their day, isolating the offending child relieves him or her of the burden of being the focus of attention—and the object of the rest of the family's frustration.

4. REVIEW THE SITUATION AND TAKE ACTION If, as we've recommended, you've made your expectations clear, stated the consequences of not complying, and issued a warning, review the situation with the child and follow through with the discipline warranted.

5. FREQUENT ACTING OUT Tantrums, of course, aren't always one-off events—kids often learn through experience that acting out will get them what they want. By scolding, admonishing, threatening, or negotiating, you further draw out the cycle, prolong the behavior, and cede control of the situation to your child. What's more, many kids, cunning devils that they are, know that pitching a fit in public is embarrassing to you, ensuring that you're more likely to cave to their demands on vacation than you would be at home.

To break the cycle, you must learn to disengage. The best ways to do this are to ignore the behavior, remove yourself from the child's presence (or vice versa), or isolate the child with a time-out. This takes discipline on your part, however: At first your child may ratchet up the tantrums until he or she realizes that you mean business.

A private place is ideal for a time-out, but it's not absolutely necessary. You can carve out space for one almost anywhere: on a theme park bench, in a park, in your car, in a restroom, or even on a sidewalk.

Finally, you can head off an impending meltdown by giving your child attention—the key motivator behind most tantrums—before things reach an explosive emotional pitch.

6. SALVAGE OPERATIONS Kids are full of surprises, and sometimes those surprises are, well, not good. What if your sweet precious pulls a stunt so beyond the pale that it threatens to derail your entire trip? In the case of one Ohio boy visiting Disney World with his family, his offense resulted in his being grounded more or less for life. For starters, his parents split up the group: One parent escorted the miscreant back to the hotel room, where he was effectively confined for the duration. That evening, Mom and Dad arranged for in-room sitters for the rest of the stay. Expensive? Yep, but better than ruining the vacation for everybody else.

In another case, a child acted out at the Magic Kingdom, though the offense was of a lesser order of magnitude. Because it was the family's last day at Disney World, the parents elected to place the misbehaver in time-out for the rest of their day in the park—one parent would monitor the culprit while the other parent and the siblings enjoyed the attractions. At agreed-upon times, the parents would switch places.

WHAT KIDS LIKE BEST IN WALT DISNEY WORLD

WHEN IT COMES TO DISNEY WORLD, what kids want is often different from what parents want: Children consistently name their hotel's pool as their favorite vacation activity, for example. Likewise, children prefer vastly different attractions in Disney's theme parks.

Elon University has offered a psychology class called "The Science of Happiness at Disney," taught by Alexis Franzese, PhD. Each student chooses a research topic that explores how Walt Disney World makes its guests happy. One student's research question asked whether boys and girls equally enjoyed meeting the Disney princesses (the short answer is yes). While looking at our reader-survey responses for this, however, we noticed something else: Kids prefer almost any character greeting, parade, or fireworks show over any ride in Walt Disney World.

The chart below lists the 10 most popular attractions in the Magic Kingdom for preschool and grade-school kids in 2019—the year before the pandemic, when Disney offered its full complement of entertainment options. The only ride that appeared in the top 10 for preschoolers was Dumbo. In fact, 18 of the top 20 attractions were parades, fireworks, or character greetings (the other ride in the top 20 was The Magic Carpets of Aladdin).

Grade-school kids enjoy Disney's thrill rides more, but 7 of their 10 favorite attractions were also parades, fireworks, and character greetings. (The same held true for teens.) While the touring plans in this edition don't include character greetings or parades (because Disney wasn't offering them when we went to press), keep these survey results in mind as you plan your days in the parks in case the events return. Each theme park chapter contains an updated list of age-group favorites too. (For more on the Disney characters, see page 397.)

RANK	KIDS' FAVORITE MAGIC KINGDOM ATTRACTIONS (pre-pandemic)	
	PRESCHOOL KIDS	GRADE-SCHOOL KIDS
1.	Mickey and Minnie Mouse Meet and Greet	Evening fireworks
2.	Pete's Silly Sideshow Character Meet and Greet	Seven Dwarfs Mine Train
3.	Cinderella and Elena Meet and Greet	Halloween/Christmas fireworks
4.	Rapunzel and Tiana Meet and Greet	Big Thunder Mountain Railroad
5.	Halloween/Christmas parades	Halloween/Christmas parades

	KIDS' FAVORITE MAGIC KINGDOM ATTRACTIONS *(pre-pandemic)* (continued)		
6.	Tinker Bell Meet and Greet	Mickey and Minnie Mouse Meet and Greet
7.	Afternoon parade	Splash Mountain
8.	Dumbo the Flying Elephant	Tinker Bell Meet and Greet
9.	Ariel Meet and Greet	Rapunzel and Tiana Meet and Greet
10.	Halloween/Christmas fireworks	Pete's Silly Sideshow Character Meet and Greet

ABOUT THE *UNOFFICIAL GUIDE* TOURING PLANS

CHILDREN HAVE A SPECIAL SKILL for wreaking havoc on a schedule. During one trip with daughter Hannah, Len is certain that she entered Peter Pan's Flight wearing two shoes, but she came out with one. It took half an hour to find replacements, and their carefully crafted touring plan required seat-of-the-pants updating.

If you're following a touring plan on the Lines app and something unexpected happens, just click "Optimize" when you're ready to get started again. Lines will redo your touring plan from that moment forward, based on current crowd conditions. (See page 24 for more information on Lines.)

If you're following a paper-based touring plan, here's what to expect regarding some common sources of interruptions:

1. CHARACTER GREETINGS CAN SLOW DOWN THE TOURING PLANS. When character greetings are offered, their lines can be as long as those for major attractions. If character greetings are offered, consider using Lightning Lane and Genie+ (see page 59).

2. OUR TOURING PLANS CALL FOR VISITING ATTRACTIONS IN A CERTAIN ORDER, OFTEN SKIPPING ATTRACTIONS ALONG THE WAY. Children don't like to skip *anything*! If something catches their eye, they want to see it right then and there. Some can be persuaded to skip attractions if parents explain their plans in advance, but other kids flip out at skipping something, particularly in Fantasyland. A mom from Charleston, South Carolina, writes:

> We didn't have much trouble following the touring plans at Hollywood Studios and EPCOT. The Magic Kingdom plan, on the other hand, turned out to be a train wreck. While we were on Dumbo, my 5-year-old saw eight dozen other things in Storybook Circus she wanted to do. Long story short: After Dumbo, there was no getting her out of there.

A mother of two from Burlington, Vermont, adds:

> My kids were very curious about the castle because we had read Cinderella at home. Whenever I wanted to leave Fantasyland, I would just say, "Let's go to the castle and see if Cinderella is there." Once we got as far as the front door to the castle, it was no problem going out to the Central Plaza and then to another land.

3. IF YOU'RE USING A STROLLER, YOU WON'T BE ABLE TO TAKE IT INTO ATTRACTIONS OR ONTO RIDES. It takes time to park and retrieve a stroller outside each attraction. Also, cast members will often move and rearrange strollers to make space, which adds to the time it takes to find yours later.

Magic Kingdom visitors often use the park's **Walt Disney World Railroad** to save on walking. The railroad, however, permits only folded strollers on board. Note that the railroad may be closed for much of 2022 to facilitate construction of a new attraction. If you're renting a Disney stroller, allow time to remove your stuff from it before boarding, and allow time at your destination to get another stroller. Read more stroller advice on page 382.

OTHER STUFF TO THINK ABOUT

OVERHEATING, SUNBURN, AND DEHYDRATION are the most common problems of younger children at Walt Disney World. Carry and use sunscreen. Apply it on children in strollers, even if the stroller has a canopy. To avoid overheating, stop for rest regularly—say, in the shade, or in a restaurant or at a show with air-conditioning. Carry bottles of water (refillable bottles with screw caps are sold in all major parks for about $5; bottled water is $3).

unofficial **TIP**
Look for sunscreen made without avobenzone, which causes stinging and burning if the sunscreen sweats off and gets in your eyes.

BLISTERS AND SORE FEET are the next most common problem that First Aid treats. In addition to wearing comfortable shoes, bring along blister bandages if you or your children are susceptible to blisters. These bandages (also available at First Aid in more shapes than you can imagine) offer excellent protection, stick well, and won't sweat off. Remember that a preschooler may not say anything about a blister until it has already formed, so keep an eye on things during the day. See page 453 for more on blister prevention.

GLASSES AND SUNGLASSES If your kids (or you) wear them, attach a strap or string to the frames so the glasses will stay on during rides and can hang from the child's neck while indoors. Check Lost and Found (page 452) if they go missing.

THINGS YOU FORGOT OR RAN OUT OF The theme parks and Disney Springs sell raingear, diapers, baby formula, sunburn treatments, memory cards, and other sundries. The water parks sell towels and disposable waterproof cameras. If you don't see something you need, ask if it's in stock.

RUNNING OUT OF STEAM When Bob was preparing to hike from the Colorado River to the rim of the Grand Canyon—a 5,000-foot ascent—a park ranger advised him to mix an electrolyte-replacement powder into his water and eat an energy-boosting snack at least twice every hour. While there's not much ascending to do at Walt Disney World, battling heat, humidity, and crowds contributes to poop-out, especially with kids in the mix. Limiting calorie consumption to mealtimes just won't cut it, as this wise grandma points out:

> *Children who get cranky during a visit often do so from all that time and energy expended without food. Feed them! A snack at any price goes a long way toward keeping little ones happy and parents sane!*

A mom from Blountville, Tennessee, says kids aren't the only ones who need an energy boost:

I offered my kid a snack every hour or so because I wanted to pre-vent hunger meltdowns. I also brought almonds for my husband and made him eat a snack when the kids did.

It's worth noting that Disney World's current guidelines require eating and drinking to be done while stationary and not while in line for an attraction.

WILD THINGS Alligators can be found in almost all bodies of water in Florida, including those at Disney World. Though attacks are very rare, adults and especially kids may become targets while swimming, wad-ing, or sitting near the water's edge. Alligators are most active when feeding in the late afternoon and evening. If you happen to see a gator in a nonthreatening situation, put as much space between you and it as possible, and keep kids close by. In case you're wondering, alligators can run 11 mph but only for a short distance.

BABY CARE

IN EACH OF THE MAJOR THEME PARKS, the **First Aid** and **Baby Care Centers** are located next to each other. In the **Magic Kingdom,** they're at the end of Main Street on the left, by Casey's Corner and The Crystal Palace. At **EPCOT,** they're on the World Showcase side of Odys-sey Center. At **Animal Kingdom,** they're in Discovery Island, on the left just before you cross the bridge to Africa, near Creature Comforts. At **Hollywood Studios,** they're at Guest Relations inside the main entrance.

Everything necessary for changing diapers, preparing formula, and warming bottles and food is available at the Baby Care Centers. A small shop at each center sells diapers, wipes, baby food, and other things you may need. Rockers and special chairs for nursing mothers are provided. Dads are welcome, too, and can use most services; in addition, many of the men's restrooms in the major parks have chang-ing stations.

If your baby is on formula, this Wisconsin mom has a handy tip:

We got hot water from the food vendors and mixed the formula as needed. It eliminated having to keep bottles cold and then warm them up.

Infants and toddlers are allowed in any attraction that doesn't have minimum height or age restrictions. But as a Minneapolis mom reports, some attractions are better for babies than others:

Theater and boat rides are easier for babies. Rides where there's a bar that comes down are doable, but harder—Peter Pan was our first encounter with this type of ride, and we had barely gotten situated when I realized my son might fall out of my grasp.

The same mom also advises:

We used a baby sling on our trip, and it was great when standing in lines—much better than a stroller, which you have to park before get-ting in line (and navigate through crowds).

NURSING Let us state unequivocally that nursing mothers are free to feed their babies whenever and wherever in Walt Disney World they choose. A Georgia mom, not sure that all nursing mothers under-stand this, writes:

Women have the right to nurse in public without being criticized. It's not necessary to sit through all of The Hall of Presidents *to feed your child.*

A Lake Charles, Louisiana, mom is more blunt:

Don't tell me that men who will do almost anything to see a boob will faint dead away at the sight of a nursing mother's breast. Ladies, feed your babies and tell the prudes to get over themselves!

FIRST AID If your child (or you) needs minor medical attention, go to a **First Aid Center.** Staffed by registered nurses, the centers treat everything from paper cuts to allergic reactions in addition to sunburns and blisters. Basic over-the-counter meds are often available free in small quantities too.

STROLLERS

THE NEED FOR STROLLERS at Walt Disney World is a hot topic among families with kids. Some parents, in fact, didn't realize just how important strollers are until they took their first trip to the World.

Walt Disney World Stroller Policy

The size limit for strollers in the theme parks is **31 inches wide by 52 inches long.** Stroller wagons, both pull and push models, are prohibited.

Strollers for Older Kids

It's not just the parents of babies and toddlers who rent strollers in the parks: Many parents tell us that they use them with kids who are well past needing them at home. If that seems odd, consider that a typical day in the parks requires at least a few miles of walking, which most kids don't do regularly (see "Building Endurance," page 374). A New Lenox, Illinois, family advocates this approach:

If your kids are 8 or under, rent strollers for all of them! My husband suggested getting a stroller for our 6-year-old and the two "babies" (ages 3 and 4). We plowed through crowds, and the kids didn't get nearly as tired since they could be seated whenever they wanted.

Other readers, like this Toronto mom, bristle at the thought:

Stop recommending that parents get strollers for kids over the age of 5. Kids who are in school can easily walk. I've never seen so many big kids in strollers in my life.

A mom from Chicago recalls:

It seemed like everyone under 8 and over 60 was being pushed around, making it much harder for us—especially our 5- and 7-year-olds—to navigate on foot.

You have three options for using a stroller in Walt Disney World:

renting or buying from Disney, bringing your own, or renting from a third party. We discuss the pros and cons of each option next.

DISNEY RENTS STROLLERS at all four WDW theme parks and at Disney Springs. To see what these strollers look like, Google "rental strollers at Walt Disney World." A single stroller costs $15 per day with no deposit, $13 per day for multiday rental; double strollers cost $31 per day with no deposit, $27 per day for multiday rental; note that stroller rentals at Disney Springs require a $100 credit card deposit. Strollers are welcome at Blizzard Beach and Typhoon Lagoon, but no rentals are available.

With multiday rentals, you can skip the rental line completely after your first visit—simply head over to the stroller-handout area, present your receipt, and you'll be wheeling out of there in no time. If you rent a stroller at the Magic Kingdom and you decide to go to EPCOT, Disney's Animal Kingdom, or Disney's Hollywood Studios, just turn in your Magic Kingdom stroller and present your receipt at the next park. You'll be issued another stroller at no additional charge.

Note that you can rent a stroller in advance; this allows you to bypass the payment line and go straight to the pickup line. Disney resort guests can pay ahead at their resort's gift shop, so hang on to your receipts.

Pick up strollers at the **Magic Kingdom** entrance; to the left of **EPCOT**'s Entrance Plaza and at EPCOT's International Gateway; and at **Oscar's Super Service,** just inside the entrance of **Disney's Holly-wood Studios.** At **Animal Kingdom,** they're at **Garden Gate Gifts,** to the right just inside the entrance. Returning a stroller is a breeze—you can ditch it anywhere in the park when you get ready to leave.

In general, Disney's strollers are too large for infants and many toddlers. If you still want to rent one, bring pillows, cushions, or rolled towels to buttress your child in. Because the strollers are large, they also provide a convenient place to tote water and snacks.

If you go to your hotel for a break and intend to return to the park, leave your rental in the stroller-parking area near the park entrance, marking it with something personal like a bandanna. When you return, your stroller will be waiting.

YOU CAN BUY A STROLLER at Walt Disney World too. Most Disney parks and hotels stock the highly rated **Kolcraft Cloud** model for around $50 (available at Target and online for $35–$45). The lightweight, collapsible Cloud has an overhead canopy for sun and rain protection, plus a mesh storage basket below the seat.

BRINGING YOUR OWN STROLLER is another option. Be aware, though, that only collapsible strollers are allowed on monorails, the Walt Disney World Railroad, parking trams, and buses.

This Secaucus, New Jersey, mom meticulously lays out the pros and cons of bringing your own stroller:

> **If your child is under age 2, bring your own stroller.** *Without one, you have to go all the way from your car to the Transportation and Ticket Center to the monorail (or ferry) to the stroller rental with your child, a diaper bag, and your own stuff in tow. But that's not half as bad as doing it in reverse on your way out, when you're exhausted, you now*

have purchases to carry, and the toddler who might have walked in wants to be carried out.

WDW strollers are simply too large for most children under age 2 *to be comfortable in without significant padding, and despite being so big, they have no place to store anything.*

If your child is past needing a diaper bag, the WDW strollers are a pretty good deal. *They're especially good for children ages 4–6 who no longer need a stroller at home but who won't make it walking all day.*

If your child is 2 or 3, it's a toss-up. *If you're a type-A mom like me who carries extra clothes, snacks, toys, diapers, etc., just in case, you've probably found a stroller that suits your needs and you'll be miserable with the WDW kind. If you're a type-B "we can get everything we need at the park" mom, then you'll probably be tickled with the WDW strollers.*

An Oklahoma mom found that bringing her own stroller was a hassle all around:

It's much easier to rent a stroller in the park. The one we brought was nearly impossible to get on the buses and was a hassle at the airport. I remember feeling dread when a bus pulled up—people look at you like you have a cage full of chickens.

If you're bringing your own stroller to save money, you're flying, and you're checking the stroller as luggage, see if the airline's luggage fees outweigh the cost of renting or buying in Orlando.

THIRD-PARTY RENTAL OPTIONS Because Disney's stroller rentals are generally expensive, a number of Orlando rental companies have sprung up, able to undercut Disney's prices, provide more comfortable strollers, and deliver them to your hotel or offer pickup and drop-off at the Orlando airport. Most of the larger companies offer the same stroller models (the Baby Jogger City Mini Single, for example), so the primary differences between the companies are price and service.

Regarding service, Disney no longer allows stroller companies to drop off and pick up at a Disney hotel without the guest being physically present. Disney requires guests to meet with delivery driver for all stroller and scooter rentals. The three companies reviewed below are part of the **Disney Featured Stroller Provider** program. Always ask any stroller company if you have to be present when the stroller is delivered.

We had mom and TouringPlans.com writer **Angela Dahlgren** rent strollers from different companies, use them in the parks, then return them. Her evaluations cover the overall experience, from the ease with which the stroller was rented to the delivery of the stroller, its condition upon arrival, usability in the parks, and the return process.

Kingdom Strollers (☎ 407-271-5301; kingdomstrollers.com) came in first on Angela's list, getting top marks for its website's ease of use along with stroller selection, condition, and overall service. The stroller she rented was much easier to use than Disney's standard model, had more storage, and had an easier-to-use braking system. A rental of one to three nights costs $50 (plus tax); four to seven nights is $70 (plus tax). That makes the break-even point for choosing Kingdom Strollers over Disney's strollers somewhere around five days.

Angela also recommends **Orlando Stroller Rentals,** LLC (☎ 800-281-0884; orlandostrollerrentals.com), which has higher prices ($65 for one to three nights and $85 for four to seven nights) but an excellent website that allows you to easily compare the features of the different strollers.

Disney's third Featured Provider is **Magic Strollers** (☎ 866-866-6177; magicstrollers.com). At the website, you enter the dates for which you'll need the stroller; then you get a list of choices and how much they cost to rent for the entire trip. Per-day prices range from about $11 for a basic single to about $14 for a deluxe double. Angela liked the stroller she reviewed, but she had a hard time getting the company to return phone calls. If you are willing to pick up the stroller from their warehouse shop located halfway between the airport and Walt Disney World, you'll get a 25% discount.

STROLLER WARS Sometimes strollers will disappear while you're enjoying a ride or watching a show. Disney staff will often rearrange strollers parked outside an attraction. This may be done to tidy up or to clear a walkway. Don't assume that your stroller is stolen because it isn't where you left it. It may be neatly arranged a few feet away—or perhaps more than a few feet away, as this Skokie, Illinois, dad reports:

> *unofficial* **TIP**
> Do **not** try to lock your stroller to a fence, post, or anything else at WDW.

> More than once, our stroller was moved out of visible distance from the original spot. On one occasion, it was moved to a completely different stroller-parking area near another ride, and no sign or cast member was around to advise where. We had to track a cast member down to find out where it had been moved.

Sometimes, however, strollers are taken by mistake or ripped off by people too lazy to rent their own. Don't be alarmed if your rental disappears: You won't have to buy it, and you'll be issued a new one at no charge. But while replacing a stroller is free, it's inconvenient. We heard from one Minnesota family who complained that their stroller was taken six times in one day at EPCOT and five times in a day at Hollywood Studios—even with free replacements, petty larceny on this scale represents a lot of wasted time.

Through our own experiments and readers' suggestions, we've developed a technique for hanging on to a rented stroller: Affix something personal but expendable to the handle. We tried several items and concluded that a bright, inexpensive scarf or bandanna tied to the handle works well as identification.

A multigenerational family from Utah went a step further and made their stroller difficult to heist:

> We decorated our stroller with electrical tape to make it stand out, and my son added a small cowbell to make it clang if moved.

A St. Louis dad pleads for tidiness:

> Please tell people not to leave food and drinks in a stroller when dropping it off. The stroller parking lots turned into buffets for crows and squirrels, which is gross.

LOST CHILDREN

ALTHOUGH IT'S AMAZINGLY EASY to lose a child (or two) in the theme parks, it usually isn't a serious problem: Disney employees are schooled in handling the situation. If you lose a child, let a cast member know, and then check at the **Baby Care Center** (see page 381 for locations in each theme park) and at **City Hall** in the Magic Kingdom, where lost-children logs are kept. Paging isn't used except in an emergency, but a bulletin can be issued throughout the park(s) via internal communications. If a Disney employee encounters a lost child, he or she will take the child immediately to the park's Baby Care Center.

unofficial **TIP**
Children under age 14 must be accompanied by someone age 14 or older when entering Disney World's theme parks and water parks.

Sew a label onto each child's shirt that states his or her name, your name, the name of your hotel, and your phone number. You can also purchase custom iron-on labels, write the information on a strip of masking tape, or attach a MagicBand to the child's clothing.

An easier and trendier option is a temporary tattoo with your child's name and your phone number. Unlike labels, ID bracelets, or wristbands, the tattoos can't fall off or get lost. Temporary tattoos last about two weeks, won't wash or sweat off, and are not irritating to the skin. They can be purchased online from **SafetyTat** (safetytat.com). Special tattoos are available for children with food allergies, hearing impairments, and autism spectrum disorder.

A Kingston, Washington, reader recommends recording vital info for each child on a plastic key tag or luggage tag and affixing it to the child's shoe. This reader also snaps a photo of the kids each morning to document what they're wearing. A Rockville, Maryland, mom shared a strategy one step short of a cattle brand:

Traveling with a 3-year-old, I was very anxious about losing him, so I wrote my cell phone number on his leg with a permanent marker. I felt much more confident that he'd get back to me quickly if he became lost.

Another good way to keep track of your family is to buy each person a Disney uniform—in this case, the same brightly and distinctively colored T-shirt. A Yuma, Arizona, family tried this with great success:

We all got the same shirts (bright red) so that we could easily spot each other in case of separation (VERY easy to do). It was a lifesaver when our 18-month-old decided to get out of the stroller and wander off. No matter what precautions you may try, it seems there are always opportunities to lose a child, but the recognizable shirts helped tremendously.

HOW KIDS GET LOST

CHILDREN GET SEPARATED FROM THEIR PARENTS every day at Disney theme parks under remarkably similar (and predictable) circumstances:

1. PREOCCUPIED SOLO PARENT The party's only adult is preoccupied with something like buying refreshments, reading a map, or using the restroom. Junior is there one second, gone the next.

2. THE HIDDEN EXIT Sometimes parents wait on the sidelines while two or more children experience a ride together. Parents expect the kids to exit in one place but the youngsters pop out elsewhere. Exits from some attractions are distant from entrances. Know exactly where your children will emerge before you allow them to ride by themselves.

3. AFTER THE SHOW At the end of many shows and rides, a Disney staffer announces, "Check for personal belongings and take small children by the hand." When dozens, if not hundreds, of people leave an attraction simultaneously, it's easy for parents to lose their children unless they have direct contact.

4. POTTY PROBLEMS Mom tells 6-year-old Tommy, "I'll be sitting on this bench when you come out of the restroom." Three possibilities: One, Tommy exits through a different door and becomes disoriented (Mom may not know there's another door). Two, Mom decides she will also use the restroom, and Tommy emerges to find her gone. Three, Mom pokes around in a shop while keeping an eye on the bench but misses Tommy when he comes out.

If you can't find a companion- or family-accessible restroom, make sure there's only one exit. One specific restroom in the Magic Kingdom, on a passageway between Frontierland and Adventureland, is the all-time worst for disorienting visitors. Children and adults alike have walked in from the Adventureland side and walked out on the Frontierland side (and vice versa). Adults realize quickly that something is wrong, but kids sometimes fail to recognize the problem.

Designate an easy-to-remember meeting spot, and provide clear instructions: "I'll meet you by this flagpole. If you get out first, stay right here." Have your child repeat the directions back to you. When children are too young to leave alone, sometimes you have to think outside the box, as our Rockville, Maryland, mom did:

> It was very scary at times to be alone with children who had just turned 1 and 2. At Epcot, I left my kids with a WDW employee outside of the restroom because [I didn't think] the stroller would fit inside with me. I later found that most WDW bathrooms can accommodate a front-and-back double stroller inside the handicapped stall.

5. PARADES There are many parades and shows at which the audience stands. Children tend to jockey for a better view. By moving a little this way and that, the child quickly puts distance between you and him before either of you notices.

6. MASS MOVEMENTS Be on guard when huge crowds disperse after a fireworks presentation or parade, or at park closing. With thousands of people at once in an area, it's very easy to get separated from a child or others in your party. Use extra caution after the evening parade and fireworks, or any other day-capping event. Plan where to meet in case you get separated.

7. CHARACTER ENCOUNTERS When the Disney characters appear, children can slip out of sight, even at a meet and greet or character meal.

8. GETTING LOST AT ANIMAL KINGDOM It's especially easy to lose a child in this theme park, particularly at The Oasis entryway, on the Maharajah Jungle Trek, and on the Gorilla Falls Exploration Trail. Mom and Dad will stop to observe an animal; Junior stays close for a minute or so and then, losing patience, wanders to the exhibit's other side or to a different exhibit. Especially in the multipath Oasis, locating a lost child can be maddening, as a Safety Harbor, Florida, mother describes:

> Manny wandered off in the paths that lead to the jungle village while we were looking at a bird. It reminded me of losing somebody in the supermarket, when you run back and forth looking down each aisle but can't find the person you're looking for because they're running around too. I was nutso before we even got to the first ride.

DISNEY, KIDS, *and* SCARY STUFF

DISNEY RIDES AND SHOWS are adventures with universal themes: good and evil, death, beauty and ugliness, fellowship and enmity. As you sample the attractions at Walt Disney World, you'll transcend the spinning and bouncing of midway rides to encounter thought-provoking and emotionally powerful entertainment.

unofficial **TIP**
If your child has difficulty coping with the ghouls of The Haunted Mansion, then think twice about exposing him to battle scenes in Star Tours at the Studios or the carnivorous prehistoric predators in Dinosaur at Animal Kingdom.

The endings are happy ones, but given Disney's gift for special effects, these adventures often intimidate and occasionally scare young children. There are attractions with menacing witches, burning towns, skeletons, and ghouls popping out of their graves—all done with humor, provided you're old enough to understand the joke.

You can reliably predict that Walt Disney World will, at one time or another, send a young child into system overload. Be sensitive, alert, and prepared for almost anything, even behavior that is out of character for your child. Most children take Disney's more macabre trappings in stride, and others are easily comforted by an arm around the shoulder or a squeeze of the hand. Parents who know that their children tend to become upset should take it slow and easy, sampling benign adventures like the Jungle Cruise, gauging reactions, and discussing with the children how they felt about what they saw.

Sometimes young children will try to rise above their anxiety in an effort to please their parents or siblings. This doesn't necessarily indicate mastery of fear, much less enjoyment. If your child leaves a ride in apparently good shape, ask if she'd like to go on it again—not necessarily now, but sometime. Her response should tell you all you need to know.

Evaluating children's capacity to handle the visual and tactile effects of Walt Disney World requires patience and understanding. If your child balks at or is frightened by a ride, respond compassionately—make clear that it's all right to be scared and that you won't think any less of your child for not wanting to ride.

What you definitely *don't* want to do is compound a child's fear and distress by coercing, belittling, or guilt-tripping, nor should you tolerate taunting or bullying from the child's siblings. A New York City psychologist speaks out on pressuring kids to ride:

> *I felt ethically torn watching parents force their children to go on rides they didn't want to ride. The Disney staff were more than willing to organize a parental swap to save these children from such abuse!*

THE FRIGHT FACTOR

WHILE EACH YOUNGSTER IS DIFFERENT, following are seven attraction elements that alone or combined could push a child's buttons and indicate that a certain attraction isn't age appropriate for that child:

1. THE NAME It's only natural that young children will be apprehensive about something called, say, The Haunted Mansion or The Twilight Zone Tower of Terror.

2. THE VISUAL IMPACT FROM OUTSIDE Splash Mountain, the Tower of Terror, and Big Thunder Mountain Railroad look scary enough to give adults second thoughts, and they terrify many little kids. A Utah grandma reports the following:

> *At 5 years old, my granddaughter was willing to go on almost everything. The problem was with the preliminary introductions to The Haunted Mansion and the Tower of Terror. Walking through and learning the stories before the actual rides were what frightened her and made her opt out without going in. The rides themselves wouldn't have been bad—she loved Splash Mountain and Big Thunder Mountain, but she could SEE those before entering.*

3. THE VISUAL IMPACT OF THE INDOOR-QUEUING AREA The caves at Pirates of the Caribbean and the dungeons and "stretch rooms" of The Haunted Mansion can frighten kids.

4. THE INTENSITY Some attractions inundate the senses with sights, sounds, movements, and even smells. Animal Kingdom's *It's Tough to Be a Bug!* show, for example, combines loud sounds, lights, smoke, and animatronic insects with 3-D cinematography to create a total sensory experience. A Johnston, Iowa, mom describes the situation well:

> *The 3-D and 4-D experiences are way too scary for even a very brave 5-year-old girl. The shows that blew things on her, shot smells in the air, had bugs flying, etc., scared the bejesus out of her. We escorted her crying from* It's Tough to Be a Bug! *and Mickey's PhilharMagic.*

A Gloucester, Massachusetts, mom had an on-the-spot solution:

> *My 3½-year-old was afraid of The Haunted Mansion. We just pulled his hat over his face and quietly talked to him while we rode.*

5. THE VISUAL IMPACT OF THE ATTRACTION Sights in various attractions range from falling boulders to lurking buzzards, from grazing dinosaurs to waltzing ghosts. What one child calmly absorbs may scare the pants off another who's the same age.

continued on page 392

SMALL-CHILD FRIGHT-POTENTIAL TABLE

THIS QUICK REFERENCE identifies attractions to be wary of if you have kids ages 3–7. Younger children are more likely to be frightened than older ones. Attractions not listed aren't frightening in any respect. For details on Rider Switch, see page 395.

The Magic Kingdom

ADVENTURELAND

- **JUNGLE CRUISE** Moderately intense with some macabre sights. A good test attraction.
- **THE MAGIC CARPETS OF ALADDIN** Could scare kids who don't like heights if you raise your ride vehicle high in the air.
- **PIRATES OF THE CARIBBEAN** Slightly intimidating queuing area; intense boat ride with gruesome (though humorously presented) sights and a short, unexpected slide.
- **SWISS FAMILY TREEHOUSE** Anyone who's afraid of heights may want to skip it.
- *WALT DISNEY'S ENCHANTED TIKI ROOM* A thunderstorm, loud volume level, and simulated explosions frighten some preschoolers.

FRONTIERLAND

- **BIG THUNDER MOUNTAIN RAILROAD** Visually intimidating from outside, with moderately intense visual effects. The roller coaster is wild enough to frighten many adults, particularly seniors. Rider Switch option provided.
- **FRONTIERLAND SHOOTIN' ARCADE** Frightening to kids who are scared of guns.
- **SPLASH MOUNTAIN** Visually intimidating from the outside, the ride culminates in a 52-foot plunge down a steep chute. Rider Switch option provided.
- **TOM SAWYER ISLAND AND FORT LANGHORN** Some very young children are intimidated by dark walk-through tunnels that can be easily avoided.

LIBERTY SQUARE

- **THE HAUNTED MANSION** The name raises anxiety, as do the sounds and sights of the waiting area. Intense attraction with humorously presented macabre sights. The ride itself is gentle.

FANTASYLAND

- **THE BARNSTORMER** May frighten some preschoolers.
- **DUMBO** Could scare kids who don't like heights if you raise your ride vehicle high in the air.
- **MAD TEA PARTY** Midway-type ride; can induce motion sickness in all ages.
- **THE MANY ADVENTURES OF WINNIE THE POOH** Frightens a few preschoolers.
- **SEVEN DWARFS MINE TRAIN** May frighten some preschoolers.
- **UNDER THE SEA: JOURNEY OF THE LITTLE MERMAID** Animatronic octopus frightens some preschoolers.

TOMORROWLAND

- **ASTRO ORBITER** Visually intimidating from the waiting area, but relatively tame.
- **BUZZ LIGHTYEAR'S SPACE RANGER SPIN** May frighten some preschoolers.
- *MONSTERS, INC. LAUGH FLOOR* May frighten some preschoolers.
- **SPACE MOUNTAIN** Very intense roller coaster in the dark; the Magic Kingdom's wildest ride and a scary coaster by any standard. Rider Switch option provided.
- **TOMORROWLAND SPEEDWAY** The noise of the waiting area slightly intimidates preschoolers; otherwise, not frightening.
- **TRON LIGHTCYCLE POWER RUN** *(opens 2022)* Intense outdoor roller coaster.

EPCOT

FUTURE WORLD

- **GUARDIANS OF THE GALAXY: COSMIC REWIND** *(opens 2022)* Intense roller coaster in the dark.
- **JOURNEY INTO IMAGINATION WITH FIGMENT** Loud noises and unexpected flashing lights startle younger children.

SMALL-CHILD FRIGHT-POTENTIAL TABLE
(continued)

EPCOT *(continued)*

FUTURE WORLD *(continued)*

- **THE LAND: SOARIN' AROUND THE WORLD** May frighten kids age 7 and under, or anyone with a fear of heights. Otherwise mellow. Rider Switch option provided.
- **MISSION: SPACE** Extremely intense space-simulation ride that has been known to frighten guests of all ages. Rider Switch option provided.
- **THE SEAS: THE SEAS WITH NEMO & FRIENDS** Sweet but may frighten toddlers.
- **SPACESHIP EARTH** Dark, imposing presentation intimidates a few preschoolers.
- **TEST TRACK** Intense thrill ride that may frighten guests of any age. Rider Switch option provided.

WORLD SHOWCASE

- **NORWAY: FROZEN EVER AFTER** Small drop at the end could scare little ones. Rider Switch option provided.
- **FRANCE: REMY'S RATATOUILLE ADVENTURE** May frighten some preschoolers.

Disney's Animal Kingdom

DISCOVERY ISLAND

- **AWAKENINGS** This nighttime show's shadows, sounds, and projections may frighten kids 5 years and younger.
- **THE TREE OF LIFE/IT'S TOUGH TO BE A BUG!** Intense and loud, with special effects that startle viewers of all ages and potentially terrify little kids.

AFRICA

- **FESTIVAL OF THE LION KING** A bit loud, but otherwise not frightening.
- **KILIMANJARO SAFARIS** The proximity of real animals makes a few young children anxious.

ASIA

- **EXPEDITION EVEREST** Can frighten guests of all ages. Rider Switch option provided.
- **FEATHERED FRIENDS IN FLIGHT** Swooping birds may frighten a few small children.
- **KALI RIVER RAPIDS** Potentially frightening and certainly wet for guests of all ages. Rider Switch option provided.
- **MAHARAJAH JUNGLE TREK** Some children may balk at the bat exhibit.

DINOLAND U.S.A.

- **DINOSAUR** High-tech thrill ride rattles riders of all ages. Rider Switch option provided.
- **TRICERATOP SPIN** This midway-type ride frightens only a handful of younger kids.

PANDORA—THE WORLD OF AVATAR

- **AVATAR FLIGHT OF PASSAGE** May frighten kids age 7 and younger, those with claustrophobia or a fear of heights, or those who are prone to motion sickness. Rider Switch option provided.
- **NA'VI RIVER JOURNEY** Dark ride with imposing animatronic figures frighten some preschoolers. Rider Switch option provided.

Disney's Hollywood Studios

SUNSET BOULEVARD

- **FANTASMIC!** Terrifies some preschoolers.
- **ROCK 'N' ROLLER COASTER** The wildest coaster at Walt Disney World. May frighten guests of any age. Rider Switch option provided.
- **THE TWILIGHT ZONE TOWER OF TERROR** Visually intimidating to young kids; contains intense and realistic special effects. The plummeting elevator at the end frightens many adults as well as kids. Rider Switch option provided.

SMALL-CHILD FRIGHT-POTENTIAL TABLE
(continued)

ECHO LAKE

- *INDIANA JONES EPIC STUNT SPECTACULAR!* An intense show with powerful special effects, including explosions, but young kids generally handle it well.
- **STAR TOURS—THE ADVENTURES CONTINUE** Extremely intense visually for all ages; too intense for kids under age 8. Rider Switch option provided.

Disney's Hollywood Studios *(continued)*

GRAND AVENUE

- *MUPPET-VISION 3-D* Intense and loud, but not frightening.

HOLLYWOOD BOULEVARD

- **MICKEY & MINNIE'S RUNAWAY RAILWAY** Track ride with wild twists and turns but benign visuals. May scare kids 6 and under.

TOY STORY LAND

- **ALIEN SWIRLING SAUCERS** Can induce motion sickness in riders of all ages. Rider Switch option provided.
- **SLINKY DOG DASH** Mild first roller coaster for most kids. May frighten preschoolers. Rider Switch option provided.
- **TOY STORY MANIA!** Dark ride may frighten some preschoolers.

STAR WARS: GALAXY'S EDGE

- *MILLENNIUM FALCON:* **SMUGGLERS RUN** Intense visual effects and movement. Rider Switch option provided.
- **STAR WARS: RISE OF THE RESISTANCE** Intense visual effects and movement for all ages.

continued from page 389

6. THE DARKNESS Many Walt Disney World attractions operate indoors in the dark, which can be scary. A child who gets frightened on one dark ride (such as The Haunted Mansion) may be unwilling to try others.

7. THE PHYSICAL EXPERIENCE Some rides are wild enough to cause motion sickness, wrench backs, and discombobulate guests of any age.

A BIT OF PREPARATION

WE RECEIVE MANY TIPS from parents telling how they prepared their young children for the Disney experience. Common strategies include reading Disney books and watching Disney videos. A Lexington, Kentucky, mom suggests watching videos of the theme parks on **YouTube:**

> *My timid 7-year-old daughter and I watched ride and show videos on YouTube, and we cut out all the ones that looked too scary.*

You can also watch one of Disney's free **vacation-planning videos** at tinyurl.com/disneyplanningvideos. As a YouTube supplement, these videos give your kids an adequate sense of what they'll see. You can also watch Walt Disney World specials produced by Disney and others on Disney+, Netflix, and YouTube.

ATTRACTIONS THAT EAT ADULTS

YOU MAY SPEND SO MUCH ENERGY worrying about the kids that you forget to take care of yourself. The attractions in the table below can cause motion sickness or other issues for older kids and adults.

POTENTIALLY PROBLEMATIC ATTRACTIONS FOR GROWN-UPS

THE MAGIC KINGDOM

- **FANTASYLAND** Mad Tea Party
- **FRONTIERLAND** Big Thunder Mountain Railroad, Splash Mountain
- **TOMORROWLAND** Space Mountain, Tron Lightcycle Power Run (*opens 2022*)

EPCOT

- **FUTURE WORLD** Guardians of the Galaxy: Cosmic Rewind (*opens 2022*), Mission: Space, Test Track

DISNEY'S ANIMAL KINGDOM

- **ASIA** Expedition Everest, Kali River Rapids
- **DINOLAND U.S.A.** Dinosaur
- **PANDORA** Avatar Flight of Passage

DISNEY'S HOLLYWOOD STUDIOS

- **ECHO LAKE** Star Tours—The Adventures Continue
- **SUNSET BOULEVARD** Rock 'n' Roller Coaster, The Twilight Zone Tower of Terror
- **STAR WARS: GALAXY'S EDGE** *Millennium Falcon:* Smugglers Run, Rise of the Resistance

A WORD ABOUT HEIGHT REQUIREMENTS

A NUMBER OF ATTRACTIONS REQUIRE children to meet minimum height and age requirements. (All Appeal by Age attraction ratings for preschoolers in the theme park chapters assume that the kids surveyed were tall enough to ride.) All rides, regardless of height requirements, require that children under the age of 7 have someone age 14 or older ride with them.

If you have children who don't meet the posted requirements, you have several options, including Rider Switch (see page 395). If those kids are resentful of their taller (or older) siblings who do qualify to ride, a mom from Virginia has some good advice:

> Our petite 5-year-old, to her outrage, was left out while our 8-year-old went on Splash Mountain and Big Thunder Mountain with Grandma and Granddad, and the nearby alternatives weren't helpful (too long a line for rafts to Tom Sawyer Island, etc.). The best areas had a nearby playground or other quick attractions near the rides with height requirements, like The Boneyard near Dinosaur at Animal Kingdom.

Another tip: Ask the cast member stationed at the entrance to the height-restricted attraction how long the wait will be. Now tack on 5 minutes of riding time to the wait time, then add 5 or so minutes for the riders to exit and reach your agreed-upon meeting point. This way you'll have a better sense of whether the kids who are too short to ride (and their supervising adults) will have time to do other stuff while the tall-enough members of your group experience the attraction.

Our guess is that even with the long line for the rafts, this mom would've had sufficient time to take her daughter to Tom Sawyer Island while the siblings rode Splash Mountain and Big Thunder Mountain Railroad with the grandparents. For sure, she had time to tour the Swiss Family Treehouse in adjacent Adventureland.

For more on height requirements, see the table on the next page.

ATTRACTION AND RIDE RESTRICTIONS

THE MAGIC KINGDOM

The Barnstormer 35" minimum height

Big Thunder Mountain Railroad 40" minimum height

Seven Dwarfs Mine Train 38" minimum height

Space Mountain 44" minimum height

Splash Mountain 40" minimum height

Tomorrowland Speedway 32" minimum height to ride, 54" to drive unassisted

Tron Lightcycle Power Run *(opens 2022)* 48" minimum height*

EPCOT

Guardians of the Galaxy: Cosmic Rewind *(opens 2022)* 44"–48" minimum height*

Mission: Space 40" minimum height (Green); 44" minimum height (Orange)

Soarin' Around the World 40" minimum height

Test Track 40" minimum height

DISNEY'S ANIMAL KINGDOM

Avatar Flight of Passage 44" minimum height

Dinosaur 40" minimum height

Expedition Everest 44" minimum height

Kali River Rapids 38" minimum height

DISNEY'S HOLLYWOOD STUDIOS

Alien Swirling Saucers 32" minimum height

***Millennium Falcon:* Smugglers Run** 38" minimum height

Rock 'n' Roller Coaster 48" minimum height

Slinky Dog Dash 38" minimum height

Star Tours—The Adventures Continue 40" minimum height

Star Wars: Rise of the Resistance 40" minimum height

The Twilight Zone Tower of Terror 40" minimum height

DISNEY SPRINGS

Marketplace Carousel 42" minimum height

BLIZZARD BEACH WATER PARK

Chairlift 32" minimum height

Downhill Double Dipper 48" minimum height

Slush Gusher 48" minimum height

Summit Plummet 48" minimum height

T-Bar *(in Ski Patrol Training Camp)* 60" maximum height

Tike's Peak children's area 48" maximum height

TYPHOON LAGOON WATER PARK

Bay Slides 60" minimum height

Crush 'n' Gusher 48" minimum height

Humunga Kowabunga 48" minimum height

Ketchakiddee Creek 48" maximum height

Wave Pool *Adult supervision required*

*Estimated

WAITING-LINE STRATEGIES *for* ADULTS *with* YOUNG CHILDREN

CHILDREN HOLD UP BETTER THROUGH THE DAY if you limit the time they spend in lines. Arriving early and using our touring plans are two ways to greatly reduce waiting. Here are other ways to reduce stress for children:

1. RIDER SWITCH (AKA SWITCHING OFF OR RIDER SWAP) Several attractions have minimum height and/or age requirements. Some couples with children too small or too young forgo these attractions, while others take turns riding. Missing some of Disney's best rides is an unnecessary sacrifice, and waiting in line twice for the same ride is a tremendous waste of time. Disney's solution to this problem is a system called Rider Switch. There must be at least two adults for this to work. Here's how to do it:

1. Adults and kids wait in line together.
2. When you approach the queue, tell the first ride attendant you see that you want to use Rider Switch.
3. The cast member will divide the group into those riding first and those riding second—that is, the nonriding child and up to three supervising adults.
4. The first group will enter the ride.
5. The cast member will scan the MagicBand or ticket of the adult riding second, who then waits with the nonriding child in a designated spot near the ride entrance.
6. When the first group returns, that adult takes over watching the nonriding child while the other adult returns to the Alternate Access line.
7. The cast member will scan the second group's MagicBands/tickets again, after which the group enters the ride's Alternate Access line.
8. The entire group reunites after the second group finishes the ride.

ATTRACTIONS WHERE RIDER SWITCH IS USED	
MAGIC KINGDOM	**DISNEY'S ANIMAL KINGDOM**
• The Barnstormer	• Avatar Flight of Passage
• Big Thunder Mountain Railroad	• Dinosaur
• Seven Dwarfs Mine Train	• Expedition Everest
• Space Mountain	• Kali River Rapids
• Splash Mountain	• Na'vi River Journey
• Tomorrowland Speedway	
• Tron Lightcycle Power Run *(opens 2022)*	
EPCOT	**DISNEY'S HOLLYWOOD STUDIOS**
• Frozen Ever After	• Alien Swirling Saucers
• Guardians of the Galaxy: Cosmic Rewind *(opens 2022)*	• *Millennium Falcon:* Smugglers Run
• Mission: Space	• Rock 'n' Roller Coaster Starring Aerosmith
• Soarin' Around the World	• Slinky Dog Dash
• Test Track	• Star Tours—The Adventures Continue
	• The Twilight Zone Tower of Terror

Rider Switch passes—which are digital entitlements scanned into your MagicBand or ticket—must be used on the same day they're issued. Guests may hold no more than one Rider Switch pass at a time—a pass must be redeemed before another one can be issued.

Cast members administering Rider Switch are very accommodating, as a Natick, Massachusetts, family attests:

At both Universal and Disney, the cast members were really nice about Rider Switch. If your child changes their mind at the last minute, no problem, and if they then decide they want to ride after the first part of the group has ridden, they let the full group ride together. I thought that was very nice and added needed flexibility. After all, it is hard to know two months in advance if your 8-year-old is up for the "mountains"!

2. LINE GAMES Anticipate that children will get restless in line, and plan activities to reduce the stress and boredom. In the morning, have waiting children discuss what they want to see and do during the day. Later, watch for and count Disney characters or play simple games such as 20 Questions. Games requiring pen and paper are impractical in a fast-moving line, but waiting in the holding area of a theater attraction is a different story—here, tic-tac-toe, hangman, drawing, and coloring can make the time fly.

A Springfield, Ohio, mom reports on an unexpected but welcome assist from her brother:

I have a bachelor brother who joined my 5-, 7-, and 9-year-olds and me for vacation. Pat surprised all of us with a bunch of plastic animal noses he had in his hip pack. When the kids got restless or cranky in line, he'd turn away and pull out a pig nose or a parrot nose or something. When he turned back around with the nose on, the kids would majorly crack up.

A Waco, Texas, dad broke out the bubbly:

I took bubbles along with us. My boys loved them and so did the other children waiting in line. (I bought wedding-size bottles that would fit into everyone's fanny pack.)

We can confirm that the bubble thing has caught on big all over the theme parks.

3. PHONE FUN If games and coloring are likely to induce eye rolls, load some age-appropriate games on your or your kids' phones. For suggestions beyond Angry Birds and Candy Crush, see tinyurl.com/bestgames apps or learn4good.com/games/mobile_phone_games.htm; you can also do a search for "best iPhone/Android games for kids" or something similar. Be aware, however, that some games that are free to download and play may have add-ons that cost extra—to prevent a surprise on your credit card bill, Google "block in-app purchases on iOS/Android."

4. LAST-MINUTE COLD FEET If your young child gets cold feet while you're waiting to board a ride where Rider Switch isn't offered, you can usually arrange a switch-off with the loading attendant. (This happens frequently in Pirates of the Caribbean's dungeon waiting area.) If you reach the boarding area and someone is unhappy, just tell an attendant that you've changed your mind and you'll be shown the way out.

5. "THROW YOURSELF ON THE GRENADE, MILDRED!" For saintly, long-suffering parents who are determined to sacrifice themselves on behalf of their kids, we provide the opposite of a waiting-line strategy: the Magic Kingdom one-day touring plan called the **Dumbo-or-Die-in-a-Day**

Touring Plan for Parents with Small Children (see page 719–720). Don't let the cutesy name fool you: This plan guarantees that you'll go home battered and exhausted. On the upside, it's cheaper than a $4,000 VIP tour—and it really works. Anyone under age 8 will love it!

The DISNEY CHARACTERS

NOTE: As we went to press, up-close character greetings were still suspended across Walt Disney World. The information in this section describes how Disney ran character greetings prior to the pandemic, and therefore how it is likely to run them again once COVID vaccines are widely administered.

While character greetings are suspended, Disney runs a series of mini-parades called cavalcades throughout the day in each theme park. These cavalcades usually consist of one or two floats with a small set of related characters, such as Mickey, Minnie, and Pluto. See each park's chapter for the cavalcade routes and characters offered.

The longest Len has ever waited in line at a theme park was 5 hours, with daughter Hannah to meet Anna and Elsa from *Frozen*. ("I've had relationships that didn't last that long," he muses.) Spontaneous group parenting took over, with adults taking turns buying food and drinks and running bathroom breaks for each other's kids.

But the thing that surprised Len most was how excited Anna was to see Hannah at the end of that 5-hour wait. Displaying the energy of a squirrel fed Cuban coffee, Anna jumped and danced around Hannah, hugging and talking to her as if it was Anna who'd been waiting to see her.

Hannah cried. Len cried. It was great.

Len's experience is repeated every day throughout Walt Disney World by cast members determined to be the Disney characters they're dressed as. We receive hundreds of reader comments telling us how much these cast members enhanced their theme park experience. This email from a Wisconsin mom is representative:

> *I can't say enough about the characters and how they react to the children and just people in general. They are highly trained in people skills and just add an extra dimension to the park.*

As we mention on page 378, meeting the Disney characters is one of the highest-rated activities among all age groups who visit Walt Disney World. To those who love them, the characters in Disney's films and TV shows are as real as family or friends; never mind that they were drawn by an animator or generated by a computer.

By extension, the theme park personifications of the Disney characters are just as real: It's not a guy in a mouse costume but Mickey himself; she's not a cast member in a sequined fish tail but Ariel, Princess of Atlantica. Meeting a Disney character is an encounter with a real celebrity—a memory to be treasured.

MEETING THE CHARACTERS

NOTE: To recount, the following discussion describes character greetings under normal, non-pandemic circumstances. If the pandemic persists,

WDW CHARACTER-GREETING VENUES
(temporarily suspended)

MAGIC KINGDOM

MICKEY AND HIS POSSE

- **Daisy, Donald, Goofy, Minnie, and Pluto** Pete's Silly Sideshow
- **Mickey** Town Square Theater

DISNEY ROYALTY (Princesses, Princes, Suitors, and Such)

- **Aladdin and Jasmine** Adventureland • **Anna and Elsa** On float during the Festival of Fantasy Parade and in *Mickey's Royal Friendship Faire* stage show • **Ariel** Ariel's Grotto • **Belle** *Enchanted Tales with Belle* • **Cinderella, Elena of Avalor, Rapunzel, and Tiana** Princess Fairytale Hall
- **Gaston** Fountain outside Gaston's Tavern • **Merida** Fairytale Garden
- **Snow White** Next to City Hall
- **The Tremaines and Fairy Godmother** In Fantasyland near Cinderella's Castle

FAIRIES

- **Tinker Bell** Town Square Theater

MISCELLANEOUS

- **Alice** (*Alice in Wonderland*) Mad Tea Party
- **Buzz Lightyear** (*Toy Story*) Tomorrowland
- **Captain Jack Sparrow** (*Pirates of the Caribbean*) Adventureland
- **Mary Poppins** Liberty Square
- **Peter Pan** Fantasyland next to Peter Pan's Flight
- **Pooh and Tigger** Fantasyland by The Many Adventures of Winnie the Pooh
- **Stitch** (*Lilo & Stitch*) Tomorrowland

EPCOT

MICKEY AND HIS POSSE

- **Daisy** World Showcase Plaza • **Donald** Mexico, at the Mexico Pavilion
- **Minnie, Mickey, and Pluto** Varies

DISNEY ROYALTY

- **Anna and Elsa** Norway • **Aurora** France gazebo • **Belle** France
- **Jasmine** Morocco • **Mulan** China • **Snow White** Germany

MISCELLANEOUS

- **Alice, Mary Poppins, and** (on rare occasions) **Bert** United Kingdom
- **Winnie the Pooh** Lawn between the Imagination and Land Pavilions in Future World West

DISNEY'S ANIMAL KINGDOM

MICKEY AND HIS POSSE

- **Daisy** DinoLand U.S.A., Lower Cretaceous Trail
- **Donald** DinoLand U.S.A., Celebration Welcome Center
- **Goofy and Pluto** DinoLand U.S.A., gas station
- **Mickey and Minnie** Adventurers Outpost on Discovery Island

DISNEY ROYALTY

- **Pocahontas** Discovery Island at Character Landing

MISCELLANEOUS

- **Chip 'n' Dale** DinoLand U.S.A., Upper Cretaceous Trail
- **Flik** (*A Bug's Life*) Discovery Island across from Creature Comforts
- **Kevin** (*Up*) Discovery Island and near *Feathered Friends in Flight*
- **Launchpad McQuack** DinoLand U.S.A., Aerial Adventure Base
- **Russell** (*Up*) Discovery Island (**Dug** may appear randomly.)
- **Scrooge McDuck** DinoLand U.S.A., near Restaurantosaurus

DISNEY'S HOLLYWOOD STUDIOS

MICKEY AND HIS POSSE
- **Chip 'n' Dale** Grand Avenue
- **Daisy and Donald** Near park entrance
- **Goofy** Grand Avenue across from BaseLine Tap House
- **Minnie and Sorcerer Mickey** Red Carpet Dreams on Commissary Lane
- **Pluto** Animation Courtyard

DISNEY CHANNEL STARS
- **Doc McStuffins and Friends** Animation Courtyard near *Disney Junior Play and Dance*
- **Vampirina** Animation Courtyard

MISCELLANEOUS
- **Buzz, Jessie, Woody, and Green Army Men** (*Toy Story*) Toy Story Land
- **Cruz Ramirez** (*Cars*) *Lightning McQueen's Racing Academy*
- **Edna Mode** (*The Incredibles*) Municiberg at Pixar Place
- **The Incredibles** Municiberg at Pixar Place
- **Mike and Sulley** (*Monsters, Inc.*) Walt Disney Presents
- **Olaf** (*Frozen*) Celebrity Spotlight in Echo Lake
- **Chewbacca, Darth Vader, and BB-8** (*Star Wars*) Star Wars Launch Bay
  Stormtroopers (*Star Wars*) Animation Courtyard

BLIZZARD BEACH
- **Goofy** Appears seasonally, usually from spring break until Labor Day, at park entrance

---

TYPHOON LAGOON
- **Lilo and Stitch** Singapore Sal's near the park entrance. They meet in the spring and summer months on a rotational basis.

---

expect character-greeting suspensions and/or necessary changes to safeguard against the virus.

Disney makes its most popular characters available in dedicated meet-and-greet venues in each theme park (see table at left and above) and at Disney Deluxe resorts that host character meals (see "Character Dining" in Part Six, page 280). As a mom from Little Rock, Arkansas, notes, this has mostly eliminated the likelihood of bumping into characters spontaneously as you walk around the parks:

> We were disappointed in Disney's system of character greetings. You must find the schedule and wait in line to meet any characters. I miss the days when they would just appear—we once saw Jafar walking through Adventureland all by himself! Now they're completely scheduled, so you have to plan your visit and queue up with all the other visitors. I can't tell you how many times we tried to get in line only to be told the line was closed.

Some characters who don't have dedicated spaces appear only in parades or stage shows, and still others appear only in a location consistent with their starring role. The Fairy Godmother is often near Cinderella Castle in Fantasyland, while Buzz Lightyear appears close to his eponymous attraction in Tomorrowland. Characters also often visit the Disney water parks and occasionally appear at Disney Springs.

A Brooklyn, New York, dad was surprised at how much time his family was willing to spend meeting characters:

The characters are now available practically all day long at different locations, according to a fixed schedule, which our son was old enough to read. We spent more time standing in line for autographs than we did for the most popular rides!

PREPARING YOUR CHILDREN TO MEET THE CHARACTERS There are two kinds of Disney characters: **fur characters,** whose costumes include face-covering headpieces (including animal characters and humanlike characters such as Captain Hook), and **face characters,** who wear no mask or headpiece, such as the Disney princesses and princes, Aladdin, Mary Poppins, and the like.

Only face characters speak. Because cast members couldn't possibly imitate the furs' distinctive cinema voices, it's more effective for them to be silent. Nonetheless, fur characters are warm and responsive, and they communicate effectively with gestures. Most of the furs are quite large; a few, like Buzz Lightyear, are huge. Small children don't expect this, and preschoolers especially can be intimidated.

On first encounter, don't thrust your child at the character; rather, allow the little one to deal with this big thing from whatever distance feels safe. If two adults are present, one should stay near the youngster while the other approaches the character and demonstrates that it's safe and friendly.

Be aware that some character costumes are quite cumbersome and make it hard for the cast members inside to see well. (Eyeholes are frequently placed in the mouth of the costume or even on the neck or chest.) Children who approach the character from the back or side may not be noticed, even if the child touches the character. It's possible in this situation for the character to accidentally step on the child or knock him down.

A child should approach a character from the front, but occasionally not even this works—Donald and Daisy, for example, have to peer around their bills. If a character appears to be ignoring your child, the character's handler will get its attention.

It's OK for your child to touch, pat, or hug the character. Understanding the unpredictability of children, the character will keep his feet still, particularly refraining from moving backward or sideways.

Most characters will pose for pictures or sign autographs, but note that costumes can make it difficult to wield a normal pen. Buzz Lightyear, in fact, can't sign autographs at all but sometimes uses a stamp; in any case, he's always glad to pose for photos.

Character-Greeting Venues

Prior to the pandemic, Walt Disney World had numerous character-greeting locations. The table on pages 398–399 lists them by park and character. *Note:* Characters are always subject to change, so check before you head to the parks.

During these meet and greets, characters often engage in dialogue appropriate to their story lines, which catches many people by surprise. Here's a letter from a Hamilton, Ohio, mom who didn't catch Cinderella's concern for missing footwear:

We went to Princess Fairytale Hall to meet a couple of princesses. Rapunzel was very cool and chatty, but Cinderella was another story. While the 6-year-old was waiting for a picture, I sat the 1-year-old on the floor so I could reach for my camera. All of a sudden, Cinderella goes ballistic, yelling in the most un-princesslike voice, "Oh no, the little princess MUST have shoes! The little princess CANNOT be in the castle without shoes!" I'm like, "Listen, Cindy, the little princess can't walk yet, so she doesn't have shoes. Just smile for the picture and we'll be on our way."

Characters in the parks will also know about the park's attractions that involve them, as this Canadian mom found out:

Immediately after watching Mickey's PhilharMagic, my daughter was so worried about Donald smashing through a wall [on film as part of the show] that we had to drop what we were going to do and stand in line just so she could kiss Donald and make sure he was OK. Fortunately, Donald knew what she was talking about and played along with the doctoring.

These parents, also from Canada, discovered their 3-year-old's depth of feeling for the Seven Dwarfs—one in particular:

We got in line early for the dwarfs (her favorites) at 5:50 p.m., waited almost 2 hours before her turn in line . . . and then she wouldn't leave. She insisted on hugging and interacting with every dwarf; she squeezed herself between the seven of them and avoided our attempts to grab her and pull her away. We eventually snagged her as she was screaming "GRUMPY! YOU HAVE TO BE HAPPY! BE HAPPY, GRUMPY!" at the top of her lungs.

CHARACTER MEALS

DISNEY CHARACTERS APPEAR at meals served in full-service restaurants at the theme parks and Deluxe resorts, among other locations. For more information, see page 280 in Part Six. At press time, modified character dining experiences were available only at **Garden Grill Restaurant, Hollywood & Vine, Topolino's Terrace—Flavors of the Riviera, Chef Mickey's,** and **Tusker House Restaurant.**

CHILDCARE

IN-ROOM BABYSITTING Kid's Nite Out (☎ 877-761-3580; kidsniteout .com) provides in-room and in-park childcare in the Walt Disney World/ Universal area. Base hourly rates (4-hour minimum) are $20 for one child, $23 for two children, $26 for three children, and $29 for four children, plus a $12 travel fee.

Sunshine Babysitting (☎ 407-421-6505; sunshinebabysitting.com) charges $16–$20 per hour for the first child, $2 for each additional child, with a 4-hour minimum plus $10 travel fee.

Sitters for both services are security-checked, bonded, and trained in CPR. See the websites above for additional services and fees.

SPECIAL KIDS' PROGRAMS

FREE ACTIVITIES

MANY DISNEY DELUXE AND DVC RESORTS offer a continuous slate of free kids' activities from early morning through the evening, from storytelling and cookie decorating to hands-on activities themed to the resort. (During the pandemic, most of these activities are outdoors.) These programs offer an inexpensive alternative to the theme parks on your first or last day of travel, or whenever parents need a quiet break by the pool.

FEE-BASED ACTIVITIES

IN ADDITION, WALT DISNEY WORLD offers a number of children's activities at an extra cost. See below for a sampler.

COVID *tip*
All fee-based kids' activities were temporarily suspended at press time.

DISNEY'S FAMILY MAGIC TOUR This is an approximately 2-hour guided tour of the Magic Kingdom for the entire family (kids age 3 and up are welcome). The tour combines information about the Magic Kingdom with a guided scavenger hunt with riddles. The tour departs Monday, Tuesday, Friday, and Saturday at 10 a.m. The cost is about $39 per person (including tax), plus a valid Magic Kingdom admission. The maximum group size is 20 people. Reservations can be made up to 180 days in advance by calling ☎ 407-WDW-TOUR (939-8687).

DISNEY'S PIRATE ADVENTURE CRUISES Children ages 4–12 get to hoist the Jolly Roger and set out on a boat trip to search for buried treasure by following a map. At the final port of call, the kids find the treasure (doubloons, beads, and rubber bugs!) and wolf down snacks. The adventure costs about $39–$49 per child with tax. Cruises, which depart from Bayside Marina at the Yacht & Beach Club Resorts and from Barefoot Bay at Caribbean Beach Resort, are offered daily, 9:30–11:30 a.m., weather permitting; call ☎ 407-WDW-PLAY (939-7529) for more information. *Note:* No parents allowed on the cruise!

MERMAID SCHOOL If you or your children are water puppies, consider the Mermaid School, held during warmer weather months at the All-Star Music, Art of Animation, Beach Club, Caribbean Beach, Riviera, and Yacht Club Resorts. The Polynesian Resort offers an adult version that includes a boozy Dole Whip. There are a number of activities, but the main attraction is learning to swim with a mermaid tail. Cost is $55 plus tax per person for age 4 and up. Reservations can be made by calling ☎ 407-WDW-PLAY (939-7529). Goggles are available on request.

A mom from The Woodlands, Texas, loved the program, writing:

> My daughter adored the Mermaid School. All of the mermaids were between ages 6 and 12, and you have never seen such ecstatically happy little girls. "This is the best day of my life!" I'd definitely consider it as an alternative to Bibbidi Bobbidi for a confident swimmer.

DISNEY'S PERFECTLY PRINCESS TEA PARTY At this Grand Floridian gathering, your little princess gets dressed up in her favorite regal attire and sips tea with Princess Aurora. A luncheon is served as well. Included in the price is an 18-inch Princess Aurora doll; other loot includes a tiara, silver bracelet, necklace, fresh rose, and more. The cost is about $334 (including tax and tip) for one guest age 10 and up and one child ages 3–9; add an additional guest age 10 and up for $99 or an additional child ages 3–9 for $234. The tea party is held every Sunday, Monday, Wednesday, Friday, and Saturday morning. Call ☎ 407-939-6983 for reservations and information.

WONDERLAND TEA PARTY Held at 1900 Park Fare restaurant in the Grand Floridian Monday–Friday at 2 p.m. for $52.19 per child (ages 4–12, including tax), this tea party consists of cupcake decorating, games, stories, a craft, and photos with characters from *Alice in Wonderland*. For reservations, call ☎ 407-WDW-DINE (939-3463) 180 days in advance.

BIRTHDAYS *and* SPECIAL OCCASIONS

WHEN YOU CHECK IN TO A HOTEL or restaurant, Disney cast members will generally ask if you're celebrating something special, such as a birthday or anniversary. A Lombard, Illinois, mom put the word out and was glad she did:

> My daughter was turning 5 while we were there; our hotel asked me who her favorite character was and did the rest. We came back to our room on her birthday and there were helium balloons, a card, and a Cinderella photo autographed in ink! When we entered the Magic Kingdom, we received an "It's My Birthday Today" pin (FREE!), and at the restaurant she got a huge cupcake with whipped cream, sprinkles, and a candle. IT PAYS TO ASK!

PART EIGHT

SPECIAL TIPS *for* SPECIAL PEOPLE

KEY QUESTIONS ANSWERED IN THIS CHAPTER

WALT DISNEY WORLD *for* GUESTS *with* SPECIAL NEEDS

DISNEY WORLD IS EXCEPTIONALLY ACCOMMODATING to guests with physical challenges. If you have a disability, Disney is well prepared to meet your needs.

DISNEY RESORTS

IF YOU'LL BE STAYING AT A DISNEY RESORT, let the reservation agent know of any special needs you have when you book your room. The following equipment, services, and facilities are available at most Disney hotels; note that not all hotels offer all items.

• Accessible vanities	• Portable commodes
• Bed and bathroom rails	• Refrigerators
• Braille on signs and elevators	• Roll-in showers
• Closed-captioned TVs	• Rubber bed padding
• Double peepholes in doors	• Shower benches
• Handheld showerheads	• Strobe-light smoke detectors
• Knock and phone alerts	• TTYs
• Lowered beds	• Wheelchairs for temporary use
• Phone amplifiers	• Widened bathroom doors

SERVICE ANIMALS

DISNEY WELCOMES DOGS AND MINIATURE HORSES that are trained to assist guests with disabilities. Service animals are permitted in most locations in all Disney resorts and theme parks, although they may not be admitted on certain theme park rides. Check disneyworld .disney.go.com/guest-services/service-animals for more information.

IN THE THEME PARKS

EACH THEME PARK OFFERS a free booklet describing disabled services and facilities at tinyurl.com/disabilitiesguide. You can also obtain these pamphlets when you enter the parks, at resort front desks, and at wheelchair-rental locations inside the parks.

For specific requests, call ☎ 407-560-2547 (voice). When the recorded menu comes up, press *1*. Limit your questions and requests to those regarding disabled services and accommodations (address other questions to ☎ 407-824-4321 or 407-827-5141 [TTY]).

DISNEY'S DISABILITY ACCESS SERVICE (DAS)

DISNEY'S DISABILITY ACCESS SERVICE is designed to accommodate guests who can't wait in regular standby lines. Register online between 2 and 30 days in advance of your trip (see tinyurl.com/wdw-das) or on the day of your visit at the **Guest Relations** window of the first theme park you visit. You only need to sign up once every 60 days, and the service carries over to each subsequent park you visit. The process is explained below. For clarity, we'll refer to the person signing up for the DAS service as the DAS enrollee. *Note:* Guests whose disability requires only a wheelchair or mobility vehicle do not need the DAS.

PREPARATION Before you sign up, make sure you have either the MagicBands, park tickets, or My Disney Experience emails of everyone in your group. All of your group's MagicBands/tickets will be linked to the DAS—this comes in handy in situations we'll describe below. The DAS is good for parties of up to six people. For parties of more than six, check with Guest Relations.

SIGNING UP FOR DAS At your video chat or Guest Relations, you'll be asked to present identification and describe the enrollee's limitations. You don't have to provide documentation of a specific condition; rather, what Disney is looking for is a description of how the condition affects the enrollee in the parks. The goal is to determine the right level of assistance, not to obligate you to prove that the enrollee qualifies. The enrollee must be present during this call or visit.

Be as detailed as possible in describing limitations. For instance, if your child has autism spectrum disorder and has trouble waiting in long lines or has sensory issues such as sensitivity to noise, let the cast member know each of these things specifically.

The DAS also requires a photograph. Pictures are taken with an iPad (the cast member will come to you if you can't make it up to the counter). If the DAS is for a child, you may use either the child's photo or substitute your own. Finally, you must agree to be bound by its rules.

DAS ADVANCE New for 2021, the DAS Advance feature allows you to select two attractions to visit on each day of your trip. For example, if you say you're visiting EPCOT on the Tuesday of your trip, then at some point before Tuesday, you'll be able to pick two attractions in EPCOT to visit using the Lightning Lane (see page 59). You'll see these DAS Advance reservations in My Disney Experience, too. Like Genie+, you'll get a 1-hour return window during which you can come back and ride those selected attractions.

USING DAS ON THE DAY OF YOUR VISIT The DAS may be used at any attraction or character-greeting venue with a queue. Anyone with a linked MagicBand or ticket can present it outside the attraction; if the standby wait time is less than 15 minutes, you'll usually be escorted through the standby entrance or the alternative access/Lightning Lane entrance. If the standby time is higher, a cast member will provide a time for you to return to ride—again, this is entered into MDE.

The return time will be the current wait time minus 10 minutes—if, say, you get to Splash Mountain at 12:20 p.m. and the standby is 40 minutes, your return time will be 30 minutes later, at 12:50 p.m. You may return at the specified time or at any time thereafter. The DAS enrollee must also return to ride. When you return, the enrollee will scan his or her MagicBand first, followed by the other members of your group. Everyone will be given access to the Lightning Lane or alternative access line.

You can have one DAS return time at a time. However, you can also use Genie+ (where offered), boarding groups, Individual Attraction Selections, and the DAS at the same time.

WHEELCHAIRS AND ELECTRIC VEHICLES

GUESTS WITH LIMITED MOBILITY may rent wheelchairs, three-wheeled electric convenience vehicles (ECVs, also known as scooters), and electric standing vehicles (ESVs). These give nonambulatory guests tremendous freedom and mobility. Most rides, shows, attractions, restrooms, and restaurants accommodate them. If you're in a park and you need assistance, go to Guest Relations.

Wheelchairs rent for $12 per day, or $10 per day for multiday rentals. Rentals are available at all Walt Disney World theme parks (see Parts Eleven through Fourteen for specific locations) and at Disney Springs. ECVs and ESVs cost $50 per day, plus a $20 refundable deposit ($100 refundable deposit at Disney Springs and the water parks). Wheelchairs are available for rent at the water parks and Disney Springs for $12 per day with a refundable $100 deposit.

Your rental deposit slip is good for a replacement wheelchair in any park during the same day. You can rent a chair at the Magic Kingdom in the morning, return it, go to any other park, present your deposit slip, and get another chair at no additional charge.

Apple Scooter (☎ 321-726-6837; applescooter.com) rents ECVs with a wide variety of options. Apple's rates are generally the most competitive. **Buena Vista Scooters** (☎ 866-484-4797 or 407-331-9147; buenavistascooters.com) also rents ECVs, for $51 (plus tax) per day for one day or $31 per day for two to six days, plus a $20 damage waiver fee (deeper daily discounts for longer rentals). Both companies include free delivery to and pickup from your Disney resort. You'll need to be present for delivery and pickup, however.

All Disney lots have close-in parking for disabled visitors; request directions when you pay your parking fee. Most (but not all) rides, shows, restrooms, and restaurants accommodate wheelchairs, as do monorails and buses, as outlined below.

Even if an attraction doesn't accommodate wheelchairs, ECVs, or ESVs, nonambulatory guests may ride if they can transfer from their wheelchair to the ride's vehicle. Disney staff, however, aren't trained or permitted to assist with transfers—guests must be able to board the ride unassisted or have a member of their party assist them. Either way, members of the nonambulatory guest's party will be permitted to ride with him or her.

Because the waiting areas of most attractions won't accommodate wheelchairs, nonambulatory guests and their parties should ask a cast member for boarding instructions as soon as they arrive at an attraction entrance.

Disabled guests and their families give Disney high marks for accessibility and sensitivity. An Arlington, Virginia, woman writes:

> My mom has mobility problems, and she was worried about getting around. Disney supplied a free wheelchair, every bus had kneeling steps for wheelchair users, and the cast members sprang into action when they saw us coming.

Much of the Disney transportation system is disability accessible. Monorails can be accessed by ramp or elevator, the Skyliner has special gondolas for wheelchairs and scooters, and all bus routes are served by vehicles with wheelchair lifts, though unusually wide or long wheelchairs (or motorized chairs) may not fit the lift. Watercraft accommodations for wheelchairs are iffier.

A large number of Disney hotel guests use scooters (ECVs). This affects commuting times by bus, as each Disney bus can accommodate only two scooters or wheelchairs. A Minneapolis woman touring with her parents shared her experience:

> I was stunned by the number of scooters this year. My parents each had one, and several times they had to wait to find a bus that had available space for scooters or wheelchairs. If people needing a scooter can make it to the bus stop on foot, they'd be better off waiting until they get to the park and renting a scooter there.

If you plan to use a wheelchair or scooter while visiting **Wilderness Lodge & Villas, Fort Wilderness Resort & Campground,** or an **EPCOT** resort, call ☎ 407-560-2547 (voice) for the latest information on watercraft accessibility.

Food and merchandise locations at theme parks, Disney Springs, and hotels are generally accessible, but some fast-food queues and shop aisles are too narrow for wheelchairs. At these locations, ask a cast member or member of your party for assistance.

A scooter user from Riverside, California, shares her experience:

> Had a great time! It wasn't easy using a scooter, though. Stores and restaurants have little room for a scooter to maneuver—I kept getting boxed in by people or had to back out of areas that had no turn-around space.

DIETARY RESTRICTIONS AND ALLERGIES

WALT DISNEY WORLD RESTAURANTS work hard to accommodate guests' special dietary needs. When you make a dining reservation online or by phone, you'll be asked about food allergies and the like. When you arrive at table-service restaurants and buffets, alert the host or hostess and your server.

Almost all Walt Disney World restaurants have dedicated allergy-friendly menus available; ask any cast member for a menu when you arrive at the restaurant. Allergy-friendly menus cover most people and offer a variety of food as diverse as the standard menu. For example, the Magic Kingdom's **Cosmic Ray's Starlight Cafe** offers at least 14 entrées for guests with seafood, nut, grain, egg, dairy, and soy allergies, as well as for Jewish guests who keep kosher.

Also, Disney chefs at many sit-down restaurants have adapted their dishes so that almost anyone with a common allergy can order off the standard menu. At **Narcoossee's**, for example, every item on the standard menu has been adapted to the allergy menu. **Touring-Plans.com** also maintains a list of Disney World restaurant menus, including most special offerings and prices—look for the words *allergy friendly* on the menu list at tinyurl.com/allergymenuswdw. For more information, email special.diets@disneyworld.com or visit tinyurl.com/wdwspecialdiets.

An Idaho mom and her teenage daughter found Disney restaurants very responsive to their dietary needs:

> My daughter and I both have a gluten allergy. I have never felt so well cared for and safe eating anywhere else in the world. From our resort (both the food court and Boatwright's) to every single quick-service or sit-down restaurant, we had several choices, and we never waited longer than 8 minutes for our special orders.

To request kosher meals at table-service restaurants, call ☎ 407-824-1391 24 hours in advance. All Disney menus have vegetarian options; most can be made vegan without having to talk to the chef, but vegetarians, vegans, and pescatarians should still speak up when making dining reservations.

Those with special diets *and* a sweet tooth should try the vegan, gluten-free, and kosher treats from **Erin McKenna's Bakery NYC,** with locations at Disney Springs and many Disney hotel food courts (they also deliver to the Disney area). Besides sweets, the bakery does a tasty line of savory breads from time to time. You can also order special-occasion cakes and baked goods (☎ 407-938-9044 or 855-462-2292; erinmckennasbakery.com).

MEDICATIONS

FOR GUESTS WHO EXPERIENCE ALLERGIC REACTIONS that can be severe or life-threatening, Disney provides epinephrine injectors (**EpiPens**) at **First Aid Centers** and other locations throughout the parks (check your park guide maps for locations). Nurses and emergency responders are trained in EpiPen use, but guests with known conditions should always travel with their own supplies.

CBD PRODUCTS In April 2019, a 69-year-old grandmother from Tennessee was arrested at a Magic Kingdom security checkpoint for possession of CBD (cannabidiol) oil, which her doctor had prescribed to treat arthritis pain. The charges against her were later dropped, but the incident highlighted a major discrepancy between federal and then-current Florida law. Federal law permits the production and sale of hemp-derived CBD products containing 0.3% THC or less, but at the time of the woman's arrest, these products were subject to the same restrictions as medical marijuana in Florida. A state law that removed these restrictions went into effect July 1, 2019. Disney guests should verify that their products' THC content falls within legal limits.

VISUALLY IMPAIRED, DEAF, OR HARD-OF-HEARING GUESTS

GUEST RELATIONS PROVIDES FREE **assistive-technology devices** to guests who are visually impaired, deaf, or hard-of-hearing ($25 refundable deposit, depending on the device). Sight-impaired guests can customize the given information (such as architectural details, restroom locations, and descriptions of attractions and restaurants) through an interactive audio menu that is guided by a GPS in the device. For deaf/hard-of-hearing guests, amplified audio and closed-captioning for attractions can be loaded into the same device.

Braille guidebooks are available from Guest Relations at all parks ($25 refundable deposit), and **Braille menus** are available at some theme park restaurants. Some rides provide **closed-captioning;** many theater attractions provide **reflective captioning.**

Disney provides **sign language interpretations** of live shows at the theme parks on certain designated days of the week:

- **MAGIC KINGDOM** Mondays and Thursdays
- **EPCOT** Fridays
- **DISNEY'S ANIMAL KINGDOM** Saturdays and Tuesdays
- **DISNEY'S HOLLYWOOD STUDIOS** Sundays and Wednesdays

Get confirmation of the interpreted-performance schedule a minimum of one week in advance by calling Disney World information at ☎ 407-824-4321 (voice) or 407-827-5141 (TTY). You'll be contacted before your visit with a schedule of the interpreted performances.

NONAPPARENT DISABILITIES

WE RECEIVE MANY LETTERS from readers whose traveling companion or child requires special assistance but who, unlike a person in a wheelchair, is not visibly disabled. Autism, for example, can make it very difficult or impossible for someone to wait in line for more than a few minutes or in queues surrounded by a crowd. A trip to Disney World can be nonetheless positive and rewarding for guests who are on the autism spectrum. And while any Disney vacation requires planning, a little extra effort to accommodate the affected person will pay large dividends. Disney's guide for guests with cognitive disabilities is available for download at tinyurl.com/wdwcognitiveguide. For information on **Disney's Disability Access Service,** which accommodates guests with nonapparent disabilities, see page 405.

FRIENDS OF BILL W.

FOR INFORMATION on **Alcoholics Anonymous** meetings in the Disney World area, including Celebration, Four Corners, Kissimmee, Lake Buena Vista, Narcoossee, and St. Cloud, visit osceolacountyintergroup.org. For information on **Al-Anon** and **Alateen** meetings in the area, visit al-anon orlando.org.

WALT DISNEY WORLD
"At Large"

YOU'VE JUST SPENT A SMALL FORTUNE for your vacation. If you're a person of size, you don't want to worry about whether you're going to have trouble fitting in the ride vehicles. Fortunately, Walt Disney World realizes that its guests come in all shapes and sizes and is quite accommodating. **Deb Wills** and **Debra Martin Koma,** experts on Walt Disney World travel for people with physical challenges, offer the following suggestions.

- You'll be on your feet for hours at a time, so wear comfortable, broken-in shoes. If you feel a blister starting to form, take care of it quickly. (Each theme park has a **First Aid Center** stocked with bandages and other necessities. For more on blister prevention, see page 453.)

- If you're prone to chafing, consider bringing an antifriction product designed to control or eliminate rubbing (**Body Glide** is a well-known brand). You can find this and similar products at most pharmacies and sporting-goods stores.

- Attractions have different kinds of vehicles and seating. Some have bench seats, while others have individual seats; some have overhead harnesses, while others have seat belts or lap bars. Learn what type of seating or vehicle each attraction has before you go so you know what to expect (check out tinyurl.com/allears-ride-gallery for details). If the attraction has a seat belt, pull it all the way out before you sit down to make it easier to strap yourself in. Note that some attractions have seat-belt extenders—ask a cast member about these.

- Several attractions (Expedition Everest, for example) offer a sample ride vehicle for you to try before you get in line. Ask a cast member for details.

- Front seats (such as those on Rock 'n' Roller Coaster and Test Track) often have more legroom; they don't on Space Mountain, however.

- In restaurants, look for chairs without arms. Check with a dining host if you don't see one.

- Request a resort hotel room with a king-size bed. The good sleep you'll get will be worth it.

Sometimes it isn't largeness in general but your particular build that can present a problem when it comes to ride vehicles. A Connecticut reader relates her experience:

Since I was a very young girl, I've dreamed of riding on a dragon, so I was extremely excited about the chance to experience Avatar Flight of Passage in Pandora. Unfortunately, though I was able to mount the ride's motorcycle-like seat without difficulty, the safety braces that came up behind would not lock due to my particular dimensions. The cast member in charge of checking the safeties was very kind and did try to coach me into a better fit, but in the end I had to get out and leave the ride as my husband and son looked on. I was absolutely mortified, though I was graciously offered two additional ride reservations as compensation.

Fast-forward to the next day at Disney's Hollywood Studios. I was determined not to repeat the experience, so when the time came to ride the Rock 'n' Roller Coaster, I asked if there were sample seats and restraints I could try before entering the line. I was ushered backstage by a cast member and was able to try out the exact seating configuration with success. I don't know how many other Disney rides have such tryout seats, but for guests such as myself, it can't hurt to ask, particularly on thrill rides with a long wait time.

Test seats can be found at Test Track at EPCOT, Flight of Passage and Expedition Everest at the Animal Kingdom, and Rise of the Resistance and Rock 'n' Roller Coaster at Disney's Hollywood Studios. Not all the test seats are out front and immediately visible.

WALT DISNEY WORLD *for* SENIORS

SENIOR CITIZENS have much the same problems and concerns as all Disney visitors. Older guests do, however, get into predicaments caused by touring with younger people. Pressured by their grandchildren to endure a frantic pace, many seniors concentrate on surviving Disney World rather than enjoying it. Seniors must either set the pace or dispatch the young folks to tour on their own.

An older reader in Alabaster, Alabama, writes:

Being a senior is not for wussies, particularly at Walt Disney World. Things that used to be easy take a lot of effort, and sometimes your brain has to wait for your body to catch up. Half the time, your grandchildren treat you like a crumbling ruin; then they turn around and trick you into getting on a roller coaster in the dark. Seniors must be alert and not trust anyone—not their children, not the Disney people, and especially not their grandchildren. Don't follow along blindly like a lamb to the slaughter. **He who hesitates is launched!**

Most seniors we interview enjoy the World much more when they tour with folks their own age. If, however, you're considering visiting with your grandchildren, we recommend making an exploratory visit without them first; this way, it'll be easier to establish limits, maintain control, and set a comfortable pace later on. Similarly, to get a sense of what kinds of problems might materialize, take the grandkids to a local theme park or fair before you extend the Walt Disney World invitation.

If you're *determined* to take the grandkids, read carefully the sections of this book that discuss family touring. (*Hint:* The Dumbo-or-Die-in-a-Day Touring Plan has been known to bring grown-ups of all ages to their knees.)

When it comes to attractions, we feel that personal taste should trump age. We hate to see seniors pass up a full-blown adventure like Splash Mountain just because it's a so-called thrill ride—it gets its appeal more from the music and visual effects than from the thrill of the ride. Use our theme park attraction profiles to help you make informed decisions.

GETTING AROUND

MANY SENIORS LIKE TO WALK, but a 7-hour visit to a theme park includes 4–10 miles on foot. Consider renting a wheelchair or mobility vehicle (see page 406).

LOOK OUT FOR STROLLERS! Given the number of wheeled vehicles, pedestrians, and tight spaces, mishaps are inevitable. A middle-aged couple from Brunswick, Maine, lobbies for a temporary ban:

> As an over-45 couple, we couldn't believe the number and sizes of strollers and those ubiquitous scooters. You had to be constantly vigilant or you would have your foot run over or path slowed down. One day a week, in one theme park, there should be a "no wheels" day.

A reader named Linda (no hometown given) would certainly agree:

> We were appalled by the Stroller Brigades. We are seniors, and twice I was actually hit—not bumped—by strollers that were guided by people on their phones racing to get somewhere. Once I was hit hard enough that a cast member actually came over. I don't know what the solution is, but there should be some kind of limit to the size of these things. This was such a serious issue for us that we very well may not go back.

In response to the concerns of readers like Linda, Disney now limits stroller sizes to **31 inches wide by 52 inches long.**

TIMING YOUR VISIT

RETIREES SHOULD MAKE THE MOST of their flexible schedules and go to Walt Disney World in the fall or spring (excluding holiday weeks), when the weather is nicest and the crowds are comparatively thinner. Crowds are also generally sparse from late January through early February. See Part Two, page 34, for more information.

LODGING

IF YOU CAN AFFORD IT, STAY IN WALT DISNEY WORLD. Rooms are among the Orlando–Kissimmee area's nicest, and transportation is always available to any Disney destination at no additional cost.

Disney hotels reserve rooms close to restaurants and transportation for guests of any age who can't tolerate much walking. They also provide golf carts to pick up and deliver guests at their rooms. Service can vary dramatically depending on the time of day and the number of guests requesting carts. At check-in time (around 3 p.m. for regular hotels, 4 p.m. for DVC), for example, the wait for a ride can be as long as 40 minutes.

Here are four good reasons to consider staying at a Walt Disney World resort:

1. The quality of the properties is consistently above average.
2. Staying in the World guarantees transportation when you need it. Disney buses run about every 20 minutes. (If you miss the last bus, though, you may need to call an Uber, Lyft, or taxi.)
3. You get free parking at the major theme parks.
4. You get preferential tee times on resort golf courses.

Walt Disney World hotels are spread out—it's easy to avoid most stairs, but it's often a long hike to your room from parking lots or bus stops. Seniors intending to spend more time at EPCOT and Hollywood Studios than at the Magic Kingdom or Animal Kingdom should consider the **BoardWalk Inn & Villas, Dolphin, Swan, Swan Reserve,** or **Yacht & Beach Club Resorts.**

The **Contemporary Resort** and **Bay Lake Tower** are good choices for seniors who want to be on the monorail system. So are the **Grand Floridian** and the **Polynesian Village,** though they cover many acres, necessitating a lot of walking. For a restful, rustic feeling, choose **Wilderness Lodge & Boulder Ridge/Copper Creek Villas.**

If you want a kitchen and the comforts of home, book **Animal Kingdom Villas, Beach Club Villas, BoardWalk Villas, Grand Floridian Villas, Old Key West Resort, Polynesian Villas & Bungalows, Riviera,** or **Saratoga Springs.** If you enjoy watching birds and animals, try **Animal Kingdom Lodge & Villas.** Try **Saratoga Springs** for golf.

RVers will find pleasant surroundings at **The Campsites at Disney's Fort Wilderness Resort.** Several independent campgrounds are within 30 minutes of Walt Disney World; see campflorida.com/regions/central -florida for listings. They're not as nice, but they cost less.

TRANSPORTATION

ROADS IN DISNEY WORLD CAN BE DAUNTING. Armed with a decent sense of direction and a great sense of humor, however, even the most timid driver can get around. Plus, you don't have to be zip code–specific to use GPS on your smartphone—if you want to go to EPCOT for example, entering "EPCOT" or "EPCOT parking" will get the job done. (See Part Nine, page 439, for GPS coordinates for the four Disney theme parks.)

Parking for the disabled is available near each theme park's entrance; toll-plaza attendants will provide a dashboard ticket and direct you to the reserved spaces. Disney requires that you be recognized officially as disabled to use this parking, but temporarily disabled persons are also permitted access.

SENIOR DINING

EAT BREAKFAST AT YOUR HOTEL RESTAURANT or have juice and rolls in your room. Carry snacks in a fanny pack supplemented by fresh or dried fruit, fruit juice, and soft drinks purchased from vendors. Make Advance Reservations for lunch before noon to avoid the crowds. Follow with an early dinner and be out of the restaurants, ready for evening touring and fireworks (if available), long before the main crowd even thinks about dinner.

WALT DISNEY WORLD *for* INTERNATIONAL VISITORS

AS WE WENT TO PRESS, the United States was still prohibiting entry to foreign nationals who had been in any of the following countries in the past 14 days: Brazil, China, India, Iran, the 26 states of the European Schengen Area, the Republic of Ireland, South Africa, and the United Kingdom and its dependencies (for example, the Isle of Man). In addition, Canada's border with the United States remains closed. We expect the US restrictions on visitors from Canada, Europe, and the UK to be lifted sooner rather than later—Disney was selling 2022 UK travel packages in summer 2021, for example. Even if you can get into the United States, check your country's return policy to ensure you can get home.

A mom from Menorca, Spain, offers advice to readers who are making the long haul to Walt Disney World:

> *You cannot predict how the time difference is going to affect you or the little people. Coming from Spain, we were looking at a 9-hour flight from the UK and a 6-hour time difference, and we spent our first few days in a haze after trying to do too much too soon.*

Londoner and *Unofficial* friend Andrew Dakoutros sent us this grab bag of tips and advice for other Disney-bound Brits:

> *(1) Jellyrolls [the piano bar at Disney's BoardWalk] doesn't accept UK driving licences as ID for entry [they accept passports]; (2) many MouseSavers codes [see page 33] can't be used from the UK; (3) the Twinings tea at The Tea Caddy at EPCOT doesn't taste as good as in London.*
>
> *Additionally, you need to emphasise how hot Florida is and the importance of sunscreen. Most Britons holiday in Spain or Greece, where the sun is nowhere near as strong.*

TRANSLATION SERVICES A wireless device called **Ears to the World** provides synchronized narration in French, German, Japanese, Portuguese, or Spanish for more than 30 attractions in the theme parks. The wireless, lightweight headsets provide real-time translation and are available for a $25 refundable deposit at Guest Relations in all parks.

WALT DISNEY WORLD *for* EXPECTANT MOTHERS

WHEN IT COMES TO PREGNANT WOMEN visiting Walt Disney World, the authors, alas, have no wisdom of their own to impart. Enter **Debbie Grubbs,** a Colorado reader. During her fifth month of pregnancy, she waddled intrepidly all over the World, compiling observations and tips for expectant moms that she shares below.

MAGIC KINGDOM Splash Mountain *is a no-go, obviously, due to the drop—or so I thought. It turns out that the seat configuration in the logs has more to do with it than the drop. The seats are made* *so that your knees are higher than your rear, compressing the abdomen (when it's this large). This is potentially harmful to the baby.*

Big Thunder Mountain Railroad *is also out of the question. It's just not a good idea to ride roller coasters when pregnant.*

Mad Tea Party *may be OK if you don't spin the cups. We didn't ride this one because my doctor advised me to skip rides with centrifugal [or centripetal] force.* **Dumbo** *in Fantasyland and the* **Astro Orbiter** *in Tomorrowland are OK, though.*

Space Mountain *is one of my favorite rides . . . but a roller coaster nonetheless.*

Tomorrowland Speedway *isn't recommended due to the amount of rear-ending by overzealous younger drivers.*

We also think Debbie would have had to pass on **Seven Dwarfs Mine Train** and its swinging cars, as well as Tron Lightcycle Power Run (when it opens).

DISNEY'S ANIMAL KINGDOM Dinosaur *is very jerky and should be avoided.*

We think Debbie would've avoided **Expedition Everest** too. **Na'vi River Journey** at Pandora might be fine, but **Avatar Flight of Passage** is probably too much.

EPCOT Mission: Space *and* Test Track *[and* **Guardians of the Galaxy: Cosmic Rewind** *when it opens] are restricted, as are all simulator rides; they're way too rough and jerky. [Nonmoving seats are available in some simulation attractions—ask a cast member.]* **Soarin'** *is fine.*

DISNEY'S HOLLYWOOD STUDIOS Tower of Terror *is out of the question for the drop alone, and* **Star Tours** *is restricted because it's a simulator.* **Rock 'n' Roller Coaster** *is clearly off-limits. In Toy Story Land,* **Slinky Dog Dash** *(the beginner coaster) is out, as are the* **Alien Swirling Saucers.**

Millennium Falcon: **Smugglers Run** at Star Wars: Galaxy's Edge is a no-go, and possibly **Star Wars: Rise of the Resistance** for its reentry segment at the end. **Mickey and Minnie's Runaway Railway** *might* be doable—there's one scene where the ride vehicle shakes side to side while you're doing the mambo (we're not making this up, we swear).

WATER PARKS Slides *are off-limits, but not the* **wave pools** *and* **floating creeks** *(great for getting the weight off your feet).*

A mother of three from Bethesda, Maryland, adds:

Go to a golf shop and buy one of those walking sticks with a seat attached to it—I would've been a goner without one. They're lightweight and easy to carry. Also, a support garment (such as a BellyBra) is a must for relieving pressure on your lower back.

A Branchburg, New Jersey, woman advises:

Moms-to-be should be really mindful of the temperature, staying hydrated, and having realistic expectations for how much you'll be able to do. We averaged 5–7 miles of walking per day during our trip, which may have been a bit too much for me (I was six months pregnant at the time). Once the temperatures started approaching 90, I found it

TIPS FOR GOING SOLO

SINGLE CAN MEAN TRAVELING ALONE as well as unmarried. Either way, being by yourself doesn't mean you can't have a great time at Disney World. **Deb Wills,** creator of the all-things-Disney website AllEars.net, offers this advice:

- One of the best parts about traveling solo is that you can be your own boss. Sleep in, have leisurely morning coffee on the balcony, relax by the pool . . . or not. If you'd rather get up and go early, who's to stop you?

- Put some spontaneity into your day. If you're taking Disney transportation, get on the first park bus that arrives.

- Get on the resort monorail (not the Express!) at the Magic Kingdom, and visit each of the resorts it stops at. Each resort has its own theme and character, with lots to see and explore.

- Did you know you can walk through the queues and view the preshows of the thrill rides even if you don't want to ride? Wander through at your own pace; then tell the cast member before boarding that you don't wish to ride. You'll be shown to a nearby exit.

- If you *do* want to experience the thrill rides, take advantage of the single-rider lines (when available) for the Rock 'n' Roller Coaster, Expedition Everest, and Test Track. They can cut your wait time significantly.

- Once you're vaccinated, if you encounter folks taking photos of each other, ask if they'd like to be in one photo, then offer to snap the picture. This is a great way to make friends.

- Get your favorite Disney snack, find a bench, and people-watch. You'll be amazed at what you see: the honeymooning couple wearing bride-and-groom mouse ears, toddlers seeing Mickey and the characters for the first time, grandparents smiling indulgently as their grandchildren smear ice cream all over their faces. If you're

difficult to catch my breath and my feet began to swell. A midday nap or swim break was 100% required—I tried to skip it on a few days, and I was miserable as a result. I was most frustrated at EPCOT, where most of the headliner attractions are restricted for pregnant guests.

MORE TIPS FOR MOMS-TO-BE

IN ADDITION TO OUR READERS' TIPS, here are a few of ours:

1. Discuss your Disney World plans with your OB-GYN before your trip.

2. Start walking at home to build up your stamina for walking in the parks. Once in the World, however, try to use in-park transportation when you can so that you're not having to walk all the time.

3. While there have been no confirmed cases of the Zika virus in the Orlando area to date, there have been a small number of cases in other parts of Florida, including one case in Osceola County, where Celebration and Kissimmee are located. You may want to carry insect repellent. Women who are or may become pregnant may want to take extra precautions.

WALT DISNEY WORLD
for SINGLES

DISNEY WORLD IS GREAT FOR SINGLES. It's safe, clean, and low-pressure. Safety and comfort are unsurpassed, especially for women traveling alone. Parking lots are well lit and constantly patrolled.

missing the smiles of your own children, buy a couple of balloons and give them away. You'll help make the kids near you very, very happy.

- Learn how some of the magic is created. Take a behind-the-scenes tour or one of the Deluxe hotel tours if they're offered.

- Visit Animal Kingdom Lodge and relax at an animal-viewing area. Find an animal keeper; they'll gladly discuss care of the wild animals at the resort.

- Don't hesitate to strike up conversations with cast members or guests in line with you. Once they return, international cast members in EPCOT's World Showcase will be happy to share stories about their homelands.

- Enjoy a leisurely shopping adventure around the World. Some stores (**Arribas Brothers** in Disney Springs and **Mitsukoshi Department Store** in the Japan Pavilion at World Showcase) have really neat displays and exhibits.

- Go to that restaurant you've always wanted to try but your picky eater has always declined. You don't have to order a full meal; try several appetizers or, better yet, just dessert.

- Special fun can be had at a Character Meal (no waiting in long lines). Which one has characters you love? Make an early or late reservation for fewer people and more character time. The Garden Grill in The Land is a hidden gem!

- Check the calendar for special events. The annual Flower and Garden Festival has lots of eye candy that you can enjoy at your own pace.

- Use common sense about your personal security. I feel very comfortable and safe traveling alone at Disney World and have done so many times, but I still don't do things that I wouldn't do at home (like announce to anyone listening that I'm traveling solo). If you aren't comfortable walking to your room alone, ask at the front desk for a security escort. Use extra caution in the parking lots at night, just as you would at home.

If you're looking for a place to relax without being hit on, Walt Disney World is perfect. The bars, lounges, and nightclubs are among the most laid-back and friendly you're likely to find. Between the Board-Walk and Disney Springs, nightlife abounds; virtually every type of entertainment is available at a reasonable price. If you overimbibe and you're a Disney resort guest, Disney buses will return you safely to your hotel.

See "Tips for Going Solo," above, for more ways to enjoy Walt Disney World on your own.

WALT DISNEY WORLD
for COUPLES

MANY COUPLES THINK Walt Disney World is strictly for kids. Not so, an Evans City, Pennsylvania, woman attests:

> *I have many friends who think I was crazy to travel to Walt Disney World without my children (ages 9 and 12). I absolutely loved it! Instead of rushing from thrill ride to thrill ride, we were able to slow down and enjoy all of the amazing details that make WDW the incredibly special place that it is. It is an entirely different experience, but equally magical.*

WEDDINGS, COMMITMENT CEREMONIES, AND VOWS RENEWALS

SO MANY COUPLES TIE THE KNOT or honeymoon in the World that Disney has a dedicated department to help arrange the day of your dreams. **Disney's Fairy Tale Weddings & Honeymoons** (☎ 321-939-4610; disneyweddings.com) offers a range of ceremony venues and services, plus honeymoon planning and registries.

You're still responsible for obtaining an officiant and a marriage certificate, but Disney maintains a list of officiants from which you can choose (or you can bring your own—if you do, he or she counts as one of your guests).

unofficial **TIP**
Contact Disney as soon as you have a date in mind for your event—popular dates may not be available on short notice. If you wish to hold your ceremony inside a theme park, you're restricted to very early in the morning or late at night, when the park is closed to guests.

LEGALITIES

TO MARRY IN THE WORLD, you need a marriage license ($93.50), issued at any Florida county courthouse. Florida residents must complete a 4-hour premarital counseling session to marry less than 3 days after applying for their license; completing the course reduces the license fee to $61. There is no waiting period for residents of other states; all weddings must occur within 60 days of getting the license. Blood tests aren't required, but both parties must present valid identification and their Social Security numbers. Finally, if you're widowed or divorced, you must also present a certified copy of the deceased spouse's death certificate or your divorce decree.

HONEYMOONS AND HONEYMOON REGISTRIES

HONEYMOON PACKAGES are adaptations of regular Walt Disney World travel packages, though you may purchase add-ons such as flowers and in-room gifts to make your trip more special. Some couples who honeymoon at Walt Disney World create a registry that allows friends and family to bestow gifts of tours, spa packages, special dinners, and the like. For more information on Disney honeymoon registries, visit disney.honeymoonwishes.com.

CELEBRATE . . . EVERYTHING!

DISNEY WORLD IS ALL ABOUT CELEBRATING—marriages, birthdays, anniversaries, the works—but only if you let somebody know. A St. Louis newlywed offers this advice:

> If you're celebrating, ask for Celebration Buttons when you check into your hotel or at any park's Guest Relations, then WEAR THEM! Cast members regularly congratulated us, and I'm relatively certain we were seated at better tables for dinner based solely on our buttons.

TIPS FOR VISITORS WHO NEED "ADULT TIME"

AS WE'VE NOTED, WALT DISNEY WORLD is a great destination for adults traveling without kids, either as solos, couples, or groups of friends. The self-contained Disney universe, with its easy transportation, security, and variety of dining, drinking, and entertainment options, makes it a fabulous place to vacation without children (don't tell ours!).

Naturally, anyone who visits The Most Magical Place on Earth is well advised to be prepared to see children—lots of them. Indeed, it would be naive to think otherwise. But that doesn't mean that you need to be around the little tykes every minute. Here are some tips.

- **Dine late.** Most families will try to eat dinner before 8 p.m. Have a late lunch and try for a reservation closer to the last seating at your restaurant. The exception to this is California Grill, where many people (families or not) will try to time their meal around the fireworks at the Magic Kingdom (when fireworks are offered).

- **Dine at Victoria & Albert's** (when it reopens). V&A is the only on-property restaurant that bans guests under age 10. Pricey? Yes. Worth it? You bet.

- **Go to the spa** (when it reopens).

- **Linger in World Showcase.** We could spend hours poring over the details of the World Showcase pavilions. Favorites include the Bijutsu-kan Gallery in Japan and the Gallery of Arts and History in Morocco.

- **Really take in the trails of Animal Kingdom.** The animal trails in Asia, Africa, and Discovery Island are peaceful and beautiful.

- **Stay up late.** Take a tip from Tom Bricker, a friend of this book, and don't leave the park until well past closing. There's something magical about having all of Main Street or Sunset Boulevard to yourself with the lights and background music still playing. Do make sure you don't miss the last bus to your resort, though, if you didn't drive.

- **Take a tour (when they're restarted).** Many Walt Disney World tours have an age limit for how young a guest can be to experience them.

- **Spend the morning at the pool.** Most families hit the parks in the morning and come back to their hotels around lunch. Do the opposite and pretend the lifeguard is your personal cabana boy or girl.

- **Use the TouringPlans.com hotel-room finder** (see page 24) to scope out the quietest parts of your Disney resort.

ROMANTIC GETAWAYS

NOT ALL DISNEY HOTELS lend themselves to a couple's getaway: Some are too family-oriented, while others swarm with conventioneers. For romantic (though expensive) lodging, we recommend **Animal Kingdom Lodge & Villas, Bay Lake Tower** at the Contemporary, **BoardWalk Inn & Villas, Grand Floridian Resort & Spa** and its **Villas, Polynesian Village & Villas,** the **Riviera, Wilderness Lodge & Villas,** and the **Yacht & Beach Club Resorts.** The Alligator Bayou section at **Port Orleans Riverside,** a Disney Moderate resort, also has secluded rooms.

◀| ODDS *and* ENDS

SMOKING All Walt Disney World theme parks and water parks, along with the ESPN Wide World of Sports Complex, are smoke-free— *smoking is allowed only outside of the park entrances.* Disney resort guests may smoke only in designated areas; smoking in your room or on your balcony is prohibited.

For a full list of places where smoking is permitted, see disneyworld .disney.go.com/guest-services/designated-smoking-areas.

LOOSE ICE AND DRY ICE are prohibited in coolers inside the theme parks and water parks. Reusable ice packs are permitted.

PART NINE

ARRIVING *and* GETTING AROUND

GETTING *to* WALT DISNEY WORLD

FROM ORLANDO INTERNATIONAL AIRPORT (MCO)

YOU HAVE FIVE OPTIONS for getting from MCO to Walt Disney World. Because most readers stay at a Disney-owned hotel, we cover **Disney's Magical Express** airport bus service first, then towncar services and ride-hailing services, then car rentals and other options. Driving directions conclude this section.

Disney's Magical Express *(ending December 31, 2021)*

This free bus service shuttles guests of Disney-owned and -operated resorts between MCO and Walt Disney World. (The Swan, the Dolphin, Swan Reserve, Shades of Green, and the hotels of Bonnet Creek Resort and the Disney Springs Resort Area don't participate.) Magical Express also provides free luggage delivery to your resort. The Magical Express service is ending December 31, 2021. See disneyworld.disney.go.com /guest-services/magical-express for more details.

Replacement for Disney's Magical Express

Behind the scenes, Disney's Magical Express bus service was operated by Mears Transportation, which also runs taxi, towncar, and shuttle services throughout Central Florida. Shortly after Disney announced it was discontinuing Magical Express, Mears announced a similar bus service, called **Mears Connect** (☎ 407-422-4561; mearsconnect.com),

ORLANDO AIRPORT–TO–DISNEY RESORT TRANSPORTATION OPTIONS			
OPTION	ROUND-TRIP PRICE	PROS	CONS
RIDE-HAILING SERVICE (LYFT, UBER)	$80–$160 plus gratuity (up to 3 adults)	• Possibly the cheapest option for 3 or 4 people • Direct service to your resort	• Price varies considerably based on demand • May be hard to find cars with child seats • Car quality ranges from acceptable to luxurious
MEARS CONNECT	$32/adult, $27/child plus small gratuity	• Cheapest option for 1 or 2 people • Mears ran Magical Express for years, so they know what they're doing • Child seats available	• Longest transportation time of any option • May drop off passengers at other resorts before yours
TOWNCAR SERVICE	$186 plus gratuity (up to 4 adults)	• Likely the fastest way to get to your resort • Direct service to your resort • Child seats available • Driver will meet at baggage claim and assist with luggage	• Most expensive option

that runs between Orlando International Airport (MCO) and Walt Disney World–area hotels.

At press time, Mears Connect's pricing was $32 per adult and $27 per child, round-trip, between MCO and Disney's hotels; one-way fares are half that. If you're traveling alone or with one other adult, and you don't mind the wait to drop off other guests at their resorts, Mears Connect is the cheapest option.

Towncar Service

Happy Limousine (☎ 407-856-1280; happylimo.com) provides towncar, minivan, and limo service between Orlando International Airport (and Sanford) and Disney World–area hotels. Child seats and boosters are available, as are wheelchair-accessible options. One-way trips start at $93 for a four-person luxury SUV, $98 for a 5-person minivan, and $108 for a 10-person transit van.

One advantage of a towncar over Uber and Lyft is that the towncar driver will meet you at baggage claim and identify themselves with a placard showing your name. If you're concerned about carrying your own luggage, finding or using a ride-hailing service, or potentially waiting on other people to fill a bus to your destination, a towncar service might be your best bet. Another advantage is that towncar services generally don't use "surge" pricing, as Uber and Lyft do, so you know in advance what the price of your transportation will be.

Towncar services are probably the best choice for groups of five or more; the direct service to your hotel and the convenience of having your driver meet you at baggage claim probably more than make up for the cost increase between Mears Connect and a towncar.

Ride-Hailing Services

We generally recommend **Lyft** and **Uber** over taxis and shuttle services. They're often significantly less expensive, and while you can't pick the specific car you'll get ahead of time, it's exceedingly rare that we're in one and find ourselves thinking a taxi or shuttle van would be cleaner or more comfortable.

Both services are cheaper than taxis when commuting within the World. On a recent trip from Saratoga Springs Resort to the Magic Kingdom via Fort Wilderness, for example, we paid $12, while the return taxi ride along the same route, in the same traffic, was $25.

Lyft and Uber can also pick you up and drop you off at the airport. The pickup location is on MCO's second level, the same level as baggage claim and where passengers are currently picked up by family and friends.

The cost of a one-way ride from the airport varies greatly depending on the number of people in your party, what kind of car you request, and the time of day you need to travel. A basic Uber or Lyft vehicle for up to three people in the middle of the day runs around $33 plus gratuity. The same ride can be $80 or more at 5 p.m. because of demand. Likewise, a vehicle with room for five costs around $50 midday but more during peak times. Fancy cars, such as Uber or Lyft Black, cost $75–$86 one-way, about the same as a towncar service. We prefer Lyft over Uber.

Before the pandemic, Disney partnered with Lyft on its own service called **Minnie Vans,** which used the Lyft app to summon a car driven by a Disney cast member. However, Disney suspended the Minnie Vans service during the pandemic, and at press time it had not announced a date when the service will resume.

A Washington, D.C., reader found Uber a welcome alternative to Disney's bus service:

> My first night at EPCOT, the bus line was so long—and so stalled—that I decided it made more sense to shell out for an Uber than to wait another hour to get back to my hotel; likewise at other busy times throughout the World. It was money well spent—less than renting a car for a week.

And from an Indianapolis couple:

> If you're using a touring plan to make the most of your day and time is tight, we can't recommend Uber enough. We used the monorail and buses during the day and evening, but when it came to making it to our breakfast reservations and getting to Animal Kingdom for rope drop, Uber was immediately our first choice vs. losing sleep to get to the bus stop early. We never waited for a car for longer than 4 minutes, and the drivers were friendly and quick.

Taxis

Taxis carry four to eight passengers, depending on vehicle type. Rates vary according to distance. If your hotel is in the World, your fare will be about $60–$72, plus tip. For the US 192 Maingate area, it will cost about $55. To International Drive or downtown Orlando, expect to pay in the neighborhood of $40–$50.

Mears (see above) provides local cab service, shuttle service, and an exclusive partnership with Uber called **Uber Taxi.** Using the Uber app, customers can book Mears taxis just as they would regular Uber rides. Mears says UberTaxi is intended to offer the convenience of Uber to customers who prefer and trust a traditional taxi service over a ride-hailing service.

FROM THE AIRPORT TO	ONE-WAY ADULT/CHILD	ROUND-TRIP ADULT/CHILD
INTERNATIONAL DRIVE	$23/$18	$35/$27
DOWNTOWN ORLANDO (leaves hourly)	$21/$17	$33/$25
DSRA RESORTS–LAKE BUENA VISTA	$25/$20	$39/$30
US 192 MAINGATE AREA	$25/$20	$39/$30

Renting a Car

Note: As we went to press, car-rental locations and logistics for Orlando International Airport's new terminal C were not available. Terminal C is separate from the airport's main facility, which houses terminals A and B. When it opens in early 2022, terminal C will offer free monorail service to terminals A and B, which may be how car-rental processing is done.

Readers staying in Walt Disney World ask us frequently if they'll need a car. If your plans don't include regular visits to restaurants, attractions, or other destinations outside Disney World, then the answer is a qualified no. That's mainly due to cost—most car-rental companies dumped huge portions of their inventory during the pandemic, resulting in sky-high prices when demand returned. Prior to the pandemic, Orlando was one of the least-expensive car-rental markets in the US, averaging under $30 per day. As we went to press, the lowest price for a weekly rental we could find for late 2021 and early 2022 was $65 per day for a car at the airport, or $49 per day if you schlep your family and luggage to and from an off-site company via shuttle. Don't forget to add your resort's nightly parking fee into that cost ($15–$25 at a Disney hotel).

That said, take into account the thoughts of this reader from Washington State:

> We rented a car and were glad we did. With a car, we could drive to the grocery store to restock our snack supply. It also came in handy for our night out.

A dad from Avon Lake, Ohio, adds:

> Although we stayed at the Grand Floridian, we found the monorail convenient only for the Magic Kingdom. Of the six nights we stayed, we used our car five days.

An Ann Arbor, Michigan, mother of three shares her experience:

> During our stay it was almost impossible to get into any of the Disney restaurants. Purely out of desperation, we rented a car so we

could eat outside WDW. We had no problem finding good places to eat at a fraction of what you'd pay inside.

PLAN TO RENT A CAR IF

1. Your hotel is outside Walt Disney World.
2. Your hotel is in the World but you want to eat someplace other than the theme parks and your hotel.
3. You plan to return to your hotel for naps or swimming during the day.
4. You plan to visit other area theme parks or water parks (including Disney's).

At **MCO,** all car-rental counters are on **Level One** of the main terminal. Level One is also where you can catch a courtesy shuttle to an off-site rental location.

Orlando is the largest rental-car market in the entire world. At last count, 36 companies vie for your business. Ten—**Alamo, Avis, Budget, Dollar, Enterprise, Hertz, National, Payless, SixT,** and **Thrifty**—have counters at terminals A and B. **Fox** and 25 other companies have locations near the airport and provide courtesy shuttles outside Level One at all terminals.

We prefer renting inside the airport for these reasons:

1. You can complete your paperwork while you wait for your checked luggage to arrive at baggage claim.
2. It's just a short walk to the garage to pick up your car.
3. The extra time and effort it takes to use the shuttle usually isn't worth the money saved, especially when you're traveling with kids.

If you rent on-site, you'll return your car to the garage adjacent to the terminal where your airline is located. If you return your car to the wrong garage, you'll have to schlep your luggage from one side of the airport to the other to reach your check-in.

Most rental companies charge about $5–$8 a gallon to fill the gas tank. If you plan to drive a lot, prepay for a fill-up so you can return the car empty, or fill up at the 7-11 on airport property just before you get to terminals A and B.

HOW ORLANDO RENTAL-CAR COMPANIES STACK UP When it comes to renting a car, most *Unofficial Guide* readers are looking for the following, as reflected in the chart on the next page:

1. Quick, courteous, and efficient processing on pickup
2. A nice, well-maintained, late-model automobile
3. A car that is clean and odor-free
4. Quick, courteous, and efficient processing on return
5. If applicable, an efficient shuttle between the rental agency and airport

On a 0 (worst) to 100 (best) scale, the chart shows how readers rate the Orlando operations of each company. Companies not listed didn't get enough surveys to rate; we strongly recommend renting from a company on the chart. To participate in our survey, visit touringplans.com/walt-disney-world/survey.

National Car Rental was named the top rental company for the 11th time in the past 12 years. If you prioritize service and car condition as much as getting a good deal, go with National. **Alamo,** the only other winner in the last 12 years, is almost always in the top two here.

COMPANY	Pickup Efficiency	Condition of Car	Cleanliness of Car	Return Efficiency	Overall Rating	Survey Rank
NATIONAL	93	94	96	91	93	1
ALAMO	91	93	95	90	92	2
ENTERPRISE	86	91	92	88	89	3
HERTZ	83	88	89	90	87	4
AVERAGE	81	89	91	86	87	N/A
AVIS	77	88	87	87	85	5
THRIFTY	70	86	88	82	81	6 (tie)
DOLLAR	72	83	88	82	81	6 (tie)
BUDGET	65	87	87	85	81	6 (tie)

Note: For any car-rental agency not shown, we didn't receive enough survey responses to analyze.

Most companies, in fact, deliver consistently good cars and service. If budget is a top priority, we're comfortable recommending any company in the top five that has the lowest price. In general, cars from less-expensive companies tend to have higher miles and fewer amenities, such as backup cameras and satellite navigation or radio (one even had crank-up windows).

Readers complain most about the hassle of off-site shuttles and the paperwork involved in picking up cars there. At **Fox,** be prepared for the customer-service desk to assume you're going to steal the car; the voluminous paperwork is to help the bounty hunters find you. Also, the pace is slow at **SixT,** even if the line is short—we suspect that's because most of their customers are visiting from outside the US, and the staff needs time to review differences in rental policies, insurance coverage, electronic tolls, and the like. Both companies' people are fantastic at what they do.

INSURANCE AND FEES Car renters should know what their auto insurance does and doesn't cover. If you have the slightest question about your coverage, call your agent. A corollary discussion pertains to added coverage from your credit card company if the rental fee is charged on the card. Usually, credit card coverage picks up deductibles and some ancillary charges that your auto-insurance policy doesn't cover. The tune is the same, however: Make sure you understand what is and isn't covered.

A 6%–7% sales tax, a $2.50-per-day airport-facility surcharge, and a vehicle-license-recovery fee of 45¢ to $2.02 per day will be added to your rental car bill. Some companies, including Alamo, add fees for tire and battery wear, plus other cryptic fees. Luckily, you can rent a car at your hotel on the day you actually need it.

OUR BEST RENTAL-CAR DISCOUNT TIP We've saved hundreds of dollars over the past couple of years with a website called **AutoSlash** (autoslash.com), which does two things very well:

1. If you haven't yet rented a car, Autoslash will help you find the lowest rates available, using every discount you're eligible for.
2. If you've already rented a car, tell AutoSlash the details, and it'll search continuously for a lower rate. If a lower rate turns up, AutoSlash will email you a link to rebook.

AutoSlash frequently finds multiple low-price deals through **Priceline.** In those cases, AutoSlash will list the car type, rental company, and price for every deal available. Use our list of the best rental companies on the previous page to weed out the ones that don't appeal to you, and book the cheapest one that does.

TOLLS If you're flying into Orlando and plan on driving extensively, consider picking up a **Visitor Toll Pass** (visitortollpass.com) when you arrive at the airport. You'll pick up a small Toll Pass device from a vending machine at Terminal A on Level 1 and link it to your credit card. The Toll Pass hangs from your rearview mirror, pays tolls automatically, and allows you to use the electronic toll and express lanes throughout Florida. If the Visitor Toll Pass program isn't working, you can pick up a normal toll transponder at most grocery stores and drugstores, such as Publix and CVS.

Interstate 4

Regardless of how you navigate to Orlando, you'll almost certainly drive on I-4, its busiest highway and one that demands a great deal of a driver's concentration.

WDW EXITS OFF I-4 East to west (in the direction of Orlando to Tampa), five I-4 exits serve Walt Disney World:

Exit 68 (FL 535/Lake Buena Vista) primarily serves the Disney Springs Resort Area and Disney Springs, including the Marketplace and the West Side. It also serves non-Disney hotels with a Lake Buena Vista address. This exit puts you on a road with lots of traffic signals, especially near I-4. A construction project to improve the I-4 exit here begins in late 2021. Avoid this area unless you're headed to one of the preceding destinations.

Exit 67 (FL 536/EPCOT/Disney Springs) delivers you to a four-lane expressway into the heart of Disney World. It's the fastest and most convenient way for westbound travelers to access almost all Disney destinations except Disney's Animal Kingdom and ESPN Wide World of Sports Complex. Be alert for road construction.

Exit 65 (Osceola Parkway) is the best exit for westbound travelers to access Disney's Animal Kingdom, Animal Kingdom Lodge, Pop Century Resort, Art of Animation Resort, the All-Star Resorts, and the ESPN Wide World of Sports Complex.

Exit 64 (US 192/Magic Kingdom) is the best route for eastbound travelers to all Disney destinations. If eastbound traffic is heavy, get off at Exit 62 instead.

Exit 62 (Disney World/Celebration) is the first Disney exit you'll encounter heading east. This four-lane, controlled-access highway connects to the Walt Disney World Maingate. Accessing Disney World via the next exit, Exit 64, also routes you through the main entrance.

I-4 DELAYS I-4 can be a mess anywhere from Tampa to Daytona. The greatest congestion is between the Universal Orlando–International Drive area and downtown Orlando, but the section to the southwest serving the Disney World exits can become a choke point at almost any time of day.

If you're going from Walt Disney World toward Orlando (east), the jam usually breaks up after you pass the FL 535 exit, but it gets congested again near Universal Orlando and northeast due to

I-4 & Walt Disney World Area

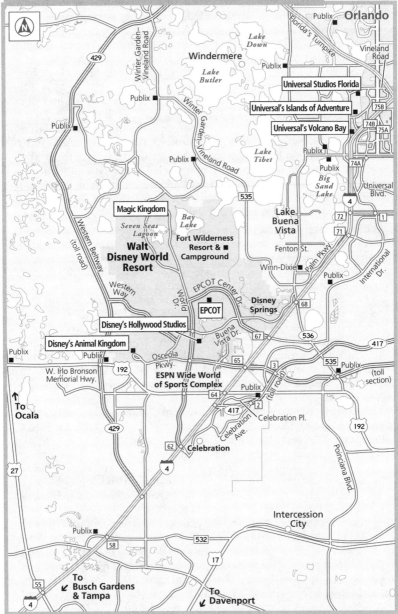

construction. As you head west toward Tampa, traffic eases up after
the US 192 interchange.

In addition to extremely heavy traffic, I-4 is finishing up (in 2022)
construction projects that affect the entire stretch of the highway from

FL 434 north of Orlando southwest past downtown Orlando, past the Universal Orlando exits, and past all of the Walt Disney World exits. The projects extend to the intersection of US 27, southwest of Disney World in Polk County. Work includes widening, paving, constructing new interchanges, improving existing interchanges, adding two express toll lanes in each direction, and adding access/egress ramps. There are also unrelated projects on I-4 extending southwest from Daytona and I-95; near Sanford north of Orlando; and from US 27 to US 92 farther southwest.

If you're considering a hotel on or near I-Drive, try to find one toward the southern end. If I-4 traffic becomes intolerable, it's pretty easy to commute from the Universal Orlando–International Drive area to Walt Disney World on (1) **Turkey Lake Road,** connecting to Palm Parkway and FL 535 on the northwest side of I-4; (2) the southernmost section of **I-Drive,** connecting to FL 536 on the southeast side of the interstate; or (3) **Daryl Carter Parkway,** which bridges I-4 just northeast of FL 535, connecting Palm Parkway and International Drive near the Orlando International Premium Outlets.

AVOIDING THE I-4 BLUES Many GPS apps and newer GPS units will automatically reroute you around delays from construction and traffic issues. Use those if you can anytime you're driving around Orlando.

For those without GPS, we provide the following alternative routes, assuming that construction in the affected areas will continue into 2022. Before you take any of these detours, however, use the websites below to verify whether the construction zones are still active.

If you're driving at low-traffic times, you might prefer to deal with I-4 construction rather than make a detour. During the day (6 a.m.–10 p.m.), most projects try to keep all lanes open, though traffic sometimes slows to a crawl (as it does in the WDW area even when no work is going on). From 10 p.m. to 6 a.m., however, there may be lane closures.

Real-time road conditions are available online at the **Interstate 4 Exit Information Guide** (i4exitguide.com/i-4-traffic), and the **FDOT Interactive Project Map** (data.fdot.gov/road/projects) shows all active construction projects in Florida. Information about construction in Orlando and the tourist areas is available at **Central Florida Roads** (cflroads.com). For info about and current conditions on area toll roads, visit the website for the **Central Florida Expressway Authority** (cfxway.com).

Traveling southwest on I-4, we recommend going around Orlando on FL 417/Central Florida GreeneWay (a toll road), exiting on West Osceola Parkway into Walt Disney World. In addition to construction in Orlando and the Disney World area, there may also be construction between Daytona and DeLand. To avoid this part of I-4, exit I-95 onto US 92 westbound, and turn south (left) onto US 17. When you hit I-4, take it west a short distance to FL 417, and bypass Orlando to the east.

*un*official **TIP**
FL 417, aka the **Central Florida GreeneWay,** is a toll road, so make sure you have about $5 in cash or change to pay the toll.

From I-95 southbound, exit onto US 92 westbound; then turn south (left) onto US 17. When you hit I-4, take it west a short distance to FL

417; bypass Orlando to the east, exiting onto West Osceola Parkway and then into Walt Disney World.

From I-95 northbound, exit onto FL 44 toward DeLand. At I-4, go southwest, exiting onto Saxon Boulevard. Take Saxon Boulevard west to US 17, and turn south (left). When you hit I-4 again, take it west a short distance to FL 417. Take FL 417, and bypass Orlando to the east.

From MCO, exit the airport on Jeff Fuqua Boulevard and proceed south to the FL 417/Central Florida GreeneWay toll road. Turn right up the ramp and take FL 417 northwest. Exit onto West Osceola Parkway and follow it to Walt Disney World.

From Sanford International Airport, take East Airport Boulevard west to the FL 417/Central Florida GreeneWay toll road and bypass Orlando to the east, exiting on West Osceola Parkway and continuing into Walt Disney World.

From Miami, Fort Lauderdale, and southeastern Florida, head north on Florida's Turnpike to Exit 249/Osceola Parkway West, and follow the signs.

From Tampa and southwest Florida, take I-75 northbound to I-4; then drive east on I-4, take Exit 64 onto US 192 West, and follow the signs.

ALTERNATIVE AIRPORTS

A SHORT DISTANCE northeast of Orlando is **Sanford International Airport (SFB;** orlandosanfordairport.com). Small, convenient, and easily accessible, it's low-hassle compared with the huge MCO and its block-long security-checkpoint lines.

The primary domestic carrier at SFB is **Allegiant Air** (☎ 702-505-8888; allegiantair.com), with service throughout the East Coast and the Midwest. **Sun Country** (☎ 651-905-2737; suncountry.com) also serves SFB and dozens of US cities. European carriers include **TUI fly** (☎ 855-808-4015; tuifly.com) and **Wamos Air** (☎ +34 912181539; wamosair.com). Another SFB carrier, **Surinam Airways** (flyslm.com), is based in South America. Two low-cost Canadian airlines also serve Sanford: **Flair Airlines** (flyflair.com) is planning to start service in October 2021 between Canada and five other US cities, and **Swoop** (flyswoop.com) offers flights to Sanford from November through April, with twice-weekly return flights to Canada.

An Uber or Lyft from Sanford to Disney property will run you $50–$125 or more one-way.

A reader from Roanoke, Virginia, uses Sanford frequently, writing:

The 45-minute drive to WDW is more than made up for by avoiding the chaos at Orlando International, and it's stress-free.

This couple from White Township, New Jersey, prefers flying into Tampa instead:

Flying from Newark to Tampa instead of Orlando saves us money and our sanity. It means significantly lower fares, fewer children on the plane, and shorter security lines.

Be aware, however, that it's a 77-mile drive from Tampa International Airport to the Magic Kingdom—about an hour and 15 minutes.

HOW *to* TRAVEL *Around the* WORLD *(or, The* Real Mr. Toad's Wild Ride)

TRYING TO COMMUTE around Walt Disney World can be frustrating, simply because of the number of transportation options available. To get between many points, your options include cars, boats, monorails, and elevated gondolas, plus walking.

Between any two points in Walt Disney World, there's almost always a free transportation option available. Some of the free options are slow enough, however, that paying for an alternative option often makes more sense. We'll walk you through those options right after some orientation.

FINDING YOUR WAY

WALT DISNEY WORLD IS HUGE—about the size of San Francisco. As with any big city, it's easy to get lost here. The easiest way to orient yourself is to think in terms of five major clusters:

1. **The Magic Kingdom area** encompasses all hotels and theme parks around Seven Seas Lagoon. This includes the Magic Kingdom; hotels connected by the monorail; Shades of Green Resort; and the Palm, Magnolia, and Oak Trail Golf Courses.

2. **The Bay Lake area** includes developments on and around Bay Lake: Wilderness Lodge & Villas, Fort Wilderness Campground, and the Four Seasons Resort Orlando and Tranquilo Golf Club.

3. **The EPCOT area** contains EPCOT and its resort hotels, Disney's Hollywood Studios, the BoardWalk, ESPN Wide World of Sports, Pop Century Resort, Art of Animation Resort, Caribbean Beach Resort, Riviera Resort, and Star Wars: Galactic Starcruiser (opening in 2022).

4. **The Disney Springs area** includes Disney Springs; Typhoon Lagoon water park; Lake Buena Vista Golf Course; the Disney Springs Resort Area; and the Port Orleans, Saratoga Springs, and Old Key West resorts.

5. **The Animal Kingdom area** includes Disney's Animal Kingdom, Blizzard Beach water park, Animal Kingdom Lodge & Villas, the All-Star Resorts, and Coronado Springs Resort.

The following section covers how to get around Walt Disney World using the Disney transportation system. Tips using non-Disney hotel shuttles and for driving yourself begin on page 439.

THE DISNEY TRANSPORTATION SYSTEM (DTS)

THE DISNEY TRANSPORTATION SYSTEM is large, diversified, and generally efficient, but sometimes it's overwhelmed, particularly at park opening and closing. If you could always be assured of getting on a bus, boat, monorail, or gondola at these critical times, we'd advise you to leave your car at home. In reality, delays are unavoidable when huge crowds want to go somewhere at once, even before the era of social distancing. In addition, some destinations are served directly, while many others require one or more transfers. Finally, it's sometimes difficult to figure out how Disney's various methods of transportation interconnect.

The DTS is a "hub and spoke" system. Hubs include the **Transportation and Ticket Center (TTC), Disney Springs,** and all four major **theme parks** (from about an hour before official opening time to 1 hour after closing). With some exceptions, direct service is available from Disney resorts to the major theme parks and Disney Springs, as well as between parks.

If you're staying at a Magic Kingdom resort that's served by the monorail (**Contemporary** and **Bay Lake Tower, Grand Floridian & Villas, Polynesian Village & Villas**), you'll be able to commute efficiently to the Magic Kingdom. If you want to visit EPCOT, you must take the monorail to the TTC and transfer to the EPCOT

unofficial **TIP**

If a hotel offers boat or monorail service, its bus service will be limited— you'll have to transfer at a hub for many destinations.

monorail. (Guests at the Polynesian Village & Villas can eliminate the transfer by walking 5–10 minutes to the TTC and catching the direct monorail to EPCOT.)

If you're staying at an EPCOT resort (**BoardWalk Inn & Villas, Dolphin, Swan, Swan Reserve, Yacht & Beach Club Resorts**), you can walk or commute by boat to EPCOT's International Gateway (rear) entrance. Although direct buses link EPCOT resorts to the Magic Kingdom and Disney's Animal Kingdom, there's no direct bus to EPCOT's main entrance or Disney's Hollywood Studios. To reach the Studios from the EPCOT resorts, you must take a boat, the Skyliner, or walk. Note that the Swan, Swan Reserve, and Dolphin use Mears Transportation, not Disney, for bus service.

The **Caribbean Beach, Pop Century, Art of Animation, Saratoga Springs, Port Orleans, Coronado Springs, Old Key West, Animal Kingdom Lodge & Villas,** and **All-Star Resorts** offer direct buses to all theme parks (though Pop and Animation may provide only the Skyliner to EPCOT and Hollywood Studios during slower times of the year). The rub is that you must sometimes walk a long way to bus stops or endure more than a half dozen additional pickups before actually heading for the park(s). Commuting in the morning from these resorts is generally easy, though you may have to ride standing. Returning in the evening, however, can be a different story. **Shades of Green** runs frequent shuttles from the resort to the TTC, where guests can transfer to their final destinations.

Hotels of the **Disney Springs Resort Area** (**DSRA**) provide shuttle service through an independent company. The DSRA shuttles constitute a negative for guests at these hotels—the service is simply substandard. Before you book a DSRA hotel, check the nature and frequency of its shuttles.

Guests staying at **Fort Wilderness Resort & Campground** must use its buses to reach boat landings or the Settlement Depot and Reception Outpost bus stops. From these points, guests can travel directly by boat to the Magic Kingdom or by bus to other destinations. Except for going to the Magic Kingdom, the best way for Fort Wilderness guests to commute is in their own car.

The Disney Transportation System vs. Driving Your Own Car

To help you assess your transportation options, we've developed a table (see pages 434–435) comparing the approximate commuting times from Disney resorts to various Walt Disney World destinations, using Disney transportation or your own car. The table represents more than 550,000 routes on which we collected data for this edition of the book, all in 2021. It includes bus, monorail, and boat options—the Skyliner system has its own table.

DISNEY TRANSPORTATION The times listed in the table in the "Disney System" columns represent an average-case and worst-case scenario. For example, if you want to go from the All-Star Resorts to the Magic Kingdom, the table indicates the times as "38 (49)." The first number, 38, indicates how many minutes your commute will take on an average day. It assumes that buses arrive every 20 minutes (see "Walt Disney World Bus Service" below), your average wait is half of that, there are no major traffic delays, and everything else is as usual. It represents the average time we observed during our research of the transportation system. For the pessimists, the number in parentheses (49) indicates the 90th percentile of trip times—90% of trips take no more than this long for the next bus to show up, load, and get you to your destination. Use this to plan for contingencies. (*Example:* The bus is pulling away as you arrive at the stop, and you must wait around 20 minutes for the next one. Once en route, the bus hits every red light on the way to the Magic Kingdom.)

Bus schedules are also adjusted based on demand and fuel costs. By far the biggest influence on your travel time between two points on the DTS is the amount of time you have to wait for your bus to arrive. Once you hop on your bus, the travel time is pretty consistent, barring any unusual traffic problems; but your time waiting for the bus can vary greatly. Most cast members will tell you that buses run every 20 minutes. Our data indicates they run slightly more often: about every 19 minutes. The mode (the most common transportation time) for a bus between any two points is 28 minutes. Service at the Value and Moderate resorts is about the same as at Deluxe resorts, something we were a bit surprised to see.

Walt Disney World Bus Service

Note: For an up-to-date look at what time buses start running at each resort, see tinyurl.com/wdw-bus-times.

The average bus transportation time increased greatly in 2021 between almost all of Disney's resorts and their theme parks. For instance, the average transportation time between the All-Star Movies resort and the Magic Kingdom increased from 25 minutes to 38 minutes, and the average time from Pop Century to Animal Kingdom from 27 minutes to 37 minutes. We believe these increases are largely because Disney hasn't been able to replace the bus drivers they laid off during the pandemic. And we think Disney is distributing its drivers not to minimize the average route time, but to keep the maximum time between any two points to 50 minutes or less. It's no wonder that throughout 2021, Disney has consistently reminded its hotel guests that they can drive their own cars for free to the theme parks.

*un*official **TIP**
If your Disney resort doesn't have direct bus service to the water parks, use Uber, Lyft, or a taxi instead.

Disney buses have an illuminated panel above the windshield that flashes the bus's destination. Theme parks also have designated waiting areas for each Disney destination. To catch the bus to the Old Key West Resort from Disney's Hollywood Studios, for example, go to the bus stop and wait in the area marked to the Old Key West Resort. At the resorts, go to any bus stop and wait for the bus displaying your destination on the illuminated panel; the **My Disney Experience** app (see page 33) displays the approximate arrival time of the next bus to your destination. Directions to Disney destinations are available at check-in or at your hotel's Guest Relations desk. Guest Relations can also answer questions about the transportation system.

Service from resorts to major theme parks is fairly direct. You may have intermediate stops, but you won't have to transfer. Service to the water parks and other Disney resorts almost always requires transfers or extra stops.

Travel between your Disney hotel and the water parks can be tricky. To travel between your Disney hotel and Blizzard Beach you must transfer at the Animal Kingdom. Traveling between your Disney hotel and **Typhoon Lagoon** will probably also require a stop (and possibly a bus transfer) at Disney Springs; if you're unlucky, this round-trip journey takes 2–3 hours per day. Our advice is to ask your hotel if direct service is available; if not, call a ride-hailing service.

The fastest way to commute among resorts by bus is to take a bus from your resort to one of the major theme parks and then transfer to a bus for your resort destination. This works, of course, only when the parks are open—actually, from 1 hour before opening until 1 hour after closing. (Disney buses stop taking passengers *to* the theme parks when they close, but they'll take passengers *from* the parks for an hour afterward.)

If you're trying to commute to another resort for a late dinner during the off-season, when parks close early, you'll have to transfer at **Disney Springs**—which Disney, in its transportation instructions, lists somewhat disingenuously as the transfer point for *all* resort-to-resort commuting, hoping you'll stop and drop some dough en route. If the theme park buses are running, though, proceed to the park closest to your resort, and then transfer to the bus going to the resort where you'll be dining.

Despite what Disney's official schedule says, bus service to the parks begins about 90 minutes before official park opening (so **7:30 a.m.** on days when official park opening is 9 a.m.). Generally, buses run every 20–25 minutes. Buses to all four parks deliver you to the park entrance.

To be on hand for Early Theme Park Entry, catch direct buses to EPCOT, Disney's Animal Kingdom, and Disney's Hollywood Studios 60–90 minutes before official park opening. Catch direct buses to the Magic Kingdom about 60–75 minutes before official park opening. If you must transfer to reach your park, such as at Fort Wilderness, leave 15–20 minutes earlier.

For your return bus trip in the evening, leave the park 40 minutes to an hour before closing to avoid the rush. If you're caught in the exodus, you may be inconvenienced, but you won't be stranded: Buses, boats, monorails, and gondolas continue to operate for 1 hour after the parks close.

continued on page 436

COMMUTING TIMES BY CAR VS. THE

Average MAXIMUM time in minutes from	to MAGIC KINGDOM		to EPCOT		to DHS		
	YOUR CAR	DISNEY SYSTEM	YOUR CAR	DISNEY SYSTEM	YOUR CAR	DISNEY SYSTEM	
ALL-STAR RESORTS	37 (47)	38 (49)	18 (23)	30 (49)	16 (20)	37 (49)	
ANIMAL KINGDOM	37 (48)	50 (68)	16 (17)	27 (38)	16 (17)	24 (34)	
ANIMAL KINGDOM LODGE & VILLAS	39 (50)	28 (44)	19 (21)	37 (45)	18 (19)	41 (50)	
ART OF ANIMATION RESORT	40 (51)	34 (49)	23 (28)	33 (50)	20 (24)	34 (50)	
BEACH CLUB RESORT & VILLAS	36 (46)	48 (66)	16 (21)	25 (49*)	14 (18)	19 (47*)	
BLIZZARD BEACH	36 (46)	28 (39)	18 (23)	—	18 (22)	39 (54)	
BOARDWALK INN & VILLAS	36 (46)	34 (45)	16 (21)	22 (40*)	14 (18)	18 (48*)	
CARIBBEAN BEACH AND RIVIERA	37 (47)	30 (47)	18 (23)	***	15 (19)	***	
CONTEMPORARY–BAY LAKE	—	—	21 (26)	30 (45)	23 (27)	34 (49)	
CORONADO SPRINGS	37 (47)	39 (44)	18 (23)	39 (45)	16 (20)	31 (44)	
DHS	36 (46)	25 (35)	19 (24)	25 (35)	—	—	
DISNEY SPRINGS	Bus service only back to your Disney resort						
DOLPHIN	35 (45)	33 (65)	15 (20)	16 (44*)	15 (19)	16 (42*)	
DISNEY SPRINGS RESORT AREA	41 (51)	69 (91)	21 (26)	47 (62)	20 (24)	45 (60)	
EPCOT	36 (46)	26 (37)	—	—	19 (23)	21 (30)	
FORT WILDERNESS	37 (47)	17 (27)	18 (23)	40 (49*)	19 (23)	29 (50)	
GRAND FLORIDIAN & VILLAS	—	—	18 (23)	43 (50*)	20 (24)	29 (50)	
MAGIC KINGDOM	—	—	26 (39)	33 (45)	22 (29)	24 (34)	
OLD KEY WEST	36 (46)	40 (48)	18 (23)	27 (44)	18 (22)	35 (40)	
POLYNESIAN VILLAGE	—	—	17 (22)	29 (50**)	19 (23)	28 (50)	
POP CENTURY RESORT	40 (51)	37 (49)	23 (28)	***	20 (24)	***	
PORT ORLEANS FRENCH QUARTER	37 (47)	26 (66)	19 (24)	25 (60)	19 (23)	28 (69)	
PORT ORLEANS RIVERSIDE	38 (48)	26 (65)	20 (25)	23 (62)	20 (24)	29 (69)	
RIVIERA RESORT	37 (47)	43 (50)	18 (23)	***	15 (19)	***	
SARATOGA SPRINGS	38 (48)	27 (66)	18 (23)	27 (45)	20 (24)	42 (44)	
SHADES OF GREEN	28 (36)	35 (49)	18 (23)	33 (45)	20 (24)	20 (28)	
SWAN	35 (45)	24 (61)	15 (20)	18 (42*)	15 (19)	14 (33*)	
TREEHOUSE VILLAS (SARATOGA SPRINGS)	37 (47)	27 (66)	18 (23)	23 (54)	19 (23)	27 (66)	
TYPHOON LAGOON	37 (47)	41 (56)	18 (23)	51 (70)	15 (19)	62 (85)	
WILDERNESS LODGE	—	24 (63)	20 (25)	43 (49)	22 (26)	45 (50)	
YACHT CLUB	36 (46)	25 (65)	16 (21)	16 (40*)	14 (18)	15 (35*)	

Note: Before 4 p.m., all transportation between the theme parks and Disney Springs requires a transfer at a nearby resort. After 4 p.m., buses run directly from the theme parks to Disney Springs. There are no buses from Disney Springs directly to the theme parks.

† Driving time vs. time on DTS. Driving times include time in your car, stops to pay tolls, time to park, and any transfers on Disney trams and monorails.

DISNEY TRANSPORTATION SYSTEM †

to ANIMAL KINGDOM		to TYPHOON LAGOON		to DISNEY SPRINGS		to BLIZZARD BEACH	
YOUR CAR	DISNEY SYSTEM	YOUR CAR	DISNEY SYSTEM	YOUR CAR	DISNEY SYSTEM	YOUR CAR	DISNEY SYSTEM
11 (12)	30 (48)	12 (13)	27 (63)	13 (14)	35 (45)	6 (7)	16 (40)
—	—	17 (19)	65 (83)	19 (21)	—	10 (13)	41 (50)
9 (10)	27 (45)	19 (21)	26 (67)	22 (24)	42 (50)	11 (14)	23 (54)
14 (16)	40 (50)	12 (14)	19 (59)	15 (16)	23 (50)	10 (12)	22 (56)
17 (18)	31 (49)	9 (10)	23 (59)	10 (11)	39 (50)	12 (13)	22 (60)
10 (13)	—	13 (14)	80 (103)	14 (15)	—	—	—
17 (18)	47 (50)	9 (10)	25 (59)	10 (11)	38 (49)	12 (13)	22 (58)
17 (18)	31 (46)	6 (7)	23 (59)	7 (8)	30 (43)	12 (13)	25 (61)
20 (21)	41 (50)	17 (18)	27 (63)	16 (17)	29 (49)	15 (16)	25 (62)
11 (12)	23 (59)	12 (13)	6 (54)	13 (14)	24 (49)	6 (7)	25 (43)
16 (17)	20 (30)	8 (9)	77 (99)	9 (10)	—	11 (12)	56 (71)
Bus service only back to your Disney resort							
16 (17)	36 (60)	10 (11)	21 (61)	11 (12)	25 (62)	11 (12)	22 (57)
21 (22)	48 (64)	9 (10)	26 (29)	6 (7)	—	16 (17)	66 (81)
16 (17)	33 (48)	12 (13)	50 (62)	13 (14)	—	11 (12)	51 (65)
24 (25)	29 (50)	10 (11)	26 (62)	11 (12)	29 (50)	19 (20)	27 (66)
18 (19)	38 (50)	15 (16)	26 (67)	16 (17)	37 (50)	13 (14)	24 (61)
17 (18)	45 (63)	23 (31)	59 (75)	27 (36)	—	12 (13)	61 (77)
19 (20)	40 (50)	8 (9)	20 (57)	9 (10)	31 (49)	14 (15)	20 (56)
17 (18)	38 (50)	14 (15)	25 (63)	15 (16)	28 (50)	12 (13)	18 (57)
14 (16)	37 (49)	12 (14)	23 (57)	15 (16)	40 (50)	10 (12)	20 (61)
19 (20)	27 (68)	9 (10)	20 (55)	10 (11)	21 (61)	14 (15)	23 (60)
20 (21)	30 (71)	10 (11)	19 (56)	11 (12)	25 (61)	15 (16)	24 (64)
17 (18)	44 (49)	6 (7)	23 (59)	7 (8)	25 (50)	12 (13)	25 (61)
21 (22)	32 (43)	9 (10)	23 (61)	6 (7)	31 (50)	16 (17)	24 (63)
18 (19)	22 (33)	15 (16)	59 (75)	18 (20)	57 (83)	13 (14)	50 (64)
16 (17)	35 (60)	10 (11)	21 (60)	11 (12)	24 (60)	11 (12)	21 (56)
17 (19)	32 (71)	9 (10)	22 (59)	6 (7)	23 (60)	13 (14)	22 (59)
20 (21)	28 (40)	—	—	8 (9)	—	15 (16)	55 (70)
20 (21)	42 (50)	17 (18)	28 (64)	18 (19)	30 (50)	15 (16)	24 (60)
17 (18)	35 (48)	8 (10)	24 (58)	10 (12)	36 (47)	12 (13)	21 (57)

* This hotel is within walking distance of EPCOT; time given is for boat transportation to the International Gateway (EPCOT's rear entrance).

** By foot to Transportation and Ticket Center and then by EPCOT monorail

*** Not enough data to calculate

continued from page 433

As you may have noticed by now, this book is replete with reader complaints about Disney's bus service. From an Ohio mom:

WDW needs to do something about the buses to and from the parks. They are the WORST! Slow, infrequent, and too small. Thank goodness we rented a car. We drove everywhere after taking the terrible buses three times—zipped in and out and got around quickly.

A Massillon, Ohio, family thinks Disney should work on its bus-tracking technology:

Several times at Saratoga Springs, we had to wait 45 minutes or more for a bus. Often two buses for the same park will arrive back-to-back, and then you may need to wait 45 minutes until they come again. They need to track how the buses are spaced—maybe have some buses close by that can jump in when needed, or track them with GPS.

A reader who stayed at Port Orleans reports:

The DTS was wildly erratic, but we were lucky more often than not. For every time we had to wait half an hour at the bus stop, there were two or three times with no wait at all.

If you're planning on riding a bus from **Port Orleans Riverside** to a park around opening time, the **West or North bus stop** may be your best option. These are the first stops on the route, and the bus is sometimes full or standing-room-only before it gets to all the stops.

As elsewhere in Walt Disney World, bus service at Disney Springs is a crapshoot. This reader found himself in bus hell:

I budgeted an hour for the return trip from Disney Springs to Animal Kingdom Lodge on the morning of our departure, and I STILL found myself on the phone with Magical Express 30 minutes before our bus was supposed to leave for the airport, asking when the next bus after that would leave Animal Kingdom Lodge. We barely made the backup bus. This was not a magical ending to my vacation.

NOT ALL HUBS ARE CREATED EQUAL All major theme parks, Disney Springs, and the TTC are hubs on the bus system. If your route requires you to transfer at a hub, transfer at the closest park or the TTC, except at park closing. Avoid Disney Springs as a transfer point—traffic around here slows everything to a crawl.

Except at Fort Wilderness, no buses run between the TTC and the Disney resorts. If you're commuting from resort to resort, you must transfer at Disney Springs or one of the major theme parks during park operating hours. If you're parked at the TTC and you want to travel to a Disney resort, go to the right of the Magic Kingdom entrance to catch a bus to your destination.

Walt Disney World Monorail Service

Picture the monorail system as three loops. **Loop A** is an express route that runs counterclockwise connecting the Magic Kingdom with the TTC. **Loop B** runs clockwise alongside Loop A, making all stops, with service to (in order) the TTC, Polynesian Village & Villas, Grand

Floridian & Villas, the Magic Kingdom, Contemporary Resort and Bay Lake Tower, and back to the TTC. The long **Loop C** dips southeast, connecting the TTC with EPCOT. The hub for all loops is the TTC (where you usually park to visit the Magic Kingdom).

The monorail that serves the **Magic Kingdom** resorts usually starts running an hour or so before official park opening. If you're staying at a Magic Kingdom resort and you wish to be among the first into the park for Early Theme Park Entry when official opening is 9 a.m., board the monorail at these times:

- **From Contemporary Resort and Bay Lake Tower** 7:45–8 a.m.
- **From Polynesian Village & Villas** 7:50–8:05 a.m.
- **From Grand Floridian & Villas** 8–8:10 a.m.

If you're a day guest, you'll be allowed on the monorail at the TTC between 8:15 and 8:30 a.m. when official opening is 9 a.m. If you want to board earlier, walk from the TTC to the Polynesian Village Resort and board there.

If you bought Disney's Park Hopper pass, you might think that means you can flit among the parks; alas, it's more complicated. For example, you can't go directly from the Magic Kingdom to EPCOT—you must catch the express monorail (Loop A) to the TTC and then transfer to the Loop C monorail to EPCOT. If lines to board either monorail are short, you can usually reach EPCOT in 30–40 minutes, but should you want to go to EPCOT for dinner (as many do) and you're leaving the Magic Kingdom in late afternoon, you may have to wait 30 minutes or longer to board the Loop A monorail. This delay boosts your commuting time to 50–60 minutes.

Disney frequently changes the monorail's operating hours to allow for daytime inspection of the track and vehicles. When the monorail is closed, Disney provides bus or boat transportation to get you where you're going. If you're going to book an expensive monorail resort, first call the resort and inquire about monorail problems. Phone numbers for the resorts can be found on pages 42–43.

Walt Disney World Boat Service

Boats are a popular, third transportation option between some theme parks and resorts, as a reader from Ames, Iowa, reminds us:

We stayed at Port Orleans French Quarter in December and took the ferry to Disney Springs several times. We also did a self-guided resort Christmas-decorations tour and had fun taking different boats around the Magic Kingdom and EPCOT resorts. These ferries were a much more pleasant option than buses for most legs of that tour.

 **COVID** *tip*
Boat routes serving Disney Springs were still suspended as of fall 2021.

The table below shows the routes served by boats. Note that most routes stop at several resorts and that service may be suspended during thunderstorms. Wheelchairs and scooters are permitted; strollers must be folded before you board and stowed while you're on the boat. Most routes run from about 45 minutes before park opening to 45 minutes after park closing.

WALT DISNEY WORLD BOAT ROUTES *(round-trip)*
Magic Kingdom → Fort Wilderness → Magic Kingdom
Magic Kingdom → Grand Floridian Resort & Villas → Polynesian Village → Magic Kingdom

WALT DISNEY WORLD BOAT ROUTES *(round-trip)* *(continued)*
Fort Wilderness Campground → Wilderness Lodge → Contemporary Resort → Fort Wilderness *Note:* Walk or take the monorail from the Contemporary to the Magic Kingdom.
EPCOT → Boardwalk Inn & Villas → Beach Club → Yacht Club → Swan → Dolphin → EPCOT
Disney's Hollywood Studios → Boardwalk Inn & Villas → Beach Club Resort & Villas → Yacht Club → Swan → Dolphin → Disney's Hollywood Studios
Disney Springs → Saratoga Springs → Old Key West → Disney Springs
Disney Springs → Port Orleans French Quarter → Port Orleans Riverside → Disney Springs

Disney Skyliner

The first phase of this new transportation system opened in fall 2019. The elevated, ski lift–like Skyliner connects the **Art of Animation, Pop Century, Caribbean Beach,** and **Riviera Resorts** with **Disney's Hollywood Studios** and **EPCOT**'s International Gateway. The Skyliner routes have been added to our Walt Disney World overview map in Part One (pages 16–17) and to the maps for the above Disney resorts in Part Five, "Accommodations."

Each gondola holds about 10 guests. **Caribbean Beach Resort** serves as the central hub for all Skyliner routes; Disney runs Caribbean Beach's internal buses between the Skyliner station and guest rooms at the resort.

As fans of both multimodal transportation and Disney, we're excited to see the Skyliner work. Our big initial concern was that the gondolas lacked air-conditioning. However, their 17-mph speed and good ventilation keep passengers cool even on very warm days.

Our one minor gripe is that riders have to get off the gondolas at the Caribbean Beach hub, then reboard another line to get to the Studios, EPCOT, the Riviera, or Pop Century and the Art of Animation (AoA). Anyone who's ever had to change trains in a major metropolitan city's subway hub, however, will take this in stride.

The table below shows typical point-to-point transportation times between any two Skyliner stations. The first pair of numbers is the average trip time assuming normal crowds, and the number in parentheses is the trip time assuming no crowds.

For example, the time to get from the Pop Century/AoA station to EPCOT reads "31–45 (15)." Thus, you should expect the trip to EPCOT to take 31–45 minutes from the time you arrive at the Pop/ AoA station. The actual time in transit will be about 15 minutes, and the rest of the time will be spent waiting to board.

The table uses the following estimates for the time it takes to board at these stations:

- CARIBBEAN BEACH 6–15 minutes
- DISNEY'S HOLLYWOOD STUDIOS 10 minutes
- EPCOT 10 minutes

SKYLINER TRAVEL TIMES *(in minutes)*					
	POP CENTURY/ ART OF ANIMATION	**CARIBBEAN BEACH**	**EPCOT**	**HOLLYWOOD STUDIOS**	**RIVIERA RESORT**
POP CENTURY/ ART OF ANIMATION	—	9-18 (3)	31-45 (15)	22-40 (10)	19-37 (7)
CARIBBEAN BEACH	9-18 (3)	—	18-27 (12)	13-22 (7)	10-19 (4)
EPCOT	28-37 (15)	22 (12)	—	35-44 (19)	18 (8)
HOLLYWOOD STUDIOS	26-35 (10)	17 (7)	35-44 (19)	—	27-36 (11)
RIVIERA RESORT	16-25 (10)	7 (4)	11 (8)	20-29 (14)	—

- **POP CENTURY/ART OF ANIMATION** 6-15 minutes
- **RIVIERA RESORT** 3 minutes

If you're riding at an off-peak time, your times may be much lower.

DRIVING TO AND AROUND WALT DISNEY WORLD

THE VAST MAJORITY of *Unofficial Guide* readers who drive to Orlando use GPS to get where they're going, either through their phone, their car, or a dedicated device. All GPS units and apps made in the last few years recognize location names such as Magic Kingdom and Pop Century. If you have an older unit, use the addresses below for the theme parks and in Part Five, "Accommodations," for hotels.

The best GPS apps will get traffic updates and route you around delays. Our favorite app is **Waze** (free; iOS, Android, and Windows Phone; waze.com), which provides real-time traffic updates along with navigation. **TomTom** GPS units do the same using an accessory cable that picks up traffic signals from HD radio broadcasts.

If you're driving without GPS, print out directions to Walt Disney World from **Google Maps** (maps.google.com) before you leave home; then, once you're in Orlando, use the overview maps in Part One (see pages 14–17) and in this chapter to find your way around. If you want to go primitive, the rental-car companies have free maps available (we like **Alamo Rent a Car**'s Walt Disney World road map, also available

DESTINATION PARKING LOT	GPS ADDRESS	LATITUDE AND LONGITUDE
THE MAGIC KINGDOM	3111 World Dr. Lake Buena Vista, FL 32830	N28° 25.124' W81° 34.871'
EPCOT	200 EPCOT Center Dr. Lake Buena Vista, FL 32830	N28° 22.869' W81° 32.964'
ANIMAL KINGDOM	2901 Osceola Pkwy. Lake Buena Vista, FL 32380	N28° 21.480' W81° 35.426'
DHS	351 S. Studio Dr. Lake Buena Vista, FL 32830	N28° 21.309' W81° 33.415'
BLIZZARD BEACH	1534 Blizzard Beach Dr. Lake Buena Vista, FL 32830	N28° 21.338' W81° 34.384'
TYPHOON LAGOON	1145 E. Buena Vista Dr. Lake Buena Vista, FL 32830	N28° 22.162' W81° 31.576'
DISNEY SPRINGS	1490 E. Buena Vista Dr. Lake Buena Vista, FL 32830	N28° 22.064' W81° 31.167'

at the front desk or concierge desk of any Disney resort). Use Disney's road signs as a supplement to any option.

GPS Coordinates for the Theme Parks

See the table on the previous page. Supplement these with Disney's road signs, which will direct you to parking as you get close.

Driving to and from the Theme Parks

1. PARKING LOT LOCATIONS The **Animal Kingdom, EPCOT,** and **DHS** lots are adjacent to each park's entrance; the **Magic Kingdom** lot is adjacent to the TTC. From the TTC, take a ferry, monorail, or bus to the park's entrance (the bus is often fastest). Electronic displays will show you the estimated transit times for the ferry and monorail.

2. PAYING TO PARK Disney resort guests and annual pass holders park free; all others pay. If you paid to park and you move your car later that day, show your receipt and you won't have to pay again at the new lot. The daily parking rate for motorcycles and standard cars is $25; a preferred parking option, with spots closer to the park entrances, costs $45–$50 per day.

3. REMEMBER WHERE YOUR CAR IS PARKED Jot down, text, or take a phone picture of the section and row where you've parked. If you're driving a rental, note the license-plate number.

4. HOW LONG IT TAKES TO PARK AND GET TO THE PARK ENTRANCE At the **Magic Kingdom,** it'll take 35–50 minutes to get to the TTC; go through the security screening; board a monorail, ferry, or bus; and reach the park entrance. Add another 20 minutes if you haven't purchased your park admission in advance. At **EPCOT** and **Animal Kingdom,** figure about 15–20 minutes to pay, park, walk, or ride to the entrance and get through the security screening. At Disney's Hollywood Studios, allow 15–20 minutes, and see the following note.

5. GETTING TO DISNEY'S HOLLYWOOD STUDIOS FROM POP CENTURY AND ART OF ANIMATION If the line to use the **Skyliner** is more than 30 minutes, consider using Uber, Lyft, or a taxi. Note that Disney also offers bus service between the two resorts and Hollywood Studios during busier times of year.

6. COMMUTING FROM PARK TO PARK Using Disney transportation or your car, allow 45–60 minutes one-way, entrance to entrance. If you plan to park-hop, leave your car in the lot of the park where you'll finish the day.

7. LEAVING THE PARK AT THE END OF THE DAY If you stay at a park until closing, expect the parking-lot trams, monorails, gondolas, and ferries to be mobbed. (The Magic Kingdom has wait-time displays showing the lines for the monorail and ferry.) If the tram is taking too long, walk to your car or walk to the first stop on the tram route, and wait there for a tram. When someone gets off, you can get on.

8. DINNER AND A QUICK EXIT One way to beat closing crowds at the Magic Kingdom is to arrange reservations for dinner at the **Contemporary Resort.** When you leave the Magic Kingdom for dinner, move your car from the TTC lot to the Contemporary lot. After dinner, walk

(8–10 minutes) or take the monorail back to the Magic Kingdom. When the park closes and everyone else is fighting to board the monorail or ferry, you can stroll back to the Contemporary, claim your car, and get on your way. Use the same strategy at EPCOT by arranging a reservation at an EPCOT resort. When the park closes after the fireworks, exit via the International Gateway and walk to the resort where you parked.

9. CAR TROUBLE Parking lots have security patrols; if you have a dead battery or minor automotive problem, they can help. For more-serious trouble, go to the **Car Care Center** (☎ 407-824-0976), near the Magic Kingdom parking lot. Prices for most services are comparable to those at home. The facility stays busy, so expect to have to leave your car unless the fix is simple. Hours are Monday–Friday, 7 a.m.–7 p.m.; Saturday, 7 a.m.–4 p.m.; and Sunday, 8 a.m.–3 p.m.

10. SCORING A GREAT PARKING SPOT If you arrive at a park after noon or move your car from park to park, check for available parking spaces close to the park entrance; these will have been vacated by early guests who have left. Instead of following signs or being directed by staff to a distant space, drive straight to the front and start hunting, or use the approach of this Coopersburg, Pennsylvania, couple:

> *After leaving EPCOT for lunch, we returned to find a fullish parking lot. We were unhappy because we had left a third-row parking spot. My husband told the attendant that we had left just an hour ago and that there were lots of spaces up front. Without a word of protest, he waved us to the front and we got our same spot back!*

Speeders Beware

Orange County law enforcement's jurisdiction extends to Disney's roads. Many readers have written us surprised after receiving citations, assuming they'd be let off with a warning at worst. Remember, it's a speed limit, not a speed suggestion.

Sneak Routes

We're constantly looking for ways to avoid traffic snarls. If you have a GPS that will route you around traffic delays, use that. If not, try these sneak routes we've discovered.

US 192 (IRLO BRONSON MEMORIAL HIGHWAY) Traffic on US 192 runs east–west south of Walt Disney World. The road is divided into east and west sections—the west section is from I-4 to Kissimmee, and the east section is from I-4 east to US 27. Traffic is bad both ways. If your hotel is along the west section, you can bypass most of the traffic by driving north on **Apopka-Vineland Road** or **Poinciana Boulevard** (a right turn if you're driving on US 192 in the direction of I-4) and accessing **Osceola Parkway,** a four-lane toll road that dead-ends in Walt Disney World. If your hotel is on the east side, head on US 192 to **Sherberth Road** at mile marker 5 and turn north to enter Walt Disney World near the Animal Kingdom.

DISNEY SPRINGS The 3-mile stretch of **Buena Vista Drive** from Coronado Springs Resort to Disney Springs has 15 traffic signals—about one every 1,000 feet—making it a major traffic bottleneck from

Disney Springs Sneak Routes

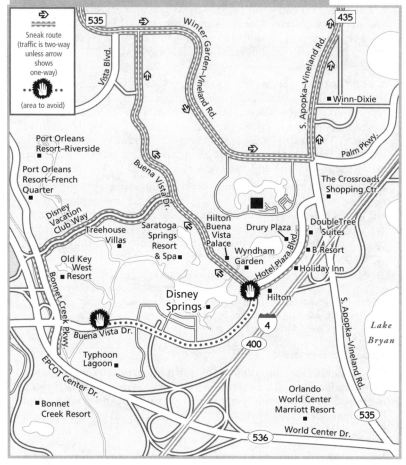

late afternoon through late evening. And it's not just around Disney Springs: Buena Vista Drive is one of Walt Disney World's most important roads, connecting the hotels of the Disney Springs Resort Area (DSRA), EPCOT, Disney's Hollywood Studios, the Magic Kingdom, Disney's Animal Kingdom, and Typhoon Lagoon.

The good news is that if you're coming by car from I-4 or on foot from the DSRA, it's easy to get to Disney Springs. Westbound **I-4** offers three exits to Disney Springs, including a direct exit to the Disney Springs parking garages—take **Exit 67** for EPCOT/Disney Springs. Guests staying at a DSRA hotel will find convenient pedestrian bridges linking Disney Springs to Hotel Plaza Boulevard and Buena Vista Drive.

Coming from the theme parks, you can bypass the mess by taking **I-4** or alternatively by looping around on **Bonnet Creek Parkway** and **Disney Vacation Club Way.** If you're going back to an EPCOT or Magic Kingdom resort from Disney Springs, it may be faster to take I-4 West and follow the signs back to Disney property.

I-Drive Area Sneak Routes

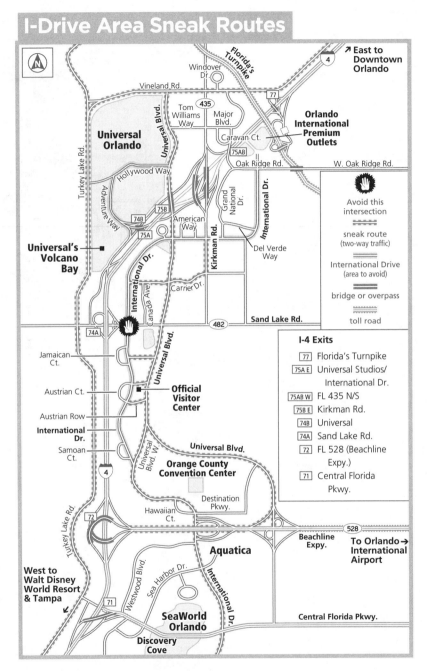

↗ East to Downtown Orlando

Florida's Turnpike

Windover Dr.

Vineland Rd.

435

Tom Williams Way

Major Blvd.

77

Universal Boulevard

Orlando International Premium Outlets

Caravan Ct.

75AB

Oak Ridge Rd.

W. Oak Ridge Rd.

Universal Orlando

Hollywood Way

Turkey Lake Rd.

Adventure Way

International Dr.

Grand National Dr.

74B

75B

75A

American Way

Del Verde Way

Universal's Volcano Bay

International Dr.

Kirkman Rd.

Canada Ave.

Carrier Dr.

74A

482

Sand Lake Rd.

Jamaican Ct.

Austrian Ct.

Austrian Row

International Dr.

Samoan Ct.

Universal Blvd.

Official Visitor Center

4

Universal Blvd. W.

Universal Blvd.

Orange County Convention Center

Destination Pkwy.

Hawaiian Ct.

72

Turkey Lake Rd.

528

Beachline Expy.

To Orlando → International Airport

Aquatica

Westwood Blvd.

Sea Harbor Dr.

International Dr.

West to Walt Disney World Resort & Tampa

71

SeaWorld Orlando

Discovery Cove

Central Florida Pkwy.

✋ Avoid this intersection

〜 sneak route (two-way traffic)

═ International Drive (area to avoid)

▦ bridge or overpass

〜 toll road

I-4 Exits

77	Florida's Turnpike
75A E	Universal Studios/ International Dr.
75AB W	FL 435 N/S
75B E	Kirkman Rd.
74B	Universal
74A	Sand Lake Rd.
72	FL 528 (Beachline Expy.)
71	Central Florida Pkwy.

I-4 Expect heavy traffic and possible westbound delays from about 7 to 9:30 a.m.; eastbound toward Orlando, expect heavy traffic from 4 to 7 p.m. If you want to avoid I-4 altogether, check out our I-4 Sneak Routes map, on page 445.

US 192–Kissimmee Resort Area Sneak Routes

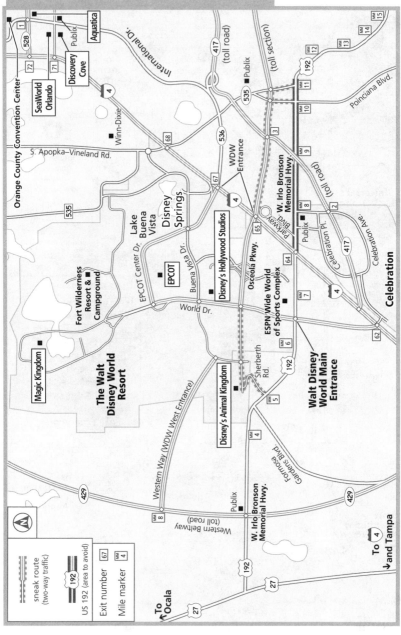

INTERNATIONAL DRIVE The I-Drive area is by far the most difficult to navigate without long traffic delays. Most hotels on I-Drive are between

I-4 Sneak Routes

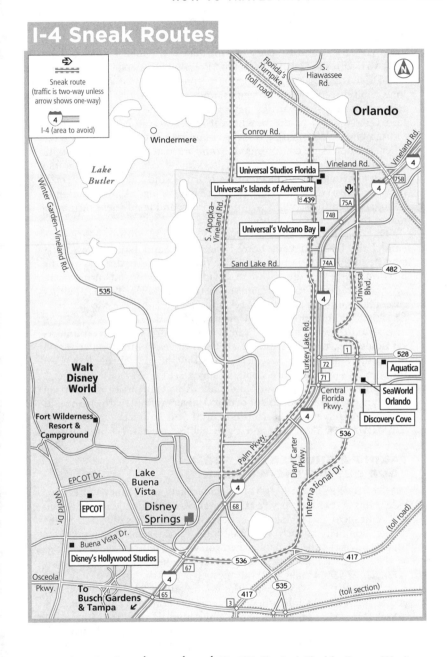

Kirkman Road to the north and **FL 417 (Central Florida GreeneWay)** to the south. Between Kirkman Road and FL 417, three major roads cross I-Drive: From north to south on I-Drive (in the direction of Disney World), the first is **Universal Boulevard**. Next is **Sand Lake Road (FL 482)**, pretty squarely in the middle of the hotel district. Finally, the **Beachline Expressway (FL 528)** connects I-4 and the airport.

The southern third of I-Drive can be accessed via **Central Florida Parkway,** which connects I-4 and Palm Parkway with the SeaWorld area of I-Drive, and by **Daryl Carter Parkway,** which connects Palm Parkway with the Orlando Vineland Premium Outlets.

I-Drive is a mess for a number of reasons: scarcity of left-turn lanes; long, multidirectional traffic signals; and, most critically, limited access to westbound I-4 (toward Disney). From the Orange County Convention Center south to the Beachline Expressway and FL 417/Central Florida GreeneWay, getting on westbound I-4 is easy, but in the stretch where the hotels are concentrated (from Kirkman to about a mile south of Sand Lake), the only way most visitors know to access I-4 westbound is to slog through the gridlock of the I-Drive–Sand Lake Road intersection en route to the I-4–Sand Lake Road interchange. A combination of a long, long traffic signal; a sea of motorists; and insufficient turn lanes makes this about as much fun as a root canal.

The object, then, is to access I-4 westbound without getting on Sand Lake Road. If your hotel is north of Sand Lake, access **Kirkman Road** by going north on I-Drive (in the opposite direction of the heaviest traffic) to the Kirkman Road intersection and turning left, or by cutting over to Kirkman via eastbound **Carrier Drive.** In either case, take Kirkman north over I-4, and make a U-turn at the first traffic signal (at the entrance to Universal Orlando). This will put you directly onto a westbound I-4 ramp. You can also go north on **Universal Boulevard,** which parallels I-Drive to the east; after you cross I-4 onto Universal property, stay left and follow the signs through two left turns to I-4—the signs are small, so stay alert.

If your hotel is south of Sand Lake Road but north of Austrian Court, use **Austrian Row** to cut over to Universal Boulevard. Turn right (south) on Universal, and continue until you intersect the **Beachline Expressway (FL 528);** then take the Beachline west to I-4 (no toll).

TAKING A SHUTTLE BUS FROM YOUR OUT-OF-THE-WORLD HOTEL

MANY INDEPENDENT HOTELS and motels near Disney World provide trams and buses. They're fairly carefree, depositing you near theme park entrances and saving you parking fees. The rub is that they might not get you there as early as you desire (a critical point if you take our touring advice) or be available when you wish to return to your lodging. Each service is different; check details before you make reservations.

unofficial **TIP**
Warning: Most shuttles don't add vehicles at park opening or closing. In the morning, you may not get a seat.

Some shuttles go directly to Walt Disney World, while others stop at other hotels en route. This can be a problem if your hotel is the second or third stop on the route. During periods of high demand, buses frequently fill up at the first stop, leaving little or no room for passengers at subsequent stops. Before booking, ask how many hotels are on the route and the sequence of the stops.

The different hotels are often so close together that you can easily walk to the first hotel on the route and board there. Similarly, if there's a large hotel nearby, it might have its own dedicated bus service that's more efficient; use that instead of the service provided by your hotel. Most out-of-the-World shuttles work on a fixed schedule instead of arriving and departing somewhat randomly like the Disney buses. Knowing exactly when a bus will depart makes it easier to plan your day.

A multigenerational family from Seattle share their experience:

> We stayed at a hotel off-site and it was fine, but I think next time we'll stay in the World. The shuttles weren't all that convenient or frequent, so we ended up taking taxis more than we thought we would.

A woman from Carlisle, Pennsylvania, adds this:

> I much prefer staying at a Disney resort so that I can use Disney transportation, but because the person I was traveling with booked the room, I reluctantly stayed off-site. The room and breakfast service were fine. The shuttle to and from the park, however, was not ideal. The only shuttles to the park were at 8:45 a.m. to EPCOT and 9:45 a.m. to the TTC, and the only shuttles back to the resort were 9 p.m. from the TTC and 10 p.m. from EPCOT. We had to call Uber to take us to Disney Springs.

At closing or during a hard rain, more people will be waiting for the shuttle than it can hold, and some will be left behind. Most shuttles return for stranded guests, but guests may wait 20 minutes to more than an hour.

If you're depending on non-Disney shuttles, leave the park at least 45 minutes before closing. If you stay until closing and you don't want the hassle of the shuttle, take Uber, Lyft, or a taxi; cab stands are located at the TTC and near the Bus Information buildings at Disney's Hollywood Studios. If no cabs are on hand, a cast member will call one for you. If you're leaving the Magic Kingdom at closing, it's easier to take the monorail to a hotel and hail a cab from there rather than at the TTC.

unofficial **TIP**
If you want to go from resort to resort or almost anywhere else, you'll have to transfer at a bus hub.

DEPARTING FROM ORLANDO INTERNATIONAL AIRPORT (MCO)

IF YOU'RE USING **Mears Connect** (see page 420), your bus will depart your hotel for the airport 3–4 hours before your flight, depending on how busy the airport is expected to be.

DRIVING Plan on leaving for the airport 2–3 hours before your flight, depending on whether you have to return a rental car, the route you take, and whether you have TSA PreCheck for security lines.

It takes about 35 minutes and around $5 in small bills and quarters to drive from Walt Disney World to MCO along the FL 417 or FL 528 toll roads. The same trip on I-4, FL 482 East, and Jeff Fuqua Boulevard is free but averages 50–60 minutes with traffic, and there's a greater chance it'll take longer.

If you're returning a rental car, allow an extra 20 minutes to complete that process for on-site car rental companies; allow an extra 60 minutes to return a car to an off-site company and catch the airport shuttle to the terminal.

MCO handled around 48 million passengers a year before the pandemic. It's not unusual to see lines from the checkpoints snaking out of the terminal and into the main shopping corridor and food court. A number of passengers have reported missing their flights even when they arrived at the airport 90 minutes before departure. System improvements have alleviated some but by no means all of the congestion. Most waits to clear security average 20 minutes or less, compared with 55 minutes or longer before the improvements.

Waits in the **TSA PreCheck** lines are almost always 5 minutes or less. If you fly frequently, PreCheck is good for five years and costs $85 per person. We wouldn't fly without it. Get more information at tsa.gov/precheck.

ELECTRIC-VEHICLE CHARGING IN WALT DISNEY WORLD

ECO-FRIENDLY READER Craig from Canada wrote us with this list of charging stations in and around the World.

In Walt Disney World

Animal Kingdom Parking Lot (2 chargers) Follow the path to disabled parking, turn left after the shelter, go to the end of the row, and double back.

Coronado Springs Resort (3 chargers) In the parking lot adjacent to the new Gran Destino Tower

Disney's Fort Wilderness Resort Campsites have 110v outlets plus 30-amp RV outlets

Disney's Hollywood Studios Parking Lot (2 chargers) Just east of the main park entrance and northwest of the lots

Disney's Riviera Resort (1 charger) West parking lot

Disney Springs Grapefruit Garage (2 chargers) Level 3

Disney Springs Lime Garage (2 chargers) Top level

Disney Springs Orange Garage (2 chargers) Level 5

Disney's Wilderness Lodge (1 charger) Halfway down the first row, near the taxi stand

EPCOT Parking Lot At the front of the Journey lot

Shades of Green (1 generic charger plus 2 Tesla Destination Chargers) Valet parking only

Transportation and Ticket Center (3 chargers) Follow the blue lines on the right lane after paying for parking.

Tesla Superchargers (Off-Property)

Applebee's (10 chargers) 6290 W. Irlo Bronson Memorial Hwy., just behind the restaurant

Wawa (6 chargers) 7940 W. Irlo Bronson Memorial Hwy.

Craig adds, "There are Level 2 (midspeed) chargers in various places around Disney property; all are run by **ChargePoint** (chargepoint.com). Each charging station has two J-1772 charging ports to accommodate two cars at a time per station."

Finally, check **PlugShare** (plugshare.com) for the locations of other chargers near Walt Disney World.

BARE NECESSITIES

MONEY, *Etc.*

CREDIT CARDS, MOBILE PAYMENTS, AND DISNEY GIFT CARDS

ACCEPTED THROUGHOUT WALT DISNEY WORLD are **American Express, Diners Club, Discover, Japan Credit Bureau, MasterCard,** and **Visa.** If you have one of these cards linked to an iPhone 6 or newer, you can use **Apple Pay** as well. **Disney Gift Cards** can be used at most Disney-owned and -operated stores and restaurants, and for recreational activities, tickets, and parking. See disneygiftcard.com for details.

 unofficial **TIP**
Note that a handful of places around WDW take only cash. We recommend carrying $20 or so for incidentals just in case.

If you're staying at an on-property Disney resort, a **MagicBand** (see page 78) can be linked to the credit card you'll put on file for incidental hotel charges. This lets you use your MagicBands as you would a credit card at most Disney-owned stores and restaurants on-property. This is useful if you're covering the expenses of others in your group, such as responsible teens or young adults, who won't be with you all the time, don't have their own credit cards, and don't want to carry cash.

BANKING SERVICES

AT THE THEME PARKS, banking is limited to ATMs, which are marked on park maps and are plentiful throughout Walt Disney World; most MasterCard, Visa, Discover, Cirrus, Plus, Star, and Honor cards are also accepted. To get cash with an American Express card, you must sign an agreement with Amex before your trip. ATMs are also at every Disney resort and throughout Disney Springs.

CURRENCY EXCHANGE

IN THE MAGIC KINGDOM, it's at **Guest Relations** in City Hall, on Main Street, U.S.A., at the park entrance. In EPCOT, it's at Guest Relations on the west side of the EPCOT Entrance Plaza. In the Studios or Animal Kingdom, exchange your euros, kroner, or zloty at Guest Relations to the left of the entrance turnstiles. Disney Springs' Guest Relations location is at the Welcome Center. Finally, all Disney resorts can do currency exchange at their front desks.

∎ IN-PARK ISSUES

CELL PHONES

BRING YOUR PHONE CABLE and wall plug to the parks. Your phone will likely get a lot of use in the parks, either from guiding you around or entertaining you during waits in line. You'll probably want to increase your phone's screen brightness, too, for easier reading in the glaring Florida sun. All of that will drain your phone's battery faster than normal.

We strongly recommend investing in an external battery pack or battery case. We're fans of **Mophie** and **New Trent** batteries; both are available at online retailers such as Amazon.

Charging stations are located near the *Tangled*-themed restrooms in Fantasyland in the Magic Kingdom; they're built into the faux-wood posts near the seating area. Also try the seating area behind Big Top Treats in Storybook Circus or the shopping area at the exit to Space Mountain. In EPCOT, look for outlets upstairs at The Land; near the restrooms at The Seas; and outside at Norway and Morocco.

Be aware that on very busy days, the park's cell towers and Wi-Fi may be overwhelmed, making it difficult to send or receive calls, texts, or data. A woman from Leawood, Kansas, spells out the problem:

> *In our group, we were using three different carriers, and we all had problems sending and receiving texts and making calls.*

A Kennesaw, Georgia, woman adds:

> *I found the Wi-Fi horrible in all the parks. Dropped out continually, drained my battery, and wasn't strong enough to run Disney's own app. Very disappointing.*

RAIN

LEN'S TWIN SISTER, LINDA, notes that when it comes to theme parks, "rain culls the weak from the herd." (She's the competitive one.) So go to the parks even in bad weather. Besides lighter crowds, most attractions and waiting areas are under cover. Showers, especially during warmer months, are short.

unofficial **TIP**
Raingear isn't always displayed in shops, so ask for it if you don't see it.

Ponchos and umbrellas cost about $12. Ponchos sold at Walt Disney World are made of clear plastic, so picking out somebody in your party on a rainy day can be tricky. Amazon sells an inexpensive orange poncho that will make your family pumpkin-colored beacons in a plastic-covered sea of humanity.

A Wilmington, North Carolina, mom thinks good raingear is worth the investment:

> *We're outdoor-sports people, so we have good raincoats. It rained every day on this trip, driving many people out of the parks and leaving others looking miserable. Meanwhile, we hardly noticed the rain from inside our high-end jackets.*

Some unusually heavy rain precipitated (no pun intended) dozens of reader suggestions for dealing with soggy days. The best came from this Memphis, Tennessee, mom:

1. Raingear should include ponchos and umbrellas. When rain isn't beating down on your ponchoed head, it's easier to ignore.

2. If you're using a stroller, bring a plastic sheet or an extra poncho to protect it from rain. (Ponchos cover Disney's single strollers only.) Carry a towel in a plastic bag to wipe off your stroller after experiencing an attraction during a rainfall.

One *Unofficial Guide* researcher advises, "Wear a baseball cap under the poncho hood. Without it, the hood never covers your head properly, and your face always gets wet."

LOST AND FOUND

IF YOU LOSE (OR FIND) SOMETHING in the Magic Kingdom, go to **City Hall.** At EPCOT, Lost and Found is behind Spaceship Earth. At Disney's Hollywood Studios, it's at **Hollywood Boulevard Guest Relations,** and at Disney's Animal Kingdom, it's at **Guest Relations** at the main entrance. If you discover that you've lost something 24 hours or more after you've left the parks, call ☎ 407-824-4245 (for all parks). The central Lost and Found is on the east side of the Transportation and Ticket Center. You can also report lost items at disneyworld.com/lostandfound.

It's unusual for readers to send us tips about Lost and Found, but a mom from Indianapolis sent two! Here's the first:

> *If you lose something on a ride and it has medication in it, Disney cast members will shut down the ride for 45 seconds to try to retrieve it. If they can't find it or it didn't contain meds, you have to come back to Lost and Found for it at the end of the day.*

LOST MAGICBANDS AND TICKETS Duplicates can be made, usually at no cost, at Guest Relations at any theme park or resort. A replacement fee may be charged depending on your situation.

Lost tickets are the subject of the second tip from our mom above:

> *If you've got plastic tickets, write down or take a picture of the serial numbers on the back. This way, a cast member can look up when the ticket was last used, giving you an idea of where it was lost.*

LOST CARS Don't forget where you parked—snap a picture with your phone or camera, send yourself a text or email, or write down your section and row.

MEDICAL MATTERS

HEADACHE RELIEF Aspirin and other sundries are sold at the **Emporium** on Main Street, U.S.A., in the Magic Kingdom (behind the counter—you have to ask); at most retail shops in EPCOT's Future World and World Showcase, Disney's Hollywood Studios, and Disney's Animal Kingdom; and at each Disney resort's gift shop.

ILLNESSES REQUIRING MEDICAL ATTENTION For the locations of the **First Aid Centers** in the theme parks, please see the "Services" sidebar of each theme park chapter. Guests who use the service are generally very positive about it. This Hickory, North Carolina, reader's experience is representative:

We visited First Aid a time or two in the parks (my wife needed her blood pressure checked because she was worried about the heat and her pregnancy). We found trained medical staff, no wait, and all the friendliness and knowledge you would expect from Disney.

Off-property, there's an **Advent Health Centra Care** walk-in clinic at 12500 S. Apopka–Vineland Road (☎ 407-934-CARE [2273]; open 24 hours. They also do COVID testing (☎ 407-938-0650).

A North Carolina family had a good experience at **Buena Vista Urgent Care** (8216 World Center Drive, Suite D; ☎ 407-465-1110):

We started day one needing medical care for our son, who has asthma and had developed croup. We found great care at Buena Vista Urgent Care. We waited 20 minutes, and then we were off to the parks.

The Medical Concierge (☎ 855-932-5252; themedicalconcierge .com) has board-certified physicians on call 24-7 to make in-person visits to your hotel room, even during the pandemic. Walk-in clinics are also available.

DOCS (Doctors on Call Service; ☎ 407-399-DOCS [3627]; doctors oncallservice.com) also offers 24-hour house-call service. The physicians are either board-certified or board-eligible. A father of two from O'Fallon, Illinois, gives them a thumbs-up:

My wife's cold developed into an ear infection that required medical attention, and DOCS was able to respond in 40 minutes. The doctor had medicine with him and was very professional and friendly.

Another option for house or video calls is **Physician Room Service** (☎ 407-238-2000; physicianroomservice.com). Like the others, they're staffed by board-certified doctors.

DENTAL NEEDS Call **Celebration Dental Group** (☎ 407-566-2222).

PRESCRIPTION MEDICINE Three drugstores located nearby are **CVS** (8242 World Center Drive; ☎ 407-239-1442), **Walgreens** (12100 S. Apopka–Vineland Road; ☎ 407-238-0600), and **Turner Drugs** (1530 Celebration Blvd., Ste. 105A; ☎ 407-828-8125; turnerdrugs celebration.com).

PREVENT BLISTERS IN FIVE EASY STEPS

1. PREPARE You can easily cover 5–12 miles a day at the parks, so get your feet and legs into shape before you leave home. Start with short walks around the neighborhood. Increase your distance gradually until you can do 6 miles without needing CPR.

2. PAY ATTENTION During your training program, your feet will tell you if you're wearing the right shoes. Choose well-constructed, broken-in running or hiking shoes. If you feel a hot spot coming on, chances are a blister isn't far behind. The most common sites for blisters are heels, toes, and balls of feet. If you develop a hot spot in the same place every time you walk, cover it with a blister bandage (such as Johnson & Johnson) or cushion before you set out.

Don't wear sandals, flip-flops, or slip-ons in the theme parks. Even if your feet don't blister, they'll get stepped on by other guests or run over by strollers.

3. SOCK IT UP Good socks are as important as good shoes. When you walk, your feet sweat, and the moisture only increases friction. To counteract friction, wear socks made from material such as Smartwool or CoolMax, which wicks perspiration away from your feet (Smartwool socks come in varying thicknesses). To further combat moisture, dust your feet with antifungal powder.

4. DON'T BE A HERO Take care of foot problems the minute you notice them. Carry a small foot-emergency kit with gauze, antibiotic ointment, disinfectant, moleskin or blister bandages, scissors, a sewing needle or something else sharp (to drain blisters), and rubbing alcohol to sterilize the needle. Extra socks and foot powder are optional.

If carrying all of that sounds like too much, stop by a park **First Aid Center** as soon as you notice a hot spot forming on your foot.

5. CHECK THE KIDS Children might not say anything about blisters forming until it's too late. Stop several times a day and check their feet. If you find a blister, either treat it using the kit you're carrying, or stop by a First Aid Center.

LODGING A COMPLAINT WITH DISNEY

COMPLAINING ABOUT A LEAKY FAUCET or not having enough towels is pretty straightforward, and you'll usually find Disney folks highly responsive. But for a complaint that goes beyond an on-site manager's ability to resolve, don't expect much—if anything.

Disney's unresponsiveness in fielding complaints is one of our readers' foremost gripes. A Providence, Rhode Island, dad's remarks are typical:

It's all warm fuzzies and big smiles until you have a problem—then everybody plays hide-and-seek. The only thing you know for sure is it's never the responsibility of the Disney person you're talking to.

A Portland, Maine, reader sums it up in classic New England style:

Lodging a complaint with Disney is like shouting at a brick.

Disney prefers to receive complaints in writing. Address your letter to **Walt Disney World Guest Communications** at PO Box 10040, Lake Buena Vista, FL 32830-0040, or email wdw.guest.communications @disneyworld.com.

Be aware, though, that by the time you get home and draft a letter, it's often too late to correct the problem. And although Disney would have you believe they're a touchy-feely lot, they generally won't make things right for you after the fact. You *may* receive an acknowledgment of the nonapology-apology sort ("we're sorry you *felt* inconvenienced"), but don't count on them actually offering to fix anything—even if you decide to take it up with Bob Chapek himself.

If you're *really* steamed, you could fire off a letter to the **Orlando Sentinel** (633 N. Orange Ave., Orlando, FL 32801-1349; insight@orlando sentinel.com) or perhaps contact the consumer-affairs reporter for one of the Orlando TV stations.

▉ SERVICES

PHOTOPASS AND MEMORY MAKER

FOR YEARS NOW, Walt Disney World has employed roving bands of photographers to take digital photos of guests as part of its **PhotoPass** service; guests may then purchase these photos online. Use the **My Disney Experience (MDE)** app to find the specific locations of PhotoPass photographers on the day of your visit. If face masks are required inside the park, you'll need to keep them on for photographs too.

Individual PhotoPass images can be purchased at disneyphotopass .com. Current prices range from $16.95 for a digital download to $20.95 for an 8-by-10–inch print. You can also buy personalized photo products such as mugs and phone cases.

Photographs are also sold in a package called **Memory Maker** (see disneyworld.disney.go.com /memory-maker). It includes not only PhotoPass pictures but also photos and videos taken by automated cameras on theme park rides (for the full list, see the next page). Memory Maker costs $169 when purchased a minimum of three days before your trip or $199 when purchased in the park. If you're planning to spend just one day in a park, you can buy a **Memory Maker One Day Entitlement** ($69), available exclusively through the MDE app. Disney annual pass holders can download photos at no charge.

unofficial **TIP** On the face of it, Memory Maker is a better deal than paying by the photo, but only if you know you want to buy lots of photos. You'll have to make the call regarding which option is best for you and your budget.

Because PhotoPass and Memory Maker are linked to your MDE account (see page 31), you can also see the photos of friends and family you've linked to there. Plus, you can perform some basic photo editing within the app. Here's how to get started:

1. Find a PhotoPass photographer to take your first picture. Photographers roam throughout the theme parks and water parks, including near park entrances, in restaurants (and during character meals), and around iconic attractions such as Splash Mountain.

2. The photographer will scan your RFID ticket, MagicBand, or (coming soon) your phone. This links your pictures to your MDE account. Onboard ride-photo systems should automatically detect your MagicBand and link the photos to your account.

3. Visit the MDE website within 45 days of your trip to view your photos. You can add decorative borders and short captions to your pictures, too, as well as share photos online.

In some areas, such as the Test Track postshow, Disney has replaced live photographers with automated cameras that capture your photos at select posing stations. Like the live photographers, these images will be linked to your MDE account. If you're already logged in to MDE, your purchase will be automatically linked to your account. If not, you'll be asked to do so (or sign up for MDE) to complete the purchase. Photos taken on the following rides will be automatically linked to your MDE account:

THE MAGIC KINGDOM
- Big Thunder Mountain Railroad • Buzz Lightyear's Space Ranger Spin
- *Enchanted Tales with Belle* • Pirates of the Caribbean
- Seven Dwarfs Mine Train • Space Mountain • Splash Mountain

EPCOT • Test Track • Frozen Ever After

DISNEY'S ANIMAL KINGDOM • Dinosaur • Expedition Everest
DISNEY'S HOLLYWOOD STUDIOS
- Rock 'n' Roller Coaster • Slinky Dog Dash • The Twilight Zone Tower of Terror

You can download Memory Maker photos as many times as you want, subject to a few restrictions: First, if you prepurchase, you must do so at least three days before your trip in order to have all of your photos included. If you prepurchase fewer than three days before you arrive, you'll have to buy separately any photos taken during that three-day window. Next, Disney will store your photos for 45 days, so you'll need to download them promptly once you return home (you can also pay for extra time). Finally, once you've downloaded the first photo, you have 30 days to download the rest. Disney grants you a limited license to reproduce Memory Maker photos for your personal use.

Because any two families can share a Memory Maker package via MDE, folks in the *Unofficial Guide* online community often split the cost with others traveling around the same time. It's a great way to get your photos at half price. Visit tinyurl.com/share-memory-maker to find a partner on our discussion boards.

We get a lot of reader comments about PhotoPass and Memory Maker, most of them positive. From a Loveland, Ohio, mom:

The PhotoPass option is awesome and so easy. Everywhere we went, we would find Disney photographers and we got a lot of great pictures, which is nice since usually when you are on vacation you have part of your family missing as he/she is taking the photo.

These honeymooners from Cambridge, Massachusetts, give Memory Maker a thumbs-up:

My wife talked me into getting Memory Maker, and we both ended up happy with the memories captured. Not having to carry a camera around was very convenient, especially when we went on water rides. Another advantage was having access to all the on-ride photos and videos—the Tower of Terror video alone made the purchase worth it.

A Silver Spring, Maryland, dad got an unexpected disappointment:

I advance-purchased Memory Maker largely because we were planning several character meals, under the apparently incorrect assumption that photographers would be there. There was no sign of any photographer at any of the four character meals we did.

In 2019 Disney installed multiple automatic cameras at character meal and greeting venues. These cameras capture numerous moments throughout the meal or meet and greet and offer guests a variety of character photos.

Tip: Call ahead of your WDW visit to verify whether photographers will be on hand at a particular character meal, and then check again closer to your trip. Participating venues change from time to time, and we've seen conflicting/inconsistent information on otherwise reliable Disney websites—including Disney's own.

In addition to the in-park photographers, there is now a Memory Maker station at **Disney Springs.** There are no characters, but if you want a photographer to take a few snaps of your family, stop by. This can be a quick alternative to a formal posed photo session, and as a bonus, the pictures will be included in your existing photo package.

PET CARE

ACROSS FROM THE PORT ORLEANS RESORTS, the plush **Best Friends Pet Care** resort accommodates up to 270 canines in its Doggy Village, which has standard and luxury suites, some with private outdoor patios and play yards; the Kitty City pavilion houses up to 24 felines in two- and four-story cat condos. There's also a separate area just for birds and "pocket pets" such as hamsters. Encompassing more than 17,000 square feet of air-conditioned indoor space plus 10,000 square feet of covered outdoor runs and play areas, the resort is open to both Walt Disney World resort guests and visitors staying off-property. We sent Rosie, the *Unofficial Guide* research poodle, and it went great. We even got emailed photos of her during her stay. For more information, call ☎ 877-4-WDW-PETS (877-493-9738) or visit bestfriendspetcare.com. (*Note:* Pet parents must provide written proof of current vaccination from a vet, either at check-in or by fax at 203-840-5207.)

In addition, dogs are welcome at four hotels on Disney property: **Art of Animation, Port Orleans Riverside, Fort Wilderness Resort & Campground,** and the **Yacht Club.** Additional fees of $50–$75 per night apply, along with a host of human- and animal-conduct rules; inquire when making your hotel reservation. This new dog-accommodating policy was poorly received by many readers, including this one:

I refuse to pay $400 to sleep in a bed where a dog previously slept.

That said, we haven't seen a single complaint regarding dogs at Disney hotels in all the reader surveys we've received since the policy was enacted.

EXCUSE ME, BUT WHERE CAN I FIND . . .

RELIGIOUS SERVICES IN THE WALT DISNEY WORLD AREA? See allears .net/btp/church.htm for a partial list.

SOMEPLACE TO PUT ALL THESE PACKAGES? Lockers are located on the right side of the entrance to the Magic Kingdom; to the right of Spaceship Earth in EPCOT, at the International Gateway; to the right of the entrance at DHS; and to the left of the entrance at Animal Kingdom. The cost is $10 per day for small lockers and $12 per day

unofficial **TIP**
Package Pickup closes 2 hours before the parks close.

for large lockers at the theme parks. Lockers at the water parks cost $10 for small and $15 for large. Jumbo lockers, at EPCOT and the Magic Kingdom only, cost $15 per day. All lockers are now keyless.

Package Pickup is temporarily suspended; when it's running, it's located near each theme park's entrance (EPCOT has two Package Pickups, near the Future World and International Gateway entrances). Ask the salesperson to send your purchases to Package Pickup; when you leave the park, they'll be waiting for you. If you're staying at a Disney resort, you can also have packages delivered to your resort's gift shop for pickup the following day. If you're leaving within 24 hours, though, take them with you or use the in-park pickup location.

If you live in the United States, the gift shop at your Disney resort will ship your items to you via standard ground shipping. We're told that the maximum shipping cost is $40, so now is the time to buy souvenirs in bulk.

GROCERY STORES THAT DELIVER? If you don't have a car or you're too slothful to drive, you have a couple of options.

Amazon Prime members can use **Amazon Pantry** to order prepackaged items, from boxed cereals and snacks to coffee, sunscreen, aspirin, and diapers, at very competitive prices and have them delivered to your resort. If you're looking for fresh foods, along with beer and wine, **Garden Grocer** (gardengrocer.com) will shop for you and deliver your groceries.

The best way to compile your Garden Grocer order is on the website before you leave home—they even offer discounts for ordering 60, 30, or 15 days ahead. Delivery arrangements are per your instructions. If you're staying at a hotel where they deliver, you can arrange for your groceries (including alcohol) to be left with Bell Services. If there's something you want that you don't see on the website, click "Request an Item" and they'll try to find it for you. If you prefer to order by phone, call ☎ 866-855-4350.

For orders of less than $200 (before tax), a $14 delivery fee applies; for orders of $200 or more, delivery is free. Same-day delivery (before 10 a.m.) costs $30, and next-day delivery is $20. Orders canceled or modified without proper notice are subject to restocking fees; check the website for details.

As of this writing, Garden Grocer doesn't deliver to the Swan, Swan Reserve, or Dolphin; delivery to Disney's EPCOT resorts may be limited to afternoon only. Finally, note that Garden Grocer's delivery schedule may fill completely around holidays, at which point they'll stop accepting orders.

WINE, BEER, AND LIQUOR? In Florida, wine and beer are sold in grocery stores; for the stronger stuff, you'll have to go to a state-licensed liquor store. The best range of booze in the Disney area is sold at **ABC Fine Wine & Spirits,** less than a mile north of the Crossroads shopping center (11951 S. Apopka–Vineland Road; ☎ 407-239-0775). We also like **Publix Liquors** in the Water Tower Shoppes (29 Blake Blvd., Celebration; ☎ 321-939-3109).

PART ELEVEN

The MAGIC KINGDOM

KEY QUESTIONS ANSWERED IN THIS CHAPTER

▌▌ OVERVIEW

OPENED IN 1971, the Magic Kingdom was the first of Walt Disney World's four theme parks, much of it built by the same people who built Disneyland in California almost two decades prior. The crown jewel of the World's parks, the Magic Kingdom is what springs to most people's mind when they think of Disney World. Its attractions, such as Cinderella Castle, Pirates of the Caribbean, and Splash Mountain, have helped set the standard for theme park attractions the world over.

▌▌ ARRIVING

FROM INSIDE WALT DISNEY WORLD If you're staying at the **Contemporary, Bay Lake Tower, Grand Floridian Resort,** or **Polynesian Village,** you can commute to the Magic Kingdom by monorail (guests at the first three can walk to the park more quickly). If you're staying at **Wilderness Lodge & Boulder Ridge/Copper Creek Villas** or **Fort Wilderness Resort & Campground,** you can take a boat or bus. Guests at other Walt Disney World resorts can reach the park by bus. All Disney

continued on page 462

The Magic Kingdom

G+ Attraction Offers Genie+

IAS Attraction Offers Individual Access

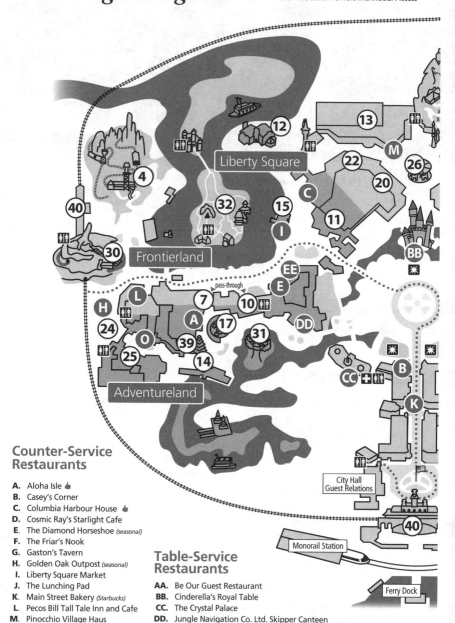

Counter-Service Restaurants

A. Aloha Isle 👍
B. Casey's Corner
C. Columbia Harbour House 👍
D. Cosmic Ray's Starlight Cafe
E. The Diamond Horseshoe *(seasonal)*
F. The Friar's Nook
G. Gaston's Tavern
H. Golden Oak Outpost *(seasonal)*
I. Liberty Square Market
J. The Lunching Pad
K. Main Street Bakery *(Starbucks)*
L. Pecos Bill Tall Tale Inn and Cafe
M. Pinocchio Village Haus
N. Tomorrowland Terrace Restaurant *(seasonal)*
O. Tortuga Tavern *(seasonal)*

Table-Service Restaurants

AA. Be Our Guest Restaurant
BB. Cinderella's Royal Table
CC. The Crystal Palace
DD. Jungle Navigation Co. Ltd. Skipper Canteen
EE. Liberty Tree Tavern 👍
FF. The Plaza Restaurant
GG. Tony's Town Square Restaurant

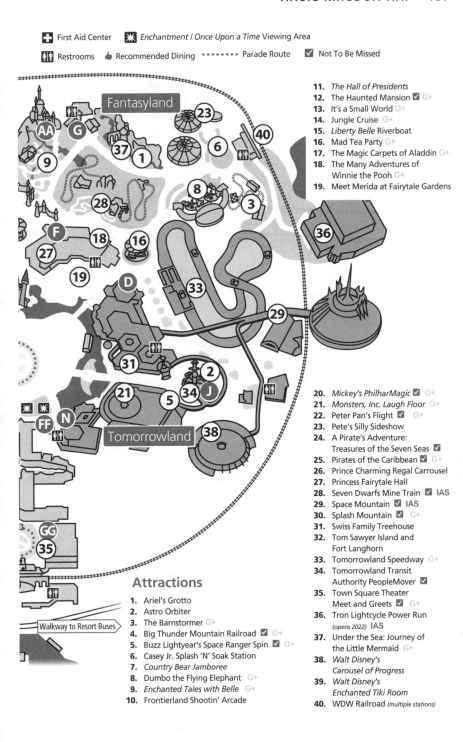

First Aid Center   Enchantment / Once Upon a Time Viewing Area

Restrooms   Recommended Dining   ········ Parade Route   ☑ Not To Be Missed

Fantasyland

Tomorrowland

Attractions

1. Ariel's Grotto
2. Astro Orbiter
3. The Barnstormer G+
4. Big Thunder Mountain Railroad ☑ G+
5. Buzz Lightyear's Space Ranger Spin ☑ G+
6. Casey Jr. Splash 'N' Soak Station
7. *Country Bear Jamboree*
8. Dumbo the Flying Elephant G+
9. *Enchanted Tales with Belle* G+
10. Frontierland Shootin' Arcade

11. *The Hall of Presidents*
12. The Haunted Mansion ☑ G+
13. It's a Small World G+
14. Jungle Cruise G+
15. *Liberty Belle* Riverboat
16. Mad Tea Party G+
17. *The Magic Carpets of Aladdin* G+
18. The Many Adventures of Winnie the Pooh G+
19. Meet Merida at Fairytale Gardens

20. *Mickey's PhilharMagic* ☑ G+
21. *Monsters, Inc. Laugh Floor* G+
22. Peter Pan's Flight ☑ G+
23. Pete's Silly Sideshow
24. A Pirate's Adventure: Treasures of the Seven Seas ☑
25. Pirates of the Caribbean ☑ G+
26. Prince Charming Regal Carrousel
27. Princess Fairytale Hall
28. Seven Dwarfs Mine Train ☑ IAS
29. Space Mountain ☑ IAS
30. Splash Mountain ☑ G+
31. Swiss Family Treehouse
32. Tom Sawyer Island and Fort Langhorn
33. Tomorrowland Speedway G+
34. Tomorrowland Transit Authority PeopleMover ☑
35. Town Square Theater Meet and Greets ☑ G+
36. Tron Lightcycle Power Run *(opens 2022)* IAS
37. Under the Sea: Journey of the Little Mermaid G+
38. *Walt Disney's Carousel of Progress*
39. *Walt Disney's Enchanted Tiki Room*
40. WDW Railroad *(multiple stations)*

Walkway to Resort Buses

continued from page 459

lodging guests, regardless of conveyance, are deposited at the park's entrance, bypassing the Transportation and Ticket Center (TTC).

DRIVING If you're thinking about driving to the Magic Kingdom, consider having a taxi or ride-hailing service drop you off at either the **Contemporary** or the **Grand Floridian Resort** instead, especially if you are arriving after park opening; it may cost slightly more than parking at the Magic Kingdom, but it's significantly faster. Otherwise, you'll encounter lines to pay for parking, to board trams (or walk) to take you to the TTC, to get through security, or to get on a monorail or ferry to take you to the park. All of this can take an hour or more on busy days.

unofficial **TIP**
Getting dropped off at the Contemporary or Grand Floridian saves off-property guests the daily $25 Magic Kingdom parking fee and virtually all of the waiting.

Have your driver go past the hotel entrance and drop you off in the far corner; from here, it's a short walk to the park, and lines at the security checkpoint there are much shorter. When you're ready to leave, just head to the Contemporary or Grand Floridian and hail a ride, making sure to wait in front of the hotel. You'll avoid the morning hassle in reverse.

This mom from Salt Lake City found using a ride-hailing service a big time-saver:

> We used Lyft to go to and from the parks every day. It was SO convenient and much quicker than using Disney buses. The tip to get dropped off at the Contemporary to go to the Magic Kingdom was a lifesaver. Saved us so much time, especially in marathon traffic one Saturday morning. And getting picked up there to go to the hotel at night was seamless.

If driving is unavoidable (see page 439 for GPS coordinates) and you're bringing a stroller, a Ridgewood, New Jersey, family recommends the ferry (which starts operating 30–90 minutes before official park opening):

> The ferry to the Magic Kingdom is a must if you're using a stroller. You can drive the stroller right onto the ferry and then just head to the back to be the first ones off when it docks.

MAGIC KINGDOM OPENING (ROPE DROP)

unofficial **TIP**
Rope drop refers to cast members using a length of rope to hold back crowds until the park opens. After the rope is dropped— or rewound, to be precise—crowds race-walk to their first rides.

ARRIVING AT THE MAGIC KINGDOM **30–60 minutes before official opening** ensures the shortest possible waits for rides.

On-site guests who want to take advantage of Early Theme Park Entry (see page 38) should arrive at the park entrance 60 minutes before official opening (that is, 30 minutes before Early Entry) on all days. Off-site guests, who aren't eligible for Early Theme Park Entry, should arrive 30 minutes before official opening on all days.

Once in the park, you'll find most of the rides in Fantasyland and Tomorrowland running. Rides in Adventureland, Frontierland, and Liberty Square may start operations closer to the park's official opening time.

Main Street's larger shops, such as the **Emporium,** will be open when you're admitted into the park, in case you need sunscreen, ponchos, or aspirin. **The Main Street Bakery (Starbucks)** will also be open for coffee and breakfast items.

Upon entering the park, most guests head for one of the headliner attractions: Seven Dwarfs Mine Train in Fantasyland gets the biggest crowds, followed by Space Mountain in Tomorrowland, with Big Thunder Mountain Railroad in Frontierland in third place. When Tron Lightcycle Power Run opens in Tomorrowland (2022), it should be the biggest draw in the park for teens and adults.

GETTING ORIENTED

AT THE MAGIC KINGDOM, **stroller, wheelchair, ECV/ESV rentals,** and **locker rentals** are on the right, just inside the entrance. On your left as you enter **Main Street, U.S.A.,** is **City Hall,** the center for information, lost and found, guided tours, and entertainment schedules.

Be sure to pick up a **guide map** at the park entrance or at City Hall. It shows all attractions, shops, and eating places; provides information about first aid, baby care, and assistance for the disabled; and provides tips for good photos. It also lists times for the day's special events, live entertainment, Disney-character parades, and concerts if they're offered; plus, it tells you when and where to find Disney characters.

The guide map is supplemented by a daily entertainment schedule, the *Times Guide.* In addition to listing performance times, the *Times Guide* provides info on Disney-character appearances (when offered) and what Disney calls **Special Hours,** or operating hours for attractions and restaurants that open late or close early. The **My Disney Experience** app (see page 33) contains this information too, but, in a rare triumph of analog over digital, it's faster to use the *Times Guide.*

Main Street, U.S.A., ends at the **Central Plaza,** from which branch the entrances to five other "lands" (clockwise from the left): **Adventureland, Frontierland, Liberty Square, Fantasyland,** and **Tomorrowland.**

Cinderella Castle, at the entrance to Fantasyland, is the Magic Kingdom's visual anchor. The castle is an excellent meeting place if your group decides to split up or gets separated.

FAVORITE ATTRACTIONS BY AGE GROUP

INCLUDING RIDES, SHOWS, PARADES, fireworks, and street performers, there are almost 80 individual attractions in the Magic

---

NOT TO BE MISSED AT THE MAGIC KINGDOM

ADVENTURELAND • Pirates of the Caribbean

FANTASYLAND • Character meet and greets (various) *(closed at press time)*
• Peter Pan's Flight • Seven Dwarfs Mine Train

FRONTIERLAND • Big Thunder Mountain Railroad • Splash Mountain

LIBERTY SQUARE • The Haunted Mansion

MAIN STREET, U.S.A. • Meet Mickey Mouse at Town Square Theater *(closed at press time)*

PARADES AND FIREWORKS • Festival of Fantasy afternoon parade *(closed at press time)* • *Disney Enchantment* fireworks • Holiday parades and fireworks (seasonal)

TOMORROWLAND • Buzz Lightyear's Space Ranger Spin • Space Mountain
• Tron Lightcycle Power Run *(opens 2022)*

MAGIC KINGDOM SERVICES
MOST PARK SERVICES are centered on Main Street, U.S.A., including:
Baby Care Center Next to The Crystal Palace, left around the Central Plaza (toward Adventureland)
Banking Services ATMs underneath the Main Street railroad station
Cell Phone Charging Space Mountain exit and behind Big Top Treats in Storybook Circus. Can drop at City Hall with cord for charging.
First Aid Center Next to The Crystal Palace, left around the Central Plaza (toward Adventureland)
Live Entertainment and Parade Information City Hall, at the railroad-station end of Main Street
Lost and Found City Hall
Lost Persons City Hall
Storage Lockers Inside the turnstiles, to the right as you face the train station
Walt Disney World and Local Attraction Information City Hall
Wheelchair, ECV/ESV, and Stroller Rentals Inside turnstiles at right as you face the train station

unofficial **TIP**
Because Cinderella Castle is so large, designate a very specific meeting spot, such as the entrance to Cinderella's Royal Table restaurant at the rear of the castle.

Kingdom. The chart on the opposite page lists the 10 most popular attractions by age group.

Parades and fireworks appear in the top 10 for every age group. Before the pandemic, character greetings were especially popular with preschool and grade-school children, and meeting Mickey Mouse in particular ranked in the top 10 park experiences for every age group except seniors (and Mickey was in the top 20 for them).

These attractions form the core of our Magic Kingdom touring plans; if you're looking for step-by-step instructions on where to go and when, start with these (see page 502 for more information). Most of the attractions listed here offer Lightning Lane to reduce waits in line; see the next section for details.

ATTRACTION RATINGS The attractions profiled in this book have two sets of ratings: an overall rating next to the attraction's name, which reflects the authors' impressions, and reader ratings broken down by age group. Both use a five-star scale, with five stars being best.

Appeal by Age ratings are rounded to the nearest half-star. To help place them in context, we also provide a label, such as Above Average, showing how that attraction stacks up to others in the park. These labels are assigned using the attraction's average number of reader ratings and incorporating a 95% confidence interval (sort of like a margin of error), similar to our restaurant ratings (see Part Six). As with restaurants, the authors' ratings for attractions don't always jibe with readers' ratings.

The average reader ratings for all Magic Kingdom attractions by age group are as follows, based on the 180,300 attraction ratings we received over the past 18 months:

PRESCHOOL	YOUNG ADULTS	GRADE SCHOOL	OVER 30	TEENS	SENIORS
4.1 stars	3.9 stars	4.2 stars	4.0 stars	3.8 stars	4.0 stars

GENIE+, LIGHTNING LANE, AND INDIVIDUAL ATTRACTION SELECTIONS AND TOURING PLANS

NOTE: See page 59 for detailed information and strategy suggestions for Genie+, Lighting Lane, and Individual Attraction Selections.

MAGIC KINGDOM MOST POPULAR ATTRACTIONS BY AGE GROUP

PRE-SCHOOL	GRADE SCHOOL	TEENS	YOUNG ADULTS	OVER 30	SENIORS
Meet Mickey Mouse at Town Square Theater*	Big Thunder Mountain Railroad	Space Mountain	Big Thunder Mountain Railroad	Evening fireworks	Evening fireworks
Meet Disney Pals at Pete's Silly Sideshow*	Buzz Lightyear's Space Ranger Spin	Big Thunder Mountain Railroad	The Haunted Mansion	The Haunted Mansion	The Haunted Mansion
Festival of Fantasy parade*	Seven Dwarfs Mine Train	The Haunted Mansion	Pirates of the Caribbean	Big Thunder Mountain Railroad	Pirates of the Caribbean
Buzz Lightyear's Space Ranger Spin	Space Mountain	Pirates of the Caribbean	Space Mountain	Pirates of the Caribbean	Big Thunder Mountain Railroad
It's a Small World	Splash Mountain	Seven Dwarfs Mine Train	Seven Dwarfs Mine Train	Seven Dwarfs Mine Train	Seven Dwarfs Mine Train
Dumbo the Flying Elephant	*Mickey's PhilharMagic*	Splash Mountain	Festival of Fantasy parade*	Space Mountain	*Mickey's PhilharMagic*
Peter Pan's Flight	Mad Tea Party	Evening fireworks	Evening fireworks	Splash Mountain	Tomorrowland Transit Authority PeopleMover
Under the Sea: Journey of the Little Mermaid	Festival of Fantasy parade*	Buzz Lightyear's Space Ranger Spin	Meet Mickey Mouse at Town Square Theater*	Tomorrowland Transit Authority PeopleMover	Splash Mountain
The Many Adventures of Winnie the Pooh	Evening fireworks	Jungle Cruise	Buzz Lightyear's Space Ranger Spin	Festival of Fantasy parade*	The Hall of Presidents
The Barnstormer	*Enchanted Tales with Belle**	*Mickey's PhilharMagic*	Jungle Cruise	Meet Mickey Mouse at Town Square Theater*	Festival of Fantasy parade*

*Closed at press time

It was easy for us to recommend using Disney's old FastPass+ ride reservation system with our touring plans because FastPass+ was free to use, had plenty of historical data to analyze, and behaved predictably. None of that is true with Genie+. So the big questions for this edition are:

1. Is Genie+ worth paying for at the Magic Kingdom?
2. If it's worth the cost, which attractions benefit most from Genie+ or Individual Attraction Selection?
3. How can you avoid paying for Individual Attraction Selections?
4. How do Genie+ and Individual Attraction Selections work with the touring plans?

Is Genie+ Worth Paying For at the Magic Kingdom?

The Magic Kingdom might be the easiest park to recommend using Genie+, but it's not an obvious yes for everyone.

One of the reasons why using FastPass+ was necessary at the Magic Kingdom was because other guests were using it. FastPass+ attractions usually allocated 75–80% of their ride capacity to guests with Fast-Pass+, leaving just 20–25% of the ride's seats available to standby guests.

GENIE+ AND INDIVIDUAL ATTRACTION SELECTIONS AT THE MAGIC KINGDOM	
ADVENTURELAND	
• Jungle Cruise	• Pirates of the Caribbean
FANTASYLAND	
• The Barnstormer	• The Many Adventures of Winnie the Pooh
• Dumbo the Flying Elephant	• *Mickey's PhilharMagic*
• *Enchanted Tales with Belle*	• Peter Pan's Flight
• It's a Small World	• Seven Dwarfs Mine Train *(Individual Access only)*
• Mad Tea Party	• Under the Sea: Journey of the Little Mermaid
FRONTIERLAND	
• Big Thunder Mountain Railroad	• Splash Mountain
LIBERTY SQUARE	
• The Haunted Mansion	
TOMORROWLAND	
• Buzz Lightyear's Space Ranger Spin	• Tomorrowland Speedway
• *Monsters, Inc. Laugh Floor*	• Tron Lightcycle Power Run *(opens 2022; Individual Access only)*
• Space Mountain *(Individual Access only)*	

Note: Character greetings were not operating when Genie+ and Lightning Lane were introduced. We think character greetings will be added upon their return. Our guess is that Tron will be Individual Access only when it opens at the Magic Kingdom too.

Because so many people used FastPass+, and FastPass+ guests were prioritized when allocating ride capacity, the waits in line at some attractions—mostly second-tier ones—went up. (Lines went down slightly at headliner rides, probably because the act of choosing three FastPasses, coupled with Disney's limitations on what you could choose, served as a way to more evenly distribute guests around the park.) Using FastPass+ was the only way to beat the lines introduced by FastPass+.

Genie+ isn't free, so fewer people will use it than FastPass+. That means the waits at both the Lightning Lane and standby lines should be shorter than with FastPass+. Fewer people will be in the Lightning Lane, making the wait to use it shorter. With fewer people in the Lightning Lane, more ride capacity can be allocated to guests in the standby line, making their waits shorter too. And because Disney can raise the price of Genie+ if it becomes popular, the use of Genie+ should be somewhat self-regulating.

The one hitch to the logic above is that FastPass+ also did a great job of getting people to ride attractions that were traditionally less popular. For example, by showing guests that FastPass+ was available for *Mickey's PhilharMagic,* more people visited it than would have otherwise. Unless Disney can convince the same number of people to visit *Mickey's PhilharMagic* without free FastPasses, the risk is that guests will concentrate on the most popular rides instead, driving up those wait times. We think this is where Genie+'s itinerary feature might come into play—if Genie+ tells guests to visit less popular attractions they wouldn't otherwise see, it'd be a way for Disney to spread out crowds more evenly throughout the park, keeping lines at the big rides lower.

We think Genie+ is worth the cost at the Magic Kingdom if you meet any of these criteria:

- You'll arrive at the park after Early Theme Park Entry begins (that is, you won't be at the park as soon as it opens). This includes off-site guests, who aren't eligible for Early Theme Park Entry, and on-site guests who want to sleep in.
- You won't be using a touring plan.
- You're visiting during a holiday, spring break, or other peak season.

The other consideration with Genie+ is the number of Genie+ ride reservations you'll be able to get in a given day. Under the old Fast-Pass+ system, we think the vast majority of guests used five or fewer FastPasses in a given day at the Magic Kingdom. We assume that Genie+ will have more reservations available than FastPass+ because fewer people will use it. While Genie+ wasn't yet running at press time, here's how much time we think it's possible to save using Genie+ with a touring plan, using different assumptions about how many Genie+ reservations it's possible to obtain in a day:

The **Typical Use** scenario assumes that you'll be able to obtain Genie+ reservations for five attractions in your touring plan, where you haven't already experienced those rides, the reservations don't conflict with any meals or breaks you've already planned, and the standby lines are long enough to justify obtaining the reservation. The **Optimistic Use** scenario assumes all of the preceding, plus that Genie+ reservations are available at almost exactly the pace at which you're going to visit the attractions. The **Perfect Use** scenario assumes that you're able to get Genie+ reservations, one-by-one, with an immediate return time, for every eligible ride on your touring plan. We think that's exceedingly unlikely to happen; we present it here to estimate the upper limit on what might be possible. Finally, remember that Seven Dwarfs Mine Train and Space Mountain may not be part of Genie+; there's a separate cost to use Lightning Lane with those attractions.

Which Attractions Benefit Most from Genie+ or Individual Attraction Selections?

For Genie+, the chart on the next page shows the top 14 attractions that might benefit most from using Genie+, based on current wait times and historical FastPass+ data. The chart goes in descending order of priority.

Regarding Individual Attraction Selections, we think Space Mountain and Seven Dwarfs Mine Train, plus Tron when it opens, will be the only Individual Attraction Selections. Whether those are worth the cost will depend on where Disney's charging for those and how that lines up on your personal time-versus-money spectrum.

How Can You Avoid Paying for Individual Attraction Selections?

There are a few strategies to avoid paying for Individual Attraction Selections. Each of them involves another cost:

1. Stay at a Disney resort, use Early Theme Park Entry over multiple days, and head to each attraction as soon as the park opens. For new attractions, such as Tron, this is likely to be the strategy recommended by our touring plan software.
2. Stay at a Disney Deluxe or DVC resort and visit the attractions during Extended Theme Park Hours.
3. Visit the attraction during an After Hours event, such as the Boo Bash Halloween party.

Clearly, Disney has thought hard about how to force consumers into an explicit time-versus-money calculation with these attractions.

MAGIC KINGDOM ATTRACTIONS THAT BENEFIT MOST FROM GENIE+ (HIGHEST PRIORITY TO LOWEST)	
1 Peter Pan's Flight	**8** Pirates of the Caribbean
2 Splash Mountain	**9** It's a Small World
3 Jungle Cruise	**10** The Barnstormer
4 Big Thunder Mountain Railroad	**11** Under the Sea: Journey of the Little Mermaid
5 Haunted Mansion	**12** Tomorrowland Speedway
6 The Many Adventures of Winnie the Pooh	**13** Mad Tea Party
7 Buzz Lightyear's Space Ranger Spin	**14** *Mickey's PhilharMagic*

Note: Character greetings were not operating at press time.

How Do Genie+ and Individual Attraction Selections Work with the Touring Plans?

FOR INDIVIDUAL ATTRACTION SELECTIONS First, obtain an Individual Attraction Selection return time from My Disney Experience. Next:

If you're using one of the touring plans from this book, follow the plan step by step until it's time to use your reservation. Suspend the touring plan while riding the attraction, then pick up the plan where you left off. If the touring plan recommends visiting the attraction before or after your return time, skip that step.

If you're using our free touring plan software, enter the reservation return time into the touring plan software. The software will organize your touring plan so that you return to the attraction at your designated return time.

FOR GENIE+ If you're using one of the touring plans from this book, keep track of the next two or three steps in your touring plan as you go through the park. In Genie+, get the first available reservation for any of those three attractions, and fit that return-time window into the plan. For example, suppose the next three steps in your touring plan are Jungle Cruise, Pirates of the Caribbean, and Big Thunder Mountain Railroad. You check Genie+ for the next available return time for those three attractions, and the return times are 11 a.m. for Jungle Cruise, 11:30 a.m. for Pirates, and 10:45 a.m. for Big Thunder. You'd select Big Thunder because it's the next available return time from among those three. Once in line for Big Thunder, scan Genie+ availability for the next three attractions in your plan. If none of the next three steps in your plan participate in Genie+, then get a reservation for the next attraction in your plan that participates in Genie+.

If you're using our touring plan software, the software will recommend which attraction to obtain a Genie+ reservation for next by analyzing your touring plan, the current Genie+ reservation distribution

ESTIMATED TIME SAVINGS USING A TOURING PLAN WITH GENIE+ FOR VARIOUS CROWD LEVELS			
CROWD LEVEL	**TYPICAL USE (5 RESERVATIONS PER DAY)**	**OPTIMISTIC USE (9 RESERVATIONS PER DAY)**	**PERFECT USE (16 RESERVATIONS PER DAY)**
Low	20 minutes saved	40 minutes saved	65 minutes saved
Medium	40 minutes saved	80 minutes saved	130 minutes saved
High	60 minutes saved	100 minutes saved	170 minutes saved

MAGIC KINGDOM RESTAURANT REFRESHER
COUNTER SERVICE
• **Aloha Isle** (✪ 98%/Exceptional), Adventureland
• **Main Street Bakery (Starbucks)** (✪ 92%/Above Average), Main Street, U.S.A.
• **Columbia Harbour House** (✪ 92%/Much Above Average), Liberty Square
• **Gaston's Tavern** (✪92%/Above Average), Fantasyland
• **Liberty Square Market** (✪ 91%/Above Average), Liberty Square
• **Casey's Corner** (✪ 88%/Average), Main Street, U.S.A.
• **The Friar's Nook** (✪ 87%/Average), Fantasyland
• **Pecos Bill Tall Tale Inn and Cafe** (✪ 86%/Average), Frontierland
• **The Lunching Pad** (✪ 83%/Below Average), Tomorrowland
• **Cosmic Ray's Starlight Cafe** (✪ 82%/Much Below Average), Tomorrowland
• **Pinocchio Village Haus** (✪ 76%/Do Not Visit), Fantasyland
FULL SERVICE
• **Jungle Navigation Co. Ltd. Skipper Canteen** (L, D) (✪ 93%/Much Above Average), Adventureland
• **Liberty Tree Tavern** (L, D) (✪ 91%/Above Average), Liberty Square
• **The Plaza Restaurant** (L, D) (✪ 80%/Much Below Average), Main Street, U.S.A.
• **Cinderella's Royal Table** (L, D) (✪ 86%/Average), Fantasyland
• **Be Our Guest Restaurant** (L, D) (✪ 81%/Do Not Visit), Fantasyland
• **Tony's Town Square** (L, D) (✪ 80%/Much Below Average), Main Street, U.S.A.
• **The Crystal Palace** (L, D) (✪ 78%/Much Below Average), Main Street, U.S.A.

rate, and likely wait times for the rest of the day. When you obtain that reservation, simply enter the return time into the software, and the software will redo your touring plan to use it.

DINING IN THE MAGIC KINGDOM

ABOVE IS A QUICK RECAP of the Magic Kingdom's major restaurants, rated by readers from highest to lowest. See Part Six for details.

MAIN STREET, U.S.A.

YOU'LL BEGIN AND END YOUR VISIT on Main Street, which closes 30 minutes–1 hour after the rest of the park. A Disneyfied version of a turn-of-the-20th-century small-town American thoroughfare, Main Street is lined with shops, character-greeting venues, places to eat, City Hall, and a fire station. In the morning, horse-drawn trolleys, fire engines, and horseless carriages transport visitors along Main Street to the Central Plaza. In the afternoon, artists in Main Street's glassware shop perform live glass blowing and sculpting.

unofficial **TIP**
The pedestrian walkway most frequently used during parades and fireworks runs from just past **Tony's Town Square Restaurant** to the Tomorrowland side of **The Plaza Restaurant;** the other runs from near the **First Aid Center,** next to The Crystal Palace, to the Main Street fire station (**Engine Co. 71**), near City Hall on Main Street.

The circular area around the Central Plaza is a paved, landscaped viewing spot for the large crowds that watch the parades and evening fireworks, when they're offered. To disperse heavy crowds during these events, the areas behind the shops on either side of Main Street can become pedestrian walkways on which guests can exit and enter the park.

The **Walt Disney World Railroad** stops at Main Street Station; get on to tour the park or ride to Frontierland or Fantasyland. It's not faster than walking, but it's easier on the feet. The railroad was closed at press time to facilitate the construction of a new attraction and will not resume operation until sometime in 2022.

KEY TO ABBREVIATIONS In the attraction profiles that follow, each star rating is accompanied by a category label in parentheses (see page 266). E means **Exceptional,** MAA means **Much Above Average,** AA means **Above Average,** A means **Average,** BA means **Below Average,** and MBA means **Much Below Average.**

AVERAGE WAIT-IN-LINE TIMES This generally uses the attractions' maximum hourly capacity as a fixed reference because ride capacity may change during the pandemic.

Main Street Characters *(not offered at press time)*

DESCRIPTION AND COMMENTS Colorful characters, including the mayor of Main Street, roam the area for photos, autographs, and lively conversation. Not as engaging as the characters who populate Hollywood Boulevard in Disney's Hollywood Studios, but still fun.

TOURING TIPS Characters are usually available from park opening until around 1 p.m. They're fun to talk to if you're in the area, but don't make a special trip.

Town Square Theater Meet and Greets: Mickey Mouse, Tinker Bell and Friends
(closed at press time) ★★★★

PRESCHOOL ★★★★★ (MAA)   GRADE SCHOOL ★★★★½ (MAA)   TEENS ★★★★½ (MAA)
YOUNG ADULTS ★★★★½ (AA)   OVER 30 ★★★★½ (MAA)   SENIORS ★★★★½ (AA)

What it is Character-greeting venue. **Scope and scale** Minor attraction. **When to go** Before 10 a.m. or after 4 p.m. **Comment** Mickey and the fairies have 2 separate queues, requiring 2 separate waits in line. **Duration of experience** 2 minutes per character. **Probable waiting time** 30 minutes. **Queue speed** Slow. **ECV/wheelchair access** May remain in wheelchair. **Participates in Genie+** Likely upon return. **Early Theme Park Entry** No. **Extended Evening Hours** No.

DESCRIPTION AND COMMENTS Children and teenagers rate character greetings among the highest of any Disney attractions, and there's no bigger celebrity than Mickey Mouse. Meet Mickey, along with Tinker Bell and her Pixie Hollow friends, throughout the day at the Town Square Theater on Main Street, to your right as you enter the park.

TOURING TIPS Lines usually recede after dinner. If Genie+ isn't available, our touring plans frequently put meeting Mickey as the first step in the day. He usually starts greeting guests at the park's official opening time, even if you're let into the park early.

Transportation Rides

DESCRIPTION AND COMMENTS Trolleys, buses, and the like.
TOURING TIPS Will save you a walk to the Central Plaza. Not worth a wait.

Walt Disney World Railroad *(closed for construction)* ★★★

PRESCHOOL ★★★★½ (MAA)   GRADE SCHOOL ★★★★½ (AA)   TEENS ★★★★ (BA)
YOUNG ADULTS ★★★★ (A)   OVER 30 ★★★★½ (AA)   SENIORS ★★★★½ (AA)

What it is Scenic railroad ride around the perimeter of the Magic Kingdom; provides transportation to Frontierland and Fantasyland. **Scope and scale** Minor attraction. **When to go** Anytime. **Comment** Main Street is usually the least congested station. **Duration of ride** About 20 minutes for a complete circuit. **Average wait in line per 100 people ahead of you** 8 minutes; assumes 2 or more trains operating. **Loading speed** Moderate. **ECV/wheelchair access** Guests must transfer from ECV to provided wheelchair. **Participates in Genie+** No. **Early Theme Park Entry** No. **Extended Evening Hours** No.

DESCRIPTION AND COMMENTS Take a relaxing ride around the perimeter of the Magic Kingdom aboard a real steam-powered locomotive, with stops in Frontierland and Fantasyland. Views from the train include a peek into each land except Adventureland (where you're apt to see more of the behind-the-scenes infrastructure). The most scenic part of the tour is between the Frontierland and Main Street, U.S.A., stations. If you're in Frontierland and headed out of the park, it's a nice way to end your visit.

TOURING TIPS The railroad remains closed due to construction of a new *Tron*-inspired roller coaster in Tomorrowland, which should open in 2022. Disney hadn't announced a date for the railroad's reopening at press time.

When it's running, we suggest saving the train until after you've seen the featured attractions, or use it when you need transportation. On busy days, lines form at the Frontierland station but rarely at the Main Street station. Wheelchair access is available at the Frontierland and Fantasyland stations.

Only folded strollers are permitted on the train, so you can't board with your rented Disney stroller. You can, however, obtain a replacement at your destination (keep your stroller name card and rental receipt with you).

A dad from Green Pond, New Jersey, points out that not all stations are equal:

Tell your readers that if they ride the railroad they should go to the Main Street station. We tried to get on in New Orleans Square, and it was a zoo—there were people shoving past other people and rolling over other people with strollers and wheelchairs. The Main Street station is much more organized, efficient, and relaxing because of the extra cast members working there.

Finally, note that the railroad shuts down immediately before and during parades and cavalcades; check your park guide map or *Times Guide* for times. Needless to say, this is not the time to get in line.

ADVENTURELAND

ADVENTURELAND IS THE FIRST land to the left of Main Street, U.S.A. It combines an African-safari theme with a tropical island atmosphere. Some of Adventureland's attractions are theme park classics. They're also among the oldest in the park, so crowds don't usually build here until late morning.

Jungle Cruise ★★★½

| PRESCHOOL ★★★★ (MBA) | GRADE SCHOOL ★★★★ (MBA) | TEENS ★★★★ (BA) |
| YOUNG ADULTS ★★★★ (BA) | OVER 30 ★★★★ (BA) | SENIORS ★★★★ (A) |

What it is Outdoor safari-themed boat ride. **Scope and scale** Major attraction. **When to go** Before 10:30 a.m., during the last 2 hours before closing, or use Genie+. **Duration of ride** 8-9 minutes. **Average wait in line per 100 people ahead of you** 3½ minutes; assumes 10 boats operating. **Loading speed** Moderate. **ECV/wheelchair access** May remain in ECV/wheelchair and wait for specially configured boats. **Participates in Genie+** Yes. **Early Theme Park Entry** No. **Extended Evening Hours** No.

DESCRIPTION AND COMMENTS Jungle Cruise is an outdoor group boat ride through some of the world's best-known simulated tropical waterways. You'll pass through forest and jungle populated entirely by animatronic animals (some hostile) and natives.

Jungle Cruise was the park's signature ride when it opened at Disneyland. With the advent of modern, highly themed, *real* zoo environments such as Animal Kingdom, the Magic Kingdom's version would surely have faded into obscurity were it not for one thing: The skippers tell jokes. OK, *jokes* is a stretch—the skippers do *the* cheesiest, most groan-inducing stand-up you've ever heard. If you dig that sort of thing, it's glorious. If not, heed this Pelham, Alabama, reader's warning:

Jungle Cruise severely needs an update. Our tour guide indulged in annoying comedy to make up for the lack of excitement. I would rather have been eaten by the animatronic hippos.

This reader's prayers have partially been answered: Disney updated the Jungle Cruise's scenery and jokes in 2021. The puns remain.

The best Jungle Cruise experience we've ever had began with all the passengers agreeing beforehand to laugh enthusiastically at whatever jokes we heard. It took about two puns for the skipper to catch on and play along. The ride ended with us chanting the skipper's name during thunderous applause, to which the skipper said, "Is this what unconditional love feels like? Take that, Mom and Dad!"

TOURING TIPS We think the ride is better at night.

The Magic Carpets of Aladdin ★★½

PRESCHOOL ★★★★½ (MAA)	GRADE SCHOOL ★★★★ (BA)	TEENS ★★★ (BA)
YOUNG ADULTS ★★★ (MBA)	OVER 30 ★★★ (MBA)	SENIORS ★★★½ (BA)

What it is Elaborate midway ride. **Scope and scale** Minor attraction. **When to go** Before 11 a.m. or after 7 p.m. **Duration of ride** 1½ minutes. **Average wait in line per 100 people ahead of you** 16 minutes. **Loading speed** Slow. **ECV/wheelchair access** Must transfer from ECV to provided wheelchair. **Participates in Genie+** Yes. **Early Theme Park Entry** No. **Extended Evening Hours** No.

DESCRIPTION AND COMMENTS This spinning midway ride is like Dumbo with magic carpets instead of elephants. A spitting camel sprays jets of water on carpet riders. Riders can maneuver their carpets up and down and side to side to avoid the water. The front seat controls vehicle height, while the back seat controls tilt—if you let the kids sit up front, prepare to get wet!

TOURING TIPS Like Dumbo, this ride has great eye appeal but an extremely slow loading time. Try to get younger kids on during the first 30 minutes the park is open, or try just before park closing. Genie+ is almost never needed.

A Pirate's Adventure: Treasure of the Seven Seas
(closed at press time) ★★★½

PRESCHOOL ★★★★ (BA)	GRADE SCHOOL ★★★★½ (A)	TEENS ★★★★ (A)
YOUNG ADULTS ★★★★ (A)	OVER 30 ★★★★ (BA)	SENIORS ★★★★½ (A)

What it is Interactive game. **Scope and scale** Diversion. **When to go** Noon–6 p.m. **Duration of experience** About 20 minutes to play the entire game. **ECV/wheelchair access** May remain in ECV/wheelchair. **Participates in Genie+** No. **Early Theme Park Entry** No. **Extended Evening Hours** No.

DESCRIPTION AND COMMENTS A Pirate's Adventure features interactive areas with physical props and narrations that lead guests through a quest to help Captain Jack Sparrow find lost treasure, all within Adventureland.

Guests begin their journey at The Crow's Nest. Your group of up to six people chooses a leader; the leader's MagicBand (or ticket or talisman) activates a video screen that assigns the group to one of five different missions. Your group is given a map and sent off to your first location.

Once at the location, the leader of the party touches the talisman to the symbol at the station, and the animation begins. Each adventure has four or five stops throughout Adventureland; each stop contains 30–45 seconds of activity. No strategy or action is required: Simply watch what unfolds on the screen, get your next destination, and head off.

We like how well each station integrates into its surroundings and how the stations' artifacts and props tie together the attraction and movie story lines. If you're not yet convinced to play, stand in Adventureland and watch the faces of the kids playing when they do something that triggers smoke, noise, or other effects.

A Maryland mom writes:

The very best thing we did with our 4-year-old was A Pirate's Adventure. It was incredible. We did all five scavenger hunts, and it took 2 hours—our most fun 2 hours at the park! It's high-tech, magical, imaginative, active, and individualized. And you can keep the beautiful maps!

And from a New York City reader:

Our girls (age 9) had a blast and were eager to complete all five stages of the journey. The maps were a fun challenge for them: easy enough to be fun but challenging enough to give them a sense that they were accomplishing something—and the surprises at each stage were lots of fun for all of us. The only caution I would add is that you should try to take part when there aren't too many other people participating. Waiting in line behind another group took the fun out of finding a stop.

TOURING TIPS Not a must if time is tight.

Pirates of the Caribbean ★★★★

PRESCHOOL ★★★½ (MBA)   **GRADE SCHOOL** ★★★★ (A)   **TEENS** ★★★★½ (MAA)
YOUNG ADULTS ★★★★½ (MAA)   **OVER 30** ★★★★½ (MAA)   **SENIORS** ★★★★½ (MAA)

What it is Indoor pirate-themed boat ride. **Scope and scale** Headliner. **When to go** Before 11 a.m., after 7 p.m., or use Genie+. **Comment** Frightens some children. **Duration of ride** About 7½ minutes. **Average wait in line per 100 people ahead of you** 3 minutes; assumes 1 Genie+ line, 1 standby line. **Loading speed** Fast. **ECV/wheelchair access** Must transfer from ECV to provided wheelchair and then from wheelchair to boat. **Participates in Genie+** Yes. **Early Theme Park Entry** No. **Extended Evening Hours** Yes.

DESCRIPTION AND COMMENTS An indoor cruise through a series of sets that depict a pirate raid on an island settlement, from bombardment of the fortress to debauchery after the victory. Arguably one of the most influential theme park attractions ever created, the Magic Kingdom's version retains the elaborate queuing area, grand scale, and detailed scenes that have awed audiences since its debut in Disneyland in 1967.

As one of the theme park's most popular rides, Pirates is scrutinized and revised often. The successful *Pirates of the Caribbean* movies have boosted the ride's popularity, and guests' demands led to the addition of animatronic figures of Captain Jack Sparrow and Captain Barbossa in scenes. The latest refresh changes a scene of raiders auctioning off women to an auction of captured townsfolk's luxury possessions and chickens, led by a gunwielding female pirate.

The cumulative effect of these additions, however, makes the ride's narrative confusing and self-contradicting. For example, while you might believe that your boat is floating past these scenes at a specific point in time, the appearance of Jack Sparrow in multiple places means that you're also in different timelines. And it's nonsense to suggest that these pirates will bombard a town, torture its inhabitants, and pillage everything in sight, but will stop all of that for an auction that determines the correct market price for chickens. The new scene just doesn't make sense in the context of the rest of the ride.

TOURING TIPS Engineered to move large crowds in a hurry, Pirates is a good attraction to see in the late afternoon.

Swiss Family Treehouse ★★★

PRESCHOOL ★★★½ (MBA)   GRADE SCHOOL ★★★½ (MBA)   TEENS ★★★ (MBA)
YOUNG ADULTS ★★★ (MBA)   OVER 30 ★★★½ (MBA)   SENIORS ★★★ (MBA)

What it is Outdoor walk-through treehouse. **Scope and scale** Minor attraction. **When to go** Anytime. **Comment** Requires climbing a lot of stairs. **Duration of tour** 10–15 minutes. **Probable waiting time** None most days, 10 minutes tops. **ECV/wheelchair access** Must be ambulatory. **Participates in Genie+** No. **Early Theme Park Entry** No. **Extended Evening Hours** Yes.

DESCRIPTION AND COMMENTS An immense replica of the Swiss Family Robinson's arboreal abode. With its multiple stories and mechanical wizardry, it's the queen of all treehouses.

TOURING TIPS A self-guided walk-through tour involves a lot of stairs up and down, but no ropes, ladders, or anything fancy. Lookie-loos or people stopping to rest sometimes create bottlenecks that slow things down. Visit in late afternoon or early evening if you're on a one-day tour, or in the morning of your second day.

Walt Disney's Enchanted Tiki Room ★★★

PRESCHOOL ★★★★ (MBA)   GRADE SCHOOL ★★★½ (MBA)   TEENS ★★★ (MBA)
YOUNG ADULTS ★★★½ (MBA)   OVER 30 ★★★★ (BA)   SENIORS ★★★★ (A)

What it is Audio-Animatronic Pacific Island musical-theater show. **Scope and scale** Minor attraction. **When to go** Before 11 a.m. or after 3:30 p.m. **Comment** Frightens some preschoolers. **Duration of presentation** 15½ minutes. **Preshow entertainment** Talking birds. **Probable waiting time** 15 minutes. **ECV/wheelchair access** May remain in ECV/wheelchair. **Participates in Genie+** No. **Early Theme Park Entry** No. **Extended Evening Hours** Yes.

DESCRIPTION AND COMMENTS This show, conceived by Walt Disney, stars four singing, wisecracking mechanical parrots: José, Fritz, Michael, and Pierre. The quartet performs songs arranged in styles from the 1940s to the 1960s, accompanied by dozens of other birds, plants, and tikis that come to life all around you.

The show was an engineering marvel when it opened in Disneyland in 1967. We suspect most millennials regard it as lame. It remains a favorite of many, including us, who enjoy the period-appropriate musical references and, frankly, Walt's idea of a building full of animatronic birds.

Readers such as this mom of three from Coleman, Michigan, caution that the attraction may frighten some younger kids:

The Tiki Room show was very scary, with a thunder-and-lightning storm and a loud volcano. Can't Disney do anything without scaring young children?

TOURING TIPS Usually not too crowded. We go in the late afternoon, when we appreciate sitting in air-conditioned comfort with our brains in park.

FRONTIERLAND

THIS "LAND" FOLLOWS ADVENTURELAND as you move clockwise around the Magic Kingdom. Frontierland's focus is on 1800s America, with stockade-type structures and pioneer trappings. If you start at Big Thunder Mountain and walk toward The Haunted Mansion in Liberty Square, you'll also be walking back in time: The different rides and buildings represent distinct eras in US history, from the settling of the frontier through the California gold rush to the antebellum South.

Big Thunder Mountain Railroad ★★★★

PRESCHOOL ★★★★ (BA)   GRADE SCHOOL ★★★★½ (MAA)   TEENS ★★★★½ (MAA)
YOUNG ADULTS ★★★★½ (MAA)   OVER 30 ★★★★½ (MAA)   SENIORS ★★★★½ (A)

What it is Western mining–themed roller coaster. Scope and scale Headliner. When to go Before 10 a.m. or in the hour before closing. Comments Must be 40" to ride; Rider Switch option provided (see page 395). Duration of ride About 3½ minutes. Average wait in line per 100 people ahead of you 2½ minutes; assumes 5 trains operating. Loading speed Moderate-fast. ECV/wheelchair access Must transfer to ride vehicle. Participates in Genie+ Yes. Early Theme Park Entry No. Extended Evening Hours Yes.

DESCRIPTION AND COMMENTS Every age group, from grade-schoolers through adults, rates Big Thunder as the best roller coaster in the Magic Kingdom. The idea is that you're on a runaway mine train careening through a gold rush frontier town. Big Thunder contains first-rate examples of Disney creativity: a realistic mining town, colorful caverns, and an earthquake, all humorously animated with swinging possums, smart-aleck buzzards, and the like. Ride it after dark if you can. Seats in the back offer the best experience.

In terms of intensity, we put this coaster at about a 5 on a scary scale of 10—it has tight turns rather than big hills or drops, and no loops or upside-down parts. Because it's outdoors and kids can see most of the ride, it's a better introduction to "real" roller coasters for young children than Space Mountain; we'd recommend trying it if your kids enjoyed Seven Dwarfs Mine Train.

TOURING TIPS Nearby **Splash Mountain** (page 477) affects traffic flow to Big Thunder Mountain Railroad—guests who ride one usually ride both. This translates to large crowds in Frontierland all day and long waits for Big Thunder. The best way to experience both rides (at least until Tron Lightcycle Power Run opens) is to ride Seven Dwarfs Mine Train and Space Mountain one morning as soon as the park opens, then Splash Mountain and Big Thunder Mountain the next morning. If you have only one day, the order should be (1) Seven Dwarfs, (2) Big Thunder, (3) Splash Mountain, and (4) Space Mountain.

A Midwestern mom offers this tip to families with kids too short to ride:

If you're rider-swapping on Thunder Mountain or Splash Mountain and have young kids to entertain, there's a fantastic little playground nearby where you can pass the time. It's completely covered and near the restrooms too! It's next to Splash Mountain, under the train tracks.

Guests experience Disney attractions differently. Consider this letter from a woman in Brookline, Massachusetts:

Being older and having limited time, my friend and I confined our activities to attractions rated as four or five stars for seniors. Because of your recommendation, we waited an hour to board Big Thunder Mountain Railroad, which you rated a 5 on a scary scale of 10. After living through 3½ minutes of pure terror, I will rate it a 15. We were so busy holding on and screaming and even praying for our safety that we didn't see any falling rocks, a mining town, or an earthquake.

A Vermont woman feels there's more to consider about Big Thunder than being scared:

Big Thunder Mountain Railroad rates high on the lose-your-lunch meter. One more sharp turn and the kids in front of me would've needed a dip in Splash Mountain!

Country Bear Jamboree ★★★½

**PRESCHOOL ★★★★ (BA) GRADE SCHOOL ★★★½ (MBA) TEENS ★★★ (MBA)
YOUNG ADULTS ★★★½ (MBA) OVER 30 ★★★½ (MBA) SENIORS ★★★★ (BA)**

What it is Corny Audio-Animatronic hoedown. **Scope and scale** Minor attraction. **When to go** Anytime. **Duration of presentation** 11 minutes. **Preshow entertainment** None. **Probable waiting time** Not terribly popular but has a comparatively small capacity. Waiting time between noon and 5:30 p.m. on a busy day will average 11–22 minutes. **ECV/wheelchair access** May remain in wheelchair. **Participates in Genie+** No. **Early Theme Park Entry** No. **Extended Evening Hours** Yes.

DESCRIPTION AND COMMENTS A charming cast of animatronic bears sings and stomps through a series of country and Western songs. On the plus side, it's an air-conditioned refuge on hot days, and the remix of "The Ballad of Davy Crockett" and "Ole Slew Foot" is genius. However, the *Jamboree* has run for so long that the geriatric bears are a step away from assisted living.

Reader comments tend to echo a desire for something new. From a Sandy Hook, Connecticut, mom:

I know they consider it a classic, and kids always seem to love it, but could they PLEASE update it after half a century?

A woman from Carmel, Indiana, put her experience in succinct perspective:

Here is a half-hour of my life that I can never get back.

But a Mississippi dad defends the show:

In my 30s I considered Country Bear Jamboree *hokey and lame, yet I thoroughly enjoyed my daughter's intense love of it at ages 3 and 8 on previous trips. This time, at age 54, I sat up fairly close with my wife and loved it—we even sang along! Of course, this was partly to embarrass my now-16-year-old daughter, who sat hunched down in the very last row. She says we have creeping senility, but I told her, "Just wait till you bring your kids!"*

TOURING TIPS On hot and rainy days and during peak seasons, the *Jamboree* draws large crowds from midmorning on.

Frontierland Shootin' Arcade *(closed at press time)* ★½

**PRESCHOOL ★★★½ (MBA) GRADE SCHOOL ★★★★ (BA) TEENS ★★★★ (BA)
YOUNG ADULTS ★★★½ (BA) OVER 30 ★★★½ (MBA) SENIORS ★★★ (BA)**

What it is Electronic shooting gallery. **Scope and scale** Diversion. **When to go** Anytime. **Comment** Costs $1 per play. **ECV/wheelchair access** May remain in ECV/wheelchair. **Participates in Genie+** No. **Early Theme Park Entry** No. **Extended Evening Hours** Yes.

DESCRIPTION AND COMMENTS One of a few attractions not included in your Magic Kingdom admission. Would-be gunslingers get around 35 shots per $1 play. Each shot is followed by a short delay before the next shot can be taken—this prevents small children from accidentally using all 35 shots in 5 seconds. Despite the arcade's low overall rating, many *Unofficial Guide* staff gladly spend a few bucks here when they visit the World. It's a small bit of you're-in-control interactivity in a park with a lot of sitting and watching.

TOURING TIPS Skip it if time is tight. The fun is entirely in the shootin'—no prizes can be won.

Splash Mountain ★★★★★

PRESCHOOL ★★★★* (BA)   GRADE SCHOOL ★★★★½ (MAA)   TEENS ★★★★½ (MAA)
YOUNG ADULTS ★★★★½ (MAA)   OVER 30 ★★★★½ (MAA)   SENIORS ★★★★½ (MAA)

Many preschoolers are too short to ride; others freak out when they see it from the waiting line. Among preschoolers who actually ride, however, most love it.

What it is Indoor-outdoor water-flume adventure. **Scope and scale** Super-headliner. **When to go** During warm weather: as soon as the park opens, during afternoon or evening parades, just before closing, or use Genie+. **Comments** Must be 40" to ride; Rider Switch option provided (see page 395). **Duration of ride** About 10 minutes. **Average wait in line per 100 people ahead of you** 3½ minutes; assumes ride is operating at full capacity. **Loading speed** Moderate. **ECV/wheelchair access** Must transfer to ride vehicle; transfer device available. **Participates in Genie+** Yes. **Early Theme Park Entry** No. **Extended Evening Hours** Yes.

DESCRIPTION AND COMMENTS Splash Mountain tells the story of Br'er Rabbit, who goes off in search of adventure and finds it . . . along with a hungry fox and bear. Steep slides and animatronics alternate with at least one special effect for each of the senses. The ride covers more than half a mile, splashing through swamps, caves, and bayous before climaxing in a five-story plunge and Br'er Rabbit's triumphant return home. More than 100 animatronic characters, including Br'er Rabbit, Br'er Bear, and Br'er Fox, regale riders with songs, including "Zip-a-Dee-Doo-Dah."

Disney will close Splash Mountain at some point in the near future to retheme the ride to the Disney movie *The Princess and the Frog.* No timeline has been announced.

TOURING TIPS This happy, adventuresome ride is one of the Magic Kingdom's most popular attractions. Crowds build faster the second hour the park is open, and waits of more than 2 hours can be expected once the park fills on busy, warm days. Get in line no later than 10:30 a.m. during warmer months. Long lines will persist all day.

If you have only a day to see the Magic Kingdom and you're eligible for Early Theme Park Entry, ride Tron Lightcycle Power Run as soon as the park opens, then hotfoot it to Frontierland to ride Big Thunder Mountain and Splash Mountain. Wait until evening to experience Space Mountain, and until the last hour the park is open to get in line for Seven Dwarfs Mine Train. If you're not eligible for Early Theme Park Entry, start with Big Thunder Mountain and Splash Mountain as soon as you're admitted into the park—crowds will not have peaked yet. Fit in Seven Dwarfs Mine Train during lunch, dinner, or any parades. Save Tron and Space Mountain for after dinner.

If you have two mornings, start with the Fantasyland and Frontierland attractions—Seven Dwarfs Mine Train, Big Thunder Mountain Railroad, and Splash Mountain—on one day, and then do Tron Lightcycle Power Run and Space Mountain the next. Spreading your visits over two mornings eliminates a lot of walking.

If you ride in the front seat, you'll almost certainly get wet; riders elsewhere get at least splashed. Since you don't know which seat you'll be assigned, go prepared. On a cool day, carry a plastic garbage bag and tear holes in the bottom and sides to make a water-resistant (not waterproof) sack dress (tuck the bag under your bum). Or store a change of clothes, including footwear, in one of the park's rental lockers.

Leave your camera or phone with a nonriding member of your group, or wrap it in plastic. For any attraction where there's a distinct possibility of getting soaked, wear Tevas or some other type of waterproof sandal, and change back to regular shoes after the ride.

The scariest part of this adventure ride is the steep chute you see when standing in line. The drop looks worse than it is; nonetheless, many children freak out when they see it. A mom from Grand Rapids, Michigan, recalls her kids' rather unique reaction:

We discovered after the fact that our children thought they would go under water after the big drop, so they tried to hold their breath throughout the ride in preparation. They were too preoccupied with that to enjoy the clever story.

Tom Sawyer Island and Fort Langhorn   ★★★

PRESCHOOL ★★★★ (A)   GRADE SCHOOL ★★★★ (A)   TEENS ★★★½ (BA)
YOUNG ADULTS ★★★½ (MBA)   OVER 30 ★★★½ (MBA)   SENIORS ★★★½ (MBA)

What it is Outdoor walk-through exhibit and rustic playground. **Scope and scale** Minor attraction. **When to go** Midmorning–late afternoon. **Comments** Closes at dusk. Great for rambunctious kids. **ECV/wheelchair access** Must be ambulatory. **Participates in Genie+** No. **Early Theme Park Entry** No. **Extended Evening Hours** No.

DESCRIPTION AND COMMENTS Tom Sawyer Island is a getaway within the park. It has hills to climb; a cave, windmill, and pioneer stockade (Fort Langhorn) to explore; a tipsy barrel bridge to cross; and paths to follow. You can watch riverboats chug past. It's a delight for adults and a godsend for children who want to cut loose after being closely supervised all day. Fort Langhorn remained closed at press time, but the rest of the island was open.

TOURING TIPS Tom Sawyer Island is underrated—we think it's one of the Magic Kingdom's better-conceived attractions. Kids revel in its frontier atmosphere, and it's a must for families with children ages 5-15. If your group is made up of adults, visit on your second day or on your first day after you've seen the attractions you most wanted to see.

Although kids could spend a whole day here, plan on at least 40 minutes. Access is by raft from Frontierland; two rafts operate simultaneously, and while the trip itself is pretty efficient, you may have to stand in line to board both ways.

A St. Clair Shores, Michigan, family made an unplanned visit:

My 5-year-old son needed to run off some energy, so we veered from the touring plan and took the raft to Tom Sawyer Island. I thought it was a playground (we never bothered to head there before), but it was the coolest area to explore for our whole family! Very few people were there, which meant I got amazing pictures of my kids without strangers in the background, and the buildings, tunnels, and fort were so fun to explore! My kids asked to go back here the next day, and we did!

Walt Disney World Railroad

DESCRIPTION AND COMMENTS Stops in Frontierland on its circuit of the park. See the description under Main Street, U.S.A. (page 470), for additional details.

TOURING TIPS Pleasant, feet-saving link to Main Street and Fantasyland, but the Frontierland station is more congested than those stations.

⚫ LIBERTY SQUARE

LIBERTY SQUARE re-creates the United States at the time of the Revolutionary War. The architecture is Federal and Colonial. The **Liberty Tree,** a live oak more than 150 years old, lends dignity and grace to the patriotic setting.

The Hall of Presidents ★★★

PRESCHOOL ★★ (MBA)	**GRADE SCHOOL** ★★★ (MBA)	**TEENS** ★★★½ (MBA)
YOUNG ADULTS ★★★½ (MBA)	**OVER 30** ★★★★ (A)	**SENIORS** ★★★★½ (MAA)

This is the lowest-rated Magic Kingdom attraction among preschoolers, grade-schoolers, and teens.

What it is Audio-Animatronic historical theater presentation. **Scope and scale** Minor attraction. **When to go** Anytime. **Duration of presentation** Almost 23 minutes. **Preshow entertainment** None. **Probable waiting time** About 15 minutes. It would be exceptionally unusual not to be admitted to the next show. **ECV/wheelchair access** May remain in wheelchair. **Participates in Genie+** No. **Early Theme Park Entry** No. **Extended Evening Hours** No.

DESCRIPTION AND COMMENTS *The Hall of Presidents* combines a wide-screen theater presentation of key highlights and milestones in the political history of the United States with a short stage show featuring life-size animatronic replicas of every US president. The figures' physical resemblances and costumes are masterful.

    In addition to Abraham Lincoln and George Washington, all presidents since Teddy Roosevelt (except George H. W. Bush) have small speaking roles in the show, either in the film or onstage. Regardless of who speaks, the inspirational, patriotic tone is a constant. For that reason, foreign visitors rate the show lower than Americans do.

    We've always had a high opinion of *The Hall of Presidents.* We also receive a lot of comments from readers who get more than entertainment from it. A young mother in Marion, Ohio, advises:

The Hall of Presidents *is a great place to breast-feed!*

    And a woman in St. Louis writes:

We always go when my husband gets cranky so he can take a nice nap.

TOURING TIPS The *Hall's* latest addition is President Joseph R. Biden, who recites the oath of office. Over the last decade or so, it's become common-place for some members of the audience to cheer or jeer, according to their political affiliation, as the current president and his contemporaries are named. These partisan displays are divisive and not in keeping with the show's positive message, but they aren't likely to go away—so skip *The Hall of Presidents* if you'd rather not be reminded of politics on vacation.

The Haunted Mansion ★★★★½

PRESCHOOL ★★★ (MBA)	**GRADE SCHOOL** ★★★★ (MBA)	**TEENS** ★★★★½ (MAA)
YOUNG ADULTS ★★★★½ (MAA)	**OVER 30** ★★★★½ (MAA)	**SENIORS** ★★★★½ (MAA)

What it is Haunted-house dark ride. **Scope and scale** Major attraction. **When to go** Before 11 a.m. or during the last 2 hours before closing. **Comment** Frightens some very young children. **Duration of ride** 7-minute ride plus a 1½-minute preshow. **Average wait**

in line per 100 people ahead of you 2½ minutes; assumes both "stretch rooms" operating. **Loading speed** Fast. **ECV/wheelchair access** Must transfer to ride vehicle. **Participates in Genie+** Yes. **Early Theme Park Entry** No. **Extended Evening Hours** Yes.

DESCRIPTION AND COMMENTS Only slightly scarier than a whoopee cushion, The Haunted Mansion—which opened with the rest of Walt Disney World in 1971—proves that top-notch special effects don't always require 21st-century technology. "Doom Buggies" on a conveyor belt transport you through the house from parlor to attic, then through a graveyard. The effects change tone with the setting: Those found in the house are generally spooky, while the graveyard effects, such as a ghostly opera singer wearing a Viking helmet, are for laughs. Some kids get anxious about what they think they'll see, but almost nobody actually gets scared.

Eve Zibart, a veteran journalist and the author of several Unofficial Guides, ranks The Haunted Mansion as one of her favorite Disney attractions:

This is one of the best attractions in the Magic Kingdom, jam-packed with visual puns, special effects, hidden Mickeys, and lovely Victorian-spooky sets. It's not scary except in the sweetest of ways, and it will remind you of the days before ghost stories gave way to slasher flicks.

A Temple, Texas, mom isn't convinced when we say it isn't scary:

You say the actual sights aren't really frightening—but what isn't frightening about a hanging corpse, a coffin escapee, and an axe-wielding skeleton bride?

A mom from Victoria, British Columbia, wishes that teens would shut their pieholes:

My 4-year-old daughter loved Space Mountain, but The Haunted Mansion really scared her. Our experience was that teenagers deliberately scream and pretend to be scared on this ride. This scares the crap out of the little ones.

Interactive elements in the left side of the outdoor queue ensure that guests have something to occupy them when lines are long. Features include a music-playing monument and a ship captain's tomb that squirts water.

TOURING TIPS Lines here ebb and flow more than those at most other Magic Kingdom hot spots because the Mansion is near *The Hall of Presidents* and the *Liberty Belle* Riverboat. These two attractions disgorge hundreds of guests when each show or ride ends, and many of these folks head straight for the Mansion. If you can't go before 11:30 a.m. or in the last 2 hours the park is open, try to slip in around dinner.

When admitted to the Mansion, you'll first enter a foyer with a fireplace, then be guided quickly into a second preshow room with wood paneling, and four paintings above you. Keeping close to the wall, find the wall panel with a small, red light at about eye level, and stand with your back to that panel while you watch the preshow.

Liberty Belle Riverboat ★★½

PRESCHOOL ★★★½ (BA)	GRADE SCHOOL ★★★½ (BA)	TEENS ★★★ (BA)
YOUNG ADULTS ★★★½ (BA)	OVER 30 ★★★½ (MBA)	SENIORS ★★★★ (A)

What it is Scenic boat ride. **Scope and scale** Minor attraction. **When to go** Anytime. **Duration of ride** About 16 minutes. **Average wait to board** 10–14 minutes. **ECV/wheelchair access** May remain in ECV/wheelchair. **Participates in Genie+** No. **Early Theme Park Entry** No. **Extended Evening Hours** No.

DESCRIPTION AND COMMENTS This large paddle-wheel riverboat navigates the waters around Tom Sawyer Island and Fort Langhorn, passing settler cabins, old mining paraphernalia, an Indian village, and a small menagerie of animatronic wildlife. A beautiful craft, the *Liberty Belle* provides a lofty perspective of Frontierland and Liberty Square.

TOURING TIPS The riverboat, which departs roughly every half-hour, is a good attraction for the busy middle of the day. If you encounter huge crowds, chances are that the attraction has been inundated by guests coming from a just-concluded performance of *The Hall of Presidents*. If it's hot outside, find a spot in the shade on the bottom deck.

FANTASYLAND

FANTASYLAND IS THE ENCHANTED HEART of the Magic Kingdom, spread gracefully like a miniature Alpine village beneath the steepled towers of **Cinderella Castle.**

Fantasyland is divided into three distinct sections. Directly behind Cinderella Castle and set upon a snowcapped mountain is **Beast's Castle,** part of a *Beauty and the Beast*–themed area. Most of this section holds dining and shopping, such as **Be Our Guest Restaurant** (reviewed in Part Six); **Gaston's Tavern,** a small quick-service restaurant; and a gift shop. The far-right corner of Fantasyland—including **Dumbo, The Barnstormer** kiddie coaster, and the Fantasyland train station—is called **Storybook Circus** as an homage to Disney's *Dumbo* films. A covered seating area with plush chairs, electrical outlets, and USB phone chargers is located behind **Big Top Souvenirs.**

The middle of Fantasyland holds the headliner, **Seven Dwarfs Mine Train,** and a secondary attraction, **Under the Sea: Journey of the Little Mermaid.** The placement of these two attractions allows good traffic flow either to the left (toward Beast's Castle) for dining, to the right for attractions geared to smaller children, or back to the original part of Fantasyland for Disney classics such as **Peter Pan's Flight** and **The Many Adventures of Winnie the Pooh.**

The original section, behind Cinderella Castle, holds an antique carousel, *Mickey's PhilharMagic,* and the popular **Princess Fairytale Hall** meet and greet (closed at press time).

Finally, when nature calls, don't miss the *Tangled*-**themed restrooms and outdoor seating,** near Peter Pan's Flight.

Ariel's Grotto *(closed at press time)* ★★★

PRESCHOOL ★★★★½ (MAA)   GRADE SCHOOL ★★★★½ (MAA)   TEENS ★★★½ (BA)
YOUNG ADULTS ★★★★ (A)   OVER 30 ★★★★ (MBA)   SENIORS ★★★½ (BA)

What it is Character-greeting venue. **Scope and scale** Minor attraction. **When to go** Before 10:30 a.m. or during the last 2 hours before closing. **Duration of experience** About 30-90 seconds. **Probable waiting time** 45 minutes. **Queue speed** Slow. **ECV/ wheelchair access** May remain in wheelchair. **Participates in Genie+** No. **Early Theme Park Entry** No. **Extended Evening Hours** No.

DESCRIPTION AND COMMENTS This is Ariel's home turf, next to her signature ride (see page 489). In the base of the seaside cliffs under Prince Eric's Castle, Ariel greets guests from a seashell throne.

An older couple from San Antonio didn't find what they were expecting at the Grotto:

The description on the park map reads, "Visit Ariel and all her treasures," which led us to believe it was some sort of walk-through gallery. Curious, we were ushered into Ariel's Treasure Room. Imagine our surprise when we saw a young woman dressed only in a clamshell bra and a fish tail. When we told her we weren't interested in a photo opportunity—I could just imagine having a picture of a scantily clad woman on my desk—she looked hurt and said, "You don't want a picture of me?"

TOURING TIPS The Grotto may close an hour before the rest of the park. The greeting area is set up almost as if to encourage guests to linger on purpose, which keeps the line long. The queue isn't air-conditioned.

The Barnstormer ★★

PRESCHOOL ★★★★½ (AA)	GRADE SCHOOL ★★★★ (MBA)	TEENS ★★★ (MBA)
YOUNG ADULTS ★★★ (MBA)	OVER 30 ★★★ (MBA)	SENIORS ★★★ (MBA)

What it is Small roller coaster. **Scope and scale** Minor attraction. **When to go** Before 11 a.m., during parades, or the last 2 hours before closing. **Comment** Must be 35″ to ride. **Duration of ride** About 53 seconds. **Average wait in line per 100 people ahead of you** 7 minutes. **Loading speed** Slow. **ECV/wheelchair access** Must transfer to ride vehicle. **Participates in Genie+** Yes. **Early Theme Park Entry** Yes. **Extended Evening Hours** Yes.

DESCRIPTION AND COMMENTS The Barnstormer is a dinky little coaster with a brief but zippy ride. Of the 53 seconds the ride is in motion, 32 seconds are consumed by leaving the loading area, being ratcheted up the first hill, and braking into the off-loading area. The actual time you spend careering around the track: 21 seconds.

A Westport, Connecticut, reader warns adults that the ride may not be as tame as it looks:

A nightmare that should have gone in your "Eats Adults" section. It looked so innocent—nothing hidden in the dark, over quickly—but it took me hours to stop feeling nauseated.

Though the reader's point is well taken, we think The Barnstormer is a good introduction to roller coasters, one that can help your kids step up to more-adventuresome rides. (**Seven Dwarfs Mine Train** would be the next to try.)

TOURING TIPS The cars are too small for most adults and tend to whiplash taller people. Parties without children should skip this one. Because the ride draws in kids visually and aurally, it subjects families to slow-moving lines. If The Barnstormer is high on your children's hit parade, try to ride within the first 2 hours that Fantasyland is open.

A Cary, North Carolina, mom offers a heads-up for solo parents:

There are some fussy rules for riding The Barnstormer. Each of the ride cars holds only two people, and every child under 7 must be accompanied by [someone age 14 or older]. That means a single parent can't take two small children on the ride alone—you either need to rustle up another adult [or older child] to help or skip it entirely.

Casey Jr. Splash 'N' Soak Station *(closed at press time)* ★★★

PRESCHOOL ★★★★½ (MAA)	GRADE SCHOOL ★★★★ (AA)	TEENS ★★½ (MBA)
YOUNG ADULTS ★★½ (MBA)	OVER 30 ★★★ (MBA)	SENIORS ★★½ (BA)

What it is Elaborate water-play area. **Scope and scale** Diversion. **When to go** When it's hot. **ECV/wheelchair access** May remain in wheelchair. **Participates in Genie+** No. **Early Theme Park Entry** No. **Extended Evening Hours** No.

DESCRIPTION AND COMMENTS Casey Jr., the circus train from *Dumbo,* plays host to an absolutely drenching experience outside the Fantasyland Train Station in the Storybook Circus area. A cadre of captive circus beasts sprays water on kids and hapless parents.

TOURING TIPS Puts all other theme park splash areas to soaking shame—bring a change of clothes and a big towel. It doesn't run during cooler weather.

Dumbo the Flying Elephant ★★½

PRESCHOOL ★★★★½ (MAA)   GRADE SCHOOL ★★★★ (MBA)   TEENS ★★★ (MBA)
YOUNG ADULTS ★★★ (MBA)   OVER 30 ★★★½ (MBA)   SENIORS ★★★½ (BA)

What it is Disneyfied midway ride. **Scope and scale** Minor attraction. **When to go** Before 11 a.m. or after 6 p.m. **Duration of ride** 1½ minutes. **Average wait in line per 100 people ahead of you** 10 minutes. **Loading speed** Slow. **ECV/wheelchair access** Must transfer to ride vehicle. **Participates in Genie+** Yes. **Early Theme Park Entry** No. **Extended Evening Hours** No.

DESCRIPTION AND COMMENTS A sweet, happy children's ride based on the lovable flying pachyderm. Parents and kids sit in small fiberglass elephants mounted on long metal arms, which spin around a central axis. Controls inside each vehicle allow you to raise the arm, making you spin higher off the ground. Despite being little different from rides at state fairs and carnivals in parking lots, Dumbo is the favorite Magic Kingdom attraction of many younger children.

Wait times average less than 30 minutes. A covered queue offers interactive elements that your kids can play with to pass the time in line. (Closed during the early days of the pandemic, it reopened in summer 2021.) This Glenelg, Maryland, mother of two preschoolers is a fan:

The Dumbo waiting area is fantastic for young kids. That's right—what my kids look forward to most is not the actual Dumbo ride but the playground that Disney created as the waiting area.

TOURING TIPS If Dumbo is essential to your child's happiness, ride after dinner; not only are the crowds smaller at night, but the lighting and effects make the ride much prettier then. Or you can try to ride following the afternoon parade, if it's performed.

If you want to ride twice with a minimal wait, have two adults get in line on the same side of Dumbo, and allow between 32 and 64 people to get between the first adult and child and the second adult. Pass the child to the second adult when the first ride is over.

Enchanted Tales with Belle (closed at press time) ★★★★

PRESCHOOL ★★★★½ (MAA)   GRADE SCHOOL ★★★★½ (AA)   TEENS ★★★ (MBA)
YOUNG ADULTS ★★★½ (MBA)   OVER 30 ★★★★ (MBA)   SENIORS ★★★★ (BA)

What it is Interactive live character show. **Scope and scale** Minor attraction. **When to go** As soon as the park opens or during the last 2 hours before closing. **Duration of presentation** Approximately 20 minutes. **Preshow entertainment** A walk through Maurice's cottage and workshop. **Probable waiting time** 30 minutes. **Queue speed** Slow. **ECV/wheelchair access** Must transfer from ECV to provided wheelchair. **Participates in Genie+** Yes. **Early Theme Park Entry** No. **Extended Evening Hours** No.

DESCRIPTION AND COMMENTS This multiscene *Beauty and the Beast* experience begins in the cottage and workshop of Belle's father, Maurice, which is filled with odd gadgets, mementos from his daughter's younger days, and a magic mirror.

Soon enough, the room gets dark and the mirror begins to sparkle. With magic and some really good carpentry skills, the mirror turns into a full-size doorway, through which guests enter into a wardrobe room. Once in the wardrobe room, the attraction's premise is explained: You're supposed to reenact the story of *Beauty and the Beast* for Belle on her birthday, and guests are chosen to act out key parts in the play.

Once the parts are cast, everyone walks into the castle's library and takes a seat. Cast members explain how the play will take place and introduce Belle, who gives a short speech about how thrilled she is for everyone to be there. The play is acted out within a few minutes, and all of the actors get a chance to take photos with Belle and receive a small bookmark as a memento.

During our visits, only guests who were chosen to act in the play got to take photos with Belle. Those so chosen received a separate Memory Maker card for their photos.

Enchanted Tales with Belle is surely the prettiest and most elaborate meet-and-greet station in Walt Disney World. For the relative few who get to act in the play, it's also a chance to interact with Belle in a way that isn't possible in other character encounters. Sure, you may have a 30-minute wait for a 20-minute play, but it's the best thing of its kind in Orlando—your kids will love it.

An enthusiastic review from an Austin, Texas, mom:

Enchanted Tales with Belle surprised us with how well it was done. My husband was a knight, my daughter was Mrs. Potts, and my son was silverware. It was so much fun, and the kids were so proud.

TOURING TIPS Because the line moves slowly, see *Enchanted Tales* early in the morning or try to visit during the last 2 hours the park is open.

It's a Small World ★★★½

PRESCHOOL ★★★½ (MAA)   GRADE SCHOOL ★★★★ (MBA)   TEENS ★★★ (MBA)
YOUNG ADULTS ★★★½ (MBA)   OVER 30 ★★★½ (MBA)   SENIORS ★★★★ (BA)

What it is World brotherhood-themed indoor boat ride. **Scope and scale** Major attraction. **When to go** Before 11 a.m. or after 7 p.m. **Duration of ride** About 11 minutes. **Average wait in line per 100 people ahead of you** 3½ minutes; assumes busy conditions with 30 or more boats operating. **Loading speed** Fast. **ECV/wheelchair access** Must transfer from ECV to provided wheelchair. **Participates in Genie+** Yes. **Early Theme Park Entry** Yes. **Extended Evening Hours** Yes.

DESCRIPTION AND COMMENTS Happy and upbeat to an almost unsettling degree, It's a Small World is guaranteed *not* to leave you asking, "How'd that song go again?" Small boats carry you on a tour around the world, with singing and dancing dolls showcasing the dress and culture of each nation represented. One of Disney's oldest entertainment offerings, Small World first unleashed its mind-numbing theme song and lethal cuteness on the big world at the 1964 New York World's Fair; the original exhibit was moved to Disneyland after the fair, and a duplicate was created for Walt Disney World when it opened in 1971.

Though it bludgeons you with its sappy redundancy, almost everyone enjoys It's a Small World—the first time, anyway. It stands, however, with *Enchanted Tiki Room,* and *Country Bear Jamboree* as monuments to an earlier age of entertainment.

A reader from Campbellton, New Brunswick, offers these handy tips for coping with the maddening repetition of the theme song:

If, like me, you can't stand It's a Small World but get dragged on anyway, (1) ask to sit at the back of the boat, then (2) once you're in the building, pull out your iPhone and headphones and blast some heavy metal. You'd be amazed at how different and deceptively funny the ride becomes!

TOURING TIPS Cool off here when it's hot. During the pandemic, lines extend outside into Fantasyland and are largely without shade. Try to visit early in the morning or after the sun starts to set. If you wear a hearing aid, *turn it off.*

Mad Tea Party ★★

PRESCHOOL ★★★½ (MAA)   **GRADE SCHOOL** ★★★½ (AA)   **TEENS** ★★★ (AA)
YOUNG ADULTS ★★★ (BA)   **OVER 30** ★★★½ (MBA)   **SENIORS** ★★★ (MBA)

What it is Midway-style spinning ride. **Scope and scale** Minor attraction. **When to go** Before 11 a.m. or after 5 p.m. **Comment** The teacup spins faster when you turn the wheel in the center. We're not sure if that's a good thing or not. **Duration of ride** 1½ minutes. **Average wait in line per 100 people ahead of you** 7½ minutes. **Loading speed** Slow. **ECV/wheelchair access** Must transfer to ride vehicle; transfer device available. **Participates in Genie+** Yes. **Early Theme Park Entry** Yes. **Extended Evening Hours** Yes.

DESCRIPTION AND COMMENTS Riders whirl feverishly in big teacups. *Alice in Wonderland*'s Mad Hatter provides the theme. Teens like to lure adults onto the teacups and then turn the wheel in the middle—making the cup spin faster—until the adults are plastered helplessly against the sides and on the verge of tossing their tacos. Don't even *consider* getting on this thing with any person younger than 21. Against our better judgment, here's a tip from a reader we've dubbed Melba the Human Centrifuge:

If you want to spin your teacup, don't put more than three people in one cup.

TOURING TIPS Mad Tea Party is notoriously slow-loading. Ride on the morning of your second day if your schedule is more relaxed.

The Many Adventures of Winnie the Pooh ★★★½

PRESCHOOL ★★★★½ (MAA)   **GRADE SCHOOL** ★★★★ (MBA)   **TEENS** ★★★½ (MBA)
YOUNG ADULTS ★★★½ (MBA)   **OVER 30** ★★★½ (MBA)   **SENIORS** ★★★★ (MBA)

What it is Indoor track ride. **Scope and scale** Minor attraction. **When to go** Before 10 a.m. or in last hour park is open. **Duration of ride** About 4 minutes. **Average wait in line per 100 people ahead of you** 4 minutes. **Loading speed** Moderate. **ECV/wheelchair access** Must transfer from ECV to provided wheelchair. **Participates in Genie+** Yes. **Early Theme Park Entry** Yes. **Extended Evening Hours** Yes.

DESCRIPTION AND COMMENTS Ride a Hunny Pot through the pages of a huge picture book into the Hundred Acre Wood, where you encounter Pooh, Piglet, Eeyore, Owl, Rabbit, Tigger, Kanga, and Roo as they contend with a blustery day. There's even a dream sequence with Heffalumps and Woozles.

A 30-something couple from Lexington, Massachusetts, thinks Pooh has plenty to offer adults:

The attention to detail and special effects make it worth seeing even if you don't have children in your party. The Pooh dream sequence was great!

A Richmond, Indiana, mom loved Pooh's interactive queue:

The queue for The Many Adventures of Winnie the Pooh was amazing! There were so many things for little kids to do, and consequently fewer meltdowns! I wish there were more queues like that.

TOURING TIPS Sunny, happy, and upbeat, Pooh is a good choice if you have small children and you're touring over two or more days.

Meet Merida at Fairytale Gardens
(closed at press time) ★★★½

PRESCHOOL ★★★★½ (MAA)   **GRADE SCHOOL** ★★★★ (A)   **TEENS** ★★★½ (MBA)
YOUNG ADULTS ★★★½ (MBA)   **OVER 30** ★★★½ (MBA)   **SENIORS** ★★★★ (A)

What it is Storytelling session plus character meet and greet. **Scope and scale** Diversion. **When to go** Check *Times Guide* for schedule. **Duration of presentation** About 10 minutes. **Probable waiting time** 30 minutes. **Queue speed** Slow. **ECV/wheelchair access** May remain in wheelchair. **Participates in Genie+** No. **Early Theme Park Entry** No. **Extended Evening Hours** No.

DESCRIPTION AND COMMENTS Merida, the flame-haired Scottish princess from *Brave,* greets guests in Fairytale Gardens, in front of Cinderella Castle on the Tomorrowland side, between the castle and Cosmic Ray's Starlight Cafe.

A mom from Shelby, North Carolina, saw red here and liked it:

Many of the princesses give red-lipstick kisses, which delighted both of my children!

TOURING TIPS Princess meet and greets tend to be exceedingly popular, so expect long lines. If meeting Merida is a must-do, get in line about 15 minutes before the next performance.

Mickey's PhilharMagic ★★★★

| PRESCHOOL ★★★★ (A) | GRADE SCHOOL ★★★★½ (AA) | TEENS ★★★★ (A) |
| YOUNG ADULTS ★★★★ (A) | OVER 30 ★★★★ (A) | SENIORS ★★★★½ (AA) |

What it is 3-D movie. **Scope and scale** Major attraction. **When to go** Anytime. **Duration of presentation** About 12 minutes. **Probable waiting time** 20–30 minutes. **ECV/wheelchair access** May remain in wheelchair. **Participates in Genie+** Yes. **Early Theme Park Entry** Yes. **Extended Evening Hours** Yes.

DESCRIPTION AND COMMENTS *Mickey's PhilharMagic* is a 3-D film with an odd collection of Disney characters, mixing Mickey and Donald with Simba and Ariel as well as Jasmine and Aladdin. Presented in a theater large enough to accommodate a 150-foot-wide screen—huge by 3-D standards— the movie is augmented by an arsenal of special effects built into the theater. The plot involves Mickey, as the conductor of the *PhilharMagic,* leaving the theater to solve a mystery. In his absence, Donald attempts to take charge, with disastrous results.

Brilliantly conceived, furiously paced, and laugh-out-loud funny, *Mickey's PhilharMagic* will leave you grinning. And where other Disney 3-D movies are loud, in-your-face affairs, this one is softer and cuddlier. Things pop out of the screen, but they're really not scary. It's the rare child who's frightened—but there are always exceptions, as was the case with the 3-year-old child of this North Carolina mom:

Our family found PhilharMagic way too violent (what seemed like minutes on end of Donald getting the crap kicked out of him by various musical instruments). I had to haul my screaming child out of the theater and submit to a therapeutic carousel ride afterwards.

Happily, an Oregon mom has an easy way to nip the willies in the bud:

My advice to parents is simply to have their kids not wear the 3-D glasses. We took my daughter's off, and she began giggling and having a good time.

TOURING TIPS Provides a nice air-conditioning break during the middle part of the day.

Peter Pan's Flight ★★★★

| PRESCHOOL ★★★★½ (AA) | GRADE SCHOOL ★★★★ (A) | TEENS ★★★½ (MBA) |
| YOUNG ADULTS ★★★★ (MBA) | OVER 30 ★★★★ (A) | SENIORS ★★★★ (A) |

What it is Indoor track ride. **Scope and scale** Minor attraction. **When to go** First or last 30 minutes the park is open. **Duration of ride** A little more than 3 minutes.

Average wait in line per 100 people ahead of you 5½ minutes. **Loading speed** Moderate-slow. **ECV/wheelchair access** Must be ambulatory. **Participates in Genie+** Yes. **Early Theme Park Entry** Yes. **Extended Evening Hours** Yes.

DESCRIPTION AND COMMENTS Peter Pan's Flight is superbly designed and absolutely delightful, combining beloved Disney characters, beautiful effects, and charming music. This indoor ride begins in the Darling family's house before embarking on a relaxing trip in a "flying pirate ship" over old London and thence to Never Land, where Peter saves Wendy from walking the plank and Captain Hook rehearses for *Dancing with the Stars* on the snout of the ubiquitous crocodile. Nothing here will jump out at you or frighten young children.

A themed queue has air-conditioning and features a walk through the Darlings' street and home, where you'll see family portraits and various rooms, play a few games, and get sprinkled with a bit of (virtual) pixie dust.

TOURING TIPS Count on long lines all day. Fortunately, the queue runs under the roof of the building, out of direct sun and rain, and has tons of art and interactive games to help pass the time. Ride in the first 30 minutes the park is open, during a parade, or just before the park closes.

Pete's Silly Sideshow *(closed at press time)* ★★★½

PRESCHOOL ★★★★★ (E)	GRADE SCHOOL ★★★★★ (E)	TEENS ★★★★ (A)
YOUNG ADULTS ★★★★ (A)	OVER 30 ★★★★ (A)	SENIORS ★★★★ (A)

What it is Character-greeting venue. **Scope and scale** Minor attraction. **When to go** Before 11 a.m. or during the last 2 hours before closing. **Duration of experience** 3 minutes per character. **Probable waiting time** Under 30 minutes each side. **Queue speed** Slow. **ECV/wheelchair access** May remain in wheelchair. **Participates in Genie+** Likely upon return. **Early Theme Park Entry** No. **Extended Evening Hours** No.

DESCRIPTION AND COMMENTS Pete's Silly Sideshow is a circus-themed character-greeting area. The characters' costumes are distinct from the ones normally worn around the parks. Characters include Goofy as The Great Goofini, Donald Duck as The Astounding Donaldo, Daisy Duck as Madame Daisy Fortuna, and Minnie Mouse as Minnie Magnifique.

TOURING TIPS When it's open, Pete's opens 1 hour later than the rest of the park and usually closes at the same time as the first evening fireworks show. The queue is indoors and air-conditioned. There's one queue for Goofy and Donald and a second queue for Minnie and Daisy; you can meet two characters at once, but you have to line up twice to meet all four.

Prince Charming Regal Carrousel ★★★

PRESCHOOL ★★★★½ (MAA)	GRADE SCHOOL ★★★★ (BA)	TEENS ★★★ (MBA)
YOUNG ADULTS ★★★ (MBA)	OVER 30 ★★★½ (MBA)	SENIORS ★★★½ (MBA)

What it is Merry-go-round. **Scope and scale** Minor attraction. **When to go** Anytime. **Duration of ride** About 2 minutes. **Average wait in line per 100 people ahead of you** 5 minutes. **Loading speed** Slow. **ECV/wheelchair access** Must transfer from ECV to provided wheelchair. **Participates in Genie+** No. **Early Theme Park Entry** Yes. **Extended Evening Hours** Yes.

DESCRIPTION AND COMMENTS One of the most elaborate and beautiful merry-go-rounds you'll ever have the pleasure of seeing, especially when its lights are on.

TOURING TIPS Unless young children in your party insist on riding, appreciate the carousel from the sidelines—while lovely to look at, it loads and unloads very slowly.

Princess Fairytale Hall *(closed at press time)* ★★★

What it is Character-greeting venue. **Scope and scale** Minor attraction. **When to go** Before 10:30 a.m. or after 4 p.m. **Duration of experience** 7-10 minutes (estimated). **Probable waiting time** Under 50 minutes (estimated). **Queue speed** Slow. **ECV/wheelchair access** May remain in wheelchair. **Participates in Genie+** Likely upon return. **Early Theme Park Entry** No. **Extended Evening Hours** No.

DESCRIPTION AND COMMENTS Fairytale Hall is Princess Central in the Magic Kingdom. Inside are two greeting venues, with each holding a small reception area for two princesses. Thus, there are four princesses meeting and greeting at any time, and you can see two of them at once. Signs outside the entrance tell you which line leads to which princess pair and how long the wait will be. Rapunzel usually leads one side, typically paired with Tiana. Cinderella and Elena of Avalor (a Disney Channel character) are the usual pair on the other.

Around 5-10 guests at a time are admitted to each greeting area, where there's plenty of time for small talk, a photo, and a hug from each princess. Enough time is given to each family, in fact, that we ran out of things to say to Rapunzel before we shuffled quietly along.

TOURING TIPS These lines can be substantial. If your kids love princesses, even the B-list ones, get Fairytale Hall out of the way first thing.

Seven Dwarfs Mine Train ★★★★

What it is Indoor-outdoor roller coaster. **Scope and scale** Headliner. **When to go** As soon as the park opens. **Comment** Must be 38" to ride. **Duration of ride** About 2 minutes. **Average wait in line per 100 people ahead of you** About 4½ minutes. **Loading speed** Fast. **ECV/wheelchair access** Must transfer to ride vehicle. **Participates in Genie+** No. **Early Theme Park Entry** Yes. **Extended Evening Hours** Yes.

DESCRIPTION AND COMMENTS Seven Dwarfs Mine Train lies somewhere between The Barnstormer and Big Thunder Mountain Railroad—that is, it's geared to older grade-school kids who've been on amusement park rides before. There are no loops, inversions, or rolls in the track, and no massive hills or steep drops; rather, your ride vehicle's seats swing side-to-side as you go through turns. And—what a coincidence!—Disney has designed a curvy track with steep turns. An elaborate indoor section shows the Seven Dwarfs' underground mining operation.

The exterior design includes waterfalls, forests, and landscaping and is meant to join together all of the various Fantasyland locations surrounding it. The swinging effect is more noticeable the farther back you're seated in the train.

The Mine Train generates a lot of reader comments. First, from a Rhode Island couple:

We give high marks to Seven Dwarfs Mine Train. It's faster than it looks in videos, and the animatronics are top-notch. Much like Big Thunder and Splash Mountain, this ride is even better at night!

A Chester, Virginia, mom offers a little cost-benefit analysis:

Seven Dwarfs Mine Train was a great ride but not worth a 90-minute wait.

A mom from Horsham, Pennsylvania, felt let down:

Our family's rating is two stars at most. The detail and activities in line were great, and I thought the animation of the characters' faces was amazing. But we were all sadly disappointed in the ride—it's over so quickly that it really isn't worth your time.

A woman from White City, Saskatchewan, was particularly irked:

One-and-a-half hours of my time for one-and-a-half minutes of disappointment.

Finally, from a Philadelphia reader:

The Guide *is correct in calling the Seven Dwarfs Mine Train underwhelming, but we found it was much, much better at night. The lighting and track layout combined to make the ride feel a little faster, and it was generally more enjoyable. I see no reason to ride it in daylight again.*

TOURING TIPS If you have children who might be interested in riding this but not Space Mountain, then head for Seven Dwarfs as soon as the park opens. Try Big Thunder Mountain or Splash Mountain next, depending on how well they do here.

See our Splash Mountain touring tips on page 477 for advice on how to see Seven Dwarfs Mine Train and the Magic Kingdom's other headliners as quickly as possible.

Under the Sea: Journey of the Little Mermaid
★★★½

| PRESCHOOL ★★★★½ (MAA) | GRADE SCHOOL ★★★★ (MBA) | TEENS ★★★½ (MBA) |
| YOUNG ADULTS ★★★½ (MBA) | OVER 30 ★★★★ (MBA) | SENIORS ★★★★ (MBA) |

What it is Dark ride retelling the film's story. **Scope and scale** Major attraction. **When to go** Before 10:30 a.m. or during the last 2 hours before closing. **Duration of ride** About 5½ minutes. **Average wait in line per 100 people ahead of you** 3 minutes. **Loading speed** Fast. **ECV/wheelchair access** Must transfer from ECV to provided wheelchair. **Participates in Genie+** Yes. **Early Theme Park Entry** Yes. **Extended Evening Hours** Yes.

DESCRIPTION AND COMMENTS Under the Sea takes riders through almost a dozen scenes retelling the story of *The Little Mermaid,* with animatronics, video effects, and a vibrant 3-D set the size of a small theater.

Guests board a clamshell-shaped ride vehicle running along a continuously moving track (similar to The Haunted Mansion's). Then the ride "descends under water," past Ariel's grotto and on to King Triton's undersea kingdom. The most detailed animatronic is of Ursula, the octopus, and she's a beauty. Other scenes hit the film's highlights, including Ariel meeting Prince Eric, her deal with Ursula to become human, and, of course, the couple's happy ending.

The attraction's exterior is attractive, with detailed rock work, water, and story elements. Our favorite effect is a "hidden Mickey" created through a special alignment of the sun's shadow and the rock work, and only at noon on November 18, Mickey's birthday.

The ride isn't Disney's most ambitious: Most of the effects throughout the ride are simple and unimaginative, such as starfish that only spin or lobsters that simply turn left and right. Also, virtually the entire second half of the story is condensed into a handful of small scenes crammed together at the end, as if the budget ran out before the ride could be finished properly.

TOURING TIPS Expect moderate waits most of the day. If you can, ride early in the morning or late at night.

Walt Disney World Railroad

DESCRIPTION AND COMMENTS The railroad stops in Fantasyland on its circle tour of the park. The leg from Fantasyland to Main Street, U.S.A., is the most scenic of the entire loop. See the description under Main Street, U.S.A. (page 470), for additional details.

TOURING TIPS Pleasant, feet-saving link to Main Street and Frontierland . . . but so crowded in the afternoon during times of peak attendance that you'll almost certainly find it faster to walk anywhere in the park.

TOMORROWLAND

AT VARIOUS POINTS IN ITS HISTORY, Tomorrowland's attractions presented life's possibilities in adventures ranging from the modern-day (If You Had Wings' round-the-world travel in the 1970s) to the distant future (Mission to Mars). The problem that stymied Disney repeatedly: The future came faster and looked different than they'd envisioned.

Today, Tomorrowland's theme makes the least sense of any area's in any Disney park. Its current attractions are based on gas-powered race cars, rocket travel (two rides), a look back at 20th-century technology, a ride with aliens, a comedy show with monsters, and, with Tron, a motorcycle race inside a computer. It's not so much a vision of the future as it is a collection of attractions that don't fit anywhere else in the park.

A new roller coaster themed to Disney's *Tron* movie franchise is expected to open in 2022. The ride sits mostly behind the Tomorrowland Speedway and outside of the current park boundary; parts of the ride building extend over the WDW Railroad, which will affect railroad operations until very close to Tron's opening.

Astro Orbiter ★★

PRESCHOOL ★★★★ (BA)	GRADE SCHOOL ★★★★ (MBA)	TEENS ★★★ (MBA)
YOUNG ADULTS ★★★ (MBA)	OVER 30 ★★★ (MBA)	SENIORS ★★½ (MBA)

What it is Retro–style rockets revolving around a central axis. **Scope and scale** Minor attraction. **When to go** Before 11 a.m. or in the last hour before closing. **Comment** Not as innocuous as it appears. **Average wait in line per 100 people ahead of you** 13½ minutes. **Loading speed** Slow. **ECV/wheelchair access** Must transfer to ride vehicle. **Participates in Genie+** No. **Early Theme Park Entry** Yes. **Extended Evening Hours** Yes.

DESCRIPTION AND COMMENTS Though visually appealing, the Astro Orbiter is at heart a slow-loading carnival ride: The fat little rocket ships simply fly in circles, albeit circles on a three-story platform above Tomorrowland. The best thing about the Astro Orbiter is the nice view when you're aloft.

TOURING TIPS Expendable on any schedule. If you ride with preschoolers, seat them first. The Astro Orbiter flies higher and faster than Dumbo and frightens some young children. It also apparently messes with some adults. A mother from Lev HaSharon, Israel, writes:

It was a nightmare—I was able to sit through all the "Mountains," the "Tours," and the like without my stomach reacting even a little, but after Astro Orbiter I thought I would be finished for the rest of the day. Very quickly I realized that my only chance for survival was to pick a point on the toe of my shoe and stare at it (and certainly not lift my eyes out of the "jet") until the ride was over. My 4-year-old was my copilot; she loved it (go figure), and she had us up high the whole time.

Buzz Lightyear's Space Ranger Spin ★★★★

**PRESCHOOL ★★★★½ (A)   GRADE SCHOOL ★★★★½ (MAA)   TEENS ★★★★ (MAA)
YOUNG ADULTS ★★★★ (A)   OVER 30 ★★★★ (BA)   SENIORS ★★★★ (A)**

What it is Whimsical space-themed indoor ride. **Scope and scale** Minor attraction.
When to go First or last hour the park is open. **Duration of ride** About 4½ minutes.
Average wait in line per 100 people ahead of you 3 minutes. **Loading speed** Fast. **ECV/
wheelchair access** Must transfer from ECV to provided wheelchair. **Participates in
Genie+** Yes. **Early Theme Park Entry** Yes. **Extended Evening Hours** Yes.

DESCRIPTION AND COMMENTS This indoor attraction is based on the
space-commando character Buzz Lightyear from the *Toy Story* film series;
the marginal story line has you and Buzz trying to save the universe from
the evil Emperor Zurg. You spin your car and shoot simulated laser cannons at Zurg and his minions. The first room's mechanical claw and red
robot contain high-value targets, so aim for these.

TOURING TIPS Each car is equipped with two laser cannons and two score-
keeping displays, enabling you to compete with your riding partner. A joy-
stick allows you to spin the car to line up the various targets. Each time
you pull the trigger, you release a red laser beam that you can see hitting
or missing the target.

   Most folks spend their first ride learning how to use the equipment (fire
off individual shots as opposed to keeping the trigger depressed) and fig-
uring out how the targets work. On the next ride, you'll be surprised by
how much better you do. If you're hopeless at games of skill, check out our
tips at tinyurl.com/buzzfortheunskilled.

   Many *Unofficial* readers praise Buzz Lightyear. Some, in fact, spend
several hours on it, riding again and again. The following comment from a
Snow Hill, Maryland, dad is representative:

*Buzz Lightyear was so much fun it can't be legal! We hit it first on early-entry
day and rode it 10 times without stopping. The kids had fun, but it was Dad
who spun himself silly trying to shoot the Z's.*

   Experience Buzz after riding Space Mountain first thing in the morning
or in the last hour the park is open.

Monsters, Inc. Laugh Floor ★★★

**PRESCHOOL ★★★★ (MBA)   GRADE SCHOOL ★★★★ (AA)   TEENS ★★★★ (AA)
YOUNG ADULTS ★★★★ (AA)   OVER 30 ★★★★ (AA)   SENIORS ★★★★ (A)**

What it is Interactive animated comedy show. **Scope and scale** Major attraction.
When to go Anytime. **Comment** Audience members may be asked to participate in
skits. **Duration of presentation** About 15 minutes. **ECV/wheelchair access** May
remain in wheelchair. **Participates in Genie+** Yes. **Early Theme Park Entry** No.
Extended Evening Hours Yes.

DESCRIPTION AND COMMENTS We learned in Disney-Pixar's *Monsters, Inc.*
that children's screams could be converted to electricity, which was used to
power a town inhabited by monsters. During the film, the monsters discovered
that kids' laughter worked even better as an energy source, so in this attraction they've set up a comedy club to capture as many laughs as possible.

   Mike Wazowski, the one-eyed green monster, emcees the club's three
comedy acts. Each act consists of an animated monster (most aren't seen
in the film) trying out various bad puns and knock-knock jokes. Using technological wizardry, behind-the-scenes Disney employees voice the characters and often interact with audience members during the skits. As with any

comedy show, some performers are funny and some are not, but Disney has shown a willingness to experiment with new routines and jokes.

A Sioux Falls, South Dakota, mom is a big fan:

Laugh Floor was great—it's amazing how the characters interact with the audience. I got picked on twice without trying. Plus, kids can text jokes to Roz.

TOURING TIPS The theater holds several hundred people, so there's no need to rush here first thing in the morning. Try to arrive late in the morning after you've visited other Tomorrowland attractions, or after the afternoon parade when guests start leaving the park.

Space Mountain ★★★★

PRESCHOOL ★★½* (MBA)	GRADE SCHOOL ★★★★½ (MAA)	TEENS ★★★★★ (E)
YOUNG ADULTS ★★★★½ (MAA)	OVER 30 ★★★★½ (MAA)	SENIORS ★★★½ (MBA)

Some preschoolers love Space Mountain; others are terrified by it.

What it is Roller coaster in the dark. **Scope and scale** Super-headliner. **When to go** When the park opens or in the last hour the park is open. **Comments** Great fun—much wilder than Big Thunder Mountain Railroad. Must be 44" to ride; Rider Switch option provided (see page 395). **Duration of ride** Almost 3 minutes. **Average wait in line per 100 people ahead of you** 3 minutes; assumes 2 tracks, dispatching at 21-second intervals. **Loading speed** Moderate–fast. **ECV/wheelchair access** Must transfer from ECV to provided wheelchair and then from wheelchair to ride vehicle. **Participates in Genie+** No (it's a separate Individual Attraction Selection). **Early Theme Park Entry** Yes. **Extended Evening Hours** Yes.

DESCRIPTION AND COMMENTS Totally enclosed in a mammoth futuristic structure, Space Mountain has always been one of the Magic Kingdom's most popular attractions. The theme is a space flight through dark recesses of the galaxy. Effects are superb, and the ride is the fastest and wildest in the Magic Kingdom: much zippier than Big Thunder Mountain Railroad but much tamer than Rock 'n' Roller Coaster at Hollywood Studios or Expedition Everest at Animal Kingdom.

Roller-coaster aficionados will tell you (correctly) that Space Mountain is a designer version of the Wild Mouse, a midway ride that's been around for more than 70 years. There are no long drops or swooping hills as there are on a traditional coaster—only quick, unexpected turns and small drops. Disney's contribution essentially was to add a space theme to the Wild Mouse and put it in the dark.

An Elburn, Illinois, reader recommends bracing yourself—literally:

They should require you to wear a neck brace on Space Mountain. That ride is painful.

TOURING TIPS People who can handle a fairly wild coaster ride will take Space Mountain in stride. What sets Space Mountain apart is that cars plummet through darkness, with only occasional lighting. Half the fun of Space Mountain is not knowing where the car will go next.

Space Mountain is a favorite of many Magic Kingdom visitors ages 7–60. Each morning before opening, particularly during summer and holiday periods, several hundred guests await the signal to head to the ride's entrance. To get ahead of the competition, be one of the first in the park. Proceed to the end of Main Street and wait at the entrance to Tomorrowland. Parents touring with children too small to ride can take advantage of **Rider Switch,** described on page 395. Many of these guests will opt for Tron Lightcycle Power Run first when that ride opens, then visit Space Mountain after.

Seats are one behind another, as opposed to side by side, which means that parents can't sit next to their kids who meet the height requirement but who might get scared.

If you don't catch Space Mountain first thing in the morning, try again during the hour before closing.

Tomorrowland Speedway ★★

PRESCHOOL ★★★★ (A)	GRADE SCHOOL ★★★★ (A)	TEENS ★★★½ (MBA)
YOUNG ADULTS ★★★ (MBA)	OVER 30 ★★★ (MBA)	SENIORS ★★★ (MBA)

What it is Drive-'em-yourself minicars. **Scope and scale** Minor attraction. **When to go** Before 10 a.m. or during the last 2 hours before closing. **Comment** Kids must be 54" tall to drive unassisted, 32" with a person age 14 or older. **Duration of ride** About 4¼ minutes. **Average wait in line per 100 people ahead of you** 4½ minutes; assumes 285-car turnover every 20 minutes. **Loading speed** Slow. **ECV/wheelchair access** Must transfer to ride vehicle; transfer device available. **Participates in Genie+** Yes. **Early Theme Park Entry** Yes. **Extended Evening Hours** Yes.

DESCRIPTION AND COMMENTS An elaborate miniature raceway with gas-powered cars that travel up to 7 mph. The raceway, with its sleek cars and racing noises, is quite alluring. The cars poke along on a guide rail, leaving drivers little to do, but teens and many adults still enjoy it.

TOURING TIPS This ride is visually appealing, and loads of the 9-and-under set love it (adults, not so much). If your child is too short to drive, ride along and allow him or her to steer the car while you work the foot pedal.

A mom from North Billerica, Massachusetts, writes:

I was truly amazed by the number of adults in line—the only reason I could think of for that would be an insane desire to go on absolutely every ride at Disney World. The cars aren't a whole lot of fun, and they tend to pile up at the end, so it takes almost as long to get off as it did to get on.

A dad from Pleasantville, New York, had this to say:

This is one attraction I wish they would replace with something better. It's boring and it smells bad.

The line for the speedway snakes across a pedestrian bridge to the ride's loading areas. Here's a tip for a shorter wait: Turn right off the bridge, and then head to the first loading area rather than continuing to the second one.

Tomorrowland Transit Authority PeopleMover ★★★½

PRESCHOOL ★★★★ (A)	GRADE SCHOOL ★★★★ (BA)	TEENS ★★★★ (A)
YOUNG ADULTS ★★★★ (A)	OVER 30 ★★★★½ (MAA)	SENIORS ★★★★½ (MAA)

What it is Scenic tour of Tomorrowland. **Scope and scale** Minor attraction. **When to go** Anytime, but especially during hot, crowded times of day (11:30 a.m.–4:30 p.m.). **Comment** A good way to check out the line at Space Mountain and the Speedway. **Duration of ride** 10 minutes. **Average wait in line per 100 people ahead of you** 1½ minutes; assumes 39 trains operating. **Loading speed** Fast. **ECV/wheelchair access** Must be ambulatory. **Participates in Genie+** No. **Early Theme Park Entry** Yes. **Extended Evening Hours** Yes.

DESCRIPTION AND COMMENTS Tramlike cars, a once-unique prototype of a linear induction–powered mass-transit system, carry riders on a leisurely tour of Tomorrowland, including a peek inside Space Mountain.

A Delafield, Wisconsin, family offers only the faintest of praise:

Tomorrowland is best at night. With the lights, it turns boring rides like the PeopleMover into something less boring.

TOURING TIPS A relaxing ride where lines move quickly. It's a good choice during busier times of day.

Tron Lightcycle Power Run *(opens 2022)*

What it is Indoor-outdoor roller coaster. **Scope and scale** Super-headliner. **When to go** As soon as the park opens, using Early Theme Park Entry if possible, or the last hour the park is open. **Comment** Estimated 48" minimum height requirement. **Duration of ride** About 2 minutes. **Average wait in line per 100 people ahead of you** About 3½ minutes. **Loading speed** Fast. **ECV/wheelchair access** Must transfer from wheelchair. **Participates in Genie+** No (it's a separate Individual Attraction Selection). **Early Theme Park Entry** Yes. **Extended Evening Hours** Yes.

DESCRIPTION AND COMMENTS Tron Lightcycle Power Run is an elevated, high-speed, indoor-outdoor roller coaster. Riders sit as if on a motorcycle while they rocket past scenes that simulate being inside a computer (and one with neon lighting at that).

Tron's ride vehicles are set up as 14 semidetached light cycles, with seven rows of two cycles each. Riders must lean forward slightly to hold onto the cycle's handlebars. Once seated and out of the ride's loading zone, riders are launched like a catapult into the ride's first set of turns. An impressive set of video effects surrounds the rider through most of the journey.

Tron is most similar to the Rock 'n' Roller Coaster at Hollywood Studios (see page 582), which is also a catapult-launched indoor coaster. Tron is by far the most intense coaster in the Magic Kingdom, although it doesn't have any loops or inversions. If Seven Dwarfs Mine Train, Splash Mountain, or Big Thunder Mountain give you pause, skip Tron.

TOURING TIPS Tron Lightcycle Power Run will be one of the Magic Kingdom's hottest rides once it comes online. Expect hundreds of theme park guests to head straight for it as soon as the park opens. If you're an off-site guest, it's possible that a thousand or more guests will already be in line ahead of you before you arrive at the attraction.

If you're staying on-site, your best bet for riding with minimal waits is to arrive at the Magic Kingdom at least an hour before official opening. As soon as you're admitted into the park for Early Theme Park Entry, head for Tomorrowland and ride Tron. Once you're done, ride Space Mountain nearby if the wait is 15 minutes or less.

If Early Theme Park Entry isn't an option, try Tron in the last hour the park is open, or during lunch or dinner. Expect long waits at almost any time of day.

Walt Disney's Carousel of Progress ★★★

PRESCHOOL ★★★ (MBA)　**GRADE SCHOOL ★★★½** (MBA)　**TEENS ★★★½** (MBA)
YOUNG ADULTS ★★★★ (BA)　**OVER 30 ★★★★** (A)　**SENIORS ★★★★½** (AA)

What it is Audio-Animatronic theater show. **Scope and scale** Major attraction. **When to go** Anytime. **Duration of presentation** 21 minutes. **Preshow entertainment**

Documentary on the attraction's long history. **Probable waiting time** Less than 10 minutes. **ECV/wheelchair access** May remain in wheelchair. **Participates in Genie+** No. **Early Theme Park Entry** Yes. **Extended Evening Hours** No.

DESCRIPTION AND COMMENTS *Walt Disney's Carousel of Progress* is a four-act play offering a nostalgic look at how electricity and technology changed the lives of an animatronic family during the 20th century. General Electric sponsored the first version of the show for the 1964 World's Fair in New York City, in keeping with the fair's theme of progress. The first scene is set around 1900 (our research indicates Thursday, February 14, 1901, on a farm outside Arkansas City, Kansas); the second around 1927; and the third in the late 1940s. The fourth scene is allegedly contemporary, but references to laser discs and car phones are not-so-subtle clues that the script hasn't been updated in over 25 years.

Although the last scene needs updating, *Carousel of Progress* is the only attraction in the park that displays Walt's optimistic vision of a better future through technology and industry. If you're interested in the man behind the mouse, this show is a must-see.

TOURING TIPS *Carousel* handles big crowds effectively and is a good choice during busier times of day. Because of its age, it seems to have more minor operational glitches than most attractions, so you may be subjected to the same dialogue and songs several times. Think of it as extra time in the air-conditioning.

MAGIC KINGDOM ENTERTAINMENT

unofficial **TIP**

Note: If you're short on time, it's impossible to see both Magic Kingdom feature attractions and live performances.

LIVE ENTERTAINMENT

MOST LIVE ENTERTAINMENT was cut during the pandemic. As we went to press, Disney had just reached an agreement with the Actors Equity union regarding vaccinations. We expect many live performances to return, but not all (due to budget cuts). For specific events the day you visit, check the live-entertainment schedule in the My Disney Experience app or in the *Times Guide,* available along with the guide map. Walt Disney World live-entertainment guru Steve Soares usually posts the Magic Kingdom's performance schedule about a week in advance at wdwent.com.

CHARACTER CAVALCADES In lieu of parades since the pandemic started, Disney runs a series of small one- or two-float cavalcades throughout the day, usually starting about an hour after the park opens. The cavalcade route is the same as the parade route: from Frontierland near Splash Mountain, through Liberty Square, then around the central hub and down Main Street, U.S.A. One cavalcade includes Disney princesses; another has Mickey, Minnie, and friends; a third hosts Goofy and his friends; and Tinker Bell gets her own float. Seasonal cavalcades for Halloween and Christmas are also run.

FIREWORKS AND OTHER NIGHTTIME ENTERTAINMENT

LIKE ITS PARADES, the Magic Kingdom's dazzling nighttime spectaculars are highly rated and not to be missed.

BAY LAKE AND SEVEN SEAS LAGOON ELECTRICAL WATER PAGEANT
★★★★ Usually performed at nightfall (8:50 at the Polynesian Village Resort, 9 at the Grand Floridian Resort, and 10:15 at the Contemporary Resort) on Seven Seas Lagoon and Bay Lake, this is one of our favorites among the Disney extras, but you have to leave the Magic Kingdom to view it. The pageant is a stunning electric-light show aboard small barges and set to nifty electronic music. Leave the Magic Kingdom and take the monorail to the Polynesian Village, the Grand Floridian, or the Contemporary.

DISNEY ENCHANTMENT FIREWORKS SHOW (not offered at press time)
Disney has run two nighttime spectaculars over the past decade: a show called *Wishes* and a show called *Happily Ever After.* Both were multisensory shows of fireworks, music, and video projections. Both ranked among the highest-rated attractions in Walt Disney World, across all age groups. It's hard to overstate just how elaborate and impressive these shows are in person. Disney's latest show, which opens on October 1, 2021, is called *Disney Enchantment* and promises even more.

Enchantment will include images projected onto Cinderella Castle, almost certainly with snippets from the usual suspects of *Frozen* and *Cinderella,* as well as scenes from *The Hunchback of Notre Dame; Monsters, Inc.; Cars;* and *Wreck-It Ralph,* among others. New for this show is the extension of projection images down Main Street, U.S.A., allowing more guests to see these fantastic animations.

Enchantment's fireworks can be enjoyed from outside the park, but with the projections so tightly integrated into the performance, be aware that you'll miss a substantial portion of the show if you're not viewing from the Main Street area inside the Magic Kingdom.

TINKER BELL'S FLIGHT
Look for this quintessentially Disney special effect in the sky above Cinderella Castle during *Enchantment* when the park is open late.

Fireworks Cruises and Dessert Parties

FIREWORKS DESSERT PARTY
Disney reserves the **Plaza Gardens** and **Tomorrowland Terrace** restaurant for paid fireworks viewing. Three options are available:

- The **Disney Enchantment Pre-Party** costs $79 per adult and $47 per child and includes all-you-care-to-eat desserts in the Plaza Gardens while you watch the fireworks. This option requires you to stand while watching the show.
- The **Disney Enchantment After-Party** is $99 per adult and $59 per child. Held in the Tomorrowland Terrace, it includes use of the restaurant to view the show, then post-show desserts, wine, and beer.
- **Disney Enchantment Treats & Seats** runs before, during, and after the show inside the Tomorrowland Terrace. It costs $114 per adult and $69 per child.

Reservations can be made 60 days in advance online or by calling ☎ 407-WDW-DINE (939-3463). A St. Louis reader who went to the dessert party pronounced it "meh":

> We did the fireworks dessert party at Tomorrowland Terrace against my better judgment. While the vantage point was pretty good and the desserts were tasty, it was definitely not worth the price.

A less expensive option ($79 adult, $47 ages 3–9) offers only non-alcoholic beverages, and the fireworks viewing area is standing-room only in the Plaza Garden. You must arrive 90 minutes before showtime.

FIREWORKS CRUISE For a different view, you can watch the fireworks from Seven Seas Lagoon aboard a pontoon boat. The cost is $425 (including tax) for up to 10 people. Chips, soda, and water are provided; sandwiches and more-substantial food items may be arranged through reservations. Your Disney captain will take you for a little cruise and then position the boat in a perfect place to watch the fireworks. (A major indirect benefit of the charter is that you can enjoy the fireworks without fighting the mob afterward.)

Because this is a private charter, only your group will be aboard. Life jackets are provided, but wearing them is at your discretion. To reserve a charter, call ☎ 407-WDW-PLAY (939-7529) at exactly 7 a.m. Eastern time about 180 days before the day you want to cruise. Because the Disney reservations system counts days in a somewhat atypical manner, we recommend that you phone about 185 days out to have a Disney agent specify the exact morning to call for reservations.

FERRYTALE FIREWORKS: A SPARKLING DESSERT CRUISE Another option for seeing the evening fireworks at an extra cost. Guests board a ferry at the TTC for desserts, souvenir glasses, and a view of the fireworks. This event includes alcoholic beverages for the adults; unlike the pontoon cruise, it's not a private charter. Pricing is $99 for adults and $69 for children. Reserve at ☎ 407-939-3463 or online at disneyworld.disney.go.com (search for "Ferrytale Fireworks").

VIEWING (AND EXIT) STRATEGIES FOR PARADES AND FIREWORKS

Vantage Points for Parades

> **Note:** *Even though there isn't a regular evening parade right now, the following advice is still generally useful for* Enchantment *and the nighttime parades and fireworks held during special events (see previous section), which follow a similar schedule.*

Magic Kingdom parades circle **Town Square,** head down **Main Street,** go around the **Central Plaza,** and cross the bridge to **Liberty Square.** In Liberty Square, they follow the waterfront and end in Frontierland. Sometimes they begin in Frontierland and run the route in the opposite direction. See the map on pages 460–461.

Because most spectators pack Main Street and the Central Plaza, we recommend watching the parade from **Liberty Square** or **Frontierland** instead. Great vantage points that are frequently overlooked are as follows:

1. **Sleepy Hollow snack-and-beverage shop, immediately to your right as you cross the bridge into Liberty Square.** If you arrive early, buy refreshments and claim a table closest to the rail. You'll have a perfect view of the parade as it crosses Liberty Square Bridge, but only when the parade begins on Main Street.

2. **The pathway on the Liberty Square side of the moat from Sleepy Hollow snack-and-beverage shop to Cinderella Castle.** Any point along the way offers an unobstructed view as the parade crosses Liberty Square Bridge. Once again, this spot works only for parades coming from Main Street.

3. **The covered walkway between Liberty Tree Tavern and the Diamond Horseshoe Saloon.** This elevated vantage point is perfect (particularly on rainy days) and usually goes unnoticed until just before the parade starts.

4. **Elevated platforms in front of the Frontierland Shootin' Arcade, Frontier Trading Post, and the building with the sign reading FRONTIER MERCANTILE.** These spots usually get picked off 10–12 minutes before parade time.

5. **Benches on the perimeter of the Central Plaza, between the entrances to Liberty Square and Adventureland,** offer a comfortable resting place and an unobstructed (though somewhat distant) view of the parade as it crosses Liberty Square Bridge.

6. **Liberty Square and Frontierland dockside areas;** spots here usually go early.

7. **The porch of Tony's Town Square Restaurant,** on Main Street, provides an elevated viewing platform and an easy exit path when the fireworks are over.

Assuming it starts on Main Street (evening parades normally do), the parade takes 16–20 minutes to reach Liberty Square or Frontierland.

On evenings when the parade runs twice, the first draws a huge crowd, siphoning guests from attractions. Many guests leave the park after the early parade, and many more depart following the fireworks (which are scheduled on the hour between the two parades).

Vantage Points for Fireworks

As noted on page 496, the nightly fireworks show includes a dazzling video-projection display on the front of Cinderella Castle and down Main Street, U.S.A. The best viewing spots for the entire presentation are **between the Central Plaza and the castle,** offering up-close views of the castle projections.

The next-best spots are in **Plaza Gardens East and West** nearest the castle. These gardens are specifically constructed for fireworks viewing. We prefer Plaza Gardens East (the same side of the park as Tomorrowland) because the configuration of light/audio poles is slightly less obtrusive when you're viewing the castle.

If those spots are already taken, your next-best alternatives are on Main Street, where you'll get to see the (smaller) projections closer. Watching from the train-station end of Main Street is the easiest way to facilitate a quick departure.

If we're staying in the park and trying to avoid the crowds on Main Street, our two favorite spots to see just the fireworks are as follows:

1. **In Fantasyland between Seven Dwarfs Mine Train and** *Enchanted Tales with Belle.* Some of the minor fireworks that float above the castle will be behind you, but all of the major effects will be right in front of you.

2. **On the bridge between the Central Plaza and Tomorrowland.** A few trees block some of the castle, but if Tinker Bell does her fireworks flight from the castle, she'll fly directly over this area.

Leaving the Park After Evening Parades and Fireworks

unofficial **TIP**
Digital displays at the Magic Kingdom exit show the wait to board the monorails and ferry—take the one with the shorter line.

With armies of guests leaving the park after evening parades and fireworks, the Disney transportation system (buses, ferries, and monorail) gets overwhelmed, causing long waits in boarding areas. (Similar situations often occur during the special holiday parades and fireworks, when they're offered.)

A mom from Kresgeville, Pennsylvania, recounts:

Our family of five made the mistake of going to the Magic Kingdom the Saturday night before Columbus Day to watch the parade and fireworks. Afterwards, we lingered at The Crystal Palace to wait for the crowds to lessen, but it was no use. We started walking toward the gates and soon became trapped by the throng, not able to go forward or back. Our group became separated, and it became a nightmare. We left the park at 10:30 p.m. and didn't get back to the Polynesian Village (less than a mile away) until after midnight. Even if they were to raise Walt Disney himself from cryogenic sleep and parade him down Main Street, I'll never go to the Magic Kingdom on a Saturday night again!

An Oklahoma City dad offers this advice:

Never, never leave the Magic Kingdom just after the evening fireworks. Go for another ride—no lines because everyone else is trying to get out!

Congestion persists from the end of the early evening parade (if it's performed) until closing time. Most folks watch the early parade and then the fireworks a few minutes later. If you're parked at the Transportation and Ticket Center (TTC) and are intent on beating the crowd, view the early parade from the Town Square end of Main Street, leaving the park as soon as the parade ends.

> *unofficial* **TIP**
> Be aware that the railroad doesn't run during parades because the floats must cross the tracks when entering or exiting the parade route in Frontierland.

Here's what happened to a family from Cape Coral, Florida:

We tried to leave the park before the parade began, but Main Street was already packed and we didn't see any way to get out of the park—we were stuck. In addition, it was impossible to move across the street, and even the shops were so crowded it was virtually impossible to maneuver a stroller through them to get close to the entrance.

If you don't have a stroller (or are willing to forgo the return refund for rental strollers), catch the **Walt Disney World Railroad** in **Frontierland** and ride to the park exit at Main Street. Again, don't cut it too close—the train stops running for the parade.

MAIN STREET PASSAGEWAYS The Magic Kingdom has two pedestrian walkways behind the shops on either side of Main Street, U.S.A., specifically for guests who want to get in or out of the park without walking down the middle of Main Street. If you're on the Tomorrowland side of the park, look for a passageway that runs from between **The Plaza Restaurant** and **Tomorrowland Terrace,** back behind the east side of Main Street, to **Tony's Town Square Restaurant** near the park exit. If you're on the Adventureland side of the park, the passageway runs from the **First Aid** area to the **Main Street Fire Station** near the park exit. However, these passageways aren't used every night, so there's no guarantee that they'll be available.

> *unofficial* **TIP**
> Instead of walking outside, you can cut through the Main Street shops—they have interior doors that let you pass from one shop to the next.

If the passageways aren't open and you're on the Tomorrowland side of the park, here's how to exit during a parade: Cut through Tomorrowland Terrace and then work your way down Main Street until you're past the Main Street Bakery (Starbucks) and have crossed a small cul-de-sac. Bear left into the side door of that corner shop. Work your way from shop to shop until you reach Town Square—easy, because people will be outside watching the parade. Then, at Town Square, bear left to reach the train station and park exit.

Note: This won't work if you're on the Adventureland side of the park. You can make your way through **Casey's Corner** to Main Street and then work your way through the shops, but when you pop out of the **Emporium** at Town Square, you'll be trapped by the parade. As soon as the last float passes, however, you can bolt for the exit.

If your car is parked at the TTC lot, you could also just watch the early parade and then leave before the fireworks show. Line up for the ferry; one will depart about every 8–10 minutes. Try to catch the ferry that will be crossing Seven Seas Lagoon while the fireworks show is in progress. The best vantage point is on the top deck to the right of the pilothouse as you face the Magic Kingdom—the sight of fireworks silhouetting the castle and reflecting off the lagoon is unforgettable.

While there's no guarantee that a ferry will load and depart within 3 or 4 minutes of the fireworks, your chances are about 50–50 of timing it just right. If you're in the front of the line for the ferry and don't want to board the boat that's loading, stop at the gate and let people pass you. You'll be the first to board the next boat.

Strollers, wheelchairs, and ECVs make navigating crowds even more difficult. If you have one of these, or if you're staying at a Disney hotel that is not served by the monorail and you have to depend on Disney transportation, watch the early parade and fireworks; then enjoy the attractions until about 20–25 minutes before the late parade is scheduled to begin. Then leave the park using one of the strategies listed previously, and catch the Disney bus or boat back to your hotel.

MAGIC KINGDOM HARD-TICKET EVENTS

THE MAGIC KINGDOM HOSTS several **holiday-themed after-hours events** from mid-August through December. Celebrating Halloween and Christmas, they require separate paid admission and can sell out. Space doesn't permit us to cover them with more than a brief mention in the book (see "The Walt Disney World Calendar," page 40), but we provide full details, including photos, best days to go, touring advice, and more, at our website, **TouringPlans.com:** Go to blog.touringplans.com and search "Boo Bash" and "Mickey's Merrytime."

TRAFFIC PATTERNS *in* *the* MAGIC KINGDOM

WHEN WE RESEARCH THE MAGIC KINGDOM, we study its traffic patterns, asking:

1. WHICH SECTIONS OF THE PARK AND WHICH ATTRACTIONS DO GUESTS VISIT FIRST? When the park opens, guest traffic is heaviest going to Fantasyland and Tomorrowland, followed by Frontierland. Seven Dwarfs Mine Train pulls people into the back reaches of the park, while Space Mountain (and, eventually, Tron) pulls people to the right.

2. HOW LONG DOES IT TAKE FOR THE PARK TO FILL UP? HOW ARE THE VISITORS DISPERSED IN THE PARK? A surge of early birds arrive before or around opening time but are quickly dispersed throughout the empty park. After the initial wave is absorbed, there's a lull lasting about an hour after opening. Then the park is inundated for about 2 hours, peaking between 10 a.m. and noon. Arrivals continue in a steady but diminishing stream until around 2 p.m. The lines we sampled were longest between 1 and 2 p.m., indicating more arrivals than departures into the early afternoon. For touring purposes, most attractions develop long lines between 10 and 11:30 a.m.

From late morning until early afternoon, guests are equally distributed among all the lands. However, guests concentrate in **Fantasyland, Liberty Square,** and **Frontierland** in late afternoon, with a decrease of visitors in Adventureland and Tomorrowland. Adventureland's **Jungle Cruise** and Tomorrowland's **Buzz Lightyear** and **Space Mountain** continue to be crowded, but most other attractions in those lands are readily accessible.

3. HOW DO MOST VISITORS TOUR THE PARK? Many **first-time visitors** are guided by friends or relatives familiar with the Magic Kingdom; these tours may or may not follow an orderly sequence. First-timers without personal guides tend to be more orderly in their touring, but they also tend to be drawn to Cinderella Castle upon entering the park, and thus they begin their rotation from Fantasyland. **Repeat visitors** usually head straight to their favorite attractions.

4. WILL GOING LEFT (OR RIGHT) HELP AVOID CROWDS? We tested a frequent claim that most people turn right into Tomorrowland and tour the Magic Kingdom counterclockwise. We found the claim to be baseless. Neither do most people turn left and start in Adventureland.

Here's why: Magic Kingdom headliner attractions are located intentionally at opposite points around the park to distribute crowds evenly: **Space Mountain** and **Tron** on the east side, **Splash Mountain** and **Big Thunder Mountain Railroad** on the west, **Seven Dwarfs Mine Train** to the north, and so on.

If, therefore, you were to start touring by heading left, you'd have low crowds in Adventureland and moderate crowds in Frontierland—but

ATTRACTIONS THAT GET CROWDED EARLY
FANTASYLAND • Peter Pan's Flight • Princess Fairytale Hall • Seven Dwarfs Mine Train
FRONTIERLAND • Big Thunder Mountain Railroad • Splash Mountain
TOMORROWLAND • Buzz Lightyear's Space Ranger Spin • Space Mountain • Tomorrowland Speedway • Tron Lightcycle Power Run *(opens 2022)*

by the time you got to Fantasyland and Tomorrowland, you'd run into the largest crowds of the day. A similar scenario would await you if you started by bearing right into Tomorrowland: packed crowds in the rest of the lands you visit.

Avoiding the biggest crowds in the park, then, requires the following:

1. Knowing which attractions to visit, and when.
2. Knowing how to make the best use of Genie+ (if you're willing to pay for it).
3. Being willing to cross the park to save time.

5. HOW DO SPECIAL EVENTS, SUCH AS PARADES AND LIVE SHOWS, AFFECT TRAFFIC PATTERNS? Parades pull huge numbers of guests away from attractions and provide a window of opportunity for experiencing the more popular attractions with less of a wait. (Cavalcades don't have this effect.) Castle Forecourt Stage shows also attract crowds but only slightly affect lines.

6. WHAT ARE THE TRAFFIC PATTERNS NEAR AND AT CLOSING TIME? On our sample days, in busy times and off-season at the park, departures outnumbered arrivals beginning in midafternoon. Many visitors left in late afternoon as dinnertime approached. When the park closed early, guests departed steadily during the 2 hours before closing, with a huge exodus at closing time. When the park closed late, a huge exodus began immediately after the early-evening parade and fireworks, with a second mass departure after the late parade, continuing until closing.

Because Main Street and transportation services remain open after the other five lands close, crowds leaving at closing mainly affect conditions on Main Street and at the monorail-, ferry-, and bus-boarding areas. In the hour before closing, the other five lands are normally uncrowded.

To get a complete view of actual traffic patterns while you're in the park, use our mobile app, **Lines** (touringplans.com/lines). It gives you current wait times as well as estimates in half-hour increments for today and tomorrow. A quick glance shows how traffic patterns affect wait times throughout the day.

MAGIC KINGDOM TOURING PLANS

unofficial **TIP**
Don't worry that other people will be following the touring plans, rendering them useless. Fewer than 4 in every 100 people in the park will have been exposed to this info.

STARTING ON PAGE 713, our step-by-step touring plans are field-tested for seeing *as much as possible* in one day with a minimum of time wasted in lines. They're designed to help you avoid crowds and bottlenecks on days of moderate to heavy attendance. You should understand, however, that there's more to see in the Magic Kingdom than can be experienced in one day.

On days of lighter attendance (see "Selecting the Time of Year for Your Visit," page 34), our plans will save you time but won't be as critical to successful touring as on busier days.

Each Magic Kingdom touring plan has two versions: one for Disney resort guests and one for off-site guests. Plans for on-site guests use Disney's Early Theme Park Entry benefit (see page 38) to minimize waits in line. Early Entry means thousands of guests will already be in lines and on rides before off-site guests step foot in the park, so the touring strategy for off-site guests must necessarily be different. Even with a perfect touring plan, Early Entry means off-site guests may wait up to an hour more in lines per day in the Magic Kingdom.

Our Magic Kingdom touring plans for this edition do not require you to use either Disney's extra-cost Genie+ ride-reservation system or Individual Attraction Selections. If you opt for either (or both) of these offerings, simply tell our free touring plan software which reservation times you have, and the software will adjust the plan.

CHOOSING THE APPROPRIATE TOURING PLAN

WE PRESENT FOUR Magic Kingdom touring plans:

- One-Day Touring Plan for Adults
- One-Day Touring Plan for Parents with Small Children
- Dumbo-or-Die-in-a-Day Touring Plan for Parents with Small Children
- Two-Day Touring Plan

Each touring plan has two versions: one for Disney resort guests and one for off-site guests.

If you have two days (or two mornings) at the Magic Kingdom, the **Two-Day Touring Plan** is *by far* the most relaxed and efficient. It takes advantage of early morning, when lines are short and the park hasn't filled with guests. This plan works well year-round and eliminates much of the extra walking required by the one-day plans. No matter when the park closes, our two-day plan guarantees the most efficient touring and the least time in lines. The plan is perfect for guests who wish to sample both the attractions and the atmosphere of the Magic Kingdom.

If you have just a single day to visit but you want to see as much as possible, then use the **One-Day Touring Plan for Adults.** Yes, it's a bear, but it gives you maximum bang for your buck.

If you have children younger than age 8, choose the **One-Day Touring Plan for Parents with Small Children.** A compromise that blends the preferences of younger children with those of older siblings and adults, this plan includes many children's rides in Fantasyland but omits the more intense rides and other attractions

*un**official* **TIP**
Rider Switch allows adults to enjoy the more adventurous attractions while keeping the group together.

that may frighten young children or are off-limits because of height requirements. You could also use the One-Day Touring Plan for Adults, and take advantage of **Rider Switch,** whereby children accompany adults to the loading area of a ride with age and height requirements but don't board (see page 395).

The **Dumbo-or-Die-in-a-Day Touring Plan for Parents with Small Children** is designed for parents who are happy to self-sacrificially stand around, sweat, wipe noses, pay for stuff, and watch the kids enjoy themselves. **You'll love it!**

"Not a Touring Plan" Touring Plans

For the type-B reader, these touring plans (see page 710) avoid detailed step-by-step strategies for saving every last minute in line. To paraphrase one of our favorite movies, they're more guidelines than actual rules. Use them to avoid the longest waits in line while having maximum flexibility to see whatever interests you in a particular part of the park.

For the Magic Kingdom, these "not" touring plans include advice for adults and parents with one day in the park, for anyone with two days, and for anyone with an afternoon and a full day to tour.

Two-Day Touring Plan for Families with Small Children

If you have young children and are looking for a two-day itinerary, combine the **Magic Kingdom One-Day Touring Plan for Parents with Small Children** with the second day of the **Magic Kingdom Two-Day Touring Plan.**

Two-Day Touring Plan: Early-Morning Touring on Day One and Afternoon, Then Evening Touring on Day Two

Many of us enjoy an early start at the Magic Kingdom on one day, followed by a second day with a lazy sleep-in morning, resuming your touring in the afternoon and/or evening. If this appeals to you, use the **Magic Kingdom One-Day Touring Plan for Adults** or the **Magic Kingdom One-Day Touring Plan for Parents with Small Children** on your early day. Stick to the plan for as long as it feels comfortable (many folks leave after the afternoon parade). On the second day, pick up where you left off. Customize the rest of the plan to incorporate parades, fireworks, and other live performances according to your preferences.

MAGIC KINGDOM TOURING PLAN COMPANION

WE'VE CONSOLIDATED A GREAT DEAL of information about the Magic Kingdom in its Touring Plan Companion, on page 737 just after the touring plans. Like the plans, the companions are designed to clip out and take with you to the park. The Magic Kingdom Touring Plan Companion recaps key information in this chapter: the best times to visit each attraction, the authors' ratings, attraction height requirements and fright potential, and quick-reference info on dining and places to take a break.

THE SINGLE-DAY TOURING CONUNDRUM

TOURING THE MAGIC KINGDOM in one day is complicated by two facts:

1. The park's average day is more than an hour shorter than it was a few years ago.
2. The premier attractions are at almost opposite ends of the park.

Splash Mountain and **Big Thunder Mountain Railroad** are in Frontierland, **Space Mountain** and **Tron** are in **Tomorrowland,** and **Seven Dwarfs Mine Train** is in the top center. It's virtually impossible to ride all five without encountering lines at one or another.

If, for example, you hit Tron and Space Mountain right as the park opens, you won't have too bad of a wait, but by the time you get to Fantasyland, the line for Seven Dwarfs Mine Train will already be substantial. Likewise, you can ride Seven Dwarfs without a problem first thing in the morning, but by the time you get to Tomorrowland, Space Mountain and Tron will already have fair-size lines. See our Splash Mountain touring tips on page 477 for our recommended one- and two-day strategies for these attractions.

PRELIMINARY INSTRUCTIONS

BECOME FAMILIAR WITH THE MAGIC KINGDOM'S **opening procedures,** as described on pages 462–463. On days of moderate to heavy attendance, follow your chosen touring plan exactly, deviating from it only as follows:

1. **When you're not interested in an attraction in the plan.** Easy-peasy: Simply skip it and proceed to the next attraction.

2. **When you encounter a very long line at an attraction.** In this case, skip to the next attraction and try again later at the one with the line.

Before You Go

1. Call ☎ 407-824-4321 or check disneyworld.com the day before you go to verify official opening time.

2. Purchase admission before you arrive.

3. Get familiar with park-opening procedures (see above), and reread the plan you've chosen so you know what you're likely to encounter.

4. At 7 a.m. on the day of your visit, make Genie+ and/or Individual Attraction Selection reservations if you bought them.

MAGIC KINGDOM TOURING PLANS AT A GLANCE

Magic Kingdom One-Day Touring Plan for Adults (four versions) (pages 713–716)

FOR Adults without young children.

ASSUMES Willingness to experience all major rides (including roller coasters) and shows that were operating at press time. Does not assume the use of Genie+ or Individual Attraction Selections.

THIS PLAN INCLUDES THE ATTRACTIONS we think best represent the Magic Kingdom, from its newest roller coasters to those created by Walt Disney himself. It requires a lot of walking and some backtracking to avoid lines. Extra walking and morning hustling will spare you hours of standing in line. How far you get depends on how quickly you move from ride to ride, how many times you rest or eat, how quickly the park fills, and what time the park closes.

Magic Kingdom One-Day Touring Plan For Parents with Small Children (two versions) (pages 717–718)

FOR Parents with children younger than age 8.

ASSUMES Periodic stops for rest, restrooms, and refreshments. Does not assume the use of Genie+ or Individual Attraction Selections.

THIS PLAN INCLUDES THE PARK'S HIGHEST-RATED ATTRACTIONS for younger children, plus many of the ones for adults and older kids. It also includes the evening fireworks.

The plan has a slower pace, with plenty of free time throughout the day. If more time is needed, though, here are the rides whose overall ratings make them the most expendable in the plan:

- It's a Small World • The Many Adventures of Winnie the Pooh

Magic Kingdom Dumbo-or-Die-in-a-Day Touring Plan for Parents with Small Children *(two versions)* *(pages 719–720)*

FOR Adults compelled to devote every waking moment to the pleasure and entertainment of their young children; rich people who are paying someone else to do the same. Does not assume the use of Genie+ or Individual Attraction Selections.

ASSUMES Frequent stops for rest, restrooms, and refreshments.

NAME ASIDE, THIS PLAN IS NO JOKE, Y'ALL. Whether you're loving, masochistic, selfless, or just unhinged, this itinerary will provide a youngster with about as perfect a day as is possible at the Magic Kingdom. Families using this plan should review the Magic Kingdom attractions in our **Small-Child Fright-Potential Table** in Part Seven (see pages 390–392).

Magic Kingdom Two-Day Touring Plan *(pages 721–722)*

FOR Those wishing to spread their Magic Kingdom visit over two days.
ASSUMES Willingness to experience all major rides and shows. Does not assume the use of Genie+ or Individual Attraction Selections.

THIS TWO-DAY TOURING PLAN takes advantage of early-morning touring. Each day, you should complete the structured part of the plan by about 4 p.m. This leaves plenty of time for live entertainment, or time for a break back at your hotel before deciding what to do in the evening.

◼ OVERVIEW

WALT DISNEY'S ORIGINAL 1960s-era vision for EPCOT was a complete rethinking of the American city. Back then, **EPCOT** was an acronym meaning "Experimental Prototype Community of Tomorrow." Among Walt's ideas for future city living were self-driving electric cars, prefab solar-powered homes electronically connected to a network of information services; and an entire city center enclosed in a giant air-conditioned dome.

After Walt Disney died in 1966, the people who took over his company considered his ideas too risky to implement. When EPCOT Center finally opened at Walt Disney World 16 years later, it was a theme park with a split personality: Half of it—called **Future World**—was based on a futuristic, semi-educational, "better living through technology" look at the world, while the other half—**World Showcase**—was a kind of permanent world's fair (another of Walt's passions).

IS EPCOT WORTH VISITING IN 2022?

EPCOT REMAINS THE DISNEY WORLD theme park most in need of refurbishment. The good news: It's happening, albeit slowly.

unofficial **TIP**
If you're visiting the World for four days or fewer, you may find more things to do by skipping EPCOT and concentrating on the Magic Kingdom, Animal Kingdom, and Disney's Hollywood Studios.

continued on page 510

EPCOT

Attractions

1. *The American Adventure* ☑
2. *Awesome Planet*
3. *Canada Far and Wide*
4. Club Cool
5. Disney & Pixar Short Film Festival G+
6. Frozen Ever After IAS
7. Gran Fiesta Tour Starring the Three Caballeros
8. Guardians of the Galaxy: Cosmic Rewind *(opens 2022/2023)*
9. *Impressions de France/Beauty and the Beast Sing-Along*
10. Journey into Imagination with Figment G+
11. Living with the Land ☑ G+
12. Meet Anna and Elsa at Royal Sommerhus
13. Mission: Space ☑ G+
14. *Reflections of China*
15. Remy's Ratatouille Adventure ☑ IAS
16. SeaBase
17. The Seas with Nemo & Friends G+
18. Soarin' Around the World ☑ G+
19. Spaceship Earth ☑ G+
20. Test Track ☑ G+
21. *Turtle Talk with Crush* ☑ G+

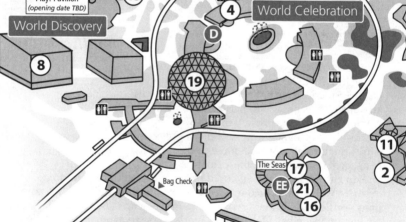

G+ Attraction Offers Genie+   ✚ First Aid Center   ✳ *Harmonious* Top Viewing Spot

IAS Attraction Offers Individual Access   🚻 Restrooms

👍 Recommended Dining   ☑ Not To Be Missed

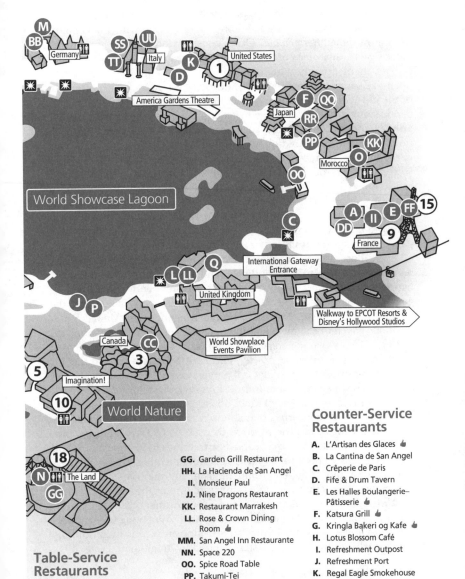

World Showcase Lagoon

Germany

Italy

United States

America Gardens Theatre

Japan

Morocco

France

International Gateway Entrance

United Kingdom

Walkway to EPCOT Resorts & Disney's Hollywood Studios

World Showplace Events Pavilion

Canada

Imagination!

World Nature

The Land

Table-Service Restaurants

AA. Akershus Royal Banquet Hall
BB. Biergarten Restaurant
CC. Le Cellier Steakhouse
DD. Chefs de France
EE. Coral Reef Restaurant
FF. La Crêperie de Paris
GG. Garden Grill Restaurant
HH. La Hacienda de San Angel
II. Monsieur Paul
JJ. Nine Dragons Restaurant
KK. Restaurant Marrakesh
LL. Rose & Crown Dining Room
MM. San Angel Inn Restaurante
NN. Space 220
OO. Spice Road Table
PP. Takumi-Tei
QQ. Teppan Edo
RR. Tokyo Dining
SS. Tutto Gusto Wine Cellar
TT. Tutto Italia Ristorante
UU. Via Napoli Ristorante e Pizzeria

Counter-Service Restaurants

A. L'Artisan des Glaces
B. La Cantina de San Angel
C. Crêperie de Paris
D. Fife & Drum Tavern
E. Les Halles Boulangerie–Pâtisserie
F. Katsura Grill
G. Kringla Bakeri og Kafe
H. Lotus Blossom Café
I. Refreshment Outpost
J. Refreshment Port
K. Regal Eagle Smokehouse
L. Rose & Crown Pub
M. Sommerfest
N. Sunshine Seasons
O. Tangierine Café
P. Traveler's Café
Q. Yorkshire County Fish Shop

continued from page 507

A new headliner attraction, **Remy's Ratatouille Adventure,** opened in World Showcase's France Pavilion in 2021, along with a new nighttime show called *Harmonious.* Other construction projects are moving more slowly. **Guardians of the Galaxy: Cosmic Rewind,** an indoor roller coaster themed to the Guardians of the Galaxy movie series, might open in 2022. The **Play! Pavilion,** "devoted to playful fun," on the site of the old Wonders of Life Pavilion, has been announced, but the pandemic seems to have delayed construction indefinitely. Likewise, other already-announced projects, such as a Mary Poppins–themed attraction in the UK Pavilion and an ambitious redo of the front half of the park, have been canceled, paused, or scaled back.

Remy's Ratatouille Adventure represents the first completely new attraction at EPCOT in 16 years, and it's good for small children. In spite of that, we hesitate to recommend EPCOT for short visits until Guardians of the Galaxy opens. For one thing, much of Future World will be a construction zone well into 2022, with convoluted walking paths and restaurants closed or operating out of temporary locations.

Even more affected is World Showcase. A few indoor restaurants remain closed due to the pandemic, and Disney sent home the international cast members who staffed each pavilion, with their local languages and style, replacing them with US cast members. In addition, the Germany, Italy, Japan, Morocco, United Kingdom, and United States Pavilions haven't been meaningfully updated since EPCOT first opened in 1982. (To put that in perspective, "Physical" was at the top of the pop charts; *Dallas, Laverne & Shirley,* and *M*A*S*H* were still on the air; and the first bricklike consumer cell phone was still a year away.) Scenes in the nearly 40-year-old film *Impressions de France,* for instance, show prices in francs—a currency France abandoned two decades ago.

Our other key concern is that a number of the attractions currently in development have little to do with what EPCOT has always purported to be about. Over the years, its attractions have entertained and informed guests about topics such as communication, energy production, space exploration, environmentalism, and the role of computers in society—topics that continue to be both important and fascinating.

With billions of dollars and many talented Imagineers at Disney's disposal, you'd think they could come up with something more appropriate for EPCOT—once Disney's most innovative, forward-thinking theme park—than a roller coaster inspired by an animated tree.

UPCOMING NAME CHANGES

IN 2019 DISNEY ANNOUNCED that the front half of EPCOT—Future World—would be subdivided into three "lands," each with its own name. **World Discovery** covers the east side of Future World, currently known as Future World East, including the Test Track, Mission: Space, Play!, and Guardians of the Galaxy Pavilions. **World Nature** incorporates attractions in Future World West, including the Imagination!, Land, and Seas Pavilions. The central part of Future World, including Spaceship Earth, will be known as **World Celebration.** The World

Showcase Pavilion will keep its name. Disney hadn't yet made the switch to these names at press time but remains committed to the change.

Until these changes are official, we'll use "Future World" to generally refer to the half of the park that isn't World Showcase, and we'll use the new land names when discussing those specific sections of Future World.

ARRIVING

ENTRANCE CHOICES EPCOT has two entrances. The larger one is in Future World, at the front of the park, and it's the one you will use if you arrive by car, bus, or monorail. The other entrance, the **International Gateway (IG)**, is located in the rear of the park, between the France and United Kingdom Pavilions in World Showcase.

unofficial TIP
Arriving at EPCOT 30–60 minutes before official opening ensures the shortest possible waits for rides.

EPCOT's Future World entrance can handle more people and is closer to headliner rides such as Soarin', Test Track, and Guardians of the Galaxy: Cosmic Rewind (when it opens). However, the IG entrance will put you closer to Remy's Ratatouille Adventure.

This Sacramento, California, reader suggests using the IG entrance:

> *The IG entrance is convenient for getting into EPCOT first thing in the morning. We entered by boat from the Dolphin and were met inside the gate by cast members who helped us set up our ride reservations for the day.*

ARRIVING FROM INSIDE DISNEY WORLD If you're staying at an EPCOT resort, it will take you about 20–30 minutes to walk the mile or so from your hotel to the IG and then from there to Future World. **Boat service** is also available from the EPCOT resorts to the IG. It's also about a 10- to 20-minute ride (20–40 minutes with crowds) on the **Skyliner** (see page 438), which links the IG with Disney's Hollywood Studios and Disney's Caribbean Beach, Riviera, Pop Century, and Art of Animation Resorts. Add another 5–8 minutes to walk to Future World from the IG.

DRIVING Arriving by car is easy and direct (see page 439 for GPS coordinates). EPCOT has its own parking lot, and unlike the Magic Kingdom, it doesn't require you to take a monorail or ferry to reach the park entrance. Take a tram or walk from the parking lot to the front gate. Monorail service connects EPCOT with the Transportation and Ticket Center, the Magic Kingdom (transfer required), and the Magic Kingdom resorts (transfer required).

If you want to drive and use the IG entrance, you'll need to pay for parking at the resorts closest to EPCOT: the **Swan, Dolphin,** or **Swan Reserve.** It may be cheaper and/or easier to use a ride-hailing service to get dropped off and picked up at those hotels instead.

EPCOT OPENING (ROPE DROP)

FUTURE WORLD AND WORLD SHOWCASE both typically open at 11 a.m. and close at 10 p.m. On-site guests who want to take advantage of Early Theme Park Entry (see page 38) should arrive at EPCOT 60 minutes before official opening (that is, 30 minutes before Early Entry) on all days. Off-site guests, who aren't eligible for Early Theme Park Entry, should arrive 30 minutes before official opening on all days.

WHICH EPCOT ENTRANCE SHOULD YOU USE? The IG is about 10 minutes closer to the family-friendly **Remy's Ratatouille Adventure,** in World Showcase's France Pavilion, than the Future World entrance, and that's a huge head start. But if the rat ride isn't a priority, then enter at Future World instead for easier access to **Soarin' Around the World, Test Track,** and **Guardians of the Galaxy: Cosmic Rewind** (when it opens).

GETTING ORIENTED

> **NOT TO BE MISSED AT EPCOT**
>
> **FUTURE WORLD** • Guardians of the Galaxy: Cosmic Rewind *(opens 2022)*
> • Living with the Land • Mission: Space • Soarin' Around the World • Spaceship Earth
> • Test Track • *Turtle Talk with Crush* • SeaBase
>
> **WORLD SHOWCASE** • *The American Adventure* • Frozen Ever After
> • *Harmonious* • Meet Anna and Elsa at Royal Sommerhus *(suspended at press time)*
> • Japan and Mexico Pavilions • Remy's Ratatouille Adventure

EPCOT'S THEMED AREAS are markedly different: World Showcase features the landmarks, cuisine, and culture of almost a dozen nations and is meant to be a sort of permanent World's Fair. Future World is in flux: Its older attractions examine where mankind has come from and where it's going, while its newer attractions are themed to Disney's make-believe universe of characters.

Navigating EPCOT is unlike getting around at the Magic Kingdom, where nearly every "land" is discrete and visually distinct from its neighbors—for example, Liberty Square and Main Street, U.S.A.

EPCOT, by contrast, is visually open. And while it might seem odd to see a Japanese pagoda and the Eiffel Tower on the same horizon, getting around is fairly simple. An exception is Future World, where construction walls hide (for now) everything on its east and west sides.

The park's architectural anchor is **Spaceship Earth,** a shiny 180-foot geosphere that's visible from almost everywhere in the park. Like Cinderella Castle at the Magic Kingdom, Spaceship Earth can help

EPCOT SERVICES

EPCOT'S SERVICE FACILITIES, most located in Future World, include:

Baby Care Center On the World Showcase side of the Odyssey Center

Banking Services ATMs outside the main entrance, on the Future World bridge, and in World Showcase at the US Pavilion and International Gateway entrance

Cell Phone Charging Outlets available in The Seas, upstairs near the women's restroom; in The Land, upstairs near the Garden Grill; and possibly a few open outlets in the Test Track postshow, depending on how displays are arranged

Dining Reservations At Guest Relations, to the left of Spaceship Earth, or through the My Disney Experience app

First Aid Center On the World Showcase side of the Odyssey Center, next door to the Baby Care Center

Live-Entertainment Information At Guest Relations

Lost and Found At the main entrance at the gift shop or Guest Relations

Lost Persons At Guest Relations and the Baby Care Center

Walt Disney World and Local Attraction Information At Guest Relations

Wheelchair, ECV, ESV, and Stroller Rentals Inside the main entrance and to the left, toward the rear of the Entrance Plaza; also at the International Gateway entrance

EPCOT Most Popular Attractions by Age Group

PRE-SCHOOL	GRADE SCHOOL	TEENS	YOUNG ADULTS	OVER 30	SENIORS
Meet Anna and Elsa at Royal Sommerhus*	Soarin' Around the World	Test Track	Soarin' Around the World	Soarin' Around the World	Soarin' Around the World
Frozen Ever After	Frozen Ever After	Soarin' Around the World	Test Track	Test Track	Living with the Land
The Seas with Nemo and Friends	Test Track	Mission: Space (Orange and Green)	Mission: Space (Orange)	Japan Pavilion	Test Track
SeaBase	Turtle Talk with Crush*	SeaBase	Japan Pavilion	Voices of Liberty	The American Adventure
Turtle Talk with Crush*	Meet Anna and Elsa at Royal Sommerhus*	Japan Pavilion	Spaceship Earth	Spaceship Earth	Voices of Liberty
Soarin' Around the World	Disney & Pixar Short Film Festival	Evening fireworks	Living with the Land	Living with the Land	Disney & Pixar Short Film Festival
Gran Fiesta Tour Starring the Three Caballeros	Spaceship Earth	Living with the Land	Mexico Pavilion	Frozen Ever After	Impressions de France
Journey into Imagination with Figment	The Seas with Nemo and Friends	The Seas with Nemo and Friends	Germany Pavilion	Mexico Pavilion	Frozen Ever After
Test Track	Gran Fiesta Tour Starring the Three Caballeros	Gran Fiesta Tour Starring the Three Caballeros	SeaBase	SeaBase	SeaBase
Spaceship Earth	Journey into Imagination with Figment	Norway Pavilion	Norway Pavilion	France Pavilion	Norway Pavilion

*Closed at press time

you keep track of where you are in EPCOT. But it's in a high-traffic area and isn't centrally located, so it's not a good meeting place.

Any World Showcase pavilion makes a good meeting place, but specifics matter. Each pavilion is a town in miniature, with buildings, gardens, and plazas. So instead of just saying "Let's meet in Japan," pick a specific place—for instance, the sidewalk side of the pagoda.

FAVORITE ATTRACTIONS BY AGE GROUP

EPCOT'S LINEUP INCLUDES more than 50 attractions, shows, fireworks, live performers, and festival and seasonal entertainment. The chart below shows the park's 10 most popular attractions by age group.

Before the pandemic, EPCOT's character greetings, fireworks, and live entertainers were popular across all age groups. Those should be part of your day at EPCOT when they return.

The average reader ratings for all EPCOT attractions by age group are as follows, based on the 108,000 attraction ratings we received over the past 18 months:

- PRESCHOOL 4.0 stars
- GRADE SCHOOL 4.0 stars
- TEENS 3.8 stars
- YOUNG ADULTS 3.9 stars
- OVER 30 3.1 stars
- SENIORS 3.9 stars

RIDER SWITCH AT EPCOT At all Disney parks, select attractions allow one parent to ride while the other stays with a nonriding child. The parents then switch roles so that the other can ride using the Alternate Access. (See page 395 for complete details.)

unofficial **TIP**
If you plan to use Rider Switch at EPCOT, plan for extra time in line for the second rider.

At EPCOT, however, long waits in the Alternate Access line may complicate Rider Switch, requiring families to spend inordinate amounts of time in line so that both parents can ride. A Tulsa, Oklahoma, dad of one elaborates:

> *Rider Switch worked out really well on every ride in every park except EPCOT. The Alternate Access lines plus ride times for Soarin' (30 minutes), Mission: Space (30 minutes), and Test Track (45 minutes) were so long that it made Rider Switch very frustrating.*

GENIE+ AND INDIVIDUAL ATTRACTION SELECTIONS AND TOURING PLANS

DISNEY'S NEW GENIE+ ride-reservation system is offered at seven EPCOT attractions, with two others designated as Individual Access:

GENIE+ AND INDIVIDUAL ATTRACTION SELECTIONS IN EPCOT	
FUTURE WORLD	
• Disney and Pixar Short Film Festival	• Soarin' Around the World
• Dumbo the Flying Elephant	• Spaceship Earth
• Journey Into Imagination with Figment	• Test Track (*Individual Access only*)
• Living with the Land	• The Seas with Nemo & Friends
WORLD SHOWCASE	
• Frozen Ever After	• Remy's Ratatouille Adventure (*Individual Access only*)

Character greetings weren't being offered when Genie+ and Lightning Lane were introduced, but we think they'll be added upon their return. Our guess is that **Guardians of the Galaxy: Cosmic Rewind** will be Individual Access only when it opens, moving **Test Track** back to the Genie+ program.

It was easy for us to recommend using Disney's old FastPass+ ride-reservation system with our touring plans, because it was free to use, had plenty of historical data to analyze, and behaved predictably. None of that is true with Genie+. So the four big questions for this edition are:

1. Is Genie+ worth paying for at EPCOT?

2. If it's worth the cost, which attractions benefit most from Genie+ or Individual Attraction Selection?

3. How can you avoid paying for Individual Attraction Selections?

4. How do Genie+ and Individual Attraction Selections work with the touring plans?

Is Genie+ Worth Paying for at EPCOT?

We think so, provided you meet any of these three criteria:

- You'll be arriving at EPCOT after Early Theme Park Entry begins (that is, you won't be at the park as soon as it opens). This includes off-site guests who aren't eligible for Early Entry and on-site guests who want to sleep in.
- You won't be using a touring plan.
- You're visiting during a holiday, spring break, or another peak season.

Regardless of the time of year you visit, arriving at park opening should allow you to see at least two of EPCOT's headliner attractions without significant waits. Because just seven attractions participate in Genie+, it's unlikely that you'd need more than three to five ride reservations per day. On days of heavy attendance, though, you'd be competing with lots of other people for reservations, pushing out return times and limiting how many reservations you can obtain per day.

The table below shows how much time we estimate you'll be able to save using Genie+ with one of our EPCOT touring plans, at three different crowd and Genie+ usage levels:

Which EPCOT Attractions Benefit Most from Genie+?

The chart below shows the top seven attractions that might benefit most from using Genie+, based on current wait times and historical FastPass+ data. The chart goes in descending order of priority.

EPCOT ATTRACTIONS THAT BENEFIT MOST FROM GENIE+ *(Highest Priority to Lowest)*	
1 Frozen Ever After	5 Spaceship Earth
2 Soarin' Around the World	6 Journey Into Imagination with Figment
3 Mission: Space	7 The Seas with Nemo and Friends
4 Living with the Land	

How Can You Avoid Paying for Individual Attraction Selections?

There are a couple of strategies, although each entails spending money somewhere else.

1. Stay at any Disney resort, use Early Theme Park Entry over multiple days, and head to each attraction as soon as the park opens. For new attractions such as Remy's Ratatouille Adventure and Guardians of the Galaxy: Cosmic Rewind, this is likely to be the strategy recommended by our touring plan software.

2. Stay at a Disney Deluxe or DVC/DDV resort, and visit the attractions during Extended Theme Park Hours.

How Do Genie+ and Individual Attraction Selections Work with the Touring Plans?

See our corresponding advice for the Magic Kingdom on page 463.

	ESTIMATED TIME SAVINGS USING A TOURING PLAN WITH GENIE+ FOR VARIOUS CROWD LEVELS		
CROWD LEVEL	TYPICAL USE (3 GENIE+ RESERVATIONS PER DAY)	OPTIMISTIC USE (3 GENIE+ RESERVATIONS PER DAY)	FULL USE (7 GENIE+ RESERVATIONS PER DAY)
Low	20 minutes saved	35 minutes saved	50 minutes saved
Moderate	40 minutes saved	60 minutes saved	75 minutes saved
High	50 minutes saved	80 minutes saved	100 minutes saved

DINING IN EPCOT

HERE'S A QUICK RECAP of EPCOT's top restaurants, rated by readers starting with the highest. There are too many EPCOT restaurants rated average or better to list here. See Part Six for details.

EPCOT RESTAURANT REFRESHER	
COUNTER SERVICE	**FULL SERVICE**
Les Halles Boulangerie–Pâtisserie (● 97%/Exceptional), France, World Showcase	**Teppan Edo** (L, D) (● 97%/Exceptional), Japan, World Showcase
Yorkshire County Fish Shop (● 97%/Above Average), United Kingdom, World Showcase	**Garden Grill Restaurant** (L, D) (● 92%/Much Above Average), The Land, Future World West
L'Artisan des Glaces (● 96%/Exceptional), France, World Showcase	**Via Napoli** (L, D) (● 92%/Above Average), Italy, World Showcase
Kringla Bakeri og Kafe (● 93%/Above Average), Norway, World Showcase	**Spice Road Table** (L, D) (● 90%/Average) Morocco, World Showcase
Refreshment Port (● 92%/Average), World Showcase between Showcase Plaza and Canada	**Tutto Gusto Wine Cellar** (● 88%/Average), Italy, World Showcase
Regal Eagle Smokehouse (● 91%/Above Average), United States, World Showcase	**Chefs de France** (L, D) (● 88%/Average), France, World Showcase
Tangierine Cafe (● 88%/Above Average), Morocco, World Showcase	

FUTURE WORLD

IMMENSE, GLEAMING FUTURISTIC STRUCTURES define the first themed area just beyond EPCOT's main entrance. Broad thoroughfares are punctuated with billowing fountains, all reflected in shiny space-age facades. Front and center is the **Spaceship Earth** geosphere. Pavilions to the east are dedicated to mankind's technological achievements; those to the west celebrate human imagination and the natural world.

At the time of this writing, Disney was in the middle of a major remodeling project for Future World. The pandemic and recession have canceled, changed, or delayed many plans, and Disney hasn't yet said exactly what's going to happen or by when. Expect construction around the front entrance, the former Innoventions areas behind Spaceship Earth, and much of the rest of Future World Plaza. Some attractions, restaurants, and shops will be closed or relocated during this project.

FUTURE WORLD EAST AND WEST

FOR NOW, FUTURE WORLD consists of these two main areas. A number of Future World attractions are grouped together in pavilions within these areas, while other attractions are islands unto themselves under the general Future World East or West umbrella. The pavilions aren't as clearly delineated as those in World Showcase, though.

We lead off with the pavilion-less attractions in the following section, beginning with the up-and-coming **Guardians of the Galaxy: Cosmic Rewind;** the others are listed alphabetically. Then we describe Future World's current pavilions and their respective attractions,

KEY TO ABBREVIATIONS In the attraction profiles that follow, each star rating is accompanied by a category label in parentheses (see page 266). E means **Exceptional,** MAA means **Much Above Average,** AA means **Above Average,** A means **Average,** BA means **Below Average,** and MBA means **Much Below Average.**

AVERAGE WAIT-IN-LINE TIMES This generally uses the attractions'

maximum hourly capacity as a fixed reference because ride capacity is subject to change during the pandemic.

Guardians of the Galaxy: Cosmic Rewind
(Future World East/World Discovery; opens 2022)

What it is Massive indoor roller coaster. **Scope and scale** Super-headliner. **When to go** As soon as the park opens, using Early Theme Park Entry if possible. **Participates in Genie+** We think this will be an Individual Attraction Selection instead of a regular Genie+ selection. **Early Theme Park Entry** Likely. **Extended Evening Hours** Likely. **Comment** Estimated 44"–48" minimum height requirement.

DESCRIPTION AND COMMENTS A roller coaster with cars capable of rotating 360 degrees, Guardians of the Galaxy: Cosmic Rewind is a new style of ride for Disney World. Guests begin in the Galaxarium, a planetarium-like exhibition that explores the similarities and mysteries of the formation of Earth's galaxy and the planet Xandar. The Guardians of the Galaxy arrive, and everything goes haywire. Cosmic Rewind includes the first reverse launch on a Disney coaster.

TOURING TIPS Cosmic Rewind will be the highest-priority attraction for most guests once it opens. Your best bet to ride without long waits in line is to (1) stay at a Disney resort to take advantage of Early Theme Park Entry, (2) arrive at EPCOT's main entrance at least an hour before official opening, and (3) head for Cosmic Rewind as soon as you're admitted into the park.

It's possible that Disney will use boarding groups to prevent long standby lines at Cosmic Rewind, as it does at Star Wars: Rise of the Resistance at Hollywood Studios. If that happens, boarding groups would be allocated each morning at 7 a.m. via Disney's My Disney Experience app.

Club Cool *(Central Future World/World Celebration)*

DESCRIPTION AND COMMENTS Attached to the Creations Shop in the center of Future World, this Coca-Cola–sponsored retail space/soda fountain provides free unlimited samples of soft drinks from around the world. Some will taste strange to Americans (such as bitter-tasting **Beverly** from Italy). Past selections have included supersweet **Inca Kola** from Peru, raspberry-flavored **Sparletta Sparberry** from Zimbabwe, and apricot-and-passion fruit-flavored **VegitaBeta** from Japan.

Perhaps because it's free and indoors, kids and teens rate Club Cool higher than most EPCOT offerings.

TOURING TIPS Club Cool can get crowded, so you may have to wait a bit before dispensing your drink during busier times. But because there's not much else to do here, people don't usually spend a lot of time inside. Don't come in expecting to fill a Big Gulp–size cup with free soda—the machines dispense just an ounce or two at a time. Finally, watch out for sticky floors.

Mission: Space *(Future World East/World Discovery)* ★★★★

What it is Space-flight simulator ride. **Scope and scale** Super-headliner. **When to go** First or last hour the park is open. **Participates in Genie+** Yes. **Early Theme Park Entry** Yes. **Extended Evening Hours** Yes. **Comments** Orange version not recommended for pregnant women or anyone prone to motion sickness or claustrophobia; must be 40″ to ride Green, the gentler nonspinning version, and 44″ to ride the Orange version. **Duration of ride** About 5 minutes plus preshow. **Average wait in line per 100 people ahead of you** 4 minutes. **Loading speed** Moderate–fast. **ECV/wheelchair access** Must transfer to ride vehicle.

DESCRIPTION AND COMMENTS Mission: Space was created as a centrifuge-based space simulator that spins riders around a central axis to simulate the g-forces of rocket liftoff and, eventually, a moment of weightlessness. It was one of the most popular rides at Disney World until two guests died after riding it in 2005 and 2006. While neither death was linked directly to the attraction, the negative publicity caused many guests to skip it entirely. In response, Disney added a tamer nonspinning version in 2006.

Disney's lawyers probably clocked as much time as the ride engineers in designing the "lite" version. Even before you walk into the building, you're asked whether you want your ride with or without spin. Choose the spinning version and you're on the **Orange** team; the **Green** team trains on the no-spin side. Either way, you're immediately handed the appropriate "launch ticket" containing the first of myriad warnings, as this *Unofficial Guide* reader discovered:

I chose the more intense version and was handed the Orange launch ticket to read. Basically, it explained that if I had ever had a tonsillectomy or even a mild case of pattern baldness, I should take the less intense ride.

Mission: Space's Orange version is a journey to Mars. The Green version, which takes you orbiting around Earth, is comparatively smooth and mild enough for first-time astronauts.

This San Antonio reader says you don't give up much by choosing the Green option:

I am 65 and have ridden the Orange version a number of times. On our latest trip, we went on the Orange version again and felt a little uncomfortable. My wife suggested that we try the Green version, which I mistakenly believed was some sort of boring mission-control exercise where we would sit behind a computer. The Green version gave us a great experience, including the feeling of lift-off and zero gravity, without the nausea.

A Nashville, Tennessee, reader tried both versions:

I felt the Green was a little lacking, but then Orange was more than I was expecting—the g-force made me want to puke.

Guests for both versions enter the International Space Training Center, where they're introduced to the deep-space exploration program and then divided into groups for flight training. After orientation, they're strapped into space capsules for a simulated flight, where, of course, the unexpected happens. Each capsule accommodates a crew consisting of a group commander, a pilot, a navigator, and an engineer, with a guest in each role. The crews' execution of their respective responsibilities has no effect on the outcome of the flight.

The capsules are small, and both ride versions are amazingly realistic. The nonspinning (Green) version doesn't subject your body to g-forces, but it does bounce and toss you around in a manner roughly comparable to other Disney motion simulators. A Bradenton, Florida, mom found motion sickness to be the least of her problems:

I'd like to see warnings here about claustrophobia—I had no clue until the capsule closed that it would be so tight in there. I went into full panic mode.

TOURING TIPS We're told that the posted wait time for the Orange version is always higher than the Green one to give those on the fence about riding a nudge toward trying the tamer version. Disney can reconfigure the ride's four centrifuges to either Orange or Green based on guest demand.

Having experienced the industrial-strength Mission: Space under a variety of circumstances, we've always felt icky when riding it on an empty stomach, especially first thing in the morning, so we looked around for an expert to tell us why. Because NASA is a codeveloper of Mission: Space and an authority on the effect of g-forces on the human body, we called them. However, they were reluctant to pass along anything resembling medical advice to the general public.

Fortunately, a longtime friend put us in touch with a real NASA astronaut who was willing to share (anonymously) some ideas on what causes the nausea, as well as some tips for preventing it. Our expert guesses, as we do, that low blood sugar is the culprit and suggests eating a normal meal 1-2 hours before experiencing the ride. Avoid milk and tomatoes—they're hard to keep down and, as our contact noted with the voice of experience, particularly unpleasant if they come back up (bananas, we hear, are a better choice.) Another trick of the astronaut trade is to suck on a piece of hard candy or a mint; it's not clear, though, whether the candy helps keep blood-sugar levels high or is just a placebo. If all else fails, each simulator has motion-sickness bags.

Hit the john before you get in line—you'll think your bladder really has been to Mars and back before you get out of this one.

Few things delight our readers more than kibitzing about rides that can make you vomit, and Mission: Space is at the top of this particular heap. From a Yakima, Washington, reader:

Mission: Space is awesome. Quite a few people we spoke to didn't ride because they were intimidated by the warnings about motion sickness.

A woman from Lisbon, Connecticut, used Mission: Space as her own personal relationship lab:

We now understand why husbands and wives will probably never go to space together, after I (the "navigator") pushed his (the "pilot's") button during the flight. I couldn't help being a backseat driver—we could have crashed!

A new restaurant, **Space 220,** opened between Mission: Space and Test Track in 2021 (see page 309). The restaurant's theme is "dine on a space station" and features video displays of Earth from orbit.

Spaceship Earth *(Central Future World/World Celebration)* ★★★★

PRESCHOOL ★★★½ (MBA)	**GRADE SCHOOL ★★★★ (A)**	**TEENS ★★★★ (A)**
YOUNG ADULTS ★★★★ (AA)	**OVER 30 ★★★★ (MAA)**	**SENIORS ★★★★ (A)**

What it is Educational dark ride through past, present, and future. **Scope and scale** Headliner. **When to go** Before noon or after 4 p.m. **Participates in Genie+** Yes. **Early Theme Park Entry** Yes. **Extended Evening Hours** Yes. **Comment** If lines are long when you arrive, try again after 4 p.m. **Duration of ride** About 16 minutes. **Average wait in line per 100 people ahead of you** 3 minutes. **Loading speed** Fast. **ECV/wheelchair access** Must transfer from ECV to provided wheelchair and then from wheelchair to ride vehicle.

DESCRIPTION AND COMMENTS EPCOT's signature landmark, Spaceship Earth spirals through an 18-story geosphere, taking visitors past animatronic scenes depicting mankind's developments in communications, from cave painting to printing to television to space communications and computer networks. The ride shows an amazing use of the geosphere's interior.

Spaceship Earth's scenes are periodically refreshed. The most recent include a home garage showing what looks like the invention of the first Apple personal computer. Interactive screens in the vehicles let you customize the ending animated video. A postshow area with games and interactive exhibits (many closed during the pandemic) rounds out the attraction.

TOURING TIPS Because it's located near EPCOT's main entrance, Spaceship Earth attracts arriving guests soon after the park opens. Your time is better spent on other Future World attractions, such as Soarin' Around the World, Test Track, or (when it opens) Guardians of the Galaxy: Cosmic Rewind. Wait times at Spaceship Earth usually fall after 4 p.m., so one option is to see it on the way out of the park.

PLAY! PAVILION
(Future World East/World Discovery; no opening date announced)

DISNEY HASN'T SAID MUCH about this new Future World pavilion since the pandemic put a hold on indoor entertainment spaces. The concept art seems to show a futuristic cityscape whose storefronts are entrances to mini-attractions. All of these should be themed around the idea of play and feature (and promote) Disney characters and films.

TEST TRACK

SPONSORED BY CHEVROLET, this pavilion (the last one on the left before World Showcase) consists of the **Test Track** ride and **Inside Track,** a collection of transportation-themed exhibits and multimedia presentations. All age groups except preschoolers rate the ride part highly; grade-schoolers, teens, and young adults rate Inside Track as Above Average.

Many readers say Test Track "is one big commercial" for Chevrolet. We agree that the promotional hype is more heavy-handed here than in most other corporate-sponsored attractions. But Test Track is nonetheless one of the most creatively conceived attractions in Disney World.

Test Track (Future World East/World Discovery) ★★★★

PRESCHOOL ★★★★ (A)   GRADE SCHOOL ★★★★½ (MAA)   TEENS ★★★★★ (E)
YOUNG ADULTS ★★★★½ (MAA)   OVER 30 ★★★★½ (MAA)   SENIORS ★★★★½ (MAA)

What it is Auto-test-track simulator ride. **Scope and scale** Super-headliner. **When to go** The first 30 minutes the park is open or just before closing, or use the single-rider line (if offered). **Participates in Genie+** No (it's an Individual Access selection). **Early Theme Park Entry** Yes. **Extended Evening Hours** Yes. **Comment** Must be 40" to ride. **Duration of ride** About 4 minutes. **Average wait in line per 100 people ahead of you** 4½ minutes. **Loading speed** Moderate–fast. **ECV/wheelchair access** Must transfer to ride vehicle.

DESCRIPTION AND COMMENTS Test Track takes guests through the process of designing a new vehicle and then "testing" their car in a high-speed drive through and around the pavilion.

As they enter the pavilion, guests pass displays of sleek, futuristic concept cars and glossy video screens where engineers discuss the work of car design and consumers explain the characteristics of their perfect car.

After hearing about auto design, guests are admitted into the Chevrolet Design Center to create their own concept car. Using a large touchscreen interface (think a giant iPad), groups of up to three guests drag their fingers to design their car's body, engine, wheels, trim, and color. The computer screen reflects each design decision's impact on the car's capability, efficiency, responsiveness, and power. (For example, designing a large truck with a huge V-8 engine increases the car's capability and power but drastically reduces its efficiency.) The entire creative experience takes 5–8 minutes.

Next, guests board a six-seat ride vehicle attached to a track on the ground for an actual drive through Chevrolet's test track. The idea here is that guests are taking part in a computer simulation designed to test their vehicle's performance characteristics. The tests include braking maneuvers, cornering, and acceleration, culminating in a spin around the outside of the pavilion at speeds of up to 65 mph.

The ride visuals are sleek and eye-catching, but trying to understand them as a coherent story is fruitless. At various points during the ride, video screens show the virtual cars designed by the guests in your vehicle and a status update on how the vehicle's tests are progressing. Most guests figure out quickly that absolutely nothing in their car's design has any effect whatsoever on their ride experience.

Test Track's postshow area continues the design process by allowing guests to create commercials for their concept cars. Farther into the pavilion are displays of actual Chevys, many of which you can sit in.

TOURING TIPS Test Track breaks down more often than any ride in Walt Disney World—roughly 4 out of every 10 days of operation. It's also one of the attractions most likely to be down at park opening. Ask a cast member whether it's operating before you trek to this corner of Future World.

When it's working properly, it's one of the park's better attractions—but for this London, Ontario, mom, such instances never materialized:

Test Track breaks down more than any ride I've ever seen. We went back there over and over again, got in line, and then had to get out.

A repeat visitor from East Aurora, New York, suggests that all is not lost when the ride malfunctions:

If the ride breaks down, tell a cast member. They'll most likely give you a slip that allows you to skip the line and ride again. This happened to us twice during the busiest time of the year, and we rode again with no problem.

Because most groups are unwilling to split up, the **single-rider line** (when it's offered) is usually much shorter than the regular standby line.

IMAGINATION!

THIS MULTIATTRACTION PAVILION is on the south side of Future World West, in what will be named **World Nature**. Outside are an "upside-down" waterfall and one of our favorite Future World landmarks: a fountain that "hops" over the heads of unsuspecting passersby. We recommend touring here in the early afternoon; see individual attractions for specifics.

Disney & Pixar Short Film Festival   ★★½

PRESCHOOL ★★★★ (A)	GRADE SCHOOL ★★★★½ (AA)	TEENS ★★★★ (AA)
YOUNG ADULTS ★★★★ (AA)	OVER 30 ★★★★ (AA)	SENIORS ★★★★½ (MAA)

What it is Short movies and trailers for Disney-Pixar films. **Scope and scale** Diversion. **When to go** Hardly ever. **Participates in Genie+** Yes. **Early Theme Park Entry** No.

Extended Evening Hours No. **Duration of presentation** About 20 minutes. **Probable waiting time** About 13 minutes. **ECV/wheelchair access** May remain in wheelchair.

DESCRIPTION AND COMMENTS This theater screens three 3-D shorts—Pixar's *Feast* and *Piper* and Disney's *Get a Horse*—all of which can be easily found online. We think the Short Film Festival's high reader ratings are more indicative of a need for new ideas and attractions in this part of EPCOT than anything else.

TOURING TIPS Rarely crowded. Not a good reason to buy Genie+. Not worth your time or money.

Journey into Imagination with Figment ★★½

PRESCHOOL ★★★★ (A)   GRADE SCHOOL ★★★★ (MBA)   TEENS ★★★ (MBA)
YOUNG ADULTS ★★★ (MBA)   OVER 30 ★★★ (MBA)   SENIORS ★★★½ (MBA)

What it is Dark fantasy-adventure ride. **Scope and scale** Major-attraction wannabe. **When to go** Anytime. **Participates in Genie+** Yes. **Early Theme Park Entry** No. **Extended Evening Hours** No. **Duration of ride** About 6 minutes. **Average wait in line per 100 people ahead of you** 2 minutes. **Loading speed** Fast. **ECV/wheelchair access** May remain in wheelchair.

DESCRIPTION AND COMMENTS Journey into Imagination takes you on a tour of the zany Imagination Institute. Sometimes you're a passive observer and sometimes you're a test subject as the ride provides a glimpse of the fictitious lab's inner workings. Stimulating all your senses and then some, it hits you with optical illusions, a room that defies gravity, and other brain teasers. All along the way, Figment (a purple dragon) makes surprise appearances. After the ride, you can adjourn to an interactive exhibit area.

Reader responses to Figment and company are pretty consistent. From a Franklin, Tennessee, family of three:

Journey into Imagination should be experienced only if you're a HUGE Figment fan. We, on the other hand, hated it.

TOURING TIPS You can enjoy the interactive postshow exhibit without taking the ride, so save it for later in the day. Skip this one if time is short.

THE LAND

THIS HUGE THEMED PAVILION in Future World East/World Nature contains three attractions and two restaurants. When The Land was built, its emphasis was on farming, but it now focuses on the environment.

This is a good place to grab a fast-food lunch. If you're coming here to see the attractions, however, stay away during mealtimes. Be forewarned that strollers aren't allowed inside the pavilion—those with babes in arms might want to bring an infant carrier.

Awesome Planet ★★½

PRESCHOOL ★★★ (MBA)   GRADE SCHOOL ★★★½ (MBA)   TEENS ★★★½ (MBA)
YOUNG ADULTS ★★★½ (BA)   OVER 30 ★★★½ (MBA)   SENIORS ★★★★ (BA)

What it is Indoor film about the environment. **Scope and scale** Minor attraction. **When to go** Anytime, but save it for later in the day. **Participates in Genie+** No. **Early Theme Park Entry** No. **Extended Evening Hours** No. **Comments** The film is on the pavilion's upper level. **Duration of presentation** About 15 minutes. **Probable waiting time** 10 minutes. **ECV/wheelchair access** May remain in wheelchair.

DESCRIPTION AND COMMENTS If *Awesome Planet* is a preview of EPCOT attractions to come, then Earth is doomed and we're all going to die.

Don't get us wrong—the film's visuals are gorgeous and comprehensively cover the planet's animals and biomes alike. And to its credit, *Awesome Planet* actually uses the word *biomes* instead of *environment.*

Also to its credit as a multinational corporation, Disney has always presented the best scientific theories of the time in its public presentations on everything from the relationship between biodiversity and evolution, to dinosaur extinction, to how the solar system and universe were formed. The beginning of *Awesome Planet* continues this, with a fantastic clip about the Giant Impact Hypothesis, which suggests that the earth and moon were formed by a collision of the early Earth and a planet about the size of Mars.

Another good point is that *Awesome Planet* doesn't shy away from showing the threats the planet is currently facing: rising temperatures, higher sea levels, more intense storms, and more wildfires. Perhaps there's some hope for us after all, even in the face of those.

The film's fatal flaw is that it doesn't mention—at all—the root cause of these problems, or what we can do to solve them. In contrast, the previous film that played here, *The Circle of Life,* had an entire segment dedicated to man's negative impacts on the environment, with an uplifting message on how to improve it. Why is this important for a theme park film? For one thing, EPCOT is (ostensibly) dedicated to making the world a better place. In that context, not explaining something as basic as a cause-effect-solution loop for environmental harm borders on negligence.

What makes this even more galling is that the film's script has narrator Ty Burrell mimicking his role as real estate agent Phil Dunphy from the ABC-Disney TV show *Modern Family.* The film's premise is that you're looking for a planet to buy and Phil is walking you through the benefits of Earth—including, yes, use of the phrase "location, location, location."

In other words, Disney thought it was more important for the *Awesome Planet* script—which is about the natural world, in a pavilion called The Land, in a land called World Nature—to have a tie-in to a character from one of its television franchises than to explain the causes of mankind's greatest environmental threats.

We may as well be saying this for EPCOT as well as for the planet: It was great while it lasted.

TOURING TIPS The theater is large enough to accommodate everyone who wants to see the film, at almost any time of year.

Living with the Land ★★★★

PRESCHOOL ★★★½ (MBA)	GRADE SCHOOL ★★★½ (MBA)	TEENS ★★★½ (MBA)
YOUNG ADULTS ★★★★ (A)	OVER 30 ★★★★ (MAA)	SENIORS ★★★★½ (MAA)

What it is Indoor boat ride chronicling the past, present, and future of farming and agriculture in the United States. **Scope and scale** Major attraction. **When to go** Before noon or after 3 p.m. **Participates in Genie+** Yes. **Early Theme Park Entry** No. **Extended Evening Hours** No. **Comments** Go early and save other Land attractions (except for Soarin') for later in the day. The ride is on the pavilion's lower level. **Duration of ride** About 14 minutes. **Average wait in line per 100 people ahead of you** 3 minutes; assumes 15 boats operating. **Loading speed** Moderate. **ECV/wheelchair access** Must transfer from ECV to provided wheelchair.

DESCRIPTION AND COMMENTS The boat ride takes visitors through swamps, past inhospitable farm environments, and through a futuristic greenhouse where real crops are grown using the latest agricultural technologies. The greenhouse exhibits change constantly: Along with familiar fruits and grains such as tomatoes, corn, and rice, recent plantings include Mickey-shaped pumpkins, hot peppers, and more-exotic foods such as Malabar nuts, pandan, caimito, and amaranth. This produce is used in restaurants throughout WDW.

Many EPCOT guests assume that Living with the Land will be too dry and educational for their tastes. A woman from Houston writes:

I had a bad attitude about Living with the Land—I just didn't think I was up for a movie about wheat farming. Wow, was I surprised!

TOURING TIPS See this attraction before the lunch crowd hits The Land's restaurants or after 3 p.m. If you have a special interest in the agricultural techniques being demonstrated, take the **Behind the Seeds at EPCOT** tour (temporarily suspended).

Soarin' Around the World ★★★★½

| PRESCHOOL ★★★★ (A) | GRADE SCHOOL ★★★★½ (MAA) | TEENS ★★★★½ (MAA) |
| YOUNG ADULTS ★★★★½ (MAA) | OVER 30 ★★★★★ (E) | SENIORS ★★★★★ (E) |

What it is Flight simulator ride. **Scope and scale** Super-headliner. **When to go** First 30 minutes the park is open or between 4 p.m. and park closing. **Participates in Genie+** Yes. **Early Theme Park Entry** Yes. **Extended Evening Hours** Yes. **Comments** Entrance on the lower level of the Land Pavilion. May induce motion sickness; must be 40" to ride; Rider Switch option provided (see page 395). **Duration of ride** 5½ minutes. **Average wait in line per 100 people ahead of you** 4 minutes; assumes 3 concourses operating. **Loading speed** Moderate. **ECV/wheelchair access** Must transfer to ride vehicle.

DESCRIPTION AND COMMENTS Soarin' Around the World is a thrill ride for all ages, as exhilarating as a hawk on the wing and as mellow as swinging in a hammock. If you've ever experienced flying dreams, you'll have a sense of how Soarin' feels.

Once you enter the main theater, you're secured in a seat not unlike those on inverted roller coasters. Then the rows of seats swing into position, making you feel as if the floor has dropped away, and you're suspended with your legs dangling. Thus hung out to dry, you embark on a simulated hang-glider tour, with IMAX-quality images projected all around you and with the flight simulator moving in sync with the movie. The images are well chosen and drop-dead beautiful. Special effects include wind, sound, and even smell. The ride itself is thrilling but perfectly smooth.

The film glides around the globe, from the Matterhorn and an Arctic glacier to the Taj Mahal and the Great Wall of China. The visuals are stunningly sharp thanks to laser IMAX projectors, and computer-animated animals create clever transitions. However, the film's display of vertical landmarks appears comically distorted from seats on the left or right side of the screen. To avoid this, once you're directed to one of the three concourses, politely request to wait an extra cycle for seats in row B1 for an ideal view.

Soarin' is a must for guests of any age who meet the height requirement—and yes, there are seniors who absolutely love it. A Lewiston, Maine, dad gives it a hearty thumbs-up:

Soarin' is amazing! Even if the "trip around the world" doesn't make a lot of sense, it's still stunning.

If heights make you nervous, you may have reservations, as did this North Carolina mom:

Soarin' was VERY cool, but also on the scary side for people who are afraid of heights or who don't like that unsteady feeling. While we were "soaring"

*up, I was fine, but when we were going down, I had to keep telling myself,
"This is only an illusion. I cannot fall out. This is only an illusion . . ."*

TOURING TIPS Soarin' Around the World, Test Track, Remy's Ratatouille
Adventure, and (eventually) Guardians of the Galaxy: Cosmic Rewind
take some crowd pressure off all four corners of the park. Keep in mind,
however, that Test Track and *Guardians* will serve up a little too much
thrill for some guests. Soarin', conversely, is an almost-perfect ride for
any age. For that reason, it's at the top of the hit parade. See it before
noon or between 4 p.m. and park closing.

THE SEAS WITH NEMO & FRIENDS

FEATURING CHARACTERS from Disney-Pixar's *Finding Nemo* and *Finding Dory,* this pavilion in Future World West/World Nature encompasses
what was once one of America's top marine aquariums, a ride that
tunnels through the aquarium, an interactive animated film, and a number of walk-through exhibits. Those exhibits need updating, but the
tank alone makes this pavilion a must-visit.

SeaBase ★★★½

PRESCHOOL ★★★★½ (MAA)	GRADE SCHOOL ★★★★ (AA)	TEENS ★★★★ (A)
YOUNG ADULTS ★★★★ (A)	OVER 30 ★★★★ (A)	SENIORS ★★★★ (A)

What it is A huge saltwater aquarium, plus exhibits on oceanography, ocean ecology, and
sea life. **Scope and scale** Major attraction. **When to go** Before 12:30 p.m. or after 5 p.m.,
especially when it gets dark early. **Participates in Genie+** No. **Early Theme Park Entry**
Yes. **Extended Evening Hours** Yes. **Comment** Watch for tank feeding times at 10 a.m.
and 3:30 p.m. **Average wait in line per 100 people ahead of you** 3½ minutes. **Loading
speed** Fast. **ECV/wheelchair access** May remain in wheelchair.

DESCRIPTION AND COMMENTS SeaBase is among Future World's most
ambitious offerings, housed in a 200-foot-diameter, 27-foot-deep main tank
containing fish, marine mammals, and crustaceans in a simulation of an
ocean ecosystem. Visitors can watch the activity through 8-inch-thick windows below the surface (including some at the **Coral Reef** restaurant). Upon
entering, you're directed to the loading area for **The Seas with Nemo &
Friends** (see next profile), an attraction that conveys you via a plexiglass tunnel through SeaBase's main tank. You disembark at **SeaBase Alpha,** where
you can enjoy the other attractions. (If the wait for Nemo & Friends is too
long, head straight for the exhibits by going through the pavilion's exit,
around back, and to the left of the main entrance.)

About two-thirds of the main aquarium is home to reef species, including sharks, rays, and a number of fish that you've seen in quiet repose on
your dinner plate. The other third, separated by an inconspicuous divider,
houses bottlenose dolphins and sea turtles. As you face the main aquarium, the most glare-free viewing windows for the dolphins are on the
ground floor to the left by the escalators. For the reef species, it's the same
floor on the right by the escalators. Stay as long as you like.

TOURING TIPS Experience the ride and *Turtle Talk* by lunchtime before the
park gets crowded, saving the excellent exhibits for later. If you see a cast
member standing near the tank's windows, ask them what kind of fish
you're looking at and whether they have names.

SeaBase is usually less crowded during the evening, making it a perfect
time to have large swaths of the aquarium to yourself.

The Seas with Nemo & Friends ★★★

PRESCHOOL ★★★½ (MAA) GRADE SCHOOL ★★★★ (BA) TEENS ★★★½ (MBA)
YOUNG ADULTS ★★★½ (MBA) OVER 30 ★★★½ (MBA) SENIORS ★★★½ (MBA)

What it is Ride through a tunnel in SeaBase's main tank. **Scope and scale** Major attraction. **When to go** After 2 pm. **Participates in Genie+** Yes. **Early Theme Park Entry** Yes. **Extended Evening Hours** Yes. **Duration of ride** 4 minutes. **Average wait in line per 100 people ahead of you** 3½ minutes. **Loading speed** Fast. **ECV/wheelchair access** Must transfer to ride vehicle.

DESCRIPTION AND COMMENTS The Seas with Nemo & Friends is a high-tech ride featuring characters from the animated hit *Finding Nemo.* The ride likewise deposits you at the heart of the pavilion, where the exhibits, *Turtle Talk with Crush,* and viewing platforms for the main SeaBase aquarium are.

Upon entering the Seas pavilion, you're given the option of experiencing the ride or proceeding directly to the SeaBase exhibit area. If you choose the ride, you'll be ushered to its loading area, where you'll be made comfortable in a "clamobile" for your journey through the aquarium. The attraction features technology that makes it seem as if the animated characters are swimming with live fish. Very cool. Almost immediately you meet Mr. Ray and his class and learn that Nemo is missing. The remainder of the odyssey consists of finding Nemo with the help of Dory, Bruce, Marlin, Squirt, and Crush. Unlike the film, however, the ride ends with a musical finale.

A mom from Asheville, North Carolina, thinks we underestimate the fright factor:

The Seas with Nemo & Friends is scary—sharks, jellyfish, and anglerfish, along with growling, and so on. My 8-year-old hated it!

TOURING TIPS The later you ride, the better (ditto for *Turtle Talk with Crush;* see next profile).

Turtle Talk with Crush ★★★★

PRESCHOOL ★★★★½ (MAA) GRADE SCHOOL ★★★★½ (MAA) TEENS ★★★½ (BA)
YOUNG ADULTS ★★★½ (BA) OVER 30 ★★★★ (A) SENIORS ★★★★ (A)

What it is Interactive animated film. **Scope and scale** Minor attraction. **When to go** After 3 p.m. **Participates in Genie+** Yes. **Early Theme Park Entry** No. **Extended Evening Hours** No. **Duration of presentation** 15 minutes. **Preshow entertainment** None. **Probable waiting time** 10–20 minutes. **ECV/wheelchair access** May remain in wheelchair.

DESCRIPTION AND COMMENTS *Turtle Talk with Crush* is an interactive theater show starring the 153-year-old surfer-dude turtle from *Finding Nemo* and Dory (the blue tang) and other characters from *Finding Dory.*

Although it starts like a typical Disney-theme-park movie, *Turtle Talk* quickly turns into a surprise interactive encounter as the on-screen Crush begins to have actual conversations with guests in the audience. Real-time computer graphics are used to accurately move Crush's mouth when forming words, and he's voiced by a guy who went to the Jeff Spicoli School of Diction.

A mom from Henderson, Colorado, has a crush on Crush:

Turtle Talk with Crush is a must-see. Our 4-year-old was picked out of the crowd by Crush, and we were just amazed by the technology. It was adorable and enjoyed by everyone from Grammy and Papa to the 4-year-old!

TOURING TIPS It's unusual to wait more than one or two shows to get in. If you find long lines at park opening, try back after 3 p.m. when more of the crowd has moved on to World Showcase.

■ WORLD SHOWCASE

EPCOT'S OTHER THEMED AREA, World Showcase is an ongoing world's fair encircling a picturesque 40-acre lagoon. The cuisine, culture, history, and architecture of almost a dozen countries (and one pretend kingdom) are permanently displayed in individual national pavilions spaced along a 1.2-mile promenade. The pavilions replicate familiar landmarks and present representative street scenes from the host countries.

World Showcase has some of the most beautiful gardens anywhere in the United States. In Germany, France, the United Kingdom, Canada, and, to a lesser extent, China, they're sometimes tucked away and out of sight on the World Showcase Promenade. They're best appreciated during the day, as a Clio, Michigan, woman explains:

> *Visit World Showcase in the daylight in order to view the beautiful gardens. We were sorry we didn't do this because we were following the guide and riding rides that we could have done later in the dark.*

In addition to the gardens, World Showcase's live entertainers were some of the most highly rated attractions in EPCOT, for all age groups. The following reviews call out those that are especially popular, and live entertainment may return in 2022. Check the *Times Guide* for performances and schedules.

Some kids find the World Showcase pavilions and live entertainment boring, so to make it more interesting, most EPCOT retail shops sell **Passport Kits** for about $14. Each kit contains a blank "passport" and stamps for every World Showcase country. As kids accompany their folks to each country, they tear out the appropriate stamp and stick it in the passport. Disney has built a lot of profit into this little product, but guests—namely, parents—don't seem to mind the cost.

As this dad from Birmingham, Alabama, relates, the Passport Kit helps get the kids through World Showcase with a minimum of impatience, whining, and tantrums:

> *Adding stamps from the EPCOT countries was the only way I was able to see all the displays with cheerful children.*

Children also enjoy **Kidcot Fun Stops**, which are usually nothing more than a large table set up somewhere in each pavilion. Tables are staffed by Disney cast members who hand out free souvenir postcards from the country. (The tables had small coloring and craft projects before the pandemic.)

A mom from Billerica, Massachusetts, is a fan of the Fun Stops:

> *The Kidcot project at EPCOT was amazing! Our 2- and 5-year-olds loved collecting stamps.*

An adult version of passport-stamp collecting, **Drinking Around the World** (see page 289) is enthusiastically endorsed by a woman from party-hearty New Orleans:

> *We drank a beer in each country at EPCOT—Dad was the designated driver—and posed for photos in each, and it quickly became hilarious, as were the progression-of-drunkenness photos that followed.*

There's another side to Drinking Around the World, though, and this dad from New Hampshire states it forcefully:

Although Disney might not be actively pushing alcohol consumption in World Showcase, they were very obviously not policing it either when we visited. I like to drink and I love a good party, but time and place are important. I know it's a huge moneymaker for Disney, but if it gets any worse than it was this year, I can see where families would start taking their vacations elsewhere—there was nothing fun or relaxing about it. This year folks were either way too drunk or having to do battle to protect their families from those who were.

We avoid EPCOT on fall weekends during the Food & Wine Festival for this reason.

World Showcase also offers some of the most diverse and interesting shopping in Walt Disney World. See Part Seventeen for details.

WORLD SHOWCASE PAVILIONS

MOVING CLOCKWISE AROUND **World Showcase Promenade,** here are the nations represented and their attractions.

For World Showcase, we list Appeal by Age ratings not just for the attractions but for the pavilions themselves. In addition to rides and films, they offer peaceful gardens; unique architecture; interesting places to eat, drink, and rest; top-notch live entertainment; and more. Note that not every pavilion has a dedicated attraction.

MEXICO

PRESCHOOL ★★★½ (BA)	GRADE SCHOOL ★★★★ (BA)	TEENS ★★★★ (A)
YOUNG ADULTS ★★★★ (AA)	OVER 30 ★★★★ (AA)	SENIORS ★★★★ (A)

PRE-COLUMBIAN PYRAMIDS dominate Mexico's architecture. One pyramid forms the pavilion's facade; the other overlooks the restaurant and plaza alongside the **Gran Fiesta Tour** indoor boat ride.

Readers rate Mexico as one of the best pavilions in World Showcase. The village scene inside the pavilion is beautiful and exquisitely detailed. A retail shop occupies most of the left half of the inner pavilion, while Mexico's **Kidcot Fun Stop** is in the first entryway inside the pyramid. On the opposite side of the main floor is **La Cava del Tequila,** a bar serving more than 200 tequilas, as well as cocktails, Mexican beer, wine, and mescal.

The pyramids contain many authentic and valuable artifacts. Take the time to stop and see these treasures.

Gran Fiesta Tour Starring the Three Caballeros   ★★½

PRESCHOOL ★★★★ (AA)	GRADE SCHOOL ★★★★ (BA)	TEENS ★★½ (BA)
YOUNG ADULTS ★★★½ (MBA)	OVER 30 ★★★½ (MBA)	SENIORS ★★★½ (MBA)

What it is Scenic indoor boat ride. **Scope and scale** Minor attraction. **When to go** Before noon or after 5 p.m. **Participates in Genie+** No. **Early Theme Park Entry** No. **Extended Evening Hours** Yes. **Duration of ride** About 7 minutes (plus 1½-minute wait to disembark). **Average wait in line per 100 people ahead of you** 4½ minutes; assumes 16 boats in operation. **Loading speed** Moderate. **ECV/wheelchair access** Must transfer from ECV to provided wheelchair.

DESCRIPTION AND COMMENTS The Gran Fiesta Tour incorporates animated versions of Donald Duck, José Carioca, and Panchito—an avian singing group called The Three Caballeros, from Disney's 1944 film of the same name—to spice up what's basically a slower-paced, Mexican-style It's a Small World.

The story line has the Caballeros scheduled to perform at a fiesta when Donald suddenly goes missing; large video screens show him enjoying Mexico's sights and sounds while José and Panchito try to track him down. Everyone is reunited in time for a rousing concert near the end of the ride.

At the risk of sounding like the Disney geeks we are, we must point out that Panchito is technically the only Mexican Caballero—José Carioca is from Brazil and Donald is from Burbank. In any case, more of the ride's visuals seem to be on the left side of the boat, so have small children sit nearer the left to keep their attention, and listen for Donald's humorous monologue as you wait to disembark at the end of the ride.

A Fanwood, New Jersey, reader feels the ride is culturally insensitive:

The Gran Fiesta Tour was dreadful. If the idea was to rid the ride of derogatory Mexican stereotypes, the designers woefully missed the mark.

A Wilmington, Delaware, woman blames Gran Fiesta Tour's lack of pizzazz on . . . who else?

Donald Duck has ruined even the minimal value of the Mexico ride.

TOURING TIPS If the line looks longer than 5 minutes, grab a margarita (or several!) at La Cava del Tequila and stagger back in 15.

"NORWAY"

PRESCHOOL ★★★½ (BA)   **GRADE SCHOOL ★★★★ (MBA)**   **TEENS ★★★½ (BA)**
YOUNG ADULTS ★★★★ (BA)   **OVER 30 ★★★★ (BA)**   **SENIORS ★★★★ (BA)**

THIS PAVILION (note the scare quotes) encapsulates both everything we love about EPCOT and everything we hate about corporate Disney. Parts of the pavilion—that is, those based on the actual country of Norway—are complex, beautiful, and diverse. Highlights include replicas of the 14th-century **Akershus Castle** in Oslo; a miniature version of a **stave church** built in 1212 in Gol (go inside—the doors open!); and other buildings that accurately represent traditional Scandinavian architecture. We were even inspired to visit Norway specifically because of how great this pavilion *used* to be.

For years after it was built, however, EPCOT's Norway sat in a state of mostly benign neglect. The boat ride, Maelstrom, was a relatively short and lightly themed float-through of the country's history. The postride film was imbued with the same tired "our spirit is our people" platitudes that are repeated, in one way or another, in every World Showcase presentation ever made. But at least it was about a real country, at a real point in time.

All of that changed in 2013 when Disney released *Frozen*, set in the mythical Scandinavian-ish kingdom of Arendelle. In an unprecedented (and, we hope, never repeated) move, Disney replaced two World Showcase attractions about a real country—Norway—with a boat ride about a fictional place in an animated movie.

Yes, we get that a hit like *Frozen* comes along only once every 20 years and that Disney has to make hay while the sun shines. But when it comes to EPCOT, putting a make-believe kingdom in the middle of World Showcase trivializes the *theme* in *theme park*.

Frozen Ever After ★★★★

PRESCHOOL ★★★★½ (MAA)   GRADE SCHOOL ★★★★½ (MAA)   TEENS ★★★★ (A)
YOUNG ADULTS ★★★★ (AA)   OVER 30 ★★★★ (A)   SENIORS ★★★★ (A)

What it is Indoor boat ride and Disney film–shilling tool. **Scope and scale** Major attraction. **When to go** Before noon or after 7 p.m. **Participates in Genie+** No (it's an Individual Access selection). **Early Theme Park Entry** Yes. **Extended Evening Hours** Yes. **Comment** Breaks down fairly often, so check if it's running before you head over. **Duration of ride** Almost 5 minutes. **Average wait in line per 100 people ahead of you** 4 minutes; assumes 12 or 13 boats operating. **Loading speed** Fast. **ECV/wheelchair access** Must transfer to ride vehicle.

DESCRIPTION AND COMMENTS Frozen Ever After is a nice boat ride through the pretend kingdom of Arendelle. The premise is that you've arrived just in time for the Winter in Summer celebration, in which Elsa will use her magical powers to make it snow during the hottest part of the year. Nearly every major and minor character from the film is represented, from Olaf the snowman to Sven the reindeer, along with much of the soundtrack's songs with brand-new lyrics.

Be aware that there's a short, mild section where you're propelled backward for a few seconds, followed by a short downhill and small splash that most kids should take in stride. The ride's detailed sets are augmented with digital projection mapping and more than a dozen animatronics sporting video-screen faces (like Seven Dwarfs Mine Train) and demonstrating some of the most spookily sophisticated movements we've ever seen; watch the fluidity of Elsa's wrists and elbows during the pivotal "Let It Go" scene, and weep for a future of robotic massage parlors.

TOURING TIPS Along with Soarin' Around the World, Test Track, and Remy's Ratatouille Adventure (and until **Guardians of the Galaxy** opens), Frozen Ever After is one of the three attractions that most guests head to first.

The ride experiences more breakdowns than most Walt Disney World attractions. If you plan to see Frozen Ever After first thing in the morning, ask a cast member if it's running before you hike all the way to Norway.

The opening of **Remy's Ratatouille Adventure** should divert much of the park-opening crowds from Frozen to France.

Meet Anna and Elsa at Royal Sommerhus
(closed at press time) ★★★★

PRESCHOOL ★★★★★ (E)   GRADE SCHOOL ★★★★½ (MAA)   TEENS ★★★½ (BA)
YOUNG ADULTS ★★★★ (A)   OVER 30 ★★★★ (A)   SENIORS ★★★★ (BA)

What it is Meet and greet with the famous Frozen princesses. **Scope and scale** Minor attraction. **When to go** At opening, at lunch or dinner, or in the last hour the park is open. **Participates in Genie+** Likely when it reopens. **Early Theme Park Entry** No. **Extended Evening Hours** No. **Duration of experience** About 3 minutes. **Probable waiting time** 15–25 minutes. **ECV/wheelchair access** May remain in wheelchair.

DESCRIPTION AND COMMENTS Royal Sommerhus is a character-greeting venue for Anna and Elsa. While Frozen was set in a fictional kingdom instead of Norway, we grudgingly concede that the meet and greet features traditional Norwegian architecture and crafts. Having visited Norway, we think Disney did a decent job when it comes to authenticity.

TOURING TIPS During times of peak meet and greet, Royal Sommerhus has multiple rooms with multiple Annas and Elsas receiving guests simultaneously. If you're visiting World Showcase in the afternoon, waits tend to be shortest around lunchtime (12:30-ish), 4 p.m., and 6–7 p.m.

CHINA

PRESCHOOL ★★★ (MBA)	GRADE SCHOOL ★★★½ (MBA)	TEENS ★★★½ (BA)
YOUNG ADULTS ★★★★ (A)	OVER 30 ★★★★ (BA)	SENIORS ★★★★ (BA)

A HALF-SIZE REPLICA of the **Temple of Heaven** in Beijing identifies this pavilion. Gardens and reflecting ponds simulate those found in Suzhou, and an art gallery features a lotus-blossom gate and formal saddle roofline.

The pavilion also hosts exhibits on Chinese history and culture. Past exhibits have covered everything from China's indigenous peoples to the layout of Hong Kong Disneyland. The current exhibit displays scaled-down replicas of the terra-cotta "tomb warriors" buried with the Qin dynasty emperor in the second century B.C. to guard him in the afterlife.

Reflections of China   ★★★½

PRESCHOOL ★★½ (MBA)	GRADE SCHOOL ★★★ (MBA)	TEENS ★★★½ (BA)
YOUNG ADULTS ★★★½ (BA)	OVER 30 ★★★½ (BA)	SENIORS ★★★★ (BA)

What it is Film about the Chinese people and culture. **Scope and scale** Major attraction. **When to go** Anytime. **Participates in Genie+** No. **Early Theme Park Entry** No. **Extended Evening Hours** No. **Comment** Audience stands throughout performance. **Duration of presentation** About 14 minutes. **Preshow entertainment** None. **Probable waiting time** 10 minutes. **ECV/wheelchair access** May remain in wheelchair.

DESCRIPTION AND COMMENTS Pass through the Hall of Prayer for Good Harvest to view this Circle-Vision 360° film. Warm and appealing (albeit politically sanitized), it's a brilliant introduction to the people and natural beauty of China. We think the film's relatively low marks are due to the theater's lack of seats, not its cinematic quality. Disney had announced an updated film, *Wondrous China,* for the pavilion by 2021, but that seems delayed into 2022 at the earliest.

TOURING TIPS The film can usually be enjoyed anytime without much waiting.

GERMANY

PRESCHOOL ★★★½ (BA)	GRADE SCHOOL ★★★½ (MBA)	TEENS ★★★½ (BA)
YOUNG ADULTS ★★★★ (A)	OVER 30 ★★★★ (AA)	SENIORS ★★★★ (A)

DOMINATED BY A CLOCK TOWER with boy and girl figures and a fountain depicting St. George's victory over the dragon, the pavilion's *platz* (plaza) is encircled by buildings in traditional architectural styles. The main attraction is **Biergarten Restaurant,** which serves rib-sticking German food and beer (see Part Six, page 316). Yodeling, folk dancing, and oompah-band music are part of the festivities.

The biggest draw in Germany may be **Karamell-Küche** ("Caramel Kitchen"), offering small caramel-covered sweets, including apples and cupcakes. We love coming here for a midday snack to tide us over until dinner. Check out the large and elaborate model railroad just beyond the restrooms as you walk from Germany toward Italy.

Germany's live entertainment is **Oktoberfest Musikanten,** who hold the stage down during meals inside the Biergarten.

Germany is pleasant and festive, so tour anytime.

ITALY

PRESCHOOL ★★★ (MBA) **GRADE SCHOOL** ★★★ (MBA) **TEENS** ★★★½ (BA)
YOUNG ADULTS ★★★★ (A) **OVER 30** ★★★★ (BA) **SENIORS** ★★★★ (BA)

THE ENTRANCE TO ITALY is marked by an 83-foot-tall campanile (bell tower) modeled after the tower in St. Mark's Square in Venice. Left of the campanile is a replica of the 14th-century Doge's Palace, also in the famous square. The pavilion has a waterfront on the lagoon where gondolas are tied to striped moorings.

Streets and courtyards in Italy are among the most realistic in World Showcase. **Via Napoli** has some of the best pizza in Walt Disney World; **Tutto Gusto Wine Cellar** serves small plates along with libations. Because there's no film or ride, you can tour Italy at any hour.

UNITED STATES

PRESCHOOL ★★½ (MBA) **GRADE SCHOOL** ★★★ (MBA) **TEENS** ★★★ (MBA)
YOUNG ADULTS ★★★½ (BA) **OVER 30** ★★★½ (BA) **SENIORS** ★★★★ (AA)

THE UNITED STATES PAVILION consists of a decent barbecue place (the horribly named **Regal Eagle**), a preshow gallery of rotating exhibits on American history (the **American Heritage Gallery**), and a patriotic show called *The American Adventure.*

The **Voices of Liberty** is a skilled and popular singing group that performs all-American and Disney classics at the America Gardens Theatre stage opposite the pavilion. All age groups from teens and up rate the Voices of Liberty's performances highly.

The American Adventure ★★★★

PRESCHOOL ★★½ (MBA) **GRADE SCHOOL** ★★★ (MBA) **TEENS** ★★★½ (MBA)
YOUNG ADULTS ★★★★ (A) **OVER 30** ★★★★ (AA) **SENIORS** ★★★★½ (MAA)

What it is Mixed-media and Audio-Animatronic theater presentation on US history. **Scope and scale** Headliner. **When to go** Anytime. **Participates in Genie+** No. **Early Theme Park Entry** No. **Extended Evening Hours** No. **Duration of presentation** About 29 minutes. **Preshow entertainment** Voices of Liberty vocal group. **Probable waiting time** 25 minutes. **ECV/wheelchair access** May remain in wheelchair.

DESCRIPTION AND COMMENTS *The American Adventure* demonstrates how good Disney theater presentations can be. It's not without it's shortcomings, though.

Housed in an imposing brick structure reminiscent of Colonial Philadelphia, the 29-minute show is a stirring, albeit sanitized, rendition of American history, narrated by an animatronic Mark Twain (who carries a burning cigar) and Ben Franklin. Behind a stage almost half the size of a football field is a 72–foot rear-projection screen on which motion picture images are interwoven with onstage action.

The production arouses patriotic emotion in some viewers but drowsiness in others. A man from Fort Lauderdale, Florida, writes:

I saw The American Adventure *about 10 years ago and snoozed through it. I tried it again and it was still ponderous. I'll try it again in 10 years.*

The American Adventure's scale is both its strength and its weakness: It takes time and money, after all, to mount a presentation this big, which explains why no new stage scenes have been added or updated since the show opened almost 40 years ago. In the meantime, our understanding of

America's history and its role in the world has evolved, but the show hasn't kept pace: Topics such as racism, gender equality, and the environment, for example, are treated as solved problems instead of the ongoing challenges they are. This Erie, Pennsylvania, couple resented what they saw as Disney's squeaky-clean take on American history:

The American Adventure glosses over America's dark points. For example, it neatly cuts out the audio about who bombed Pearl Harbor (at EPCOT, after all, Japan is right next door). Why not focus on the natural beauty of America, its ethnic diversity, its contributions to world society?

TOURING TIPS *The American Adventure* is Disney's best patriotic attraction. The largest crowds usually appear from around 2:30 to 4:30 p.m., but it isn't hard to get into: Because of the theater's large capacity, it's highly unusual not to be admitted to the next performance.

JAPAN

PRESCHOOL ★★★½ (BA)	GRADE SCHOOL ★★★★ (BA)	TEENS ★★★★ (MAA)
YOUNG ADULTS ★★★★½ (MAA)	OVER 30 ★★★★½ (AA)	SENIORS ★★★★ (A)

A FIVE-STORY, BLUE-ROOFED PAGODA, inspired by an eighth-century shrine in Nara, sets this pavilion apart. A hill garden behind it features waterfalls, rocks, flowers, lanterns, paths, and rustic bridges. On the right, as one faces the entrance, a building inspired by the ceremonial and coronation hall at Kyoto's Imperial Palace contains restaurants and a branch of Japan's **Mitsukoshi** department store (in business since 1673). Through the center entrance and to the left, **Bijutsu-kan Gallery** exhibits colorful displays on Japanese pop culture. Recent subjects have included everything from comics to *kawaii,* Japan's "culture of cute."

Japan blends simplicity, architectural grandeur, and natural beauty. Tour anytime.

MOROCCO

PRESCHOOL ★★★ (MBA)	GRADE SCHOOL ★★★½ (MBA)	TEENS ★★★½ (BA)
YOUNG ADULTS ★★★★ (A)	OVER 30 ★★★★ (A)	SENIORS ★★★★ (A)

A BUSTLING MARKET, WINDING STREETS, lofty minarets, and stuccoed archways re-create the romance and intrigue of Marrakesh and Casablanca. The pavilion also has a museum of Moorish art and three restaurants, one of which was closed at press time. Of the restaurants that are open, the counter-service **Tangierine Cafe** is one of the highest-rated restaurants in EPCOT.

A Northfield, Minnesota, mother of two exploring Morocco found, of all things, peace and quiet:

We found an awesome resting place in Morocco—an empty air-conditioned gallery with padded benches. No one came in during the 15 minutes that we rested, which was quite a difference from the rest of the park! Look for the red doors on your left when you enter.

Morocco has neither a ride nor a theater. Tour anytime.

FRANCE

PRESCHOOL ★★★ (MBA)	GRADE SCHOOL ★★★½ (MBA)	TEENS ★★★½ (A)
YOUNG ADULTS ★★★★ (A)	OVER 30 ★★★★ (MAA)	SENIORS ★★★★ (AA)

A REPLICA OF THE EIFFEL TOWER is, *naturellement,* this pavilion's centerpiece. The restaurants, along with the bakery and ice-cream shop, are very popular.

In 2020 France introduced a new *Beauty and the Beast***–themed sing-along show,** which plays 11 a.m.–6 p.m., alternating performances in the same theater as *Impressions de France* (see below), which now plays from 6:30 p.m. to park closing.

Beauty and the Beast Sing-Along ★★

PRESCHOOL ★★★★ (A)	GRADE SCHOOL ★★★★ (A)	TEENS ★★★ (MBA)
YOUNG ADULTS ★★★ (MBA)	OVER 30 ★★★½ (BA)	SENIORS ★★★½ (BA)

What it is Film retelling of the story, with singing. **Scope and scale** Minor attraction. **When to go** 11 a.m.–6 p.m. **Participates in Genie+** No. **Early Theme Park Entry** No. **Extended Evening Hours** No. **Duration of presentation** About 15 minutes. **Preshow entertainment** None. **Probable waiting time** 15 minutes.

DESCRIPTION AND COMMENTS This is the third current Walt Disney World attraction to tell the *Beauty and the Beast* story, along with the Magic Kingdom's *Enchanted Tales with Belle* and Hollywood Studios' *Beauty and the Beast—Live on Stage.* It's also the lowest-rated version, lacking the intimate charm of *Enchanted Tales* and the production value of *Live on Stage.*

For this show, Disney's script writers threw a small twist into the original *Beauty* story, presumably to entice people who have seen the other, better attractions to give this one a chance. That twist is that LeFou, Gaston's sidekick during the film, was secretly working behind the scenes to bring Belle and Beast together. Extra animation scenes were created to tell this (tiny) part of the story, and these scenes serve as glue between clips from the original movie.

Speaking of the original movie, this new idea of LeFou as matchmaker doesn't add up. For one thing, LeFou is the one who tries to persuade angry villagers that Belle's father is crazy, and it's that assembled mob that Gaston leads to kill Beast. If Disney wants us to believe that LeFou was a genius and that attempted homicide was all part of his plan, they're going to need a better script than this.

What's even more confusing is that Mrs. Potts starts the film by saying that this is the true story of Beauty and the Beast. Viewers are left to decide whether everything they thought they knew was wrong or if Angela Lansbury is lying.

Sadly, Disney doesn't take advantage of the full 200-degree screen—the entire film plays on just one of the five screens that can be used.

TOURING TIPS The film rarely plays to full theaters; see anytime.

Impressions de France ★★★½

PRESCHOOL ★★½ (MBA)	GRADE SCHOOL ★★★ (MBA)	TEENS ★★★ (MBA)
YOUNG ADULTS ★★★★ (A)	OVER 30 ★★★★ (A)	SENIORS ★★★★½ (AA)

What it is Film essay on France and its people. **Scope and scale** Major attraction. **When to go** 6:30 p.m.–park closing. **Participates in Genie+** No. **Early Theme Park Entry** No. **Extended Evening Hours** No. **Duration of presentation** About 18 minutes. **Preshow entertainment** None. **Probable waiting time** 15 minutes (at suggested times).

DESCRIPTION AND COMMENTS *Impressions de France* is an 18-minute movie with beautiful scenery, beautiful music, beautiful people, and beautiful towns, all projected over 200 degrees onto five screens.

While we think this is the best film in World Showcase, it was outdated way before the horrific Notre-Dame fire in the spring of 2019. (The film's scenes of the cathedral are particularly poignant now.) Unlike at China and Canada, the audience sits to view the film.

TOURING TIPS Usually begins on the half hour. France's streets are small and become congested when visitors queue for the film.

Remy's Ratatouille Adventure ★★★★

READER-SURVEY RATINGS   TOO NEW TO RATE

What it is Indoor dark ride. **Scope and scale** Major attraction. **When to go** As soon as the park opens. **Participates in Genie+** No (it's an Individual Access selection). **Early Theme Park Entry** Yes. **Extended Evening Hours** Yes. **Duration of ride** About 4½ minutes. **Average wait in line per 100 people ahead of you** About 3 minutes; assumes hourly capacity of around 2,200 riders. **Loading speed** Moderate. **ECV/wheelchair access** Must transfer to ride vehicle.

DESCRIPTION AND COMMENTS In Remy's Ratatouille Adventure, you're shrunk to the size of a rat and whisked through Paris for a quick retelling of the *Ratatouille* film's story. As one of Remy's vermin pals, you watch him ascend from a rodent with a dream to become one of Paris's most celebrated chefs running his own kitchen.

Remy's storytelling combines 3-D films on room-size screens with large, detailed ride-through sets that include water and heat effects. Along with the ride and film, Remy's building and show scenes feature more three-dimensional depth than we expected, adding to the illusion you're in Paris.

A couple of frenetic scenes, such as one in which Remy is chased with a cleaver, may frighten small children.

TOURING TIPS Remy's is the first all-new major attraction at EPCOT in more than a decade and the first in World Showcase since 1988. It's family-friendly, with good theming and a lead character who's as lovable as any disease vector could hope to be. Remy will offer boarding groups when it opens, but that may change. The tips below cover both possibilities.

WITH BOARDING GROUPS Remy may run boarding groups like Rise of the Resistance at Disney's Hollywood Studios. A traditional standby line isn't offered with boarding groups. If Remy uses boarding groups, you'll need to obtain one exactly at 7 a.m. to ride (see page 595 for details). If you can't get one, your other option is to pay for an Individual Attraction pass.

WITH STANDBY LINES If Remy is using a standby line, your best bet is to arrive at EPCOT's International Gateway entrance at least an hour before opening. (If you're driving, park at one of the EPCOT resorts—the Swan and Dolphin are the closest; parking is $35 a day.) That gives you a 10-minute head start on folks walking from the park's front entrance.

Ride Remy's as soon as the park opens. If you have small children, head next to Frozen Ever After in Norway, about 0.5 mile either way around World Showcase. After experiencing Frozen, you'll have completed two of the park's four headliner rides, with Test Track and Soarin' remaining.

UNITED KINGDOM

PRESCHOOL ★★★½ (BA)	GRADE SCHOOL ★★★½ (MBA)	TEENS ★★★½ (MBA)
YOUNG ADULTS ★★★★ (A)	OVER 30 ★★★★ (MAA)	SENIORS ★★★★ (A)

A HODGEPODGE OF PERIOD ARCHITECTURE attempts to depict Britain's urban and rural sides. One street alone has a thatched-roof cottage, a four-story Tudor half-timber building, a pre-Georgian plaster building, a formal Palladian facade of dressed stone, and a city square with a Hyde Park bandstand (whew!). The pavilion consists mostly of shops. The **Rose & Crown Pub** and **Rose & Crown Dining Room** offer dining on the water side of the promenade. For fish and chips to go, try **Yorkshire County Fish Shop.** There are no attractions here, so tour anytime. Reservations aren't required for the Rose & Crown Pub, making it a nice place to stop for a beer.

CANADA

PRESCHOOL ★★★ (MBA)	**GRADE SCHOOL** ★★★ (MBA)	**TEENS** ★★★ (MBA)
YOUNG ADULTS ★★★½ (MBA)	**OVER 30** ★★★½ (MBA)	**SENIORS** ★★★★ (BA)

THE DIVERSITY OF CANADA—cultural, natural, and architectural—is reflected in this large, impressive pavilion. Thirty-foot-tall totem poles embellish an Indian village at the foot of a replica of a magnificent château-style hotel. **Le Cellier** is a steakhouse on Canada's lower level (see page 320 for our review).

Canada Far and Wide ★★★½

PRESCHOOL ★★½ (MBA)	**GRADE SCHOOL** ★★★ (MBA)	**TEENS** ★★★ (MBA)
YOUNG ADULTS ★★★½ (BA)	**OVER 30** ★★★★ (BA)	**SENIORS** ★★★★ (A)

What it is Film essay on Canada and its people. **Scope and scale** Major attraction. **When to go** Anytime. **Participates in Genie+** No. **Early Theme Park Entry** No. **Extended Evening Hours** No. **Comment** Audience stands. **Duration of presentation** About 14 minutes. **Preshow entertainment** None. **Probable waiting time** 9 minutes. **ECV/wheelchair access** May remain in wheelchair.

DESCRIPTION AND COMMENTS The third film shown in this pavilion since EPCOT opened, *Canada Far and Wide* is the best one yet. It combines all of the visual majesty that you'd want in a 360-degree film with a faster, more modern script that works its way from one end of the country to the other. As in the previous films, Montreal, Calgary, and Vancouver get their own segments (some of which have been repurposed from the old films). *Far and Wide* has additional clips of Canada's capital, Ottawa, and specifically mentions its three territories—Yukon, Northwest Territories, and Nunavut—and highlights their Indigenous peoples and cultures.

TOURING TIPS This large-capacity attraction (guests must stand) gets moderate late-morning attendance, as Canada is the first pavilion encountered as you travel counterclockwise around World Showcase Lagoon.

EPCOT ENTERTAINMENT

THIS SECTION describes the live entertainment currently available in Future World and World Showcase throughout the day.

Harmonious

DESCRIPTION AND COMMENTS Disney says this show will integrate music, fireworks, and other special effects with floating sets and projection videos featuring Disney characters. Harmonious Dining Packages are available to see the show at either of two lagoon-side venues: the **Rose & Crown Dining Room** in the United Kingdom and **Spice Road Table** in Morocco. Check-in for dinner starts 45 minutes before the show begins, meaning your meal should end around the same time the show ends. Both restaurants feature fixed-price dinners: $89 per adult and $39 per child at Rose & Crown, and $72 per adult and $31 per child at Spice Road Table. Reservations are strongly encouraged.

VIEWING (AND EXIT) STRATEGIES FOR *HARMONIOUS*

We're told that the best viewing location for *Harmonious* will be in **Showcase Plaza**—the area where Future World meets World Showcase—between the Disney Traders and Port of Entry shops.

The best place on World Showcase Lagoon for any presentation is in a seat on the lakeside veranda of **La Cantina de San Angel** in Mexico. Come early—at least 90 minutes before the show—and relax with a cold drink or snack while you wait for the show.

A woman from Pasadena, California, nailed down the seat but missed the relaxation:

Stake out a prime site for the fireworks at least an hour and a half ahead—and be prepared to defend it. We got a lakeside table at Cantina de San Angel at 6:30 p.m.; unfortunately, we had to put up with troops of people asking us to share our table and trying to wedge themselves between our table and the fence.

La Hacienda de San Angel in Mexico, the **Rose & Crown Pub** in the United Kingdom, and **Spice Road Table** in Morocco also offer lagoon views. The views at the Rose & Crown aren't quite as good as at the other restaurants.

If you want to combine dinner at these sit-down locations with viewing the show, make a reservation for about 1 hour and 15 minutes before showtime. Report a few minutes early for your seating, and tell the host that you want a table outside where you can watch the show. Our experience is that the staff will bend over backward to accommodate you.

Because most guests run for the exits after a presentation and islands in the southern (US Pavilion) half of the lagoon block the view from some places, the most popular spectator positions are along the **northern waterfront,** from Norway and Mexico to Canada and the United Kingdom. Although the northern half of the lagoon offers good views, you must usually claim a spot 60–100 minutes before the show begins.

For those who are late finishing dinner or don't want to spend an hour or more standing by a rail, here are some good viewing spots along the **southern perimeter** (moving counterclockwise from the United Kingdom to Germany) that often go unnoticed until 10–30 minutes before showtime:

1. **International Gateway Island** The pedestrian bridge across the canal near the International Gateway spans an island that offers great viewing. This island normally fills 30 minutes or more before showtime.

2. **Second-Floor (Restaurant-Level) Deck of the Mitsukoshi Building in Japan** An Asian arch slightly blocks your sight line, but this covered deck offers a great vantage point, especially if the weather is iffy. Only La Hacienda de San Angel in Mexico is more protected. If you take up a position on the Mitsukoshi deck and find the wind blowing directly at you, you can be reasonably sure that the smoke from the fireworks won't be far behind. May be reserved by Disney for private viewings.

3. **Gondola Landing at Italy** An elaborate waterfront promenade offers excellent viewing. Claim a spot at least 30 minutes before showtime. May be reserved by Disney for private viewings.

4. **Boat Dock Opposite Germany** Another good vantage point, the dock generally fills 30 minutes before the show. Note that this area may be exposed to more smoke from the fireworks because of EPCOT's prevailing winds.

5. **Waterfront Promenade by Germany** Views are good from the 90-foot-long lagoonside walkway between Germany and China.

None of these viewing locations are reservable (except by Disney), and the best spots get snapped up early on busy nights. Most nights, you can still find an acceptable vantage point 15–30 minutes before the show. Don't position yourself under a tree, an awning, or anything that blocks your overhead view.

A New Yorker who staked out his turf well in advance made this suggestion for staying comfortable until showtime:

> Your excellent guide also served as a seat cushion while I waited seated on the ground. Please make future editions even thicker for greater comfort.

Getting Out of EPCOT After *Harmonious*

Harmonious ends the day at EPCOT—when it's over, everyone leaves at once. It's important, then, to not only decide how quickly you want to flee the park after the show but also to pick a vantage point that will help you do that most efficiently.

The **Skyliner** gondola system connects EPCOT with Disney's Hollywood Studios as well as the **Caribbean Beach, Riviera, Pop Century, and Art of Animation Resorts.** EPCOT's Skyliner station is just beyond the International Gateway exit.

If you're staying at (or you parked at) an EPCOT resort (**Swan, Dolphin, Swan Reserve, Yacht & Beach Club Resorts,** or **BoardWalk Inn & Villas**), watch the show from somewhere on the southern (**United States Pavilion**) half of World Showcase Lagoon; then leave through the **International Gateway** between France and the United Kingdom. You can walk or take a boat back to your hotel from the International Gateway.

If you're staying at any other Disney hotel and you don't have a car, the fastest way home is to join the mass exodus through **the main Future World gate** after the show and catch a bus or the monorail.

Those who've left a car parked in the EPCOT lot have a stickier situation. To beat the crowds, find a viewing spot at **the end of World Showcase Lagoon nearest Future World** (and the exits). Leave as soon as the show wraps up, trying to exit ahead of the crowd (but noting also that thousands of people will be doing exactly the same thing).

If you want a good vantage point **between Mexico and Canada** on the northern end of the lagoon, stake out your spot 60–100 minutes before the show (45–90 minutes during less-busy periods). Otherwise, you may squander more time holding your spot before the show than you would if you watched from the less-congested southern end of the lagoon and took your chances with the crowd upon departure.

More groups get separated and more kids get lost following the evening fireworks than at any other time. In summer, you'll be walking in a throng of up to 30,000 people. If you're heading for the parking lot, anticipate this congestion and pick a spot in the main EPCOT entrance area where you can meet if someone gets separated from the group. We recommend the **flower beds just behind Spaceship Earth,** but check for construction there during the day, and select an alternative location if it's not accessible.

For those with a car, the hardest part is reaching the parking lot: Once you've made it there, you're more or less home free. If you've paid close attention to where you parked, consider skipping the tram and walking. But if you do, watch your children closely and hang on to them for all they're worth—the parking lot can get dicey at this time of night, with hundreds of moving cars.

This Salt Lake City mom hailed a ride out of Dodge, um, EPCOT:

> We watched the fireworks from the bridge at the International Gateway by the United Kingdom; then we just walked straight to the BoardWalk Inn and got a ride from Lyft. It took us 10 minutes from leaving the fireworks to getting to our ride to getting dropped off at our hotel. Super convenient, and we didn't have to leave with the 30,000 people exiting EPCOT in the front of the park!

▌ TRAFFIC PATTERNS *in* EPCOT

WITH REMY'S RATATOUILLE ADVENTURE open, we expect larger crowds at EPCOT's International Gateway entrance because of its proximity to Remy's in France. Remy's should pull crowds from Frozen Ever After in Norway at park opening, although many of those folks will make Frozen the second stop of the day. It should also pull crowds from older attractions in Future World, such as Test Track. It may also help distribute crowds more evenly between Future World and World Showcase at park opening.

When **Guardians of the Galaxy: Cosmic Rewind** opens, it should shift the EPCOT crowd's center of gravity back to Future World. Remy's Ratatouille Adventure will still draw loads of parents with small children, who aren't able to experience Test Track or *Guardians.* That should moderate crowds even more at Frozen Ever After.

▌ EPCOT TOURING PLANS

TOURING EPCOT IS MUCH MORE STRENUOUS than touring the other theme parks. EPCOT requires about twice as much walking, and unlike the Magic Kingdom, it has no effective in-park transportation—wherever you want to go, it's always quicker to walk.

Our plans will help you avoid crowds and bottlenecks on days of moderate to heavy attendance, but they can't shorten the distance you have to cover. (Wear comfortable shoes.) On days of lighter attendance, when crowds aren't a critical factor, the plans in this book will help you organize your tour. We offer two **One-Day Touring Plans:**

- EPCOT One-Day Touring Plan (without Guardians of the Galaxy: Cosmic Rewind)
- EPCOT One-Day Touring Plan (with Guardians of the Galaxy: Cosmic Rewind)

These pack as much as possible into one long day and require a lot of hustle and stamina.

Each EPCOT touring plan has two versions: one for Disney resort guests and one for off-site guests. Plans for on-site guests use Disney's **Early Theme Park Entry** benefit (see page 38) to minimize waits in line. Early Entry means thousands of guests will already be in lines and on rides before off-site guests step foot in the park, so the touring strategy for off-site guests must necessarily be different.

The most straightforward way to convert these one-day plans to two-day plans is to see the attractions on the east side of the park on one day, and the west side on the other.

An alternative strategy for converting the one-day plans to two-day plans is to tour Future World's attractions on one day and World Showcase's attractions on the other. That strategy has a couple of disadvantages: One is that Future World will have three headliner attractions once *Guardians* opens, while World Showcase will have one (Remy's); the second is that World Showcase has better dining choices for dinner.

Our EPCOT touring plans for this edition do not assume use of **Genie+** or **Individual Attraction Selections.** If you opt for either or both of these, simply use our free software to adjust your plan.

"Not a Touring Plan" Touring Plans

For the type-B reader, these touring plans (see page 710) dispense with detailed step-by-step strategies for saving every last minute in line. For EPCOT, these "not" touring plans include advice for adults and parents with one day in the park, for anyone with two days, and for anyone with an afternoon and a full day to tour.

BEFORE YOU GO

1. Call ☎ 407-824-4321 or check the day before you go to verify official opening time.

2. Make reservations at the EPCOT full-service restaurant(s) of your choice 60 days before your visit.

3. At 7 a.m. on the day of your visit, make Genie+ and/or Individual Attraction Selection reservations if you bought them.

EPCOT TOURING PLANS AT A GLANCE

EPCOT One-Day Touring Plan *(four versions)* *(pages 723–726)*

FOR Adults and children age 8 or older.
ASSUMES Willingness to experience all major rides and shows.

THE FIRST TWO VERSIONS OF THIS PLAN include just **Soarin' Around the World, Frozen Ever After, Test Track,** and **Remy's Ratatouille Adventure;** the last two add **Guardians of the Galaxy: Cosmic Rewind.**

PART THIRTEEN

DISNEY'S ANIMAL KINGDOM

KEY QUESTIONS ANSWERED IN THIS CHAPTER

◼◼ OVERVIEW

> **unofficial TIP**
> Disney's Animal Kingdom is four times the size of the Magic Kingdom and almost twice the size of EPCOT, but most of it is accessible only on guided tours or as part of attractions.

WITH ITS LUSH FLORA, WINDING STREAMS, meandering paths, and exotic settings, Disney's Animal Kingdom is stunningly beautiful. The landscaping alone conjures images of rainforest, veldt, and formal gardens. Soothing, mysterious, and exciting, every vista is a feast for the eyes. Add to this loveliness a population of some 1,700 animals, replicas of Africa's and Asia's most intriguing architecture, and a singular array of attractions, and you have Disney's most distinctive theme park.

Animal Kingdom comprises six "lands"—**The Oasis, Discovery Island, DinoLand U.S.A., Africa, Asia,** and **Pandora—The World of Avatar**—but it offers relatively few attractions in its 500 acres: eight rides, several walk-through exhibits, an indoor theater, three amphitheaters, a conservation exhibit, and a children's playground.

Once upon a time, Disney's idea of animals in theme parks was limited to cartoon characters and Audio-Animatronic figures. Meanwhile, 84 miles away in Tampa, **Busch Gardens** had been slowly building on a successful combination of natural-habitat zoological exhibits and thrill rides since it opened in 1959.

Of course, there's nothing like competition to make Disney change its tune, and in 1989, shortly after the opening of what is now Disney's Hollywood Studios, then-Imagineer Jim Rohde presented then-CEO

continued on page 544

Disney's Animal Kingdom

9

11

18

D

C

CC

Africa

8

A

Discovery Island

E

15

BB

B

H

17

2

14

F

Pandora—The
World of Avatar

The Oasis

7

DD

G

13

AA

Bag Checks

Restrooms

First Aid Center

G+ Attraction Offers Genie+

IAS Attraction Offers Individual Access

Recommended Dining

Not To Be Missed

Attractions

1. The Animation Experience at Conservation Station G+
2. Avatar Flight of Passage ☑ IAS
3. The Boneyard
4. Conservation Station and Affection Section
5. Dinosaur ☑ G+
6. Expedition Everest ☑ IAS
7. *Feathered Friends in Flight*
8. *Festival of the Lion King* ☑
9. Gorilla Falls Exploration Trail
10. Kali River Rapids G+
11. Kilimanjaro Safaris G+
12. Maharajah Jungle Trek
13. Meet Favorite Disney Pals at Adventurers Outpost
14. Na'vi River Journey ☑ G+
15. Tree of Life/ *Awakenings/ It's Tough to Be a Bug!*
16. TriceraTop Spin
17. Wilderness Explorers ☑
18. Wildlife Express Train

Rafiki's Planet Watch

Asia

Finding Nemo— The Musical *(opening 2022)*

DinoLand U.S.A.

Counter-Service Restaurants

A. Creature Comforts *(Starbucks)* 👍
B. Flame Tree Barbecue 👍
C. Harambe Market 👍
D. Kusafiri Coffee Shop & Bakery 👍
E. Pizzafari
F. Restaurantosaurus
G. Royal Anandapur Tea Company
H. Satu'li Canteen 👍
I. Yak & Yeti Local Food Cafes 👍

Table-Service Restaurants

AA. Rainforest Cafe
BB. Tiffins
CC. Tusker House Restaurant 👍
DD. Yak & Yeti Restaurant 👍

continued from page 541

Michael Eisner with his proposal for a zoological park. Disney went public with its plans for Animal Kingdom in 1995, and the park opened three years later.

Even if Disney largely copied its recipe from Busch Gardens, Animal Kingdom serves up more than its share of innovations. For starters, there's lots of space, allowing for sweeping vistas worthy of *National Geographic* or the Discovery Channel. Then there are the enclosures—natural in appearance, with few or no apparent barriers between you and the animals. The operative word, of course, is *apparent:* That flimsy stand of bamboo separating you from a gorilla is actually a neatly disguised set of steel rods embedded in concrete.

Animal Kingdom has gotten mixed reviews since it opened in 1998. The animal exhibits, along with the architecture and the landscaping, consistently draw praise, but guests also complain about the park's layout—in particular, the necessity of backtracking through Discovery Island to reach the themed areas—as well as its congested walkways and lack of shade.

Yet in spite of its weaknesses, Animal Kingdom works. It's a place to linger in, to savor. Of course, Disney, with its crowds, lines, and regimentation, has conditioned its theme park guests to do just the opposite of that; nevertheless, many visitors understand instinctively that Animal Kingdom must be approached differently from, say, the Magic Kingdom.

A mother of three (ages 5, 7, and 9) from Hampton Bays, New York, writes:

> *To enjoy Animal Kingdom, you must have the right attitude. It's an educational experience, not a thrill park. We spoke to a cast member who played games with the kids—my daughter found a drawer full of butterflies, and the boys located a hidden ostrich egg and lion skull.*

We agree: Animal Kingdom's best features are its animals, nature trails, and cast members. The **Wilderness Explorers** scavenger hunt

ANIMAL KINGDOM SERVICES

MOST PARK SERVICES are inside the main entrance and on Discovery Island, as follows:

Baby Care Center On Discovery Island

Banking Services ATMs at the main entrance, by the turnstiles, and near Dinosaur in DinoLand U.S.A.

Cell Phone Charging Outlets available at Pizzafari, Restaurantosaurus, Tusker House, and Conservation Station

Entertainment Information In the *Times Guide,* available at Guest Relations

First Aid Center On Discovery Island

Guest Relations/Information Inside the main entrance to the left

Lost and Found Inside the main entrance to the left

Lost Persons Can be reported at Guest Relations and the Baby Care Center

Magic Bands Just inside the main entrance at Garden Gate Gifts, in Africa at Mombasa Marketplace, and at other retail shops throughout the park

Storage Lockers Inside the main entrance to the left

Wheelchair, ECV/ESV, and Stroller Rentals Inside the main entrance, to the right (see page 552) ties together all of the park's best elements, and it's part of our Animal Kingdom touring plan described on page 727–728. It's a lot of fun to play, and you just might learn something along the way.

Pandora—The World of Avatar is Animal Kingdom's newest "land." It completes an expansion project begun in 2011, when Disney signed *Avatar* filmmaker James Cameron to a development deal. Pandora has two attractions: **Avatar Flight of Passage,** a state-of-the-art flight simulator, and **Na'vi River Journey,** a slow-moving boat ride through colorful forests and swamps. Readers rate Flight of Passage as one of the best attractions at any Disney *or* Universal theme park in the US.

Like other Disney parks, many Animal Kingdom shows, character greetings, and dining locations were closed during the pandemic. We've noted in this chapter the attractions and restaurants closed at press time and updated the Animal Kingdom touring plan accordingly.

ARRIVING

FROM INSIDE WALT DISNEY WORLD, Disney buses are the only free option for getting to Animal Kingdom from on-property resorts, but service from many resorts is erratic.

DRIVING Animal Kingdom is in the southwest corner of Walt Disney World; from I-4, take **Exit 65** for Osceola Parkway. (For GPS coordinates, see page 439.) **Animal Kingdom Lodge** is about a mile from the park on its west side; **Blizzard Beach** water park, **Coronado Springs Resort,** and the **All-Star Resorts** are also in the vicinity.

> *unofficial* **TIP**
> If you want to beat the lines at Pandora, arrive well before opening or wait until the last hour the park is open.

Animal Kingdom has its own vast pay parking lot with close-in parking for the disabled. Disney usually opens the parking lot about an hour before official park opening. Once parked, you can walk or catch a tram to the entrance.

ANIMAL KINGDOM OPENING (ROPE DROP)

ANIMAL KINGDOM IS USUALLY the first Disney World park to open in the morning, and the first to close. Expect it to open at 8 a.m. daily, and possibly earlier during holidays and other times of peak attendance.

On-site guests eligible for Early Theme Park Entry should arrive at the entrance 60 minutes before official opening (30 minutes before Early Entry) on all days. Off-site guests should arrive 30 minutes before official opening on all days.

Once you're in the park, you'll usually find all of Pandora, along with *It's Tough to be a Bug,* **Expedition Everest, Kilimanjaro Safaris, Dinosaur,** and **TriceraTop Spin,** already open.

> *unofficial* **TIP**
> If you want to ride Avatar Flight of Passage without paying for Genie+ or Individual Attraction Selections during summer and holidays, your best chance to avoid a long wait in line is to stay at a Disney hotel and arrive at the Animal Kingdom entrance 1 hour before official opening.

Because **Avatar Flight of Passage** is among the hottest tickets in all of Walt Disney World, Animal Kingdom adjusts its opening procedures based on crowd levels, catching some guests by surprise. Here's what a Fort Wayne, Indiana, reader experienced while trying to beat the morning crush:

If you plan to tour Animal Kingdom, arrive as early as possible, then 30 minutes earlier. We arrived at 7:20 expecting to be in the crowd for rope drop, but the crowd had already been admitted and we immediately had a 90-minute wait—before 7:40 a.m.—for Avatar Flight of Passage.

unofficial **TIP**
To confirm the official park-opening time, check online the night before you go. To stay abreast of ride closures, delays, and the like, also check the daily *Times Guide*, the My Disney Experience app, and/or our app, **Lines.**

Because the park has relatively few attractions, most guests who arrive at park opening have left the park by midafternoon. The lack of attractions also means Animal Kingdom can get swamped from midmorning to early afternoon during holidays.

During slower or colder periods, the park may delay opening its secondary attractions: **Kali River Rapids** and **Maharajah Jungle Trek** in Asia, as well as **The Boneyard** in DinoLand U.S.A. The **Wildlife Express Train** and **Conservation Station** may either open late or remain closed for the day.

GETTING ORIENTED

AT THE ENTRANCE PLAZA, the security checkpoint and ticket kiosks front the main entrance. To your right, before the turnstiles, is an ATM. After you pass through the turnstiles, **wheelchair and stroller rentals** are to your right. **Guest Relations**—park headquarters for information, guide maps, entertainment schedules (*Times Guide*), lost and found, and lost persons—is to the left. Nearby are **restrooms and lockers.** Beyond the entrance plaza, you enter **The Oasis,** a lush green network of converging pathways winding through a landscape punctuated with streams, waterfalls, and misty glades and inhabited by what Disney calls "colorful and unusual animals."

Animal Kingdom is arranged somewhat like the Magic Kingdom, in a hub-and-spoke configuration. Similar to Main Street, U.S.A., The Oasis funnels visitors to **Discovery Island,** at the center of the park. Dominated by the park's central icon, the 14-story hand-carved **Tree of Life,** Discovery Island is the park's retail and dining center. From here, guests fan out to access the themed areas: **Africa, Asia, DinoLand U.S.A.,** and **Pandora.** Discovery Island also hosts a theater attraction in the Tree of Life and several short nature trails.

You should be able to take in all of Animal Kingdom in one day—but we encourage you to take your time.

NOT TO BE MISSED AT DISNEY'S ANIMAL KINGDOM
DISCOVERY ISLAND • Tree of Life • Wilderness Explorers
AFRICA • *Festival of the Lion King* • Kilimanjaro Safaris
ASIA • Expedition Everest
DINOLAND U.S.A. • Dinosaur • *Finding Nemo—The Musical (reopens in 2022)*
PANDORA—THE WORLD OF AVATAR • Avatar Flight of Passage

ANIMAL KINGDOM
Most Popular Attractions by Age Group

PRESCHOOL	GRADE SCHOOL	TEENS	YOUNG ADULTS	OVER 30	SENIORS
Meet Favorite Disney Pals at Adventurers Outpost*	Avatar Flight of Passage	Avatar Flight of Passage	Avatar Flight of Passage	Avatar Flight of Passage	Kilimanjaro Safaris
Kilimanjaro Safaris	Kilimanjaro Safaris	Expedition Everest	Expedition Everest	Expedition Everest	*Festival of the Lion King*
Festival of the Lion King	Expedition Everest	Kilimanjaro Safaris	Kilimanjaro Safaris	Kilimanjaro Safaris	Avatar Flight of Passage
TriceraTop Spin	*Festival of the Lion King*	*Festival of the Lion King*	*Festival of the Lion King*	*Festival of the Lion King*	Expedition Everest
Kali River Rapids	Kali River Rapids	Kali River Rapids	Tree of Life/ *Awakenings*	Gorilla Falls Exploration Trail	Gorilla Falls Exploration Trail
The Boneyard*	The Boneyard*	Dinosaur	The Animation Experience	Kali River Rapids	Maharajah Jungle Trek
Na'vi River Journey	Wilderness Explorers	Gorilla Falls Exploration Trail	Dinosaur	Tree of Life/ *Awakenings*	Na'vi River Journey
Gorilla Falls Exploration Trail	Meet Favorite Disney Pals at Adventurers Outpost*	Maharajah Jungle Trek	Kali River Rapids	The Animation Experience	*It's Tough to Be a Bug*
Wilderness Explorers	Na'vi River Journey	*Finding Nemo—The Musical*	Gorilla Falls Exploration Trail	Meet Favorite Disney Pals at Adventurers Outpost*	Kali River Rapids

*Closed at press time

FAVORITE ATTRACTIONS BY AGE GROUP

ANIMAL KINGDOM HAS ABOUT TWO DOZEN RIDES, shows, fireworks shows, live performers, and seasonal entertainment. The table below shows the park's most popular attractions by age group.

Kilimanjaro Safaris and *Festival of the Lion King* appear in the list of every age group. All groups except preschoolers and seniors put **Avatar Flight of Passage** at No. 1, and all but preschoolers include Expedition Everest in their top attractions. Every age group's list includes at least one animal-centered attraction.

The average reader ratings for all Animal Kingdom attractions by age group are as follows, based on the 70,000 attraction ratings we received over the past 18 months:

- **PRESCHOOL** 3.9 stars
- **GRADE SCHOOL** 4.1 stars
- **TEENS** 3.8 stars
- **YOUNG ADULTS** 3.8 stars
- **OVER 30** 4.0 stars
- **SENIORS** 4.0 stars

GENIE+, LIGHTNING LANE, AND INDIVIDUAL ATTRACTION SELECTIONS AND TOURING PLANS

AS A REMINDER, the big questions for these new programs are:

1. Is Genie+ worth paying for at the Animal Kingdom?
2. If worth the cost, which attractions benefit most from Genie+ or Individual Attraction Selections?
3. How can you avoid paying for Individual Attraction Selections?
4. How do Genie+ and/or Individual Attraction Selections work with the touring plans?

GENIE+ AND INDIVIDUAL ATTRACTION SELECTIONS AT DISNEY'S ANIMAL KINGDOM	
AFRICA	
• Kilimanjaro Safaris (*Individual Access only*)	• The Animation Experience at Conservation Station
ASIA	
• Expedition Everest (*Individual Access* only)	• Kali River Rapids
DINOLAND U.S.A.	
• Dinosaur	
PANDORA—THE WORLD OF AVATAR	
• Avatar Flight of Passage (*Individual Access only*)	• Na'vi River Journey

Character greetings were not operating when Genie+ and Lightning Lane were introduced. We think character greetings will be added upon their return.

Is Genie+ Worth Paying For at Animal Kingdom?

WE THINK GENIE+ IS WORTH the cost at Animal Kingdom if you meet any of these criteria:

- You'll arrive at the park after Early Theme Park Entry begins (that is, you won't be at the park as soon as it opens). This includes off-site guests who aren't eligible for Early Theme Park Entry and on-site guests who want to sleep in.
- You won't be using a touring plan.
- You're visiting during a holiday, spring break, or other peak season.

Regardless of the time of year you visit, arriving at park opening should allow you to see at least two of the Animal Kingdom's headliner attractions without significant waits. Since only six attractions participate in the Genie+ program, it's unlikely that you'd need more than two or three Genie+ reservations per day. On days of heavy attendance, though, the lack of attractions at Animal Kingdom means you'll be competing with lots of other people for Genie+ reservations, pushing out the Genie+ return times, and limiting how many you can obtain per day.

ESTIMATED TIME SAVINGS USING A TOURING PLAN WITH GENIE+ FOR VARIOUS CROWD LEVELS			
CROWD LEVEL	**TYPICAL USE (2 GENIE+ RESERVATIONS PER DAY)**	**OPTIMISTIC USE (4 GENIE+ RESERVATIONS PER DAY)**	**FULL USE (6 GENIE+ RESERVATIONS PER DAY)**
Low	20 minutes saved	40 minutes saved	60 minutes saved
Moderate	30 minutes saved	50 minutes saved	85 minutes saved
High	40 minutes saved	70 minutes saved	125 minutes saved

Which Attractions Benefit Most from Genie+ or Individual Attraction Selections?

For Genie+, the chart below shows the top six attractions that might benefit most from using Genie+, based on current wait times and historical FastPass+ data. The chart goes in descending order of priority.

ANIMAL KINGDOM ATTRACTIONS THAT BENEFIT MOST FROM GENIE+ (HIGHEST PRIORITY TO LOWEST)	
1 Na'vi River Journey	**4** Kali River Rapids
2 Expedition Everest	**5** Animation Experience
3 Dinosaur	
Note: Character greetings were not open at press time.	

Regarding Individual Attraction Selections, we think Flight of Passage and Kilimanjaro Safaris will be the only Individual Attraction Selections. Whether those are worth the cost will depend on where Disney's charging for those and how that lines up on your personal time-versus-money spectrum.

How Can You Avoid Paying for Individual Attraction Selections?

Animal Kingdom may not participate in Disney's Extended Theme Park Hours program. Even if it did, we think it's unlikely that Kilimanjaro Safaris would operate that late. So your best option to see both Flight of Passage and the Safaris is to stay at a Disney resort and use Early Theme Park Entry: Head to Flight of Passage as soon as the park opens, then ride Kilimanjaro Safaris.

How Do Genie+ and Individual Attraction Selections Work with the Touring Plans?

See our advice for the Magic Kingdom on page 463.

DINING IN ANIMAL KINGDOM

HERE'S A QUICK RECAP of Animal Kingdom's top restaurants, rated by readers, starting with the highest rated. See Part Six, "Dining In and Around Walt Disney World," for details.

ANIMAL KINGDOM RESTAURANT REFRESHER	
COUNTER SERVICE	**FULL SERVICE**
Satu'li Canteen (⊕ 97%/Exceptional), Pandora	**Nomad Lounge** (⊕ 97%/Exceptional), Discovery Island
Creature Comforts (Starbucks) (⊕ 96%/Exceptional), Discovery island	**Yak & Yeti Restaurant** (⊕ 95%/Much Above Average), Asia
Pongu Pongu (⊕ 96%/Exceptional), Pandora	**Tusker House** (⊕ 90%/Average), Africa
Flame Tree Barbecue (⊕ 95%/ Exceptional), Discovery Island	**Tiffins** (⊕ 89%/Average), Discovery Island
Harambe Market (⊕ 95%/Much Above Average), Africa	**Rainforest Cafe** (⊕ 72%/Do Not Visit), Animal Kingdom entrance
Thirsty River Bar & Trek Snacks (⊕ 94%/Much Above Average), Asia	
Royal Anandapur Tea Company (⊕ 91%/Average), Asia	

The OASIS

THOUGH THE FUNCTIONAL PURPOSE of The Oasis is the same as that of Main Street, U.S.A., in the Magic Kingdom—that is, to direct guests to the center of the park—it also serves as what Disney calls a transitional experience. In plain English, this means that it sets the stage and gets you in the right mood for enjoying Disney's Animal Kingdom. The minute you pass through the turnstiles, however, you'll know that this isn't just another central hub.

Rather than consisting of a single broad thoroughfare, The Oasis encompasses multiple paths. Whereas Main Street, Hollywood Boulevard at the Studios, and the Future World entrance plaza at EPCOT direct you like an arrow straight into the heart of their respective parks, The Oasis immediately envelops you in an environment replete with choices. Nothing obvious clues you in to where you're going: There's no fairy-tale castle or giant golf ball to beckon you. Instead you'll find a lush, green, canopied landscape dotted with streams, grottoes, and waterfalls.

The zoological exhibits in The Oasis are representative of those throughout Animal Kingdom. A sign identifies the animal(s) in each exhibit, but be aware that there's no guarantee they'll be immediately visible. Because most of the habitats are large and provide their occupants ample terrain in which to hide, you must linger and concentrate, looking for small movements in the vegetation. When you do spot the animal, you may make out only a shadowy figure, or perhaps only a leg or a tail.

The Oasis is a place to savor and appreciate—if you're used to blitzing at warp speed to queue up for the big attractions, plan to spend some time here, on your way in or out of the park. The Oasis usually closes 30–60 minutes after the rest of Animal Kingdom.

DISCOVERY ISLAND

DISCOVERY ISLAND COMBINES TROPICAL GREENERY with whimsical equatorial African architecture. Connected to the other lands by bridges, the island is the hub from which guests can access the park's various themed areas. A village is arrayed in a crescent around the base of Animal Kingdom's iconic landmark, the **Tree of Life**. Towering 14 stories above the village, it's this park's version of Cinderella Castle or Spaceship Earth. Flanked by pools, meadows, and exotic gardens populated by a diversity of birds and animals, the Tree of Life houses a theater attraction inspired by Disney-Pixar's *A Bug's Life*.

As you enter Discovery Island over the bridge from The Oasis and the park entrance, you'll see the Tree of Life directly ahead, at 12 o'clock. The bridge to **Asia** is to the right of the tree at 2 o'clock, with the bridge to **DinoLand U.S.A.** at roughly 4 o'clock. The bridge connecting The Oasis to Discovery Island is at 6 o'clock, the bridge to **Pandora—The World of Avatar** is at 8 o'clock, and the bridge to **Africa** is at 11 o'clock.

Discovery Island is also the park's central headquarters for shopping and services. Here you'll find the **First Aid** and **Baby Care Centers**. For Disney merchandise, try **Island Mercantile**. Counter-service food and snacks are available, as is upscale full-service dining at **Tiffins**.

KEY TO ABBREVIATIONS In the attraction profiles that follow, each star rating is accompanied by a category label in parentheses (see page 266). E means **Exceptional**, MAA means **Much Above Average**, AA means **Above Average**, A means **Average**, BA means **Below Average**, and MBA means **Much Below Average**.

AVERAGE WAIT-IN-LINE TIMES This generally uses the attractions' maximum hourly capacity as a fixed reference because ride capacity may change during the pandemic.

Discovery Island Trails

PRESCHOOL ★★★½ (BA)   GRADE SCHOOL ★★★★ (A)   TEENS ★★★½ (BA)
YOUNG ADULTS ★★★★ (A)   OVER 30 ★★★★ (A)   SENIORS ★★★★ (A)

Participates in Genie+ No. Early Theme Park Entry Yes. Extended Evening Hours No.

DESCRIPTION AND COMMENTS Winding behind the Tree of Life, a network of walking trails offers around a dozen animal-viewing opportunities, from otters and tortoises to lemurs, storks, and porcupines. One end of the path begins just before the bridge from Discovery Island to Africa, on the right side of the walkway; the other is to the right of the entrance to the Tree of Life. In addition to the animals, you'll find verdant landscaping, waterfalls, and quiet spots to sit and reflect on your relationship with nature. Or nap. As we think Henry David Thoreau once said, "Not until we have dozed do we begin to understand ourselves."

Meet Favorite Disney Pals at Adventurers Outpost
(closed at press time) ★★★½

PRESCHOOL ★★★★★ (E)   GRADE SCHOOL ★★★★½ (AA)   TEENS ★★★★ (A)
YOUNG ADULTS ★★★★ (A)   OVER 30 ★★★★½ (AA)   SENIORS ★★★★½ (AA)

What it is Character-greeting venue. Scope and scale Minor attraction. When to go First thing in the morning or after 5 p.m. Duration of experience About 2 minutes. Probable waiting time About 20 minutes. Queue speed Fast. ECV/wheelchair access May remain in wheelchair. Participates in Genie+ Likely upon return. Early Theme Park Entry No. Extended Evening Hours No.

DESCRIPTION AND COMMENTS An indoor, air-conditioned greeting location for Mickey and Minnie, Adventurers Outpost is decorated with photos and other memorabilia from the Mouses' world travels.

TOURING TIPS The Outpost has two greeting rooms with two identical sets of characters, so lines move fairly quickly.

Tree of Life ★★★★½ / It's Tough to Be a Bug! ★★★ / Awakenings ★★★★

It's Tough to Be a Bug!

PRESCHOOL ★★★½ (BA)   GRADE SCHOOL ★★★★ (BA)   TEENS ★★★½ (MBA)
YOUNG ADULTS ★★★½ (MBA)   OVER 30 ★★★★ (MBA)   SENIORS ★★★★ (BA)

Awakenings

PRESCHOOL ★★★★ (A)   GRADE SCHOOL ★★★★ (A)   TEENS ★★★★ (A)
YOUNG ADULTS ★★★★½ (A)   OVER 30 ★★★★½ (A)   SENIORS ★★★★½ (AA)

What it is 3-D theater show/nighttime projection show. Scope and scale Major attraction. When to go Anytime. Comment The theater is inside the tree. Duration of presentation About 8 minutes. Probable waiting time Under 20 minutes. ECV/wheelchair access May remain in wheelchair. Participates in Genie+ No. Early Theme Park Entry Yes. Extended Evening Hours No.

DESCRIPTION AND COMMENTS The Tree of Life, apart from its size, is a work of art—the most visually compelling structure in any Disney theme park. Although it's magnificent from afar, it's not until you get up close that you can truly appreciate the tree's rich detail. What appears from a distance to be ancient gnarled bark is, in fact, hundreds of carvings depicting all manner of wildlife, each integrated seamlessly into the trunk, roots, and limbs of the tree. Look for these carvings on the front left side of the tree, along the Discovery Island walkway to Africa.

In sharp contrast to the grandeur of the tree is the subject of the attraction housed within its trunk. Called *It's Tough to Be a Bug!,* this humorous, intense 3-D presentation is about the difficulties of being small and creepy-crawly. The show is similar to *Mickey's PhilharMagic* at the Magic Kingdom in that it combines a 3-D film with an arsenal of tactile and visual special effects. But where *Mickey's PhilharMagic* stars familiar Disney characters in zany situations, *It's Tough to Be a Bug!* can do a number on anybody, young or old, who's squeamish about insects. A mom of two from Williamsville, New York, shared this experience:

It's Tough to Be a Bug! *was my girls' first Disney experience, and almost their last. The story line was difficult to follow—all they were aware of was the torture of sitting in a darkened theater being overrun with bugs. A constant stream of parents headed to the exits with terrorized children. Those who were left behind were screaming and crying as well. The 11-year-old refused to talk for 20 minutes after the fiasco, and the 3½-year-old wanted to go home. Not back to the hotel, but* **home.**

From a Louisville, Kentucky, reader:

My 12-year-old son and I laughed at the comments from concerned parents about It's Tough to Be a Bug!, *so we thought it would be fun to [go to the show to] watch families leave early with crying kids. Our particular show didn't disappoint, even in ways beyond my expectation—as the show progressed, my son became eerily quiet. In fact, only a matter of time later, I found him hunkered under his seat after he saw and "felt" the bugs coming at him. Needless to say, he was a good sport, and we were able to put it behind him after spending several hours with the on-site child psychologist. (Just kidding!)*

The Tree of Life also hosts **Awakenings,** a child-friendly nighttime show projected onto the tree's trunk and canopy. Shown several times a night (when the park is open that late), *Awakenings* combines digital video projections with music and special effects. We've seen four different 3-minute shows; in each, special projection effects make it appear that some animals carved into the tree trunk have come alive. Other special effects happen in the leaves and branches. We rate *Awakenings* as not to be missed.

TOURING TIPS *It's Tough to Be a Bug!* is rarely crowded even on the busiest days. Go in the morning after the Pandora attractions, Kilimanjaro Safaris, Kali River Rapids, Expedition Everest, and Dinosaur. If you miss the bugs in the morning, try again in the late afternoon. The best viewing spots for *Awakenings* are directly in front of the tree on Discovery Island, across from Island Mercantile.

Wilderness Explorers ★★★★

PRESCHOOL ★★★★ (A)   **GRADE SCHOOL ★★★★½** (AA)   **TEENS ★★★½** (BA)
YOUNG ADULTS ★★★½ (BA)   **OVER 30 ★★★★** (BA)   **SENIORS ★★★½** (BA)

What it is Parkwide scavenger hunt and puzzle-solving adventure game. **Scope and scale** Diversion. **When to go** Sign up first thing in the morning and complete activities throughout the day. **Comment** Collecting more than 25 badges takes 3–5 hours, which can be done over several days. **ECV/wheelchair access** May remain in wheelchair. **Participates in Genie+** No. **Early Theme Park Entry** No. **Extended Evening Hours** No.

DESCRIPTION AND COMMENTS Walt Disney World may offer several interactive games in its theme parks, and Wilderness Explorers is the best of the bunch—a scavenger hunt based on Russell's Scout–like troop from the movie *Up.* Players earn "badges" (stickers given out by cast members) for completing predefined activities throughout the park. For example, to earn the Gorilla Badge, you walk the Gorilla Falls Exploration Trail to observe how the primates behave, then mimic that behavior back to a cast member to show what you've seen.

Sign up near the bridge from The Oasis to Discovery Island. You'll be given an instruction book and a map showing the park location for each badge to be earned.

Cast members have been specially trained for this game and can tailor the activities based on the age of the child playing: Small children might get an explanation about what deforestation means, for example, while older kids may have to figure out why tigers have stripes. It's tons of fun for kids and adults, and we play it often when we're in the park.

The Wilderness Explorers program is a big hit with kids, as a Melbourne, Australia, mom relates:

Wilderness Explorers was the highlight of my son's day. Much time is spent collecting badges, but it is well worth the investment of time!

TOURING TIPS Activities are spread throughout the park, including areas to which many guests never venture. You have to ride specific attractions to earn certain badges, so visiting those at our suggested times will save time.

AFRICA

COVID *tip*
Live entertainment was not offered at press time.

THE LARGEST OF ANIMAL KINGDOM'S LANDS, Africa is entered through **Harambe,** a Disneyfied take on a modern rural African town. A market is equipped with modern cash registers; dining options consist of a sit-down buffet, a few counter-service options, and snack stands. What distinguishes Harambe is its understatement: Far from the stereotypical great-white-hunter image of an African town, Harambe is definitely (and realistically) *not* exotic. The buildings, while interesting, are architecturally simple. Though better maintained and more idealized than the real McCoy, Disney's Harambe would be a lot more at home in Kenya than the Magic Kingdom's Main Street would be in Missouri.

Harambe serves as the gateway to Animal Kingdom's largest and most ambitious zoological exhibit: the African veldt habitat. Guests access the veldt via the **Kilimanjaro Safaris** attraction, at the end of Harambe's main drag near the fat-trunked baobab tree. Harambe is also the departure point for the train to **Rafiki's Planet Watch** and **Conservation Station** (the park's veterinary headquarters), as well as the home of *Festival of the Lion King,* a long-running live show performed in its own theater. A walkway by the theater connects Africa with Pandora.

Festival of the Lion King ★★★
(reduced version playing during pandemic)

PRESCHOOL ★★★★½ (MAA)   GRADE SCHOOL ★★★★½ (MAA)   TEENS ★★★★½ (MAA)
YOUNG ADULTS ★★★★½ (MAA)   OVER 30 ★★★★½ (MAA)   SENIORS ★★★★★ (E)

What it is Theater-in-the-round stage show. **Scope and scale** Major attraction. **When to go** Before 11 a.m. or after 4 p.m. Check your park map or *Times Guide* for showtimes. **Duration of presentation** 30 minutes. **Preshow entertainment** None. **When to arrive** 20–30 minutes before showtime. **ECV/wheelchair access** May remain in wheelchair. **Participates in Genie+** No **Early Theme Park Entry** No. **Extended Evening Hours** No.

DESCRIPTION AND COMMENTS Inspired by the Disney animated feature, *Festival of the Lion King* is part stage show and part parade; the theater is behind and to the left of Tusker House restaurant. Guests sit in four sets of bleachers surrounding the stage and organized into cheering sections, which are called on to make elephant, warthog, giraffe, and lion noises. (You won't be alone if you don't know what a giraffe or warthog sounds like.) There's a great deal of strutting around and a lot of singing and dancing. By our count, every tune from *The Lion King* is belted out— some more than once. If you didn't know the words to the songs before the show, you definitely will after.

Festival of the Lion King is one of the few stage shows Disney had restarted at press time. In order to get it to run safely, *Festival* had to cut its audience participation, acrobats, and some special effects. While the remaining singers and dancers are absolute professionals, they can't make up for a show that's now too small and too slow for its stage.

Unofficial Guide readers are almost unanimous in their praise of the original *Festival of the Lion King*. This letter from a Naples, Florida, mom is typical:

> Festival of the Lion King *was the best thing we experienced at Animal King-dom. The singers, dancers, fire twirlers, acrobats, and sets were spectacular.*

TOURING TIPS *Festival of the Lion King* is still a big draw, so try to see the first show in the morning or one of the last two shows at night. For mid-day performances, you'll need to queue up at least 35–45 minutes before showtime; to minimize waiting in the hot sun, don't hop in line until cast members give the word. The bleachers can make viewing difficult for the height-deficient—if you have small children or short adults in your party, snag a seat higher up.

Gorilla Falls Exploration Trail ★★★★

**PRESCHOOL ★★★★ (A)   GRADE SCHOOL ★★★★ (A)   TEENS ★★★★ (A)
YOUNG ADULTS ★★★★ (A)   OVER 30 ★★★★½ (A)   SENIORS ★★★★½ (AA)**

What it is Walk-through zoological exhibit. **Scope and scale** Major attraction. **When to go** Before or after Kilimanjaro Safaris. Also check the *Times Guide* for early off-season closures. **Duration of tour** About 20–25 minutes. **ECV/wheelchair access** May remain in wheelchair. **Participates in Genie+** No. **Early Theme Park Entry** No. **Extended Evening Hours** No.

DESCRIPTION AND COMMENTS As the trail winds between the domain of two troops of lowland gorillas, it's hard to see what, if anything, separates you from the primates. Also on the trail is a hippo pool with an underwater viewing area, plus a naked-mole-rat exhibit. A highlight is an exotic-bird aviary so craftily designed that you can barely tell you're in an enclosure.

TOURING TIPS The Gorilla Falls Exploration Trail is lush, beautiful, and filled with people much of the time. Guests exiting Kilimanjaro Safaris can choose between returning to Harambe or walking the Gorilla Falls Exploration Trail. Many opt for the trail. Thus, when the Safaris are operating at full tilt, it spews hundreds of guests every couple of minutes onto the Exploration Trail.

The trail's hours are cut during fall and winter, closing as early as 4:30 p.m. Check the *Times Guide* for the schedule.

Kilimanjaro Safaris ★★★★★

**PRESCHOOL ★★★★½ (MAA)   GRADE SCHOOL ★★★★½ (MAA)   TEENS ★★★★½ (MAA)
YOUNG ADULTS ★★★★½ (MAA)   OVER 30 ★★★★½ (MAA)   SENIORS ★★★★★ (E)**

What it is Simulated ride through an African wildlife reservation. **Scope and scale** Super-headliner. **When to go** As soon as the park opens or after 3 p.m. **Duration of ride** About 20 minutes. **Average wait in line per 100 people ahead of you** 4 minutes; assumes full-capacity operation with 18-second dispatch interval. **Loading speed** Fast. **ECV/wheelchair access** Must transfer from ECV to provided wheelchair. **Participates in Genie+** No (it's a separate Individual Attraction Selection). **Early Theme Park Entry** No. **Extended Evening Hours** No.

DESCRIPTION AND COMMENTS Animal Kingdom's premier zoological attraction, Kilimanjaro Safaris offers an exceptionally realistic, albeit brief, imitation of an actual African photo safari. Thirty-two guests at a time board tall, open vehicles and are dispatched into a simulated African veldt habitat. Animals such as zebras, wildebeests, impalas, Thomson's gazelles, giraffes, and even rhinos roam apparently free, while predators such as lions, as well as potentially dangerous large animals like hippos, are separated from both prey and guests by all-but-invisible, natural-appearing barriers. Although the animals have more than 100 acres of savanna, woodland, streams, and rocky hills to call home, careful placement of watering holes, forage, and salt licks ensures that the critters are hanging out by the road when safari vehicles roll by.

Having traveled in Kenya and Tanzania, I (Bob) can tell you that Disney has done an amazing job of replicating the sub-Saharan east-African landscape. As on a real African safari, what animals you see, and how many, is pretty much a matter of luck. We've experienced Kilimanjaro Safaris more than 100 times and had a different experience on each trip.

Animal Kingdom may offer a **nighttime version** of Kilimanjaro Safaris. Before the first safari truck rolled into the setting sun, Disney spent more than a year acclimating the existing animals, as well as nocturnal species such as hyenas, to life in a theme park. For the nighttime version, Disney also installed a baseball stadium–size wall of graphics displays at the far end of the attraction's savanna grasslands.

Turned on late in the day, the displays are programmed to simulate a gradually setting sun for hours on end—providing enough light for guests to see the animals that are still roaming around. It's hard to predict which ones you're likely to see, however: On one nighttime tour, we found that the rhinos were noticeably more active at night, while other animals, such as hippos, crocodiles, and elephants, became virtual recluses. A Wilmington, Delaware, man had a different experience, though:

Animal Kingdom at night was the hit of our trip, and Kilimanjaro Safaris was great. We saw more animals in action than we had ever seen in the daytime, and the nighttime added just a hint of danger to the entire proceeding that made it fun.

TOURING TIPS Kilimanjaro Safaris is one of Animal Kingdom's busiest attractions, along with **Expedition Everest** and the two **Pandora** attractions. From a touring standpoint, this is a good thing: By distributing guests evenly throughout the park, those other attractions make it unnecessary to run to Kilimanjaro Safaris first thing in the morning.

Waits for Kilimanjaro Safaris diminish around midafternoon, sometimes as early as 3 p.m. but more commonly somewhat later. We recommend taking the nighttime safari after you've experienced the daytime version.

If you want to take photos, note that the vehicle isn't guaranteed to stop at a given location. Drivers try their best to accommodate guests and stop when big animals come into view, but be prepared to snap at any time. As for the ride, it's not that rough.

RAFIKI'S PLANET WATCH

NOT A TRUE "LAND" in scope or scale, this section of Animal Kingdom—named for a beloved character from *The Lion King*—consists of **Conservation Station** (the animal-care center), the petting zoo, and environmental exhibits, all accessible from Harambe via the **Wildlife Express Train.** Rafiki's Planet Watch may operate seasonally.

The Animation Experience at Conservation Station ★★★

PRESCHOOL ★★½ (MBA)	GRADE SCHOOL ★★★★ (A)	TEENS ★★★★½ (MAA)
YOUNG ADULTS ★★★★½ (MAA)	OVER 30 ★★★★½ (MAA)	SENIORS ★★★★½ (MAA)

What it is Character-drawing class. **Scope and scale** Minor attraction. **When to go** Check *Times Guide* for hours. **Comments** Accessible only by the Wildlife Express Train. Fun but out of place in this theme park. **Participates in Genie+** Yes. **Early Theme Park Entry** No. **Extended Evening Hours** No.

DESCRIPTION AND COMMENTS The Animation Experience, which opened in July 2019, provides information about the history of Disney animation and gives guests a chance to draw their favorite characters from *The Lion King* with the help of an instructor.

TOURING TIPS The Animation Experience is located in a remote section of the park, so crowds shouldn't be large during the early and late part of the day.

Conservation Station and Affection Section ★★★

PRESCHOOL ★★★½ (A)	GRADE SCHOOL ★★★★ (A)	TEENS ★★★ (MBA)
YOUNG ADULTS ★★★ (MBA)	OVER 30 ★★★½ (BA)	SENIORS ★★★½ (BA)

What it is Behind-the-scenes educational exhibit and petting zoo. **Scope and scale** Minor attraction. **When to go** Anytime. **Comments** Opens later and closes earlier than the rest of the park. Check *Times Guide* for hours. Accessible only by the Wildlife Express Train. **Probable waiting time** None. **ECV/wheelchair access** May remain in wheelchair. **Participates in Genie+** No. **Early Theme Park Entry** No. **Extended Evening Hours** No.

DESCRIPTION AND COMMENTS Conservation Station is Animal Kingdom's veterinary and conservation headquarters. Here guests can meet wildlife experts, observe ongoing projects, and learn about the behind-the-scenes operations of the park. The Station also serves as a rehabilitation center for injured animals and a nursery for recently born (or hatched) critters.

While there are several permanent exhibits, including Affection Section (an animal-petting area), what you see at Conservation Station will largely depend on what's going on when you arrive. On most days when we've visited, there isn't enough happening to justify waiting in line twice (coming and going) for the train.

Most of our readers agree that Conservation Station isn't worth the hassle. A Tinley Park, Illinois, mom writes:

Skip Conservation Station. Between the train ride to get to it and being there, we wasted a precious 1½ hours!

A Denver family had a better experience:

We really enjoyed Conservation Station. We saw a 13-foot python eating a rat!

And a reader from Kent, England, was amused by both the goings-on and the other guests:

The most memorable part of Animal Kingdom for me was watching a veteri-nary surgeon and his team at Conservation Station perform an operation on a rat snake that had inadvertently swallowed a golf ball, presumably believ-ing it to be an egg! This operation caused at least one onlooker to pass out.

TOURING TIPS Because Conservation Station is so removed from the rest of the park, you won't see it unless you take the train. Conservation Station typically opens 90 minutes after the rest of the park and closes an hour or more earlier.

Wildlife Express Train   ★★

PRESCHOOL ★★★★ (A)	GRADE SCHOOL ★★★½ (BA)	TEENS ★★★ (MBA)
YOUNG ADULTS ★★★½ (MBA)	OVER 30 ★★★½ (MBA)	SENIORS ★★★½ (MBA)

What it is Scenic railroad ride to Rafiki's Planet Watch and Conservation Station. **Scope and scale** Minor attraction. **When to go** Anytime. **Comments** Opens 90 min-utes after rest of park; last train departs at 4:30 p.m. **Duration of ride** About 7 minutes one-way. **Average wait in line per 100 people ahead of you** 9 minutes. **Loading speed** Moderate. **ECV/wheelchair access** May remain in wheelchair. **Participates in Genie+** No. **Early Theme Park Entry** No. **Extended Evening Hours** No.

DESCRIPTION AND COMMENTS This ride snakes behind the African wildlife reserve as it makes its loop connecting Harambe to Rafiki's Planet Watch and Conservation Station. En route, you see the nighttime enclosures for the animals that populate Kilimanjaro Safaris. Similarly, returning to Harambe, you see the backstage areas of Asia. Regardless of which direction you're heading, the sights aren't especially stimulating.

TOURING TIPS Most guests who head to Conservation Station do so after experiencing Kilimanjaro Safaris and the Gorilla Falls Exploration Trail. Thus, the train begins to get crowded between 10 and 11 a.m.

ASIA

CROSSING THE ASIA BRIDGE FROM DISCOVERY ISLAND, you enter Asia through the village of **Anandapur,** a veritable collage of Asian themes inspired by the architecture and ruins of India, Indo-nesia, Nepal, and Thailand. Situated near the bank of the Discovery River and surrounded by lush vegetation, Anandapur provides access to a gibbon exhibit and Asia's two feature attractions: the **Kali River Rapids** raft ride and **Expedition Everest.**

Expedition Everest—yep, a mountain and, at 200 feet, the tallest in Florida—is a super-headliner roller coaster. You board an old moun-tain railway destined for the base camp of Mount Everest and end up racing both forward and backward through caverns and frigid can-yons en route to paying a social call on none other than the Abomi-nable Snowman.

Expedition Everest   ★★★★½

PRESCHOOL ★★½ (MBA)	GRADE SCHOOL ★★★★½ (MAA)	TEENS ★★★★★ (E)
YOUNG ADULTS ★★★★★ (E)	OVER 30 ★★★★★ (E)	SENIORS ★★★★½ (AA)

What it is High-speed outdoor roller coaster through Nepalese mountain village. **Scope and scale** Super-headliner. **When to go** First or last hour the park is open. **Comments** Must be 44" to ride; Rider Switch option provided (see page 395); has single-rider line. **Duration of ride** 4 minutes. **Average wait in line per 100 people ahead of you**

4 minutes; assumes 2 tracks operating. **Loading speed** Moderate–fast. **ECV/wheelchair access** Must transfer to ride vehicle. **Participates in Genie+** No (it's a separate Individual Attraction Selection). **Early Theme Park Entry** Yes. **Extended Evening Hours** No.

DESCRIPTION AND COMMENTS The only true roller coaster in Animal Kingdom, Expedition Everest vies with Avatar Flight of Passage for the park's longest waits in line—and for good reason. Your journey begins in an elaborate waiting area modeled after a Nepalese village; then you board an old train headed for the base camp of Mount Everest. Throughout the waiting area are posted notes from previous expeditions, some with cryptic observations regarding a mysterious creature said to guard the mountain. These ominous signs are ignored (as if you have a choice!), resulting in a high-speed encounter with the Abominable Snowman himself.

The ride consists of tight turns (some while traveling backward), hills, and dips but no loops or inversions. From your departure at the loading station through your first high-speed descent, you'll see some of the most spectacular panoramas in Walt Disney World: On a clear day, you can see the buildings of Coronado Springs Resort, EPCOT's Spaceship Earth, and possibly downtown Orlando. But look quickly because you're immediately propelled, projectile-like, through the inner and outer reaches of the mountain. The final drop and last few turns are among Disney's very best coaster effects.

Disney bills Expedition Everest as a "family thrill ride"—more akin to Big Thunder Mountain Railroad than Rock 'n' Roller Coaster—but it's an exciting experience nonetheless, and as is typical of a super-headliner attraction, it generates lots of reader comments. A Seattle family of four gives Expedition Everest a thumbs-up:

Expedition Everest is tremendous. It has enough surprises and runaway speed to make it one of the more enjoyable thrill rides in the whole Orlando area.

A Macon, Georgia, teen successfully recruited Grandma to ride:

Expedition Everest was so smoooooth! I went right out and brought my granny back to ride it. She didn't throw up or anything!

TOURING TIPS A touring strategy that doesn't require much backtracking is to start with Dinosaur, then see Expedition Everest and Kali River Rapids as part of a counterclockwise tour of the park.

Expedition Everest reaches a top speed of around 50 mph, about twice that of Space Mountain, so expect to see the usual safety warnings for health. Ask to be seated up front—the first few rows offer the best front-seat experience of any Disney coaster, indoor or outdoor. Also, note the animal poop on display in the Lightning Lane if you use it—a deliberate attempt at verisimilitude, or did Disney run out of money for ride props and use whatever they could find?

Feathered Friends in Flight ★★★★

PRESCHOOL ★★★★ (A) **GRADE SCHOOL** ★★★★½ (MAA) **TEENS** ★★★★½ (MAA)
YOUNG ADULTS ★★★★½ (MAA) **OVER 30** ★★★★½ (MAA) **SENIORS** ★★★★½ (MAA)

What it is Stadium show about birds. **Scope and scale** Major attraction. **When to go** Anytime. **Special comment** Performance times listed in park map and *Times Guide*. **Duration of presentation** 30 minutes. **Preshow entertainment** None. **When to arrive** 10–15 minutes before showtime. **ECV/wheelchair access** May remain in wheelchair. **Participates in Genie+** No. **Early Theme Park Entry** No. **Extended Evening Hours** No.

DESCRIPTION AND COMMENTS Asia's theater has presented a show featuring live birds for years. *Feathered Friends in Flight* debuted in summer 2020 and is the best—and highest-rated—version ever done. The show's hosts are some of Disney's animal trainers, who explain different bird species' habitats and characteristics. A number of species are represented, with plenty more flying overhead. The show is fast-paced, informative, and entertaining for everyone. In many ways the show is a model of how other shows in the park might work.

Like its predecessor, *Feathered Friends* focuses on the birds' natural talents and characteristics, which far surpass any tricks learned from humans—don't expect parrots riding bikes or cockatoos playing tiny pianos. A Brattleboro, Vermont, reader found the birds extremely compelling:

The birds are thrilling, and we especially appreciated the fact that their antics were not the results of training against the grain but actual survival techniques that the birds use in the wild.

TOURING TIPS *Feathered Friends* plays at the stadium near the bridge on the walkway into Asia. Though the stadium is covered, it's not air-conditioned; thus, early-morning and late-afternoon performances are more comfortable. To play it safe, get to the stadium about 10–15 minutes before showtime.

Kali River Rapids ★★★½

PRESCHOOL ★★★★ (A)   **GRADE SCHOOL ★★★★½** (MAA)   **TEENS ★★★★** (A)
YOUNG ADULTS ★★★★ (A)   **OVER 30 ★★★★** (A)   **SENIORS ★★★★** (BA)

What it is Whitewater raft ride. **Scope and scale** Headliner. **When to go** Before 11 a.m. or the last hour the park is open. **Comments** You're likely to get wet; may open 30 minutes after the rest of the park and close early on off-peak or cold days; must be 38″ to ride; Rider Switch option provided (see page 395). **Duration of ride** About 5 minutes. **Average wait in line per 100 people ahead of you** 5 minutes. **Loading speed** Moderate. **ECV/wheelchair access** Must transfer to ride vehicle; transfer device available. **Participates in Genie+** Yes. **Early Theme Park Entry** No. **Extended Evening Hours** No.

DESCRIPTION AND COMMENTS Kali River Rapids is an unguided trip in a circular rubber raft down an artificial river; each raft has a top-mounted platform that seats 12 people. The raft essentially floats free in the current and is washed downstream through rapids and waves. Because the "river" is fairly wide, with various currents, eddies, and obstacles, each trip is different and exciting.

What distinguishes Kali River Rapids from other theme park raft rides is Disney's trademark attention to visual detail. Whereas some raft rides are just an unadorned plunge down a concrete ditch, Kali River Rapids flows through a dense rainforest and past waterfalls, temple ruins, and bamboo thickets, emerging into a cleared area where greedy loggers have ravaged the forest, and finally drifting back under the tropical canopy as the river cycles back to Anandapur. Along the way, your raft runs a gauntlet of raging cataracts, logjams, and other dangers.

The queuing area, which winds through an ancient Southeast Asian temple, is one of the most striking and visually interesting settings of any Disney attraction; the sights on the raft trip itself are also first-class.

That said, Kali River Rapids is marginal in two important respects: First, you get only about 3½ minutes on the water, and second . . . well, it's a weenie ride. Sure, you get wet, but the drops and rapids aren't all that exciting, as this Kansas family points out:

It was boiling hot, so we were happy about the prospect of being drenched. At the end, we all looked at each other and said, "Is that IT?" We couldn't believe we'd stood in line, sweating half to death, for 75 minutes just for that.

TOURING TIPS Kali River Rapids is hugely popular on hot summer days. Ride before 11 a.m. or during the last hour the park is open.

Disney has toned down the amount of water splashed at you during the ride. We've still gotten wet but not soaked through. Because you'll probably get wet, we recommend wearing shorts and sport sandals (such as Tevas) to the park, as well as bringing along a jumbo trash bag *plus* a smaller plastic bag. Before you board, punch a hole in the big bag for your head. *Note:* You'll stay drier if you don't cut holes for your arms; the downside is that it'll make fastening your seat belt awkward, so it's your call. If you're wearing closed shoes and socks, take them off, put your shoes back on minus the socks, and then wrap the smaller bag around your shoes. If you're worried about mussing your coiffure, bring a third bag for your head.

A Shaker Heights, Ohio, family who donned our *couture de garbage* discovered that staying dry on Kali River Rapids is not without its social costs:

Cast members and the other people in our raft looked at us like we'd just beamed down from Mars. (One cast member asked if we needed wet suits and snorkels.) Plus, we didn't cut arm holes in our trash bags because we thought we'd stay drier that way—once we sat down, though, we couldn't fasten our seat belts. After a lot of wiggling and adjusting and helping each other, we finally got belted in, and off we went, looking like sacks of fertilizer with heads poking out. Very embarrassing, but we stayed nice and dry.

A family from Humble, Texas, who rode early in the morning on a cool day, shares this:

We didn't read your precautions for Kali River Rapids until after we rode. The 6-year-old and Mom were COMPLETELY drenched—so much so that we had to leave the park and go back to our room at Port Orleans to change clothes. Since the temperature was around 60 degrees that morning, we were pretty miserable by the time we got back to our room. Needless to say, our schedule was shot by then.

Riding later in the day would have been a better option in this case.

Kali River Rapids offers free 2-hour locker rentals to the left of the attraction entrance, near the restrooms. Store a change of dry clothes here or, alternatively, wear as little as the law and Disney will allow. If you're wearing closed shoes, prop up your feet above the bottom of the raft—slogging around in wet shoes is a surefire ticket to Blisterville.

Maharajah Jungle Trek ★★★★

PRESCHOOL ★★★★ (A)	GRADE SCHOOL ★★★★ (A)	TEENS ★★★★ (A)
YOUNG ADULTS ★★★★ (A)	OVER 30 ★★★★ (A)	SENIORS ★★★★½ (A)

What it is Walk-through zoological exhibit. **Scope and scale** Headliner. **When to go** Anytime it's open. **Comment** May open later and close earlier than rest of park. **Duration of tour** About 20–30 minutes. **ECV/wheelchair access** May remain in wheelchair. **Participates in Genie+** No. **Early Theme Park Entry** No. **Extended Evening Hours** No.

DESCRIPTION AND COMMENTS This walk is similar to the Gorilla Falls Exploration Trail (page 554) but with an Asian setting and Asian animals. You start with Komodo dragons and work up to Malayan flying foxes. Next is a cave with fruit bats. Ruins of the maharajah's palace provide the setting for Bengal tigers. From the top of a parapet in the palace you can view a herd of blackbuck antelope and Asian deer. The trek concludes with an aviary.

Labyrinthine, overgrown, and elaborately detailed, the temple ruin would be a compelling attraction even without the animals. Look for a plaster trip-tych just after the tiger exhibit that shows (right to left) a parable about man living in harmony with nature. Throw in a few bats, bucks, and Bengals, and you're in for a treat. Most readers, like this Washington, D.C., couple, agree:

The Maharajah Jungle Trek was absolutely amazing. We were able to see all the animals, which were awake by that time (9:30 a.m.), including the elusive tigers. The part of the trek with the birds was fabulous; you could spot hundreds, some of which were eating on the ground a mere 3 feet away from us.

TOURING TIPS The Maharajah Jungle Trek doesn't get as jammed up as the Gorilla Falls Exploration Trail and is a good choice for midday touring when most other attractions are crowded. The downside, of course, is that the exhibit showcases tigers, bats, and other creatures that might not be very active in the heat of the day. Finally, the Jungle Trek's operating hours may be shorter than the park's, especially during fall and winter, so check your *Times Guide* for the latest information.

▮▮ DINOLAND U.S.A.

THIS MOST TYPICALLY DISNEY of Animal Kingdom's lands crosses an anthropological dig with a quirky roadside attraction. Accessible via the bridge from Discovery Island, DinoLand U.S.A. is home to a children's play area, a nature trail, a 1,500-seat amphitheater, and **Dinosaur,** one of Animal Kingdom's three thrill rides.

Also in DinoLand are a couple of natural-history exhibits, including **Dino-Sue,** an exact replica of the largest, most complete *Tyrannosaurus rex* skeleton discovered to date. Named for fossil hunter Sue Hendrickson, the skeleton is 40 feet long and 13 feet tall. Dino-Sue doesn't dance, sing, or whistle, but she'll get your attention nonetheless.

The Boneyard ★★★½

PRESCHOOL ★★★★½ (MAA)   GRADE SCHOOL ★★★★½ (MAA)   TEENS ★★½ (MBA)
YOUNG ADULTS ★★ (MBA)   OVER 30 ★★★ (MBA)   SENIORS ★★½ (MBA)

What it is Elaborate playground. **Scope and scale** Diversion. **When to go** Anytime. **Comment** Opens 1 hour after rest of park. **Duration of experience** Varies. **Probable waiting time** None. **ECV/wheelchair access** May remain in wheelchair. **Participates in Genie+** No. **Early Theme Park Entry** No. **Extended Evening Hours** No.

DESCRIPTION AND COMMENTS With an open-air "dig site" as its centerpiece, this elaborately themed playground appeals to kids age 10 and younger but is visually appealing to all ages. Decorated with dinosaur skeletons, the "dig site" is a sandpit where kids can scrounge for bones and fossils. There's also a ropes course, as well as slides, swings, climbing areas, and caves to play in.

TOURING TIPS Not the most pristine of Disney attractions, but certainly one where younger kids will want to spend some time. Aside from being dirty (or at least sandy), The Boneyard gets mighty hot in the Florida sun, so keep your kids well hydrated, and drag them into the shade from time to time. Try to save this until after you've experienced the main attractions.

Because The Boneyard is so close to the center of the park, it's easy to drop in whenever your kids get antsy. While the little ones clamber around on giant femurs and ribs, you can sip a tall cool one in the shade (still keeping an eye on them, of course).

As a Michigan family attests, kids love The Boneyard:

The highlight for our kids was The Boneyard, especially the dig site. They just kept digging and digging to uncover the bones of the woolly mammoth.

Be aware, however, that The Boneyard rambles over about 0.5 acre and is multistoried, making it easy to lose sight of a small child. Fortunately, there's only one entrance and exit. A mother of two from Stillwater, Minnesota, found the playground too large for her liking:

If you're a parent who likes to have your eyes on your kids at all times, you won't like The Boneyard. Kids climb to the top of the slides; then you can't see them and you don't know what chute they'll be exiting from.

From the mother of a 3-year-old:

If your child is quite young, make sure you have two people in The Boneyard— one to help them up all the stairs, the other to stay at the bottom and watch them as they exit the slide. By the time you get from the top of the structure to the bottom, they're off who-knows-where getting into mischief of one kind or another without adult supervision.

Dinosaur ★★★★

PRESCHOOL ★★★ (BA) **GRADE SCHOOL ★★★★** (AA) **TEENS ★★★★** (A)
YOUNG ADULTS ★★★★ (A) **OVER 30 ★★★★** (A) **SENIORS ★★★½** (MBA)

What it is Motion-simulator dark ride. **Scope and scale** Headliner. **When to go** Before 10:30 a.m. or after 4 p.m. **Comment** Must be 40" to ride; Rider Switch option provided (see page 395). **Duration of ride** 3½ minutes. **Average wait in line per 100 people ahead of you** 3 minutes; assumes full-capacity operation with 18-second dispatch interval. **Loading speed** Fast. **ECV/wheelchair access** Must transfer to ride vehicle. **Participates in Genie+** Yes. **Early Theme Park Entry** Yes. **Extended Evening Hours** No.

DESCRIPTION AND COMMENTS Dinosaur is a combination track ride and motion simulator. In addition to moving along a cleverly hidden track, the ride vehicle also bucks and pitches (the simulator part) in sync with the visuals and special effects.

The plot has you traveling back in time on a mission of rescue and conservation. Your objective: to haul back a living dinosaur before the species becomes extinct. Whoever is operating the clock, however, cuts it a little close, and you arrive on the prehistoric scene just as a giant asteroid is hurtling toward Earth. General mayhem ensues as you evade carnivorous predators, catch Barney, and get out before the asteroid hits.

Dinosaur serves up nonstop action from beginning to end, with brilliant visual effects. Elaborate even by Disney standards, the tense, frenetic ride is embellished by the entire Imagineering arsenal of high-tech gimmickry.

A mother from Kansasville, Wisconsin, liked Dinosaur a lot:

Dinosaur is the best ride at WDW. Our group of 10, ranging in age from 65 (grandma) to 8 (grandson), immediately—and unanimously!—got back in line after finishing.

That said, the menacing dinosaurs, along with the overall intensity of the experience, make Dinosaur a no-go for younger kids, as this Michigan family discovered:

Our 7-year-old son withstood every ride Disney threw at him, from Space Mountain to Tower of Terror. Dinosaur, however, did him in. By the end, he was riding with his head down, scared to look around.

TOURING TIPS Disney situated Dinosaur in such a remote corner of the park that you have to poke around to find it. This, in conjunction with the overwhelming popularity of Pandora's rides, along with Kilimanjaro Safaris and Expedition Everest, makes Dinosaur the easiest headliner attraction at Walt Disney World to get on. Lines should be relatively light through midmorning. A decent strategy for avoiding backtracking and long waits is to start a counterclockwise tour of the park here, saving Pandora's attractions for last.

Theater in the Wild/*Finding Nemo—The Musical* (reopens 2022)

What it is Enclosed venue for live stage shows. Scope and scale Major attraction. When to go Anytime. Comment Check your park map or *Times Guide* for showtimes. Duration of presentation N/A. When to arrive 30 minutes before showtime. ECV/wheelchair access May remain in wheelchair.

DESCRIPTION AND COMMENTS Before the pandemic, *Finding Nemo—The Musical* was arguably the most elaborate live show in any Disney World theme park. Incorporating dancing, special effects, and sophisticated digital backdrops of the undersea world, it featured onstage human performers retelling Nemo's story with colorful, larger-than-life puppets. To be fair, *puppets* doesn't adequately convey the size or detail of these props, many of which were as big as a car and required two people to manipulate.

The show didn't reopen with the park in 2020. In late 2021, Disney announced that the show would be revamped for a return in 2022. We expect the new show to run much shorter than the original's almost 35 minutes, to boost the number of performances per day. We wouldn't be surprised to see performers and effects cut as well.

TOURING TIPS To get a seat, show up 20–25 minutes in advance. Access to the theater is via a relatively narrow pedestrian path—if you arrive as the previous show is letting out, you'll feel like a salmon swimming upstream.

TriceraTop Spin ★★

| PRESCHOOL ★★★★½ (MAA) | GRADE SCHOOL ★★★★ (BA) | TEENS ★★★ (MBA) |
| YOUNG ADULTS ★★★ (MBA) | OVER 30 ★★★ (MBA) | SENIORS ★★★ (MBA) |

What it is Hub-and-spoke midway ride. Scope and scale Minor attraction. When to go Before noon or after 3 p.m. Duration of ride 1½ minutes. Probable wait in line per 100 people ahead of you 10 minutes. Loading speed Slow. ECV/wheelchair access Must transfer from ECV to provided wheelchair. Participates in Genie+ No. Early Theme Park Entry Yes. Extended Evening Hours No.

DESCRIPTION AND COMMENTS Another Dumbo-like ride for young children. Here you spin around a central hub until a dinosaur pops out of the top of the hub. You would think Disney could come up with something a bit more creative.

TOURING TIPS Come back later if the wait exceeds 20 minutes.

■ PANDORA—*The World of Avatar*

IN AN ATTEMPT TO COUNTER Universal Orlando's wildly popular Harry Potter lands that opened in 2010 and 2014, Disney signed director James Cameron to a theme park development deal in 2011 based on his blockbuster 2009 film *Avatar*. It was a decision that puzzled many Disney theme park fans—including us.

While *Avatar* is the second-highest-grossing film of all time, having earned almost $3 billion since it was released, we've always joked that it was the movie everybody saw about characters nobody liked. Clearly, the reason for *Avatar*'s success wasn't the script or the acting: It was the movie's then-revolutionary 3-D digital effects.

We shouldn't have worried. Pandora's headliner attraction, Avatar Flight of Passage, opened as (and is still) one of the highest-rated attractions in any US Disney or Universal theme park.

The opening of Pandora marked the end of 20th-century Disney Imagineering. The next generation of blockbuster theme park attractions—including the ones later introduced at Star Wars: Galaxy's Edge at Disneyland and Hollywood Studios—starts with Pandora's scale and detail as the standard.

In addition to a wildly popular super-headliner attraction, Pandora boasts an awe-inspiringly immersive setting, officially called the **Valley of Mo'ara.** *Unofficial Guide* readers rate this themed environment among the top 20 attractions in Animal Kingdom.

In the *Avatar* universe, Pandora is a planetary moon in a star system 4.3 light-years from Earth. But rather than tie this Pandora to *Avatar* characters or story lines, Disney chose to set the scene a generation after the events in the movie: The Indigenous Na'vi have made peace with the humans who had exploited Pandora for its natural resources, and Pandora is now an ecotourism destination and a center for scientific research.

What Disney built in Pandora is a world more beautiful than nature produces on its own. The colors are more vibrant, the sounds more alive, the landscaping entirely more interesting, and the details more, well, *detailed* than what you can probably see out your window right now. It's intersected by perfectly placed waterfalls, and in the middle of it all is a giant floating mountain.

The exquisite detail extends to the ride queues. The one for Na'vi River Journey showcases the weaving skills of Pandora's Indigenous peoples, while the seemingly endless line for Avatar Flight of Passage wends through cave dwellings, nocturnal jungle scenes, and high-tech laboratories on its way to the ride itself.

Avatar Flight of Passage ★★★★½

PRESCHOOL ★★★ (MBA)   GRADE SCHOOL ★★★★½ (MAA)   TEENS ★★★★★ (E)
YOUNG ADULTS ★★★★★ (E)   OVER 30 ★★★★★ (E)   SENIORS ★★★★½ (MAA)

What it is Flight simulator. **Scope and scale** Super-headliner. **When to go** As soon as the park opens or after 3 p.m. **Comments** One of Disney's most advanced rides; must be 44″ to ride. **Duration of ride** About 6 minutes. **Average wait in line per 100 people ahead of you** About 5 minutes. **Loading speed** Moderate. **ECV/wheelchair access** Must transfer from ECV to provided wheelchair and then from wheelchair to ride vehicle; transfer device available. **Participates in Genie+** No (it's a separate Individual Attraction Selection). **Early Theme Park Entry** Yes. **Extended Evening Hours** No.

DESCRIPTION AND COMMENTS Avatar Flight of Passage is one of the most technologically advanced rides Disney has ever produced: a flight simulator in which you hop on the back of a winged, dragonlike Pandora banshee for a spin to take in the planet's scenery.

Your journey begins with a long walk from the base of Pandora, up an inclined path, and into abandoned cave dwellings. Wall paintings and markings inside the caves tell the story of the Na'vi. From there, you walk through jungle and more rocks to reach the research laboratory of the humans who have settled on Pandora and are studying the planet's wildlife.

The lab's star exhibit is a Na'vi avatar lying in suspended animation. Encased in a giant water-filled tube, the sleeping apparition floats gently, its rest briefly interrupted by a finger twitch or leg movement. (People we've toured with have described it as either mesmerizing or vaguely unsettling.)

Once through the queue, you're brought to a 16-person chamber to prepare for your flight. A video explains the concept of an avatar: a way to project your consciousness onto another being—in this case a Na'vi riding astride a banshee—and feel everything it feels. Your preparation includes a "parasite decontamination procedure" and other quasi-scientific processes, mainly to help pass the time until your ride vehicles are ready.

When it's time to ride, you're led into a small room holding what looks like 16 stationary bicycles without pedals. You're handed 3-D goggles and told to approach the "bike," swing one leg over, mount it, and scoot as far forward as you can. Once you're seated, padded restraints are deployed along your calves and lower back, ensuring that you don't fall off during your flight. (The snugness of the restraints, coupled with the somewhat confined space holding the vehicles, makes some claustrophobic guests exit before riding.)

Then the room goes dark, there's a flash of light, and suddenly your brain is "linked" to the Na'vi surfing a banshee. You swoop up and down, left and right, on this flying dragon, going over the Pandora plains, through the mountains, and across its seas, all through a high-definition video projected onto a giant screen in front of you. As you fly, airbags at your legs inflate and deflate to simulate the banshee's breathing below you.

The flying effects are very well done. You can turn your head almost 90° either way, and about 45° up and down, to survey the Pandora landscape. Riders toward the middle of the room (seats 4–8 in one group and 9–12 in the other) have, we think, better range of vision.

If you've experienced Soarin' at EPCOT, the technology at work here is similar, with the individual "bikes" replacing the grouped seats. Likewise, the ebb and flow of the flight reminds us of the Soarin' film's pacing, right down to the finale over the beach. The video is clear and well synchronized with the ride vehicles, and we've heard very few reports of motion sickness—which is unusual for screen-based motion simulators.

The word *rave* hardly does justice to how Flight of Passage has been received. First, from an Indiana family of four:

Our favorite ride in all of Walt Disney World is Avatar Flight of Passage. The experience is magical. It really does feel like you're flying because of the wind, smells, and movement of the banshee. A lot of people compare it to Soarin', but after riding Flight of Passage first, Soarin' was a letdown.

An Edmonton, Alberta, couple had this to say:

Flight of Passage is one of the best rides we've ever been on. We would gladly wait 3 hours to ride this. A MUST-DO!

And from a Freehold, New Jersey, mom:

From the "breathing" ride vehicle to the unbelievable visuals to (my favorite) the wafting aromas, this ride is absolutely amazing. I love Forbidden Journey at Universal, but aside from Hogwarts Castle being a better queueing area, the Avatar ride is by far superior.

Flight of Passage is super, provided you can ride. A tall Oklahoman who couldn't complains:

I am 6'6", and I was too tall to ride. Two other individuals from my pod were also too tall/large. Very disappointing, and Disney did not handle it very well.

TOURING TIPS Flight of Passage is the first ride most people head for at Animal Kingdom. The good news is that when the park opens by 8 a.m., most guests leave Animal Kingdom well before closing. Thus, lines for Flight of Passage drop considerably near park closing. A Napa, California, reader recounts a very typical experience:

We did rope drop at Animal Kingdom during spring break on a day with park opening at 7 a.m. for resort guests. By 6:30 a.m., the line to get in was out in the parking lot. It's also kinda stressful with everyone bumping into each other trying to get to Flight of Passage.

Park opening is erratic at Animal Kingdom for several reasons, but it's mainly a matter of safety and traffic control. To forestall a mob at the entrance—and a Pamplona-like stampede to Pandora—Disney modulates the crowds as they arrive, ushering guests safely into a queue. Making crowd control even more critical is the fact that Animal Kingdom's walkways are the narrowest in all of the Disney World parks, which can create choke points.

If you intend to be among the first in the park:

1. Check online or call ☎ 407-824-4321 the night before your visit to confirm official park-opening time.

2. On-site guests should arrive 60 minutes before official opening; off-site guests should arrive 30 minutes before official opening.

3. If you're staying on-site, use Disney transportation; Disney's buses get into the parking lot before cars. If you're driving, consider a cab or use Uber or Lyft rather than driving yourself—this way you won't get stuck waiting to pay for parking.

4. Have your admission in hand, thus avoiding the ticket booth.

5. Look for a turnstile that seems to be processing people quickly and smoothly.

6. If you need to use the restroom, use the facilities to the left of the park entrance. Disney has a process for letting you rejoin your party in the queue later on if you need to take a bathroom break, but it's not nearly as convenient as getting that out of the way first thing.

Na'vi River Journey   ★★★½

PRESCHOOL ★★★★ (A)	GRADE SCHOOL ★★★★ (BA)	TEENS ★★★½ (MBA)
YOUNG ADULTS ★★★½ (MBA)	OVER 30 ★★★★ (BA)	SENIORS ★★★★ (BA)

What it is Boat ride. **Scope and scale** Headliner. **When to go** Before 9:30 a.m. or during the last 2 hours before closing. **Comments** Very pretty but needs a plot; no height requirement. **Duration of ride** 5 minutes. **Average wait in line per 100 people ahead of you** About 5 minutes. **Loading speed** Moderate. **ECV/wheelchair access** Must transfer to ride vehicle; transfer device available. **Participates in Genie+** Yes. **Early Theme Park Entry** Yes. **Extended Evening Hours** No.

DESCRIPTION AND COMMENTS Na'vi River Journey is a 4½-minute boat ride through the Pandora jungle. You begin by boarding one of two small, hewn rafts joined together. Each raft has two rows of seats, so four people go in each boat. That might seem small, but it's likely a nod to authenticity: The Na'vi are unlikely to have invented technology like fiberglass to make larger vessels like those in, say, It's a Small World.

Off you go into the nighttime jungle, past glowing plants and exotic animals. To create these, Disney has used traditional 3-D sets for the flora, coupled with video screens showing the movement of the fauna. These video screens are semitransparent, though. What's past them are more screens, with background scenes that also move. That means you're seeing action in the foreground and background simultaneously, all surrounded by densely packed landscaping.

Another bit of technology put to great use is video projection mapping like that used in the Magic Kingdom's nighttime shows. Here it's used to project three-dimensional bugs crawling on tree trunks in one of the middle scenes.

The big star, however, is displayed in the ride's culminating scene: the Shaman of Songs, easily the most lifelike animatronic figure Disney has ever created. The shaman's arms move with astonishing grace—we certainly don't know any real people who are that coordinated. Yet another nice touch: The shaman sings off-key rather than professionally pitch-perfect.

The main problem with Na'vi River Journey has to do with storytelling: You go in not knowing anything about the character, and not enough story unfolds during the ride to get you excited about meeting the shaman.

TOURING TIPS We don't think that it's worth waiting longer than 30 minutes (the queue only has enough shade to cover maybe 30 minutes' worth of guests).

ANIMAL KINGDOM ENTERTAINMENT

ANIMAL ENCOUNTERS Throughout the day, Animal Kingdom staff members conduct impromptu short lectures on specific animals at the park. Look for a cast member in safari garb holding a bird, reptile, or small mammal.

Winged Encounters—The Kingdom Takes Flight, a small, interactive event featuring macaws and their handlers, takes place on Discovery Island in front of the Tree of Life. Guests can talk to the animals' trainers and see the birds fly around the middle of the park.

Most other live entertainment in the park, including musical acts and acrobats, is suspended during the pandemic.

CHARACTER CAVALCADES In place of parades and other live entertainment, small boats whisk Disney characters on the waterway around Discovery Island, each to its own soundtrack. Characters include Chip 'n' Dale, Donald and characters from *DuckTales,* Pocahontas, the *Lion King* cast, and Mickey Mouse. Characters don't appear at specific times, but they appear regularly starting about an hour after park opening. The spot where you can see the characters closest is under the bridge on the walkway between Pandora and Africa.

DONALD'S DINO-BASH! ★★½ Regular character greetings are a welcome addition to DinoLand U.S.A. In this case, Donald has discovered that birds are evolutionary descendants of dinosaurs, so he's brought out his friends to celebrate. Characters usually appear intermittently starting at 10 a.m. as follows: **Chip 'n' Dale** across from TriceraTop Spin until 4:30 p.m.; **Daisy, Donald,** and **Goofy** until 5:30 p.m. at Chester and Hester's Dino-Rama; and **Launchpad McQuack** and **Scrooge McDuck** at The Boneyard until 4 p.m. Because the venues are outdoors, the Dino-Bash may shut down temporarily if it's raining.

COVID *tip*
Donald's Dino-Bash was not offered at press time.

TRAFFIC PATTERNS
in ANIMAL KINGDOM

THE PARK'S MAIN DRAWS are the **Pandora** attractions, **Kilimanjaro Safaris** in Africa, and **Expedition Everest** in Asia.

During busy times of year, guests will start lining up outside the Animal Kingdom entrance an hour before opening to be close to the front of the standby line for Flight of Passage. For now, plan on arriving 45–60 minutes before park opening.

Pandora, the Safaris, and Everest are at opposite sides of the park, which allows for even guest distribution. Waits at Dinosaur remain low until 10:30 or 11 a.m. Likewise, crowds don't peak at Expedition Everest until about an hour after park opening, and even later than that at Kali River Rapids. As the day wears on, guests who've experienced the headliners turn their attention to other rides, animal exhibits, and shows, further distributing crowds across the entire park.

unofficial **TIP**
Wait times at the Pandora attractions often peak in the 2 hours after park opening. Less popular attractions generally don't get high traffic until 11 a.m.

Many guests who arrive at opening will leave after having completed their tour of the park by late afternoon. Wait times at the headliners historically dip as the afternoon wears on, usually bottoming out between 3 and 6 p.m. If evening hours return to the Animal Kingdom, crowds will pick back up after sunset for the nighttime Kilimanjaro Safaris and for Pandora's attractions as guests stay to see the land's "bioluminescent" landscaping.

Our mobile app, **Lines** (touringplans.com/lines), gives you current wait times and future estimates in half-hour increments for the day of and the day after your visit.

ANIMAL KINGDOM TOURING PLAN

OUR ANIMAL KINGDOM TOURING PLAN has two versions: one for Disney resort guests and one for off-site guests. Plans for on-site guests use Disney's Early Theme Park Entry benefit (see page 38) to minimize waits in line. Early Entry means thousands of guests will already be in lines and on rides before off-site guests step foot in the park, so the touring strategy for off-site guests must necessarily be different.

Our Animal Kingdom touring plans for this edition do not assume use of Genie+ or Individual Attraction Selections. If you opt for either (or both) of these, just use our free touring plan software to enter your return times.

"Not a Touring Plan" Touring Plans

For the type-B reader, these touring plans (see page 710) dispense with detailed step-by-step strategies for saving every last minute in line. For

Animal Kingdom, these "not" touring plans include advice for adults and parents with one day in the park, arriving either at park opening or later in the morning.

BEFORE YOU GO

1. Call ☎ 407-824-4321 or check online the day before you go to verify official opening time.
2. Make reservations at the Animal Kingdom full-service restaurant(s) of your choice 60 days before your visit.

ANIMAL KINGDOM TOURING PLAN AT A GLANCE

Disney's Animal Kingdom One-Day Touring Plan (two versions) (pages 727–728)

THIS TOURING PLAN ASSUMES a willingness to experience all major rides and shows. If you have children under age 8, refer to the **Small-Child Fright-Potential Table** on pages 390–392. When you're following a printed touring plan, simply skip any attraction that you don't wish to experience.

PART FOURTEEN

DISNEY'S HOLLYWOOD STUDIOS

KEY QUESTIONS ANSWERED IN THIS CHAPTER

OVERVIEW

DISNEY'S HOLLYWOOD STUDIOS has added two new lands and five new rides in the past five years. **Toy Story Land** opened in 2018 with two new child-friendly rides. The other land, **Star Wars: Galaxy's Edge,** opened in 2019 with two cutting-edge rides geared to older kids, teens, and adults. And the Studios launched the family-friendly ride **Mickey & Minnie's Runaway Railway** in early 2020 to rave reviews.

PANDEMIC EFFECTS

NO DISNEY WORLD PARK has been more affected by the pandemic than Hollywood Studios. Live entertainment, character greetings, and stage shows are central to the park's movies-and-television theme. Several live shows remain closed, and no character greetings or live performers have returned. As we went to press, the Studios offered nine rides, three live shows, two movies, and one walk-through exhibit. *Fantasmic!,* the Studios' nighttime spectacular, remained closed despite the return of similar shows at the Magic Kingdom and EPCOT.

In past editions of this book, a similarly small number of things to do was enough for us to say that the Studios wasn't worth your time or money. For older children, teens, and adults, that's not the case today because several of the latest rides at the Studios are among Disney's best and most popular. Star Wars: Rise of the Resistance is arguably the best ride Disney has made in decades, while Runaway

Railway is so immersive, colorful, and full of Mickey's personality that it's impossible not to come out with a smile on your face.

Parents with small children may want to opt for a second day at the Magic Kingdom or Animal Kingdom rather than visit the Studios. At present, the Studios has just four child-friendly rides, three musicals (one of them not worth your time), a Muppets film that's 30 years old, and two walk-through exhibits unlikely to appeal to most small children.

PARK RESERVATIONS AND BOARDING GROUPS

THE STUDIOS HAS LIMITED CAPACITY, as well as many of Walt Disney World's most popular attractions, so getting park reservations for it is more difficult than for any other park. Our suggestion is to obtain park reservations as soon as you know your travel dates. If you're an annual pass holder not staying at a Disney resort, make reservations at least 30 days in advance.

A park reservation is required to obtain a boarding group (i.e., a spot on the waiting list) if Rise of the Resistance is using boarding groups. You must use the My Disney Experience app to obtain a boarding group on the day of your visit because they're not available in advance. See the Rise of the Resistance review on page 594 for more details.

ARRIVING

ARRIVING FROM INSIDE DISNEY WORLD If you're staying at an EPCOT resort, it'll take you 20–30 minutes to walk the mile or so from your hotel to the Studios' entrance. **Boat service** is also available from the EPCOT resorts to the Studios, and it's about a 20-minute ride on the **Skyliner** system (see page 438), which links EPCOT's International Gateway with Hollywood Studios and Disney's Caribbean Beach, Riviera, Pop Century, and Art of Animation Resorts. In addition to the Skyliner, Disney may offer bus service to the Studios from these hotels on days with high attendance. Guests at other Disney resorts access DHS by **bus.**

As we went to press, guests at Pop Century were lining up for the Skyliner to the Studios up to 2 hours before official opening. While the Skyliner is free, that's not a great use of time. A better option is to use Disney's bus service (if available) or a ride-hailing service, described in the next section.

DRIVING The DHS parking lot is located next to the park (for GPS coordinates, see page 439). The parking lots open about an hour before official park opening. Take a tram or walk from the parking lot to the front gate. There can be traffic delays in the morning while everyone waits for the lot to open.

If you want to drive while avoiding traffic, consider using **self-parking** ($27 per day) at the **Swan and Dolphin**, and then walking the 0.5 mile to the Studios entrance. Doing this avoids having to wait for Disney transportation. The cheapest, easiest, and least risky option of all, however, might be to use a **ride-hailing service** to drop you off and pick you up at these hotels instead.

continued on page 574

Disney's Hollywood Studios

G+ Attraction Offers Genie+

IAS Attraction Offers Individual Access

☑ Not To Be Missed

👍 Recommended Dining

🚻 Restrooms

➕ First Aid Center

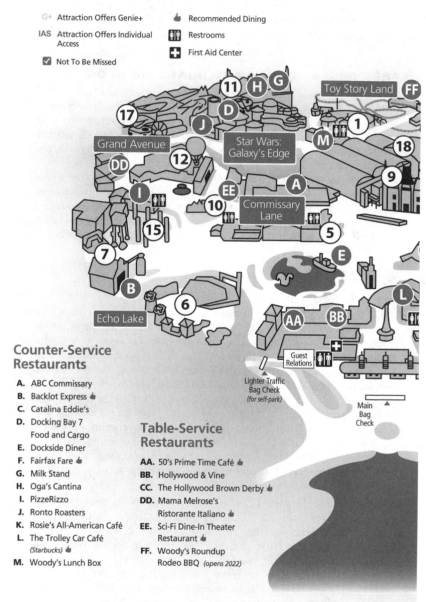

Toy Story Land

Grand Avenue

Star Wars: Galaxy's Edge

Commissary Lane

Echo Lake

Guest Relations

Lighter Traffic Bag Check *(for self-park)*

Main Bag Check

Counter-Service Restaurants

A. ABC Commissary
B. Backlot Express 👍
C. Catalina Eddie's
D. Docking Bay 7 Food and Cargo
E. Dockside Diner
F. Fairfax Fare 👍
G. Milk Stand
H. Oga's Cantina
I. PizzeRizzo
J. Ronto Roasters
K. Rosie's All-American Café
L. The Trolley Car Café *(Starbucks)* 👍
M. Woody's Lunch Box

Table-Service Restaurants

AA. 50's Prime Time Café 👍
BB. Hollywood & Vine
CC. The Hollywood Brown Derby 👍
DD. Mama Melrose's Ristorante Italiano 👍
EE. Sci-Fi Dine-In Theater Restaurant 👍
FF. Woody's Roundup Rodeo BBQ *(opens 2022)*

Attractions

1. Alien Swirling Saucers G+
2. *Beauty and the Beast—Live on Stage!*
   Theater of the Stars
3. *Disney Junior Dance Party! / Disney Junior*
   Play and Dance
4. *Fantasmic!* ☑
5. *For the First Time in Forever:*
   A Frozen Sing-Along Celebration
6. *Indiana Jones Epic*
   Stunt Spectacular!
7. *Jedi Training: Trials of the Temple*
8. *Lightning McQueen's Racing Academy*
9. Mickey and Minnie's Runaway Railway
   ☑ G+
10. Mickey & Minnie Starring in *Red Carpet*
    Dreams
11. *Millennium Falcon:* Smugglers Run G+
12. *Muppet-Vision 3-D* ☑ G+
13. Rock 'n' Roller Coaster Starring
    Aerosmith ☑ G+
14. Slinky Dog Dash ☑ IAS
15. Star Tours—
    The Adventures Continue ☑ G+
16. Star Wars Launch Bay
17. Star Wars: Rise of the Resistance ☑ IAS
18. Toy Story Mania! ☑ G+
19. The Twilight Zone
    Tower of Terror ☑ G+
20. *Walt Disney Presents*

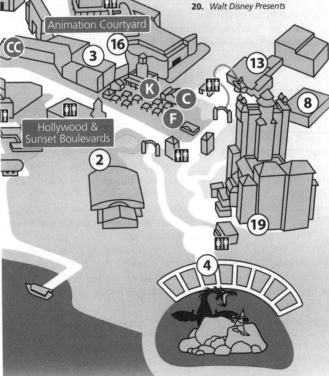

Animation Courtyard

Hollywood &
Sunset Boulevards

continued from page 571

DHS OPENING PROCEDURES (ROPE DROP)

VIRTUALLY ALL RIDES will begin operation as soon as guests are admitted into the park. Shows normally begin running an hour or more after the rest of the park.

On-site guests wishing to use Early Theme Park Entry should arrive at the Studios entrance 60 minutes before official opening on off-peak days and 90 minutes before official opening on days with high attendance.

When Early Entry begins, on-site guests should arrive at the Studios entrance 60 minutes before official opening (that is, 30 minutes before Early Entry) on all days. Off-site guests should arrive 30 minutes before official opening on all days.

HOW MUCH TIME TO ALLOCATE

DEPENDING ON WHEN YOU ARRIVE, the time of year you tour, and how big a *Star Wars* fan you are, a comprehensive tour of the park takes 7–8 hours with lunch and breaks. Allow more time if you want to enjoy the lightsaber- or droid-building experiences in Galaxy's Edge. At press time, Disney's Hollywood Studios did not participate in Disney's Extended Evening Theme Park Hours.

GETTING ORIENTED

ON YOUR LEFT AS YOU ENTER, **Guest Relations** serves as the Studios' headquarters and information center. Go there to pick up a park map or entertainment schedule (*Times Guide*), to report lost persons, or to access the **Baby Care Center**. To the right of the entrance are **locker, stroller, and wheelchair rentals; Package Pickup;** and **Lost and Found.**

As at the Magic Kingdom, you enter the park and then pass down a main street. In this case, it's the **Hollywood Boulevard** of the 1930s and '40s. At the end is a replica of the iconic **Grauman's Chinese Theatre,** home of **Mickey & Minnie's Runaway Railway.**

As you face the Chinese Theatre, two themed areas, **Sunset Boulevard** and **Animation Courtyard,** branch off Hollywood Boulevard to the right. Branching left off Hollywood Boulevard is **Echo Lake. Grand Avenue** holds *Muppet-Vision 3-D* and **Mama Melrose's,** a full-service Italian restaurant.

NOT TO BE MISSED AT DISNEY'S HOLLYWOOD STUDIOS
HOLLYWOOD AND SUNSET BOULEVARDS • *Fantasmic! (closed at press time)* • Mickey & Minnie's Runaway Railway • Rock 'n' Roller Coaster • The Twilight Zone Tower of Terror
ECHO LAKE • Star Tours—The Adventures Continue
COMMISSARY LANE • Mickey and Minnie Starring in *Red Carpet Dreams* *(closed at press time)*
TOY STORY LAND • Slinky Dog Dash • Toy Story Mania!
STAR WARS: GALAXY'S EDGE • *Millennium Falcon:* Smugglers Run • Star Wars: Rise of the Resistance

Toy Story Land's attractions are located behind the Chinese Theatre and to the left of Animation Courtyard. Finally, **Star Wars: Galaxy's Edge** is in the upper-left corner of the park, accessible from Grand Avenue and Toy Story Land.

FAVORITE ATTRACTIONS BY AGE GROUP

THE STUDIOS ENCOMPASSES some four dozen rides, shows, live performances, and fireworks. The chart below shows the park's 10 most popular attractions by age group.

Here are the average ratings for DHS attractions, by age group, for the 82,000 attraction ratings we received in the past 18 months:

- **PRESCHOOL** 4.0 stars
- **GRADE-SCHOOL** 4.4 stars
- **TEENS** 4.1 stars
- **YOUNG ADULTS** 4.2 stars
- **OVER 30** 4.1 stars
- **SENIORS** 4.1 stars

DISNEY'S HOLLYWOOD STUDIOS
Most Popular Attractions by Age Group

PRE-SCHOOL	GRADE-SCHOOL	TEENS	YOUNG ADULTS	OVER 30	SENIORS
Toy Story Mania!	Toy Story Mania!	Rise of the Resistance	Rise of the Resistance	Rise of the Resistance	Rise of the Resistance
Star Wars Launch Bay character greetings*	Slinky Dog Dash	Rock 'n' Roller Coaster	Rock 'n' Roller Coaster	Rock 'n' Roller Coaster	The Twilight Zone Tower of Terror
Mickey & Minnie's Runaway Railway	Star Wars Launch Bay character greetings*	The Twilight Zone Tower of Terror	The Twilight Zone Tower of Terror	The Twilight Zone Tower of Terror	Toy Story Mania!
For the First Time in Forever	Mickey & Minnie's Runaway Railway	Toy Story Mania!	Toy Story Mania!	Toy Story Mania!	Slinky Dog Dash
Disney Junior Play and Dance	For the First Time in Forever	Mickey & Minnie's Runaway Railway	Slinky Dog Dash	Slinky Dog Dash	Mickey & Minnie's Runaway Railway
Celebrity Spotlight (Olaf meet & greet)*	Celebrity Spotlight (Olaf meet & greet)*	Slinky Dog Dash	Millennium Falcon: Smugglers Run	Millennium Falcon: Smugglers Run	Star Wars Launch Bay character greetings*
Beauty and the Beast—Live on Stage*	Star Tours: The Adventures Continue	Star Wars Launch Bay character greetings*	Mickey & Minnie's Runaway Railway	Mickey & Minnie's Runaway Railway	Fantasmic!*
Alien Swirling Saucers	Jedi Training*	Star Tours: The Adventures Continue	Star Wars Launch Bay character greetings*	Star Wars Launch Bay character greetings*	Star Tours: The Adventures Continue
Slinky Dog Dash	Fantasmic!*	Fantasmic!*	Star Tours: The Adventures Continue	Fantasmic!*	For the First Time in Forever
Star Tours: The Adventures Continue	Rise of the Resistance	Millennium Falcon: Smugglers Run	For the First Time in Forever	Star Tours: The Adventures Continue	Beauty and the Beast—Live on Stage*

*Closed at press time

GENIE+, LIGHTNING LANE, AND INDIVIDUAL ATTRACTION SELECTIONS AND TOURING PLANS

IT WAS EASY FOR US to recommend using Disney's old FastPass+ ride-reservation system with our touring plans, because FastPass+ was free to use, had plenty of historical data to analyze, and behaved predictably. None of that is true with Genie+. So the big questions for this edition are:

1. Is Genie+ worth paying for at the Disney's Hollywood Studios?
2. If it's worth the cost, which attractions benefit most from Genie+ or Individual Attraction Selections?
3. How can you avoid paying for Individual Attraction Selections?
4. How do Genie+ and Individual Attraction Selections work with the touring plans?

GENIE+ AND INDIVIDUAL ATTRACTION SELECTIONS IN DHS	
ECHO LAKE	
• Star Tours—The Adventures Continue	
GALAXY'S EDGE	
• *Millennium Falcon:* Smugglers Run	• Rise of the Resistance *(Individual Access only)*
GRAND AVENUE	**HOLLYWOOD BOULEVARD**
• Muppet-Vision 3-D	• Mickey & Minnie's Runaway Railway
SUNSET BOULEVARD	
• Rock 'n' Roller Coaster	• The Twilight Zone Tower of Terror
TOY STORY LAND	
• Alien Swirling Saucers	• Toy Story Mania!
• Slinky Dog Dash *(Individual Access only)*	

Note: Character greetings were not offered when Genie+ and Lightning Lane were introduced. We think character greetings will be added to this list upon their return.

Is Genie+ Worth Paying For at Disney's Hollywood Studios?

Along with the Magic Kingdom, the Studios might be the easiest park to recommend Genie+, especially if you meet any of these criteria:

- You'll arrive at the park after Early Theme Park Entry begins (that is, you won't be at the park as soon as it opens). This includes off-site guests who aren't eligible for Early Theme Park Entry and on-site guests who want to sleep in.
- You won't be using a touring plan.
- You're visiting during a day of moderate or high crowds

Regardless of the time of year you visit, arriving at park opening should allow you to see one or two of the Studios' headliners without significant waits. Since only eight attractions participate in the Genie+ program, it's unlikely that you'd need more than four or five Genie+ reservations per day. On days of heavy attendance, though, you'll be competing with lots of other people for Genie+ reservations, pushing out the Genie+ return times, and limiting how many you can obtain per day.

ESTIMATED TIME SAVINGS USING A TOURING PLAN WITH GENIE+ FOR VARIOUS CROWD LEVELS			
CROWD LEVEL	**TYPICAL USE (3 RESERVATIONS PER DAY)**	**OPTIMISTIC USE (5 RESERVATIONS PER DAY)**	**PERFECT USE (8 RESERVATIONS PER DAY)**
Low	30 minutes saved	50 minutes saved	90 minutes saved
Medium	70 minutes saved	100 minutes saved	140 minutes saved
High	90 minutes saved	150 minutes saved	200 minutes saved

HOLLYWOOD STUDIOS SERVICES

MOST PARK SERVICES are on Hollywood Boulevard, including:

Baby Care Center At Guest Relations; baby food and other necessities also available at Oscar's Super Service, on the right just inside the park

Banking Services ATM on the right just inside the park

Cell Phone Charging Outlets in the Hollywood Brown Derby lobby, inside Backlot Express, and near the restrooms next to Toy Story Mania!

ECV/Scooter Rentals At Package Pickup, outside and to the left of the park entrance

First Aid Center At Guest Relations

Live Entertainment and Character Information Available in the *Times Guide* schedule and at Guest Relations

Lockers On the right just inside the park

Lost and Found At Guest Relations

Lost Persons Report at Guest Relations/Baby Care Center

Magic Bands At The Darkroom on the right side of Hollywood Boulevard as you enter the park, just past Oscar's Super Service

Wheelchair and Stroller Rentals To the right of the entrance, at Oscar's Super Service

Which Attractions Benefit Most from Genie+ or Individual Attraction Selections?

For Genie+, the chart below shows the top eight attractions that might benefit most from using Genie+, based on current wait times and historical FastPass+ data. The chart goes in descending order of priority.

DHS ATTRACTIONS THAT BENEFIT MOST FROM GENIE+ (HIGHEST PRIORITY TO LOWEST)	
1 *Millennium Falcon:* Smugglers Run	5 The Twilight Zone Tower of Terror
2 Rock 'n' Roller Coaster	6 Alien Swirling Saucers
3 Mickey & Minnie's Runaway Railway	7 Star Tours—The Adventures Continue
4 Toy Story Mania!	8 *Muppet-Vision 3-D*

Note: Character greetings were not offered at press time.

How Can You Avoid Paying for Individual Attraction Selections?

The easiest way to avoid paying for Individual Attraction Selections at Slinky Dog Dash is to head for that ride as soon as you enter the park. That doesn't work if Rise of the Resistance is using boarding groups, however. If you are unable to get a boarding group for Rise of the Resistance, purchasing Individual Attraction Selections for it is the only way to experience the best ride Disney's done in years. It's a blatant money-grab made possible by executives who've never had to explain to a disappointed child why only the well-heeled or lucky get to go on the attraction.

How do Genie+ and Individual Attraction Selections Work with the Touring Plans?

See our advice for the Magic Kingdom on page 468.

DINING IN DISNEY'S HOLLYWOOD STUDIOS

HERE'S A QUICK RECAP of the Studios' top restaurants, rated by readers from highest to lowest. See Part Six for details. An opening date has not yet been announced for **Roundup Rodeo BBQ,** a new restaurant coming to Toy Story Land.

DHS RESTAURANT REFRESHER	
COUNTER SERVICE	**FULL SERVICE**
Ronto Roasters (⊕ 96%/Exceptional), Galaxy's Edge	**The Hollywood Brown Derby** (⊕ 93%/Above Average), Hollywood Boulevard
Docking Bay 7 (⊕ 93%/Above Average), Galaxy's Edge	**50's Prime Time Cafe** (⊕ 87%/Average), Echo Lake
The Trolley Car Cafe (Starbucks) (⊕ 93%/Average), Sunset Boulevard	
Woody's Lunch Box (⊕ 91%/Average), Toy Story Land	
Backlot Express (⊕ 90%/Average), Echo Lake	
ABC Commissary (⊕ 90%/Average), Commissary Lane	

DISNEY'S HOLLYWOOD STUDIOS ATTRACTIONS

HOLLYWOOD BOULEVARD

THIS PALM-LINED THOROUGHFARE re-creates Tinseltown's main drag during the Golden Age of Hollywood. Most of the Studios' service facilities are located here, interspersed with eateries and shops. The merchandise sold here includes everything from Disney trademark items to movie-related souvenirs.

SUNSET BOULEVARD

EVOKING THE GLAMOUR OF THE 1940s, Sunset Boulevard—the first right off Hollywood Boulevard—provides another venue for dining, shopping, and street entertainment.

KEY TO ABBREVIATIONS In the attraction profiles that follow, each star rating is accompanied by a category label in parentheses (see page 266). **E** means **Exceptional, MAA** means **Much Above Average, AA** means **Above Average, A** means **Average, BA** means **Below Average,** and **MBA** means **Much Below Average.**

AVERAGE WAIT-IN-LINE TIMES This is the attractions' maximum hourly capacity in passengers per hour.

Beauty and the Beast—Live on Stage / Theater of the Stars
★★★★

PRESCHOOL ★★★★½ (AA)	GRADE SCHOOL ★★★★ (BA)	TEENS ★★★★ (MBA)
YOUNG ADULTS ★★★★ (BA)	OVER 30 ★★★★ (A)	SENIORS ★★★★½ (AA)

What it is Live Hollywood-style musical with Disney characters, performed in an open-air theater. **Scope and scale** Major attraction. **When to go** Anytime, but not as hot after sunset. **Comment** Check *Times Guide* for showtimes. **Duration of presentation** 25 minutes. **Preshow entertainment** None. **When to arrive** 25-35 minutes in advance. **ECV/wheelchair access** May remain in wheelchair. **Participates in Genie+** No. **Early Theme Park Entry** No. **Extended Evening Hours** No.

DESCRIPTION AND COMMENTS The long-running *Beauty and the Beast* show combines a shortened (but complete) retelling of the story with all of the major musical numbers, with tons of characters and good set decoration. The theater affords a clear field of vision from almost every seat. Best of all, a canopy protects the audience from the Florida sun (or rain), but the theater still gets mighty hot in the summer.

TOURING TIPS *Beauty and the Beast* usually runs from midmorning to around 4 p.m. The show is so popular that you should arrive 25–35 minutes early to get a good seat. If you can't make it in time, look for overflow seating outside: Two sets of bleachers offer perfect views of the stage. The seating isn't covered, though, so drink plenty of water and use sun protection as needed.

Fantasmic! *(closed at press time)*   ★★★★½

PRESCHOOL ★★★★ (A)   GRADE SCHOOL ★★★★½ (AA)   TEENS ★★★★½ (AA)
YOUNG ADULTS ★★★★½ (AA)   OVER 30 ★★★★½ (AA)   SENIORS ★★★★½ (AA)

What it is Mixed-media nighttime spectacular. **Scope and scale** Super-headliner. **When to go** Check *Times Guide* for schedule; if 2 shows are offered, the second will be less crowded. **Comment** One of Disney's best nighttime events. **Duration of presentation** 25 minutes. **Probable waiting time** 50–90 minutes for a seat, 35–40 minutes for standing room. **ECV/wheelchair access** May remain in wheelchair. **Participates in Genie+** No. **Early Theme Park Entry** No. **Extended Evening Hours** No.

DESCRIPTION AND COMMENTS Off Sunset Boulevard behind the Tower of Terror, this mixed-media show is staged on an island opposite the 7,900-seat Hollywood Hills Amphitheater. By far the largest theater facility ever created by Disney, it can accommodate an additional 2,000 standing guests for an audience of nearly 10,000.

Fantasmic! is one of the most innovative outdoor spectacles we've seen at any theme park. Starring Mickey Mouse in his role as the Sorcerer's Apprentice from *Fantasia,* the production uses lasers, images projected on a shroud of mist, fireworks, lighting effects, and music in combinations so stunning you can scarcely believe what you're seeing. The theme is simple: good versus evil. The plot gets lost in all the special effects at times, but no matter: It's the spectacle, not the story line, that's powerful.

A Pearland, Texas, mom found *Fantasmic!* too intense for her young child:

Fantasmic! should come with a warning. The larger-than-life laser visages, loud and ominous music, and thundering explosions sent hordes of parents with screaming children fleeing for the exits.

We don't receive many reports of young children being terrified by *Fantasmic!*, but the reader's point is well taken. Spend some time preparing your kids for what they will see. You can mitigate the fright factor somewhat by sitting back a bit. Also, hang on to your kids after the show, and give them instructions for regrouping should you get separated.

TOURING TIPS Before the pandemic, *Fantasmic!* was presented one or more times most evenings, but Disney was known to change the schedule, so check before you go. *Fantasmic!* is to the Studios what *Happily Ever After* is to the Magic Kingdom: While it's hard to imagine a 10,000-person amphitheater running out of space, that's exactly what happens almost every time the show is staged. On evenings when there are two shows, the second will always be less crowded. If you attend the first (or only) scheduled performance, then arrive at least an hour in advance; if you opt for the second, arrive 50 minutes early.

A Cross Junction, Virginia, woman offers this planning tip:

Buy deli sandwiches outside the park, pack them with snacks and water, and get an early seat.

A multigenerational family from Barrie, Ontario, makes this suggestion for guests who are short on nature's upholstery:

Bring pillows or towels to sit on. We were sitting on those benches from 6 p.m. for the 7:30 show, and boy, did our rears hurt by the end!

Rain and wind sometimes cause *Fantasmic!* to be canceled; unfortunately, Disney usually doesn't make a final ruling about whether to proceed or cancel until just before showtime. We've seen guests wait stoically for over an hour with no assurance that their patience and sacrifice will be rewarded. In any case, we don't recommend arriving more than 20 minutes before showtime on rainy or especially windy nights. On nights like these, pursue your own agenda until 10–20 minutes or so before showtime; then head to the stadium to see what happens.

Our own researcher David, a dad of two, notes that the Magic Kingdom's Halloween and Christmas parties affect *Fantasmic!* crowds:

As a kid-friendly nighttime show, Fantasmic! *is a hot mess on nights when the Magic Kingdom closes early.*

When this happens, plan to arrive about 90 minutes before the show to ensure good seats.

A veteran of both Disneyland and Walt Disney World notes:

Disneyland's [crowd-control] cast members push throngs of guests through the park like clockwork, even when it's bursting at the seams. At Disney World, it's basically every man for himself as the cast members retreat, leaving very tired, very cranky guests to duke it out. Such is the case at Fantasmic!—*thankfully, a backstage corridor was open for a quick reroute, but the presence of cast members was rare.*

Finally, a couple from Alberta, Canada, sums things up:

For a show so deservedly hyped, I would hope that WDW finds ways to make seeing it less stressful.

FANTASMIC! DINING PACKAGE If you're planning to eat at **The Hollywood Brown Derby, Hollywood & Vine,** or **Mama Melrose's Ristorante Italiano,** you can obtain a voucher for the members of your dining party to enter *Fantasmic!* via a special entrance and sit in a reserved section. This saves you 30–90 minutes of waiting in the regular line to be admitted. If you know you're going to eat at one of these locations, the dining package is a better way to see *Fantasmic!* than lining up in advance.

You must call ☎ 407-WDW-DINE (939-3463) up to 60 days in advance and request the package for the night you want to see the show. *Note:* This is a real reservation, not an Advance Reservation, and it must be guaranteed with a credit card at the time of booking. There's no additional charge for the package itself, but there is a $10-per-person charge for canceling with less than 48 hours' notice.

Included in the package are fixed-price menus for all three restaurants as follows; respective prices are the most recent available for adults and kids ages 3–9: *Hollywood & Vine:* breakfast $50/$32, lunch and dinner $63/$41; *The Hollywood Brown Derby:* lunch and dinner $65/$24; *Mama Melrose's:* lunch and dinner $43/$18. Nonalcoholic drinks are included; tax, tips, and park admission are not. Some Disney dining plans are accepted. Prices may vary seasonally, so call ☎ 407-WDW-DINE (939-3463) to confirm.

You'll receive your vouchers at the restaurant during your meal; if you're eating dinner, you'll need to arrive no later than 2½ hours before showtime. Then, about half an hour before the show, you'll report to the Highlands Gate on Sunset Boulevard, between Theater of the Stars and the Once Upon a Time store. A cast member will collect your vouchers and escort you to the reserved-seating section of the amphitheater. Though you're required to arrive early, you can be seated immediately. The reserved seats are in the center of the stadium; you won't have assigned seats—it's first come, first served—so arrive early for the best choice. Finally, if *Fantasmic!* is canceled due to weather or other circumstances, you'll get a voucher for another performance within five days.

Weather notwithstanding, a Waldorf, Maryland, couple thinks the dining package is the only way to go:

We booked dinner at Hollywood & Vine, got our passes for the package, and waltzed on in to the show. We felt like VIPs, and it was so relaxing to see the show without the rush of the crowds.

Lightning McQueen's Racing Academy   ★★½

PRESCHOOL ★★★★ (A)	GRADE SCHOOL ★★★½ (BA)	TEENS ★★★ (BA)
YOUNG ADULTS ★★★ (BA)	OVER 30 ★★★ (MBA)	SENIORS ★★★½ (BA)

What it is Wide-screen movie of Lightning McQueen's racing tips. **Scope and scale** Minor attraction. **When to go** Anytime. **Duration of presentation** Continuous 10 minutes. **Preshow entertainment** None. **ECV/wheelchair access** May remain in wheelchair. **Participates in Genie+** No. **Early Theme Park Entry** No. **Extended Evening Hours** No.

DESCRIPTION AND COMMENTS This theater show features *Cars* superstars Lightning McQueen, Cruz Ramirez, and Tow Mater. While the last two appear only on the massive wraparound screen, Lightning McQueen is front and center as a full-size animatronic.

The show starts slowly, with Lightning explaining why he developed a racing academy, but it becomes impressive once the simulation starts. Using the huge screens, Lightning mimes racing as a track flies by around you. As usual, things don't go quite as planned when an old adversary shows up, but it's all settled by a race, of course.

For a relatively short show, the visuals and the wonderfully subtle movements of Lightning on the stage make this a worthwhile stop in the Studios.

TOURING TIPS Added to increase the park's capacity, *Lightning McQueen's Racing Academy* is located in one of the most remote corners of the park: past the end of Sunset Boulevard, then past the end of the Rock 'n' Roller Coaster plaza. Because it's hard to find and requires backtracking to get anywhere else, it's rarely crowded. A photo opportunity with Cruz Ramirez is outside the show.

Mickey and Minnie's Runaway Railway   ★★★★

PRESCHOOL ★★★★½ (AA)	GRADE SCHOOL ★★★★½ (AA)	TEENS ★★★★½ (AA)
YOUNG ADULTS ★★★★½ (AA)	OVER 30 ★★★★½ (AA)	SENIORS ★★★★½ (AA)

What it is Indoor dark ride through the new Mickey Mouse cartoon universe. **Scope and scale** Headliner. **When to go** As soon as the park is open or in the last hour before park closing. **Duration of ride** 5 minutes. **Average wait in line per 100 people ahead of you** 4 minutes; assumes all trains operating. **Loading speed** Moderate. **ECV/wheelchair access** Must transfer to ride vehicle. **Participates in Genie+** Yes. **Early Theme Park Entry** No. **Extended Evening Hours** No.

DESCRIPTION AND COMMENTS Disney restarted regular production of Mickey Mouse cartoons in 2013. Mostly written and directed by Paul Rudish, these 7-minute vignettes—more than 100 have been made so far—are minor masterpieces of storytelling, animation, and humor; Mickey and Minnie sport a retro-1930s look, complete with "pie eyes." In settings across the world, and sometimes entirely in languages other than English, the Mouses, Goofy, Donald, and the rest of the gang embark on crazy adventures that always seem to end up just fine. If you haven't seen them yet, plan on binge-watching them with your kids (they're all on YouTube and Disney+).

Runaway Railway places you in the center of one of those cartoons. The premise is that you're on an out-of-control railroad car, courtesy of Goofy. You careen, gently, through 10 large cartoon show scenes, from tropical islands to cities to out-of-control factories. In each scene, Mickey and Minnie attempt to save you from disaster, with mixed results.

In each scene, Disney uses a mix of traditional, three-dimensional painted sets and the latest in video projection technology to show movement and special effects. It's all done very well, and there are so many things to see on either side of the ride that it's impossible to catch everything in one or two rides. For more Mickey, the Mickey Shorts Theater near *Indiana Jones Epic Stunt Spectacular!* at Echo Lake shows a montage of the new cartoons too.

TOURING TIPS Runaway Railway is the Studios' sleeper hit of the decade, so expect long lines throughout the day. Your best bet is to get in line as soon as the park opens or late in the afternoon.

Rock 'n' Roller Coaster Starring Aerosmith ★★★★

PRESCHOOL ★½ (MBA)　**GRADE SCHOOL ★★★★½** (MBA)　**TEENS ★★★★★** (E)
YOUNG ADULTS ★★★★★ (E)　**OVER 30 ★★★★½** (MBA)　**SENIORS ★★★★** (BA)

What it is Rock music–themed roller coaster. **Scope and scale** Headliner. **When to go** First 30 minutes the park is open or after 4 p.m. **Comments** Must be 48" to ride; Rider Switch option provided (see page 395). **Duration of ride** Almost 1½ minutes. **Average wait in line per 100 people ahead of you** 2½ minutes; assumes all trains operating. **Loading speed** Moderate-fast. **ECV/wheelchair access** Must transfer from ECV to provided wheelchair and then from wheelchair to ride vehicle; transfer device available. **Participates in Genie+** Yes. **Early Theme Park Entry** Yes. **Extended Evening Hours** No.

Motion Sickness

DESCRIPTION AND COMMENTS Way wilder than Space Mountain or Big Thunder Mountain Railroad in the Magic Kingdom, Rock 'n' Roller Coaster is an attraction for fans of high-speed thrill rides. Although the presence of Aerosmith and the synchronized music add measurably to the experience, the ride itself is what you're here for. Rock 'n' Roller Coaster's loops, corkscrews, and drops make Space Mountain seem like It's a Small World. What really makes this metal coaster unusual, however, is that first, it's in the dark (like Space Mountain, only with Southern California nighttime scenes instead of space), and second, you are launched up the first hill like a jet off a carrier deck. By the time you crest the hill, you'll have gone from 0 to 57 mph in less than 3 seconds. When you enter the first loop, you'll be pulling almost 5 g's—2 more than astronauts used to experience at liftoff on a space shuttle.

Reader opinions of Rock 'n' Roller Coaster are predictably mixed, and invariably colored by how the reader feels about roller coasters. First, from a mother of two from High Mills, New York:

You can't warn people enough about Rock 'n' Roller Coaster. My daughter and I refused to go on it at all. My 9-year-old son, who had no problems with any ride, including Tower of Terror, went on with my husband and came off so shaken he was "done for" the rest of the day. My husband just closed his eyes and hoped for the best.

From a Longmont, Colorado, dad:

The first 15 seconds are spectacular. I've never experienced anything like the initial take-off.

From an Australian couple who traveled a long way to ride a coaster:

My wife and I are definitely not roller-coaster people. However, we found Rock 'n' Roller Coaster quite exhilarating—and because it's dark, we didn't always realize that we were being thrown upside down. We rode it twice!

TOURING TIPS Rock 'n' Roller Coaster is not for everyone—if Space Mountain or Big Thunder pushes your limits, skip it. The attractions in Galaxy's Edge, along with Slinky Dog Dash and Mickey & Minnie's Runaway Railway, draw crowds away from Rock 'n' Roller Coaster. If you can't ride first thing in the morning, waits after 4 p.m. should be manageable.

The Twilight Zone Tower of Terror ★★★★★

PRESCHOOL ★★½ (MBA)	GRADE SCHOOL ★★★★ (MBA)	TEENS ★★★★★ (MAA)
YOUNG ADULTS ★★★★★ (MAA)	OVER 30 ★★★★½ (MAA)	SENIORS ★★★★½ (AA)

What it is Sci-fi-themed indoor thrill ride. **Scope and scale** Super-headliner. **When to go** First 30 minutes the park is open or after 4 p.m. **Comments** Must be 40" to ride; Rider Switch option provided (see page 395). **Duration of ride** About 4 minutes plus preshow. **Average wait in line per 100 people ahead of you** 4 minutes; assumes all elevators operating at full capacity. **Loading speed** Moderate. **ECV/wheelchair access** Must transfer from ECV to provided wheelchair and then from wheelchair to ride vehicle. **Participates in Genie+** Yes. **Early Theme Park Entry** Yes. **Extended Evening Hours** No.

DESCRIPTION AND COMMENTS The Tower of Terror is a different species of Disney thrill ride, though it borrows elements of The Haunted Mansion at the Magic Kingdom. The story is that you're touring a once-famous Hollywood hotel gone to ruin. As at Star Tours, the queuing area here immerses guests in the adventure as they pass through the hotel's once-opulent public rooms. From the lobby, guests are escorted into the hotel's library, where *Twilight Zone* creator Rod Serling, speaking from an old black-and-white TV, greets them and introduces the plot.

The Tower of Terror is a whopper, at 13 stories tall. Breaking tradition in terms of visually isolating themed areas, it lets you see the entire Studios from atop the tower . . . but you have to look quick.

The ride vehicle, one of the hotel's service elevators, takes guests to see the haunted hostelry. The tour begins innocuously, but at about the fifth floor things get pretty weird. Guests are subjected to a full range of eerie effects as they cross into the Twilight Zone. The sudden drops and ascents begin when your ride vehicle travels horizontally across the building, into a second elevator shaft.

The Tower of Terror is an experience to savor. Though the plunges—yep, plural—are calculated to thrill, the meat of the attraction is its extraordinary visual and audio effects. There are several different lift-and-drop sequences that are selected randomly, making the attraction faster and keeping you guessing about when, how far, and how many times the elevator will fall.

A senior from the United Kingdom tried the Tower of Terror and liked it very much:

I was thankful I had read your review of the Tower of Terror, or I certainly would have avoided it. As you say, it's so full of magnificent detail that it's worth riding even if you don't fancy the drops involved.

A Washington state reader thinks the randomness is a net negative:

The last time I rode the Tower of Terror was almost 20 years ago, and I remember a HUGE drop initially. This time it was just kind of up-down, up-down, up-up-down. Bummer.

The Tower has great potential for terrifying young children and rattling more-mature visitors. If you have teenagers in your party, use them as experimental probes: If they report back that they really, really liked the Tower of Terror, run as fast as you can in the opposite direction.

TOURING TIPS The attractions in Galaxy's Edge, along with Slinky Dog Dash and Mickey & Minnie's Runaway Railway, draw crowds away from Tower of Terror. If you can't ride first thing in the morning, waits should be shorter in the last hour the park is open.

To save time once you're inside the queuing area, when you enter the library waiting room, stand in the far back corner across from the door where you entered and at the opposite end of the room from the TV. When the doors to the loading area open, you'll be the first admitted.

If you have young children (or anyone) who are apprehensive about this attraction, ask the attendant about **Rider Switch** (see page 395).

ECHO LAKE

AN ACTUAL MINIATURE LAKE near the middle of the Studios, to the left of Hollywood Boulevard, Echo Lake pays homage to its real-life California counterpart, which served as the backdrop to many early motion pictures.

For the First Time in Forever: A Frozen Sing-Along Celebration ★★★½

PRESCHOOL ★★★★½ (MBA)	GRADE SCHOOL ★★★★½ (AA)	TEENS ★★★★ (BA)
YOUNG ADULTS ★★★★ (BA)	OVER 30 ★★★★ (A)	SENIORS ★★★★½ (A)

What it is Sing-along stage show retelling the story of *Frozen*, with appearances by Anna and Elsa. **Scope and scale** Minor attraction. **When to go** Check the park map or *Times Guide* for showtimes. **Duration of presentation** 30 minutes. **When to arrive** 25 minutes before showtime. **ECV/wheelchair access** May remain in wheelchair. **Participates in Genie+** No. **Early Theme Park Entry** No. **Extended Evening Hours** No.

DESCRIPTION AND COMMENTS This 30-minute musical recap of the chilly Disney hit includes songs from the original movie and a visit from Anna and Elsa. Scenes from the movie, projected on a drive-in-size screen in the background, provide continuity and bring those who haven't seen the film up to speed. Live performers, including two "royal historians" and several supporting characters from *Frozen*, retell the story with corny and sometimes punchy humor.

Most of the show unfolds at a leisurely pace, but the ending is presented in a nanosecond, leaving much of the audience stupefied. Of course, the finale features Anna and Elsa and another rousing belting of "Let It Go." If you're a fan of the movie, you probably won't care about the weak points. And even if you're not a fan, you'll enjoy the show's spirit as well as that of a theater full of enraptured kids. Yes, it's contagious.

Most readers really like the sing-along, including this mom from Houston:

I'm glad we didn't skip it, because it was a total hoot—my husband and I loved it, and it turned out to be the highlight of our DHS visit! When we got home, my husband and 9-year-old son, neither of whom had seen the movie before, watched Frozen *with my daughter.*

But a Connecticut reader was less impressed:

The sing-along was extremely disappointing—most of the time, you're just watching scenes from the movie.

TOURING TIPS The indoor theater is one of Disney World's largest and most comfortable, with excellent sight lines from every seat. Crowd management when entering the theater is a little confusing, but once you're inside it sorts itself out.

Indiana Jones Epic Stunt Spectacular! *(closed at press time)*
★★★½

PRESCHOOL ★★★½ (MBA)	GRADE SCHOOL ★★★½ (A)	TEENS ★★★ (BA)
YOUNG ADULTS ★★★★ (BA)	OVER 30 ★★★★ (MBA)	SENIORS ★★★★½ (A)

What it is Movie-stunt demonstration and action show. **Scope and scale** Headliner. **When to go** First two shows or last show. **Comment** Performance times posted on a sign at the entrance to the theater. **Duration of presentation** 30 minutes. **Preshow entertainment** Selection of "extras" from audience. **When to arrive** 20–30 minutes before showtime. **ECV/wheelchair access** May remain in wheelchair. **Participates in Genie+** No. **Early Theme Park Entry** No. **Extended Evening Hours** No.

DESCRIPTION AND COMMENTS Educational though somewhat unevenly paced, the popular production showcases professional stunt men and women who offer behind-the-scenes demonstrations of their craft. Sets, props, and special effects are very elaborate.

TOURING TIPS The Stunt Theater holds 2,000 people; capacity audiences are common. The first performance is always the easiest to see. If the first show is at 11 a.m. or earlier, you can usually walk in, even if you arrive 5 minutes late. For the second performance, show up about 15–20 minutes ahead of time; for the third and subsequent shows, arrive 20–30 minutes early. If you plan to tour during late afternoon and evening, attend the last performance of the day. To beat the crowd out of the stadium, sit on the far right (as you face the staging area) and near the top.

Before the pandemic, the key to being chosen from the audience to be an extra in the stunt show was to arrive early, sit down front, and display unbridled enthusiasm. A woman from Richmond, Virginia, explains:

After the first performance, I realized the best way to get picked was to stand up, wave my arms, and shout when the "casting director" called for volunteers. (Sitting toward the front helps too.)

Jedi Training: Trials of the Temple *(closed at press time)*
★★★½

PRESCHOOL ★★★★ (A)	GRADE SCHOOL ★★★★½ (MBA)	TEENS ★★★ (MBA)
YOUNG ADULTS ★★★★ (BA)	OVER 30 ★★★★ (BA)	SENIORS ★★★★ (BA)

What it is Outdoor stage show. **Scope and scale** Minor attraction. **When to go** First 2 shows of the day. **Comments** To sign your children up to go onstage, visit the Indiana Jones Adventure Outpost early in the morning. Spots are first come, first served. **Duration of show** About 15 minutes. **When to arrive** 15 minutes before showtime. **ECV/wheelchair access** May remain in wheelchair. **Participates in Genie+** No. **Early Theme Park Entry** No. **Extended Evening Hours** No.

DESCRIPTION AND COMMENTS *Jedi Training: Trials of the Temple* is staged several times daily to the left of the Star Tours building entrance, opposite Backlot Express. If you want your young Skywalkers-in-training to appear onstage, visit the sign-up area at the Indiana Jones Adventure Outpost as early in the morning as possible. Spots go quickly and are first come, first served.

A Windham, New Hampshire, mom describes a common conundrum:

Many families will have to choose between racing to Slinky Dog Dash to ride or racing to sign up for Jedi Training: Trials of the Temple *(children MUST be present at sign-up). We hopped on Slinky Dog, then crossed the park to sign up for* Jedi. *By the time we got there, we were pushed to the 2:20 p.m. show, which eliminated the possibility of leaving for a nap after lunch.*

A Melbourne, Australia, mom laments the investment of time:

Jedi Training can quickly derail a touring plan. It requires that the kids be there more than 30 minutes before the show; add in the show and the time to sign up in the morning, and you're looking at a 90-plus-minute investment. That wasn't in the plan, but it was my son's favorite part of our last visit.

Once onstage, these miniature Jedi are trained in the ways of The Force and do battle against the likes of Darth Vader and Kylo Ren. If all this sounds too intense, it's not: Stormtroopers provide comic relief, and just as in the movies, the good guys always win.

TOURING TIPS The show is surprisingly popular, given that Disney hasn't promoted it with the same level of hype as other shows. In the summer, grab drinks at Backlot Express, right next door, about 20 minutes before the show starts.

If *Jedi Training: Trials of the Temple* is at the top of your child's hit parade, a mom from Camp Hill, Pennsylvania, suggests checking the weather before you head to the park:

Because the show is on an outdoor stage, the show gets canceled if it rains, and because all shows are filled, there is no chance to rebook the same day. Disney needs to rethink this show and put it under some kind of cover. Nothing makes for a more unhappy day than disappointed kids and parents after a lot of anticipation and waiting around.

Mickey and Minnie Starring in *Red Carpet Dreams*
(closed at press time)   ★★★★

PRESCHOOL ★★★★½ (AA)   **GRADE SCHOOL** ★★★★½ (AA)   **TEENS** ★★★★ (A)
YOUNG ADULTS ★★★★ (A)   **OVER 30** ★★★★ (A)   **SENIORS** ★★★★ (A)

What it is Character-greeting venue. **Scope and scale** Diversion. **When to go** First or last hour the park is open or during mealtimes. **Duration of experience** About 2 minutes. **Comments** Everybody loves Mickey and Minnie; not to be missed. **Average wait in line per 100 people ahead of you** 60 minutes. **Queue speed** Slow. **ECV/wheelchair access** May remain in wheelchair. **Participates in Genie+** Likely upon return. **Early Theme Park Entry** No. **Extended Evening Hours** No.

DESCRIPTION AND COMMENTS This is the venue for meeting Mickey and Minnie Mouse at Disney's Hollywood Studios. The idea is that you're visiting both of them while they're working on their latest films. Minnie's greeting area is the set of her latest film, a musical blockbuster. Mickey is reprising his role from *Fantasia,* so he's dressed as the Sorcerer's Apprentice.

TOURING TIPS The meet and greet entrance is on Commissary Lane, between the entrance to the ABC Commissary and the entrance to the Sci-Fi Dine-In. Long lines form once the park is full but drop considerably during lunch and dinner.

Star Tours—The Adventures Continue ★★★½

PRESCHOOL ★★★★ (BA) **GRADE SCHOOL** ★★★★½ (AA) **TEENS** ★★★★½ (AA)
YOUNG ADULTS ★★★★½ (A) **OVER 30** ★★★★ (A) **SENIORS** ★★★★½ (AA)

What it is Indoor space-flight-simulation ride. **Scope and scale** Major attraction. **When to go** During lunch or after 4 p.m. **Comments** Expectant mothers and anyone prone to motion sickness should not ride. Too intense for many children younger than age 8; must be 40" to ride; Rider Switch option available (see page 395). **Duration of ride** About 7 minutes. **Average wait in line per 100 people ahead of you** 5 minutes; assumes all simulators operating. **Loading speed** Moderate–fast. **ECV/wheelchair access** Must transfer from ECV to provided wheelchair and then from wheelchair to ride vehicle. **Participates in Genie+** Yes. **Early Theme Park Entry** Yes. **Extended Evening Hours** No.

DESCRIPTION AND COMMENTS Based on the *Star Wars* saga, this was Disney's first modern simulator ride. Guests ride in a flight simulator modeled after those used for training pilots and astronauts, experiencing dips, turns, twists, and climbs. The ride film, projected in high-definition 3-D, has more than 50 combinations of opening and ending scenes, including clips from *The Force Awakens.* You could ride Star Tours all day without seeing the same scenes twice. The downside to Star Tours is that it's not in Galaxy's Edge.

TOURING TIPS Wait-in-line times are lowest during lunch and after 4 p.m.

Mickey Shorts Theater ★★★½

PRESCHOOL ★★★★ (A) **GRADE SCHOOL** ★★★★½ (AA) **TEENS** ★★★★ (A)
YOUNG ADULTS ★★★★ (A) **OVER 30** ★★★★ (A) **SENIORS** ★★★★ (A)

What it is Cartoon featuring Mickey Mouse. **Scope and scale** Diversion. **When to go** Anytime. **Duration of presentation** 10 minutes. **Preshow entertainment** None. **Probable waiting time** 9 minutes. **ECV/wheelchair access** May remain in wheelchair. **Participates in Genie+** No. **Early Theme Park Entry** No. **Extended Evening Hours** No.

DESCRIPTION AND COMMENTS The Mickey Shorts Theater shows a new 10-minute Mickey Mouse cartoon called *Vacation Fun,* which pastes together clips from several of the newer, best Mickey Mouse cartoons into one. If you've seen *Couple Sweaters, O Sole Minnie, Amore Motore,* or *Potatoland,* you'll recognize the scenes.

If you loved Mickey & Minnie's Runaway Railway, here's your chance to see more of the new-style cartoons. And if you've not yet seen the new cartoons, this is the place to get familiar with them.

TOURING TIPS Even if you've seen some of the clips, the theater is large, comfortable, and air-conditioned. It's the perfect short break in the middle of a hot day.

GRAND AVENUE

THIS THEMED AREA has just one attraction, two restaurants, and a bar. The street sets serve as a pedestrian thoroughfare to Galaxy's Edge.

Muppet-Vision 3-D ★★★★

PRESCHOOL ★★★★ (A) **GRADE SCHOOL** ★★★★ (MBA) **TEENS** ★★★½ (MBA)
YOUNG ADULTS ★★★★ (MBA) **OVER 30** ★★★★ (MBA) **SENIORS** ★★★★ (BA)

What it is 3-D movie starring the Muppets. **Scope and scale** Major attraction. **When to go** Anytime. **Duration of presentation** 17 minutes. **Preshow entertainment** The Muppets on TV. **Probable waiting time** 15 minutes. **ECV/wheelchair access** May remain in wheelchair. **Participates in Genie+** Yes. **Early Theme Park Entry** Yes. **Extended Evening Hours** No.

DESCRIPTION AND COMMENTS *Muppet-Vision 3-D* provides a total sensory experience, with wacky 3-D action augmented by auditory, visual, and tactile special effects. If you're tired and hot, this zany show will make you feel brand-new. Arrive early to enjoy the hilarious video preshow.

A New Brunswick, Canada, reader thinks the Muppets are heaven-sent:

> *I think* Muppet-Vision 3-D *is a godsend for five reasons: (1) It NEVER has a line (even on our visit on New Year's Day!). (2) Everyone ages 1–100 gives the show high marks. (3) Between the preshow and the movie, it's half an hour of sitting comfortably in an air-conditioned theater. (4) Between the live actors and animatronics, it's so much more than just another silly 3-D movie. (5) IT'S THE MUPPETS!*

TOURING TIPS Waits generally peak around lunchtime, and with the Studios' other attractions returning to pre-pandemic capacities, it's unusual to find a wait longer than one show. If you do encounter a long line, try again later.

THE AREA FORMERLY KNOWN AS PIXAR PLACE

THE TINY DEAD-END STREET on the way to Toy Story Land holds a few food stands, along with photo opportunities, and in pre-pandemic times, character greetings and occasional live performances. Check your *Times Guide* for showtimes.

TOY STORY LAND

THE 11-ACRE Toy Story Land opened in 2018. The idea behind it is that you've been shrunk to the size of a toy and placed in Andy's backyard, where you get to play with other toys he's set up.

Toy Story Land's attractions are designed to appeal to young children. This is a great thing that DHS has needed more of for years (and still does), but because two of the rides have relatively low capacity, you should expect long waits throughout the day.

Toy Story Land is one of two ways to access Galaxy's Edge, the other being **Grand Avenue** (see 587).

Alien Swirling Saucers ★★½

PRESCHOOL ★★★½ (MAA) **GRADE SCHOOL ★★★★ (MBA)** **TEENS ★★★½ (MBA)**
YOUNG ADULTS ★★★½ (MBA) **OVER 30 ★★★½ (MBA)** **SENIORS ★★★½ (MBA)**

What it is Spinning car ride. **Scope and scale** Minor attraction. **When to go** First 30 minutes the park is open or after 3 p.m. **Comment** Must be 32" to ride. **Duration of ride** 3 minutes. **Average wait in line per 100 people ahead of you** 10 minutes. **Loading speed** Slow. **ECV/wheelchair access** Must transfer to ride vehicle.

DESCRIPTION AND COMMENTS Alien Swirling Saucers is themed around *Toy Story*'s vending-machine aliens and their obsession with The Claw. About a dozen ride cars move, whiplike, in an elongated figure-eight around three circular tracks embedded in the ground. The ride experience is actually much milder than the Magic Kingdom's Mad Tea Party.

TOURING TIPS For the shortest waits, ride during the first 30 minutes or last hour the park is open. Consider skipping the Saucers if the wait exceeds 20 minutes.

Slinky Dog Dash ★★★★

PRESCHOOL ★★★★ (A) **GRADE SCHOOL ★★★★★ (E)** **TEENS ★★★★½ (MAA)**
YOUNG ADULTS ★★★★½ (MAA) **OVER 30 ★★★★½ (MAA)** **SENIORS ★★★★½ (AA)**

What it is Mild outdoor roller coaster. **Scope and scale** Major attraction. **When to go** As soon as the park opens or just before closing. **Comment** Must be 38" to ride. **Duration of ride** 2 minutes. **Average wait in line per 100 people ahead of you** 4 minutes. **Loading speed** Moderate. **ECV/wheelchair access** Must transfer from ECV to provided wheelchair and then from wheelchair to ride vehicle. **Participates in Genie+** Yes. **Early Theme Park Entry** Yes. **Extended Evening Hours** No.

DESCRIPTION AND COMMENTS Slinky Dog Dash is a long outdoor children's roller coaster designed to look as if Andy built it out of Tinkertoys. The trains are themed to *Toy Story*'s Slinky Dog, complete with bobbing tail. As for intensity, it's something along the lines of the Magic Kingdom's Barnstormer or Seven Dwarfs Mine Train—lots of turns, dips, and hills but no loops or high-speed curves—and not nearly as rough as Big Thunder Mountain Railroad. For adults, it's probably more fun than you'd expect, but not worth a very long wait.

TOURING TIPS Slinky Dog Dash gets crowded as soon as the park opens and stays that way all day. Visit at park opening or right before the park closes.

Toy Story Mania! ★★★★½

PRESCHOOL ★★★★½ (MAA)   GRADE SCHOOL ★★★★★ (E)   TEENS ★★★★½ (MAA)
YOUNG ADULTS ★★★★½ (MAA)   OVER 30 ★★★★½ (MAA)   SENIORS ★★★★½ (AA)

What it is 3-D ride through indoor shooting gallery. **Scope and scale** Headliner. **When to go** At park opening or after 4:30 p.m. **Duration of ride** About 6½ minutes. **Average wait in line per 100 people ahead of you** 4½ minutes. **Loading speed** Fast. **ECV/wheelchair access** Must transfer from ECV to provided wheelchair. **Participates in Genie+** Yes. **Early Theme Park Entry** Yes. **Extended Evening Hours** No.

DESCRIPTION AND COMMENTS Toy Story Mania! ushered in a new generation of Disney attraction: the virtual dark ride. Since Disneyland opened in 1955, ride vehicles have moved past 2-D and 3-D sets often populated by Audio-Animatronic figures. At Toy Story Mania!, the elaborate sets and endearing characters are gone. Instead, imagine long, empty corridors covered with reflective material. There's almost nothing there—until you put on your 3-D glasses. Instantly, the corridor is brimming with color and activity, thanks to projected computer-graphic images (CGI).

Conceptually, this is an interactive shooting gallery much like Buzz Lightyear's Space Ranger Spin (see page 491), but in Toy Story Mania!, your ride vehicle passes through a totally virtual midway, with booths offering such games as ring tossing and ball throwing. You use a cannon on your vehicle to play as you move from booth to booth. Unlike the laser guns in Buzz Lightyear, though, the pull-string cannons in Toy Story Mania! take advantage of CGI technology to toss rings, shoot balls, and even throw eggs and pies. Each booth is manned by a *Toy Story* character who's right beside you in 3-D glory, cheering you on. In addition to 3-D imagery, you experience vehicle motion, wind, and water spray.

The ride begins with a training round, then continues through a number of "real" games in which you compete against your riding mate. The technology has the ability to self-adjust the level of difficulty, and there are plenty of easy targets for small children to reach. *Tip:* Let the string retract all the way back into the cannon before pulling it again.

TOURING TIPS Waits at Toy Story Mania! were reduced significantly with the opening of Slinky Dog Dash and Mickey & Minnie's Runaway Railway.

ANIMATION COURTYARD

THIS AREA IS TO THE RIGHT of Mickey & Minnie's Runaway Railway in the middle of the park. It holds two large theaters used for live stage shows (one is closed at press time), a walk-through display of *Star Wars* movie props (closed at press time), and several character-greeting locations (closed at press time).

Disney Junior Dance Party!/Disney Junior Play and Dance ★★

PRESCHOOL ★★★★½ (MAA)   **GRADE SCHOOL** ★★★★ (AA)   **TEENS** ★★½ (MBA)
YOUNG ADULTS ★★★ (MBA)   **OVER 30** ★★★ (MBA)   **SENIORS** ★★½ (MBA)

What it is Live show for preschool children. **Scope and scale** Minor attraction. **When to go** Check *Times Guide* for showtimes. **Comment** Audience sits on the floor. **Duration of presentation** 25 minutes. **When to arrive** 20–30 minutes before showtime. **ECV/wheelchair access** May remain in wheelchair. **Participates in Genie+** No. **Early Theme Park Entry** No. **Extended Evening Hours** No.

DESCRIPTION AND COMMENTS This high-energy music-and-videos show features characters from Disney Channel's *The Lion Guard*, *Doc McStuffins*, and *Vampirina*, along with Mickey Mouse. A simple narrative serves as the platform for all the singing, dancing, and audience participation.

The pre-pandemic *Dance Party* included two actors, a host, and a DJ, who rally the kids as if this were a CrossFit class for preschoolers. The audience sits on the floor so that kids can spontaneously erupt into motion when the mood strikes. *Note:* They do, and it does.

The post-pandemic *Play and Dance* version of the show keeps only the DJ and characters and provides plenty of room between groups for preschoolers to get their groove on.

TOURING TIPS Staged in a huge building on the right side of the courtyard. Get here at least 25 minutes before showtime, pick a spot on the floor, and chill until the action begins.

Star Wars Launch Bay *(closed at press time)* ★★★
Exhibits

PRESCHOOL ★★★½ (BA)   **GRADE SCHOOL** ★★★★ (MBA)   **TEENS** ★★★★ (BA)
YOUNG ADULTS ★★★★ (BA)   **OVER 30** ★★★★ (MBA)   **SENIORS** ★★★★ (BA)

Character Greetings

PRESCHOOL ★★★★ (AA)   **GRADE SCHOOL** ★★★★½ (A)   **TEENS** ★★★★½ (A)
YOUNG ADULTS ★★★★½ (AA)   **OVER 30** ★★★★½ (A)   **SENIORS** ★★★★ (AA)

What it is Displays of a few *Star Wars* movie models and props, a movie trailer, and character greetings. **Scope and scale** Diversion. **When to go** Anytime. **Comment** The movie trailer includes plot spoilers from the entire *Star Wars* oeuvre. **Probable waiting time** 20–30 minutes each for the movie trailer and character greetings. **ECV/wheelchair access** May remain in wheelchair. **Participates in Genie+** No. **Early Theme Park Entry** No. **Extended Evening Hours** No.

DESCRIPTION AND COMMENTS Launch Bay opened when the Studios needed more things for guests to do while new rides were being built; now it's essentially a walk-through commercial for the latest *Star Wars* films. There are a few interesting models on display for the serious fan to admire, along with a short movie that summarizes the whole franchise, but the real draw is the character greetings.

Three characters hold court, currently Chewbacca, Darth Vader, and BB-8. Waits in line for Chewie and Vader usually run about 20–30 minutes. The line for the movie trailer—which, again, just summarizes the existing films—runs 15–30 minutes.

TOURING TIPS Visit first thing in the morning for shorter lines.

Walt Disney Presents ★★★

PRESCHOOL ★★½ (MBA)	GRADE SCHOOL ★★★½ (MBA)	TEENS ★★★½ (MBA)
YOUNG ADULTS ★★★★ (BA)	OVER 30 ★★★★ (BA)	SENIORS ★★★★½ (A)

What it is Disney-memorabilia collection plus a short film about Walt Disney. **Scope and scale** Minor attraction. **When to go** Anytime. **Duration of presentation** 25 minutes. **Preshow entertainment** Disney memorabilia. **Probable waiting time** For the film, 7 minutes. **ECV/wheelchair access** May remain in wheelchair. **Participates in Genie+** No. **Early Theme Park Entry** No. **Extended Evening Hours** No.

DESCRIPTION AND COMMENTS *Walt Disney Presents* consists of an exhibit area showcasing Disney memorabilia and recordings, followed by a film about Walt Disney's life and achievements, narrated by Julie Andrews. On display are various innovations in animation developed by Disney, along with models and plans for Disney World and other Disney theme parks.

TOURING TIPS Every minute spent among these extraordinary artifacts will enhance your visit, taking you back to a time when the creativity and vision that created the park you're in were personified by one struggling entrepreneur. The standard film is sometimes replaced with previews of current Disney movies.

STAR WARS: GALAXY'S EDGE

STAR WARS HAS SO MANY DEDICATED FANS that the Jedi Code constitutes a government-recognized religion in several countries (including tax-exempt status in the United States).

In 2015, Disney announced its plans for Galaxy's Edge, arguably the biggest bet made on their US theme parks since EPCOT in 1982. Two virtually identical 14-acre versions were built, the other at Disneyland; together they're rumored to have cost more than $2 billion. By way of comparison, Disney bought the entire *Star Wars* franchise for $4 billion, and building the entire 500-acre Animal Kingdom cost $1.5 billion in today's dollars when it opened in 1998.

Disney's goal with Galaxy's Edge was to redefine the entire theme park experience. It put more money, technology, and storytelling effort into this one project than it had put into anything in a long, long time. Disney incorporated the *Star Wars* alphabet of Aurebesh to spell out signage. Disney cast members were provided background stories about their lives in Galaxy's Edge and used invented terminology and idioms in conversation with guests: "Hello!" became "Bright suns!" and restrooms were called refreshers.

Fans couldn't wait to experience Galaxy's Edge: Disney's then-CEO Bob Iger joked that the entire marketing campaign for the land would consist of him tweeting, "It's open."

The expectations were impossible to live up to. The first ride to open in Galaxy's Edge was *Millennium Falcon*: Smugglers Run, to mixed reviews. The land itself, while looking reasonably like a *Star Wars* planet's outpost, lacks visual elements such as movement and water found in Pandora and the Wizarding Worlds. Guests didn't appreciate having to navigate the land's language idioms when all they wanted was directions to the nearest bathroom. Most cast members have abandoned their stories and verbiage. And while Rise of the Resistance is the best ride Disney has built in decades, it exhibits more operational delays and problems than almost any other Disney World ride. Rise of the Resistance is incredibly popular. That popularity, coupled with its unsteady operation, means Disney had to implement yet another way of standing in line: the boarding group. As we went to press, Rise was one of two attractions to offer these. When offered, they're mandatory to ride without purchasing Individual Attraction access. An explanation of how they work is on page 594.

Perhaps the biggest gamble with the land was Disney's decision to place Galaxy's Edge at a specific time in the *Star Wars* canon: in the third trilogy, between *The Last Jedi* and *Rise of Skywalker*. That means the land doesn't have any characters from the original trilogy, such as Luke Skywalker, Han Solo, Obi-Wan Kenobi, Princess Leia, or Darth Vader. Nor have we seen any characters from the hit Disney+ series *The Mandalorian*. Disney's thinking here was that the land would be future-proof, able to host new stories and new characters that are written into subsequent films in the *Star Wars* franchise. And the problem, of course, is that not only do those stories or characters not exist yet, but most *Star Wars* fans love the characters from the original three films most.

THE LAND Galaxy's Edge is an outpost in the village of Black Spire Outpost, on the planet of Batuu. Formerly a busy trading port and waypoint before the invention of light speed–capable transportation, it's now a dusty backwater filled with bounty hunters, smugglers, and those who make a living by not being recognized. As if that weren't enough, members of the Resistance and the First Order live in and around the town in an uneasy coexistence (at least they did before Earth's pandemic).

Galaxy's Edge has two access points: on **Grand Avenue** and in **Toy Story Land**. Entering through Grand Avenue puts you in the middle of the Resistance's encampment, while the side closest to Toy Story Land is controlled by the First Order.

DISNEY DISH WITH JIM HILL

MINI-*MILLENNIUM* One of the worst-kept secrets in Galaxy's Edge is that there's a mini version of the *Millennium Falcon* on the full-size *Millennium Falcon*. To see it, stand facing the *Falcon* straight on, with the entrance to Smugglers Run on your left. Locate the cockpit (the round circle thing with glass windows) on the left side of the *Falcon*. Directly under that is a dark-gray grated exhaust that leads down to a set of two pipes that head right. Follow those pipes until you see what looks like a boxed radiator. Directly in front of that radiator is the mini *Millennium Falcon*.

Galaxy's Edge Attractions
Millennium Falcon: Smugglers Run ★★★★

PRESCHOOL ★★★½ (BA)   GRADE SCHOOL ★★★★½ (AA)   TEENS ★★★★½ (AA)
YOUNG ADULTS ★★★★½ (AA)   OVER 30 ★★★★½ (AA)   SENIORS ★★★★ (A)

What it is Interactive simulator ride. **Scope and scale** Super-headliner. **When to go** As soon as it opens or after 6 p.m. **Comments** Could've been great; 38" height requirement; Rider Switch option available (see page 395). **Duration of ride** 4½ minutes. **Average wait in line per 100 people ahead of you** 3½ minutes. **Loading speed** Moderate–fast. **ECV/wheelchair access** Must transfer to ride vehicle. **Participates in Genie+** Yes. **Early Theme Park Entry** Yes. **Extended Evening Hours** No.

DESCRIPTION AND COMMENTS Smugglers Run lets guests fly Han Solo's *Millennium Falcon,* the "fastest hunk of junk in the galaxy." Guests approaching the attraction will see a life-size *Millennium Falcon* parked outside the spaceport, periodically venting gas as technicians tinker with the temperamental craft. (You can look at the replica, but you can't walk under or touch it.)

To board, you're recruited by Hondo Ohnaka, an animatronic pirate who has cut a deal with Chewbacca to use the *Falcon* for some sketchy transportation business. After ascending to a second-story catwalk with wraparound views of the ship, visitors enter Ohnaka's command center, where Hondo explains the mission, while the *Falcon* can be seen on a video screen preparing for launch. Ohnaka is one of Disney's most advanced animatronics, with electric motors capable of 50 functions, and his movements are eerily fluid.

At this point, you enter the *Falcon* through an umbilical bridge and are assigned to a flight crew of up to six people. While awaiting your turn, you can relax in the ship's instantly recognizable main hold, complete with a holographic chess board from the movies.

When the time arrives, your flight crew walks down the ship's curving corridors and appears to enter the *Falcon*'s one and only cockpit, thanks to a patented carousel system that keeps the small simulator cabins hidden from each other. Your mission has you stealing supplies from the First Order to sell on the black market. Each rider is assigned his or her own station: a pilot and copilot up front to steer around obstacles and activate the hyperdrive, two gunners in the middle to shoot down enemy fighters, and a pair of engineers in the rear to repair the ship when the pilots and gunners mess up. Computer-generated scenery is projected on an ultra-HD dome outside the windshield. By far, the best role is that of pilot.

What separates this ride from other simulators (such as Star Tours) are 200 buttons, switches, and levers in the cockpit, each of which does something when activated: Watch for indicator rings to illuminate around certain controls, clueing you in to the correct moment to punch them.

Another difference between Smugglers Run and other simulators is that the video screens displaying the action aren't attached to the ride vehicle. This not only allows for a more realistic display of the action but also reduces the potential for motion sickness.

At the end of the day, however, in spite of the amount of money, time, and technology that Disney has invested in this attraction, the Smugglers Run ride experience is a disappointment. Seats for the gunners and engineers are situated far enough back from the video screens that it's like watching a drive-in movie through a tunnel. Worse, the controls for those four seats are mounted at a 90° angle from the action on-screen: If you're in one of these seats, you can either look at the screen or the controls you're supposed to be working—but not both. It's so hard to work the controls, in fact, that we gave up halfway through our rides.

The experience for the pilots is no better—one pilot controls left and right movements while the other, inexplicably, controls up and down. The real *Millennium Falcon* doesn't work this way, and nobody with any sense would design actual controls like this.

Terrible ergonomics are only part of the problem, though. *Star Wars* fans have known since 1977 exactly how the *Falcon*'s guns and gunners are supposed to look and work. What Disney has built here captures none of that—the thrill of combat has been reduced to push-button data entry. It's an inexcusable design compromise, one that undercuts the entire land's claim at realism.

Finally, the script that our rides followed was so comically predictable that it actively distracted from the experience. If you've ever been on any other Disney simulator, say, Star Tours or Mission: Space, you'll recognize the exact same plot points, at the exact same pace.

The *Millennium Falcon* enjoys a beloved, unique place in American cinema. We think it deserved better. That said, opinions among the *Unofficial* team aren't uniform: Seth Kubersky, author of *The Unofficial Guide to Disneyland,* describes it as "a four-star ride in a five-star wrapper."

TOURING TIPS Disney's posted wait time for this ride might be the most accurate estimate of how long you'll actually wait than any other major ride in Walt Disney World. Smugglers Run wait times drop off after 6 p.m. Ride early in the morning, immediately after Slinky Dog Dash.

Star Wars: Rise of the Resistance ★★★★★

PRESCHOOL ★★★½ (BA)	GRADE SCHOOL ★★★★½ (E)	TEENS ★★★★★ (E)
YOUNG ADULTS ★★★★★ (E)	OVER 30 ★★★★★ (E)	SENIORS ★★★★½ (E)

*Rise of the Resistance is the highest-rated attraction in any Disney or Universal theme park in the United States.

What it is Next-generation dark ride. **Scope and scale** Super-headliner. **When to go** When your boarding group is called. **Comments** Get a boarding group on the My Disney Experience app at exactly 7 a.m. or 1 p.m. on the day of your visit; not to be missed; 40" height requirement; Rider Switch option available (see page 395). **Duration of ride** About 25 minutes with all preshows; about 5 minutes for ride. **Average**

wait in line per 100 people ahead of you 4 minutes. **Loading speed** Moderate–fast. **ECV/wheelchair access** Must transfer to ride vehicle. **Participates in Genie+** No (it's Individual Attraction access only). **Early Theme Park Entry** No. **Extended Evening Hours** No.

DESCRIPTION AND COMMENTS A mobile Resistance gun turret tucked into a scrubland forest marks the entrance to the most epic indoor dark ride in Disney theme park history. Rise of the Resistance is an innovative attempt to integrate at least four different ride experiences—trackless vehicles, a motion simulator, walk-through environments, and even an elevator drop—into Disney's longest attraction ever.

The adventure begins as you explore the Resistance military outpost, laser-carved out of ancient stone. An animatronic BB-8 rolls in, accompanied by a hologram of Rey, who recruits you to strike a blow against the First Order. Fifty guests at a time exit the briefing room to board a standing-room-only shuttlecraft piloted by Nien Nunb from *Return of the Jedi.* As the ship breaks orbit, you can feel the rumble and see Poe Dameron accompanying you in his X-Wing, until a Star Destroyer snags you in its tractor beam and sucks you into its belly.

When the doors to your shuttlecraft reopen, you've been convincingly transported into an enormous hangar, complete with 50 Stormtroopers, TIE Fighters, and a 100-foot-wide bay window looking into outer space. Cast members clad as First Order officers brusquely herd captive guests into holding rooms to await their interrogation by black-clad baddie Kylo Ren.

Before long, you're making a break for it in an eight-passenger (two four-seat rows) troop transport with an animatronic droid as your driver; the car is capable of traveling without a fixed track and simulating movement. The ride blends dozens of robotic characters and enormous sets with video projections to create some of the most overwhelming environments ever seen in an indoor ride. One sequence sends you in between the legs of two towering AT-ATs while dodging laser fire from legions of Stormtroopers, while another puts you face-to-face with the Solo-slaying Ren. In the epic finale, you'll survive an escape pod's dramatic crash back to Batuu, a heart-stopping multistory plunge enhanced by digital projections. The drop at the end isn't quite as intense as the one on the Tower of Terror—but don't underestimate its ability to loosen your lunch.

TOURING TIPS We think Rise of the Resistance is the best ride Disney has produced in decades. It's the most popular ride in the park, and the most complex ride Disney has ever made. That complexity makes it prone to breakdowns—daily, on average, and sometimes more than once. Those breakdowns led Disney to introduce a new way of waiting to experience the ride, called boarding groups.

Boarding groups function like mandatory Genie+ reservations without a specific return time. You obtain a boarding group for everyone in your party through the My Disney Experience (MDE) app at exactly 7 a.m. or exactly 1 p.m. on the day of your Studios visit. If you're successful, you'll get a boarding group number. Once you have a boarding group, MDE will tell you which boarding groups are currently eligible to ride (for example, "Groups 40 to 45 now boarding") or give you a rough estimate of how long your wait will be to ride. If your phone is set up to receive alerts from MDE, you'll also get one when your group is ready.

Disney is reasonably flexible if you're doing something else, such as eating lunch, when your boarding group is called—showing up late shouldn't be a problem unless the ride is about to close.

You and everyone in your group must have a park reservation for the Studios on the day you attempt to get a boarding group. That is, you can't start at another park, hop to the Studios, and get a boarding group.

The good news is that you don't have to be in the park (or even in Florida) to request a boarding group at 7 a.m. The bad news is that you *must* be in the Studios to request a boarding group at 1 p.m. Further, all boarding groups will be snapped up within a few seconds after 7 a.m., so there's no room for delay or error. And that's a problem because MDE, and the Wi-Fi at Hollywood Studios, are not completely reliable either.

We tested the network speed and reliability of Disney's Wi-Fi in locations around Hollywood Studios, as well as via the T-Mobile cellular network, to see how fast we could connect to MDE servers. Disney's Wi-Fi speeds were two to nine times faster than our cellular network.

However, Disney's Wi-Fi was much less reliable than our cell service. See tinyurl.com/rotr-networks for more details on our tests. The fastest, most reliable Wi-Fi spot seems to be in Animation Courtyard near the entrance to *Disney Junior Play and Dance.*

The fast but unreliable nature of Disney's Wi-Fi means that you should have as many people as possible try to obtain boarding groups for your entire party at 7 a.m. and at 1 p.m. If you're in the park, half of you should be on Disney's Wi-Fi and half should be on a cellular network.

Even if you're able to submit a boarding group request exactly at 7 a.m. or 1 p.m., the flood of requests from thousands of other people is enough to overwhelm the MDE computers. It's common to have MDE respond with a message like "Oh no! Something went wrong!" to your request. By the time you've received the error and resent your request, all boarding groups are likely to be taken.

Disney's implementation of boarding groups is essentially a lottery—some people win, and some people lose, through no fault of their own. And because the process fails for hundreds of people every morning, Disney is unlikely to do anything to make it up to you.

Disney's second supply of boarding groups, handed out at 1 p.m., is generally considered a "backup" supply that only gets to ride if the attraction has run reliably and on time throughout the day. As we went to press, Rise of the Resistance was calling around 165 boarding groups per day (at around 100 people per boarding group). Your odds of getting on the ride decrease as that number rises above 165.

If Rise of the Resistance is using a traditional standby line instead of boarding groups, then the best way to experience Rise without a long wait is to stay at a Disney resort and use Early Theme Park Entry to get in line as soon as the park opens.

Galaxy's Edge Shopping, Dining, and More

SHOPPING Outside of the area's two headliner rides, **Batuu** boasts a Marrakech-esque marketplace of shops selling unique in-universe merchandise, some of which are practically attractions themselves. None of the items for sale bear the standard *Star Wars* or Disney logos, to maintain the illusion that everything on offer was actually crafted by and for the Black Spire Outpost villagers.

At **Savi's Workshop,** small groups are led by "Gatherers" through the process of building their own lightsabers, from picking a colorful kyber crystal to selecting customizable handles. The cost of this experience is around $235 including tax; we also endured a 2½-hour wait because the experience can handle just a few dozen people per hour. Despite the steep price tag, it's one of the best things we experienced in Galaxy's Edge: The finished lightsaber feels substantial, balanced, and elegant in your hands. We'd do it again.

unofficial **TIP**
Costumes are forbidden at Galaxy's Edge for guests age 14 and older.

If you want to build a lightsaber of your own, make park reservations and reservations for Savi's up to 60 days in advance. You can proudly pair your saber with a screen-accurate Jedi tunic ensemble from **Black Spire Outfitters**—but you may wear it only outside of Galaxy's Edge.

Dok-Ondar's Den of Antiquities is overseen by a surly Ithorian (or hammerhead) who's the local godfather of black market goods; if you want to buy a historical character's lightsaber or Sith holocron, you may need to barter with this animatronic bimouthed bigwig, who haggles with guests through his human helpers. Sharp-eyed fans will spot Easter eggs from practically every *Star Wars* film and TV show, including a 12-foot-tall taxidermic Wampa from *The Empire Strikes Back.*

Two shops allow guests to take an interactive pal back to their home planet. At **Droid Depot,** you can pick robot parts off of conveyor belts to build your own pint-size R-series or BB-series droid, which will then communicate with its counterparts around the land; preassembled droids, including a chatty C-3PO and a DJ R3X Bluetooth speaker, are also available. Reservations for Droid Depot can be made 60 days in advance and are strongly recommended.

Creature Stall allows guests to adopt a plush Porg puppet; a disgustingly adorable writhing baby Rathtar; or a shoulder-sitting, monkey lizard–like Salacious Crumb. All the creatures react to your touch with sound and movement.

For kids young and old, **Toydarian Toymaker** sells plush dolls of legendary characters that seem handcrafted from upcycled fabric scraps, along with other unconventional playthings. For T-shirts, hats, pins, and the like, you can either report to **First Order Cargo,** a spaceport hangar selling Dark Side propaganda, or sign up at the makeshift **Resistance Supply** stall and show your support for the freedom fighters. Finally, **Jewels of Bith** has pins, patches, and trinkets from across the Outer Rim.

DINING When you get hungry, you'll find that just as much attention has gone into the food and drink of Galaxy's Edge as everything else; even the Coca-Cola sodas come in unique spherical bottles emblazoned in Aurebesh, the *Star Wars* alphabet. There's no sit-down service, but Galaxy's Edge has the two highest-rated counter-service restaurants in the park: rustle up galactic food-truck grub from **Docking Bay 7** or grab a sausage grilled under a Podracer engine at **Ronto Roasters.** Wash it all down with a cold glass of (nondairy) blue or green milk from the **Milk Stand. Oga's Cantina** pours exclusive adult drinks, from Spice Runner cider to Jet Juice cocktails. Reservations are strongly recommended; see Part Six, page 291, for more on dining in the park.

INTERACTIVITY IN GALAXY'S EDGE Perhaps the most intriguing elements of Galaxy's Edge are its experiments in live interaction, both digital and analog. Live performers, actor-controlled creature puppets, and roving droids can engage with guests and selected souvenirs. Characters include Rey, Chewbacca, Kylo Ren, and various Stormtroopers.

THE HOTEL Disney is building a themed hotel, called **Star Wars: Galactic Starcruiser,** adjacent and connected to Galaxy's Edge. It will be a separate, fully immersive experience from the park. What we've heard so far is that you'll sign up for two-day live-action role-playing adventures, most of which will happen inside the hotel but which could spill out into Galaxy's Edge. What you do in each location will become part of your running narrative: Along with regular guests, the 100-room hotel will be filled with *Star Wars* characters with whom you'll have to interact (and occasionally outwit) as part of your adventure. Disney hasn't announced an opening date, but we expect it to open in 2021 or early 2022. We wouldn't be surprised if rates started above $600 per person, per night (in a pricing structure used on Disney Cruise Line ships), with a two-night stay—no more, no less. And, as on cruise ships, there will be scheduled "departure" and "arrival" days where everyone in the hotel checks in at the same time.

unofficial **TIP**
If you're not staying at a Disney resort, consider booking a room at a Value resort the night before your Galaxy's Edge visit so you can take advantage of Early Theme Park Entry.

GALAXY'S EDGE TOURING TIPS Make park reservations for Hollywood Studios as soon as your travel dates are known. If Rise of the Resistance is using boarding groups, obtain one at 7 a.m. on the date of your visit; try again at 1 p.m. if you weren't successful at 7 a.m.

Ride *Millennium Falcon:* Smugglers Run early in the morning, after you've experienced Slinky Dog Dash, or try riding in the last hour the park is open.

Save shopping and dining for after you've done the rides. Note, however, that there may also be long lines for the restaurants and certain shops. Make reservations for Savi's Workshop, the Droid Depot, and Oga's Cantina 60 days before your visit.

As of summer 2021, booking a Disney VIP tour (at up to $850 per hour with a 7-hour minimum) will get you access to one ride on Rise of the Resistance without a boarding group.

DISNEY'S HOLLYWOOD STUDIOS ENTERTAINMENT

IN ADDITION TO THE SHOWS and performances profiled earlier in this chapter, the Studios offers the following. Check your *Times Guide* for showtimes.

CHARACTER CAVALCADES At random times throughout the day, starting about an hour after park opening, Disney characters ride in automobiles down Hollywood Boulevard from near the park entrance to just behind Star Tours. Three different character groups alternate appearances: Mickey, Minnie, and their pals are in one group; Vampirina and other Disney Junior characters form another group; and Pixar characters are the third.

JINGLE BELL, JINGLE BAM! This nighttime holiday spectacular has projections, seasonal music, and snow. Hosted by Wayne and Lanny, the comical elves from ABC's *Prep & Landing,* the show also features holiday scenes from *Mickey's Christmas Carol, Beauty and the Beast, Pluto's Christmas Tree, Bambi,* and *The Nightmare Before Christmas.*

DISNEY'S HOLLYWOOD STUDIOS TOURING PLAN

OUR HOLLYWOOD STUDIOS TOURING PLAN (see pages 729 and 730) has two versions: one for Disney resort guests and one for off-site guests. Plans for on-site guests use Disney's Early Theme Park Entry benefit (see page 38) to minimize waits in line. Early Entry means thousands of guests will already be in lines and on rides before off-site guests set foot in the park, so the touring strategy for off-site guests must necessarily be different.

Our Hollywood Studios touring plans for this edition do not assume use of Genie+ or Individual Attraction Selections. We also assume that shows such as *Indiana Jones Stunt Spectacular* and *Voyage of the Little Mermaid* will remain closed. Should those shows open, or you opt for Genie+ and/or Individual Attraction Selections, just use our free touring plan software to adjust the plan.

UNIVERSAL ORLANDO

OVERVIEW

UNIVERSAL ORLANDO is a complete destination resort: A system of roads and two multistory parking facilities is connected by moving sidewalks to **CityWalk,** a shopping, dining, and nighttime-entertainment complex that also serves as a gateway to **Universal Studios Florida (USF)** and **Universal's Islands of Adventure (IOA)** theme parks, as well as **Universal's Volcano Bay** water park (see Part Sixteen, page 653, for a description).

LODGING AT UNIVERSAL ORLANDO

UNIVERSAL HAS EIGHT RESORT HOTELS. The 750-room **Portofino Bay Hotel** is a gorgeous property set on an artificial bay and themed like an Italian coastal town. The 650-room **Hard Rock Hotel** is an ultra-cool "Hotel California" replica, and the 1,000-room, Polynesian-themed **Royal Pacific Resort** is sumptuously decorated and richly appointed. These three resorts are on the pricey side, but guests get free Universal Express Unlimited passes for the length of their stay, including check-in and checkout day (see page 604 for details).

The retro-style **Cabana Bay Beach Resort,** Universal's largest hotel, has 2,200 moderate- and value-priced rooms, plus amenities (bowling alley, lazy river) not seen at comparable Disney resorts. **Loews**

continued on page 602

Universal Orlando

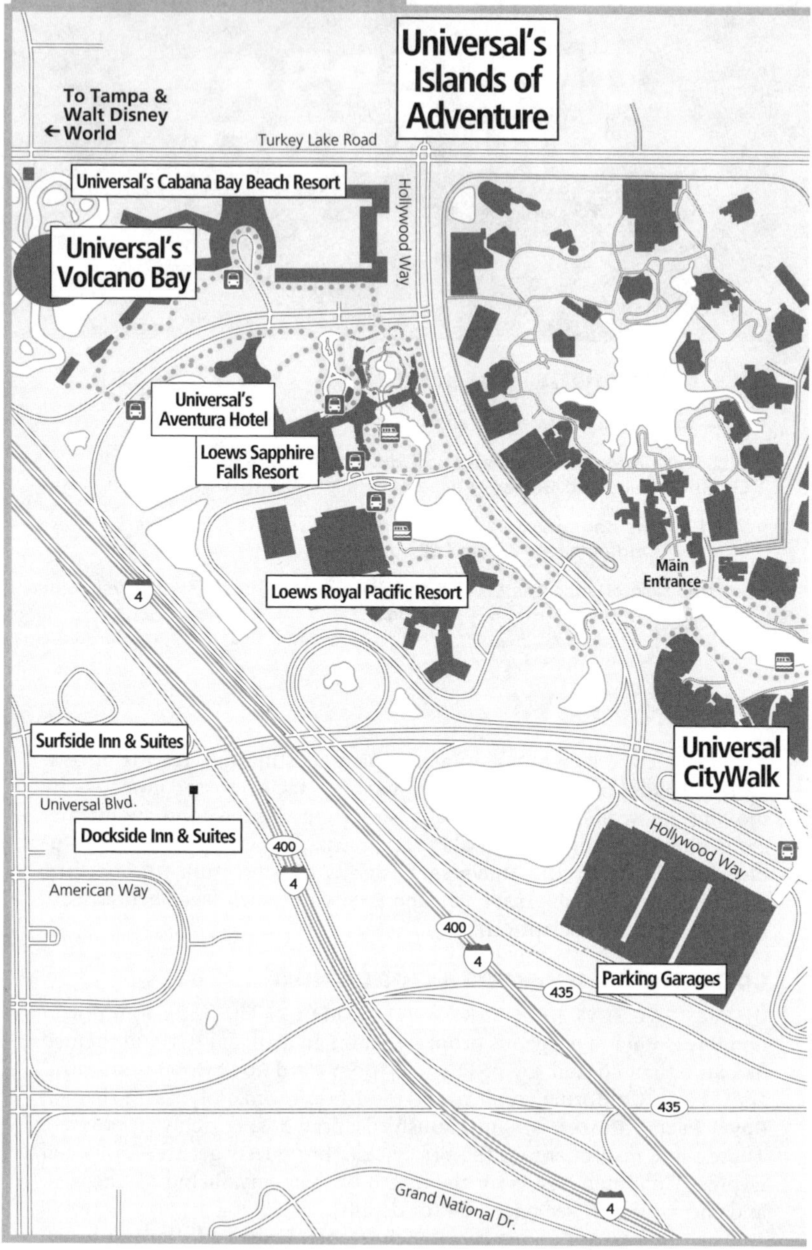

To Tampa &
Walt Disney
← World

Turkey Lake Road

Hollywood Way

Universal's Islands of Adventure

Universal's Cabana Bay Beach Resort

Universal's Volcano Bay

Universal's Aventura Hotel

Loews Sapphire Falls Resort

Loews Royal Pacific Resort

4

Main Entrance

Surfside Inn & Suites

Universal CityWalk

Universal Blvd.

Dockside Inn & Suites

400

4

American Way

Hollywood Way

400

4

435

Parking Garages

435

Grand National Dr.

4

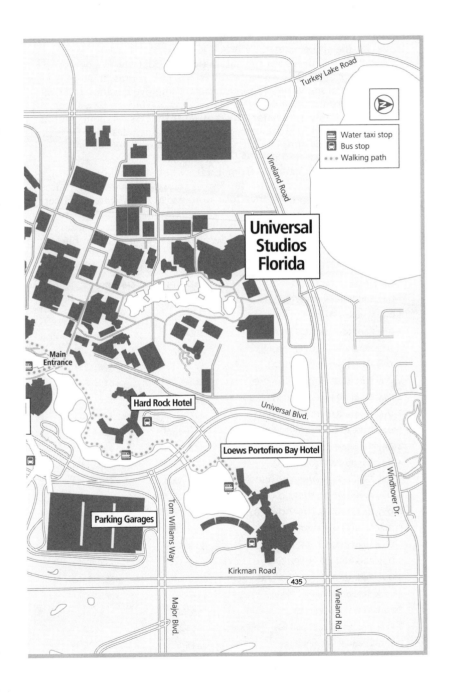

Turkey Lake Road

Vineland Road

Water taxi stop
Bus stop
Walking path

Universal Studios Florida

Main Entrance

Hard Rock Hotel

Universal Blvd.

Loews Portofino Bay Hotel

Windhover Dr.

Parking Garages

Tom Williams Way

Kirkman Road

435

Major Blvd.

Vineland Rd.

continued from page 509

Sapphire Falls Resort has a Caribbean theme and is priced between the Royal Pacific and Cabana Bay Beach Resorts.

A sixth hotel, **Universal's Aventura Hotel,** is adjacent to Loews Sapphire Falls Resort. The 16-story tower has 600 rooms, including 13 Kids' Suites, along with a food hall showcasing five cuisines and Universal's first rooftop bar and grill with a view of Volcano Bay. The seaside-themed **Endless Summer Resort,** just off Universal's main campus on the former Wet 'n Wild water-park property, includes both Surfside Inn and Dockside Inn; combined, the duo offers 2,800 value-priced rooms (including 1,450 two-bedroom suites).

Bus service is available from Endless Summer, while Aventura and Cabana Bay connect to the rest of the resort via shuttle buses and walking paths; the other four hotels also offer water-taxi service. All hotel guests get Early Park Admission to The Wizarding World of Harry Potter (one or both theme parks, depending on the season) and Volcano Bay up to 1 hour before the general public.

UNIVERSAL ORLANDO ADMISSIONS		
TICKET TYPE	**ADULTS**	**CHILDREN (Ages 3–9)**
1-Day Single-Park (USF/IOA)	$109–$159	$104–$154
1-Day Volcano Bay	$70–$85	$65–$80
1-Day Park-to-Park (USF/IOA)	$164–$214	$159–$209
2-Day Single-Park (USF/IOA)	$213–$291	$203–$281
2-Day Park-to-Park (USF/IOA)	$273–$361	$263–$341
2-Day Park-to-Park (USF/IOA/VB)	$313–$386	$303–$376
3-Day Single-Park (USF/IOA)	$233–$316	$223–$306
3-Day Single-Park (USF/IOA/VB)	$273–$351	$263–$341
3-Day Park-to-Park (USF/IOA)	$293–$376	$283–$366
3-Day Park-to-Park (USF/IOA/VB)	$333–$411	$323–$401
4-Day Single-Park (USF/IOA)	$247–$328	$237–$318
4-Day Single-Park (USF/IOA/VB)	$297–$373	$287–$363
4-Day Park-to-Park (USF/IOA)	$312–$393	$302–$323
4-Day Park-to-Park (USF/IOA/VB)	$362–$438	$352–$428
5-Day Single-Park (USF/IOA)	$259–$340	$249–$330
5-Day Single-Park (USF/IOA/VB)	$319–$395	$309–$385
5-Day Park-to-Park (USF/IOA)	$329–$410	$319–$400
5-Day Park-to-Park (USF/IOA/VB)	$389–$465	$379–$455
2-Park Seasonal Annual Pass	$350	$350
2-Park Power Annual Pass	$400	$400
2-Park Preferred Annual Pass	$450	$450
2-Park Premier Annual Pass	$625	$625
3-Park Seasonal Annual Pass	$450	$450
3-Park Power Annual Pass	$510	$510
3-Park Preferred Annual Pass	$560	$560
3-Park Premier Annual Pass	$815	$815

ARRIVING AT UNIVERSAL ORLANDO

THE UNIVERSAL ORLANDO COMPLEX can be accessed from eastbound I-4 by taking **Exit 75A** and turning left at the top of the ramp onto Universal Boulevard. Traveling westbound on I-4, use **Exit 74B** and then turn right onto Hollywood Way. Entrances are also off Kirkman Road to the east, Turkey Lake Road to the north, and Vineland Road to the west. Universal Boulevard connects the International Drive area to Universal via an overpass bridging I-4. Turkey Lake and Vineland Roads are good alternatives when I-4 is gridlocked.

unofficial **TIP**
If you want to ensure you arrive at Universal Orlando before park opening, we advise using a ride-hailing service.

Once on-site, you'll be directed to park in one of two multitiered parking garages. Parking runs $26 for cars and $32 for RVs. Prime parking is $50 ($40 during slower seasons), and valet is $75 ($26 for under 2 hours, or free for 2 hours with CityWalk lunch validation). From the garages, (sometimes) moving sidewalks deliver you to Universal CityWalk; it takes about 8–20 minutes to get from the garages to the parks. From CityWalk, you can access the main entrances of both USF and IOA. Volcano Bay guests park in the same garages and are shuttled to the water park. Parking is free for everyone after 6 p.m. (except during Halloween Horror Nights).

If you don't have your own car, **Mears Transportation** (☎ 855-463-2776 or 407-423-5566; mearstransportation.com) operates a shuttle between Walt Disney World and Universal Orlando that stops three times a day at Disney hotels; cost is $23 for guests age 3 and older. Better yet, use a ride-hailing app; at the day's end, an Uber-branded pickup area awaits on the parking garage's roof.

Universal offers one- to five-day tickets for one or two theme parks; adding Volcano Bay to a multiday ticket costs $25–$60 plus tax, depending on length, and upgrading from one-park-per-day to Park-to-Park access costs $55–$70. Single and multiday tickets are date-specific, and prices can vary by up to $30 depending on the date you select during purchase for its first use. Flexible date tickets are also available for $14–$29 less than the cost of the most expensive equivalent date-specific passes, but they do not guarantee admission if the parks reach maximum capacity. Examine Universal's ticket calendar carefully, because in certain seasons you may save a few dollars by buying multiple one-day tickets instead of a multiday pass. All multiday tickets expire five to eight days after their first use, depending on pass type and length. Universal also sells a range of two- and three-park annual passes, some of which include sizable discounts on hotels, food, and merchandise. Children ages 3–9 are charged $5 less than adults on single-day tickets and $10 less on multiday passes; there's no kids' discount on annual passes. Unlike Walt Disney World, Universal Orlando does not require advance reservations to visit its parks, although the turnstiles may close if the capacity limit is reached; date-specific tickets do not guarantee admission.

unofficial **TIP**
Visit **MouseSavers** (mousesavers.com/universal-orlando-discounts-and-deals) for a convenient list of current ticket prices at Universal Orlando. All prices include tax.

The prices in the table on page 602 are what you'll pay at Universal's website, not including 6.5% sales tax. Buy your passes in advance at ☎ 800-711-0080 or universalorlando.com, or through Universal Orlando's official mobile app for iOS or Android.

Be sure to check Universal Orlando's website for seasonal deals and specials. You will pay $20 more than the online price by buying your multiday tickets at the gate. Consider using an online ticket wholesaler such as **Tripster** (☎ 888-590-5910; tripster.com) or Orlando Ticket Connection (☎ 855-473-7987; orlandoticketconnection.com). All tickets are brand-new. Vendors will provide you with electronic tickets just like Universal does.

The main Universal Orlando information line is ☎ 407-363-8000; the website is universalorlando.com. Reach **Guest Services** at ☎ 407-224-4233. To file a report with **Lost and Found**, visit tinyurl.com/uorlostandfound.

UNIVERSAL EXPRESS

SIMILAR TO DISNEY WORLD'S FORMER FASTPASS+, Universal Express is a system whereby any guest can "skip the line" and experience an attraction via a special queue with little or no waiting. While Disney's system required scheduling your ride reservation hours or days ahead of time, Universal Express involves no planning; you simply visit any eligible operating attraction whenever you choose, with no return-time windows required. In addition, unlike FastPass+, Universal Express is not free for everyone, but it is still available, while FastPass+ is currently suspended and is being supplanted by Disney Genie and Lightning Lane (which may require additional fees).

Unlimited Universal Express access at the two theme parks is a complimentary perk (valued at $129.99 per person, per day) for guests at Universal's top three hotels: **Hard Rock, Portofino Bay,** and **Royal Pacific.** Guests may use the Express lines all day long simply by flashing the pass they get at check-in. This perk far surpasses any benefit accorded to guests of Disney resorts and is especially valuable during peak season.

Day guests, along with guests staying at **Cabana Bay, Sapphire Falls, Endless Summer,** and **Aventura,** can buy Universal Express Passes for the theme parks for an extra $85.19–$287.54 (including tax, depending on the season), which provides line-jumping privileges at each Universal Express attraction at a given park. You can buy Universal Express for one or both theme parks and for either single (one ride only on each participating attraction) or unlimited use.

unofficial **TIP**
If you use Universal Express, be careful not to lose your pass. We recommend bringing a lanyard (or buying one from Universal for $12 and up) so you can wear the pass around your neck.

Universal Express at **Volcano Bay** is not free for hotel guests but can be purchased by anyone for $21.29–$106.49, depending on the season and included slides.

More than 90% of rides and shows are covered by Universal Express, a much higher percentage than those covered by FastPass+ at Walt Disney World; the notable exceptions are **Pteranodon Flyers** and (for now) **Jurassic World VelociCoaster** and **Hagrid's Magical Creatures Motorbike Adventure** at IOA.

You can also buy Universal Express at the theme parks' ticket windows, just outside the front gates, but it's faster to buy inside. Express Passes are sold at most gift shops, as well as from freestanding kiosks that proliferate around the parks during peak seasons; Express is also available up to eight months in advance at universalorlando.com. You'll need to know when you plan on using it, though, because prices vary depending on the date.

IS UNIVERSAL EXPRESS WORTH IT? It depends on when you visit, hours of park operation, and crowd levels. If you want to sleep in and arrive at a park after opening, Express is an effective, albeit expensive, way to avoid long lines at the headliner attractions, especially during holidays and busy times.

If, however, you arrive 30 minutes before park opening and you use our Universal touring plans (see pages 731–734), you should experience the lowest possible waits at both parks. We encourage you to try the touring plans first, but if the waits for rides become intolerable, you can always buy Express in the parks.

VIRTUAL LINES

AT CERTAIN TIMES, SELECT ATTRACTIONS may offer—or even require—the use of Virtual Line reservations instead of the standard standby queue. These 30-minute timed-return windows can be secured for free through the official Universal Orlando smartphone app (or at vltest.universalorlando.com for Hagrid's); upon redemption, guests should be able to board the ride after a brief wait (typically 15 minutes or less). You must be on Universal property to claim a spot in a Virtual Line, but you don't have to be inside the parks. The lineup of participating attractions can change daily (or hourly) based on attendance, and additional return times may be released throughout the day, so keep checking the app periodically. Guests with Universal Express Passes don't need a return time to use Express at participating attractions.

SINGLE-RIDER LINES

SEVERAL ATTRACTIONS HAVE THIS SPECIAL LINE for guests riding alone. As Universal employees will tell you, this line is often just as fast as the Express line—it will decrease your wait and leave more time for repeating rides or just bumming around. Note, though, that some queues (particularly Forbidden Journey's and Escape from Gringotts's) are attractions in themselves and deserve to be experienced during your first ride.

LOCKERS

UNIVERSAL ENFORCES A MANDATORY locker system at its big thrill rides. On most rides, all bags, purses, and other objects too large to be secured in a pocket must be placed in a locker. A strict "no loose items" policy is enforced at **The Incredible Hulk Coaster** and **Hollywood Rip Ride Rockit.** At these rides, guests must pass through an airport-style security screening to ensure that no phones, keys, or even spare change enters the queue.

*un*official **TIP**
You must scan your park ticket before receiving a locker number or retrieving your valuables from a locker, so keep your pass with you while you ride.

Small lockers outside these attractions are free to use for an amount of time that depends on the length of the standby line. If the line is 30 minutes, for example, and the ride itself is 10 minutes, you get 40 minutes plus a small cushion of about 15 minutes. If you need to stow something larger than a small purse or fanny pack, larger lockers are available for a fee. The small mandatory lockers then cost $3 for each half-hour after the free period, with a $20 maximum; large lockers cost $2 while you ride and then $3 for each additional half-hour, up to $20.

Adjacent to IOA's soaking water rides are optional lockers that cost $4–$5 for the first 90 minutes and $3 for each additional hour, up to $20. And at the front of each park are paid all-day lockers in standard and family sizes for $10–$15; these can be opened and relocked with your park ticket as many times as you like.

UNIVERSAL DINING PROGRAMS

CHARACTER DINING A weekly character breakfast with Despicable Me's Minions is offered at **The Tahitian Room** at Royal Pacific Resort on Saturdays ($35 adults, $21 kids ages 3–9, plus tax), and a Marvel Super Hero dinner is held at **Cafe 4** in IOA Thursday–Sunday ($50 adults, $25 kids ages 3–9, plus tax). For information and reservations, call ☎ 407-224-3663.

COVID *tip*
Character dining was temporarily suspended at press time.

A character breakfast is also held during the holiday season at IOA with The Grinch ($35 adults, $21 kids ages 3–9, plus tax). After purchasing your dining experience online, you must call ☎ 407-224-7554 up to 24 hours before arriving to confirm your table. Separate theme park admission is required.

COCA-COLA FREESTYLE SOUVENIR CUP This perk entitles you to a souvenir sipper cup with one day of unlimited fountain soft drinks at all participating Coca-Cola Freestyle locations at both USF and IOA. Cost is $18.09 for one cup or $14.90 each for three or more. The price includes the first day of refills; each additional day costs $11.70.

UNIVERSAL, KIDS, AND SCARY STUFF

THOUGH THERE'S PLENTY FOR YOUNGER CHILDREN to enjoy at the Universal Orlando parks, most major attractions can potentially make kids under age 8 wig out.

At **Universal Studios Florida,** forget **Fast & Furious: Supercharged, Hollywood Rip Ride Rockit, Men in Black Alien Attack, Revenge of the Mummy, The Simpsons Ride,** and **Transformers: The Ride 3-D.** The first part of the E.T. Adventure ride is a little intense for a few preschoolers, but the end is all happiness and harmony.

Although these are billed as family rides, both **Hogwarts Express** trains running between the two parks have some scary visuals, as does **Harry Potter and the Escape from Gringotts.** Interestingly, very few families report problems with *Universal Orlando's Horror Make-Up Show.* Anything we haven't listed here is probably a safe bet.

At **Universal's Islands of Adventure,** watch out for **The Amazing Adventures of Spider-Man, Doctor Doom's Fearfall, Hagrid's Magical Creatures Motorbike Adventure, Harry Potter and the Forbidden**

Journey, **The Incredible Hulk Coaster, Jurassic Park River Adventure, Jurassic World VelociCoaster,** and *Poseidon's Fury.* **Skull Island: Reign of Kong** is visually and psychologically intense; it may be too much for little ones. **Popeye & Bluto's Bilge-Rat Barges** is wet and wild, but most younger kids handle it pretty well. **Dudley Do-Right's Ripsaw Falls** is a toss-up, to be considered only if your kids really like water-flume rides. No other attractions should pose a problem.

At **Volcano Bay,** the **Ko'okiri Body Plunge** and **Kala and Tai Nui Serpentine Body Slides** feature a fall through a drop door before you plunge down twisting, winding tubes. The **Puihi and Honu Round Raft Rides** and the **Ohyah and Ohno Drop Slides** are also not for the faint of heart.

CHILD SWAP Universal's Child Swap is similar to Disney's Rider Switch (see page 395), but it's superior in several respects. The entire family goes through the whole line together before being split into riding and nonriding groups near the loading platform. The nonriding parent and child(ren) wait in a designated room, usually with some sort of entertainment (for example, Forbidden Journey at IOA shows the first 20 minutes of *Harry Potter and the Sorcerer's Stone* on a loop), a place to sit down, and sometimes restrooms with changing tables. At any theme park, the best tip we can give is to ask the greeter in front of the attraction what you're supposed to do.

UNIVERSAL CITYWALK

AT CITYWALK you'll find a variety of restaurants, clubs, shops, outdoor entertainment, a concert hall (**Hard Rock Live**), the **Hollywood Drive-In** minigolf course, and the **Universal Cinemark** movie theater. CityWalk also has a number of combination restaurants and clubs. Open to families with kids until 9 p.m., many of these venues offer live entertainment.

Recent eatery additions include **Bigfire,** specializing in wood-grilled meats; the **Toothsome Chocolate Emporium & Savory Feast Kitchen,** a sweet shop and restaurant in a 19th-century-inspired steampunk building; and **Voodoo Doughnut,** part of an Oregon chain that bakes dozens of over-the-top varieties. For more information, see Part Six, "Dining in Universal CityWalk" (page 362).

Entertainment options include **CityWalk's Rising Star,** a karaoke joint where singers are backed by a live band; reggae at **Bob Marley—A Tribute to Freedom;** a **Pat O'Brien's** dueling-pianos club; **Fat Tuesday,** specializing in New Orleans–style daiquiris; a **Hard Rock Cafe** and **Hard Rock Live** concert venue; **Jimmy Buffett's Margaritaville;** the **Red Coconut Club,** a two-story upscale cocktail lounge with live music and dancing; and a dance club called **The Groove,** with high-tech lighting and visual effects. If you want to go clubbing, $12.77 (tax included) admits you to all of the clubs. For details, call Universal CityWalk information at ☎ 407-224-2691.

COVID *tip*
Party pass sales and cover charges were suspended at press time, and some venues are temporarily closed.

CityWalk is open daily, 8 a.m.–2 a.m. (until midnight during slower seasons). Parking, located in the same garages that serve the

continued on page 610

Universal's Islands of Adventure

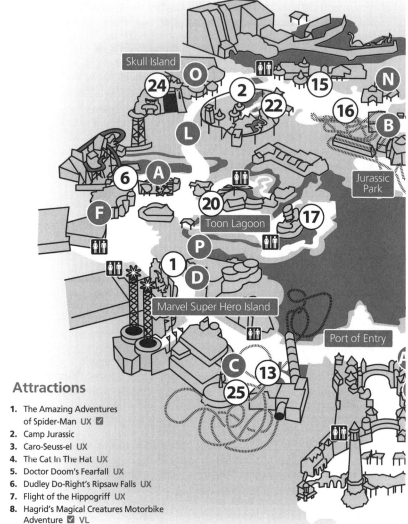

Attractions

1. The Amazing Adventures
   of Spider-Man UX ☑
2. Camp Jurassic
3. Caro-Seuss-el UX
4. The Cat In The Hat UX
5. Doctor Doom's Fearfall UX
6. Dudley Do-Right's Ripsaw Falls UX
7. Flight of the Hippogriff UX
8. Hagrid's Magical Creatures Motorbike
   Adventure ☑ VL
9. Harry Potter and the Forbidden Journey UX ☑
10. The High in the Sky Seuss Trolley Train Ride! UX
11. Hogwarts Express: Hogsmeade Station UX ☑
12. If I Ran The Zoo
13. The Incredible Hulk Coaster UX ☑
14. Jurassic Park Discovery Center
15. Jurassic Park River Adventure UX ☑
16. Jurassic World VelociCoaster (opening 2021)
17. Me Ship, The Olive
18. Ollivanders
19. One Fish, Two Fish, Red Fish, Blue Fish UX
20. Popeye & Bluto's Bilge-Rat Barges UX ☑

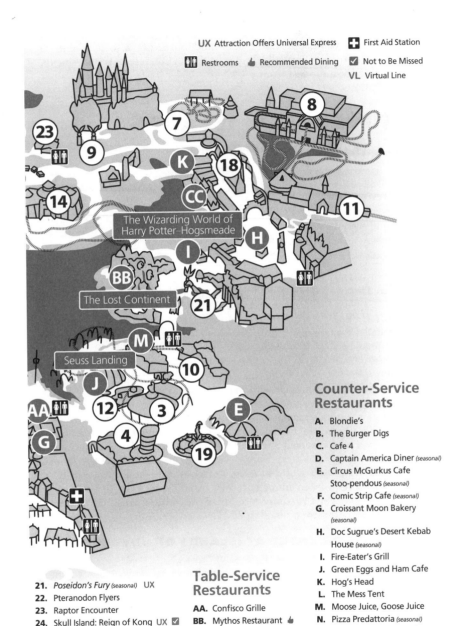

UX Attraction Offers Universal Express
Restrooms 👍 Recommended Dining
➕ First Aid Station
☑ Not to Be Missed
VL Virtual Line

The Wizarding World of Harry Potter–Hogsmeade

The Lost Continent

Seuss Landing

21. *Poseidon's Fury (seasonal)* UX
22. Pteranodon Flyers
23. Raptor Encounter
24. Skull Island: Reign of Kong UX ☑
25. Storm Force Accelatron *(seasonal)* UX

Table-Service Restaurants

AA. Confisco Grille
BB. Mythos Restaurant 👍
CC. Three Broomsticks
    (counter service) 👍

Counter-Service Restaurants

A. Blondie's
B. The Burger Digs
C. Cafe 4
D. Captain America Diner *(seasonal)*
E. Circus McGurkus Cafe
    Stoo-pendous *(seasonal)*
F. Comic Strip Cafe *(seasonal)*
G. Croissant Moon Bakery
    (seasonal)
H. Doc Sugrue's Desert Kebab
    House *(seasonal)*
I. Fire-Eater's Grill
J. Green Eggs and Ham Cafe
K. Hog's Head
L. The Mess Tent
M. Moose Juice, Goose Juice
N. Pizza Predattoria *(seasonal)*
O. Thunder Falls Terrace 👍
P. Wimpy's *(seasonal)*

continued from page 607

theme parks, is free after 6 p.m. If you're staying at a Universal resort, it's a short walk, but water taxis and buses are also available to transport you to CityWalk. To get back to your resort, try a pedicab, available for a modest tip. Call ☎ 407-224-F O O D (3663) for dinner reservations.

UNIVERSAL'S ISLANDS *of* ADVENTURE

NOT TO BE MISSED AT UNIVERSAL'S ISLANDS OF ADVENTURE
• The Amazing Adventures of Spider-Man • The Incredible Hulk Coaster
• Hagrid's Magical Creatures Motorbike Adventure • Jurassic Park River Adventure
• Harry Potter and the Forbidden Journey • Popeye & Bluto's Bilge-Rat Barges
• Hogwarts Express–Hogsmeade Station • Skull Island: Reign of Kong
• Jurassic World VelociCoaster

OPENED IN 1999, ISLANDS OF ADVENTURE is a direct competitor to Disney's Magic Kingdom, the most-visited theme park in the world. IOA has kid-friendly rides and cartoon characters (like Fantasyland), thrill rides in a sci-fi city (like Tomorrowland), and a jungle river with robot creatures (like Adventureland). Its layout—a central entry corridor leading to a ring of connected lands—even mimics the classic Disney model, with one major exception: Instead of a hub and castle in the center, Universal built a large lagoon whose estuaries separate the park's thematically diverse "islands" (actually peninsulas).

 unofficial **TIP** Consider yourself warned: Several attractions at Islands of Adventure will drench you to the bone.

In 2007 Universal made a very bold bet: securing the rights to build a Harry Potter–themed area within IOA. Universal went all-out to create a setting and attractions designed to be the envy of the industry. The **Wizarding World of Harry Potter–Hogsmeade** opened at IOA in 2010 and was an immediate hit. In summer 2019, IOA opened **Hagrid's Magical Creatures Motorbike Adventure**, and the **Jurassic World VelociCoaster** opened in 2021.

GETTING ORIENTED AT ISLANDS OF ADVENTURE

unofficial **TIP** Due to a smaller pool of reader data for Universal Orlando versus the Disney parks, we provide only basic appeal by age reader-survey ratings for the attractions in this chapter.

BOTH UNIVERSAL THEME PARKS are accessed from Universal CityWalk. Crossing CityWalk from the parking garages, bear left to Universal's Islands of Adventure or right to Universal Studios Florida.

IOA is arranged much like EPCOT's World Showcase—that is, in a large circle surrounding a lake—but its themed areas are self-contained "lands" reminiscent of those at the Magic Kingdom. **Port of Entry** is where you'll find Guest Services, lockers, stroller and wheelchair rentals, ATM banking, lost and found, and shopping.

From Port of Entry, moving clockwise around the lagoon, you first access **Marvel Super Hero Island;** then **Toon Lagoon, Skull Island, Jurassic Park, The Wizarding World of Harry Potter–Hogsmeade,** and **The Lost Continent;** and finally **Seuss Landing.**

ISLANDS OF ADVENTURE ATTRACTIONS

MARVEL SUPER HERO ISLAND

WITH ITS FUTURISTIC DESIGN and comic book signage, Marvel Super Hero Island offers attractions themed to Marvel Comics characters.

The Amazing Adventures of Spider-Man
(Universal Express) ★★★★★

PRESCHOOL ★★★½	GRADE SCHOOL ★★★★½	TEENS ★★★★½
YOUNG ADULTS ★★★★½	OVER 30 ★★★★	SENIORS ★★★★

What it is Indoor adventure simulator ride based on Spider-Man. **Scope and scale** Super-headliner. **When to go** During the first 40 minutes the park is open. **Comments** Single-rider line available; must be 40″ to ride. **Duration of ride** 4½ minutes. **Loading speed** Fast.

DESCRIPTION AND COMMENTS The Amazing Adventures of Spider-Man combines moving ride vehicles, 3-D film, and live action. It's frenetic, fluid, and considered by many to be the best theme park attraction on the planet.

The story line is that you're a reporter for the *Daily Bugle* newspaper (where Peter Parker, also known as Spider-Man, works as a mild-mannered photographer) when it's discovered that evildoers have stolen—we promise we're not making this up—the Statue of Liberty. You're drafted on the spot by your cantankerous editor to go get the story. After speeding around and being thrust into a battle between good and evil, you experience a 400-foot "sensory drop" from a skyscraper roof all the way to the pavement. Spidey is less frantic than the similar Transformers ride at USF and features more dialogue and humor.

TOURING TIPS If you were on hand for Early Park Admission, ride after experiencing The Wizarding World and Skull Island: Reign of Kong. If you skip the Wizarding World, ride after Hulk.

Doctor Doom's Fearfall *(Universal Express)* ★★★

PRESCHOOL ★½	GRADE SCHOOL ★★★½	TEENS ★★★★
YOUNG ADULTS ★★★½	OVER 30 ★★★½	SENIORS ★★★

What it is Vertical ascent and free fall. **Scope and scale** Major attraction. **When to go** First 40 minutes the park is open or after 3 p.m. **Comments** Single-rider line available; must be 52″ to ride. **Duration of ride** 40 seconds. **Loading speed** Slow.

DESCRIPTION AND COMMENTS Here you're strapped into a seat with your feet dangling, blasted 200 feet up in the air, and then allowed to partially free-fall back down. The scariest part of the ride by far is the apprehension that builds as you sit, strapped in, waiting for the ride to launch; blasting up and falling down are actually pleasant.

TOURING TIPS We've seen glaciers that move faster than the line for Doctor Doom's Fearfall. If you want to ride without a long wait, be on hand at park opening or try after 3 p.m.

The Incredible Hulk Coaster *(Universal Express)* ★★★★½

PRESCHOOL ★	GRADE SCHOOL ★★★★½	TEENS ★★★★★
YOUNG ADULTS ★★★★★	OVER 30 ★★★★½	SENIORS ★★★★

What it is Roller coaster. **Scope and scale** Super-headliner. **When to go** During the first 40 minutes the park is open or after 3 p.m. **Comments** Single-rider line available; must be 54″ to ride. **Duration of ride** 2¼ minutes. **Loading speed** Moderate.

DESCRIPTION AND COMMENTS The Hulk is one of the best coasters in Florida, providing a ride comparable to Kumba at Busch Gardens. You'll be shot like a cannonball from 0 to 40 mph in 2 seconds; then you'll be flung upside down 100 feet off the ground. Then it's a mere six rollovers, punctuated by two plunges into holes in the ground, before you're allowed to get out and throw up.

TOURING TIPS Ride Hulk first thing, or immediately after you've enjoyed early entry at the Potter attractions; otherwise, wait until late afternoon. Mandatory free lockers are provided for stowing phones and other unsecured objects. There's a separate line for those who want to ride in the first row.

Storm Force Accelatron *(Universal Express)* ★★½ *(seasonal)*

PRESCHOOL ★★★★	GRADE SCHOOL ★★★½	TEENS ★★★½
YOUNG ADULTS ★★★½	OVER 30 ★★★	SENIORS ★★★

What it is Covered spinning ride. **Scope and scale** Minor attraction. **Comment** If you're prone to motion sickness, keep your distance. **When to go** Anytime. **Duration of ride** 1½ minutes. **Loading speed** Slow.

DESCRIPTION AND COMMENTS Storm Force is a spiffed-up version of Disney's nausea-inducing Mad Tea Party. A story line loosely ties this midway-type ride to Marvel Super Hero Island, but it offers no useful advice on keeping your lunch down.

TOURING TIPS When open, the ride is typically a walk-on, and even on the busiest days, the wait rarely tops 20 minutes.

TOON LAGOON

WHIMSICAL AND GAILY COLORED, this land translates cartoons into real buildings and settings. **Comic Strip Lane,** the main street of Toon Lagoon, is the domain of Beetle Bailey, Blondie, and Dagwood—among other characters that your kids have probably never heard of.

Dudley Do-Right's Ripsaw Falls *(Universal Express* ★★★½

PRESCHOOL ★½	GRADE SCHOOL ★★★★½	TEENS ★★★★½
YOUNG ADULTS ★★★★	OVER 30 ★★★★	SENIORS ★★★★

What it is Flume ride. **Scope and scale** Headliner. **When to go** Before 11 a.m. **Comment** Must be 44″ to ride. **Duration of ride** 5 minutes. **Loading speed** Moderate.

DESCRIPTION AND COMMENTS Inspired by characters from the *Rocky and Bullwinkle* cartoons, this ride features Canadian Mountie Dudley Do-Right as he tries to save his girlfriend, Nell Fenwick, from the nefarious Snidely Whiplash. Story line aside, it's a flume ride with the inevitable big drop at the end.

TOURING TIPS Make no mistake—this ride *will* get you wet, though not as soaked as Popeye. Ride the Ripsaw Falls after you've experienced the Marvel Super Hero rides and Skull Island: Reign of Kong.

Me Ship, *The Olive*   ★★★ *(temporarily closed)*

PRESCHOOL ★★★★½	GRADE SCHOOL ★★★★	TEENS ★★★
YOUNG ADULTS ★★½	OVER 30 ★★★	SENIORS ★★★½

What it is Interactive playground for kids. **Scope and scale** Minor attraction. **When to go** Anytime.

DESCRIPTION AND COMMENTS *The Olive* is Popeye's three-story boat come to life as an interactive playground. Younger kids can scramble around in Swee'Pea's Playpen, while older sibs shoot water cannons at riders trying to survive the adjacent Bilge-Rat Barges.

TOURING TIPS If you're into the big rides, save this for later in the day.

Popeye & Bluto's Bilge-Rat Barges
(Universal Express) ★★★★

PRESCHOOL ★★★	GRADE SCHOOL ★★★★½	TEENS ★★★★½
YOUNG ADULTS ★★★★½	OVER 30 ★★★★½	SENIORS ★★★★

What it is Whitewater raft ride. **Scope and scale** Headliner. **When to go** Before 11 a.m. **Comment** Must be 42" to ride. **Duration of ride** 4½ minutes. **Loading speed** Moderate.

DESCRIPTION AND COMMENTS This family raft ride is engineered to ensure that everyone gets drenched. The rapids are rougher and more interesting, and the ride longer, than Animal Kingdom's Kali River Rapids, but Disney wins for theming hands-down.

TOURING TIPS You'll get a lot wetter from the knees down on this ride, so use your poncho or garbage bag, and ride barefoot with your britches rolled up. This ride often opens an hour after the rest of the park. Experience the barges in the morning after the Marvel Super Hero attractions and Dudley Do-Right.

SKULL ISLAND

THIS IS BOTH AN ATTRACTION and an entire "island" unto itself, between Dudley Do-Right's Ripsaw Falls and Thunder Falls Terrace.

Skull Island: Reign of Kong *(Universal Express)* ★★★★

PRESCHOOL ★★★	GRADE SCHOOL ★★★½	TEENS ★★★★
YOUNG ADULTS ★★★★	OVER 30 ★★★★	SENIORS ★★★★

What it is Indoor-outdoor truck safari with 3-D effects. **Scope and scale** Super-headliner. **When to go** Immediately after park opening or just before closing. **Comments** Single-rider line available; must be 34" to ride. Probably not a good choice for little ones. **Duration of ride** About 6 minutes; 4 minutes when exterior is bypassed in inclement weather. **Loading speed** Fast.

DESCRIPTION AND COMMENTS Skull Island: Reign of Kong is an original adventure set in the 1930s, casting guests as jungle explorers with the 8th Wonder Expedition Company. The spooky queue experience features an ancient temple inhabited by lifelike animatronic figures that may startle the unwitting.

Your transportation is an oversize 72-seat open-sided "expedition vehicle" helmed by one of five different animatronic tour guides. You pass through a maze of caves, where you're swiftly assaulted by icky prehistoric bats, bugs, and beasties, brought to gruesome life through a mix of detailed physical effects and razor-sharp 3-D screens. You're then thrust into the center of a raging battle between vicious V-Rex dinosaurs and the big ape himself. Finally, just when you think it's all over, you'll have one last face-to-face encounter with the "eighth wonder of the world," only this time in the fur-covered flesh.

TOURING TIPS Skull Island is epic in every sense—including its lines. Ride first thing in the morning or immediately following the Hogsmeade attractions if you're using Early Park Admission. Finally, if you or your little one is afraid of the dark, insects, or man-eating monsters, you may want to forgo the monkey.

JURASSIC PARK

JURASSIC PARK, and its *Jurassic World* follow-up trilogy, is a Steven Spielberg film franchise about a fictitious theme park with real dinosaurs. Jurassic Park at IOA is a real theme park (or at least a section of one) with *fictitious* dinosaurs. A bridge from Lost Continent allows guests to bypass Hogsmeade on busy days and head directly to the Jurassic World VelociCoaster.

Camp Jurassic ★★★½

PRESCHOOL ★★★★½	GRADE SCHOOL ★★★★½	TEENS ★★★
YOUNG ADULTS ★★★	OVER 30 ★★★	SENIORS ★★★

What it is Kids' play area. **Scope and scale** Minor attraction. **When to go** Anytime.

DESCRIPTION AND COMMENTS One of the best theme park playgrounds you'll find anywhere. A sort of dinosaur-themed Tom Sawyer Island minus the rafts, it allows kids to explore lava pits, caves, mines, and a rainforest. It's big enough for many kids to spend a solid hour just running around.

TOURING TIPS Camp Jurassic will fire the imaginations of the under-13 set—if you don't impose a time limit on the exploration, you could be here awhile.

Jurassic Park Discovery Center ★★½

PRESCHOOL ★★★★	GRADE SCHOOL ★★★★	TEENS ★★★
YOUNG ADULTS ★★★½	OVER 30 ★★★	SENIORS ★★★

What it is Interactive natural-history exhibit. **Scope and scale** Minor attraction. **When to go** Anytime.

DESCRIPTION AND COMMENTS This interactive educational exhibit mixes fiction from *Jurassic Park,* such as using fossil DNA to bring dinosaurs to life, with various skeletal remains and other paleontological displays. The best exhibit here lets guests watch an animatronic raptor being hatched, with a young witness getting to name the newborn.

TOURING TIPS The lower level of the Discovery Center also doubles as a post-ride gift shop and oversize locker area for the VelociCoaster, but most of the exhibits are still accessible. Tour after seeing the park's major rides and attractions, or on your second day in the park. Most folks can digest this exhibit in 10–15 minutes.

Jurassic Park River Adventure
(Universal Express) ★★★★

PRESCHOOL ★★★	GRADE SCHOOL ★★★★	TEENS ★★★★
YOUNG ADULTS ★★★★	OVER 30 ★★★★	SENIORS ★★★★

What it is Indoor-outdoor river-raft adventure ride based on the Jurassic Park movies. **Scope and scale** Headliner. **When to go** Before 11 a.m. **Comments** Must be 42″ to ride; single-rider line available. **Duration of ride** 6½ minutes. **Loading speed** Fast.

DESCRIPTION AND COMMENTS Guests board boats for a water tour of Jurassic Park. Everything is tranquil as the tour begins, but the tour boat is then accidentally diverted into Jurassic Park's maintenance facilities. Here, the boat and its riders are menaced by an assortment of hungry meat-eaters. At the climactic moment, the boat and its passengers escape by plummeting over an 85-foot drop.

TOURING TIPS Though the boats make a huge splash at the bottom of the drop, you can stay relatively dry if you sit in an interior seat. Because Jurassic Park River Adventure is situated next to The Wizarding World of Harry Potter–Hogsmeade, the boat will experience heavy crowds earlier in the day. Try to ride before 11 a.m. Unless your kids are fairly hardy, wait a year or two before you spring the River Adventure on them.

Jurassic World VelociCoaster ★★★★★

What it is Roller coaster. **Scope and scale** Super-headliner. **When to go** Immediately after park opening, late morning, or just before closing. **Comment** Must be 51" to ride; single-rider line available. **Duration of ride** About 2 minutes. **Loading speed** Medium-fast

DESCRIPTION AND COMMENTS Universal Orlando's most extreme roller coaster to date blurs the line between the original film franchise and its *Jurassic World* follow-ups with queue cameos from actors Chris Pratt (as Owen Grady), Bryce Dallas Howard (as Claire Dearing), and B. D. Wong (as Dr. Henry Wu). Apparently, none of them have paid attention to the movies in which they starred because they're offering guests scenic tours of the maximum-security paddocks where Blue and her carnivorous pals camp out. What could possibly go wrong?

Riders board 24-passenger trains to experience two high-speed launches, an 80-degree dive down a towering 155-foot-tall "top hat," and close encounters with realistic rockwork and sculpted dinosaurs. With a top speed of 70 mph and an astounding 12 moments of out-of-your-seat air time (including a first-of-its-kind zero-g inverted stall), VelociCoaster boasts the kind of statistics that make coaster nerds salivate. However, you merely need to look at how the Intamin-built track twists and turns along the waterfront to know that this is one of the most intense scream machines in town, if not on Earth.

VelociCoaster delivers nonstop adrenaline from the first burst of acceleration until you hit the final brake run. Thankfully, the restraints rest comfortably across your hips and upper thighs, holding you securely as you're flung helplessly through the finale's heart-stopping "Momasaurus roll" above the lagoon. (Loose-fitting eyeglasses or facemasks may not be so lucky.) Other roller coasters may have a taller drop or greater maximum velocity, but nothing else strings together so many exhilarating elements into 4,700 feet of relentlessly paced track.

TOURING TIPS VelociCoaster quickly overtook The Incredible Hulk Coaster as the hard-core thrill junkies' favorite ride, but Hagrid's continues to attract bigger crowds, since it's accessible to a wider range of guests. If you can fight the urge to be among the first riders of the day, try to hit VelociCoaster in late morning after experiencing the other top attractions. Otherwise, make it your last ride of the night; it's even scarier in the dark.

Unlike at the Hulk or Rip Ride Rockit, guests here can hold onto their cell phones, wallets, and other loose items until just before boarding, when they can stash their stuff in double-sided lockers for retrieval immediately after disembarking.

Pteranodon Flyers ★★★

| PRESCHOOL ★★★★½ | GRADE SCHOOL ★★★★ | TEENS ★★★ |
| YOUNG ADULTS ★★½ | OVER 30 ★★★ | SENIORS ★★ |

What it is Suspended kiddie coaster. **Scope and scale** Minor attraction. **When to go** In the first or last 30 minutes of the day, or use Virtual Line. **Comment** Adults and older children must be accompanied by a child between 36″ and 56″ tall. **Duration of ride** 1¼ minutes. **Loading speed** More sluggish than a hog in quicksand.

DESCRIPTION AND COMMENTS This ride swings you along a track that passes over a small part of Jurassic Park. The queue moves at a glacial pace, and the ride itself lasts barely 75 seconds, but you get a gorgeous view of the island's greenery, and the swinging cars deliver a surprisingly satisfying snap as they negotiate the track's curves.

TOURING TIPS Look for kiosks outside Camp Jurassic's entrance that dispense timed-return tickets. You'll still have to wait awhile to come back, but it beats stewing in the standby queue.

Raptor Encounter ★★★½

| PRESCHOOL ★★★½ | GRADE SCHOOL ★★★★ | TEENS ★★★★½ |
| YOUNG ADULTS ★★★★½ | OVER 30 ★★★★½ | SENIORS ★★★★½ |

What it is Photo op with lifelike dinosaur. **Scope and scale** Minor attraction. **When to go** Before noon. **Duration of encounter** About a minute. **Queue speed** Slow-ish.

DESCRIPTION AND COMMENTS Blue from *Jurassic World*, IOA's semi-tame velociraptor star (actually an amazingly realistic puppet), makes regular appearances in her paddock next to the River Adventure. A game warden briefs one family at a time regarding proper safety procedures—convey calm assurance, move in slowly, don't smell like meat—before they step up for a photo. Selfies are encouraged; just don't be surprised if the dino snaps when you say, "Smile!"

TOURING TIPS The Raptor Encounter is quite popular, so ask a team member stationed outside the paddock entrance approximately how long your wait will be before queuing. When the full-grown dino needs a break, an adorable handheld baby velociraptor may take her place.

THE WIZARDING WORLD OF HARRY POTTER-HOGSMEADE

unofficial **TIP**
The only restrooms in The Wizarding World at IOA, labeled PUBLIC CONVENIENCES, are in the middle of Hogsmeade. Remember where they are—especially if you're planning to ride Forbidden Journey and you're prone to motion sickness.

IN 2007, UNIVERSAL INKED A DEAL with Warner Brothers Entertainment to create a fully immersive Harry Potter-themed environment based on the best-selling children's books by J. K. Rowling and the companion blockbuster movies from Warner Brothers.

Depicted in winter, the village of **Hogsmeade** is rendered in exquisite detail: The stone cottages and shops have steeply pitched slate roofs; bowed multipaned windows; gables; and tall, crooked chimneys.

Wizarding World–Hogsmeade Attractions

Flight of the Hippogriff (*Universal Express*) ★★★

| PRESCHOOL ★★★★ | GRADE SCHOOL ★★★★ | TEENS ★★★½ |
| YOUNG ADULTS ★★★½ | OVER 30 ★★★½ | SENIORS ★★★½ |

What it is Kids' roller coaster. **Scope and scale** Minor attraction. **When to go** First 90 minutes the park is open or after 4 p.m. **Comment** Must be 36″ to ride. **Duration of ride** 1 minute. **Loading speed** Slow.

DESCRIPTION AND COMMENTS Below and to the right of Hogwarts Castle, next to Hagrid's Hut, the Hippogriff is short and sweet but not worth much of a wait. Potter nerds will want to ride to see Hagrid's Hut and a charming animatronic of Buckbeak.

TOURING TIPS Have your kids ride soon after the park opens while older sibs enjoy other Wizarding World attractions.

Hagrid's Magical Creatures Motorbike Adventure ★★★★★

PRESCHOOL ★★	GRADE SCHOOL ★★★★½	TEENS ★★★★★
YOUNG ADULTS ★★★★★	OVER 30 ★★★★★	SENIORS ★★★★½

What it is Indoor–outdoor roller coaster. **Scope and scale** Super-headliner. **When to go** First thing during Early Park Admission, or whenever possible using Virtual Line. **Comments** Single-rider line occasionally available; must be 48″ to ride. **Duration of ride** About 3 minutes. **Loading speed** Medium.

DESCRIPTION AND COMMENTS This family-friendly thrill ride is a highly themed roller coaster without huge hills or upside-down loops. Instead, it focuses on thrilling launches through forested terrain during outdoor segments, as well as close encounters with animatronic creatures inside and between the ride's indoor buildings.

Guests board 14-passenger trains inspired by Hagrid's motorcycle and sidecar for an adventure that includes a vertical climb leading into a backward helix, followed by a free-fall drop into darkness. Fantastical creatures and familiar figures from the Potter world make appearances during your experience, such as the flying Ford Anglia, Fluffy the three-headed dog, and old Hagrid himself (an impressively lifelike animatronic).

If you think Universal's attractions are too dependent on video screens and simulated movement, Hagrid is here to answer your prayers with richly detailed scenery, spectacular practical effects, and accelerated air time that's exhilarating but not too extreme for tweens and parents to enjoy together. While the coaster's 50-mph top speed might not sound terribly swift, it feels far faster when you're navigating ground-hugging twists and turns through a grove of 1,200 real trees. Move over, Everest, and step aside, Seven Dwarfs: Hagrid's is the best "story coaster" in Orlando, and a strong contender for the best ride at Universal Orlando.

TOURING TIPS The ride receives a huge rush of guests every morning at Early Entry rope drop and often experiences a delayed opening; standby waits are shortest at lunchtime and in the early evening, and the effects look best after dark. Universal is currently testing a new Virtual Line system for Hagrid's Magical Creatures Motorbike Adventure, which is accessed by visiting vltest. universalorlando.com. You'll need to sign in with an email and password, and select the number of people in your party, in order to receive an estimated wait before returning to enter Hagrid's physical queue. Try to join the Virtual Line as soon as the park has officially opened for the day, and keep checking back periodically if the queue is at capacity. Hagrid's doesn't currently offer Universal Express access but may in the future. A single-rider queue is sometimes available when Virtual Line is not active, but it doesn't save that much time. The sidecar sits lower than the cycle but closer to the effects, so every rider gets a good view. Larger guests (40-inch waists and above) should test the sample seats before lining up and then request a motorbike seat, which affords a little more breathing room than a cramped sidecar.

Harry Potter and the Forbidden Journey
(Universal Express) ★★★★★

PRESCHOOL ★★	GRADE SCHOOL ★★★★½	TEENS ★★★★½
YOUNG ADULTS ★★★★½	OVER 30 ★★★★½	SENIORS ★★★★

What it is Motion-simulator dark ride. **Scope and scale** Super-headliner. **When to go** Immediately after Hagrid's during Early Entry, or in the last hours before closing. **Comments** Single-rider line available; must be 48″ to ride. **Duration of ride** 4¼ minutes. **Loading speed** Fast.

DESCRIPTION AND COMMENTS This ride provides the only opportunity at Universal Orlando to come in contact with Harry Potter, Ron Weasley, Hermione Granger, and Dumbledore as portrayed by the original actors. Half of the attraction is a series of preshows that sets the stage for the main event, a dark ride.

After entering through the castle dungeons, you ascend through the greenhouse into a multistory gallery of magically moving portraits; then you proceed to Dumbledore's office, where the chief wizard (a realistic Musion EyeLiner hologram) appears on a balcony and welcomes you to Hogwarts. After his welcoming remarks, Dumbledore dispatches you to the Defence Against the Dark Arts classroom, where Harry, Ron, and Hermione pop out from beneath an invisibility cloak and invite you to a Quidditch match.

All of this leads to the Room of Requirement. Here, you board a four-passenger bench attached to the end of a Kuka robotic arm, which can be programmed to replicate all the sensations of flying, including broad swoops, steep dives, sharp turns, sudden stops, and fast acceleration. The ride vehicle moves you through a series of alternating sets and domes where scenes are projected all around you. The movement of the Kuka arm is synchronized to create the motion that corresponds to what's happening in the set or film. When everything works correctly, it's mind-blowing: You'll soar over Hogwarts Castle, narrowly evade an attacking dragon, spar with the Whomping Willow, get tossed into a Quidditch match, and fight off Dementors inside the Chamber of Secrets.

TOURING TIPS Try not to ride on an empty stomach if possible. If you start getting queasy, fix your gaze on your feet and try to exclude as much from your peripheral vision as possible.

unofficial **TIP**
Parents, take note: Because the seats on the benches are compartmentalized, kids can't see or touch Mom or Dad if they get frightened.

Each bench has modified seats at either end for larger guests; try the test seat outside the entrance before queueing to make sure you'll fit.

At Forbidden Journey, the wait in the single-rider line (when available) can be as much as one-tenth the wait in the standby line. You'll miss much of the interior of the castle, however.

Hogwarts Express *(Universal Express)* ★★★★½

PRESCHOOL ★★★★½	GRADE SCHOOL ★★★★½	TEENS ★★★★½
YOUNG ADULTS ★★★★½	OVER 30 ★★★★½	SENIORS ★★★★½

What it is Transportation attraction. **Scope and scale** Headliner. **When to go** Immediately after park opening until midafternoon. **Comment** Park-to-Park Ticket required to ride. **Duration of ride** 4 minutes. **Loading speed** Moderate.

DESCRIPTION AND COMMENTS See page 635 for a full review.

TOURING TIPS Lines are usually less than 20 minutes through the morning but can build later in the day, so ride before midafternoon if experiencing the train is important.

Note: You must have a Park-to-Park Ticket to ride. Single-park tickets can be upgraded at Guest Services or at either train station.

Ollivanders ★★★★

PRESCHOOL ★★★★	GRADE SCHOOL ★★★★½	TEENS ★★★★½
YOUNG ADULTS ★★★★½	OVER 30 ★★★★	SENIORS ★★★★½

What it is Combination wizarding demonstration and shopping op. **Scope and scale** Minor attraction. **When to go** In the first or last 30 minutes of the day. **Comments** Audience stands; identical to USF version but with a much slower line. **Duration of show** 6 minutes.

DESCRIPTION AND COMMENTS Next to the Owl Post is Ollivanders, offering the same wand-choosing ceremony as the Diagon Alley attraction of the same name (see page 635). It's great fun, but the tiny shop can accommodate only a handful of guests at a time. After the show, the whole group is dispatched to the Owl Post and Dervish and Banges to buy stuff. An interactive wand, which triggers special effects hidden inside shop windows throughout Hogsmeade and Diagon Alley, costs $62.83; a basic model that doesn't do any tricks costs $58.58.

TOURING TIPS Because of the shop's very low capacity, long waits for the show at Ollivanders can form. If you need to see this show and you can't go to the USF Ollivanders, go first thing in the morning or as late as possible. If you just want to buy a wand, enter the store directly rather than waiting for the show; you can also buy wands at an outdoor cart near the *Frog Choir* stage, or in the large gift shop near the park's entrance, usually with little to no wait.

Wizarding World Entertainment

Nearly every retail space sports some sort of animatronic or special-effects surprise. At **Dervish and Banges,** the fearsome *Monster Book of Monsters* rattles and snarls at you as Nimbus 2001 brooms strain at their tethers overhead. At the **Hog's Head** pub, the titular porcine part, mounted behind the bar, similarly thrashes and growls. (The pub also serves The Wizarding World's signature nonalcoholic brew, Butterbeer. Outdoor vendors also sell it, but the wait at the Hog's Head is generally 10 minutes or less, versus half an hour or more in the lines outside.)

Roughly across the street from the pub, you'll find benches in the shade at the **Owlery,** next to the **Owl Post,** where you can have snail mail stamped with a Hogsmeade postmark before dropping it off for delivery (an Orlando postmark will also be applied by the real USPS).

Street entertainment at the Forbidden Journey end of Hogsmeade includes the *Frog Choir* (★★★), composed of four singers, two of whom are holding large amphibian puppets sitting on pillows; and the *Triwizard Spirit Rally* (★★★), showcasing dancing and martial arts. Performances run about 6–15 minutes.

On select evenings, the *Nighttime Lights at Hogwarts Castle* show (★★★½) brings the Forbidden Journey facade to life with video projections synchronized to the films' scores. Best viewing is from in front of the *Frog Choir* stage or on the bridge to Jurassic Park. The 10-minute show is repeated several times from sunset to park closing; the first showing is the most crowded, so stay for the last. During the Halloween and holiday seasons, special *Dark Arts* and *Magic of Christmas* versions are shown.

THE LOST CONTINENT

THIS AREA IS AN EXOTIC MIX of Silk Road bazaar and ancient ruins, with Greco-Moroccan accents. The best (and often only) attraction may be the **Mystic Fountain,** an interactive talking fountain with an attitude, so keep your umbrella handy.

Poseidon's Fury
(Universal Express) ★★★½ *(seasonal)*

PRESCHOOL ★★	GRADE SCHOOL ★★★	TEENS ★★★
YOUNG ADULTS ★★★½	OVER 30 ★★★	SENIORS ★★★½

What it is High-tech theater attraction. **Scope and scale** Headliner. **When to go** After experiencing all the rides. **Comment** Audience stands throughout. **Duration of show** 17 minutes, including preshow.

DESCRIPTION AND COMMENTS The Greek god Poseidon tussles with an evil wizardish guy using fire, water, lasers, and smoke machines. The plot unfolds in installments as you pass from room to room and finally into the main theater. Though the premise is kind of silly, the special effects are still amazing, and while the production plods a bit at first, it wraps up with an impressive flourish.

TOURING TIPS Catch *Poseidon* after getting your fill of the rides. Frequent explosions, dark, and noise may frighten younger children.

SEUSS LANDING

THIS 10-ACRE THEMED AREA is based on Dr. Seuss's famous children's books. The buildings and attractions display a whimsical, brightly colored cartoon style with exaggerated features and rounded lines. Seuss Landing has four rides; an interactive play area, **If I Ran the Zoo,** populated by Seuss creatures; and *Oh! the Stories You'll Hear!* (★★★), a live musical show featuring the Lorax, the Cat in the Hat, and other beloved characters.

Caro-Seuss-el *(Universal Express)* ★★★

PRESCHOOL ★★★★½	GRADE SCHOOL ★★★½	TEENS ★★★
YOUNG ADULTS ★★★	OVER 30 ★★★	SENIORS ★★★½

What it is Merry-go-round. **Scope and scale** Minor attraction. **When to go** Anytime. **Comment** Ride is outside but covered. **Duration of ride** 2 minutes. **Loading speed** Slow.

DESCRIPTION AND COMMENTS Totally outrageous, this full-scale, 56-mount merry-go-round is made up entirely of Dr. Seuss characters.

TOURING TIPS Waits usually aren't too long, even in the middle of the day.

The Cat in the Hat *(Universal Express)* ★★★½

PRESCHOOL ★★★★½	GRADE SCHOOL ★★★★	TEENS ★★★
YOUNG ADULTS ★★★	OVER 30 ★★★½	SENIORS ★★★★

What it is Indoor cartoon dark ride. **Scope and scale** Major attraction. **When to go** Before 11:30 a.m. or after 4 p.m. **Comment** Must be 36" to ride. **Duration of ride** 3½ minutes. **Loading speed** Moderate.

DESCRIPTION AND COMMENTS Guests ride on "couches" through 18 different sets inhabited by animatronic Seuss characters, including The Cat in the Hat, Thing 1 and Thing 2, and the beleaguered goldfish who tries to maintain order in the midst of bedlam.

TOURING TIPS Fun for all ages. Try to ride early or late in the day.

The High in the Sky Seuss Trolley Train Ride!
(Universal Express) ★★★½

PRESCHOOL ★★★★½	GRADE SCHOOL ★★★½	TEENS ★★★
YOUNG ADULTS ★★★	OVER 30 ★★★½	SENIORS ★★★★

What it is Elevated train. **Scope and scale** Major attraction. **When to go** Before 11:30 a.m. or just before closing. **Comment** Oddly, kids must be 40″ to ride. **Duration of ride** 3½ minutes. **Loading speed** Molasses.

DESCRIPTION AND COMMENTS Trains putter along elevated tracks while a voice reads one of four Dr. Seuss stories over the train's speakers. As each train makes its way through Seuss Landing, it passes a series of animatronic characters that are part of the story being told. A strangely stringent minimum height requirement means that many in the Trolley's target demographic are too short to ride.

TOURING TIPS The trains are small, fitting about 20 people, and the loading speed is glacial. Ride at the end of the day or first thing in the morning.

If I Ran the Zoo (Universal Express) ★★★

PRESCHOOL ★★★★½	GRADE SCHOOL ★★★★	TEENS ★★½
YOUNG ADULTS ★★½	OVER 30 ★★★½	SENIORS ★★★½

What it is Interactive play area and outdoor maze. **Scope and scale** Diversion. **When to go** Anytime. **Comment** Kids may get wet.

DESCRIPTION AND COMMENTS This play area is themed to Dr. Seuss rhymes and filled with the fantastic animals and gizmos from the beloved author's stories.

TOURING TIPS Tour anytime. Note that much of the play area is unshaded— bring cold drinks, hats, and sunscreen for the little ones.

One Fish, Two Fish, Red Fish, Blue Fish
(Universal Express) ★★★

PRESCHOOL ★★★★½	GRADE SCHOOL ★★★★★	TEENS ★★★
YOUNG ADULTS ★★★	OVER 30 ★★★½	SENIORS ★★★½

What it is Wet version of Dumbo the Flying Elephant. **Scope and scale** Minor attraction. **When to go** Before 10 a.m. **Comment** Plan on getting wet. **Duration of ride** 2 minutes. **Loading speed** Slow.

DESCRIPTION AND COMMENTS Imagine Dumbo with Seuss-style fish instead of elephants and you have half the story—the other half involves another opportunity to get soaked. Guests steer their fish up or down 15 feet in the air while traveling in circles. At the same time, they try to avoid streams of water projected from "squirt posts."

Wet

TOURING TIPS You'll get wetter on this thing than at a full-immersion baptism. Lines can build in the afternoon, so try to ride early, while you'll still have time to dry off.

DINING AT UNIVERSAL'S ISLANDS OF ADVENTURE

OF IOA'S DINING OPTIONS, we like **Three Broomsticks,** The Wizarding World of Harry Potter's counter-service restaurant, which serves Boston Market–style rotisserie chicken plus fish-and-chips, shepherd's pie, and barbecue ribs; a similar menu (minus the Potter theming and crowds) is available at **Thunder Falls Terrace** in Jurassic Park. The **Hog's Head** pub, attached to Three Broomsticks, serves beer, wine, mixed

continued on page 624

Universal Studios Florida

Attractions

1. *Animal Actors on Location!* UX
2. *The Bourne Stuntacular* ☑
3. Despicable Me Minion Mayhem UX
4. E.T. Adventure UX
5. Fast & Furious: Supercharged *(seasonal)* UX VL
6. *Fear Factor Live (seasonal)* UX
7. Fievel's Playland
8. Harry Potter and the Escape from Gringotts UX ☑
9. Hogwarts Express: King's Cross Station UX ☑
10. Hollywood Rip Ride Rockit UX
11. Kang & Kodos' Twirl 'n' Hurl *(seasonal)* UX
12. Men in Black Alien Attack UX ☑
13. Ollivanders
14. Race Through New York
    Starring Jimmy Fallon UX VL
15. Revenge of the Mummy UX ☑
16. *Shrek 4-D* UX
17. The Simpsons Ride UX ☑
18. Transformers: The Ride–3-D UX ☑
19. *Universal Orlando's Horror*
    Make-Up Show UX ☑

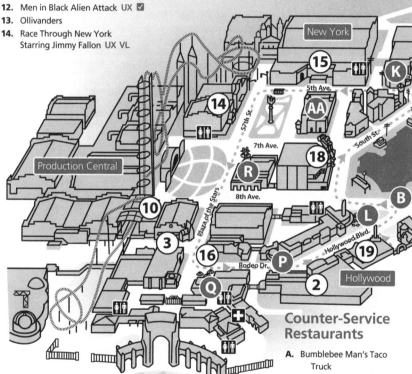

Counter-Service Restaurants

A. Bumblebee Man's Taco
   Truck
B. Central Park Crepes
C. Chez Alcatraz
D. Duff Brewery
E. Fast Food Boulevard 👍
F. Florean Fortescue's
   Ice-Cream Parlour 👍
G. Fountain of Fair
   Fortune *(seasonal)*

20. *Universal Orlando's Cinematic Celebration (seasonal)*

21. Woody Woodpacker's Nuthouse Coaster **UX**

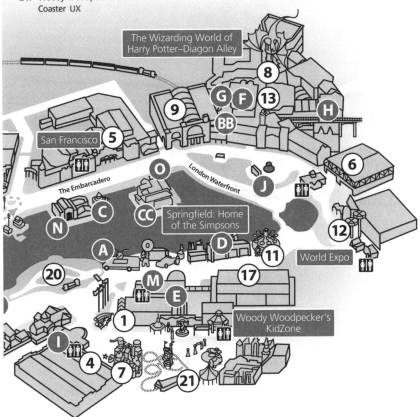

The Wizarding World of Harry Potter–Diagon Alley

San Francisco

The Embarcadero

London Waterfront

Springfield: Home of the Simpsons

World Expo

Woody Woodpecker's KidZone

Table-Service Restaurants

H. The Hopping Pot
I. KidZone Pizza Company *(seasonal)*
J. London Taxi Hut *(seasonal)*
K. Louie's Italian Restaurant
L. Mel's Drive-In
M. Moe's Tavern

N. Richter's Burger Co.
O. San Francisco Pastry Company *(seasonal)*
P. Schwab's Pharmacy *(seasonal)*
Q. Today Cafe 👍
R. Universal Studios' Classic Monsters Cafe *(seasonal)*

AA. Finnegan's Bar & Grill
BB. Leaky Cauldron *(counter service)* 👍
CC. Lombard's Seafood Grille

UX Attraction Offers Universal Express   **VL** Virtual Line   ✚ First Aid Station   🚻 Restrooms

👍 Recommended Dining   ✅ Not to Be Missed   ▪ ▪ ▪ Parade Route

continued from page 621

drinks, and the obligatory Butterbeer. We're also fond of the gyros at **Fire Eater's Grill** and the kabobs at **Doc Sugrue's.**

IOA has two sit-down restaurants: **Confisco Grille,** in Port of Entry, and **Mythos Restaurant,** in The Lost Continent. Confisco is fine for appetizers, sandwiches, and drinks. Despite its Hellenic-sounding name, Mythos isn't really a Greek restaurant; it offers spanakopita and souvlaki but also serves something for everyone, including Italian risotto, Thai noodles, and Japanese sushi rolls, plus steaks and burgers. That said, some of the entrées (cranberry-crusted pork, pan-seared salmon) are excellent, and the prices are similar to quick-service.

ISLANDS OF ADVENTURE TOURING PLANS

Decisions, Decisions

When it comes to touring IOA efficiently in a single day, you have two basic choices:

If you're intent on experiencing The Wizarding World first thing during Early Park Admission, be at the turnstiles at least 30–60 minutes before the park opens. Once you're admitted, hurry to Hogsmeade and ride **Hagrid's Magical Creatures Motorbike Adventure,** followed by **Forbidden Journey** and then **Flight of the Hippogriff.** Next head to other must-experience attractions before the park gets crowded. The catch? Ride difficulties could have you stuck in a long line while crowds—and more lines—spread to other areas of IOA.

If you don't have Early Park Admission privileges at IOA, we recommend skipping Potterville first thing. Instead, try to grab a Virtual Line reservation for Hagrid's while enjoying other attractions in the meantime, starting at **Marvel Super Hero Island** and then heading for **Skull Island.** The Wizarding World usually clears out in the afternoon and is often empty in the last hour, even on busy days, meaning you can ride Forbidden Journey with a minimal wait if you get in line shortly before closing time.

Universal's Islands of Adventure One-Day Touring Plan (page 731)

THIS TOURING PLAN IS for guests without Park-to-Park Tickets and is appropriate for groups of all sizes and ages. It includes thrill rides that may induce motion sickness or get you wet. If the plan calls for you to experience an attraction that doesn't interest you, simply skip it and go to the next step. If you have young children in your party, customize the plan to fit their needs and take advantage of Universal's Child Swap at thrill rides.

The Best of Universal Studios Florida and Islands of Adventure in One Day (pages 733 and 734)

THIS TOURING PLAN IS for guests with One-Day Park-to-Park Tickets who wish to see the highlights of Universal Studios Florida and Islands of Adventure in a single day. The plan uses Hogwarts Express to get from one park to the other and then back again; you can walk back to the first park for the return leg if the line is too long. The plan includes a table-service lunch at Mythos (make reservations online a few days before your visit) and dinner at the Leaky Cauldron; during holiday periods, you may need to substitute a quick-service snack for one or both meals to fit in all of the plan's attractions.

UNIVERSAL STUDIOS FLORIDA

NOT TO BE MISSED AT UNIVERSAL STUDIOS FLORIDA	
• *The Bourne Stuntacular*	• Revenge of the Mummy
• Harry Potter and the Escape from Gringotts	• The Simpsons Ride
• Hogwarts Express–King's Cross Station	• Transformers: The Ride 3-D
• Men in Black Alien Attack	• *Universal Orlando's Horror Make-Up Show*
• Ollivanders	

UNIVERSAL STUDIOS FLORIDA OPENED IN JUNE 1990. At the time, it was almost four times the size of Disney's Hollywood Studios, and much more of the facility was accessible to visitors.

USF is laid out in a *P*-configuration, with the rounded part of the *P* sticking out disproportionately from the stem. Beyond the main entrance, a wide boulevard stretches past several shows and rides to the park's New York area. Branching off this pedestrian thoroughfare to the right are four streets that access other areas of the park and intersect a promenade circling a large lake.

The park is divided into eight areas: **Hollywood, Production Central, New York, San Francisco, The Wizarding World of Harry Potter–Diagon Alley, World Expo, Springfield: Home of the Simpsons,** and **Woody Woodpecker's KidZone.** Because most USF attractions aren't thematically integrated into the areas of the park in which they reside, we present them alphabetically rather than by area, with the exception of The Wizarding World.

USF offers all standard services and amenities, including stroller and wheelchair rentals, lockers, baby-care facilities, car assistance, and foreign-language assistance. Most of the park is accessible to disabled guests, and TDDs are available for the hearing-impaired. Almost all services are in the **Front Lot,** just inside the main entrance.

HOW MUCH TIME TO ALLOCATE

TOURING UNIVERSAL STUDIOS FLORIDA, including one meal and a visit to Diagon Alley, takes about 10–12 hours. Some theater attractions don't schedule performances until 11 a.m. or after. This means that early in the day, all park guests are concentrated among the limited number of attractions in operation.

You won't have to worry about any of this if you use our USF touring plan. We'll keep you a step ahead of the crowd and make sure that any given attraction is running by the time you get there.

UNIVERSAL STUDIOS FLORIDA ATTRACTIONS

Animal Actors on Location! (Universal Express)   ★★★½

PRESCHOOL ★★★★	GRADE SCHOOL ★★★★½	TEENS ★★★½
YOUNG ADULTS ★★★½	OVER 30 ★★★★	SENIORS ★★★★

What it is Animal tricks and comedy show. **Scope and scale** Major attraction. **When to go** After you've experienced all rides. **Duration of show** 25 minutes.

DESCRIPTION AND COMMENTS This show integrates video segments with live sketches, jokes, and animal tricks performed onstage. Live animals, some of which are veterans of TV and movies (and many of which were rescued from shelters), take part, and kids are invited to participate.

TOURING TIPS Sit in the center of the stadium about halfway up for the best chance to be picked. Check the entertainment schedule for showtimes.

The Bourne Stuntacular (Universal Express) ★★★★½

PRESCHOOL ★★	GRADE SCHOOL ★★★★	TEENS ★★★★½
YOUNG ADULTS ★★★★½	OVER 30 ★★★★½	SENIORS ★★★★

What it is Live-action stunt show. **Scope and scale** Headliner. **When to go** Scheduled showtimes; after you've experienced all rides. **Duration of show** 25 minutes.

DESCRIPTION AND COMMENTS This replacement for the revered *Terminator 2: 3-D* show once again blurs the line between stage and screen, blending flesh-and-blood stunt actors and automated moving props—including full-size vehicles and buildings—against a massive 130-foot-wide LED display. You don't need to know the first thing about Matt Damon's amnesiac assassin to enjoy watching Jason Bourne battle bad guys across Moroccan rooftops, or dangle beneath a helicopter flying above the streets of Dubai. Fast-paced, faithful to the film franchise, and filled with show-stopping special effects, this is easily the best stunt show in Orlando.

TOURING TIPS Shows start about every 45 minutes, but the theater tends to fill up, so arrive at least 15 minutes prior to the performance you wish to attend. Seats in the front row are great for fight choreography aficionados, but we prefer the view of the screen from the rear. The *Stuntacular* features earsplitting gunfire and brutal violence (including choke holds) but no blood or guts.

Curious George Goes to Town ★★½ (temporarily closed)

PRESCHOOL ★★★★★	GRADE SCHOOL ★★★★	TEENS ★★½
YOUNG ADULTS ★★	OVER 30 ★★½	SENIORS ★★

What it is Interactive playground. **Scope and scale** Minor attraction. **When to go** Anytime. **Comment** The place for rambunctious kids.

DESCRIPTION AND COMMENTS This interactive playground exemplifies the Universal obsession with wet stuff. In addition to innumerable spigots, pipes, and spray guns, two giant roof-mounted buckets periodically dump a thousand gallons of water on unsuspecting visitors below. Kids who want to stay dry can mess around in the foam-ball playground, also equipped with chutes, tubes, and ball blasters.

TOURING TIPS Visit after you've experienced all the major attractions.

Despicable Me Minion Mayhem (Universal Express) ★★★½

PRESCHOOL ★★★★	GRADE SCHOOL ★★★★½	TEENS ★★★★
YOUNG ADULTS ★★★★	OVER 30 ★★★★	SENIORS ★★★★

What it is Motion-simulator ride. **Scope and scale** Major attraction. **When to go** Immediately after park opening or just before closing. **Comment** Expect *long* waits in line. **Duration of ride** 5 minutes. **Loading speed** Moderate–slow.

DESCRIPTION AND COMMENTS Despicable Me Minion Mayhem involves high-tech motion simulators moving and reacting in sync with a cartoon projected onto an IMAX-like high-definition screen. The story line combines elements from the animated movie *Despicable Me,* starring Gru, the archvillain, along with his adopted daughters and his diminutive yellow Minions. During the queue and preshow, you visit Gru's house and are then ushered into his laboratory, where you're turned into a Minion. Guests disembark the ride into a disco party with a Minion meet and greet before making the obligatory exit through the gift shop.

TOURING TIPS Despicable Me Minion Mayhem is unfortunately situated at the very front of the park, within a few yards of the turnstiles. As a result, and because it's a popular attraction, long lines develop as soon as the park opens. If you're among the first to enter and the wait is 20 minutes or less, get in line for Despicable Me; then ride Hollywood Rip Ride Rockit, but if the line for Despicable Me exceeds 20 minutes, try late afternoon or the hour before the park closes. Stationary seating is available for those prone to motion sickness and for children less than 40 inches tall.

E.T. Adventure *(Universal Express)* ★★★½

PRESCHOOL ★★★★	GRADE SCHOOL ★★★½	TEENS ★★★
YOUNG ADULTS ★★★½	OVER 30 ★★★½	SENIORS ★★★★

What it is Indoor adventure ride based on the beloved movie. **Scope and scale** Major attraction. **When to go** Within 30 minutes of ride opening or late afternoon. **Comment** Must be 34" to ride. **Duration of ride** 4½ minutes. **Loading speed** Moderate.

DESCRIPTION AND COMMENTS Board a bicycle-like conveyance to escape with E.T., The Extra-Terrestrial, from earthly law enforcement officials and journey to his home planet. Concerning the latter, where E.T. is reunited with family and friends, Len likens it to *The Wizard of Oz*'s Technicolor scene, only reenacted with a cave full of naked mole rats. (C'mon, Len, where's the love?) Even so, E.T. is one of Universal's only family-friendly dark rides that relies on sets and robotics instead of screens, so we hope it sticks around for a long time to come.

TOURING TIPS Most preschoolers and grade-school children love E.T. Ride in the morning or late afternoon. On peak days, a time-saving single-rider line is occasionally opened.

Fast & Furious: Supercharged *(Universal Express)* ★★★

PRESCHOOL ★★	GRADE SCHOOL ★★★	TEENS ★★★
YOUNG ADULTS ★★★	OVER 30 ★★½	SENIORS ★★½

What it is Car chase 3-D motion simulator. **Scope and scale** Headliner. **When to go** After experiencing the other headliners. **Comments** Single-rider and Virtual Lines available; must be 40" to ride. **Duration of ride** 5 minutes. **Loading speed** Fast.

DESCRIPTION AND COMMENTS Inspired by the $5 billion box office behemoth that is Universal's *Fast & Furious* franchise, Fast & Furious: Supercharged begins in a queue themed to an industrial warehouse; here, you can check out some of the high-performance cars showcased in the films. Two preshows, in which live hosts interact awkwardly with prerecorded clips of Jordana Brewster (Mia) and Chris "Ludacris" Bridges (Tej), establish the backstory for anyone who hasn't seen the nine-and-counting *Furious* films.

After boarding specially designed tramlike "party buses," you're taken to an underground club, where a postrace rave party is in full swing until the feds crash the party in search of a crucial crime witness who's hiding among the guests. Lead characters Dom Toretto (Vin Diesel), Luke Hobbs (Dwayne "The Rock" Johnson), Letty Ortiz (Michelle Rodriguez), and Roman Pearce (Tyrese Gibson) appear in holographic form to rescue you from Owen Shaw (Luke Evans), the bad guy from *Fast & Furious 6*. In the attraction's climax, a 360-degree projection tunnel with hydraulic platforms, 400-foot-long screens, and 4K projectors makes it seem as if your ride vehicle is in the middle of a high-stakes car chase, speeding at 100-plus mph through a West Coast urban jungle.

Fast & Furious: Supercharged is similar to Skull Island: Reign of Kong at IOA, but without the immersive 3-D or impressive animatronics. The dialogue and visual effects are shockingly cheesy, even by theme park standards—Len considers this a feature, not a bug—but it all goes by in such a nitro-fueled blur that it may not matter to fans of the flicks.

TOURING TIPS Supercharged periodically offers a free Virtual Line system that lets you select your ride time using the Universal Orlando mobile app (see page 605); you can also grab a paper ticket from the ride's kiosks. You'll save time only if the standby wait is more than 30 minutes, though. Standard standby, Universal Express, and single-rider lines are also available.

The best views are from the center/right seats in the first bus—stay to the left if the queue splits before the loading dock. Though less scary than the King Kong ride, Supercharged has a slightly higher height requirement; luckily, the slot-car-racing game in the Child Swap room may be more fun than the actual attraction.

Fear Factor Live (Universal Express)
★★½ (seasonal)

PRESCHOOL ★★½	GRADE SCHOOL ★★★★	TEENS ★★★½
YOUNG ADULTS ★★★½	OVER 30 ★★★½	SENIORS ★★★

What it is Live version of the gross-out-stunt TV show. **Scope and scale** Headliner. **When to go** 3–5 shows daily; crowds are smallest at the first and second-to-last shows. **Comments** Too intense for kids age 8 and younger. Contestants for the stage show must be 18 years or older (photo ID required) and weigh at least 110 pounds. Anyone who doesn't wish to compete in the main show can sign up for the Critter Challenge or the Food Challenge; with an adult's permission, volunteers as young as age 16 can compete in the latter. **Duration of show** 30 minutes.

DESCRIPTION AND COMMENTS *Fear Factor Live* is a stage version of the reality show that originally aired on NBC and was then revived for MTV. In the theme park iteration, six volunteers compete for a prize package that contains Universal swag like T-shirts.

Contestants must hang from a bar two-and-a-half stories in the air while heavy-duty fans blast their faces; grab beanbags out of a tank full of eels; and, for the grand finale, scramble up a wall, jump into a car that is lifted in the air, and then hit a target with a rocket launcher.

Between rounds, intermission entertainment includes the Desert Hat Ordeal, where a lunatic audience member has spiders, snakes, roaches, or scorpions placed on his or her face, and the Food Challenge, in which volunteers try to chug a "smoothie" made of curdled milk, mystery meat, and various live bugs without vomiting.

TOURING TIPS The contestants for the physical stunts are chosen early in the morning and between performances outside of the theater; anyone demented enough to volunteer should arrive at least 75 minutes before showtime to sign papers and complete some obligatory training. The contestants for the Critter and Food Challenges are selected directly from the audience. *Fear Factor Live* mercifully goes on hiatus in the fall to turn its stadium over to Halloween Horror Nights.

Fievel's Playland ★★★

PRESCHOOL ★★★★½	GRADE SCHOOL ★★★★	TEENS ★½
YOUNG ADULTS ★½	OVER 30 ★★★	SENIORS ★★★½

What it is Children's play area with waterslide. **Scope and scale** Minor attraction. **When to go** Anytime. **Loading speed** Slow for the waterslide.

DESCRIPTION AND COMMENTS This playground features ordinary household items reproduced on a giant scale: a huge boot, a sardine-can fountain, huge spoons, and such. Most of the playground is reserved for preschoolers, but a combination waterslide–raft ride is open to all ages. Except for that, there's no waiting in line, and you can stay as long as you want.

TOURING TIPS The water ride is extremely slow to load and carries just 300 riders an hour. With an average wait of 20–30 minutes, the 16-second ride isn't worth the trouble, and, yes, you *will* get soaked. A lack of shade ensures that the playground is scorching during the summer.

Hollywood Rip Ride Rockit (*Universal Express*) ★★★★

PRESCHOOL ★	GRADE SCHOOL ★★★★	TEENS ★★★★½
YOUNG ADULTS ★★★★½	OVER 30 ★★★★	SENIORS ★★★

What it is High-tech roller coaster. **Scope and scale** Headliner. **When to go** The first hour after park opening or late afternoon. **Comments** Single-rider line available; must be 51" to ride. **Duration of ride** 2½ minutes. **Loading speed** Moderate.

DESCRIPTION AND COMMENTS A sit-down X-Car coaster, Rip Ride Rockit runs on a 3,800-foot steel track, with a maximum height of 167 feet and a top speed of 65 mph. You ascend—vertically—at 11 feet per second to crest the 17-story-tall first hill, the second-highest point reached by any roller coaster in Orlando (only Mako at SeaWorld is higher). The drop is almost vertical, too, and launches you into Double Take, a 136-foot-tall loop inversion in which you begin on the inside of the loop, twist to the outside at the top (so you're upright), and then twist back inside the loop for the descent. You next hurtle into a stretch of track shaped like a musical treble clef, followed by a spiraling negative-gravity maneuver: You feel like you're in a corkscrew inversion, but you never actually go upside down.

Like Rock 'n' Roller Coaster at Hollywood Studios, this coaster has a musical soundtrack. With Rip Ride Rockit, however, you get to choose the genre of music you want to hear as you ride: classic rock, country, disco, pop, or rap. When it's all over, Universal sells photos and a DVD of your ride that intercuts stock coaster footage with clips of you screaming.

The "Triple R" isn't as smooth as it used to be, subjecting you to lots of side-to-side jarring. A Wisconsin reader warns:

I've ridden coasters over 400 feet tall and with speeds in excess of 120 mph, but I've never ridden one as rough as Rip Ride Rockit. With the beating my head and neck took, I'll never ride it again.

TOURING TIPS Because the ride is so close to the USF entrance, it's a crowd magnet. Your only chance to ride without a long wait is to be one of the first to enter the park when it opens.

Kang & Kodos' Twirl 'n' Hurl (*Universal Express*) ★★★

PRESCHOOL ★★★★	GRADE SCHOOL ★★★½	TEENS ★★★
YOUNG ADULTS ★★★	OVER 30 ★★★	SENIORS ★★★

What it is Spinning ride. **Scope and scale** Minor attraction. **When to go** Before 11 a.m. or whenever there are 50 people or fewer in line. **Comment** Rarely has long lines but loads slowly. **Duration of ride** 1½ minutes. **Loading speed** Slow.

DESCRIPTION AND COMMENTS The Twirl 'n' Hurl is Dumbo with Bart Simpson's sense of humor. Tentacled aliens Kang and Kodos hold pictures of *Simpsons* characters; you make the characters speak and spin by steering your craft to the proper altitude. All the while, Kang exhorts you (loudly) to destroy Springfield while haughtily insulting humans. Preschoolers enjoy the ride; older kids love the snarky narration.

TOURING TIPS Twirl 'n' Hurl rarely attracts long lines, but slow loading speeds ensure a long wait. It usually opens at 10 a.m., so try to ride before 11 a.m. If you want to enjoy the jokes without the wait, you can easily hear them from the sidelines.

Men in Black Alien Attack *(Universal Express)* ★★★★

PRESCHOOL ★★★	GRADE SCHOOL ★★★★	TEENS ★★★★
YOUNG ADULTS ★★★★	OVER 30 ★★★★	SENIORS ★★★★

What it is Interactive dark thrill ride. **Scope and scale** Headliner. **When to go** During the first 2 hours the park is open or anytime using the single-rider line. **Comments** Single-rider line available; must be 42" to ride. **Duration of ride** 4½ minutes. **Loading speed** Moderate–fast.

DESCRIPTION AND COMMENTS In this ride based on the movie of the same name, you volunteer as a Men in Black (MIB) trainee. MIB Chief Zed briefs you on the finer points of alien spotting and familiarizes you with your training vehicle and your weapon, an alien "zapper." Then you load up and are dispatched on an innocuous training mission that immediately deteriorates into a situation where only you are in a position to prevent aliens from taking over the universe.

If you saw the movie, you understand that the aliens are mostly giant bugs and that zapping them makes them explode into myriad gooey body parts. Thus, the meat of the ride (no pun intended) consists of careening around Manhattan in your MIB vehicle and shooting aliens.

TOURING TIPS Each of the 120 or so alien figures has sensors that activate special effects and respond to your zapper—aim for the eyes and keep shooting until the aliens' eyes turn red. Targets above you score the most points; look for aliens behind second-story windows. Avoid a long wait and ride during the first 2 hours the park is open, or try the single-rider line if you don't mind splitting your group.

Race Through New York Starring Jimmy Fallon
(Universal Express) ★★★½

PRESCHOOL ★★★½	GRADE SCHOOL ★★★★	TEENS ★★★★
YOUNG ADULTS ★★★½	OVER 30 ★★★½	SENIORS ★★★½

What it is Comedic 3-D simulator ride. **Scope and scale** Headliner. **When to go** First 2 hours of the day or according to your Virtual Line return time. **Comments** Virtual Line may be required; must be 40" to ride. **Duration of ride** 4 minutes. **Loading speed** Moderate.

DESCRIPTION AND COMMENTS Race Through New York is housed in a replica of NBC's historic 30 Rock offices in Manhattan. Guests, except for those with Universal Express, are assigned a Virtual Line reservation time via Universal Orlando's mobile app or an automated kiosk (see page 605).

When your appointed time arrives, you return to the ride entrance, where you'll be directed up to a fancy lounge outfitted with couches and touchscreen tables with video games inspired by *The Tonight Show Starring Jimmy Fallon*. The main attractions, however, are live appearances by some *Tonight Show* regulars: the Ragtime Gals, a male vocal quintet that performs tongue-in-cheek barbershop interpretations of pop hits, and Hashtag the Panda, a goofy dancer in an animal costume.

When the color of the lights changes to match your card, it's time to make your way to Jimmy Fallon's studio. The Roots, Fallon's house band, rap the safety instructions before you enter a 72-seat theater with a large screen; here, you'll don 3-D glasses and race against Fallon in his souped-up "Tonight Rider" roadster. Starting at the *Tonight Show* studio, the competition sends you careening through the streets and subways of New York and eventually to, yes, the moon.

The queueless experience and preshow areas get a lot of points, and the ride itself has some of the sharpest visuals and smoothest movement in the Universal repertoire. But it breaks no new technical ground for the genre, and it relies on guests recognizing Fallon's stable of characters (like Ew! Girl and Tight Pants Man) for its jokes—which grow stale after several viewings.

TOURING TIPS Reserve your Virtual Line pass through the Universal mobile app for early afternoon, when other attractions generally have their longest lines. If return times have run out for the day, check at the attraction an hour or two before park closing to see if they're taking walk-ins.

Revenge of the Mummy *(Universal Express)* ★★★★½

PRESCHOOL ★½	GRADE SCHOOL ★★★½	TEENS ★★★★½
YOUNG ADULTS ★★★★½	OVER 30 ★★★★½	SENIORS ★★★★

What it is Combination dark ride–roller coaster. **Scope and scale** Headliner. **When to go** The first 2 hours the park is open or after 4 p.m. **Comments** Single-rider line available; must be 48″ to ride. **Duration of ride** 3 minutes. **Loading speed** Moderate.

DESCRIPTION AND COMMENTS In this indoor dark ride based on the *Mummy* flicks, you fight off "deadly curses and vengeful creatures" while you fly through Egyptian tombs and other spooky places on a high-tech roller coaster. The special effects are showing their age but are still pretty good: video effects, animatronics, lighting, and enough fire-spewing gas vents to roast a chicken.

The ride begins slowly, passing through various chambers, including one where flesh-eating scarab beetles descend on you. Suddenly your vehicle stops, then drops backward and rotates. The next thing you know, you're shot at high speed up the first hill of the roller coaster. Though it's a wild ride by anyone's definition, the emphasis remains as much on the visuals, robotics, and special effects as on the ride itself.

TOURING TIPS Try to ride during the first 2 hours the park is open. If lines are long, the singles line is often faster than Universal Express. While most grade-schoolers we surveyed who were plucky enough to ride the Mummy like it, one dad feels we underestimate the fright factor:

My second-grader (who wasn't scared at all on Space Mountain) was terrified during this ride and cried afterward. Even I thought it was quite scary, and other adults on our ride echoed the same.

Shrek 4-D *(Universal Express)* ★★★½

PRESCHOOL ★★★½	GRADE SCHOOL ★★★½	TEENS ★★★
YOUNG ADULTS ★★★	OVER 30 ★★★	SENIORS ★★★½

What it is 3-D movie. **Scope and scale** Major attraction. **When to go** Anytime after you've experienced the rides. **Duration of show** 20 minutes.

DESCRIPTION AND COMMENTS The preshow has the villainous Lord Farquaad describing his posthumous plan to reclaim his lost bride, Princess

Fiona, who married Shrek. (The plan is posthumous since Lord Farquaad ostensibly died in the movie and it's his ghost making the plans, but whatever.) Guests then move to the main theater, don their 3-D glasses, and recline in seats equipped with "tactile transducers" and "pneumatic air propulsion and water spray nodules capable of both vertical and horizontal motion." As the 3-D film plays, guests are also subjected to smells relevant to the on-screen action (hoo boy).

This attraction is a mixed bag. It's irreverent, frantic, laugh-out-loud funny, and iconoclastic (Disney gets skewered, with Pinocchio, the Three Little Pigs, and Tinker Bell all sucked into the mayhem). But the video quality is dated by today's 4K standards, the story is incoherently disconnected from the clever preshow, and the bucking seats swiftly become a pain in the butt.

TOURING TIPS If lines are longer than 20 minutes, try visiting during mealtimes or in the last 2 hours the park is open. *Shrek 4-D* shuts down one of its two theaters in the fall to hold a haunted house for Halloween Horror Nights, greatly increasing wait times.

The Simpsons Ride   *(Universal Express)*   ★★★★

PRESCHOOL ★★½	GRADE SCHOOL ★★★★	TEENS ★★★½
YOUNG ADULTS ★★★½	OVER 30 ★★★½	SENIORS ★★★½

What it is Mega-simulator ride. **Scope and scale** Headliner. **When to go** During the first 2 hours the park is open or after 4 p.m. **Comments** Must be 40" to ride; not recommended for pregnant women or anyone prone to motion sickness. **Duration of ride** 4⅓ minutes, plus preshow. **Loading speed** Moderate.

DESCRIPTION AND COMMENTS This simulator ride is similar to Despicable Me Minion Mayhem and Star Tours at Disney's Hollywood Studios, but it has a larger screen more like that of Soarin' at EPCOT.

Two preshows have *Simpsons* characters speaking sequentially on different video screens in the queue; their comments help define the characters for guests who are unfamiliar with the TV show. The story line has the conniving Sideshow Bob secretly arriving at Krustyland amusement park and plotting his revenge on Krusty the Clown and Bart, who once revealed that Sideshow Bob had committed a crime for which he'd framed Krusty. Sideshow Bob gets even by making things go wrong with the attractions that the Simpsons (and you) are riding.

TOURING TIPS Like the TV show on which it's based, The Simpsons Ride has a definite edge—some parents, in fact, may find the humor a little crass for younger kids. Expect large crowds all day. Because the screen you sit in front of is a giant curved dome, sitting outside the central sweet spot may worsen motion sickness. For the best experience, ask the attendant at the bottom of the ramps for Level 2; then ask the next attendant you see for Room 6.

Transformers: The Ride 3-D   *(Universal Express)*   ★★★★

PRESCHOOL ★★★	GRADE SCHOOL ★★★★	TEENS ★★★★
YOUNG ADULTS ★★★★	OVER 30 ★★★★	SENIORS ★★★½

What it is Multisensory 3-D dark ride. **Scope and scale** Super-headliner. **When to go** First hour the park is open or after 4 p.m. **Comments** Single-rider line available; must be 40" to ride. **Duration of ride** 4½ minutes. **Loading speed** Moderate-fast.

DESCRIPTION AND COMMENTS Hasbro's Transformers—those toy robots from the 1980s that you turned and twisted into trucks and planes—have been, er, transformed into director Michael Bay's blockbuster movie franchise and then into a theme park attraction.

The story line: Decepticon baddies are after the Allspark, source of cybernetic sentience. Your job is to safeguard the shard with the help of your Autobot allies Optimus Prime and Bumblebee.

The plot amounts to little more than a giant game of keep-away, and the uninitiated will likely be unable to tell one meteoric mass of metal from another, but you'll be too dazzled by the debris whizzing by to notice. Transformers: The Ride 3-D is very intense and immersive, but it doesn't hold up as well after repeated rides as The Amazing Adventures of Spider-Man, whose humor, heart, and moving props it lacks.

TOURING TIPS This ride draws crowds—your only solace is that The Wizarding World of Harry Potter-Diagon Alley draws even larger throngs. The single-rider line will get you on board faster, but it closes when it gets backed up. Front-row seats may be too close to the screen for you to focus on the action.

Universal Orlando's Horror Make-Up Show
(Universal Express) ★★★★½

PRESCHOOL ★★	GRADE SCHOOL ★★★½	TEENS ★★★★
YOUNG ADULTS ★★★★	OVER 30 ★★★★	SENIORS ★★★★½

What it is Theater presentation on the art of movie makeup. **Scope and scale** Major attraction. **When to go** Scheduled showtimes and after you've experienced all rides. **Comment** May frighten some young children. **Duration of show** 25 minutes.

DESCRIPTION AND COMMENTS Lively, well-paced look at how makeup artists create film monsters, realistic wounds, severed limbs, and other assorted grossness. The *Horror Make-Up Show*'s humor and tongue-in-cheek style transcend the gruesome effects, and most folks (including preschoolers) take the blood and guts in stride.

TOURING TIPS Look for the second-story windows to the left of the theater marquee for a touching tribute to victims of the 2016 Pulse nightclub tragedy.

Woody Woodpecker's Nuthouse Coaster
(Universal Express) ★★½

PRESCHOOL ★★★★½	GRADE SCHOOL ★★★★	TEENS ★★★
YOUNG ADULTS ★★★	OVER 30 ★★★	SENIORS ★★★½

What it is Kids' roller coaster. **Scope and scale** Minor attraction. **When to go** Anytime. **Comments** Must be 36″ to ride; children 36″–48″ must be accompanied by a supervising companion. **Duration of ride** 1 minute. **Loading speed** *Slooow.*

DESCRIPTION AND COMMENTS This children's roller coaster is virtually identical to the Magic Kingdom's Barnstormer: It's small enough for little ones to enjoy but sturdy enough for adults, though its moderate speed might unnerve some younger kids (the minimum height to ride is 36 inches). The entire ride lasts about a minute, and at least 20 of those 60 seconds are spent cranking the train up the first (and only) lift hill.

TOURING TIPS Visit after you've experienced the major attractions. If your young child has never before experienced a roller coaster, this would be an appropriate first attempt.

THE WIZARDING WORLD OF HARRY POTTER-DIAGON ALLEY

SECRETED BEHIND A LONDON STREET FACADE that features **Grimmauld Place** and **Wyndham's Theatre,** Diagon Alley is accessed through a secluded entrance in the middle of the facade. As in the Harry Potter books and films, the unmarked portal is concealed within a magical brick wall that is ordinarily reserved for wizards and the like. The endless procession of Muggles in tank tops and flip-flops will leave little doubt where that entryway is, however.

When Early Park Admission is in effect, USF admits eligible on-site resort guests 1 hour before the general public, with the turnstiles opening 75–90 minutes before the official opening time. Arrive at least 30 minutes before early entry starts; during peak season, we recommend showing up on the very first boat or bus from your hotel. If you're a day guest visiting on a busy Early Park Admission day, Diagon Alley may already be packed when you arrive.

Even when Early Park Admission isn't offered, all guests may enter Diagon Alley from the front gates 15–30 minutes before park opening, and hotel guests in IOA will arrive via Hogwarts Express a little after that, though Harry Potter and the Escape from Gringotts doesn't begin operating until close to official opening time.

Wizarding World–Diagon Alley Attractions

Harry Potter and the Escape from Gringotts
(Universal Express) ★★★★★

PRESCHOOL ★★½	GRADE SCHOOL ★★★★½	TEENS ★★★★½
YOUNG ADULTS ★★★★★	OVER 30 ★★★★½	SENIORS ★★★★½

What it is Super-high-tech 3-D dark ride with roller-coaster elements. **Scope and scale** Super-headliner. **When to go** Immediately after park opening or just before closing. **Comments** Single-rider line available; must be 42" to ride. **Duration of ride** 4½ minutes. **Loading speed** Moderate–fast.

DESCRIPTION AND COMMENTS Like Harry Potter and the Forbidden Journey at IOA, Harry Potter and the Escape from Gringotts incorporates a substantial part of the overall experience into its elaborate queue, which (like Hogwarts Castle) even nonriders should experience. You enter through the bank's lobby, where you're critically appraised by glowering animatronic goblins before visiting with Bill Weasley, Ron's curse-breaking big brother. Then you take a simulated 9-mile plunge into the earth aboard an "elevator" with a bouncing floor and ceiling projections. All this is before you pick up your 3-D goggles and then ascend a spiral staircase into the stalactite-festooned boarding cave where your vault cart awaits.

Escape from Gringotts merges Revenge of the Mummy's indoor-coaster aspects with The Amazing Adventures of Spider-Man's seamless integration of high-resolution 3-D film and massive sculptural sets, while adding a few new tricks such as independently rotating cars and motion-simulator bases built into the track. The result is a ride that combines favorite innovations from its predecessors in an exhilarating new way, making it one of the greatest themed thrill attractions of all time.

As far as physical thrills go, Gringotts falls somewhere between Disney's Seven Dwarfs Mine Train and Space Mountain, with only one short (albeit unique) drop and no upside-down flips.

TOURING TIPS If you're a Universal resort guest and you qualify for Early Park Admission, take advantage, or use Universal Express or the single-rider line (which bypasses all preshows). Otherwise, try the attraction around lunchtime or in the late afternoon; wait times usually peak after opening but become reasonable later in the day. Note that you must leave your bags in a free locker.

Hogwarts Express *(Universal Express)* ★★★★½

| PRESCHOOL ★★★★½ | GRADE SCHOOL ★★★★½ | TEENS ★★★★½ |
| YOUNG ADULTS ★★★★½ | OVER 30 ★★★★½ | SENIORS ★★★★½ |

What it is Transportation attraction. **Scope and scale** Headliner. **When to go** Late morning or just before park closing. **Comment** Requires a Park-to-Park Ticket to ride. **Duration of ride** 4 minutes. **Loading speed** Moderate.

DESCRIPTION AND COMMENTS As in the Harry Potter novels and films, Diagon Alley at USF is connected to Hogsmeade at IOA by the Hogwarts Express train. The counterpart to Hogsmeade Station in IOA is USF's King's Cross station, located a few doors down from Diagon Alley's hidden entrance. (Note that King's Cross has a separate entrance and exit from Diagon Alley—you can't go directly between them without crossing through the London Waterfront.)

The passage to Platform 9¾, from which Hogwarts students depart on their way to school, is concealed from Muggles by a seemingly solid brick wall, through which you'll witness guests ahead of you dematerializing. The train itself looks authentic to the nth degree, from the billowing steam to the brass fixtures and upholstery in your eight-passenger private cabin.

Along your one-way journey, moving images projected beyond the windows of the car simulate the streets of London and the Scottish countryside rolling past. You experience a different presentation coming and going; plus, there are surprise appearances by secondary characters (Fred and George Weasley, Hagrid) and threats en route (Dementors, licorice spiders), augmented by sound effects in the cars.

TOURING TIPS You must have a valid Park-to-Park Ticket to ride; disembarking passengers must enter the second park and, if desired, queue again for their return trip. You'll be allowed (nay, encouraged) to upgrade your 1-Park Base Ticket at the station entrance. If the posted wait is more than 15 minutes, it's typically quicker to walk to the other Wizarding World than to take the train.

Ollivanders ★★★★

| PRESCHOOL ★★★½ | GRADE SCHOOL ★★★★½ | TEENS ★★★★½ |
| YOUNG ADULTS ★★★★½ | OVER 30 ★★★★ | SENIORS ★★★★ |

What it is Combination wizarding demonstration and shopping op. **Scope and scale** Major attraction. **When to go** After riding Harry Potter and the Escape from Gringotts. **Comment** Audience stands to watch the show. **Duration of show** 6 minutes.

DESCRIPTION AND COMMENTS Unlike the branch location in Hogsmeade (see page 619), the Diagon Alley Ollivanders is in its rightful location per the books, and in much larger digs. The shop has multiple separate choosing chambers, where wands choose a wizard (rather than vice versa).

TOURING TIPS Check out the self-sweeping broom (shades of *Fantasia*) while waiting for the show. If your young 'un is selected to test-drive a wand, be forewarned that you'll have to buy it if you want to take it home. Ollivanders may distribute free return-time reservations when the standby wait becomes excessive; these can all be claimed by midmorning on busy days. Ask an employee at the attraction entrance for details.

Wizarding World Entertainment

Take a moment to spot **Kreacher** (the house elf regularly peers from a second-story window above 12 Grimmauld Place) and chat with the

Knight Bus conductor and his Caribbean-accented shrunken head. Look down the alley to the rounded facade of **Gringotts Wizarding Bank,** where a 40-foot fire-breathing Ukrainian Ironbelly dragon (as seen in *Harry Potter and the Deathly Hallows: Part 2*) perches atop the dome.

To the right of Escape from Gringotts is **Carkitt Market,** a canopy-covered plaza where short live shows are staged every half hour or so. *Celestina Warbeck and the Banshees* (★★★½) showcases the swinging sorceress, who sings jazzy tunes titled and inspired by J. K. Rowling herself, and *Tales of Beedle the Bard* (★★★½) recounts the Three Brothers fable from *Deathly Hallows* with puppets crafted by Michael Curry (*Festival of the Lion King, Finding Nemo—The Musical*).

Intersecting Diagon Alley near the Leaky Cauldron is **Knockturn Alley,** a labyrinth of twisting passageways where the Harry Potter bad guys hang out. A covered walk-through area with a projected sky creating perpetual night, it features spooky special effects in the faux shop windows (don't miss the creeping tattoos and crawling spiders).

UNIVERSAL STUDIOS FLORIDA ENTERTAINMENT

IN ADDITION TO THE SHOWS profiled earlier, USF offers a range of street entertainment. Costumed comic-book and cartoon characters, along with movie star look-alikes, roam the park for photo ops. Dream-Works Destination (★★½), a dance party and photo op with characters from *Shrek, Kung Fu Panda, Trolls,* and other DreamWorks films, has taken over the former Barney theater in KidZone. The Universal app notes times and places for character greetings and shows.

The Blues Brothers Show (★★★½) is a 12-minute R&B concert held in the New York area, featuring Jake and Elwood performing hit songs from the classic 1980 movie musical. The concert is a great pick-me-up, and the short run time keeps the energy high. **Marilyn Monroe and the Diamond Bellas** (★★½) perform a 4-minute song-and-dance routine in front of the *Horror Make-Up Show,* and the **Beat Builders** (★★★) are a *Stomp*-style quartet of beefy guys who drum on the scaffolding outside Louie's Italian Restaurant.

The Disney-like **Universal's Superstar Parade** (★★★) features dancers and performers, four large and elaborate floats inspired by cartoons, and a very mixed bag of street-prowling Universal characters. The parade isn't very long, and the two stops that previously featured choreographed ensemble numbers have been eliminated, so the whole procession takes a little over 5 minutes to pass by any particular point along its path.

The parade begins at the Esoteric Pictures gate in Hollywood between the *Horror Make-Up Show* and Cafe La Bamba. It turns right; immediately makes a hard left around Mel's Drive-In; and then follows the waterfront past Transformers: The Ride 3-D, toward San Francisco. From here, it turns left at Louie's Italian Restaurant and proceeds along 5th Avenue, past Revenge of the Mummy. At the end of 5th Avenue, the parade takes a left onto 57th Avenue/Plaza of the Stars and heads toward the front of the park, where it makes another left onto Hollywood Boulevard, from whence it disappears backstage through the gate where it entered. The best viewing spots are along 5th Avenue, on the front steps of faux buildings in New York.

Universal Orlando's Cinematic Celebration (★★★★), USF's big night-time spectacular, is performed seasonally at park closing on the lagoon in the middle of the park. The 19-minute presentation pays tribute to favorite film franchises featured in the Universal parks, including *Jurassic Park/Jurassic World, Despicable Me, Transformers,* and *Harry Potter.* The scenes are projected onto enormous "screens" made by spraying water from the lagoon into the air (similar to *Fantasmic!* at Disney's Hollywood Studios) and augmented by more than 120 illuminated fountains. Fireworks, moving lights, and lasers are also used to good effect throughout the presentation. It's easily the best nighttime show USF has offered this century and well worth sticking around to see.

The terraced **Central Park,** across the lagoon from San Francisco, is the primary viewing location for this show, with additional viewing between **Mel's Drive-In** and Transformers: The Ride 3-D, and near Duff Brewery. No reservations are required, and you should be able to get a good view by arriving about 15 minutes before showtime.

DINING AT UNIVERSAL STUDIOS FLORIDA

SPRINGFIELD: HOME OF THE SIMPSONS has a number of wacky *Simpsons*-inspired eateries: **Krusty Burger, The Frying Dutchman** for seafood, **Cletus' Chicken Shack, Luigi's Pizza, Lard Lad Donuts, Lisa's Teahouse of Horror, Bumblebee Man's Taco Truck, Duff Brewery,** and **Moe's Tavern.** Portions are large and the quality is good.

The best quick-service food in USF is served at the **Leaky Cauldron.** Diagon Alley's flagship restaurant serves authentically hearty British pub fare such as bangers and mash (sausages and mashed potatoes), cottage pie, toad-in-the-hole, Guinness stew, and a ploughman's platter for two of Scotch eggs and imported cheeses. When you're done, head over to **Florean Fortescue's Ice-Cream Parlour** and cap off your meal with some delicious Butterbeer ice cream.

USF's two sit-down restaurants are **Finnegan's Bar and Grill,** in New York, and **Lombard's Seafood Grille,** in San Francisco. Finnegan's serves burgers and wings as well as fish-and-chips and other takes on Irish cuisine. Lombard's is the better restaurant, but it's not in the same league (in terms of price or quality) as, say, DHS's Hollywood Brown Derby.

UNIVERSAL STUDIOS FLORIDA TOURING PLANS
Universal Studios Florida One-Day Touring Plan *(page 732)*

THIS PLAN IS FOR GUESTS without Park-to-Park Tickets and includes every recommended attraction at USF. If a ride or show is listed that you don't want to experience, skip that step and proceed to the next. Move quickly from attraction to attraction, and if possible, hold off on lunch until after experiencing at least six rides.

The Best of Universal Studios Florida and Islands of Adventure in One Day *(pages 733 and 744)*

SEE PAGE 624 for the description of this plan.

The WATER PARKS

YOU'RE SOAKING *in* IT!

DISNEY AND UNIVERSAL ORLANDO operate water parks alongside their Orlando theme parks. Disney's water parks are **Blizzard Beach** and **Typhoon Lagoon,** and Universal's is **Volcano Bay.**

Disney's and Universal's water parks are much larger and more elaborately themed than the local or regional water parks you may have visited. Almost all of the waterslides, wave pools, and lazy rivers at these parks are larger and longer than those at local and regional water parks too.

COST One day of admission to either of Disney's water parks costs around $73 for adults and $68 for kids, including tax. Peak season is late May–late September. If you visit outside of that window, Disney offers a discount of around $5 per ticket.

If you buy your Walt Disney World admission tickets before leaving home and you're considering the **Water Park and Sports** (WPS) add-on (see page 71), you might want to wait until you arrive and have some degree of certainty about the weather during your stay. You can add the WPS option at any Disney resort or Guest Relations window at the theme parks. This is true regardless of whether you purchased your Base Tickets separately or as part of a package. Also note that if you're planning to visit only one theme park per day and you're planning only one day to visit a water park, buying separate water-park admission is almost always cheaper than buying the PHP add-on.

Admission to Volcano Bay (including tax) costs $75–$91 per adult ($69–$85 for kids ages 3–9) for one day or $59–$80 as an upgrade to any multiday ticket.

GETTING THERE Disney provides regular daily bus service between its resorts and water parks. Likewise, Universal runs shuttle buses between most of its resort hotels and Volcano Bay; Universal's Aventura and Cabana Bay hotels are adjacent to Volcano Bay, so walking is usually faster.

The best way to get to these parks from off-site is to drive if you have a car. Parking is free and close by at Disney's water parks; Universal's parking fee is $28 (including tax), and you'll take a shuttle bus from the parking structure to the water park. If you don't have a car, then a ride-hailing service, taxi, or shuttle can drop you off at the park entrance.

WHEN TO GO

DISNEY AND UNIVERSAL generally open their water parks every day of the year. Orlando-area temperatures can vary from the high 40s to the low 80s during December, January, and February. When it's warmer out, these off-season months can serve up a dandy water-park experience, as this Batavia, Ohio, reader confirms:

unofficial **TIP**
If your schedule is flexible, a good time to visit the water parks is midafternoon to late in the day, when the weather has cleared after a storm.

> *Going to Blizzard Beach in December was the best decision ever! They told us at the entrance that if the park didn't reach 100—yes, I said 100—people by noon, they would be closing. I guess they got to 101, because it stayed open but was virtually empty. There was no wait for anything all day! In June we waited in line for an hour for Summit Plummet, but in December it was just the amount of time it took to walk up the stairs. We had the enormous wave pool to ourselves. We did everything in the entire park and ate lunch in less than 3 hours. It was perfect. The weather was slightly chilly at 71°F and overcast with very light rain, but the water was heated, so we were fine.*

We've had experiences similar to this reader's: We visited Volcano Bay on a Saturday in September when the daily high temperature was "only" 72°F. So few people were in the park with us that we were able to count all of them. We never encountered a line longer than 10 people for any slide.

That said, the water parks may close if the daytime high temperatures dip much below 60°F or so. If you're visiting during late fall, winter, or early spring and temperatures are low, check the park's website the day before you visit.

AVOIDING LINES The best way to avoid standing in lines is to visit the water parks when they're least crowded. Our research, conducted before the pandemic over many weeks in the parks, indicates that tourists, not locals, make up the majority of visitors on any given day. And because

COVID *tip*
Blizzard Beach and Volcano Bay are open. At press time, there was no reopening date for Typhoon Lagoon.

weekends are popular travel days, the water parks tend to be less crowded then. In fact, of the weekend days we evaluated, the parks never reached full capacity; during the week, conversely, one or both

Disney parks closed every Thursday we monitored, and both closed at least once every other weekday. Therefore, we recommend going on a Monday or Friday.

A mom from Manlius, New York, describes what *crowded* means:

We visited Typhoon Lagoon, arriving before opening so we could stake out a shady spot. The kids loved it until the lines got long (11 a.m.–noon), but I hated it. It made Coney Island seem like a deserted island in the Bahamas. Floating on Castaway Creek was really unpleasant. Whirling around in a chlorinated concrete ditch with some stranger's feet in my face, periodically getting squirted by water guns, passing under cascades of cold water, and getting hung up by the crowd is not at all relaxing for me. My husband and I then decided to bob in the Surf Pool. After about 10 minutes of being tossed around like corks in boiling water, we sought the peace of our shady little territory—which in our absence had become much, much smaller.

A visitor from Middletown, New York, had a somewhat better experience at the same park:

On our second trip to Typhoon Lagoon, we dispensed with the locker rental (having planned to stay for only the morning when it was least crowded) and at park's opening just took right off for the Storm Slides before the masses arrived—it was perfect! We must have ridden the slides at least five times before any kind of line built up, and then we were also able to ride the tube and raft rides (Keelhaul and Mayday Falls) in a similar uncrowded, quick fashion because everyone else was busy getting their lockers!

When Typhoon Lagoon or Blizzard Beach reopens after inclement weather has passed, you almost have a whole park to yourself.

WHICH WATER PARK TO VISIT?

WE ASK *UNOFFICIAL GUIDE* READERS to rate water-park attractions, just as they do those at the theme parks. Taken in aggregate, readers rank **Volcano Bay** first, with **Blizzard Beach** and **Typhoon Lagoon** tied for second.

Volcano Bay's big advantage is that it's open up to 4 hours more per day than Disney's water parks, including later closings. If you're looking for the best choice for a diverse group, Blizzard Beach is probably your best bet because it's rated first or second by every age group. A couple from Woodridge, Illinois, agrees:

If you have time to go to only one water park, definitely go to Blizzard Beach. It seems like they took everything from Typhoon Lagoon and made it better and faster. Summit Plummet was awesome—a total rush. The toboggan and bobsled rides were exciting—the bobsled really throws you around. The family tube ride was really good—much better and longer than the one at Typhoon Lagoon.

A hungry reader from Aberdeen, New Jersey, notes that Blizzard Beach's dining options are lacking:

At Blizzard Beach, there's only one main place to get food (most of the other spots are more for snacks). At lunchtime, it took almost 45 minutes to get some sandwiches and drinks.

Finally, a mother of four from Winchester, Virginia, gives her opinion on choosing between Typhoon Lagoon and Blizzard Beach:

At Blizzard Beach, the family raft ride is great, but the kids' area is poorly designed. As a parent, when you walk your child to the top of a slide or the tube ride, they're lost to your vision as they go down because of the fake snowdrifts. There are no direct ways down to the end of the slides, so little ones are left standing unsupervised while parents scramble down from the top. The Typhoon Lagoon kids' area is far superior in design.

PLANNING YOUR DAY *at* DISNEY WATER PARKS

DISNEY WATER PARKS are almost as large and elaborate as the major theme parks. You must be prepared for a lot of walking, exercise, sun, and jostling crowds. If your group really loves the water, schedule your visit early in your vacation. If you go at the beginning of your stay, you'll have more flexibility if you want to return.

To have a great day and beat the crowds, consider:

1. GETTING INFORMATION Call ☎ 407-WDW-MAGIC (939-6244) or check disneyworld.com the night before to verify when the park opens.

2. TO PICNIC OR NOT TO PICNIC Decide whether you want to carry a picnic lunch. Guests are permitted to take lunches and beverage coolers into the parks, but alcoholic beverages, glass containers, and loose ice and dry ice are prohibited; reusable ice packs are permitted. Only one cooler per family is allowed. The in-park food is comparable to fast food, but the prices are a bit high.

3. GETTING STARTED If you're going to Blizzard Beach or Typhoon Lagoon, get up early, have breakfast, and arrive at the park 40 minutes before opening. If you have a car, drive instead of taking a Disney bus.

4. FOLLOW A GOOD TOURING PLAN We have two touring plans designed to help you avoid crowds and bottlenecks at Disney water parks (see pages 735 and 736). If you're attending on a day of moderate to heavy attendance (see the Crowd Calendar at **TouringPlans.com**), consider using one of these tested plans. More are available on the site.

5. ATTIRE Wear your swimsuit under shorts and a T-shirt so you don't need to use lockers or dressing rooms. Regarding women's bathing suits, be advised that it's extremely common for women of all ages to

Most Popular Water Parks by Age Group					
PRE-SCHOOL	**GRADE SCHOOL**	**TEENS**	**YOUNG ADULTS**	**OVER 30**	**SENIORS**
Blizzard Beach	Blizzard Beach	Volcano Bay	Typhoon Lagoon	Volcano Bay	Typhoon Lagoon
Typhoon Lagoon	Typhoon Lagoon	Blizzard Beach	Blizzard Beach	Blizzard Beach	Blizzard Beach
Volcano Bay	Volcano Bay	Typhoon Lagoon	Volcano Bay	Typhoon Lagoon	Volcano Bay

accidentally part company with the top of their two-piece suit on the slides. Both the paths and beach sand get incredibly hot during the summer, so some form of foot protection is a must. Socks will do in a pinch, but water socks or sandals that strap to your feet are best. Shops in the parks sell sandals, Reef Runners, and other protective footwear that can be worn in and out of the water.

6. WHAT TO BRING You'll need a towel, sunscreen, and money. If you don't have towels, they can be rented for $2 each. Sunscreen is available in all park shops. Because wallets and purses get in the way, lock them in your car's trunk, or leave them at your hotel. Carry your Disney resort ID (if you have one) and enough money for the day in a plastic bag or other waterproof container, or use your MagicBand to pay for stuff.

Though nowhere is completely safe, we felt comfortable hiding our plastic money bags in our cooler. Nobody disturbed our stuff, and our cash was much easier to reach than if we'd stashed it in a locker across the park. If you're carrying a wad or you worry about money anyway, rent the locker.

A Canadian reader suggests the following option if you don't feel totally comfortable stashing your valuables in a locker, a cooler, or the like:

> As our admission was from an all-inclusive ticket [not a MagicBand], I was concerned about our passes being stolen or lost, yet I didn't want the hassle of a locker. I discovered that the gift shop sells water-resistant plastic boxes (with strings to go around your neck) in two sizes for around $5, with the smallest being just big enough for passes, credit cards, and a bit of money. I would've spent nearly as much on a locker rental, so I was able to enjoy the rest of the day with peace of mind.

Finally, a limited number of **wheelchairs** are available for rent for $12 per day with a $100 refundable deposit. Personal flotation devices (life jackets) are free.

7. WHAT NOT TO BRING Personal swim gear (fins, masks, rafts, and the like) isn't allowed. Everything you need is provided or available to rent. If you forgot your swimsuit, you can buy one.

8. ADMISSION Buy your admission in advance or about 45 minutes before official opening. Guests staying five or more days should consider the **Park Hopper Plus** add-on, which provides admission to either Blizzard Beach or Typhoon Lagoon.

9. LOCKERS Rental lockers are $10 per day for a standard size and $15 per day for a large (lockers are keyless). Standard-size lockers are roomy enough for one person or a couple, but a family will generally need a large locker. Though you can access your locker freely all day, not all lockers are conveniently located.

Getting a locker at Blizzard Beach or Typhoon Lagoon is truly competitive. When the gates open, guests race to the locker-rental desk. The rental procedure is somewhat slow; if you aren't among the first in line, you can waste a lot of time waiting. We recommend skipping the locker. Carry a MagicBand or only as much cash as you'll need for the day in a watertight container that you can stash in your cooler. Ditto for personal items, including watches and eyeglasses.

10. TUBES Tubes for bobbing on the waves, floating in the creeks, and riding the tube slides are available for free.

11. GETTING SETTLED Establish your base for the day. There are many beautiful sunning and lounging spots scattered throughout both Disney water parks—arrive early and you can almost have your pick.

The breeze is best along the beaches of the surf pools at Blizzard Beach and Typhoon Lagoon. At Typhoon Lagoon, if there are children younger than age 6 in your party, choose an area to the left of Mount Mayday (ship on top) near the children's swimming area.

Also available are flat lounges (nonadjustable) and chairs (better for reading), shelters for guests who prefer shade, picnic tables, and a few hammocks. If you have money to burn, private cabanas are available at both water parks for up to six guests. Called **Polar Patios** at Blizzard Beach and **Beachcomber Shacks** at Typhoon Lagoon, they come outfitted with lounge chairs, tables, towels, private lockers, a refillable drink mug, and an attendant who'll be at your beck and call. Available by reservation at ☎ 407-WDW-PLAY (939-7529), the cabanas run from around $234 to $345 (including tax), depending on the season.

We think the best spectator sport at Typhoon Lagoon is the body-surfing in the Surf Pool—it's second only to being out on the waves yourself. With this in mind, position yourself to have an unobstructed view of the waves.

12. A WORD ABOUT THE SLIDES Waterslides come in many shapes and sizes. Some are steep and vertical, and some are long and undulating. Some resemble corkscrews, while others imitate the pool-and-drop nature of whitewater streams.

unofficial **TIP**
When lines for the slides become intolerable, head for the surf or wave pool or the tube-floating streams.

Depending on the slide, swimmers ride mats, inner tubes, or rafts. With body slides, swimmers slosh to the bottom on the seat of their pants.

Though Typhoon Lagoon and Blizzard Beach are huge parks with many slides, they're overwhelmed almost daily by armies of guests. If your main reason for going to Typhoon Lagoon or Blizzard Beach is the slides and you hate long lines, be among the first guests to enter the park. Go directly to the slides, and ride as many times as you can before the park fills.

For maximum speed on a body slide, cross your legs at the ankles, and cross your arms over your chest. When you take off, arch your back so almost all your weight is on your shoulder blades and heels (the less contact with the surface, the less resistance). Steer by shifting most of your upper-body weight onto one shoulder blade. For top speed on turns, weight the shoulder blade on the outside of each curve. If you want to go slowly, distribute your weight equally, as if you were lying on your back in bed. For curving slides, maximize speed by hitting the entrance to each curve high and exiting the curve low.

Some slides and rapids have a minimum height requirement. Riders for **Humunga Kowabunga** at Typhoon Lagoon and for **Slush Gusher** and **Summit Plummet** at Blizzard Beach, for example, must be 4 feet tall. Pregnant women and people with back problems or other health difficulties shouldn't ride.

SOGGY TIPS FROM A WATER-PUPPY FAMILY

A Bow, New Hampshire, family who are evidently working on a PhD in Disney water parks were kind enough to share their knowledge:

IF YOU'RE GOING TO THE WATER PARKS, train on your StairMaster prior to going, especially if you visit Blizzard Beach. For Runoff Rapids, you climb 125 stairs (yes, I counted). Imagine doing that three times in a row, trying to keep up with kids who want to go down the slide multiple times. In addition, there are at least (and here, I'm guessing) 300 stairs if you choose the Alpine Path instead of the chairlift to get to Summit Plummet. At Typhoon Lagoon, each slide, except Miss Adventure Falls, has about 60 steps, so at either park you have quite a bit of stairs to climb or go down.

We were at Blizzard Beach 15 minutes before park opening in late August, and we felt that this was plenty of time to beat the crowds. We noticed crowds building [about an hour after opening]. If you are there at park opening, stash your things as quickly as possible (or send a member of your party to do so) while you take the chairlift to Summit Plummet. We were first in line for the chairlift, and we were at the top with no lines. The chairlift is definitely faster if you are one of the first in line, and you won't get winded from walking the Alpine Path. However, if you arrive later in the day, the line for the chairlift builds, and you'll be left having to climb the Alpine Path—great if you're in shape, but not so much if you're not!

Check the closing time of the water parks if you plan on arriving in late afternoon. When Typhoon Lagoon closed at 8 p.m. and we arrived shortly after 2 p.m., lines tended to thin out by 4 p.m. However, when we tried that same tactic (arriving in the afternoon) when Typhoon Lagoon closed at 6 p.m., we noticed that the lines were still long, and it seemed like the crowd wasn't thinning at all. On those days, we wished that we had been there for park opening and left when crowds started to build.

We enjoyed the water parks, but we only stayed about 3 hours max. Though the water parks are big (as in spread out), there weren't enough attractions to keep us there the entire day. Yes, they have slides, but not as many as I expected a Disney park to have. When lines started to build, it became less fun to wait 15-plus minutes for a slide that takes less than 2 minutes to go down. Also,

13. LAZY RIVERS Each of the water parks we cover here offers mellow lazy rivers. A great idea, the floating streams are long, tranquil inner-tube rides that give you the illusion that you're doing something while you're being sedentary.

Disney's lazy rivers flow ever so slowly around the entire park, through caves, beneath waterfalls, past gardens, and under bridges. They offer a relaxing alternative to touring a park on foot.

Lazy rivers can be reached from several put-in and take-out points. There are never lines; just wade into the creek and plop into one of the

the less-popular attractions, such as the lazy river, got really busy, and there were hardly any tubes to be found.

Water shoes or water sandals are a good bet in the water parks, as the paths can get really hot in the summer, and only a few water jets are near the pathways to keep them cool. However, on some slides (such as the body slides), water shoes aren't allowed, so stash your water shoes at the base of the path where you exit, and grab them on your way out.

Some slides at Blizzard Beach, such as the Downhill Double Dipper, take FOREVER in line because you're waiting for a tube to make it from the pool up the conveyor belt to the slide stairs. Once the tube finally arrives, you still have to wait for both parties to go down together and to exit the pool. This process takes a long time. If this slide is important to you, make it one of the first things you do. The toboggan rides can also take a while because there is no clear system of who can take the mat when it finally arrives at the top (two mat rides are at the top of the mat conveyor belt: Toboggan Racers and Snow Stormers). Also, some slides aren't very comfortable. At Typhoon Lagoon, the Humunga Kowabunga should be called the Wedgie Maker. If your family is going to both water parks (like we did), I suggest skipping Gangplank Falls at Typhoon Lagoon and doing Teamboat Springs at Blizzard Beach instead. Not only is Teamboat Springs a LOT longer than Gangplank Falls, but it's also more fun.

Also, the wave pools at both parks are very different. At Typhoon Lagoon, it's "The Wave" pool—as in, there's only one HUGE wave that you can try to bodysurf (good luck with that!). At Blizzard Beach, it's more like "The Waves" pool, where waves are put out at a continual rate, at all times, like a gentle rocking motion, and there are tubes you can use. Typhoon Lagoon has no flotation devices of any kind because, well, they'd be dangerous to everyone involved.

If you have something electronic like a smartphone or tablet that you need to stay dry at the water parks, buy a waterproof container BEFORE you go. The water parks sell only water-resistant containers, and even though the one we bought didn't seem to leak, it would have given us more peace of mind to have a waterproof bag/container.

inner tubes floating by. Ride the current all the way around, or get out at any exit. It takes 30–35 minutes to float the full circuit.

14. BAD WEATHER Thunderstorms are common in Florida. On summer afternoons, storms can occur daily. Water parks close during a storm. Most storms, however, are short-lived, allowing the parks to resume normal operations. If a storm is severe and prolonged, it can cause a great deal of inconvenience: In addition to the park's closing, guests compete aggressively for shelter, and Disney resort guests may have to joust for seats on a bus back to the hotel.

You should monitor the local weather forecast the day before you go, checking again in the morning before leaving for the water park. Scattered thundershowers are no big deal, but moving storm fronts are to be avoided.

15. ENDURANCE The water parks are large and require almost as much walking as one of the theme parks. Add to this wave surfing, swimming, and all the climbing required to reach the slides, and you'll be pooped by day's end. Unless you spend your hours like a lizard on a rock, don't expect to return to the hotel with much energy. Consider something low-key for the evening. You'll probably want to hit the hay early.

16. LOST CHILDREN AND LOST ADULTS It's easier to lose a child or become separated from your party at one of the water parks than it is at a major theme park. Upon arrival, pick a very specific place to meet should you get separated. If you split up on purpose, set times for checking in. Lost-children stations at the water parks are so out of the way that neither you nor your lost child will find them without help from a Disney cast member. Explain to your children how to recognize cast members (by their distinctive name tags) and how to ask for help.

WATER-PARK TOURING PLANS

ONE-DAY TOURING PLANS for Typhoon Lagoon and Blizzard Beach can be found on pages 735 and 736, respectively. These plans are for parents with small children; touring plans for adults, along with our online reader survey, are available at **TouringPlans.com**. We'd love to hear from families who have tried these plans.

The plans presented here include all the slides, flumes, and rides appropriate for kids in both parks. Having brought our own children to these parks, we've also included tips on which slides to try first in case this is your child's first water-park experience. For example, at **Typhoon Lagoon** we suggest the family whitewater raft ride **Miss Adventure Falls** as the first attraction. If your child enjoys that, we list **Gangplank Falls** and then **Keelhaul Falls** as the next steps up in waterslides. If that seems a bit much, however, the touring plan recommends the **Ketchakiddee Creek** play area as an alternative.

BLIZZARD BEACH

unofficial **TIP**
Picnic areas are scattered around the park, as are pleasant places for sunbathing.

BLIZZARD BEACH IS DISNEY'S more exotic water-adventure park, and it arrived with its own legend. The story goes that an entrepreneur tried to open a ski resort in Florida during a particularly savage winter. Alas, the snow melted; the palm trees grew back; and all that remained of the ski resort was its alpine lodge, the ski lifts, and, of course, the mountain. Plunging off the mountain are ski slopes and bobsled runs transformed into waterslides. Visitors to Blizzard Beach catch the thaw—icicles drip and patches of snow remain. The melting snow has formed a lagoon (wave pool), which is fed by gushing mountain streams.

Both Disney water parks are distinguished by their landscaping and the attention paid to executing their themes. As you enter Blizzard Beach, you face the mountain. Coming off the highest peak and bisecting the area at the mountain's base are two long slides. To the left of the slides is the wave pool. To the right are the children's swimming area and the ski lift. Surrounding the layout like a moat is a tranquil stream for floating in tubes.

On either side of the highest peak are tube, raft, and body slides. Including the two slides coming off the peak, Blizzard Beach has 19 slides. Among them is **Summit Plummet,** Disney World's longest speed slide, which begins with a 120-foot free fall, and the **Teamboat Springs** 1,200-foot-long water-bobsled run.

unofficial **TIP**
If you're into slides, Blizzard Beach is tops among the Disney water parks.

One reader reports that the Blizzard Beach slides picked her husband's pocket:

> *Our family absolutely loved Summit Plummet, but it claimed all four of our park passes/room-key cards as its victims. My husband had the four cards in an exterior pocket of his swimsuit, secured closed by Velcro AND a snap. But after doing Summit Plummet and Slush Gusher twice apiece and Teamboat Springs once, he looked down, noticed the pocket flapping open, and found all four cards missing! So we had to cancel all the cards (they had charging privileges) and couldn't purchase any food or drinks while we were there (we didn't bring any cash because we planned to charge with our cards)!*

We've worn MagicBands at the water parks, and they're much more secure. The point is that anything in your pockets—cash, keys, and the like—may come out. A couple from Bowie, Maryland, came away with battle scars:

> *Summit Plummet gave me a bunch of bruises. Even my husband hurt for a few days. It wasn't a fun ride. Basically, you drop until you hit the slide, and that is why everyone comes off rubbing their butts. They say you go 60 mph on a 120-foot drop. I'll never do it again.*

For our money, the most exciting and interesting slides are the **Slush Gusher** and **Teamboat Springs** on the front right of the mountain, and **Runoff Rapids** on the back side of the mountain. Slush Gusher is an undulating speed slide that we consider as exciting as the more vertical Summit Plummet but not as bone-jarring. On Teamboat Springs, you ride in a raft that looks like a children's round blow-up wading pool.

Runoff Rapids is accessible from a path that winds around the far left bottom of the mountain. The rapids consist of three corkscrew tube slides, one of which is enclosed and dark. As at Teamboat Springs, you'll go much faster on a two- or three-person tube than on a one-person tube. If you lean so that you enter curves high and come out low, you'll really fly. Because we like to steer the tube and go fast, we much prefer the open slides (where we can see) to the dark, enclosed tube. We thought crashing through the pitch-dark tube felt disturbingly like being flushed down a toilet.

The **Snow Stormers'** mat slides on the front of the mountain are fun but not as fast or as interesting as Runoff Rapids or **Downhill Double Dipper** on the far left front. **Toboggan Racers,** at the front and center

Blizzard Beach

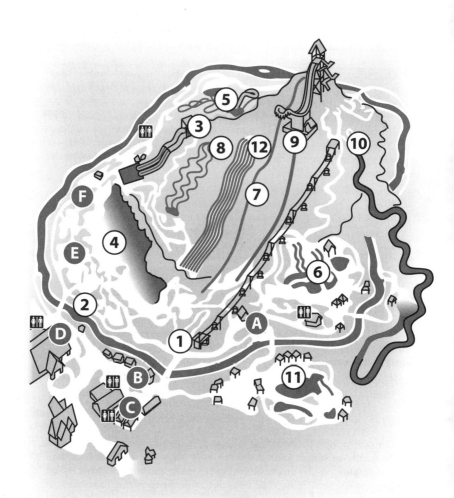

Attractions

1. Chairlift
2. Cross Country Creek
3. Downhill Double Dipper
4. Melt-Away Bay
5. Runoff Rapids
6. Ski Patrol Training Camp
7. Slush Gusher
8. Snow Stormers
9. Summit Plummet
10. Teamboat Springs
11. Tike's Peak
12. Toboggan Racers

Restaurants

A. Avalunch
B. Cooling Hut
C. Frostbite Freddy's
D. Lottawatta Lodge
E. Polar Pub
F. Warming Hut

 Restrooms

BLIZZARD BEACH ATTRACTIONS

CHAIRLIFT UP MOUNT GUSHMORE Height requirement: 32". Great ride even if you go up just for the view. When the park is packed, use the singles line.

CROSS COUNTRY CREEK No height requirement. Lazy river circling the park; grab a tube.

DOWNHILL DOUBLE DIPPER Height requirement: 48". Side-by-side tube-racing slides. At 25 mph, the tube zooms through water curtains and free falls. It's a lot of fun, but it's rough.

MELT-AWAY BAY No height requirement. Wave pool with gentle, bobbing waves. Great for younger swimmers.

RUNOFF RAPIDS No height requirement. Three corkscrew tube slides to choose from. The center slide is for solo raft rides; the other two slides offer one- or two-person tubes. The dark, enclosed tube gives you the feeling of being flushed down a toilet.

SKI PATROL TRAINING CAMP Height requirement: 60" for T-Bar. Place for preteens to train for the big rides.

SLUSH GUSHER Height requirement: 48". 90-foot double-humped slide. Ladies, cling to those tops—all others, hang on for your lives.

SNOW STORMERS No height requirement. Three mat-slide flumes; down you go on your belly.

SUMMIT PLUMMET Height requirement: 48". 120-foot free fall at 60 mph. Needless to say, this ride is very intense. Make sure your child knows what to expect; being over 48 inches tall doesn't guarantee an enjoyable experience. If you think you'd enjoy being washed out of a 12th-floor window during a heavy rain, then this slide is for you.

TEAMBOAT SPRINGS No height requirement. 1,200-foot group whitewater raft flume. Wonderful ride for the whole family.

TIKE'S PEAK Height requirement: 48" and under only. Kid-size version of Blizzard Beach. This is the place for little ones.

TOBOGGAN RACERS No height requirement. Eight-lane race course. You go down the flume on a mat. Less intense than Snow Stormers.

of the mountain, consists of eight parallel slides where riders are dispatched in heats to race to the bottom. The ride itself is no big deal, and the time needed to get everybody lined up ensures that you'll wait extra long to ride. A faster, more exciting race venue can be found on the side-by-side slides of the undulating Downhill Double Dipper. Competitors here can reach speeds of up to 25 mph.

A ski lift carries guests to the mountaintop (you can also walk up), where they can choose from **Summit Plummet, Slush Gusher,** or **Teamboat Springs.** For all other slides at Blizzard Beach, the only way to reach the top is on foot. If you're among the first in the park and don't have to wait to ride, the ski lift is fun and provides a bird's-eye view of the park. After riding once to satisfy your curiosity, however, you're better off taking the stairs to the top. The following attractions have a minimum height requirement of 48 inches: **Slush Gusher, Summit Plummet,** and **Downhill Double Dipper.**

unofficial **TIP**
Blizzard Beach fills early during hotter months. To stake out a nice sunning spot and to enjoy the slides without long waits, arrive at least 35 minutes before the official opening time (check disneyworld.com the night before you go).

The wave pool, called **Melt-Away Bay,** has gentle, bobbing waves. The float creek, **Cross Country Creek,** circles the park, passing through the mountain. The children's areas (**Tike's Peak** and **Ski Patrol Training Camp**) are creatively designed, nicely isolated, and—like the rest of the park—visually interesting.

The layout of Blizzard Beach (and Typhoon Lagoon, described next) is a bit convoluted. With slides on both the front and back of the mountain, it isn't always easy to find a path leading to where you want to go.

At the ski resort's now-converted base area are shops; counter-service food; restrooms; and tube, towel, and locker rentals. Blizzard Beach has its own parking lot but no lodging, though Disney's All-Star and Coronado Springs Resorts are almost within walking distance.

TYPHOON LAGOON

TYPHOON LAGOON is comparable in size to Blizzard Beach. The park has 15 waterslides, some as long as 420 feet, and two streams. Most of the slides drop from the top of a 100-foot-tall artificial mountain. Landscaping and a typhoon-aftermath theme add interest and a sense of adventure to the wet rides.

Guests enter Typhoon Lagoon through a misty rainforest and then emerge in a ramshackle tropical town where the park's concessions and services are situated. Special sets make every ride an odyssey as swimmers encounter bat caves, lagoons and pools, spinning rocks, formations of dinosaur bones, and many other imponderables.

Typhoon Lagoon has its own parking lot but no lodging. Disney resort guests can commute to the water park on Disney buses.

If you indulge in all features of Typhoon Lagoon, admission is a fair value. If you go primarily for the slides, you'll have just 2 early-morning hours to enjoy them before the wait becomes prohibitive.

Typhoon Lagoon provides water adventure for all ages. Activity pools for young children and families feature geysers, tame slides, bubble jets, and fountains. For the older and more adventurous are the enclosed **Humunga Kowabunga** speed slides, the corkscrew **Storm Slides,** and three whitewater raft rides: **Gangplank Falls, Keelhaul Falls,** and **Mayday Falls. Crush 'n' Gusher,** billed as a "water roller coaster," consists of a series of flumes and spillways that course through an abandoned tropical fruit–processing plant. It features tubes that hold one or two people, and you can choose from three routes—Banana Blaster, Coconut Crusher, and Pineapple Plunger—ranging from 410 to 420 feet long. Only Crush 'n' Gusher and the Humunga Kowabunga speed slides (where you can hit 30 mph) have a minimum height requirement of 48 inches.

A Waterloo, Ontario, mom found Typhoon Lagoon more strenuous than she'd anticipated:

> I wish I'd been prepared for the fact that we'd have to haul the tubes up the stairs of Crush 'n' Gusher. My daughter was not strong enough to carry hers, so I had to lug them up by myself. I was EXHAUSTED by the end of the day, and my arms ached for a couple of days afterward. Had I known that was the case, I would have started lifting weights several months before our trip in preparation!

A New Jersey reader agreed:

> Thumbs WAY DOWN to the designer who made several places in the queue for Storm Slides where the stairs go DOWN then back UP then back DOWN then UP again—leading to all guests walking UP extra needless fights of stairs. BOO!

Those of you who share the sentiments of the readers quoted above will appreciate Typhoon Lagoon's **Miss Adventure Falls,** near Crush 'n' Gusher. Riders hop in a four-person, circular raft at the bottom of the slide then ride a conveyor belt up to the top in about a minute. (The conveyor belt is, let's be honest, not a bad shiatsu massage for your butt.) Though the rafts hold four, the ride works just as well for singles and couples.

The queuing area at the bottom of the conveyor is inadequate, making for major jam-ups on busy days. Because the attraction is suitable for all ages, expect big crowds and long waits unless you ride just after park opening.

Slower metabolisms will also enjoy the meandering, 2,000-foot-long **Castaway Creek,** which floats tubers through hidden grottoes and rainforests. And, of course, the sedentary will usually find plenty of sun to sleep in. Typhoon Lagoon's **Surf Pool** is the world's largest inland surf facility, with waves up to 6 feet high (enough, so Disney says, to "encompass an ocean liner").

SURF POOL

WHILE BLIZZARD BEACH AND VOLCANO BAY have wave pools, Typhoon Lagoon has a Surf Pool. Most people will encounter larger waves here than they have in the ocean. The surf machine puts out a wave about every 90 seconds (just about how long it takes to get back in position if you caught the previous wave). Perfectly formed and ideal for riding, each wave is about 5–6 feet from trough to crest. Before you join the fray, watch two or three waves from shore. Because each wave breaks in almost the same spot, you can get a feel for position and timing. Observing other surfers is also helpful.

The best way to ride the waves is to swim about three-fourths of the way to the wall at the wave-machine end of the pool. When the waves come—trust us, you'll feel and hear them—swim vigorously toward the beach and try to position yourself one-half to three-fourths of a body length below the breaking crest. The waves are so perfectly engineered that they'll either carry you forward or bypass you. Unlike ocean waves, though, they won't slam you down.

A teenage girl from Urbana, Illinois, notes that the primary hazard in the Surf Pool is colliding with other surfers and swimmers:

The Surf Pool was nice except I kept landing on really hairy guys when the big waves came.

A Gate City, Virginia, mom was caught off-guard by the size and power of the waves:

I had forgotten how violent the wave pool is at Typhoon Lagoon. Thinking I'd be able to hold on to two young(ish) nephews is a mistake I made only once before getting them back to shallower water.

A reader from Somerset, New Jersey, alerted us to another problem:

Typhoon Lagoon is a great family water park—our unexpected favorite. However, please tell your readers not to sit on the bottom of the wave pool—I got a horrible scratch/raspberry and saw about five others with similar injuries. The waves are stronger than they look.

Typhoon Lagoon

Restaurants

A. Leaning Palms
B. Lowtide Lou's
C. Snack Shack
D. Typhoon Tilly's

Attractions

1. Bay Slides
2. Castaway Creek
3. Crush 'n' Gusher
4. Gangplank Falls
5. Humunga Kowabunga
6. Keelhaul Falls
7. Ketchakiddee Creek
8. Mayday Falls
9. Miss Adventure Falls
10. Storm Slides
11. Surf Pool

Restrooms

TYPHOON LAGOON ATTRACTIONS

BAY SLIDES Height requirement: 60″ and under only. Miniature two-slide version of Storm Slides, specifically designed for small children. The kids splash down into a far corner of the Surf Pool.

CASTAWAY CREEK No height requirement. Half-mile lazy river in a tropical setting with cool mists, waterfalls, and a tunnel through Mount Mayday. Wonderful!

CRUSH 'N' GUSHER Height requirement: 48″. Water roller coaster where you can choose from three slides—Banana Blaster, Coconut Crusher, and Pineapple Plunger—ranging from 410 to 420 feet long. This thriller leaves you wondering what exactly happened, if you make it down in one piece, that is; it's not for the faint of heart. If your kids are new to water-park rides, this is not the place to break them in, even if they're tall enough to ride.

GANGPLANK FALLS No height requirement. Whitewater raft flume in a four-person tube.

HUMUNGA KOWABUNGA Height requirement: 48″. Speed slides that hit 30 mph. A five-story drop in the dark rattles even the most courageous rider. Women should ride this one in a one-piece swimsuit.

KEELHAUL FALLS No height requirement. Fast whitewater ride in a single-person tube.

KETCHAKIDDEE CREEK Height requirement: 48″ and under only. Toddlers and preschoolers love this area reserved only for them. Say "splish-splash" and have lots of fun.

MAYDAY FALLS No height requirement. Wild single-person tube ride. *Hang on!*

MISS ADVENTURE FALLS No height requirement. Gentle family raft ride down a well-themed slide.

STORM SLIDES No height requirement. Three body slides plunge down and through Mount Mayday.

SURF POOL No height requirement. World's largest inland surf facility, with waves up to 6 feet high. Adult supervision is required. Surfing lessons are offered Monday–Friday, in the early morning before the park opens or in the evening after the park closes (hours vary); surfboard provided. Cost is $190 for 2½ hours (tax included); minimum age is 8; class size is 12. Call ☎ 407-WDW-PLAY (939-7529). The price does not include park admission, and lessons may not be offered when the park reopens.

The best way to avoid collisions while surfing is to paddle out far enough that you'll be at the top of the wave as it breaks. This tactic eliminates the possibility of anyone landing on you from above and ensures maximum forward visibility. A corollary to this: The worst place to swim is where the wave actually breaks. You'll look up to see a 6-foot wall of water carrying eight dozen screaming surfers bearing down on you. This is the time to remember every submarine movie you've ever seen . . . *Dive! Dive! Dive!*

Either in the early morning before the park opens or in the evening after the park closes (hours vary), you can take **surfing lessons,** with an actual surfboard. Practice waves range from 3 to 6 feet tall; most students are first-timers. The cost is $190 per person including tax, and equipment is provided. For details, and to see if they're being offered, call ☎ 407-WDW-PLAY (939-7529).

▌█ UNIVERSAL'S VOLCANO BAY

UNIVERSAL'S WATER PARK (universalorlando.com/web/en/us/theme -parks/volcano-bay), Volcano Bay, on Universal Orlando property next to Cabana Bay Beach Resort, features a scenic, man-made mountain and a colorful atmosphere that goes toe-to-toe with those of Typhoon Lagoon and Blizzard Beach. The thrill, scope, and diversity of its 18 attractions make Volcano Bay an excellent alternative to the Disney swimming parks.

There is no guest parking at Volcano Bay itself; visitors will park in the same parking garages as other Universal theme park guests and pay the usual rates (see page 603). Special shuttle buses transport guests along dedicated lanes to the front gate of Volcano Bay, which is also accessible on a walking path from the neighboring **Cabana Bay Beach Resort** and **Aventura Hotel.**

unofficial **TIP**

Don't try to park at Cabana Bay or Aventura if you're not staying there—you'll get hit with a $45/day fee.

Buy your tickets at the Volcano Bay bus stop inside the parking structure, at any on-site hotel, at the park entrance, or at universal orlando.com. Buying your ticket and setting up an online account in advance will greatly speed your entry into the park. The park opens at 10 a.m. (9 a.m. in the summer, with 30–60 minutes of early admission daily for all on-site hotel guests) and stays open as late as 8 p.m. during the summer. Disney water parks typically close by 6 or 7 p.m., but Volcano Bay was designed for nighttime operation, with special lighting effects activated after sunset.

Universal Orlando describes Volcano Bay's 28 acres as "a lush tropical oasis that unfolds before you, instantly transporting you to a little-known Pacific isle." The park's icon, visible to passing cars on I-4, is a colossal volcano rising above a pristine beach, with majestic waterfalls transforming into blazing lava by night.

Universal also replaced queues with Virtual Lines and built conveyor belts for all the rafts. Every visitor is issued a waterproof TapuTapu wristband that you use to claim your place in the Virtual Lines, as well as reserve and open lockers and make payments throughout the park when it's linked to your credit card (with a secure PIN) using the Universal Orlando website or app. The TapuTapu bands also trigger special effects throughout Volcano Bay, such as controlling streams of water in **Tot Tiki Reef** or shooting water cannons at other guests who are enjoying the **Kopiko Wai Winding River.**

Tap your TapuTapu band against a tiki totem outside a ride, and you'll be given an approximate time before you can return; your wait may be shorter than expected if other guests skip their return times, or it could be longer if the attraction temporarily closes due to weather or technical problems. You can hold a reservation for just one ride at a time, and TapuTapu will alert you when it's time to return with a minimal wait. Note that you can't get in another Virtual Line until you use or cancel your first ride.

In theory, this system allows guests to enjoy the wave pool and lazy river instead of standing in hot queues, but peak days can be plagued by multihour waits for most of the slides, with some popular attractions completely filling up for the day by midday. Universal Express passes can be purchased online or inside the park on select days; they start at $21 per person for one use per ride. Your best bet is to arrive as early as possible and secure a spot on **Krakatau Aqua Coaster,** followed by **Honu, Ko'okiri Body Plunge,** and **Puihi,** in that order. Also look for slides advertising RIDE NOW during early and late hours; you can hop on without losing your place in a Virtual Line.

VOLCANO BAY AT A GLANCE

VOLCANO BAY IS DIVIDED into four primary areas (lands), each with a unique theme, but because all of the areas sport the same lush South Seas scenery, it's impossible to tell where one section ends and another begins without a map.

The park's backstory is based on the fictional story of the Waturi, an ancient Polynesian people who set out on outrigger canoes to find a new home. The Waturi visited many Polynesian islands, drawing elements from each culture, until they caught sight of the legendary fish Kunuku playing in the waves of Volcano Bay and settled there.

In practical terms, the park looks like an upscale resort in the South Pacific, with lush palm trees, tiki carvings, and thatched cabanas; as long as you're at ground level, you'd hardly guess there's a busy interstate only yards away. The Waturi legend also influenced the unpronounceable names of most of the attractions, but that's about as far as the theming goes on the slides—don't expect any indoor scenes or dark ride–style effects.

Guests enter the park at **Wave Village,** which is dominated by the **Waturi Beach** multidirectional wave pool and the **Reef** leisure pool. Paths from there lead clockwise to **Rainforest Village,** housing the park's densest collection of thrill rides, including **TeAwa the Fearless River,** and **River Village,** which features family-friendly attractions like the **Kopiko Wai** lazy river. The heart of the park is the *volcano* in Volcano Bay: 200-foot **Krakatau,** home to the signature **Krakatau Aqua Coaster** as well as three drop-capsule body slides, plus hidden caverns with cascading waterfalls and special effects triggered by your TapuTapu band.

Each area of the park offers amenities such as concierge locations and lockers ($10–$17 for all-day access). The themed restaurants and bars throughout Volcano Bay are particularly noteworthy, far exceeding what we've come to expect from water-park grub with light, refreshing meals perfect for a day at the beach. Caribbean and island-inspired foods are on the menu, and even less-adventurous fare like pizza and hot dogs has been upgraded with flatbread crusts and pretzel buns.

At **Bambu,** in Rainforest Village, we love the quinoa-edamame burger, topped with roasted shiitake mushrooms, lettuce, tomato, and Sriracha mayo, with a side of fries. Also at Rainforest Village is **The Feasting Frog;** try the tacos or poke tuna, both served with plantain chips. At River Village, **Whakawaiwai Eats** is home to the Hawaiian Pizza, with caramelized pineapple, diced ham, and pickled jalapeños. In Wave Village, at **Kohola Reef Restaurant and Social Club,** the slow-smoked glazed chicken, served with mango slaw and fries, doesn't disappoint. For dessert, try the chocolate lava cake. **Dancing Dragons Boat Bar** (Rainforest Village) and **Kunuku Boat Bar** (Wave Village) serve a variety of exotic signature cocktails, but these are far too sugary for our taste. Stick with the locally brewed Volcano Blossom beer instead.

You can upgrade your visit with reserved padded loungers ($32–$159 per pair), 6-person cabanas ($170 and up), or 16-person Family Suite cabanas ($320–$640); all prices depend on the date. While they're not a necessity, we recommend the private loungers for their included

continued on page 658

Universal's Volcano Bay

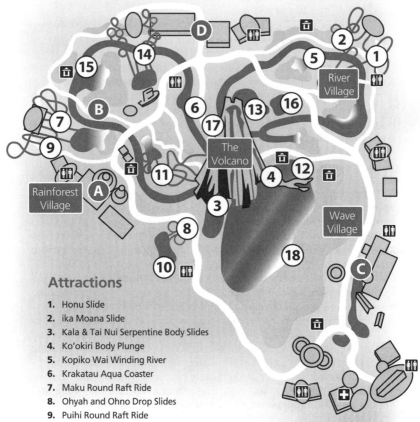

Attractions

1. Honu Slide
2. ika Moana Slide
3. Kala & Tai Nui Serpentine Body Slides
4. Ko'okiri Body Plunge
5. Kopiko Wai Winding River
6. Krakatau Aqua Coaster
7. Maku Round Raft Ride
8. Ohyah and Ohno Drop Slides
9. Puihi Round Raft Ride
10. Puka Uli Lagoon
11. Punga Racers
12. The Reef
13. Runamukka Reef
14. Taniwha Tubes: Tonga & Raki
15. TeAwa the Fearless River
16. Tot Tiki Reef
17. Vol's Caverns
18. Waturi Beach

Restaurants

A. Bambu
B. The Feasting Frog
C. Kohola Reef Restaurant & Social Club
D. Whakawaiwai Eats

 First Aid Station   Restrooms   🛏 Cabanas

VOLCANO BAY ATTRACTIONS

Rainforest Village

KALA AND TA NUI SERPENTINE BODY SLIDES **Height requirement: 48".** After falling through a drop door, two riders go down 124-foot body slides simultaneously. Their paths cross several times as they hurtle down translucent intertwining tubes. The green side is like the Incredible Hulk Coaster of slides: It starts fast and somehow gets faster as it goes.

MAKU AND PUIHI ROUND RAFT RIDES **Height requirement: 42", 48" if riding alone.** *Maku* and *Puihi* mean "wet" and "wild," and that's no exaggeration. North America's first "saucer ride," the six-person Maku raft plunges riders through bowl-like formations before landing them in a pool surrounded by erupting geysers. Puihi is the far more frightening slide of the pair: A six-person raft launches down into a dark, winding tunnel before shooting up a banked curve; riders glimpse the highway below and momentarily experience zero gravity prior to sliding back down.

OHYAH AND OHNO DROP SLIDES **Height requirement: 48".** Two short but intense twisting slides that launch guests 4 and 6 feet above the water at the end; Ohno is the taller of the two.

PUNGA RACERS **Height requirement: 42", 48" if riding alone.** Guests go feet-first down four side-by-side body slides, passing through "underwater sea caves," also known as enclosed plastic tubes.

PUKA ULI LAGOON **No height requirement.** Tranquil leisure pool.

TANIWHA TUBES **Height requirement: 42", 48" if riding alone.** One tower sports four Easter Island–inspired waterslides with rafts for single or double riders. Along the way, tiki statues make sure that you don't stay dry. The slides are similar but not identical—bear left to the green Tonga slides with more-open sections if you get claustrophobic.

TEAWA THE FEARLESS RIVER **Height requirement: 42", 48" if riding alone.** Guests hang tight in their flotation vests amid roaring whitewater rapids as they surf beneath the slides inside Krakatau. If you're looking for a lazy river, this ain't it!

River Village

HONU AND IKA MOANA SLIDES **Height requirement: Ika Moana, 42"; Honu, 48" if riding alone.** Honu and Ika Moana are two separate slides attached to the same tower, where guests board multiperson animal-themed rafts (a sea turtle and a whale, respectively) before speeding down into a pool. Honu is a blue raft slide that sends you vertically up two giant sloped walls before sliding back down—it's the scariest group ride in the park. Ika Moana is a much gentler journey in and out of twisting green tunnels.

KO'OKIRI BODY PLUNGE **Height requirement: 48".** Hop on this 125-foot slide, featuring a drop door with a 70-degree-angle descent, straight through the heart of the mountain. Drumbeats building up to the drop get your heart pounding, but the plunge itself is over before you have time to scream.

KOPIKO WAI WINDING RIVER **No height requirement.** A gentle lazy river that passes through the park's landscape and into the volcano's hidden caves.

KRAKATAU AQUA COASTER **Height requirement: 42", 48" if riding alone.** Guests board a specially designed canoe that seats up to four. The ride uses linear induction motor technology, which launches the canoe uphill as well as downhill as you twist and turn around the volcano's blown-out interior. It's similar to Crush 'n' Gusher at Typhoon Lagoon, but far longer and more thrilling. Krakatau is the park's most popular ride, so get your TapuTapu reservation as early as possible.

RUNAMUKKA REEF **For children under 54" tall.** A three-story water playground for older children inspired by the coral reef, featuring twisting slides, sprinklers, and more.

TOT TIKI REEF **For children under 48" tall.** A toddler play area with spraying Maori fountains, slides, and a kid-size volcano.

Wave Village

THE REEF **No height requirement.** Leisure pool with calm waters and its own waterfall. Relax and watch braver souls shoot down the Ko'okiri Body Plunge.

WATURI BEACH **Children under 48" must wear a lift vest.** Features a multidirectional wave pool, situated at the foot of Krakatau Lagoon and fed by waterfalls cascading off the volcano's peak.

continued from page 655

shade canopy, locking storage box, and attendant to deliver food and drink orders. The cabanas get all that, plus towel service, free fruit and bottled water, and a private kiosk for making TapuTapu reservations.

Though Volcano Bay experienced more than its share of growing pains during its first year of operations, the park has worked out most of the bugs and offers a good variety of activities. If you can adjust your attraction-riding expectations to fit TapuTapu's quirks and relax into the park's immersive atmosphere, Volcano Bay is a relaxing, enjoyable way to spend a day outside the theme parks.

PART SEVENTEEN

DISNEY SPRINGS, SHOPPING, *and* NIGHTLIFE

KEY QUESTIONS ANSWERED IN THIS CHAPTER

- How do I get to Disney Springs? *(see 662)*
- What are the best shops and experiences at Disney Springs? *(page 663)*
- Where are the best bars and nightclubs at Disney Springs? *(page 666)*
- Where is the best shopping in the Disney theme parks? *(page 667)*
- Where is the best shopping outside the theme parks? *(page 671)*
- Which are the best bars and nightclubs at the Disney resorts? *(page 672)*
- Where can I find free concerts in Walt Disney World? *(page 673)*

A DISNEY WORLD VACATION isn't just theme parks and attractions: Many people also want to shop, see live entertainment, or just let loose in the evening. This chapter is for you.

Walt Disney World has a huge outdoor mall complex with restaurants, shopping, and theaters, so its hotel and theme park guests never need to spend money outside its borders. This chapter covers that complex, called **Disney Springs.** In addition, it explores the best **shopping** in the theme parks and nearby in Orlando. Finally, it lists great **nightlife** options in the Disney resorts and elsewhere in the World.

All things considered, the pandemic has had less impact on Disney Springs than on the parks. As at the parks, guests must wear a mask while indoors.

As we went to press, most Disney Springs restaurants were operating at close to full capacity—any remaining limits were likely due as much to lack of staff as anything else. Some retail shops limit the number of guests who can be in the store at any time. If you can't get in immediately, it's a wait of a couple of minutes at most.

continued on page 662

Disney Springs

Disney's Saratoga
Springs Resort
& Spa

Strawberry
Parking Lot

Lake Buena Vista

water taxi

water taxi

water taxi

West Side
Dock

The
Landing
Dock

N

Virgin
Atlantic
Check-In

CC

D

DD

West Side

AA

T

Q J
Q U
K

10

B

E

A

C

F

W

Parking

3 4

G 6 5 8 1 9 7 2

GG

M

BB

ZF

ZC

Orange Garage

14 ZI 23

WEST SIDE
Shopping
1. Disney's Candy Cauldron
2. DisneyStyle
3. Fit2Run
4. M&M Store
5. Pelé Soccer
6. Sosa Family Cigars
7. Star Wars Galactic Outpost
8. Sunglass Icon
9. Super Hero Headquarters

Dining
A. Beatrix
B. City Works Eatery & Pour House
C. Food Trucks at Exposition Park
D. House of Blues Restaurant & Bar/
The Smokehouse
E. Jaleo/Pepe by José Andrés
F. Starbucks
G. Salt & Straw

THE LANDING
Shopping
10. The Art of Shaving
11. Chapel Hats
12. Group 1: Erwin Pearl,
The Ganachery, Oakley, Sanuk,
Savannah Bee Company
13. Havaianas

Dining
H. The Boathouse
I. Chef Art Smith's
Homecomin'
J. The Edison
K. Enzo's Hideaway
L. Erin McKenna's
Bakery NYC
M. Everglazed Donuts &
Cold Brew
N. Gideon's Bakehouse
O. Jock Lindsey's
Hangar Bar
P. Joffrey's Coffee & Tea
Q. Maria & Enzo's
R. Morimoto Asia/
Morimoto Street Food
S. Paddlefish
T. Paradiso 37
U. Pizza Ponte
V. Raglan Road/
Cookes of Dublin
W. STK Orlando
X. Terralina Crafted Italian
Y. Vivoli il Gelato
Z. Wine Bar George

TOWN CENTER
Shopping
14. Coca-Cola Store
15. Group 1: American Threads,
Johnston & Murphy, Tommy
Bahama, Ugg
16. Group 2: Columbia Sportswear,
Everything but Water, Free People,
Johnny Was, Kate Spade New York,
Lilly Pulitzer, Sperry, Sugarboo,
Vera Bradley
17. Group 3: Coach, MAC, Jo Malone
18. Group 4: Lacoste, Luxury of Time,
Sephora, Shore, Stance, Superdry
19. Group 5: Levi's, Orlando Harley
Davidson, TUMI, Volcom
20. Group 6: Alex and Ani, Anthropologie,
Ever After Jewelry Co., Francesca's,
Kiehl's, Kipling, lululemon, Melissa Shoes
L'Occitane en Provence, Rustic Cuff,
Under Armour, UNOde50
21. Group 7: Edward Beiner, Na Hoku,
Pandora

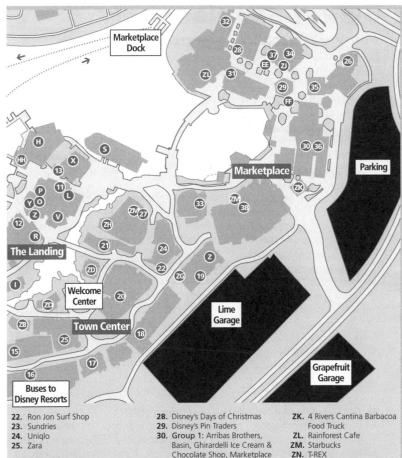

22. Ron Jon Surf Shop
23. Sundries
24. Uniqlo
25. Zara

Dining

ZA. Amorette's Patisserie
ZB. Blaze Fast-Fire'd Pizza
ZC. Chicken Guy
ZD. D-Luxe Burger
ZE. Frontera Cocina
ZF. Planet Hollywood
ZG. The Polite Pig
ZH. Sprinkles
ZI. Wolfgang Puck Bar & Grill

MARKETPLACE Shopping

26. Bibbidi Bobbidi Boutique
27. Build-A-Dino/Dino Store

28. Disney's Days of Christmas
29. Disney's Pin Traders
30. Group 1: Arribas Brothers, Basin, Ghirardelli Ice Cream & Chocolate Shop, Marketplace Co-Op, Tren-D
31. Group 2: The Art Corner, Goofy's Candy Co., Star Wars Trading Post
32. Group 3: The Art of Disney, Disney's Wonderful World of Memories
33. LEGO Store
34. Mickey's Pantry
35. Once Upon a Toy
36. PhotoPass Studio
37. The Spice & Tea Exchange
38. World of Disney

Dining

ZJ. Earl of Sandwich

ZK. 4 Rivers Cantina Barbacoa Food Truck
ZL. Rainforest Cafe
ZM. Starbucks
ZN. T-REX

Entertainment and Attractions

AA. Aerophile
BB. AMC Disney Springs 24 Dine-In Theatres
CC. Cirque du Soleil
DD. House of Blues
EE. Marketplace Carousel
FF. Marketplace Train Express
GG. Splitsville Luxury Lanes
HH. Vintage Amphicar & Italian Water Taxi Tours

continued from page 659

DISNEY SPRINGS

ARRIVING AT DISNEY SPRINGS

BY CAR Guests driving to Disney Springs will take Buena Vista Drive from Disney property, and Hotel Plaza Boulevard from the Disney Springs resorts and FL 535. I-4 westbound offers direct access to the complex via Exit 67. There are three parking garages and four surface lots. The **Lime** garage serves The Landing, Town Center, and Marketplace areas of Disney Springs. The **Orange** garage is closest to the West Side, the AMC 16 movie theater, and Planet Hollywood. The third garage, **Grapefruit,** sits opposite the Lime garage on the other side of Buena Vista Drive. It is connected to Disney Springs via a raised walkway. There is no charge to park in the garages.

An LED display on each level of the garages indicates how many open spaces there are on each level. As rule, the lower levels fill up first, with more open spaces available on each successive level up. The Orange garage can be reached directly from westbound I-4 via Exit 67. All three garage entrances are accessed from Buena Vista Drive.

Because these garages are immense, what you want to do is find a parking space near an elevator bank—this is much more important than scoring a space on a lower level. When we park, we make a beeline to the top level, locate the elevators, and then park as close to them as possible. During the day, it's not unusual to find a space within 20–30 feet. Conditions change as the day progresses, but you're all but guaranteed to find the closest available space to the elevators on the top level. There's also "preferred" parking available in the Lemon and Mango parking lots for $10. We're not sure why you'd pay this much to park, but, hey, it's there if you can't find a spot and you're desperate. All other parking is free.

BY DISNEY TRANSPORTATION All Disney resorts and theme parks offer **bus transportation** to Disney Springs; some bus routes also include a pickup or drop-off at **Typhoon Lagoon.** The Disney bus area is centrally located between the Orange and Lime garages. **Saratoga Springs, Old Key West**, and the **Port Orleans Resorts** offer boat transportation (not operating as we went to press) to the Disney Springs dock at The Landing.

BY TAXI/RIDE-HAILING SERVICE Drop-off and pickup are at the **Cirque du Soleil** theater on the far west side of Disney Springs and at the far east side of the Marketplace.

ON FOOT Saratoga Springs Resort has walking paths to the West Side and Marketplace. Guests staying at hotels in the **Disney Springs Resort Area** (see page 192) can walk to Disney Springs on walkways and pedestrian bridges to avoid traffic.

COVID *tip*
The water taxi was not available at press time.

DISNEY SPRINGS WATER TAXI Guests who don't wish to walk the length of Disney Springs can take a water taxi between points of interest. Docks are at the **Marketplace** close to Rainforest Cafe, **The Landing** close to Paradiso 37, and the **West Side** close to House of Blues and the Strawberry parking lot.

GETTING ORIENTED

DISNEY SPRINGS IS DIVIDED INTO FOUR AREAS, each with its own theme. **Marketplace,** on the east side of Disney Springs, is the most Disney and most kid-friendly, with World of Disney and many activities for children. It has a small carousel and mini-train rides for a nominal fee. A free splash area is great for cooling down, and free concerts take place across from World of Disney in the amphitheater.

The Landing is the waterfront section of Disney Springs. Open, winding paths offer sweeping views of the water and Saratoga Springs as you walk between the Marketplace and West Side.

The third area is the Old Florida–style **Town Center,** which has most of the well-known retail outposts of Disney Springs (**Zara** and **Uniqlo** are the largest). If you've ever found yourself at Pirates of the Caribbean and thought, "What this place needs is a Wetzel's Pretzels," you'll love shopping here. Town Center sits between The Landing and the parking lot.

On the **West Side,** a new Disney-themed **Cirque du Soleil** production named *Drawn to Life* is scheduled to open in 2021. **Jaleo by José Andrés** (page 332), an **AMC** multiplex theater, and **Starbucks** are the biggest draws. A huge entertainment area—The NBA Experience— opened in 2019 and closed in 2020.

COMING SOON

DISNEY SPRINGS EXPECTS to open at least two new venues soon: **Jo Malone,** selling perfumes, and **Salt & Straw,** an ice-cream parlor.

DISNEY SPRINGS SHOPPING AT A GLANCE

Marketplace

BIBBIDI BOBBIDI BOUTIQUE (*temporarily closed; also at the Magic Kingdom and Grand Floridian***)** BBB, located at the far eastern end of the Disney Springs Marketplace next to Once Upon a Toy, is a salon for kids ages 3–12 that will give princess hopefuls a royal makeover, all of which includes so much hair spray that we suspect the place has an ozone hole hovering over it. Packages range from $70 to $480 plus tip. While we may balk a bit that there's no PhD Princess or Med School Maiden package, we can't deny how popular Bibbidi Bobbidi Boutique is with both the kids getting the makeovers and their parents. Photo packages, a Knight Package (for the brothers who have to sit around waiting for the princesses), and other add-ons are available for an extra charge.

BBB can be reserved up to 60 days in advance (70 days for Disney resort guests); call ☎ 407-939-7895 for information or reservations. Allow 30 minutes–1 hour for the whole makeover.

DISNEY'S DAYS OF CHRISTMAS This shop is just plain fun, with hundreds of holiday decorations, from ornaments to stockings to stuffed animals wearing their Christmas best. We especially like the station for ornament personalization. There's also a section dedicated to *The Nightmare Before Christmas.*

GOOFY'S CANDY CO. An interactive show kitchen with lots of sweets. Enjoy create-your-own pretzel rods, marshmallows, and candy apples.

THE LEGO STORE This is an ideal rest stop for parents, and you don't even have to go inside the store. A hands-on outdoor play area has bins of Legos that the kids can go crazy with while Mom and Dad take a break. Inside is all the latest Lego paraphernalia. Photo ops with life-size Disney characters surround the shop.

MARKETPLACE CO-OP The Co-op is loved among Disney fans for its six pop-up-style retail experiences within one shop. Areas include **Cherry Tree Lane** (character-themed women's clothing and accessories), **Disney Centerpiece** (home and kitchen items), **D-Tech on Demand** (custom electronics accessories), **Twenty Eight & Main** (men's goods), **WonderGround Gallery** (Disney-inspired original art), and **Disney Tails** (Disney-themed pet accessories).

*un*official **TIP**
At **Ghirardelli Soda Fountain & Chocolate Shop,** you can smell the chocolate when you walk in. Chocolate souvenirs abound, but treat yourself to a "world famous" sundae topped with hot fudge made daily at the shop. The line for ice cream often winds out the door—it's that good.

ONCE UPON A TOY This is the place to find toy sets and a huge selection of plush; it's also the best place for books, video games, and other media. All the Disney franchises, from the Pixar titles to Marvel and *Star Wars*, are well represented here. We also appreciate that Once Upon a Toy is far less crowded than World of Disney.

THE SPICE AND TEA EXCHANGE Carries flavored salts and sugars, teas, and spice mixes. You can also purchase wines and cookbooks.

TREN-D A fun, hip, urban-inspired boutique for women, with fashion apparel and accessories, plus exclusive items from cutting-edge designers and Disney merchandise you won't find anywhere else.

WORLD OF DISNEY With the largest selection of Disney merchandise on-site or anywhere else, World of Disney can get oppressively crowded at night. It has a little bit of everything. On especially busy days, you may be required to make reservations to enter World of Disney. If so, signage in front of the store will provide instructions on how to do so.

Town Center

AMORETTE'S PATISSERIE Beautiful cakes and pastries; Disney character–themed cakes, large and small, that you won't see anywhere else; and Champagne by the glass. Amorette's will deliver a cake to your Disney Springs restaurant for special occasions with 72 hours notice. *Note:* They don't deliver outside of Disney Springs.

COCA-COLA STORE Not a "best of" unless you're just really obsessed with Coke, but the roof deck has a bar and views of Disney Springs.

JO MALONE Perfumes, candles, and other scented lifestyle items.

KATE SPADE What sets this location apart from the one at your local mall is that it often has Disney-themed bags and accessories you can otherwise find only online.

LILLY PULITZER Bright, fun prints for the country club and sorority girl sets. Sadly, there are no exclusive Disney Lilly prints here—a missed opportunity, if you ask us.

PANDORA The jewelry retailer has an agreement with Walt Disney World that includes another shop on Main Street, U.S.A., and sponsorship of the evening fireworks at Magic Kingdom. Many Disney-exclusive charms sell out quickly.

SUPERDRY Fun casual wear for teens and young adults. We can't put our finger on why we like Superdry, but we do.

TOMMY BAHAMA One of the few shops at Disney Springs with a decent selection of casual menswear. Also has a nice selection of swimwear for both men and women.

UNIQLO Fast fashion along with a nice selection of exclusive Disney apparel. Uniqlo is handy if you need to buy basics such as socks, underwear, and T-shirts.

VERA BRADLEY The ubiquitous quilted bags with a fanatical following. You'll find both Disney-exclusive and mainline prints here.

The Landing

THE ART OF SHAVING Sells shaving gear and offers men's barber and shaving services, including a $50 haircut. Let us know if you try it.

THE GANACHERY Exquisite handmade chocolates in gourmet flavor combinations. This is a Disney-run shop. The candy may be more pricey than you're expecting, but the quality is solid. Makes a nice late-night treat in your hotel room.

GIDEON'S BAKEHOUSE This new addition serves cookies that weigh almost half a pound, admirably attempting to redefine the phrase *single serving*.

JOFFREY'S COFFEE & TEA COMPANY You can purchase leaves to take home or enjoy a hot or cold tea at the counter. Very pleasant and less hectic than Starbucks for your beverage needs.

You'll also find a variety of kiosks selling everything from wind chimes to yo-yos as you walk through The Landing.

Disney Springs West Side

DISNEY'S CANDY CAULDRON Watch as gooey treats are made in the open kitchen. Dipped candy apples (befitting the Snow White–Evil Queen theme) are the specialty of the house. There is also a decent selection of bulk candies.

EVERGLAZED DONUTS & COLD BREW In addition to cold-brew coffee, this brand-new addition to the West Side also serves doughnuts with fruit cereal, s'mores, and peanut butter cups.

M&M'S A large store selling everyone's favorite melt-in-your-mouth chocolates in every flavor imaginable, along with clothing, mugs, and other merchandise.

SALT & STRAW A premium ice-cream parlor.

SOSA FAMILY CIGARS They hand-roll 'em and carry premium imports, including Arturo Fuente, Cuesta-Rey, Diamond Crown, La Gloria Cubana, Macanudo, Padrón, Partagas, Puros Indios, and Sosa. A walk-in humidor stores the top brands.

MAGIC KINGDOM SHOPPING SAMPLER	
I WANT . . .	**FIND IT AT . . .**
• One-stop shopping	• **The Emporium,** Main Street
• Candy, pastries, fudge	• **Main Street Confectionery,** Main Street • **Big Top Treats,** Fantasyland
• Disney art and collectibles	• **The Art of Disney,** Main Street
• Holiday decor	• **Olde Christmas Shoppe,** Liberty Square
• Memory cards and batteries	• **Box Office Gifts,** Main Street
• Personalized mouse ears	• **The Chapeau,** Main Street • **Fantasy Faire,** Fantasyland
• Princess wear	• **The Emporium,** Main Street
• Tech gifts	• **Space Mountain Gift Shop,** Tomorrowland
• Women's jewelry, handbags, accessories	• **Main Street Jewelers** (has a **Pandora** shop)

STAR WARS GALACTIC OUTPOST A large selection of *Star Wars* souvenirs, from T-shirts to Stormtrooper helmets. See page 671 for more on *Star Wars* swag.

BARS AND NIGHTLIFE AT DISNEY SPRINGS

DISNEY SPRINGS IS A POPULAR DESTINATION after dark for folks who aren't ready to be in for the night but don't want to burn park admission for just a few hours in the evening. You'll find street entertainment, including singers, musicians, and performance artists spread throughout Disney Springs (it sometimes feels like they're spaced such that as soon as one is out of earshot, you can hear the next one). There's even more entertainment at many of the restaurants, including bands and singers at **Splitsville** (page 349) and **House of Blues** (page 673) and music and Irish dancers at **Raglan Road** (page 343).

Some of our favorite places to grab a drink are at Disney Springs. The aforementioned Raglan Road has multiple bars and a fantastic menu of appetizers. **Wine Bar George** (page 359) and **Jaleo** (page 332) have excellent drinks and tasty small-plate menus. **Morimoto Asia** (page 338) and **The Boathouse** (page 317) both have bars worth a visit. Reader ratings for **Enzo's Hideaway, The Edison,** and **STK Orlando** are so low that we can't recommend them.

TAKE IT ON THE RUN, BABY

FOR AN EVENING OF DRINKING and strolling, Disney Springs has you covered. Starting with the **AmphiBar** outside the entrance to **The Boathouse,** the restaurants quickly figured out that there was a market for cocktails to go. Find Guinness outside **Raglan Road** and margaritas at **Frontera Cocina** and **Dockside Margaritas.**

SHOPPING *in* WALT DISNEY WORLD *and* ORLANDO

WE ALMOST TITLED THIS SECTION "Exit Through the Gift Shop," but that would've been a cliché (and Banksy beat us to it). Retail is a

EPCOT SHOPPING SAMPLER	
I WANT . . .	**FIND IT AT . . .**
• One-stop shopping	• **Creations Shop,** Future World
• Disney art and collectibles	• **The Art of Disney,** Future World
• Disney comics and books	• **ImageWorks,** Imagination! Pavilion
• Eco-friendly gifts	• **Outpost,** World Showcase
• Kitchen supplies and decor	• **Port of Entry,** World Showcase
• Memory cards and batteries	• **Camera Center,** Future World
• Personalized mouse ears	• **Creations Shop,** Future World
• Princess wear	• **The Wandering Reindeer** (*temporarily closed*), Norway Pavilion
• Tech gifts	• **Creations Shop and Camera Center,** Future World

huge revenue source for Disney. If you enjoy shopping, we recommend setting aside some time and money to do so. And even if you don't enjoy it, you may be traveling with someone who does.

SHOPPING AT DISNEY WORLD

EACH THEME PARK has at least one major retail space, several minor ones, and space attached to most attractions. While we occasionally bemoan the homogenization of the merchandise selection, this does mean that if something catches your eye, you'll most likely see it again. Ditto for sale prices. Pricing is consistent throughout the resorts, and an item on sale in one location will be the same price at all locations.

See the following pages for a quick-reference guide to which theme park shops carry what you're looking for.

EPCOT Shopping

Retail is a huge part of the **World Showcase** experience at EPCOT, much more so than at the other theme parks. This is one of the few times on your vacation that you won't be able to say "I'll see it again later" if something catches your eye. With a selection that ranges from affordable trinkets to Mikimoto pearls, the shops in World Showcase have something for everyone. Walking clockwise around World Showcase, you'll find the following:

★ **MEXICO** Probably the most immersive shopping experience in all of World Showcase, **Plaza de los Amigos** is a re-creation of a Mexican shopping village at dusk. You'll find all manner of sombreros, Day of the Dead items, Oaxacan carved wooden animals, and blankets. Along the side of the shopping area is **La Princesa de Cristal,** with crystal jewelry and trinkets, and another shop with leather items, women's dresses and blouses, and other accessories. If you need a break from shopping, the **San Angel Inn Restaurante** (page 346) and *Unofficial* favorite watering hole **La Cava del Tequila** (page 289) are located just off the shopping area.

★ **NORWAY The Fjording** and **The Wandering Reindeer** (temporarily closed) are a series of small shopping galleries with popular imports such as trolls (from $15) and wooden Christmas ornaments (from $5). Other

DISNEY'S ANIMAL KINGDOM SHOPPING SAMPLER	
I WANT ...	**FIND IT AT ...**
• One-stop shopping	• **Discovery Trading Company,** Discovery Island
• African souvenirs	• **Mombasa Marketplace,** Harambe, Africa
• Dinosaur kitsch and toys	• **Chester and Hester's Dinosaur Treasures,** DinoLand U.S.A.
• Memory cards and batteries	• **Island Mercantile,** Discovery Island
• Personalized mouse ears	• **Island Mercantile,** Discovery Island
• African wines, cookbooks, and Flame Tree barbecue sauce	• **Zuri's Sweets Shop,** Africa
• My own shoulder-top banshee or glowing Pandora merch	• **Windtraders,** Pandora— The Land of Avatar

hard-to-find imports include Scandinavian foods and candies, Laila perfume and body lotion, and Helly Hansen and Dale of Norway clothing, including thick woolen sweaters. You'll also find all things *Frozen* here.

★ **CHINA** This pavilion features one of our favorite shops, piled with such imports as real silk kimonos, cloisonné, and thick silk rugs. **House of Good Fortune** is more like a rambling department store than a shop. You'll find everything here, from silk fans to $4,000 jade sculptures to antique furniture. The silk dresses and robes are competitively priced in the $100 range. Darling handbags are $10 and up, and silk ties are around $20. We always admire the handwoven pure-silk carpets, starting around $300 for a 2-foot rug and topping out around $2,500 for a 4-by-8–foot rug. The prices are comparable to what you'd pay in a retail shop—if you could find one that imports carpets like these.

Village Traders, a shop between China and Germany, sells African woodcarvings that are as unusual as they come. Another specialty here is bead jewelry, crafted in Uganda from repurposed Disney paper products such as old handout guides.

★ **GERMANY** Shops interconnect on both sides of the cobblestoned central plaza and purvey an impressive collection of imports. Tiny **Das Kaufhaus** (temporarily closed) stocks a nice selection of Adidas

---

TIPS FOR AVOIDING BUYER'S REMORSE

1. Know ahead of time how much things cost. Many theme park items are available at disneystore.com.

2. Be specific. Disney collecting can spiral out of control if you don't narrow your focus. Pick a character or movie you love, and stick to that.

3. Don't buy dated merchandise. That Walt Disney World 2019 T-shirt you buy to commemorate your vacation is going to look awfully silly on January 1, 2020. There's a reason this stuff is the number-one seller at Disney outlets.

4. The local big-box stores will have a selection of low-priced Disney and Universal souvenirs. Look for them at the front of the stores.

5. Don't fall for "limited editions." If they make 2,000 of something, is it really limited?

6. Wait. Don't make your purchases until you've been to more than one shop.

7. Consider comestibles as souvenirs. There's no buyer's remorse if you consume the evidence.

8. Some of the best things in life are free. Consider our favorite freebies at Walt Disney World (see 670), and skip the cash register.

DISNEY'S HOLLYWOOD STUDIOS SHOPPING SAMPLER	
I WANT . . .	**FIND IT AT . . .**
• One-stop shopping	• **Mickey's of Hollywood,** Hollywood Blvd.
• Candy, pastries, fudge	• **Beverly Sunset** (temporarily closed), Hollywood and Sunset
• Holiday decor	• **It's a Wonderful Shop,** Streets of America
• Magic Bands and other Disney gifts	• **The Darkroom,** Hollywood Blvd.
• Personalized mouse ears	• **Legends of Hollywood,** Sunset Blvd.
• Princess wear	• **Legends of Hollywood,** Sunset Blvd.
• Retro men's clothing and gifts	• **Keystone Clothiers,** Hollywood Blvd.
• Women's jewelry, handbags, and accessories	• **Keystone Clothiers,** Hollywood Blvd.
• *Star Wars* souvenirs	• **Black Spire Outfitters,** Galaxy's Edge

sportswear. Next door is **Volkskunst** (temporarily closed), where the walls are covered with Schneider cuckoo clocks and the shelves are stocked with limited-edition steins and glassware. Next is **Der Teddybär** (temporarily closed), featuring Engel-Puppen dolls and Steiff plush toys, among other delights for children. Across the plaza, **Kunstarbeit in Kristall** carries a fabulous collection of Swarovski crystal, including pins, glassware, and Arribas Brothers collectibles (check out the limited-edition $37,500 replica of Cinderella Castle, blinged out with more than 20,000 Swarovski crystals). Next is the **Weinkeller,** with nearly 300 varieties of German wine. Step through the door to **Die Weihnachts Ecke,** where Christmas ornaments and handmade nutcrackers are on display year-round. Anyone with a sweet tooth will go crazy just smelling the most delicious store in Germany's lineup, **Karamell-Küche.** Treats are made in-house with Werther's Original caramel, from caramel apples to cookies and candies made or drizzled with caramel. You'll also find an impressive selection of Werther's Original candies.

★ **ITALY Il Bel Cristallo** showcases Puma sportswear, Bulgari and Emilio Pucci fragrances, Murano figurines, elaborate Venetian masks, and a small selection of Christmas decorations in the back room.

★ **JAPAN** An outpost of Japan's 300-year-old **Mitsukoshi Department Store** stretches along one entire side of the pavilion. Kid-friendly merchandise (Hello Kitty, Naruto, and Yu-Gi-Oh!) fills the front, with kimonos, slippers, handbags, and lots more at the back. Mitsukoshi's expanded culinary display includes a sake-tasting bar, along with chopsticks, pretty rice bowls, a large variety of teas and teapots, and imported snacks. The selection of products related to anime (the uniquely Japanese style of animation) is great as well. Tourists line up for an oyster guaranteed to have a pearl in its shell (pearls are polished for you by the salesperson).

★ **MOROCCO** Several shops wend through this pavilion: **Tangier Traders** sells traditional Moroccan clothing, shoes, and fezzes; **The Brass Bazaar** features brass, of course, and ceramic and wooden kitchenware (not dishwasher safe); and **Casablanca Carpets** offers a wide variety of Moroccan rugs, as well as decorative pieces such as abstract-shaped lamps, sequined pillows, and incense holders.

★ **FRANCE** The courtyard at the France Pavilion has some *merveilleux* shopping opportunities. A dedicated Guerlain shop, **La Signature,** offers cosmetics and fragrances from the French house. **Plume et Palette** has fragrances, cosmetics, and women's accessories from Christian Dior, Givenchy, Kenzo, Le Tanneur, and Thierry Mugler, to name a few.

Find wines and kitchen goods, including a Champagne-tasting counter, at **Les Vins de Chefs de France** and **L'Esprit de la Provence,** which are connecting shops. And finally, at the back of the pavilion, **Souvenirs de France** sells a smattering of everything French, from berets and Eiffel Tower models to T-shirts and language books.

★ **UNITED KINGDOM** A handful of interesting imports from across the pond are scattered throughout half a dozen small shops. **The Toy Soldier** (temporarily closed) stocks costumes, books, and plush toys featuring English characters from favorite films and television shows, such as *Dr. Who* and *Downton Abbey,* as well as British rock and roll–themed items, including Beatles merchandise. You'll find plenty of Alice in Wonderland, Peter Pan, and Winnie the Pooh merchandise too. Stop at **The Crown & Crest** (temporarily closed) to look up your family name in the coat-of-arms book, and the shop will create your family's insignia in a beautiful frame of your choice. At the adjacent **Sportsman's Shoppe** (temporarily closed), you'll find plenty of football (soccer) apparel, balls, and books.

Across the street, you'll find **The Queen's Table,** a gift shop with UK-themed clothing, glassware, and more. **Lords and Ladies,** a quaint store, offers lotions, soaps, scarves, jewelry, and perfume from the United Kingdom. **The Tea Caddy** stocks Twinings tea, biscuits (cookies to us Yanks), and candy.

★ **CANADA** There's not much shopping here, but **Northwest Mercantile** (temporarily closed) has a wide selection of merchandise, including NHL jerseys, T-shirts, sweatshirts, aprons, and pajamas. Bottles of ice wine and maple syrup make nice souvenirs for foodies.

Our Favorite Free Souvenirs from Walt Disney World

CELEBRATION BUTTONS Just married? Just graduated? Just happy to be nominated? There's a button for that.

KIDCOT FUN STOPS Sometimes the best souvenir is the one you get for free (or at least it's a good line to tell your kids).

BIRTHDAY TREATS Be sure to mention any special occasions you're celebrating when you check in for your meal at a full-service restaurant. You may get a surprise dessert.

STICKERS Cast members give out so many of these, we're afraid there might be an adhesive shortage.

TRANSPORTATION TRADING CARDS Did you know that monorail and bus drivers have trading cards to give out?

TOILETRIES We may or may not have hoards of Disney resort shampoos, bath gels, and soaps in our own homes.

The Force Is Strong . . . on Your Wallet

Since before the release of *Star Wars: The Force Awakens* in 2015, virtually every store of size in Walt Disney World has had some sort of *Star Wars* merchandise available. If you're looking for the galaxy's best selection of unique gifts, the stores of **Galaxy's Edge** in Disney's Hollywood Studios are where you'll want to look. **Black Spire Outfitters** carries general *Star Wars* clothing, toys, and gifts; **Creature Stall** sells toys and plush, as does **Toydarian Toymaker;** and **Dok-Ondar's Den of Antiquities** has clothing and toys, as well as food, housewares, and art and collectibles. You'll be able to get your own droid, plus *Star Wars*–themed Mickey ears, at **Droid Depot. First Order Cargo** stocks a bit of everything, done in the fashion of futuristic military dictatorships. **Resistance Supply** is similar, for the good guys. You'll need a lightsaber if you plan to join the Resistance—pick one up at **Savi's Workshop.**

More Tips for Disney Shopping

Don't want to carry your stuff around? If you're staying at a Disney hotel, you can have your packages delivered to your resort from any of the four Disney parks. Packages will be delivered to the gift shop by noon the following day, so this service is unavailable if you're checking out of your room the same day. Same-day pickup inside the theme parks is available. For a nominal charge, you can ship items to your home.

A New Brunswick, Canada, reader spread the news:

> *I can't help but wonder how well known the parks' delivery services are. In EPCOT I overheard two shoppers discussing whether they should buy a large pint glass; a major point of discussion was "How would we get it home?" I chimed in to tell them all about Disney's Package Pickup service.*

If you realize on your flight home that you forgot to buy mouse ears for your niece, don't worry. **ShopDisney** online (shopdisney.com) has a dedicated section of parks merchandise.

SHOPPING OUTSIDE DISNEY WORLD

Upscale Shopping

The Mall at Millenia is anchored by **Bloomingdale's, Macy's,** and **Neiman Marcus.** You'll find designer boutiques, such as **Burberry, Chanel, Gucci, Hermès, Louis Vuitton, Salvatore Ferragamo,** and **Yves Saint Laurent** as well. Millenia also has the closest **Apple Store** to Universal or Walt Disney World. It isn't entirely high-end, however, with fast-fashion staples such as **H&M** and **Forever 21,** as well as the usual suspects, including **Gap, Victoria's Secret,** and **J.Crew.** Visit mallatmillenia.com for a full directory.

Midscale Shopping

The Florida Mall is home to **Dillard's, JC Penney, Macy's,** and **Sears.** Apart from the anchors and high-end designer shops, it has much the same stores as The Mall at Millenia. Visit simon.com/mall/the-florida-mall.

Outlet Shopping

If you think the crowds at the parks can be overwhelming, avoid the two **Orlando Premium Outlets** (premiumoutlets.com/outlet/orlando -vineland) at International Drive and Vineland Avenue. Tourists arrive here by the busload, and the experience will leave you questioning everything from consumer culture to your own judgment in dropping by. For the theme park visitor, the only redeeming aspect of these two shopping malls is the **Disney Character Warehouse** (there are locations at both outlets).

Disney Shopping Outside of Walt Disney World

The Disney outlet at Vineland is about twice the size of the location on I-Drive. To get an idea of what you'll find there, check out Derek Burgan's past **"The Magic, The Memories, and Merch!"** entries on the **TouringPlans.com** blog (blog.touringplans.com/author/derek), in which he gives the scoop on what Disney made too much of.

Fans seeking one-of-a-kind souvenirs, including costumes, props, and local art, should head to **TD Collectibles** (11920 W. Colonial Dr., Ste. 30, Ocoee; ☎ 407-347-0670; tdcollectibles.net). Store hours are Tuesday–Saturday, noon–4:30 p.m.

Orlando International Airport has two Disney shops, one at each terminal, for purchases you need to make on the way home. The shops are fairly large and well themed for what they are; plus, they're run by Disney. They're good spots to kill time while you wait for your flight.

NIGHTLIFE *at* WALT DISNEY WORLD RESORTS

DISNEY'S BOARDWALK OFFERS two adult-oriented venues, Jellyrolls and Atlantic Dance Hall. **Jellyrolls** (temporarily closed) is a dueling-piano bar that's open 7 p.m.–2 a.m. nightly (cover charge applies). It's one of the few 21-and-up places you'll find at Walt Disney World. The entertainment is outstanding here. Across from Jellyrolls is **Atlantic Dance Hall** (temporarily closed). It's often booked for private events, but on weekends it's generally open in the evenings (and has free admission). The house DJ spins everything from '70s disco to top 40 and EDM. Like Jellyrolls, Atlantic Dance Hall is 21-and-up.

At Coronado Springs, you'll find **Rix Sports Bar & Grill**. It usually isn't busy unless there's a convention at the resort. Other Walt Disney World resort bars with live entertainment are **Scat Cat's Club** (temporarily closed) at Port Orleans French Quarter and **River Roost** (temporarily closed) at Port Orleans Riverside.

Trader Sam's Grog Grotto (inspired by the bar at the Disneyland Hotel in California) at the Polynesian Village is a delight. If you've

*un*official **TIP**
Nightlife doesn't just mean stuff for the olds to do. There are plenty of kid-friendly activities after dark for the young ones. Check your resort's recreation schedule for campfires, movies on the beach or at the pool, and more.

ever found yourself at the *Enchanted Tiki Room* and thought to your-self, "You know, booze would really make this better," this is your place. See page 354 for a detailed review.

Our favorite nightspot at Walt Disney World, **Top of the World** at Bay Lake Tower, is for Disney Vacation Club members and their guests. If you're a member, or you can talk one into letting you in, try to stay after the Magic Kingdom fireworks—the view and setting are outstanding.

Free Concerts at Walt Disney World

EPCOT FESTIVAL OF THE ARTS This festival takes place in January and February and includes concerts at the America Gardens Theatre. The Disney on Broadway series is often featured.

GARDEN ROCKS Held during the Flower & Garden Festival in the spring, this series features acts from the 1960s onward. Many bands are more or less in their original lineup, while others have one member from a more famous group.

EAT TO THE BEAT Classic and once-in-the-news acts accompany your trip around the World Showcase during the fall Food & Wine Festival. Groups tend to be from the 1980s and later.

House of Blues

COVID *tip*

Most concerts are temporarily suspended.

Type of show Live concerts with an emphasis on rock and blues. **Tickets and information** ☎ 407-934-BLUE (2583); hob .com. **Admission cost with taxes** From $11 for club nights to $25 and up, depending on who's performing. **Nights of lowest attendance** Monday and Tuesday. **Usual showtimes** Vary between 7 p.m. and 9:30 p.m., depending on who's performing.

DESCRIPTION AND COMMENTS Developed by Blues Brother Dan Aykroyd, House of Blues consists of a restaurant and blues bar, as well as a concert hall. The restaurant is one of the few late-night-dining options in Walt Disney World. Live music cranks up every night at 10:30 p.m. in the restaurant and blues bar, but even before then, the joint is way beyond 110 decibels. The music hall next door features concerts by an eclectic array of musicians and groups. Genres have included gospel, blues, funk, ska, dance, salsa, rap, zydeco, hard rock, groove rock, and reggae.

TOURING TIPS Prices vary from night to night according to the fame and drawing power of the featured band. Tickets ranged from $19 to $80 during our visits but go higher when a really big name is scheduled.

The music hall is set up like a nightclub, with tables and barstools for only about 150 people and standing room for a whopping 1,850. The tables and stools are first come, first served, with doors opening an hour before showtime on weekdays and 90 minutes before showtime on weekends. All shows are all ages unless otherwise indicated.

READERS' QUESTIONS *and* COMMENTS

READERS' QUESTIONS *to the* AUTHORS

FOLLOWING ARE SOME FREQUENTLY ASKED questions and comments from *Unofficial Guide* readers.

QUESTION: *When you do your research, are you admitted to the parks for free? Do the Disney people know you're there?*

ANSWER: We pay regular admission; usually Disney doesn't know we're on-site. We pay for our own meals and lodging, both in and out of Walt Disney World.

QUESTION: *How often is the* Unofficial Guide *revised?*

ANSWER: We publish a new edition in hard copy and e-book formats once a year, with at least one reprint/e-update to account for changes at the theme parks. (Take it from us: The only constant at Walt Disney World is change.)

QUESTION: *Where can I find information about what's changed at Walt Disney World in between published editions of the* Unofficial Guide?

ANSWER: We post important information online at **TouringPlans.com.**

QUESTION: *Do you write each new edition from scratch?*

ANSWER: Nope. When it comes to a destination the size of Walt Disney World, it's hard enough to keep up with what's new. Moreover, we put a lot of effort into communicating the most useful information in the clearest possible language. If an attraction or hotel hasn't changed, we try not to tinker with its coverage for the sake of freshening the prose.

QUESTION: *I've never read any other* Unofficial Guides. *Are they all as critical as* The Unofficial Guide to Walt Disney World?

ANSWER: What some readers perceive as critical we see as objective and constructive. Our job is to prepare you for both the best and worst of Walt Disney World. As it happens, some folks are very passionate about what one reader calls "the inherent goodness of Disney." These readers might be more comfortable with press releases or the *Official Guide* than with the strong consumer viewpoint represented in our guide. That said, some readers take us to task for being overly *positive*.

QUESTION: *How many people have you surveyed for your age-group ratings regarding the attractions?*

ANSWER: Since the first *Unofficial Guide* was published in 1985, we've interviewed or surveyed **more than 700,000** Walt Disney World patrons.

QUESTION: *Do you stay in Walt Disney World? If not, where?*

ANSWER: We stay at Walt Disney World lodging properties quite often. Since we began writing about Walt Disney World in 1982, we've stayed at all the Disney resorts and more than 100 different properties in various locations around Orlando, Lake Buena Vista, and Kissimmee.

QUESTION: *Bob, what's your favorite Florida attraction?*

ANSWER: What attracts me (as opposed to my favorite attraction) is **Juniper Springs,** a stunningly beautiful stream about 1½ hours north of Orlando in the Ocala National Forest. Originating in a limestone aquifer, the crystal-clear water erupts from the ground and begins a 10-mile journey to the creek's mouth at Lake George. Winding through palm, cypress, and live oak, the stream is more exotic than the Jungle Cruise, and alive with birds, turtles, and alligators. Put in at the Juniper Springs Recreation Area on FL 40, 36 miles east of Ocala. The 7-mile trip to the FL 19 bridge takes about 4½ hours. Canoe rentals and shuttle service are available at the recreation area. Call ☎ 352-625-3147 for more information.

READERS' COMMENTS

A WOMAN FROM SUWANEE, GEORGIA, offers a suggestion for the perfect Disney vacation:

> *Your book made our trip a much more successful one. It also frustrated our male adults, who erroneously believed this was a trip for their enjoyment. We followed your advice to get up early and see as much as possible before an early lunch. But the men refused to go back to the hotel for a nap and a meal outside the park, so we fought the crowds until 3 or 4 p.m., by which time everyone was exhausted and cranky. My mother and I decided our next trip will include your guidebook and the children—but no men!*

A Midwestern mom loved getting in the game, writing:

> *It was a thrill for me to [be at the official] park opening—to hear the music and announcements, then hurry with the throngs to the first ride. It was so exciting! My husband teased me for days about running over old ladies and little children—I didn't run! I was speed-walking!*

A woman from Mount Gretna, Pennsylvania, had some questions about theme park attire:

> *I don't believe there was a section that addressed whether or not you could wear dresses on the rides. Quite a few amusement parks have*

security straps or bars that come up between one's knees, making it very difficult and immodest to wear dresses or skirts. Many women want to wear dresses for convenience, comfort, or cultural/religious convictions. I was concerned as I was packing whether this would limit any rides I could get on. I was quite pleased that it did not.

An Atlanta reader relates the story of a dirty bird and a solicitous cast member:

While riding Splash Mountain, a teenage boy in our boat had brought a poncho (smart move), and he took it off before we got out of the boat . . . just in time for a bird to poop on him. He went to buy a shirt in the gift shop, and when the cast member found out what had happened, he gave the kid a free shirt. I thought that was very nice!

A Columbia, Missouri, woman offers advice for wives with anxious husbands:

A smartphone is the best thing in the world for keeping your husband busy in line. As long as mine had that phone, he could check email, check dinner plans, and take and send pictures of the kids to family back home. He never complained about waiting in line, ever.

A Denver reader bursts our bubble (hey, we thought we were Disney's favorites):

WDW cast members have an interesting reaction to the Guide. With the book in hand, we got an almost vampire-vs.-holy-water reaction from one cast member (who then asked if he could take a quick peek).

From an exhausted mother:

Make sure moms are prepared for the fact that their kids will throw tantrums . . . and so will their husbands. Disney is a magical, wonderful thing, but it was also the most exhausting thing I have ever done. It required more patience than I've needed so far as a parent.

From an opinionated Georgia family of four:

My 13-year-old son's one-word description of Space Mountain: "Awesome." My husband's one-word description: "Hell." My 10-year-old's best comment: "Here's a Disney motto no one talks about: 'Bleed 'em dry.' " My 13-year-old's best comment, as I was trying to get everyone to stop and pose in front of the topiaries: "Keep movin', Mom! There's no time for memories!"

A Somerville, Alabama, woman is succinct if nothing else:

Everything, other than my husband, was perfect.

The weather is always, um, a hot topic with *Unofficial Guide* readers. First from a Poulsbo, Washington, reader:

Holy hell, the Florida humidity is NO JOKE!

From a woman who is more receptive after a couple of drinks:

We found (as an adult couple) that arriving early and leaving the parks for an afternoon drink or three in the monorail resorts was our saving grace! It also allowed my husband to convince me to go on more of the roller coasters!

And so it goes. . . .

UNDERSTANDING DISNEY WORLD ATTRACTIONS

CUT YOUR TIME IN LINE *by* UNDERSTANDING *the* RIDES

WALT DISNEY WORLD HAS MANY TYPES OF RIDES. Some, such as **Pirates of the Caribbean** at the Magic Kingdom, can carry more than 3,000 people an hour. At the other extreme, **TriceraTop Spin** at Animal Kingdom can handle only around 500 people an hour. Most rides fall somewhere in between. Many factors figure into how long you'll wait to experience a ride: its popularity; how it loads and unloads; how many persons can ride at once; how many units (cars, rockets, boats, flying elephants, and the like) are in service at a time; and how many cast members are available to operate the ride.

To develop an efficient touring plan, it's necessary to understand how rides and shows are designed and function. Let's examine both.

1. How Popular Is the Ride?

Newer rides, such as the two new attractions at **Star Wars: Galaxy's Edge** in Disney's Hollywood Studios, attract a lot of people, as do such longtime favorites as Animal Kingdom's **Expedition Everest.** If a ride is popular, you need to know how it operates in order to determine the best time to ride. But a ride need not be especially popular to generate long lines; in some cases, such lines are due not to a ride's popularity but to poor traffic engineering. This is the case at the **Mad Tea Party** and **The Barnstormer** (among others) in Fantasyland. Both rides serve only a small percentage of any day's attendance at the Magic Kingdom, yet because they take so long to load and unload, long lines form regardless.

2. How Does the Ride Load and Unload?

Some rides never stop—they're like conveyor belts that go around and around. These are **continuous loaders.** Examples include **The Haunted Mansion** and **Under the Sea: Journey of the Little Mermaid** at the Magic Kingdom, along with **Spaceship Earth** at EPCOT. The number of people who can be moved through in an hour depends on how many cars— "doom buggies" or whatever—are on the conveyor. The Haunted

Mansion and Spaceship Earth have lots of cars on the conveyor, and each consequently can move more than 2,000 people an hour.

Other rides are **interval loaders.** Cars are unloaded, loaded, and dispatched at set intervals (sometimes controlled manually, sometimes by computer). **Space Mountain** in Tomorrowland is an interval loader: It has two tracks (the ride has been duplicated in the same facility). Each track can run as many as 14 space capsules, released at 36-, 26-, or 21-second intervals. (The bigger the crowd, the shorter the interval.)

In one kind of interval loader, empty cars, as in Space Mountain's space capsules, return to where they reload. In a second kind, such as Splash Mountain, one group of riders enters the vehicle while the previous group departs. Rides of the latter type are referred to as **in-and-out** interval loaders. As a boat docks, those who have just completed their ride exit to the left; at almost the same time, those waiting to ride enter the boat from the right. The reloaded boat is released to the dispatch point a few yards down the line, where it's launched according to the interval being used.

Interval loaders of both types can be very efficient people-movers if (1) the dispatch (launch) interval is relatively short and (2) the ride can accommodate many vehicles at one time. Because many boats can float through Pirates of the Caribbean at one time, and the dispatch interval is short, almost 3,000 people can see this attraction each hour.

The least efficient rides, in terms of traffic engineering, are **cycle rides,** also called **stop-and-go rides.** Those waiting to ride exchange places with those who have just ridden. Unlike in-and-out interval rides, cycle rides shut down during loading and unloading. While one boat is loading and unloading in It's a Small World (an interval loader), many other boats are advancing through the ride. But when **Dumbo** touches down, the whole ride is at a standstill until the next flight launches (ditto **Prince Charming Regal Carrousel** and the **Mad Tea Party**).

With cycle rides, the time in motion is **ride time,** and the time the ride idles while loading and unloading is **load time.** Load time plus ride time equals **cycle time,** or the time from the start of one run of the ride until the start of the next. The only cycle rides in Disney World are in the Magic Kingdom and Disney's Animal Kingdom.

3. How Many People Can Ride at One Time?

This figure expresses **system capacity,** or the number of people who can ride at one time. The greater the carrying capacity of a ride (all other things being equal), the more visitors it can accommodate per hour. Some rides can add extra units (cars, boats, and such) as crowds build, to increase capacity; others, such as the **Astro Orbiter** in Tomorrowland, have a fixed capacity (it's impossible to add more rockets).

4. How Many Units Are in Service at a Given Time?

Unit is our term for the vehicle in which you ride. At the **Mad Tea Party,** the unit is a teacup; at **Peter Pan's Flight,** a pirate ship. On some rides (mostly cycle rides), the number of units operating at one time is fixed. There are always 32 flying elephants at Dumbo and 90 horses on Prince Charming Regal Carrousel. There's no way to increase the capacity of such rides by adding units. On a busy day, the only way to carry more people each hour on a fixed-unit cycle ride is to shorten the loading time or decrease the ride time.

The bottom line: On a busy day for a cycle ride, you'll wait longer and possibly be rewarded with a shorter ride. This is why we steer you away from cycle rides unless you're willing to ride them early in the morning or late at night. These are the cycle rides:

- **MAGIC KINGDOM** Astro Orbiter, The Barnstormer, Dumbo the Flying Elephant, Mad Tea Party, The Magic Carpets of Aladdin, Prince Charming Regal Carrousel
- **DISNEY'S ANIMAL KINGDOM** TriceraTop Spin

Many other rides throughout Walt Disney World can increase their capacity by adding units as crowds build. For example, if attendance is light, **Big Thunder Mountain Railroad** in Frontierland can start the day by running only one of its five mine trains from one of two available loading platforms. If lines build, the other platform is opened and more mine trains are placed into operation. At capacity, the five trains can carry about 2,400 persons an hour. Likewise, **Star Tours** at Disney's Hollywood Studios can increase its capacity by using all its simulators, and the **Gran Fiesta Tour** boat ride at Mexico in EPCOT can add more boats. Sometimes a long queue will disappear almost instantly when new units are brought online. When an interval loader places more units into operation, it usually shortens the dispatch intervals, allowing more units to be dispatched more often.

5. How Many Cast Members Are Available to Operate the Ride?

Adding cast members to a ride can allow more units to operate or additional loading or holding areas to open. In the Magic Kingdom, **Pirates of the Caribbean** and **It's a Small World** can run two waiting lines and loading zones. **The Haunted Mansion** has a 1½-minute preshow staged in a "stretch room." On busy days, a second stretch room can be activated, permitting a more continuous flow of visitors to the actual loading area.

Additional staff makes a world of difference to some cycle rides. Often, the **Mad Tea Party** has only one attendant. This person alone must clear visitors from the ride just completed, admit and seat visitors for the upcoming ride, check that each teacup is secured, return to the control panel, issue instructions to the riders, and finally activate the ride (whew!). A second attendant divides these responsibilities and cuts loading time by 25%–50%.

CUT YOUR TIME IN LINE *by* UNDERSTANDING *the* SHOWS

THE FEATURED ATTRACTIONS at Walt Disney World also include theater presentations. While they aren't as complex as rides, understanding them from a traffic-engineering standpoint may save you touring time as well.

Most theater attractions operate in three phases:

1. Guests are in the theater viewing the presentation.

2. Guests who have passed through the turnstile wait in a holding area or lobby. They will be admitted to the theater as soon as the show in progress concludes. Several attractions offer a preshow in their lobby to entertain guests until they're admitted to the main show. Examples include *Enchanted Tiki Room* in the Magic Kingdom and *Muppet-Vision 3-D* at DHS.

3. A line waits outside. Guests in line enter the lobby when there's room and will ultimately move into the theater.

The theater's capacity, the presentation's popularity, and park attendance all determine how long the lines will be at a show. Except for holidays and other days of heavy attendance, the longest wait for a show usually doesn't exceed the length of a single performance. Because almost all theater attractions run continuously, stopping only long enough for the previous audience to leave and the waiting audience to enter, a performance will be in progress when you arrive. For example, the **Canada Far and Wide** movie at EPCOT's Canada Pavilion in World Showcase lasts 12 minutes; your longest wait under normal circumstances is about 12 minutes if you arrive just after the show has begun.

ACCOMMODATIONS INDEX

Note: Page numbers in **bold** indicate a resort's main entry.

See also the Restaurant Index on pages 687–690 and the Subject Index on pages 691–709.

See also the Restaurant Index on pages 687–690 and the Subject Index on pages 691–709.

See also the Restaurant Index on pages 687-690 and the Subject Index on pages 691-709.

See also the Restaurant Index on pages 687–690 and the Subject Index on pages 691–709.

See also the Restaurant Index on pages 687–690 and the Subject Index on pages 691–709.

RESTAURANT INDEX

Note: Page numbers in **bold** indicate a restaurant's main entry.

See also the Accommodations Index on pages 682–686 and the Subject Index on pages 691–709.

See also the Accommodations Index on pages 682–686 and the Subject Index on pages 691–709.

See also the Accommodations Index on pages 682–686 and the Subject Index on pages 691–709.

See also the Accommodations Index on pages 682-686 and the Subject Index on pages 691-709.

SUBJECT INDEX

See also the Accommodations Index on pages 682–686 and the Restaurant Index on pages 687–690.

See also the Accommodations Index on pages 682-686 and the Restaurant Index on pages 687-690.

See also the Accommodations Index on pages 682–686 and the Restaurant Index on pages 687–690.

See also the Accommodations Index on pages 682–686 and the Restaurant Index on pages 687–690.

See also the Accommodations Index on pages 682–686 and the Restaurant Index on pages 687–690.

See also the Accommodations Index on pages 682–686 and the Restaurant Index on pages 687–690.

See also the Accommodations Index on pages 682–686 and the Restaurant Index on pages 687–690.

See also the Accommodations Index on pages 682–686 and the Restaurant Index on pages 687–690.

See also the Accommodations Index on pages 682–686 and the Restaurant Index on pages 687–690.

See also the Accommodations Index on pages 682–686 and the Restaurant Index on pages 687–690.

See also the Accommodations Index on pages 682–686 and the Restaurant Index on pages 687–690.

See also the Accommodations Index on pages 682-686 and the Restaurant Index on pages 687-690.

See also the Accommodations Index on pages 682-686 and the Restaurant Index on pages 687-690.

See also the Accommodations Index on pages 682–686 and the Restaurant Index on pages 687–690.

TOURING PLANS

"Not a Touring Plan" TOURING PLANS

FOR ALL PLANS, make park reservations as soon as you know your travel dates.

MAGIC KINGDOM

FOR ALL GUESTS If using Genie+, get the first available reservation for any of the first three attractions to visit, and fit that return-time window into the plan. If none of the next three steps participates in Genie+, then get a reservation for the next attraction in the plan that *does* participate. Get your "next" Genie+ reservation once you've gotten in line for your current Genie+ reservation. If Tron is using boarding groups, pause your tour to ride when your boarding group is called.

FOR GUESTS USING EARLY THEME PARK ENTRY Arrive at the park entrance 40 minutes–1 hour before official opening. If Tron Lightcycle Power Run is using boarding group reservations, obtain one before you arrive.

FOR OFF-SITE GUESTS ARRIVING AT OFFICIAL OPENING TIME Arrive at the park entrance 30–60 minutes before official opening. If Tron Lightcycle Power Run is using boarding group reservations, obtain one before you arrive.

FOR PARENTS WITH ONE DAY TO TOUR AND USING EARLY ENTRY See Fantasyland first, starting with Seven Dwarfs Mine Train and then Peter Pan's Flight. See Frontierland and then Adventureland. Consider a mid-day break if the park is open past 8 p.m. Then tour Tomorrowland and Liberty Square.

FOR PARENTS WITH ONE DAY TO TOUR AND ARRIVING AT OFFICIAL OPENING Begin a clockwise tour of the park in Fantasyland, except for Seven Dwarfs Mine Train and Peter Pan's Flight. After Fantasyland, tour Tomorrowland, then Adventureland, Frontierland, and Liberty Square. Experience Seven Dwarfs Mine Train and Peter Pan's Flight in the late afternoon or evening.

FOR ADULTS WITH ONE DAY TO TOUR AND USING EARLY ENTRY If Tron Lightcycle Power Run is open and not using boarding groups, see that first, then the rest of Tomorrowland. Tour the headliner attractions in Frontierland and Adventureland next, saving shows for the middle of the day. Tour Liberty Square around dinner. End the day with Fantasyland, saving Seven Dwarfs and Peter Pan's Flight for as late as possible.

FOR ADULTS WITH ONE DAY TO TOUR AND ARRIVING AT OFFICIAL OPENING Start touring in Frontierland, then tour Adventureland and

Liberty Square. Visit Fantasyland in late afternoon, and Tomorrowland after dinner.

FOR PARENTS AND ADULTS WITH TWO DAYS TO TOUR AND USING EARLY ENTRY On Day One, tour Fantasyland's headliner rides first, starting with Seven Dwarfs Mine Train. Tour Frontierland next, then Liberty Square. Finish up with Fantasyland's secondary rides. Start Day Two in Tomorrowland, then tour Adventureland and Liberty Square.

FOR PARENTS AND ADULTS WITH TWO DAYS TO TOUR AND ARRIVING AT OFFICIAL OPENING On Day One, tour Frontierland first, then tour Liberty Square. Finish up the day with Peter Pan's Flight and Seven Dwarfs Mine Train in Fantasyland. Start Day Two in Adventureland, then tour Tomorrowland.

FOR PARENTS AND ADULTS WITH AN AFTERNOON AND A FULL DAY For the afternoon, tour Frontierland and Tomorrowland. On your full day of touring, see Fantasyland, Liberty Square, and Adventureland.

EPCOT

FOR ALL GUESTS If Disney is using boarding groups at either Remy's Ratatouille Adventure or *Guardians of the Galaxy,* obtain a boarding group reservation for that ride on the day of your visit. Pause your tour to ride when your boarding group is called.

FOR GUESTS USING EARLY ENTRY If Remy is not using boarding groups, enter EPCOT at the International Gateway (IG) entrance, and ride Remy's Ratatouille Adventure in France as soon as the park opens. If Remy *is* using boarding groups, enter EPCOT via the main entrance. Next, head to Future World East/World Discovery and tour those attractions, then visit Future World West/World Nature. Begin a counterclockwise tour of World Showcase at Canada. For dinner, snack at the food booths in World Showcase. Finish the day with a viewing of *Harmonious.*

FOR GUESTS ARRIVING AT OFFICIAL OPENING TIME Enter EPCOT at the main entrance, and head for Soarin' Around the World in Future World West/World Nature. Tour the rest of Future World West, then head for Future World East/World Discovery. Begin a clockwise tour of World Showcase at Mexico. For dinner, snack at the food booths in World Showcase. If Remy is using a standby line, finish the day with a ride on Remy in France; otherwise, fit it in whenever your boarding group is called. End the day with a viewing of *Harmonious.*

FOR GUESTS USING EARLY ENTRY WITH REMY'S AND *GUARDIANS OF THE GALAXY* OPEN Enter EPCOT at the main entrance, and ride *Guardians of the Galaxy:* Cosmic Rewind as soon as the park opens. Tour Future World East, then Future World West. Tour World Showcase clockwise starting with Mexico. For dinner, snack at the food booths in World Showcase. Finish your day with a ride on Remy's Ratatouille Adventure in France and a viewing of *Harmonious.*

FOR GUESTS ARRIVING AT OFFICIAL OPENING WITH REMY'S AND *GUARDIANS OF THE GALAXY* OPEN Enter EPCOT at the IG entrance, and ride Remy's Ratatouille Adventure in France as soon as you're admitted to the park. Head to Future World West and tour those attractions, then visit Future World East. Begin a counterclockwise tour of World Showcase at Mexico. For dinner, snack at the food booths in World Showcase. Finish the day with a viewing of *Harmonious*.

DISNEY'S ANIMAL KINGDOM

FOR PARENTS AND ADULTS USING EARLY ENTRY Begin a land-by-land, counterclockwise tour of the park, starting at Dinosaur in DinoLand. Work in shows like *Feathered Friends in Flight* as you near them. If the park is open past dark, eat dinner, and end the night with *Awakenings* at the Tree of Life and a tour of the Valley of Mo'ara in Pandora.

FOR PARENTS AND ADULTS ARRIVING AT OFFICIAL OPENING TIME Begin a land-by-land, counterclockwise tour of the park starting at Kilimanjaro Safaris in Africa. Work in shows like *Feathered Friends in Flight* as you near them. Save the attractions in Pandora for last. If the park is open past dark, eat dinner, and end the night with *Awakenings* at the Tree of Life and a tour of the Valley of Mo'ara in Pandora.

FOR PARENTS AND ADULTS ARRIVING LATE MORNING Begin a clockwise tour of the park, starting in Africa and saving Pandora for last. If the park is open past dark, eat dinner, and end the night with *Awakenings* at the Tree of Life and a tour of the Valley of Mo'ara in Pandora.

DISNEY'S HOLLYWOOD STUDIOS

FOR GROUPS WITH OLDER CHILDREN, TEENS, AND ADULTS USING EARLY ENTRY If Rise of the Resistance is using boarding group reservations, obtain one at exactly 7 a.m. on the day of your visit, or try again at 1 p.m. If not using boarding groups, ride Rise of the Resistance as soon as you're admitted into the park. Next, begin a clockwise tour of the park in Toy Story Land, then head to Galaxy's Edge. Try the attractions on Sunset Boulevard after lunch. Ride Mickey & Minnie's Runaway Railway later in the day, when crowds have started to thin.

FOR ADULTS ARRIVING AROUND LUNCHTIME Make park reservations for the Studios as soon as you know your travel dates. If boarding groups are offered, obtain a reservation for Rise of the Resistance at exactly 7 a.m. on the day of your visit, or try again at 1 p.m. Next, begin a clockwise tour of the park in Galaxy's Edge, then visit the attractions on Sunset Boulevard. Ride Mickey & Minnie's Runaway Railway midafternoon, and save Toy Story Land for last, when crowds have started to thin. If Rise of the Resistance is *not* using boarding groups, get in line during the last 2 hours the park is open.

The Magic Kingdom

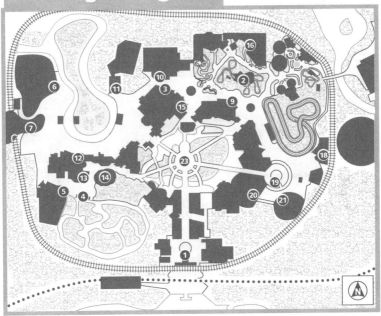

MAGIC KINGDOM EARLY-ENTRY
ONE-DAY TOURING PLAN FOR ADULTS
*(Assumes Tron Lightcycle Power Run is **not open**)*
Make park reservations for the Magic Kingdom as soon as you know your travel dates.

1. Arrive at the Magic Kingdom entrance 40 minutes before official opening on days of normal attendance and 1 hour before official opening during holidays and busy times. Get guide maps and the *Times Guide* while waiting to enter the park.
2. As soon as the park opens, ride Seven Dwarfs Mine Train in Fantasyland.
3. Take Peter Pan's Flight in Fantasyland.
4. In Adventureland, take the Jungle Cruise.
5. Experience Pirates of the Caribbean.
6. Ride Big Thunder Mountain Railroad in Frontierland.
7. Ride Splash Mountain. While you're in line for Splash Mountain, use Mobile Ordering to order lunch. The best spot nearby is Pecos Bill Tall Tale Inn & Cafe, also in Frontierland.
8. Eat lunch.
9. Ride The Many Adventures of Winnie the Pooh.
10. Take the It's a Small World boat ride.

11. Tour The Haunted Mansion around the corner in Liberty Square.
12. See the *Country Bear Jamboree* in Frontierland.
13. Experience *Walt Disney's Enchanted Tiki Room* around the corner in Adventureland.
14. Tour the Swiss Family Treehouse.
15. See *Mickey's PhilharMagic* in Fantasyland.
16. Ride Under the Sea: Journey of the Little Mermaid. If you're staying in the park for dinner, order using Mobile Ordering.
17. Eat dinner.
18. Ride Space Mountain in Tomorrowland.
19. Ride the Tomorrowland Transit Authority PeopleMover.
20. Try Buzz Lightyear's Space Ranger Spin.
21. If time permits, see *Walt Disney's Carousel of Progress*.
22. If time permits, revisit favorite attractions, try new ones, or tour the park.
23. See the *Enchantment* fireworks show.

To use Genie+ with this plan: Get the first available reservation for any of the next three attractions to visit, and fit that return-time window into the plan. If none of the next three steps participate in Genie+, then get a reservation for the next attraction in the plan that *does* participate.

If using Individual Attraction Selections, try to get a Space Mountain reservation for around 5 p.m.

See tinyurl.com/free-tplans to customize this plan at no charge—you can customize the attractions along with your walking speed, plus get real-time updates while you're in the park.

The Magic Kingdom

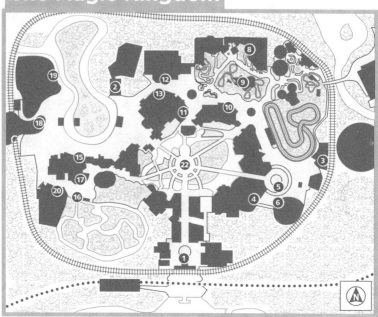

MAGIC KINGDOM NON-EARLY-ENTRY
ONE-DAY TOURING PLAN FOR ADULTS

*(Assumes Tron Lightcycle Power Run is **not open**)*

Make park reservations for the Magic Kingdom as soon as you know your travel dates.

1. Arrive at the Magic Kingdom entrance 30 minutes before official opening on days of normal attendance, and 1 hour before official opening during holidays and busy times. Get guide maps and the *Times Guide* while waiting to enter the park.

2. As soon as you're admitted to the park, tour The Haunted Mansion in Liberty Square.

3. Ride Space Mountain in Tomorrowland.

4. Try Buzz Lightyear's Space Ranger Spin.

5. Ride the Tomorrowland Transit Authority PeopleMover.

6. See *Walt Disney's Carousel of Progress.* While you're in line, use Mobile Ordering to order lunch. The best spot nearby is Cosmic Ray's Starlight Cafe, also in Tomorrowland.

7. Eat lunch.

8. In Fantasyland, ride Under the Sea: Journey of the Little Mermaid.

9. Ride Seven Dwarfs Mine Train.

10. Ride The Many Adventures of Winnie the Pooh.

11. See *Mickey's PhilharMagic.*

12. Take the It's a Small World boat ride.

13. Take Peter Pan's Flight in Fantasyland. While you're in line, order dinner using Mobile Ordering. The best nearby spot is Pecos Bill Tall Tale Inn & Cafe, in Frontierland.

14. Eat dinner.

15. See the *Country Bear Jamboree* in Frontierland.

16. In Adventureland, take the Jungle Cruise.

17. If time permits, experience *Walt Disney's Enchanted Tiki Room.*

18. Ride Splash Mountain in Frontierland.

19. Ride Big Thunder Mountain Railroad.

20. Experience Pirates of the Caribbean.

21. If time permits, revisit favorite attractions, try new ones, or tour the park.

22. See the *Enchantment* fireworks show.

To use Genie+ with this plan: Get the first available reservation for any of the next three attractions to visit, and fit that return-time window into the plan. If none of the next three steps participate in Genie+, then get a reservation for the next attraction in the plan that *does* participate.

If using Individual Attraction Selections, try to get a Space Mountain reservation for around 9:30 a.m., and a Seven Dwarfs Mine Train reservation for around 1 p.m.

See tinyurl.com/free-tplans to customize this plan at no charge—you can customize the attractions along with your walking speed, plus get real-time updates while you're in the park.

The Magic Kingdom

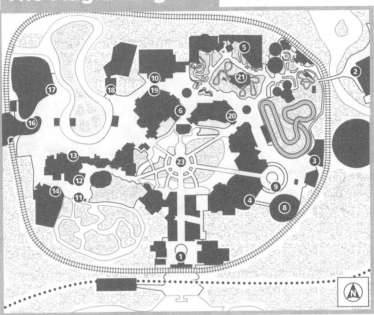

MAGIC KINGDOM EARLY-ENTRY
ONE-DAY TOURING PLAN FOR ADULTS

*(Assumes Tron Lightcycle Power Run is **open**)*

Make park reservations for the Magic Kingdom as soon as you know your travel dates.

1. Arrive at the Magic Kingdom entrance 40 minutes before official opening on days of normal attendance, and 1 hour before official opening during holidays and busy times. Get guide maps and the *Times Guide* while waiting to enter the park.

2. As soon as the park opens, ride Tron Lightcycle Power Run in Tomorrowland.

3. Ride Space Mountain.

4. Try Buzz Lightyear's Space Ranger Spin.

5. Ride Under the Sea: Journey of the Little Mermaid in Fantasyland.

6. See *Mickey's PhilharMagic.* If you're staying in the park for lunch, order using Mobile Ordering while waiting for the show to start.

7. Eat lunch.

8. If you're staying to see the fireworks, see *Walt Disney's Carousel of Progress* in Tomorrowland.

9. Ride the Tomorrowland Transit Authority PeopleMover.

10. Take the It's a Small World boat ride in Fantasyland.

11. In Adventureland, take the Jungle Cruise.

12. See *Walt Disney's Enchanted Tiki Room.*

13. See the *Country Bear Jamboree* around the corner in Frontierland.

14. Experience Pirates of the Caribbean in Adventureland. If you're staying in the park for dinner, order using Mobile Ordering while you're in line.

15. Eat dinner.

16. Ride Splash Mountain in Frontierland.

17. Ride Big Thunder Mountain Railroad.

18. Tour The Haunted Mansion in Liberty Square.

19. Take Peter Pan's Flight in Fantasyland.

20. Ride The Many Adventures of Winnie the Pooh.

21. Ride Seven Dwarfs Mine Train.

22. If time permits, revisit favorite attractions, try new ones, or tour the park.

23. See the *Enchantment* fireworks show.

To use Genie+ with this plan: Get the first available reservation for any of the next three attractions to visit, and fit that return time window into the plan. If none of the next three steps participate in Genie+, then get a reservation for the next attraction in the plan that *does* participate in Genie+.

If using Individual Attraction Selections, try to get a Space Mountain reservation for around 9:30 a.m., and a Seven Dwarfs Mine Train reservation for around 8:30 p.m.

See tinyurl.com/free-tplans to customize this plan at no charge—you can customize the attractions along with your walking speed, plus get real-time updates while you're in the park.

The Magic Kingdom

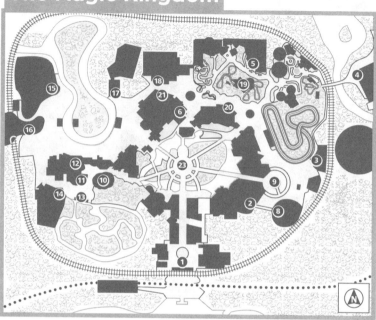

MAGIC KINGDOM NON-EARLY-ENTRY ONE-DAY TOURING PLAN FOR ADULTS

*(Assumes Tron Lightcycle Power Run is **open**)*

Make park reservations for the Magic Kingdom as soon as you know your travel dates.

1. Arrive at the Magic Kingdom entrance 30 minutes before official opening on days of normal attendance, and 1 hour before official opening during holidays and busy times. Get guide maps and the *Times Guide* while waiting to enter the park.

2. As soon as you're admitted to the park, ride Buzz Lightyear's Space Ranger Spin in Tomorrowland.

3. Ride Space Mountain.

4. Ride Tron Lightcycle Power Run.

5. In Fantasyland, ride Under the Sea: Journey of the Little Mermaid.

6. See *Mickey's PhilharMagic*. While you're in line, use Mobile Ordering to order lunch. The best spot nearby is the Columbia Harbour House in Liberty Square.

7. Eat lunch.

8. See *Walt Disney's Carousel of Progress* in Tomorrowland.

9. Ride the Tomorrowland Transit Authority PeopleMover.

10. Tour the Swiss Family Treehouse in Adventureland.

11. See *Walt Disney's Enchanted Tiki Room*.

12. See the *Country Bear Jamboree* around the corner in Frontierland.

13. In Adventureland, take the Jungle Cruise.

14. Experience Pirates of the Caribbean. While you're in line, order dinner using Mobile Ordering. The best nearby spot is Pecos Bill Tall Tale Inn & Cafe, in Frontierland.

15. Ride Big Thunder Mountain Railroad.

16. Ride Splash Mountain in Frontierland.

17. Tour The Haunted Mansion in Liberty Square.

18. In Fantasyland, take the It's a Small World boat ride.

19. Ride Seven Dwarfs Mine Train.

20. Ride The Many Adventures of Winnie the Pooh.

21. Take Peter Pan's Flight in Fantasyland.

22. If time permits, revisit favorite attractions, try new ones, or tour the park.

23. See the *Enchantment* fireworks show.

To use Genie+ with this plan: Get the first available reservation for any of the next three attractions to visit, and fit that return-time window into the plan. If none of the next three steps participate in Genie+, then get a reservation for the next attraction in the plan that *does* participate.

If using Individual Attraction Selections, try to get a Space Mountain reservation for around 9:30 a.m., and a Seven Dwarfs Mine Train reservation for around 8 p.m.

See tinyurl.com/free-tplans to customize this plan at no charge—you can customize the attractions along with your walking speed, plus get real-time updates while you're in the park.

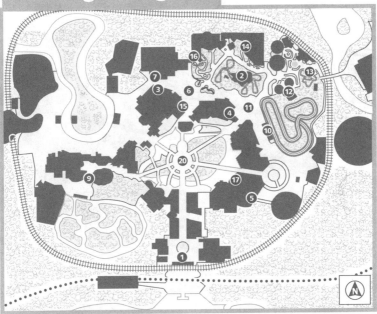

MAGIC KINGDOM EARLY-ENTRY ONE-DAY TOURING PLAN
FOR PARENTS WITH SMALL CHILDREN

Review the Small-Child Fright-Potential Table on pages 390–392. Make park reservations for the Magic Kingdom as soon as you know your travel dates. Interrupt the plan for meals, rest, and a cocktail or two.

1. Arrive at the Magic Kingdom entrance 40 minutes before official opening on days of normal attendance, and 1 hour before official opening during holidays and busy times. Get guide maps and the *Times Guide* while waiting to enter the park.
2. As soon as the park opens, head toward the right-hand side of Cinderella Castle and follow the path to Seven Dwarfs Mine Train in Fantasyland. Ride.
3. Take Peter Pan's Flight.
4. Ride The Many Adventures of Winnie the Pooh.
5. Ride Buzz Lightyear's Space Ranger Spin in Tomorrowland.
6. In Fantasyland, ride Prince Charming Regal Carrousel.
7. Try the It's a Small World boat ride. Use Mobile Ordering to order lunch while in line. The best nearby dining location is Columbia Harbour House in Liberty Square.

8. Eat lunch.
9. Ride the Magic Carpets of Aladdin in Adventureland.
10. Take a spin on the Tomorrowland Speedway in Tomorrowland.
11. Give the Mad Tea Party a whirl in Fantasyland.
12. Ride Dumbo the Flying Elephant.
13. Try The Barnstormer.
14. Ride Under the Sea: Journey of the Little Mermaid.
15. See *Mickey's PhilharMagic*.
16. See *Enchanted Tales with Belle*.
17. If time permits, see *Monsters Inc. Laugh Floor* in Tomorrowland.
18. If time permits, revisit favorite attractions, try new ones, or tour the park.
19. Eat dinner.
20. See the *Enchantment* fireworks show.

To use Genie+ with this plan: Get the first available reservation for any of the next three attractions to visit, and fit that return-time window into the plan. If none of the next three steps participate in Genie+, then get a reservation for the next attraction in the plan that *does* participate.

Individual Attraction Selection reservations shouldn't be needed for Seven Dwarfs Mine Train. If using IAS, try for a reservation around the park's official opening time.

See tinyurl.com/free-tplans to customize this plan at no charge—you can customize the attractions along with your walking speed, plus get real-time updates while you're in the park.

The Magic Kingdom

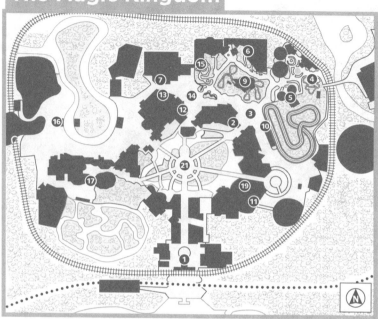

MAGIC KINGDOM NON-EARLY-ENTRY ONE-DAY TOURING PLAN FOR PARENTS WITH SMALL CHILDREN

Review the Small-Child Fright-Potential Table on pages 390–392. Make park reservations for the Magic Kingdom as soon as you know your travel dates. Interrupt the plan for meals and rest.

1. Arrive at the Magic Kingdom entrance 30 minutes before official opening on days of normal attendance, and 1 hour before official opening during holidays and busy times. Get guide maps and the *Times Guide* while waiting to enter the park.

2. As soon as the park opens, head to Fantasyland and ride The Many Adventures of Winnie the Pooh.

3. Give the Mad Tea Party a whirl.

4. Try The Barnstormer.

5. Ride Dumbo the Flying Elephant in Fantasyland.

6. Ride Under the Sea: Journey of the Little Mermaid.

7. Try the It's a Small World boat ride. Use Mobile Ordering to order lunch while in line. The best nearby dining location is Columbia Harbour House in Liberty Square.

8. Eat lunch.

9. Ride Seven Dwarfs Mine Train in Fantasyland.

10. Take a spin on the Tomorrowland Speedway.

11. Ride Buzz Lightyear's Space Ranger Spin in Tomorrowland.

12. See *Mickey's PhilharMagic* in Fantasyland.

13. Take Peter Pan's Flight.

14. In Fantasyland, ride Prince Charming Regal Carrousel.

15. See *Enchanted Tales with Belle*.

16. If time permits, take the raft over to Tom Sawyer Island in Frontierland.

17. Ride the Magic Carpets of Aladdin in Adventureland. Use Mobile Ordering to order dinner while in line. The best nearby location is Pecos Bill's, in Frontierland.

18. Eat dinner.

19. See the *Monsters Inc. Laugh Floor* in Tomorrowland.

20. If time permits, revisit favorite attractions, try new ones, or tour the park.

21. See the *Enchantment* fireworks show.

To use Genie+ with this plan: Get the first available reservation for any of the next three attractions to visit, and fit that return-time window into the plan. If none of the next three steps participate in Genie+, then get a reservation for the next attraction in the plan that *does* participate.

If using Individual Attraction Selections, try to get a reservation for Seven Dwarfs Mine Train for around noon.

See tinyurl.com/free-tplans to customize this plan at no charge—you can customize the attractions along with your walking speed, plus get real-time updates while you're in the park.

The Magic Kingdom

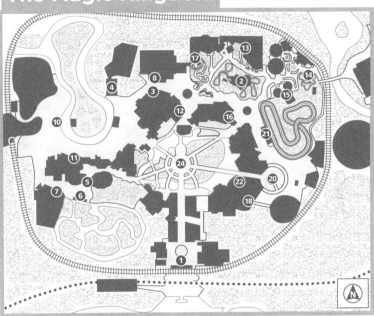

MAGIC KINGDOM EARLY-ENTRY DUMBO-OR-DIE-IN-A-DAY TOURING PLAN FOR PARENTS WITH SMALL CHILDREN

Review the Small-Child Fright-Potential Table on pages 390–392. Make park reservations for the Magic Kingdom as soon as you know your travel dates. Interrupt the plan for meals, and rest.

1. Arrive at the Magic Kingdom entrance 40 minutes before official opening on days of normal attendance, and 1 hour before official opening during holidays and busy times. Get guide maps and the *Times Guide* while waiting to enter the park.
2. As soon as the park opens, ride Seven Dwarfs Mine Train in Fantasyland.
3. Take Peter Pan's Flight.
4. Tour The Haunted Mansion in Liberty Square.
5. Ride the Magic Carpets of Aladdin in Adventureland.
6. Ride the Jungle Cruise.
7. Experience Pirates of the Caribbean.
8. Take the It's a Small World boat ride. While you're in line, use Mobile Ordering to order lunch. The closest good spot is Pecos Bill Tall Tale Inn & Cafe in Frontierland.
9. Eat lunch.
10. Take the raft over to Tom Sawyer Island in Frontierland.
11. See the *Country Bear Jamboree*.
12. See *Mickey's PhilharMagic* in Fantasyland.
13. Ride Under the Sea: Journey of the Little Mermaid.
14. Try The Barnstormer.
15. Ride Dumbo the Flying Elephant twice.
16. Ride The Many Adventures of Winnie the Pooh.
17. If time permits, try *Enchanted Tales with Belle*.
18. Try Buzz Lightyear's Space Ranger Spin in Tomorrowland. While you're in line, use Mobile Ordering to order dinner. The closest spot is Cosmic Ray's Starlight Cafe.
19. Eat dinner.
20. If time permits, ride the Tomorrowland Transit Authority PeopleMover.
21. Take a spin on the Tomorrowland Speedway.
22. If time permits, see the *Monsters, Inc. Laugh Floor* in Tomorrowland.
23. Circle back to any skipped attractions, or revisit favorites.
24. See the *Enchantment* fireworks show.

To use Genie+ with this plan: Get the first available reservation for any of the next three attractions to visit, and fit that return-time window into the plan. If none of the next three steps participate in Genie+, then get a reservation for the next attraction in the plan that *does* participate.

Individual Attraction Selection reservations shouldn't be needed for Seven Dwarfs Mine Train.

See tinyurl.com/free-tplans to customize this plan at no charge—you can customize the attractions along with your walking speed, plus get real-time updates while you're in the park.

The Magic Kingdom

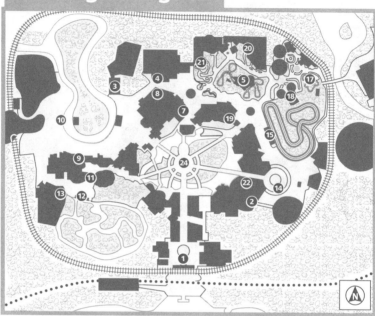

MAGIC KINGDOM NON-EARLY-ENTRY DUMBO-OR-DIE-IN-A-DAY TOURING PLAN FOR PARENTS WITH SMALL CHILDREN

Review the Small-Child Fright-Potential Table on pages 390–392. Make park reservations for the Magic Kingdom as soon as you know your travel dates. Interrupt the plan for meals, and rest.

1. Arrive at the Magic Kingdom entrance 30 minutes before official opening on days of normal attendance, and 1 hour before official opening during holidays and busy times. Get guide maps and the *Times Guide* while waiting to enter the park.
2. As soon as you're admitted to the park, try Buzz Lightyear's Space Ranger Spin in Tomorrowland.
3. See The Haunted Mansion in Liberty Square.
4. Take the It's a Small World boat ride in Fantasyland.
5. Ride Seven Dwarfs Mine Train. While in line, use Mobile Ordering to order lunch. The best spot nearby is Columbia Harbour House in Liberty Square.
6. Eat lunch.
7. See *Mickey's PhilharMagic* in Fantasyland.
8. Take Peter Pan's Flight.
9. See *Country Bear Jamboree* in Frontierland.
10. Take the raft over to Tom Sawyer Island.
11. Ride the Magic Carpets of Aladdin in Adventureland.
12. Ride the Jungle Cruise.
13. Experience Pirates of the Caribbean.
14. If time permits, ride the Tomorrowland Transit Authority PeopleMover.
15. Take a spin on the Tomorrowland Speedway. While in line, use Mobile Ordering to order dinner. The best spot nearby is Cosmic Ray's Starlight Cafe.
16. Eat dinner.
17. Try The Barnstormer.
18. Ride Dumbo the Flying Elephant twice.
19. Ride The Many Adventures of Winnie the Pooh.
20. Ride Under the Sea: Journey of the Little Mermaid.
21. If time permits, try *Enchanted Tales with Belle*.
22. If time permits, see the *Monsters, Inc. Laugh Floor* in Tomorrowland.
23. Circle back to any skipped attractions, or revisit favorites.
24. See the *Enchantment* fireworks show.

To use Genie+ with this plan: Get the first available reservation for any of the next three attractions to visit, and fit that return-time window into the plan. If none of the next three steps participate in Genie+, then get a reservation for the next attraction in the plan that *does* participate.

If using Individual Attraction Selections, try to get a Seven Dwarfs Mine Train reservation for around 10:30 a.m.

See tinyurl.com/free-tplans to customize this plan at no charge—you can customize the attractions along with your walking speed, plus get real-time updates while you're in the park.

The Magic Kingdom

MAGIC KINGDOM EARLY-ENTRY TWO-DAY
TOURING PLAN FOR ADULTS: DAY ONE

Make park reservations for the Magic Kingdom as soon as you know your travel dates.

1. Arrive at the Magic Kingdom entrance 40 minutes before official opening on days of normal attendance, and 1 hour before official opening during holidays and busy times. Get guide maps and the *Times Guide* while waiting to enter the park.
2. As soon as the park opens, ride Seven Dwarfs Mine Train in Fantasyland.
3. Ride Peter Pan's Flight.
4. In Frontierland, ride Big Thunder Mountain Railroad.
5. Experience Splash Mountain if temperatures permit.
6. In Liberty Square, ride The Haunted Mansion.

7. See *The Hall of Presidents*. Order lunch using Mobile Ordering. The best nearby spot is Columbia Harbour House, next door to the Hall.
8. Eat lunch.
9. Explore Tom Sawyer Island in Frontierland.
10. Work in a viewing of *Country Bear Jamboree* in Frontierland.
11. Ride It's a Small World in Fantasyland.
12. See *Mickey's PhilharMagic* in Fantasyland.
13. Revisit any favorite attractions or ones that were skipped.
14. If time permits, see the *Enchantment* fireworks show.

(continued on next page)

To use Genie+ with this plan: Get the first available reservation for any of the next three attractions to visit, and fit that return-time window into the plan. If none of the next three steps participate in Genie+, then get a reservation for the next attraction in the plan that *does* participate.

Individual Attraction Selection reservations shouldn't be needed for Seven Dwarfs Mine Train.

See tinyurl.com/free-tplans to customize this plan at no charge—you can customize the attractions along with your walking speed, plus get real-time updates while you're in the park.

The Magic Kingdom

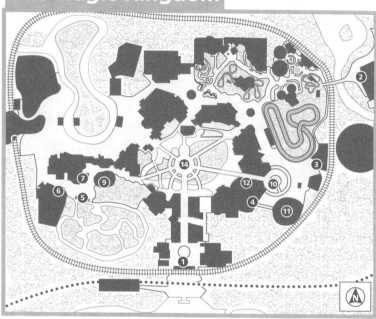

MAGIC KINGDOM EARLY-ENTRY TWO-DAY TOURING PLAN FOR ADULTS: DAY TWO

Make park reservations for the Magic Kingdom as soon as you know your travel dates.

1. Arrive at the Magic Kingdom entrance 40 minutes before official opening on days of normal attendance, and 1 hour before official opening during holidays and busy times. Get guide maps and the *Times Guide* while waiting to enter the park.
2. As soon as the park opens, head to Tomorrowland. If Tron Lightcycle Power Run is open, ride it.
3. Ride Space Mountain.
4. Ride Buzz Lightyear's Space Ranger Spin.
5. In Adventureland, take the Jungle Cruise.
6. Ride Pirates of the Caribbean.
7. See *Walt Disney's Enchanted Tiki Room.*

Use Mobile Ordering to order lunch ahead of time.
8. Eat lunch.
9. Tour the Swiss Family Treehouse.
10. Ride the Tomorrowland Transit Authority PeopleMover.
11. See *Walt Disney's Carousel of Progress.*
12. See the *Monsters, Inc. Laugh Floor* if time permits.
13. Revisit any favorite attractions, or tour the rest of the park.
14. If you haven't already done so, see the *Enchantment* fireworks show.

To use Genie+ with this plan: Get the first available reservation for any of the next three attractions to visit, and fit that return-time window into the plan. If none of the next three steps participate in Genie+, then get a reservation for the next attraction in the plan that *does* participate.

Individual Attraction Selection reservations shouldn't be needed for Tron.

See tinyurl.com/free-tplans to customize this plan at no charge—you can customize the attractions along with your walking speed, plus get real-time updates while you're in the park.

EPCOT **EARLY-ENTRY ONE-DAY TOURING PLAN**

(Assumes Guardians of the Galaxy: Cosmic Rewind *is* **not open***)*

Make park reservations as soon as you know your travel dates. If Remy's Ratatouille Adventure is using a virtual queue (see page 60), obtain a reservation at 7 a.m. on the day of your visit, and interrupt the plan to ride when it's time to ride. If EPCOT opens at 11 a.m., eat a late breakfast before arriving, so you don't have to stop for lunch as soon as the park opens.

1. Arrive at EPCOT 50 minutes before official opening (70 minutes on busy days and holidays). If Remy's Ratatouille Adventure in France is using a virtual queue, use EPCOT's main entrance; if Remy is not using a virtual queue, arrive use EPCOT's International Gateway entrance.

2. If Remy is not using a virtual queue, ride it as soon as the park opens.

3. Ride Soarin' Around the World at The Land Pavilion in Future World West/World Nature.

4. Ask a cast member if Test Track is operating. If it is, ride it in Future World East/World Discovery. Use the single-rider line if it's open and your group is willing to use it.

5. Ride Mission: Space in Future World East/ World Discovery if time permits and your group is interested.

6. Ride Spaceship Earth in World Celebration.

7. Eat a light, late lunch. Sunshine Seasons in The Land is the closest, best option.

8. Walk through the *Moana—Journey of Water* exhibit, in World Nature, if it's open.

9. Tour The Seas' main tank and exhibits.

10. Begin a tour of World Showcase at the Canada Pavilion and see *Canada Far and Wide*. A good strategy for dinner is to stop at any of the food booths around World Showcase.

11. In France, watch *Impressions de France* if it's offered. Skip the *Beauty and the Beast* film if that's the one shown, and consider ice cream at L'Artisan des Glaces instead.

12. Tour the Morocco Pavilion and exhibits.

13. Tour the Japan Pavilion and exhibits.

14. See *The American Adventure*.

15. Tour the Italy Pavilion.

16. Check out the Germany Pavilion.

17. See the China Pavilion and its film.

18. Tour the Norway Pavilion and ride Frozen Ever After if time permits.

19. See the Mexico Pavilion and ride the Gran Fiesta Tour if time permits.

20. See *Harmonious*. Good viewing locations should be available around the Mexico Pavilion, in front of World Showcase where it meets Future World, and between Canada and France.

To use Genie+ with this plan: Get the first available reservation for any of the next three attractions to visit, and fit that return-time window into the plan. If none of the next three steps participate in Genie+, then get a reservation for the next attraction in the plan that *does* participate.

If using Individual Attraction Selections, try to get a Remy reservation for around 11 a.m. and a Test Track reservation for around 12:30 p.m.

See tinyurl.com/free-tplans to customize this plan at no charge—you can customize the attractions along with your walking speed, plus get real-time updates while you're in the park.

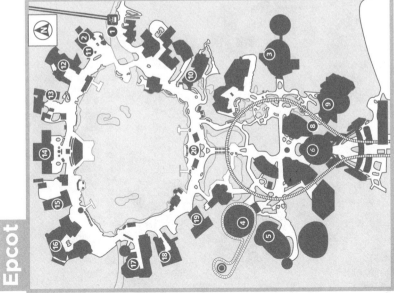

Epcot

EPCOT NON-EARLY-ENTRY ONE-DAY TOURING PLAN

*(Assumes Guardians of the Galaxy: Cosmic Rewind is **not open**)*

Make park reservations as soon as you know your travel dates. If Remy's Ratatouille Adventure is using a virtual queue (see page 60), obtain a reservation at 7 a.m. on the day of your visit, and interrupt the plan when it's time to ride. If EPCOT opens at 11 a.m., eat a late breakfast before arriving, so you don't have to stop for lunch as soon as the park opens.

1. Arrive at EPCOT's main entrance 30 minutes before official opening (50 minutes on busy days and holidays). Get guide maps and the *Times Guide*.

2. As soon as the park opens, ride Soarin' Around the World at The Land Pavilion in Future World West/World Nature.

3. Ask a cast member if Test Track is operating. If it is, head to Future World East and ride Test Track. Use the single-rider line if it's open and your group is willing to use it.

4. Ride Mission: Space if time permits and your group is interested.

5. Ride Spaceship Earth in World Celebration.

6. Ride Living with the Land in the Land Pavilion.

7. Eat a light, late lunch. Sunshine Seasons is the closest, best option.

8. Tour The Seas main tank and exhibits.

9. Walk through the *Moana—Journey of Water* exhibit in World Nature, if it's open.

10. Begin a tour of World Showcase at the Mexico Pavilion. Skip the boat ride to save time. A good strategy for dinner is to stop at one of the food booths around World Showcase.

11. Tour the Norway Pavilion and ride Frozen Ever After.

12. See the China Pavilion, but skip the film— it's not rated highly by any age group.

13. Check out the Germany Pavilion.

14. Tour the Italy Pavilion.

15. See *The American Adventure*.

16. Tour the Japan Pavilion and exhibits.

17. Tour the Morocco Pavilion and exhibits.

18. In France, ride Remy's Ratatouille Adventure. To save time, skip either film being shown.

19. If you have more than 2 hours before the park closes, tour the Canada Pavilion and see *Canada Far and Wide*. Otherwise, skip Canada.

20. See *Harmonious*. Good viewing locations should be available around the Mexico Pavilion, in front of World Showcase where it meets Future World, and between Canada and France.

To use Genie+ with this plan: get the first available reservation for any of the next three attractions to visit, and fit that return time window into the plan. If none of the next three steps participate in Genie+, then get a reservation for the next attraction in the plan that *does* participate.

If using Individual Attraction Selections, try to get a Test Track reservation for around 11:30 a.m. and a Remy reservation for around 6 p.m.

See tinyurl.com/free-tplans to customize this plan at no charge, including the attractions and your walking speed, plus real-time updates while you're in the park.

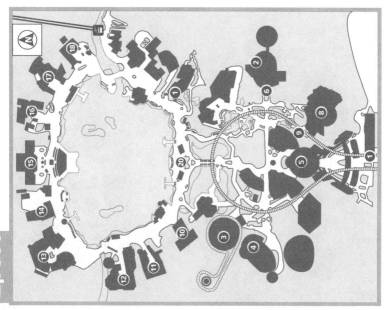

EPCOT EARLY-ENTRY ONE-DAY TOURING PLAN

*(Assumes Guardians of the Galaxy: Cosmic Rewind is **open**)*

Make park reservations as soon as you know your travel dates. If Guardians is using a virtual queue (see page 60), obtain a reservation at 7 a.m. on the day of your visit, and interrupt the plan when it's time to ride. If EPCOT opens at 11 a.m., eat a late breakfast before arriving, so you don't have to stop for lunch as soon as the park opens.

1. Arrive at EPCOT's main entrance 50 minutes before official opening (70 minutes on busy days and holidays). Get guide maps and the *Times Guide*.

2. If Guardians of the Galaxy is not using a virtual queue, ride Guardians of the Galaxy: Cosmic Rewind in Future World East/World Discovery as soon as the park opens.

3. Ride Soarin' Around the World at The Land Pavilion in Future World West/World Nature.

4. Ask a cast member if Test Track is operating. If it is, ride Test Track in Future World East. Use the single-rider line if it's open and your group is willing to use it.

5. If your group includes teens, ride Mission: Space in Future World East, and skip Living with the Land in step 7.

6. Ride Spaceship Earth in World Celebration.

7. Ride Living with the Land in the Land Pavilion. Skip if you have teens, to save time.

8. Eat a light, late lunch. Sunshine Seasons in The Land is the closest, best option.

9. Tour The Seas main tank and exhibits.

10. Walk through the *Moana—Journey of Water* exhibit, if it's open.

11. Begin a tour of World Showcase at the Mexico Pavilion. Skip the boat ride to save time.

12. Tour the Norway Pavilion, and ride Frozen Ever After.

13. See the China Pavilion, but skip the film—it's not rated highly by any age group.

14. Check out the Germany Pavilion.

15. Tour the Italy Pavilion.

16. See *The American Adventure*.

17. Tour the Japan Pavilion and exhibits.

18. Tour the Morocco Pavilion and exhibits.

19. In France, ride Remy's Ratatouille Adventure. To save time, skip either film being shown.

20. Tour the Canada Pavilion and see *Canada Far and Wide*.

21. See *Harmonious*. Good viewing locations should be available around the Mexico Pavilion, in front of World Showcase where it meets Future World, and between Canada and France.

To use Genie+ with this plan: Get the first available reservation for any of the next three attractions to visit, and fit that return-time window into the plan. If none of the next three steps participate in Genie+, then get a reservation for the next attraction in the plan that *does* participate.

If using Individual Attraction Selections, try to get a Guardians reservation for around 11 a.m. and a Remy reservation for around 7 p.m.

See tinyurl.com/free-tplans to customize this plan at no charge—you can customize the attractions along with your walking speed, plus get real-time updates while you're in the park.

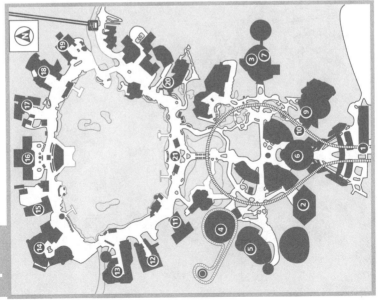

Epcot

EPCOT NON-EARLY-ENTRY ONE-DAY PLAN

(Assumes Guardians of the Galaxy: Cosmic Rewind is **open**)

Make park reservations as soon as you know your travel dates. If Guardians is using a virtual queue (see page 60), obtain a reservation at 7 a.m. on the day of your visit, and interrupt the plan when it's time to ride. If EPCOT opens at 11 a.m., eat a late breakfast before arriving, so you don't have to stop for lunch as soon as the park opens.

1. Arrive at EPCOT's main entrance 30 minutes before official opening (50 minutes on busy days and holidays). Get guide maps and the *Times Guide*.
2. As soon as the park opens, ride Soarin' Around the World at The Land Pavilion in Future World West/World Nature.
3. Ask a cast member if Test Track is operating. If it is, ride Test Track in Future World East/World Discovery. Use the single-rider line if it's open and your group is willing to use it.
4. If your group includes teens, ride Mission: Space in Future World East, and skip Living with the Land in step 6.
5. Ride Spaceship Earth in World Celebration.
6. Ride Living with the Land in the Land Pavilion. Skip if you have teens, to save time.
7. Eat a light, late lunch. Sunshine Seasons in The Land is the closest, best option.
8. Tour The Seas main tank and exhibits.
9. Walk through the *Moana—Journey of Water* exhibit, if it's open.
10. Begin a tour of World Showcase at Mexico.

Skip the boat ride to save time.
11. Tour the Norway Pavilion, and ride Frozen Ever After.
12. See the China Pavilion, but skip the film—it's not rated highly by any age group.
13. Check out the Germany Pavilion.
14. Tour the Italy Pavilion.
15. See *The American Adventure*.
16. Tour the Japan Pavilion and exhibits.
17. Tour the Morocco Pavilion and exhibits.
18. In France, ride Remy's Ratatouille Adventure. To save time, skip either film being shown.
19. If you have more than 2 hours before the park closes, tour the Canada Pavilion, and see *Canada Far and Wide*. Otherwise, skip Canada and ride Guardians of the Galaxy.
20. Return to Future World East and ride Guardians of the Galaxy: Cosmic Rewind.
21. See *Harmonious*. Good viewing locations are around the Mexico Pavilion, in front of World Showcase where it meets Future World, and between Canada and France.

To use Genie+ with this plan: get the first available reservation for any of the next three attractions to visit, and fit that return-time window into the plan. If none of the next three steps participate in Genie+, then get a reservation for the next attraction in the plan that *does* participate.

If using Individual Attraction Selections, try for a Guardians reservation for around 2 p.m.—it'll save you a walk back from World Showcase later; get a Remy reservation for around 6 p.m.

See tinyurl.com/free-tplans to customize this plan at no charge—you can customize the attractions along with your walking speed, plus get real-time updates while you're in the park.

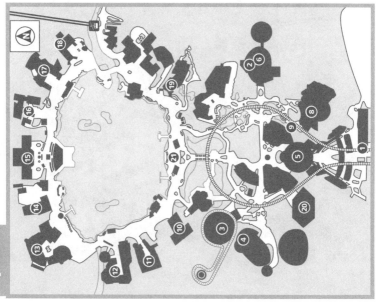

Disney's Animal Kingdom

ANIMAL KINGDOM NON-EARLY-ENTRY ONE-DAY TOURING PLAN

Make park reservations for the Animal Kingdom as soon as you know your travel dates.

1. Arrive at the Animal Kingdom main entrance 30 minutes before official opening on days of normal attendance, and 50 minutes before official opening during holidays and busy times. Follow cast member instructions to line up for Flight of Passage. Get guide maps and the *Times Guide* while you're waiting to enter the park.

2. As soon as you're admitted into the park, take the Kilimanjaro Safaris tour in Africa.

3. Get wet on Kali River Rapids in Asia if temperatures permit.

4. Ride Expedition Everest.

5. Ride Dinosaur in Dinoland U.S.A. Use Mobile Ordering to order lunch in advance. The best restaurants in the park are Satu'li Canteen in Pandora and Flame Tree Barbecue on Discovery Island.

6. Eat lunch. On your way to lunch, sign up for

Wilderness Explorers on the bridge from Discovery Island to The Oasis. Play a few games as you tour the rest of the park.

7. Walk the Maharajah Jungle Trek.

8. See *Feathered Friends in Flight* in Asia.

9. Walk the Gorilla Falls Exploration Trail.

10. See *Festival of the Lion King.*

11. Tour the Discovery Island Trails and any other animal exhibits that interest you.

12. Ride Avatar Flight of Passage in Pandora.

13. Take the Na'vi River Journey boat ride.

14. See *Finding Nemo—The Musical* in Dinoland, U.S.A., if it's open.

If the park is open past dark:

15. Eat dinner in the park.

16. See *Awakenings* at the Tree of Life. Check the *Times Guide* for start time.

17. Tour the Valley of Mo'ara in Pandora.

To use Genie+ with this plan: get the first available reservation for any of the next three attractions to visit, and fit that return time window into the plan. If none of the next three steps participate in Genie+, then get a reservation for the next attraction in the plan that *does* participate.

If using Individual Attraction Selections, obtain a reservation for Kilimanjaro Safaris at 9 a.m. and for Flight of Passage for around 4 p.m.

See tinyurl.com/free-tplans to customize this plan at no charge, including the attractions and your walking speed, plus real-time updates while you're in the park.

Disney's Animal Kingdom

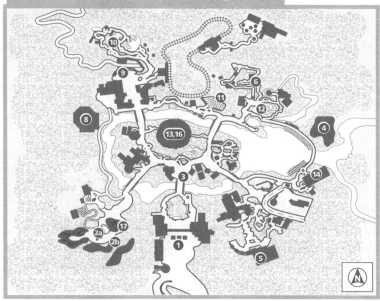

ANIMAL KINGDOM EARLY-ENTRY ONE-DAY TOURING PLAN

Make park reservations for the Animal Kingdom as soon as you know your travel dates.

1. Arrive at the Animal Kingdom main entrance 50 minutes before official opening on days of normal attendance, and 70 minutes before official opening during holidays and busy times. Follow cast member instructions to line up for Flight of Passage. Get guide maps and the *Times Guide* while waiting to enter.
2. Ride Avatar Flight of Passage (**2a**), then Na'vi River Journey (**2b**) in Pandora.
3. Sign up for Wilderness Explorers on the bridge from Discovery Island to The Oasis, on your way to Asia. Play a few games as you tour the park.
4. Ride Expedition Everest in Asia.
5. Ride Dinosaur in Dinoland U.S.A.
6. Walk the Maharajah Jungle Trek. Use Mobile Ordering to order lunch in advance. The best restaurants in the park are Satu'li Canteen in Pandora and Flame Tree Barbecue on Discovery Island.

7. Eat lunch.
8. Work in the next show of *Festival of the Lion King* in Africa around the next two steps.
9. Take the Kilimanjaro Safaris tour in Africa.
10. Walk the Gorilla Falls Exploration Trail.
11. See *Feathered Friends in Flight* in Asia.
12. Get wet on Kali River Rapids in Asia, if temperatures permit.
13. Tour the Discovery Island Trails and any other animal exhibits that interest you.
14. See *Finding Nemo—The Musical* in Dinoland, U.S.A., if it's open.

If the park is open past dark:

15. Eat dinner in the park.
16. See *Awakenings* at the Tree of Life. Check the *Times Guide* for start time.
17. Tour the Valley of Mo'ara in Pandora.

To use Genie+ with this plan: get the first available reservation for any of the next three attractions to visit, and fit that return time window into the plan. If none of the next three steps participate in Genie+, then get a reservation for the next attraction in the plan that *does* participate.

If using Individual Attraction Selections, you shouldn't need one for Flight of Passage. Try to get an Expedition Everest return time of around 9 a.m.

See tinyurl.com/free-tplans to customize this plan at no charge, including the attractions and your walking speed, plus real-time updates while you're in the park.

Disney's Hollywood Studios

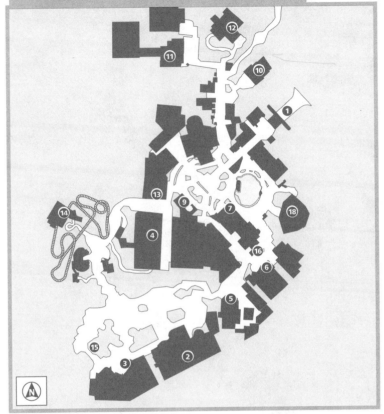

DHS EARLY-ENTRY ONE-DAY TOURING PLAN

Make park reservations for DHS as soon as you know your travel dates. If Rise of the Resistance is using boarding groups, obtain a reservation at exactly 7 a.m. on the day of your visit, or try again at 1 p.m. Stop the tour when your boarding group is called. Make reservations 60 days in advance for Savi's Workshop, the Droid Depot, and Oga's Cantina. Check tinyurl.com/dhs-swge before your trip for the latest information.

1. Check park hours the night before, and plan to arrive 50 minutes before opening on non-peak days, and 70 minutes before opening during holidays and other busy times.
2. If Rise of the Resistance isn't using boarding groups, ride as soon as the park opens.
3. Ride *Millennium Falcon: Smugglers Run*.
4. Ride Toy Story Mania!
5. See *Muppet-Vision 3-D*.
6. Experience Star Tours in Echo Lake.
7. Work in *For the First Time in Forever* around the next two steps. Use Mobile Ordering to order lunch at Docking Bay 7.
8. Eat lunch.

9. Try Mickey & Minnie's Runaway Railway.
10. Work in *Beauty and The Beast Live on Stage* around the next two steps.
11. Ride the Rock 'n' Roller Coaster.
12. Experience the Twilight Zone Tower of Terror.
13. See *Walt Disney Presents*.
14. Ride Slinky Dog Dash in Toy Story Land.
15. Explore the rest of Galaxy's Edge.
16. See the Mickey Mouse film *Vacation Fun*.
17. Revisit any favorite attractions, or tour the rest of the park.
18. See the evening fireworks and/or *Fantasmic!* (if they're performed).

To use Genie+ with this plan: Get the first available reservation for any of the next three attractions to visit, and fit that return-time window into the plan. If none of the next three steps participate in Genie+, then get a reservation for the next attraction in the plan that *does* participate.

If using Individual Attraction Selections, you shouldn't need one for Rise of the Resistance. Try to obtain one for Slinky Dog Dash around 4 p.m.

See tinyurl.com/free-tplans to customize this plan at no charge, including the attractions and your walking speed, plus real-time updates while you're in the park.

Disney's Hollywood Studios

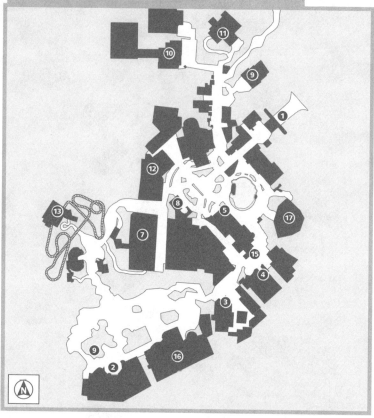

DHS NON-EARLY-ENTRY ONE-DAY TOURING PLAN

Make park reservations for DHS as soon as you know your travel dates. If Rise of the Resistance is using boarding groups, obtain a reservation at exactly 7 a.m. on the day of your visit, or try again at 1 p.m. Stop the tour when your boarding group is called. Make reservations 60 days in advance for Savi's Workshop, the Droid Depot, and Oga's Cantina. Check tinyurl.com/dhs-swge before your trip for the latest information.

1. Check park hours the night before, and plan to arrive 50 minutes before opening on non-peak days, and 70 minutes before opening during holidays and other busy times.

2. As soon as you're admitted, ride *Millennium Falcon: Smugglers Run* in Galaxy's Edge.

3. See *Muppet-Vision 3-D* in Grand Avenue.

4. Experience Star Tours in Echo Lake.

5. Work in a showing of *For the First Time in Forever* around the next few steps.

6. Use Mobile Ordering to order lunch at Docking Bay 7 in Galaxy's Edge.

7. Ride Toy Story Mania! in Toy Story Land.

8. Try Mickey & Minnie's Runaway Railway.

9. Work in *Beauty and The Beast Live on Stage* around the next two steps.

10. Ride the Rock 'n' Roller Coaster.

11. Experience the Twilight Zone Tower of Terror.

12. See *Walt Disney Presents.*

13. Ride Slinky Dog Dash in Toy Story Land.

14. Revisit any favorite attractions, or tour the rest of the park.

15. See the Mickey Mouse film *Vacation Fun.*

16. Ride Rise of the Resistance in Galaxy's Edge, and explore the remainder of the land.

17. See the evening fireworks and/or *Fantasmic!* (if they're performed).

To use Genie+ with this plan: Get the first available reservation for any of the next three attractions to visit, and fit that return-time window into the plan. If none of the next three steps participate in Genie+, then get a reservation for the next attraction in the plan that *does* participate.

If using Individual Attraction Selections, try to obtain one for Slinky Dog Dash for around 4 p.m. and for Rise of the Resistance for around 5 p.m.

See tinyurl.com/free-tplans to customize this plan at no charge, including the attractions and your walking speed, plus real-time updates while you're in the park.

Universal's Islands of Adventure

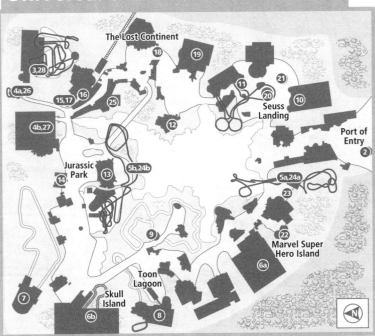

UNIVERSAL'S ISLANDS OF ADVENTURE ONE-DAY TOURING PLAN

1. Buy admission in advance. Call ☎ 407-363-8000 or visit universalorlando.com the day before for the official opening time.

2. Arrive 90–120 minutes before opening if Early Park Admission is offered and you're eligible, or 30–45 minutes before opening if you're a day guest. Check Universal's app for showtimes, and check vltest.universal orlando.com for Virtual Line reservations for Hagrid's Magical Creatures Motorbike Adventure starting at official park opening; if available, deviate from this plan when it's your turn, and return to it after riding.

3. Early-entry guests should ride Hagrid's Magical Creatures Motorbike Adventure only if they are at the front of the pack.

4. Early-entry guests may ride Flight of the Hippogriff (**4a**), followed by Harry Potter and the Forbidden Journey (**4b**), if at least 30 minutes remain in early entry.

5. Guests without early entry should first ride The Incredible Hulk Coaster (**5a**). Early-entry guests should enter Jurassic Park before the park officially opens and ride the Jurassic World VelociCoaster (**5b**).

6. Ride The Amazing Adventures of Spider-Man. Day guests should start with Spider-Man (**6a**), followed by Skull Island: Reign of Kong (**6b**). Early-entry guests may ride Reign of Kong (**6b**) on their way to Spider-Man (**6a**) while walking from Jurassic Park. Both early-entry and day guests continue as follows.

7. Take the Jurassic Park River Adventure. Leave your belongings in a pay locker here through the next two rides.

8. Ride Dudley Do-Right's Ripsaw Falls.

9. Ride Popeye & Bluto's Bilge-Rat Barges. Retrieve your property from Jurassic Park.

10. Experience The Cat in the Hat.

11. Experience The High in the Sky Seuss Trolley Train Ride!

12. Eat lunch. A good sit-down choice is Mythos. Make reservations at zomato.com.

13. Explore the Jurassic Park Discovery Center.

14. Meet Blue at the Raptor Encounter.

15. Watch the Frog Choir or *Triwizard Spirit Rally* on the stage outside Hogwarts Castle.

16. See the wand ceremony at Ollivanders, and buy a wand if you wish.

17. See the other show on the stage outside Hogwarts Castle, time permitting.

18. Chat with the Mystic Fountain.

19. See *Poseidon's Fury* (seasonal).

20. Enjoy the Caro-Seuss-el.

21. Ride One Fish, Two Fish, Red Fish, Blue Fish.

22. Ride Doctor Doom's Fearfall.

23. Ride Storm Force Accelatron (seasonal).

24. Ride The Incredible Hulk Coaster (**24a**) or Jurassic World VelociCoaster (**24b**), whichever you didn't ride earlier.

25. Have dinner at Three Broomsticks.

26. Ride Flight of the Hippogriff (if you haven't).

27. Ride Harry Potter and the Forbidden Journey.

28. Ride Hagrid's Magical Creatures Motorbike Adventure after sunset, if possible.

29. Watch the last Hogwarts Castle light show (if scheduled), or revisit any favorite attractions.

Universal Studios Florida

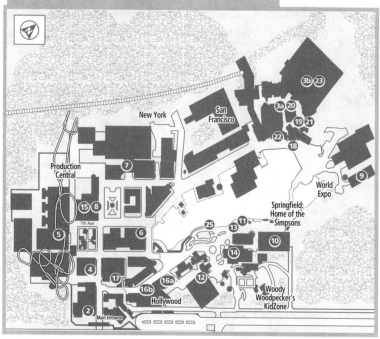

UNIVERSAL STUDIOS FLORIDA ONE-DAY TOURING PLAN

1. Buy admission in advance. Call ☎ 407-363-8000 or visit universalorlando.com the day before for the official opening time.

2. Arrive at USF 90–120 minutes before the official opening time if Early Park Admission is offered and you're eligible, or 30–45 minutes before opening if you're a day guest. Check Universal's app for daily show-times, and look for Virtual Line reservations for select attractions starting at official park opening.

3. Early-entry guests should visit Ollivanders (**3a**) and ride Harry Potter and the Escape from Gringotts (**3b**). If Gringotts isn't operating, enjoy the rest of Diagon Alley but don't get in line.

4. Before early entry ends, ride Despicable Me Minion Mayhem. Day guests should begin their tour here.

5. Ride Hollywood Rip Ride Rockit.

6. Experience Transformers: The Ride 3-D.

7. Ride Revenge of the Mummy in New York.

8. Ride Race Through New York Starring Jimmy Fallon, or get a Virtual Line return time for early afternoon if the standby entrance isn't available.

9. Experience Men in Black Alien Attack in World Expo.

10. Ride The Simpsons Ride in Springfield.

11. Try Kang & Kodos' Twirl 'n' Hurl.

12. Ride E.T. Adventure in Woody Woodpecker's KidZone.

13. Eat lunch at Fast Food Boulevard.

14. Work in *Animal Actors on Location!* around lunch, according to the daily entertainment schedule.

15. Experience Race Through New York Starring Jimmy Fallon according to the Virtual Line reservation you made, if you didn't ride earlier.

16. See *Universal Orlando's Horror Make-Up Show* (**16a**) and *The Bourne Stuntacular* (**16b**) according to the daily entertainment schedule.

17. See *Shrek 4-D* in Production Central.

18. Chat with the Knight Bus conductor and his shrunken head outside of Diagon Alley. Also look for Kreacher in the window of 12 Grimmauld Place, and dial MAGIC (62442) in the red phone booth.

19. See *Celestina Warbeck and the Banshees*.

20. See the wand ceremony at Ollivanders, and buy a wand if you wish.

21. See *Tales of Beedle the Bard*.

22. Tour Diagon Alley. Browse the shops, explore the dark recesses of Knockturn Alley, and discover the interactive effects. If you're hungry, try the Leaky Cauldron or Florean Fortescue's Ice-Cream Parlour.

23. Ride Harry Potter and the Escape from Gringotts.

24. Revisit favorite attractions, if time permits.

25. If it's scheduled, watch *Universal Orlando's Cinematic Celebration* from Central Park (between Hollywood and Woody Woodpecker's KidZone).

Universal Studios Florida

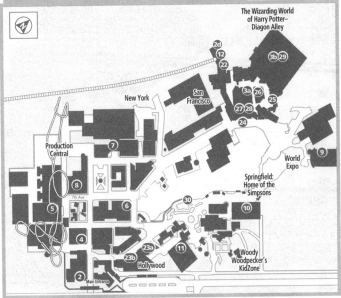

UNIVERSAL ORLANDO HIGHLIGHTS
ONE-DAY/TWO-PARK TOURING PLAN: PART ONE
(Assumes: 1-Day Park-to-Park Ticket)

1. Buy admission in advance. Call ☎ 407-363-8000 or visit universalorlando.com the day before for the official opening time.

2. Arrive at USF 90–120 minutes before official opening if Early Park Admission is offered and you're eligible, or 30–45 minutes before opening if you're a day guest. Check Universal's app for daily showtimes, and check vltest.universalorlando.com for Virtual Line reservations for Hagrid's Magical Creatures Motorbike Adventure starting at official opening; if available, deviate from this plan when it's your turn, and return to it after riding. **Alternative:** If only IOA is open for Early Park Admission and you're eligible, arrive at IOA 90–120 minutes before official opening. Ride Hagrid's Magical Creatures Motorbike Adventure (**2a**), Harry Potter and the Forbidden Journey (**2b**), and Flight of the Hippogriff (**2c**). Then take the first Hogwarts Express (**2d**) of the morning to USF, and continue at the next step. **(See map on next page for steps 2a–2d.)**

3. Early-entry guests should head to Diagon Alley to visit Ollivanders (**3a**) and ride Harry Potter and the Escape from Gringotts (**3b**). If Gringotts isn't operating, enjoy the rest of Diagon Alley but don't get in line.

4. Return to the front of the park to ride Despicable Me Minion Mayhem. Day guests should begin here.

5. Ride Hollywood Rip Ride Rockit.

6. Experience Transformers: The Ride 3-D in Production Central.

7. Ride Revenge of the Mummy in New York.

8. Ride Race Through New York Starring Jimmy Fallon if the standby entrance is open.

9. Ride Men in Black Alien Attack in World Expo.

10. Experience The Simpsons Ride in Springfield.

11. Ride E.T. Adventure in Woody Woodpecker's KidZone.

12. Ride Hogwarts Express to IOA. Have your park-to-park ticket ready.

Tour Islands of Adventure using Part Two of this plan (see next page); then return to USF and resume at step 23 below.

23. See *Universal Orlando's Horror Make-Up Show* (**23a**) and/or *The Bourne Stuntacular* (**23b**) according to the daily entertainment schedule.

24. Chat with the Knight Bus conductor outside of Diagon Alley. Also look for Kreacher in the window of 12 Grimmauld Place and dial MAGIC (62442) in the red phone booth.

25. See *Celestina Warbeck and the Banshees* or *Tales of Beedle the Bard* in Diagon Alley.

26. See the wand ceremony at Ollivanders, and buy a wand if you wish.

27. Eat dinner at the Leaky Cauldron.

28. Tour Diagon Alley. Browse the shops, explore the dark recesses of Knockturn Alley, and discover the interactive effects.

29. Ride Harry Potter and the Escape from Gringotts.

30. If scheduled, watch *Universal Orlando's Cinematic Celebration* from Central Park (between Hollywood and Woody Woodpecker's KidZone).

(continued on next page)

Universal's Islands of Adventure

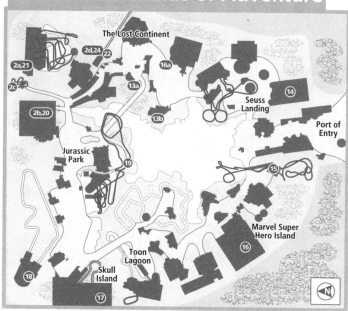

UNIVERSAL ORLANDO HIGHLIGHTS
ONE-DAY/TWO-PARK TOURING PLAN: PART TWO
(continued from previous page)

13. Break for lunch. We suggest Fire Eater's Grill in Lost Continent (**13d**) for a quicker meal or Mythos (**13b**) for sit-down dining.
14. Ride The Cat in the Hat in Seuss Landing.
15. Ride The Incredible Hulk Coaster on Marvel Super Hero Island.
16. Ride The Amazing Adventures of Spider-Man.
17. Ride Skull Island: Reign of Kong.
18. Take the Jurassic Park River Adventure
19. Ride the Jurassic World VelociCoaster.

20. Ride Harry Potter and the Forbidden Journey.
21. Experience Hagrid's Magical Creatures Motorbike Adventure, using your Virtual Line reservation if available.
22. Return to USF via Hogwarts Express, or walk back to the other park if the posted wait exceeds 20 minutes.

Resume Part One starting with step 23 (see previous page).

Typhoon Lagoon

TYPHOON LAGOON ONE-DAY TOURING PLAN
FOR PARENTS WITH SMALL CHILDREN

1. Arrive at the park entrance 30 minutes before opening. Take care of locker and towel rentals at Singapore Sal's, to your right after you've walked along the winding entrance path and emerged into the park. Find a spot to stow the remainder of your gear, noting any nearby landmarks to help you find your way back.
2. Ride Miss Adventure Falls as many times as you like.
3. Ride Gangplank Falls as many times as you like.
4. If your kids enjoyed Gangplank Falls, try Keelhaul Falls if it seems appropriate.
5. Enjoy the Ketchakiddee Creek kids' play area.
6. Grab some tubes and ride Castaway Creek. A complete circuit takes 20–25 minutes.
7. Swim in the Surf Pool as long as you like.
8. Ride the Bay Slides in the Surf Pool.
9. Repeat your favorite attractions as desired.

Blizzard Beach

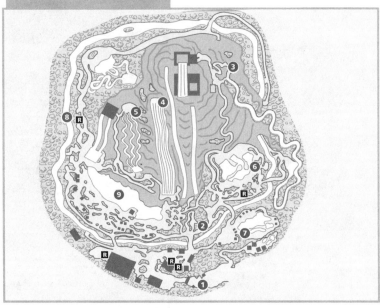

BLIZZARD BEACH ONE-DAY TOURING PLAN
FOR PARENTS WITH SMALL CHILDREN

1. Arrive at the park entrance 30 minutes before opening. Take care of locker and towel rentals at Lottawatta Lodge, to your left as you enter the park. Find a spot to stow the remainder of your gear, noting any nearby landmarks to help you find your way back.
2. Take the chairlift up Mount Gushmore to the Green Slope. *Note:* It might be faster—though more tiring—to walk to the top.
3. Raft down Teamboat Springs. Repeat as much as you like while the park is still uncrowded.

4. If your kids are up for it, try the Toboggan Racers.
5. If the kids enjoyed the Toboggan Racers, try the Snow Stormers next.
6. Visit the Ski Patrol Training Camp.
7. Visit Tike's Peak.
8. Grab some tubes and go floating in Cross Country Creek.
9. Swim in Melt-Away Bay's Wave Pool for as long as you like.

MAGIC KINGDOM Touring Plan Companion

Attraction | Recommended Visitation Times | Authors' Rating

Ariel's Grotto *(closed at press time)* | Before 10:30 a.m. or in the 2 hours before closing | ★★★

Astro Orbiter | Before 11 a.m. or in the hour before closing | ★★

The Barnstormer *(Genie+)* | Before 11 a.m., during parades, or in the 2 hours before closing | ★★

Big Thunder Mountain Railroad *(Genie+)* | Before 10 a.m. or in the hour before closing | ★★★★
  Comments 40" minimum height; expectant mothers should not ride

Buzz Lightyear's Space Ranger Spin *(Genie+)* | First or last hour the park is open | ★★★★

Casey Jr. Splash 'N' Soak Station *(closed at press time)* | When it's hot | ★★★

Country Bear Jamboree | Anytime | ★★★½

Dumbo the Flying Elephant | Before 11 a.m. or after 6 p.m. | ★★★½

Enchanted Tales with Belle *(Genie+, closed at press time)* | At opening or in the 2 hours before closing | ★★★★

Frontierland Shootin' Arcade *(closed at press time)* | Anytime | ★½

The Hall of Presidents | Anytime | ★★★

The Haunted Mansion *(Genie+)* | Before 11 a.m. or in the 2 hours before closing | ★★★★½
  Comment Fright potential

It's a Small World *(Genie+)* | Before 11 a.m. or after 7 p.m. | ★★★½

Jungle Cruise *(Genie+)* | Before 10:30 a.m. or in the 2 hours before closing | ★★★½

Liberty Belle **Riverboat** | Anytime | ★★½

Mad Tea Party *(Genie+)* | Before 11 a.m. or after 5 p.m. | ★★ | *Comments* Expectant mothers should not ride; motion sickness potential

The Magic Carpets of Aladdin *(Genie+)* | Before 11 a.m. or after 7 p.m. | ★★½

The Many Adventures of Winnie the Pooh *(Genie+)* | Before 10 a.m. or in the hour before closing ★★★½

Meet Merida at Fairytale Gardens *(closed at press time)* | Check *Times Guide* for schedule | ★★★½

Mickey's PhilharMagic *(Genie+)* | Anytime | ★★★★

Monsters, Inc. Laugh Floor *(Genie+)* | Anytime | ★★★

Peter Pan's Flight *(Genie+)* | First or last 30 minutes the park is open | ★★★★

Pete's Silly Sideshow *(Genie+ likely, closed at press time)* | Before 11 a.m. or in the 2 hours before closing | ★★★½

A Pirate's Adventure: Treasure of the Seven Seas *(closed at press time)* | Available noon–6 p.m. | ★★★½

Pirates of the Caribbean *(Genie+)* | Before 11 a.m., after 7 p.m., or use Genie+ | ★★★★

Prince Charming Regal Carrousel | Anytime | ★★★

Princess Fairytale Hall *(Genie+ likely, closed at press time)* | Before 10:30 a.m. or after 4 p.m. | ★★★

Seven Dwarfs Mine Train | At opening | ★★★★

Space Mountain *(IAS)* | At opening or in the hour before closing | ★★★★ | Comments 44" minimum height; expectant mothers should not ride

Splash Mountain *(Genie+)* | At opening, during parades, just before closing, or use Genie+ | ★★★★★
  Comments 40" minimum height; expectant mothers should not ride

Swiss Family Treehouse | Anytime | ★★★ | *Comment* Fright potential due to height

Tom Sawyer Island and Fort Langhorn | Midmorning–late afternoon | ★★★

Tomorrowland Speedway *(Genie+)* | Before 10 a.m. or in the 2 hours before closing | ★★
  Comment 54" minimum height requirement for kids to drive unassisted

Tomorrowland Transit Authority PeopleMover | Anytime, but especially during hot, crowded times of day (11:30 a.m.–4:30 p.m.) | ★★★½

Town Square Theater Meet and Greets *(Genie+, closed at press time)* | Before 10 a.m. or after 4 p.m. | ★★★★

Tron Lightcycle Power Run *(IAS, opens 2022)* | At opening or in the hour before closing

Under the Sea: Journey of the Little Mermaid *(Genie+)* | Before 10:30 a.m. or in the 2 hours before closing ★★★½

Walt Disney's Carousel of Progress | Anytime | ★★★

Walt Disney's Enchanted Tiki Room | Before 11 a.m. or after 3:30 p.m. | ★★★

Walt Disney World Railroad *(closed for construction)* | Anytime | ★★★

DINING INFORMATION—Counter Service

Restaurant | Location | Quality | Value | Selections

Aloha Isle | Adventureland | Excellent | B+ | Soft-serve, ice-cream floats, pineapple juice

Be Our Guest Restaurant | Fantasyland | Excellent | C | *Breakfast (not offered at press time):* Cured meats and cheeses, bacon-and-egg sandwich, croissant doughnuts. *Lunch and dinner* are full service.

Casey's Corner | Main Street, U.S.A. | Good | C | Hot dogs, plant-based hot dogs, corn dog nuggets, fries, brownies

Columbia Harbour House | Liberty Square | Good | B+ | Grilled salmon with rice, fried fish and shrimp, lobster roll, fried chicken, New England clam chowder, grilled shrimp, salads, kids' meals

Cosmic Ray's Starlight Cafe | Tomorrowland | Fair–Poor | C- | Burgers, hot dogs, Greek salad, chicken sandwich, chicken strips, bacon cheeseburger, plant-based burger; some kosher

DINING INFORMATION—Counter Service *(continued)*

The Diamond Horseshoe *(seasonal)* | Frontierland | Fair-Poor | D | Sandwiches (pulled pork, grilled chicken, brisket, turkey salad); Cowboy Mac (mac and cheese with beef brisket and jalapeño cornbread); Chuck Wagon platters and Saloon Feasts with pulled pork, brisket, or grilled chicken; cake, banana pudding, and cheesecake; wine and beer

The Friar's Nook | Fantasyland | Good | B | Hot dogs; bacon-mac-and-cheese, sausage-and-gravy, or Buffalo chicken tots, bacon mac and cheese

Gaston's Tavern | Fantasyland | Good | C | Cinnamon rolls, cupcakes, LeFou's Brew (frozen apple juice with toasted-marshmallow flavoring)

Golden Oak Outpost *(seasonal)* | Frontierland | Good | B+ | Chili-cheese fries, chicken strips, chocolate chip cookies, bottled water and soft drinks

Liberty Square Market | Liberty Square | Good | C | Fresh fruit, packaged drinks and snacks

The Lunching Pad | Tomorrowland | Fair | C | Breakfast sandwich, all-beef hot dogs, barbecue pork sandwich, cheese-stuffed pretzels, frozen sodas

Main Street Bakery (Starbucks) | Main Street, U.S.A. | Good | B | Coffees, pastries, breakfast sandwiches

Pecos Bill Tall Tale Inn and Cafe | Frontierland | Good | C | Pork carnitas and chicken fajita platter, nachos, rice bowl with veggies, salad with or without chicken, churros, doughnut holes, yogurt

Pinocchio Village Haus | Fantasyland | Fair-Poor | D | Flatbread pizzas, chicken strips, Caesar salad, kids' meals

Tomorrowland Terrace Restaurant *(seasonal)* | Tomorrowland | Fair | C- | Varies

Tortuga Tavern *(seasonal)* | Adventureland | Fair | B | Turkey legs, hot dogs, brisket sandwiches, rum cake

DINING INFORMATION—Full Service

Restaurant | Meals Served | Location | Price | Quality | Value | Selections

Be Our Guest Restaurant | L-D | Fantasyland | Expensive | ★★★★ | ★★ | Breakfast, when offered, is counter service. *Lunch and dinner:* French onion soup or charcuterie plate appetizers, roasted pork tenderloin with seasonal vegetables, filet mignon with Robuchon potatoes, pan-seared scallops with risotto

Cinderella's Royal Table | L-D | Fantasyland | Expensive | ★★★ | ★★ | Charcuterie plate appetizer, beef tenderloin with Bordelaise sauce, chicken breast, duck two ways, pan-seared scallops, chickpea "fingers"

The Crystal Palace | L-D | Main Street, U.S.A. | Expensive | ★★★½ | ★★★ | Family-style platters of fried chicken, fried cauliflower, prime rib, seasonal salads

Jungle Navigation Co. Ltd. Skipper Canteen | L-D | Adventureland | Expensive | ★★★ | ★★★ | Char siu pork, Korean barbecue–inspired crispy fried chicken, grilled steak with adobo, corn pancakes with pork and avocado cream; chocolate cake with caramelized bananas; plant-based options; kids' menu

Liberty Tree Tavern | L-D | Liberty Square | Expensive | ★★★ | ★★★ | All-you-can-eat family-style dining with turkey breast, pork roast, mashed potatoes, stuffing, vegetables, and mac and cheese; toffee cake

The Plaza Restaurant | L-D | Main Street, U.S.A. | Moderate | ★★ | ★★ | Old fashioned diner and ice-cream shop fare: roast beef sandwich, fried chicken sandwich, turkey club sandwich, sundaes, kids' menu

Tony's Town Square Restaurant | L-D | Main Street, U.S.A. | Expensive | ★★★ | ★★ | Pasta (gluten-free and multigrain options), pizza, shrimp fettuccine Alfredo, chicken parmigiana, Roman-style steak

Advance Reservations recommended for Magic Kingdom full-service restaurants; call ☎ 407-WDW-DINE (939-3463) or visit disneyworld.disney.go.com/reservations/dining.

GOOD REST AREAS IN THE MAGIC KINGDOM

Back of Storybook Circus, between Big Top Treats and the train station | Fantasyland | Covered plush seating with electrical outlets and USB phone-charging stations

Covered porch with rocking chairs on Tom Sawyer Island | Frontierland | Across the water from the *Liberty Belle* Riverboat dock; bring refreshments from Frontierland; closes at sunset

Cul-de-sac | Main Street, U.S.A. | Between the china shop and Main Street's Starbucks on right side of street as you face the castle; refreshments nearby

Picnic tables | Fantasyland | Near the *Tangled*-themed restrooms, between Peter Pan's Flight and The Haunted Mansion; outdoors but has phone-charging stations

Quiet seating area | Tomorrowland | Near restrooms on the right as you approach Space Mountain—look for pay phones, and there's a covered seating area farther back in that corridor; refreshments nearby

Second floor of train station | Main Street, U.S.A. | Refreshments nearby; crowded during fireworks and parades

Upstairs at Columbia Harbour House | Liberty Square | Grab a beverage and relax upstairs; restrooms available

EPCOT Touring Plan Companion

Attraction | Location | Recommended Visitation Times | Authors' Rating

The American Adventure | United States, World Showcase | Anytime | ★★★★

Awesome Planet | The Land, Future World | Anytime | ★★½

Beauty and the Beast Sing-Along | France, World Showcase | 11 a.m.–6 p.m. | ★★

Canada Far and Wide | Canada, World Showcase | Anytime | ★★★½

Disney & Pixar Short Film Festival (Genie+) | Imagination! Pavilion, Future World | Hardly ever | ★★½

Frozen Ever After (Genie+) | Norway, World Showcase | Before noon or after 7 p.m. | ★★★★

Gran Fiesta Tour Starring the Three Caballeros | Mexico, World Showcase | Before noon or after 5 p.m. | ★★½

Guardians of the Galaxy: Cosmic Rewind (opens 2021) | Future World East/World Discovery | At opening | *Comments* Estimated 44"–48" minimum height

Harmonious | World Showcase Lagoon | Arrive at least 90 minutes before showtime

Impressions de France | France, World Showcase | 6:30 p.m.–park closing | ★★★½

Journey into Imagination with Figment (Genie+) | Imagination! Pavilion, Future World | Anytime | ★★½

Living with the Land (Genie+) | The Land, Future World | Before noon or after 3 p.m. | ★★★★

Mission: Space | Future World East/World Discovery | First or last hour the park is open | ★★★★ *Comments* 40" minimum height; expectant mothers should not ride; motion sickness potential

Reflections of China | China, World Showcase | Anytime | ★★★½

Meet Anna and Elsa at Royal Sommerhus (Genie+ likely, closed at press time) | Norway, World Showcase | As soon as it opens, at lunch or dinner, or last hour the park is open | ★★★★

Remy's Ratatouille Adventure (IAS, opens 2021) | France, World Showcase | At opening

SeaBase | The Seas with Nemo & Friends, Future World | Before 12:30 p.m. or after 5 p.m. | ★★★½

The Seas with Nemo & Friends (Genie+) | Future World | After 2 p.m. | ★★★

Soarin' Around the World (Genie+) | The Land, Future World | First 30 minutes the park is open or between 4 p.m. and park closing | ★★★★½ | *Comments* 40" minimum height; motion sickness potential

Spaceship Earth (Genie+) | Central Future World/World Celebration | Before noon or after 4 p.m. | ★★★★

Test Track (IAS) | Future World East/World Discovery | First 30 minutes the park is open or just before closing | ★★★★ *Comments* 40" minimum height; expectant mothers should not ride; breaks down frequently

Turtle Talk with Crush | The Seas with Nemo & Friends, Future World | After 3 p.m. ★★★★

DINING INFORMATION—Counter Service

Restaurant | Location | Quality | Value | Selections

L'Artisan des Glaces | France, World Showcase | Excellent | C | Gourmet ice creams and sorbets

La Cantina de San Angel | Mexico, World Showcase | Good | B | Tacos, Mexican salad, grilled chicken with rice and corn, fried cheese empanadas, guacamole, margaritas, kids' meals, churros, fruit pops

Fife & Drum Tavern | United States, World Showcase | Fair | C | Turkey legs, hot dogs, popcorn, soft-serve ice cream, slushies, beer, alcoholic lemonade, root beer floats

Les Halles Boulangerie-Pâtisserie | France, World Showcase | Good | A | Pastries, niçoise salad, cheese plates, sandwiches, quiches, soups

Katsura Grill | Japan, World Showcase | Good | B | Basic sushi; udon noodle bowls; chicken, beef, or shrimp teriyaki; chicken curry; edamame; miso soup; green tea cheesecake; beer, sake, plum wine; teriyaki chicken kids' plate

Kringla Bakeri og Kafe | Norway, World Showcase | Good–Excellent | B | Pastries, desserts, iced coffee, imported beer and wine

Lotus Blossom Café | China, World Showcase | Fair | C | Egg rolls, pot stickers, orange chicken, chicken fried rice, Mongolian beef with rice, caramel-ginger or lychee ice cream, plum wine, Tsingtao beer

Refreshment Outpost | Between Germany and China, World Showcase | Good | B– | Hot dogs, slushies, soda, beer

Refreshment Port | Near Canada, World Showcase | Good | B– | Poutine, chicken nuggets; unusual alcoholic drinks, beer

Regal Eagle Smokehouse | United States, World Showcase | Good | B | Regional barbecue specialties, burgers, salads, and vegetarian options; beer, hard cider, wine, and cocktails

Rose & Crown Pub | United Kingdom, World Showcase | Good | C+ | Fish-and-chips, sausage roll, beer, wine, liquor, coffee drinks, pub blends

Sommerfest | Germany, World Showcase | Fair | C | Bratwurst, jumbo pretzel, cold beer

Sunshine Seasons | The Land, Future World | Excellent | A | Rotisserie and wood-fired meats and fish; salads, sandwiches, soups

Tangierine Café | Morocco, World Showcase | Good | B | Chicken and lamb shawarma, lentil and couscous salads, hummus, tabbouleh, vegetarian platter, kids' meals, Moroccan wine and beer

Traveler's Café (Starbucks) | West side of the border of World Showcase and Future World | Good | B | Coffee drinks, teas, breakfast sandwiches, pastries

Yorkshire County Fish Shop | United Kingdom, World Showcase | Good | B+ | Fish-and-chips, draft ale

DINING INFORMATION—Full Service

Restaurant | Meals Served | Location | Price | Quality | Value | Selections

Akershus Royal Banquet Hall | B–L–D | Norway, World Showcase | Expensive | ★★ | ★★★★ | *Breakfast:* Dilled salmon, mackerel, goat cheese. *Lunch and dinner:* Smorgasbord of meats, cheeses, seafood, salads; roast chicken; stuffed pasta; grilled salmon; kjottkake (Norwegian meatballs); kids' menu; full bar; character meals

Biergarten Restaurant | L–D | Germany, World Showcase | Expensive | ★★ | ★★★★ | Traditional German sausages, potato salad, homemade spaetzle, roast chicken, braised red cabbage, full bar

Le Cellier Steakhouse | L–D | Canada, World Showcase | Expensive | ★★★½ | ★★★ | Charcuterie plate appetizer with edible beef-fat candle, Canadian Cheddar soup, steaks, seafood, five-cheese mac and cheese, loaded mashed potatoes, poutine, warm pecan–brown butter tart, full bar and Canadian wines

Chefs de France | L–D | France, World Showcase | Expensive | ★★★ | ★★★ | Boeuf Bourguignon, French onion soup topped with Gruyère, vegetarian options, beer and wine

Coral Reef Restaurant | L–D | The Seas with Nemo & Friends, Future World | Expensive | ★★ | ★★ | Lobster bisque, steak and seafood; kids' menu; full bar

La Crêperie de Paris *(opens 2021)* | B–L–D | France, World Showcase | Cuisine from the Brittany region of France

Garden Grill Restaurant | B–L–D | The Land, Future World | Expensive | ★★★ | ★★★ | Beef filet, turkey with stuffing and gravy, salads, BBQ ribs, plant-based options; kids' menu; wine, beer, and mixed drinks; character meals

La Hacienda de San Angel | D | Mexico, World Showcase | Expensive | ★★★½ | ★★½ | Queso fundido, guacamole, carne asada-style NY strip, fried-shrimp tacos, flank steak fajitas, flautas appetizer, full bar with specialty tequilas

Monsieur Paul *(closed at press time)* | D | France, World Showcase | Expensive | ★★★★½ | ★★★ | Black-truffle soup, black sea bass in potato "scales," roasted duck breast, kids' menu, full bar

Nine Dragons Restaurant | D | China, World Showcase | Moderate | ★★ | ★★ | Crispy duck bao buns, honey-sesame chicken, salt-and-pepper shrimp, full bar

Restaurant Marrakesh *(closed at press time)* | L–D | Morocco, World Showcase | Expensive | ★★½ | ★★ | Goat cheese-and-olive spread with tabbouleh appetizer, beef brewat roll, lemon chicken, fish tagine, kebabs; full bar

Rose & Crown Dining Room | L–D | United Kingdom, World Showcase | Moderate | ★★★½ | ★★ | Fish-and-chips, bangers and mash, shepherd's pie, Welsh Pub Burger, English trifle, Scotch eggs, full bar

San Angel Inn Restaurante | L–D | Mexico, World Showcase | Expensive | ★★★ | ★★★ | Tlayuda or queso fundido appetizers, ribeye tacos, vegetarian tqavos, sweet corn ice cream, full bar

Space 220 *(opens 2021)* | L–D | Future World East | International space station theme with digital "windows" showing a view of Earth and stars

Spice Road Table | L–D | Morocco, World Showcase | Expensive | ★★★★ | ★★★ | Mediterranean-style small plates including fried calamari and hummus fries, lamb kefta, spiced shrimp and chicken, chocolate mousse, full bar

Takumi-Tei *(closed at press time)* | D | Japan, World Showcase | Expensive | ★★★★★ | ★★★½ | Frequently changing menus showcasing traditional Japanese kaiseki cuisine: crab appetizer, Wagyu beef, sushi, Japanese water cake for dessert

Teppan Edo | L–D | Japan, World Showcase | Expensive | ★★★★ | ★★★ | Chicken, shrimp, beef, scallops, and veggies stir-fried on teppanyaki grill; full bar

Tokyo Dining | L–D | Japan, World Showcase | Moderate | ★★★★ | ★★★ | Sushi and sashimi, full bar

Tutto Gusto Wine Cellar | L–D | Italy, World Showcase | Expensive | ★★★★ | ★★★ | Cheese plates, charcuterie, marinated vegetables; tiramisu, gelato and sorbet, Torta della Nonna, cannoli; wine flights

Tutto Italia Ristorante | L–D | Italy, World Showcase | Expensive | ★★★★ | ★★ | Pasta, steak, salmon, chicken, fried calamari; Torta della Nonna, tiramisu, cannoli, and gelato for dessert; beer and wine

Via Napoli Ristorante e Pizzeria | L–D | Italy, World Showcase | Expensive | ★★★½ | ★★★ | Wood-fired pizzas, pastas, beef filet, Mediterranean sea bass, chicken parmesan, tiramisu, cannoli, beer and wine

Advance Reservations recommended for EPCOT full-service restaurants; call ☎ 407-WDW-DINE (939-3463) or visit disneyworld.disney.go.com/reservations/dining.

Good Rest Areas in EPCOT

Benches | Mexico, World Showcase | Inside the pavilion against the inside of the wall that forms the walking ramps to the retail space; air-conditioned

Benches | The Seas with Nemo & Friends, Future World | Air-conditioned

Japan gardens | Japan, World Showcase | To the left of Katsura Grill, a set of tables overlooking a lovely garden and koi pond; outdoors but shaded, with refreshments nearby

Rotunda and lobby | United States, World Showcase | Ample room; air-conditioned; refreshments nearby; usually quiet

UK Rose Garden benches | United Kingdom, World Showcase | A small town square and manicured gardens behind the pavilion

DISNEY'S ANIMAL KINGDOM Touring Plan Companion

Attraction | Recommended Visitation Times | Authors' Rating

The Animation Experience at Conservation Station *(Genie+)* | Check *Times Guide* for hours | ★★★

Avatar Flight of Passage *(IAS)* | At park opening or after 3 p.m. | ★★★★½ | *Comments* 44″ minimum height; expectant mothers should not ride

The Boneyard | Anytime | ★★★½

Conservation Station and Affection Section | Anytime | ★★★

Dinosaur *(Genie+)* | Before 10:30 a.m. or after 4 p.m. | ★★★★ | *Comments* Fright potential; 40″ minimum height; expectant mothers should not ride

Expedition Everest *(IAS)* | First or last hour the park is open | ★★★★½ | *Comments* 44″ minimum height; expectant mothers should not ride

Feathered Friends in Flight | Anytime | ★★★★

Festival of the Lion King (reduced version playing during pandemic) | Before 11 a.m. or after 4 p.m.; check *Times Guide* for showtimes | ★★★

Gorilla Falls Exploration Trail | Before or after Kilimanjaro Safaris | ★★★★

Kali River Rapids *(Genie+)* | Before 11 a.m. or last hour the park is open | ★★★½ | *Comments* You'll get wet; 38″ minimum height; expectant mothers should note that ride is bouncy

Kilimanjaro Safaris *(Genie+)* | At opening or after 3 p.m. | ★★★★★

Maharajah Jungle Trek | Anytime | ★★★★

Meet Favorite Disney Pals at Adventurers Outpost *(closed at press time)* | First thing in the morning or after 5 p.m. ★★★½

Na'vi River Journey *(Genie+)* | Before 9:30 a.m. or in the 2 hours before closing | ★★★½

The Oasis | Anytime | N/A

Theater in the Wild/*Finding Nemo—The Musical (reopens 2022)* | Check *Times Guide* for showtimes

Tree of Life/*It's Tough to Be a Bug!/Awakenings (Genie)* | Anytime | ★★★★ | *Comment* Fright potential

TriceraTop Spin | Before noon or after 3 p.m. | ★★

Wilderness Explorers | Sign up first thing in the morning and complete activities throughout the day. | ★★★★

Wildlife Express Train | Anytime | ★★

DINING INFORMATION—Counter Service

Restaurant | Location | Quality | Value | Selections

Creature Comforts (Starbucks) | Discovery Island near Africa | Good | C | Coffee drinks, teas, breakfast sandwiches, and pastries

Flame Tree Barbecue | Discovery Island | Excellent | B- | Pulled-pork sandwich, ribs, smoked half-chicken, smokehouse chicken salad, fries and onion rings; child's plate of baked chicken drumstick, hot dog, or PB&J sandwich; beer and wine, Mandarin orange vodka lemonade

Harambe Market | Africa | Good | B | Grilled chicken or ribs served over rice and salad greens; salads; plant-based "sausage"; kids' meals

Kusafiri Coffee Shop and Bakery *(closed at press time)* | Africa | Good | B | Elephant ear pastries, giant cinnamon rolls, croissants and other pastries; sausage, egg, and cheese biscuit; fruit; yogurt; coffee, cocoa, and juice; some kosher

Pizzafari | Discovery Island | Fair | C | Cheese, pepperoni, and sausage personal pizzas; shrimp flatbread; pasta; Caesar salad; kids' meals; cannoli cake

Restaurantosaurus | DinoLand U.S.A. | Fair | C | Burgers, chili-cheese hot dog, chicken nuggets, Cobb salad, breaded shrimp, plant-based Southwestern burger, kids' meals

Royal Anandapur Tea Company | Asia | Good | B | Hot and iced teas, coffees, lattes, frozen chai, pastries

Satu'li Canteen | Pandora | Good | A | Customizable bowls with chicken, beef, shrimp, or fried tofu; steamed "pods" (stuffed bao buns); kids' options

Yak & Yeti Local Food Cafes | Asia | Fair | C | Honey chicken with steamed rice, cheeseburger, teriyaki chicken salad, veggie tikka masala, Korean fried chicken sandwich, tempura shrimp, egg rolls, fried rice; kids' meals; American-style breakfast fare

DINING INFORMATION—Full Service

Restaurant | Meals Served | Location | Price | Quality | Value | Selections

Rainforest Cafe | L-D | Park entrance | Moderate | ★★ | ★★ | Crab dip, coconut shrimp, burgers, ribs, brownie cake with ice cream; full bar

Tiffins | L-D | Discovery Island | Expensive | ★★★★ | ★★★ | Appetizers of charred octopus and sweet corn soup; entrées include whole fried sustainable fish and butter chicken; passion fruit tapioca; full bar

Tusker House Restaurant | B-L-D | Africa | Expensive | ★★★ | ★★★ | Roast pork, beef, and chicken; character meals; full bar next door

Yak & Yeti Restaurant | L-D | Asia | Expensive | ★★½ | ★★ | Lo mein noodle bowls, coconut shrimp, chicken tikka masala, Korean fried chicken tenders, firecracker shrimp; full bar

Advance Reservations recommended for Animal Kingdom full-service restaurants; call ☎ 407-WDW-DINE (939-3463) *or visit* disneyworld.disney.go.com/reservations/dining.

GOOD REST AREAS IN DISNEY'S ANIMAL KINGDOM

Gazebo behind Flame Tree Barbecue | Discovery Island | Follow the path toward the water, along the left side of Flame Tree Barbecue; gazebo has ceiling fans

Outdoor covered benches near exit from Dinosaur | DinoLand U.S.A. | Gazebo-like structure with nearby water fountain

Seating area adjacent to Dawa Bar | Africa | Refreshments nearby; outdoors and can be noisy from street performers

Walkway between Africa and Asia | Plenty of shaded rest spots, some overlooking streams; refreshments nearby; a favorite of *Unofficial Guide* researchers

DISNEY'S HOLLYWOOD STUDIOS Touring Plan Companion

Attraction | Recommended Visitation Times | Authors' Rating

Alien Swirling Saucers (Genie+) | First 30 minutes the park is open or after 3 p.m. | ★★½ |
Comment 32" minimum height

Beauty and the Beast—Live on Stage/Theater of the Stars | Anytime but not as hot after sunset | ★★★★

Disney Junior Dance Party!/Disney Junior Play and Dance | Check *Times Guide* for schedule | ★★

Fantasmic! | Check *Times Guide*; if 2 shows are offered, the second will be less crowded. | ★★★★½

For the First Time in Forever: A Frozen Sing-Along Celebration | Check Times Guide for showtimes;
arrive 15 minutes before showtime | ★★★½

Indiana Jones Epic Stunt Spectacular! *(closed at press time)* | First 2 shows or last show | ★★★½

Jedi Training: Trials of the Temple *(closed at press time)* | First 2 shows | ★★★½

Lightning McQueen's Racing Academy | Anytime | ★★½

Mickey & Minnie's Runaway Railway (Genie+) | At opening or in the last hour before closing | ★★★★

Mickey and Minnie Starring in *Red Carpet Dreams* (Genie+ *likely, closed at press time*) | First or last hour the park is
open or during mealtimes | ★★★★

Mickey Shorts Theater | Anytime | ★★★½

Millennium Falcon: Smugglers Run (Genie+) | At opening or after 6 p.m. | ★★★★ | *Comments* 38" minimum
height; expectant mothers should not ride

Muppet-Vision 3-D (Genie+) | Anytime | ★★★★

Rock 'n' Roller Coaster Starring Aerosmith (Genie+) | First 30 minutes the park is open or after 4 p.m. | ★★★★ |
Comments 48" minimum height; expectant mothers should not ride

Slinky Dog Dash (Genie+) | At opening or just before closing | ★★★★ | *Comment* 38" minimum height

Star Tours—The Adventures Continue (Genie+) | During lunch or after 4 p.m. | ★★★½
Comments Fright potential; 40" minimum height; expectant mothers should not ride; motion sickness potential

Star Wars Launch Bay *(closed at press time)* | Anytime | ★★★

Star Wars: Rise of the Resistance (IAS) | When your boarding group is called. Get a boarding group on the
My Disney Experience app at exactly 7 a.m. or 1 p.m. on the day of your visit | ★★★★★ | *Comments* 40"
minimum height; expectant mothers should not ride

Toy Story Mania! (Genie+) | At opening or after 4:30 p.m. | ★★★★½

The Twilight Zone Tower of Terror (Genie+) | First 30 minutes the park is open or after 4 p.m.
★★★★ | *Comments* 40" minimum height; expectant mothers should not ride

Walt Disney Presents | Anytime | ★★★

DINING INFORMATION—Counter Service

Restaurant | Location | Quality | Value | Selections

ABC Commissary | Commissary Lane | Fair | D | Pork carnitas or shrimp tacos, salads (vegetarian option available),
sandwiches and burgers, rice bowls, plant-based burger; kids' meals; some kosher; wine and beer

Backlot Express | Echo Lake | Fair | C | Angus bacon cheeseburger, chicken strips, Cuban sandwich, Southwest salad,
red pepper hummus with pita bread

Catalina Eddie's | Sunset Boulevard | Fair | C | Cheese and pepperoni pizzas, Caesar salad with or without chicken;
kids' meals; strawberry shortcake terrine

Docking Bay 7 Food and Cargo | Star Wars: Galaxy's Edge | Excellent | A | Smoked ribs served with blueberry corn
muffins, roasted chicken served on salad or with mac and cheese and roasted veggies, vegan menu, tuna poke

Dockside Diner | Echo Lake | Fair | C | Hot dogs with various toppings, Parmesan chips, pickled vegetables

Fairfax Fare | Sunset Boulevard | Fair | B | Assorted hot dogs, Chicago-style hot dog salad

Milk Stand | Star Wars: Galaxy's Edge | Fair | D | Frozen nondairy drinks, with or without alcohol

Oga's Cantina | Star Wars: Galaxy's Edge | Fair | D | Alcoholic and nonalcoholic cocktails; wine and beer; Batuu Bits
snack mix, sampler platter with cured and roasted meats, cheese, and pork cracklings | *Comment* Online reserva-
tions available

PizzeRizzo | Grand Avenue | Poor | D | Personal pizzas, meatball subs, salads | *Comment* Not recommended

Ronto Roasters | Star Wars: Galaxy's Edge | Good | B | Pita wrap filled with roast pork and grilled Portuguese sau-
sage, pork rinds, nonalcoholic fruit punch, breakfast wraps

Rosie's All-American Cafe | Hollywood Boulevard | Fair | C | Burgers, chicken nuggets, fries, plant-based "lobster" roll;
child's turkey sandwich or chicken nuggets with a smoothie and fruit; strawberry shortcake verrine

The Trolley Car Cafe (Starbucks) | Hollywood Boulevard | Good | B | Coffee, tea, breakfast sandwiches, pastries

Woody's Lunch Box | Toy Story Land | Excellent | A- | *Breakfast:* Lunch Box Tarts; breakfast bowl with scrambled
eggs, potato barrels, and country gravy. *Lunch and dinner:* Sandwiches (barbecue brisket, smoked turkey,
grilled three-cheese), tomato-basil soup, "totchos" (potato barrels with chili, queso, and corn chips)

DINING INFORMATION—Full Service

Restaurant | Meals Served | Location | Price | Quality | Value | Selections

50's Prime Time Cafe | L-D | Echo Lake | Moderate | ★★★ | ★★★ | Pot roast, meat loaf, fried chicken; PB&J milkshake, warm apple crisp, and chocolate-peanut butter layer cake for dessert; full bar

Hollywood & Vine | B-L-D | Echo Lake | Expensive | ★★★ | ★★★ | Caramel monkey bread for breakfast, beef tenderloin, roasted turkey, mac and cheese with shrimp, roasted pork, plant-based options (menu changes often); character meals; full bar

The Hollywood Brown Derby | L-D | Hollywood Boulevard | Expensive | ★★★★ | ★★★ | Cobb Salad (named after the owner of the original restaurant); signature burger with pastrami, Gruyère, tomato, and fried egg; chicken breast with red pepper-and-Toma cheese polenta cakes and Madeira jus; grapefruit cake; kids' menu. Patio lounge serves cocktails and small plates.

Mama Melrose's Ristorante Italiano | L-D | Grand Avenue | Moderate | ★★★ | ★★ | Seasonal pastas, fresh mozzarella, flatbread "pizzas," charred strip steak; tiramisu, chocolate-and-cherry torte, and cannoli; full bar

Sci-Fi Dine-In Theater Restaurant | L-D | Commissary Lane | Moderate | ★★½ | ★★ | Sandwiches, burgers (plant-based burger available), salads, pasta; shakes and sundaes; full bar

Advance Reservations recommended for DHS full-service restaurants; call ☎ **407-WDW-DINE (939-3463)** *or visit* disneyworld.disney.go.com/reservations/dining.

Good Rest Areas in Disney's Hollywood Studios

Animation Building | Animation Courtyard | Benches in and around Star Wars Launch Bay; refreshments nearby

Benches along Echo Lake | Some are shaded; refreshments nearby

Covered seating behind Sunshine Day Bar | Sunset Boulevard | Refreshments nearby; ample seating

Tune-In Lounge | Echo Lake, next to 50's Prime Time Cafe | Air-conditioned bar; nonalcoholic drinks and food from 50's Prime Time Cafe also available (Thanks to Matt Hochberg of studioscentral.com for this tip.)

UNOFFICIAL GUIDE USE #37
DEAD WEIGHT TO KEEP YOU GROUNDED DURING HURRICANES.